Jan. 1943

W. G. Falk, 3.70

FOUNDATIONS OF
MODERN WORLD
SOCIETY

STANFORD BOOKS IN WORLD POLITICS

Graham Stuart, Editor

✤

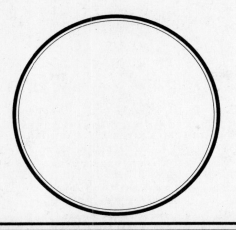

FOUNDATIONS OF MODERN WORLD SOCIETY

By

Linden A. Mander

Professor of Political Science
University of Washington

STANFORD UNIVERSITY PRESS
Stanford University, California
HUMPHREY MILFORD :: OXFORD UNIVERSITY PRESS
London

STANFORD UNIVERSITY PRESS
STANFORD UNIVERSITY, CALIFORNIA

LONDON: HUMPHREY MILFORD
OXFORD UNIVERSITY PRESS

———

THE BAKER AND TAYLOR COMPANY
55 FIFTH AVENUE, NEW YORK

THE MARUZEN COMPANY
TOKYO, OSAKA, KYOTO, SENDAI

———

COPYRIGHT 1941 BY THE BOARD OF TRUSTEES
OF THE LELAND STANFORD JUNIOR UNIVERSITY

PRINTED AND BOUND IN THE UNITED STATES
OF AMERICA BY STANFORD UNIVERSITY PRESS

PREFACE

PERHAPS it may appear futile to discuss the foundations of international and world society at a time when Europe is engulfed in deadly struggle. Surely if there were any foundations of an inter- or trans-national character, they are being destroyed. Surely it is a refusal to look at obvious facts to assert that human life today rests upon anything but naked force, or to claim that there is anything left but international disorganization.

However black the outlook may be, and however hopeless the task may seem, it is nevertheless the urgent business of the scientist to look beyond immediate appearances—to see whether the sun does actually go around the earth or whether in truth it is the earth which revolves around the sun. The sun appears to rise in the east and travel across the sky; but closer observation leads to a correction of first impressions. Or, to adopt another figure of speech, however devastating and disastrous an epidemic may be, the task of the scientist and the doctor is to continue diagnosis and examination as calmly and as accurately as possible, and to make clear what are the causes of disease and what are the remedies. How many panics in past ages have been due to superstitious beliefs concerning demons! How many lives have been lost through a refusal to look more closely into the facts which have produced plagues and other visitations!

If we look at the world today, we shall be astonished at the amount of human activity that cannot be described except on an international or trans-national or world basis. But human beings in the last few years have shut out the picture of the world as it is and have put on blinkers which have prevented them from seeing beyond a number of short-term interests, national myths, party symbols, and primitive emotions. Dean Pound has written that the political and legal theories of the nineteenth century were developed by men who looked at the facts of the world of the eighteenth and nineteenth centuries, but that later thinkers drew their deductions from these nineteenth-century theorists and not from looking at the changing world in which they lived. We are pay-

v

ing a heavy penalty for this mischievous practice of theorizing from the theories of predecessors. Francis Delaisi, in his *Political Myths and Economic Realities,* traces the consequences to civilized life of the myth of political sovereignty. H. G. Wells, in a recent volume, has reminded us that the League of Nations failed because it was too much political and legal. And, in an address at the University of Washington, Professor A. H. Compton told an audience that the simple experiment of Faraday about a hundred years ago concerning the electromagnetic field has meant more to Europe than the campaigns of Napoleon. But how many people consider Faraday and Pasteur and the other scientists who have helped us to conquer distance and triumph over disease as basically affecting the problem of government? The majority are still dominated by sentimental political and national appeals, and misinterpret the nature of the society in which we live.

The evidence contained in the following chapters should make it quite clear that nations as isolated units of government are unable any longer to perform their tasks as sovereign independent entities except at ruinous cost. The present war is an indication of the frightful sacrifices demanded in the attempt to maintain security by national effort alone or with the help of allies. And the evidence also shows unmistakably that these nations cannot by themselves adequately organize shipping, radio, properly continuous railroads, air travel, health, conservation, the prevention of crime, and a host of other activities. For what purpose then are they fighting? Looked at from this angle, the tragedy of Europe may be seen in a new light—the tragedy of countries fighting to defend themselves with a system of government which has worked well in its day but which is no longer adequate for the purposes of the present world. Blood and treasure are being sacrificed because of the retention of an instrument which should now play a subordinate (but still important) role in government but which people have vainly striven to continue as an exclusive and dominant political entity. The utmost loyalty has been demanded for a form of society which is less and less able to handle the business which confronts it. Europe and, for that matter, the world are resisting a necessary change in the structure of government and in the loyalties which governments demand. It should seem obvious that, as life changes and new problems arise, new methods of government must come into existence to meet changed conditions—otherwise disaster ensues. Feudalism played its part and gave way in the fullness of time to a new kind of society. So must present forms of government in turn change their functions.

Seen from this standpoint, international government is not a luxury but a necessity. At the present moment the danger exists that the war may be fought for the wrong things and that men may be asking and answering with terrible intensity the wrong questions. They may not see that the essential need of the world today is constitutional building—to find the political form of society which is best suited to control the vast forces which modern science has released—and that nationalism, by attempting to maintain itself in the center of the stage, is overplaying its part, is weakening itself, and, indeed, is threatening itself with destruction. A second world war in our generation will have been fought in vain unless mankind can realize quickly the deepest problem which confronts it.

In truth, the central question is not, as so many assert, nationalism versus internationalism. The fundamental issue is what kind of nationalism can best serve the interests of the people of the world, and what kind of international organization can most efficiently minister to man's needs. It is an intensely practical question and one which demands for its answer, not the easy theorizing of the armchair philosopher, or the facile classifications of the passionate conservative and still more passionate radical partisan, or the verbal schematic products of the platitudinous theologian; on the contrary, it requires a description of things as they are, and an estimate of the significance of things as they are, and as they are developing, inasmuch as things not only *are,* but are in the process of *becoming.* And these estimates will lead to general judgments which in one sense may appear theoretical but which in another sense are the practical everyday things seen in their wider relations.

A British scholar[1] has recently criticized what he calls political utopianism and denounced many writers for their armchair and wishful thinking. He quotes from Lord Bacon, who said: "Philosophers make imaginary laws for imaginary commonwealths, and their discourses are as the stars which give little light because they are so high," and urges that "on account of the pernicious and inveterate habit of dwelling on abstractions, it is safer to begin and raise the sciences from those foundations

---

[1] E. H. Carr, *The Twenty Years' Crisis* (The Macmillan Company, Ltd., London, 1940).

which have relation to practice, and let the active part be as the
seal which prints and determines the contemplative counterpart."
Carr spends much time in demonstrating the futility which results from indulging in theoretical speculations based upon ra-
tionalism, utilitarianism, internationalism, *laissez faire,* overeasy
synthesis of interests, and naïve assumptions of international
economic harmony. He then attempts a "realistic criticism," and
speaks of the foundations of realism. Interestingly enough, Carr
falls victim to the very evils which he denounces; his analysis
operates within the framework of concepts which are different
from the concepts of his victims but are equally theoretical. He
erects a false antithesis between utopia and reality and between
man as an egoist and man as a social being. He takes the concept of national interests as fundamental, is dominated by the
idea of power, and unduly contrasts realism and idealism as if
these were wholly antithetical terms. Nevertheless Carr is profoundly right in urging us to beware of trying to compress a complicated world into a few simple principles, even though he himself
does not escape from the danger against which he warns.

The present volume is an attempt to avoid building utopias
in disregard of the tremendous complexities of the contemporary
world. It is an attempt at "realism," in that it sets out to show
how much the evidence compels us to see that the foundations
of human life are broader than such terms as "national power"
and "national interests" imply. It does not trace the course of
modern international diplomacy—not because the question of national power is not urgent, but because this question has been
already discussed in many other volumes and because so much
else must be included here. It does attempt to show the great
contradiction which exists between the requirements of human
welfare and the demands being made by the sovereign state and
the "New Order" based upon force; in the final chapter it considers the significance of the present war and the principles upon
which a stable peace must be built. It does not say that human
beings will accept the necessary changes in political society; it
does assert that unless those changes are accepted there can be
little but continued and deepening anarchy in the modern world.

A word of explanation concerning the order of the chapters
in the present volume may be added. Writers on international
relations usually begin by discussing the modern state or nationality and emphasize political questions and the international
organization of sovereign states. Because the welfare of human

beings constitutes the great aim of democracy, it has seemed desirable to the present writer to begin instead with world conditions which directly affect the well-being of individuals and societies. Contemporary civilization has become over-political-minded, and many fine values have become subordinated to the idea of national power and prestige. If we are sincere in proclaiming that welfare rather than power is the democratic goal, it would seem logical to begin by considering those things which minister to man's physical, economic, mental, and spiritual welfare. Sovereignty and political organizations enter the picture eventually.

What is a nation or a state but a group of people associated for certain purposes? And the more purposes the people have in common as a nation or as a state, the stronger their sense of unity. But the state or nation provides only certain elements of life, not all of them. It may supply certain elements at one time and not at another. National and state institutions may be more efficient at one period than another in performing this function or that. The content of nationalism and of a state changes. It is not a closed system but may be added to, contracted, and combined with other agencies of government in order to meet human needs. Americans should not have to be told that many constitutional amendments were adopted in order to prevent the state from invading certain areas of private life. If, in order to achieve individual freedom and to insure that governments should be the servant and not the master, the nation became limited in its power over individuals within its boundaries, should it not have limitations imposed upon it in relation to peoples without? If there are certain things which can be better done by co-operation, it is the height of folly to retain a spurious sovereignty and a false sense of independence when the burdens of new tasks become too great for separate national action.

Without denying the logic of established institutions, this volume attempts to emphasize the urgent need of developing an attitude of political discovery, so as to adapt political institutions to meet new and unprecedented tasks, to demonstrate that the full promise of contemporary civilization depends upon man's political inventiveness in this time of rapid change, and to present international relations not so much in terms of power politics as in terms of constitution building and of establishing political units more in accordance with the facts of life.

I wish to thank my wife, and also Mr. Dan Blom, Miss Thelma Williams, Miss Rose Doyle, and especially Mrs. Helen McCauley,

Miss Helen Hodges, Mr. Glen Wood, Mr. Richard Rader, and Mr. Donald Urquhart for their assistance in preparing the manuscript. To Dr. Charles E. Martin I owe a debt of gratitude for many kindnesses and for his encouragement and his part in making possible the publication of the present work. I am also anxious to acknowledge the invaluable help given to me by Professor Graham H. Stuart and the Stanford University Press staff.

L. A. M.

SEATTLE, WASHINGTON
    June 20, 1941

CONTENTS

Chapter I

HEALTH AS AN INTERNATIONAL AND WORLD PROBLEM

MANY people underestimate the part played by nonpolitical forces in the development of the human race. It is probable that the great majority of those who bemoan the failure of the League of Nations to prevent war and aggression do not adequately appreciate the significance of its Health Organization, which may yet do more for mankind than all that a purely political League could have accomplished. Those who have been already saved through the activities of the Health Section probably far outnumber those who have been killed by reason of the breakdown of collective security.

A glance at history will show the vast suffering and ruin caused by disease which has frequently modified, and even destroyed, the social and political institutions of great civilizations.

In 430 B.C., plague attacked Athens; the population died by hundreds, and the Athenian armies were unable to drive out the forces of Sparta. The disease not only weakened Athens as a political power but demoralized and debased the very character of the people. Not forty years later, the Carthaginian army which was invading Sicily had to withdraw because of an epidemic of disease which devastated its ranks, and, as Zissner in his *Rats, Lice, and History* (from which much of the material of the next few paragraphs is borrowed), points out, was thereby prevented from establishing control over Sicily. Had Carthage been able to accomplish this end, it is possible that Rome would not have gained the victory which finally eliminated Carthage and its "commercial, Semitic culture," and that Roman military power, organizing ability, and legal methods would not have become a decisive influence in the future development of Europe.

The Roman Empire in turn became the victim of several devastating epidemics. The causes of the decline of Rome are many; but among them disease must rank as one of the most powerful.

1

In the second and third centuries, A.D., plague swept the Roman world intermittently and took the lives of scores of thousands, weakened still more the political authority of the government, and disintegrated an economic life which was already manifesting symptoms of decay. The very efficiency of communications in the Empire made the spread of the disease all the easier, with the result that even faraway Scotland did not escape its ravages, which depopulated large areas and added to the ruin of civic and rural life.

The fifth century witnessed an intensification of the barbarian invasions; they undoubtedly helped to spread disease throughout Europe. Britain experienced a plague during the Saxon invasion between 440 and 450. Vienna also suffered heavily from the outbreak of disease. Within a decade Rome fell victim, then Gaul, then North Africa. These visitations formed the prelude to the most disastrous "pandemic" of all, the great plague of Justinian, which began in Egypt in A.D. 450. At its height the plague took more than 10,000 people a day in Byzantium; corpses were emptied into the towers of forts and were placed on ships which were then abandoned. Gibbon notes that Justinian's reign was marked by a heavy decline of population and without question the plague, which lasted for half a century, weakened the rule of Byzantium in Italy and in Africa and diminished its power of resistance against Persian and Arabic invasions.

Several centuries later the Crusades added to the melancholy story of the triumph of microbes over man. From 1096 until after 1300, hundreds of thousands of Crusaders died, not at the hands of their Moslem foes, but from the attacks of an invisible enemy against which their armed might was of no avail. The First, Second, Third, and Fourth Crusades suffered frightful losses from plague and famine; the expedition of the Emperor Frederick II in 1227 failed because of outbreak of disease; and readers of Sire de Joinville will recall that in 1250 King Louis IX of France and his troops while in Egypt were attacked by the dread army sickness, scurvy. Louis' attempt collapsed, and twenty years later he and his son died of dysentery in the course of his second Crusade.

The consequences of the Black Death which broke out in Europe about 1350 are well known. Probably over twenty-five million people (about one-quarter of the whole population) died; historians say that the breakdown of the feudal system was hastened by its ravages. For over thirty years the disease spread in epidemics which were calamitous to European society. Writers state that forces already at work modifying the feudal structure of England were "strengthened by the Pestilence"; the labor legislation required to cope with the new situation led to important constitutional changes, including the appointment of "Justices of Laborers." In the next century England and France suffered epidemics of sweating sickness. In 1456 the Turks had to lift the siege of Belgrade and relax their hold upon Hungary because of the spread of typhus, a disease which showed its indifference to both armies by killing the Hungarian deliverer, Hunyadi. For the next hundred years and more, typhus decimated the armies which moved into Hungary and the Balkan States, regions which are still the home stations from which typhus may spread across Europe.

Toward the end of the fifteenth century, the same dread disease struck Spain. It originated in the civil wars of Granada, spread throughout the whole country, and depopulated large areas. Within two generations it had helped to overturn the political balance of power in Europe. The French army which had invaded Italy had surrounded the Spanish Imperial army. Diseased and disorganized, the latter had no hope of withstanding the forces of Francis I, until in 1528 typhus attacked the French and compelled them to retreat. The French army then rapidly disintegrated and was destroyed by the Imperial troops. In this way Italy came under the rule of Spain and Emperor Charles V triumphed over France in the Mediterranean.[1]

The Thirty Years War (1618–48) decisively altered the map of Europe, and is commonly regarded as marking the beginning of the modern period. Yet its outcome depended more upon disease than upon military factors. Time after time the prospects of victory on the field of battle faded and the whole situation was transformed by the appearance of an invisible enemy, hostile alike to both of the armed adversaries. Likewise in the late eighteenth century, the Prussian forces which marched against the French Revolutionary armies had to retreat because of dysentery. Moreover, Napoleon's campaign into Russia ended disastrously, not only because of distance and Russian military resistance but also because of the ravages of typhus and dysentery. And the Crimean War provides eloquent evidence of the relative destructive power

---

[1] H. W. Haggard's *Devils, Drugs, and Doctors,* Part IV, "The Passing of Plague and Pestilence" (Halcyon House, New York, 1929), gives a vivid description of the effects of disease in the centuries prior to 1800.

of disease and armaments; in the French, English, and Russian armies the number of sick far outstripped the number of wounded, and, except in the case of the Russians, more men died of disease than of wounds.

Disease and epidemics have taken their toll of millions; they have killed them directly and left society impoverished, disorganized, or at least weakened and with resistance lowered. But disease has also controlled the destinies of mankind by affecting rulers and others "whose physical frailties and moral delinquencies" have profoundly influenced the course of human events.

Would English history have been the same if Henry VIII had not been syphilitic? Perhaps Queen Catherine would not have lost four children (including three sons) in childbirth or early infancy. If Henry had had a son, the Reformation in England might have taken a different course. Possibly Joan of Arc would not have seen visions and led the French army if she had come to physical maturity earlier. The course of Spanish and European history might have been substantially altered if the Emperor Charles V had not retired from the throne in 1556 on account of wretched health due to arteriosclerosis. And what political results came from Philip II's gout and diabetic gangrene? MacLaurin writes, "when we consider that the destinies of nations are commonly held in the hands of elderly gentlemen whose blood-pressures tend to be too high owing to their fierce political activities, it is not too much to say that arteriosclerosis is one of the greatest tragedies that afflict the human race."[2] Nor is it unreasonable to assume that, despite the discoveries of medical science, illness and disease may be playing their part among the modern political leaders of the world with disastrous consequences to their subjects.

Nineteenth-century Europe, which witnessed a decline in the virulence of some epidemics, had to face a new scourge—cholera. Duguet writes, "Le choléra a toujours eu son berceau dans l'Inde, où les plus anciens textes signalent sa présence. Il y rester cantonné jusqu'au début du XIXe siècle . . . . En 1830, 1837, c'est la première invasion européenne." In 1831, *"année fatale,"* cholera appeared at Mecca and introduced a new problem for the European nations. They had long known of the danger of disease spreading from the Orient to the West—Venice, in 1328, had created the first *"organisation quarantenaire,"* an example followed later by Genoa and Marseilles. But the Italian cities had

[2] C. MacLaurin, *Post Mortems of Mere Mortals* (Doubleday, Doran and Company, New York, 1935), p. 159.

no co-ordinated plans; a disease which one government thought dangerous enough to necessitate quarantine efforts another government lightly ignored; some imposed burdensome periods of observation, which caused much hardship to navigation interests. Duguet observes: "En somme, défense incohérente, contradictoire, et ce qui est aussi grave, fort onéreuse pour le trafic maritime, réelement victime de cet arbitraire."[3]

The appearance of cholera at Mecca made Europe realize that the thousands of Moslems who made their holy pilgrimages from Asia, North Africa, and southeastern Europe, and traveled and lived under most unsanitary conditions, constituted a major threat to its health. Readers of Richard Burton's *Pilgrimage to Meccah,* which appeared in 1855, will recall the vivid description of the effects of the overcrowding and the dirty habits of the pilgrims, and especially of the shocking conditions under which thousands of sacrificial animals were slaughtered under the tropical sun.

In 1847 France created medical posts in the Near East—in Constantinople, Beyrouth, Damascus, Alexandria, and Cairo and later at Suez, Teheran, and Smyrna. Such individual efforts were inadequate: "Mais il fallait faire plus, introduire dans la lutte contre les épidémies le principe de la solidarité et de la collaboration entre États."[4] Otherwise Europe ran the risk of illustrating Carlyle's dictum that, while the rich might deny their brotherhood with the poor in life, they might experience it in a death spread by the diseased and the outcasts whom they had shunned.

In 1838 some of the European nations compelled Turkey to establish a Superior Health Council comprising four Turkish representatives and one representative from each major power. The committee adopted measures to prevent the spread of epidemics into Turkey and supervised quarantine service at the Turkish ports and elsewhere. (The Council was abolished in 1923, owing to the desire of Turkey to enjoy complete independence.)

In 1851, twelve powers attended the first International Health Conference at Paris, and signed a Treaty.[5] The terrible cholera epidemic of 1865 induced the powers to meet at Constantinople

---

[3] F. Duguet. *Le Pilgrimage de la Mecque au point de vue religieux, social et sanitaire* (Rieder, Paris, 1932), p. 120.

[4] *Ibid.,* p. 121.

[5] Only three nations ratified the Convention, and of these Portugal and Sardinia denounced it a few years later. C. Vitta, "Le Droit Sanitaire International," in *Académie de Droit International* (Recueil des Cours, 1930), XXXIII, 565.

in the following year, and at Vienna in 1874. In 1881 a council was set up at Alexandria for the purpose of preventing epidemics spreading from Egypt. Four Egyptian and fourteen non-Egyptian representatives met in regular monthly meetings, examined suspected ships, set up quarantine stations in the Red Sea, and assisted in developing special health measures for Egypt.

An International Sanitary Council was established also at Teheran in order to prevent the spread of epidemics from the Orient to Europe by way of Persia. And by an additional provision of the Act of Navigation of the Danube, of May 28, 1881, an International Sanitary Council was stationed at Bucharest to act in co-operation with the European Commission of the Danube to guard against the introduction of diseases by way of that river.[6]

Meanwhile, health and sanitation had become an important problem at Tangier.[7] In 1792, foreign consuls met, thereafter collectively made representations to the Sultan of Morocco, and were at length empowered to take measures to safeguard the public health of the port. In 1892 the Sanitary Council, which comprised the members of the diplomatic corps, acquired increased authority from the Sultan to clean the streets, pave the roads, improve means of sewage disposal, build slaughterhouses (with three divisions, for Jews, Moslems, and Christians), and make provision for a pure water supply.

The Washington Convention of 1881 marked an outstanding achievement in international co-operation for health. Delegates realized that they must attempt to reconcile two things—the maximum guaranty against the spread of disease, and the minimum delay to shipping and commerce. They agreed that nations had the sovereign right to prevent the introduction of diseases by ships coming from other countries, and therefore their representatives could rightly claim to inspect the ship before it left the foreign port. Such inspection, however, might be regarded as a limitation upon the sovereignty of the country from whose port the ship would sail.

Another question arose; suppose that a vessel were sailing from a country with a low, to a country with a high, standard of public health; ought the latter to insist that its medical representatives give a bill of clearance to the ship in question? The United

---

[6] C. Vitta, *op. cit.,* pp. 589–90.

[7] G. H. Stuart. *The International City of Tangier* (Stanford University Press, California, 1931), pp. 31–39.

States wished to adopt the principle that its consuls and medical experts should be empowered to inspect ships destined for United States ports and not merely accept a bill of health granted by local authorities. But the proposal encountered resistance. The delegates also realized that, however important political organization might be, the fundamental need was for further scientific knowledge concerning the nature and course of some of the major diseases, especially (for the Americas) yellow fever.

Thus the task of preventing the spread of disease carried with it a greater need than international co-operation in the political field: it involved more than common action against disease after its appearance; it meant striking at the source, co-operating in the realm of prevention as well as in the realm of quarantine.

The Convention of 1881 finally agreed that: (1) Ships were to undergo sanitary inspection at their point of departure by the port health authorities and were to obtain a visé by the consul of the country of destination. (2) Health certificates were to be issued, free of charge. (3) An elaborate form of an international bill of health should be adopted so to make more uniform the basic requirements of international shipping. (4) In order to gather adequate information on health conditions the conference set up two international sanitary agencies to which the signatory powers would report all details which would assist in maintaining as complete a knowledge of the public health situation as possible. The office at Vienna was to serve Europe, Asia, and Africa; and the Havana Office was to deal with the Western Hemisphere. These offices were to issue health bulletins, and expenses were to be defrayed by the signatories in proportion to their population and shipping. (5) A resolution concerning the publication of health statistics bore witness to the importance of accurate information for medical purposes. (6) The Convention, realizing that certain areas were particularly susceptible to yellow fever, adopted a resolution calling for a temporary international sanitary commission to be established at twenty-two cities, and the signatories agreed to bear the expense of sending physicians to these areas.

The governments of the New World decided to set up an international sanitary bureau with headquarters at Washington, D.C., and, in 1902, adopted the first Pan-American sanitary convention. By this time medical knowledge had advanced considerably, and the conference was able to adopt more specific measures dealing with yellow fever, extermination of mosquitoes, control of plague, destruction of rodents which carried the plague, and purification of water and food so as to minimize the danger of cholera and typhus.

Meanwhile Europe found itself compelled to take further action because the Moslem pilgrimages to Mecca continued to spread disease. At first Great Britain appeared to be unsympathetic toward international health co-operation in Egypt, the Red Sea, and the Suez Canal. Other countries, jealous of their sovereignty, or suspicious of co-operation, also held back. It was not until thousands of lives had been sacrificed that the European states realized the folly of pitting a political theory against the grim realities of epidemics and recognized that more far-reaching international efforts were necessary if each country was to escape the ravages of disease. Cholera epidemics afflicted Europe almost every year between 1880 and 1892. In the last-named year, 157,000 perished in European Russia, 70,000 in the Caucasus, 4,500 in France; in Hamburg shops and hotels were closed, trains ceased to run, and hundreds of people died. And yet Turkey protested, at the 1894 Paris Conference, that an international attempt to improve conditions at Djeddah constituted *"une ingérence dans les affaires intérieures de la Turquie."* Add to these political obstinacies the religious fanaticisms of pilgrims, and one has some idea of the irrational obstacles to human progress.

The 1892 Conference at Venice realized the need for sanitary supervision at Suez and adopted regulations reorganizing the council at Alexandria and reapportioned European representation there. The Conference at Dresden in 1893 and those at Paris in 1894 and at Venice adopted further measures, including provision for medical inspection of ships from the Far East, the establishment of sanitary police in ports of debarkation, and the extension of these controls to countries on the Persian Gulf. In 1903 the International Sanitary Convention at Paris made more definite rules for the quarantine and disinfecting of ships. Steamship companies and captains of the vessels faced severe penalties for violation of the rules. The establishment of sanitary stations at various ports in the Middle East, combined with the general policy adopted at Paris, did much to lessen the danger of plague and cholera to Europe.

At Washington, D.C., in 1905 the American states decided to hold periodic health conferences and to permit only medical and sanitary officers to attend as delegates. This step showed the increasingly specialist nature of the problem of public health: no longer would the vague generalities of diplomatists suffice; with the progress of science, experts were needed; the problem was fundamentally a scientific, and only secondarily a political, one.

Such were the main "legislative achievements" of the international conferences. They had been important, but it now became necessary to provide permanent machinery in order to insure continuity of effort. Progress in governmental efficiency has increasingly depended upon the unostentatious daily routine of administrative officials. In international affairs, also, the importance of a "civil service" was gradually recognized, and the sanitary convention of 1903 provided for the establishment of an International Office of Public Health. The office was set up in 1907 with headquarters in Paris. The main duty of the new organization was to collect information relative to public health matters, to keep nations informed of recent developments, and to act as a co-ordinating agency. The participating governments, of whom there were thirty-seven in 1920, jointly bore the expenses and provided a committee of officials to supervise the work of the office. One writer notes that the French delegate cast "the suspicious eye of sovereignty on the new organization. No single one of its powers may be allowed to interfere with the right of sovereignty of which every state is so jealous." The Office International d'Hygiène Publique was to exercise only an "exclusive moral" influence!

This brief historical survey should make clear the persistent problem of disease and how long mankind has battled its uncompromising and inveterate enemy. The nineteenth century marked the beginnings of international effort. The twentieth century was to witness its extension. The World War of 1914–1918 revealed the necessity of close co-operation between the Allied armies, and during it an Inter-Allied Sanitary Commission met frequently at Paris. The specialists on the Commission did a great amount of policy making, and successfully provided an object lesson in international health co-operation.

During the Paris Peace Conference the International Red Cross Society urged the necessity of further permanent international action; its influence helped toward the inclusion of Articles 23, 24, and 25 in the Covenant of the League of Nations. Under Article 23 League members promised *inter alia* to "take steps in matters of international concern for the prevention and control of disease"—a clause inserted at the request of the British government, which desired to make "the duty and responsibility of governments more clear." Article 24 provided that, should they so consent, the international bureaus already established might be placed under League control. Under Article 25 "The members of the League agree to encourage and promote the establishment and co-operation of duly authorized voluntary national Red Cross organizations having as purposes the improvement of health, the prevention of disease, and the mitigation of suffering throughout the world"—an indication of the great importance of nongovernmental agencies in matters of human welfare.

A conference in 1920 drew up a scheme for the League of Nations Health Organization, which, after sôme delay, was adopted by the 1923 League Assembly in a lengthy resolution. The Organization comprises: (1) A General Advisory Health Council, which contains representatives of more than fifty governments and of the standing committee of the International Public Health Office. (2) A standing Health Committee of twelve medical experts, who are appointed in their capacities as individual scientists, and not as governmental representatives (the Health Committee meets three times a year, the members receive a three-year appointment and need not be citizens of countries that are members of the League) and frequently appoints subcommittees which can co-opt outside specialists. (3) The Permanent Secretariat of the Health Organization, which comprises a number of medical men and their assistants and forms part of the general League Secretariat.

The Health Organization of the League aims primarily to co-ordinate the governmental and other organized health activities of the world. It does not pretend to be a superstate health agency. Its work has been extraordinarily diversified and far-reaching, in contrast to the achievements of international health organization in prewar days, which did little more than co-ordinate efforts against the most serious epidemics and diseases. Postwar health work has been more positive, more continuous, and more effective. It may be summarized under several headings:

EPIDEMICS

The battle against epidemics.—Early in 1920 Eastern Europe was in the grip of terrible epidemic conditions; typhus and relapsing fever, originating in Russia, were attacking millions of people. The League Council requested the London Health Conference to take action. A few weeks later the League Epidemic Commission began its work. Within fifteen months it had spent about one million dollars in co-ordinating remedial measures, and succeeded in preventing the Russian danger from spreading. The commission then proceeded to Greece, where it organized a staff of nearly eighty medical officers, who set up vaccination stations and took other measures to combat smallpox, cholera, and typhoid. The 1922 Russian famine sent scores of thousands of people fleeing in desperation toward Western Europe carrying with them the further danger of disease. Poland appealed to the League for assistance, and requested that a European health conference be held to consider measures to stay the menace. The League responded, and at Warsaw in March 1922 the first all-European conference of the postwar period was held. Representatives of twenty-seven governments attended and agreed upon methods of strengthening the health defenses of countries bordering on Russia. Special sanitary-training conferences were held, provisions were made for adequate inspection and examination, and special regimes were set up in frontier zones extending five kilometers each side of the boundary. The threat of epidemics set aside theoretical discussions of sovereignty, and human political pretensions paled into insignificance in the face of the microbic enemies of all mankind.

The Health Committee in 1923 appointed a malaria subcommittee, which in 1924 became the Malaria Commission.[8] This disease is endemic in areas inhabited by six hundred and fifty million people, approximately one-third of the world's population. Malaria is not only widespread but is extremely difficult to control. In postwar years it spread with renewed activity in Russia, Albania, Greece, Yugoslavia, and Bulgaria. A special subcommittee investigated these and other areas and prepared a report in 1927. It found that measures which were successful in one country might not prove effective elsewhere. Many costly methods were found to be useless, and resulted in discrediting the work of health services in less medically minded countries. The organization therefore established special courses in malariology in London, Paris, and Hamburg, after attending which health officers took practical work in malaria districts in different areas. League officers visited the Mississippi, the Danube, and other rivers to see what relations might exist between conditions on these rivers and malaria itself. They investigated the effects of rice fields, of animals, and drainage measures and considered a

[8] Valuable material may be found in the Minutes of the Various Sessions of the Health Committee.

number of other highly technical subjects. In 1928 the Malaria Commission issued its further findings and in 1929 visited India to report on the methods of stamping out the disease there. Close co-operation between the League and national government health officials has been maintained. Moreover, the Commission has been investigating the world's quinine needs, and hopes to discover some remedy which will be as effective as but less expensive than quinine.

Millions of people have died or have suffered blindness and deformity from smallpox. League experts are working on this problem. The League Health Organization has also turned its attention to leprosy. The three million or more lepers in the world, especially in India, China, and Japan, and also in South America, and elsewhere, constitute a challenge to the co-operative work of the world. Dr. Carlos Chargas in 1925 asked that the Health Organization take up the problem of leprosy, and himself became chairman of a special committee. At Rio de Janeiro an international center under the auspices of the League was established to study this disease. The Health Organization, in paying tribute to Chargas at the time of his death, rejoiced that the American continent possessed a leprosy institute as well equipped as that which exists in the Far East, and the government of Brazil has placed this institute at the disposal of the League.

The spread of syphilis constitutes a serious problem. In 1928 the League Health Organization began a detailed study. Over 25,000 cases were analyzed, and the findings were embodied in a long report in 1934. The Health Committee responded to a request from Bulgaria to co-operate in anti-syphilis measures in that country.

Any person who has watched ships unloading and has seen rats scurrying along the ropes can appreciate the importance of adequate measures to prevent infected rats from carrying disease into port cities. Buell writes that "a rat infected with the bubonic plague which climbs on board a ship at Calcutta may carry the disease to Liverpool." It was an important step for the Health Organization Commission on ship fumigation to make a tour of leading ports of the world in order to study the most effective methods of disinfection and of quarantine. Visits of these medical officers have enabled co-operation to develop among the directors of port health services.

The Annual Report of the Public Health Commissioner of India contains information which reveals the growing importance of international quarantine and sanitary provisions in an age of aerial navigation. The health authorities of India have been concerned over the danger of the introduction of yellow fever, and, the report suggests, "With the development of air traffic the question has become one of urgent importance." Now that an airline is operating between Lagos in West Africa and Khartoum, where it joins the Cape-Cairo line, it is possible for infected persons and mosquitoes to be carried "from endemically infected areas in West and Central Africa to India within the incubation period of the disease." A new kind of "jungle yellow fever," which chiefly affects land workers, has been recognized; the virus can be transmitted from monkey to monkey by the *Aedes Aegypti* mosquito, and Indian authorities realize the extreme consequences which would follow for millions of people if the disease obtained a hold in India, the home of millions of monkeys "which could by no practical means be eliminated or controlled."

In September 1936 the Indian government issued orders forbidding the entry into India "of any aircraft which has started from or alighted in a yellow fever endemic or 'silent' area, except such aircraft which have obtained at Alexandria or Cairo a certificate of disinsectisation with 'Pyrocide 20' in the manner prescribed." Nor may a passenger or member of the crew enter India within nine days of having been in an endemic or "silent" area unless protected by inoculation or by a previous attack of yellow fever. Most significant is the fact that India was represented at a Pan-African Health Conference held at Johannesburg in November 1935. For health purposes it may be truly said that India is part of Africa; for the mosquito makes the two continents members one of another, and national sovereignty in the popular sense becomes little more than a grim jest in the presence of the threat of yellow fever.

Lack of space prevents more than a passing reference to the Health Committee's work on sleeping sickness, tuberculosis, cancer, infant mortality, rabies, and welfare of the blind. No one who reads the official documents can fail to be impressed by the great amount of intergovernmental and privately endowed effort which is being made in these fields of public health.

Although attention has been primarily directed to the work of the League, it would be an error to underestimate the part played by the countries of the American continent (some of which have also signed the more universal international sanitary conventions), or to fail to emphasize the excellent work of the Pan-

American Sanitary Bureau established at Washington. In 1924 at Havana another Pan-American Sanitary convention was signed; it is a document of sixty-three articles, which can only briefly be summarized here: The objects of the code are to prevent spread of disease, to promote co-operative measures, to standardize the collection of statistics, to encourage interchange of information, and as far as possible to standardize preventive methods. Each signatory agrees to notify the other parties and the Pan-American Sanitary Bureau, at intervals of not over two weeks, of its position with reference to public health; and it undertakes obligatorily to report on twelve specified diseases and upon such other diseases as the Pan-American Sanitary Bureau may add to the list. Each government will publish immediately the measures which it regards as necessary to prevent the spread of diseases, and to establish a central statistical office and regional statistical offices as soon as possible. Detailed provisions follow, dealing with bills of health and other sanitary documents which ships must carry, and with the treatment of vessels suspected of and those infected with diseases.

In June 1926 a sanitary convention was signed at Paris; it came into force in March 1928. Under it the signatory governments undertake to notify the International Office of Public Hygiene of the first cases of plague, cholera, or yellow fever and the existence of an epidemic of typhus or smallpox. The list of communicable diseases is not as extensive as that contained in the Pan-American Sanitary Convention, the reason apparently being that authorities consider that insufficient uniformity and efficacy of preventive measures have been attained.[9] The notifying telegrams are to have precedence over ordinary telegrams, and provision is made for notification of all bureaus connected with public health and not merely those connected with the League. Detailed measures provide for inspection of vessels, the condition of drinking water, the disinfection of apparel and bedding, special arrangements for emigrants, the issuance of certificates, etc. No fewer than forty-four articles refer to this phase of the problem. Several articles deal with measures at land frontiers, in railroad frontier zones, and on river ways. Special provisions for the Suez Canal and the neighboring countries occupy over twenty articles, and a lengthy section of seventy-one articles deals with the health problem raised by pilgrims entering and leaving the

[9] C. Vitta, *op. cit.*, p. 606.

Hedjaz, where the holy cities of the Moslem world are situated. A short section deals with modification in the position of the Sanitary, Maritime, and Quarantine Board of Egypt.

A number of powers signed an international convention for their mutual protection against dengue fever at Athens, July 25, 1934.[10] The instrument came into force March 25, 1935. The signatories agreed to notify the sanitary authorities of the other powers on the appearance of dengue fever in epidemic form and to keep the International Office of Public Hygiene informed of the course of the epidemic.

Medical authorities fear that the present war may set loose another epidemic comparable to the great influenza epidemic during the years 1918–1919 which resulted in the death of more than twenty million people and which affected practically every country and even every family on the earth. George W. Gray writes that devastating disease "almost invariably follows war, famines, political and economic collapse, and other violent upheavals of society"; and history furnishes sufficient evidence of this truth. Gray quotes Major Greenwood, professor of epidemiology and vital statistics in the London School of Hygiene and Tropical Medicine, as saying that it may well be that influenza rather than typhus or plague will reap a rich harvest following another war. Even now influenza is prevalent in many parts.

One may briefly note the international character of the efforts made toward finding remedies against this disease. Two German physicians, Hirsch in 1888, and Pfeiffer in 1892, made initial discoveries; but only within the last few years has substantial advance been made. During this period, an extraordinary amount of experimental work has gone on. Drs. Wilson Smith, Andrewes, and Laidlaw in 1933 at the British Medical Research Council at Hampstead found that the ferret was useful for experimental purposes. Dr. Shope at the Princeton Laboratory of the Rockefeller Foundation in New York carried the work further, and in 1936 the Rockefeller Foundation set up a special laboratory in New York for the study of influenza. One of its members, Dr. R. M. Taylor, studied the disease in Budapest in 1939. Medical investigations are proceeding in Canada, Australia, and elsewhere. "Thus the research front against the disease is truly international and worldwide."[11]

[10] *League of Nations Treaty Series,* Vol. 197 (1937), No. 4080, p. 59.
[11] George W. Gray, "The Problem of Influenza," *Harper's Magazine,* January 1940, p. 169.

Epidemiological intelligence service.—Epidemics spread so quickly that the ordinary official channels of information may be too slow to enable countries to put their health defenses into emergency operation with sufficient rapidity to safeguard themselves in the event of disease breaking out elsewhere. Effective action along the Russo-Polish frontier depended on quick and adequate information. Hence the importance of the League of Nations Health Organization Intelligence Service, organized in 1921, which made special reports on the disease situation in Eastern Europe, with special reference to typhus, relapsing fever, and cholera. After 1922 the publications took the form of a periodical, which appeared in July 1923 as the first monthly *Epidemiological Report*. The step was made possible by the help of an annual grant of $32,840 from the Rockefeller Foundation. The *Report,* which has increased in value and accuracy, has been bound into annual volumes, and has provided medical statistics and information to the profession throughout the world.

In 1922 the Japanese member of the Health Committee asked the Organization to consider the establishment of a center in the Far East, an area which is liable to frequent and severe epidemics. In 1925 a conference of Far Eastern health administrators agreed to set up a bureau in Singapore; it began operations during the same year, assisted by a five-year grant of $25,000 from the Rockefeller Foundation. The Bureau in its early period distributed telegraphic information from thirty-five ports, but its service rapidly increased; and in 1928 it received information from 140 ports, and broadcast in code each Friday from a number of wireless stations in the East, and by telegraph from Geneva, to more than 124 public health administrations. Many technical radio difficulties had to be overcome before the service reached its present high level of efficiency. Governments are now warned in advance of epidemics and can take precautions against ships coming from infected areas. "They know, too, that they can dispense with such measures for shipping from non-infected areas. The feeling of security is thus increased and unnecessary quarantine restrictions are eliminated."[12]

EDUCATIONAL ACTIVITIES

Science has flourished in proportion to the co-operative efforts of scientists. It knows no national boundaries, and health promo-

[12] V. Heiser, *Millions of Patients* (League of Nations Association, Chicago, 1937), p. 14.

tion and disease prevention depend largely upon effective interchange of the results of research. The Health Committee, quick to appreciate this truth, first published monographs dealing with public health organization and activity in European countries. The publications developed into the *International Health Yearbook,* which contains information on statistics, legislation, administrative regulations, and the general health policy of various countries. Special studies dealing with particular disease have been printed and, as Heiser suggests, the League of Nations' library is becoming a great international storehouse of useful scientific information, accessible to all who may be interested, regardless of nationality or race.

The Health Organization has done more; it has supplemented statistical and academic research with collective study tours during which health officials meet their co-workers from other countries. Collective interchange began in 1922; and again the Rockefeller Foundation showed its wise generosity by subsidizing the project. Up to 1930, 600 officials had participated in these interchanges. In addition, many independent tours were organized which resulted in strengthening the "scientific ties between Europe and the distant countries like Japan, India, and South America." The Health Committee also appointed a commission to collect information on courses in public health given in various countries, and about ten years ago began sessions which were really conferences between directors of schools of public health. It can be appreciated that the dissemination of information and the interchange of officers have helped to raise the prestige of the local services and to induce governments to improve their own public health work.

BIOLOGICAL STANDARDIZATION

The use of sera against disease[13] has greatly increased throughout the world; it is therefore important to have international agreement on "methods for measuring the anti-toxic strength of such sera." Heiser points out that during the World War of 1914–1918 English and American doctors in France often had to use French anti-tetanus serum which differed widely from their own

[13] The September 1935 issue of the *Quarterly Bulletin* of the League of Nations Health Organization contains a lengthy article written by Dr. R. Gautier, then secretary of the Permanent Commission on Biological Standardization; from it much of the following material is drawn.

products. "Counting the German unit as one, it required sixty-seven units of American, or 2,500 units of French serum to equal it." Sometimes doctors injected quantities of serum which they believed adequate but which were in fact insufficient, "since the assay had been effected in terms of a unit of lesser potency than that to which they were accustomed." Gautier asserts that many deaths might have been averted if the sera then used had been assayed in relation to a single standard. The League Health Committee, in 1921, decided to undertake the study of biological standardization. Between then and 1935, no fewer than ten international standardization conferences were held, and in 1924 a Permanent Commission on Biological Standardization was established.

The Commission, if it believes that conditions are ready for the standardization of a serum, requests some national or private laboratories of outstanding reputation to conduct a preliminary investigation. The results are co-ordinated at the Copenhagen Institute in Denmark or the Hampstead Institute in England.[14] The experimenters meet in conference, adjust their findings, and the Commission makes its recommendations. The technical problems involved, and the extraordinary amount of scientific knowledge which is thus brought together, lie far beyond the province of this work. It is impossible, however, even for one with no knowledge of medicine to read through the *Quarterly Bulletin* of the Health Organization without being deeply impressed by the remarkable results of international co-operation in this branch of science. Outstanding authorities known to medical circles the world over have together been able to render an immeasurable service to mankind. So great and so rapid have been the achievements that Dr. Gautier suggests that many medical authorities are unaware of the progress that has been made.

The International Conference on Biological Standardization, which met at Geneva, October 1–4, 1935, to review the results obtained and discuss steps which might be taken to insure the wider utilization of the standard units recommended by the Permanent Commission on Biological Standardization, set up two technical committees to consider (*a*) the standards adopted for sera and bacterial products, and (*b*) the standards for certain therapeutic substances, vitamins, and hormones. Finally it adopted the following recommendations:

[14] This work has now been interrupted by the war.

(1) . . . . that the use of international standards adopted by the Permanent Commission of Biological Standardization of the Health Organization will be made effective by the competent authorities of all countries. (2) . . . . that the League of Nations should place the necessary funds at the disposal of the Health Organization for it to continue to meet the expense entailed by the free distribution of such standards. (3) That each country should have a national centre or centres, recognized by the competent authority, to take charge of the international standards and equivalent national standards ; (4) . . . . Having been informed that patents protecting the preparation of streptococcus antitoxin [anti-scarletina serum] and of the toxin used for its assay have been granted in certain countries ; believing that this practice constitutes an obstacle to progress in the standardization of this serum ; Draws the attention of the Health Committee of the League of Nations to this state of affairs, and suggests that the Committee might usefully consider what means could be employed to avoid the serious drawbacks which ensue. (5) . . . . that, in view of the progress achieved in the field of biological standardization, intergovernmental conferences on this subject be summoned periodically at intervals not exceeding three years.

The National Institute for Medical Research at Hampstead, London, acts on behalf of the Health Organization in distributing international standards for various products and in maintaining a Biological ·Standards Department which sends free samples of international standards to any public health service or scientific institute which makes application.

Dr. Madsen, President of the Permanent Commission of the League of Biological Standardization, writes :

. . . l'œuvre de standardisation est une des fonctions permanentes de la Société des Nations. Tandis que d'autres tâches que l'Organisation d'hygiène de la Société des Nations a assumées peuvent être plus ou moins occasionnelles. . . , ce travail de standardisation revêt un caractère différent : celui d'un centre international et d'autorité internationale.[15]

NUTRITION

In recent years medical discoveries have revealed the great importance of diet in promoting and maintaining health. Carbohydrates, proteins, minerals, and vitamins are essential to normal physical well-being. Foods are classified as energy-producing and

[15] *Le Nord*, II (1939), 193.

protective. The latter contain much protein, minerals, and vitamins, without which people suffer from scurvy, beriberi, pellagra,
and similar diseases. Recent investigations have shown that different groups of people require different types of diet, and careful
calculations have been made in order to ascertain the needs of
children, mothers, men in heavy and light industry, and other
special groups.

From the point of view of adequate nutrition, most countries
have a poor record. In Great Britain one-half the people, and
in the United States almost 75 per cent of the city population, are
below the minimum standard of health and fitness. Almost everyone in China and India is undernourished, and it is probable that
Central and Southeastern Europe suffer heavily from malnutrition.

The causes of this unfortunate condition have been traced to
bad food habits and economic conditions. Political rivalry and
the growth of armaments have recently deflected expenditure from
protective and energy foods to fighting materials. "Guns for
butter" is a bad dietary program. Lack of purchasing power,
due to economic maladjustment, and the commercial policies
adopted by national governments during the last twenty years
have operated to accentuate the difficulty. Under the influence of
economic nationalism, tariff barriers have mounted. Many nations have turned to the production of wheat and other energy-
producing foods at the expense of the protective foods; they have
sacrificed their dietary needs, with the result that their standard
of health is falling. Further, agricultural conservatism and ignorance of physiology and dietetics have caused farmers in many
places to cling to old methods and to traditional crops. Even if
they wished to adopt new agricultural habits, the people of Central and Eastern Europe and in Asia lack necessary capital and
credit and suffer from difficulties of marketing their products.
They do not possess adequate refrigeration facilities; and their
cost of getting products from producer to consumer is too high.

The economic policies of many governments have increased
the evil for another reason. Because the so-called energy foods,
such as bread, possess relatively little elasticity of demand, the
rise and fall in their price has no appreciable effect upon the demand for them. The demand for protective foods, on the other
hand, is very elastic. People buy less milk, butter, and citrus fruits
when prices rise. Consequently, any tariff measure which increases the price of bread does not lower the consumption of that

article to any great degree but does reduce the amount of purchasing power available for the protective foods; the dietary condition of the population therefore suffers.

These considerations suggest why the League Health Organization has conducted investigations into the question of nutrition and standards of living.[16] Most people readily appreciate the importance of economic forces in international affairs; they may not see that a movement to improve nutrition carries economic analysis one step farther, to the point of inquiring what is the ultimate purpose of economic activity. For what end does mankind produce unless, as John Ruskin eloquently asserted many years ago, it is to produce better men and women and not merely to produce "an endless series of inanimate objects"?

Two members of the Health Section of the League, Drs. Burnet and Aykroid, published a report, "Nutrition and Public Health," in the *Health Quarterly,* in 1935. In the same year delegates from Australia and New Zealand to the International Labor Conference proposed that an inquiry be made into the nutrition of workers. This inquiry the Labor Office undertook, and published in 1936 *Workers' Nutrition and Social Policy.* In 1935 the League Assembly urged a more active policy, and the Health Committee thereupon appointed a technical commission of authorities on physiology and biochemistry, which later issued a report, *The Physiological Bases of Nutrition.*

An adequate standard of nutrition depends upon a sufficiency of both protective and energy foods, but this in turn depends upon the agricultural system. The League Council therefore set up a mixed committee comprising experts in medical science, economics, agriculture, and public welfare, which issued five reports dealing with the problem of nutrition and the physiological bases of nutrition, the standard of nutrition in various countries, the statistics of food production, consumption, and prices, and the relation of nutrition to agricultural and economic policy. Because the problem is related to that of rural hygiene, the League sponsored a European conference on rural life to be held in 1939.[17]

We describe elsewhere[18] how in the government of dependencies the dietary needs of native people have become an important

[16] See F. L. McDougall, *Food and Welfare* (Geneva Studies, Geneva Research Centre), Vol. IX, No. 5, November 1938.

[17] Canceled on account of the war.

[18] See chapter xi, below.

question. The *International Labor Review* of September 1936 contains an article, "Workers' Nutrition in Africa," which outlines the factors involved in providing adequate diet facilities for dependent peoples whose civilization is being profoundly modified by contact with the Western World.

Sufficient time has not yet elapsed for international co-operation to do more than initiate measures which are designed to improve the diet of the peoples of all nations. Obviously, while governments spend so much on armaments, the physical well-being of individuals must suffer; consequently a fundamental requirement for better health is the establishment of political institutions fitted to modern world needs. Even if this problem were settled, there would remain many difficult questions—the provision of adequate capital and credit for agricultural producers, more efficient marketing schemes on a continental scale, the eradication of antiquated methods of farming, the promotion of rural life in its wider aspects, the encouragement of co-operative movements, and the breaking down of tariff barriers, quotas, and other restrictive schemes. These measures all require international effort. Even if they in turn were adopted, the educational task of awakening the millions of people of all lands to a consciousness of the importance of diet and of its place in the promotion of human welfare would tax the abilities of leaders. But if nations would consider life in terms of national and international health instead of national power, if they would think less in terms of politics and more in terms of welfare, the whole emphasis of international politics might be changed. Instead of forcing industrial and agricultural policies to fit the requirements of military security and making each country, in a futile attempt to become self-sufficient, sacrifice its protective foods with disastrous consequences to health, the world would so organize itself that (1) the industrial areas would concentrate upon the production of industrial goods for which they are best fitted, (2) the New World with its great spaces and opportunities for large-scale agriculture would specialize in wheat and other energy-producing foods, and (3) the small countries of Europe would devote more attention to market-garden products which could be sent to the neighboring industrial countries in return for industrial or grain products. In such a vast multilateral system of international trade, a consideration of the dietary needs of the modern world would carry still farther the ideal of production by countries according to the economic law of comparative advantage.

HOUSING

The problem of housing provides a meeting ground for the economist and the public health official. The building trade is among the most important in a country's economy, in that its prosperity promotes the prosperity of many other industries—electric light, gas, lumber, painting, water supply, etc. Experience has so clearly demonstrated the economic role of housing that no further comment is necessary here. Nor need we do more than state in general terms the vital importance of housing to national health. Dr. O. E. W. Olsen, upon whose study, *Post-War Housing Problems*,[19] the following section is largely based, points out that adequate housing demands sufficient protection of people against heat and cold (a matter upon which considerable research has been conducted in recent years), sufficient air space, sunshine, and light, community recreational areas, protection against noise, the abatement of air pollution, and satisfactory disposal of sewage and refuse. Further, wise policy will make provision for public loans and subsidies, differential rents, and slum clearance so as to overcome present evils and implement a comprehensive welfare program for the future.

In what way does international co-operation come into the picture? We might assume at first sight that, inasmuch as houses constitute immovable property, little or nothing can be done by the League of Nations or any other international authority to promote improved housing conditions. Such a view would be mistaken; for one of the most important elements in any policy is the collection of evidence and the utilization of the experience gained by the people of other countries. It was because of this and because the housing question so intimately affects the position of workers that the International Labor Office in 1922 began an investigation of governmental policies relating to workers' houses and later published three studies: *The Housing Problem in Europe since the War* (1924), *The Housing Problem in the United States of America* (1925), and *The Housing Policy in Europe; Cheap Home Building* (1930). It conducted inquiries into rent paid by workers, and brought together a vast mass of statistics dealing with housing matters. It gave considerable attention to the question of public works as a factor in mitigating economic depressions and advocated an energetic housing policy toward this end;

---

[19] O. E. W. Olsen, *Post-War Housing Problems* (Geneva Studies. Geneva Research Centre), Vol. XI, No. 6, October 1940.

and it made surveys of the lodging and sleeping accommodations of agricultural workers. The Economic and Financial Organization of the League undertook studies of the financial aspects of housing. M. Helger, of Sweden, carried out an inquiry into the housing policies of ten countries—Belgium, Great Britain, Denmark, Finland, France, the Netherlands, Norway, Sweden, the United States, and Canada—and endeavored "on the basis of a comparison of national expenditures, to derive general principles for application according to different national and local conditions."[20] The special committee of statistical experts then communicated its conclusions to the national governments.

Meanwhile the Health Organization of the League was doing valuable work. In addition to its technical inquiries, it associated itself with the European Conference on Rural Hygiene held in 1931, with similar conferences in Africa and the Far East, and with the important Housing Exhibition at the International Paris Exhibition in 1937. It established a special Housing Commission in 1935 which began planning types of houses based upon the necessary hygienic conditions of light, sunshine, population density, air sufficiency, water supply, and general community planning. It is difficult to convey an adequate sense of the importance of these meetings of the Housing Commission because so little of the dramatic and sensational can be reported. However, those with even the minimum of appreciation of public health policy will see the significance of this work. In 1937 the Commission planned a three-year program, which, unfortunately, has been interrupted by the war now going on. Its activities were enjoying the co-operation of national committees in Great Britain, Czechoslovakia, France, Mexico, the Netherlands, Poland, and the United States. Although no regular channels of co-operation have as yet been established, methods of co-ordination will at length undoubtedly be facilitated by the existence of these national committees.

It is not too much to believe that international co-operation in housing may play a great role at the conclusion of the present conflict. As a result of bombing from the air and other military activities, many cities will have been partially, and perhaps largely, destroyed. Consequently Europe will require the services of its best town-planning and architectural experts and its economists and financial organizations, if it is to rebuild the most suitable

[20] O. E. W. Olsen, *op. cit.*, p. 49.

houses in the most desirable surroundings at the cheapest possible cost for the greatest number of people. Whether Europe soon adopts a federal union or not, considerable scope will be left for international co-operation, in large-scale production, fabricated houses, sound financing, and modern town planning.

Fortunately, the tradition of co-operation in these matters has not been confined to the League of Nations. Between July 27 and August 1, 1914, the first International Congress of Towns was held at Ghent; and, if the first World War had not intervened, the International Union of Local Authorities would have been set up shortly afterward. As it was, the International Congresses were not resumed until 1924. Since then six conferences have been held, and the International Union has published several volumes dealing with matters of local government. In June 1935 the first issue of its *International Quarterly Review, "Local Government Administration,"* appeared. Increasingly the Union has become a central clearinghouse of information upon many questions, not a few of which deal with public health and housing. A glance at the *International Quarterly Review* will show that articles have appeared and conferences have been held dealing with such subjects as town planning for both cities and rural areas, municipal swimming baths, surfaces of school playgrounds, methods of street lighting, central heating for city buildings, playgrounds, and recreational parks, control of smoke and dust, the planning of slaughterhouses and sewage disposal for small and large communities, the treatment of trade-waste waters and the prevention of river pollution, the planning and control of camping as a means of promoting and insuring public health, and many other matters relating to general welfare.

The existence of vigorous local governments and their organization into an International Union for purposes of exchanging information and arranging conferences should facilitate the co-operation of national governments, for local authorities may continue to act as valuable sources of local information and supply the local initiative which is so important if centralization of decision is not to produce bureaucratic domination. Close consultation between local and national authorities should continue, and the international affiliations of local bodies and professional associations should be encouraged. In this way vocational education and rich local community life can make possible a large degree of creativeness and local freedom which must form the more intimate bases of a widespread international co-operation.

TOWARD INTERNATIONAL HEALTH
CO-OPERATION

The League and national health authorities.—National governments have requested the Health Organization to send experts to help them in problems of a specialized character. In 1928 Greece wished to reorganize its sanitary services. The League's Health Committee toured the country and drew up a report which recommended unification of public health services, the establishment of a central sanitary administration and a school of hygiene, and the development of certain technical services. Following these recommendations the Greek government drew up new legislation, and several of its public health officials received assistance from the Health Organization to study abroad.

The League has done much to assist China in building up its public health organization. In 1929 the national government requested the medical director of the League Health Organization to become a member of its advisory council. A few months later it asked that a commission of experts survey the conditions of Chinese port, health, and maritime quarantine. In 1930 the experts presented a series of recommendations, including the organization of a central health station which should become the nucleus of a national health service, the establishment of a national institute of medical training for undergraduates and postgraduates, special measures to deal with the problems of smallpox and cholera in Shanghai, and methods of improving port health administration.

Although civil war and Japanese aggression have interposed many obstacles, the Chinese government has been able to take important steps. It set up a provisional central health station which for two years worked in temporary premises and then moved into a new modern building. The station began a course of training for sanitary inspectors and hospital internes, and some postgraduate courses for doctors. Its malariology section organized study centers for malaria in the Yangtze valley; and the field station, fearing that the vast road-construction program would facilitate the spread of malaria into other areas, took various preventive measures. The station distributes sera of international standards and vitamin and medicinal substances to substations. Provincial authorities, realizing its great value, are increasingly requesting the central health station for advice and for health programs. The national quarantine service has made excellent progress, and health supervision of Chinese rivers and maritime ports has "already inspired with confidence the officers of vessels of many countries entering Chinese waters." The three sections of Shanghai—Greater Shanghai, the French Concession, and the International Concession—although independent, have co-operated closely in health matters.[21]

The League Health Organization has rendered special service to Latin America, in many parts of which health conditions are extremely bad. In 1927 the League sponsored a conference of South American experts on child welfare at Montevideo, and arranged for investigations in Argentina, Brazil, and Uruguay. It suggested that an international school for infant and child welfare be established at Buenos Aires, and an international school of public health at Rio de Janeiro (which later added leprosy to its work). In August 1929, in response to a request from Bolivia, the Health Organization sent two experts to help the government in reorganizing its health service. In March 1932 Chile asked the League for assistance in its technical organization, particularly to study nutrition.

After the 1931 International Conference on Rural Hygiene, Czechoslovakia requested the League Health Organization to co-operate with it by placing a member of the Health Section at the disposal of its own Institute of Hygiene for two years, so as to enable special commissions to work with the Czechoslovakian Ministry of Health and to arrange for health experts to visit Slovakia where rural health conditions were especially poor. The health survey undertaken by various authorities resulted in three public health reforms. Outstanding foreign medical authorities, including Dr. Stampar, ex-director of the Public Health Service in Jugoslavia, co-operated with the government, and the League Health Organization granted scholarships to several Czechoslovakian officials.

In February 1932 South Africa requested the League Committee to call a regional health conference to discuss health problems confronting Africa. The most serious diseases in that continent are yellow fever and sleeping sickness. The automobile, the railroad, and the airplane have rendered liable to infection many regions of Central, East, and South Africa which until now have been free from these diseases. Yellow fever is disseminated from human cases in the first three days of the attack; the incubation period does not go beyond six days, and the mosquito

---

[21] The present Sino-Japanese hostilities have of course affected this policy.

which carries the disease is a domestic variety which remains in or near the house where it has fed. After twelve days it can transmit the virus to another person. The conference so arranged discussed methods of preventing the spread of yellow fever, and to that end suggested setting up laboratories at places where immunization tests and vaccination could be carried out; it emphasized the need for pipe-drawn water supplies and other local measures, and commended the International Sanitary Convention for Aerial Navigation of 1932, the acceptance of which "would form an invaluable safeguard against the spread of yellow fever to other countries when air trunk routes were established."

The regional conference also considered the fact that plague was spreading with alarming rapidity in South Africa; the spread was due not to infection through ports but to the action of wild rodents inland. The rodents infected domestic species of mice, which transmitted the disease to man. Governments to the north of South Africa feared the spread of the disease and recognized the need of co-operation to meet the menace. Smallpox next received attention. The medical authorities realized the disadvantages resulting from the different requirements of the East and South African government in the vaccination of immigrants from India, and after long discussion they agreed on a procedure which would provide adequate protection. Rural hygiene found a place on the agenda, and recommendations were made. The delegates realized the value of interchange of views, and suggested that the League Health Organization consult the governments in Africa with a view to calling further conferences.

The foregoing survey indicates the importance of the League of Nations and of intergovernmental co-operation in health matters; but the record would be incomplete without reference to the remarkable services rendered by nonofficial organizations such as the International Red Cross, medical schools and research foundations, and welfare and charitable societies. International progress depends upon the ability, the disinterestedness, and the vision of nongovernmental agencies as well as upon the efficiency of governments. Frequently the great stimulus for social advance has come from a private group or organization, and only after long effort has its work been taken over by or co-ordinated with governmental institutions. This truth is well illustrated by the work of the Rockefeller Foundation, which has rendered invaluable service to the health of the world. It has truly been an international institution ministering, in the words of its motto, to "the wellbeing of mankind throughout the world." In this respect, it is typical of many other organizations whose work cannot be summarized here.

The Rockefeller Foundation.—In 1909 Mr. John D. Rockefeller established a commission[22] for the purpose of controlling hookworm disease. In 1913 the Foundation was enlarged and received a new endowment of one hundred million dollars. Soon afterward its Sanitary Commission was reorganized as the International Health Board, and a subsidiary, the China Medical Board, was set up five years later. The trustees also established a division of medical education to aid medical schools throughout the world.

The outbreak of the war of 1914–1918 interrupted the major objectives, and for some time the Foundation had to devote itself to emergency war work. It gave financial assistance to the American Red Cross, administered anti-tuberculosis campaigns in France, provided funds for military hospitals, supported the Carrel-Dakin method of sterilizing wounds (a treatment which healed injured tissues much more rapidly than previous methods), and prepared and distributed sera to government hospitals.

Important as its war work was, the major contributions of the Foundation were made in the postwar period. In 1913–1914 the officials outlined the scope of its work: (a) to assist in the relief and control of hookworm disease and other controllable diseases; (b) to aid in following up such treatment and to cure controllable diseases by promoting the establishment and development of agencies to promote sanitation and public health; and (c) to spread knowledge of scientific medicine. It proposed to carry out its program by inviting the co-operation of governmental and other agencies, as far as possible working through existing public health agencies so as to avoid duplication, grafting new agencies wherever possible upon existing agencies, and undertaking work on the assumption that governments would ultimately take over the burden of responsibility; the Foundation would limit itself to setting forces in motion and leave the permanent work in the hands of the governments concerned.

When Mr. Rockefeller died in 1937 his gifts to mankind had totaled 530 million dollars; 446 million went to four funds, of which the medical research was one. In 1938 the Foundation medical staff comprised 60 doctors, 5 sanitary engineers, 2 public health nurses, 2 entomologists, a biochemist, a psychiatrist, and

---

[22] The material in this section is adapted from the *Annual Review* published by the Foundation.

a zoölogist—72 people in all. Of these officials 29 were in the
United States, Canada, and Mexico, 16 in Europe, 12 in South
America, and the rest in other parts of the world. A director-
general and twenty-one departmental directors formulate policy.

The Foundation realized that medicine was an international
agency—that no one country had produced the great surgeons,
doctors, and medical scientists throughout the centuries. It saw
the importance of maintaining communication of ideas between
medical specialists, and attempted to meet the serious interruption caused by the World War by distributing medical periodicals
in Europe and sending aid to European medical scientists who
were deprived of journals and reviews in the tragic postwar years.
Library funds were provided, journals were supplied, and emergency laboratory aid was given to medical schools at Vienna,
Gratz, Budapest, and other places. The Foundation took steps
to minimize the losses sustained through the interruption of training of medical men during the War, and provided fellowships for
foreign study.

Impressed with the need of developing more uniform standards of medicine throughout the world, it encouraged international
co-operation among medical schools and gave generously to them
in all countries. It emphasized the need of training public health
officers. Its grants helped to establish in 1921 the London School
of Hygiene, an institution which by reason of its important position wields a great influence within and beyond the British Empire.
It has maintained a world-wide research staff which has investigated diseases in all countries and has assisted governments to
assume responsibility for controlling various diseases, stating that
otherwise its own work would at best "be palliative, ephemeral,
and in the end futile." It has co-operated with nongovernmental
agencies in the five continents in an endeavor to realize the ideal
enunciated by Dr. Wickliffe Rose, a generation ago, that "unless
public health is conceived in international terms, the strategic opportunity of our generation will be lost."

The Foundation attacked hookworm by encouraging research
and by making communities "public-health-conscious." It spent
millions of dollars in fighting yellow fever. The heroic conduct of
great scientists like Noguchi, Stokes, and Young, who laid down
their lives in the cause of science, provides a thrilling chapter in
medical history. The Foundation believed that victory had been
won; but the jungle "struck back in the late twenties, and a new
and more deadly type of yellow fever appeared as a threat to the

world." The Foundation established laboratories in Bahia, Rio de Janeiro, New York, and Lagos, which made remarkable experiments and did extraordinary preventive work. It fought influenza, scarlet fever (one report makes special reference to Rumania), yaws, rabies, diphtheria, cancer, and especially malaria; gave assistance to institutions in the United States, Central America, Europe, South America, Asia, Puerto Rico, Jamaica, and the Philippines; and granted aid to the malaria experiment station in Rome with its branches all over Italy. In 1936 it ended seven years' work in Greece and planned to adopt the same policy in other countries.

In the field of public health the Foundation has studied specific diseases, given fellowships for the training of public health doctors, established training centers, carried out demonstrations to ascertain the best methods to be followed by governments, and undertaken intensive research in a limited number of fields by public health laboratories. It has supported public health nursing, given financial assistance for the establishment of health centers, buildings, equipment, maintenance, and personnel of nursing schools, aided nursing schools in Prague, East Holland, Brussels, and many other places, encouraged public health centers to improve village life (for instance, in Jugoslavia), and supported a state hygienic institute in Budapest and a co-operative health center in Athens.

All public health depends upon the progress of medicine. The Foundation has been active in assisting medical schools throughout the world, and has given special attention to psychiatry. The 1934 annual report lists such activities as: granting money to universities and other institutions for research and teaching in psychiatry and associated subjects; granting money for individual research in mind diseases; giving fellowships for advanced training; support for the study of neurology and related subjects (including the growing and regeneration of the peripheral nerves and virus diseases of the nerve system); a grant to the Lister Institute of Medicine in London for an instrument with which to study the biophysical aspects of body fluids; and a grant to the State Institute of Public Health in Stockholm for biochemical research.

Mental behavior is closely associated with physiological conditions, and the Foundation has made grants for the study of biochemistry, the biology of sex, embryology, general physiology, genetics, internal secretions, and nutrition, to many institutions throughout the world. Space does not permit discussion of the wider fields of the Foundation's work in social science and the humanities which are related to the major problem of health here discussed.

In 1937 the president of the Foundation, Raymond B. Fosdick, told the following story:

Some twenty years ago in a Central American city a revolution developed while the Foundation was engaged in a study of yellow fever control measures. Dr. Emmett Vaughn, who was in charge of the work, determined to continue his research. Every morning with a flag of truce he crawled through the barricades to collect mosquitoes on one side of the fighting line, and in the afternoon he crawled back again to gather up his specimens on the other side. He was molested by neither army. Both sides thought him somewhat crazy—a man who, when great issues of human destiny were being fought out, spent his time catching mosquitoes. Today in that Central American country the revolution has been largely forgotten, but Dr. Vaughn is remembered as the man who helped to stamp out an age-long pestilence.

This incident not only illustrates the close connection between international health and international relations but also shows how unsound is the habit of drawing too hard and fast a line between national and international affairs. Certain important phases of human life apply to all nations, and their effective regulation requires an appreciation of the scope of the problem and also the need of institutions adequate to cope with it—institutions which can facilitate co-operation of governments, specialists, and other interested parties and which can speak and act with authority. History strengthens the belief that persons with ability and enthusiasm can set in motion forces which will ultimately influence the widest policies of governments and international organizations.

Nor should one fail to draw attention to the splendid work of the National Public Health Services of many of the governments of the world.[23] An appreciation of what is done by them is necessary in order to obtain a full view of the many-sided political aspects of the problem of health and the prevention of disease. All units of government—local, county, state, national, and international—doctors, Red Cross societies, the Universities, the great Foundations and other organizations too numerous to mention

[23] See *Fortune,* May 1941, for a description of the United States Public Health Service.

here[24]—can co-operate in building a highly integrated and healthy world, combining co-operation in the larger aspects of research and administration with national and local initiative in spheres in which such initiative can best function.[25]

Prevention of plant and animal diseases.—Disease attacks not merely human beings but also animals and plants upon which human welfare so largely depends, and nations have therefore recognized the advantage of co-operation in the realm of entomology and mycology.

Within the British Empire a substantial amount of joint action has been undertaken by the British and the Dominion governments. Two examples may be given.

The Imperial Bureau of Entomology was reorganized in 1913 to encourage and co-ordinate throughout the Empire work on human and animal diseases. To its upkeep the Imperial Government, the governments of the self-governing Dominions, India, the Colonies and other Dependencies, the Sudan, and the North Borneo Company contribute. The Bureau publishes a monthly and a quarterly review, identifies insects for official entomologists all over the Empire, and has set up a laboratory for the purpose of breeding beneficial parasites for export to the overseas Empire.

The Imperial Bureau of Mycology, founded in 1920, encourages and co-ordinates Empire research concerning plant diseases. It is supported by Great Britain, the Dominions, India, the Sudan, and the non-self-governing colonies and Protectorates. Its functions are similar to those of the Bureau of Entomology, "distributing information in all matters connected with plant diseases, and undertaking the identification of specimens." That the battle is by no means a light one is evident from the fact that something like ten per cent of the world's crops are destroyed every year by insects.

[24] The work of the Rockefeller Foundation is typical of the work done by many other splendid organizations. It is to be hoped that one of these institutions will publish a volume which will give a vivid yet accurate account of health as an international problem. Such a volume written by medical experts in co-operation with authorities or governments would prove of great value not only to the general public but also to those who are concerned with the changing relations between governments and professional, social, and economic associations.

[25] To take but one example: The Commonwealth Fund in New York has published a series of volumes—*Mosquito Control, Public Health Law, Ways to Community Health Education, Recording of Local Health Work, Community Health Organization, Rural Health Practice*—which should prove valuable to health officials all over the world.

It was inevitable that wider international measures would be necessary for effective action. As early as 1878 a convention was signed at Berne concerning measures to be taken against the plant lice, *Phylloxera vastatrix*. Modifications were made in 1881 and 1889. In 1929 a convention for the protection of plants was signed at Rome and came into force in January 1932. The signatory powers, "having recognized the usefulness of international regulation and co-operation in the control of plant diseases and pests, and of closer collaboration to this end," undertook to supervise areas within their jurisdiction which supplied plants, to report the appearance of plant diseases in those areas, to take measures to prevent such diseases and pests, and to regulate all transport and packing of plants and plant parts. They each agreed to establish an official organization for plant protection with scientific, technical, and applied research branches and with a service responsible for inspection of areas and consignments of plants. They undertook to issue health certificates (which would conform to a model certificate annexed to the convention), to accompany exported plants. The contracting parties were requested to supply the International Institute of Agriculture at Rome[26] with a list of the plant diseases and pests against which they particularly desired to protect themselves.

After considerable preparatory work by the Institute of Agriculture at Rome a convention on the organization of the fight against locusts was signed at Rome in October 1920 and came into effect April 3, 1922. The contracting parties undertook to adopt necessary measures to prevent by the most rapid means the movement of locusts across national borders and especially to conclude particular agreements with neighboring countries to facilitate common measures. They agreed to furnish to the Institute at Rome at least once a year, and more often if necessary, all information of technical, scientific, legislative, and administrative character in order that the Institute might give it the widest publicity. In 1926 the governments of Palestine, Transjordania, Iraq, Turkey, and Syria, "having considered it advantageous to institute an International Bureau of Intelligence on Locusts," agreed to main-

[26] This institute was established by the International Convention of June 7, 1905, for the purpose of collecting statistical, technical, and economic information concerning agriculture, "to record any new diseases of crops which may have appeared in any part of the world, showing the countries affected by such diseases, their progress and, where possible, any effective measures for their control," and to study questions concerning agricultural co-operation and insurance and many other matters.

tain, at common expense and on equal shares, an office at Damascus. The agreement was to last for three years, and would be renewed automatically for an equal period, unless notification to the contrary was delivered at least one year in advance. The organic statute of the International Bureau of Intelligence on Locusts went into effect at the same time. Under Article 4 the main objects of the Bureau were to receive and register information received concerning the area and locality of breeding grounds, the known or probable movements of locusts, and the methods of controlling and combating them, to furnish any information of a special nature which might be called for, and to try to obtain exemption from post and telegraphic charges for communications so made. The Bureau was to be placed under the authority of an international committee of technical representatives, one for each state.

In 1935 a number of governments signed an international convention[27] concerning the transit of animals, meats, and other products of animal origin, in order to establish a fair balance between the health interests of transit countries and the legitimate interests of international trade. They recognized the need of affording the transit the fullest measure of freedom consistent with the requirements of veterinary health inspections and of public health. The parties agree that the existence of cattle plague justifies absolute refusal of transit, and that swine fever, foot-and-mouth disease, sheep pox, or contagious peri-pneumonia will justify refusal of transit. Certificates of origin and health drawn up in accordance with principles issued by the International Office for Contagious Diseases of Animals will be sufficient to permit transit of animals. Signatories agree that twenty-four hours' notice should be given to competent veterinary authorities for frontier inspection, except where there is a permanent inspection service. The contracting parties agree to take all measures necessary to prevent overloading, and, if diseases are found, the transit countries may at the forwarder's expense slaughter the infected assignments.

The convention is to last for two years and for subsequent periods of four years, unless denounced at least six months before the expiration of the period. It came into force December 6, 1938.

An international convention[28] concerning the export and im-

[27] *League of Nations Treaty Series,* 1938–39, Vol. 193, No. 4486, p. 37.
[28] *Ibid.,* No. 4487, p. 59.

port of animal products (other than meat preparations, fresh animal, milk and milk products) which had been signed in 1935 also came into force at the same time.

Within the last few years the locust menace in Africa has reached alarming proportions. In 1928 the so-called desert locust swarmed over Kenya; within three years East Africa suffered from a devastating invasion of the tropical migratory locust, until by 1932 all this region was overrun. In 1930 the red locust appeared in Northern Rhodesia and soon spread over the area to the south and east, reaching the Union of South Africa. An official report describes the great losses sustained by the territories and emphasizes that international measures alone can suffice to overcome the evil. Since 1931 the Imperial Institute of Entomology has been acting as a center for anti-locust research, and periodic international conferences, notably those at Rome (1931), Paris (1932), and London (1934), have brought together eminent specialists to discuss their results and plan further work. Representatives of thirteen countries have united to fight the locust, which has "proved to be notoriously disrespectful towards intercolonial and even international boundaries, and it follows that an efficient anti-locust policy should also be developed without any regard for such boundaries."[29]

The foregoing survey should make clear how intimately the problem of health has become, or should have become, a part of the problem of government; and one of the tragedies of the present time lies in the inadequate appreciation of the importance of technical questions in the field of political science. Indeed international co-operation for health, as well as national policies for the prevention of disease and the promotion of physical welfare, touch the very foundations of civilization. Haggard has well written that if we were deprived of the discoveries and inventions of the chemist, the physicist, and the engineer we would suffer considerable inconvenience, but if modern medical science were lost to us the great cities of the world would go back in civilization, not fifty but probably five hundred years. Pestilences and epidemics would reduce urban populations to a mere fraction of their present size. "Large sections of the world which are now prosperous would become uninhabitable." Forgotten diseases would return and communications would spread disease with rapidity. "It is no mere imagination, but the cold and literal

[29] Owen Clough (ed.), *Report on African Affairs for the Year 1933* (Billings and Sons, Ltd., Guildford and Esher), Vol. V, p. 38.

truth, to say that modern civilization and the use of the inventions and discoveries of physical science would be utterly impossible were it not for medical protection."[30]

But modern medicine depends upon education and the intelligent control of man's instincts and emotions. It is not too much to say that the political hatreds and prejudices that dominate the world today endanger the scientific spirit, and bid fair to check the growth of public health in many parts of the world. Not only the present war with its wholesale destruction but also the great and long-continued diversion of money to military defense threaten to starve the social services and to place public health in serious jeopardy. The world may well have to choose between indulging its political emotions and co-operating to promote the physical welfare of all.

[30] Haggard, *op. cit.*, p. 382.

Chapter II

THE INTERNATIONAL PREVENTION OF CRIME

WITH the growth of communications, the problem of preventing crime and of apprehending criminals is becoming increasingly an international one. If terrorists, murderers, slave raiders, forgers, traffickers in women and children, opium smugglers, and other lawbreakers escape across national boundaries and beyond the jurisdiction of a state to which they are subject, the ends of justice will be defeated unless the receiving country is willing to assist in bringing the offenders to trial.

In the sphere of law and order the question is not one of nationalism versus internationalism; it is a question of both national and international organization, a division of powers for the more efficient prevention of actions harmful to society. When criminals and lawbreakers build up international methods for antisocial ends, they must be met by equally wide but more effectively organized force. Otherwise an insistence upon a formal sovereignty may assist smugglers, terrorists, and others to weaken the foundations of law. Indeed, we shall see plentiful evidence of criminal activities being protected in the name of sovereignty and national interests.

PIRACY

Freedom of the seas would be a doubtful boon if robbery and disorder made it impossible for merchant ships to travel in safety. If nations renounced their sovereign claims to great oceanic areas and in so doing would no longer accept responsibility for keeping order in those parts, the last condition of affairs might be worse than the first. History has shown that piracy can make the position of merchant ships even more intolerable than discrimination under responsible national governments has done. International anarchy could inflict greater loss to maritime trade than a system of competing claims of oceanic jurisdiction.

Piracy and robbery are almost as old as history itself. In ancient times sea robbers attacked Phoenician and Greek merchants. Rome, for a while, was able to insure the safety of ships; but after the third century of the Christian era it was so occupied with guarding its land frontiers that the Mediterranean again lapsed into piracy. During the Middle Ages the evil flourished; in the Mediterranean and the Adriatic, and especially along the African and Spanish coasts, pirates pursued their ruthless trade. For almost a thousand years the western Mediterranean was dangerous to the shipping of the Christian states. In the northern seas of Europe pirates were equally active, and even the English Channel swarmed with them, a situation explainable in part by the fact that the line between the ordinary merchant and the pirate was frequently very narrow; many merchants turned to robbery, if they thought that by this means they could reap greater gain than by legitimate commerce.

After the discovery of the Americas, the expansion of trade, and the discovery of new and more valuable cargoes, such as spices, gold, and silver, piracy became even more attractive; and in the sixteenth, seventeenth, and eighteenth centuries it spread to the Caribbean area. English, Dutch, and French financiers who opposed the colonial exclusiveness of Spain in America helped to set up ships to plunder Spanish trading vessels; and in the eighteenth century, freebooting and privateering flourished in the Americas until competition became so intense that many of the pirates were driven out of business, changed their location, and moved to the Pacific.

The Barbary States in North Africa—Morocco, Algiers, Tunis, and Tripoli—were for a long period, and especially during the eighteenth century, the center of extensive piratical activities. The rulers and chieftains raided the islands and neighboring coasts, took hundreds and thousands of people captive, and held them for ransom; they confiscated vessels and cargoes; they forced their captives to do the most laborious tasks, deprived them of food, placed them in disease-ridden detention houses, and in other ways treated them with great cruelty. Not only did the governments obtain money by robbery, plunder, and kidnaping, but they blackmailed European governments and exacted great sums from them "for immunity from future attacks."[1] Espe-

---

[1] R. W. Irwin, *The Diplomatic Relations of the United States with the Barbary Powers* (The University of North Carolina Press, 1931), p. 11.

cially did the weaker governments have to pay heavily. Even the great powers—Britain, France, and Holland—paid tribute; and, soon after it gained its independence, the United States had to face the demands of the pirates. Curiously enough, the individual governments seemed content to acquiesce in the humiliations to which they were subjected, and for a long time made little or no attempt to take concerted action against the forces of lawlessness. In part, their attitude was due to a dog-in-the-manger policy. Some of them calculated that if they suppressed the tribute-exacting Barbary governments their commercial competitors might obtain the greater benefit from the resulting regime of peaceful maritime trade.

In 1786 the question was widely discussed in the United States. John Adams favored buying off the Barbary pirates, saying that it was worth while to pay two hundred thousand pounds in order to save one million dollars' worth of commerce and to avoid waging war for the purpose of enforcing the rights of Americans. Jefferson advocated a strong policy on grounds of justice and honor and the need of obtaining respect abroad, and insisted that forcible suppression of the piratical nuisance would in the long run be an economical measure. Benjamin Franklin hinted at the possibility of a European combination to abolish piracy; and in 1785 Jefferson proposed joint action by the United States and France upon Algiers, if the latter would not forego its exactions upon France.[2] Other public men favored international co-operation; and Jefferson drew up a series of "proposals for concerted action": (*a*) a confederacy to wage war against the pirate states should be formed; (*b*) its members should contribute to a naval force to operate along the African Coast; (*c*) the resulting fleet should be directed by a committee; and (*d*) the contracting parties should not permit even hostilities among themselves to interfere with their joint action against the Barbary States.

These proposals Jefferson submitted to a number of European governments. Several of the smaller ones were favorable, but the doubtful attitude of France and Britain and other factors caused the plan to be dropped. At the Conference of Aix-la-Chapelle in 1818 Great Britain proposed that measures be taken against the Barbary pirates. But it refused to agree to any Russian forces being stationed in the Mediterranean to form part of an international police; that is, considerations of national power out-

[2] R. W. Irwin, *op. cit.*, pp. 47–53.

weighed considerations of safety of commerce. W. Alison Phillips writes:

The Barbary pirates were the scourges of the whole continental sea-board; they held up trading vessels at the mouth of the Elbe, and in the Mediterranean no vessel was safe that did not sail under the British or the Ottoman flag; yet it was found impossible to concert measures against them because of British jealousy of Russian intervention in the Mediterranean.[3]

Thus international action accomplished little. National states had long taken action against piracy: England from the fourteenth century to 1536 tried piracy offenses in the admiralty courts, and after that date in the common law courts; she also passed many acts which defined and punished piracy (1536, 1670, 1698, 1721, 1744) as well as several against the slave trade in the nineteenth century. France made an anti-piracy ordinance in 1681 and another in 1718, issued a decree in 1798, and passed laws in 1803 and 1858. Spain published an ordinance in 1628; and an ordinance of the Spanish royal navy in 1748 declared that pirates should be punished with death as enemies of the human race. Argentina, Bolivia, Chile, Greece, Peru, and other governments likewise passed national laws against pirates in the nineteenth century.

It is often said that piracy is a crime against international law; but, as Bingham points out, it is not an easy matter to define piracy, which may not have the same meaning under the law of nations as it has under municipal law.[4] If one believes that international law is substantially the same as municipal law, except that it possesses no enforcing agencies, and that all persons are or should be "subject to one legal order," then piracy may be considered a crime "punishable wherever encountered." But if the law of nations is between states only and does apply directly to individuals, the answer will be different. In fact, several states do not have common law provisions for the prosecution of all pirates. No international agency exists to punish them, and in many states there are no laws enabling punishment of foreign pirates. In the strict sense, Bingham concludes, piracy is not an offense against the law of nations. What the phrase really means

[3] W. Alison Phillips, *The Confederation of Europe* (Longmans, Green & Co., London, 1914), p. 190.

[4] Joseph Walter Bingham, "Piracy," supplement to *The American Journal of International Law*, Vol. 26 (1932), pp. 755–65.

is that "a special common basis of jurisdiction beyond the similar grounds of personal allegiance, territorial domination, domination over ships, and injuries to interests under states protection" has been created. That is, piracy under international law is only a special ground of "state jurisdiction." States may or may not exercise their jurisdiction—the law of nations "is permissive only." "It justifies state action within limits and fixes those limits. It goes no further."

The decline of piracy has been due more to the general advance of international trade, the greater size of vessels, the more regular sailing schedules, the development of cables, and later radio, than to the effective national or concerted international action.

During the nineteenth century the American continent and the Caribbean had to deal with the problem of American filibusters, who for some years indulged in lawless expeditions against Nicaragua and Honduras. The filibusters used the United States as a base of operations, and the American government for some time took few or no preventive measures. The British authorities were deeply concerned because the adventurers threatened the Mosquito territory, caused much unrest in Central America, and thereby adversely affected the position of British subjects. Owing to the somewhat delicate diplomatic situation which prevailed between the United States and Great Britain, the latter did not raise the question "whether filibusters were pirates," and the law officers of the British government did not claim that British naval commanders had any "'right to interfere with them on the high seas."[5] Even when President Buchanan designated the filibusters as criminals under American law it did not follow that they were pirates or criminals—"enemies against humanity"—and therefore outside the protection of all law. Lord Palmerston recognized this fact, and wrote that the American President would probably strongly protest if Britain attempted to deal with the criminals as pirates— "he would probably turn upon us and say that we had no right to shoot American citizens, merely because we had declared that they had violated American laws or even international law. They were American citizens still, and answerable only to the government to which they owed allegiance, or to the government whose country they had invaded, but that we had no jurisdiction over them, and no right to put them to death."[6] In 1858 the British

---

[5] Richard W. Van Alstyne, "American Filibustering and the British Navy," *The American Journal of International Law,* January 1938, p. 141.   [6] *Ibid.*

government decided to take firmer action against filibusters, and notified the United States of its intention. Fortunately the situation cleared and Anglo-American diplomatic relations were not disturbed by further incidents. But just as pirates had profited because of the military and naval rivalries of nations, so filibustering for a time flourished because of the international complications arising out of power politics.

In 1922 the five naval powers—Great Britain, the United States, France, Italy, and Japan—drew up a treaty with the object of forbidding submarine attacks against merchant vessels; Article 3 provided that any person who should violate the rules set down, "whether or not such person is under orders of a governmental superior, shall be deemed to have violated the laws of War and shall be liable to trial and punishment as if for an act of piracy and may be brought to trial before the civil or military authorities of any power within the jurisdiction of which he may be found." The article attracted much attention but was not incorporated in either the 1922 or the later 1930 Naval Treaties. "The idea . . . . of incorporating into piracy *jure gentium* inhuman violations of the rules of warfare by naval commanders acting under the orders of their government was definitely abandoned."[7]

This situation prevailed until 1937, when the submarine attacks against merchant shipping during the Spanish Civil War caused nine states to meet at Nyon and sign an agreement which provided for special measures against the sinking of merchant ships by submarines "contrary to the most elementary dictates of humanity"; such actions "should justly be treated as acts of piracy." Submarines guilty of attacks might be counterattacked and, if possible, destroyed by the naval forces of the powers signatory to the agreement. Considerable discussion took place as to whether or not the Nyon Arrangements made these illegal attacks equivalent to piracy. The general view is that they did not do so, because, although attacks on merchant vessels were designated "piratical acts," the agreements made no provision for the trial and punishment of guilty individuals but authorized naval vessels to take preventive action of a deterrent nature. Norman Padelford notes that the Nyon Arrangements are rather to be regarded "as important experiments in, and contributions to, international cooperation and administration," and as significant attempts to bring

[7] "The Nyon Arrangements, Piracy by Treaty?" *The British Year Book of International Law,* 1938, p. 201.

some of the international aspects of civil war within the realm of international regulation and law.[8]

LIQUOR

Liquor has been a more serious international problem than one may have imagined, and like other social questions has proved to be too complex to be solved by national action alone. International co-operation was found necessary in Africa soon after the advent of modern colonization there.[9] The great powers, by the Brussels Act of 1890, attempted to control the liquor trade in Central Africa. Before this time slave traders had exchanged European spirits for Negro slaves. Although English feeling was already becoming aroused, the Berlin Conference of 1884 took no action, and only six years later were the first international steps taken.

The Brussels Act divided certain regions into prohibition and non-prohibition zones. In the former the powers prohibited liquor, except for strictly limited quantities for medicinal purposes and for use by white people. Each government was permitted to decide the boundaries of its prohibited zones, with the result that although France and Portugal failed to proclaim any, other governments extended prohibition over an area of 2,782,400 square miles. In the non-prohibition regions the governments promised to impose minimum duties of 13 cents per gallon for a period of three years, after which time each power might individually increase the amount of duty. But the Act failed to distinguish between higher-grade liquor and the "trade spirits" usually sold to natives, and as all the seaports in West Africa lay in the non-prohibition area (which amounted in all to 5,370,700 square miles) it was important to insure that the duties be high enough to prevent the importation of poor-grade liquor. Unfortunately, some of the powers, especially Holland and Germany, were interested in exporting large quantities of trade gin and rum, and even Britain supplied a diminishing amount. Experience soon showed that the duties were too low to prevent imports. Moreover, if one colonial government increased its duties, and its neighbor did not, the trade moved to the port where the duties were

[8] Norman J. Padelford, "Foreign Shipping during the Spanish Civil War," *American Journal of International Law*, XXXII (1938), 279.

[9] A. McPhee, *The Economic Revolution in British West Africa* (George Routledge & Sons, London, 1926), pp. 66–68, 92–93.

the lowest; from there the liquor could be smuggled across the land frontiers. Since there were several colonies on the west coast of Africa, any effective increase of duties required international agreement, and independent national action was not sufficient.

In 1899 another conference met at Brussels and agreed to increase minimum duties to 60 cents per gallon, an amount which the British government believed to be too low. The agreement lasted until the 1906 conference, called at the request of Great Britain, raised the duty to 86 cents per gallon. During this period, higher wages and economic progress had enabled the natives to increase their income and to pay the higher duties and liquor continued to flood the African colonies.

Another international conference met in 1912 to consider raising the duties and extending the area of prohibition zones. France, taking a negative position, refused to proclaim further prohibition zones, claimed that higher duties would merely encourage the production of domestic native alcohol, and argued that where the African people were Mohammedans the duties were unnecessary, since Mohammedanism forbade use of liquor. In consequence, Britain took individual action and increased its duties and added prohibition areas.

After the World War of 1914–1918 the powers made a renewed attack upon the problem. They signed a treaty far more comprehensive than the Brussels Act of 1890. Under the convention of St. Germaine-en-Laye, the governments (a) prohibited the importation and sale of trade spirits, for the first time distinguishing the cheaper liquor from the higher-grade article, (b) extended the area of control, (c) forbade the manufacture of distilled beverages by natives and whites in the area governed by the convention, (d) placed an import duty of $7.00 a gallon on pure alcohol, and (e) provided for a report from each government to a central international office under the control of the League of Nations.

The League of Nations established the Permanent Mandates Commission, which was to receive annual reports from mandatory powers, and, *inter alia,* to watch over the liquor problem in mandated territories. The Commission has tried (1) to equalize import duties by scaling them up to the highest level possible, (2) to obtain annual reports from mandatory authorities which can be used as a basis of comparison, (3) to frame a generally acceptable definition of "trade spirits," "spirituous liquors," and "spirits."

Since the Mandates Commission deals with only a part of the world's colonial territory, despite its activity and that of other agencies, serious difficulties remain. Among these difficulties may be listed the following:

1. The policy of high import duties and, in the case of France and British colonies, the introduction of the "negative principle of excluding all spirits except those specifically admitted," has not met with unqualified success. Some authorities claim that it has insured that present liquor imports are of better quality, that less has been consumed since than before the war, and that, at least, liquor can no longer be used in exchange for goods. Critics assert that more and not less liquor has been imported into the French colonies, Togoland, Dahomey, and the Ivory Coast, and into British Nigeria, Sierra Leone, and especially the Gold Coast.

2. The question is complicated by the fact that here, as well as elsewhere in tropical areas, Europeans desire to have liquor.

3. Natives manufacture their own beverages, some of which, according to A. C. Burns, for many years in the government service of Nigeria, are extremely powerful. In a section of Nigeria, according to him, the natives are tapping and injuring palm trees in order to obtain palm wine.

4. Many governments obtain considerable revenue from duties on liquor. In 1913, Nigeria derived over one million pounds from this source. The amount declined during the war, but Lugard pertinently asks why the West African dependencies, rich in palm oil, kernels, cocoa, tin, and gold, which "render them by universal consent among the wealthiest of our tropical colonies, should claim that a revenue from trade spirits, which is possessed by no other colonies, should be indispensable to balance their budget."[10]

5. Authorities differ as to the effects of imported liquor on natives. The 1909 Royal Commission which was sent to Nigeria examined many witnesses and concluded that "there is absolutely no evidence of race deterioration due to drink,"[11] a conclusion with which Lord Lugard and others profoundly disagree.

6. Complete prohibition would undoubtedly create problems of smuggling and domestic manufacture. To meet these, Lugard suggests the imposition of heavy duties on spirits, the importa-

[10] Sir F. D. (now Lord) Lugard, *The Dual Mandate in British Tropical Africa* (W. Blackwood & Sons, Ltd., London, 1926), p. 605.

[11] Quoted in A. C. Burns, *History of Nigeria* (George Allen & Unwin, Ltd., London, 1929), p. 244.

tion or local manufacture of very light beer, the "compulsory dilution of spirits to fixed maximum strength before issued from bond," a system of rationing by which the total quantity imported each year would be fixed in advance, and the "extension of prohibition zones in those areas where spirits are little drunk."

The liquor question has affected international relations not only in dependencies but also in Europe and America. As early as 1887 six powers signed a treaty to forbid the sale of liquor to men engaged in fishing in the North Sea, where floating cabarets had given rise to many abuses, because fishermen were tempted to exchange their catches for liquor. To maintain order the governments agreed to give their cruisers power to arrest any vessel suspected of violating the treaty, take it to port, and hand it over to its national authorities for trial.[12]

After the World War of 1914–1918 liquor producers exerted influence on their governments to increase liquor sales abroad, and in consequence the smaller countries, Iceland and Norway, which had adopted prohibition, suffered considerable pressure from more powerful nations. In 1921 Spain threatened to triple the duty on fish from Iceland unless the latter country modified its prohibition policy relative to Spanish wines; and Iceland, rather than lose its important market for fish in Spain, gave way, in April 1922, "suspended its prohibition law for one year," and later extended the period indefinitely.

In 1916 Norway's prohibition law brought forth a strong protest from France, with the result that Norway agreed to permit the importation of French wines to an unlimited degree. Spain and, later, Portugal exercised similar pressure on Norway, which had to repeal its prohibition law because the wine-producing countries which consumed a large portion of Norway's fish threatened to close their markets. Buell remarks that the threat of a trade embargo by one country against another for adopting prohibition "is certainly a most questionable procedure."[13]

The prohibition policy of the United States also gave rise to serious international controversy. The situation was really one of long standing. Smugglers had been active before the country had gained its independence in 1783, and continued to operate even after that date. In a number of cases, notably Church v. Hubbart,

[12] R. L. Buell, *International Relations* (Henry Holt & Co., New York, 1929), p. 270.
[13] Buell, *op. cit.,* pp. 271–72.

1804, Hudson *v.* Guestier, 1810, and the Betsey case, 1818, the courts had to consider whether or not nations possessed the right to take action against foreign vessels engaged in smuggling but actually outside the three-mile limit. Chief Justice Marshall upheld the right of a government to secure itself from injury by exercising power outside the range of cannon fire, adding that "the right given to our own revenue cutters to visit vessels four leagues from our coast" was evidence that the United States accepted the principle.

However, before 1920 the United States had little difficulty with foreign "hovering vessels" and very few international questions arose concerning jurisdiction over smugglers operating from beyond the three-mile limit. But after the adoption of prohibition in 1919 rum-running afforded great chances for profit. Vessels brought liquor from all parts of the globe. They kept just outside the three-mile limit and sent liquor ashore by means of boats sent out from hiding places along the shore. The Attorney General's report for 1925 showed that in that year 38 foreign and 753 American vessels had been seized. Masterson quotes from the *London Times* of December 17, 1924, that $120,000,000 worth of liquor had been sent into California, Washington, and Oregon from British Columbia during the year, "and that a fleet of vessels ranging from thirty-foot motor launches to schooners of from two hundred to three hundred tons, were plying regularly out of Vancouver, ostensibly headed for South American ports";[14] lying twelve miles out at sea, "waiting to deliver their cargo to vessels from the shore, some of them carried cargoes valued at $3,000,000." This instance is only one of many. "The liquor smuggling business is the most gigantic criminal problem the United States has ever faced on the high seas."

Not only did traffickers smuggle liquor directly into the United States, but ships obtained two clearances "so that the master could produce the one calling for a foreign port if boarded and examined on the high seas by custom officers, while if he succeeded in unloading his illicit cargo without detection, he could go into the American port named in the other clearance for a return cargo." The Canadian government permitted these practices and gave clearances to vessels obviously too small to reach the destination named in their application. This evil was reme-

---

[14] W. E. Masterson, *Jurisdiction in Marginal Seas* (The Macmillan Company, New York, 1929), pp. 212–13.

died in 1925, when Canada by treaty undertook to refuse clearance to such vessels.

Some American shipowners tried to transfer their vessels to a foreign registry after the Attorney General had decided that American citizens possessing liquor on American vessels were guilty of violating the law. The owners planned to use these vessels in the liquor traffic, and to ask the protection of the foreign government of registry should the United States authorities seize the ship outside the three-mile limit. To meet this effort to defeat the law, the United States Shipping Board, before granting such a permit, insisted on a warrant clause that the purchaser of the vessel (and his successor) would not use it for liquor-trade business, on penalty of forfeiture to the United States. The Canadian government refused to recognize the right of the United States to insert such a clause, claiming that such action was "a projection of sovereignty" without parallel, and declined to register American vessels under these conditions.

International controversy increased when the United States passed the 1922 Tariff Act empowering revenue authorities to search for smugglers within a distance of four leagues from the shore. The courts, in interpreting this act, laid down the principle that a vessel hailed beyond the three-mile limit but within a four-league distance from the shore, pursued and caught beyond the four-league limit, was justifiably captured on the high seas under the doctrine of "continuous hot pursuit." Great Britain, however, took its stand on the three-mile limit, and claimed that seizure of vessels outside this limit was contrary to international law: "Any attempt on the part of the United States authorities to seize a British ship outside the three-mile limit would be regarded by His Majesty's Government as creating a very serious situation."

Under the Prohibition Law, as interpreted by the Supreme Court in Cunard v. Mellon (1922), foreign vessels could not bring liquor into the United States or its territorial waters even if kept under seal and not intended for delivery in the United States. This decision threatened to inflict serious injury on foreign shipping; for vessels returning from the United States to Europe had to travel "dry," whereas vessels from Canada could carry wines and liquors. Moreover, France, Italy, and Spain had laws which required their ships to carry a certain amount of liquor. Buell writes that foreign powers thus "aided the violation of the prohibition policy of America, while the United States forced prohibition upon foreign states! Such were the international problems created by what international law calls a purely 'domestic' question!"[15]

The United States desired to obtain Britain's consent for extension of its powers of search beyond the three-mile limit. Great Britain wished to gain the right for its ships to carry liquor under seal within American territorial waters. Both parties were willing to compromise, and in 1924 signed a treaty which (1) accepted three marine miles as the limit of territorial waters; (2) stipulated that Great Britain should not object to the search of vessels flying the British flag outside the territorial waters, but within one hour's steaming distance, if they were suspected of trying to evade the liquor laws of the United States; (3) provided that the United States should not search or penalize British vessels which were carrying liquor in United States territorial waters if the liquor was kept under seal; (4) provided for claims for loss or injury through seizure.

The United States signed similar treaties with other powers and was thereby enabled better to eliminate smuggling from the high seas. These included treaties with Germany, the Netherlands, Cuba, Panama, Italy, Sweden, Norway, Denmark, Spain, France, and Belgium.

The famous "I'm Alone" case which arose in March 1929 raised questions of far-reaching importance. This vessel, a smuggler, was sighted near the United States coast, refused to stop when ordered by an American Coast Guard vessel, and was chased for two hundred miles and at length sunk by a Coast Guard boat, though not the vessel which had first hailed her. The Canadian government claimed that the smuggler was beyond an hour's sailing from shore when hailed, that the United States had no right to exercise the doctrine of "hot pursuit" from beyond the three-mile limit, that in this case the doctrine did not apply because the cutter which had hailed the smuggler had been unable to carry on the chase and the substitute vessel had no right to sink the suspected ship. The United States denied the Canadian contentions, and asserted that the "I'm Alone" was within an hour's sailing of shore when hailed and that the doctrine of hot pursuit did apply under the circumstances.

The two governments could not settle the matter by diplomatic means, and accordingly submitted the question to a joint

[15] Buell, *op. cit.,* p. 273.

commission, which after exhaustive investigation gave no final answer to the question of the right of hot pursuit but found that the sinking of the vessel "could not be justified by any principle of international law." It considered that "the United States ought formally to acknowledge its illegality and to apologize to his Majesty's Canadian Government," and recommended accordingly. Fortunately, recourse to the peaceful method of a joint commission solved a problem which threatened to cause much ill will.

Canada took the view that the United States in extending its search for smugglers beyond the traditional limits acknowledged by international law was threatening the doctrine of freedom of the seas. Masterson deals interestingly with this contention. He suggests that the hovering laws, or laws dealing with smugglers hovering just outside the three-mile or twelve-mile limit waiting to dispatch liquor to the shore, do not interfere with "rights of innocent passengers"; legitimate commerce, therefore, suffers no injury. Nor do the laws involve any claim of sovereignty or of territorial waters over an area which is policed solely for anti-smuggling purposes. They do not exclude foreign vessels and do not assert a general jurisdiction over vessels. He asks what other interest can be weighed against "this tangible interest of the littoral state," the welfare of which depends upon the adequate enforcement of its laws. And he denies that the doctrine of the freedom of the seas opens the high seas to all vessels at all times. The rights of action against pirates, of "hot pursuit," and of search of neutral vessels in wartime constitute recognized limitations. It would seem, therefore, that a more satisfactory method of dealing with the question would be to balance interests rather than to argue from abstract principles.[16]

Other international problems arose from the fact that it was lawful to export liquor from Canada and at the same time unlawful to import liquor into the United States; along the St. Lawrence River, and the United States–Canadian land boundary generally, people tried to run liquor across the border. The Canadian policy of granting clearances to ships or boats crossing the St. Lawrence River made prohibition enforcement more difficult for the United States. How extensive were the shipments can be seen from figures which show that during the year ending March

[16] See W. E. Masterson, op. cit., pp. 380–401, for a discussion of this question and of the possibility of international legislation.

31, 1928, Canada received $18,000,000 from duties imposed on liquor exported to the United States. The latter country made repeated requests to Canada for assistance in the solution of this border problem. At a conference held in 1929 the United States maintained that its smuggling problems could in large measure be traced to Canada; the Canadian supply encouraged bootleggers in the United States to indulge in fraudulent reproduction of Canadian stamps and labels, leading to the sale of much liquor ostensibly, but not actually, of Canadian origin; and the United States had been able to reduce the amount of liquor smuggling from the high seas but found it more difficult to solve the Canadian border problem. It therefore asked Canada to prohibit traffic from the Canadian side by refusing clearances and by preventing the release from distilleries of duty-paid spirits destined for export to the United States. It suggested that each country "should refuse to allow its instrumentalities to be used by persons engaged in breaking the laws of the other country." It asserted that the proposal would benefit Canada, because the liquor traffic, if long tolerated, would corrupt Canadian life and any measures which would lessen law-breaking activities should be accepted.

The Canadian reply was not unsympathetic, but it indicated a different viewpoint. It claimed that there was bound to be difficulty when two countries with a 3,000-mile border separating them adopted radically different liquor policies; that smuggling might be reduced, but was bound to continue in some degree; that the amount of liquor smuggled from Canada to the United States constituted only a small part of the amount actually for sale in the United States, possibly not more than 5 per cent to 10 per cent; that, therefore, the Canadian supply was a relatively minor factor, a consideration which should be kept in mind in contemplating the policy which Canada was asked to adopt. The Canadian representatives suggested that the United States authorities take more adequate steps to enforce the law along the border by requiring vessels under five tons to register with the collector of the district before engaging in foreign trade, so that a more adequate control could be effected; and stated that the United States authorities could easily capture many of the boats making trips in the open daylight along the Detroit and the Niagara frontier. Canada had already done more than was required of her under the 1924 treaty, having supplied information concerning the clearances issued to vessels as the treaty had provided, increased the bond required, taken steps to close export houses and agreed not to issue additional licenses for distilleries or breweries without the Department of National Revenue first consulting the provincial authorities, reduced the number of docks from which boats could leave to cross the river from forty to ten, and prohibited the importation of liquor into Canada, with minor exceptions, except by government agencies. Canada doubted also if the refusal of clearances would be of great help, since it might simply cause the liquor traffic to be diffused along the whole border and, once Canada made the export to the United States illegal, the burden of enforcing the law would fall upon Canada—"so far as the smuggling of Canadian liquor did continue the blame for non-enforcement would be shifted to Canadian patrols." The proposal, too, might involve unexpected consequences if the general principle were admitted of refusing clearances to any goods "the importation of which was forbidden or restricted by another country." Subsequently the Canadian government modified its policy and introduced legislation making it illegal to export liquor into the United States.

The nations bordering the Baltic signed a treaty in 1925 under which each signatory power agreed to prohibit small vessels under 100 tons from carrying liquor from its territory unless it had obtained special official authority. The powers agreed to permit each other to search vessels suspected of engaging in contraband liquor traffic beyond the three-mile limit up to a distance of twelve nautical miles. Similar treaties for the prevention of smuggling have been signed by the United States and Mexico, Sweden and Norway, and Mexico and Germany.

In August 1935 Congress passed an anti-smuggling act empowering the President to proclaim an enforcement area at any place on the high seas for purposes of preventing the unlawful introduction of merchandise. The area is not specifically defined, and may vary from time to time and from place to place. The act authorizes the seizure of vessels, foreign or domestic, up to ninety miles from the coast, but also provides that the act will not be enforced against a foreign vessel "in contravention of any treaty with a foreign government."

SLAVERY

There are two distinct but related aspects of the problem of slavery: (a) Slave trading, which has involved the transport of slaves from one country or one continent to another, the suppression of which required international action; and (b) slavery as a domestic institution, which may perhaps be considered as a purely national issue but which has international ramifications because the existence of domestic slavery constitutes a standing invitation to raiders to indulge in slave trading.

Europeans began slave trading several centuries ago. After the expulsion of the Moors and Jews from Spain, Portuguese merchants imported African Negroes for labor purposes. They made great profits, and justified their nefarious trade on the plea that Negroes belonged to a lower order of beings and that because slavery existed in Africa it would be better to bring them as slaves to Christian lands where they could enjoy the benefit of Christianity. Slave traders carried off hundreds of thousands of Negroes each year. In 1713 Great Britain undertook to bring into the West Indies 144,000 Negroes within a period of thirty years. McPhee estimates that over 100,000 per year were shipped from West Africa alone;[17] Lugard writes that it is impossible to estimate the number of people killed or enslaved, but suggests that probably 100,000 slaves reached the east coast of Africa yearly; and authorities believe that about 1,000,000 people were taken slaves each year, at least ten having been killed or left to starve for every person who reached the coast alive. The figure may be doubled for the rest of Africa. And this appalling set of affairs "had been going on for centuries!"[18] In the Sudan the population was reduced from eight and one-half millions to under two millions within a few years.[19] These instances will give some impression of the magnitude of the traffic.

In the eighteenth century the British conscience awoke to the evil. The great Wilberforce and his colleagues began the abolition movement, and in 1807 they succeeded in ending the slave trade within the Empire; but they soon realized that as long as slavery itself remained, foreign vessels, which British authorities could not arrest on the high seas, could carry slaves and smuggle them into the colonies. Domestic slavery and the slave trade were parts of the same problem.

The reformers first considered whether the slave system might not be reformed and "purged of its cruelties." By 1830 they had decided that "all attempts at gradual evolution are wild and

[17] A. McPhee, *The Economic Revolution in British West Africa* (George Routledge & Sons, Ltd., London, 1926), p. 29.

[18] Sir F. D. Lugard, *The Dual Mandate in British Tropical Africa* (W. Blackwood & Sons, Ltd., London, 1929), p. 355.

[19] *Ibid.*, p. 356.

visionary," and, in May, Buxton proposed its abolition. Three years later, in 1833, success came, and slavery was ended within the Empire. But the fight had not been won. Indeed, it became apparent that only the first battle had been fought. Slavery existed in other countries, and the call of idealism and humanity prevented the English reformers from being content with merely freeing slaves in one nation. Moreover, the abolition of slavery in one form led to its reappearance in another. Plantation owners sent out recruiters to obtain "indentured" labor, and indenture at its worst was scarcely distinguishable from slavery. Conditions of servitude akin to slavery (mui-tsai, debt slavery, peonage, and forced labor) brought new tasks to the reformers, who established the Protection of Aborigines Society to guard and promote the welfare of native peoples. In large measure the members were responsible for fighting the evils of slavery as they appeared in new guises, and ultimately for having written into the 1926 slavery convention, as its objective, "the abolition of slavery in *all its forms.*" Action against the slave trade had logically led to efforts against slavery and conditions akin to slavery, and to a positive conception of building up native society so as not merely to save it from injustice and exploitation, but also to enable it to develop along the lines of its own genius, and thereby to realize its highest potentialities.

Great Britain ended the slave trade in 1807 by unilateral action. Other nations followed—the United States in 1808, Sweden in 1813, Holland in 1814. But because the ocean is free to ships of all nations, unilateral action on even a wide scale did not serve substantially to reduce the traffic; slave traders continued their infamous work under the flags of nations which had not declared the traffic to be illegal. Great Britain at first attempted to fight the traffic singlehanded by ordering her cruisers to visit suspected vessels. But in 1817 Sir W. Scott ruled that the British Government had no legal right in time of peace to visit and search vessels belonging to other sovereign states. Britain thereupon sought to obtain some form of international agreement.

Already at the Congress of Vienna, the British Foreign Minister, Castlereagh, had unsuccessfully urged the powers to set up a permanent committee of surveillance. He then proposed an economic boycott against countries which refused to abolish the slave trade. "At Paris in 1814, and at Vienna in 1815, every resource of Great Britain was used to secure general abolition by the Powers. West Indian islands were offered, subsidies were promised, commercial boycotts were threatened to those countries whose flags were principally resorted to by the trade; but without much success. There was a marked distrust of British motives."[20] This distrust served to ruin Castlereagh's scheme for "the vigilant superintendence of an armed and international police on the coast of Africa." The European nations did not intend to support "proposals which promised to strengthen" Britain's maritime supremacy, which the Napoleonic wars had served to increase. The governments also rejected Castlereagh's second plan and merely adopted a general declaration

that, regarding the universal abolition of the trade in negroes as a measure particularly worthy of their attention . . . . they are animated by a sincere desire to co-operate in a most prompt and a most effective execution of this measure by all the means at their disposition and to act in the employment of these means with all the zeal and all the perseverance which they owe to so great and admirable a cause.

The high-sounding eloquence of the Congress resulted in no effective multilateral action, and progress for the next thirty years took the form of bilateral treaties by which certain nations granted each other the right to visit and search vessels suspected of engaging in the slave traffic. However, the result was quite unsatisfactory, because a vessel could be detained only provided that slaves were actually found on board. Nor did the treaties provide against the possibility of selling the condemned vessel; hence the owner could transfer his ship to someone else and suffer little loss. France, Denmark, Sardinia, and Sweden accepted the right of search; but Spain obstinately refused, with the result that slave traders flew the Spanish flag, and made advance in eliminating the traffic extremely difficult. Unfortunately, too, Brazil and the United States for a long time refused the right of search, and slavers "flocked" to the flags of those countries.[21]

Great Britain approached the United States and suggested that it agree to the policy of a reciprocal right of search of vessels suspected of slave trading. But what should have been a question of humanitarian rights became tangled up with the problems of war policy. During the Napoleonic struggles, Great Britain had searched American vessels and impressed seamen whom

[20] H. G. Soulsby, *The Right of Search and the Slave Trade in Anglo-American Relations, 1814–1862* (The Johns Hopkins Press, Baltimore, 1933), p. 13.

[21] W. L. Mathieson, *Great Britain and the Slave Trade, 1839–1864* (Longmans, Green & Co., London, 1929), p. 27.

it claimed to be of British nationality. The United States therefore feared that Great Britain, which according to American opinion had abused its belligerent rights in wartime, might in a similar
manner abuse its right of search in time of peace.

What appeared to be a simple question of fundamental rights
of Negroes became involved in an elaborate and "often vigorous
discussion of commerce at sea." Once more we see the progress
of human welfare affected by the necessities or imagined necessities of military and naval defense. The suspicion that what on
the surface seemed a matter of social reform was in reality an instrument which might be used to the detriment of neutral rights
or for the promotion of belligerent advantage served to postpone
the abolition of the slave trade for many years. Piracy and traffic in slaves alike profited from the inability of governments to
consider them apart from the problem of security.

In 1841 the first international treaty relating to the slave trade
was signed at London by England, France, Prussia, Russia, and
Austria. These governments undertook to prevent their subjects
from engaging in the slave trade. They branded the trade as piracy
(which they had refused to do in 1815), and conceded the right
of mutual search. Cruisers of government A could search a slaver
belonging to country B and bring it to the national courts of B
for trial and condemnation. Palmerston hoped to induce all the
Continental powers to ratify the treaty, but his scheme failed.
General Cass, the American ambassador to Paris, suspected that
England was attempting to extend the right of policing the high
seas for selfish purposes and began an agitation against the proposal, with the result that the French refused to sign the treaty.

Great Britain made a distinction between search and visit; the
former was to be permitted only under treaty; the latter should
be accepted without special treaty consent. The United States, on
the other hand, claimed that "visit was as great an outrage as
search" and that the principle of freedom of the seas was at stake.
Next year some of the differences were settled, and the two countries by the Webster-Ashburton Treaty of 1842 agreed to keep
a squadron each off the coast of Africa and "to carry out its laws
against slave ships flying its flag." In 1862 they went farther
and allowed the cruisers of either country to search the merchant
ships of the other and established mixed courts which could condemn slavers. The mixed courts, however, were abolished by the
Convention of June 3, 1870, "which obliged the cruisers to bring
suspected slavers in for condemnation to the courts of the country

of the suspected vessel." Already some governments had declared
slave trading a crime to be punished as piracy. The cruiser system
adopted by Great Britain, which cost many hundred thousand
pounds a year, consisted in stationing a number of war vessels off
the west coast of Africa and intercepting the suspected slavers.
By subsequent legislation, cruisers could seize the traffickers if
they possessed the typical equipment of these vessels, and not
merely if they were found with slaves aboard. For a time the
naval officers adopted the policy of what was called inshore blockade, so as to catch the slavers soon after leaving the African ports.
They also destroyed the barracoons or depots "where the traders
kept the slaves brought from the interior," as well as the goods
with which to pay the chiefs who supplied the unfortunate victims. But this method was declared illegal and, until the courts
reversed this decision, the cruiser forces were deprived of the
advantage of attacking the evil on land.

After 1840 there came a reaction in England and a determined
movement took place against the use of British naval forces for
the suppression of the slave trade. Buxton's book published in
1839 caused considerable comment.[22] The author argued that (1)
the cruiser system had failed to achieve its object and a "vast slave
trade still went on"; (2) action by one or two nations was useless,
because without an extensive international agreement there were
too many loopholes; (3) the traffic was too profitable to be stopped
by these means; (4) the use of force merely added to the cruelties
of the slave trade at sea because the traffickers, on being pursued
by a cruiser, would be tempted to throw the slaves overboard so
as to escape being caught in the act of carrying slaves. Influential
people joined Buxton in his campaign.[23] Some were opposed to
the use of force on principle, and used arguments similar to those
employed today against imposing sanctions upon an aggressor
nation. Others asserted that it was unfair that Great Britain
should bear so great an expense and risk the lives of her sailors
in the unhealthy tropics in attempting a thankless and impossible
task. The free-trade movement brought another obstacle to the
anti–slave trade movement. Cobden, Bright, and their followers
moved to have sugar imported into England free of duty, even
though grown by slave labor. They argued that it was necessary
for the industrial welfare of England to import sugar at the

[22] W. L. Mathieson, *op. cit.,* pp. 36–41.
[23] *Ibid.,* chapter iii.

lowest possible cost, and denied that the horrors of slavery were as great as had been pictured.

Opponents of slavery and the slave trade argued that the evil was so terrible that it would be criminal to wait upon the slow course of natural social evolution. If forceful methods were used against criminals within the nation, why not a similar drastic action against those traffickers who sinned against God and man by indulging in this unholy enterprise of profiting from the misery of millions?

In the 'seventies new forces appeared. The measures hitherto taken were directed against the slave trade at sea, but new problems arose with the opening up of Africa by explorers and missionaries. In large sections of Africa, in Moslem countries, Turkey, Arabia, and Zanzibar, the institution of slavery formed a part of the social system, "sanctioned alike by religion and civil law." Many of the interior tribes of Zanzibar conducted slave raids on behalf of the Arab chieftains, some of whom became practically independent of Zanzibar. By 1888 slave traders had built up a formidable military power in the central parts of Africa, and even formed a threatening political system. European opinion was again aroused, and many prominent individuals took up the cause of antislavery. The scramble for colonies in Africa fastened new masters upon the unfortunate Negro people; but at least the Western imperialist powers were theoretically opposed to the institution of slavery and in some cases took active steps to destroy the traffic in slaves.

The first international effort to deal with Africa's inland slave trade was made at the 1885 Berlin Conference, which Bismarck convened (1) to obtain recognition of the International Association of the Congo as a state, (2) to define the general policy of occupation in central Africa, and (3) to insure equal opportunities for traders and missionaries of all nations. The Conference adopted the Berlin Act, which contained two articles dealing with slavery. Under Article 6 the powers undertook to preserve the native tribes, promote their moral and material well-being, and assist in suppressing slavery and especially the slave trade. Under Article 9 they promised not to permit their colonies to be used as either markets or means of transit for the trade in slaves, and agreed "to employ all means . . . . for putting an end to this trade and for punishing those who engage in it."

The Berlin Act applied only to the conventional basin of the Congo but did not touch the slave trade in East Africa. For that purpose an antislavery conference met at Brussels in 1889, and from it came the General Act for the Repression of African Slave Trade, July 2, 1890.

In this act the powers recognized that the most effective means of counteracting the slave trade in the interior of Africa were to (1) organize efficient government within their colonies; (2) establish strongly occupied stations to serve as centers of attack against slave hunting; (3) build roads, and especially railroads, so as to eliminate the system of human porterage; (4) establish steamboats on inland waters and lakes, and telegraph lines to maintain rapid communication; (5) maintain expeditions and flying columns to insure the safety of the high roads; and (6) restrict imports of firearms and of ammunition. Governments undertook to free slaves rescued from the traders and to keep a strict watch over the roads in order to stop convoys on the march, and over ports and places near the coast to prevent the shipment of slaves brought from the interior. Chapter iii prescribed measures for the repression of the slave trade at sea, especially off the east coast of Africa; in this zone the governments agreed to the reciprocal right of visit of search and seizure of suspected vessels of less than five hundred tons. The powers undertook to set up at least one international bureau at Zanzibar for the collection of information and documents likely to assist in the suppression of the slave trade. The signatories recognized that there were countries in which domestic slavery was a traditional institution closely bound up with social structure but promised to stop the slave trade to these parts; and the rulers of Turkey and Persia agreed that slaves shipped to their ports should be freed. France refused to ratify that part of the treaty which referred to the right of mutual search, fearing that it would enable Great Britain to increase its maritime strength in an area where it already possessed great influence—another example of how international power politics operated to hinder social reform.

Lord Lugard calls this act the Magna Carta of the African slave; with its ratification, he writes, a new era dawned. Nevertheless, many loopholes remained. Meanwhile, the future of the native races was receiving much consideration in the light of new standards of administration and the findings of modern anthropology. At the end of the World War the powers which signed the Treaty of St. Germain revised the Act of Berlin by promising to secure "the complete suppression of slavery in all its forms and of the slave trade by land and sea." This statement was the most comprehensive ever adopted in an international agreement on slavery; it embodied a recognition of the fact that there were conditions analogous to slavery which the governments should take steps to remedy. The League of Nations Covenant contained the principle of international co-operation against slavery by prohibiting slave trading in the mandated territories. The mandatory powers agreed to forbid traffic in slaves and gradually to eliminate slavery in the B and C mandates.

The League of Nations took its first major step in 1922 when it adopted a resolution placing the question of "recrudescence of slavery" on the agenda for the following session. Sir Arthur Steele-Maitland, representing New Zealand, drew the attention of the Assembly to the undoubted increase in the slave trade in Africa during recent years. He specifically mentioned Abyssinia as the "stronghold of slavery," and argued that the importation of arms into Africa was largely responsible for the magnitude of the evil. Sir John Harris mentions that Steele-Maitland met with considerable opposition from certain representatives, and for a time little progress was made. However, the Fourth Assembly (1923) asked the Council to permit a competent body of experts to carry out an extensive investigation and report to the next session. In June 1924 the Council established the Temporary Commission on Slavery which held its first meeting soon after. From a great amount of material which it collected, it presented its report one year later.

The Commission faced many difficulties. It realized that the slave trade was definitely international in character, but that slavery and the analogous institutions presented a more complicated problem, because, in so far as they lay within the sovereign jurisdiction of particular countries, "they might be outside of the realm of international relations as strictly defined."

The Commission had to obtain information on which to base its conclusions and recommendations. The question arose, Should it have power to use information derived from private sources, or should it be restricted to the use of official reports? If it relied upon private information, what guaranty was there that such information would be responsible and trustworthy in character? If it relied solely upon governmental information, what guaranty was there that official reports would reveal the true state of affairs? For was it not natural to assume that a government would be tempted to hide the full facts relating to slavery within its borders?

The Commission realized its delicate situation, and attempted to escape from the dilemma by proposing the following procedure: The Commission should consult individuals and organizations designated by governments, receive communications from organizations or individuals other than those indicated by governments, and if it considered such communications worthy of consideration, should then ask the government concerned whether it considered the organization or the individuals competent and reliable. All communications concerning slavery conditions were to be forwarded "to the Government under whose administration the facts alluded to are alleged to take place or prevail." Some governments did not relish the prospect of having nonofficial agencies report to the League on slavery within their territory. The Commission tried to reassure them by emphasizing that "it was not a tribune, but merely a body of experts entrusted with the task of proposing measures to facilitate the eradication of slavery."

The majority of the Commission agreed to recommend a new slavery convention, although M. Van Rees believed that such a step was unnecessary. However, his colleagues insisted that a more inclusive instrument should be adopted, and to that end made several observations and recommendations. They realized that the institution of slavery could not be abolished at one stroke: the process must be gradual. The first step proposed was that slavery should no longer be regarded as legal. Slaves might claim their freedom, if they wished, without having to pay ransom, but the master would not be guilty of breaking the law if he kept slaves who wished to remain under his authority. The Commission believed that Ethiopia might take special measures: (*a*) encourage the principal chiefs to free their slaves and thereby set an example to the smaller masters; (*b*) enact that all slaves must be registered by a certain date, otherwise to be freed; (*c*) possibly abolish the legal status of slavery. In order to avoid the economic dislocation due to suddenly throwing many ex-slaves on the free market, the emancipated persons should work for their masters for a definite period. Governments might also enact that children of slaves were to be free, courts might free slaves who had been ill-treated, owners must no longer sell their slaves or inflict bodily punishment, and slaves should obtain certain elementary civil rights.

The Commission, after reviewing the slave-raiding conditions which still existed in the Sahara Desert and the southern parts of Morocco and Tripoli, suggested that increased patrols, the right of pursuit across frontiers, and imposition of the severest penalties would be required to wipe out the evil.

Slave trading was confined mainly to Ethiopia and some Mohammedan states on the Arabian peninsula. The Commission recommended that foreign consuls and diplomatic agents should be permitted to revive the right of asylum; and that stricter passport regulations should be required before pilgrims could go to the Holy City of Mecca, so as more effectively to safeguard them from being seized and sold into slavery.

Concerning conditions analogous to slavery, the Commission recommended measures to stop abuses arising from the practice of "purchase" permitted under certain marriage customs. Provisions were urgently required (1) to combat the traffic in young people which developed from the practice of buying them, ostensibly to improve their mental and moral condition; and (2) to prevent people from enslaving themselves in order to pay their debts. It suggested that a debtor should be freed once he had worked off the principal of the loan, instead of having to remain in servitude because of an inability to pay the ever increasing debt resulting from abnormally high interest rates. The Commission believed that domestic slavery and serfdom must be abolished gradually in order to avoid a social crisis which would follow from wholesale liberation, and made certain observations on the practice of forced labor which should be permitted only for essential public works. It condemned all forms of "direct or indirect compulsion aimed at forcing natives into private employment."

The report made clear that the evils of slavery existed on a wide scale, and, true to its century-old policy, the British Government presented the draft of a new convention for the consideration of the Assembly, setting forth the minimum standards which, it hoped, would meet with the approval of the League members. The draft was considered by the Sixth Committee, submitted to governments for their examination and comment, and reconsidered by the Committee. The revised draft was submitted to the 1926 Assembly, which approved what came to be known as the Slavery Convention.

The Convention strengthened the attack upon slavery by making more specific the general obligations imposed by the 1919 Convention. The signatories undertook to prevent and suppress the slave trade and "to bring about, progressively and as soon as possible, the complete abolition of slavery in all its forms." The word "progressively" was inserted because, as pointed out above, it was considered unwise for governments to abolish domestic slavery at a stroke of the pen, in view of the intimate way in which the institution is wrapped up with the whole life of certain tribes. By Article III the powers agreed "to adopt all appropriate measures with a view to preventing and suppressing the embarkation, disembarkation, and transport of slaves in their territorial waters and upon all vessels flying their respective flags"; they promised to negotiate a general convention to specify more definitely the rights and duties in this matter, and to give each other every assistance in securing the abolition of slavery and the slave trade. Two important methods were suggested: (1) governments should permit a neighboring government to pursue slave traders across inland boundaries into their own territories; and (2) they should agree to permit each other to grant the right of asylum so that consular or other officials might liberate any slave asking for freedom "and repatriation to his country of origin."

The Convention laid down an important principle (to be analyzed below) that compulsory or forced labor might be exacted only for public purposes. This clause attacks an evil very closely connected with slavery, and attempts to abolish what is in effect slavery under another name. Finally, the signatory powers promised to impose severe penalties for infraction of laws—a desirable and important provision.

Although the Convention was a forward step, it disappointed the British delegation. Sir Austen Chamberlain had proposed that Article III be amended to read,

The act of conveying slaves on the high seas shall be deemed as between the high contracting parties to be the equivalent of an act of piracy and the public ships of the signatory States shall have the same rights in relation to vessels and persons engaged in such act as in relation to vessels and persons engaged in piracy.

France, Portugal, and Italy opposed the amendment, with the result that the Convention merely obliged the powers to consider the matter at a future date. It is regrettable that three nations, two of them great powers, should still so far defend the principle of slave trading as to refuse to accept a drastic method for its abolition.

More than forty governments signed the Convention; but experience had shown that without some permanent commission to watch over the application of treaties many proposed reforms failed to materialize. Since the 1926 Convention made no provision for such a commission, Lord Cecil proposed that an expert body be set up to replace the Temporary Slavery Commission, which had been disbanded. But the matter was postponed until the 1932 Assembly called for the appointment of a permanent committee of experts. The Council agreed, and finally the committee was established.

Seven expert advisers assist the League Council. Members are appointed for an indefinite period. They meet every second year, and will continue their labors until the campaign against slavery has been successful. The Commission is purely an advisory body; it has no powers of supervision. It will consider possibilities of financial assistance to states desirous of combating slavery and will study the documents supplied to the League by the various governments; indeed, it can make use only of information submitted by governments—an interesting restriction in view of the earlier discussions. Its proceedings are to be confidential, but the League Council may at its discretion publish the committee's report to the Council. The League's Secretariat provides the clerical staff required for its work.

The committee of experts drew up its rules of procedure in January 1934 and submitted them to the League Council. The Spanish representative on the Council regretted that the committee was confined to advisory work and had no powers of supervision, that it was not given authority to deal with forced or compulsory labor, and that it was able to receive only information forwarded by governments. Sir John Simon remarked that it would depend upon the effectiveness of the present machinery whether or not the Assembly would have to enlarge the scope and the powers of the committee.

It is perhaps too early to judge whether the experts, under existing conditions and restrictions, can effectively combat the age-old evils of slavery, the slave trade, and conditions analogous to slavery. The world may yet realize that the principle of national sovereignty should not be used to defend policies which involve the perpetuation of such vicious institutions as slavery, and that international organization does not necessarily detract from national efficiency and welfare—it may even add to them.

FORCED LABOR

The Temporary Slavery Commission recognized that forced labor is closely akin to slavery; and the 1926 Convention bound the contracting parties to abolish compulsory labor for other than public purposes as soon as possible. In 1929 there appeared the *Report and Draft Questionnaire* of the International Labor Conference, which contained a valuable discussion of the whole question. From it the following sections are largely drawn.

In dependencies much pioneering work has to be done in building up organized government, providing elementary services in health and education, and raising the standards of living. Often the government of a dependency has not the necessary revenue to perform services normally undertaken in the Western World; there is little native wealth to tax; and external loans are limited by reason of the small amount of security available. If the administration wishes to undertake essential services, it must make use of the one great resource which is available, namely, native labor. Probably some great territories, Mozambique, for example, could not have been developed so quickly without such methods.

Some people defend the policy of forced labor. They claim that contact with white civilization brings benefits to backward peoples. Natives become accustomed to the idea of law; they receive money payments which enable them to purchase more goods than they otherwise would be able to do; by the use of forced labor governments can extend the area of effective rule, extinguish tribal warfare, develop and expand native production, and discipline the people and promote the virtues of punctuality and regularity. While admitting the possibility of abuses, advocates of forced labor regard them as an incidental defect which may be remedied.

Other observers claim that the social effects of forced labor have been almost uniformly bad. Excessive forced labor in the collecting of rubber and in railroad construction has caused depopulation in the Lower and Middle Congo, where thousands have fled from the terrible conditions. In many cases the mortality rate has been appalling and little concern has been shown for native welfare. Too much routine, especially in tasks which have no real interest for him, robs the native of his joy in living and, far from being educative, tends to build up a mental resistance to and dislike of wholesome work. Not infrequently natives are called away when they are preparing their land for planting, and compulsory labor is on these occasions most unpopular; it is detrimental to the economic interests of the locality, and "tends to disrupt the village life and upset the whole native economy."

The question arises as to what amount of forced labor is justified. If certain work must be done, what principle shall be used to judge its necessity? The International Labor Office report suggests the following criterion: The public works on which forced labor is employed must directly benefit the native community supplying the labor, and be "clearly demonstrable to that native community itself." The work should be of public interest. It should be of urgent necessity. Forced labor should be used only when it is impossible to obtain voluntary labor and only after it is quite clear that the physical burden will not be too heavy for the native workers. Moreover, the responsibility of supervision and enlistment should rest with the competent central authorities and not be left to local officials or native chiefs. The emergency cases which would justify forced labor are fires, floods, earthquakes, violent epidemics, invasions of locusts, war—crises which threaten, or endanger, part or whole of the population. Important public works such as railroads, drainage, irrigation may have some claim, for these measures make possible the opening up and basic development of a country; in this case, however, the government must be most careful not to push the plea of public welfare too far and make excessive demands upon the time and energy of the natives.

Wherever large bodies of workers are removed from their villages for forced-labor purposes, a number of serious problems arise. Away from the milieu to which they are accustomed, native morale is apt quickly to degenerate. The absence of the workers' wives tends to encourage abnormal sexual habits; the cessation of the tribal authority which they respect, and which provides the sanction of their social conduct, leaves them unguided amid strange circumstances; they lose their own standards without gaining new ones; and their "religion" fails them. They suffer severely from climatic change, and even more severely from change of diet. Usually they are most susceptible to attack by diseases with which they come in contact for the first time. Herded together, they fall victims to highly infectious diseases which play havoc with them. Hence the importance of careful medical and social supervision.

Above all, women and children and the aged and medically unfit should not be recruited for forced labor; men should undergo medical examination to insure that they possess the physique necessary for the particular work in view, and only a limited proportion of the adult male population should be taken. While they are away from home they should be medically examined at stated intervals. An adequate medical staff, dispensaries, and hospitals should be provided. Sanitation facilities, water supply, and suitable food and housing conditions should be insisted upon. If the men are taken into a different climate and given food to which they are little accustomed, the change in diet "should be introduced gradually and every possible measure should be adopted to mitigate the effects" from the change of climate.

Natives should not be forced to perform unaccustomed labor except by gradual habituation. They should not be required to work more than eight hours a day and forty-eight hours a week; sixty days a year should constitute the normal period, with a possible extension to six months. Natives should be paid the wage normally given for the same type of work in districts in which they are employed; a work day should include the time consumed in traveling to and from the job; overtime should be paid at a higher rate. The natives should be paid accident and sickness compensation, and the administration should provide for the dependents "of dead and incapacitated workers."

The report suggests that governments should not require forced labor from natives while the men are sowing and cropping in their villages: forced labor should not interfere with essential native agricultural production. Above all, governments should provide adequate inspection in order to prevent the abuses which can all too easily occur.

One of the most hated forms of forced labor is porterage. In countries where roads and railways are inadequately developed, human carriers have been widely used. The amount of labor required for carrying goods has been enormous, and hundreds of thousands of working days have been consumed in this manner. The report urges that women and children, the sick, and the aged should be exempt from all porterage; as with other types of forced labor, compulsory porterage should provide the same wage rates as volunteer porterage; the normal day should not exceed eight hours, and the government should carefully prescribe the maximum load that the natives may carry; men should not be required to go more than four days' journey from their villages unless absolutely necessary, and should not have to do more than fifteen days a month, or twenty-five days for the year.

Some governments formerly required natives to cultivate part of their land and grow trees or crops. They justified the policy on the ground that such agricultural cultivation provided insurance against famine, helped to raise the standard of living, and inculcated habits of discipline. These things may be true, the International Labor Office suggests; but it recommends that any food produced under a system of compulsory cultivation should be the property of the producers (not the government) "or, where production is on the communal system, it should remain the property of the community which produces it." From this standpoint, it is not easy to justify compulsory cultivation of crops for market, since no question of insurance against famine is involved. The International Labor Office report did not deny the importance of agricultural education but questioned whether compulsory labor, unless limited to insurance against famine or an inadequate food supply, would not defeat the purpose of education by creating resentment and opposition.

Local labor should be required in "minor services connected with cleanliness, sanitation, and the maintenance of paths and tracks in the immediate vicinity of the village, of watering places, of washing places, of latrines, cemeteries, etc." Forced labor for local public works should be limited to maintaining and keeping clean local, but not main or metaled, roads, and constructing local administration buildings and village schools. Only adult able-bodied males should have to perform this kind of labor for a period not to exceed sixty days a year, and only when they do not have to sow and harvest their crops.

The report took a strong stand against forced labor for the benefit of private individuals or companies; where it still existed, it should be ended as soon as possible. Nor should natives be compelled to furnish certain products (such as timber, rubber, palm oil, copra, etc.) to individuals or companies; where such conditions exist, they should be removed as quickly as possible. Natives should not be taxed for the purpose of forcing them to work for private employers, nor should they be subjected to vagrancy or "pass" laws, the deprivation of their lands, or restriction of lands or cattle-owning for the same purpose.

The International Labor Office incorporated many of these findings into a draft questionnaire which was designed to prepare a convention and series of recommendations for consideration by the 1929 session of the International Labor Conference.

Following these recommendations the International Labor Organization considered the question of forced labor at its 1930 annual conference. Its action did not go unchallenged. The International Colonial Institute at Brussels resolved that there was only a limited room for international agreements on this matter. The

main French colonial institutions went on record against "the international control of native administration, an intervention it considers unnecessary and dangerous." Several chambers of commerce also protested against "any interference on the part of the
International Labor Office in the regulation of labor in the colonies." And Belgian and Portuguese organizations threw their
influence against the move. But the International Labor Office,
and especially its Director, took up the challenge and vigorously
asserted the competence of the organization, which received the
support of many bodies, especially those connected with Christian
missions.

The 1930 Convention concerning forced or compulsory labor
provided that each member of the International Labor Organization which ratified it undertook to diminish and humanize forced
labor in its dependencies.

In 1936 the International Labor Organization adopted a further draft convention relative to special conditions of "recruiting"
workers and a recommendation concerning the progressive elimination of recruiting. We shall see in another chapter that abuses in recruiting may result in something closely akin to slavery, and the
convention in attempting to eradicate this evil provides that (1)
recruiting should not involve constraint upon native peoples; (2)
it should not endanger native society by withdrawing an excessive
percentage of adults and thereby breaking up family life; (3) public officers may not recruit for private undertakings, nor may chiefs
act as recruiting agents; (4) employers and employers' associations must be licensed before they may recruit, and licenses may
be withdrawn as a penalty for misconduct; (5) before being engaged, workers must be brought before a public officer, who must
be satisfied that no abuse has occurred and that adequate provision for medical examination has been made; (6) the workers
must be protected in specially prescribed ways while on their journeys to and from their homes, and the cost is to be borne by the
recruiter and the employer. If recruiting or employment takes
place in a territory under a different administration, detailed agreements must be made between the governments of the territory of
recruiting and of the territory of employment.

The recommendation concerning progressive elimination of
recruiting declares that this should be a cardinal principle to be
followed by member states; in order to hasten such elimination
each member is invited to improve labor conditions, develop transport, promote settlement of workers in areas of employment, en-

courage the voluntary movement of labor, and raise the standard of life of native peoples.

These measures against slavery and forced labor not only are important as humanitarian efforts toward elementary justice but are vitally connected with the problem of maintaining labor standards in the more advanced industrial countries of the world. It is pointed out in the section dealing with labor as an international problem that the workers' standard of life is threatened by the importation of goods made from sweated labor; and, as backward areas become accessible, the exploitation of helpless and unorganized people by conscienceless profit-seekers may proceed unaffected by the standards prescribed by civilized communities and thereby the gains already won in such areas by organized effort may be destroyed. International control is here of importance to all concerned.

COUNTERFEITING CURRENCY

In 1925 the League of Nations was contemplating the withdrawal of its financial control over Hungary, and the victorious powers were considering closer relations with its ex-enemy, when a great scandal, involving the forging of one-thousand-franc notes, arose. Three Hungarians were arrested in Amsterdam and investigation showed that not only Hungarians of official rank were involved but also important German, Austrian, and Rumanian persons. The head of the Hungarian cartographical department where the notes were printed, the chief of the Hungarian police, and a number of Hapsburg supporters were the most prominent figures.[24] The incident, the most important of many attempts to counterfeit currency, convinced several governments that some form of international action was necessary. They realized (to quote from the proceedings):

that purely national action against counterfeiters of currency was insufficient and that international action was fraught with many difficulties and was often impossible. Sometimes these difficulties were to be found in legislation. In many countries, for instance, punishment of the forging of foreign money was very much lighter than that of national money, and in several the forging of foreign money was not a punishable offense at all. Again—there were wide differences in the punishment given to the various phases of the crime, such as the simple uttering of counterfeits, participation in counterfeiting, or possessing the instruments of counterfeiting. And the rules govern-

[24] A. J. Toynbee, *Survey of International Affairs, 1926* (Oxford University Press, London, 1928), pp. 178–90.

ing extradition were such that it was usually most difficult and often impossible, to get counterfeiters who had escaped from the country brought to justice.

After preliminary investigations by a mixed committee, an International Conference in 1929 adopted a draft convention which became effective February 22, 1931. The high contracting parties undertook to co-operate to prevent the illegal issue of currency; each agreed to organize a central office of investigation which should keep in close contact with currency-issuing institutions, with the police authorities of its own country, and with the central offices of other countries. The last-named should correspond directly with each other. The central offices were to exchange full information on forgeries of notes, including photostatic reproductions, and specimens, suspected persons, fingerprints, and other evidence likely to lead to detection. Detailed provisions for letters of request were provided in Article XVI. It was agreed that whenever fifteen central offices had been created by the signatory powers, and before the convention entered into force, the League of Nations should call the first conference of representatives of the central offices and other authorities involved to work out the more technical details. Pending the creation of an international office, the international bureau should continue to act as a co-ordinating body.

The first Conference of representatives from central police offices met in March 1931. Its recommendations went beyond the 1929 Convention which dealt with the offense of counterfeiting or falsifying paper money (including bank notes) and metallic currency, for they dealt with other kinds of financial instruments. In view of the great growth in the international use of checks, bills of exchange, letters of credit, state bonds, shares and bonds, international co-operation had to be extended to include these items. In May 1937, the League Council set up a committee of jurists to consider the question at length, and to prepare a draft additional protocol to the 1929 Convention, "the object of which was to extend to the suppression of the falsification of documents of value the provisions of this Convention." International co-operation in this field was fast becoming a necessity.

TRAFFIC IN WOMEN AND CHILDREN

The organized exploitation of vice has not confined itself within national boundaries. As communications have improved, vice profiteers have widened their activities, and the traffic in women and children for immoral purposes has become increasingly an international problem. About 1869 Josephine Butler began the struggle against licensed houses or brothels, which subjected prostitutes "to a system of slavery and deprivation of rights." In 1877 an International Abolitionist Federation Congress met at Geneva, after which Alexander Coote and Senator Bérenger stimulated national committees and governments to take action against the nefarious traffic. In 1899 voluntary organizations held a congress to consider ways of lessening the evil and formed the International Bureau for the Traffic in Women and Children.

In 1904 a diplomatic conference convened by France drew up an agreement by which governments undertook to appoint central authorities to collect information concerning the traffic, to watch ports and assist victims of the trade. In 1910 an international convention was adopted by which countries agreed to punish those engaging in the traffic even though they had committed the offense in another country. Unfortunately there was no international central agency to follow up the work of the conferences and to stimulate governments to action, and only sixteen states had ratified the 1904 agreement and nine states the 1910 Convention when war broke out in 1914.

In 1919 the efforts of private organizations and especially of Alexander Coote were successfully devoted to including the question of traffic in women and children in the work of the League of Nations. The League Council, in May 1920, appointed an official of the Secretariat to keep in touch with matters relating to the white-slave traffic, and in 1921 summoned a conference which was attended by representatives of thirty-four states. The Conference drew up a final act which strengthened the provisions of the 1904 and 1910 conventions by raising the age of consent from twenty to twenty-one, making it a punishable offense not only to procure but to attempt to procure women for the traffic, urging governments to make annual reports to the League and recommending the establishment of a League Advisory Committee, and improving the machinery of extradition.

The Council set up the Advisory Committee on Traffic in Women and Children, which was reorganized in 1924 into two advisory committees—Traffic in Women and Children, and Child Welfare. The two committees meet immediately after each other, and on each there are advisory members who represent the most

important international private organizations interested in these
questions. They include the International Catholic Organization,
the International Women's Associations, the International Federation of Girls' Friendly Societies, and a large number of others.

One of the weaknesses inherent in previous conventions had
been the lack of co-ordinating machinery. The Traffic in Women
and Children Committee set up after 1921 remedied this defect.
It did important work by bringing agencies into touch with one
another, examining annual reports, and providing private organizations in various countries with information of methods adopted
abroad.

Sound policy requires adequate and accurate information. For
this reason the League, with the assistance of the American Social Hygiene Bureau, undertook an extensive inquiry into the
traffic in Europe and America. The report showed the widespread character of the evil; how traffickers used forged passports and forged birth, marriage, and death certificates supplied
by regular criminal agencies, how they not only transported abroad
professional prostitutes but also induced girls to join music halls
and cabarets and forced them into prostitution by paying inadequate wages and by other means.

Some years later the League followed up the foregoing inquiry by appointing a committee to inquire into the traffic in the
Far East. This committee reported in 1933, and its main findings
were as follows:

1. Ignorance and poverty are the great causes of the traffic in
the Orient. Out of 50,000 prostitutes recruited from Japan for
China, 1,654 were illiterates, nearly 3,000 had not attended school,
and almost 40,000 had not gone beyond the primary school.

2. In the Orient more men than women had emigrated to
Siam, Malaya, and the Philippines; this serious sex disproportion
stimulated the international traffic.

3. In the East as in the West the great explanation was to be
found in human greed—"greed to make large profits out of human
misery and human sex hunger." The methods of recruitment were
much the same as in the West, perhaps even more blatant, and
the typical evasion of migration restrictions took place.

4. The abuse of Moslem marriage and divorce law and customs
enabled traffickers to take women from the Dutch East Indies to
Singapore: "They could marry their victims an hour before their
departure, take them to Singapore as legal wives and divorce them
an hour after arrival."

The committee recommended (a) the appointment of central authorities in China and Persia, and a more thorough collaboration and exchange of information by central authorities throughout the East; (b) the appointment of more women officials; (c) closer co-operation between Chinese officials and the authorities of foreign settlements in China, especially Shanghai; (d) preventive work with women of Russian origin in the Far East, including direct help and the founding of workshops and other organizations; (e) the abolition of licensed or recognized brothels which provide the surest market for foreign women, enable traffickers to keep close control over them, and "ensure in a country of transit a depot where the victim may be housed without cost and even at a profit pending a decision as to her ultimate disposal"; and (f) collaboration of government authorities with missions and private organizations.

Meanwhile the delegate from Poland had urged the League of Nations to take steps toward forbidding licensed houses in any country. The proposal involved a question which "had hitherto been considered a matter of domestic jurisdiction," and was connected with another proposal to make the repatriation of foreign prostitutes compulsory.

In 1927 a special body of experts suggested that, "in view of the number of minor girls who are exploited on the pretense that they are over age," the age limit be abolished and it be made an offense to procure or attempt to procure any woman of whatever age. They claimed that the frequent use of false papers made it difficult to ascertain whether a woman was or was not under twenty-one years of age, that many who consented to go abroad were not "fully aware of the disaster" to which they were being led, and that "even if the victim over age had been a prostitute" the law should not permit anyone to derive financial benefits from such a traffic. After considerable discussion and diplomatic correspondence the conference of October 1933 adopted the International Convention for the Suppression of the Traffic in Women of Full Age. Thus all women, whether over or under twenty-one years, were to be protected.

Attempts have been made to strengthen co-operation among central authorities. In 1932 a League inquiry revealed that

1. The central authorities do not come under the same service in every country and are not always attached to an executive service;
2. In practically no country does there appear to exist a specialised staff for the work of the central authorities;

3. Inter-communication between the central authorities is not yet co-ordinated or standardised;

4. Relations between the central authorities and the League of Nations are not sufficiently developed.[25]

In February 1937 the Conference of Central Authorities in the Far East met at Bandoeng, Java. (a) It considered the general proposals of the Commission of Enquiry, and recommended the creation of a Bureau of the League in the Far East to receive reports from all participating countries, which should deal confidentially with various aspects of the traffic. (b) It urged closer co-operation among the police authorities of all governments and regional or local conferences to consider in greater detail what more effective steps might be taken. (c) Considering the position of Hongkong as the strategic point for the traffic in women and children, it recommended that the Hongkong government be requested to strengthen its inspection provisions in migration matters—a task of great difficulty in view of the fact that about 10,000 persons enter and leave Hongkong each day, necessitating a large staff of officials if stricter control were to be instituted. (d) The Conference dealt at length with the problem of licensed brothels and considered the medical, ethical, and social aspects of the question. For reasons too numerous to analyze here, it did not recommend immediate abolition of licensed houses, but declared itself in favor of abolition as a final goal, recommended that educational measures be taken toward forming public opinion against such houses, and emphasized the need of complementary administrative medical and social action. (e) Finally, the Conference recommended that governments should welcome the co-operation of voluntary organizations and, in view of the success "which has attended the appointment of women officials in the East," urged

that governments should consider the possibility of employing a larger number of women officials on work connected with the welfare of women and children as women with the necessary attainments and training become available.

THE CONTROL OF NARCOTICS

The word narcotic is derived from the Greek ναϱϰάω, "to make numb," or νάϱϰη, "stiffness," "numbness." Opium, one

---

[25] *League of Nations; Traffic in Women and Children Committee,* C. 504, M. 245, 1932, Vol. IV, p. 8.

of the narcotic drugs, was early known to possess medicinal properties, but its abuse has produced untold physical suffering and moral degradation from ancient times to the present day.

The first country to attempt to control, and even to stamp out, the evil was China. The opium-smoking habit had spread so widely in China that the authorities had become alarmed, and the Emperor issued the first anti-opium edict in 1729. During the next century the opium trade grew, in spite of the government's action, and European carriers made great profits. Out of the disputes which arose, not only over opium but concerning the whole basis of Western relations with China, came the so-called Opium War. As a result of the conflicts of 1840 and 1858, the trade was legalized, on the theory that regulation would stop the illicit traffic and that orderly production and sale were preferable to inefficient prohibition. Whatever the theoretical merit of the argument, the opium evil grew to such magnitude by 1900 that the Chinese government again attempted to prohibit it.

Already in 1880 China and the United States had signed a treaty by which the two powers had agreed to prevent the opium trade. In 1906 the Chinese government issued an edict to suppress poppy-growing within a period of ten years. By 1917 considerable improvement had taken place. Great Britain had agreed with China to limit the export of opium from India, and this bilateral accord was a step in the right direction.

Meanwhile, the problem had grown more complicated and baffling owing to the discoveries of modern science and their prostitution to financially advantageous but socially ruinous ends. Although opium had been used for a long time, its derivatives, as well as drugs made from the leaves of the coca shrub, came into prominence only about the middle of the nineteenth century. Morphine, which is made from opium and is from four to six times as strong, was used, after the invention of the hypodermic syringe in 1853, during the American Civil and Franco-Prussian wars. In 1898 Dreser, by combining morphine and acetic acid, produced heroin. Cocaine, made from the leaves of the coca shrub, appears to have been first used about 1855; it became valuable for surgery, and was also much in demand for popular cures and for use by drug addicts.

Morphine makes people contented and produces an optimistic attitude toward life; cocaine causes an aggressive and hostile attitude. In the absence of morphine the addict suffers considerable distress; there is nothing that he will not do in order to obtain

the drug. He will lie and steal and utterly debase himself. Authorities are generally agreed that the dope habit is a menace to society
and that much criminality can be traced to it. The high profits
from the illicit traffic enable peddlers to bribe officials and intensify
political corruption. Probably four-fifths to nine-tenths of the
trade in drugs is unnecessary for medicinal and health purposes
and can be classified as illicit traffic.

It is this illicit traffic which constitutes one of the world's
major problems. Colonel Woods[26] has stated that once the drugs
have been manufactured and have left the factory the police have
the utmost difficulty in tracking them down because of the amazing variety and ingenuity of the methods adopted by traffickers.
Smugglers send packages of drugs with bills of lading made out
"to order" or to some bank, and if any accident occurs and detection ensues the traffickers leave the goods unclaimed. For this
reason many seizures of opium and morphine do not lead to the
discovery of those engaged in the traffic. Sometimes the forward-
ers make false declarations by describing packages of drugs to be
(for example) rice powder. Frequently drugs are shipped from
free ports where customs officials and other authorities do not
inspect the goods. Sometimes substitutions are made—Colonel
Woods tells that some bowling balls and pins were to be reshipped
at Kobe, but that from there duplicates which had been made and
filled with drugs were shipped on to the port of destination. Often
traffickers are in league with dishonest officials. D'Erlanger[27]
explains that a great amount of drugs came into Egypt because
of false official papers made out by a subordinate Italian consular official. Traffickers use the postoffice and send thousands
of doses by registered letters. Colonel Woods tells that $70,000
worth of narcotics were seized in Los Angeles. Chinese have long
complained that drugs have been forwarded from the foreign-
controlled postoffices in their country. In Egypt, girls who came to
visit incoming ships were found to be carrying off small packages
of drugs concealed in their clothing. Even more ingenious was
the method of concealing narrow packages under the hair of cam-
els in order to smuggle opium across the long desert boundaries.
Only by accident did an official discover that traffickers were
using caravans for this purpose, since the extended frontiers make

[26] Arthur Woods, *Dangerous Drugs* (Yale University Press, New Haven,
1931).

[27] Baron Harry d'Erlanger, *The Last Plague of Egypt* (Lovat Dickson and
Thompson, Ltd., London, 1936).

detection extremely difficult because of the absence of an adequate police force.

Other methods of concealing drugs include the use of trunks with false bottoms, bedsteads with hollow legs, water closets, fountain pens, umbrellas, artificial flowers, barrels of pickles and dried fish, Holy Bibles with squares cut out from the pages, life belts, coal bunkers, hollow canes, etc. If drugs are "once launched in the channels of trade, their chances of a prosperous voyage and safe arrival in the haven where they would be are good."

Inadequate systems of national inspection and control assisted the traffickers. Some governments had required exporters to obtain an import certificate from the government of the place of destination; but governments which required no export or import license played into the hands of the opium rings. Even where an export certificate was required, it might be loosely drawn and prove to be ineffective. Inadequate penalties were an additional incentive to the illicit traffic. The complaint has been made that Japan has imposed absurdly small penalties. "Fines for illicit trafficking are sometimes less than the profit gained from merely a week's sale of smuggled heroin."[28] Finally, the manufacture of "esters," or combinations of morphine and cocaine with acetic acid which can be made so as to have the same effect as morphine itself, brings added problems. Any legal regulation of one combination will encourage the illicit traffickers to make a new combination, which, in the absence of frequent adaptations of legislative measures, can be freely bought and sold.

The first international effort to cope with the problem took place at Shanghai in 1909. The United States found that the Spanish government's opium monopoly in the Philippines had led to an extensive illicit traffic. The investigations of Dr. Hamilton and Bishop Brent and the desire of the American authorities to suppress the evil caused President Theodore Roosevelt to invite fourteen governments to consider the question. The resulting Shanghai conference did little, beyond adopting some general resolutions and urging the importance of drastic action by each government both in its own homeland and in its possessions. But the representatives were not plenipotentiaries with full powers to frame a convention and their work, therefore, was merely of a preliminary character. The nine resolutions had little direct in-

[28] Helen H. Moorhead, "International Administration of Narcotic Drugs, 1928–1934," *Foreign Policy Association Reports* (1935), p. 302.

fluence, and only the United States and China took any action later. Eisenlohr notes that

morphine was apparently the only narcotic whose abuse was causing concern. To the harassed anti-narcotic reformer and administrative official of today the pristine simplicity of the problem in 1909, as opposed to the infinite complexity to which neglect has permitted it to grow today, is a subject upon which he does not like to dwell.[29]

The conference had no immediate success; nevertheless it marked the first step in international effort, and its recommendations formed the basis of the first Opium Convention adopted three years later.

The Hague Opium Conference met in 1912. Twelve governments sent twenty-nine plenipotentiaries, who possessed much greater authority than the representatives who had met at Shanghai. They adopted a convention which urged the passage of effective legislation to control the production and distribution of raw opium; the manufacture, sale, and use of derivatives were to be limited to medicinal and legitimate purposes; manufacturing establishments were to be licensed, or at least recorded; lists should be kept of amounts that had been manufactured, imported, and sold, also a record of total purchase and export; exports were to be permitted only to individuals who possessed licenses or permits of the importing countries. Any other government might sign the convention, and the signatories undertook to exchange information through channels provided by the Dutch government.

Unfortunately, these measures were considerably weakened by several omissions. The Convention did not indicate how far and by what methods the control of production and distribution was to be effected, or whether limitation of the manufacture and sale of derivatives was to be by direct or by indirect means. The signatory powers undertook only to use their "best endeavors" to adopt the use of licenses for exports; and a similar qualifying clause weakened the whole attempt to restrict imports to licensed purchases.

The Hague Conference was more successful in declaring principles than in presenting effective methods of control. It rejected the United States' proposal for an international commission to supervise the agreement. It set forth no definite program. Many

[29] L. E. S. Eisenlohr, *International Narcotics Control* (George Allen & Unwin, Ltd., London, 1934), pp. 19–20.

loopholes for differing interpretations existed; and no international co-ordinating machinery was created. And yet this Convention had not been ratified by December 31, 1912, the date agreed upon, and six months later the governments sent representatives to examine the possibility of depositing their ratification. After a third conference in June 1914, the International Opium Convention finally came into force. The United States, China, the Netherlands, Honduras, and Norway ratified in 1915, and Belgium and Luxemburg in 1919. But it was not until the Peace Conference that the Hague Opium Convention came into force generally. Eisenlohr writes:

In short, the Shanghai Conference and the Hague Convention were fatally conservative and fatally weak. If the reduction of opium cultivation and limitation of drug manufacture had been undertaken in 1909 and 1912 in a vigorous, systematic, and scientific manner, the enormous growth of the manufactured drugs industry during the war would have been checked and controlled at its close, and the tremendous wave of narcotic addiction which since the war has been the chief preoccupation of the narcotics fight need not have occurred—the fact remains that the most critical moment in the history of the narcotics fight was passed unheeded, and the opportunity of preventing the unchecked spread of drug addiction was lost when at Shanghai and The Hague the represented powers failed to pursue a strong and determined policy against the production of opium and to carry out promptly and vigorously the measures agreed upon at the Conference.[30]

One may regard the Shanghai and the Hague Conferences in a more favorable light by considering that they were the first steps and that, without this preliminary work, the League would have been unable to make such progress in recent years in fighting the drug evil.[31]

The Treaty of Versailles contained two parts which dealt with the drug question: (a) a clause ratifying the 1912 Convention and providing for the enactment of legislation within one year; and (b) the Covenant of the League of Nations, Article 23 of which reads: "Subject to and in accordance with the provisions of international conventions existing or hereafter to be agreed upon, the members of the League . . . . will intrust the League

[30] Eisenlohr, op. cit., p. 22.

[31] See also R. L. Buell, "The International Opium Conferences," World Peace Foundation, Vol. 8, 1925, and W. W. Willoughby, Opium as an International Problem (Johns Hopkins Press, 1925), for accounts of the prewar conferences and the early work of the League.

with the general supervision over the execution of agreements with regard to the traffic in opium and other dangerous drugs." On December 15, 1920, the League Assembly adopted a resolution authorizing the Council to set up an advisory committee which should report to the Council three months before each session of the Assembly on matters concerning the traffic in opium and other dangerous drugs. The committee, which met in 1921, represented the principal drug-manufacturing and opium-growing countries and was the first international machinery at all adequate to deal with the opium problem. It had permanence, breadth of membership, and "generous terms of reference," and was much more comprehensive than any which had been set up in the prewar period. Its first task was to formulate the basic issues at stake, and decide the principles which should guide general policy. Three possible methods may be used: The first is to regulate and control the trade in drugs, and by ascertaining the amount needed for legitimate medical and scientific purposes and by controlling the import and export trades to eliminate smuggling and illicit traffic. It is more immediate and, apparently, the easiest method. But, as we shall see, the ease with which illicit traffic may be carried on makes the effort of regulating legitimate trade much less simple than at first sight appears. The high profits derived from the sale of narcotics make traffickers willing to take all kinds of risks, and once the drugs get into circulation, it is well-nigh impossible to trace them.

The second method is to limit the amount of manufactured drugs. Proponents of this scheme say that a limitation of manufacture will eliminate illicit traffic, because, if all the drugs that are made are required for legitimate purposes no surplus will remain for diversion into illicit channels. They assert that the manufacture of narcotics can be supervised without great difficulty, since the process requires a great deal of technical skill, expensive machinery, and practiced operators. It is easier to find unregistered factories than to seize the relatively small packages of prepared drugs after they have found their way into the channels of trade.

The basic weakness of limiting manufactures is that, unless all countries come into the scheme, manufacturers will move to countries where production is unregulated; from there they will continue to flood the world with drugs, leaving the countries which rigidly control manufactures to face the threat of smuggling on a large scale.

For these reasons some authorities favor the most far-reaching measure of all, limitation of production. It was estimated that in 1933 fifteen hundred tons of opium were produced for a world which needed only one hundred tons for legitimate purposes. In addition, the heroin production was far in excess of world requirements. It would seem, therefore, that, if the total amount of poppy leaves grown is strictly limited, there can be no possible surplus for illicit manufacture and none for illicit trade. Difficulties in carrying out the scheme are: (1) the scattered nature of agricultural production, for it is not as simple a matter to regulate thousands of individual growers in many countries as to control factories where workers and machinery are concentrated; (2) the problem of obtaining accurate figures of the amount produced, which, although a serious obstacle, should not be insuperable; (3) the dependence of certain countries, like Turkey and Persia, upon opium, not only as a source of government revenue but also as a means of livelihood for large numbers of peasants. Some years ago the Persian representative argued that thousands of people would be ruined if production of the opium poppy were suppressed unless the country could obtain a large loan to enable it to train experts to assist in introducing new crops.

These are the outstanding methods which the Advisory Committee has considered. Which one to adopt led to much controversy, and together with conflicting governmental policies caused so much ill-feeling as to threaten to wreck more than one international gathering, and did cause the withdrawal of the United States from the 1925 Conference.

The Committee's first task was to ascertain the legitimate needs of the world; this information was necessary for any intelligent scheme of regulation. It sent out a questionnaire to sixty-three governments, only four of which replied within the time set by the Committee. Even worse was the record in the cocaine inquiry. Not one government of the countries which were important producers of cocaine even sent an answer. The Committee had persistently to remind governments of their obligations under the Hague Convention. Only after many efforts was it successful in persuading governments to send in more adequate annual reports. Because the Advisory Committee was unable to obtain adequate information from the governments, it turned to the League Secretariat and requested it to make estimates of the medicinal and scientific needs of the world.

Part of the difficulties lay in the inadequacy of national administrative systems. Many governments did not have the machinery to deal satisfactorily with drug problems.

The effective control of the production and trade in drugs necessitates the services of more than one administrative department as well as definite location of responsibility in one particular branch. From the time a consignment of opium is imported, manufactured into morphine or heroin, exported, or distributed among the pharmacies and dispensaries of a country, the customs agents, sometimes the revenue officials, the health officers and medical inspectors and not infrequently the police and the judiciary are called in to lend their respective services to its control. This necessary diversity of function has to be reconciled with the equally essential centralization of responsibility.[32]

Great Britain, the first to create a special department, in 1920 set up a new division in the Home Office. Later, several other governments brought their administration to a point of efficiency in dealing with the drug evil; but for some time international organization had to wait upon the development of adequate national administrative machinery.

By 1924 it was realized that the control of drug traffic was largely a question of controlling the illicit trade carried on by persons bent on defying the law and indulging in "bootleg" activities. The import certificate system established by the Hague Conference assisted governments somewhat, but there were many loopholes. A certificate system, in order to function adequately, required a permanent central organ to collect information as to the drug needs of the world, the amount of imports and exports, and the extent of the illegal traffic. Moreover, close co-operation with police forces the world over was necessary to combat the lawbreakers. Unfortunately, few institutions existed to provide the necessary information. One government might apprehend a criminal or be suspicious of trafficking; but in the absence of an international research bureau and national facilities for providing all interested countries with the most complete facts, the League was severely handicapped.

The traffickers often paid absurdly small penalties for breaking the law. Some authorities believed that it was more important to provide a greater "certainty of detection" than the "prospect of heavy penalty which with luck" the trafficker "might escape altogether." Sir Malcolm Delevigne proposed that the Secretariat keep a Black List containing names of individuals or firms en-

[32] Eisenlohr, *op. cit.,* p. 69.

gaged in illicit traffic. The idea was excellent, but the question then arose—should the list be confidential or be available to the public? Those who did not wish to have the light of publicity turned upon the drug traffic said that it would be unfair to a firm which had lapsed from virtue once to be branded before the world for all time; and the Advisory Committee, in a spirit of what many people believed to be overcaution, decided not to adopt a public list.

The existence of more than thirty free ports or zones, including such important cities as Rio de Janeiro, Danzig, Hamburg, Salonika, Naples, Genoa, Fiume, Stockholm, Istanbul, Barcelona, and Vladivostok, made possible a flourishing illicit trade. These cities, which do not possess custom regulations or inspection as do the ordinary ports, have constituted a haven of refuge and base of operations for smugglers.

To deal with these many questions the Advisory Committee in 1923 proposed that a new opium conference be called. The suggestion was adopted by the Assembly and the Council. The Assembly also requested the Council to invite governments to a conference for the purpose of limiting (a) the manufacture of morphine, heroin, or cocaine, and (b) the amounts of raw opium and coca leaves to be imported for manufacturing purposes.

In accordance with these resolutions the first Opium Conference met from November 3, 1924, to February 11, 1925. Eight countries (the British Empire, India, China, France, Japan, the Netherlands, Portugal, and Siam) were represented at the gathering, which was primarily a meeting of governments with territories and possessions in the Far East.

The President of the Conference in his opening speech noted the growing menace of illicit traffic and remarked that "never . . . . has the aspect of clandestine trade been so alarming and threatening as it is now." After a number of violent controversies between the Chinese and the other delegates an agreement was finally reached. The powers declared that they were determined to effect "a gradual and effective suppression" of the manufacture of and trade in prepared opium, and desired to suppress opium smoking as quickly as possible. They agreed to make the sale of prepared opium and its distribution a government monopoly, to exclude children from smoking dens, to limit the number of retail shops as far as possible, to restrict the export of opium to territories where it was used for smoking, to initiate an educational campaign in schools and disseminate literature to strengthen public opinion against the use of opium, and to assist one another in suppressing illicit traffic by exchanging information and examining their respective legislative measures "in the most favorable spirit."

The second Opium Conference was a much larger gathering. Forty-one delegates attended it in contrast to the eight governments represented at the first conference. The agenda provided for consideration of measures to give effect to the 1912 Opium Convention in limiting (1) the manufacture of morphine, heroin, or cocaine, (2) the imports of raw opium, and (3) the production of raw opium and coca leaf for export to the amount required for medicinal and scientific purposes. Early in the session controversy broke out, the course of which cannot be dealt with here. Suffice it to say that the United States and China withdrew from the Conference. The United States, which talked of isolation in political matters, retired in disgust because the Opium Conference would not go fast enough along the lines of international control.

The need for a central administrative board was obvious, but the delegates disagreed concerning the extent of its power. The problem has been well summarized by the *Foreign Policy Report* of February 27, 1935:

First, must a government submit full and frequent statistics to this board?

Second, should the board have the right to question these statistics, to ask for further details, to question discrepancies arising between the figures of different governments, to comment on the statistics and explanations given?

Third, should each country be required to submit estimates to the board of its needs of drugs for medical and scientific use, or should these estimates be made by the Board? It had been conceded that such estimates must be available to some central clearing house, so that standards might be obtained against which information could be checked and a global total for world needs ascertained. Another fundamental difference arose over the question whether these estimates should be binding on governments, and whether publicity should be given to the estimates.

Fourth, should the board be given the right to communicate directly with governments, and not be compelled to communicate through an organization essentially political in character, such as the Council of the League? Even more important was the question whether the board should be given the right to make public the facts of the world situation and the position of governments with relation to it.

Fifth, would governments agree in advance to follow the recommendation of the board, even to the point of imposing an embargo on exports of narcotics to the countries whose governments refused to follow the board's recommendations? Authority for action on the basis of information must be granted, otherwise the international organ will become ineffective.

Great Britain (as the United States had done) urged that the production and manufacture of drugs should be limited to the amount required for medicinal purposes; that the countries at present manufacturing drugs should send to a central body an annual estimate of its requirements; and that these estimates should form a basis of total world needs. Great Britain and the United States favored a comprehensive plan of international supervision in opium but not in armaments. France, which had advocated considerable international control in armaments, when it came to the question of drugs, urged that each government should decide its own needs and that its figures could be trusted. The French also opposed the plan of directly limiting the manufacture of drugs, and preferred to limit the volume of trade. Opponents of the British and the American plan argued that international control would limit national sovereignty, would be too complicated, and would involve undue administrative complexities. Some objected that the proposal would lead to a monopoly of manufacture with the danger of excessive prices to the consumers. Japan denied the right of an international body to "revise estimates supplied by a government." The governments, it argued, should retain sufficient power to protect themselves from the board's decisions. The Netherlands insisted that the board have the power simply to collect and to publish statistics. The French delegation objected very strongly to giving the board power to communicate directly with governments, and suggested that its questions and recommendations be made through the Council of the League or the Secretary-General.[33]

Mrs. Moorhead correctly writes that "out of the hodgepodge of ideas and debates during the Geneva Conference of 1925 emerged a convention which represented a definite advance over the Hague Convention of 1912, although it fell far short of providing the stringent measures recommended by the American and British delegations."[34]

Under the convention the signatory powers: (1) agreed to

---

[33] Helen H. Moorhead, in *Foreign Policy Association Reports* (1935), p. 333.
[34] *Ibid.*

limit the trade and use of drugs and their derivatives exclusively
"to medical and scientific purposes"; (2) strengthened the import
and export certificate system by making it much more extensive;
(3) adopted anti-opium control measures for free ports and zones;
(4) provided for heavier penalties; (5) facilitated the extradition
of offenders against narcotic laws and regulations; (6) increased
the number of derivative drugs to which international regulation
should apply; (7) agreed that if a narcotic was deemed by the
Health Committee to be habit-forming, it would automatically
come within the scope of the convention. This measure met the
difficulty caused by the manufacture of new compounds which
otherwise would have escaped regulation.

The convention also provided for a permanent central board
to be composed of eight technical experts, who were not to represent governments. The board was to receive quarterly import and
export statistics, annual estimates of imports and domestic consumption, annual statistics of the amount of raw material produced, of manufactured drugs, and of illicit seizures. The board
was empowered to ask governments to explain any apparent excessive stock or traffic in drugs. But it

lost the most important of the powers originally proposed for it, chiefly
because France would not agree that estimates of need should be binding in character, nor that the Board should be allowed to supply
missing estimates, modify the estimates, or use them except "as a
guide in the discharge of its duties." Moreover, estimates were not
to include all requirements for manufacture and consumption. A most
important point was that the estimates were not to be made public.
The proposed independence of the Board in its relations with governments was limited in that its formal requests for explanations must be
made through the Secretary-General of the League of Nations. The
statistical information concerning manufacture and stocks was to be
submitted annually, instead of every six months as the Advisory Committee had proposed. A government objecting to a recommendation
that exports to another country should be stopped might simply inform the Council and the Board of its objections and offer its explanation.[35]

Thus the Geneva Convention failed directly to limit the manufacture of drugs and to that degree reflected the general temper
of the Advisory Committee which since 1920 had rejected direct
limitation and attempted to deal with the problem by measures to
control the trade. Nevertheless, some members of the Committee

[35] Helen H. Moorhead, *op. cit.*, p. 334.

wished to take more drastic action. Their proposals included (1) various types of monopoly control, and (2) more stringent police organization. In the former class we find Signor Cavazzoni's plan for strengthening national administrative machinery by keeping all imported narcotics in national warehouses, to be released only "upon presentation of the proper government certificate," and by adopting a comprehensive statistical system. The plan was not accepted because it involved the appearance of a government monopoly, and the Advisory Committee contented itself with drawing up a model code providing for a unified and centralized drug administration. Colonel Woods went farther than Signor Cavazzoni and advocated that governments own or adequately control all factories manufacturing dangerous drugs, and rigidly control exports, especially to countries which had not adopted the import certificate system. Dr. Anselmino suggested that governments should permit only "a definitely restricted group of producers" to operate, and proposed a syndicate of drug manufacturers. Colonel Woods also proposed that national administrative officials whose duty it was to enforce the narcotic laws "should meet to discuss ways and means of carrying out their duties."

The proposals to establish more effective organization of police are of interest. Eisenlohr pays tribute to the work of the police in its fight against the drug traffic:

In the first place the police assessors on the Committee have contributed much to the Committee's achievements; secondly, the international police organization has dealt energetically with the problems of the illicit traffic; and, thirdly, it has made every effort to cooperate directly with the Committee and to establish a recognized and official relationship with it.[36]

The attitude of a police official is seen in the statement of Colonel Woods, formerly New York City Police Commissioner, to the Advisory Committee:

I have not been able to escape the impression in the few days during which I have had the privilege of sitting with this Committee, that there may be too much diplomacy and too little rough-shod direct police action in the fight against these narcotic outlaws. It is not a diplomatic question, gentlemen, but a pure police task, and in the contest with lawbreakers as rich, as powerful, as well-organized, and as far-reaching as these the police must act strongly, and must be free from diplomatic entanglements.[37]

[36] L. E. S. Eisenlohr, *op. cit.*, p. 109.
[37] *Ibid.*, p. 110.

The International Police Commission which was set up after the first International Police Congress in 1923 turned its attention to the drug problem. The 1926 Congress recommended the establishment of national central police offices "to facilitate the campaign against the drug traffic." The 1928 Congress requested that a member of the Commission be permitted to attend the sessions of the Opium Advisory Committee. In 1929 the League Assembly invited it "to assist in framing a convention for the suppression of counterfeit currency and the falsification of cheques," and through the Council to help the League's "technical committees."

In 1930 the police assessor of the Advisory Committee, Mr. Sirks, proposed the following plan of police organization in order to fight the narcotics problem:

1. The establishment in each country of a central narcotics bureau to unify administration and police control over the narcotics trade.

2. The establishment of co-operative relations with like authorities of other countries.

3. The establishment of a central bureau at the Secretariat of the League of Nations for the international Police Bureau at Vienna.

4. Provision for the extradition of offenders against narcotics laws.

The Committee at first did not show great enthusiasm for these proposals but later accepted much of a draft convention for the suppressing of the illicit traffic which the International Criminal Police Commission submitted to it in 1931.

It provided for the strict and uniform application of police measures against crimes committed in connection with the illicit traffic in drugs, defined these crimes, called for the extradition of criminals, or their detention and punishment in whatever country they might have sought refuge, and provided for the centralized organization of the police and periodical conferences of the police chiefs of the several countries.[38]

The fourteenth Assembly and later several governments approved the Convention.

In spite of the steps taken in the Geneva Conference and during subsequent years the narcotics situation grew worse. Impressed by the alarming nature of the evidence presented to it, the League Assembly in 1929 took further action. (Through defects

[38] L. E. S. Eisenlohr, *op. cit.*, pp. 117–18.

in the Dutch system of control one firm in eighteen months had exported four tons of heroin and morphine—equal to four times the world's needs.) It went on record as favoring a scheme to limit the manufacture of drugs and requested the Advisory Committee to draw up plans to that end. Following action by the latter, a preliminary meeting of the manufacturing countries to consider in advance the allocation of quotas was held in London on October 27, 1930. A fundamental question soon arose. The countries which were already manufacturing drugs desired to keep a monopoly by dividing the future market among themselves and maintaining existing ratios; countries which hoped to enter the field of manufacture of a highly lucrative article wished a flexible scheme of ratios. The preliminary conference adopted a draft scheme, but did not come to an agreement on quotas.

The general conference held at Geneva from May 27 to July 13, 1931, adopted a Convention which was embodied in seven chapters.[39] It drew up a more comprehensive definition of dangerous drugs so as to include synthetically manufactured esters. To prohibit the evasion of regulations by the use of new drugs it prescribed that if a special body of experts of the League of Nations Health Committee found that a new drug was habit-forming, it automatically would become subject to the 1931 Convention on notification to the signatory powers. The signatories agreed to limit the amount of raw materials to the amount actually needed for the supply of legitimate medical and scientific needs for a period not exceeding six months. The Convention provided for a Supervisory Body which was to watch over the estimates of amount of drugs needed. Governments undertook to supply their estimates for one year in advance. These estimates were to be binding. Should a government fail to send its estimates to the League authorities, the Supervisory Body (made up of four members chosen by the Advisory Committee, the Permanent Central Board, the League of Nations Health Committee, and the Office Internationale d'Hygiène Publique) would adopt a figure; it was empowered to amend the estimates with the consent of the governments concerned. Supplementary estimates were permitted in case of emergency, and to obviate the danger of undue fluctuation of prices. The signatories also agreed to create special administrative machinery to apply the provisions of the Convention and to

[39] See *League of Nations, Conference for Limiting the Manufacturing and Regulating the Distribution of Narcotics, Geneva, May 27–July 13, 1931.* Official No. 455, N. 193, 1931, XI.

undertake campaigns against the use of drugs and suppression of illicit traffic.

The Convention (which can be denounced after five years) marks a step forward in international government by providing a supra-national authority which can lay down the amount of drugs permitted to national authorities. By means of its efficient statistical department, it enables governments to co-operate to prevent the accumulation of huge quantities of manufactured drugs beyond amounts specified in the estimates.

In 1931 a conference was held at Bangkok to consider the further suppression of opium smoking in the Far East. Under the 1925 Opium Agreement the signatory powers had agreed to review from time to time the position of opium smoking. Seven powers attended the sessions, which lasted from November 9 to 27, 1931. A review of the existing conditions showed that smoking had not decreased in the six years since the last conference. After considering the report of the commission of inquiry, the delegates realized the need of adopting stronger measures, and drew up the Bangkok Agreement, which provided that the retail sale and distribution of opium should take place only in government-owned, -managed, or -supervised shops. Persons handling narcotics must be paid a fixed salary, and not a commission on sales. The signatories agreed to introduce compulsory legislation to sell opium for cash only and to reduce the number of factories. Eleven recommendations followed dealing with other aspects of the opium question, including such technical matters as the control of dross, the cure of addicts, and the aftercare of persons who had been cured. The agreement was not to go into effect until ratified by all the signatory powers, a condition realized on April 22, 1937, ninety days after ratification by Japan.[40]

In 1936 the Advisory Committee of the League reported that certain additional narcotic substances should be brought under international control, and proposed a conference to draw up a draft convention to suppress illicit traffic. The conference was held at Geneva in June 1936, and concluded an agreement to strengthen the penalties for offenses against the Conventions of 1912, 1925, and 1931. It provided that any action contrary to the Conventions must be punished by imprisonment or some

---

[40] League of Nations, *Conference on the Suppression of Opium Smoking,* Bangkok, November 9 to November 27, 1931, *Minutes and Documents, Geneva, 1932.* Official C. 577, M. 284, XI; also . . . . *Agreement and Final Act,* Official No. C. 70, M. 36, XI.

forfeiture of liberty. Criminals convicted of violating the various articles may have their convictions used against them in territories belonging to the other signatory powers, who agree, with certain exceptions, to make the offenses as described in the agreement "extradition crimes," to set up a central office of supervision to co-ordinate all work connected with the suppression of illicit drug traffic, and to keep in close touch with similar institutions of the other governments. The conference recommended that, where necessary, governments create a specialized police force to the purpose of the present Convention, which was to come into force ninety days after the Secretary-General had received ten ratifications.[41]

In 1936 the Advisory Committee began preparatory work for a conference to "consider the possibility of limiting and controlling the cultivation of the opium poppy." In its resolution to the League Council it recommended that the two questions, the cultivation of the opium poppy and the cultivation and harvesting of the coca leaf, because of the different problems involved, be separated, and that attention be concentrated upon continuing the studies, and collecting documentary material relating to the control of the opium poppy "with a view to convening at as early a date as possible a conference for the limitation and control of this raw material," and "to adjourn to a later date the problem of control of the coca leaf, while nevertheless considering that the studies relating to this problem should be continued."

What have been the results of the League action in the field of opium? The Advisory Committee, in June 1936, reported that all together fifty-four clandestine factories had been discovered between 1929 and 1936, and that the control of narcotics had been very successful. Many of the illicit manufacturing plants had been shifted to other parts of the world. Baron d'Erlanger noted that Egypt had been largely freed from the drug menace. The Advisory Committee also reported that many drugs which had gone into the illicit traffic had been abandoned because of the efficacy of the police and the marked rise in price in several countries. Moreover, many drugs were being adulterated—a proof that international control had been extremely effective.

For these results the co-operation of governments and police

---

[41] League of Nations, *Conference for the Suppression of the Illicit Traffic in Dangerous Drugs,* Official No. C. 286, M. 174, 1936, XI.

authorities and the work of the League have been responsible.
The international conventions have been ratified by an increasing number of governments and, considering the scope of the
problem and the many technical difficulties involved, as well as
the necessity of establishing national agencies, the League may
well claim high praise for what it has done. Nevertheless much
of the field remains unconquered—sufficient indeed, to enable
Margaret Goldsmith, in her volume *The Trail of Opium,* to make
many criticisms of the League for its failure to do more. Undoubtedly, it is a question of emphasis. The League has failed
badly in many respects; which is another way of saying that
groups and nations have preferred their immediate advantages
over the long-term advantages to be derived from building a
firm foundation of common interests. Undoubtedly many abuses
have continued; it is equally true that they would have been
worse had there been no concerted attack by the League of
Nations.

One last point remains to be considered. Just as slavery and
piracy continued to flourish in an atmosphere of international
political rivalry which prevented effective international co-operation from overcoming these evils, so in the Far East today the
institution of war is helping to nullify collective efforts toward
the suppression of opium and other dangerous drugs. The charge
is freely made by responsible authorities that Japan is deliberately
using drugs as an instrument of war and that the fight against
China is being waged, not merely with bullets, bombs, and shells,
but with the deadly weapon of narcotics which undermine the
morale and physical health of the Chinese people. The United
States representative on the League Opium Committee brought
forth considerable evidence to show how the drug traffic is flourishing in the areas of China under Japanese control. The representative of Egypt, while carefully pointing out that at the
moment he had no firsthand evidence, asserted that the secondhand information was of such an alarming character that the
situation could only be described as most serious.[42]

In the growing intensity of modern wars, we find that every

[42] The League of Nations Advisory Committee on Traffic in Opium and
Other Dangerous Drugs, *Minutes of the Twenty-fourth Session,* pp. 37–43,
Geneva, 1939. See also Marcus Mervine, *Japanese Concessions in Tientsin and
the Narcotic Trade* (Council of International Affairs, Nanking, February 1937);
Haldore Hanson, "Smuggler, Soldier, and Diplomat," *Pacific Affairs,* December 1936, p. 545; Frederick T. Merrill, "The Opium Menace in the Far East,"
Foreign Policy Association Reports, March 1, 1937, and other pamphlet material.

possible instrument is being brought into use in order to defeat
the enemy; and we may expect, if the struggles become increasingly
bitter and unrestrained, that still more grim methods of catastrophic consequence to human welfare will be employed.

EXTRADITION

If a state should refuse to deliver a criminal who had entered
its territory to the state from which he had escaped, it would be
aiding and abetting actions detrimental to law and order. In an
effort to prevent crime, states have co-operated to a limited extent
by signing extradition treaties providing for the manner and conditions under which one country will deliver a criminal to another. Extradition treaties were not common before 1800; until
then they were directed toward returning political offenders to
their own government for punishment. But by the middle of the
nineteenth century states began to adopt the modern practice of
extradition for nonpolitical offenses.

The older type of treaty specified the particular offenses which
should lead to extradition.[43] The 1794 Jay Treaty between Great
Britain and the United States provided for extradition in cases
of murder and forgery. The 1842 treaty enlarged the list to
include murder, assault with intent to murder, piracy, arson,
robbery, and forgery. The 1891 treaty further expanded the list
to cover twenty-six offenses. The more modern type of treaty is
general in character and provides for extradition for actions
which are punishable in both states. Most of the treaties are
bilateral in character, but a few multilateral conventions have been
signed—one at Montevideo in 1902, another at Caracas in 1911,
a third at Montevideo in 1933 and now in force between some
American states, and a Convention signed at Guatamala in 1935
by a number of Central American states.

Several difficulties have arisen in applying the general rules of
extradition. Should a government extradite one of its own citizens who has escaped to his own land from a country where he
committed a crime? Great Britain and the United States normally
are willing to extradite their citizens, but most states refuse to
do so. It can be readily appreciated that serious injustice might
be done to a person holding objectionable political views in the
eyes of governing authorities if he were extradited for one crime

[43] Manley O. Hudson, *Cases on International Law* (West Publishing Company, St. Paul, Minnesota, 1937), pp. 408-19.

and then tried for another. As a general rule, therefore, states accept the principle of speciality, i.e., an individual shall be tried only for the crime which has been named in the warrant of extradition.

A country may hesitate to hand over an offender to another country if it believes that the penalties in the latter are too severe. The question of capital punishment causes particular difficulty. Some states in Latin America and Europe have abolished this mode of punishment, and a number of them have enacted laws "limiting extradition so as to avoid surrender where the death penalty might follow." Many countries have signed treaties agreeing not to impose the sentence of death on extradited criminals. Typical of these treaties are those: between Spain and Brazil, 1872; between Portugal and Switzerland, 1873; between the United States and Costa Rica, 1922; and between the United States and Rumania, 1924.

The most difficult are the cases which involve political offenses. In 1830 Austria and Prussia refused to deliver some Polish political refugees to Russia; but in 1833 Austria, Prussia, and Russia signed agreements which provided that individuals guilty of high treason, conspiracy, or revolt against a throne or a legitimate government should be surrendered. Belgium, however, in the same year passed an extradition law which included a liberal article that Belgian treaties with other states "should contain the provision that a foreigner should not be tried or punished for any political offense committed previously to his extradition, nor for any act connected with such an offense." Its first treaty along these lines was signed with France in 1834, and was followed during the next thirty years by forty-six similarly worded conventions. In 1856 Belgium found reason to modify its extradition law as follows:

An attempt (*attentat*) against the person of the head of a foreign government or against the members of his family, when this attempt constitutes the act of murder, assassination or poisoning, shall not be considered a political offense or an act in connection with a political offense.

Thus Belgium, a liberal state, recognized that there were limits to the methods by which people might legitimately attempt to reform a constitution; other countries followed the Belgian example, and extradited those guilty of political actions of the type just quoted. Many of them, too, agreed to extradite anarchists,

on the ground that they were opposed to all forms of government, and persons whose political crime was of "a gross and
outrageous character." A 1922 Finland law provides that the
government will grant extradition if the crime is a particularly
cruel one. Hershey suggests that communists and socialists are in
a different class from anarchists because their efforts are not
"directed against the bases of all social organization," but "aim
at re-organization of society on a juster and sounder foundation,"
a view with which several states will heartily disagree. He adds
that journalism offenses "are usually regarded as political, but
not necessarily so."[44]

A crime may be committed from a double motive, in part
political and in part personal. These are what the French call
délits connexes (mixed). Switzerland has had most experience
and, incidentally, most difficulty in dealing with this type of
problem.

. . . . that country, by reason of its geographical position and the traditions and character of its people, early became a haven for political
refugees . . . . Many and vigorous were the protests dispatched to
the Swiss government, in 1834, and later, when it appeared that political refugees were using Swiss soil as a base from which to carry on
their revolutionary activities.[45]

Switzerland, in 1892, adopted the principle of "predominance," i.e., treating an offense as political if its predominant
character is political.[46] It made no attempt to set forth general
rules of predominance, but left it to the federal tribunal to decide
as particular cases arose. In 1908 the federal tribunal enunciated
three general principles "which it considered determined the predominantly political character of an offense"; the act (1) must
have been committed to help a purely political program, (2) must
have really served a political end and if the murder of a public
official did not directly modify the political system, the offense
would be deemed primarily nonpolitical in character, and (3)
must not be unduly atrocious in character. It is important to

[44] Amos Hershey, *Essentials of International Public Law and Organization* (The Macmillan Company, New York, 1927), p. 384.

[45] Lora L. Deere, "Political Offenses in the Law and Practice of Extradition," *American Journal of International Law,* 1933, p. 256.

[46] In the same year, l'Institut de Droit international, at its meeting in Geneva, adopted "une résolution en vue de l'élimination des actes de terrorisme
de la catégorie des délits politiques." A. Sottile, "Terrorisme international,"
Académie de Droit International, Recueil des Cours, Vol. 65 (1938), p. 103.

note that an accused person who claims that he has committed a political, and therefore nonextraditable, offense must assume the burden of proof.

The outstanding fact is that governments have found it almost impossible to draw the line between (*a*) political and nonextraditable and (*b*) common and extraditable offenses. Deere remarks that "the universal opinion is to the effect that such a definition is both impossible and undesirable," and that it is important to entrust the determination of what is a political offense to a judiciary which, more than an executive body, can be relied upon to do justice. And the same writer made (in 1933) the penetrating observation that:

the future of the rule of no extradition of political offenders depends partly upon the political offenders themselves and partly upon the future of the states making up the present world order . . . .

There may develop an integration of political organization to such an extent that each state or division in the organization would feel an interest in itself punishing attacks directed at any one of the group regardless of where the act might be committed. At present, however, in view of the strong feeling of nationalism and the principle of territorial sovereignty, there seems to be no trend in this direction, and the problem of what constitutes a political offense for extradition purposes will therefore frequently present itself for solution.[47]

The events of the next year provided an eloquent commentary upon this judgment. The Italian court of appeal at Turin in 1934 refused the request of the French government for the extradition of two persons accused of assassinating King Alexander of Jugoslavia and M. Barthou, the French Minister of Foreign Affairs, at Marseilles in France. The court based its decision upon Article 3 of the 1870 Franco-Italian extradition treaty, which excluded political crimes from the process of extradition. The incident focused attention upon the new international atmosphere within which political crimes were being committed. The peace treaties had ended the formal state of war after 1918, but great passions remained; and the defeated countries, charging that the peace terms were unjust and tyrannical, continuously thought in terms of revenge. The advent of dictatorships brought the expulsion of many political opponents; persons who would not conform were denied a voice in the government, and even the right to reside in their native land. Many of the political exiles plotted

[47] Deere, *op. cit.*, pp. 169–70.

against the dictators, and, in this way what was essentially a domestic difference of one party against another became an international problem. Political refugees from the Soviet Union, Italy, Germany, and other countries swelled the list of political malcontents. Political assassinations of important officials added to the already complex problems of international relations. In 1927, a Russian youth murdered the Soviet minister at Warsaw. The Soviet Union accused Poland of being part of a world-wide conspiracy against the U.S.S.R.; and Poland indignantly denied the charge. While the controversy was at its height, Soviet officials arrested a Pole who had entered Russia allegedly for purposes of terrorism. Each country claimed to be innocent and held the other responsible for the action against itself.

The same phenomenon appeared elsewhere in Europe. Hundreds of Fascist refugees fled to Paris, and Italy accused France of encouraging underground political intrigue. An Italian charged with murder escaped to Paris; this and other incidents caused Italy to pass an act depriving of citizenship those who harmed Italy's interests and Italy's good name abroad. In 1926 the French discovered a plot by which Spain was to be raided from the French side of the border from points where arms and munitions were to be stored. The French police published the plan, and its exposure seriously affected French-Italian relations. France interpreted the conspiracy as an effort on the part of Italy to endanger Franco-Spanish friendship.

In 1928 some machine parts were found at Szent Gotthard on the Austro-Hungarian frontier. Five trucks had been falsely declared, and the Succession States feared lest the arms were destined for Hungary, which had been disarmed under the Treaty of Trianon. Moreover, such action might set a precedent for arms smuggling to other defeated powers. The League Council took no definite action, but the governments of Europe remained considerably perturbed.

During subsequent years many outrages occurred in Jugoslavia. No fewer than twenty terrorist crimes took place, culminating in 1934 in the murder of King Alexander and M. Barthou, the French foreign minister at Marseilles. The Jugoslav authorities claimed that the crime was committed by men who had been trained in special camps in Hungary. They accused Hungary of assisting Jugoslav émigrés to obtain arms and ammunition, of issuing false passports to them, and of drilling them in the methods of professional terrorism. The Czechoslovakian statesman,

Beneš, stated that Hungary had tolerated the existence of a veritable school of terrorists at Janka Puszta only a few miles from the Jugoslav border.

In 1925 Professor Pella published an important volume, *La criminalité collective des Etats,* in which he foreshadowed a plan of international co-operation and even the creation of an International Penal Court. The first International Conference for the unification of penal law, held at Warsaw in 1927, considered the problem, and at the Third Conference at Brussels in 1930, the Fourth Conference at Paris in 1931, the Fifth Conference at Madrid in 1932, and the Sixth Conference at Copenhagen in 1935, reports were discussed. The last gathering drew up a draft of eight articles and added a *vœu*

que, lorsque l'extradition n'est pas accord'ée, les délinquants puissent être déférés à une juridiction pénale internationale, à moins que l'Etat requis ne préfère les faire juger par ses propres tribunaux.[48]

It was Rumania which in 1926 first brought the matter before the League of Nations by proposing that a study be undertaken for the elaboration of International Conventions for a Concerted Repression of Terrorism. But only after the assassination of King Alexander and M. Barthou in 1934 did the League, on the initiative of France, take action. After considerable discussion the Council called an intergovernmental conference, which met at Geneva, November 1, 1937.

These instances indicate the demoralizing forces at work in a Europe rendered emotionally unstable by the cataclysm of the World War of 1914–1918, the grievances arising from the Peace Treaties, the disappointments suffered by minorities, the apprehension of the majorities, the intolerance of the dictatorships, and the resentments persisting among persons expelled from their country. The decline of liberalism, and of the spirit of tolerance within and between nations, caused many domestic problems to take on an international aspect. People who could not use the ballot at home were tempted to use the bullet abroad. In an effort to stem the growing tide of international violence, governments discussed methods for the repression of terrorism, and considered two conventions—one for the prevention of terrorism and the other for the establishment of an international criminal court.

Opinion was seriously divided as to the desirability of any convention along these lines. Great Britain urged that her exist-

[48] Quoted by A. Sottile, *op. cit.,* p. 115.

ing arrangements were sufficient to take care of terrorist activities, and that it would be difficult to persuade Parliament to change Britain's methods. It claimed that the time was not ripe for the creation of an international criminal court, because such a court would be seldom used, and because of the great diversity in national criminal law systems. Norway also announced its unwillingness to join an international criminal court. The Netherlands and Hungary approved both conventions. Haiti approved the convention for the suppression of terrorism, stating that extradition should be subordinated to such an agreement because terrorism was in reality a crime against civilization. But Haiti feared that the proposed international court would be too slow in its action and too expensive to be very useful. Czechoslovakia, Belgium, and France supported both conventions. The last-named stressed the inadequacy of extradition measures in political crimes. The Belgian representative asserted that an international convention was necessary even though nations claimed that their domestic laws provided adequate punishment for acts of terrorism, and pointed out that although traffic in women and children and the counterfeiting of currency are regulated by national law it was found desirable to supplement these measures by international organization because of the inadequacy of unco-ordinated national actions. But terrorism was assuming an even more international character than the traffic in women and the counterfeiting of currency. Extradition treaties were not effective enough because of insufficient international police organization and the lack of adequate facilities for the exchange of information concerning suspicious characters, the slow execution of letters of request, and the lack of agreements between countries involved as to the real nature of the outrages.

The Spanish representative supported both conventions, although he believed that the criminal court had little chance of survival; however, since adherence to the court was not to be compulsory, experience would show whether the court was a fundamental necessity or not. Other representatives spoke for and against the conventions.[49]

After much discussion and correspondence the draft convention for the prevention and punishment of terrorism was adopted in 1938. It defined acts of terrorism and obligated the signatory powers to co-operate as fully as possible in preventing all activi-

[49] The objections are analyzed by A. Sottile, *op. cit.,* pp. 136–39.

ties suspected of being terrorist in nature. Under Article 15, each signatory undertook to establish an appropriate service in close contact with its own police authorities and with the corresponding services of the other states for the purpose of bringing together all information calculated to facilitate the prevention of terrorist offenses and for their punishment when committed.

The convention for the creation of an international criminal court was drawn up in the same year. It provides for a permanent court of judges chosen from acknowledged authorities on criminal law; it is to consist of five regular judges and five deputy judges, no two of the same nationality, chosen by the Permanent Court of International Justice from a panel nominated by the interested countries. Judges are to hold office for ten years, and one regular and one deputy judge are to retire every two years. The court is to apply the substantive criminal law which is the least severe. It shall determine what that law is by considering the law of the territory in which the offense is committed and the law of the country which commits the accused for trial.

The many detailed provisions of the fifty-six articles cannot be analyzed here. Suffice it to say that they represent an ambitious attempt to overcome the weaknesses of the present system of extradition. It may well be open to doubt whether any considerable measure of success will attend these conventions for some time,[50] and whether we may expect any substantial relief from international terrorism until two fundamental conditions are realized: (1) a restoration of widespread political, religious, and social tolerance within all countries, especially the dictatorships (but can dictatorships be tolerant?); and (2) a substantial degree of international security to permit a lessening of the abnormal fears and sensitivities now rampant in the world. International terrorism is, in large measure, the outcome of political anarchy and repression, both national and international. Its solution will depend upon reforms which will eradicate the conditions which lead to terrorism, rather than upon erecting international machinery to suppress what a wiser and more enlightened domestic policy could have prevented from arising.

Nor can one ignore the considerable amount of evidence which exists of the fact that terrorism has been increasingly made a weapon of waging international war, by undermining the author-

[50] See Sottile, *op. cit.*, pp. 175–78, for a general estimate, and especially a discussion of the wisdom of not tying the Conventions more closely to the League of Nations.

ity of rival governments and thereby paving the way for ultimate penetration and conquest. There can be little real success in having an international court to try terrorists if these men and women are merely the instruments of governmental forces arrayed against each other in bitter opposition. Until international individual terrorism is divorced from the international struggle for national supremacy over other nations, it cannot be treated separately as a simple question of crime prevention. The major question of international security and order must be solved first: only after that is done can effective steps be taken to deal with a problem which will then be reduced to relatively solvable proportions. The widespread nature of "fifth column" methods which the present war has revealed—spies in all kinds of preliminary work to weaken the future enemy, trusted people worming their way into confidence only to betray it, people guiding enemy parachutists—places the question of international crime in a sinister light, and shows the way in which modern war is breaking down the distinction between public and private activities.

Chapter III

MONETARY ISSUES AS WORLD PROBLEMS

THE INTERNATIONAL nature of monetary organization was clearly realized before 1914; and now, after twenty-five years of uncertainty and disequilibrium, we can appreciate the advantages to the prewar world of a remarkable mechanism which functioned across national boundaries. The history of the period 1914–1940 is largely the history of nations which preferred for one reason or another to narrow their financial foundations in an attempt to support a purely national economy. The following account is therefore a description of the tragic consequences of a continuous breakdown of international co-operation. As a blind man may be said to appreciate the beauty of light in a negative way, so modern world society is learning or should be learning through bitter experience the truth of the necessity of building economic institutions on foundations wider than that of the sovereign state.

GOLD

During the nineteenth century an increasing number of countries adopted the so-called gold standard. Under this system banks must hold a certain amount of gold as a basis for paper money; depositors might ask for payment in gold at any time, and it was therefore necessary, in order to maintain their solvency, that banks should maintain a substantial gold reserve. Moreover, gold served the further purpose of readily adjusting the balance of international trade.

Economic life responds very quickly to changes in price levels. A sharp rise or fall in prices affects economic enterprises in a very direct manner. And it is generally admitted that stability of prices is most desirable. But stability of prices depends upon the relation between the amount of business done and the amount of money available. One may take a simple illustration. Suppose fifty people, who are seated in fifty chairs, possess a total of fifty dollars with which they wish to purchase the chairs. Each chair would be worth one dollar. If another fifty chairs are available for them to buy, but the amount of money remains the same, each chair must be priced at fifty cents. The illustration neglects many complicating factors but it may serve to introduce the general problem.

On the basis of this example, one may deduce that if the total amount of world economic activity increases by an average of 3 per cent a year, there must be a similar percentage increase in the amount of currency available in order to maintain stability of price levels. Increased economic activity without an increase of currency will lead to a fall in general prices. It follows that if gold is regarded as a necessary basis of currency, an expansion of trade activity which requires an expansion of currency will also necessitate an increase in the world's gold supply.

Economists have made elaborate estimates of world gold production figures, and equally elaborate calculations of the annual increase in the world's gold supplies which would be required in order to maintain stable prices. The estimates vary from less than 1 per cent to over 3 per cent, according to whether the estimates are based upon nineteenth-century or twentieth-century needs. The outlook for price stability is not bright if the assumptions stated are sound. Mr. Joseph Kitchin in 1930 stated that ". . . on 1850 to 1910 experience, an increase in the gold in central banks and treasuries of somewhere between 3.1 per cent and 3.4 per cent is required to keep prices stable if the world's rate of development is not slowed down, and I cannot conceive of anything like this rate of increase being attained . . . . a fall in the trend of wholesale commodity prices for an indefinite period (moderate at first but increasing with time) is in prospect."[1]

There seemed, when he wrote this, to be every reason for assuming that sooner or later the world must suffer from an inadequate supply of gold. It did not seem possible that the great mines in South Africa, which accounted for more than one-half of the world's production, could last indefinitely; mines all over the world were experiencing higher costs of production as they went deeper; most lands had been surveyed, and mankind could no longer expect more than an occasional new gold discovery of any substantial magnitude. Mr. Kitchin's warning did not stand

[1] Joseph Kitchin, "Gold Production," in *The International Gold Problem* (Royal Institute of International Affairs, Oxford University Press, 1931), p. 68.

alone. The Gold Delegation of the League of Nations Financial Committee, in its interim report of 1930, expressed the fear that the world would soon experience a shortage of gold.

This line of reasoning naturally led to suggestions of methods of economizing gold so as to enable the same quantity to do a greater amount of work. Such suggestions were made by the Gold Delegation, and by the experts who drew up the agenda for the World Economic Conference of 1933. They included: (*a*) a better distribution of gold among countries; (*b*) international agreements to lessen the minimum ratio of gold to other currency; (*c*) the replacement of small notes by subsidiary coin "which will to some extent reduce the strain on gold reserves through the decrease in note circulation."

It may be noted that the increasing use of gold in ordinary life for dental purposes, jewelry, and other ornamentation led to a further demand upon the gold supplies of the world; and this fact was present in the minds of economists when they contemplated the general gold problem.

The gloomy prognostications of what might be called monetary Malthusianism have not thus far been fulfilled. A number of factors have offset the forces at work making for a gold shortage. The fall in prices which followed the world depression raised the value of gold. The increased price of gold as a result of government action—notably that of the United States, which raised the price from twenty to thirty-five dollars an ounce—gave a great stimulus to gold mining and resulted in a great increase in production. The use of platinum instead of gold for jewelry purposes, the falling off in the gold consumption of other industrial activities, and especially the departure of certain nations from the gold standard and the use of managed paper currencies have altered the whole emphasis of the problem, at least for the time. Indeed, C. O. Hardy suggests that, if and when the gold standard is again adopted, the problem will rather be one of absorbing the surplus and not of "compensating for a deficiency," so rapidly has the situation changed. In the meantime the rapid increase in the gold supply has not been turned to full economic use, because national governments, even those which have (or had!) large supplies of gold, have gone off the gold standard and have prohibited the free international movement as well as the unrestricted domestic redemption of gold. Moreover, circumstances have so altered as to lessen the use of gold in mitigating international exchange fluctuations. We shall see later that the postwar period has been characterized by an extreme nervousness of capital, due to abnormal political instability both within nations themselves and in their international relations. This nervousness finds expression in a great amount of short-term investments which "do not correspond to shifts in trade, in interest rates, or attractiveness of genuine investment opportunity" and are therefore not subject to the ordinary economic controls of central banking policy. When capital is panicky and political crises are numerous, and when confidence is shaken in a country's credit structure, "no gold supply can be adequate to meet" the drain of gold which follows a rush by investors to find a haven of safety for their money. Gold reserves cannot withstand a prolonged attack of political jitters. Hardy points out that the German Reichsbank in 1931 held a very strong position, having the fourth largest gold reserve in the world, but that a short period of panic sufficed to force Germany off the gold standard.

Thus the question of adequacy of gold supplies turns in large measure upon two further questions: (1) whether or not the world will go back to the gold standard, and (2) whether or not the existing distribution of gold is satisfactory. Should the world again adopt the gold standard, it is theoretically arguable that the quantity of gold would again become a question of great urgency. And if we find that the gold which is already available is so badly distributed that it is shut off from countries which need it, we must ask whether this maldistribution is a cause or an effect of economic abnormality.

Theorists who blame maldistribution of gold for much of the world's present dislocation say that the World War of 1914–1918 created an abnormal situation and plunged several countries into debt; the necessity of paying such debts in gold diminished the gold basis of currency, forced down prices in the debtor countries, created serious crises, and made it necessary for the debtor countries to (1) export more of their products at still lower prices, or (2) send out more gold, thus still further endangering their national currency structure, or (3) go into default and suspend payments. These critics alleged that the countries which received large quantities of gold, especially France and the United States, did not permit the gold to raise their price levels by being used as the basis of an expanded note issue, but that they "sterilized" it, by segregating it or in some other manner refusing to allow it to play its traditional role. In this way the maldistribution of gold caused a disequilibrium of currencies, threw national price levels out of gear, and prevented a restoration of the gold standard. Countries in an unfavorable economic position and finding themselves short of money had to depreciate their currency and adopt schemes of exchange control. Theorists who write along these lines emphasize the importance of monetary policy in causing the world depression, and naturally believe that monetary methods may alleviate the present ills. They say that if central banks will increase their purchase of securities and thus create more money, new capital developments will take place which will increase employment and add to purchasing power.

Policy along their lines would lead to action which normally can take place only within national limits. If that is so, what will avail the smaller and economically weaker countries which need capital? They cannot sufficiently create purchasing power merely by an inflationist policy by their central banks. What can be done in their case?

Two lines of action are possible: (1) Further loans to them from the creditor countries, and (2) a lowering of tariff barriers by the creditor nations so that the latter will receive more goods and supplies from the debtor countries; in this way economic activity in those debtor countries will be stimulated and will permit them to lessen their indebtedness. The difficulty with the first course, that is, further loans from creditor nations, is that it intensifies the problem of repayment. Very quickly the question would again arise, How can the debtors pay their creditors if the latter persists in maintaining their high tariff walls?

The foregoing discussion has moved from a consideration of the maldistribution of gold to questions of investments and tariff policy. And according to another group of economists this is inevitable, because in their view the so-called maldistribution of gold is an effect rather than a cause of the world's present economic dilemma. They ask why the maldistribution of gold should have occurred, and reply that nonmonetary factors have been largely responsible in bringing about the monetary disequilibrium. These factors include: the rigidity of interest rates; the growing burden of debt structure, both national and international; the contradictory policy of those countries which loaned money abroad but persisted in keeping up high tariffs; the growing economic nationalism due to alleged necessities of defense; and the desire of agricultural countries to "balance" their economy by encouraging some degree of industry. And these factors have combined to make the maintenance of the gold standard impossible and to force debtor countries to part with their gold. Maldistribution of gold, therefore, is a symptom, rather than a cause. Professor T. E. Gregory has remarked that, even if all the world's gold reserves were miraculously handed back to countries so as to restore the position of 1913, with present economic forces at work gold would soon again be maldistributed.

Economists are not agreed whether or not it is desirable to return to the gold standard.[2] The Gold Delegation of the League of Nations in 1932 considered it of the utmost importance for the world's economic and financial development to return to gold as soon as possible, and urged that national policies should include "the restoration of a reasonable degree of freedom in the movement of goods and services," a solution of the reparations and war debts problem, which involved heavy outpayments from countries unable to live up to their obligations without overgreat financial strain, and co-operation among the central banks of the world so that gold moving to and from countries should be enabled to influence the level of prices. Countries receiving gold should use it in order to expand their currency and so raise prices; countries losing gold would normally experience a decline of prices, and their cheaper goods would cause the higher-price-level countries to buy from them and in this manner gradually restore the price level and the normal processes of international trade. Governments also should balance their budgets and economize the use of gold. Professors Lionel Robbins and Hayek wrote along similar lines, urging that the gold standard was a semiautomatic mechanism "less open to political pressure than any other standard," and that with its restoration the current exchange fluctuations would be minimized and confidence again restored.

Experts who opposed the early return of the gold standard insisted that its restoration and maintenance would depend upon many conditions which at present cannot be realized and that, should a "premature restoration" take place, it might have extremely unfortunate consequences, comparable to those which befell Great Britain after returning to the gold standard in 1925. Sir Arthur Salter, in his *World Trade and Its Future,* noted that within ten years of the Peace Treaty most national monetary systems had been restored but the international political crises which developed after 1930—the Japanese invasion of Manchuria, the

---

[2] See *Monetary Policy and the Depression,* issued by the Royal Institute of International Affairs (Oxford University Press, 1933).

breakdown of the Disarmament Conference, the disturbing effects of Hitler's advent to power—and certain economic factors such as falling prices, the growing rigidity of economic life, the unwise investment policies of creditor countries, and the increase of tariffs, broke the gold standard. The 1920 Brussels Financial Conference organized by the League of Nations had recommended balanced budgets, cessation of inflation, establishment of central banks of issue, the organization of international agencies for new credits, and the restoration of the gold standard. But monetary re-establishment alone was insufficient. As Sir Arthur puts it, money and finance are only the servants of trade, and the newly restored gold currencies of the postwar period depended upon the maintainence of equilibrium in the general system of international payments.

Opponents of the early return to the gold standard argue that, if these adverse factors destroyed the gold standard in the last decade, there is little ground for believing that present conditions will permit the political and economic stability required for the working of the gold-standard system. Professor Cassel, the Swedish economist, in his dissenting memorandum in the report of the League of Nations Gold Delegation of 1932, asserted that an attempt at this time to return to gold would be doomed to failure, because it would be impossible to obtain

the fulfillment of a number of essential conditions, among which the following should be mentioned here; a great reduction in the value of gold, a radical redistribution of the world's gold reserve, the resumption of a systematic gold economizing policy, cancellation of all claims upon reparation and war debt payments, definite guarantees against the repetition of such extraordinary demands for gold as have occurred during the last few years, and, finally, restoration of a reasonable freedom of international trade and of international capital movement.

The same authority in 1936 published his *The Downfall of the Gold Standard* and, in a chapter entitled "The Illusion of a Return to Gold," strongly urged the necessity of making monetary policy independent of gold reserves and concluded that "for all practical purposes the gold standard is a thing that belongs to the past." The almost continuous instability in international relations during the last few years bears out Cassel's statement. The invasion of the Rhineland, the absorption of Austria, foreign intervention in Spain, the Italian conquest in Abyssinia, the tension in the Mediterranean, the crisis over Czechoslovakia, the conflict in China, and the present war are too disturbing to permit the functioning of "a semiautomatic mechanism." Until some form of international security has been attained we shall look in vain for the restoration of the gold standard, even assuming that its return is theoretically desirable—an assumption which many economists are not disposed to admit. The reasons of J. M. Keynes, C. R. Whittlesey, and R. T. Harrod involve considerations which lie beyond the province of the present work. Nevertheless, the judgment may be ventured that the alternatives which now appear possible all will require more and not less international regulation, and a greater subservience of national to international needs.

SILVER

Great Britain adopted the gold standard in 1816. Until 1873 most countries remained on either a bimetallic or a silver basis. The difficulties of bimetallism led to its general discontinuance and the demonetization of silver in the year just mentioned. The price of silver thereupon fell sharply and silver producers suffered great hardship. In the United States they organized to defend their interests and in 1878 succeeded in having the Bland-Allison Act passed, under which the Treasury was ordered to purchase large amounts of silver for conversion into silver coinage. The act was strengthened by the Sherman Purchase Act in 1890, but was repealed during the financial crisis of 1893. The silver interests were prominent in the 1896 elections; but from that time until the end of the World War in 1918 silver dropped from world attention.

Two principal arguments had been employed to justify the use of silver as currency: (1) The continuous fall in world prices after 1873 might be offset by using either a silver or a bimetallic currency, which would increase the supply of money and thereby keep up price levels. This argument lost its force after the 'nineties, when an upswing of prices took place. And (2) a bimetallic standard would offset the ups and downs of silver and gold production and would assist in stabilizing exchanges—an argument not without some theoretical force.

About a decade ago the silver question came into renewed prominence. The average price of silver had dropped from 58.2 cents an ounce in 1928 to 25 cents in December 1932, the lowest in its history. This catastrophic decline occurred because: (1) Several countries sought gold as a basis for their re-established postwar currencies. (2) The fall in the price of silver did not result in a decline in its output, because much silver "is normally produced as a by-product of copper, lead, and zinc, and, therefore, as long as the prices of these principal products are maintained at a reasonably profitable level for the producers, this production will be kept up and their by-product, silver, will continue to be thrown on the market, even though its own price is low and declining."[3] (3) Many countries substituted paper, nickel, bronze, and copper money for silver, and others lessened the amount of silver in their coins, partly to stop the process of melting down and partly for reasons of economy. (4) India, which, although on the gold standard since 1899, had used an enormous amount of silver rupees for everyday currency, decided to reduce the amount of its silver reserves. The 1926 Royal Commission recommended that within ten years the government should reduce its silver holdings from 247 to 73 million ounces. The sale of over one hundred million ounces between 1927 and 1932 gave the final blow to the silver market.

At this time the arguments in favor of reintroducing silver into currency reserves used toward the end of last century reappeared, namely, that only by adopting bimetallism or otherwise using silver can the world restore equilibrium in the relative prices of silver and gold and in the foreign exchanges, and insure a rise in price levels. But another argument now appeared, namely, that the use of silver by the Western nations would help to raise the purchasing power of the Orient, especially China, which, it was asserted, was suffering heavily from the low price of silver. In vain, economists pointed out that the fall in the price of silver was actually helping China's exports, which a high exchange rate would adversely affect, and that, if the world doubled the gold price of silver, the currency of China would be endangered because her people would export silver and not goods in order to pay for imports and in this way China would deplete her silver reserves.

The 1933 World Economic Conference considered the silver question. The experts had reported that silver was not an important factor in the world's monetary situation; but, owing to pressure of the silver states in America, the matter received attention. In fact, the only resolution passed by the Conference dealt with

[3] E. W. Kemmerer, *Kemmerer on Money* (J. C. Winston, Philadelphia, 1934), p. 119.

silver. The resolution and subsequent arrangements provided for an international agreement between the silver-producing and the silver-using countries in order to mitigate price fluctuations. Signatory governments undertook not to debase their silver coinage "below a fineness of 800/1000" and to use silver for their subsidiary coinage; India agreed not to sell more than one hundred forty million ounces of silver during the years 1934–38; Australia, Canada, the United States, Mexico, and Peru agreed not to sell any silver and to withdraw 35,000,000 ounces of silver a year from their mines between 1934 and 1938. Moreover, China was not to sell silver "resulting from demonetized coins for four years, and Spain must limit her sales to 20,000,000 ounces per year for the same period."

This international agreement was overshadowed by the United States domestic policy. In March 1933 President Roosevelt placed an embargo on silver exports. An act of May 1933 gave him authority to introduce bimetallism, to permit the unlimited coinage of silver should he so choose, and for six months to accept silver in payment of war debts. A joint resolution of June 5, 1933, provided that all coins and currencies could be legal tender for public and private debts in the United States. In December 1933 the Treasury was ordered to purchase newly mined domestic silver at 64.64 cents an ounce, and this price was raised later. The Silver Purchase Act of June 1934 ordered the Secretary of the Treasury to purchase silver at home or abroad at a price not to exceed $1.29 per ounce—the object being to have one quarter of the money reserve consist of silver and so to raise the domestic price.

These national and international efforts to restore silver and to stabilize its price were not very successful. Professor John Park Young writes that the silver fluctuations in 1935 were greater than at any previous time. Nor did the American silver policy succeed in its aim of encouraging foreign nations "to utilize more silver in their monetary systems." Indeed, it operated to force China and Mexico to demonetize silver.[4] It failed to raise the purchasing power of the Eastern countries, just as the experts had prophesied; and it intensified China's difficulties. Professor Young is not alone in his judgment that "a rising silver price was the principal factor responsible for China's grave economic troubles after early 1933, culminating in the breaking down of its

---

[4] *Foreign Policy Report,* July 1, 1936.

currency system.''[5] China at first attempted to stop the export of silver to the United States by imposing an export tax, but extensive smuggling made it difficult to carry out this policy; then, realizing that it could hope for no modification in the American silver policy, it went off the silver standard on November 4, 1935, and substituted a managed currency. By so doing it seriously affected the very United States silver interests which had clamored for action, because China which had previously imported the metal for currency purposes now ceased to be a purchaser. A later agreement between the United States and China was made; but it was the outcome of political rather than economic considerations.

From all this we can see that silver has become an international problem mainly because the advice of expert economists was rejected, and because certain governments, particularly the United States, attempted, under the pressure of mining interests, to take unsound positive action instead of maintaining a negative, or at least a relatively passive, policy. Stabilization involves many nations.

SHORT-TERM LOANS

One serious consequence of the world's political instability and frequent crises has been the abnormal growth of short-term loans and what has been picturesquely called "hot money." A certain amount of short-term credit is always necessary because of seasonal fluctuations. Farmers normally require loans for a few months, and merchants need advances to tide them over certain periods. These normal factors, however, have been overshadowed by other short-term loans, some of which have been used by borrowing countries for capital construction. Funds so expended are tied up and cannot be easily liquidated. One cause of Great Britain's going off the gold standard in 1931 was that several Continental banks had a large amount of money on short call in London, much of which London had reinvested in Europe. When the Austrian Credit Anstalt crashed, confidence vanished and European investors rushed to their banks to withdraw their deposits;

[5] See, for example, R. B. Westerfield, *Our Silver Debacle* (The Ronald Press, New York, 1936), chapters ix–xi. Westerfield believes that no solution of the silver question as an economic or monetary question is possible, either nationally or internationally, now that India, Mexico, and China are off the silver standard. He would stop the purchase of foreign silver and put domestic silver on a national dole, because silver is obsolescent, a fact which we should recognize (pp. 199–207).

and the banks pressed London, which could not stand the strain of such a sudden and huge demand for gold.

No normal banking system can function in an atmosphere of crisis and panicky withdrawal of funds. If, therefore, they lend too great a proportion of their deposits on short loans, they jeopardize their stability and solvency, for they are at the mercy of sudden demands for gold by frightened investors in the event of a panic.

Short-term loans have increased so markedly because the frequent international crises have made investors unwilling to lend their capital abroad for long periods. Unable to see far ahead, they fear to undertake long-time loans in a kaleidoscopically changing world. Borrowing countries are unable to obtain funds for long-term construction projects, and may take a risk and use short-term loans for that purpose. The political conditions for sound investment are lacking, and should banks succumb to the temptation of issuing too many short-term loans they play a dangerous game. Economists agree that a reduction in the amount of these short-term loans is necessary if financial stability is to be re-established.

There is another aspect of the question. Capital movements today seem to bear less relation to economic and banking factors than they do to political conditions. Hardy writes that they "do not correspond to shifts in trade, in the interest rate, or in the attractiveness of genuine investment opportunity" and are therefore "not subject to control through the ordinary mechanism of central bank policy."[6] Capital has been more concerned "to seek safety rather than profit" and, in the search for safety, funds have been "shuttled from one land to another." It has become "hot money," and it has introduced many complicating issues.

Europe's monetary uncertainty in 1932–33, the great pressure upon the gold currencies of France, Switzerland, and Holland, the upturn in American business, and fears in France that the Blum government would unduly penalize French capitalistic interests combined to produce a remarkable migration of capital from Europe, which sorely needed it, to the United States, which already had extraordinary amounts of gold and securities. This flow of capital had serious consequences for the European countries, and created embarrassing problems for the United States. Authorities feared that large foreign investments in this country would send

---

[6] Charles O. Hardy, *Is There Enough Gold?* (The Brookings Institution, Washington, D.C., 1936), p. 99.

the prices of stock to new heights and would "generate a speculative boom with results as disastrous as those in 1929," and also that gold imports would unduly expand the bank reserves of the United States and thus inflate the credit structure. "The importation of about four billion dollars in gold during the last three years, therefore, created the basis for an enormous expansion of credit which would undoubtedly have led to serious inflation."[7] The Federal Reserve Board, in order to offset the effect of gold imports, "twice raised the legal requirements," by 50 per cent in July 1936 and by another 33⅓ per cent in the first half of 1937. The government also "sterilized" the gold imports by holding much of it "in an inactive account in the general fund." Sterilization is a costly business; according to Bratter, "if gold has to be acquired by the Treasury at the same rate as in the last few months, it will involve an increase in the public debt of over $1,898,000,000 a year. Such an increase is particularly embarrassing at a time when the government bond market is manifesting growing concern over continued government deficits."[8] Curiously enough, this gold influx, far from enriching the country, seemed to add to its financial difficulties, and the government attempted to find means of stopping, and even reversing, the inward movement of capital and gold.

One suggestion is to impose further taxation upon foreign capital invested in this country, but there are difficulties in this method. The United States might "offset the influx of capital by renewed foreign lending . . . . but Americans are unlikely to invest money abroad so long as foreigners themselves see better prospects for profits and greater safety for their capital in the United States."[9] It might be possible to reduce the price of gold, but such a step would cause many difficulties of a domestic and international character. The United States and European countries could co-operate to devise banking measures to lessen the volume of "hot money." These measures might help, but the basic evil is political insecurity. Until the world solves this problem, all the lesser measures will be of minor importance and are likely to be swamped in a tidal wave of political panic. Given a minimum degree of political security, it should be possible to work out methods to remedy the evils of "hot money" and excessive short-term loans, and by international co-operation to promote sound international capital investment.

[7] H. M. Bratter, "Hot Money and International Problems," *Foreign Policy Report,* June 15, 1937, p. 84.   [8] *Ibid.,* p. 85.   [9] *Ibid.,* p. 86.

First it should be noted that the problem of investment is related to the question of gold distribution and of bank reserves. In a discussion on a paper entitled, "For What Objects do Central Banks Hold Gold?" J. M. Keynes writes that it is unnecessary for central banks to keep so much gold in reserve in order to secure their paper issues, and that their gold reserves need not bear any particular ratio to the note issue. If this idea "were accepted in the world at large . . . . it would be an enormous gain." The main function of gold should be to enable a country to pursue a sound policy of international lending, especially to countries suffering from gold shortage. "The important thing is that creditor nations should regularly lend their surplus, and that there should not be tension in the gold market arising out of their willingness to do that."[10]

Great Britain's readiness to lend abroad was largely restricted by reason of her gold situation; and the unwillingness of American and French banks to participate in foreign loans was unfortunate, however natural it was under the circumstances.

The breakdown in international lending intensified the world economic crisis, because the debtor countries, and countries which suffered from the catastrophic fall in agricultural prices and from the effects of tariffs placed upon their exports not only could not get financial help to relieve their distress, but even had to export gold which they could ill afford to lose.[11] Keynes concludes that the solution of the problem requires "some sort of international policy by an international institution toward international lending—something a little remote from the gold problem. Gold comes in as a symptom, as a sort of barometer but you will not get real stability unless you cast your eyes beyond gold to the irregularity of the international loan market. That is perhaps the most fundamental cause of serious upsets such as we are suffering from today." We must therefore examine the possibilities of international organization in this matter.

INVESTMENTS

Undoubtedly international investment played a most important part in the development of international trade between 1800

[10] R. H. Brand, "For What Obects Do Central Banks Hold Gold?" in *The International Gold Problem* (Royal Institute of International Affairs), p. 187.

[11] M. A. Heilperin, *International Monetary Organization* (International Institute of Intellectual Co-operation, Paris, 1939), p. 30.

and 1914. It made possible the use of capital from Europe to promote the great agricultural, pastoral, mining, lumber, railroad, and other activities of the New World. Without it the new markets for Europe's manufactures and the new openings for the increased population of the nineteenth century could not have developed so rapidly.

Many economists doubt that international investment will ever again have the same great opportunities as it had several years ago. These considerations indicate that it will not: (1) The United States and other creditor countries have suffered heavy losses by reason of defaults on the part of debtor countries and will not readily regain confidence. (2) The scope for foreign investment has diminished owing to the growth of economic nationalism; many of the debtor countries wish to free themselves from the "imperialism" of their powerful neighbors, and are taxing foreign investments in order to weaken the financial hold of the foreign capitalist. (3) The declining rate of population growth in many parts of the world will lessen the demand for food supplies; agricultural countries will therefore not increase their areas of cultivation and borrow so much capital. (4) Agricultural methods have made great progress—"All over the world, the scientific breeding of animals, the increasing use of mechanical appliances, the development of new methods of farming, artificial fertilizers, improved transport, and biological discoveries have helped to increase the output of agricultural products per unit of labor and land employed."[12] Europe will therefore not require to import so much agricultural produce from abroad. The agricultural countries of the New World are setting up their own industries, in keeping with the general growth of economic nationalism. All these developments lessen the scope for international investment. (5) The growth of tariffs, especially in creditor countries, has made the problem of repayment of loans extremely difficult. It seems unlikely that there can be a marked resumption of international lending as long as debtor countries find it difficult to surmount existing tariff walls and cannot pay their interest and sinking fund by means of goods. Further lending without careful consideration of methods of receiving interest and amortization payments would seem to be unwise. Sound investment will necessitate serious attention to the problem of repayment.

[12] *The Problem of International Investment* (Royal Institute of International Affairs), p. 30.

And yet a considerable need of foreign loans still exists.[13] Many countries which possess ample resources have a low standard of living. They require capital in order to permit them to develop their resources, improve communications, promote public health, and extend their educational facilities. But the problem will require much more careful handling than it has received in the past. And organization will be needed to prevent the type of reckless lending which characterized the period 1920 to 1930. Sir Arthur Salter writes:

It is . . . . impossible to measure specifically the evil of wasteful expenditure by public authorities of funds obtained from foreign loans. But it is very great indeed and will remain a cancer in the whole of the world's financial and political system until it is dealt with. I venture to challenge a denial, from any responsible person acquainted with the public borrowings of the years 1925–28, of the assertion that, with the exception of loans recommended by the League of Nations and the Central Banks, the *bulk* of the foreign loans in these years to public authorities in debtor countries would better not have been made.

If this is true, it is clearly a grave indictment of the world's credit system as regards the immense sphere of its operations comprised by foreign loans to public authorities.

Nor is this all. The dead-weight of these wasteful loans, involving an annual charge represented by no adequate yield of a public enterprise, was a major factor in causing the financial crisis of the same kind as reparations and war debts, and may in future years prove a heavier and more enduring burden upon the world's economy. And the end is not yet. The defaults which have taken place, and those which will come soon, will have destroyed the confidence of the investor in foreign lending of all kinds, including that which is most sound and most vitally needed. When the turn in economic depression is reached, the resiliency of the recuperative forces which should come from new lending will this time be lacking.

Commercial loans do not involve the same dangers as public loans; and when they are unwise the consequences usually extend only over a limited range. This is not the case, however, when the banks of a country assume responsibility for loans from abroad. When this practice extends, the whole of a national banking system may be endangered; and a substantial part of the difficulties of some central and eastern European countries has been so caused.[14]

We see, then, that resumption of international lending is desirable, and since, even though the amount of international invest-

[13] This need will be intensified by the destruction suffered in the present war.
[14] Sir Arthur Salter, *Recovery, the Second Effort* (The Century Co., New York, 1932), pp. 123–24.

ment may not reach prewar figures, there still remain considerable fields for it; that it must be carefully planned so as to permit opportunity of repayments; and that loans must be made for genuinely economic and productive purposes.

State regulation of international investment.—Governments for some time have taken action to regulate international investment. The British authorities exercise their control persuasively rather than according to some law, by "requesting" financial houses to refrain from making certain loans on grounds of public policy. Through the Bank of England it can if necessary exert sufficient pressure; the Bank may refuse to rediscount bills of lending houses which do not respond to the government's request. It is most rare that such action is necessary. In April 1936 the British government established a Foreign Transactions Advisory Committee, whose duty it was to investigate the problem of foreign loans.

The Committee is to consider applications for loans from foreign governments and other public authorities; offers of share or loan capital to the public, which involve the remittance of funds directly or indirectly to countries outside the British Empire; offers of this kind, not to the public, but in respect of which permission to deal may be sought from the Stock Exchange Committee; and the acquisition of blocks of securities from abroad.[15]

The Royal Institute of International Affairs study group suggested that if London were to contemplate a permanent control of the capital market, "which seems very likely," it will be desirable to set up a Foreign Transactions Advisory Committee with even wider powers.

The United States also exercises a measure of government control over foreign investments. In 1922 the Department of State required would-be investors in the foreign field to consult the Department "on account of the bearing of such operations upon the proper conduct of foreign affairs." The Johnson Act, passed in 1934, to prevent financial transactions with foreign defaulting governments, imposed further official control. Germany has carried governmental action to the greatest lengths. Her nationals may not export currency or purchase foreign securities and her exporters must obtain permits before they can send goods abroad; many kinds of "blocked" currency exist, and

---

[15] *The Problem of International Investment* (Oxford University Press, for the Royal Institute of International Affairs, 1937), p. 79.

in general it may be said that no freedom remains in Germany in the sphere of foreign investment.

The governments of debtor countries have also established official supervision of international loans. The Commonwealth of Australia set up an Australian Loan Council in 1923–24 to co-ordinate borrowing and to prevent competition between the states and the Commonwealth and between states themselves, in the international money market. Other countries have imposed methods of direct exchange control by limiting the amount of foreign exchange which importers can obtain in order to pay for purchases from abroad.

Governments have not merely taken action to control the amount of investment abroad or loans from abroad as the case may be; they have taken steps to "encourage or promote overseas investments" in several ways. Sometimes the government makes a direct investment; or guarantees export credits and "loans for stabilization and relief purposes." The Export Credits Guarantee Department of the British Board of Trade may grant credits for periods up to ten years. Similar bodies have been set up by at least a dozen other countries. The departments carefully investigate the nature of the proposed exports and the economic soundness of the importing country. The governments then by means of guaranties cover "the risks of default, of undue delay, and of transfer difficulties." Their backing provides to exporters the element of confidence which otherwise might be lacking in an age of political and economic instability, which frequently makes the fulfillment of contracts a difficult matter.

The advantages of a careful consideration of foreign investments by responsible national agencies are obvious. The public authority brings an impartial view to economic openings, and is likely to discourage unsound and reckless loans. Such precautions would seem to be desirable. On the other hand, governmental supervision over foreign loans is open to two objections: the first is the one which attaches to all governmental activity in economic matters—red tape, undue delay, bureaucratic methods, and, especially in the loan field, usurpation of "functions which properly belong to acceptance houses, insurance companies, and certain other institutions."[16] A consideration of these charges lies outside the scope of the present work. The second criticism is pertinent to a volume dealing with international relations: However

[16] *Ibid.*, p. 93.

necessary governmental backing and investigation may be for sound international investment, the danger is that the government will exercise control over investments primarily for political ends and will subordinate the economics of welfare to considerations of national power and prestige. Who can doubt that German official interference in foreign trade has been dictated largely by rearmament factors? And who will deny that a similar charge can be made against other governments in these days of international instability? Thus we appear to face a dilemma. The unregulated flow of capital may produce further economic dislocation; but governmental control, in the attempt to avoid this evil, may add to the international tension by increasingly associating capital investment policy with political objectives.

Is there a way out? The answer is yes, provided that governmental intervention to regulate investments is divorced from considerations likely to lead to political rivalry and therefore to international war. Only by the establishment of international security sufficient to remove the fear of war, lessen preparations for war, and eliminate the partnership between economic activity and armament strength can state regulation of investments guarantee sound loans for productive purposes and sound methods of repayment. Until sufficient international organization exists to maintain peace, state activity in international investment will heighten rather than lessen international political and economic confusion. Merely to have state-directed competing policies offers no solution.

International organization and investment.—Some degree of international co-operation in investment policy is indispensable. The need for it has been admirably expressed by Sir Arthur Salter:

> The lenders of the different countries, even if united nationally, must act together or they will break down one another's standards. And they would most conveniently use the two international institutions at their disposal, the Financial Committee of the League of Nations and the Bank of International Settlements. These two institutions might usefully cooperate, or form a joint committee, the League specializing rather more on the governmental side, the public finances, and the bank on that of the Central Banks and on what touches currency. Such a joint committee might begin by drawing up a kind of Charter of Public Loans, the principles upon which such loans should be arranged, and the precautions desirable in different classes of cases.[17]

[17] Salter, *op. cit.*, pp. 129–30.

The Committee of Experts who drafted the program for the World Economic Conference also suggested the establishment of an international credit institute which would grant credits, under sound conditions but with strict supervision, so as to prevent inflation, in order "to set in motion capital which is at present lying idle." The Committee referred to the need of a monetary normalization fund which could be used to relieve pressure upon, or to strengthen, the finances of a country in difficulties. During the previous years, nations had taken unilateral action in attempting to overcome their financial difficulties: Great Britain in resuming the gold standard in 1925 and in leaving it in 1931; France in stabilizing the franc in 1928; and the United States in its financial measures in 1933–34. All these separate steps caused serious repercussions in other countries. Governments had set up their equalization funds to protect their own currencies; but on September 26, 1936, France, the United States, and England agreed to operate their stabilization funds in close consultation so as to avoid disruptive competition in currency depreciation.

France had suffered severely in its attempt to remain on the gold standard. In the previous eighteen months, it had lost over 2000 million dollars in gold, and within seven weeks, in August and September, 1936, the Bank of France lost an additional 320 millions. But many Frenchmen, who remembered the great upset caused by inflation in the 'twenties, feared to abandon the gold standard. Moreover, there was a question of prestige involved. The authorities also realized that if the devaluation of the franc precipitated a currency war and caused other countries to engage in "competitive currency depreciation," France would gain little or no permanent benefit. For two years informal conversations took place, after which Great Britain agreed to use her equalization funds to avoid a disturbance of exchange rates and added that in her opinion a further development of international trade was desirable. Finally, Great Britain, France, and the United States signed the agreement and invited other countries to join. Switzerland, Belgium, and the Netherlands later accepted. Thus, the devaluation of the franc "was not an isolated act but a part of a new international alignment." Premier Blum, over-optimistically as events showed, regarded the agreement between the three countries "as the beginning of a new era in international monetary relations."[18]

[18] W. H. Shepardson and W. O. Scroggs, *The United States in World Affairs in 1936* (Harper & Brothers, New York, 1937), p. 183.

Sir Walter Layton in 1937 warned that the equalization funds must be used in collaboration and not in competition. Otherwise, he said, trouble will result. There must be, to quote his words, "a new international effort. If it is not an international effort, it is nothing."[19] Collaboration in the use of equalization funds will probably assist in some measure to iron out short-term disturbances in exchange rates, although economists are not unanimous in their judgment on this point.

THE PROBLEM OF INTEREST RATES

We have seen that one of the great causes of instability is the excessive amount of short-term loans, particularly if they are applied to long-term projects. Until political confidence is restored, investors will be reluctant to trust their capital abroad for long periods. The need of peace is nowhere more obvious than in the field of international investment. Until investors and entrepreneurs can calculate for a sufficient time ahead and can have a reasonable hope of international security in a world of rapid technological change, the flow of capital will be greatly impeded. On the other hand, long-term loans require not only the means of repayment but also an assurance of reasonable price stability, or a lowering of interest rates if prices should fall. The Polish economist, Mlynarski, in 1933, pleaded for elasticity of interest rates.[20] He pointed out that economic progress is based principally on credit, which is a fundamental necessity in our economic civilization. But fixed interest rates on loans floated for a period of twenty to thirty years constitute a serious obstacle in a world where changes in price levels may render the burden of interest and amortization payments an excessive one. "Is there any producer today who, in a long-term contract for supplying water, gas or electric current, would agree to fix the price" for 20 to 30 years ahead? "Why, therefore, is only the price of capital in long term contracts to remain inelastic?" He proposed, instead, a law providing a fixed, guaranteed rate of interest, plus a rate which would vary according to changes in the wholesale price index level. A permanent committee of creditors holding securities should cooperate with public authorities in calculating the changes in index numbers and applying them to the interest payments falling due.

[19] Sir Walter Layton, "The End of the Gold Bloc," *International Affairs,* January–February, 1937, p. 31.

[20] F. J. Mlynarski, *Credit and Peace* (George Allen & Unwin, London, 1933), *passim.*

This general principle was adopted in the 1924 Dawes Reparations Plan; it applied not to interest rates, it is true, but to reparation payments, which were to vary according to an index of Germany's production. There appears to have been no attempt as yet to follow Mlynarski's suggestion in the realm of foreign loans.

BANK FOR INTERNATIONAL SETTLEMENTS

Co-operation among central banks was an important factor in rebuilding the financial structure of Europe in the postwar period; the rehabilitation of Austria and of Hungary and the granting of financial assistance to Danzig, Estonia, Albania, and Rumania was in no small measure the result of the co-operation of national central banks associated with the League of Nations. To avoid a "scramble for gold" in an attempt to solve their currency difficulties, the central banks agreed not to withdraw gold from each other's vaults without mutual consent; and a number of them undertook not to purchase gold from South Africa without the approval of the Bank of England. These arrangements did not go very far, and despite the growing importance of central banks in the postwar period their early conversations were limited and informal in character.

The International Conference of Brussels, 1920, urged that the League of Nations investigate the possibilities of establishing an international clearinghouse. The Financial Commission of the International Economic Conference at Genoa in 1922 proposed a general convention to "centralize and co-ordinate the demand for gold, and so . . . . avoid those wide fluctuations in the purchasing power of gold which might otherwise result from the simultaneous and competitive efforts of a number of countries to secure metallic reserves"; it would require the establishment of adequate machinery for collaboration among central banks. Already in 1921 the late Mr. F. A. Vanderlip, the American financier, had proposed a scheme for a "gold reserve bank for the United States and Europe." These and other ideas received attention during the decade after the World War of 1914–1918. Many people realized that the financial and monetary needs of the world required a more systematic basis of co-operation, and a definite location for an institution which would (1) make easier and more regular the personal intercourse of central bank officials, (2) render more efficient and economical the use of gold, (3) facilitate the interchange of statistical and other banking information, (4) assist in the consideration of transfer problems, (5) help to maintain the gold standard, and (6) provide assistance to countries suffering from temporary financial embarrassment.

However logical these principles, they would probably not have sufficed of themselves to set up the Bank for International Settlements. Something more immediate and urgent was needed, and a decisive factor appeared during the years 1929–1930. Germany had been forced to pay large reparation sums. The Allies had not appreciated the problems of transfer and of exchanges, and had forgotten that heavy demands upon national currencies might have a serious effect upon international monetary stability. In 1924 the Dawes Plan set up machinery to handle this problem, and the late Mr. S. Parker Gilbert and the Transfer Commission did valuable work in maintaining reparation payments without injuring Germany's exchanges. By 1929 the general economic situation had made it impossible for Germany to continue to meet her payments, and the representatives of interested governments met to arrange a new schedule of payments. They decided to replace the Agent General and the Transfer Committee by a new institution which would enable the main central banks of the world to co-operate in assisting Germany "during a period of transfer difficulties." The Young Plan enumerated the advantages of such an institution. The experts believed that a Bank for International Settlements would simplify the reparations problem by bringing the existing organizations into an efficient unity. It could facilitate the reparations deliveries in kind by granting financial accommodation to firms which were making these deliveries of goods. It would constitute an impartial authority to decide whether a German declaration of inability to pay some of the postponable annuities was justified and whether Germany might temporarily suspend part of the payments, pending a solution of exchange or other difficulties. The Bank was to devote part of its profits to assist in paying Germany's last twenty-two annuities, and by enabling Germany to co-operate with the Allies as an equal would remove the sting of political inequality which remained while the Agent General and the Transfer Committee remained on German soil.

The experts had presented the case for an international institution which would more efficiently handle the immediate problem of German reparations, but they also had in mind the wider part to be played by a Bank for International Settlements. They realized that co-operation among central banks for world economic purposes would become increasingly important, and that this new institution would be the instrument through which such co-operation could be effected.

An organizing committee at Baden-Baden in 1929 and an international conference at The Hague in 1930 drew up the details which dealt with the location of the bank, its relation with governments, the currency in which funds should be accounted, and its objects and functions.

The bank entered upon the following tasks: buying, selling, earmarking and holding gold in custody; purchasing and discounting bills; buying and selling securities, except shares; buying and selling exchange; opening deposits and receiving deposits; acting as an agent for central banks; acting as trustee in the matter of reparations; undertaking special agreements to facilitate international settlements; and maintaining a high degree of liquidity. It was not permitted to issue notes to bearer and, therefore, was prohibited from creating an international currency. It might not accept bills and thus compete with the ordinary banks, which at this time were suffering from a decline of commission rates gained in this branch of activity; nor to open current account for governments (though apparently it could open time deposit accounts) nor grant loans to governments nor acquire predominant interests in business undertaking or in real estate. Each of the central banks might veto any transaction in its own country or in its own currency.

The economic blizzard which followed 1931 and the widespread suspension of the gold standard dealt a heavy blow to the Bank for International Settlements. Exchanges were disrupted; every country ran for cover and became a victim of the philosophy and practice of economic nationalism. Central-bank co-operation suffered with the rest of international organization, and the shares of the Bank of International Settlements fell in price. Eleanor Dulles lists five ways in which the bank was affected: Under Article XXI of its statute, its operations were to be effected in gold or gold-exchange currency, a condition which "prohibited new investments or deposits, in countries which had definitely abandoned the gold standard."[21] Central banks withdrew much of their deposits from the Bank for International Settlements. It suffered from the maze of national regulations which impeded exchange transactions. The depression halted the co-operation among central banks

[21] E. L. Dulles. *The Bank for International Settlements at Work* (The Macmillan Company, 1932), p. 25.

and correspondingly restricted the role of the Bank for International Settlements. And it had to adapt itself to the whole changed situation due to the departure of the world from the gold standard.

The proposed International Agricultural Mortgage Company. —In May 1931 the League Council approved a scheme to create an International Agricultural Mortgage Company.[22] It proposed a convention containing a charter and statutes which the national governments might sign. The purpose was to provide capital to enable agriculturists, particularly in eastern and southeastern Europe, to effect changes in their crop systems and to plant crops which had not glutted the market. The company was to make long-term loans, and because of its international backing it was expected that it could do so at lower rates of interest.

The bank was to be situated at Geneva and to operate under a charter granted by the Swiss government. Each participating country was to subscribe to a special reserve fund and to participate in the authorized capital. The mortgage bank was to keep on deposit with the Bank of International Settlements or other banks of high standing a sum equal to that advanced by the governments. The League Council was to appoint the president and the vice-president of the board, and the permanent committee of the International Institute of Agriculture and the Bank for International Settlements were also each to name a director. The mortgage company was to make loans to national companies, the loans to be repayable by annual amortization within thirty years. The national companies were to undertake to use the loans exclusively for first mortgages secured on real property. Loans were not to exceed 50 per cent of the estimated value of the property offered as security. The 1932 Stresa conference recommended that the convention be put into force as soon as possible, but in the same year it was decided for political and general reasons to postpone the date of operation.

PUBLIC WORKS

The possibility of stimulating international public works as a means of encouraging capital exports has received much attention. The International Labor Conferences considered the problem in 1919 and 1926 and at the request of the European Commission, the International Labor Office made a report in January 1931

[22] Wallace McClure, *World Prosperity as Sought through the Economic Work of the League of Nations* (The Macmillan Company, New York, 1933), has a convenient summary, pp. 529–31.

in which it suggested some economically productive enterprises which might be undertaken in Europe and which would afford opportunities for international capital investment and promotion of long-term credit. The projects included a new European road system, international navigable waterways, the transmission of electrical current from one country to another, and the substitution of automatic couplings instead of screw couplings on all European railroads. Several countries in Europe—Austria, Belgium, Bulgaria, Slavonia, Esthonia—had plans dealing with roads, rivers, electric power, municipal work projects, land improvements, forestry, housing, and ports. In 1932 certain projects were referred back to the experts, and were examined more in detail—a Jugoslavian waterway to the Aegean, water supply and sanitation for Poland, modern traffic and transportation methods for Jugoslavia, and irrigation schemes for Greece (a plan which received attention because of the heroic Greek efforts to take care of the flood of refugees which had swept the country). The rapid deterioration of the international political and economic situation made progress along these lines difficult, if not temporarily out of the question.

In 1937 the International Labor Conference passed a recommendation concerning international co-operation in respect of public works that each member of the International Labor Organization should inform the office what public works it had undertaken or planned during each year, and should co-operate in the work of any international committee which the governing body of the International Labor Office might set up for the purpose of studying the whole problem. It also passed a recommendation concerning the national planning of public works, and recommended: that each member should time its public works so as to increase the volume of employment during periods of depression, and that special attention should be paid to public works which stimulate heavy industries or which create a more direct demand for consumers' goods; that the financing of public works should be carried out by placing resources in reserve during periods of prosperity and by means of expansion of credit at the right time; and that certain classes of workers, such as young workers, women, and nonmanual workers, should be especially considered. The discussions in the thirteenth sitting revealed an almost unanimous view on these matters, and both the United States government adviser and the employers' adviser warmly supported the plan.

In June 1938 the first session of the new international public works committee was held. Twenty-five countries were officially represented; employers' and workers' representatives appointed by the International Labor Office, representatives of the Economic Committee, the Finance Committee, and the Communications and Transit Committee of the League of Nations also attended. The committee engaged in a general discussion of the principles involved, and examined in detail the information which had been received; it classified public works (1) according to their kind (roads, bridges, tunnels, railways, agricultural land reclamation, land irrigation, canals, forestry work, construction of dams for reservoirs, provision of water supplies, the construction of ports, airports, coast protection work, administrative buildings, public utilities, etc.), (2) according to the body responsible for carrying out the work, or subsidizing or supervising it (central, regional or local authorities, public utility undertakings), and (3) according to bodies or individuals in receipt of subsidy or loans granted with a view to increasing the volume of employment. A second part of the plan indicated the kind of information to be supplied by the governments.

The present war has interrupted this as well as many another experiment, and has made it impossible to estimate how far the Committee would be able to make headway in this type of international economic co-operation.

THE LEAGUE LOANS

Meanwhile the economic depression had made the repayment of international loans issued under the auspices of the League of Nations almost impossible. The League had been able to render great service in the reconstruction of Austria after its collapse in 1921–22. Through the action of the Financial Committee a loan of £26,000,000 was underwritten by ten countries. A loan of £10,000,000 to Hungary followed for economic restoration. The Financial Committee also supervised loans for Danzig, gave assistance to Estonia in establishing a new banking system, provided for a loan to Greece and Bulgaria for refugee settlement, helped China to re-establish its currency, and gave technical assistance to Rumania.

The loans amounted to £30,000,000, and defaults by the debtor countries raised doubts as to the efficacy of international co-operation in capital investments. In 1932, the Austrian, the Hungarian, and two Greek loans defaulted, and only 50 per cent of the amount due on Bulgarian loans was being paid to bond-holders. These defaults tended to discredit the financial organization of the League. Critics pointed out that many investors took up the loans because of the League's guaranty that the loans were sound and that sufficient revenues had been allotted by the borrowing country to provide adequate security for interest and sinking-fund repayments. The loans therefore commanded a higher price than similar governmental loans not issued under the authority of the League; some of them admittedly could not have been raised at all but for the League's backing.

Supporters of the principle of international co-operation in financial matters replied that the defaults resulted from the great fall in world prices and the cessation of international lending after the world economic crisis of 1931, which made the debt burdens too heavy for the borrowing countries to carry. They admitted that in some cases the League's economic experts might have over-estimated the ability of the debtor countries to carry a loan, and asked whether, if the League Financial Organization had demanded stricter conditions, some of the later difficulties might not have been avoided.

A committee set up in London during April 1932 to protect the bondholders of League loans reminded the League Council and the British government that the investing public had subscribed to the League loans "in the faith that a special security attached to them" and that these League loans, therefore, had a "moral claim to special consideration." The defaults were consequently having a "deplorable effect on the influence of the League of Nations both in financial and in other fields" and the committee urged the British government to use its influence on the Council "to take such steps as will best serve to restore confidence in League issues and enable the League to continue its work of European reconstruction."[23]

SUMMARY

The survey given shows that monetary factors have exerted a profound influence upon international life. How far international organization can remedy many of the financial ills from which the world is suffering is therefore an important question. Some enthusiasts have argued that further international measures

[23] *Annual Survey of International Affairs* (Oxford University Press, London, 1933), pp. 73-77.

will be necessary, and even go so far as to advocate an international currency based upon an international gold reserve and managed by some supra-national agency. Such a scheme, while theoretically possible, may be ignored as long as the national state remains. (Although Stresemann in 1929 asked of the League Assembly, "Where is the European coinage that we need?") Nor are countries likely to agree to pool their gold reserves, for they will cling to gold not only from force of habit but also to meet national emergencies. Until peace is firmly secured and economic organization is much more solidly established, the idea of pooling gold reserves will remain in the realm of theory. Nor can we hope that nations will make a voluntary redistribution of gold, unless it occurs as the normal consequence of trade; for it will be impossible to find an acceptable principle on which such a redistribution should take place.

Einzig[24] correctly judges that under present international conditions there is only a limited scope for financial co-operation. Does this mean that the attempts at international co-operation which have been described above have been futile? By no means. It is probable that without them many of the European countries in the early postwar period could not have balanced their budgets or even have borrowed money at all. International co-operation gave them an opportunity to recover from the ravages of war and to place their finances in a sounder condition. The international loans led to a temporary international control which forced governments to introduce economies which they might not have been able to effect alone. It is doubtful whether Central Europe would have enjoyed any economic recovery without the action of the League of Nations, the Bank of England, and other central banks. Probably the League and its partners in international co-operation made errors of judgment in "bolstering up" certain economic conditions which were essentially unsound. Perhaps postwar monetary policy, both national and international, was mistaken in attempting to return to 1914 currency valuations. Nevertheless, one should not forget that more important countries, like Belgium, Italy, and Great Britain, owed a great deal to international financial co-operation during periods of monetary difficulties.

Einzig believes that in normal times it would not have been

[24] Paul Einzig, *World Finance, 1914–1935* (The Macmillan Company, New York, 1935), especially the concluding chapter.

a difficult matter for the central banks to co-operate. As it was, political factors and economic contradictions which went beyond the limits of elasticity prevented this co-operation from being as effective as it might have been under more fortunate conditions. When the crisis came in 1931 the three major financial countries, the United States, Great Britain, and France, could not agree even on the fundamental principles of action: The United States preached price stability; Britain advocated a rise in the world price level; France tried to maintain the existing level so as to gain the maximum advantage for French commodity prices. In the absence of basic political agreements, international financial co-operation served only to postpone and not to solve economic difficulties. The Bank of International Settlements had barely been established when the economic earthquake shook the world. It was an instrument of potential importance, and in more normal times might have assisted in channelizing the international flow of money and relieving countries under pressure. After 1931, however, the position was so serious that each nation ran to adopt a day-to-day, hand-to-mouth policy which was little more than a scramble to keep its own organization intact. When Britain went off the gold standard and the United States depreciated the dollar and Germany indulged in financial unorthodoxies, the scope of international financial co-operation was diminished. But the desperate need remained.

However, technical co-operation continues and methods are being improved which may serve as efficient instruments for carrying out larger policies of co-operation if and when the world regains some degree of economic and political equilibrium. One cannot, therefore, pass final judgment on the efforts of international monetary co-operation, because the basic factor, political stability, has been missing. A French Minister of Finance once said: "Faites-moi une bonne politique et je vous ferai de bonnes finances."[25] The Minister's wise remark needs to be remembered today. Monetary stability cannot co-exist with political instability, and economic confidence cannot develop in an atmosphere of political chaos. Political policies and aims which had little to do with the economics of welfare played a large part in wrecking the international economic structure of Europe and the world. Until they give way to other political policies which will permit the development of international security, international financial and

[25] Quoted in Einzig, *op. cit.,* p. 359.

economic co-operation will be confined to a role inadequate to fulfill the world's genuine requirements.

What of the future? The breakdown of the gold standard has not constituted the only tragedy in international finance. Conceivably the world might have adopted a monetary system independent of gold and still have maintained a large degree of monetary unity. In practice, monetary blocs have appeared which have marked off the world into a series of relatively independent and even hostile groups. As national financial systems became more and more badly strained after the collapse of 1931, regional groups emerged in an attempt to offset "the breakdown of monetary equilibrium." Great Britain and the Dominions and other countries most intimately associated with her in trade relations formed the sterling bloc. Japan expanded into Asia and sought to build up a yen bloc. A number of European countries held to gold for several years, until they were forced off in the years 1935 and 1936.[26] Germany developed an intricate system of exchange control based upon bilateral trade agreements in which the exchange rates were manipulated according to an immediate purpose in view. The United States remained on the dollar but did not attempt to build up a dollar bloc, trusting rather to the policy of reciprocal trade agreements. Condliffe well points out that the Tripartite Agreement between France, Britain, and the United States in a sense represented

an attempt to form a bridge between the dollar and sterling blocs and to afford an opportunity for the gold bloc countries to join with Great Britain and the United States in the gradual re-establishment of monetary equilibrium upon the basis of which freer trade might be promoted over a widening area. Though this purpose was not achieved, the method of the agreement offers an instructive illustration of the way in which a bridge might be built between great regional trading blocs organized around leading currencies.[27]

The same author points out that the financial policies pursued by these various blocs corresponded to different commercial policies, and emphasizes, not only that there is a great difference between a regional system which develops trade "on a basis of exchange stability by price competition within a free market" and the regional system dominated by "monopolistic State barter trans-

[26] See above, p. 123.

[27] J. B. Condliffe, *The Reconstruction of World Trade* (W. W. Norton and Co., New York, 1940), p. 325.

actions on a bi-lateral clearing basis," but also that there can be no compromise between a system which serves the purpose of economic welfare (however well or badly it fulfills that function) and a system in which the economic purposes are subordinate to military power and conquest.

The discussion of economic policy directed toward war or peace should enable us to see the limits of international economic organization. During the last few years national economic systems have become more diverse, owing to the strain of war and war preparation, the weaknesses of capitalism, and the growth of totalitarian doctrines. In a relatively peaceful world, international organization might enable considerable co-operation to take place between the relatively liberal and the totalitarian economies. Indeed, as J. E. Meade points out, an International Authority should not attempt "to impose uniform patterns" upon national states, because the task would be too great, and uniformity is not necessarily desirable, since the world needs to benefit by experimentation in economic life. But, under conditions of peace, certain "connecting principles" might enable measures of co-operation to be worked out between the planned and the liberal economies.

These considerations have been rendered necessary in a discussion of currency as an international problem, for currency is an instrument for trade and commerce and the subordination of trade and commerce to military objectives necessarily affects monetary policies.[28] If we assume a return to more normal political relations,[29] the conditions of which are discussed in chapter xv below, the question arises as to what is the minimum amount of international organization which will be required to help stabilize currency conditions throughout the world, in view of the fact that the self-regulating character of foreign exchanges has disappeared.

Meade believes that an International Central Bank must have the power to issue an international currency, and to straighten out exchange fluctuation rates by financing the export of international currency notes in such a way as to control the price levels within various states and thereby prevent price deflation and business depression. But such control might not be sufficient, because national banks could possibly weaken the international monetary control by sterilizing their supplies; hence the international au-

[28] See Herbert Feis, *The Changing Pattern of International Economic Affairs* (Harper & Bros., 1940), pp. 68, 69, 76, 77.

[29] *Ibid.*, pp. 123–30, where Feis emphasizes the need for sound political conditions in order to permit effective economic collaboration in the postwar world.

thority must possess the power "to plan and control a significant part of the total public expenditure throughout the Member States."[30] It is obvious that this amount of control would involve a considerable curtailment of national sovereignty in economic affairs. Meade also suggests that an international monetary authority might have to exercise the power to compel a national central bank to depreciate the value of its currency, if it were losing a considerable portion of its monetary reserves; and might help to smooth out variations in exchange rates by dealing in forward exchanges of various currencies: "The bank could offer to buy and to sell the various currencies for delivery at specified dates in the future at prices to be fixed now."[31] Moreover, it could counteract the evil consequences of excessive short-term flights of capital by itself operating an international-exchange equalization fund. It might have to forbid the abuse of the equalization funds set up by national authorities.

Financial stability cannot be attained as long as excessive tariff barriers and other economic rigidities remain, and the international authority would therefore have to assume much control over other aspects of economic life. It would need: to have a "real power" of regulating international trade; to appoint representatives with final power of decision on national boards of control over the foreign trade of member states with planned economies; to supervise (a) the production, price, and sale of important raw materials "such as tin, rubber, and tea," (b) international cartels, (c) international migration, (d) the issue of foreign loans and purchase of foreign securities; and it would need to compel the principle of the Open Door in colonial trade (which might necessitate direct international administration of colonies).

As Condliffe well remarks, these "are heroic suggestions which, if adopted even in part, would result in the creation of an International Authority vastly different from that of the League of Nations which throughout its twenty years of existence had to rely upon persuasion and the force of public opinion."[32] The same authority adds that even if these suggestions which raise visions not only of "a world-state, but what looks very like a

---

[30] J. E. Meade, *The Economic Basis of a Durable Peace* (Oxford University Press, 1940), p. 52.

[31] J. E. Meade, *op. cit.*, p. 68.

[32] J. B. Condliffe, *op. cit.*, pp. 390–91.

totalitarian world-state," are not practicable "there is every reason to believe that centralized powers of the type outlined by Mr. Meade must be established within great trading regions. They must, for example, form the basis for any real organization of a federated Europe,"[33] and will call for the exercise of great political imagination, if other parts of the world are to bring their political units of government into closer line with the economic realities of the day. Perhaps Streit's federalism will involve fewer complexities after all!

[33] J. B. Condliffe, *op. cit.,* p. 391.

Chapter IV

LABOR AND LABOR STANDARDS

LABOR also has become an international problem. John B. Andrews, Secretary of the American Association for Labor Legislation, tells how, soon after graduation, he joined that organization, which had as one of its purposes the promotion of greater uniformity in state labor legislation. By 1910 he had completed a study of poisoning caused by the use of yellow phosphorus in the match industry. The workers who dipped the splints into the phosphorus paste breathed the fumes and sometimes contracted the occupational disease, phosphorus necrosis, which caused their teeth to drop out and their jaw bones to decay. To the proposal that the matter be regulated by state legislation requiring improved ventilation, employers "protested that the first state law, on account of the expensive safeguards required, would drive the industry from the state." Nor could they use physically harmless substitutes, because they were more expensive. Mere state legislation would be insufficient; a wider "uniform regulation was essential." Andrews accordingly worked for a national bill.

"But when the Congressional hearings opened, these same industrialists protested that even under uniform national regulation their American product would be put at a disadvantage in competition with matches imported from certain foreign countries which were using low-paid labor." It was the fact that a number of countries had ratified a treaty prohibiting the manufacture of poisonous matches which finally enabled Congress to pass a bill in 1912 "placing a prohibition tax upon matches made with poisonous phosphorus, and also prohibiting their importation and exportation." What at first sight appeared to be a problem of local labor legislation turned out to be a problem requiring comprehensive international action.

Even in the early nineteenth century, while the industrial revolution was yet young, and foreign competition was comparatively undeveloped, a few farseeing men realized that labor conditions would exercise a great influence upon the conditions of international trade. Outstanding among them was Robert Owen, the British employer-socialist, who became manager in David Dale's factory in Larnack, married Dale's daughter, introduced the silent monitor in the factory by which workers were exalted to higher efficiency by nothing more than an appeal to their better nature, made money, and later attempted to realize a socialist commonwealth in America.

In 1818 Owen placed his views before an international conference; he urged that high wages in one country and low wages in another, bad conditions here and good conditions there, would make sound development of international trade impossible. If production of goods by sweated labor was to be avoided, the labor standards must be raised by international action. If this were done, one country would not be exposed to competition from the lower-paid labor of another, the purchasing power of the workers would be raised, and in this way a wider market for an expanding industrial system, being revolutionized in its output capacity by the application of coal and iron and scientific technique, would be provided.

Other individuals took up the matter during the century; the labor movement formed its First International in the 'sixties and the Second International in 1889. All advocated a betterment of working conditions through international organization. The German Emperor called a Conference in Berlin in 1890. It adopted several recommendations, which had no practical effect. Success could not come from an occasional conference but demanded much "careful technical preparation and continuous and regular action." Mere general resolutions did not suffice in a competitive and complicated world.

A number of economists and interested scholars in 1900 formed an International Association for Labor Legislation. This body studied labor questions in all countries, prepared an agenda, set up an international office in Basle, and persuaded the Swiss government to call a conference at Berne in 1905. Here representatives from twenty countries met and adopted two resolutions, one limiting the use of white phosphorus in the match industry and the other limiting night work of women in factories. The delegates possessed no official standing, but an official conference met later and transformed these resolutions into international conventions; there were held "two successive conferences, the first technical and the second diplomatic—such was the method invented to get around a double difficulty arising from the fact that the experts were not empowered to sign conventions, and the diplomats lacked the technical knowledge to draft them."[1]

A second conference of experts held in Berne in 1913 agreed on limitation of hours of work for women and young people and prohibited night work for children; but hostilities in August 1914 prevented further action. The International Association for Labor Legislation did splendid pioneer work. It had sixteen autonomous national sections; twenty-two governments co-operated with it; and, although its budget was extremely limited, its leaders, many of whom later were to help in setting up the International Labor Organization as we know it today, were men of fine idealism and great practical ability and experience. Under its auspices seven international Conferences were held. Its members used their influence to urge nations to enter into bilateral treaties for the purpose of improving workers' conditions. France, Italy, Germany, the Netherlands, Switzerland, Austria-Hungary, Luxembourg, Belgium, Hungary, Sweden, Denmark, Great Britain, Spain, and the United States signed one or more bilateral agreements (twenty-three in number), which dealt with such questions as social insurance, worker's compensation, and employment of women and children. Typical of these was the Franco-Italian treaty of 1904. It granted to French workers in Italy and to Italian workers in France reciprocal insurance and banking facilities and the protection of their respective labor laws. Italy undertook to set up a system of labor inspection as effective as that in France, and gradually to reduce the length of the working day for women; both governments promised to prepare an annual report on the application of labor legislation to women and children.

The first step had been taken and labor aspirations became more clearly formulated, but much remained to be done before the world could expect to have an institution capable of functioning on a scale commensurate with the magnitude of the world's labor problems. Only two conventions resulted from a century of effort. Other methods were required if legislation was to keep pace with social necessity.[2]

---

[1] Preface by Albert Thomas, *The International Labour Organization, The First Decade* (George Allen & Unwin, Ltd., London, 1931), p. 24.

[2] For nineteenth-century developments, see Albert Vabre, *Le Droit international du travail* (Marcel Giard, Paris, 1923), pp. 11–72. Also L. L. Lorwin, *Labor and Internationalism* (The Macmillan Company, 1929), and G. A. Johnston, *International Social Progress* (The Macmillan Company, 1924).

THE INTERNATIONAL LABOR ORGANIZATION

During the World War of 1914–1918 the working class did not lose sight of their objective—an international organization for the improvement of labor conditions—and between 1914 and 1918 the trade unions and other groups of workers in Europe and America passed several resolutions to the effect that a lasting peace must include provisions for social justice and methods of eliminating the economic causes of war. At the Peace Conference, therefore, the labor question received prominent attention. A Commission of sixteen was set up to investigate the international aspects of employment and to recommend a permanent organization which should be able to provide a means of continuous consultation and investigation. The Commission, during its work of almost two months, met extraordinarily difficult questions which involved deep-seated problems of political and economic theory, some of which will be examined here later. Finally, after exhaustive sessions, articles were adopted and the International Labor Organization was incorporated in Part XIII of the Peace Treaty. The preamble, which many people regard as the international charter of labor, sets forth the objectives so effectively that it is reproduced in full:

WHEREAS, the League of Nations has for its object the establishment of universal peace, and such a peace can be established only if it is based upon social justice;

AND WHEREAS conditions of labour exist involving such injustice, hardship and privation to large numbers of people as to produce unrest so great that the peace and harmony of the world are imperilled; and an improvement of those conditions is urgently required: as, for example, by the regulation of the hours of work, including the establishment of a maximum working day and week, the regulation of the labour supply, the prevention of unemployment, the provision of an adequate living wage, the protection of children, young persons and women, provision for old age and injury, protection of the interests of workers when employed in countries other than their own, recognition of the principle of freedom of association, the organization of vocational and technical education and other measures;

WHEREAS also the failure of any nation to adopt humane conditions of labour is an obstacle in the way of other nations which desire to improve the conditions in their own countries;

THE HIGH CONTRACTING PARTIES, moved by sentiments of justice and humanity as well as by the desire to secure the permanent peace of the world, agree to the following. [Then follow the clauses providing for the organization.]

The philosophy underlying the new world experiment may be summarized as follows: (1) Low labor standards in any country constitute a danger to standards, elsewhere and, to avoid cut-throat competition arising from low-paid labor abroad, the erection of tariff barriers would be insufficient; and only an approach to more nearly uniform conditions could provide a sound solution. (2) By raising the purchasing power of workers all over the world, large-scale industry would be enabled to find more extensive markets and in this way avoid crises of overproduction. (3) Intelligent legislation, agreed upon by member countries, could secure the necessary conditions and improve the efficiency of labor. (4) Organized labor should have not merely the right of association but also a voice in the determination of labor policy. And (5) these economic factors enter deeply into the problem of world peace.[3]

These views did not pass unchallenged, and opposition arose especially from the employer class. Critics argued thus: (1) Society should trust to "natural" economic forces and avoid governmental intervention in business; the proposed international labor legislation would lead toward increased governmental direction and control. (2) Labor had no right to demand a voice in industrial policy nor (according to some) to organize itself into unions and engage in collective bargaining. (3) Countries which adopted the international standards set by the International Labor Organization would experience heavier costs of production and would have to raise prices; whereas nonmembers of the Organization and those which had not ratified the labor conventions would be able to sell at a lower price in the world market. (4) Any attempt to adopt universal labor legislation ignored the basic fact of wide national differences in physical and economic conditions. Take, for example, child-labor legislation: To protect young children from over-early factory work may be desirable; but how would it be possible to establish a satisfactory world-wide minimum age since children mature earlier in one climate than another? Or, take the problem of night work: In general, it may be good to prohibit this class of labor; but in the tropics night work might be less exhausting than toiling during the day under a blazing sun. (5) Labor legislation is more a domestic than an international question, in view of different degrees of economic

[3] The arguments pro and con are summarized in P. Perigord, *The International Labor Organization* (Appleton & Co., New York, 1926).

organization and social advancement; national life constitutes something of a unity, and it would be impossible to legislate on labor matters without affecting the whole course of a nation's life. International efforts would be unable to take into account the many effects upon individual countries which a given piece of labor legislation would have. (6) The International Labor Organization, with its international methods, threatened national sovereignty and therefore must be regarded with suspicion and misgiving.

The International Labor Organization under the energetic leadership of its first Director, M. Albert Thomas, began its activities prior to the League of Nations and soon had its agencies in active operation. The three instruments of the Organization are: the General Conference, the Governing Body, and the Labor Office.

THE GENERAL CONFERENCE

The General Conference is a permanent organ; it holds annual meetings at Geneva which "are regarded as a continuous session." We shall examine the main problems which arise: (1) national representation and the selection of delegates; (2) legislative scope and capacity of the Conference; (3) ratification of Conference action by national members; (4) the revision of conventions; and (5) the enforcement of standards.

Each member state sends four representatives—two government, one worker, and one employer. In the peace negotiations this question of representation occasioned much controversy. Many workers desired to have a greater number of worker representatives at the Annual Conference. They pointed out that if the Conference were to be dominated by government officials, labor would not be interested; it wished to have a real voice in establishing new conditions for the working class. However understandable their viewpoint, it was evident that if the Conference were to carry weight and pass resolutions likely to result in action by the respective national governments, sufficient governmental representation was not only desirable—it was imperative.

The association of nongovernmental with governmental representatives in international conferences has far-reaching implications. First, a conference organized along these lines implies that labor conditions are a matter for more than governments alone. International relations are not confined, as hitherto supposed, to public authorities.[4] Furthermore, if the workers' and

[4] See Etienne Antonelli, Preface to Albert Vabre, *op. cit.,* pp. v–vi.

employers' organizations are to have a real voice in choosing their representatives, the state must guarantee freedom of association. When Russia went communist and Italy and Germany adopted dictatorships, they created awkward problems for the International Labor Organization. There are no employers' organizations in the Soviet Union; and trade unions of the orthodox type do not exist in Germany and Italy. The workers' delegates at the Annual Conference challenged the credentials of the "labor" representatives from Germany and Italy; and employers questioned the right of an "employer" to be in the Soviet delegation. Undoubtedly the problem of representatives of dictator countries is a difficult one to solve along the lines of the original theory of the International Labor Organization, that of tripartite representation of government, workers, and employers. The organization realized that it must recognize the fundamental changes in government which have occurred, and in 1937 accepted the argument of the Soviet "employer," a manager of a textile industry, who told the Conference that he had to face problems similar to those which confronted private employers—the hiring and firing of labor, promotions, purchase and disposal of goods, etc.

Yet the presence of worker and employer representatives presupposes the existence of the capitalist system. Many workers who advocate international labor action criticize the International Labor Organization because it admits employers—it "compromises" with capitalism, and is merely revisionist. Supporters of the Organization assert that it does not ignore, but frankly recognizes, the inevitability of conflicts between labor, capital, and government. It believes, however, that these conflicts can be peacefully settled by continuous research, by a capacity for give and take, and by each proposal having to run the gantlet of the threefold criticism—worker, employer, and government. The first task is to find the facts upon which "imagination and inventiveness can operate. . . . . To this extent, the I.L.O. is neither pro-capitalistic nor pro-socialistic, but does appear to be inconsistent with doctrines of class warfare, and committed to the policy of gradual amelioration of economic conditions by co-operation between labor, capital, and government."

By Article 389 of the Treaty of Versailles nongovernmental delegates are to be appointed from a member's most representative body of workers and employers. Did this mean that the government must choose a representative from the organization with the greatest membership? Disputes between rival unions have occurred as to which one should be consulted in sending the national workers' representative. After much controversy an appeal went to the Permanent Court in 1922. It ruled that the article did not mean that any one trade union or employers' association should be considered exclusively.

The International Labor Conferences scrutinize credentials of delegates and their advisers and may refuse to admit any person deemed not to have been nominated in accordance with Article 389. It is on this basis that the Italian workers' and the German Nazi delegates were challenged. The Conference has had to face the question what to do in the case of countries where workers' organizations are little developed, and where governments consult the workers directly (and not through organized bodies), as Japan did in the early years of the International Labor Organization. To select a workers' representative in countries where there is no central organization, but only a number of loosely related trade unions, is a difficult matter.

Incomplete delegations form the other serious problem of representation. If a government persistently refuses to appoint a workers' or an employers' delegate it upsets the balance which was designed by the Peace Treaty to give effective representation to nongovernmental delegates. The volume issued by the International Labor Office correctly notes that "if the workers had had any expectation in 1919 that this provision would remain a dead letter, they certainly would never have placed their confidence in the new institution; they would rather have turned their backs on it and tried other means of obtaining satisfaction for their demands."[5] The workers' delegates accordingly made a strong protest when at the first International Labor Conference at Washington they found that sixteen out of forty states had sent incomplete delegations. But the Conference could do little more than bring moral pressure to bear upon the recalcitrant or careless governments and request them to forward reasons for their action. This procedure, as the International Labor Office points out, served to remind states of their obligations and brought to light some genuine difficulties and also occasionally suggested remedies. Apparently the number of states which send complete delegations to the Conference has increased.

The Annual Conference considers labor conditions throughout the world with a view to adopting either conventions or recom-

[5] *The International Labour Organization, The First Decade,* p. 56.

mendations, which are then submitted to governments of member states. A two-thirds vote of the Conference is necessary for such action, the delegates voting individually and not as national units. This procedure is of interest for two reasons: (1) The two-thirds rule marks an exception to the general rule that international conventions require a unanimous vote of the participating sovereign countries. (2) Because delegates can vote as individuals and not merely as representatives in a national unit, workers and employers have an independent voice which they otherwise would not possess. The founders of the International Labor Organization correctly gauged modern needs when they realized that no longer could international relations "be confined to diplomacy, with diplomacy having as it did, a limited concept of the personal relations of heads of state and of representatives of governments in their simple political dealings with one another." The complexities of life today require the collaboration of many interests—governmental, technical, producer, consumer, employer, labor—according to the particular problem to be solved.

The Annual Conference, although it performs a legislative function, does so indirectly rather than directly; it is not the organ of a superstate, but is primarily an instrument for formulating and defining labor standards and principles. It does not supersede national legislatures, but initiates measures which member states of the International Labor Organization can apply "through national and domestic legislation." Each member undertakes within eighteen months of the Conference to bring the recommendations or draft conventions there adopted before the authority or authorities within whose competence the matter lies for legislative or any other such action as may be deemed desirable. A member is not obligated to adopt the conventions or recommendations, but merely to consider them. Its discretion remains unfettered, and its independence unimpaired.

A "draft convention" is usually regarded as involving a more definite obligation than a "recommendation," but the line between the two is not entirely clear. Francis G. Wilson suggests that recommendations serve the purpose of formulating more general principles which governments might not be ready as yet to put into a convention. He continues: "perhaps the essential function of the recommendation is the enunciation of an international standard which is above or beyond the possibilities of international agreement, such as are included in the more meticulously formulated conventions. When such a standard is formulated in a recommendation, it is hoped that the practice of states will enable the Conference at a later date to embody the principles of the recommendation in a convention."[6]

The founders of the International Labor Organization were anxious to maintain the principles of universality and continuity, so that the Conferences would be regarded not as occasional meetings of governments but rather as an unbroken effort toward the achievement of better world conditions. The ideal was excellent, but it ran into several obstacles. If Conferences dealt only with general subjects they ran the risk of not considering the conditions of the more specialized industries. If they concentrated upon the specialized industries they ran the risk of losing sight of the more general standards; conferences of experts would tend to become absorbed in merely technical problems and "would be in danger of losing sight of the general principles on which international labor legislation is based." It was also important to obtain a reasonable degree of continuity of government, workers', and employes' delegates in the Annual Conferences in order that new representatives would be able to obtain the benefit of accumulated experience in Conference technique and procedure.

In a few instances an exception has been made to the principle of universal participation. Maritime matters concern only a few countries; and it would be superfluous to have governments which because of their inland position have no labor problems affecting seamen attend a conference dealing with specialized matters in which they have no interest. So with labor conditions in coal mines. Here, too, the problem concerns only a few countries. Nevertheless, in an endeavor to preserve the principle of universality the Governing Body called a preparatory technical conference in January 1930 which was to be advisory in character and whose decisions were to be sent to the Annual Conference later, there (it was expected) to be adopted as a regular Convention. The International Labor Organization was not certain whether this procedure would be the solution to a problem which was likely to increase rather than to decrease in future years, but it realized that it would have to find some means of "reconciling the general and universal character of the Conferences." It admitted that its procedures were still in the formative stage and that the organization had to adapt itself to a "diversity of situations and circumstances"; it was necessary, how-

[6] F. G. Wilson, *Labor in the League System* (Stanford University Press, 1934), p. 73.

ever, to "safeguard the general authority, the homogeneity and continuity" of the Conference in accordance with the letter and spirit of Part XIII of the Peace Treaty and also "to guarantee by the most appropriate procedure the fullest possible technical and specialized study of the problems under consideration."[7]

A legislature may have wide or narrow powers; its scope may be strictly confined or practically unlimited by the constitution under which it operates. At first sight we might assume that the International Labor Organization would have to limit its activities to labor matters connected with industry, and, indeed, a number of employers and other critics, jealous of the International Labor Organization, have taken this view; and the question has on three occasions been referred to the Permanent Court of International Justice.

What is the competence of the Organization? In the preamble to Part XIII of the Peace Treaty, the objects of the International Labor Organization are defined in broad terms such as the attainment of "social justice" and the "improvement of conditions of labor which involve injustice, hardship, and privation to large numbers of people"; the methods suggested to attain these ends include the regulation of hours of work and conditions of labor supply, the prevention of unemployment, the provision of an adequate living wage, and several other specific means. The preamble ends with the words "and other measures," thus suggesting that the International Labor Organization is not to be limited to the detailed methods enumerated above. In Article 427, which set forth certain general principles, the final paragraph begins: "Without claiming that these methods and principles are either complete or final, the High Contracting Parties are of opinion that they are well fitted to guide the policy of the League of Nations." Those who drew up the Constitution evidently intended that the Organization should have ample powers, that the social justice toward which it should work should be regarded as a movement and not as something static, and that economic policy should be understood as requiring not merely emergency measures but rather a continuous program and an unwearying application of foresight to economic problems as they arise, and a conception of a social goal toward which a conscious economic policy is directed.

This broad interpretation did not pass unchallenged; and in

[7] *The International Labour Organization,* p. 83.

the early years, as suggested above, the competence of the International Labor Organization was called in question. Some critics attempted to exclude from its consideration so-called national questions and domestic matters; others argued that the organization could not deal with conditions of work and methods of production in the field of agriculture, or attempt to prohibit night work in bakeries if the measure sought to regulate the personal work of the employers themselves. These questions came before the Permanent Court of International Justice for advisory opinions. In all cases the Court upheld the right of the International Labor Organization to deal with these matters, and thus gave support to the theory of "extended competence." It noted that if the Organization had possessed power to bind member states, a restrictive view of its competence would be justified. But such was not the case, and because national sovereignty was protected and nations remained free to ratify or not ratify a convention as they pleased, there was no reason for denying a wide field to the International Labor Organization in its adoption of draft conventions and recommendations.

The International Labor Office itself has adopted the social approach to problems of industrial relations and international economic co-operation and believes that it is no longer sufficient to limit governmental policy to emergency measures against unemployment and other social evils. Industrial legislation is not to be regarded "as a sort of humanitarian excrescence on the economic question."

This view has been well expressed by Harold B. Butler, at that time director of the Office, in his annual report to the 1935 Conference:

The protection of the worker against the hazards and abuses to which he was exposed in industry was the basic notion upon which social policy was directed during the hundred years ending with the termination of the war. It is hardly too much to say that in its essence social legislation was regarded even by many of its protagonists as a sort of humanitarian excrescence on the economic system. The intervention of the State, however necessary in the general interest of the community, was assumed to be anti-economic in so far as it restricted the free play of the law of supply and demand. A fundamental antithesis was believed to exist between the social and the economic objectives, wherever the demands of the two appeared in conflict. As has been pointed out in the first chapter of this report, a different view is now gaining ground. The purely protective conception of social action is now giving way to the wider conception of social security.

The negative aim of guarding the worker against social risks and abuses is being replaced by the positive aim of affording him adequate opportunities both of achieving a decent level of material comfort and of ensuring his individual development.

As a result of this new approach to social questions, social and economic policy are now seen as complementary aspects of a single problem. Unemployment insurance and relief, public works in times of depression, hours of labour, the organization of industry, cannot be judged in social terms alone or in economic terms alone. . . . . Unemployment itself is seen not simply as a social evil, but also as an economic evil. The growth of technical efficiency and the consequent replacement of human by mechanical labour present problems of the greatest complexity, which can only be correctly approached if their social and economic implications are kept simultaneously in view.

Elsewhere, Mr. Butler explained why the International Labor Office must adapt its methods to changing conditions:

As social policy has become more inextricably involved in the discussion and solution of the broad economic issues, the Conference has been inevitably led to consider matters which had hitherto seemed to lie on the extreme border-line of its jurisdiction or beyond it. The progressive abandonment of the self-adjusting system has vitally altered the situation. The introduction of any measure of planned economy at once raises the questions of the goal towards which it is directed. It is impossible for the Conference to ignore the fundamental questions upon which social progress or reaction are now seen to depend. As the most representative body in the social field, it is increasingly its duty to keep the social repercussion of economic measures constantly in review. By so doing it can make an invaluable contribution to the international discussion of the real issues which are now perplexing and dividing the economic world.

The world economic depression helped to widen the scope of activity engaged in by the Organization. The prolonged period of unemployment, the extraordinary dislocation of international trade, the many and various governmental interventions in economic life, and the uncertainty of economists concerning the significance of industrial and agricultural changes have led the Annual Conferences, the Governing Body, and the Office to give attention to some of the more basic economic problems of modern life.

RATIFICATION

An international convention must be ratified by the competent national authorities of a member state before it becomes effective. We have considered elsewhere some of the more general problems of ratification; but in labor matters a number of constitutional difficulties arose because the draft conventions of the International Labor Organization (unlike international conventions which are signed by diplomats especially designated as plenipotentiaries) are adopted in Annual Conference by a two-thirds majority vote in which workers and employers, as well as government delegates, take part.

The technical problems of a constitutional nature need not concern us here. Suffice it to say that the International Labor Office by patient effort was able to persuade the governments to abandon their unduly restrictive legal interpretations of constitutional procedures.[8] But the removal of these obstacles did not of itself clear the way for universal ratification. Indifference, preoccupation with national issues, and fear of the consequences of nonratification by other states were the excuses given for failure to consider and ratify International Labor conventions. It is obvious that if one government ratifies a convention, and another does not, the former state will be placed "at a disadvantage in trade competition." In order to meet this difficulty, a number of governments agreed to undertake a joint examination of conventions each year so that they might simultaneously adopt them. Denmark, Finland, Norway, and Sweden tried this method; but the International Labor Office felt that the result was not satisfactory because a small difference of opinion between two or more of the states might be used as an excuse for nonratification by all of them. Other countries indulged in "conditional" ratification, stipulating that their ratifications would come into force only when certain other states took similar action. The method is understandable, for a government of one country exposed to the competition of another will want to make certain that a major competitor will be subject to the same obligations. On the other hand, conditional ratification can be easily abused; it is possible for a government to insert such unreasonable "conditions" as to preclude the likelihood that its own ratification will ever come into effect. The Labor Office exerted its influence to persuade governments to minimize the use of conditional ratifications, and in general met with an encouraging response.

One of the chief difficulties in the way of ratification lay in

[8] A. Vabre, *op. cit.*, p. 298. The author criticizes *"le byzantinisme"* of the French government in its attitude toward the problem of ratifying labor conventions.

the great number of conventions and recommendations which the early conferences had succeeded in passing. International action was outstripping the capacity of nations to adjust their economic structures to the new standards set. Clearly a revised procedure was desirable so that there could be more time for the Labor Office to prepare, and for parliaments to consider and adopt, conventions and recommendations. In 1922 Switzerland suggested that the Conference should meet less frequently; but this proposal ran into the difficulty that to adopt biennial conferences would have required a revision of the Peace Treaty which had prescribed annual meetings.

After considerable experimentation, including a two-reading and a double-discussion method, the Organization finally adopted the system of preparatory conferences. The last-named method was first used in connection with maritime questions, textiles, labor inspection, etc., and then "was given a definite place in the machinery of the Organization." The Office now feels that the present methods of adopting conventions gives them "a better prospect of being translated into national law and practice than in the past."

ENFORCEMENT

It is not sufficient to sign and ratify conventions: adequate steps must be taken to enforce them. Uniform standards result only when all participating states efficiently administer the labor treaties which they have signed. At the Berlin Conference in 1890, at the International Labor Congress at Zurich in 1897, and at subsequent conferences, delegates drew attention to the importance of law enforcement. Without it international labor conventions would serve "merely to voice expressions of good will without much practical value."[9] The International Association for Labor Legislation in 1911 made an inquiry into the methods of administering labor laws in the various countries. In 1919, Arthur Fontaine argued that "it was useless to adopt a program of international labour legislation if there was nobody charged with supervising its application. It would in fact be to the detriment of those States who applied such legislation in a loyal spirit."[10]

Although the International Labor Office recognized the impor-

[9] Quoted in *International Labour Conference, Twenty-sixth Session, Geneva, 1940, The Organization of Labour Inspection, in Industrial and Commercial Undertakings, Preliminary Report,* p. 16.
[10] *Ibid.*

tance of this question, for some years it concentrated its attention upon obtaining ratifications of its conventions. By 1927–28, it realized that ratification of itself did not provide sufficient guaranties. The Director, M. Thomas, declared that some governments were complaining that other governments were treating ratification as "merely a scrap of paper" and adopting labor legislation which was "a mere caricature of the international rules laid down." Some of these states gave various reasons for not applying conventions which they had ratified—that there were constitutional difficulties, that the general economic situation was unpropitious and the financial condition of the country unfavorable, that the measure was unimportant, or that "special circumstances" justified the noninclusion of some provisions of a ratified convention. To these excuses a special committee of the Organization replied in no uncertain fashion:

> The I.L.O. has no use for ratifications of principle, not to say window-dressing ratifications. The moral advantage which might result from merely platonic ratifications is entirely negligible in comparison with the discredit which such ratifications are liable to bring upon the work of the I.L.O. in the eyes of States which regard the conclusions of international Conventions and their scrupulous application as a sure method of promoting social progress.[11]

The constitution of the International Labor Organization provides three methods for insuring enforcement of conventions which have been ratified: (*a*) annual reports, in which member governments describe the measures which they have taken "to give effect to the provisions of Conventions" which they have ratified; (*b*) formal representations by employers or workers that they have been unable to obtain from their governments "the effective observance" of a convention to which the government is a party; and (*c*) the right of any government, a member of the International Labor Organization, to lodge a complaint against another member if it believes that the latter is ineffectually applying a convention which it has signed.

Each of these three methods requires further examination. One must realize at the outset that any attempt to force national governments to live up to their treaty obligations is a matter of the utmost delicacy and difficulty. The failure of economic sanctions against Italy, the unwillingness of governments to strengthen

---

[11] Quoted in J. B. Andrews, *Labor Laws in Action* (Harper & Bros., New York, 1938), p. 222.

the League machinery to protect minorities or increase the powers of the Permanent Mandates Commission, the reluctance of certain states to agree to the establishment of a Permanent Slavery Commission with even limited channels of obtaining information, all are evidence of the extreme jealousy with which governments guard their national sovereignty.

The *Annual Reports* have been the most effective means of providing "mutual supervision" over the application of conventions. Article 408 provides that the reports "shall be made in such form and shall contain such particulars as the Governing Body may request. The Director shall lay a summary of these reports before the next meeting of the Conference."

In January 1926 the Governing Body appointed a committee to consider ways and means of making the best and fullest use of information contained in the reports, which were so detailed as to make it difficult if not impossible for the average member of a General Conference to read and digest them. It was desirable to have a summary and an analysis which would enable members to concentrate upon "those points which can most usefully and profitably be discussed." The committee recommended that a technical Committee of Experts be appointed to condense the annual summaries to a much briefer report. Some persons feared that the appointment of the committee—a modest step— would be interpreted by governments as an additional measure of international control and would therefore "hinder further ratifications." But those who argued that it was necessary to know the real facts, and not be content with a large number of un- or ill-digested reports, won the day. The committee was appointed and first met in May 1927; a decade later it comprised ten persons (including three non-European), each of whom specialized on the conventions in which he had special interest and competence.

The Committee of Experts has become an important instrument in bringing the pressure of publicity and explanation upon governments which have been slow in applying the conventions which they have ratified, or have not ratified conventions which the Annual Conference has adopted. The committee makes a condensed summary of the annual reports. The Conference Committee on the Application of Conventions holds a general discussion on the experts' summary and examines the application of conventions "country by country," and "convention by convention." It draws attention in careful but definite language to missing, incomplete, and late reports and to ratifications which appear not to have been accompanied by sufficient national legislation, and emphasizes the desirability of "appropriate national measures" to give effect to the conventions. Its deliberations give governments an opportunity to state their reasons for nonenforcement or nonratification, while in the General Conference the workers can criticize governmental authorities for not living up to their obligations.

Wilson points out that the "diplomatic observations of the experts" become in the hands of the workers "criticisms of nonenforcement in the Conference." Wilson's judgment is that "the annual reports under Article 408 have given rise to an evolution of procedure which has been far more successful than could reasonably have been anticipated in the early days of the Organization."[12] The International Labor Office has not been able to examine the enforcement of national legislation "in a direct way" but rather by the processes of "indirection and conciliation." The Committee does not regard its work as unimportant. Quite the contrary; in 1935 it said in its report: "The Committee cannot state too strongly its belief that its task is a regular and integral part of the work of each session of the Conference and not a supplementary item on the agenda of the Conference." In 1936 it frankly emphasized that the center of gravity of its task was shifting from establishing legislative conformity to securing effective administration. And in 1937 it spoke of the need of strengthening factory inspection and law enforcement.[13]

The founders of the International Labor Organization added another method which, they hoped, would help to secure a more effective enforcement of conventions which had been ratified. Under Article 409 the workers or employers of a country might make "representation" to the International Labor Office that their government had "failed to secure . . . . effective observance" of a convention; the Governing Body was then to ask the government to comment upon the charge. If no statement was received within a reasonable time, or if the statement when received was deemed unsatisfactory, the Governing Body should have the right to publish the representation and the reply (if any) made by the government. The method has been used on two occasions: in the case of the Japanese Seamen's Union complaint in 1924, and in that of the Latvian Union's complaint in 1931–32.

[12] F. G. Wilson, *op. cit.,* p. 241.
[13] J. B. Andrews, *op. cit.,* p. 225.

LABOR LAW ADMINISTRATION

In recent years the International Labor Organization has become increasingly concerned with labor law administration. In 1936 the Governing Body decided that in the future members appointed to the Expert Committee must possess a practical knowledge of administrative problems. The Organization sponsored a western European factory-inspection conference held at The Hague in 1935, and a similar conference for the countries of eastern Europe in 1937. In the latter year the Office established a new division on labor law and administration. Two years later the International Labor Organization submitted a number of conclusions to a Preparatory Technical Conference. The report adopted by the Conference urged the desirability of international regulation, the need of placing each national inspection service under the direct and exclusive control of a central authority, the necessity of appointing inspectors solely on the basis of qualifications and of protecting them from dismissal except for good cause, also that the inspectors should have adequate powers specifically defined, that they should have the right to apply to the competent authorities for the issue of orders or for the taking of measures with immediate executive force, that penalties should be prescribed for obstructing inspectors, and that adequate penalties should be inflicted for breaches of the laws and regulations which the inspectors have to enforce.[14]

We have here another illustration of the fact that international organization may stimulate national action in countries with lower standards. Undoubtedly the need for factory inspection grows greater with the development of more intricate and dangerous processes and the organization of economic production on a more impersonal basis. From the point of view of human welfare few things are likely to be more important than the strict and impartial enforcement of labor standards, and the work of the Organization in this connection must be regarded as possessing unusual significance.

ACCOMPLISHMENTS OF THE ORGANIZATION

What has the International Labor Organization accomplished? To give an adequate answer would carry the analysis beyond the limits of this volume. Here one can only suggest in barest outline

---

[14] See the *Preliminary Report on The Organisation of Labour Inspection,* International Labor Office, Geneva, 1939.

the types of activity undertaken. It may be pointed out that the Organization has considered many questions and adopted a great number of conventions and recommendations, including those dealing with the eight-hour day; the hours of work in maritime occupations and in agriculture, conditions in agricultural production (in an appeal to the World Court its competence was upheld); hours of work in commerce, offices, and mines; a weekly rest for all workers; annual holidays with pay; the abolition of night work for women and children; the prohibition of night work in bakeries; the protection of children, young people, and women in industry; and a draft convention on the employment of women before and after childbirth so that a six-weeks' rest is granted before and after confinement and adequate benefit payment is made during that period. It has attempted to extend this protection to women wage earners in agriculture and to prohibit the employment of women in unhealthful industries.

It has turned its attention to industrial hygiene, has brought out special studies on economic questions which are veritable storehouses of information, and has produced a remarkable piece of work, *The Encyclopedia of Industrial Hygiene,* the preparation of which required the work of ninety-five collaborators from fifteen countries. It has engaged in research for the prevention of industrial accidents, emphasized the importance of factory inspection, and passed an important recommendation on accident prevention in 1929. It has adopted a convention for the protection of dockers employed in loading and unloading ships. Realizing that industry cannot afford to dispense with a sound system of social insurance, the International Labor Organization made a prolonged study of the question and drew up two draft conventions and three recommendations concerning compensation for industrial accidents, and in 1927 considered the problem of sickness insurance.

Economists are agreed that an adequate system of statistics is indispensable in assisting to determine sound economic policy and to forecast effects. The Organization has sponsored international conferences of labor statisticians and issued special studies of wage statistics because it realizes the importance of insuring that comparisons between different countries are not invalidated by inadequate or noncomparable systems of statistics. It has worked toward the establishment of a minimum wage and adopted a draft convention to that end in 1928. It has studied the family wage system which has been adopted in some countries and has investigated the doctrine of high wages to discover how far they are a factor in economic prosperity.

No person these days can fail to be impressed by the extent and burden of unemployment. The causes of unemployment have occupied the attention of economists for many years, and the International Labor Organization not only has published statistics of the numbers of unemployed but has made an inquiry into the national and international aspects of the matter. Its various studies have been valuable to experts, but it has not limited its work to theoretical study. The International Labor Conference of 1919 adopted a recommendation for the establishment of unemployment insurance. It realized the importance of efficient national employment exchanges operated on a nonprofit basis. In an endeavor to promote employment and to place people in occupations best suited to them, it undertook studies in vocational guidance, apprenticeship, and technical education. It co-operated in making studies of migration problems and published important volumes on migration statistics, and its representatives took part in several international conferences. Its studies in the so-called lean years between 1929 and 1936 were of great assistance to the international conference held in 1937 to draw up schemes for promoting emigration to South America.

The Organization turned its attention to maritime labor, and considered the possibility of drawing up an international seamen's code in the form of a collection of laws and regulations which might be used throughout the world. It adopted a convention for the establishment of seamen's employment agencies on a nonprofit basis, and three separate conventions to prohibit the employment of young persons at sea. It attempted to apply the eight-hour day to seamen, but for various reasons the matter was postponed; and in 1929 it considered the question of protecting seamen against sickness and accident. Between 1920 and 1926 the conference suggested measures for the welfare of seamen in port.

It is studying the question of the representation and organization of agricultural workers, and has adopted a convention concerning sickness insurance for this group. But the problem of agricultural workers is an extremely difficult one, and much study and effort will be required in this connection. Lack of space forbids more than a reference to the efforts made on behalf of professional workers, salaried employees, and native and colonial labor. Nor is it possible to do more than refer to other lines of activities, such as recommendations concerning the utilization of workers' spare time, the housing problem, studies dealing with the workers' right of association, collective agreements, arbitration and conciliation systems, and studies in profit-sharing and workers' participation in management. These and other endeavors engaging the attention of the Conferences and the Labor Office comprise a great part of the field of economic relations.

Rather than attempt to analyze the many problems which confronted the Organization in dealing with the scores of labor questions which it considered, or to compress an analysis of each convention into even one or two pages apiece, it will be preferable to consider one problem, namely, the rights of performers in broadcasting, television, and the mechanical reproduction of sounds, in order to show the way in which the welfare of one class of people is affected by international action.

In chapter vii we discuss the protection of nationals abroad, their property and investments; one section of the chapter deals with the part played by international conventions in protecting literary and artistic property. With the coming of phonographs and broadcasting an artist's work could be heard by a more permanent audience since the records could be played many times, and by a more extended audience because broadcasting made possible national and even worldwide audiences. A combination of gramophone and wireless intensified the problem of authors' rights, and later conventions expanded the original Berne Convention of 1886. But gramophones and broadcasting deeply affected the welfare of performers as well as authors. The number of musicians thrown out of work by the mechanical reproduction of sound ran into scores of thousands. The International Labor Organization notes that more than 5,000 musicians were unemployed in France in 1932, over 15,000 in the United States in 1935, and over 90 per cent of the members of the musical profession in Vienna in 1937.

To meet the new situation the National and International Federations of Performers tried to find new openings for work and also to obtain certain rights in respect to broadcasting and gramophone recording. They claimed that performers as well as authors should have the exclusive right to authorize the recording, reproduction, or transmission of their performances on the ground that they gave a distinctive interpretation without which the ideas or music of the author would remain either unexpressed or badly rendered. They also claimed "nonmaterial rights" which meant "performer's rights to respect for the personal contribution that he makes to a work of art when interpreting it": he should have his name placed on records and announced on broadcasts; he should be protected against the alteration or distortion of his performance. The professional artists also claimed pecuniary rights in the form of extra compensation when their performances were broadcast or recorded.

When the performers attempted to have their rights included in the Berne Convention they met with opposition from the authors and composers, who voiced their objections at the International Congresses held at Copenhagen in May 1923 and at Seville in 1935. The performers then turned to the International Labor Organization for help. As early as 1926 the Congress of the International Union of Musicians requested the Office to study the problem of performers' rights. After several years of investigation the matter was ripe for consideration by the International Labour Conference and the question was put on the agenda for the 1940 session. A committee of experts drew up a number of recommendations which included the following: (*a*) no record or broadcast of an original performance may be made without the consent of the performer; (*b*) the performer is entitled to have his name indicated on records of his performances and when his performances are broadcast; (*c*) he should have separate remuneration if his performance is broadcast "even when his contract contains no provisions to that effect"; (*d*) broadcasting organizations should be entitled to record artists' performances for broadcasting at a later date without making additional payments unless subsequent use is made of the record; (*e*) the performer's name should be mentioned as long as record of the performance lasts; and (*f*) disputed questions should be submitted to arbitration.[15]

The war has interrupted the work of the International Labor Organization, but when peace is restored we may expect to find that the rights of performers will be one of the first subjects to be considered by the General Conference.

If we keep in mind the fact that the question which has just been briefly analyzed constitutes only one of more than one hundred labor problems which have been the subject of conventions and recommendations adopted by over fifty nations of the world, we may form some idea of the remarkable amount of research and

[15] See *Report on Rights of Performers in Broadcasting, Television and the Mechanical Reproduction of Sounds,* International Labour Organization, Geneva, 1939.

expert knowledge, of discussion by governments, workers, and employers which has been expended and will be expended in the international effort to promote the welfare of labor.

The Organization has therefore considerably extended the scope of its work. In 1919 some of its founders believed that it should consider only industrial problems; but the leaders now realize that the welfare of workers in all branches of employment must be the goal. The International Labor Organization has improved its technique of making conventions and encouraging their ratification. It has added to its permanent machinery, and there now exist permanent International Agricultural and Public Works Committees. Recommendations have been passed for a Permanent International Tripartite Committee on the Textile Industry, and for a Permanent Committee on Migration Questions.

The visits of International Labor Office officials to various countries have helped governments to prepare and improve social legislation. Specialists have gone to Egypt to advise on matters of industrial hygiene, to Turkey to assist in social insurance questions, and to Venezuela to help in colonization and social insurance policy and in drafting a labor code. Father LeRoy traveled in Brazil, Uruguay, Argentina, and Chile, and the Director, accompanied by three experts, visited the Dutch East Indies, Ceylon, Malaya, French Indo-China, and British India to study conditions at first hand and to see in what directions the International Labor Organization could help to hasten economic reform.

The research work of the Organization has enabled it to do much pioneer work. Many years ago it urged long-range planning of public works to cope with depressions. Today this policy is accepted in many countries. Its technical findings have been of immense service to international conferences such as those held in Johannesburg in 1930 and in Geneva in 1938 to consider measures against silicosis.

All of these activities, important as they are, are subordinate to the main purpose of the Organization which is to build up what may be described as an International Labor Code. Its success in this direction depends upon the ratification of the various conventions by the member states, and the record shows that as of March 15, 1939, no fewer than 63 conventions had been adopted and 839 ratifications received. Theoretically this number equals about one-quarter of the number which would have been received had there been a 100 per cent ratification by all countries. However, it is important to remember that some conventions, as, for example, those dealing with forced labor, hours of work in coal mines, minimum age at sea, medical examination of young persons at sea, protections of dockers against accidents, and sickness insurance for those working at sea do not concern countries which have no colonies, or coal mines, or merchant marine, as the case may be, and that the record of ratifications is therefore better than at first sight appears. To secure over eight hundred ratifications by more than fifty countries within the space of twenty years is no small achievement; and probably were it not for the disturbing effects of the political anarchy of the last ten years the achievements of the International Labor Organization would stand out still more clearly.

It is interesting to note that the curve of ratifications has been a steady one throughout the whole period, and that in the twelve months ending March 15, 1939, fifty-seven new ratifications were received. The Director, Mr. Winant, in his report issued on May 10, 1939, added that the conventions exercised an indirect as well as a direct influence:

Their existence sets up a standard which public opinion gradually tends to accept as normal; and one result of this is that they act as a check on any tendency to allow conditions of work to be depressed below that level in times of difficulty. This indirect influence is very hard to measure; but if the differences which exist in labour legislation now and twenty years ago are studied in relation to the conventions, there is little doubt that it is considerable.[16]

For example, although the 1919 Convention concerning the eight-hour day and the forty-hour week in industry has received only 28 ratifications, it has provided a standard for the rest of the world and "inspired many laws and regulations." The Director shows that maternity benefit, minimum age for admission to employment in industry, on board ships, and in agriculture, social insurance, seamen's conditions, native labor, and other questions have been more actively considered by many countries as a result of the stimulus given by the work of the International Labor Organization.

In addition to the 63 conventions, the Conferences have adopted 56 recommendations, which, although they do not impose a formal international obligation, set forth general prin-

[16] *Report of the Director to the Twenty-fifth Session of the International Labour Conference,* June 1939, p. 83.

ciples and point the way to more detailed action. They include recommendations concerning unemployment, anthrax prevention, lead poisoning (women and children), labor inspection, hours of work in fisheries and in inland navigation, unemployment in agriculture, night work of women, children, and young persons in agriculture, vocational education, living-in conditions and social insurance in agriculture, workers' compensation, hours of work in hospitals, hotels, and theaters, vocational education, etc. Not the least service which an institution can render is to create an awareness of better standards and to indicate specific measures by which those standards can be attained, and the International Labor Organization through the general principles contained in the recommendations has exerted a wide influence in many countries.

It cannot be too strongly emphasized that the Organization has given a splendid demonstration of democracy in action. Conferences have taken place, not between governments acting with a minimum of consultation with interested parties, but between workers and employers and governments, who have considered in detail and from the broadest viewpoint what a proposed measure will involve. Not one of the three groups can ignore the claims and criticisms of the other two. Similarly, the representatives of one nation cannot consider matters from only a national vantage point; they come to realize that a particular policy which might be adopted with profit by one country alone would, if undertaken by all countries, produce disaster. And it is not without significance that the Organization has been able to maintain a large part of its civil service of economic experts drawn from all over the world; even now at Montreal about one-fourth of the members are still engaged in research and in preparation for extended activity when peace shall have been re-established.

The present war has of course seriously affected the position and work of the International Labor Organization. In October 1938 the Governing Body made plans in case hostilities should break out, and a few months later set up an emergency committee to consider practical measures to give effect to a policy of postwar reconstruction. Mr. Winant writes that the committee reported to the June 1939 Conference "that war would create new labor and social problems demanding urgent solution, and that the Organization must remain in a position to offer its experience as a guide in working out social policies in both belligerent and neutral countries."[17] He adds that the Office has received even more inquiries since the war than in the preceding period, and that it "has continued to serve as a world center for comparison and analysis of the experience of various nations with regard to social problems, whether of war or of peace."[18] Countries removed from the theater of the European war were able to carry on a fairly normal economic life for some time and looked to the Organization "to continue to render normal peacetime services to them." Despite the existence of war in Europe, the second American International Labor Conference met in Havana in November 1939. It urged the Office to continue its work and promised the support of both governments and people of the American continent.

The defeat of Belgium, Holland, Norway, and France profoundly affected the Organization, which was now left isolated in a continent dominated by totalitarian powers who had announced their hostility to the League of Nations and to the International Labor Organization. If the institution was to survive and play a useful part, it would have to transfer itself to a more protected location. As a result of negotiations between the Canadian government, McGill University, and the International Labor Office, fifty members of the staff moved to McGill and are carrying on publication of the *International Labor Review,* the *Legislative Series,* and special studies and reports. One may note especially the volume entitled *Studies in War Economics,* which appeared early in 1941, which contained the following articles: "Economic Organisation for Total War, with Special Reference to the Workers," by E. F. Penrose; "Who Shall Pay for the War? An Analysis of the Keynes Plan," by E. J. Riches; "Relative Wages in Wartime," by E. J. Riches; "Control of Food Prices," by A. S. J. Baster; "The Place of Housing Policy in War Economy," by Carl Major Wright; and "The Effect of War on the Relative Importance of Producing Centres, with Special Reference to the Textile Industry," by Edith Tilton Denhardt. Two articles on Nazi labor policy and the labor situation in Great Britain, which show how the two governments have adapted their administrative machinery and their "labor and social policies and practices" to the needs of intensive rearmament and total war, were also announced. An Inter-American Committee to Forward Social Security has been created under the auspices of the Organization, and technical assistance to governments and social and economic

[17] John G. Winant, "The I.L.O. in Wartime and After," *Foreign Affairs,* April 1941, p. 638.   [18] *Ibid.*

bodies is being continued. The officials realize the necessity of maintaining the active co-operation of governments, workers, and employers, not merely to help solve the economic and social problems arising from the prosecution of the war, but also to maintain in full vigor the habit of democratic consultation and policy-making, so that the fullest energies and utmost technical skill may be available at the end of the war to repair the damage caused by the conflict, and to rebuild foundations on a more secure basis.

Smith Simpson has a number of interesting judgments on the International Labor Organization, and makes certain proposals for its future working. He points out that the national branch offices which the Organization has—eight at one time and four at present—have served to relieve the strain of the central office and have helped to develop a loyalty to the institution in Geneva. He suggests that the branch-office system may help to preserve the universality of the institution "by meeting in a relatively inexpensive way certain demands for regional developments, and also in enabling the Organization at the end of the war to deal more adequately than it did at the end of the first World War with the urgent problems of peace."[19] Simpson proposes that the co-operatives might well find a place within the International Labor Organization, especially as they play as important a part in some countries as do labor unions and employers' associations.

The period of the Labor Conference is too short; it is impossible to consider freely the many questions which arise in a session of three weeks. Possibly we shall find in the future a more permanent conference at Geneva supplemented by regional conferences, such as those which have considered problems of the American continent, and by technical conferences such as the Washington Textile Conference of 1937. Since labor conditions and costs cannot be separated from the wider industrial, financial and social problems, the International Labor Organization should be recognized as being more than a "labor" organization. It "could certainly be criticized for interpreting its functions too narrowly, if it conceived labor standards as capable of progressive increase without any relation to the difficulties which these standards sometimes raise for employers and investors."[20]

[19] Smith Simpson, *The International Labour Organization: Retrospect and Forecast* (Committee to Study the Organization of Peace, Preliminary Report and Monographs, Carnegie Endowment for International Peace, 1941), p. 321.
[20] *Ibid.*, p. 331.

As international labor legislation increases, the question of factory inspection will become more important; and advance in this direction may perhaps be sought in the utilization of more adequately staffed branch offices, regional secretariats of regional conferences, permanent committees of special industries, and other "appropriate administrative bodies." Simpson believes that the conventions should become "automatically binding unless voted otherwise by the competent authority of a member," which would still retain the right to reject a convention but would then assume the burden of proving the unsuitability of the convention. But most important of all must be the recognition that labor problems can no longer be regarded as merely technical problems; they involve political considerations just as much as any other major problem of the day. "If that is true, to what extent can the International Labour Organization in the future remain aloof from 'politics'?"[21]

If Great Britain wins the present war, the Organization will again have an important role to play. The long experience of the members of the Office, the Governing Body, and the representatives at the Annual Conferences will be invaluable for the great tasks of reconstruction which lie ahead. If any form of regional or world federation is adopted, the Organization will continue to be an indispensable instrument of economic co-operation.

[21] *Ibid.*, p. 336.

Chapter V

INTERNATIONAL TRADE AND COMMERCE

Previous to 1914 international trade moved with surprising ease. We who live today under a mass of restrictions and prohibitions may well envy its delicate and self-adjusting nature. The law of supply and demand seemed to work over a large field of economic effort: if prices rose because of an inadequate supply of goods, production increased in the hope of higher profits; the resultant higher output caused prices again to fall. In international trade, the gold standard operated to keep international prices reasonably stable. If over a long period of time country A exported more to B than B did to A (we neglect triangular trade relations for the moment), it would cost more for B to buy foreign exchange in order to pay for goods coming from A. If the exchange moved beyond the gold points—i.e., the figure at which it paid a buyer to purchase gold at a bank, insure it, and have it transported, the price level of country B would tend to fall because a diminution of gold reserves would lead to a restriction of paper currency. On the other hand, country A, which had received the gold, would expand its currency and its prices would rise; the rise in prices in country A would lead to a diminished demand from B; the fall in prices in B would cause a heightened demand from A; and gradually trade would be restored to equilibrium. Thus the two distinguishing features, the law of supply and demand and an almost self-regulating currency adjustment, were such that international trade took place with comparatively little interference.

Tariff treaties were signed for fairly long periods of time, and the most-favored-nation clause, by which two nations promised to grant each other any further lowered tariff rates which might be extended to a third country on certain goods, enabled the benefits of tariff reductions to be considerably generalized. Moreover, Great Britain and Holland threw open their colonial trade to foreigners, who were subject to very few restrictions. Governments kept law and order, and there was little or no repudiation of international contracts.

BREAKDOWN OF INTERNATIONAL TRADE

Economists point out that this happy state of affairs depended upon a number of conditions which were undergoing gradual change. International trade took place between "complementary rather than competitive" countries. Many countries still concentrated upon agricultural production, and although they produced some manufactured goods they had not gone very far in doing so. Germany, the United States, France, and Britain were becoming industrial rivals, but not at an unduly alarming rate. The system worked well because there were expanding markets in two directions—nations enjoyed an increase of population at home, which absorbed a great deal of their products, and the opening up of new countries provided new markets and opportunities of capital investment. London, still the financial center of the world, dominated monetary policy and unity of direction was comparatively easy to obtain.[1]

Nevertheless, some ominous signs were appearing. Already the economic system had begun to suffer from a growing rigidity —governmental costs were rising, involving heavier taxation; trade unions were demanding higher wages and were resisting wage reductions in times of depression and thus, according to some economists, were preventing a necessary lowering of costs; monopolies were holding up prices, preventing the operation of the law of supply and demand and thus denying the masses the purchasing power they would otherwise have had. Agricultural countries were wanting to go into industrial production, and tariffs were rising. Nevertheless, it was generally true that prewar commerce was surprisingly self-regulating.

The World War of 1914–1918.—The war interrupted and profoundly affected the mechanism of international trade. Owing to immediate war necessities, the state entered economic life to an unprecedented degree, and intensified the governmental interference which, on humanitarian grounds, had already begun to produce better wages and conditions for the working class. The submarine and the blockade forced nations to a war policy of self-sufficiency; vested interests grew up and gained such great strength that their dislodgment became almost impossible when the war

---

[1] Sir Arthur Salter, *World Trade and Its Future* (University of Pennsylvania Press, 1936), pp. 10–27.

had ended. Organized labor received concessions from some governments which it was not willing to lose. Organized capital grew in power, and tended toward monopoly. Great war loans were causing national debts to mount and placing a heavy interest burden upon the postwar generation. Economic rigidity was increasing.

The destructive effects of the war were more far-reaching than this brief analysis suggests. It diverted scientific research to purposes of destruction, disrupted the world's credit system, and lowered the standard of living for all peoples. Between 1914 and 1918 people of belligerent countries suffered from the shortage of many things which make for health and civilized living. World prices were forced out of line and within nations, too, the price structure was distorted; supplies were rationed and uneconomic substitutes were called into play. After the war was over, it was found that great stocks of munitions, manufactures, and raw materials had accumulated in the wrong places. Too many ships had been built; millions of dollars worth of transport materials had to be scrapped; the problem of reabsorbing into industry many millions of soldiers presented infinite difficulties; and, as Condliffe notes, the task of readjustment.

was greatest in precisely those industries the overstimulation of which is the normal sign of the unbalancing of production that leads to an industrial crisis. . . . . To many people the paradox of poverty and distress in the face of enormous productive capacity appears almost beyond explanation; but the problem is largely one of wrong capacity in the wrong places, aggravated by a breakdown of the distributive system.[2]

The collapse of the world's credit system involved disastrous consequences, the causes of which were not readily appreciated by the man in the street. Credit inflation produced changes in income; the collapse of prices in the postwar period brought much suffering because of the difficulty of adjusting debt structure to new price levels. The breakdown of the gold standard and the maladjustments of national currencies, one to the other, made it difficult to exploit to the utmost the specialized production which depended largely upon "a common monetary measure for the whole trading world."[3]

In a recent volume James T. Shotwell shows something of the

[2] J. B. Condliffe, *War and Depression* (World Affairs Pamphlets, World Peace Foundation, Boston, 1935), pp. 13–14.
[3] *Ibid.,* p. 19.

direct costs of the World War.[4] The editor of the famous series, *The Economic and Social History of the World War,* in one hundred and fifty volumes, quotes some of the evidence there presented: The war cost Austria-Hungary five times as much as its annual income, and almost four-fifths of its total national wealth. It impoverished Germany's economic system by forcing everything into military service, with the result that, when the collapse came, disorder and disruption were complete. Much of the normal life was set aside as being militarily "non-essential"; consequently, when Germany came to re-establish her peaceful life, her whole economy was inadequate for the normal international trade so essential to her welfare. While not denying the many mistakes made by Allied statesmen, Shotwell estimates that the war itself cost Germany four times the amount of the reparations figures. What Germany forgot was the *destruction of the future,* a destruction which was not evident at the time of hostilities. Hitler, in Shotwell's judgment, has done Germany and the world a great disservice by concentrating attention unduly upon the effects of the peace and ignoring the profound effects of the war: "Germany's attempt to escape from the continuing economic disturbances due to the War can only succeed if it can enslave the rest of the world in the same kind of economic fetters as it wears today." That is the negative side of the truth. The other side is that there can be no sound economic development unless war is eliminated. Unfortunately, the world misread the evidence, as the following chapters will show.

The peace treaties.—The peace treaties further disrupted the prewar economic unity of Europe. The terms which the victors imposed upon the vanquished may have been necessary from a military point of view, but from an economic point of view they were disastrous. In particular, the Treaty of Versailles dealt Europe a heavy blow by dislocating the economy of the leading industrial country of the continent.

The Treaty deprived Germany of (1) 79 per cent of her iron ore supply, through the loss of Alsace-Lorraine; (2) about one-third of her coal—20,000,000 tons of coal a year, in addition to the difference between the prewar and the postwar production of northern France; (3) important potash supplies in Alsace, thereby diminishing the productivity of German soil as much as 40 per cent; (4) large areas of agricultural land in Posen and West

[4] James T. Shotwell, *What Germany Forgot* (The Macmillan Company, New York, 1940), pp. 129–30.

Prussia which had produced about a quarter of Germany's grain and potatoes and one-tenth of its domestic animals; (5) 140,000 milch cows, despite the fact that the shortage of milk had created a grave food problem; (6) all Germany's overseas colonies; (7) German rights in Morocco and Siam and Liberia, and also other rights;[5] (8) 8,000 locomotives and 150,000 railroad wagons (under the Armistice terms), and all the locomotives and rolling stock of railroads in the provinces; (9) all merchant ships of sixteen hundred tons and upwards, one-half of its merchant ships between a thousand and sixteen hundred tons, and one-quarter of the steam trawlers and other boats, while Germany further agreed to build for the Allies up to two hundred thousand tons a year for the next five years as required. Germany's full use of her main river communications were placed under Allied control. Heavy demands were made upon her chief industries such as 35,000 tons of benzol, 50,000 tons of coal tar, 30,000 tons of ammonia sulphate. The Reparations Commission might take 50 per cent of dyestuffs and chemical drugs under German control at the time of the Treaty, and until 1925 demand one-quarter of the German production of dyestuffs and chemical drugs—the Commission to determine the method of delivery and the price "having regard to cost." Germany was denied most-favored-nation treatment, though she was compelled to give it. Preliminary payments of £1,000,000,000 in cash or the equivalent were required by May 1921, the final amount of reparations to be decided later. By the subsequent plebiscite in Upper Silesia, Germany lost an area which in 1912 had produced over 70 per cent of its zinc supply.[6]

Reparations.—Germany, upon whom these great burdens were placed, had suffered (like other countries) from four years of exhausting warfare. Its internal situation in 1919 was terrible, and foreign observers corroborated Dr. Starling's report that industries were without raw materials and that little food was available. Hundreds of adults and children had died "as a direct result of slow starvation." In Berlin two-thirds of the people "are living on a low level of vitality." Tuberculosis in Prussia had

[5] The Allies also had the option of confiscating all German concessions in Russia, China, Turkey, Hungary, and Bulgaria, and in former German territory; at the same time the rights of all German subjects might be canceled, thus threatening to wipe out the accumulated fruit of years of individual German effort abroad.

[6] For a German view of the economic effects of the Peace Treaty and Reparations, see Carl Rothe, *Weltkrieg Gegen Deutsche Wirtschaft* (Hanseatische Verlagsanstalt, Hamburg, 1932).

increased about 250 per cent. The death rate had mounted and the birth rate had dropped by almost one-half. The German people were utterly exhausted; the productivity of the land had diminished; industry was disorganized, and the morale of the nation almost broken.

It is important to realize these facts; they made fulfillment of the reparations clauses more difficult, if not impossible; and one can understand more readily the psychological reaction of a despairing and defeated people.

Sir Arthur Salter writes that the story of reparations is the story of postwar Europe. Reparations constituted a "principal obstacle to every attempt at recovery. It has disturbed the relations of old allies no less than of old enemies. It has thus been a principal factor in the tendency of countries to realign themselves into opposing groups and alliances, the alternative to the 'collective' system of the League and the Kellogg Pact, on which the future peace of the world depends. The cash results have not been proportionate to these consequences."[7]

Why, then, did the victors undertake so disastrous a policy? The answer is clear. War passions were at their height. The French had suffered appalling damage in the north of France and demanded fullest satisfaction. Popular opinion held that Germany was responsible for the war; and this belief was written into Article 231 of the Peace Treaty. Passion found a powerful ally in ignorance—ignorance of the essential economic problems of the modern world. The average person believed that wealth could be transferred from one nation to another, in much the same way as one might transfer coins from one pocket to another. This misunderstanding of the nature of international trade and of the world economic organization upon which it rested helped to intensify the dislocation of Europe by demands for payments which could only distort the already disturbed operations of economic life.

Instead of primarily looking to the future and repairing the dislocations wrought by the war, individual nations scrambled to get what they could immediately grab, irrespective of the total effect upon world, and especially upon European, economy. They refused to see that Germany was overstrained in attempting to pay reparations. They ignored transfer problems. They turned a blind eye to the dangerous inflation in central Europe in the early post-

[7] Salter, *Recovery, The Second Effort* (The Century Co., New York, 1932), p. 141.

war years. They did not realize that after 1924 Germany was able to pay reparations only because she could borrow from abroad. They did not see that the change in price level was making debt repayment almost twice as heavy as during the time when the debts were originally imposed. The war had disrupted the world economic organization; nationalist prejudice and ignorance prevented the world from rebuilding it. It preferred to indulge its emotions rather than intelligently plan to prevent in the future what had brought political and economic disaster between 1914 and 1918.

War debts.—The war debts question has aroused considerable discussion and caused much misunderstanding. On both sides of the Atlantic keen emotions have developed, making it difficult for even educated persons to approach the problem in a spirit of detached analysis and to see how it has helped to throw the world economic system out of gear.

By 1918, intergovernmental debts amounted to twenty-one billion dollars; five years later the total had reached twenty-eight billion dollars. Little attempt was made until 1922 to settle the debts question. Europe was in such a condition of uncertainty and disorganization that little good could have resulted from raising the issue. But in 1921 President Wilson informed Mr. Lloyd George that Congress and the American people would probably not consent to canceling war debts in order to facilitate a settlement of reparations in Europe. Thus early did the United States deny any relation between war debts and reparations. The French saw the matter in a very different light. They claimed that since Germany was responsible for the war, it should pay for the war— it was absurd to ask France to pay war debts to the United States if Germany paid no reparations to France. The French argument was logical, but it was a logic on a plane which the United States would not or could not appreciate.

Meanwhile Great Britain, realizing the need of freeing the world from a debt burden which threatened to prevent a revival of international trade, hinted at general cancellation; but at this stage she did not press the matter.

When negotiations began, American opinion was divided. Many economists and others, on grounds of economic theory, favored at least a partial cancellation of the debts. Firms which engaged in international trade, or had loaned money abroad, spoke on similar lines, saying that to load Europe with war debts would delay its economic reconstruction and prevent its regaining effective purchasing power, with the result that American foreign trade would suffer. Others pointed out that some countries (England especially) were already paying very high taxes and that the burden of governmental debt in those lands was seven to eleven times higher in relation to national income than in the United States. Paying the war debts would impose great hardships on these countries, while what they would pay to the United States would benefit the latter to only a small degree, since its annual receipts from debt payments would amount to less than 5 per cent of its imports—less than one-third or one-half of one per cent of the national income. The burden upon the debtors would be out of all proportion to the benefits which the United States would receive.

Nevertheless the majority of the American public demanded repayment. They spoke of the sanctity of contracts and said: Europe must pay for a war which it had voluntarily undertaken; debt repayment would do more to create confidence in governments and to re-establish credit than any other single factor; also, if Europe could afford to spend so many millions on armaments after a "war to end war," and if France could make loans to the Little Entente and Poland, they could afford to pay for the last war. For these reasons American public opinion opposed cancellation, and Congress was so united on this point as to force the Administration to demand repayment in full. Europeans retorted that the armament expenditure was largely due to the failure of the United States to join the League of Nations or to give any security guaranties by which Europe could be freed from the fear of war. To this United States isolationists replied that the European nations could, if they wanted to, develop a sound European security system. Thus the war-debts question turned out to be part of the problem of security!

In February 1922 Congress set up the World War Debt Commission, and forbade cancellation of debts—they were to be repaid by 1947 at not less than 4.1 per cent interest. By 1924 the American attitude had undergone some modification, and people began to talk in terms of what the debtors could pay rather than what they should pay, just as the Allied Powers had had to take economic realities into account and shift their demand from what Germany must pay, to what Germany could pay. The Debt Funding Commission made this admission in October 1925, and added that the problem was to decide on what basis it would be possible to determine a nation's capacity to pay over a period of time.

The agreements which the United States made maintained its

theoretical stand on no reduction of principal, but took into account the economic position of the debtors by reducing interest rates. Angell calculated that the interest reductions meant a reduction in war debts of 18 per cent for Britain, 46 per cent for Belgium, and 74 per cent for Italy. Moulton estimated that if the original 5 per cent interest rate be taken as a basis, the twelve debtor countries enjoyed a cancellation of 64.8 per cent; if one took instead the 4½ per cent interest rate authorized by the Debt Commission, the American cancellation amounted to 43 per cent; and on the basis of the average interest rate that the United States Treasury would have to pay to the loans subscribers over a period of sixty-two years, the cancellation would amount to about 20 per cent. Curiously enough, the United States action did not win much gratitude abroad. Foreigners remembered the maintenance of the principal and forgot the reduction of the interest rate! Many Americans, on the other hand, were keenly sensitive to the allowance that had been made and denounced the ungrateful Europeans. The latter claimed that the war loans of the United States represented America's war effort while the Allies held the trenches against the Germans before the American soldiers reached the front, that the loans were part of the common contribution toward the fight for freedom. The United States alleged that the contract was clear for all who would read; the Allies had promised to pay, "had they not?"

The situation became still more complicated from the postwar private loans made by American firms to Germany and to other parts of Europe. As the world economic situation became more strained, the clash of interests within the United States became more pronounced. For if Germany could not pay both reparations and interest and sinking fund on private loans, the question arose which should have precedence: if Germany defaulted on reparations payments, and France in turn defaulted on her debts to the United States, the American taxpayer would have to foot a big bill to enable the government to pay the interest on the war loans; if German reparations payments took precedence over private loans and the latter went by default, then the private lenders would find their interest coupons unpaid. The United States had thus to decide whether in case of a German inability to pay, it would be better for private lenders to Germany, or for the general taxpayer, to lose. One group asserted that the bankers had taken a risk and should not expect privileged treatment; an opposing group replied that the economic situation would be worse if private lenders suffered loss—the extra taxation required to meet the default of war debts could be spread thinly over the whole nation and would scarcely be felt, but a collapse of banking institutions would have very serious consequences by shaking business confidence and ruining certain sections of economic life.

As time went on, the connection between war debts and reparations became more obvious. The United States, while maintaining its theoretical position that war debts and reparations were independent questions, in reality admitted their connection in the Young Plan of 1929, which provided that the new reparations agreement should extend over a period of 58 years. The number of annual repayment payments thus coincided with the number of annual war-debt payments which the United States was still to receive. Also, the signatories of the Young Plan promised Germany a two-thirds reduction of reparations payments if they were granted war-debt reductions during the first 37-year period, and a total reparations cancellation to the extent of war-debt cancellation in the final 22-year period.

As conditions grew worse in Germany, the task of meeting both reparations payments (especially the unconditional quotas, most of which went to France) and the service on private loans (taken up mostly in Great Britain and the United States) became increasingly heavy. On June 20, 1931, President Hoover proposed a suspension of all intergovernmental payments, including war debts and reparations. France opposed the idea, and its resistance served to delay the inevitable outcome of reparations.

The American public still refused to consider any fundamental change. The world economic depression and the advent of Hitler soon made reparations a thing of the past, and one by one the debtors to the United States defaulted. At first they made token payments but later did not trouble even to maintain the appearance of repayment. Finland alone stood out as a shining example of strict observance of obligations. Congress replied by passing the Johnson Act in 1934 forbidding loans to countries which had defaulted, and thereby made it still more difficult for some of the debtors to maintain their currency on a gold standard.

After 1936 a great amount of European capital fled to the United States, seeking refuge and safety from a continent which was beginning to suffer from almost continuous political upsets. Many Americans could not help asking whether this vast amount of capital did not show that Europe could have paid its debts, in substantial measure at least, if it had wanted to do so. The spectacle of the insane expenditure on arms completed their sense of injury. A continent which would do that, and not pay its debts, deserved no consideration.

The war-debts question thus showed how little the countries involved were willing to take a comprehensive view of the question. Given a reasonable will to compromise, it should have been possible to work out a fair solution. With the future of world trade and of international politics at stake, a few hundred million dollars a year should not have been so great an obstacle. Had the United States seen more broadly and been more ready to adjust and had the European countries shown more willingness to meet their obligations, the result might have been different. The temper of all parties on what was after all a relatively minor problem compared with the greater questions at stake boded ill for the chances of adequate statesmanship in a tangled world. Lack of comprehensiveness stands out as the most evident fact in the war-debts question. The same characteristic was to mark the United States postwar tariff policy.

The United States tariff policy.—The postwar tariff policy of the United States was a major factor in the breakdown of international trade. The tradition of a high tariff is a long one in American history and dates back to Hamilton's famous *Report on Manufactures*. The 1816 and 1828 treaties were important initial steps in the direction of protecting home industries. The United States (in an economic sense) was a young country and borrowed heavily from abroad in order to finance its new industrial developments, its great railroad construction programs, and its agricultural expansion; for several decades it followed a policy of low tariffs, which permitted the imports necessary for its capital development.

After 1890 a sharp change took place. The high tariff of the McKinley Act was followed by the higher tariff of the Dingley Act of 1897 and the Payne-Aldrich Tariff of 1909. The Underwood Tariff of 1913, which reversed the mounting tendencies, was the last step before the World War of 1914–1918. During that conflict the United States changed rapidly from a debtor to a creditor country. Normally this transition occupies a comparatively long period of time: First, a country which is an immature borrower imports more than it exports, because the amount which it borrows annually exceeds the amount which it pays out in interest. After a certain time the accumulated interest will exceed in annual payments the amount borrowed each year;

the country then becomes a mature borrower whose annual exports exceed its annual imports. In similar fashion an immature creditor will export more annually than it imports, because its interest earnings are as yet small; but, as years pass, the interest earnings increase, until a point is reached when the country becomes a mature creditor whose annual imports will exceed its annual exports. Obviously a country which has loaned a great deal abroad must sooner or later be prepared to accept a so-called adverse trade balance if it is to have its loans repaid. It is a question of simple mathematics. If one sends more goods abroad at one time, he must receive more goods at another; otherwise he gives something for nothing.

The United States within a few years had loaned, publicly and privately, thousands of millions of dollars abroad in the form of war loans and other economic advances. Logically it should have modified its tariff and shipping policy, so as to have enabled the debtor countries to discharge their obligations. Unfortunately, it took a different course and adopted a series of inconsistent measures. It increased its tariffs in 1922 and 1930; it took energetic steps to expand its export trade; it subsidized its merchant marine and thereby deprived foreign ships of the opportunity of increasing their earnings; it sterilized the gold which came in payment from abroad; it insisted upon collecting war debts; and, after the boom of 1927–28, it curtailed further loans abroad because American investors hoped to gain greater profits at home than from abroad. In a word, it made repayment of loans by goods and services a most difficult matter.

The tariff policy requires further examination. The 1922 Fordney-McCumber Act, while disappointing to Europeans, did not produce the great outburst of indignation which met the Smoot-Hawley Tariff of 1930, because people expected that the flexible provisions of the 1922 measure would be used to reduce the level of duties on many commodities.

Percy W. Bidwell, writing in *Foreign Affairs* in October 1930, tells why the 1930 tariff was received with such bitterness in Europe. He suggests that it is difficult for citizens of the United States to understand how important external markets have been to European industry: 25 per cent of Germany's silk goods, 25 per cent of its rolling-mill products, and 50 to 60 per cent of its metal wares found their markets abroad; 90 per cent of Belgian plate and window glass and 60 per cent of its cement, 95 per cent of Swiss watches and 98 per cent of Swiss embroideries had to be exported. Other examples might be added; but the general situation is clear. European countries which needed the American market now found the door closed more tightly against them. The average increase of new duties amounted to 20 per cent, and affected important exports from Switzerland, Germany, France, Italy, Belgium, Spain, and Great Britain, as well as other countries within and outside of Europe.

The height of the tariff was not the only cause of dissatisfaction. The United States modified the principle of equalization of costs of production which had been adopted in the Fordney-Mc-Cumber Tariff Act, and in the 1930 act raised the duty on many products considerably above the figure which would have been sufficient to equalize costs. Moreover, it changed the tariff without giving other countries an opportunity to negotiate. Technically, the tariff is a national question and comes under the sovereign jurisdiction of a state; but in practice it has great influence upon the everyday life of people abroad. In the words of J. M. Jones, "Tariffs are international in their incidence and interest."

These larger questions of principle occupied the attention of only a few scholars. The more practical results were seen in Europe's reaction to the Smoot-Hawley measure. Spain retaliated by withdrawing the most-favored-nation treatment from the United States for the first time since 1906, and imposed duties which affected American automobiles, tires, and tubes, motion-picture films, and other products. Italy expressed its opposition by carrying on a popular campaign against American automobiles, and the more emotional elements of the population indulged their feelings by breaking the windows of American cars and cursing their drivers; the Italian government imposed prohibitive tariffs on United States automobiles, radios, and radio equipment; and the Ford Company closed its assembly plant at Trieste. Switzerland, urged on by the propaganda of foreign competitors, boycotted American products, and American automobiles, typewriters, tires, tools, washing machines, electric and household appliances, gasoline, vacuum cleaners, and other products suffered a sharp decline in sales. France put many American goods on a quota basis, and Canada and the rest of the British Empire replied by adopting the Ottawa system of imperial preference.[8]

The Smoot-Hawley Tariff completed the contradiction of

[8] See J. M. Jones, *Tariff Retaliation: Repercussions of the Hawley-Smoot Bill* (University of Pennsylvania Press, Philadelphia, 1934).

American economic policy. It made repayment of foreign debts still more difficult. It weakened the debtors' will to pay, and re- acted most unfavorably against the interests of United States ex- porters and branch factories abroad. The income of the cotton farmers in the South declined from 1,535 millions of dollars in 1928 to 483 millions of dollars in 1934. One-sixth of the culti- vated area in the United States was producing commodities for which no domestic market existed. Wheat, cotton, tobacco, and corn, also industrial machinery and many other manufactured goods all needed foreign markets. Francis B. Sayre estimated that 10,000,000 people of the United States depended upon exports for their livelihood; the high tariff was, therefore, "a voluntary abandonment of foreign markets," the extent of which may be judged from the fact that the United States exports dropped from 5,241 million dollars in 1929 to 2,133 million dollars in 1934, and its imports dropped from 4,400 million dollars in 1929 to 1,655 million dollars in 1934.

Obviously the American tariff was not the only cause of this disastrous fall in foreign trade. Such a claim would be absurd. But that the anomalous economic policy of the United States—a powerful creditor country maintaining high tariffs and developing a merchant marine—did seriously distort the world economic structure cannot be doubted. The debtor countries, finding it dif- ficult to repay in goods, exported their gold; their prices fell in consequence, and the failure to find markets depressed the prices of their commodities; in order to protect their national currencies they forbade the export of any more gold and ultimately defaulted on their debt payments. In addition to the war, the war debts, the economic clauses of the Versailles and other treaties, and the growing rigidity of the economic system, the United States tariff policy from 1922 to 1932 must be regarded as a fundamental cause of the world's economic disequilibrium and as contributing to the breakdown of its peace machinery. The "battles without bullets" which have been waged during the last decade can be traceable in no small measure to the contradictions of the United States economic policy.

Between 1930 and 1932 President Hoover tried to overcome these contradictions. He saw that the combination of tariffs, gov- ernment encouragement of exports, and government insistence upon the repayment of war loans was imperiling the whole system of international payments and he therefore worked toward a re- duction of reparations and war debts, the limitation of armaments (so as to lessen the amount of uneconomic expenditure), and a resumption of lending abroad. However, he approved the Smoot-Hawley Tariff and did not attempt to restore international trade by lowering the barriers imposed by high duties.

Mr. Roosevelt, on his accession to office in March 1933, proposed to balance international accounts, not by a resumption of lending, but by a reduction of the tariff and by a degree of planned economy. These two objectives proved to be somewhat contradictory, and the failure of the World Economic Conference in June 1933 destroyed the international elements of both the Hoover and the Roosevelt programs. For a time the United States moved toward economic nationalism by reducing exports and attempting to plan an insulated national economy.

Many writers set forth a theoretical justification for the closed system. Charles A. Beard wrote *The Open Door at Home,* and Samuel Crowther, Dean Donham, and others reproduced the arguments which are analyzed under the theory of economic nationalism; they pointed out that it was more important to maintain the stability of domestic prices than the stability of foreign exchange, that political instability abroad made long-term commercial and industrial plans difficult, that foreign trade accounted for less than 10 per cent of the whole of the United States trade, and that because of the diversity of its resources and the inventiveness of modern science the United States could make the transition to practical economic self-sufficiency with relatively little disruption. They identified themselves with economic nationalism, now to be discussed.

Economic nationalism.—The theory and practice of economic nationalism have developed with great rapidity and intensity during recent years.[9] There are several reasons: The younger countries, largely agricultural in their economy, have suffered from the fall in the price level of primary products. The law of comparative advantage—that countries should produce those things for which they possess the greater skill and national advantage—has received a heavy blow. Of what use is it to produce more primary products if the effect is to depress the price level still further? Why not turn to industry which has not suffered

[9] The effects of the noneconomic aspects of nationalism upon the liberal theories of international trade, and the triumph of politics over economics, may be studied in several works, e.g., J. B. Condliffe, *The Reconstruction of World Trade,* Part I; Peter Drucker, *The End of Economic Man;* Pierre Lucius, *L'Agonie du liberalisme;* and Frank Munk, *The Economics of Force.*

so serious a price collapse as agriculture has done? It is better, so the argument runs, to diversify one's economic life, to avoid putting all the economic eggs in one basket, and to establish an economic balance. Thus a nation will avoid being at the mercy of world conditions and of undue fluctuations in the price of any one commodity. The disastrous consequences to Cuba and Brazil, which have been mono-culture countries, specializing in sugar and coffee, is a sufficient example of the hazard of entrusting a nation's economic life to the uncertainties of a specialized international trade. The younger countries, moreover, did not feel that they should permanently remain merely agricultural and in a position of dependence upon older industrial nations. They did not wish to accept the existing economic status quo but desired to build up their own industries and make use of their own skills. They protested against the imperialism of the great powers, and aimed to achieve a genuine economic as well as political independence.

The troubled international situation, the desperate armaments race, and the emphasis placed upon security provide another explanation of the growth of economic nationalism. Countries wish to be self-sufficient, so that in wartime they may be independent of foreign supplies. Hence industrial nations turn to agriculture to insure adequate home production of foodstuffs, and agricultural nations develop industries in order to build up their military power. In both cases there is a loss in economic efficiency. People have been willing to sacrifice material welfare for noneconomic purposes. There has come about a subordination, even if not the end, of "economic man."

The peace treaties of 1919 set up new nations which in the first flush of national self-consciousness, and for reasons of defense, adopted high tariffs, currency restrictions, and government subsidies.[10] The old larger imperial economic units, as, for example, the Austro-Hungarian and Russian Empires, disappeared; in their place arose small, hostile units which destroyed the possibility of extensive international trade.

Some theorists assert that modern invention has lessened the need for international trade. Japan now produces many things hitherto made by Great Britain, Germany, France, and Italy; and other countries by importing machinery and developing technical skill can make for themselves things which they previously had

[10] L. Pasvolsky, *Economic Nationalism of the Danubian States* (The Macmillan Company, New York, 1928), pp. 70 ff.

to import. When Japan, India, and Australia can make their own textiles as well as produce their foodstuffs, the need for international trade is correspondingly lessened. So runs the argument.

Other writers claim that, in spite of the great growth of international trade during the nineteenth and twentieth centuries, by far the greater amount of interchange of goods still takes place within national boundaries. Trade is still mostly intra- and not inter-national. The foreign trade of the United States is less than 10 per cent of its total trade; even Great Britain, the leader in world commerce, enjoys a greater volume of trade in its home market than in its foreign market. Why, then, should a nation not develop the market within its own boundaries to its utmost capacity? Why not raise the purchasing power of those millions at home who are still living in poverty and want? Many socialists long ago pointed out that under modern capitalism industry was searching markets abroad because the workers at home were not given sufficient wages with which to buy the products which they had helped to create. When the economic crash came, and debtor countries one by one defaulted, people began to speak of the hazardous nature of international trade, which placed the fortunes of people at the mercy of political and economic forces beyond their control, and to ask whether it would not be better to adopt a planned economy within the nation itself, in an endeavor to overcome the periodic economic crises which have long afflicted human society. A nation, they maintained, just because it had political control over its own affairs, and because its internal trade was so much greater than its external trade, could set to work to build up and expand its own internal market. Planned economy thus became the ally of economic nationalism. By nationalizing economic life within the nation and adopting the open door at home, a country could escape from dependence upon an unstable and unpredictable international world.

If the internal market is more important for a nation, it follows that stability of internal prices is more important than stability of foreign exchanges. Sir Basil Blackett and others argued along this line; they pointed to the catastrophic effects of falling prices, and claimed that it was the violent fluctuation in internal prices, and of purchasing power within the nation, more than the instability of foreign exchanges which constituted the fundamental problem.[11] It would not be difficult to keep the

---

[11] Sir Basil Blackett, *Planned Money* (Constable & Co., London, 1932), p. 86.

national price level under control, because central banks which had had long experience in keeping foreign exchanges stable could, by controlling the discount rate and through open market operations, maintain essential stability. (One may note in passing that this theory was adopted by President Roosevelt in the early years of his administration.[12])

Dean Donham claimed that an indefinite expansion of the export trade would lead to a trade war between the capitalist countries and would run the risk of ruining some of the competitive nations and of hastening foreign bankruptcies. While much foreign trade is desirable, the theories that tariffs should be reduced "appear to give far too little attention to social stability" and overlook the danger that many domestic industries would be wiped out.[13]

Finally it was pointed out that the self-regulating and automatic character of the nineteenth-century capitalist system had largely broken down. The law of supply and demand no longer freely operated, and competition no longer directly affected the level of prices. Several things had happened to make the modern economic system more rigid: the state had intervened to raise and maintain wages, which were not allowed to fall below a certain level; industrial monopolies had retarded the reduction of prices previously established through competition; tariffs had prevented the free flow of goods; the great national debts had necessitated heavy fixed interest payments; and dictatorships had still further stratified society in the large and had restricted still more the free actions of economic forces.

Criticisms of the theory of economic nationalism will follow presently. It remains to consider how economic nationalism has been put into operation.

Methods of attaining self-sufficiency.—The methods adopted to attain self-sufficiency are four in number:

First, a country may launch a campaign to avoid waste. In Germany this movement has gone to remarkable lengths.[14] German regulations for avoiding waste apply to dozens of materials including men's and women's hair, food scraps, bones, bottles, scrap metal, and potato peelings.

Second, a government may require its people to do without

---

[12] See his message to the World Economic Conference, 1933.

[13] W. B. Donham, *Business Adrift* (McGraw-Hill Book Company, New York, 1931), pp. 77–97.

[14] Even before the outbreak of the new war in September 1939.

certain goods or at least to be satisfied with smaller amounts. In Germany children may not have toy balloons at Christmas time; women's skirts and men's shirts are shortened; "even stage magicians are asked to do their part in the conservation of food" and "are forbidden to use eggs, milk, or other edibles in their performance"; photographers are limited as to the amount of photographic paper they may purchase.

Third, a vigorous attempt to use substitutes may be made in countries which desire to free themselves from dependence upon foreign supplies. In 1936, regulations appeared in Germany that men's clothes and uniforms were to contain 15 to 25 per cent of artificial and a certain percentage of local wool. Cheese was not to contain more than 20 per cent cream. Builders were forced to use substitutes for, or to do without, lead, nickel, zinc, copper, and their alloys. Shopkeepers were not permitted to advertise butter, margarine, or lard. In Germany and Italy synthetic rubber was made.

Fourth, the autarchic-minded countries may produce foods at home even though resulting costs may be greater and prices higher for the consumer. Quantitative restriction of imports—butter, poultry products, sugar, oils and fats, coffee—the enforced use of domestic raw materials, as noted above, and foreign exchange restrictions all prevent the importation of goods hitherto purchased from abroad. Land irrigation and reclamation, mining for low-grade coal and for oil, and the establishment of manufactures may make for a degree of self-sufficiency, though at the expense of the general standard of living. In Italy, railway rolling stock is made domestically and experiments are being made to dispense with materials which have to be imported. Railroads are being electrified in order to reduce the importation of coal, and natural gas is being used as fuel. Scientists are experimenting with charcoal and with wood and grain alcohol for fuel purposes. By these means both Germany and Italy have hoped to become independent in many respects. Hitler proclaimed to the nation in September 1936 that

in four years, Germany must be wholly independent of foreign countries in respect to all those materials which can in any way be produced through German capability, through German chemistry, or by our machine and mining industries. The creation of this Great German raw material industry will employ productively those masses freed by the completion of rearmament.

Italy took similar measures, although not to the same degree, announcing that it hoped to attain the maximum degree of economic independence.

The Fascist government began its so-called "battle for bread" in 1925 and set up a wheat commission which was to plan the campaign, to study the question in its technical aspects, and to make recommendations. The government in its desire to make Italy independent of the rest of the world in its wheat supply attempted various well-known experiments. It engaged in scientific research, reclaimed land, distributed free seed, set up sales agencies, encouraged the building of machinery for agricultural purposes, and reduced taxes on gasoline used by farm machines; it imposed a tariff on wheat and introduced regulations in 1931 for the compulsory use of a certain amount of Italian wheat in milling operations. Some of these methods are justifiable; some have resulted in considerable loss. It is true that Italy has become more self-sufficient in its wheat supply; it has extended its wheat area and has improved the average yield per acre. But there is another side to the picture. The government has caused other commodities than wheat to be neglected. Fruits, wines, and vegetables of South Italy have had to give way to this enthusiasm for wheat. Animal husbandry has suffered, for there has been a reduction of livestock. The tariff on wheat has "upset the balance between the various branches of agricultural production" and Italy has had to import its butter and wool, its eggs, and even its live animals. More generally it can be said that the Fascist policy has attempted to utilize the soil of South Italy for purposes to which it is not suited, and that the combined effects of tariffs and high prices has been to make the Italian consumer pay considerably more for his domestically grown wheat than he would have had to pay in the world market.

The effect of the measures outlined here has been to produce what Marchand has called "the renaissance of mercantilism" in the contemporary era. Mercantilism, whether of the period lasting from the fifteenth to the eighteenth century or of the present day, is more than a purely economic doctrine; it involves the whole life of a people. It embraces a great number of forces and tendencies, and cannot be easily defined in clear and succinct terms. What is common to the various forms of mercantilism is the strong state which dominates the many phases of economic life, for purposes of political power as well as for economic welfare.[15]

[15] Jacques Marchand, *La Renaissance du Mercantilisme* (Librairie technique et économique, Paris, 1937), pp. 5–9.

Marchand points to many similarities between the earier period and our own. In both cases the state formed corporations on the assumption that it alone by its strength and organization was able to co-ordinate the many complex and frequently conflicting forces. Indeed, the corporative state of Italy is typical of the extent to which state intervention can go. Moreover, just as Colbert in the seventeenth century helped to create many new manufactures, just as the state in those days proclaimed a monopoly over certain industries, so the state today dictates as to mines, hydroelectric power, oil, armaments, and many other economic activities. In both epochs the state encouraged research, rewarded inventors, and built technical schools, all with the object of promoting national power and welfare. Other present-day examples are too numerous to be listed here. In the earlier mercantilist era Great Britain took strong steps to protect its agriculture; today all countries by tariffs and other means try to make themselves self-sufficient in wheat and other raw materials.

The traditional mercantilist theory was much concerned with a favorable balance of trade, as are many peoples today. Both ages were notable for the use of tariffs to discourage imports so as to protect home markets. The navigation acts of the seventeenth century are paralleled by the merchant-shipping acts of the last few years. We have seen that countries have recently limited imports in order to maintain their currency stability, just as earlier governments limited imports to prevent the drain of treasure. Both times witnessed price control, the establishment of boards to watch over capital investment, and the classification of industries and of imports in terms of their value in promoting national strength. The nineteenth-century indifference to colonies proved to be an interval between the two periods, which emphasized the importance of colonies as sources of raw materials, markets for home products, and outlets for surplus population. In the seventeenth century governments were concerned to increase population; and Marchand gives instances of the attempts to encourage large families in Canada by bonuses. One Canadian governor, Tallon, forbade bachelors to hunt and fish. In France, Colbert fought against the ideal of the celibate priesthood.[16] In both cases economic and military reasons dictated the attempts to prevent a decline in the birth rate; and the policy reappears today. Parallels are also seen in the field of finance. The state tightened its hold over money; today we see the development of central banks and

[16] Marchand, *op. cit.*, pp. 117, 118.

an emphasis upon the role which money has to play. In both times there were writers who emphasized the world aspects of monetary policy, the most important of whom in the seventeenth century was perhaps Emeric Crucé, who linked his monetary proposals to a plan for world peace.

Thus the state in the eighteenth as well as in the twentieth century dominated economic and political life, and intervened in the private affairs of individuals. The question arises as to whether the attempt to fit preindustrial-revolution doctrines into the present economic age is not unwise and even fatal. The fact that a system of ideas, or a policy, is of an earlier age does not necessarily prove it to be wrong, any more than an attempt to reconcile Christian doctrine or Plato's ethics with the modern mechanical age is necessarily doomed to failure. But we are justified in asking whether mercantilist ideas are in practice producing a better world and whether they cannot even now be judged by their bitter fruits. In so far as the mercantilist system is predominantly one of power politics, it stands or falls by the adequacy or inadequacy of the balance-of-power system, which, as we shall analyze elsewhere, stands revealed as a system which intensifies war and contains within itself essentially unresolvable contradictions. From the point of view of formal analysis we must ask whether the theory and practice of mercantilism as an economic phenomenon are sound.

It is important to note that seventeenth- and eighteenth-century mercantilism arose in part as an attempt to widen the base of medieval society and to harness the expanding forces which made the small feudal community too limited an instrument for the economic and social life which was emerging. The invention of gunpowder rapidly made the castles useless as instruments of defense; the mariner's compass enabled ships to sail to other lands and to develop a greater trade which in turn necessitated larger units of economic co-operation; the invention of printing led to wider appreciation of common intellectual, social, economic, and political ideas. In a sense, therefore, mercantilism was the reply of the growing state to the requirements of social growth, although it did impose restrictions as between states. But today we witness an attempt to go back upon a further development which occurred in the nineteenth century, namely, the great increase of trade across the boundaries of nations and states. The present-day mercantilism is not an attempt to find a larger unit to take care of these new forces, which are much more powerful than the forces which broke through the feudal bonds. Instead of printing for a few, we have printing and radio for the multitude; the mariner's compass has given way to many refinements of sea navigation and to lighthouse developments, which make travel so much easier; the airplane has lessened distance still more; on land the railroad and the automobile have made small states restrictive and not enlarging units. The further development of scientific warfare has made the modern state as little competent as an instrument for security as the feudal castles were in the face of the first developments of gunpowder. World conditions are so different from what they were when mercantilism arose that it is justifiable to question the wisdom of trying to retain the national state and to return to it as the prime instrumentality of ordering economic life. The analogy between the eighteenth and twentieth centuries simply does not hold.

It is impossible to deny that there are some important truths contained in the doctrine of economic nationalism. There is need to banish the fear of national insecurity and to raise the purchasing power of the masses at home. The less economically developed countries do have a claim to develop their own economic life as fully as possible. To some degree the theoretical advantages of international trade are offset by the precarious nature of present-day international political relations, and a certain lowering of the standard of living may be a small price to pay if it could really contribute to a country's security.[17]

Unfortunately, the facts show that the practical consequences of self-sufficiency have not been so attractive as the theory might suggest. In the first place those industries and agrarian interests which were geared to export markets lost their customers as foreign trade declined. Next, the business interests connected with former imports suffered depression, and profits and wages declined. Many substitute articles required new factories and the outlay of capital, thereby necessitating, in some cases at least, heavier imports. And the incontrovertible fact remains that, under modern conditions, no nation can be self-sufficient. The United States and the Soviet Union supply 80 per cent of twelve of their most important commodities; but both countries must import goods vital to their industrial efficiency, although relatively small in volume. Consider, for example, the effect upon the automobile industry of the United States if foreign supplies of rubber were shut off.

[17] Lewis L. Lorwin, "Economic Nationalism and World Co-operation," *Pacific Affairs,* August-September, 1933, pp. 361–67.

Nor can one rightly deduce that because foreign trade is only 8 or 10 per cent of a nation's total trade, it is only 8 or 10 per cent important. The human body requires the presence of vitamins which constitute a very small percentage of the food which it consumes each day, and in industry a particular product may have an importance far out of proportion to its percentage of the whole, in either amount or value.

Some industrial and agricultural units depend largely upon foreign markets; their foreign trade constitutes a high percentage of their total trade; if they lose it, they face depression and possible bankruptcy, their workers are rendered idle, their creditors cannot realize, and they in turn cannot buy goods; a serious decline of general purchasing power therefore results. These losses affect the domestic industries, and, like a stone thrown into a pool, a failure in foreign trade spreads in ever widening circles.

Nor has the attempted autarchy eased international tension. Some of the enthusiastic exponents of self-sufficiency soon began to complain of being have-nots and of being shut out from raw materials. Hitler, who had turned from international trade, after six years proclaimed that Germany must export or perish, and energetically preached *Lebensraum*. And, as forecast by more than one economist, the practice of autarchy has led to ever greater international rivalry and danger of war, because nations which could not obtain their necessary materials by peaceful trading have tried to get them by belligerent means. The American isolationist preached autarchy as a method of keeping out of war. The German autarchist spoke of it as an instrument of war! The former feared that international trade would lead to war; the latter feared that it would lead to weakness and military dependence!

The belief that mechanical and technical methods can be easily transferred from one country to another, and that such easy transference reduces "the need for and advantages of specialization," rests upon extremely doubtful foundations, as Ellsworth admirably demonstrates:

Since the benefits of international trade rest upon cost differences, the spread of technical knowledge will reduce the need for and the advantages of specialisation only so far as it tends to equalise costs of production everywhere. Unless costs are equalised, the basis for specialisation and trade remains. Unless cost differences are reduced, the benefits of trade are as great as ever . . . . the mere spread of technical knowledge in itself proves nothing with respect to the advantages of specialisation . . . . Cost differences may be increased, altered little or not at all, or largely eliminated. Any a priori generalisation as to what will always happen is unwarranted.[18]

The same author goes on to remark that as technical advance spreads throughout the world, particular specialization on the new technical level takes place, and he quotes an important passage from Ohlin's *International Economic Reconstruction:*

Technical progress is still continuing. It is possible for any country to forge ahead of others, but only in a limited number of branches of industrial activity. Hence it is only by concentration and national specialization that technical progress can be maintained and the most up-to-date technique be utilized.

That is, new bases for specialization will be developed, and "gains from specialization will shift to different commodities." The claim made in Italy that modern science has destroyed the basis of the distinction between "natural" and "artificial" industries, important for international trade, is therefore not sound.[19]

In addition, one must include the increased costs of armaments as one of the items to be charged against autarchy. Whether it be cause or effect, the deliberate attempt to make oneself economically independent has resulted in much international friction, and has helped to intensify the armament race. Instead of buying and selling peacefully, nations threaten to fight in order to obtain markets and raw materials. Well may Secretary Hull say that there is no more disastrous illusion than the belief in isolation.

The facts bear out the accuracy of the theoretical analysis just given. A secret memorandum signed by important German industrial leaders in 1937 bears eloquent testimony to the failure of the attempt at autarchy.[20] It pointed out that Germany lacked 40 to 60 per cent of its necessary raw materials, which, in the absence of German exports to pay for imports, must be acquired by more extensive recourse to substitute goods—an enormous task. Even required foodstuffs were inadequate. Moreover, an "ordered budget" was impossible while people did not know the extent of military preparations; costs of state administration were very high, because of the new governmental agencies made neces-

[18] P. T. Ellsworth, *International Economics* (The Macmillan Company, New York, 1938), pp. 514–17. Quoted by permission.

[19] *Ibid.*, p. 519.

[20] R. W. Seton-Watson, *Britain and the Dictators* (The Macmillan Company, New York, 1938), pp. 279–83.

sary by the labor front, youth organizations, and control over imports and exports and over industry and labor. Exports at a loss and the uncertainty of the rate of interest added to the difficulties. Only exports could maintain the financial and currency stability; but large exports were not compatible with the 1936 Declaration of Autarchy. German policy had reached an impasse.

The recent experience of the world has shown that, in spite of theories to the contrary, international trade is not only desirable and advantageous but, under present conditions, absolutely indispensable. The German and Italian autarchists found it impossible to live within the area which they inhabited, and turned to forcible expansion (by incorporating Austria, part of Czechoslovakia, Abyssinia, Albania, etc., into their political systems) or to special methods of international trade which must now be examined. What had begun in autarchy developed into expansionism. Economic arguments became hopelessly entangled with noneconomic arguments, with a resultant conspicuous confusion of thought. International trade could not be dismissed; rejected in one form, it reappeared in another, less efficient indeed, and weighted under a load of official restrictions.

It is significant that in a recent study on employment, wages, and international trade, the International Labor Office found that, although in a few cases the foreign trade movements of countries showed a substantial difference from the "movements of employment and real payrolls," in general changes in national employment and payrolls showed a striking power to change the volume of imports and exports. This is due to the fact that production is "the chief factor determining, through the medium of employment, the aggregate real income of industrial labour," that production is intimately affected by international movements of capital, gold, merchandise, and services; and that, in so far as trade restrictions affect international gold and short-term capital movements, they tend to accentuate "fluctuations in employment and the aggregate income of labour." The conclusion reached is that the benefits to society from the specialized production made possible by world markets still holds good despite all the theories to the contrary: "In a greater exchange of goods between countries lie prospects for improving working conditions and raising the real income of workers in the mutual interests of all economic classes of society and all countries."[21]

[21] International Labour Office, *Studies and Reports,* Series B, 1932, *Employment, Wages, and International Trade* (Geneva, 1940), p. 11.

METHODS DESIGNED TO RESTORE INTERNATIONAL TRADE

What have been the methods by which countries have attempted either to restore the prewar system of international trade and finance, or to offset the disadvantages which have attended their overemphatic adoption of economic nationalism? They may be classified as: (1) general world and special commodity conferences; (2) bilateral agreements, including quotas, compensations, and clearing agreements; (3) regional agreements; (4) imperial preference; (5) military imperialism; and (6) the United States Reciprocal Trade Agreements policy. Each has had certain theoretical and practical advantages and disadvantages.

Conferences.—It was natural, after the Peace Conference, and in view of the establishment of the League of Nations, to attempt to restore the prewar economic system by general measures of international co-operation.

Currencies.—The war had produced a tremendous dislocation of national currencies and a great excess of expenditure over income. The first international step toward reconstruction was the International Financial Conference held in Brussels, in 1920, under the auspices of the League of Nations. Thirty-nine governments were represented, and their economic experts brought together a great amount of material on economic and financial subjects.

The importance of this Conference cannot be overestimated. It set forth clearly the existing situation and the remedies which were necessary. It pointed out that there was still a large gap between the income and the expenditure of most states; inflation remained unchecked in several European countries, most of which imported more than they were exporting; exchanges which had been artificially pegged during the war had deteriorated when those controls were removed after 1919; the purchasing power of national currencies had diminished and the cost of living had gone up; international trade had been dislocated and diverted from normal channels.

The Conference stressed the limitation of financial remedies and urged that finance was only a part of the mechanism of economic life. It strongly emphasized the need of world peace, and warned that the continuance of a war atmosphere and of war preparations was fatal to the resumption of normal trade relations. It then made its specific financial recommendations:

1. It insisted upon balanced national budgets in order to put public finances on a sound basis. In order to balance these it was

important drastically to reduce the expenditure on armaments and war preparations: "The conference desires to affirm with the utmost emphasis that the world cannot afford this expenditure."

2. It urged a policy of relentless taxation in order to keep expenditure within the limits of revenue.

3. It warned against the growth of inflation, and recommended a return to the gold standard.

4. It advised that a country which possessed no central bank of issue should establish such an institution even if it required some form of international control and the help of foreign capital.

5. It recommended an international organization to provide credit to countries which needed it in order to pay for their essential imports.

6. It suggested extending along international lines the existing system of export credit insurance for countries then suffering from lack of confidence because of uncertain political and social conditions.

7. A number of miscellaneous proposals were added, and the Conference unanimously affirmed that national action alone was not sufficient, that international co-operation was necessary, and that in this the League of Nations "must take the initiative." It concluded by pointing out that experts of thirty-nine countries were unanimous in their recommendations. "Whatever may be the future of our positive proposals, the Conference cannot have been in vain. It has been a gathering unequalled in the history of the world. It has not been a gathering of statesmen, working on the solutions of political difficulties in the interest of their particular countries; it has been a gathering of experts from all nations working for the solution of the common problem of the whole world."

Despite these recommendations, currency difficulties continued; but in 1923 stabilization began in certain nations. By 1925, it had made considerable headway, and by 1928, most countries were financially stable. The restored gold standard, it was hoped, would maintain the stability of international exchanges and internal prices; but, as analyzed elsewhere, it had to meet conditions other than those which had prevailed before 1914. Also within the postwar nations the circulation of gold and convertibility of paper money almost disappeared. Gold became less important as a basis of domestic currency and more important as a reserve to balance "external liabilities" of short-term loans. Much gold had flowed to the United States and to France, and national currencies had been revalued at different levels. The English pound was overvalued; the French franc was undervalued and gained advantages in world trade.

Other causes, some monetary and some nonmonetary, combined to wreck the restored gold standard. High tariff barriers interfered with international payments. The United States, as a great creditor country, made it difficult for its debtors to repay because of its mounting tariff walls, its energetic export trade, and its subsidized merchant marine. Excessive interest rates made the economic structure more rigid. The French financial system was more inflexible than that of Britain, and capital flowed less freely into international channels. The growing boom from 1925 led many Americans to cease sending their capital abroad, and caused foreigners to invest in the United States. Countries which needed capital found it difficult to obtain it. Reparations and war debts made it difficult for Germany and other powers to adjust their payments. Political uncertainties and the failure to reach any disarmament agreement prevented the re-establishment of that confidence which is the indispensable foundation of commercial and economic stability. Hence the alarming development of short-term loans. Investors feared to lend money for long terms; consequently, millions of dollars were invested for 60-, 90-, or 120-day periods. Not a little of this money was devoted to capital expenditures, which meant that in case of a sudden break in confidence and a rush for funds it would be impossible for borrowers to find money at such short notice in order to repay. Political distrust and the lack of confidence played a decisive part in postwar economy; short-term capital movements (caused by political crises) became more important than factors based upon commodity prices and trade; and if the short-term reaction developed violently enough, a condition would ensue which long-run forces could not correct.

The attempt to restore the world's currency system by general international effort, as well as by national effort, succeeded for a time, but ultimately broke down.

Tariffs.—The second type of world conference had to do with tariffs. After the war many countries erected tariff duties to protect themselves against a flood of goods from nations which had depreciated their currency. The tariffs were designed also to act as a check to internal currency depreciation by cutting down

imports. The unstable currency conditions were remedied in the
middle 'twenties, but many tariff restrictions remained. We have
seen that the newly established countries desired to guarantee
what they hoped to be their security by encouraging industry
and thereby diversifying their economic system; in so doing they
built up an excess of productive capacity. They then turned to
foreign markets and intensified competition in the international
sphere. Other countries imposed high tariffs for budgetary reasons, hoping in this way to restore equilibrium—a dangerous
method. The net result was that nations undertook economic activities for which they were not best suited, and produced substitute goods at high costs. The domestic consumer suffered in
consequence and "an uneconomic stimulus to exports" created
artificial competition in foreign markets, endangering the position
of producers who by reason of natural advantages were most
efficiently organized for lower-cost production.

In an effort to overcome these conditions, the World Economic
Conference met in 1927. It made its recommendations in a clear
and forceful manner. It urged nations immediately to remove or
diminish tariff barriers which were gravely hampering trade and
to begin with those tariffs "which have been imposed to counteract the effects of disturbances arising out of the War." States
should move along three lines: individual action, bilateral action
through the conclusion of suitable commercial treaties, and collective action. It urged the wide adoption of unconditional most-
favored-nation treaties which should be interpreted in the widest
and most liberal terms. The League Council should entrust the
Economic Organization of the League to undertake the necessary
discussion, consultation, and inquiries in order to work out the
most efficient methods of tariff reduction. States should refer
commercial disputes to arbitration and preferably to the Permanent Court of International Justice. They should not place internal duties upon foreign goods, nor should they impose export
duties on raw materials; but, if such duties were unfortunately
necessary, they should "never discriminate between different foreign destinations."

The next year the Economic Consultative Committee set up
by the League of Nations made a report which expressed a degree
of modified optimism. It noted that some states had reduced their
customs duties " by autonomous action" and that during the year
1927–28 many bilateral commercial treaties had been concluded,
the most important of which was the Franco-German treaty of

August 1927. Others were the German-Jugoslavian, the German-Greek, the Austrian-Hungarian, and the Hungarian-Czechoslovakian treaties. All of them, it noted with satisfaction, were based upon the unconditional most-favored-nation clause. Little or no collective action had been taken and the committee urged that "a continuous effort should be made . . . . to reach a general agreement."[22]

An attempt was made at this time to mitigate the consequences of absolute prohibitions upon exports adopted after the war for emergency purposes. France, for example, maintained an export prohibition upon foodstuffs until August 1927. The Danubian states had also perpetuated many restrictions which shut off essential supplies to their neighboring countries. The 1927 Conference adopted a convention recommending the abolition of prohibitory measures except on grounds of public security, moral welfare, health, and defense. By Article 5 it made an exception in favor of "extraordinary and abnormal circumstances" and vital interests, and even for temporary and special purposes. Many critics believed that these modifications destroyed the whole value of the convention. Even so, countries continued to add to the list of particular exceptions, and a disappointingly small list of ratifications showed how difficult it was even at this time to take the first steps. In 1929 the Economic Organization of the League suggested to the Council that a conference be held to consider a preliminary draft of a convention for purposes of establishing a customs truce. The conference met in 1930; but meanwhile commodity prices had fallen catastrophically, and the representatives, dominated by fear and anxiety, preferred the immediate, short-term security which economic nationalism and emergency measures seemed to promise. Thus, instead of a truce for two or three years, the negotiators merely promised in March 1930 not to denounce any of their bilateral treaties before April 1, 1931. The second conference on concerted economic action, in November 1930, served only to keep discussion alive, and finally admitted practical failure.

Textiles.—The Tripartite Technical Conference held in Washington, D.C., April 2–17, 1937, was an attempt by governments, workers, and employers to find a solution for the difficulties which confronted the textile industry of the world. Twenty-seven countries were represented, and officials from the governing body

[22] League of Nations, *Economic Organization. Report of the Economic Consultative Committee* (c. 217, m. 73, 1928), p. 12.

of the International Labor Office also attended. The 209 delegates knew intimately the conditions of the textile industry and brought expert knowledge to bear upon the technical problems. They did not have to consider so wide a range of subjects as the delegates to the World Economic Conferences in 1927 and 1933. Nevertheless, the record of proceedings clearly shows that the Conference could not discuss the particular problems of the textile industry without at the same time considering the general economic and social problems of the day. Delegates realized that the improvement of the cotton and woollen industries depended upon expanding the purchasing power of the great mass of the people and upon raising their standards of living. If all the world enjoyed a per capita consumption of the population of Western Europe, "it would call for approximately forty million bales of cotton for piece goods alone instead of the present consumption of twenty-six million bales to cover all uses." The Conference disagreed as to whether the expansion of consumption should take place by increasing the purchasing power, by raising wages, or by reducing prices.

Discussion took place concerning the need of improving agricultural conditions because of the millions of people engaged in agriculture who had suffered from a disproportionate fall in prices. The Conference concluded that unreasonable trade barriers should be reduced, that minimum wage-fixing machinery and trade boards should be established where they do not at present exist, that conditions of fair competition both nationally and internationally should be established, that weekly rest and annual holidays with pay should be considered by all governments, that a minimum age should be fixed by law in all countries, and that the International Labor Office should attempt to "bring about a solution of the problem of regulation of labor conditions in the International Settlements in China."[23] These and other recommendations show that in addition to the special technical problems which confront the textile industry, there are certain more general factors which must be considered, and that it is impossible for any one section of economic life to rise beyond a certain limit above the general level of industry.

[23] International Labour Office, *Tripartite Technical Conference on the Textile Industry* (Washington, D.C., April 1937, *Record of Proceedings,* first part, Geneva, 1937), pp. 2–17. For the general significance of the Conference, see Lewis L. Lorwin, "The World Textile Conference," *World Affairs Pamphlet No. 19* (National Peace Conference, New York, 1937).

Customs formalities and nomenclature.—Efforts have been made to reduce barriers to international trade and commerce by investigating the results of undue hindrances imposed by customs departments, and the unnecessary complications which arise from different classifications of goods. The administration of customs may cause serious loss and inconvenience to those engaged in international trade. Merchants may have to face arbitrary and unfair procedures imposed by customs officials. Sudden changes in tariff rates published after goods have already been shipped, excessive requirements in description of goods, the use of health regulations in such a way as to delay delivery and even involve the rejection of goods, arbitrary evaluation of goods with no right of appeal, excessive consular fees—these and other methods constitute some of the problems under the general heading of customs formalities.

As early as 1900 the matter had received attention at an International Congress, and again in 1913. The League of Nations Council, in September 1921, passed a resolution favoring action upon that part of Article 23 of the Covenant which related to the equitable treatment of commerce. At the 1922 Genoa Conference the matter was again considered. The Economic Committee of the League submitted a draft to the governments for consideration and suggestion. Two groups of officials from the customs administrations of seventeen countries then examined the draft and brought their technical knowledge to bear upon the problem. The International Chamber of Commerce considered the draft at its Rome Congress in March of 1923.

The Geneva Conference of 1923 which drew up and adopted a convention therefore had a large amount of data upon which to work. The President of the Conference summarized the aims of the Convention as: (1) Publicity—customs regulations should be published at the earliest possible moment for the convenience of traders and others interested. (2) Simplicity in customs rules and procedure—in order to reduce prohibitions, restrictions, and formalities to a minimum. (3) Expedition—customs rules and procedures should be imposed in such a manner as to cause as little delay as possible to the rapid passage of goods and passengers from one country to another. (4) Equality—formalities should not be used to impose arbitrary or discriminating burdens or restrictions. (5) Redress—states should provide adequate means to enable traders and others to appeal against alleged abuses at the hands of customs authorities.

The amount and number of customs do not constitute the only obstacles to international trade. What is called the problem of nomenclature has raised serious difficulties. As countries increase their industrialization, they tend to add to the number of goods which are protected by tariffs; the growth of tariffs, in turn, means a greater "particularization" in describing the goods which appear on a tariff schedule. Now, different countries have different specifications, and this practice causes confusion to exporters and importers, who must exercise great care in comparing duties on goods differently specified. Not only that. Countries divide their tariffs "by entirely different systems," which "are classified according to entirely different standards." Some countries classify goods according to natural divisions, such as animal, vegetable, and mineral. Others use the different branches of production, such as agriculture, forestry, cattle-breeding, and the various industries. The French tariff combines these two methods. A glance at the table prepared for the International Economic Conference in 1927 which shows the classification adopted by five European countries—Belgium, Germany, France, Italy, and Czechoslovakia—gives some idea of the complexities involved.

Some countries still retain the method of classification by material, but they do not seem to have done this consistently. "Thus most tariffs have special sections for machines, irrespective of whether the machines are made of iron, steel, copper, wood, or leather. Similarly, the majority of tariffs have a special category for vehicles, and notably for motor-cars, these articles being made of iron, steel, aluminum, leather, wood, rubber, textiles, and glass."[24] Further, governments adopt different methods in determining the grade or quality of articles. Czechoslovakia divided cotton tissues into three classes—common, fine and very fine—and then "according to the number of the yarn," and also the number of threads in a given amount of cloth. German, Swiss, and French tariffs differ in their methods, and other countries introduce further complexities too technical to be treated here.

In textiles generally, and especially silks and woollens, these differences have placed great obstacles in the way of importers and exporters, and have been causes of many controversies over what should be the right customs rate to pay. For example, an importer, hoping to export a product to a foreign market, might

[24] *Customs Nomenclature and Customs Classification* (League of Nations Economic and Financial Section, 1927), p. 12.

find that an unexpected classification would increase the duty to such a degree that it would seriously impair his chances of a reasonable profit. When does a piece of furniture become an antique? What thickness of paper is necessary to make it into cardboard? These and hundreds of similar questions are involved in the problem of nomenclature.

Dr. Trendelenburg, a member of the Preparatory Committee for the International Economic Conference, in the document referred to, remarks that a greater unification of schedules is necessary for the following reasons: to enable progress in the sphere of trade statistics, to introduce greater certainty into the importing and exporting business, to permit a greater rationalization of production, and to facilitate commercial treaty negotiations. "It constantly happens that differences of opinion arise with regard to the duties imposed upon the goods by the other party owing to the fact that each of the parties is basing its arguments on a different type of goods and that a comparison between the respective tariff items is not possible because they only correspond in rare cases." It thus follows that one cannot easily compare the level of customs duties, for it is

impossible to say, for instance, that one country has a duty of X per cent and another a duty of Y per cent on silk tissues, as long as the classification of silk items is different in each country. The unification of schedules is therefore also a necessary preliminary to the conclusion of any international treaties for the equalisation of duties. As long as the schedule is not uniform, any agreement regarding the equalisation of duties or their reduction to a particular level must give rise to interminable disputes as to whether the duties correspond to the limits agreed upon.[25]

As early as 1853, the International Statistical Congress of Brussels tried to find a solution to overcome the differences of schedules so as to make possible more efficient statistical methods. The question was much simpler then, because industry was much less developed than now. Later rapid industrial and tariff changes caused the problem to be considered frequently, and resolutions were passed at international gatherings in 1889 (Paris), 1900 (Paris), 1905 (Mons), 1906 (Milan), 1910 and 1913 (Brussels), and the Central European Economic Conference at Brussels in 1912.

Little was accomplished before the war, but after 1919 some

[25] *Ibid.*, p. 19.

progress was made. In 1923 France and Italy signed a customs treatment of silk and silk wares convention, "an agreement which uniformly regulates the question of silk production." At the European Silk Congress at Paris in 1925, a committee was established to work upon the unification of the silk tariff schedule. The International Chamber of Commerce, in its final report (1927), recommended that unification of customs nomenclature be sought; that governments should first attempt limited agreements dealing with important classes of products or goods; that the application of this method be left at first to industries most powerfully organized internationally, or those which have already attended international gatherings to discuss their common interests; that not merely governments and manufacturers and producers but also ordinary traders should participate in the agreements; and that general lines only should be laid down so as not to prevent states from adopting new specifications in case of the creation of new products or of new methods of manufacture (in this case, further international agreement would be necessary). And it authorized its subcommittee on customs to take the initiative in co-ordinating previous scattered efforts and to give an impetus to the work on a broader basis.

The 1927 World Economic Conference urged the simplification of customs tariffs and the unification of tariff nomenclature. It recommended (1) that the League Council take steps toward this end; (2) that a beginning be made with these types of goods which most easily lend themselves to such treatment; (3) that governments be consulted at each stage of the preparation and that they in turn transmit the proposals to "the producing and commercial circles concerned"; (4) that by bilateral agreements, or a multilateral convention, governments should apply this common nomenclature; (5) that governments should not be bound to use all the subdivisions but should undertake in the headings they use to conform to the rules of classification and description internationally agreed upon; (6) that the League of Nations should propose further measures of publicity, information, friendly settlement, and arbitration. The economic committee appointed an expert subcommittee which in the following year suggested a revised tariff classification.

Quarantine restrictions.—Arbitrary use of quarantine and other restrictions on agricultural and animal products have led to difficulties in international trade and have created much ill will and, on occasion, reprisals. Two or three examples will suffice.

In 1897, France limited the importation of meat products and drew a protest from the United States. More recently, England, Germany, and Holland refused to admit potatoes and other vegetables, fruits or plants, "harvested in France within two hundred kilometers of a spot infested by doryphora. Germany even demands that the product be accompanied by a certificate declaring that the products are uninfested and that they have been harvested more than 200 kilometers from a doryphora focus." This regulation is described by M. Augé-Laribé as "pure arbitrariness."[26] J. M. Jones described the resentment felt in Spain owing to the refusal of the United States to admit Spanish grapes and oranges, ostensibly on the plea that the Mediterranean fruit fly might be introduced into this country, despite the safeguards afforded by refrigeration.[27] Canned fish was also excluded on grounds of health.[28]

In a recent volume [29] Percy W. Bidwell discusses the problems raised by the imposition of sanitary restrictions, particularly when they conceal motives of economic protectionism. He describes many of the measures imposed by European powers against American meat products in the last part of the nineteenth century. The hardships resulting to the American meat industry led to the passage of laws in the United States which required that meat destined for export must be inspected by United States authorities. The inspection service became so efficient that the European governments accepted the American certificates, and several of them "removed their prohibitions on pork products with resulting increase in American exports."[30]

The United States began its sanitary control of imported meats in 1903, and strengthened this measure of protection by the 1913 Tariff Act, which gave to the Secretary of Agriculture considerable power in issuing regulations. Similar federal control was enforced on imports of milk by the 1927 Act, which, together with state law requirements, helped to diminish the American market for Canadian milk. In order to prevent the spread of

[26] Quoted from a report of the Commission of Inquiry into National Policy in *International Economic Relations* (University of Minnesota, 1934), p. 52.

[27] J. M. Jones, *Tariff Retaliation Repercussions of the Hawley-Smoot Bill* (University of Pennsylvania Press, 1934), pp. 37–39.

[28] *Ibid.,* p. 41.

[29] Percy W. Bidwell, *The Invisible Tariff* (Council on Foreign Relations, New York, 1940). Part two, *passim.*

[30] *Ibid.,* p. 170.

animal diseases, Congress passed a law in 1865 limiting the importation of cattle to animals which passed required health tests. As veterinary science developed, and international trade increased, redoubled efforts were made to prevent the entry of diseased animals. The measures culminated in the embargo provisions of the 1930 Tariff Act under which the Bureau of Animal Industry by administrative order prohibited imports of live cattle and meats from about sixty countries. "In effect, this order allows imports of live animals and meats only from North America, countries in the Caribbean area, a few countries in northern Europe, Japan and Australia."[31] Bidwell criticizes the embargo, saying that it is unnecessary for biological purposes, and has been introduced primarily to protect the economic interests of the American livestock industry. The embargo has had serious effects upon United States–Argentine political relations. Argentina resents the use of sanitary devices to serve the purpose of economic protectionism, and alleges that not only does it lose markets within the United States but its meat trade with other countries is "endangered by the stigma laid upon it by the American embargo." It claims that a large area of the country, especially Patagonia, is free from the foot-and-mouth disease (a contention denied by American meat interests) and that justice requires a modification of the present situation.

Similar restrictive measures have been imposed upon the exports and imports of plants and plant products. The details are too numerous to mention here except to say that under the 1912 Act regulations have been imposed, especially Quarantine 37, which considerably limits the import of foreign plants; economic purposes, in the opinion of several experts, in addition to the ostensible purpose of preventing the spread of disease, have been responsible for these measures.

No one will deny that quarantines are necessary. Animal and plant diseases have cost governments many millions of dollars, and it is mere elementary wisdom to take adequate protective action. The officials in charge of plant and animal quarantine are experts in entomology, biology, silviculture, and animal husbandry, and do their best to enforce the laws so as to "protect agriculture from its biological enemies."[32] Nevertheless economic considerations have entered into sanitary protection, and have

[31] Percy W. Bidwell, *The Invisible Tariff*, p. 212.

[32] W. G. Campbell, "Quarantine Measures as Trade Barriers," *The Annals of the American Academy of Political and Social Science,* January 1929, p. 34.

given rise to much dissatisfaction through suspicion that, disguised as biological safeguards, certain restrictions are in reality animated by interested economic-pressure groups. Consequently a great field for international co-operation exists wherein countries may assist each other in preventing the spread of animal and plant diseases and at the same time eliminate the abuse of such measures.

In 1927 the World Economic Conference recommended that

International agreements which establish sanitary supervision, if they provide the contracting countries with adequate guarantees, should, without infringing sovereign rights, remove from the regulations any suspicion of disguised protection and should add to the stability of trade relations, which is one of the conditions of successful production.

The Economic Organization of the League of Nations set up a body of experts to study the question, recommended bilateral treaties between countries for joint inspection by representatives of both contracting parties, and proposed that laws which unnecessarily hindered trade should be modified. It also prepared draft multilateral conventions, which found expression in the Convention of February 20, 1935. This instrument was signed by several countries and came into force in March 1938, after having been ratified by Belgium, Bulgaria, Iraq, Latvia, Rumania, and later by the Soviet Union.

Since 1934, when the Trade Agreements Act was passed, the United States has discussed the question with many countries, so as to "reduce the international friction which sanitary restrictions, foreign as well as American, have caused. A section is now uniformly inserted in the agreements providing for consideration of objections made by the party that feels injured, and for consultation by a joint technical committee in order to reduce trade disturbances to a minimum."[33] In 1935 the United States signed a sanitary convention with Argentina which would have considerably mitigated the difficulties arising from the blanket legislation of the 1930 Act. Article 3 provided that neither party might prohibit the import of animal or plant products from areas of the other country which the importing country found to be free from diseases or pests or exposure to such diseases or pests. Other articles provided for the exchange of technical information, for the right of mutual visits for study of diseases and pests, and

[33] Bidwell, *op. cit.*, p. 252.

also for the meeting of committees of technical experts so as to minimize injuries which might arise from the application of the sanitary provisions. Bidwell notes that the 1935 convention from many points of view "was a model of its kind."[34] It went beyond the 1935 League Convention, but, unfortunately, the opposition of agricultural and livestock interests within the United States was sufficient to prevent the Senate from ratifying the measure.

International co-operation in these matters will depend almost entirely upon the willingness of economic groups within nations to refrain from pushing their group interests at the expense of general welfare. In this respect as in many others, what at first sight seems to be a conflict between nations turns out on closer examination to be a conflict between group interests utilizing national machinery and projecting into the international sphere their own class rivalries. These class conflicts then take on a national cloak and masquerade as national interests pitted against one another. If these interests will not voluntarily restrain themselves it will then be necessary by study, publicity, and other forms of pressure to compel them to subordinate their aims and methods to the requirements of the more general welfare.

Bills of lading.—Ridgeway writes that it would be difficult "to exaggerate the confusion under which goods were carried by sea" before recent international co-operation resulted in a reform of the rules governing bills of lading. In 1920 the International Chamber of Commerce proposed action to simplify the rules; the Brussels Financial Conference in the same year endorsed the movement, and the I.C.C. urged the carriers themselves to give support to the adoption of a uniform bill of lading by promising to use it and no other. Considerable research was initiated. The International Law Association, the British Bankers' Association, and other bodies joined in the campaign. Their activity resulted in the drafting of a code under a committee headed by Sir Norman Hill, and the Hague rules which were adopted in 1921 at the International Law Association Conference were accepted by the Brussels Diplomatic Conferences of 1922, 1923. Twenty-four nations signed a convention. Thirteen years later the United States ratified the instrument, following the lead of Great Britain and Australia in 1924, India in 1925, Belgium in 1928, and New Zealand in 1930. The United States' ratification was followed by those of France and Sweden, which "brought seventy per cent of

[34] Percy W. Bidwell, *The Invisible Tariff,* p. 218.

the world's tonnage under the regulation of this international code of uniform law."[35]

Ridgeway writes as follows:

The successful fight for the establishment of this bill of lading "League of Nations" is one of the brightest pages of international cooperation. The bill of lading had become a symbol of uncertainty and distrust to all international traders. Every country had a different law on the obligations of this contract. Every steamship company had a different form of bill of lading, and sometimes as many as a dozen different forms. The forms themselves were so long and so ineffectual that no one would have read them—had they been readable. But reading was impossible, for they were printed in type so small as to require a magnifying glass. And in any case they were not worth the reading for the conditions of limitation and regulation were subject to overnight change.

The Hague rules have supplanted this chaos with a rule of law. The debt of all international traders to the I.C.C. for its leadership in this achievement was well stated by Sir Norman Hill in a letter to the chairman of the bill of lading committee, "You have saved from the scrap heap one of the few really big steps that have been taken since the War to promote and facilitate international trade. We are all—both producers and consumers—your debtor."[36]

Most-favored-nation clause.—In the nineteenth century governments adopted the theory and practice of the "most-favored-nation" clause, by which country A in a commercial treaty with country B would undertake to give B the benefit of any lower duties which it might subsequently grant to country C. If a number of governments adopted this method, the result would be a general lowering of tariff barriers. Unfortunately, the clause which once served to liberate and extend foreign trade has now become an obstacle for the following reason: If some countries raise their tariffs to great heights and two other countries lower their duties one to the other, a third country which enjoyed the most-favored-nation clause may claim the benefit of the lower duties without itself making any corresponding step. Thus it is possible for a move toward tariff reduction to be defeated by one or more governments which insist upon having their cake and eating it, too. They can maintain their high tariffs and yet claim the benefits of lower tariffs on the part of other countries. The Scandinavian countries were defeated in their attempt by Great Britain's insisting upon its privileges under the most-favored-nation clause. Can

[35] G. L. Ridgeway, *Merchants of Peace* (Columbia University Press, New York, 1938), p. 315.   [36] *Ibid.,* p. 316.

any way out of the difficulty be found? It is suggested that the problem is not insoluble. In earlier days, exceptions used to be inserted in the most-favored-nation-clause agreements. Certain countries were permitted to form blocs with special low duties among themselves—say, the Scandinavian countries, or Spain, Portugal, and Latin America. Great Britain and her Dominions claimed a similar preferential treatment, although this claim was criticized by other countries. It should be possible for contracting parties in signing new most-favored-nation treaties to prescribe that the benefits of most-favored-nation clauses shall accrue only to countries which do not increase their tariffs or which adopt certain other measures. Sir Arthur Salter suggested that countries which had tariffs as low as the lowest of the contracting parties should be given the advantage of the lower duties accruing under the most-favored-nation treatment. Measures along these lines would permit the retention of the most-favored-nation clause, together with modifications which would make it the instrument of liberalizing trade, instead of being as now a hindrance to the lowering of trade barriers.[37]

The International Chamber of Commerce has also considered the difficulties in the way of bilateral treaties created by the most-favored-nation clause and has recommended "courageous experimentation in an endeavor to lower tariffs," presumably meaning that states may well take the risk of having benefits extended to third parties who maintain high tariffs. It favored multilateral agreements with an "adhesion clause" by which they would be opened to signature of other countries, and with an equity clause which would extend the benefits of the most-favored-nation clause to states which fulfilled the conditions of the general treaty even without formally adhering to it. It realized that treaty obligations should be observed, and that third states would be justified in availing themselves of their rights if they so wished; but the I.C.C. saw no reason why states should not propose modifications of the original most-favored-nation-clause relationship, or why third states should regard any such proposal as an unfriendly act. Finally, it should be possible for an international conference to draft an international convention binding the contracting parties to interpret the most-favored-nation clause of their bilateral treaties as not obstructing the application of multilateral agreements intended to bring down the general level of tariff barriers.

[37] Sir Arthur Salter, *The United States of Europe* (George Allen & Unwin, Ltd., London, 1933), pp. 92–102.

The Committee of Experts who drew up the program for the World Economic Conference in the form of a Draft Annotated Agenda urged extreme caution in permitting permanent exceptions to the principle of the most-favored-nation clause even with the end in view just described, in that such action might provoke "the formation of mutually opposed groups of countries, thus aggravating the very evils which it is sought to mitigate."[38] The agreements containing such exceptions must be kept open to the adhesion of all interested states, should be concluded "under the auspices of the League of Nations or of organizations dependent upon the League" and should not involve "new hindrances to international trade *vis-à-vis* countries having most-favored-nation rights."

Proposals were also made to grant temporary exceptions to the principle of a most-favored-nation clause. These came largely from southern and eastern Europe, which had suffered from the catastrophic fall of world prices. The Conference with a view to Concerted Economic Action in November 1930 gave qualified approval to the idea of granting a temporary exception for cereals and their derivatives and for quantities limited by quotas or other methods. The experts in 1933 agreed that the World Conference to be held at London should further examine the question, although certain members of the Commission believed that temporary exceptions would constitute a bad precedent and should not be granted.[39]

Bilateral and clearing agreements.—The impossibility of developing and maintaining absolute autarchy and the equal impossibility of restoring general world trade because of the disordered conditions due to chaotic finances, disturbed price levels, high tariff barriers, and unsettled political situations led to bilateral and clearing agreements, which were first used in November 1931 by Switzerland and Hungary. The fashion soon spread. Countries, instead of permitting the free exchange of goods by private importers and exporters who settled their balances by international payments negotiated through banks, now required that import and export transactions between the two countries should balance so as to avoid the necessity of any international transfer of funds. Importers now had to obtain prior licenses for all im-

[38] J. W. Angell, *The Program for the World Economic Conference* (World Peace Foundation, Boston, 1933), pp. 69–72.

[39] For a general discussion of the most-favored-nation clause since 1931, see Margaret S. Gordon, *Barriers to World Trade* (The Macmillan Company, New York, 1941), pp. 370–82.

ports and had to pay into a special office the sums with which to pay for them. From this money the clearing office paid the exporters, and attempted as far as possible to equalize the amounts of goods imported and exported. It followed that some goods would be more essential than others, and a complicated system of priorities grew up. Frequently the central offices determined the amount of foreign exchange which might be available for certain classes of trade, how it should be divided between foreign countries, and to which companies or individuals it should be available. Special financial methods also developed. Instead of permitting foreign exchange to be bought and sold on the open market, countries developed what the League of Nations Economic Committee called compulsory conventional clearing systems, or artificial returns of exchange. Germany brought this method to a high point. Its blocked marks were depreciated currency "made available to anyone for certain authorized purposes, but without distinction as to the nationality of the user or the commodities for which used." In addition, compensation or aski marks were adopted which were balances which could be used only within Germany itself "for certain specified commodities."

Undoubtedly these expedients were, as the League Committee and the governments which reported to it recognized, a necessary evil, and grew up as a desperate attempt to restore international trade under highly unfavorable world conditions. They permitted the financially weak debtor countries to buy goods from each other with the minimum of financial complications in a financially disordered society. In a sense it was a re-emergence of the barter system in a highly complicated commercial world. They permitted countries whose gold basis was threatened to engage in a certain amount of financial trade with less danger to their own currency systems. To this degree they helped to reduce the obstacles which had been placed in the way of foreign trade, and somewhat offset the adverse effects of quotas, high tariffs, embargoes, etc. Apologists for the scheme also claimed that it tended to reduce dumping and exchange dumping, and helped to pave the way to better political relations. But to put the matter in this way was to show the weaknesses of the system and to reveal the appalling contradictions into which modern international trade had fallen.

Critics noted that bilateral trade and clearing agreements distorted trade, and forced it into artificial channels. Frequently, countries had to accept goods which they did not need in order to market their own produce abroad. Sometimes the creditor country drove a hard bargain and asked higher prices for its own goods than it could have obtained on the world market. The system could operate only as long as a country had an adverse balance of trade. To balance every bilateral agreement meant to lose advantages of multilateral trade, to lessen its volume. It served to divert trade from one part to another, and not to increase it. There was a serious danger that agricultural nations would increase their industrialism and industrial countries engage in agriculture beyond the margin of efficiency. The system led to regimentation and to great power in the hands of political officials. Bureaucracy reared its ominous head, and traders in an effort to evade the mass of rules were tempted to indulge in smuggling and other unlawful activities. The rapidity of turnover was lowered, and stocks piled up, leading to depreciation of prices. The bilateral trade agreements also tended to lower the quality of trade. Finally, in the struggle for raw materials, governments were tempted to try to take by force that which they could not obtain by ordinary peaceful trading. Whatever the merits of the bilateral system might have been as an emergency measure, they were of such limited value when compared with the efficiency which might have been re-established in a politically stable world that the best that could be said for them was, to repeat, that they were a necessary evil. But an emergency measure prolonged beyond a certain period tends to become a normal measure, and, to that degree, instead of assisting to bring back health, it may perpetuate the very evil which, theoretically, it was supposed to cure.

Moreover, the purposes behind much of the bilateral bargaining methods are primarily political rather than economic, and have been used by Germany especially in order to bring smaller powers within the German politico-economic orbit, and are therefore related to conquest economics, discussed in a later section.[40]

Regional agreements.—Some countries which could not be or did not desire to be self-sufficient made regional agreements with their neighboring countries in an attempt to stop the rising tide of tariffs and even to reduce their level. In December 1930, Belgium, Luxemburg, the Netherlands, Norway, Sweden, and Denmark undertook not to increase their tariff duties without giving notice to each other. If after such notice a party felt that its interests were in any way prejudiced, it might propose modifications within ten days. If the first party was unable to agree to the modi-

[40] See J. B. Condliffe, *The Reconstruction of World Trade,* pp. 288–94.

fications proposed, it could put its original program into effect within one month. This agreement, known as the Oslo Convention, entered into effect on February 7, 1932, and was to last for six months, with the right of denunciation by any party after a further six months.

In July 1932, Belgium, Luxemburg, and the Netherlands concluded the Ouchy Convention,[41] under which each agreed not to increase its customs duties beyond the level then prevailing nor to increase duties to third states unless the latter by heightening their tariffs should cause grave difficulties to the signatories; and, what was particularly important, the three governments agreed immediately to reduce duties 10 per cent, to reduce them 20 per cent after one year, 30 per cent after two years, and 50 per cent by the end of the fourth year, and to give each other unconditional most-favored-nation treatment. Unfortunately this laudable attempt was wrecked by Great Britain, which demanded the most-favored-nation treatment which it enjoyed by reason of prior treaties with one or the other of the signatories. Britain's action was criticized by many economists as a regrettable insistence upon a legal right, without a corresponding willingness to enter into the spirit and practice of the agreement.

In 1932 the Stresa Conference met to consider whether a regional agreement might not help to remedy the deplorable wheat situation in southeastern Europe. An interesting proposal was made resembling somewhat the processing tax adopted in the United States. The manufacturing powers of western Europe would pay a price above the market level for wheat from southeastern Europe; the extra income would serve to rehabilitate the farmers in that area, who then would use their heightened purchasing power to buy products from the European manufacturing countries. This step failed because of the opposition of the non-European countries—Canada and Australia and Argentina had no desire to see Great Britain pay higher prices for European wheat than for their own.

By the Oslo Agreement signed at The Hague in May 1937,[42] Belgium, Luxemburg, the Netherlands and Netherlands India, Norway, Sweden, Finland, and Denmark agreed not to raise their tariffs. Belgium, Luxemburg, and the Netherlands, which had

[41] A. J. Toynbee, *Survey of International Affairs, 1932* (Oxford University Press, 1933), pp. 38–40.

[42] League of Nations, *World Economic Survey, 1936–1937* (Geneva, 1937), p. 148.

quotas, undertook to remove them from certain commodities; and the other signatories to the agreement promised not to adopt quotas. Unfavorable conditions prevented the renewal of the agreement after its expiration in July 1938.[43]

Regional agreements have an important but limited significance, depending largely upon the size and economic resources of the area in question. A small area will not radically change the course of world affairs, and if it is only partially a self-sustaining unit it will be much influenced by forces outside its boundaries. It cannot rise very far above the level of world conditions, nor can it hope to become an island of economic sanity in a sea of world trouble. The relative simplicity of regional agreements, owing to the limited area to which they apply, is offset by the interdependence of the intra- and extra-regional factors.

Imperial preference.—Countries which possess colonies have attempted to develop a system of imperial economics and, by preferential tariffs and quotas, to widen their economy beyond a purely national area to include their imperial possessions and dominions. This method is a revival of mercantilist economics and had already been preached and, to some extent, practiced before the World War of 1914–1918. The great world depression, which began in 1931, led to a renewed development of the empire policies, as illustrated by Great Britain and France.

Great Britain sought relief from the ravages of the economic nationalisms which swept the world and wiped out important markets by attempting to build up a compensating system of empire trade and financial agreements. Before 1914, Britain was "the most international of all countries," the "most completely merged . . . . in the world's economy," and the "most dependent upon overseas trade." The World War of 1914–1918 disrupted its markets, and for five years British merchants lost the important day-to-day contact with their customers. After 1919 the United States, Japan, and Germany became ever more serious competitors, and tariff barriers for economic and political purposes arose throughout the world. The strain upon British economy became marked; the great woollen, cotton, coal, metal, and shipbuilding industries which had enabled Britain to rise to supremacy now faced a major crisis; and it was more than doubtful whether new industries,

---

[43] League of Nations, *World Economic Survey, 1937–1938* (Geneva, 1938), p. 169. See also H. J. Procopé, *Economic Co-operation between the Northern Countries and the Joint Delegations for Its Promotion,* and H. Koht, "The Oslo Convention and After," *Le Nord,* 1938, Nos. 1–2.

such as the automobile, the radio, artificial silk, and electrical appliances, would make up for losses sustained in the older fields of economic effort.

It was natural for Great Britain to attempt to restore the world economic conditions which had been favorable to them in prewar days. In 1925, it returned to the gold standard, but unfortunately at a level which economists now generally agree was too high and which operated to penalize the British exporter. It supported measures to free the channels of world trade, and hoped that the 1927 World Economic Conference would assist toward this end by a comprehensive reduction of tariff duties. Internally it adopted a policy of rationalization. The railroads, though handed back to private enterprise in 1921, were combined into four large units instead of remaining in the 119 prewar units. In 1930 the Coal Mines Act set up machinery to regulate the production and sale of coal, to fix quotas, and prepare reorganization schemes. In 1926 a Conservative Government established the central electricity board, which proceeded to construct high-tension distributing lines all over the country. An industrial transference board somewhat unsuccessfully attempted to shift labor from the depressed areas.

These measures did not suffice to restore prosperity; and already world conditions were suggesting to many Britishers that reliance upon restoration of the prewar type of international trade and internal rationalization was not enough, and demands for tariffs against foreign goods and for imperial preference became more outspoken. During the war, the government had imposed the 1915 McKenna duties on automobiles and accessories, films, watches, clocks, and musical instruments. The Labor Government repealed them in 1924; but the Conservative Government restored them in 1925, and gave them a definitely protective character. Imperial preference was given to Dominions by means of a rebate of one-sixth on empire goods. However, the step was not very important. J. H. Richardson points out that the McKenna duties applied to only 2.3 per cent of British imports and thus, although they mark a theoretical departure from free trade, their practical significance was not great. The Dyestuffs Act of 1920 and the Safeguarding of Industries Act of 1921 represented a second step toward protection. The latter act was designed to restrict imports of certain military necessities from abroad, and also to stimulate production of these goods in Great Britain. In 1925 the Key Industries Act was extended so as to apply to unemployment arising from foreign competition: a firm could complain that certain imports were causing unemployment and ask for tariff assistance. These acts also did not cut very deep; by 1930 less than one-fifth of the imports into Britain paid duties. As Richardson puts it, the stream of free trade had been only slightly contaminated.

The world economic crisis of 1931 caused a profound change in British policy. The Abnormal Importations Act (1931) added duties which were not to exceed 100 per cent on many classes of manufactured goods. Because there was no definition of "abnormal," the Board of Trade had considerable liberty in applying the Act. The Horticultural Products Act of 1931 provided for duties not to exceed 100 per cent on many agricultural products. The two acts were of an emergency nature; but in 1932 the government introduced the Import Duties Act, which imposed the first permanent tariff. It provided for a 10 per cent tariff except for goods already under duty or on the free list. It set up an independent Imports Advisory Committee with power to recommend increased duties or the removal of articles from the free list, and it gave the Treasury power to raise duties to 100 per cent on imports from countries which discriminated against British goods and to lower or remove them from countries with which reciprocal trade agreements were made.

A movement arose to protect the farmer. In 1925 an act providing for subsidy on sugar beets benefited 40,000 farmers but cost the Exchequer about $200,000,000 in ten years. A Wheat Act (1932) provided for deficiency payments to wheat growers, and under its stimulus the acreage in wheat rose by one-third. The government applied a whole set of import quotas to chilled beef, frozen mutton and lamb, bacon and ham, condensed milk and milk powder, cream, potatoes, eggs, and oats. These quotas were applied to non-empire countries and also by agreement to some of the Dominions.

The new protective measures applied also to capital investments. In prewar days British capital had been loaned abroad with little or no governmental interference. In the postwar period the government took a more active part in influencing the investment of British funds abroad, especially encouraging the placement of funds within the Empire and on occasion during the first decade discouraging certain foreign loans. After the 1931 crisis the government appealed to the capital market to refrain from making new issues until the great War Loan Conversion Operation had been completed. For a time it practically prohibited foreign lending; but after July 1934 it relaxed the restrictions and permitted loans (*a*) to countries within the Sterling Bloc which required funds to minimize exchange fluctuations, (*b*) to countries which undertook to use the loans to benefit British industry, and (*c*) especially to countries within the Empire.

In 1932 an Imperial Economic Conference was held at Ottawa to see if it would be possible within the British Empire to lower tariff barriers and stimulate the flow of trade. Many imperialists had talked of a self-sustaining exclusive empire which could dispense with the rest of the world; but the great majority of serious economists knew that Britain, which exported 60 per cent of its goods to foreign lands and had almost one-half of its capital investments placed outside the Empire, could never make such revolutionary adjustments. The question was whether it would be possible to come to agreements to encourage intra-empire trade without diminishing the foreign trade of Britain and the rest of the Empire.

The Conference concluded several agreements between Britain and the Dominions which gave preferences on certain goods, and extended many of them to the non-self-governing colonies. The Conference agreed that British interests should have the right of appearing before the tariff board of a Dominion and vice versa. That is, tariffs within the Empire were not to be imposed without giving manufacturers from other parts an opportunity of stating their case. The purpose was to enable Great Britain to have a full opportunity of "reasonable competition" in the Dominions on the basis of relative costs and efficient production. Five committees (on customs administration, on commercial relations with foreign countries, on monetary and financial questions, on methods of economic co-operation, and on existing machinery for economic co-operation), also four subcommittees (on industrial standardization, on grading and standards of agricultural products, on industrial co-operation, and on films and radio) made various recommendations.

A full examination of the outcome of the imperial preference policy lies outside the scope of this volume. Several writers have made analyses, but it will be sufficient for our purpose to summarize the careful statement of Frederic Benham, of the University of London, who concludes that "it can hardly be claimed that the tariff played a major part in the British recovery."[44] Indeed,

[44] Frederic Benham, *Great Britain under Protection* (The Macmillan Company, New York, 1941), p. 220. Quoted by permission.

it adversely affected the export trades, and most of the employment increase took place in the nonprotected occupations. The great factor in recovery was the building boom, and "clearly its connection with protection was extremely slight." The issue of cheap money played a modest part; technical progress and the low prices of imported foodstuffs served to increase purchasing power in other fields; the rearmament program played a prominent part, and it too owed little to protection. On the other hand, the continued high level of unemployment was largely due to the depression in the exporting industries, and the fall in the value of the English pound adversely affected the same important branch of economic life.

Benham's conclusion is as follows:

The prosperity of Great Britain depends on her international trade. In the long run she is bound to lose by a greater movement towards greater self-sufficiency on the part of other countries. Yet her own economic policy during recent years has inevitably fostered such a movement . . . .

With the signature of the Anglo-American trade treaty in November 1938 it seemed possible that Great Britain was preparing to adopt a more liberal trade policy, and was coming to realize that her true interests lay in a general revival of world trade. But the outbreak of war temporarily put an end to all such hopes.[45]

Conquest economics, or military imperialism.—Countries which found national autarchy inadequate and which had no empire which they could organize into a larger economic unit were tempted to draw the sword in order to carve out such an empire. World trade had broken down; markets abroad were being shut out through mounting tariffs, currency restrictions, and other obstacles. What was more natural than for Japan to try to create an empire in Asia so as to plan a more rational economic order satisfactory for an allegedly overcrowded country? Hitler and his followers, after the initial enthusiasm for national autarchy had evaporated in the face of economic realities, talked of *Lebensraum* and set out to dominate a large part, and perhaps the whole, of Europe. Germany must break through the "encirclement policy" of Britain and France, because in a hundred years "there will be 250 million Germans living on this continent." Italy has defended its invasions of Ethiopia and Albania on similar economic grounds, and Japan talks of a new order in Asia. This military

---

[45] *Ibid.*, p. 249.

imperialism has two aspects: (*a*) colonial, in the narrower sense
of the term; and (*b*) conquest of other sovereign countries. Each
must be discussed separately.

Colonies.—The same arguments for colonies as were used fifty
to sixty years ago are being heard today—that nations need colonies as population outlets, as sources of raw materials, as markets
for trade, and to retain as political subjects those emigrants who,
finding conditions of life at home economically unfavorable, seek
their fortunes abroad. Between 1870 and 1914 the imperialist
powers acquired great areas of land in non-European countries—
France, four million square miles; England, three and a quarter
million; Germany, one million; Japan, one hundred and twenty-
two thousand; the United States, over seven hundred thousand;
and Belgium, nine hundred thousand square miles; and Russia secured a large territory and vast spheres of influence in Asia.

We are led to inquire if colonies possess so great a value as is
popularly supposed, if their economic significance is correctly appreciated, and if there is not a great deal of false sentiment attached to them. Most students agree that colonies have afforded
little or no outlets for surplus population. Peffer in an article,
"The Fallacy of Conquest," points out that in 1914 more Italians
lived in New York than in all the Italian colonies which were conquered by war; there were more Germans in ten blocks of Man-
hattan Island than in the whole of the German Colonial Empire
in Africa; and Japan, after having lost a quarter of a million men
to obtain South Manchuria in 1904–1905, took twenty-five years
to settle 200,000 people there! Grover Clark[46] notes that over a
period of fifty years German emigration to the whole of Africa
did not amount to 300,000 people, while the colonial struggles of
modern times, costly and provocative of deep-seated jealousies and
antagonisms, gave the European powers territories to which less
than 1.5 per cent of the permanent emigrants from Europe went.
Sweden, with fewer colonies, and with a population less than one-
tenth that of Japan, had a larger emigration than Japan, whose
net emigration to foreign countries and colonies in the years 1925–
1933 amounted to 35,000, whereas her population during this time
increased over seven and three-quarter millions.

Clark does not believe that emigration from England had any

[46] Grover Clark, *The Balance Sheets of Imperialism: Facts and Figures
on Colonies* (Columbia University Press, New York, 1936). The evidence presented to the International Studies Conference in 1937 fully bears out Clark's
view; see F. G. Wright, *Population and Peace,* chapters vii and viii.

noticeable effect upon unemployment figures. Belgium's level of unemployment in 1934 rose even though her emigration exceeded her immigration at that time, while the United Kingdom had more unemployed in the same year in spite of some emigration. In other words, emigration is only one factor in the total economic situation of any country; and Clark is undoubtedly right in claiming that it is a weak argument to suggest that economic opportunity for people remaining at home has any direct relation to the amount of emigration.

If colonies are not important as reservoirs for surplus population, how essential are they as sources of raw materials and fuels? Culbertson classifies such materials as follows: energy resources, such as coal, oil, and water power; reproducible raw materials, such as silk, cotton, jute, and nitrates; nonreproducible but partially recoverable raw materials, such as iron, which can be recovered in the form of scrap; and nonreproducible and nonrecoverable raw materials which need conservation, such as magnesium used for cement, graphite for lubricants and paint, fluor spar for use as a flux in steel manufacture, and asbestos and mica as insulators. The Royal Institute of International Affairs classifies essential industrial materials under the headings of metals, nonmetals, rubber, textile fibers, and vegetable oils. Whichever classification is adopted, the United States stands out pre-eminently as the producer of many of these necessary things; the British Empire as a whole is fortunately situated, and the U.S.S.R. takes third place; but Germany, Japan, and Italy need to import a great amount of raw materials. The United States, the British Empire, and the Soviet Union would still remain indispensable to the three powers just mentioned as sources of raw materials whatever the changes in ownership of colonial possessions. Without supplies from the major nations, the so-called "have-nots" might enjoy an emotional thrill in adding to their empires; they would obtain little economic comfort.

The fact is that the ex-German colonies in Africa are quite poor in resources, and it is misleading to say that Germany's economic situation is in any substantial measure due to the loss of her colonies,[47] or that their return would make any appreciable differ-

---

[47] However, H. D. Henderson writes that, although the colonies of all powers produce only 3 per cent of the total of the world's commercially important raw materials, they produce over one-half the tin, one-quarter the copper, and practically all the rubber. See "Colonies and Raw Materials," *Pamphlets on World Affairs,* No. 7 (Farrar & Rinehart, New York, 1939), pp. 9–10.

ence to Germany's economic welfare. As one English author puts it, it is a "cruel fraud" to persuade people that any effective economic solution can come from colonial redistribution.

A question arises, however, whether countries like Germany and Italy do not have to pay higher prices because they must buy from other countries which may impose special duties. We have seen that some nations have imposed duties upon colonial products in recent years. Most of the raw materials required for industry, however, come from areas outside of what we normally regard as colonies; and, although there are restrictions such as we have noted above, they appear not to be serious enough to justify undue emphasis on the question. In general, noncolonial nations do not particularly suffer from difficulties of getting raw materials at average market prices. The helium which Germany has been vainly trying to obtain comes not from colonies; it is produced in the United States. If it is for purposes of supplying the home countries with essential materials in wartime that colonies are demanded, the answer is that such colonies would be worthless during hostilities unless the nation had control of the seas.

We have also seen that nations desire to invest capital abroad[48] and to make profit from the development of hitherto unexploited areas. How far have nations the opportunity to invest in colonial territories belonging to other nations? In the class A and class B mandated territories, the League Covenant, and in the Congo Basin, the General Acts of Berlin 1885 and Brussels 1890, revised by the Convention of St. Germain in September 1919, provide for equality of commercial investment. In British and Dutch colonies foreign capital may be freely invested, except for the mining of petroleum ("in British Honduras, Brunei, the Cayman Islands, Fiji, Nigeria, Nyas Island, and Trinidad, oil leases or licences are only granted to British subjects,"[49] although British colonies are more naturally disposed to grant preference to British nationals); a similar attitude toward the mother country doubtless exists with the French, Dutch, and Belgian empires. The Royal Institute of International Affairs points out that France imposes many restrictions on the investment of foreign capital in French colonies unless

[48] H. D. Henderson notes that, although prewar British investors invested money freely in all parts of the world, the investments within the Empire are, in the present disordered state of international relations, worth more than foreign securities.

[49] Royal Institute of International Affairs, *Raw Materials and Colonies* (London, 1936), p. 47.

French nationals retain two-thirds of the control of the company. Portugal, on the other hand, appears to have maintained a relatively open door to investors. Japan does not encourage foreign investments within its empire. The Spanish and Italian colonies are not important as outlets for placing capital abroad. From these facts it seems that the "have not" countries do not suffer a serious economic handicap; not sufficient, indeed, to warrant "much ado about little."

In addition to these factors, which appear to have small economic significance, there remains the question of colonies as markets. Grover Clark notes that between 1894 and 1932 the Italian trade with Italian colonies amounted to less than one one-hundredth of Italy's total trade, and that twenty years of colonial administration cost a greater sum than the whole amount realized by her colonial trade in a period of forty years. Both Germany and Japan have paid heavily for their colonial adventures, for in each case the administrative costs have outweighed the economic benefits. Indeed, it is arguable that in all colonial expansion the taxpayer has suffered more than the merchant has profited.[50] Nevertheless, colonies may have a certain negative value. If all possessions were open to the trade of all nations, ownership would have no importance.[51] But if nations are shut out from the markets of colonies belonging to others, they may have a real grievance. If they are told that they can buy raw materials almost anywhere in the world at world prices, they reply that, because of tariff barriers, they cannot sell their products and that therefore they suffer from lack of foreign exchange with which to buy the materials which they need. For example, Japan has experienced difficulty in British colonial markets and India in recent years, and the Ottawa Agreements of 1932 took the very questionable step of giving preference to British over foreign goods in British colonies. Japan prohibits the importation of cotton and rayon piece goods into several of its colonies. The traditional "open door" was modified, and gave cause for complaint by those who claimed that England was excluding countries like Italy, Japan,

[50] Norman Angell's *The Great Illusion*, Conrad Gill's *National Power and National Prosperity*, and Leonard Woolf's *Empire and Commerce in Africa* stressed this point.

[51] ". . . . the real advantages of territorial possessions are negative rather than positive. They are a safeguard against certain ills rather than a means of positive advancement." L. C. Robbins, "The Economics of Territorial Sovereignty," in C. R. W. Manning (ed.), *Peaceful Change* (The Macmillan Company, New York, 1936), p. 54.

and Germany from colonial markets, and thus helping to stifle the economic life of these "have-not" powers.

On the other hand, it must not be forgotten that (1) the A and B class mandates guarantee "open door" privileges to foreign countries (although the mandatory powers do possess certain advantages in the matter of currency and government purchase of materials), (2) the countries in the Congo Basin and certain British and French West African colonies permit a substantially "open door" policy, and (3) the causes of the world economic collapse were primarily due to tariff restrictions and other obstacles to trade between the major countries. Consequently the answer to the economic problem is to be sought not primarily in the direction of colonial expansion but by a liberation of international trade. The solution of population problems depends not on the size of a nation's empire, but upon its natural resources, its economic efficiency, and its opportunities for the exchange of goods.

The evidence thus adduced supports the general conclusions of Etienne Dennery in his *Le Problème des matières premières* (1939),[52] that, although an inequality in the distribution of raw materials does exist, the question has been considerably oversimplified, and perhaps falsified, by the division of countries into "haves" and "have-nots." Dennery suggests: (1) that all countries suffer from insufficiency of raw materials; (2) that there are degrees of richness, poverty, and resources; (3) that one must consider whether potential or actual needs are to be considered; (4) that some raw materials are key products, and their importance depends upon their function rather than their quantity; (5) that some raw materials are threatened with exhaustion because they are not replaceable, while others can be replaced; (6) that changes occur in the relative importance of raw materials as a result of invasions by chemists and engineers (Switzerland's sources of power have successively been wood, coal, and water power); (7) that there is a growing decentralization of the production and the consumption of raw materials; (8) that all countries, even the so-called "satisfied ones," have to import materials; (9) that the great raw-material-producing countries have had their economic crises too (Cuba, Brazil, Australia and New Zealand, Canada, etc.), thus suggesting that raw materials constitute only one factor in the total economic situation; (10) that a nation

[52] Institut International de Coopération Intellectuelle, Société des Nations (Paris, 1939).

may be an industrial country without possessing raw materials,[53] and hence the idea of raw material "needs" is highly subjective in character; and (11) that colonies play only a minor role as a source of "matières premières."

In truth, the question of colonies seldom remains within the field of economic analysis. It quickly moves into the realm of politics and national emotion. A former British Secretary for Colonies, Mr. Amery, in opposing the return of colonies of Germany, argued that Great Britain should retain them, otherwise Germany would be able to menace the security of the British Empire. Fifty years ago English statesmen were apprehensive of German colonization on the ground that the security of their empire would be threatened—presumably adequate security of the Empire would only be realized when all colonies were under the Union Jack! As long as colonies possess a strategic value, nations will resist surrendering them to potential rivals and other nations will strive to obtain them. Any solution of the colonial problem, any redistribution of possessions, including the return of the German colonies, to be lasting, must insure against the possibility of their being used to strengthen a nation's military, naval, or air power. And such a solution can come only under a genuine system of world security which would deprive colonies of any military significance.

The question of the return of colonies to Germany brought forth considerable discussion before 1939. Opponents of their return argued that the mandatory powers extended freedom of conscience and worship to their native wards and undertook not to establish military or naval bases there, or to organize native military forces except for local police and defense purposes; and they asked whether, in view of the totalitarian philosophy and race theory prevalent in Germany, any guaranty would exist that she would join in a mandate system of "preparing the population for eventual, increased participation of self-government"? And not a few English people, sympathetic though they were to German colonial claims, hesitated to advocate a policy of handing over native populations to the Nazi government. Some believed that if Germany were to receive her colonies back as a mandatory power, Britain should be willing to place under the mandatory

[53] "La Suisse a pourtant la réputation d'un pays 'satisfait' et prospère. Son exemple souligne la multitude des attitudes qui existent à l'égard des matières premières et la variété des solutions qui ont pu être apportées en fait au problème du ravitaillement en matières premières."

system those non-self-governing colonies which have little immediate prospect of attaining self-rule and should thus openly accept
the principle of trusteeship which British imperialists claimed that
it observed in practice. A memorandum signed by four hundred
representative people was presented to the English Prime Minister
requesting that English policy be set along these lines. The so-
called "have-not" countries would then have access to raw materials and markets under the principle of the "open door" and
would not be handicapped by the existence of hostile colonial
tariffs. Other writers believed that if such a policy were adopted
the Mandates Commission should be given greater powers than
it possesses at the present time.[54]

The more conservative English imperialists, however, claimed
that it was of the utmost importance to retain the unity of national tradition and the British spirit of colonial administration.
The more liberal of them believed that it would be preferable to
avoid the expense and complication of a mandatory system and to
that degree favored national control; but they urged that England
make clear that her colonies would be open to the trade of all the
world (thus reversing the policy adopted at Ottawa in 1932).
There would thus be "equality on a low tariff basis." Some writers
proposed that chartered companies of the "have-not" countries be
given extensive rights of economic enterprise and even of administration in English and French colonial territories. But the British Government refused to consider modifications and merely made
some vague promises in 1938.

The new conquest economics.—Under Hitler a new kind of
military economics has been devised by which the conquered
peoples are to play a role subordinate to that of the victorious
German race. The ultimate goal is to reduce the conquered nations
to an agrarian status in order (*a*) to weaken them militarily, since
agrarian economies cannot be productive of efficient war machines,
and (*b*) to have them serve as sources of foodstuffs and raw materials for German and Italian factories and as markets for the
manufactures of these powers. Already Germany has begun this
policy in eastern Europe and the Balkans, of

systematically reducing industrial production, by closing down plants
which compete with their own, sending the workers thus thrown out
of employment to the Reich; and excluding the Jews who, owing to
their previous exclusion from agricultural pursuits, had played a domi-

---

[54] See below, chapter xi, "Mandates: Their Strength and Weakness."

nant part in the commercial and the financial life of relatively backward agrarian countries.[55]

Germany is pursuing the same policy in western Europe, and followers of Marshal Pétain in France seem content to accept a new agrarian destiny for France, contending that "the inherent virtues of a nation reside in its peasantry, and that only by returning to the land will industrial countries shake off the intellectual and spiritual vices allegedly produced by urban existence."[56]

Munk vividly portrays the German policy of subjecting Czechoslovakia, Poland, and France to an intense program of forced labor. He estimates that at least one and one-half million persons have been carried off to Germany for labor purposes, "subjected to military discipline, cut off from their families and homes [one of the Nazi methods of reducing the number of future Czechs, Poles, and Frenchmen], and at the same time cut off from every normal social contact, even with German co-workers. They are the new caste of untouchables, the 'underman' according to German theory."[57]

In order to destroy the Czechoslovakian economy, Germany gradually replaced leading businessmen with Nazi agents in government offices, in the National Bank, and in other important businesses such as communication and transportation. The new officials then instituted a strict control over deposits and current accounts, and forced the Czechs to sell their controlling interests in heavy industries to German banks, thereby turning them into sources of armament supply for Hitler's military machine. Germany then took control over the consumption industries by expropriating the Jews and replacing them with agents of the German government. Many Czechs had to sell out at ridiculously low prices, and received payment in a blocked account with a German bank. By clever methods Germany has introduced its currency into all the conquered territories—Poland, Denmark, Belgium, Holland, Luxemburg, and France—in such a way as to tie the native currencies to the German mark so that they "can be manipulated freely from Berlin,"[58] and finally incorporated the Czech area into the Customs Territory of the Reich.

[55] Vera Micheles Dean, "Europe under Nazi Rule," *Foreign Policy Reports,* October 15, 1940, p. 180.

[56] *Ibid.*

[57] Frank Munk, *The Economics of Force* (George W. Stewart, New York, 1940), p. 115.

[58] Munk, *op. cit.,* p. 172. And see especially chapter xvii, "Total Conquest."

Many of the leaders of the conquered areas have been shot, many others have fled the countries, with the result that it may be more than difficult for them, even should Britain win the war, to find sufficient technical experts to rebuild their destroyed economy. It is also to be noted that, in addition to bringing farm laborers into Germany, the Hitler regime has planned to settle German colonists in the eastern parts of the continent so as to insure the German domination of central Europe.

In this way does the Nazi government hope to make war pay, not necessarily in economic terms alone but also in terms of prestige, leadership, and Continental dominance. Because of this fact, it is an error to interpret Nazi economic expansion in economic terms alone. Its expansion is part of a philosophy of life which includes power as the central element. It marks, if not the end of economic man (to use Drucker's phrase), his probable subordination, or at least his incorporation into a society in which leadership, power, race, blood, and soil are merged in a political faith which constitutes the most serious challenge to the economics of welfare and the assumptions on which democracy is built which the last hundred years has witnessed.

Japan is also following the path of military economic conquest, or what Edgar Snow calls "military fascist imperialism." Snow contrasts this type of imperialism with the older laissez-faire kind, indicating that in prewar days economic expansion developed from a country's surplus capital and surplus commodities, whereas, present-day Japan's imperialism has been dominated by the conception of war and empire, by investments on the part of a country which only recently had become a creditor nation, and which had established heavy industry to only a moderate degree.

After taking Manchuria, Japan in effect confiscated "all mines and other resources, developed communications, railways, and industries." It "grabbed an enormously valuable accumulation of resources and raw materials, plus cheap labor, and needed only operating capital to make it genuinely productive."[59] The army, by taking control of capital securities, dictated the nature of investment, and seized "as much existing wealth as possible."

Japanese military imperialism seems to need to capitalize itself ever more speedily by skipping the intermediary stage of massing profits through trade and uses the simple expedient of expropriating

---

[59] Edgar Snow, *The Battle for Asia* (Random House, New York, 1941), p. 375.

the investment and accumulation of others. In China it aims to seize capital not only in money but by total expropriation of all existing wealth, resources, and means of production, including a monopoly of labor power, which can be harnessed to the military machine while the same process is completed at home. Japan must, in the end, eliminate all capital holders in China, first the Chinese, and finally the foreigners. No attempt to balance the books of Japanese imperialism can be realistic if it ignores this basic aim of expropriation of capital.[60]

Japan has seized the holdings of the Chinese government and has expropriated many millions of dollars' worth of foreign-owned property. It has taken capital from the Chinese merchants and moneyed classes. It has destroyed China's universities and colleges in an attempt to wipe out China's intellectual and technical leadership. It has attempted to eliminate China's currency and thereby obtain control over Chinese economic life.[61] It has driven Chinese from office and replaced them by subservient officials. It has encouraged the smuggling of opium and other drugs as well as the smuggling of commodities used in normal life, thereby hoping to disrupt Chinese government and Chinese morale.[62] In commenting upon the policy of Japan, Snow warns that we may be in error if we consider it in terms of our Western economic values:

The thing about Japanese economy is that since the Manchurian occupation it has been constantly changing and enlarging and reconstructed within a framework in which the military becomes the main consumer, while the people "consume" only in proportion to their relationship with the military purposes. This economy does not envisage the restoration of a peaceful society in our lifetime. It is based frankly and *inevitably* upon continuous expansion and continuous wars as the solution to all its own contradictions.[63]

George E. Taylor correctly describes the 1937 war as an attempt by Japan to control China "on a frankly monopolistic basis,"[64] with new techniques for accomplishing its purpose. But here as in

[60] *Ibid.*, pp. 376–77.

[61] Guenther Stein, "The Yen and the Sword," *Pacific Affairs,* March 1939; also D. K. Lieu, "The Sino-Japanese Currency War," *Pacific Affairs,* December 1939.

[62] H. Hanson, "Smuggler, Soldier, and Diplomat," *Pacific Affairs,* December 1936.   [63] Snow, *op. cit.,* p. 378.

[64] George E. Taylor, *The Struggle for North China* (Institute of Pacific Relations, New York, 1940), p. 16.

the case of Germany we have moved from the nineteenth-century economic imperialism to a new set of values in which the economic factors play only a part and, in the opinion of many able scholars, a minor part in determining policy.

The bearing of all this upon a better organization of modern world society is obvious.

United States Reciprocal Trade Agreements policy.—The United States policy of Reciprocal Trade Agreements represents another method of trying to reverse the tendency to economic nationalism. After the failure of the 1933 World Economic Conference, President Roosevelt's administration leaned in the direction of national self-containedness. Perhaps the word "self-containedness" is too strong, "intranationalism" may be more accurate. The President in his message to the Conference on July 3, 1933, wrote: "The sound internal economic system of a nation is a greater factor in its well-being than the price of its currency in changing terms of the currencies of other nations."

In 1934 the pendulum began to swing the other way. In January Mr. Roosevelt announced to Congress that "all of us" are seeking the restoration of foreign commerce in ways which would preclude the building of large favorable trade balances of any one nation. Already in November 1933, Secretary Henry Wallace had warned that, unless there was a fundamental tariff revision to permit imports, the United States must resign itself to a permanently reduced output. Criticisms of "The Open Door at Home" appeared. They were to the effect that (1) the financial and tariff policies of a so-called self-contained America would hurt other countries dependent upon United States trade and would force them into a painful economic readjustment and provoke their ill will; (2) no "feasible" compression of American economic interests could possibly give economic isolation; (3) self-containedness in Russia, Germany, and Bulgaria had not smoothed the foreign relations of those countries or made for peace; (4) although international trade is "often disturbing and irritating," it has conferred many benefits upon the world and a large part of it is carried on with comparatively little friction; the essential problem is to "minimize the irritating factors" and expand rather than restrict trade; (5) pressure of sectional interests upon a government would not cease in case of self-containedness; (6) although international trade produces friction, an extraordinarily large part of it operates with comparative ease and smoothness; and (7) in the words of Herbert Feis, who criticized Beard's views, there are compelling reasons to believe that in the actual economic conditions of today, the pursuit of the policy which he advocates would not produce a newer and better type of nationalism, but one given over even more to excitement and hostility, one more easily led in a direction contrary to his own intentions.[65]

Writers pointed out that the tariff had burdened the American consumer to the extent of several hundred million dollars on twenty-one products, that the South had suffered from high tariffs, and that the cotton area would be ruinously affected by a rigorous program of economic nationalism. Secretary Wallace in his pamphlet, *America Must Choose,* claimed that it would be necessary to take up to 100 million acres out of cultivation, perhaps to resettle elsewhere a large part of the population of the South, and almost certainly to undergo a great amount of regimentation if we failed to restore international trade. Secretary Hull claimed that "instead of increasing as our foreign trade decreased, our domestic trade decreased at a suicidal rate," and insisted that a twofold economic program was necessary—domestic trade and foreign trade. Concentration on one and not on the other was not enough: what was needed was action on both fronts.

The Reciprocal Trade Agreements Act of 1934 was technically an amendment to the 1930 tariff act. It empowered the President to enter into agreements with foreign countries for a period of three years and to reduce duties up to 50 per cent. These benefits were to be denied to any country which discriminated against United States commerce.

The President might act without senatorial confirmation, provided that reasonable public notice was given to interested parties within the United States so that they might present their views. The executive was to seek information and advice from the Tariff Commission, the Department of State, the departments of Agriculture and Commerce, and such other sources as he might deem necessary. The 1890 McKinley Tariff Act had empowered the President to enter into an agreement with other countries without having to refer the matter to Congress. The principle thus established was upheld by the Supreme Court in the case of Field *vs.* Clark. Defenders of the new act argued that Congress, having laid down the general policy, should leave the administration to work out the details; this method would be more democratic than the log-rolling procedures which usually accompanied Congressional consideration of tariff proposals.

[65] Herbert Feis, "The Open Door at Home," *Foreign Affairs,* July 1935.

However, sectional interests which stood to lose by a reduction of tariff duties opposed the measure. Mr. Hoover and others alleged that inadequate notice was given to the public when new agreements were contemplated—a charge strongly denied by Administration supporters. The foreign trade adviser to the President, Mr. Peek, resigned because he believed that the tariff reductions would threaten the American standard of living, although he approved reciprocal tariff bargaining in principle; and he opposed extending the unconditional most-favored-nation treatment to third-party nations, believing that the so-called conditional most-favored-nation principle should be adopted. Others criticized the plan because it "put the cart before the horse." Without currency stability, they said, tariff agreements would be precarious and ineffective.

In spite of all opposition the trade agreements act went into effect in 1934. Mr. Roosevelt warned the country not to expect too much because of the great financial instability of the world at that time. The first year witnessed no great change; but at least a halt had been called to the mounting tariff barriers. Even by 1936 it was difficult to see clearly the full effects of the move because of the complexity of cause and effect in modern international life.

The most important agreements were those with Canada, France, the European manufacturing countries, and especially with Britain in 1937. The arrangement with Cuba was not unimportant; but those with Latin America did not bring any "drastic changes" in United States tariff policy. By 1937 the United States was enjoying 11.8 per cent of the world international trade, compared with 14 per cent in 1929 and 9.5 per cent after the Smoot-Hawley Tariff Act of 1930. Between 1934 and 1937 its exports increased 55 per cent and its imports 65 per cent. These figures by themselves are not conclusive, because they may have reflected only a general advance in international trade. Significant, however, are the figures given by Brockway, in a Foreign Policy Association *Headline Book,* of exports to the agreement countries which "were in the year 1937–38 66% higher [than in the years before the program went into effect] while our exports to non-agreement countries were only 47% higher."

The importance of the Hull trade agreements lies not merely in terms of increased exports from the United States. Three other aspects may be noted:

1. Will trade agreements help toward a general restoration of

world trade? Are they significant contributions in an age characterized by a serious diminution of international trade? True, they are bilateral (and not multilateral) agreements and are not the ideal method favored by classical economists; but they contain the most-favored-nation clause and make possible a generalization of tariff reduction if the definition of goods is not too narrowly drawn. It must be admitted, however, that various devices can be employed to render a true most-favored-nation policy almost impossible. Since the United States is a creditor nation, its part in restoring international trade can best be played by modifying its tariff policy so as to import more goods than it exports. (Obviously if A lends to B he must sooner or later receive payment in some form from B unless he is willing to cancel the debt.) In so far as the Hull trade program can realize this end, it will assist to correct the contradictions in American economic policy from 1920 to 1934 and to a lesser degree from 1934 to the present time. A successful foreign trade policy for the United States must bring not only an increase of exports but a still greater increase of imports.

2. The agreements have a political aspect. Cassel, the Swedish economist, Hansen, Secretary Hull, Secretary Wallace, and others have emphasized that international trade is necessary for the maintenance of the democratic way of life, since a highly regimented national economy, which a self-sufficiency program compels, is incompatible with free democratic institutions. Foreign trade is therefore necessary as a political safety valve as well as an important element in maintaining the standard of economic life in the democracies.

3. Many economists have pointed out that economic nationalism does not diminish international friction. No country contains all the raw materials it needs, and the growth of tariffs and other obstacles placed in the way of obtaining raw materials serves to intensify the world's political problems. Nations will fight to get necessary goods if they cannot acquire them peacefully. The so-called "have-not" countries have created almost uninterrupted international tension; their excuse is that they cannot sell their goods in order to gain essential raw materials, and they must conquer what they cannot exchange. To the degree that the Hull trade treaties open up the channels of international trade, they will assist in lessening international friction. But it should be emphasized that a much more fundamental modification of the American tariff structure will be required if the United States is

to make a major contribution to the restoration of world trade. The Reciprocal Trade Agreements are a step in the right direction, but only a step.

ATTEMPTS AT INTERNATIONAL COMMODITY CONTROL

We have now to consider the attempts, by international co-operation, to prevent dislocation and possible collapse of special agricultural and other primary industries. The day of free competition has passed, and the necessity of concerted action has become obvious. The following examples will show how far international co-operation has gone in this direction. The story is not one of great success, owing to the relative newness of the problem, the counter-working of the theory and practice of economic nationalism, and the struggle to seize raw materials for purposes of power politics. If, however, the economics of welfare is to make headway, the following examples must be taken to indicate the general path along which international policy must proceed.

The question of raw materials has had several changes of fashion since the end of the World War of 1914–1918. At first there was considerable scarcity following the wastage and the dislocation caused by the world conflict. Italy proposed a policy of international control of raw materials, but without success. The League Economic Committee in 1921 considered the question and made a number of general recommendations, particularly urging that measures of restriction or prohibition and export duties were bad. The 1927 World Economic Conference also recommended freedom of access to raw materials as much as possible and the minimization of export duties and other restrictions. But by this time the world was witnessing an overproduction and a slump in the price of wheat, sugar, coffee, tin, and other raw materials, and the question was not so much how to insure a sufficiency of supplies as how to gain adequacy of profitable markets.

As pointed out elsewhere, several restriction schemes were adopted by governments to prevent a collapse of the whole structure of the primary producing economy. Recently the have-and-have-not fashion of thought has spread, and once more the charge is made that certain countries must have access to raw materials and that they are being denied the legitimate opportunities which they require for their existence. But it is most important to emphasize that, strictly speaking, there is not a particular problem of raw materials. It is merely one phase of the whole question of international exchange, and "it is only by re-establishing the normal currents of trade and finance, that there is any hope of bringing a remedy to the present difficulties of international economic relations, one of the special aspects of which is the difficulty of procuring raw materials."[66]

Wheat farmers have suffered greatly from the adoption of economic nationalism and from the desire of nations to insure an adequate food supply in time of war. In recent years the doctrine that agriculture is important in building up a strong and healthy nation has become allied with the desire of countries to offset the disadvantages of a monoculture. Some governments have seen in the peasantry a bulwark against radical doctrines. Practically every government has taken some step to encourage wheat growing. In consequence, overproduction is rife and farmers are threatened with ruin. The Institute of Agriculture at Rome called two conferences to see what might be accomplished. The 1931 Wheat Conference at Rome did little more than survey the complexities of the problem. A later conference of eleven exporting countries at London produced many proposals but little agreement on policy: "The United States would have nothing to say to a quota; Russia would have nothing to do with restricted acreage." The Conference adopted a few general recommendations, and set up a permanent consultative committee. A scheme by which manufacturing countries would pay higher prices for wheat to enable the southeast part of Europe to get on its feet failed.

In 1931 Canada called a wheat conference, which accepted "the principle of reduction of acreage"; but the Soviet Union refused to consider a quota export system. At the World Economic Conference in 1933, Canada, Australia, Argentina, and the United States agreed to a policy of regulated production so as to prevent a further fall in price. They also agreed to co-operate with producers in Europe. The Secretary General of the League of Nations then called another conference which included twenty European countries, the United Kingdom, and the four countries just mentioned. The conference concluded an international wheat agreement which "provided for the reduction of exports on a

[66] Michael A. Heilperin, *The Monetary Aspect of the Raw Materials Problem* (International Studies Conference, International Institute of Intellectual Co-operation, Paris, 1938), p. 30.

quota basis and pledged its adherence to reduced wheat acreage to 15 per cent beginning with the season of 1933–34." When prices rose to the higher figure, the countries agreed to reduce tariffs and other barriers. The signatories undertook not to encourage production but to do what they could to heighten the consumption of wheat. An international wheat committee was established with equal membership from importing and exporting countries; it was limited to advisory work and was to have no control over policy.

Unfortunately, prices continued to fall, and tariff and other barriers continued to rise. The agreement made no provision for the disposal of existing surplus stocks. Consequently it was difficult to get the machinery of co-operation in motion. The principle is sound, and without doubt co-operation between governments and farming and consumer interests will be increasingly important; but until two things happen, international organization for wheat will have limited success: there must be a lessening of the fear of war and a strengthening of the authority of any international wheat committee.

Such is the view of M. Paul de Hevesy of Hungary, who in 1934 advocated a World Wheat Entente. His thesis was that the world market for wheat did not possess the elasticity of some other products; that while national harvests of wheat were variable, the world yield was remarkably stable; that although the consumption of bread was giving way to other foods in some countries, world consumption varied but little; that the price of wheat was too low and the accumulated stocks were too great to be solved without international measures. He therefore proposed an International Council of Wheat. It should have an International Office and each member nation would have a National Office of Wheat, which would possess a monopoly of buying and selling the commodity and would work in close harmony with the international office. The latter would fix the price for the world market. Other detailed recommendations followed which need not be noted here. M. de Hevesy anticipated that the Entente would be consistent with a large degree of freedom of action and that, having achieved its purpose of overcoming the disequilibrium existing in the wheat market of the world, it could be dissolved.[67]

The Food Research Institute in 1935 noted that little progress had been made "toward a genuine economic equilibrium in the world wheat economy," and doubted if sufficient skill had yet been

[67] Paul de Hevesy, *Le Problème mondial du blé* (Librarie Felix Alcan, Paris, 1934).

acquired to enable national or international agencies to make accurate forecasts of market conditions, acreage requirements, and weather and other natural conditions.[68] Its view reflects that of those who are suspicious of "planning," whether national or international.

The great increase in coal production after the World War, and the demand for reparations in the form of coal from Germany, upset the whole industry. Overproduction resulted and, in order to offset the low prices which were making production uneconomic, governments had recourse to subsidies. Europe faced a coal crisis. The League Economic Committee suggested international measures; but the countries turned to national remedies. They rationalized the industry, and in the case of Great Britain appointed a central council of coal owners to "allocate production quotas among the various districts." They made trade agreements, and also restricted imports—France, for example, limited imports to 80 and later to 72 per cent of the average for the years 1928–1930. But national restriction plus national rationalization helped rather to intensify the gap between expanded production and diminished markets. It shifted the incidence of the depression but increased its intensity. In 1928 the coal subcommittee of the League Economic Committee considered rationalization on an international scale, and the International Miners Conference made similar proposals. The League Assembly of 1927 considered the question, and a committee of experts published a report in 1929. It recommended that the League should study further the problem of tariff barriers but not international organization of coal production. The situation grew worse, and the Assembly in 1931 again was discussing the problem of coal; the economic committee resumed its studies,[69] and in January 1932 another conference of experts was held. It decided that the League should assist in drawing up an agreement. The 1933 World Economic Conference appointed a coal subcommittee, which resolved that the main producing nations should come to an agreement, that the League should watch the interests of the consumers, and that the League Council should call a conference of producing and consuming countries in the event of a failure of the producers to reach an agreement.

These proposals did not result in substantial action. Competi-

[68] R. F. Martin, *International Raw Commodity Price Control* (National Industrial Conference Board, New York, 1937), pp. 50–55.

[69] League of Nations, Economic Committee, *The Coal Problem* (Geneva, 1932).

tion became most intense, and in the disorganized political and economic state of the world the industries preferred to scramble for themselves. Nevertheless, experienced people in industry realize the necessity of a comprehensive approach to the whole problem. Greaves suggests that an effective international organization of coal would require:

1. The granting of monopoly and rationalizing powers to national bodies. For it must be realized that coal, unlike oil, must be based on national or, at least, regional units. Such national bodies would naturally be subject to their international superior, acting where its decisions were concerned merely as its agent.
2. An international producers' agreement providing for an international coal board to replace the separate national authorities.
3. Representation of the consuming countries and labour on this board.
4. Submission to an I.L.O. convention on hours of work, conditions of employment, and wages.
5. A common marketing scheme for countries inside and outside the group.[70]

In 1934 Poland and Great Britain reached an agreement, renewed in 1937 for two years, to regulate the sale of coal in export markets; and Germany, Belgium, Great Britain, the Netherlands, and Poland agreed for four years from April 1937 to regulate coke exports.

The Miners' International Federation and the Governing Body of the International Labor Organization in 1936 urged the Economic Committee of the League to take action toward an international coal agreement. But the committee preferred not to intervene "for the time being, in the hope that an agreement may be reached between the producing countries."

In January 1938 the Governing Body of the International Labor Organization invited representatives of governments, owners, and miners of the chief coal-producing countries to a technical Tripartite Conference at Geneva in the following May.

The International Labor Office in a two-volume study, *The World Coal-Mining Industry,* published in 1938, stated its conclusions thus:

The facts presented in this chapter reveal clearly that the coal-mining industry in all countries has passed out of the era of "free competition" into one of economic and social "control" in which pro-

---

[70] H. R. G. Greaves, *Raw Materials and International Control* (Methuen, London, 1936).

duction, marketing and prices are largely governed by combines, cartels, etc., which are subject to the regulation of public and semi-public bodies. Despite their differences, the schemes of control have this in common, that they all aim at developing rules and regulations which would minimise the effects of differences of mining, transportation and distribution costs upon prices and upon the relative competitive status of mining districts or exporting countries.

What is also clear from the record is that the efforts, described in Chapter VII, to restrict import shipments and to protect domestic collieries as well as the movement, reviewed in this chapter, towards integration and the regulation of output, sales and prices, do not form a harmonious system nor are they entirely complementary to one another. In some measure, it is true, the control of coal mining in individual countries presupposes the regulation of the import and export trade in coal, while such regulation promotes, to some extent, the movement towards national control. On the other hand, the piling up of obstacles to the world trade in coal during recent years represents a short-run reaction to emergency conditions, while the various control schemes arise out of a desire to deal with the economic and social problems of coal mining on a long-run basis. To evolve a policy which would meet the short-run problems of the industry in individual coal-mining countries while satisfying, at the same time, the long-run needs of the industry as a whole, is one of the basic problems which the transition from "free competition" to "economic control" in coal mining has accentuated. A particular aspect of this general problem arises from the fact that any measures taken on behalf of the coal-mining industry must be devised in full recognition of their possible effects upon the further use of substitutes for coal and further economies in the use of coal. The final suggestion which emerges is that the growth of combination and public regulation in coal mining, by protecting the competitive equilibrium against the differentials of labour costs, should act to facilitate the international regulation of labour standards in the industry.[71]

The great growth in the use of sugar in the latter part of the nineteenth century, combined with the extensive development of beet-sugar growing in Europe, led to overproduction, and growers in the West Indies and elsewhere were threatened with ruin. In 1902 several governments agreed to an international sugar convention, the first to give an international committee power to dictate policy. The organization worked well for a time, but even before the World War of 1914–1918 difficulties arose, and the agreement lapsed in 1920.

[71] International Labour Office, *The World Coal-Mining Industry* (Studies and Reports, Series B, No. 31, Geneva, 1938), I, 251–52.

238   Foundations of Modern World Society

The same phenomenon of overproduction appeared soon after the end of the World War in 1918. The 1927 economic conferences recommended that the problem be studied, but no steps were taken. Greaves notes that in 1928 seven-eighths of the world's total sugar output "was being produced behind protective barriers, or with the help of subsidies and bounties." In 1930 a gentleman's agreement was reached between the United States and Cuba, and for a period of five years Cuba limited its exports to the United States, which in turn limited its output to the 1928–29 level. But Java, the Philippines, and Europe were important producers. After negotiations with them a conference met at Brussels in December 1930; negotiations were interrupted, and another general conference met at Paris in March 1931; finally a convention was signed at Brussels in May of that year. The Chadbourne scheme, as it was called, established an International Sugar Council which was to permit a 5 per cent increase in export quotas when the world price rose to two cents a pound, and further exporting increases when the price rose to 2.45 and 2.5 cents. On the International Sugar Council each of the three countries had three members, whose voting power was weighted in proportion to the extent of the sugar interests involved. This scheme is interesting because it represented not an agreement between governments, as had the Brussels Sugar Convention of 1902, but an agreement between national bodies of producers to secure regulation of the raw sugar supplies of the world through commercial channels."[72] The attempt at allocating exports for a period of five years failed because when some countries curtailed their production other countries increased theirs, with the result that prices did not rise and even tended to fall. Consequently the plan lasted less than four years. In 1937 the continued unsatisfactory position of sugar, which did not respond very markedly to the improvement in general economic conditions, led to another international sugar conference, which met in London April 5, 1937, was attended by twenty-two nations, and adopted an agreement providing for an adjustment between the total exports to the free markets and the total requirements. The plan of export quotas was supplemented by the appointment of an International Sugar Council with an Executive Committee and a Secretariat.

Great Britain attempted to overcome the postwar rubber slump

[72] Royal Institute of International Affairs, *World Agriculture* (Oxford, 1932), p. 221.

in Malaya by adopting the Stevenson plan in 1922, which restricted the output in Ceylon and Malaya. The attempt failed after being in force for a few years because it held the price of rubber to a higher level, penalized consumers, especially in the United States, and caused interested parties to seek new plantations. The Dutch expanded their area of planting, and Firestone opened up areas in Liberia.

The renewed struggle which occurred after removal of restrictions led to difficulties, both in the Dutch Indies and in British Malaya. In 1934 the governments of Holland and Britain discussed the matter; and the next year France, Great Britain, India, the Netherlands, and Siam drew up an official agreement which was to last until 1938, and was to apply to the regions belonging to these countries in southeast Asia. South America and Liberia were not included. The agreement was designed to regulate the production export of rubber so as to reduce existing world stocks to a normal level by means of fixed quota allotments and limiting the area of planting. An international rubber-regulation committee was established to determine the export quotas of the signatory powers. The committee comprises government appointed delegates and of panels nominated by the manufacturers to advise the committee. The scheme was more extensive than the Stevenson plan had been, but it still lacked universality because important outside interests were not included.

Timber also suffered from a combination of overproduction and a decline of markets. Canada, the United States, Austria, Finland, Poland, Rumania, Sweden, Jugoslavia, and the Soviet Union have been the principal victims. Most countries have developed a national organization in order to systematize their exports, and this fact should make international co-operation simpler, in view of the difficulty of organizing unco-ordinated private groups on a continental or world basis. At a conference held in June 1931, timber exporters accepted the principle of international-quota distribution and suggested the establishment of international statistical research. Sweden was to call a later conference to "embody these measures in a convention." The central and eastern countries of Europe met at the Vienna conference in 1932, and agreed to restrict exports. In 1931 the League Economic Committee appointed a committee of timber experts from fifteen major timber-producing countries. The committee agreed that no international organization of timber production was then possible, because of the lack of enforcing authority, but that exporting countries should agree on the amount of timber that should be exported each year and that nations should agree to reduce the cuttings of timber to an amount which would not exceed the annual growth. But thus far little has been done to carry these recommendations into practice.

It was realized that the world trade was "utterly disorganized"[73] and that the situation of the timber industry is paradoxical. Despite the reduced demand for lumber due to smaller-sized houses, the use of substitutes, and the decline in the use of wood for fuel, the normal demand would still exceed the possibilities of national forests which are economically capable of exploitation. And the decline in consumption has not stopped the decline in prices—there is "wild competition," as the League report puts it. However, it is becoming recognized that "timber problems have ceased to be purely national economic questions and have become international problems," and that "no remedies can be effective henceforward without international co-operation." Unfortunately, there is no substantial agreement as yet on the form of this co-operation. At the 1932 Vienna Conference the proposal to establish a Central International Timber Office, possibly connected with the International Institute of Agriculture at Rome, met with no success.

Depression affected the tin industry as well. Great Britain has interests in the Malay States, Nigeria, Siam, and Burma; the Bolivian-American Company operates mines in Bolivia; while Dutch interests control the mines in the Dutch East Indies. Despite national amalgamations, the industry continued to suffer loss at the end of the decade following the war. In 1931 an international conference representing British Malayan, Nigerian, Bolivian, and Dutch East Indian interests met at London. They drew up the international tin agreement, providing for the reduction of output by several thousand tons a year. Each country had one member upon the committee whose main duty it was to determine the quotas of production. An international syndicate was formed in August 1931 and took charge of disposition of surplus stocks. In 1933 the agreement was renewed for a period of three years, the output quota being increased by several per cent. During the next year French Indo-China, Portugal, the Belgian Congo, and Cornwall acceded to the plan. The long-term success of such an

[73] League of Nations, Economic Committee, *The Timber Problem* (Geneva, 1932), p. 7.

agreement will depend upon maintaining satisfactory prices to consumers and the adjustment of the labor standards of workers in the Orient to those in the West.

The policy of the international tin committee gave grounds for disquietude. Charges were made that it unduly held up the price of tin, and that it created a buffer stock of several thousand tons in order to await a rise in the market price. Great Britain apparently favored maintaining high prices so as to obtain foreign exchange in order to prosecute the war which broke out in December 1939. United States consumers, however, were paying higher prices, and the continuation of such a policy caused dissatisfaction. The low quota assigned to Malaya caused unemployment among the Chinese workers, and in 1937 an expert of the League of Nations criticized the conditions in the Yunnan tin mines, thus confirming to some degree the charges which had been brought against the international committee.[74]

We may summarize by saying that the serious condition in which all these products now find themselves is due in the case of some of them to an apparent overproduction, which, in turn, is traceable (1) in part to the effects of the last war, which called into cultivation large areas which, after peace was restored, could no longer find satisfactory markets, in view of the resumption of cultivation by the warring countries; (2) in part, to the discovery of low-cost sources of supply, such as the copper mines in Africa; (3) in part, to monopolistic tendencies of groups desiring to make undue profit; and (4) in part, to the attempt of nations to make themselves self-sufficient in case of war.

Attempts at international organization constitute a reply (1) to the disturbances created by war and the threat of war, (2) to the inability of groups and individuals to see the political and economic problems as a whole and to sacrifice a temporary advantage to a long-term stability, and (3) to groups which do not hesitate to use national policies and emotions for their own group ends. Any satisfactory solution of the problem of raw materials therefore depends upon remedies in these three fields. The question of preventing war is examined in another chapter. We conclude this chapter by considering the organization and attitude of mind necessary for a solution of the economic contradictions which now confront the nations of the world.

[74] Alvin Barber, "Tin Control in a Major War," *Far Eastern Survey*, November 22, 1939, pp. 267–72.

INTERNATIONAL ORGANIZATION AND
ECONOMIC GROUPS

The problem is to conserve the advantages of large-scale production, and to see if trusts and combines can be purged of their evil features and transformed into acknowledged instruments of public and private welfare. The Marxist may well say that they cannot be regulated under a capitalist system and that the only remedy is a radical transformation of economic society. Palme Dutt, for example, writes that there is no longer a united international capitalism, that society has reached the point where monopolistic blocks are curtailing production and trade, that there are currency wars, and that the contradictions of modern society are so great that the trusts must develop more intense conflicts and ever more desperate methods.[75] The answer to this charge lies hidden in the future. Efforts are being made, however, to reform monopolies. These attempts are foredoomed to failure if the Marxists are right; they have a chance of success if the Marxist analysis is, as the writer believes, inadequate to explain modern economic and political phenomena.

Trusts have restricted trade and held up prices unreasonably and have depressed wages and cornered markets. These have been the evils. But the trusts have rendered some fine services.[76] They have helped to stabilize economic conditions against the ravages of dumping, cutthroat competition, and currency depreciation. They have been replies to excessive tariff barriers; and, by regulating markets according to distance and transportation facilities, effecting savings and heightening efficiency through combinations of sales forces, curtailing advertising costs, and co-operating in shipping and other distributing services, and by exchanging patents and processes, they have done good. Some of the international combines have attempted to bring about political understandings among the governments. They have frequently exercised a restraining influence during an upswing of prices, and by keeping a uniform scale have enabled small purchasers to benefit. Rousiers notes that maritime conferences have given small clients a better chance than they would have in a fiercely competitive system: "All shippers are sure that their most powerful competi-

[75] R. Palme Dutt, *World Politics, 1918–1936* (Victor Gollancz, Ltd., London, 1936), pp. 85–107.
[76] League of Nations, *General Report on the Economic Aspects of International Industrial Agreements* (Geneva, 1931).

tors have to pay the same freights, that they do not receive higher rebates—in a word, that they are treated in exactly the same way." And Hirsch also, reporting to the Preparatory Committee for the 1927 International Economic Conference, notes that international cartels did help to bring together economic groups that were divided into hostile political camps under the influence of the World War of 1914–1918. Staley well says that the world commodity controls have today a special significance: "In all the welter and confusion of new efforts at conscious control of economic activity, they are among the few that are *super-national*." He admits that many of them have been guilty of bad practices, but correctly notes that the world very much needs "the habit of working out economic policies on a wider than national basis." And the controls "represent a trend towards the broadening of economic policy to fit the new conditions of world-wide economic inter-dependence, despite their origin in producers' demands for restriction of output."[77]

How can the trusts and combines be adapted to serve the wider public needs? First, they must be supervised and registered in such a way that their operations will be carried out in full publicity. Hirsch proposed that the League of Nations "might establish a general observation post to see how far the combines represented a legitimate trend toward rationalization of industry for the European economic system as a whole"; the International Management Institute at Geneva could perhaps undertake this task. Moreover, the League could publish reports on the unfavorable effects of monopolies, and might establish an independent body to which a party could appeal for a report on the effect of particular international agreements.

This general recommendation was also made by William Oualid, who proposed that League Members should adopt a draft convention containing a declaration of principles, including the need of normal equilibrium between production and consumption, stable prices, stable supply, and regular work; and that cartels, by abusing their economic power, act to endanger public interest. An international cartel desiring official recognition from the League and its members should be required to make a declaration concerning the enterprises belonging to it, "the States under whose laws they exist, the nature of their products or of their operations, the

[77] Eugene Staley, *World Economy in Transition* (Council of Foreign Relations, New York, 1939), pp. 146–47.

conditions of the cartel, its aims, its means, its statutes or contracts specifying these matters."[78] The League would be authorized to invite member states to take action against unregistered
cartels. All member states should create national commissions or
bureaus of control to investigate cartels and to centralize and
verify "the justice of complaints made against the actions of irregular international cartels operating in their territory, or themselves to take the initiative of inquiries into such actions,"[79] and
submit the results of the inquiries to their governments and to the
League. These national organs should include administrative and
legal experts, employers and workers in equal numbers, and representatives of consumers, co-operatives or other consumer organizations. The League should have a similar agency composed of
government, employer, and worker representatives of the International Labor Organization, whose task it would be to examine the
national reports and bring complaints to the attention of member states.

Staley draws attention to the need for such a type of international control and suggests that the International Economic Organization should have authority

to require reports from international cartels and commodity control
schemes, like those in copper, aluminum, steel, tin, rubber, sugar, tea.
It might eventually charter public corporations for the construction
of international public works, or for the administration of international
public utilities—canals, radio facilities, aviation lines and the like.[80]

Thus the problem of controlling economic groups leads to the
wider problem of world economics, of which it is a part. Staley
suggests a world economic conference, not for the purpose of trying to bring in detailed recommendations, but merely to adopt
certain principles—not as a substitute for action but as "a useful
prelude to a positive and dynamic program."[81] He advocates an
autonomous international organization representative of economic
groups as well as governments within a reorganized League of
Nations. This organization could launch a "world development
program by studying the needs of capital, labor, raw materials,
technical training of experts for relatively undeveloped areas." It
would be something of a "permanent world economic conference,"

[78] W. Oualid, *International Raw Materials Cartels* (International Studies
Conference, International Institute of Intellectual Co-operation, Paris, 1938),
p. 51.
[79] Eugene Staley, *World Economy in Transition*, p. 52.
[80] Staley, *op. cit.*, p. 310.   [81] *Ibid.*, p. 302.

an "international planning commission designed to facilitate co-operation between countries."[82] The experience of the International Labor Organization over twenty years shows that such an organization is not beyond the bounds of possibility and of efficient action. Needless to add, such an organization, more in keeping with the world's economic needs, can come into being only when the present lamentable war situation has ended and steps have been taken to remove the terrible burden of armaments and the constant fear of political insecurity.

It is interesting to note that Senator O'Mahoney, Chairman of the United States Temporary National Economic Committee in his final statement at the closing public session (March 11, 1941) to consider recommendations on the question of industrial monopoly, recommended the expansion of government control over national corporations through a system of national charters. Only in this way, according to O'Mahoney, can we expect to prevent the evasion of the antitrust laws and reduce the difficulties of their enforcement. Cartels and monopolies constitute both a national and an international problem, and national as well as international governments must face the task of utilizing the energies of, and preventing abuses by, large-scale business. The Senator adds the following significant words:

In an hour of political uncertainty one hundred and fifty-three years ago, the Continental Congress called a national convention to draft a national political constitution. That conference of American leaders was successful beyond the dreams of any of those who authorized it. Our need today is a national economic constitution which shall abolish the economic uncertainties which seem to threaten even our political system.

And he stated that to this end

a national conference called by Congress of the various organizations, representative of business, labor, agriculture and consumers which have for years been working on diverse phases of this central problem might concentrate public thought and action on the objectives on which there is general agreement instead of, as now, on the objectives concerning which there is only misunderstanding, suspicion and disagreement.

The same general principles apply to international economic relations.

[82] *Ibid.,* p. 305.

SUMMARY

What is the present situation? Even before the present war the international currency system based upon the gold standard had broken down, the world as a unit of relatively free trade had gone, and the fluidity of economic life had given place to more rigid organization, both national and international. The theory and practice of economic nationalism had become widespread; but these things had led to insuperable difficulties, and therefore to an attempt to break through the barriers which they had helped to build.

We have seen the various methods which have been tried. The World Economic Conferences of 1927 and 1933 failed because the problems were too complex to be solved together at one time. Conferences devoted to one commodity—wheat, coal, timber, sugar, textiles—have each had a doubtful success, partly because the economic system is enough of a unity to make it difficult to isolate one or two items. Regional conferences have done a little; but they also have been unable to free themselves from the world community. The same criticism applies to imperial preferences. Bilateral clearing agreements help as an emergency measure in order to restart trade which has been paralyzed by a breakdown in currency relations; but, carried very far, they threaten to cripple multilateral trade for reasons given above. The United States Reciprocal Trade Agreements, with their unconditional most-favored-nation clauses, are definitely a small step in the right direction. The present war has further disrupted international economy until one wonders if the limit of elasticity has not been exceeded. If the world is to extricate itself from the present mountainous contradictions which confront it, a greatly expanded view of what economic welfare and political freedom mean, a widespread appreciation of the tremendous adaptations of political and economic organization which will be necessary, and a deep feeling of the need of raising the moral intelligence of nations, groups, and individuals will be required. The difficulties which will face us at the end of the present war will be ten times greater than they were in 1920; and at that time mankind rejected adjustments which were simple compared with the conditions which will now be necessary for world stability.

It will be important to realize that international trade still remains a vital necessity. Even Hitler was compelled to admit that "Germany must export or die," and attempted to break through the limitations of national autarchy by military conquest. For democracies which wish to trade on a peaceful basis, the words of Lewis Lorwin are to the point:

As the world economy based on increasing geographic specialization and relative free trade is giving way to a world economy based on controlled national economies, it is necessary to devise methods of regulating world trade. The supreme task of the twentieth century is the organization of the world market.

Even greater national and regional self-sufficiency cannot dispense with world trade. It may and will mean a change in the content and direction of international economy, but not its disappearance. What we shall see is a new world economy based on greater co-ordination and on more regional and world planning.

First, the world will need continuous and careful co-operative research "by all nations" in world economic problems. "This method calls for the organization of permanent bodies and committees which would pursue specific programs continuously." These permanent committees should serve the worldwide economy and also special regions. Lorwin proposed the establishment of a Pacific Development Council that should promote co-operation in the economic development of countries bordering on the Pacific. The research departments of the Economic and Financial Sections of the League of Nations must continue to play an important part.

This truth was emphasized by the Bruce Committee. Modern economic and social welfare, it wrote, demands day-to-day co-operation in scientific research, education, economic organization, and, indeed, every department of human life. Government would be impossible without the routine and unostentatious activities of hundreds of thousands of people. In a world which has become "for all its political severance . . . . daily closer knit," the same day-by-day adaptation to changing conditions must take place. The Secretary-General of the League has well said: " . . . . the abundance of life cannot be compressed within rigid limits. There are too many factors of change." As the League special committee has pointed out, industry is growing within agricultural states and all governments now are facing much the same type of problem. Therefore, "the opportunities of each country to gain by the experience of others are increased." Many of the problems need scientific study, careful and continuous co-operation, the exchange of experience, and the co-ordination of national policies. We have already traced in various fields of human endeavor the forces of human life which have necessitated organization transcending national boundaries. Indeed, international government has become a necessity for national survival. The League of Nations, despite its failure to prevent war, realized the need of "the interchange of experience and the co-ordination of action between national authorities," and over one-half of its budget was devoted to economic and social work.

And at the time when the League was being politically eclipsed, its members were planning for a development and an expansion of work in the economic and social field. The Bruce Committee in its report[83] of August 22, 1939, suggested that the League's resources are of the utmost value in this work because they enabled it, in the most economical way,

a) To collect and sift evidence drawn from all over the world;
b) To obtain the services of the best experts in the world working without reward for the good of the cause;
c) To arrange meetings between experts working in the same fields, enabling them to discuss their preoccupation, their successes, their failures;
d) To provide the essential links between the experts and those responsible for policy;
e) To provide constant and automatic opportunities for statesmen to meet and discuss their policy;
f) To provide thereby means for better understanding of the aims and policies of different nations;
g) To provide machinery for the conclusion of international conventions.

Finally, and perhaps most important of all, governments which desire expert advice or help can get it, not from the outside or as a favor, but from an institution which they themselves maintain, and on the services of which they have a right to call.

The work outlined above, the Committee believes, "is not performed elsewhere and . . . . its expansion does not involve overlapping with other international activities." It therefore proposes to bring all of the economic and social work of the League under an effective and representative agency which can co-ordinate the activities of the organization which has become increasingly interconnected, and by this reorganization to add "fresh efficiency and vigor to the work itself," and by separating the economic and the

[83] League of Nations, *The Development of International Co-operation in Economic and Social Affairs* (Report of the Special Committee, Geneva, 1939)

social from the political activities of the League to give states which are not members of the League "the opportunity of the fullest possible co-operation in the work itself as well as in its direction and supervision."

In pursuance of these objectives, it submitted to the Assembly a draft constitution for a Central Committee for Economic and Social Questions. The Committee should comprise representatives of twenty-four states, chosen for one year by the Assembly. After the first election it should comprise "such number for such period as may be determined in the light of experience." The Committee should co-opt not more than eight members appointed in a personal capacity on grounds of special competence and authority. It should study the conditions under which states which desired to participate in the economic and social work of the League should be able to do so. The Central Committee should meet at least once a year and submit the annual report to the Assembly, and should draw up its own rules of procedure, approve its agenda, elect its own president and bureau, etc. All matters "shall be decided by a majority of the members present."

Second, unless and until a worldwide financial order has been restored, clearinghouse agreements and barter methods must continue between countries whose currency systems have been disrupted from the common world system. But these should be systematized so as to enable increased world trade to take place; they should not be allowed progressively to diminish the international exchange of goods. Therefore a "World Exchange Board might be organized to serve as a clearinghouse for the study and promotion of exchange between countries of surplus products with a minimum dependence on gold and monetary movements."[84] See also chapter iii, above, "Monetary Issues as World Problems," for an analysis of other proposals.

Third, the area of freer trade must be extended. In 1938, before the present war, Alvin H. Hansen noted that there existed several major preferential trading areas—the United States, the British Empire, the French Empire, the Soviet Union, the Scandinavian countries; the totalitarian bloc, Italy and Germany, and their dependent countries; Japan and its controlled area in Asia.[85] These preferential areas, he remarked, had a "tendency toward a

---

[84] L. Lorwin: "Economic Nationalism and World Co-operation," *Pacific Affairs,* August-September, 1933, p. 370.

[85] See J. B. Condliffe, *The Reconstruction of World Trade,* for a good discussion.

minimization of commercial relations"; between them the price system does not function; "one preferential area breeds another"; and the world "becomes inmeshed in a vicious circle."

All countries are driven to act on the economic defensive. The countries with a great amount of raw materials are suffering economic depression because they cannot sell them; and the countries which need raw materials cannot buy them because the tariff barriers erected by other countries prevent them from selling goods in order to acquire exchange to buy the raw materials. Obviously some way out of the vicious circle should be found. Only by the re-establishment of a larger area of monetary stability and exchange of goods can we expect progress. The British area, the French area, the United States area enlarged by its bilateral trade agreements, the Soviet area, and the Scandinavian area should become progressively less exclusive. Because they contain the major part of the world's resources, they ought to take the lead in further breaking down the trade barriers which remain. In order to do this, Hansen proposed a multilateral convention by which the United States, Great Britain (the Empire and the Dominions), the Scandinavian countries, and those countries with which the United States has signed bilateral trade agreements would undertake to reduce their tariffs 10 per cent each year for three years on commodities of which "75% of the total imports come from the combined countries joining the convention." "Desperate conditions call for bold action," but only by some such means can a workable international system be restored. The convention should be open to any other country which cared to sign. He continues:

These reduced rates would . . . . be made available to all countries with which the contracting parties now have de facto most-favored-nation relations. This plan amounts in fact to the application of the principle of the leading supplier, which has already been made the guiding rule in the bilateral agreements concluded by this country. Such an arrangement would enable the contracting parties to reduce the tariffs chiefly to the advantage of each other without resorting to discrimination, with respect to the commodities in question, against non-contracting countries. At the same time, it would give a powerful incentive to non-contracting countries to join the multilateral agreement in order that tariff reductions might also be made on those commodities for which they are the leading suppliers.[86]

This step would have considerably modified the preferential ar-

[86] A. H. Hansen, *Full Recovery or Stagnation?* (W. W. Norton & Co., New York, 1938), p. 242.

rangements which were dividing the world into six or seven areas, insufficiently co-ordinated and causing much international tension.

Hansen wrote that a heavy responsibility rested upon the United States and Great Britain. That responsibility still exists. The two countries have the raw materials, and can take the lead in reconstructing an international monetary standard, in reducing tariffs and removing other trade barriers: "The markets of this great area must be made reasonably free and accessible to all nations. We cannot face reality without accepting these economic necessities." Only by such action can the economic difficulties of Germany, Italy, and Japan be eased, and the economic excuse (if indeed there be any), or the semblance of an economic excuse for their military policies, be eradicated. What must be done to insure that nations will not use the economic improvement for power politics will be discussed in a later chapter. Here it suffices to note that the United States and Great Britain, and indeed all countries, need to look at tariffs in a new light and to adopt customs duties on a more scientific basis. The nations with the preponderance of economic resources must build their policy on two fundamental principles: (1) long-term investments abroad must be provided; and (2) creditor countries must receive more than they export. The Executive Commercial Policy Commission in 1934 recommended that American industries should be divided into six major categories: (a) those requiring foreign outlets; (b) those requiring little government aid to enable them to compete in domestic markets with foreign goods; (c) those necessary for national defense; (d) those "well-suited" to the American environment; (e) those with a partial foothold in the United States but which have no hope of being able to supply the whole domestic market; and (f) those quite unsuited to America. Each of these categories should receive a different degree of tariff protection.

These proposals represent a step in the right direction, for they point to a more systematic classification and evaluation of domestic productive forces in terms of necessity and efficiency.

Fourth, the world fundamentally needs a solution of the problem of unemployment, the assurance of industrial stability within nations, the development of the highest efficiency in industry, and a rising standard of living based upon an increase in the real incomes of all countries. Spencer Miller tells that three hundred youth leaders came to Geneva in 1936 "bearing the petitions of 950,000 unemployed European youth." The spokesman who addressed a special session of the International Labor Organization

Annual Conference "made a most moving and prophetic appeal in behalf of the seven and a half million unemployed youth in Europe." Said he: "Give us work, or we must go to war."[87] But no solution was found, and today most of the youth are employed in war industries, or are in active war service at the front. Unemployment helped dictators to power; it created disillusionment in democracy and in the capitalistic system; and it paved the way to war. "Without security, the rights of liberty and democracy become more and more meaningless. A psychology of despair easily becomes transformed into a psychology of war."[88]

In the light of this outstanding fact, the importance of national antidepression policies becomes obvious. Alvin H. Hansen warns against the easy assumptions that international measures, such as removal of tariff barriers, of themselves will suffice, and emphasizes that the 1929 economic collapse in the United States, and the sharp depression of 1937–38 had catastrophic economic effects upon the world, with consequent political upheavals disastrous to world peace. The same writer adds that

this country could make no greater contribution toward the solution of the international political as well as economic problems than that of achieving a higher degree of internal economic stability at a level of fairly full employment of labor and other resources. It is, I think, a fact that an extraordinary instability of the American economy presents one of the most serious problems confronting Europe . . . .

Europe, and also the primary producing countries from whom we import so heavily, and whose prosperity or depression is, therefore, in large measure a reflection of our own, have every reason to fear the impact of America upon world affairs if we are to continue (a) a high degree of economic instability or (b) chronically depressed conditions, or (c), as of recent years, a combination of both.[89]

Unemployment thus threatens international peace, as well as democracy and the system of free economic enterprise; and unless it is conquered, a victory over Naziism may be a barren triumph. "Today the practical controlling fact is that hundreds of millions of people throughout the world have been persuaded, to the point of evangelistic conviction, that the capitalistic system is the

[87] Spencer Miller, Jr., *Unemployment and War* (Carnegie Endowment for International Peace, Commission to Study the Organization of Peace. Preliminary Reports and Monographs. International Conciliation, April 1941), p. 435.
[88] *Ibid.*
[89] Alvin H. Hansen, "The Importance of Antidepression Policy in the Establishment and Preservation of Sound International Relations," *ibid.*, p. 425.

cause of the economic insecurity of the common man and that, as the root of his economic ills, this system must be drastically modified or, failing that, destroyed." These words were spoken by Mr. Charles E. Wilson, president of the General Electric Company; and he added that the promise of economic security to the masses by the leaders of all nations—the dictatorships as well as the democracies—constituted the most significant fact in modern society.[90] For if that promise is not realized, the masses will destroy the system which fails them. Mr. Wilson then raises the question, How the system of free enterprise can meet this crisis, and answers that

the financial and managerial components of our Free Enterprise System must prove, by deeds as well as by words, their full comprehension of their social responsibilities—their deep sense of public service—and their unmatched capacity to positively plan—to put into effect—and, if you will, to police, by self-imposed rules, a constitution for industrial and commercial progress acceptable to the majority of our people—people whose economic security and destiny are vitally affected by the decisions of these controlling components of the system.[91]

This policy must lead to a clear definition of the obligations of the system, of the leaders of industry, and the adoption of an economic constitution for the free enterprise system, of the enforcement of such obligations by the industrial leaders, and of a close co-operation between government and business.

In this suggestion, I present no thought of arm's length co-operation, overshadowed by suspicion between government and business. Instead I seek arm-in-arm concord and co-ordinated effort in the common good—the kind of concord and effort which can, in my judgment, eliminate the causes of conflict, competition, and confusion between government and business.[92]

Fifth, the practical consequences of such a policy as outlined by the President of the General Electric Company are suggested by H. G. Moulton and his associates in the Brookings Institution. Moulton[93] notes that the United States has adequate raw materials, manufacturing capacity, market and merchandising facilities, fuel,

[90] *Total Security, A Challenge,* An address by Charles E. Wilson, January 2, 1941, p. 5.

[91] *Ibid.,* p. 7.   [92] *Ibid.,* p. 10.

[93] H. G. Moulton, *Income and Economic Progress* (Brookings Institution, Washington, D.C., 1935).

transportation, labor supply, and money and credit. It is not because of lack of resources that prosperity does not return. He is
not hopeful that taxation for the support of idle people, unless
it results in increased production, will solve the problem. Nor will
raising money wages achieve the desired end, because: (*a*) prices
often outstrip wage increases; (*b*) employees in industries where
wages are not raised will be adversely affected by price increases;
(*c*) higher wages result in higher costs to varying degrees in different industries. It is probable that the costs of a particular
business man will be raised more than the demand for his products will be increased, because his employees spend only a small
part of their wages for the products they have helped to create.
His market will not expand rapidly enough to offset his increased
costs resulting from higher wages. Certain labor groups will benefit from higher wages but may, in so doing, do injury to other
labor groups. Indeed, Moulton adds, a study of labor struggles
for better conditions shows how small have been the results compared with the energy and effort expended by organized unions
to gain higher wages.

Not all economists will agree that progress within the capitalist system lies in lowering prices as industry becomes more efficient. But the evidence is difficult to refute. The benefits of
technological improvements and operating efficiency must be
passed on to the consumer. In this way real purchasing power
will be raised, and on a more universal scale than if wages alone
were increased. Moreover, if industrial monopolists and trade
unionists will cease from exacting the utmost that they can get and
will co-operate to lower prices, the conflict between industry and
agriculture will be lessened. Agricultural prices have fallen much
more than industrial prices, and farmers are suffering heavily in
consequence.

The attempts to raise agricultural prices in the United States
by means of the AAA and the Bankhead Act, and elsewhere in
the world by quotas, subsidies, etc., tend to cause foreigners to
plant new areas of cotton, wheat, etc., and thereby intensifies competition. But, if industrial prices were lowered, agriculturists
would benefit by a direct increase in purchasing power, and moreover, price reduction would strengthen the competitive position
of the nation in foreign markets: "Success in international competition will in the long run depend upon productive efficiency and
not upon the level of money wages." Moreover, rising tariffs and
higher prices will force nations which need foreign markets to

lower their costs still further in order to surmount the tariff walls; this action will in turn create demands for yet higher tariffs. The progressively lower standards caused by reduction of wages and depreciated currency abroad will be paralleled by a reduction of standards of living within the tariff country itself owing to growing rigidities, higher costs, industrial inefficiency, and economic unbalance. Twenty years ago the founders of the International Labor Organization built up the I.L.O. on the theory that raising labor standards and purchasing power of all peoples was a necessary condition for the economic welfare of the modern world; today we are experiencing negatively the truth of their philosophy, as a man who has lost his sight may appreciate by contrast the beauty of light.

Sixth, in so far as the conditions here enumerated are due to the profit motive, an improvement can be effected only by a modification of man's whole attitude toward industry. A self-centered desire to make as much profit as possible, irrespective of the welfare of society, must ruin the competitive economic system. The exploiter who in the name of capitalism holds up prices, or holds down wages, betrays the system to which he gives lip-service. Neither national nor international recovery is possible so long as the monopolistic or selfishly individualist attitude on the part of laborer, employer, banker, manager, farmer, or consumer persists. It may or may not be true that the "system" prevents a change of attitude. If it is true, as the socialist avers, then a restoration of international trade even with a degree of state co-ordination, will not take place. If, however, self-interest can be sufficiently enlightened by an intelligent understanding of the meaning of "self" and of "interest" in a closely knit world, there may be ground for optimism.

The capitalist by his organizing ability may have done great service to his community; but without the technical skill of inventors, the protection of the laws, and the efforts of hundreds and thousands of workers and of others who are only remotely connected with his industry, he would have done very little. However much his own initiative and skill have counted, they are only a part of the picture and deserve only a part of the reward.

Nor is the owner justified in thinking of his business as a property. Mr. Justice Holmes has penetratingly remarked that an industry is a process rather than a property, and therefore should be open to regulation like any other social process. Consider the futility of a factory without workers and without markets. The

employer may own a plant, but without laborers the plant is useless. An industry, which embraces ownership, capital investment,
management, other labor, etc., must be considered as a social thing
and not exclusively as a private property. Only the most prejudiced view can fail to recognize the social character of what is
commonly called private enterprise. By all means we need to encourage the greatest amount of initiative, and to free all social
processes—industry, education, transportation, etc.—from useless
and arbitrary interference; but every action must be judged in the
light of its relation to social welfare.

We already recognize that few of us defend the night work of
women, the employment of small children in mines, and the other
grosser evils which have existed or do exist. Moreover, regulation
has operated not merely to prevent the most crude and savage exploitation of workers but also to assist industry and capitalists to
build up their own plants and factories. Many who denounce governmental control have lobbied for tariff protection and for other
government aids. Government has been not only a restraining
force but also an agency positively promoting industrial and commercial welfare by means of research agencies, grants, road construction, harbor works, conservation measures, and many other
methods. Business, therefore, however much it may disagree with
this governmental action or that, should appreciate the constructive
role of government and should realize that for its own welfare it
should co-operate with government instead of regarding the government as necessarily an impediment and a hostile force. The
last United States election campaign was too full of vague talk
about individualism and unrestricted private enterprise. There
may or may not have been excessive governmental action in this
or that field under the New Deal; but, if we are to serve democracy
instead of emotionally talking about it, we must first correct the
prevailing temper. People must be willing to look at the elementary fact that, in a very complicated world, government co-ordination is necessary. If we accept this truism, we shall have abolished
one mental hazard and shall be ready to take the first steps of
examining, industry by industry, what can be the most efficient
kind of relations between government and business.

At present the undue devotion of private and group interests
to their own immediate profit irrespective of others threatens the
whole structure of what one might call relatively free capitalism.
Indeed one may say that those who refuse to make possible an
expanding economy through restrictive practices and holding up

prices are the real enemies of the economic order which they profess to serve. John T. Flynn in a Town Meeting of the Air broadcast on February 13, 1939, eloquently described the situation:

Now let us look at the building industry. It is all tied up and crippled by endless agreements, practices, abuses of financiers, manufacturers, contractors, dealers, laborers. The manufacturers and the dealers—particularly the dealers—are organized into institutes and combines to put prices up and keep them there, to limit supplies, to crush competition. The sub-contractors are bound together in combines to do away with competitive bidding, to jump production costs outrageously, to parcel out jobs and business among themselves and to keep others out of the business. The laborers in their unions have three abuses—an inflexible wage scale which keeps labor costs up and the workers' total earnings down, innumerable rackets by labor leaders who levy tribute on building operations, and a ceaseless and senseless fight upon all forms of labor-saving methods and materials. There is no profit in putting up buildings. There is no profit in owning them. Why, then, should anyone build? You can pour government money into the stream of spending until you are exhausted, but it will never move into private building operations while these abuses linger. They are the abuses of business and not of the Government. The Government should have started out to correct them in 1933, but it didn't; it started out to consolidate them and validate them and to perpetuate them by means of NRA.

Take the manufacturing industry. Once on a time a man could start a new enterprise for himself. A manager of a lumber yard could go in the lumber business. Let him try now. The lumber institute, made up of his competitors, will not admit him as a recognized dealer, and the manufacturers dare not sell him or they will be blacklisted by the members of the lumber institute. It is the same in many other industries. The guild system which the NRA tried to perpetuate has ruined a man's chance of setting up in business for himself. If he saves a few thousands, therefore, he leaves it in the bank and the bank will not lend it because no one wants to borrow. The economic system is frozen by bigness on one hand and the monopolistic practices on the other.

Take the railroads. They cannot make the innumerable changes and improvements demanded by modern developments and necessary to successful competition with other forms of transportation. They haven't paid for all the junk they are operating with now. They are busted because they are crushed under the load of debt. We should have dealt with the railroads in 1933. They should have been forced through effective bankruptcies. They should have been rationally reorganized. Instead, Congress passed a fake reorganization law which enabled the bankers and managers who have wrecked the roads to hold on to them while the RFC loaned them more money to perpetuate the burden of debt which is crushing them. You can pile up in the banks and savings of the people another ten billions through government spending but none of it will take that next step into that vast tangle of old iron and debt known as the railroads.

This quotation makes clear three outstanding things: (1) that our slump is due in part to the desire for excessive profits by a number of concerns which have an economic monopoly or advantage; (2) that it is also due to an attempt to keep alive overcapitalized and inefficient industries when losses should have been cut years ago; and (3) that labor has frequently been guilty of the same profiteering motives and the same monopolistic tendencies as many capitalists. The profit-seeking motive is not confined to employers. Unions which strike for higher wages when the condition of industry is such that higher wages involve higher costs at the expense of sales, university professors who insist upon high fees for outside lectures, advertisers who charge too much, printers who ask two dollars when one dollar and a half would be sufficient, plumbers, carpenters, and all the other small independent workmen, doctors who charge excessively for operations and consultations, dentists who charge too much for inlays, lawyers whose fees are too heavy, and every other professional person who does not make the utmost effort to keep his charges down is guilty of increasing the difficulties of our economic system. For the consumer is the group which is penalized, and while many consumers are also producers, the truth is that some people can get much more than others from their professional services and thus are able more easily to absorb the higher consumption costs resulting from higher prices. The disequilibrium of society increases when capitalists, laborers, and professional classes make excessive charges.

If private property and private and corporate enterprise are to avoid increasing governmental regulation, they must themselves become increasingly conscious of the whole economic and social setting in which their action takes place. Employers, for example, can no longer expect to have a flourishing business if there exists an inadequate number of consumers; the welfare of consumers is obviously a matter of direct business concern. No amount of devotion to an exclusively private-profit motive can solve the problem; and the person guilty of such action does not see even his own position fully. He takes his own immediate plunge, extracts the utmost from it he can, but neglects to consider the many outside factors which are necessary to enable him to keep his business running. However immediate his success may be in his own factory, it avails little if the rest of the community falls to pieces. The same consideration holds true for labor and the professional classes.

Our immediate concerns, therefore, and our own private property are part of a whole human society, and the attempt to think in terms of absolute ownership prevents us from seeing how many tentacles of our own house or factory or our professional or labor skill reach out and draw sustenance from, and give sustenance to, the community. From this point of view, private property is a much more relative and a much less absolute concept than at first sight appears. If a factory is a property but the business within it is a process, then our factory in one sense is our own and we are entitled to expect a reasonable living from it; but in another sense the persons who work there are participants in a process, and if everyone is to obtain a fair share everyone becomes at the same time a trustee for the welfare of everybody else and a direct agent of his own welfare.

We thus see that the private-profit motive which each person has a right to have—because everyone needs shelter, clothing, leisure and cultural opportunity—must be tempered by the realization that the private profit is relative, and not absolute, in character. One's professional skill, as well as the factory, must be used with the realization that its advantage depends upon co-ordination with other people's advantage. Industrial, economic, and professional life thus fulfills two purposes: (1) the immediate advantage which must serve personal and family welfare; and (2) the harmonization of personal and family and group welfare. The fine art of living demands that we appreciate the elastic character of property and of professional and labor skill. Property is both a possession and a social trust. And though we talk of the superiority of the private-profit motive, we know in our best moments that we are bound by professional, ethical, and religious standards which prevent us from letting the private-profit motive dominate everything else. We know, too, that the robber, the burglar, and the gangster are those who allow the private-profit motive to outweigh all other considerations; and none of us is so foolish as to believe that a society can be built upon the philosophy of robbers, burglars, and gangsters.

Perry has recently written that if private enterprise is to justify its plea to remain private, and not be absorbed by governmental regulation and control, it must demonstrate that it can do a better and more efficient job not only for itself but also for society. If this is true, it means that private industry must be very honest with itself and the public and must prove that it means what it says and that it is doing the utmost to make sounder machines, materials of the best quality, and all at the lowest possible prices. The alternative is clear: Weaknesses must be remedied either by industries themselves, and by every person within that industry doing his honest part toward this end; or this objective will be sought by external regulation, with the consequent danger of bureaucracy.

It would be a serious error to overlook the many weaknesses and evils in the labor movement as well as those in the management of industry. No impartial student of economic history can deny that the working class has suffered, and in many cases still suffers, from grievous poverty and injustice. The workers too often have been the first to suffer from economic slumps, through losing their jobs or suffering reduction of wages or having to work only part of the time; they have had to struggle for minimum wages, minimum hours, accident compensation, decent hygienic conditions, and the elimination of unnecessary hazards in dangerous trades. Many of them still contract occupational diseases; they have lacked many of the advantages and amenities enjoyed by the upper and middle classes; they have had to fight for recognition of their unions and against labor spies and unscrupulous employers' opposition. These and many other things must be admitted if we are to begin to come to a common attitude of mind in solving our problems involving capital and labor. On the other hand, labor has not been guiltless; frequently it has been provocative, suspicious, and unreasonable, despite much unfortunate and bitter opposition.

The working class has a right to adequate wages, good working conditions, decent housing, accident and health insurance, and opportunity for education and social intercourse. Under modern conditions, especially, it needs to combine into unions, so that the individual worker will not be at the mercy of those who have great wealth behind them. In a word, labor has the right to be regarded as an integral part of modern industry, and not as mere labor power. And it has not yet obtained many of the rights which it should have.

But if labor has these rights it has its responsibilities to society no less important than those of capital. Unfortunately there is much evidence to show that many of the working men today are suffering from the same shrinkage of social motive which they condemn in the capitalist. No social group is free from the danger of self-seeking and of vocational exclusiveness; and labor today has given the community many grounds for legitimate criticism. The present controversy between the C.I.O. and the A.F.L. is a tragedy. Whatever the internal difficulties concerning jurisdiction may be, they are not so serious but that they can be settled if the rival leaders and followers have a genuine love of the working class. They should see that labor is losing prestige in a disastrous manner. No one would deny that the working-class movement in Europe and even in Great Britain has lost much ground in the last few years. But the British labor movement has an incomparably higher morale, and is almost entirely free from the rackets and unscrupulous deals which have been made or have reportedly been made between certain employers and labor leaders in various parts of this country. Charges of corruption and personal gain are frequently made; union entrance fees and dues are often overheavy; and without doubt reforms could be introduced so as to bring back genuine democracy into many unions.

To those who believe that apart from the problem of war no satisfactory relation can be worked out between capital and labor, between government and industry, and between the individual and the community, the example of the Scandinavian countries may be cited. In Norway, Sweden, and Denmark a happy arrangement was worked out which gave a substantial control to the government but reserved a wide range of freedom to private enterprise. Technical experts worked in close collaboration with the government and with co-operative societies and private corporations. The spread of adult education by means of folk high schools and public lectures developed a high degree of public intelligence; culture was widely diffused; governments could thus maintain constant communication with their people on a high level of economic and political discussion. The result was to make this area one of the most civilized in the modern world and one which provided an answer to the theoretical objection that the transition cannot be made from the highly competitive industrial system of the nineteenth to a more co-operative industrial system of the twentieth century. It is important to note that part of this success was due to the fact that there was comparatively little expenditure upon military preparations to distort the more normal structure of economic life. All the more tragic then is the spectacle of this region being invaded by the demon of modern war and having to suffer a set-back in progress for many decades.

It may be argued that this relatively simple society had not the complicated problems of larger and more industrialized nations. The objection is not entirely convincing. It may be admitted that industrialism and complexity make problems more difficult; it is obvious that they do not call into play essentially different factors.

The foregoing analysis should make clear the truth of Hansen's observation that national economic stability and welfare is the very stuff and fiber of international economic welfare, and that national and international economics are different aspects of the same reality.

Chapter VI

COMMUNICATIONS

COMMUNICATIONS have a local, national, imperial, and international significance. Roads, rivers, railroads, airplanes, cables, and radio serve to unite all kinds of society. We may expect, therefore, to find no clear-cut picture in attempting to estimate the part which communications play in modern international affairs.

The unity of nations needs a material basis, and historians point to the great service rendered by railroads in promoting the national unity of Germany, the United States, and Russia during the nineteenth century. Railroads have also helped to build empires by enabling colonial settlement to go inland instead of being confined, as the earlier empire settlements were, to the coastal regions. They were not susceptible to the diseases which destroyed animals used for transport purposes; they enabled revolts to be put down more easily; they made possible the exploitation of inland resources; and in areas visited by famine they facilitated relief measures. In these ways considerable constructive work was done. The same holds true of shipping, cables, radio, and airplanes. Cheaper postage, the development of refrigeration, the exchange of tropical products and raw materials for manufactured goods, made possible by better shipping, have led to a higher standard of living.

Just as better means of communication made for national unity, so they later made for national expansion. But in the course of the expansion, rivalry developed on an international scale, just as on a smaller scale there had been rivalry between railroad companies, shipping groups, and providers of other forms of transportation. The difference now was that governments were tempted to place their armed forces back of the expansionist forces. Within their own boundaries they had developed national security; but, in a world of power politics, communications served not only economic welfare but also military security and striking power. A railroad could be used to transport troops and munitions as well as consumers' goods; and so long as the threat of war existed, so long would governments view projected railroads (and, of course, other forms of communication) from a military as well as an economic point of view, and on many occasions the military considerations outweighed the economic.

In a world of growing international trade, however, the demands of ordinary economic life went far beyond national and empire channels, and the interests of governments as imperial instruments clashed with their interests as rulers of citizens with economic interests all over the world. The latter demanded organization which would more efficiently minister to international shipping, railroads, cables, radio, and air traffic, and the normal communications incidental to international trade led to wider systems of international co-operation. A contradiction thus developed, growing more pronounced every year; on the one hand the institution of war demanded an ever increasing amount of independent national effort, and on the other hand the need of efficient international organization for everyday purposes became apparent. The following survey will show in more detail the effects of the growingly incompatible purposes which communications have had to serve.

WATER TRANSPORTATION

SEAS AND STRAITS

The freedom of the seas which vessels enjoy today in time of peace came only after centuries of effort and struggle. Ancient historians relate how Phoenicians, Greeks, and Romans fought many a naval battle to gain sovereignty over the Mediterranean. Hundreds of years later at different times Venice claimed dominion over the Adriatic Sea, British monarchs asserted jurisdiction over waters "belonging to the King of England," and other rulers took such titles as "lord of the ocean" and "king of the seas"; each of these units treated the waters around it as its own possession and deliberately penalized foreign ships.

In the sixteenth century, the international lawyer, Gentilis, advocated a modification of the traditional policy and suggested that all countries should enjoy the use of the sea, "but without violation of another's jurisdiction." We refer elsewhere to the close connection between fishery questions and the problem of the high seas. Here it is sufficient to note that the expanding commerce of the seventeenth century brought a challenge to the monopolistic pretensions of national monarchs, and that, following many controversies on the law of the sea, the doctrine developed that the sea was free to all nations and claims of national sovereignty over the open ocean were discarded. Nations now possess jurisdiction over their territorial waters, which, generally speaking, extend for three miles from the shore line. Beyond these limits modern international shipping no longer meets with obstacles imposed by nationalistic claims of jurisdiction. The oceans are free to all, and cargoes and passengers may proceed without let or hindrance. The sea has become internationalized.[1]

This freedom of the seas in peace time is a precious right; but its value would be considerably diminished if nations which are in a position to control certain straits and canals could block international shipping at their will and pleasure. Thus freedom of ocean commerce in order to play its full part requires freedom of commerce in such narrow seas and connecting waters, as the Dardanelles and the Bosporus, the Straits of Gibraltar, the Great Belt and the Little Belt, and the Kiel, the Suez, and the Panama canals.

In earlier years Denmark claimed jurisdiction over the Danish Sounds and Belts; these were not strictly territorial waters, but Denmark claimed a prescriptive title deriving from the days of *mare clausum,* when a nation regularly claimed jurisdiction over the ocean surrounding or adjoining it. It was only in 1857 that Denmark, by international agreement, surrendered the right of collecting tolls on ships passing the Great Belt and the Little Belt, undertook not to substitute taxes, and promised "to maintain in good condition existing lights to the entrance of her ports, harbors, and roadsteads and those along her shore as well as existing buoys, beacons, and markers that served to facilitate the navigation of the Cattegat, the Sound and the Belts."[2] The King of Sweden and Norway agreed to maintain the lights on the shores of his countries "without imposing any dues upon the ships that passed the Sound and the Cattegat."[3] Denmark in return was to receive special sums from the powers, each of which was to make

---

[1] Certain limitations involved in national claims over bays, gulfs, and other waters are discussed in several volumes dealing with international law. See also P. M. Ogilvie, *International Waterways* (The Macmillan Company, New York, 1920), pp. 116–49.

[2] Charles E. Hill, *The Danish Sound Dues and the Command of the Baltic* (Duke University Press, 1926), p. 261.

[3] *Ibid.,* p. 262.

a special convention with Denmark "to regulate the rate of exchange of foreign into Danish money." The United States, which had given one year's notice in 1855 to terminate the Treaty, made a special arrangement in 1857 and contributed in no small measure to bringing about the freedom of the seas through the Danish Straits. International requirements had triumphed over national claims.

In 1850 the Clayton-Bulwer Treaty between the United States and Britain provided that if a canal were to be built in Central America separating North from South America, it would be by joint effort. The United States subsequently attempted to free itself from this provision, and on grounds of national interest claimed the right to modify the treaty by unilateral action. Considerable diplomatic correspondence ensued, in which Great Britain successfully asserted her position under international law. Finally, in 1901, the Hay-Pauncefote Treaty modified the 1850 Treaty, leaving the United States free to build a canal, in return for which it promised equal treatment for the ships of all nations. Soon after the opening of the Panama Canal, Congress passed a bill exempting United States coastwise traffic from canal tolls. The measure aroused considerable resentment in Great Britain; many people felt that the bill was inconsistent with the treaty commitments of 1901; others feared that to place tolls on foreign ships and exempt American vessels would unduly penalize foreigners and seriously affect their carrying trade, since they would have to charge higher freight and passenger rates or accept a lower rate of profit. Fortunately, Congress accepted the recommendations of President Wilson in 1914, and the canal, although constructed, administered, and fortified by the United States, is now open to ships of all nations without discrimination.

The Suez Canal is of paramount importance as an artificial waterway. It has assisted a revolution in sea transport, namely, the rise to supremacy of the steamship and the decline of the sailing vessel, which was frequently becalmed in the Red Sea. Before the canal was built, European nations had to use the route around Africa. When companies found that by using the Suez Canal they could save many days in sailing time, make great economies in wages and fuel costs, and increase their income through more frequent journeys, the canal rapidly grew in importance. In 1870, there were 486 vessels that passed through it; in 1913 the figure had risen to 5,000; in 1930, there were 5,761 vessels, of 31,000,000 tonnage, which used this great waterway. A purely national control of the waterway would carry with it the threat of discrimination against foreign vessels. Nevertheless, Great Britain, in view of its empire in India and the Pacific, felt that it had a special strategic and economic interest in the canal, and fought against the principle of international control in Egypt, and finally gained a predominant political position in that country. The other nations, however, were not minded to permit Britain to monopolize or dominate the waterway, and agreed in 1888 to a convention which still regulates the status of the canal. Under this convention the canal is free in peace and war to all vessels, and it must never be used for the purpose of blockade. Belligerent powers undertake not to take warlike action against it, and war vessels must not remain in its waters. Only in case of a legitimate self-defense exercised by Egypt and its protector, Britain, can the canal be closed. Article 11 of the convention provides that in the exercise of the right of defense the free use of the canal shall not be interfered with. In fact, on only two occasions has the canal been closed—the first before the convention was signed, the second for a period during the World War of 1914–1918.

This important canal, then, is open to the trade and commerce of all nations. The Suez Canal Company, governed by a Board of Directors, 32 in number, of whom 21 are French, 10 are British, and one is a Dutchman, administers an area which transcends all national importance and has become a matter of concern to the whole world.

However, it is impossible to regard the Suez Canal merely as a great waterway for the world's commerce in time of peace. It is for Great Britain an important line of defense, vital to maintaining her lines of communication with India, her other Asiatic possessions, Australia, and New Zealand. Consequently, the neutralization provided for in the convention of 1888 does not constitute a strong guaranty. And until the danger of international war is considerably lessened, the Suez Canal will not be an unmixed blessing to the world; for, as Hallberg[4] suggests, while it does fulfill an important civilizing mission in promoting trade and commerce, and in bringing the Orient and the Occident near to one another, it has also caused many international rivalries, played its part in bringing on the war of 1914, and in the present struggle is a factor of no small importance, as the war in North Africa and in eastern Mediterranean countries testifies.

[4] Charles W. Hallberg, *The Suez Canal* (Columbia University Press, New York, 1931).

THE BOSPORUS AND THE DARDANELLES

The Straits question has occupied Europe for several hundred years, and well illustrates the conflicting claims of imperialistic power policies and the requirements of the world's and especially Europe's economic welfare. In its modern form it dates from the decline of Turkey and the rise of Russia. The Bosporus and the Dardanelles are at the intersection of a north-south line connecting Russia with the Mediterranean and an east-west line joining Europe and Asia; and on this cross the peace of Europe has more than once been sacrificed. The reason is not difficult to find. The power which controls the east-west axis can prevent a Russian move to the south; if Russia dominates the north-south line, it can block the eastern expansion of rival powers, strengthen its position in the Mediterranean, and threaten India. The European significance of the Straits was revealed in the World War of 1914–1918, when the Allies sacrificed many thousands of men in an effort to break through the Dardanelles and the Bosporus for the purpose of transporting troops into the Black Sea, so as to assist Russia and thereby strengthen the attack on the Austro-German eastern frontiers.

Before Turkey took Constantinople in 1453, merchant traders from Italian cities sailed through the Straits into the Black Sea. After the fall of Constantinople, Turkish rulers placed obstacles in the way of the Italians, and with the extensions of their empire, claimed that the Black Sea was a Turkish lake. They assumed the right of prohibiting foreign war vessels and merchantmen from passing through the Straits; and, although they granted capitulations to foreigners, this privilege did not include the right of free navigation in the Black Sea.

The growth and expansion of Russia introduced a new factor. Peter the Great, in 1696, conquered Azof and launched Russian warships in the Black Sea. Turkey, by the Peace of 1699, lost several provinces and agreed that Christian states need not pay further tribute to her, but still insisted on excluding all foreign vessels from the Black Sea. Russia, despite her defeat in 1711, persisted in her attempt to move south; in the 1774 Treaty she gained considerable power over the Turkish Empire, and even claimed the right to intervene in Turkey's internal affairs.

These advantages, however, did not satisfy Russia, which by the 1779 Convention gained an extension of Russian navigation privileges in the Black Sea. In 1784 she annexed the Crimea, and by the end of the eighteenth century was in an excellent position to take advantage of Turkey's weakened condition.

The early nineteenth century saw the Russian advance continue. By the 1805 Treaty, Russian warships gained the right to go through the Straits to the Ionian Islands. This concession aroused European fears, and France attempted to persuade Turkey to renounce the treaty. A little later France and Russia negotiated a treaty to partition Turkey, whereupon the latter turned to England. The 1809 Anglo-Turkish Treaty expressly upheld the ancient rule of the Ottoman Empire, which forbade all warships from entering its waters, and confirmed Turkish sovereignty. Phillipson and Buxton bring out the significance of this Treaty in the following words:

> Great Britain undertook to respect a rule which, in view of Ottoman sovereignty, she was in any case bound to respect: she merely agreed in an express unconditional form to refrain from doing what she was not entitled to do under the common law. On the other hand Turkey, considering her sovereignty, was not bound to engage herself to permit or exclude the passage of this or that vessel. But having deliberately undertaken to exclude all warships, she thereby limited her liberty of action. . . . . This engagement . . . . contributed much to transform what was originally a rule of Ottoman internal administration into a rule of international law.[5]

Russia did not remain long content with the Anglo-Turkish arrangement. In 1828 it blockaded the Dardanelles and then forced Turkey to sign the Peace of Adrianople (1829). The Treaty guaranteed the freedom of trade to Russian subjects, the right of passage of Russian merchant vessels through the Straits to the Mediterranean, the immunity of Russian ships from seizure by Ottoman authorities, and the freedom of trade and navigation in the Black Sea. By this step the Czar gained a great triumph for Russian commercial navigation and, moreover, forced into the Treaty a provision that any interference with the freedom of trade would give Russia the right to have recourse to reprisals. Nevertheless, the Russians were still not satisfied; they desired and worked for the freedom of passage for their military vessels.

After secret negotiations with Turkey which aroused British fears, Russia signed the Treaty of Unkiar Skelessi (1833), by which the Dardanelles were to be closed to foreign warships during a war between Russia and any other foreign power. This de-

[5] C. Phillipson and N. Buxton, *The Question of the Bosphorus and the Dardanelles* (Stevens & Haynes, London, 1917), p. 44.

fensive but one-sided alliance practically converted the Black Sea into a Russian base, and made Turkey almost a dependency of Russia. The other powers made strong protest. Turkey as a sovereign power had the legal right to grant to Russia whatever privileges it desired; but France and Great Britain had obvious political reasons for their objections.

The increasing rivalry between Britain and Russia made the Straits ever more important, and British diplomacy attempted to preserve Turkey against the Egyptian attacks from the south and Russian penetration from the north. In 1840 the Treaty of London, reversing the Unkiar Skelessi provisions, re-established the rule that the Straits were to be closed to foreign ships of war. The position was now that "four of the leading powers of Europe jointly recognize in a formal international instrument, the applicability of the rule of closing the Bosphorus and the Dardanelles to warships of all States, whilst the Sultan, engaging to observe this rule in general, formally surrenders his former right in opening the Straits at his discretion." The Straits Convention of 1841 to which France adhered strengthened the London Treaty by making its observance a matter of "indivisible and solidary obligation" on the part of the signatory powers; and the rule of closing the Straits now became a matter of international agreement, and no longer merely the expression of the Sultan's sovereign power.

Anglo-Russian rivalry continued. Russian troops in June 1853 advanced to the River Pruth and refused the Franco-British demand to evacuate the Danubian principalities. In the Crimean War which followed, Russia suffered defeat and had to submit to the Treaty of Paris (1856), which not only neutralized the Black Sea but "denavalized it." Because foreign warships might not enter the Black Sea, victorious powers insisted that Russian military vessels and arsenals be forbidden. Russia, of course, regarded this restriction as an intolerable limitation upon her sovereign power. For two hundred years she had struggled to establish her power on the Black Sea, and now the 1856 Treaty had swept away all her gains. Little wonder that she took the first opportunity to denounce these clauses. By the "Pontus Treaty" of 1871, Articles 11, 13, 14 of the 1856 Treaty were abrogated and the position of 1841 was re-established.

The twentieth century brought the Straits question prominently to the front. In the Russo-Japanese War, Russia was handicapped through being unable to send her Black Sea squadrons to fight against Japan. She had ample reason for regarding the rule of the

Straits as unfair and discriminatory. In 1912, during the war between Turkey and Italy, the Turkish government placed mines in the Dardanelles in order to block the entrance of Italian war vessels. Its action constituted a breach of the treaty conditions, since foreign commercial vessels had the right of navigation in the Straits; and Turkey, under pressure, consented to remove the mines and permit the resumption of neutral commerce.

The rise of Germany to power led Britain to modify its attitude toward the demands of Russia, and during the war the Allied Powers signed a treaty in 1915 agreeing to place Constantinople under Russian control. The outbreak of the Bolshevist Revolution introduced new factors, and the Allies ultimately refused to be bound by their commitments made in the early months of the war.

The Treaty of Sevres (1920) imposed heavy burdens upon Turkey and weakened its position in the Straits. The Turkish Nationalist Movement under Mustapha Kemal managed to free the country from the most onerous terms; but, at Lausanne in 1923, Turkey had to submit to the demilitarization of the Straits, and to permit the free passage of warships. The signatory powers set up an International Commission comprising representatives of interested governments, which was to carry out its functions under the auspices of the League of Nations.

Turkey was permitted a maximum garrison of 12,000 men and an arsenal and a naval base at Constantinople. The Soviet representative strenuously opposed the demilitarization of the Straits, realizing that if the Dardanelles could not be closed to warships the Black Sea would remain open to any powerful naval aggressor. The only concession which Chicherin could obtain was that the strength of any foreign war fleet coming through the Straits should not exceed the strength of the strongest fleet in the Black Sea. This concession, as Slocombe points out, may have had some value in time of peace but not during war; since Turkey, with the Straits demilitarized, had no power to prevent a strong fleet from entering the Black Sea, if it chose to break the provisions of the Lausanne Treaty. Great Britain, by supporting the principle of liberty of passage for neutral warships, reversed her century-old policy. Up to now, she had advocated closing the Straits because she believed that she stood to gain less by attacking Russia in the Black Sea than by preventing Russian ships from getting into the Mediterranean and threatening British communications with India.

The new demilitarized regime lasted for thirteen years. But in

1935 and 1936 a number of events took place which altered the situation. The Italo-Ethiopian crisis had revealed the inability of the League of Nations to enforce collective security; Germany under Hitler's leadership had scrapped both the Locarno Treaty and the Treaty of Versailles by entering and remilitarizing the Rhineland. The Soviet Union had entered the League and claimed that its obligations under the Covenant obliged it to "think of the Straits in terms of offensive strategy" and to intervene in any European dispute should the Covenant be violated. For these reasons the Soviet Union was no longer content with a fleet in the Black Sea "barely adequate for defensive purposes."

Turkey asked for a revision of the demilitarization clauses of the Lausanne Treaty. Circumstances had changed; because international organization had failed to prevent aggression, nations had to look to their own armed forces for security, and Turkey was no exception. At the Conference of Montreux, June 22, 1935, Turkey proposed (1) her resumption of the right of fortifying and garrisoning the Straits and the islands guarding them; (2) the abolition of the International Straits Commission; (3) closing the Straits to all military or civilian aircraft; (4) recognition of her right to grant or withhold permission for naval forces from states on the Black Sea to pass into the Mediterranean (up to 14,000 tons at a time), as well as for other naval forces to pass through the Straits into the Black Sea, and for a Black Sea state (for example, the Soviet Union, Rumania, Bulgaria) to send a vessel up to 25,000 tons through the Straits into the Mediterranean, but no such privilege to similar-sized ships to pass from the Mediterranean into the Black Sea.

The British representative agreed to the principle of recognizing Turkish sovereignty over and remilitarization of the Straits, but claimed that because the Straits were an international waterway international supervision should be maintained. Great Britain "wished to increase the tonnage permitted to foreign warships coming into the Black Sea, proposed that Turkey be given the right to close the Straits on decision of two-thirds vote of the League Council, and suggested that, in case of war, belligerents might pursue their enemies through the Straits into the Black Sea." The last proposal involved an obvious threat to Turkey and Russia, and so angered the Soviet representatives that at one time they threatened to leave the conference. The Russian view was that, as the Black Sea was a closed sea, there was no excuse for naval vessels of other countries to enter it. Such entry could be interpreted only as aggression. But, since the Soviet Union had interests outside of the Black Sea, her ships should not be confined therein and cut off from her Baltic and Pacific ports. On this view, Soviet security required the right of unlimited passage for Russian ships going out of and restricted passage for non-Russian ships coming into the Black Sea. Obviously these rival arguments show little difference in principle from the position over one hundred years ago.

After prolonged discussion the representatives signed the convention of the remilitarization of the Straits on July 17, 1935. The details need not be considered here. Suffice it to say that power politics still dominate the question of the Straits, and will continue to do so until international organization successfully solves the problem of war.

TECHNICAL CO-OPERATION FOR SAFETY AT SEA

Adequate freedom of the seas requires not merely an abandonment of national claims to ocean highways and the suppression of piracy but also freedom from the dangers of shipwreck occasioned by fogs, collisions at sea, and inadequate lighthouse facilities at dangerous points. It is obvious that if a shore line under the jurisdiction of an economically backward or inefficient government were dangerous to shipping of all nations it would constitute a challenge to international action.

As early as 1865 the major European nations, the United States, and Morocco signed the Tangier agreement, by which the governments agreed to co-operate in the establishment of an international lighthouse at Cape Spartel in Morocco. The lighthouse itself and the surrounding land remained under the sovereignty of the Sultan of Morocco; but the contracting parties undertook the administration of the lighthouse and shared the expenses of its upkeep. Stuart writes that it was essential that the lighthouse which protects "one of the world's most important trade routes, should be kept at the highest degree of efficiency"[6] and to this end the International Commission approved the installation of a semaphore in 1892 and a fog signal in 1905. In 1914 a technical commission recommended an increase in the candle power of the beacon from 20,000 to 320,000, but the World War of 1914–1918 prevented the step from being taken. Other proposals were made in 1922, 1923, and 1926, but they had to do primarily with political

[6] G. H. Stuart, *The International City of Tangier* (Stanford University Press, 1931), p. 44; also pp. 39–49.

questions arising out of the changed international situation in Europe and the desire of the Shereefian government to exercise greater control over the administration of the lighthouse. The benefits to world commerce from the relatively small amount of international co-operation necessary to establish the lighthouse have been out of all proportion to the costs involved.

In 1889 the first International Marine Conference met at Washington. It proposed various rules to prevent collisions, and suggested uniform action in the matter of sound signals, lights, and buoys. Over twenty years passed before the International Council for the Exploration of the Sea was set up for purposes of scientific research. In 1910 twenty-four nations accepted uniform regulations concerning assistance and salvage at sea "and providing for equitable remuneration when such assistance is given." After the "Titanic" disaster in 1912, when 1,490 lives were lost through an iceberg collision, an international conference in London drew up a convention for safety of lives at sea. The convention provided for the destruction of derelict ships, the study of ice conditions, and the establishment of an ice patrol. The signatory powers were to join in defraying the expenses of the service, and agreed upon international signals, life boats, safety devices, etc. "Next to submarines icebergs are the greatest menace to international shpiping. Each spring ships of the International Ice Patrol, supported by fourteen nations, rove the North Atlantic, charting the course of giant floes, destroying some, and warning merchant ships of the presence of others, in or near heavily traversed northern routes." In 1940, for the first time in twenty-six years, United States Coast Guard cutters engaged in the work from a United States port or base (Boston); hitherto Halifax, Nova Scotia, had been the Atlantic base.

In 1921 an International Hydrographic Bureau to co-ordinate the efforts of nations to insure greater safety at sea was established. In 1929 a League Committee at Genoa met to consider proposals to unify maritime signals, and drew up detailed rules dealing with

(a) unification of buoyage regulations; (b) unification of lighthouse signs; (c) unification of various coast and port signals; (d) the desirability of a certain concordance between the characteristics of lighthouses and the associated fogsignals; (e) wireless lighthouses.

It also recommended international collaboration between air and sea navigation in the matter of signaling from shore and the enlargement of the international signaling code, and that a special maritime conference should deal with the question of local storm-warning signals.

In 1930 a general conference at Lisbon for the unification of buoyage and lighting of coasts adopted several agreements in conformity with these principles. The recommendations were designed to make uniform the various rules concerning lighthouses and safety signals, and were adopted because of the need of developing radio beacons throughout the world.

The experience of the World War of 1914–1918, new inventions, and further shipping collisions induced governments to meet and sign a general convention in May 1929. It became effective on January 31, 1933.

Among the topics dealt with are ship construction, life-saving appliances, methods of detecting and extinguishing fire, radio signal devices such as automatic alarm receivers, various phases of the art of navigation, including the collection and dissemination of meteorological data, and inspection and certification of ocean-going vessels.

In 1930 another London conference succeeded in formulating an International load-line convention which

deals with the extent to which ships may be loaded with cargo without interfering with security during the voyage. The importance of a precise location of the load line is obvious: safety first, indeed; but economic considerations dictate a parallel prudence in avoiding unnecessary abstinence in the use of cargo space.[7]

One further condition had to be realized if freedom of the seas for international commerce was to be reasonably complete. Ships might travel the ocean, be free from pirates, and avoid shipwreck by reason of the precautions just enumerated; but if they found themselves on their arrival at a foreign port discriminated against by higher taxes, or subjected to delay in unloading in favor of other ships, they would suffer serious loss. The advantages of freedom of the seas might be entirely wiped out at the very end of the voyage. Foreign shipping companies could easily be ruined by a government which claimed that, under the doctrine of sovereignty, it had a right to discriminate against foreign vessels in its own ports. Because nations are put to considerable

---

[7] Wallace McClure, *World Prosperity, as Sought through the Economic Work of the League of Nations* (The Macmillan Company, New York, 1933), p. 429.

expense in maintaining harbors, lighthouses, and port facilities, it is natural and just that they should charge harbor dues; but these dues should be equal to all shipping, and no favor should be granted in the use of ports to vessels of the home government. Otherwise international shipping would soon be entangled in endless complications.

Many bilateral treaties were signed during the nineteenth century to insure such equality of treatment; and at Paris in 1919, Barcelona in 1921, and at Genoa in 1922, these matters received further international attention. The three conferences were a prelude to the 1923 Convention and the Statute on the International Regime of Maritime Ports, which guaranteed freedom of access to seaports, and accepted the principle of equality in charges and port facilities, including "facilities of all kinds, such as allocation of berths, loading and unloading facilities, as well as dues and charges of all kinds levied in the name or for the account of the Government, public authorities, concessionaries or undertakings of any kind."[8] The signatory powers agreed that in levying customs, local or consumption duties, or incidental charges, the flag of the vessel must not be taken into account, although nation X might suspend the equality of treatment to a vessel from nation Y if Y did not adequately apply the statute; furthermore, the equality rule might be temporarily disregarded in emergency cases, or in matters of vital interest—a dangerous exception owing to the elastic nature of these phrases.

Already in 1919 the Treaty of Versailles had afforded to Czechoslovakia, a landlocked state, the privilege of free ports at Hamburg and Stettin; Germany was to lease to Czechoslovakia "areas which shall be placed under the general regime of free zones and shall be used for the direct transit of goods." The Maritime Ports statute clarified certain matters connected with this area.

A problem which may not at first sight seem important concerns the different methods of measuring the cargo capacity of vessels. Taxes or dues paid by a ship varied according to the system of measurement adopted by various ports; and many disputes arose in consequence. The Communications and Transit Organization of the League appointed a technical committee to examine the rules which were in force. After some effort the committee, in 1931, drew up a set of regulations. As to it McClure well remarks:

[8] Wallace McClure, *op. cit.*, p. 424.

Real saving would result from their acceptance by all maritime states, not the least element of which would be the avoidance of disputes growing out of different tonnages in use for the same ship, which thus may pay on different bases at each of the ports it visits. The wide utilization of the British rules has shown how necessary is internationalism in this seemingly small and technical, but by no means to be despised, detail in the vast complex of world economy.[9]

SHIPPING POLICY

Shipping has been an international problem for several hundred years, and the reason is obvious. The mercantile marine provides the means of carrying on commerce and is thus an economic agency of the first importance; it is necessary for carrying troops and supplies in wartime and therefore forms a vital element in national defense. The English Navigation Acts, which began in 1651, had as their object the building up of a strong merchant fleet in order (1) to provide a link between the mother country and the colonies, (2) to insure a means of defense in wartime, and (3) to enable England to develop as a distributing center and engage in a profitable carrying trade. Whether because of these Navigation Acts or not (economic historians are not agreed), British merchant shipping made great progress after the seventeenth century; it outstripped Dutch and French competitors, both of which were destroyed during the Napoleonic Wars. The industrial revolution in Britain led to a demand for cheaper freight rates, and the navigation laws were at first modified by the signing of reciprocity treaties concerning shipping and were then repealed between 1849 and 1854.[10] British ports and British sea trade were henceforth open to the ships of all nations. For the next thirty or forty years there was little or no state control over the mercantile marine; the period was one of tremendous expansion and of technical revolution in ocean transport. The iron steamship, the compound engine, the opening of the Suez Canal, the use of steel, and the growth of specialization of shipping whereby vessels were specially built to carry frozen meat, oil, fruit, and other products, combined to give merchant shipping a great impetus. Because of the amazing growth of its manufactures and agriculture which followed the scientific and industrial revolutions, Great Britain took

[9] Wallace McClure, *op. cit.,* p. 430. See League of Nations Organisation for Communications and Transit, *Draft Regulations for Tonnage Measurement of Ships,* C.176.M.65.1931, VIII; and *Report to the Advisory and Technical Committee,* C4.M4.1936, VIII.

[10] H. Heaton, *Modern Economic History* (The Macmillan Company, Ltd., Melbourne, 1925), p. 154.

the lead in the shipping life of the world. It was a lead built up mainly by private enterprise. The government gave subsidies to a few companies in order to insure that mails would be carried on the fastest ships; but only about 3 per cent of the vessels received this form of assistance. The private companies did not need government aid, because the one rival, the United States, which might have been a serious competitor, had dropped behind in the race. The American Civil War had adversely affected American shipping; the decline of wooden ships occurred before America had acquired the engineering skill to perfect the new type of iron and steel vessels; and the years following the Civil War witnessed the expansion to the West and a great industrial development which absorbed much of the nation's energy. Hence Great Britain stood unchallenged for the time, and her remarkable shipping developments helped to build up and consolidate the new British Empire, which was drawn closer in trade relations by the new transportation facilities and cheap freight rates.

The other nations did not view the British good fortune without a feeling of envy. The political condition of Europe and its growing emphasis upon nationalism added to the desire of governments to free themselves from a dependence upon British shipping. These governments developed industry by the use of tariffs and then assisted shipping by granting subsidies. The great battle of subsidized shipping had begun. For about thirty years before the World War, the competition grew more intense, and official subsidies took increasingly varied forms. Governments granted mail subsidies to companies and paid larger sums than the actual services rendered by the companies warranted. They reserved their own coastal shipping for their national vessels, gave loans at low rates of interest to shipping companies, and permitted materials for use in shipbuilding to be imported at low rates of duty or to be carried over railroad lines at unusually favorable charges. These and other forms of assistance enabled the shipping companies to indulge in price cutting. The practice of subsidization grew rapidly. Mrs. Knowles states:

France started this elaborate bounty system in 1881 and was followed in 1885 by Germany, Italy, Austria, Hungary, Japan, Russia, Denmark, Spain, Belgium, and the United States, all of whom adopted some of these forms of State encouragement to national mercantile marines and they were still in force in 1914.[11]

[11] L. C. A. Knowles, *Industrial and Commercial Revolutions in Great Britain during the Nineteenth Century* (E. P. Dutton & Co.), p. 305.

Companies set out to build better and faster ships, and between 1912 and 1914 Britain and Germany competed in such luxury liners as the "Lusitania," the "Mauretania," the "Imperator," the "Vaterland," the "Bismarck," the "Olympic," and the "Titanic." Germany made great progress, because it could concentrate much of its shipping in two ports, Hamburg and Bremen, where the import and export cargoes were well balanced and involved little uneconomic sailing; and because Germany's rapid advance in the iron and steel industries gave the shipping companies large supplies of low-priced raw materials.

The keen international competition brought the inevitable result—a great fall in freight rates, heavy losses to the companies, and a period of extreme uncertainty for the whole industry. It became, as Mrs. Knowles put it, "a sheer gamble." In order to offset the losses, companies formed combinations and met in conferences. Their actions took both a national and an international form. Some national lines, closely tied to the national state, agreed to stabilize their rates and bring some kind of order out of the confusion. They held conferences which divided the shipping trade into various spheres of influence. These understandings managed to obviate the more extreme fluctuations and the worst effects of the uneconomic cutthroat competition. But national arrangements did not suffice, and a number of international arrangements developed by which British and German lines apportioned the shipping routes, each national line retaining a given area in which the other would not compete. Agreements concerning timetables, passenger rates, interchangeability of tickets, etc., were common in days of peace.

Between 1900 and 1914 world shipping increased from 29,-000,000 tons to 49,000,000 tons, a remarkable development in a relatively short period of time, and one which will largely explain the unstable condition of world shipping.

The World War of 1914–1918 had disastrous consequences for the merchant marine. During that period about 12,500,000 tons were destroyed; but so efficient and determined were the national building programs that by 1920 the world possessed 57,000,000 tons. Meanwhile a new international realignment of forces had appeared: The United States, which had possessed less than 3,000,000 tons in 1900 and somewhat more than 5,000,000 tons in 1914, by 1920 had over 16,000,000 tons. Japan also had increased her tonnage, but to a lesser extent. And the stage was set for another great international shipping race. Substantially the same results appeared as had occurred in prewar days, and in 1933 the world saw the shipping industry with a capacity of 68,000,000 tons facing a world economic depression and a shrunken international trade. The inevitable consequence followed, and nearly 11,500,000 tons of vessels were rendered idle.

The question arises: Why did the nations, with the experience of the prewar days to guide them, follow the same policies even more intensely, when it must have been evident that these policies would lead to similar conditions of cutthroat competition, low freight rates, and bankruptcies? In order to find an answer it will be necessary to analyze the extent of, and the reasons for, national shipping policies.

Nations desire to possess mercantile marines for a number of reasons: By carrying goods, ships add to the national income, although the direct amount received for this service is a very small item compared with the total national dividend of most nations. An efficient mercantile marine assists a country in its foreign trade. The United States found that its trading opportunities with South America were more limited when it was dependent upon British shipping, because materials from certain ports in the United States could not be carried direct to their South American destinations; owing to the necessity of transshipment, time was lost and freight costs were heightened, and the American exporter consequently suffered in business competition with his British rival. When international competition tends to become keener, and the amount of profit narrower, direct contact with a market may constitute a decisive element. Moreover, the agents of a shipping line at the foreign end do their best to stimulate the foreign demand for the goods of their own country, because they realize that the prosperity of their merchant fleet depends upon adequate cargo and passengers. Shipping representatives thus tend to become important commercial agents.

The charge is sometimes made that foreign nations have discriminated against the ships of another country; but the United States Maritime Commission in 1937 found that Americans, at least, had not, in a highly competitive age, suffered substantially from discrimination. The Commission added that "the trend toward nationalized shipping may increase the potentialities of discrimination in the future—a consideration that should not be ignored," and that a national fleet would enable a country to engage in retaliatory action in case of discrimination against its own shipping.

It is important for a country to maintain continuity of its economic life and to guard against any interruption of transportation services. If war breaks out, the merchant ships of combatants will be required for war purposes, and the economic life of the neutral powers may suffer severely in consequence. But neutrals are anxious to maintain as much of their normal trade as possible; if they are dependent upon the merchant ships of the belligerents they may be unable to ship their goods abroad. The United States had this experience during the World War of 1914–1918 when "the withdrawal of alien vessels resulted in a serious dislocation of our foreign trade at a time when we enjoyed an unprecedented opportunity to expand our business with other nations." Referring to this, the Maritime Commission has recently stated:

Today we are faced with the threat of a recurrence of the conditions of the last war. Political uncertainty and international tension are on the increase. If the present antagonisms should result in war, we would be confronted again with the problems which beset our commerce in 1914. The disruption of our trade probably would be much greater in the future, as a larger percentage of our trade is now being transacted with nations not having their own shipping facilities.

A large mercantile marine may therefore be an insurance, and the extra cost of maintaining a merchant fleet greater than is required for normal commerce may be justified on this ground.

Another reason for merchant shipping remains to be analyzed, i.e., its importance in time of war; for a navy is impotent without a supporting mercantile marine. The Maritime Commission estimated that the United States, in the event of war with a major power, would require at least 1,000 merchant ships aggregating about six million gross tons for transportation purposes. In 1937 there were more than that number available, although most of them were relatively old and slow and the merchant marine was deficient in tankers and rapid vessels suitable for troops transport. The services which a merchant marine can render in wartime cannot receive detailed attention here; but the question arises whether or not a merchant fleet which is adequate for wartime needs can be profitably employed in normal periods of peace. Will not many of the vessels remain idle or have to be run at a loss? The Maritime Commission has admitted that national defense requirements increase both the construction and the operating costs of vessels, but believed that the nation should be informed how much of the expenditures were for reasons of defense and how much for normal economic pursuits. The point is well taken; nations should clearly distinguish the functions, defensive and economic, of a merchant marine, and should realize that the more politically disorganized the world is the more will the normal requirements of peacetime economic agencies be distorted.

We have already seen that, as a result of the World War of 1914–1918 and the great building programs of the postwar period, there were 67,000,000 tons of shipping in the world in 1933, of which nearly 11,500,000 tons lay idle. The world had an excess of shipping facilities, and ocean freight rates were so depressed as to make shipping a most unprofitable venture. The shipping companies appealed for government aid, and subsidies grew still more numerous. Countries which had hitherto given little governmental assistance joined in the subsidization race. From a short-term nationalist viewpoint subsidies were urgent if national shipping was not to be ruined by subsidized foreign competition. But the combined effect of well-nigh universal subsidization was to stimulate a worldwide uneconomic competition, which found expression in larger and more luxurious liners, on the one hand, and in cutthroat competitive rates, on the other. The vicious shipping circle cannot be broken by intensifying subsidies on all sides; this policy can lead only to progressively heavier burdens for taxpayers everywhere and further disorganization of international shipping.

The problem is rendered more serious by two other factors: the intensified economic nationalism, and the high protective tariffs which are a common feature of today. The result of the attempt by governments to reduce their dependence upon foreign trade, combined with subsidized encouragement to greater merchant fleets to carry the lessened amount of goods internationally exchanged, must be obvious. There is a downright contradiction between tariff policies designed to curtail international trade and an expanding merchant marine policy which for its profitable use requires an increased foreign trade. The contradiction becomes even more obvious if we remember that a tariff is a type of subsidy. Manufacturers at home receive tariff protection at the cost of the taxpayer in order that they may keep foreign goods out; the shipping company receives subsidies to carry more goods abroad which can be paid for only by receiving gold or goods or services from abroad!

We thus see that the question of subsidized merchant shipping is closely connected with the question of balance of payments. If the United States, a creditor country, desires repayment for its exports, it should not make the task of the debtors overburdensome by imposing high tariffs and by participating over-heavily in the shipping trade, so that other countries which can build and operate ships more cheaply cannot use their shipping services to help repay their debts.

Subsidized shipping, like tariffs, if carried beyond a certain point, results in keeping inefficient companies in existence, tends to promote wastefulness and extravagance, and adds to the burden of the taxpayer. The growing intensity of subsidized international competition leads to an aggravation of the condition of merchant shipping throughout the world; and before 1939 a French authority feared that nothing would be able to "save the fleets of commerce from complete general bankruptcy now approaching."[12]

The system of subsidies has received criticism at the hands of various bodies. In its final report the Trade Barriers Committee of the International Chamber of Commerce, in 1927, considered "the continuance of the wide-spread practice of subsidizing shipping to be undesirable as introducing an uneconomic element into business and disturbing markets," but recognized that this objection did not apply to payments by governments to shipping companies at a prevailing transportation rate for services actually rendered. The economic experts who drew up the program for the 1933 World Economic Conference stated:

In the case of shipping, the most urgent questions arise in connection with direct or indirect subsidies to national mercantile marines and premiums on national shipbuilding. This policy has certainly contributed towards the creation and maintenance of much greater tonnage than is required by existing international trade, so that in many countries shipping has become a burden on the national economy instead of a contribution to its prosperity.

We agree with the meeting of shipowners recently held at the International Chamber of Commerce that it is impossible to return to sound conditions in the shipping industry so long as the uneconomic policy of government subsidies continues. This policy of excessive intervention requires to be checked by agreement between the governments. At the same time, certain possibilities of agreement might be

---

[12] *Foreign Policy Report,* "Ship Subsidies and the Future of World Shipping," March 14, 1934; see also *League of Nations Publications VIII, Transit 1934,* for a description of the increase in tonnage, the decrease in sea-borne goods and passenger traffic, and the fall in freights in the years 1929–1934, with the consequent loss of profits and the laying-up and scrapping of part of the surplus tonnage. The report considers many proposals for international action, some of which are considered here.

considered with regard to the scrapping of old tonnage, the utilization of existing tonnage and the laying down of new ships.

At the Conference Great Britain proposed that governments should move as quickly as possible toward the ultimate abolition of state assistance to shipbuilding. Norway, Holland, Sweden, and Denmark took a similar stand. But the United States argued that the term "uneconomic subsidies" was too vague, that subsidies could not be considered the only cause of the crisis in shipping, and that it was important for the United States to have its own merchant marine.

The *Foreign Policy Report* of March 1934 well remarks that it may not be feasible to tackle the subsidy question directly, because government assistance takes so many forms. These complexities would make it extremely difficult to draw up "an international agreement sufficiently comprehensive." One of the basic troubles is that shipping is as much a political as it is an economic matter, and that, while the danger of war exists, it will be impossible to treat shipping merely as an economic problem. Until international organization has guaranteed adequate security, nations will be unable to think in terms of economic efficiency and welfare alone; they will sacrifice lower costs to considerations of safety; and as in the case of sugar and other raw materials, so in shipping, unsubsidized or modestly supported organizations will be driven out by the overwhelming pressure of more heavily subsidized foreign competition. One may say, then, that the future of the world's shipping depends upon the solution of the problem of war.

If such a solution is found, it will not necessarily cause the abandonment of all subsidies. There will then be less need for defense, but undoubtedly shipping companies will continue to exercise pressure for government assistance, just as is the case today with tariffs; and, in any case, the bewilderingly complex forms of subsidies will make their abolition extremely difficult. The *Foreign Policy Report* suggests that it might be desirable to plan shipping on an international scale in such a manner as to "assure to every one of the chief maritime powers a fair proportion of the world's shipping, while leaving each free to grant such subsidies as it deems necessary for the maintenance of its share." Such a scheme would tend to cause freight rates to rise, because it would eliminate the surplus tonnage which has forced freight rates to an abnormally low and unremunerative figure.

The French government recently proposed that there should be international agreements to limit future construction, a joint operation of vessels sailing the great ocean routes, and a joint account to cover the whole of the working receipts and expenditures. The proposal would carry farther the present practice of steamship companies which hold rate-fixing conferences but which by themselves cannot guarantee that competition of outsiders and internal disputes may not seriously upset the agreements reached. John C. De Wilde, in the *Foreign Policy Report* already referred to, has admirably summarized the situation as follows:

Furthermore, no conference can tackle the fundamental problem of surplus tonnage and the competitive building of bigger and faster liners unless assured that rational scrapping and replacement programs would meet with almost universal adoption. Intergovernmental action might make this possible. The governments of the countries interested in each trade route covered by a steamship conference might call on the lines serving the route to draw up agreements on freight rates, sailings, the scrapping and replacement of old vessels and, possibly, division of the traffic. If these agreements meet with approval, the governments concerned could guarantee them against infringement.

Before effective planning through steamship conferences can be carried out, some way of fitting tramp shipping into the scheme must be devised. Tramp vessels do not operate on regular routes, but are available for the carriage of bulk cargo to any part of the world. They perform a particularly useful economic function in supplementing regular line services during seasonal freight movements. A separate international arrangement applying to tramp shipping would therefore be necessary. Presumably such an agreement would need to provide for the scrapping of old and excess tonnage and to regulate the conditions on which "tramps" could operate on conference routes.

The technical and political obstacles to the conclusion of international shipping conventions are many. Yet there is widespread conviction that a determined attempt must be made to overcome them. The alternative is the continuation and aggravation of the nationalist policies and wasteful competition which have long been the bane of world shipping.

The present war has resulted in a shortage of shipping, and a great building program has therefore been devised in an effort to supply Great Britain with the materials which she so desperately needs. Undoubtedly shipping losses will be heavy owing to airplane and submarine attacks, and for purposes of winning the war an expanded shipbuilding program is undoubtedly needed, particularly in view of the obsolescence and obsoleteness of many of the American ships. But it should be remembered that the world merchant marine was about fifty per cent larger in 1939 than it was in 1914, that merchant vessels had an increased speed of about twenty per cent, and that improved loading and unloading facilities further added to the carrying capacity, with the result that peacetime shipping exceeded what was normally required by nearly three million tons.

Unless some international shipping agreement is made at the conclusion of the present war, the world may expect to witness for the third time in this century an excess of shipping capacity, cutthroat competition, and demands for national subsidies, with the necessary consequence of idle tonnage and added burdens to the taxpayer. Until the fear of war has been eliminated, a considerable amount of uneconomic tonnage must be kept in reserve as part of the price of security; and it would seem reasonable to expect that, with increased airplane and submarine efficiency, the nations of the world will be compelled to increase, rather than decrease, the amount of reserve shipping for emergency war use. The contradictions between peacetime and wartime shipping requirements will become greater, unless a sound world political system obviates the need of excess merchant ships required for "security" purposes. If we are to continue to live in a war world, shipping will become primarily a political problem, with the merchant marine regarded as essentially an instrument of defense; if a stable international political organization emerges, shipping problems may be treated as being fundamentally economic in character.

INTERNATIONAL RIVERS

If the doctrine of national sovereignty were strictly carried out, rivers flowing through more than one country would be subject to several exclusively national jurisdictions. It can be imagined that country A, having control over the mouth of a river, might prohibit the passage of goods from country B through its section. Country A, moreover, need not take such drastic action in order to place serious obstacles in the way of international commerce. If it were inefficient and neglectful, and permitted the river to silt up, or did not erect adequate wharving facilities, or charged onerous transit duties, it could seriously affect commerce, and produce international friction. With the growth of modern trade, countries have realized that some rivers possess so great an importance that exclusive national control is no longer consistent with general international welfare.

Grotius held that the use of rivers should be free; and from the early seventeenth century bilateral treaties which opened certain rivers to both contracting parties became increasingly common; but it was not until the Treaty of Paris in 1814 that nations made the first general declaration of freedom of international rivers. For forty years riparian states used international rivers freely; nevertheless, there still remained a strong tendency to exclude the nonriparian states. The Treaty of Paris in 1856 extended the principle of liberty and equality to the Danube, and set up the European Danube Commission comprising representatives of both riparian and nonriparian states. A treaty between riparian states at Dresden in 1821 had already opened the Elbe to general commercial navigation, and the Rhine in 1868 was thrown open to international traffic. The General Act of Berlin, in 1885, guaranteed free navigation of the Congo, the Niger, and affluent rivers, and these provisions were applied by Great Britain and Portugal to the Zambesi River in 1891. By the end of the nineteenth century the right of free navigation extended to most of the great waterways of Africa.

The United States urged that in South America the Amazon River be opened to foreign vessels; but Brazil opposed the suggestion for several years, and not until 1867 did it open the river to all nations. In fact Bolivia obtained the right of river passage across Brazilian territory only in 1903. In 1852 Argentina opened the Rio de la Plata system to all nations; Uruguay and Paraguay took similar action in the following year.

These examples—which do not give the whole list of internationalized rivers—show that the forces of modern commerce were instrumental in modifying the exclusive and impeding claims of national sovereignty.

The Danube.—The European Danube Commission is the greatest example of international organization to improve river traffic. Between 1829 and 1854 Russia controlled the mouth of the Danube. Owing to her neglect, navigators found this section of the river extremely dangerous. After the Crimean War, the great powers, believing that Turkey would be equally incompetent, decided to extend the principle of free navigation to the Danube and set up a European Commission for the purpose of making it a safe and navigable waterway. Great Britain, France, Austria, Rumania, Sardinia, and Turkey each had one representative on the Commission, which was empowered to levy dues on boats using the river. The Commission could determine the amount of the dues by majority vote, but was required to guarantee equality of treatment to all nations. Its first major task was primarily an engineering one, that of dredging to improve the navigability of the Danube. Subsequently a second commission, with representatives from only the riparian states, was set up to introduce regulations for the whole of the river. This second commission, however, broke down through attempting to levy excessive tolls and to exclude nonriparian ships. But the European Commission continued to function and by an agreement in 1865–66 obtained authority to erect further permanent works along the lower Danube, as well as to establish navigation rules. In 1865 the powers agreed to confer the status of neutralization on the works constructed by the Commission, in order to prevent their confiscation or destruction by belligerent nations in time of war. In 1871 the administrative and technical personnel also came under the status of neutralization. Three years earlier the powers had agreed to permit the Commission to borrow funds, and most of them guaranteed loans which it floated. In 1878 the Commission's authority was extended to Galatz, and five years later to Braila. In 1882 it was given a special flag, and its employees wore a distinctive armband.[13]

Writers pay tribute to the successful work of the Commission. Before it came into existence the Danube was a difficult and dangerous river with shoals and sandbars which made navigation extremely hazardous. Under the new authority, the river was deepened, wrecks were reduced, lighthouses built, floating elevators erected, and pilot and police services made more efficient. Interestingly enough, these improvements coincided with a decline in the amount of dues which vessels were required to pay.

The Commission had wide powers. It fixed the navigation duties and collected them and expended hundreds of thousands of dollars annually. A large amount of Danubian navigation was under its control, and governments had no right to interfere; it licensed tugs, lighters, and pilots, appointed and controlled its many employees, and maintained two hospitals. It exercised judicial or quasi-judicial powers, and could impose fines for breaches of its regulations. But, as Chamberlain points out, the Commission, in spite of its extensive powers, was "not an example of an

[13] F. B. Sayre, *Experiments in International Administration* (1919).

independent international body acting on its own initiative in important matters."[14] It could not punish crimes or hear civil suits for damages. Only Rumanian policemen might board ships and arrest criminals; only Rumanian police courts might punish them for crime or try civil cases. The Commission had "no police force of its own, but depends upon the guard ships which the Powers represented in the commission are authorized to keep at the mouth of the Danube."[15] Its members might be removed at any time if their governments so wished, and the matters to be considered at their semi-annual meetings were communicated to each commissioner, "thus giving the Governments an opportunity to instruct their commissioners in case of need."[16]

At the conclusion of the World War of 1914–1918 the Allied Powers made provision for the regulation of the Danube in Articles 331 and 347 of the Treaty of Versailles. The European Commission resumed its prewar powers, with British, French, Italian, and Rumanian representatives provisionally constituting the Commission. International regulation was extended to Ulm, and by Article 347 a new international commission with headquarters at Bratislava was given charge of that part of the Danube not under the control of the European Commission. Several difficult questions arose concerning the respective competences of the two commissions, as well as of the Rumanian government. The question was submitted to the Permanent Court of International Justice, which gave a decision affirming the wide authority of the international commissions as against the national claims of Rumania.

The League Committee for Communications and Transit appointed Mr. W. D. Hines to report on navigation questions of the Danube. The report, which appeared in 1925, discussed the history and administration of that river and contained proposals for co-ordinating river and railroad transportation. Mr. Hines stressed that an outstanding need for the improvement of the Danubian system was the investment of capital at reasonable rates for both public and private purposes, and noted that until international friction was lessened foreign capital would not be attracted to the area. The international political situation was here once more found to be an obstacle to the promotion of general human welfare. At the moment of writing, the international

[14] J. P. Chamberlain, *The Regime of the International Rivers; Danube and Rhine* (Columbia University Press, 1923), p. 98.

[15] *Ibid.*, p. 96.   [16] *Ibid.*, p. 97.

machinery has been discarded and replaced by a German-dominated Commission.

The Rhine.—The Rhine is another great international river. Until 1814 a large number of local arrangements were made, but at the Congress of Vienna the principle that international rivers should be administered in the interests of international commerce was enunciated. A Rhine Commission was established to put these principles into practice along this waterway. Changes were made in 1831 and 1869, but in general it may be said that the Commission comprised one member from each state along the river and that each state had one vote—except that in certain administrative and technical matters votes were given according to the length of the river which passed through each state. The Commission developed navigation facilities and special courts for interpreting the regulations which were adopted. Appeals were possible to a court in each Rhine state, or to the Commission.

After 1918 the Allied Powers changed the constitution of the Commission to include four French members and a French chairman. Chamberlain criticizes the latter appointment, and suggests that French interests in the Rhine were so far overshadowed by German and Dutch interests that no valid reason existed for giving France undue representation.

Mr. W. D. Hines also reported for the League on Rhine navigation, and found that certain obstacles to traffic had developed because of a French tax on goods which were subject to rebate in case the cargoes went through Antwerp. This provision involved discrimination against Rotterdam and other ports. German customs authorities were alleged to have discriminated against French traders who used a certain warehouse at Cologne. But the most serious question arose from competition between railways and river vessels. The League committee considered the problem and made a number of recommendations concerning this question, including the interesting proposal that the ports, railroads, and waterways of a country should be placed under a single governmental authority in order that a harmonious development of communications could be effected.

Other Rivers (German).—By Article 331 of the Treaty of Versailles, the Elbe, the Oder, and the Niemen were declared to be international rivers. International commissions were established for them. Unfortunately Germany had sufficient ground for believing that political feeling as well as the desire for efficiency in transport dictated this step, and in 1936 Hitler denounced the arrangements and proclaimed Germany free from the hated foreign domination.

The Scheldt.—The problem of the river Scheldt has exercised the statesmen of Western Europe for a considerable length of time. The 1814 Treaty of Paris provided for the freedom of navigation of the Scheldt; after a troubled period a conference of five powers met in 1831 and drew up rules providing for the joint supervision by Belgium and Holland of the pilotage and buoying of the estuary.

Because the navigable channel shifts, the bottom must be constantly dredged and the sandbanks removed. By a treaty signed in 1839 the two nations agreed that each should control its own part of the river, but certain provisions were inserted to safeguard Belgium's navigation interests in the stretch from Antwerp to the sea which was under Dutch sovereignty. Belgium claimed that the safeguards were inadequate and continually requested Holland to undertake the engineering works necessary to keep the channel open. The competition between the two cities, Antwerp and Rotterdam, added to the complexities of the problem, and until the World War of 1914–1918 the question of the Scheldt remained a source of irritation to Dutch-Belgian relations.

In 1919–20 representatives of the two countries met at Paris and devised a scheme by which the river was to be kept in suitable condition for navigation by a commission composed of equal numbers of Belgian and Dutch members. This commission was to make rules for navigation; in emergency it might make decisions without referring to the respective governments; in other cases, the governments must approve or reject its decisions within two months; and if the commission or the governments should disagree, the matter must be referred to an arbitrating body. In urgent cases three referees were to give decision within one week. Thus a type of international control was envisioned. However, the treaty remained unratified owing to unbridgeable differences: (a) the dispute as to whether the Wielingen Channel is part of Belgian territorial waters or "part of the estuary of the Scheldt and therefore subject to the sovereignty of Holland" continued;[17] (b) the fear persisted that Antwerp might gain at the expense of Rotterdam; (c) complicated questions over canal construction in neighboring parts of Holland and Belgium did not help to simplify this particular problem. Pintor observes that there is much

[17] G. W. T. Omond, "The Scheldt and the Wielingen," *Transactions of the Grotius Society,* 1921, p. 87.

to be said on both sides, but it would seem that the establishment of an international commission with adequate authority would benefit the two countries.

The Peace Treaties.—The 1919 Peace Conference followed the precedent established in 1814, and drew up a number of general principles regarding river transportation. Article 23 of the League Covenant provided that League members would take steps toward greater freedom of communications and transit. Pintor[18] claims that the Treaty of Versailles constituted a remarkable step forward in acknowledging the principle of freedom of river navigation and asserting the interests of the international community as against those of the sovereign states. McClure suggests that the attitude of the French prevented the adoption of the "liberal and far-reaching proposals" of Great Britain for freedom of communications, and that, while exacting this policy from the enemy powers, they were unwilling to "bind themselves to grant on their part similar rights either to friend or former foe."[19]

The League of Nations summoned a General Conference on Communications and Transit to meet at Barcelona in March 1921. The Conference laid down special rules for the Danube River, but its larger task was to lay down more general rules for river and other forms of communication. The problems were not easy. Much time was consumed in discussing what constituted an international waterway, and finally for the term was substituted the phrase, "waterways of international concern"—a change which Pintor believes marked the triumph of the nationalist over the internationalist viewpoint.[20] The states through which rivers passed desired to minimize the amount of international control, fearing that they would be forced to expend overburdensome amounts in keeping the navigable channel open for traffic. "It was necessary therefore to work out a formula under which such states could demand contributions from other riparians towards the upkeep or construction of works, or other riparians even demand the right to undertake such works at their own expense."[21] Conflicting interests manifested themselves—irrigation against transport, and hydroelectric power against the others. States demanded that their own sub-

[18] M. S. Pintor, "Le Régime International de L'Escaut," *Académie de Droit International, Recueil des Cours,* Vol. XXI (1928), pp. 320–21.

[19] Wallace McClure, *op. cit.,* p. 80.   [20] Pintor, *op. cit.,* p. 324.

[21] G. E. Toulmin, "The Barcelona Conference on Communications and Transit and the Danube Statute," *The British Yearbook of International Law,* 1922–23, p. 176.

jects enjoy the exclusive right of *petit cabotage,* i.e., intra-national transport of passengers' goods. Moreover, states claimed the right to object to the building of works on rivers if they threatened "vital interests"—an exception which destroys much of the value of the convention, in the opinion of H. A. Smith, who points out that very few states have ratified the convention. It therefore would appear, he writes, that the convention is not "a very valuable contribution to the general body of international law, either upon the problem of navigation rights or in connection with the other uses of rivers."[22] A somewhat more favorable estimate is made by G. E. Toulmin, who suggests that the general Barcelona Conventions constitute "a respectable if unambitious code to govern commercial movements throughout the world." And "hedged around by compromise and conditions, the right of navigation of vessels of all flags is safely guaranteed, though the task of simplifying the Statute will be a worthy object to which future generations of international lawyers may devote themselves."[23]

It is important to note that rivers serve many other purposes as well as that of transportation, and statesmen must harmonize the interests of irrigation, hydroelectric power, fisheries, public health (problems arising from the pollution of waters), and navigation. Rather than attempt a survey of even a relatively few of the international bodies which have been established to deal with these questions, it will be preferable here to concentrate attention upon an outstanding example, in order to show the methods employed and the possibilities of this type of international government. The example selected is that of the International Joint Commission established by the United States and Canada in 1909.

We may note in passing that an international technical commission has been doing admirable work in allocating the waters of the Nile River in such a manner as to afford the maximum benefit to the Sudan and to Egypt. H. A. Smith lists about fifty bilateral and multilateral treaties, some of them more successful than others, which deal with joint proposals, and methods adopted, to permit co-operation in matters of irrigation, power, transportation, etc., affecting more than one state.[24]

The International Joint Commission of Canada and the United States.—This Commission was established by the 1909

---

[22] H. A. Smith, *The Economic Uses of International Rivers* (P. S. King & Son, London, 1931), p. 192.

[23] G. E. Toulmin, *op. cit.,* pp. 177, 178.

[24] H. A. Smith, *op. cit.*

Treaty (ratified in 1911), which provided that the navigation of all navigable boundary waters shall be free and open to both parties; this right extends to the waters of Lake Michigan and all canals connecting boundary waters. Each country maintains its jurisdiction and control within its territory over the use and diversion of waters flowing across the boundary or into boundary waters; however, should any action within the United States or Canada injuriously affect the welfare of citizens in the other country, remedies are provided; for Canadians may seek redress in the courts of the United States, and United States residents may appeal to the courts of Canada. In this way international co-operation sets up more adequate machinery in order to protect private rights. Any diversions of boundary waters or obstructions or uses, must have the approval of the International Joint Commission. Both countries agree not to permit the construction or maintenance, on their respective sides of the boundary, of any remedial or protective works which would affect the natural level of waters on the other side, unless with the approval of the Commission. Provision is also made for prohibiting pollution of boundary waters and waters flowing across the boundary. Diversion of water from the Niagara River above the Falls is permitted at the rate of 20,000 cubic feet per second for the United States and 36,000 cubic feet per second for Canada. The St. Mary and Milk rivers, which rise in Montana and flow across the boundary into Alberta, the latter returning to Montana after about one hundred miles, are to be treated as one stream for purposes of irrigation and power, and the waters are to be apportioned equally. An International Joint Commission of six members, three from each country, is appointed. Jurisdiction is conferred on the Commission to act in cases arising under Articles III and IV. The Commission in considering the allocation of water is to consider public needs in the following order: Public Health, Navigation, Power, and Irrigation.

Questions involving rights, obligations, or interests, or inhabitants along the common frontier may be referred to the Commission, which is authorized to report on such questions; but the reports shall not be regarded as decisions. Any question of difference between Canada and the United States may be referred to the Joint Commission. The governments have not, in practice, utilized this article, which could be invoked to cover a wide field of disputes.

The Commission of six members has its permanent offices at

Ottawa and Washington; the two secretaries act as joint secretaries of the Commission when it sits in joint session. Regular sessions are held at Washington in April and at Ottawa in October; and provision is made for special meetings when necessary. A majority of the Commission may undertake hearings; but all the Commission must be present in order to give a final conclusion in any matter or proceeding. Neither section can act independently of the other. The Commission, of course, acts only when the United States or Canadian governments submit complaints or requests, either on their own behalf or on behalf of individual or corporate interests.

The Commission has dealt with a wide range of problems, of which some are here given. Furthermore, it considered the possible injury to settlers in Idaho upon an application in 1927 from the Creston Reclamation Company for permission to construct certain permanent works in the channel of the Kootenay River, which begins in British Columbia and flows south into the state of Idaho. It dealt with the setting up of rules concerning the establishment of gauging stations for portions of water from the St. Mary's and the Milk River to be delivered to each party during particular seasons; and it recommended a joint irrigation scheme to be constructed partly in the United States and partly in Canada. An application from the Greater Winnipeg Water District in 1913 to divert for domestic and sanitary purposes waters from the Shoal Lake was approved to the extent of 100,000 gallons per day, in order to meet the needs of the Winnipeg District without injury to navigation and power interests on the Lake of the Woods and the Winnipeg River.

As regards the Lake of the Woods:

In June 1912, the two governments requested the Commission to investigate and report upon certain questions relating to the levels and overflow of this Lake through which the international boundary passes. As a great many interests, national and international, were affected, including those of navigation, agriculture, forestry, fisheries, and waterpower, the matter was gone into with unusual care. The Commission submitted its report in 1917, recommending certain levels which it was believed would best serve all the interests concerned in both countries. Provision was made for an International Board of Control, and also for a Domestic Board to look after purely Canadian interests. At the request of the two governments, the Commission drafted a treaty which was subsequently signed and put into operation.

The Commission investigated questions relating to the levels of Rainy Lake. St. Mary's River, which connects Lake Superior with Lake Huron, is the outlet of Lake Superior, some 34,000 square miles in extent. Congress and Canada had both authorized certain diversions for power purposes. Since many conflicting interests were affected, the Commission held hearings in 1913, and then ordered diversion of waters for power purposes and compensatory works to safeguard the interests of navigation. The whole scheme was placed under an international board of engineers, which reported periodically to the Commission.

In 1912–13 the Commission investigated projected works in the Livingston Channel in the Detroit River to "prevent cross currents dangerous to navigation." The two governments agreed to widen the channel and to guard the levels of the waters. In December 1916 the United States government applied to the Commission "for approval of the dredging of the channel in the St. Clair River near the town of Port Huron, Michigan." Approval was granted on condition that a submerged weir be constructed. (The St. Clair River connects Lake Huron and Lake St. Clair.)

An extensive investigation on the extent and causes of the pollution of boundary waters occupied the Commission for about six years. It was perhaps the most thorough search of its kind ever attempted. The regulations concerning pollution of waters which it drew up were embodied in a draft treaty. The Commission presented a long report in December 1921 on the problem and possibilities of a St. Lawrence River navigation proposal. In 1925 it granted the application of the New Brunswick Electric Power Commission for authority to develop power at Grand Falls. In 1926 the St. John River Power Company, having taken over the rights of New Brunswick Electric Power Commission, sought and obtained authority to carry out the same work. As to the St. Croix River, the Commission approved an application made in 1914 for certain power works at Grand Falls, and in 1923 the state of Maine requested authority to erect and repair fishways in this river. The application was approved.

Other examples might be given. But these show that the Commission has had to regulate not merely traffic problems but also problems involving health, power, and conservation of waters. Its great significance lies in the fact that two nations have created an international body on which they are equally represented and to which they have transferred a considerable amount of authority. It is an instrument of government more in keeping with the modern needs of Canada and the United States than the old-fashioned method of treaty negotiations between sovereign powers could have been.

Summary.—H. A. Smith has suggested a number of principles which should govern the international law of rivers. The following summary is based upon his analysis: (1) Since every river system is an indivisible physical unit, it should be the duty of all governments concerned to co-operate as far as possible in developing the river to serve the whole community, however many political jurisdictions there may be, although no nation should be compelled to endanger its vital interests or to sacrifice its other interests without full compensation. (2) No state should take unilateral action to use the waters of an international river in such a way as to endanger the interests of another riparian state. (3) No state should oppose the action of another state in utilizing river waters unless its own interests are appreciably threatened. (4) If the interests of one state are greatly served, and of another state are only to a small extent injured, the latter should acquiesce in the project, subject to compensation. (5) If a proposed use of waters by one state threatens the vital and legitimate interests of another, the latter is justified in opposing the step; but "any difference as to the existence or nonexistence of such vital interests should be regarded as a justiciable dispute, suitable for arbitration, judicial settlement, or reference to the Council of the League of Nations." (6) Differences of a technical nature, if no direct agreement is possible, should be referred to competent technical international commissions. (7) If a river system is such that disputes are likely to be frequently permanent, international commissions should be constituted. (8) Disputes concerning the priority between navigation and other uses should be settled by reference to arbitration, judicial settlement, or the League Council. (9) All riparian states should consult freely and fully with each other.

These principles[25] in Smith's judgment do not imply that state sovereignty over its territories and waters in the territories is "in any way divided or qualified," or that other states have "any rights in the nature of servitudes," but only that states should not unilaterally exercise their sovereign power in an unfriendly and improper way.

To no small degree the International Transit and Communications Organization of the League and the Permanent Court and the League itself provide much of the machinery suggested by the principles just outlined. The Barcelona Convention of Navigable

[25] H. A. Smith, *op. cit.*, p. 152.

Waterways of International Concern, as we have seen, provides an unambitious statement of international law. Steps have been taken to unify river law and to unify tonnage measurement in inland navigation. The investigations of Mr. Hines and others have been of value in clarifying certain technical problems relating to the Danube and other navigable waterways of Poland. The advisory and technical committee of the Transit and Communications Organization acts as a conciliation body in disputes arising out of conventions. And this section of the League Secretariat acts as a continuing body to prepare for future conferences. Theoretically, a great advance has been made, but unfortunately some of the achievements still remain on paper, owing to many obstacles of a political and technical nature.

It is important not to swing to an opposite extreme and become unduly captivated by the concept of internationalization. J. P. Chamberlain utters a note of warning when he suggests that the opening of a river to vessels of all nationalities might not have entirely beneficial effects: "Whether freedom of river navigation to all flags is advisable depends on whether the practical value outweighs the consequent interference with the individual rights of the riparian states to regulate their interior navigation." He suggests that one should not draw an analogy between river and ocean traffic; that the open sea connects many countries, but that a river "is a pathway of trade only to the states bordering it and can be of interest only to them and the countries to which they traffic"; and that any undue extension of the rights of freedom of river navigation might involve excessive interference with the legitimate interests of national states.

LAND TRANSPORTATION

RAILROADS

The considerable amount of daily railroad traffic which takes place across national boundaries in time of peace necessitates much technical and political railroading co-operation in order to avoid delays and consequent financial loss. In a valuable article,[26] Ruth D. Masters shows how international co-operation has increased railroad efficiency in Europe, and has lessened some of the difficulties which a strict adherence to the doctrine of sovereignty would in-

---

[26] Ruth D. Masters, "International Organization of European Rail Transport," *International Conciliation*, May 1937. For a discussion of co-operation on the American continent see William J. Wilgus, *The Railway Interrelations of the United States and Canada* (Yale University Press, 1937).

volve. The following section, based upon her study, describes the situation as of 1937.

Europe is criss-crossed by political frontiers, and one wonders how the great network of European lines "could ever have been built, and, particularly, how railway services can function smoothly over it, when national frontiers seem to exist principally for the purpose of obstructing traffic in persons and goods." National states, supreme in their own borders, decide upon the directions and gauge of the lines, the organization of the companies, and the relations between carrier and public. They may even refuse to permit foreign trains to pass over their territory. And yet today "to the traveling public, Europe's railroads appear to act as if they were part of a single administrative unit." Were it not for frequent customs examinations and passport inspections, one would be little aware of frontiers. Not only do passengers move with relative ease, but "we may ship goods from Budapest to Stockholm on a single bill of lading which is in all essentials subject to a single code of law."

As Europe's economic life long ago expanded beyond the confines of national boundaries, hindrances to transport became a serious threat to her general welfare. Nevertheless, national states hugged their sovereignty; there was no guaranty that railroad lines would be built of the same width, or that rolling stock could be used on different lines. The fact that a single nation, England, constructed many of the continental lines in the early and middle nineteenth century made for some uniformity; but the possibility of different gauges, different rails, and unco-ordinated timetables increased with the growth of the number of independent states. Those who have known the inconvenience of changing trains can appreciate the immense importance of avoiding undue transshipment. But such an avoidance presupposes standardized equipment; if cars of one company or country are to run on the lines of another, the companies "must agree on uniform rules concerning compensation for the use of hired cars, liability of the railroads for damage to such cars, methods of tracing cars, etc."; in other words, "a considerable degree of technical and administrative unity is essential merely to eliminate the delays incident to transshipment."

Moreover, companies and countries, if they insist on an unqualified independence, will require a new bill of lading at every frontier; and this procedure is likely to cause considerable delay and expense.

The organization which did much to establish European railroad co-operation was the Association of German Railroads (VDEV) ; twenty-one Prussian railroad companies by June 1847 had formed a permanent union, which other lines joined later. Subsequent conferences drew up uniform rules relating to bills of lading, the division of freight receipts, and the payment of compensation for damages sustained by goods in transit. Tracks and rolling stock were standardized, and an 1850 Conference adopted "basic rules for the construction of German railroads, which dealt with the gauge, curves, rails, sleepers, minimum distance between double tracks, grade crossings, safety tracks, sidings and switches, the permanent way, construction and dimensions of locomotives, tenders and cars, safety devices, etc. It also submitted "uniform regulations for transit traffic" in which minimum technical conditions were laid down for cars in inter-VDEV traffic. The basic rules and the uniform regulations were subsequently combined in a single document, the "Technical Agreement of the VDEV for the Construction and Administration of Railroads"; this became binding on all members in 1867 and "served to insure technical uniformity of VDEV railroads."

In 1881, the members drew up a convention for the more effective interchange of railroad cars by standardizing railroad equipment, and "regulating the methods to be used to locate freight cars which were intended to pass custom barriers under seal." A 1907 conference appointed experts to study the problem of brakes on international freight trains, and devised "uniform specifications for the transverse dimensions of freight cars." A convention, "Technical Unity of Railroads, 1913 Text," at present applies to almost twenty European nations; it prescribes in detailed manner the rules which apply the principles just mentioned.

The benefits of co-operative action induced many railroad companies outside of the German Confederation to seek membership. At the outbreak of the war in 1914 the Association of German Railroads included most of the main lines in Germany, Austro-Hungary, Luxemburg, the Netherlands, some in Belgium and Rumania, and one Russian line. Although the war adversely affected it, there are still nearly 50,000 miles of track which belong to its members. In 1929 it changed its name to the Association of Middle European Railroads. This organization had great influence on railroad development in other countries, and itself developed into a more powerful and unified agency.

At the beginning, its members accepted only the rules which

they all wished to adopt; decisions had to be unanimous. Later they agreed to accept the verdict of the majority, and after 1875 a nine-tenths vote became binding on members "unless after notification of the decision one-tenth of all members protested in writing." In the earlier years the general conference drew up and altered rules; subsequently, various committees took over "much of the semilegislative function of the conference"; by 1875 they had become permanent, and in most cases their decision on a majority vote was final. The railroads in the union also agreed that their disputes should be settled by arbitration, so as to avoid the costs of litigation. At first a neutral railroad had power to give a final decision, but after 1881 permanent committees adjudicated disputes by majority decision. Even when the nationalization of railroads took place in the latter part of the nineteenth century, the international organization continued to function.

Other international organizations exist to promote more efficient railroad service: (1) The International Rail Congress Association, founded in 1885, which acts as a clearinghouse for technical information; (2) The International Railroad Union, founded in December 1922 to find remedies for the European rail organization which had become completely disrupted by the war, and to serve purposes similar to those of the Central European Union, but on a wider European scale; (3) The International Chamber of Commerce, with its railroad committee, and (4) the League's Advisory and Technical Committee on Communications and Transit, set up by the Barcelona Conference in 1920, also work toward similar ends.

Ruth Masters discusses the developments of railroad administrative unity. The International Railway Wagon Union, founded April 1920, "regulates the exchange of freight cars," and the International Union for the Use of Carriages and Vans in International Traffic, founded in October 1921, "regulates the exchange of passengers, baggage, ambulance, and mail cars." The author points out that it was a remarkable achievement to have founded two such European unions, including victor and vanquished powers, soon after 1918 when national hatreds were so intense.

For many years experts had attempted to draw up a convention for a uniform bill of lading; success finally came in 1893. The rules which were adopted prescribed the responsibility of carriers, the collection of charges, and methods of paying damages for injury to goods or delay in transport. The signatory powers formed the Berne Union for the Transport of Goods by Rail, and "established a central office for the union." The railroads agreed to give up their autonomy and accept the "principle of collective responsibility" for damages. This step resulted in lessening the amount of litigation and eliminating the former tedious and irritating border inspections. Improvements in the Berne Convention were made; its provisions were later extended to steamship and motor lines; and a new expert commission was set up.[27]

Up to this time, international agreements had been reached on freight traffic, but did not cover passengers. In 1924 the states which were members of the Berne Union met and drew up a passenger convention which went into force in October 1928.[28] It applied to damages to the passengers' baggage, and in its general principles, resembled the freight provisions just summarized. However, as with air traffic, the states could not agree on uniform rules relative to the responsibility of the carrier for injury or death of passengers, and the laws of individual states where injury or accident occurred remained applicable in each case.

For over sixty years international conferences to integrate the timetables for passenger trains had been held, and in January 1923 a permanent organization was set up for that purpose. Also a new organization was formed, in January 1930, to arrange semi-annual timetable conferences for freight trains. International clearinghouses balanced railroad accounts, and in 1936 another step forward was taken when, after the expenditure of five million dollars, train ferries across the English Channel were introduced, enabling passengers from London to Paris to remain in their railroad berths. The inconvenience of having to dismount from the train, catch a boat at an English port, and reboard a train in France has been eliminated.

Europe had become highly organized internationally for railroad purposes; but much remained to be done. For example, each railroad company still continued to charge its own passenger fares and freight rates, leaving open the possibility of ruinous cutthroat competition which, because of the close relationship existing between railroad transport and national security, might have serious international consequences. Perhaps Europe will find it desirable

[27] *League of Nations Treaty Series,* Vol. 77, No. 1778, p. 367. The 1924 Treaty, Annexes and Signatures occupy 166 pages in two languages.

[28] *Ibid.,* Vol. 78, No. 1779, p. 17. In order to revise these two conventions, two new conventions concerning the transport by rail of (*a*) passengers and baggage and (*b*) goods were signed at Berne on November 23, 1933, and came into force November 17, 1937. *Ibid.,* Vol. 192, Nos. 4483–4484.

to set up a body resembling the United States Interstate Commerce Commission, which has jurisdiction over charges which can be made by railroads.

The League of Nations has attempted to develop and codify international law on communications. It summoned the Barcelona Conference of 1921 to deal with the problem of freedom of transit, and the 1923 Geneva Conference, which drew up a convention and statute on the international regime of railways. The International Convention and Statute on Freedom of Transit was designed to guarantee freedom and equality to international transport in transit: i.e., transport which crosses one state, "its points of departure and destination being outside that state." If country A, situated between B and C, obstructs traffic between B and C, it can inflict injury upon these two countries; and in the past many disputes have arisen over transit questions. The convention provides that countries shall facilitate through transit by rail or waterway on routes in use for international transit. "No distinction is to be made on grounds of nationality of persons, the national flag flown by vessels, or the place of origin, departure or destination of goods or persons." Such traffic in transit shall not be required to pay any special dues, but only those dues intended to defray necessary expenses of supervision and administration. Some delegates noted that freedom of transit would remain merely a theoretical matter as long as nations could charge heavy rates for through or transit traffic. If a country charged less for local traffic than for through traffic, it would penalize the latter, and perhaps in practice deny freedom of transit. Other delegates claimed that, since their governments supported their railroads by taxation, they not only must have control over their own rates but must also possess the right to grant special rates designed to foster national industry or national ports. "The Italians, for example, wanted to retain their specially reduced rates for fruits from southern Italy shipped to the north for export and the Germans their low rates to Hamburg and Bremen, through which they hoped to build up their own North Sea ports at the expense of Rotterdam and navigation on the Rhine. These special rates were in effect burdens on the transit traffic, inasmuch as they favored national routes over international routes."[29] In other words, governments looked at their own railroads "not merely as means of transportation, but also as instruments of economic policy, if not of economic war." The confer-

[29] Ruth D. Masters, *op. cit.,* p. 524.

ence, therefore, had to adopt a compromise resolution agreeing that governments should maintain the right to impose differential rates, "provided these were based on economic considerations." Exceptions to equality, then, are permitted in the name of emergency, vital interest, national security, and the need to adapt the convention to local conditions. Only with the growth of international, or supra-national organization to guarantee security, may railroads serve economic functions primarily.

ROADS

The advent of the automobile restored the importance of highway transportation which had been eclipsed by the railroads. Motor vehicles "created a demand for greatly improved roads, and improved roads, in turn, greatly increased the possibilities of the new means of transportation."[30] In the United States local bodies had complete control over building and financing of roads until 1891 when New Jersey introduced the principle of state aid; by 1917 every state in the Union had a state highway department. But the needs of interstate travel and commerce called for federal action, and in 1916 Congress enacted a federal aid law. The development from exclusively local to state and federal aid has some significance for Europe: the difference is that, whereas in the United States the federal government has a constitutional power to act in assisting road-building programs, in Europe any co-ordination of road-building involves the action of sovereign states.

The construction and financing of roads constitutes only one side of the picture. After the highways have been built, governments must take steps to protect them and keep them in repair by prescribing weight limitation of vehicles, etc. They have to introduce safety regulations concerning brakes, lights, and accident insurance. They find it necessary to regulate the business of transportation for hire in the matter of stability of rates, prevention against discrimination, financial responsibility, dependability of service and co-ordination of transportation.[31] The growing scope of these problems finally led the United States Congress to pass the Motor Carriers Act of 1935, which places carriers by motor vehicle engaged in interstate and foreign commerce under the jurisdiction of the Interstate Commerce Commission. Continental transportation had required regulation on a continental scale.

[30] D. Philip Locklin, *The Economics of Transportation* (Business Publications, Inc., Chicago, 1938), p. 750.
[31] *Ibid.*, pp. 786–88.

Europe experienced the same growth of highway transportation, although at a slower rate, and it also realized the need of wider planning and regulating than independent national action alone could supply. But, whereas in the United States national unity obviated questions of national defense in highway matters between the states, in Europe the military aspects had to be kept constantly in mind. Nevertheless, much international co-operation on that continent was helping to promote plans for trans-national road construction and to free highway traffic from obstacles, dangers, and undue frontier formalities. Although some action was taken before the World War of 1914–1918, the really significant efforts did not begin until after it had ended.

A Permanent Committee on Road Traffic which was established within the Transit and Communications Section of the League of Nations spent much time preparing the ground for the first European Conference on Road Traffic which met at Geneva, March 16–30, 1931, and kept the delegates to the General Conferences and Communications and Transit Conferences informed on road matters. One cannot summarize in a short space the many technical problems which were discussed, nor do more than pay tribute in general terms to the great ability and reputation of the experts who were in attendance. A perusal of the documents compels one's admiration for the quality of the discussions carried on.

The 1931 Conference adopted a Convention on the Unification of Road Signals, providing for danger signals (△) ; signs prohibiting passage (○) ; and information signs (□). Those who have motored in foreign lands will appreciate the significance of a uniform set of symbols, for it is unlikely that motorists will know more than one or two languages; and safety as well as convenience indicates the need of as nearly universal agreement as possible on road signs. Within this threefold classification many other problems arose and were discussed—signaling by traffic police, instruction of school children, signs indicating direction to be followed, parking space, paths for cyclists only, prohibited passage, caution signs (for schools, churches, hospitals, etc.), and proximity to customs houses. The Conference requested the Permanent Committee on Road Traffic to continue its study of road signs and consider the possibility of establishing an international code of signals.

The Conference also adopted a Convention on the Taxation of Foreign Motor Vehicles which provided that touring cars visiting a foreign country shall be exempt from taxes and charges for a period of ninety days in the year. Vehicles which are used commercially for the public conveyance of passengers for payment or for transportation of persons and goods on a commercial basis are not to enjoy exemption. The minutes of the Conference reveal that the same fundamental problems had to be faced internationally as had been considered locally and nationally. Who should pay for the construction and upkeep of highways, the user or the person along whose property the road lay? Could a general rule be adopted in view of the divergent tax systems? Should not agreements be made on a bilateral basis as the German representative claimed? On the other hand, the desire of stimulating tourist traffic made it obviously important to attract foreigners by reducing formalities and expense to a minimum. The Conference was unable to agree upon a convention on international commercial motor transport. Some delegates believed that the complexities of motor versus railroad competition made any attempt at a general international agreement premature, although the Belgian representative indicated that his country with one of the densest railway systems in the world thought that a multilateral convention was possible and desirable. But the delegates realized that many different legal problems were involved and decided to postpone the matter until further investigations had been made. The Conference recommended that, "pending the conclusion of an international convention, separate agreements should be made between States on as liberal a basis as possible."

The Conference concluded an agreement between customs authorities to facilitate the procedure relating to undischarged or lost triptychs (the identifying documents) in order to remove "certain practical difficulties" of automobile tourists.

The Permanent Committee on Road Traffic considered many other matters. It urged the abolition of level-crossings in the interests of safety of traffic. It did considerable work on the unification of statistics relating to road traffic accidents. It investigated the possibility of unifying the direction of road traffic by the adoption of the rule of traffic on the right side, and recommended that those countries which keep to the left should when renewing transport material—tramways, motor omnibuses, etc.—"take the necessary preparatory steps in order that the direction of traffic might be changed with a minimum of expense when the time came." It proposed the standardization of national driving licenses and national registration cards (which had been urged by the International Association of Recognized Automobile Clubs).

As travel increases, the question of insurance of motorists

against payment of damages to third parties becomes more important. Some countries compel foreigners to take out compulsory insurance, others exempt foreigners and treat them more formally than national tourists. The task of drawing up an international convention on this question bristles with legal difficulties. A Committee of Enquiry for the civil liability of motorists was set up by the International Institute for the Unification of Private Law, and was requested to continue its study. Undoubtedly the matter will come up for reconsideration at the end of the present war.

The League of Nations Organization for Communications and Transit afforded technical assistance to the Chinese government in road-building, in transportation by road, and in hydraulic works, and sent out an elaborate questionnaire to the governments of the world concerning the co-ordination of rail, road, and inland navigation. The document comprises 348 pages and gives a valuable picture of the methods being adopted by governments to meet one of the most serious problems in present-day transportation.

This section may close with a reference to certain other bodies. The Permanent International Association of Road Congresses which began in 1908, and which at the close of 1937 had fifty-five member states, held its eighth Congress at The Hague in June 1938. A permanent international committee for the London–Istanbul Highway was created in 1935. The International Chamber of Commerce has three committees: (1) on barriers to international commercial motor transport, (2) on automobile insurance, and (3) on highway transport. A committee of experts for the codification of road law held its first meeting at Geneva in 1938. Mention must be made also of the growing importance of the Pan-American highway, which bids fair to become a factor of major importance in the relations of the countries of the American continent.

AIR TRANSPORTATION

Although the French used a balloon in the war against Austria in 1794, and balloons figured in international conflicts during the nineteenth century, the great problems of air traffic have developed only in recent years.

No one can fail to appreciate the extraordinary aeronautical progress of the last thirty years; nor can he be insensitive to the grave risks which technical achievement has brought. The airplane has introduced new factors in warfare and helped to intensify the race in armaments; it has brought new problems in empire communications and further complicates the imperialistic struggle for power. Great Britain, France, the United States, Italy, Holland, Japan, and the Soviet Union realize the extreme importance of adequate and efficient inter-empire air forces, and have spent huge sums for that purpose. And the airplane and the airship have provided new forms of service transport, and are becoming increasingly important in surveying and developing inland areas, bringing medical aid to hitherto inaccessible parts, opening up Arctic regions, maintaining order in outlying sections, speeding up mail deliveries, and increasing the tempo of life generally. Hundreds of millions of dollars have been invested, and the industry is now an indispensable part of economic life. Finally, the new airways intensify the need for renewed vigilance in the realm of public health; continents are brought closer together, and disease may be more easily spread, unless national and international health authorities redouble their precautionary efforts.

Thus air transportation has international significance, and requires analysis as an international problem.

The first international air congress met at Paris in 1889. The delegates did not have official status, but they considered many questions which later were to demand the attention of governments in the fields of both public and private law. Other conferences were held in Paris (1900), Milan (1906), Brussels (1907), Nancy (1909), and Turin (1911). Private organizations, such as the Institut de Droit International, the International Law Association, the Congrès Juridique d'Aviation, and the Comité Juridique International de l'Aviation, held several meetings in the prewar years.

The basic question that arose was whether the air was universally free or whether nations possessed sovereignty over the air space above the land within their own boundaries. One school of thought claimed that the air was free. It argued from analogy: since the sea was open to all nations, the air also should be free; and air is necessary to life, irrespective of state or nation. Defenders of state sovereignty over the air replied that there were fundamental differences between air space and the sea—the force of gravity enters into air travel, and airplanes constitute a potential danger to the land below, which is not true of ships at sea. "Other things being equal, the potential menace of a war vessel at sea decreases with its distance from shore. The reverse is true of war aircraft. The threat from war planes is far too serious to permit the development of the idea that the air can be universally free."

Further: "Civil air transport involves greater danger to innocent life and property below, and because of the speed and height of air travel it is more difficult to establish facts concerning responsibility for aerial than for marine accidents; and also, civil planes may threaten the safety of people in so far as there is need of forced landing." For these reasons many jurists asserted that a state has the right of sovereignty over the air space above its soil. Some international lawyers suggested that the nation should possess air sovereignty up to a certain height, beyond which the air space should be common to all nations. But critics pointed out that it would be almost, if not absolutely, impossible to determine whether a foreign plane was or was not at a given moment beyond the established height. Other writers declared that the nation should exercise sovereignty over its air space but should grant the right of innocent passage to foreign airships and planes. This doctrine found expression in the International Air Conference of 1919.

Even before the World War of 1914–1918, governments tended to ignore the theories of jurists, and the British, French, and Austrian legislatures proceeded on the assumption of absolute sovereignty over the air above their soil. And at the International Conference on Air Navigation in 1910 the jurists of the world were so divided on the question that the Conference broke up without reaching any agreement.

That war dealt a still heavier blow to the theories of internationalism in matters of air transport. Any lingering hopes of a world-wide view were dissipated by the immediate necessities of military action. The movement toward a national theory of air space coincided with the tremendous impetus to air transport during the war period. Before 1914 relatively few planes were in use. During the war, the possibilities of air attack were not fully realized, and the air force remained merely an auxiliary unit; nevertheless, the years of conflict witnessed rapid progress in engine construction and other technical matters, the number of machines built, and the number of pilots trained. By 1918 it was clear that a new and powerful factor had appeared in international relations.

In March 1919 an Aeronautical Commission of the Peace Conference began to draft the air clauses of the Peace Treaty and also a general convention for international aviation. Five great powers and seven powers "of limited interests" were represented on the Commission, which drew up the 1919 International Air Convention. The Convention formed the basis of much subsequent national air law and of bilateral treaties and served as the model for the Ibero-American and the Pan-American air conventions.

It lays down three fundamental principles : (1) each state possesses sovereignty over the air space above its territory; (2) other nations have a qualified freedom of innocent passage which, however, "is granted as a privilege instead of being conceded as a natural right"; (3) nations may proclaim prohibited zones over which foreign aircraft may not fly.

Each aircraft possesses the nationality of state on the register of which it is entered and must bear a nationality mark. It must belong wholly to nationals of that state or to a company therein registered. Every month states must notify the other signatory powers as to new registrations or cancellations. The signatory powers agree to recognize the validity of certificates issued by each other.

The fourth chapter of the Convention deals with the important problem of admission to air navigation above national territory. Article 15 provides that "every aircraft of a contracting State has the right to cross the air space of another State without landing. In this case it shall follow the route fixed by the State over which the flight takes place." It must land if ordered to do so by officials of the government over whose territory it may be passing. No aircraft of a contracting state capable of being flown without a pilot shall, except by special authorization, fly without a pilot over the territory of another contracting state. The sixth chapter concerns the question of prohibited transport, Articles 26–29 forbidding the carriage by aircraft of explosives and arms or munitions of war; also states may prohibit or regulate the use of photographic apparatus.

Chapter viii of the Convention sets up an International Commission for Air Navigation, which is to have important powers : (1) Administratively it is to receive proposals for amending the convention and to collect and publish information of every kind relating to international air navigation, especially wireless, meteorology, maps, etc. (2) Legislatively the Commission may propose changes in the articles of the convention, but it may itself modify the first seven annexes to the convention which are the technical regulations. (3) The Commission acts in a judicial capacity; it may settle disputes of a technical nature—disputes arising from the articles of the convention themselves go to the Permanent Court of International Justice. (4) The Commission has advisory powers, since it must give its opinion on questions which the signatory powers may send it for examination.

This convention represented a distinct step forward; in some respects it was a remarkable piece of work. Nevertheless a number of factors militated against its full success. The Peace Treaties contained clauses directed against the defeated enemy powers—Germany, Austria, Bulgaria, Hungary, and Turkey. Neutral powers labored under disadvantages, and not until certain modifications were made in 1926, and also later revisions of several articles became effective in May 1933, were the difficulties finally removed.

CODIFICATION OF PRIVATE AIR LAW

Differences in state and national laws may seriously injure trade and commerce. Manufacturers, exporters, and wholesale dealers need accurate knowledge of economic and legal conditions. The wider the area of their business connections the more they benefit from uniformity of law. Conflicting state requirements in wages and working conditions place many obstacles in the way of commerce. In a similar manner, diversity of national laws relating to contracts, insurance, damages, and other matters will adversely affect international trade. Uniformity of legislation, therefore, is a matter of great importance, particularly in the field of transportation.

In 1910 the Comité Juridique International de l'Aviation was formed for the purpose of developing a code of private air law. The World War of 1914–1918 increased both military and commercial aviation; and after 1919 especially many problems arose, the most acute of them being in the realm of insurance and the legal position of the carrier. Colegrove cites a typical example:

. . . . a firm in Berlin consigns a case of surgical instruments to a London physician by way of an air traffic company. En route over Holland the consignment is damaged through the negligence of the pilot. Who, then, stands the loss, the Berlin firm, the London physician, the shipping company or the insurance company?[32]

National laws relating to the liability of the shipper differ in many respects and cause great inconvenience to commerce. In 1922 the League Advisory and Technical Committee for Communications and Transit suggested the desirability of considering

[32] K. W. Colegrove, *International Control of Aviation* (World Peace Foundation, Boston, 1930), p. 16.

whether an agreement, "if only of a very elastic nature and in the form of recommendations or a model code," might not be possible. The International Chamber of Commerce Air Transport Committee also urged an international conference, pointing out the serious inconveniences arising from conflicting judgments of national civil courts. The French government took the initiative and, as a result, the first International Conference on Private Air Law met in Paris in October and November, 1925. Representatives from forty-three states attended and evolved a draft convention dealing with the liability of air carriers. The Conference expressed the wish that a special committee of experts with headquarters at Paris should be empowered to continue the work in greater detail and study the following questions: damage caused by aircraft to property and persons on the ground; compulsory insurance; establishment of air registers; ownership of aircraft, vested rights, and mortgages; seizure; renting of aircraft; air collisions; legal status of the commanding officer of an aircraft; bill of lading (air-consignment note); uniform rules for the determination of the nationality of aircraft.

This committee, the Comité International Technique d'Experts Juridiques Aériens (C.I.T.E.J.A.), was set up in Paris on May 17, 1926, with representatives from twenty-eight countries. At its first session it established its bylaws and set up four commissions to deal with: nationality of aircraft; air register; ownership, co-ownership, construction, and transfer; vested rights, mortgages, privileges, and seizure; category of transport (commercial, touring, etc.); bills of lading; liability of carrier toward consignors of goods and toward passengers; jettison of cargo and general average; renting of aircraft; damage and liability toward third parties (landing, collision, and jettison); limits of liability (contractual limitation, abandonment); insurance; legal status of commanding officer and crew; accidents to the crew and insurance; status of passengers; law governing acts committed on board aircraft.

The committee first considered the question of the responsibility of the carrier for passengers and goods, for efficiency in transport depends upon establishing conditions binding upon the responsible parties throughout the whole of the transaction. It compared the drafts submitted by interested parties, after which the Polish government convened the second private air law conference in October 1929. Twenty-three states signed the Warsaw Convention for the unification of certain rules relating to the carriage by air, which came into force in February 1933 as between

eight nations and was subsequently ratified by several other governments. The convention "applies to all international carriage
of persons, baggage, or goods performed by aircraft for hire" and
also to "gratuitous carriage by aircraft"; it establishes the liability
of the carrier and the amounts which must be paid. It is impossible
here to summarize the many technical articles, or do more than
refer to the third International Conference on Private Air Law
which met at Rome in May 1933 and adopted two measures: (1)
relating to a precautionary attachment of aircraft, an act

whereby an aircraft is seized, in a private interest, through the medium
of agents of justice or of the public administration for the benefit
either of a creditor, or of the owner, or of the holder of a lien on the
aircraft, where the attaching claimant cannot invoke a judgment and
execution, obtained beforehand in the ordinary course of procedure, or
an equivalent right of execution. . . . .[33]

(2) a convention for the unification of certain rules relating to
damage caused by aircraft to third parties on the ground. One
country might exact very heavy damages, and another impose only
a relatively small fine. With such different laws, air companies
would have to have legal advisers to study the legal systems and
court decisions of all the countries over which their airplanes
passed. The present convention is designed to remove some of
these complexities and uncertainties.

A convention which accepts the principle of absolute liability
and prescribes the general amounts which may be recovered, depends for its wide acceptance on the settlement of insurance:

The most deplorable deficiency is the lack of any international
regulation of insurance made by the convention . . . . the texts of
policies vary between states and, whereas in one country many restrictive clauses are allowed in the policy, in another country there are
only a few . . . . It is unsupportable that the chances of the injured
person to secure compensation depend on the nationality of the aircraft
which caused the injury.[34]

To remedy this defect representatives from many European insurance companies met in June 1934 and formed the International
Union of Aviation Insurers.

Another aspect of international air navigation is the International Sanitary Convention for Air Navigation, signed at The

[33] L. C. Tombs, *International Organization in European Air Transport* (Columbia University Press, New York, 1936), p. 137.
[34] *Ibid.,* p. 140.

Hague in 1933. It prescribes the special precautions to be taken against the carrying of plague, cholera, yellow fever, typhus, and fariola. In the same year the International Office of Public Hygiene set up a quarantine commission on air navigation.

Other international agencies which have been fulfilling the requirements of air navigation include: (1) the International Meteorological Organization, formed in 1872, which, in 1929, adopted an international code for meteorological messages; (2) the International Commission on Illumination, formed in 1913, with a secretariat in England, which in recent years has been studying such problems as international standards in signaling, light strength, and color and type of illumination for airport and airway lighting; (3) The International Hydrographic Bureau, set up in June 1921 under the League of Nations, which is doing important work in standardizing maps used in air navigation.

Unfortunately, these developments, excellent in themselves and along sound lines, are offset by the exaggerated sense of nationalism which in Europe stands in the way of a fully efficient international civil air transportation system.

In the first place, most European governments have granted heavy aviation subsidies and have subordinated civil aviation to military needs. M. Henri Bouché, in a report published by the League of Nations in 1935, noted that Great Britain, France, Italy, and Germany in 1932 had an air-navigation-carrying capacity of 19,000,000 tons-kilometers but actually used only 9,000,000. The French income from air transport was 428,000,000 francs, of which 322,000,000 came from state subsidy. Italy's civil air service earned only 6 per cent of its total receipts; Great Britain's earned 64 per cent. The air services of Europe in one year carried an amount equal to that which three or four ten-ton freight trucks, operating daily, could transport over 625 miles of railroad, and cost Europe the amazing sum of $100,000 a day!!

Thus Europe's air transportation, because of the needs of defense and political prestige, has proved most expensive.

In Bouché's judgment[35] Europe needs much greater uniformity of landing grounds and of meteorological safeguards. Such equipment requires large expenditures, but many of the European nations are too small and too poor to undertake the financial

[35] H. Bouché, "Present Economic Conditions of Civil Air Navigation," in *Enquiries into the Economic, Administrative and Legal Situation of International Air Navigation,* Series of League of Nations Publications, VIII, *Transit* (1930), p. 70.

burdens involved. Between June and December, 1929, the United States spent 330,000,000 dollars in the establishment and upkeep of airdromes. Expenditure on a similar scale in Europe would almost certainly require international co-operation. Indeed, M. Bouché has proposed the creation of a "common fund" into which each country should pay a part of the money which at present goes into national subsidies. This fund would enable the smaller countries to obtain adequate ground organization at lower cost, and permit European civil aviation to be freed from its present reliance upon military construction. Bouché even suggested considering the setting up for aviation purposes of a European banking organization which could grant subsidies or loans to air companies or public agencies engaged in civil transport.

The future of European civil aviation will depend upon international co-operation. Authorities differ as to what form that co-operation should take. Some hold that it will be necessary to abolish military aircraft and to internationalize civil air transportation. Others believe that such steps are far beyond immediate adoption and are open to grave objections. Most admit that the present state of European aviation is unsatisfactory and agree that it would be wise to withdraw national subsidies; the national companies would then have to co-operate and "put an end to a great deal of the building and operation of small numbers of aircraft in the smaller countries." Mr. Handley Page believes that a European commercial air transport company could be organized on much the same lines as the sleeping cars on the railroads.[36] One thing is clear. Europe's civil aviation needs cannot be efficiently met while international tension continues. Until defense becomes a subordinate and not an all-engrossing concern, air transportation cannot develop along the lines which are logically possible.

THE INTERNATIONAL POSTAL UNION

The situation which led to the establishment of the International Postal Union has often been described. Business men and others who wished to communicate with people abroad had to face a bewildering variety of regulations which combined to produce uncertainty and delay. A person in the United States sending a letter to a foreign destination would pay the domestic rate, plus "sea postage," plus a transit rate imposed by each government through whose territory the letter passed, plus the do-

[36] *New Commonwealth*, August 1935, p. 386.

mestic rate in the country of destination. Nor was that all—he had to pay different rates according to the sea route used. A letter from the United States to Austria cost 15 or 30 or 42 cents per half-ounce according to whether it went via Hamburg direct or via England or via France. There were six different rates to Australia, five to Greece, Turkey, Egypt, or Hongkong.

These conditions were typical. Dr. Reinsch wrote that "mail service was by no means frequent, but the fact that a letter was prepaid for a certain route often prevented it from taking advantage of a quicker means of transportation. It might just have missed the mail for which it was prepaid by a few hours, but would have to wait until another mail left by the same route before it would be forwarded." Units of weight varied, and it was therefore difficult to calculate postal rates in three or four countries through which the mail would pass. This confusing array of complications produced still others; every country had to keep a set of accounts for each country with which it had postal relations; each had to be credited with its portion of the sum prepaid on *each* article (not on the aggregate weights of the mails). Little wonder that men and firms engaged in international trade concluded that national sovereignty in postal matters was too expensive a luxury to be retained. They also realized that bilateral treaties could not bring a sound solution and that, if postal communication was to help and not hinder international trade, it would be necessary to regard the world as one great postal territory.

The International Postal Convention was not the result of the development of an international outlook so much as that of a more realistic conception of national interest. This is significant because it reveals the fact that international organization of international interests may be the only satisfactory way of conserving the national interest.[37]

Postmaster-General Blair of the United States, in August 1862, proposed an international conference to discuss the postal problems of the world. In May 1863, delegates of several governments met at Paris, not to conclude a binding convention, but rather to discuss general factors. Nevertheless, the conference adopted a number of principles designed to facilitate postal relations between countries and to serve as a basis for international conventions in the future. For the next decade, improvements

[37] H. M. Vinacke, *International Organization* (F. S. Crofts & Co., New York, 1934), p. 405.

went on slowly. Rates were reduced, but little progress was made in overcoming the serious handicaps due to lack of uniformity. After considerable delay, the Congress of Berne, attended by representatives of twenty-two states, met on September 15, 1874, and formed what later came to be known as the Universal Postal Union.

Members of the Union constitute a single area for purposes of postal communication; each one guarantees freedom of transit through its own territory. The national sovereign states no longer impose transit charges on foreign mails which they carry, and the Postal Union authorities fix the rates according to the weight of the mails and the distance to which they are carried. For this purpose "the mails are weighed for a period of six weeks during each sixth year." International postal disputes come before an arbitral board set up according to provisions of the Postal Convention.

The actual machinery of the International Postal Union need not be considered here. The Union has adopted the important principle that decisions are made by majority vote. Theoretically, each nation must ratify a decision made by a Postal Congress; but in practice the national postal authorities appear to accept the decisions of the International Congress and do not wait for their confirmation by the several governments.[38]

The amount of international organization required to insure the efficiency of our everyday postal arrangements is not generally appreciated. Turkel remarks that an International Postal Congress is attended by "about 180 delegates representing all nations of the world" who

consider between 200 and 2,000 propositions embodying technical rules for the exchange of letters, parcel post, letters with value declared, money orders, air mails and two other auxiliary services, the so-called "collection of bills" service (*virements postaux*) and the service of subscription to journals.[39]

These proposals, about one year prior to a congress, are sent to the various national postal authorities for consideration; counter proposals and other communications produce such a mass of material that a new "study commission" has been appointed to prepare a digest and draw up projects which can be more efficiently considered at the general congress, which usually passes from ten to fifteen "acts" each session.

[38] *Ibid,* p. 407.
[39] H. R. Turkel, "International Postal Congresses," in *British Year Book of International Law, 1929,* p. 171.

The same general problems of representation arise in the Postal Union as in the major international conferences (disarmament, tariffs). The governments of the small powers complain that they do not receive adequate representation on the committees, and the question of votes for Dominions and colonies has caused controversy. In 1878 British India and the French colonies were admitted. In 1895 Canada obtained a vote and Portugal succeeded in gaining voting power for her colonies. Two years later the states of Australia came in, and Germany, Denmark, Spain, and the Netherlands received votes for their colonial possessions. "The race for votes was on." It was natural for countries without colonies to protest against the increased voting powers given to powers which had colonial possessions. Turkel quotes from the document of the 1924 Congress:

Many of the countries without colonies, among whom are some very important ones, begin to feel a certain unrest. The atmosphere which results from this situation aroused certain protests and painful discussions at Madrid which disrupted the harmony of the common work and finished by having a disorganizing effect.[40]

The question of letters in transit continues to create difficulties. In the early days of the Union nations agreed to grant "liberty of transit" to foreign letters passing through their territory. But not all of them wished to grant "gratuity of transit." It was obvious that international postal efficiency would be heightened by the elimination of the varying rates of transit postage described above. But was it fair that a country (France or Belgium, for example) which had previously gained much revenue from carrying foreign mails on its railroads should now have to transport these mails for nothing? If they are so geographically situated that a great amount of foreign mail goes through their territory, they will "perform far more services for other countries than they receive in return." If they form crossroads of international communication they will wish to receive some recompense for the effort imposed upon them in transporting foreign mails, and will oppose the gratuity of transit which many countries advocate. In practice, transit rates have been lowered; and in some parts of the world, notably in Latin America and the United States, gratuity of transit (except for Panama) is accepted. Turkel writes: "It is impossible to predict what the outcome will be . . . . all one can say for the future is that this question is bound to occur again and again."[41]

[40] Turkel, *op. cit.*, p. 177.   [41] *Ibid.*, p. 175.

The arbitration machinery which has been established by the Union has been successful in settling disputes which inevitably arise in an organization of such dimensions. The Union, however, has not been able to find a solution for the problem of neutral mails in wartime. Twenty of the American republics signed a declaration to the effect "that closed despatches and open correspondence in transit are inviolable both at sea and on land, and that consequently no country in the Union may submit them to the censor or sequestrate them in time of war." The European Powers and Japan opposed the declaration "on the ground that a Postal Congress is not competent to deal with the questions of military censorship."[42]

After fifty years the Universal Postal Union reported that over 3,000,000,000 pieces of postal material were handled each year, an increase of more than 2,000 per cent in a half-century. The insured articles rose from 685,000 to more than 4,000,000 and the money orders from 918,000 to approximately 20,000,000 a year. Sharp and Kirk comment upon these figures thus: "It is no exaggeration to say that the conduct of the business, social, and political life of the present-day world would be impossible without that degree of interstate co-operation which is necessary for the maintenance of efficient postal service."[43]

The advent of the airplane brought new technical problems in mail transportation. The Paris Peace Conference did nothing effective, in spite of an Italian proposal to include an annex "dealing with postal questions" to the 1919 Air Convention.[44] The next year, at the Madrid Congress, the Universal Postal Union considered the problem of airmail but, regarding it as "an extraordinary service," left details to the member states. The next few years witnessed a great expansion of air transport, and consequently the Stockholm Congress in 1924 added several provisions —airmail rates were not to be the same as ordinary mail rates but were "to be uniform in all countries which used the service without sharing the working expenses"; and rules were made "for the transfer of mails carried by more than one service and for warehousing before further transmission."[45] These regulations proved

[42] *Ibid.*, p. 180.
[43] W. R. Sharp and G. Kirk, *Contemporary International Politics* (Farrar & Rinehart, New York, 1940), p. 174.
[44] L. C. Tombs, *International Organization in European Air Transport* (Columbia University Press, New York, 1936), p. 161.
[45] K. W. Colegrove. *International Control of Aviation* (World Peace Foundation, Boston, 1930), p. 110.

to be inadequate, and the International Chamber of Commerce petitioned the Postal Union to call a special conference at The Hague. This conference drew up an optional agreement which, in turn, was adopted in 1929 by the Postal Union Congress. The major improvements effected (1) unification of surtaxes to be charged the public and (2) the simplification of remuneration to the carrier.[46] Meanwhile the International Chamber of Commerce investigated many subjects which included:

Transmission of mail by the most rapid route; rapid and direct transmission of air mail; through transmission of mail by air and rail; rapid transmission of mail before it is sent by air; increase in aerodrome post offices and rapid transmission from city to aerodrome; publicity for air mail facilities; priority for telephone and telegraph communications in case of forced landing; simplification and unification of extra mail rates; collective agreements for the transmission of parcel post; constant study of the development of air transport in order to provide both administrations and carriers with indispensable factors for mutual agreements; night flying; closer co-operation between air navigation companies and postal administrations; postal prohibitions; samples; enclosure, in single envelope, of letters, invoices, etc., addressed to third parties; postal money orders and C.O.D. packets; technical facilities; rate uniformity; payment of claims for lost parcels; and general acceptance of the C.O.D. system.[47]

Meetings of national officials were held at Brussels in 1930 and 1931; and at Prague, in June of the latter year, eleven countries sent representatives which considered the possibility of creating a regular nightly airmail service. For various reasons the Conference agreed that only a summer months' program could be initiated in the immediate future, and it believed that although a number of governments desired to abolish the special air fee it was not yet possible to do so. It acknowledged with regret that government subsidies were still necessary for the airmail service.

At Cairo in 1934 a convention was adopted which reduced the maximum charges for airmail service and even permitted countries to abolish the surcharge altogether. But it did not act upon several recommendations of the International Chamber of Commerce relating to lower rate levels, improved provisions for liability "for loss, damage and delay," and other technical matters too detailed for consideration here. In spite of advances, the regulation of airmail is, as Colegrove notes, "still in an experimental stage."

[46] K. W. Colegrove, *International Control of Aviation,* p. 111.
[47] G. L. Ridgeway, *Merchants of Peace* (Columbia University Press, New York, 1938), pp. 306, 307.

Both he and Ridgeway pay tribute to the work of the International Chamber of Commerce, and Colegrove speaks of the collaboration between the I.C.C. and the Universal Postal Union as "a conspicuous example of effective co-operation between a private and a public international agency."[48]

CABLES, TELEGRAPH, AND RADIO

The evolution in communications has not been limited to ships, roads, railroads, mail, and airplanes. The cable, the telegraph, and the radio have added to the complexities of international relations by producing what Charles Hodges has picturesquely described as "the staccato impact of events." Two illustrations will suffice: The message which opened the British Empire Exhibition in 1924 was cabled around the world in eighty seconds; and radio can circle the earth seven and one-half times per second. This "instantaneous transmission of the spoken word" has intensified the political problem of communications to even a greater degree than the also relatively recent cables and telegraphs. Modern states are battling not only to gain control over goods and power but also over the very thought and soul of man.

Great Britain early recognized the vital importance of cables to international commerce and took the lead in laying and controlling transoceanic lines. As Hodges and Riegel both point out, its monopoly of gutta percha, the raw material used in cable insulation, gave it an initial strangle hold. London became the center of the cable world, as it had already become the center of the world's stock market and currency quotations; financial control and news control in combination provided an instrument of unparalleled strength.

Other governments might lament this monopoly; but until 1898 the British supremacy remained unchallenged. From that time American competition became important across the Atlantic, down to Latin America, and to a lesser degree in the Pacific.

Efforts to mitigate the rivalry and friction due to national control of telegraph and cable communications met with little success in the prewar period. An international conference held in St. Petersburg in 1875 adopted a convention dealing with the operation of cables in peacetime, but it did little to guarantee international freedom of cable communications in the face of national censorship. Subsequent conferences, at least five of them, brought relatively little additional success. Although the 1884 Berlin Con-

[48] Colegrove, *op. cit.,* p. 102.

vention made provision for penalties for those who deliberately or
negligently injured a cable, it contented itself with laying down
the broad principle only and left specific legislation to individual
governments. It is not surprising that little effective progress was
made.

The Hague Convention of 1907, relating to laws and customs
of war on land and the rights and duties of neutral powers, dealt
with the protection of international cables during wartime but
merely expressed the hope that cables would not be destroyed or
seized "unless absolutely necessary," a loophole which permitted
belligerents in the World War of 1914–1918 to do whatever they
pleased, especially as the Convention made no provision for compensation in the event of seizure and interruption of cables during
hostilities.

During that war the vital importance of cables was soon illustrated. Four hours after Britain had entered the war she isolated
her enemy by cutting the German cables. Within three months
the British government informed Mr. Hearst that he must print
all dispatches exactly as they were released to him by the British
censor, otherwise the British-controlled cables and mails would
be closed to him. Hearst's reply was characteristic: "I am going
to tell them to go hell"; apparently he did so, for he had to secure
his news from other and more devious channels! Allied control
of cables meant that Germany could not influence public opinion in
the neutral countries—the United States, Latin America, and the
Far East—which thereafter had their attitudes and opinions
molded according to Allied propaganda.

The nations which had so deeply experienced the strategic
importance of cables in wartime met soon after the peace to consider the future of the twenty thousand miles of cables previously
owned by Germany. The Versailles Treaty made provision for an
international conference on communications, which was held in
Washington in 1920. Despite lip service to internationalism, and
the establishment of the League of Nations, the Washington Conference did nothing to rescue cables from the clutches of national
policies. Great Britain obtained the cable from the Azores to
Halifax, and France the line from the Azores to New York as
well as the German–South Atlantic system. In the Pacific a bitter
rivalry developed. President Wilson hoped to internationalize the
Island of Yap where three German lines met: one from the Dutch
East Indies, one from Shanghai, and one from Guam which connected with a cable between the United States and China. But

Japan had already obtained a mandate over the ex-German islands north of the Equator and flatly refused to consider the internationalization of "this cable crossroads of the Pacific."

Subsequently, the United States and Japan effected a compromise. The United States recognized Japan's mandate; and Japan, in turn, agreed to the United States' demand for equal cable and radio rights at Yap. Not until a further conference in 1922 was the final disposition of the German cables made. Japan gained the cable from Yap to China, the United States took the line between Yap and Guam, and the Netherlands obtained the Dutch East Indies part. Hodges has summarized the results thus:

America's trans-Pacific influence was hindered; Japan tightened her grip on the admittedly inadequate communications between China and the outside world; and the Mikado's Land, with the support of the British, cleverly opposed all efforts to open the closed door in Far Eastern communications. The much-needed extension of trans-Pacific cable facilities has remained in abeyance because of Tokyo's apparent intention to control any further development as the middleman in ideas between the East and the West.[49]

The invention of radio had far-reaching effects upon cable communications and indeed upon the whole of international life. Although an international radio-telegraphy conference was held in 1912, it concerned itself mainly with technical matters and did little to restrain the nationalism which was already making ominous claims. Nationalist rivalries which were to become so intense in the postwar period had begun. However, since technical developments had not reached their present high standard of efficiency, the prewar rivalry was somewhat confined to the realm of theory.

The World War of 1914–1918 left the United States practically isolated, or at the mercy of Allied cables for news service. American inventors therefore redoubled their energies to develop the radio. After long research, scientists produced the Alexanderson high-frequency alternator, which introduced great technical improvements and gave to the United States a new and unprecedented advantage: "American business saw the end of its commercial isolation and wanted to compete aggressively for world markets. It was in no mood to accept a 'party line' arrangement in international communications," as stated by O. W. Riegel.[49a]

[49] Charles Hodges, *The Background of International Relations* (John Wiley & Sons, New York, 1931), p. 477; see also L. B. Tribolet, *The International Aspects of Electrical Communications in the Pacific Area* (The Johns Hopkins Press, 1929). [49a] *Mobilizing for Chaos* (Yale University Press, 1934), p. 44.

President Wilson realized the strategic importance of the radio. When the British Marconi Company placed a five-million-dollar order, Wilson requested General Electric not to sell the new high-frequency-alternator invention to a foreign company. Admiral Bullard, Director of Naval Communications, interviewed the high officials of General Electric, and the British offer was declined. Imperialism had entered into the realm of radio. By way of reply, the British Marconi developed "beam," or directional wireless, which by the use of short waves could be operated over a distance of more than two thousand miles. Hodges notes that this beam-wireless system was able to handle thirty-five million words annually and at rates which made it difficult, if not impossible, for the cables to compete. In order to straighten out intra-imperial rivalries and to strengthen British communications in a highly competitive world an imperial wireless and cable conference in 1927–28 was held. Out of it came a unification of cable and wireless under the title of Cable and Wireless, Limited, which brought into one great monopoly the leading telegraph, cable, and wireless companies of the British Empire.

This British consolidation move caused many people in America to press for a similar merger in the United States. President Hoover proposed that such a plan be studied, and the Roper Report emphasized the "requirements of national defense" and urged the establishment of a central governmental agency which should regulate all the communications systems. The Dill-Rayburn bills introduced into Congress had a similar objective.

Government control has been strengthened in most countries of the world. And the use of radio by the dictator countries is too well known to need further description at this point. The radio rivalry indulged in by great powers in South America is mentioned in the section dealing with Pan-Americanism; and radio propaganda in the Middle East became a problem of major importance between Great Britain and Italy.

Telegraph and wireless, however important for military purposes, serve wider interests which themselves necessitate international action. The demands of ordinary trade and commerce required at first bilateral treaties between neighboring countries. In 1850 Austria and Prussia signed a telegraph treaty; other countries followed, and in 1852 several of the European states adopted a multilateral convention. In 1865 twenty states were represented at an international conference at Paris which established the International Telegraphic Union and set up a permanent bureau at Berne, Switzerland, in order to gather information concerning telegraphic activities. The convention was revised in 1875 and again in 1908, and provides for the guaranty of telegrams being transmitted from one country to another and for setting aside special wires for international telegraphic service. As with other technical unions, periodic conferences are held in order to revise the agreement as necessity arises.

We have already mentioned the international agreements relating to cables, and refer here to the efforts made to organize international wireless communications. In 1906 twenty-nine states attended a conference at Berlin and signed a convention setting up the International Radio Telegraphic Union. Many rules were adopted, including the rule that coastal wireless stations and ship radios must exchange radiograms and providing for periodic conferences of revision. The second conference met in 1912—the year the steamer "Titanic" sank through colliding with an iceberg in the North Atlantic—and devoted special attention to wireless communication on ships. Until these conferences were held radiotelegraphy was a matter of private contract so that in the event of a crisis stations were unable to communicate with one another unless the message was sent by the Marconi system; each state attempted to keep a monopoly of radio communication. But the logic of events clearly showed the advantage of co-operation in these matters. The remarkable development of broadcasting in the United States and Europe immediately after 1918, led to great confusion. Companies jammed the programs of rival companies, and it became clear that international as well as national regulation had become necessary if commercial radio was to play a useful role in international society.[50]

The United States government, which had consistently refused to become entangled in international political arrangements, called together the Washington Conference of 1927 to draw up a new convention to allocate radio wave lengths to various services. Seventy-four governments signed the agreement, which covered all "forms of radio communication, from ship to ship and from land to land." Wave lengths were assigned to the different radio services (aviation, amateur broadcasting, fixed, maritime, and mobile). The signatory states might assign any type of wave to any radio stations within their jurisdiction, but undertook not to cause interference with the radio service of other nations. Before

[50] The international aspects of radio control in China caused much debate at the Washington Conference, 1921–22.

assigning frequencies as to stations likely to produce interference the signatories agreed to give notice to the International Bureau at Berne, which was then to notify other interested parties. In the event of actual interference provision was made for arbitration.

In 1929 a conference of experts met at The Hague to adopt a plan for allocating wave lengths on an international basis for Europe. Several American countries have signed a regional agreement establishing frequency assignments, and in 1937 the first inter-American Radio Conference was held at Havana. It drafted an Inter-American Convention and signed an agreement for the establishment of an Inter-American Radio Office which is designed "to facilitate co-operation on technical and legal matters." American countries are reported to be planning the establishment "of an international police radio system," an important step in the prevention of crime and the promotion of order.[51]

International telephone communications have come into prominence within the last generation. More than 37,000,000 telephones were in use in 1937, and by using radio, submarine cables, and land wire the United States could converse with practically every part of the world over seventy-four different telephone circuits. The use of radio for telephone as well as for broadcasting suggested the need of bringing these two services under one set of international regulations. The 1932 Madrid Conference of the Telegraphic Union undertook this task and revised and expanded the conventions already in force. Regulations for telegraph, telephone, and radio communications were attached to the new convention, to any one of which the signatory powers might adhere. The International Bureau at Berne was to prepare for subsequent conferences, provide technical information, and publish a monthly journal of telecommunication.

The next Telecommunication Conference, held at Cairo in 1938, had to consider the effect of the rapid expansion of broadcasting services and the great demand for additional radio frequencies which necessitated "a further tightening of existing rules to make the most economical use possible of facilities at present available." The Conference

adopted a plan for radio channels for the world's seven main intercontinental air routes; widened the high frequency broadcast bands to a total of 300 kilocycles; fixed special bands for regional use in the

---

[51] For description of the Havana Conference (1937) and the North American Regional Radio Engineering meeting (Washington, 1941), see *The American Journal of International Law,* Vol. 32 (1938), p. 569, and Vol. 35 (1941), p. 363.

tropics; extended the allocation table for the European region; and brought up to date the regulations relative to maritime and aeronautical services.[52]

It is unnecessary to describe in detail the remarkable role played by radio in modern life. Its importance as an instrument of news, of comment, and of propaganda is so obvious as to make extended illustration superfluous. One outstanding conclusion emerges— that, although great progress has been made in the technical field, the great opposition between radio communication as an instrument of military power and as an agency of general welfare will remain until the problem of international security is solved. Whether mankind will succeed in harnessing this remarkable invention for constructive ends or will continue to place it at the disposal of the destructive demon of war, time alone can tell.

SUMMARY

It was the hope of the founders of the League of Nations that by establishing a section of the Secretariat devoted to communications and transit, a co-ordinating agency of world significance would be able to play a substantial part in helping nations to plan transportation of all kinds in the most efficient manner. Closely connected with the section is the Advisory and Technical Committee set up by the League Council in June 1921 on the recommendation of the Barcelona Conference and chosen in part by the Permanent Members of the League Council and in part by the general conferences. The committee in its work and procedure is largely autonomous; it appoints expert committees to deal with special questions—there have been as many as twenty of which half a dozen were permanent committees on railroad, road, maritime, inland water traffic, electricity, and legal questions. The general conferences are called periodically in order to consider the adoption of conventions; but it is the committee and the Secretariat which provide the continuity of international effort. We may note that the committee "is not appointed by or directly responsible to any organ of the League. It owes its appointment to a conference at which delegates may be present from countries not members of the League."[53]

In the Americas a great amount of discussion has taken place on the promotion of inter-American communications and facilities.

[52] Sharp and Kirk, *op. cit.*, p. 183.

[53] H. R. G. Greaves, *The League Committees and World Order* (Oxford University Press, London, 1931), p. 155.

Committees of experts on port problems, highways, railroads, and aviation have been formed and general conferences dealing with these questions have been held. A detailed consideration of these activities would not bring to light any new questions of principle; and, interesting and valuable though the study would be, lack of space prevents further treatment of it here. The student is referred to the various publications issued by the Pan-American Union, if time permits more extensive study of international organization of transportation and communication on the American continent.

The foregoing analysis has revealed something of the need for international action in order to secure efficient transportation to serve the everyday economic and social needs of continents and even of the world itself. It has shown that institutions have grown up in response to definite needs and that if the way were clearer a great deal more might be done. But the great obstacle is the necessity for nations in an anarchical political world to look at communications primarily from the point of view of military, naval, and air power and only secondarily from the point of continental welfare. It has not been the purpose of this volume to deal with this phase of the question in detail; but one cannot emphasize too strongly the obvious fact, so tragically demonstrated in the last world war, the desperate preparations of the last few years, and the present struggle in Europe, that without communications efficient to the nth degree national authority is relatively powerless to guarantee security from immediate attack by a potential enemy. Countries therefore have increasingly subordinated the requirements of civil life which could have been largely met by co-operative international technical effort to the urgencies of individual national military, naval, and air power. Instead of providing capital to improve European transportation in many needed fields of effort, rival governments have built roads and railroads, airports, and shipping facilities where they can be of the greatest service for one immediate purpose, namely, war preparation. And until new units of government are developed which will drastically alter the present balance of effort, and until communications can safely be planned with an eye more to general human welfare and less to national power, international institutions for technical co-operation in transit and communication will exist on sufferance. In this as in the other chapters of the present volume the evidence seems clear that world political reorganization is a fundamental necessity.

Chapter VII

THE PROTECTION OF NATIONALS ABROAD, THEIR PROPERTY AND INVESTMENTS

GOVERNMENTS, as economic interests spread to wider fields, have to decide whether, and how far, they will protect their citizens who engage in foreign trade and investments. On the one hand, it may be argued that an individual in going to a distant part of the world should trade at his own risk and not involve his government; if he is willing to search for higher profits, well and good, but he need not expect to have the protection of his government in what is, after all, a private venture. On the other hand, it may be claimed that the investor at home enjoys the benefit of law and order and should be guaranteed at least certain minimum conditions of justice and security when he goes abroad. Moreover, countries cannot remain in watertight compartments and the resources of the world should be exploited for the benefit of the human race. Backward countries, so this argument runs, ought not to lock up their raw materials and let them go to waste or remain unused. They have rights, of course; but, since nature has distributed raw materials unequally, people must go beyond their political boundaries for the satisfaction of their economic needs. From this angle the trader or investor in foreign lands is not a mere profit-seeker venturing abroad for private gain when he should be investing his money at home; he is the enterpriser who by taking risks makes available the products of distant forests and mines, of far-flung plains and the seven seas, to make possible a higher standard of life for others. He is also part of a nation which requires economic wealth in order to maintain its political power and security. If, therefore, in going to countries with less-organized governments, he suffers unjust treatment, or is threatened with violence and danger, it is only right and just that he receive adequate protection.

329

We consider elsewhere[1] how the rights of the native inhabitants should be protected against abuse by foreign investors and traders. That is a problem of great magnitude; unfortunately, the imperialist powers have engaged in many ugly and indefensible methods in acquiring wealth which should have been made available for mankind as a whole. For the moment, we shall assume that capital is being invested in countries where law and order are either absent or inadequate, and that legitimate economic activity there is being hindered by conditions of political disorder and defective organization. Imperialist powers, in order to overcome these obstacles to the extension of trade and commerce, may take measures (1) to prevent disorder and revolution and (2) to guarantee fairness in the content and method of law.

In the attempts to maintain political stability the more powerful governments can bring pressure to bear upon the smaller and less-organized countries by refusing recognition to a government which comes into power by violence and revolutionary means. Modern commerce depends upon the stability of political and economic conditions; fighting and disorder disrupt the normal processes of daily life. Investors become frightened; capital is withdrawn, property is endangered, and markets are disturbed. President Wilson, in an effort to discourage political revolutions in Central and South America, and to encourage democracy— "ballots for bullets"—adopted the nonrecognition policy which was not reversed until the Franklin D. Roosevelt administration. Unfortunately such a recognition policy of itself does not distinguish between revolutions which are mere struggles for political power, the "ins" versus the "outs," and legitimate popular revolts against the injustices of a corrupt and oligarchic rule. In South and Central America many governments maintained themselves in power by dishonest means, and in the absence of fair elections it was impossible to dislodge the tyrannical officeholders by legal and constitutional means. The United States finally reversed the Wilson recognition policy, having experienced too much difficulty in trying to distinguish between the legitimate and the mere "in versus out" types of revolution; it had become the arbiter of internal affairs of other nations, laid itself open to the charge of meddlesomeness and partisanship, and provoked resentment from nations jealous of their independence and national sovereignty.

Governments may refuse recognition to revolutionary governments not because they are revolutionary but because they repu-

[1] See chapter xi.

diate the obligations of previous governments. Such a policy was directed against the Soviet Government, which had canceled the debts of the Czarist regime and prior private loans. In 1922, at the Conference of Genoa, the Allied Powers attempted to reach an agreement with the Bolshevists by which the latter would acknowledge debts contracted by the Czarist regime and in return the Allies would recognize the new government. The United States refused diplomatic recognition to the Obregon Government which assumed power in Mexico in 1920 on the grounds that it had not resumed debt payments which had been suspended in 1914, and that Article 27 of the 1917 Constitution empowered Mexico unjustly to confiscate certain lands and oil properties which had been acquired by American citizens. In 1923 an agreement was reached over the land and oil questions; the governments also signed two claims conventions, after which the United States extended recognition to Obregon.[2]

Recognition is a matter of great importance to weaker countries; without it financial loans are usually more difficult to obtain and private contracts and loans are on a less secure basis; investors and traders for that reason hesitate to make large commitments. Capital responds very rapidly to political conditions, welcoming security, and becoming extremely nervous at the first signs of disorder.

The protection of commercial interests abroad in areas where political disorder and inefficiency are rife has frequently brought strong action from the creditor countries, which may: (1) send naval patrols to places where piracy has not entirely disappeared (the Persian Gulf, China, and the Indian Ocean) to insure that ships of commerce shall not be attacked; and (2) land military forces in areas in which foreign lives and property are endangered. All the great powers have indulged in this practice. The United States at different times sent troops or marines into Nicaragua, Haiti, the Dominican Republic, and Cuba; Great Britain took similar action in Egypt and in China; France made disorders in Morocco the excuse for a military occupation which proved to be the forerunner of a protectorate; Russia landed troops in North Persia and in China; and the recent actions of Japan are too well known to need comment. These illustrations are but a few of many which might be quoted.

---

[2] See G. H. Stuart, *Latin America and the United States* (D. Appleton-Century Co., New York, 1938), pp. 162–66. The oil question was even more important than the land problem.

The landing of troops is a more drastic step than the use of naval patrols. In 1861 France, Great Britain, and Austria claimed that Mexico "had defaulted in its foreign obligations" and jointly intervened. In 1902 Germany, Great Britain, and Italy, on the plea that Venezuela was deliberately refusing to meet the legitimate claims of their nationals, blockaded Venezuelan ports and seized gunboats; the German ships even resorted to bombardment. And in 1913 "Great Britain threatened to send a warship to Guatemala if the latter government continued to misappropriate the coffee duties which in an agreement of 1895 it had promised to set aside as security for a British loan."[3] Military occupation involves an unpleasant and dramatic affront to the sense of national dignity and national sovereignty, which is lively enough in all countries and not least among the weaker powers. Moreover, there is always a possibility that some of the occupying forces will get out of hand, become unruly, or at least offend the feelings of the inhabitants by inconsiderate and sometimes rude behavior. And there is no guaranty that the extent of the military occupation will bear any just relation to the amount of danger which threatens the foreign inhabitants or will not be used as a pretext to cover imperialist aims of a far-reaching kind. Two examples will suffice here. The French taking of Fez in Morocco in 1911 and the Japanese invasion of Manchuria in 1931 were believed by many people to have been unwarranted by the facts of the case; certainly the scope of the military occupations was out of all proportion to the protection needed by French and Japanese citizens in those parts.

Small and weak countries may be subjected to another form of intervention—the declaration of neutral zones by foreign governments. If a civil war breaks out in a country, and threatens the security and safety of the foreign inhabitants, the government of the latter may inform the government of the strife-torn country that the conflict must not extend to towns or other areas in which the foreigners live. Such a measure of neutralization gives protection to the non-native residents and in theory is sound enough. But it may be that in a civil war a particular town is of great importance to one side or the other and its possession may be a decisive factor. In that case the foreign action may appear as an unjustifiable piece of partisanship and be deeply resented by at least one of the contending factions. In 1910, for example, the

[3] R. L. Buell, *International Relations* (Henry Holt & Company, New York, 1929), p. 415.

United States declared the Bluefields area in Nicaragua a neutral zone and by this step assisted the conservatives and handicapped the liberals. It is difficult to formulate a general rule, since circumstances vary so much in periods of civil disorder. The two conflicting viewpoints—that of the foreign inhabitants demanding protection, and caring little for legal niceties of the sovereign status of the country in which they live, and the view of the national government anxious to preserve its independence and jealous of its political dignity—stand out clearly enough. We shall inquire later whether methods exist, or may be devised, to resolve them.

Landing parties and naval patrols are in reality only emergency measures. They do not provide a permanent method of preventing disorder and instability in a weaker country. Hence it is not surprising that countries which possess economic interests in other lands may feel that a temporary intervention designed to meet an immediate crisis will not be enough and may consequently take steps to prevent the recurrence of such outbreaks—by insisting upon helping to create an adequately trained constabulary or gendarmerie capable of maintaining order and security. An outstanding example is provided in the 1914 Treaty between Haiti and the United States, Article X of which reads:

The Haitian Government obligates itself, for the preservation of domestic peace, the security of individual rights and full observance of the provisions of this treaty, to create without delay an efficient constabulary, urban and rural, composed of native Haitians. This constabulary shall be organized and officered by Americans, appointed by the President of Haiti, upon nomination by the President of the United States. The Haitian Government shall clothe these officers with the proper and necessary authority and uphold them in the performance of their functions. . . . . The high contracting parties agree that the stipulations in this article are necessary to prevent factional strife and disturbances.

Similar arrangements were made for American officers to take charge of native constabularies in the Dominican Republic, in Nicaragua, and in Panama. The last-named government in 1910 and 1913 asked the United States for assistance in training its local police force. These examples are typical of many instances of foreign aid in reorganizing native constabulary forces. In so far as the experiments are successful, they result in building up an efficient local body animated by a sense of *esprit de corps* and able to maintain order. When this happy result is achieved, foreign governments may feel that they can withdraw their supervision of police organization.

European traders living in less-developed countries have reason to be conscious of the dangers of disease; the absence of sanitation, the liability to epidemics, and the inadequacy of medical facilities make life in these parts a matter of some risk. Again we may draw examples from the experience of the United States. At the end of the last century yellow fever in Cuba rendered Havana notoriously unsafe for foreigners and a constant menace to near-by ports of the United States. The United States, therefore, insisted upon inserting into the Platt Amendment of 1901 Article V, which reads:

That the Government of Cuba will execute, and as far as necessary, extend, the plans already devised or other plans to be mutually agreed upon, for the sanitation of the cities of the island, to the end that a recurrence of epidemic and infectious diseases may be prevented thereby assuring protection to the people and commerce of Cuba, as well as the commerce of the Southern ports of the United States and the people residing therein.

A few years later the United States expressed dissatisfaction at the delay in the paving and in installing the sewerage system of Havana. Secretary Hay wrote that American ports and commerce had suffered "immense losses" because of the yellow fever in Cuba and its spread from there into this country. The American intervention in 1906 arrested the deteriorating sanitary condition of Cuba, a national board of sanitation was created to replace the ineffective local municipal boards, and the paving and sewerage work of Havana was completed.

In 1915 Haiti agreed to execute measures necessary "for the sanitation and public improvement of the Republic under the supervision and direction of an engineer or engineers to be appointed by the President of Haiti upon nomination by the President of the United States and authorized for that purpose by the Government of Haiti." The Haitian Public Health Service under American supervision did extraordinarily fine work. It built modern hospitals, established rural clinics, set in motion infant welfare work, vaccinated schoolchildren, distributed quinine, drained and filled swamps, cleaned streets, and performed a great number of other services.

We have given only one or two examples of this type of protection of foreign interests abroad. Of all the services rendered, the medical contribution has probably aroused the least criticism among the smaller powers and has often given splendid results in the improved health of the native community.

The great powers may also attempt to stabilize economic conditions in small debtor countries by imposing, with or without the consent of the latter, various types of financial supervision. They may justify this enforced assistance by arguing that the more-experienced countries have developed efficient economic and financial methods and that their financial control, if well and honestly exercised, may not only save the smaller countries from financial difficulty and even bankruptcy but also provide a valuable education in modern business methods; the assisted country may thereby be ultimately enabled to take over its own affairs and manage them more efficiently.

Williams describes[4] five main types of foreign financial control. The first of these is customs collection or receivership. A great deal of the revenue obtained by smaller countries is derived from customs revenues. Inefficient collection will lessen their value as security for foreign loans. Hence the creditor country often stipulates that an agent of the banking house which makes the loan, or an official appointed by its government, shall supervise the collection. The agent deducts from the total receipts the amount needed to pay for the actual collection of the duties and for the interest and sinking fund on the foreign debt; the rest goes to the native government. Williams notes that the Dominican Republic, which in 1905 accepted a general receiver of customs, in 1933 had 172 employees, of whom five of the chief officials were Americans. In Haiti also the fiscal representative received his appointment at the hands of the President of Haiti "upon the nomination of the President of the United States." In other countries—for example, Liberia, Nicaragua, Bolivia, and Salvador—foreign officials have supervised the customs revenues.

Such control has frequently resulted in improving the credit of debtor countries, thus enabling them to borrow money more cheaply, and the native treasury has received a greater income than if it had remained under the inefficient management of its own nationals. Because there are only a few ports at which officials may be stationed, the foreign control is not unduly obvious to the people at large.

Nevertheless the debtors are liable to receive unpleasant reminders of their subordinate position, for the creditor country or

[4] B. J. Williams, *American Diplomacy* (McGraw-Hill Book Company, New York, 1936), pp. 234–39.

countries may refuse to allow an alteration of tariff rates, on the ground that to raise the tariff will adversely affect the security of foreign investments. For many years China vainly attempted to persuade the foreign powers to permit her to raise her customs rates. The United States on one occasion refused to allow Haiti to issue decrees lowering the tariff without American consent. Especially if the debtor country must accept a formal agreement giving to the foreign creditor the right of intervention to protect the foreign control over customs, it lives under a constant reminder of its dependent political and financial status.

A second type of government control may be described thus: Collection of internal revenues may be taken over by a foreign power. So many influences affect international trade that in some years the income from duties on imports may be so small that foreign creditors who have relied upon this source for their interest and sinking fund may not receive payment. The debtors will be unable to meet their obligations. Naturally, a foreign investor wishes to have adequate security and will inquire if other revenues may be pledged by a debtor country as an additional guaranty. Hence we find that certain portions of the internal revenue may be handed over as security, as were the proceeds of the Portuguese tobacco monopoly in 1891 or those of the 1890 Persian tobacco monopoly, or the duties collected from a salt tax or from public lotteries, or taxes on mining proceeds, and so forth.

As in the case of customs, so with internal revenues the debtor country may have to submit not only to pledging a part of its income but also to a more direct foreign control because of the insistence by the creditor that these internal revenues be collected in the most efficient manner. In 1914 Secretary Bryan agreed that the Dominican Republic might receive a loan provided that it would hand over the collection of the alcohol and tobacco receipts to a general receiver nominated by the United States. Efficient business methods often produce extraordinary results; but even so it is surprising to learn that the United States' financial adviser to Haiti reported that $1,000,000 might have been collected by the use of adequate methods, whereas, because of the inefficient native administration, not more than $360,000 had reached the Treasury. In the light of facts such as these, Haiti agreed in 1924 to place its internal revenue bureau under a United States Receiver of Customs. In Nicaragua a United States plan to supervise internal revenues met with opposition until a compromise was reached: if the internal revenues fell below $180,000 for a three months' period, the United States Collector General should take charge of the duty of collecting.

In the Dominican Republic and Haiti the foreign control of internal revenue collectorships has now been discontinued, although in the latter country the American fiscal representative "has power to inspect the Internal Revenue Service and make recommendations as to its proper operation."[5]

A third such control may be needed. A foreign banker, in his search for sound opportunities for profitable investment, will not be entirely reassured, even when the control of customs and of internal revenue receipts of a financially backward country are placed under the supervision of agents named by himself or his government. He will be interested not only in the adequacy of that income but also in the amount of expenditure undertaken by the debtor country. In these days of unbalanced budgets, of huge public expenditures, and wholesale defaults on foreign loans, we can readily appreciate the fact that a cautious investor and his protecting government will ask for some control both of revenue and of indebtedness and expenditure. Unwise expenditure may ruin the results of sound income collection. Foreign control over a government's expenditure was provided for under Article II of the Platt Amendment, signed in 1901, by which Cuba promised not to increase its public debt until its ordinary revenues were sufficient to guarantee the payment of interest and sinking funds. The United States thereby claimed the right to be consulted before Cuba borrowed abroad. By the 1924 convention with the Dominican Republic, the United States was to agree to any increase in that country's public debt. In 1914 the two countries had disagreed as to whether the words "public debt meant bonded indebtedness or included floating expenditures." In 1916 the United States intervened in the Dominican Republic, one reason being that it had violated Article III of the 1907 convention relating to consultation in the matter of indebtedness.

A fourth such control was tried. In order to insure that expenditures should not be excessive, the United States claimed the right to supervise the framing of budgets in the Dominican Republic and in Haiti, although in the latter case, the right of supervision was withdrawn in 1931. An American officer exercised this type of control in Liberia, under the provision of a 1926 loan agreement between the two countries.

[5] B. J. Williams, *op. cit.*, p. 235.

And, fifth, to supervise the budget may not be sufficient, because governments may divert funds "from the purpose for which they were appropriated." To prevent such action in most modern countries an auditor is given the power to examine an account before it is paid and thus to make certain that the numbers within the authorization are of valid appropriation, his signature to the warrant being necessary for the disbursement of funds. This system has been applied by the United States: to the Dominican Republic, although now discontinued; to Haiti from 1918 to 1931; and to Liberia under the loan contract of 1926. Similar arrangements were made in the case of Nicaragua and Panama.

If, in spite of the measures described, debtor countries default, or if no previous controls have been imposed, and no other means are available, the stronger powers may have resort to military measures in order to compel payment.[6]

The action of Germany in sinking Venezuelan ships in 1902 brought to a head the question of armed force in the collection of debts. The question was, and still is, one of peculiar difficulty. The creditors are acutely aware of the losses which they sustain through the inability or unwillingness of debtor countries to meet their obligations. But the debtor governments are even more conscious of a sense of injury. Forcible measures against them appear as violations of their sovereignty, likely to weaken internal authority and thereby promote local disorder; the feeling of resentment may even cause the debtor to evade payment as much as possible. On the other hand, if a country is permitted to escape its normal obligations, respect for contracts will decline and governments will be encouraged to persist in a course of irresponsible behavior. If creditors would limit themselves to a just demand for reparation for real damages sustained, the problem would be relatively easy. Unfortunately, the stronger powers have often used coercive measures in order to gain advantages out of all proportion to the original grievance, and weak debtor countries are led to believe that these coercive demands are part of an imperialistic system of extortion.

Several methods have been proposed by which both creditors and debtors will obtain justice. Dr. Luis Drago, the Argentinian Minister of Foreign Affairs, on December 29, 1902, wrote a note which has since become famous. In it he argued that creditors know in advance the financial condition of the borrowing country

6 See above, pp. 331–33.

and the amount which they pay for securities depends upon their estimate of a government's financial soundness. Professor E. M. Borchard writes: "The investor . . . . buys with full notice and assumption of the risks, and has weighed the probabilities of large profit against the danger of loss." It is therefore unfair "that the government of the creditor should make the breach of such a contractual obligation to a citizen who accidentally holds a foreign public bond a cause for armed international action involving the whole nation in the burden."[7] Drago believed that governments should meet their obligations but that they should be permitted to choose the occasion—if economic adversity should place upon them an over-heavy burden they ought to be able to "default respectably," to use a phrase uttered by Professor T. E. Gregory a few years ago. Debtor countries, Drago continued, do not willingly default; they realize that such action damages their credit and reflects upon their national honor. Normally they will pay when they can. Therefore, to collect debts by force is wrong. It threatens the sovereignty of the debtor country, inasmuch as a forceful collection "presupposes territorial occupation to make it effective and occupational authority signifies the suppression or subordination of the local governments." Drago concluded that public debts should give no occasion for armed intervention nor for the actual occupation of the territory of American nations by European powers.

Authorities on international law differ as to the extent to which governments of creditor countries may go in forcibly collecting debts from defaulters. Their judgments vary according to the fundamental meaning which they attach to the idea of "sovereign states." Does sovereignty mean primarily that governments possess complete freedom of action even to the point of repudiating promises, or does the fact that sovereign states belong to the family of nations mean that they owe duties toward one another, that they must perform these duties, and that, if they are unable or unwilling to do so, it may be justifiable for other states to use force against them? Most scholars agree that more than a "mere non-payment of public debts" must be present in order to justify armed intervention. If a country is honestly in default, the creditor should not take military action. Only "when *bad faith* may be considered the moving cause of the non-payment" are governments

---

[7] E. M. Borchard, *The Diplomatic Protection of Citizens Abroad* (The Banks Law Publishing Co., New York, 1927), pp. 308–9. The following sections are based upon this excellent work.

justified in enforcing their demands. Unfortunately, governments have often used their armed forces against debtor countries without observing this principle and they have exerted pressure on behalf of outrageously exaggerated claims.

The United States has attempted to avoid using armed force for the collection of ordinary contract debts due to its citizens by other governments. Secretary Elihu Root, in 1906, stated the principle that

it is doubtless true that the non-payment of public debts may be accompanied by such circumstances of fraud and wrong-doing or violation of treaties as to justify the use of force. This government would be glad to see an international consideration of the subject which shall discriminate between such cases and the simple non-performance of a contract with a private person, and a resolution in favor of reliance upon peaceful means in cases of the latter class.

The resolution of the Rio de Janeiro Conference which was submitted to the Hague Conference of 1907 by General Porter proposed that governments refrain from employing force in the collection of ordinary public debts arising from contracts until the amount and the justice of the debt should have been determined by arbitration. After considerable discussion the Hague Conference adopted the following:

The contracting powers agree not to have recourse to armed force for the recovery of contract debts claimed from the government of one country by the government of another country as being due to its nationals. This undertaking is, however, not applicable when the debtor state refuses or neglects to reply to an offer of arbitration, or, after accepting the offer, prevents any *compromis* from being agreed on, or, after the arbitration, fails to submit to the award.

The resolution does not entirely rule out the forcible collection of public debts, but it does lessen the occasions on which such forcible action should be undertaken. Only if the debtor country refuses to arbitrate, or formulates an impossible set of conditions after theoretically accepting arbitration, or refuses to carry out the award, can another government justifiably have recourse to armed force. The resolution does not cover private debts, and no general convention similar to the one quoted has yet been made to cover debts of a nonpublic character. Borchard notes that this latter type of claim is often unjust and that it is desirable, as the number of international transactions and obligations increases, that their fulfillment and enforcement should be divorced from matters of high politics—private claims should not have to depend upon the international situation, with its conglomeration of alliances, diplomatic situations, incidents, and general considerations of political and strategic advantage. For these reasons he gives emphatic support to the proposal which several German authorities had urged in the years immediately before the World War of 1914–1918 for an international court to adjudicate claims between the debtor state and the unpaid creditor.

The individual should be given the right to bring suit against the debtor nation before this international tribunal, as has been done in the convention for the establishment of an international prize court and in the treaty of Washington for the establishment of a Central American Court of Arbitration. The creditor will thus be assured of a hearing, the debtor state will be secured against the pressure of exorbitant claims accompanied by disagreeable diplomatic coercion, the government of the claimant will avoid what is always a potential germ of international difficulty and ill-will, with the incidental expense of pressing a diplomatic claim, and the peace of the world will be fostered by the removal of one great source of international conflict. The details of the organization and operation of this international court may be left to the delegates of the Third Hague Peace Conference, who may profitably examine the proposals of several learned Germans. The prospect and opportunity for thus advancing the cause of international justice, toward which goal the Porter proposition makes only a slight forward step, must command universal support.[8]

The South American international lawyer, Calvo, also opposed the recovery of debts and the pressing of private claims by the armed intervention of governments. He proposed to obviate such intervention by making a foreigner who was about to enter into a contract with a government sign a statement that he would not call upon his own government for diplomatic protection but would accept as final the decision of the local courts in all cases of dispute which might arise. Several South American countries have incorporated this provision into their constitutions, and some international lawyers have expressed their approval on the ground that a sovereign country has complete jurisdiction over individuals within its own boundaries. Certainly, strong, well-established governments do not hesitate to assume jurisdiction over aliens within their territory, and seldom do serious complications arise in consequence. The smaller and less powerful governments wish to enjoy the same power; but, because they are physically weaker,

[8] E. M. Borchard, *op. cit.*, pp. 328–29.

they must attempt to buttress their position by invoking the aid of legal theory and obtaining from foreign investors and concession-aires an explicit declaration that they will renounce all claims of diplomatic protection. They hope in this way to take from imperialist governments the traditional right of intervening on behalf of their subjects.

The stronger nations have not taken kindly to this attempt to force the individual to renounce the privilege of receiving protective aid from his government. They argue that a person is more than a person. He is a citizen; and, while he may be prepared to renounce any assistance which his own government may render to him personally, he cannot bind his sovereign government to forego its allegedly "inalienable" right to protect him as a citizen. For an injury to a citizen may affect the welfare and prestige of his government; and it is a matter of public policy for that government to maintain and defend its fundamental interests. The citizen as an individual may be relatively unimportant, but he is the symbol of a national state which far transcends his wishes or desires.

Some international tribunals have accepted the renunciatory clause and upheld it as valid; other tribunals have denied its validity; and some governments, while they consider that the renunciation will weaken "the moral if not the legal right" of the government to intervene, nevertheless have accepted the Calvo clause as binding. Borchard mentions that we have an analogy in municipal law: a provision in a private contract which renounces judicial remedies will be held invalid; "as in municipal law the private agreement cannot oust the jurisdiction of municipal courts, so in international law the private agreement cannot oust the interposition of international remedies." And the same writer states that the more authoritative opinion among international lawyers seems to be "that the renunciatory clause is without any effect so far as any changes or modifications in the ordinary rules of international law are concerned."[9]

The problem is a difficult one, and we may expect that the debtor states will continue to object to the use of armed force for the collection of claims and that creditor countries will still be disinclined to trust the courts of the less stable governments abroad. Two general methods will help to reconcile these opposing views: (1) greater stability and better government in the weaker coun-

[9] E. M. Borchard, *op. cit.,* pp. 809–10.

tries will remove complaints concerning denial of justice and lessen the occasions for armed intervention; and (2) suitable international machinery for impartial arbitration when disputes between debtor and creditor arise may be established.

The foregoing analysis has shown how diplomatic protection is used as an instrument of promoting and safeguarding the rights of citizens abroad. But, as Eugene Staley points out, the method is inadequate and unsound for the following reasons:

a) National diplomatic protection violates the fundamental requirement of justice that an interested party shall not be a judge of his own cause. A government which protects its citizens abroad without submitting the matter to a third party may force a weaker country to make reparations by reason of power and might and not of right. The danger is not all on one side, however: a weak government may be able to inflict injustice on foreign citizens because the government of the latter may be

unwilling to incur the trouble and expense, perhaps the political risk and the odium, of effective *ex parte* enforcement of its rights . . . . In either case the orderly and equitable adjustment of conflicts is impeded by this vital defect in the method of diplomatic protection.[10]

b) National diplomatic protection frequently complicates a quarrel and leads to more serious disputes; commercial differences of private parties become mixed up with questions of national prestige.

Thus the institution of diplomatic protection operates to enlist on the two sides of a conflict, which may be basically the clash of rival private economic interests, all the formidable apparatus of armed sovereign powers, with their bellicose manifestations of nationalism, their jingoistic presses, their sensitive prides, and their constant concern for the maintenance of prestige.[11]

Thus a clash between unscrupulous traders in Samoa "brings battleships to the scene and becomes a conflict between the Great Powers." What is needed is an institution which will mitigate rather than intensify differences, and which will *minimize the influence of extraneous factors* by "localizing" and "dissociating" the point at issue. This is precisely what diplomatic protection does not do.

c) Closely related to this defect is the fact that questions of

[10] Eugene Staley, *War and the Private Investor* (Doubleday, Doran, New York, 1935), p. 442.
[11] *Ibid.*

high policy and political expediency may jeopardize the chances of individual redress for injury sustained. A government may decide that it is not expedient to back the claims of its citizen abroad; even after presenting a claim to a foreign government, it may decide to abandon the claim or take other steps which cannot be predicted. The private citizen, relying upon his government, may obtain less than he is entitled honestly to expect because his claim, if pressed, might compromise a delicate political situation. His private interests will therefore be sacrificed for a governmental advantage not in any way connected with the question of his individual rights. On the other hand, a government may take advantage of a private claim to take an arbitrary stand, pressing the claim unduly because it

desires to pick a quarrel in order to complete a territorial conquest, because internal opposition to the party in power seems to call for a foreign diversion, or because a navy bill is about to come up and it seems desirable to impress the legislature with the usefulness of naval power. Legal rights may provide the formal basis for diplomatic protection, but political expediency has in practice been a more than significant motivator.[12]

This blurring and intermingling of power politics with individual rights is a serious matter. What would happen if our law courts permitted similar methods? Has it not been the separation of legal and political matters which has made possible our enjoyment of liberty today? Is it not true that one of the reasons for the insistence upon extraterritorial rights in China lay in the belief that Chinese law permitted an over-intimate relationship between the executive and the judiciary? Is not one of the most ominous developments of the present day the subordination of the courts to political forces in the dictatorships of Europe, where the existence of politicized law is no guaranty for the preservation of human rights and liberty? If these questions supply their own answers, then may we not deduce that we have permitted in the international sphere a state of affairs which has been recognized as basically unsound within the domestic sphere of democratic states?

d) Diplomatic protection depends upon the discretion of a national government, and cannot be invoked automatically or as a matter of right by an injured party; consequently interested or aggrieved private parties engage in press and radio propaganda

[12] Eugene Staley, *op. cit.*, p. 445.

to stir up popular emotion and bring pressure to bear upon the government. A private dispute abroad may thus lead to the creation of mutually hostile national feelings, which become inflamed by distorted and unfair criticism. It is true that governments have set up claims commissions on which both sides are represented and to this extent the danger of disputes is lessened; but too frequently the delay in establishing the commissions and the slowness of their deliberations have worked injustice upon individuals seeking redress for injury sustained.

e) Often the stronger powers have utilized the plea of protecting private investments abroad in order to strengthen their policies of "political penetration." The history of modern "imperialism" is full of examples of governments employing disputes involving private corporation interests as excuses for enlarging their political empires: Italy's conquest of Abyssinia; the German acquisition of Sudetenland; the Japanese control over North China; and, in earlier days, British expansion in Egypt, and in East, West, and South Africa; America's policy in Central America and in Hawaii; and Russia's designs in China and Persia. A survey of imperialist expansion gives ample evidence, and fully bears out Staley's judgment: "Needless to say, an institution which operates so frequently in such a way is seriously defective as a device for orderly adjustment of investment conflicts."[13]

f) The danger of political intervention by strong powers has caused the weaker powers to attempt self-protection by introducing measures designed to keep foreign capital from entering their country or to permit it to come in only on condition that the investor renounce his country's protection. In the absence of satisfactory alternatives the great powers have at times been unwilling to permit their private investors to divest themselves of diplomatic protection. This action, while understandable, has actually interfered with legitimate nonpolitical enterprise and, as Staley puts it, "stimulates injurious treatment of aliens and generates causes of controversy" because in their attempts at self-protection the weaker countries create obstacles and intensify difficulties for business men "who are citizens of a state whose political power is feared."

g) The last weakness of diplomatic protection arises from the fact that, while it "takes the form of a legal process" cast in the terminology of international law, there are too few legal cate-

[13] *Ibid.*, p. 447.

gories and precedents and inadequate legal machinery to embrace the differences of culture and the complexities which arise.[14] The fundamental fact is the discrepancy between the kind of problem to be solved, and the "institutions of adjustment." The conflicts are international, sometimes extra-governmental, often supra-national; but diplomatic protection is a national instrument only. To attempt to settle supra-national problems by the use of national instruments is manifestly unwise. A sound solution demands other methods which will approximate more closely the basic condition of justice in the settlement of disputes—that no party be a judge in his own cause.

It was logical to hope that rules might be developed which would be satisfactory to both debtor and creditor nations in the matter of protection of citizens abroad, and that gradually international law would be able to devise methods and procedures which would eliminate arbitrary action by the strong and insure adequate justice by the weaker powers. We have already touched upon certain of the proposals—the Calvo, Drago, and Porter resolutions. But it is desirable to put the problem in the more general setting of international institutions.

Frederick Sherwood Dunn suggests that Grotius wrote little concerning the protection of foreigners and their property interests abroad, because international law in those days governed personal sovereigns and not impersonal states, and because these sovereigns ruled over subjects who "for the most part stayed at home."[15] Vattel developed the thesis that an injury to a person constituted an injury to his state, which must protect that citizen; but since commercial relations in the eighteenth century took place between European states which constituted a "fairly homogeneous international society," no great difficulties arose. Foreigners going abroad met substantially the same legal ideas as at home, and their protection gave rise to comparatively few disputes. Moreover, there was still not a great deal of international trade and commerce.

When European citizens and European investments invaded South American states during the nineteenth century, a new and complicated problem arose. The Latin-American countries were unsettled and subject to frequent revolutions and the domination

[14] O. J. Lissitzyn, "The Meaning of Denial of Justice in International Law," *The American Journal of International Law,* October 1936.

[15] Frederick Sherwood Dunn, *The Protection of Nationals* (The Johns Hopkins Press, Baltimore, 1932), p. 48.

of the judiciary by the executive. Naturally enough, the foreign powers complained of inadequate legal protection, and sought to attain the ends of justice by diplomatic and, if necessary, armed intervention. But, as we have already seen, the Latin-American countries had reason to believe that the stronger countries were taking advantage of the situation to further imperialistic aims and not merely to protect individual rights.

The fundamental basis of Calvo's doctrine was that foreigners should not expect any better legal treatment than that enjoyed by the citizens of the local state, and that therefore they should regard the judgments of the local courts as final. The European and United States' view was that there existed an international standard of justice to which the local governments must conform and in the absence of which foreign powers might insist upon redress. Dunn writes that the diplomatic protection of citizens abroad, while it undoubtedly gave rise to abuses, did under the circumstances serve "as a substitute for territorial conquest in bringing the Latin-American states within the orbit of international trade and commerce."[16] Such negative virtue did not satisfy those who desired a sounder basis, and many jurists attempted to refine the system and purge it of its abuses. Outstanding works appeared by Heilborn, John Bassett Moore, Treipel, Tchernoff, Anzilotti, and later by Borchard, and Eagleton, who attempted to systematize the subject and set forth its rules and principles.

Such efforts seemed all the more desirable in view of the growth of international arbitration for the settlement of claims arising out of injuries suffered by foreigners. Many treaties with this end in view were signed between the Latin-American states on the one hand and the European powers on the other, as well as between the United States and Great Britain, the commissioners acting as judges and supporting their decisions by references to international law. It seemed imperative to clarify these rules and principles.

After 1918 the League of Nations appointed a committee to consider the progressive codification of international law. One of the subjects selected by the committee was that of the responsibility of states for injury to foreigners within their borders. The rapporteur, Señor Guerrero, from Salvador, brought in a report which substantially followed the views of Calvo and called for a great reduction in the sphere of diplomatic protection. At the first

[16] *Ibid.*, p. 58.

Conference for the Codification of International Law held at The Hague in 1930, the committee was unable to agree upon the fundamental question already mentioned—that is, whether foreigners should enjoy a greater measure of protection than native citizens, and also upon the question whether or not a definite standard of "due diligence" could be found by which to measure the extent of alleged failure to give a foreigner adequate protection and reparation.

The matter has remained at substantially the same level since the Hague Conference and, as suggested above, there is little hope that agreement will be reached until the creditor countries cease using the diplomatic protection of nationals abroad as an excuse for pursuing other ends, and until the smaller and weaker countries so improve their internal judicial systems as to take away from foreign residents and their governments a sense of legitimate grievance. Legal reforms within and political restraint without, together with an appreciation of the fundamentally common interest that all parties have in the peaceful settlement of all disputes by arbitration instead of by force or evasion, will combine to produce a recognition of the larger aspects of the problem. Dunn is undoubtedly right in suggesting that, without denying the importance of legal studies, and attempts to systematize legal principles, what is most needed today is to clarify the practical ends and common interests of nations, "to make these common interests articulate, and to look upon international law simply as an instrument for fostering and safeguarding them."[17] Presumably for the better, the United States, under its "good neighbor" policy, has definitely obligated itself not to intervene under any circumstances in the internal domestic politics of the Latin-American republics.[18]

PRIVATE INTERNATIONAL LAW

It would be a mistake to assume that diplomatic protection constitutes the only method of obtaining justice for merchants and others engaged in business and enterprises abroad. So great is the amount of international economic and social intercourse that the diplomatic agencies of government would be overwhelmed by the amount of work to be done. Moreover, a regular system based upon rules and one capable of speedier justice is essential for the requirements of commerce. Carter well writes: "For eight hun-

---

[17] F. S. Dunn, *op. cit.*, p. 203.

[18] G. H. Stuart, *Latin America and the United States* (1938), pp. 30–37.

dred years merchants have cried for speedy justice. Mercantile men must be about their business, for trade will not wait."[19]

Indeed, even in early medieval times, the merchant could not afford lengthy and costly formal proceedings of the courts of law. He would rather "cut his loss than have his case hung up indefinitely." Merchants therefore developed a mercantile law which was truly international and was administered in local and popular courts of *mercatores et marinarii*. The famous Laws of Oleron contained judgments concerning the rights and duties of ships and their personnel, and other divisions of the Law Merchant dealt with other phases of trade and commerce. It was administered, not by professional judges belonging to a particular nation, but by tribunals of experts in trade matters. Despite many variations, the law was essentially the same in different parts of Europe: "the same people met each other in succession at the great fairs where the same questions must have constantly arisen. . . . . To the great fairs such as those at Lyons, Besançon, Antwerp, Winchester, Stourbridge, and St. Ives, merchants came from afar."[20]

The Courts of Pie Powder (*Piepoudre*) attached to the fairs gave speedy justice. The guild merchants developed a remarkable system of mutual arbitration which enabled commerce to be carried on more easily. But with the rise of national courts and the decline of the guild merchants, the local courts lost ground. The Courts of Admiralty usurped their jurisdiction, and the Courts of Common Law were to eclipse both the local mercantile courts and the Admiralty Courts. The result was not an unmixed blessing. Lord Campbell wrote that the English courts of the eighteenth century were so ignorant of many legal questions concerning commercial affairs that merchants often settled their disputes by private arbitration.

Mention of national courts brings to the front the new factors which were to influence trade and commerce. We have referred to the many differences of language, custom, religion, art, and other forms which characterize modern nations. It would be surprising if these differences did not include marked differences of law. As national sovereignty asserted itself, the desire to be free from the legal control of outside authority became pronounced. Territorial law, i.e., complete jurisdiction within the boundaries of a state, gained in power, and personal law based upon blood

[19] A. T. Carter, *A History of English Legal Institutions* (Butterworth & Co., London, 1906), p. 270.

[20] *Ibid.*, p. 266.

relationship tended to decline. Now no theory can be carried out without making allowance for other principles. A state claiming absolute control over persons within its own boundaries (including foreigners who are residing or trading there) cannot claim control over its own citizens if they reside within the jurisdiction of another state. But states claim that their citizens still owe allegiance even when they are abroad. And out of the conflicting claims of jurisdiction (those of allegiance and of territory) arise the problems of private international law frequently designated the conflict of laws.

A few of the problems may be summarized. Which national law should prevail in determining the domicile of a person who has a residence in more than one country? What principles shall be adopted to regulate the conflict of laws? Countries have different rules concerning legal procedure, as for example, the evidence required in order to constitute legal proof. Rules of evidence differ. The period of limitation of legal action is not the same. Some countries require stricter proof of foreign law when introduced as evidence. The weight given to judgments of foreign courts constitutes another problem. Persons may have the legal capacity to marry at one age in one country and at another age in other countries. Forms of marriage differ; what is deemed incestuous marriage in one part is not so regarded in another. Property rights connected with marriage show many variations. Divorce is easier to obtain in one country than in another; alimony constitutes a problem because of different requirements. The capacity of corporations to carry on business is a matter of extreme importance in these days, but the differences of national laws provide many obstacles. National laws differ concerning the rights and duties of parents and children in such things as custody, support, legitimacy, adoption, and guardianship. In property matters questions concerning ownership and transfer of land, of jurisdiction over and rights in vessels, the assignment of foreign debts, and the use of negotiable instruments raise a bewildering maze of problems. National requirements in the realm of contracts, show marked variations; form of contracts, legality of performance, and rights of action are urgent questions as international agreements grow in number and in scope. The list might be widely extended did space permit.

In order to overcome the delay and confusion which result from differing and often contradictory requirements of the respective national systems, two general lines of approach have been made: (1) international conferences and bilateral treaties to bring greater uniformity, or to make clearer the rules which should prevail in the event of disputes; and (2) movements toward unofficial arbitration and conciliation by merchants and others engaged in foreign trade and commerce—a modern edition, as it were, of the Law Merchant of medieval times.

In 1893, 1894, 1900, and 1925 conferences were held in Europe to consider the adoption of conventions dealing with private international law, and a number of measures were agreed upon. A convention signed in November 1896 and effective in May 1899 concerned questions of civil procedure, such as judicial assistance in the service of documents, security for costs, and the execution of judgments for costs. The Hague Conference on Private International Law considered the questions of divorce and separation. The 1902 Convention, ratified in 1904, dealt with the conflict of laws in regard to (1) marriage, (2) divorce and separation, and (3) guardianship of minors. These conventions regulated many of the conflicts in ways[21] too technical to be discussed here.

The 1910 and 1912 Hague Conferences for the unification of the law of negotiable instruments drew up a protocol which was not ratified because of the ensuing World War. But in 1930, after considerable work by the League of Nations, a conference at Geneva adopted three conventions dealing with the unification of the law of bills of exchange and promissory notes. In the following year three conventions were adopted relating to checks (the provisions are too technical to be presented here). Governments have also adopted uniform legislation in the matter of transit. International conferences drew up rules for the prevention of collisions by ships at sea, the unification of rules relating to collisions and salvage (1910), the unification of rules relative to the limitation of liability of owners of vessels (1924), to maritime liens and mortgages (1924–1926), to bills of lading (1924), and to immunities of government-owned vessels (1926). We have referred elsewhere to the developments in international air navigation and railroad communications.

Efforts to codify private international law rules have also been prominent on the American continent. In 1889 seven Latin-American governments attended a conference at Montevideo and drew up conventions dealing with conflicts in civil, commercial, and penal law and the law of procedure, but relatively little further action

---

[21] See A. K. Kuhn, *Comparative Commentaries on Private International Law, or Conflict of Laws* (The Macmillan Company, New York, 1937), pp. 59–60.

was taken for several years. At Rio de Janeiro in 1906 the Third
Inter-American Conference appointed a committee of jurists to
work out projects for codification. It was not until 1925, when
the great Cuban jurist, de Bustamante, published his *Projet de
Code de Droit International Privé,* that a considerable advance
was made. The code with some modifications was adopted by the
Pan-American Conference in 1928, and was ratified by fifteen
American states.

The difficulty of obtaining multilateral conventions, in view
of the great differences between national legal systems, has led
countries to sign bilateral or regional treaties for the purpose of
reciprocal aid in overcoming the many divergencies. Typical of
these is the Anglo-French treaty of 1934 for the reciprocal execution of judgments. A 1931 Inter-Scandinavian Convention uni-
fies the private international law rules dealing with marriage,
adoption, and guardianship. Admirable work has also been done
by law societies and other bodies in attempting a restatement of
the law of the conflict of laws. This latter movement has been
especially important within the United States.

Despite the progress made in these matters, a considerable
amount of diversity, complexity, and uncertainty still remains to
create many obstacles to merchants and others engaged in international trade and commerce. Change has been slow, and something more was needed if the rapidly developing international economic relations were not to be seriously impeded. Sir Cecil Hurst
wrote in the 1925 British *Yearbook of International Law* an article entitled, "Wanted an International Court of Pie Powder."
Other writers took the same view and the movement toward nongovernmental arbitration and conciliation about to be described
have in view the same essential purpose, namely, speedy justice
with the minimum of formality and expense.

COMMERCIAL ARBITRATION

The many disadvantages of an international system in which
the protection of industrial and commercial interests abroad rests
with national diplomacy must now be evident. Governments have
often used the plea of obtaining justice for their subjects as a
cloak for imperialist designs, and smaller countries have suffered
unfair treatment at the hands of great powers. But the latter have
not been invariably in the wrong, and business interests have frequently suffered from the long delay in the presentation of their
claims because politically it might have been inexpedient for their

government to take action at the time. The same business interests also were unable to obtain substantial justice, because it was often impossible to secure the enforcement of foreign judgments after an award had been made. The disadvantages and complexities of private international law have also been mentioned.

Naturally, individuals and organizations engaged in foreign trade sought ways to remedy these defects. Even before 1914 some steps had been taken toward the development of private commercial conciliation and arbitration. The London Court of Arbitration, the London Corn Trade Association, the Liverpool Cotton Association, and certain French and German organizations existed for the purpose of settling commercial disputes without becoming involved in governmental and diplomatic formalities. In 1914 an International Congress drew up a resolution concerning proposed rules of private business arbitration and the desirability of securing legal sanction for the decisions of foreign arbitrators. Unfortunately the war interrupted these developments, but after the cessation of hostilities the International Chamber of Commerce again took the matter in hand.

Sir Lynden L. Macassey has summarized the present machinery of international commercial arbitration under six heads: (1) Means developed by treaties and international agreements, such as those between France and Belgium (1899), Austria and Italy (1922), Italy, Yugoslavia, and Czechoslovakia, etc., providing for reciprocal enforcement of arbitral awards; (2) international agreements between nongovernmental organizations, the most important of which is the Inter-American Commercial Arbitration Commission established by the Pan-American Union; (3) organizations established by national chambers of commerce to promote international commercial arbitration among their members (especially notable is the Bradford Chamber of Commerce in Yorkshire, the organization of which became the basis of the International Wool-Textile Arbitration Agreement of October 27, 1926, which covers English, French, Belgian, German, and Italian woollen and textile manufacturers and merchants; several other such organizations exist); (4) arrangements by merchants of different countries for adopting forms of contracts which provide for commercial arbitration (forms used by the London Corn Trade Association, the Liverpool Cotton Association, the Merchants Silk Union of Lyon, etc.); (5) several courts and tribunals which determine cases in accordance with procedures, agreed upon internationally, as, for example, the court of arbitration of the International Chamber of Commerce in Paris (which has national committees in many countries in Europe, the United States, and Japan; it recommends that in all contracts an article be inserted providing that disputes arising out of the contract should be settled under the rules of conciliation and arbitration of the International Chamber of Commerce) ; (6) arbitration, by arbitrators appointed *ad hoc,* or by some specified appointing authority, accounting for the settlement of a growing number of international commercial disparities.[22]

It will be seen that two types of commercial arbitration exist. One is the national system referred to above. The London Corn Trade Association, for example, might set up a committee which would render a decision in a dispute between nationals of different countries engaged in the corn trade. Such a national system, although it marks a step forward and is suited to disputes concerning the quality of merchandise or similar questions of a technical nature, is open to the charge that it operates to strengthen the position and influence of the economically stronger states—a national agency does not possess a sufficiently broad character for permanent international needs.

Arbitration and conciliation machinery on an international basis can avoid the charge of serving a particular national interest, and for that reason has gradually grown in importance. Indeed at first sight there seems to be no reason why business interests should not set up their own private associations for the settlement of commercial disputes; yet on closer examination we find several formidable obstacles: The first is the problem of enforcement. Various governments have accepted the principle that an arbitral award has no binding force without confirmation by a court. Some examples drawn from the *International Yearbook on Civil and Commercial Arbitration*[23] will illustrate this point. In 1892 the German Reichsgericht upheld an action to obtain judgment on a foreign award made by an arbitration body. But the English High Court of Justice in 1911 ruled that a German arbitral award which was not declared executory in Germany was not enforceable in England. An English firm had failed to comply with the award of the Bremen cotton merchants, and the latter applied to the Liverpool Cotton Association to expel the defaulter from its ranks. The

[22] Sir Lynden Macassey, *International Commercial Arbitration: Its Origin, Development and Importance (Transactions of the Grotius Society, 1938,* Sweet & Maxwell, Ltd., London), Vol. XXIV (1939), pp. 193–96.

[23] Edited by Dr. Arthur Nussbaum (Oxford University Press, 1928).

firm in question brought action in court to set aside the award and to establish the invalidity of the expulsion. The German firm counterclaimed for an order to comply with the award. The Court had to determine whether or not the award was a decision which it could recognize as a foreign judgment; the learned judge wrote that in his opinion it was not, and accordingly he refused to issue an order of expulsion. An Italian decision in 1925 laid down that an arbitration clause agreed upon in Italy by which all disputes arising from a contract were to be decided by a foreign arbitral award was contrary to articles in the Italian Code of Civil Procedure and was therefore invalid. The Supreme Court of Austria in 1904 considered the case of an Austrian merchant who had contracted to deliver eggs to a Berlin merchant and had failed in his delivery. He was sued by the Berlin merchant before an arbitral tribunal in Berlin. The tribunal declared itself competent, but the Austrian Supreme Court ruled that the decisions of German arbitral tribunals were not final and refused to enforce the award. Similarly the Supreme Court of Czechoslovakia in 1925 ruled that a German arbitral award needed an order for enforcement granted by the German court before the Czechoslovakian court could in turn issue its order for enforcement of the award.

These examples show the uncertainty which confronts merchants engaged in foreign trade when they attempt to set up their own commercial arbitration and conciliation system.[24] Until the awards of the commercial arbitral bodies are recognized by the law courts of the land, a merchant may disregard the associational decisions and thereby bring arbitral agencies into disrepute; for if he chooses to break his contract, knowing that the law courts will not uphold any arbitral judgments rendered against him, he can render the whole system of professional awards ineffective.

The International Chamber of Commerce in 1920 set up a committee to study ways and means of gaining legal recognition of arbitration awards.[25] The findings of the committee were discussed by a congress held at London in 1921, which passed a resolution urging governments (1) to secure legal recognition of the validity of arbitration clauses and of persons designed as arbitrators without distinction of nationality, (2) to develop uniform

[24] For a good discussion of this question, see P. Brachet, *De l'Execution International des sentences arbitrales* (Rousseau et Cie, Paris, 1928).

[25] R. Vulliemin, *De l'Arbitrage commercial* (Librairie Arthur Rousseau, Paris, 1931), pp. 184–215.

national legislation to render executory the awards of foreign arbitrators "regardless of the nationality of the parties," and (3) to adopt uniform national rules of procedure in commercial arbitration.

Meanwhile the International Chamber of Commerce had also considered the possibility of drawing up regulations to organize international commercial arbitration on a more comprehensive basis. In facing this problem the Chamber met two conflicting theories. The Anglo-American group placed emphasis upon "moral sanctions"; the Continental representatives stressed the importance of "legal sanctions." Mr. Owen D. Young put the case strongly for procedures based upon persuasion. He suggested that there were three different methods which should be discussed: (1) Arbitration within the law, where national laws already enforced the decisions of private arbitration bodies; the International Chamber of Commerce could formulate a more complete code which would then have legal sanction. (2) Arbitration outside the law; here it would be necessary to establish a separate code of arbitration based upon moral sanctions exercised by the International and the various national Chambers of Commerce "with all the force that business men of a country can bring to bear upon a recalcitrant neighbor." This type of arbitration should be adopted only in cases where there were well-organized national business groups capable of dealing with a member guilty of taking advantage of legal technicalities to disregard the award of an International Chamber of Commerce tribunal or a similar body. (3) A system of conciliation to be developed by the International Chamber of Commerce, under which it would "tender its good offices," to see if the differences between the two parties could not be resolved by persuasive means. It was pointed out that in many cases involving disputes between United States and Argentine merchants conciliatory measures had sufficed to settle the matters quickly and inexpensively. Mr. Young therefore urged a cautious program of conciliation outside the law. Progress should come as a result of experience and not be based on mere theoretical reasoning.

As a result of these deliberations in 1920–1922, the Council of the International Chamber of Commerce published its rules of conciliation and arbitration in July 1922. They formed a compromise between the moral-sanction and the legal-sanction schools, with a strong leaning toward enforcement by moral means. Ridgeway regards the foundation of this world court of arbitration as one of the great achievements of postwar economic statesmanship.[26] The Court held its first case in June 1923, and by the end of that year forty-eight disputes had been submitted to it. Since that time it has continued its excellent work.

The International Chamber of Commerce then turned its efforts toward promoting national legislation which would recognize the validity of arbitration clauses inserted in international commercial contracts, and passed a resolution to that effect at its Rome Congress in March 1923. The League of Nations Economic Committee summoned a meeting of a Committee of Experts in July 1922 and, after accepting its recommendations, prepared a draft protocol which on September 24, 1923, was approved by the Assembly.[27] Within two years twenty-eight nations had signed and ten had ratified the protocol, by which the signatory powers undertook to enforce arbitral awards which were made "within the territory of the state in which execution is sought"; that is, if a Chamber of Commerce "court" in country A made an award, the government of A would see to it that the judgment was enforced within its own territory.

A third problem remained to be settled, that of enforcing arbitral awards made in a foreign territory. It will be recalled that the Supreme Court of Czechoslovakia ruled that a German arbitral award needed an enforcement order from a German court before it would grant the order for enforcement in Czechoslovakia, and that the Austrian Supreme Court had refused to enforce in Austria an award which had been rendered by German arbitral tribunals. These two incidents were typical of many which brought home to business men the necessity of reaching an international agreement which would guarantee enforcement of awards made in a foreign land. We should carefully note the distinction between a foreign award of private arbitrators and foreign judgment of a court, and the International Chamber of Commerce realized that two separate questions were involved. The legal systems of the world differ considerably, and to reconcile them is a difficult matter. The International Chamber believed that it could develop a system of arbitration which would avoid many of the complications arising from these differences.

In March 1926 the Economic Committee of the League studied

[26] G. L. Ridgeway, *Merchants of Peace* (Columbia University Press, New York, 1938), p. 325.

[27] *Report on the Economic Work of the League of Nations, Economic and Financial Section* (1927. II, 43. C.E.I. 41), pp. 30–32.

the question exhaustively and concluded that a great deal of effort
and study were still needed. The World Economic Conference in
1927 considered the matter and the League set up a committee of
jurists to draft a protocol, which the Assembly adopted in September of that year. Article I of this protocol states that the contracting parties will recognize as binding an arbitral award made in
another contracting state, and that it will be executed in accordance with the laws of that state provided (1) that the arbitration
is valid and the award is capable of settlement under the laws of
the state, (2) that the award has been given by the arbitral tribunal
in the manner agreed upon by the parties, (3) that it has become
final in the state in which it has been made, and (4) that it is not
contrary to public policy.[28]

Ridgeway well summarizes the situation:

The importance of a functioning International Court of Commercial Arbitration in the evolution of this regime of international
arbitration can readily be seen. The founding of the I.C.C. Court of
Commercial Arbitration, the steady extension of its usefulness and
its authority in the business world, the growth of national legislation
favorable to international commercial arbitration, and the final drafting
and ratification of two great multilateral treaties mark successive steps
in the extension of peace-making in international commerce. The
ratification of the protocol by leading commercial states firmly establishes this privileged regime of international arbitration over against
the chaotic territory of legal judgments preempted by conflicting national systems of law.[29]

One further judgment may be added, that of James S. Carson,
vice-president of the American and Foreign Power Company,
who in a radio address on December 6, 1937, said:

The maintenance of peace between governments is the highest
achievement that may be expected from arbitration. In order to attain
it, we should recognize that one cannot begin to build at the top. A
wide, sound basis of national knowledge of arbitration is necessary
before the international field can be developed to its fullest capacity.
A man who will not arbitrate small questions, will not arbitrate big
ones. The man who does not arbitrate at home, will not arbitrate
abroad. An aggregation of men who will not arbitrate, make for a
government that will refuse arbitration. Two such governments in
conflict lead to war.[30]

[28] *Report on the Economic Work of the League of Nations* (cited above).
p. 32.   [29] G. L. Ridgeway, *op. cit.*, pp. 330–31; R. Vulliemin, *op. cit.*, pp. 123–27.
[30] Quoted in James S. Carson, "Can International Arbitration Work?" *The
Arbitration Journal,* Vol. II (1938), p. 56.

DOUBLE TAXATION

Taxation has become increasingly important in recent years. The costs of government have been rising rapidly because of added expenditure made necessary by the tremendous increase in armaments and the unprecedented extension of social services. Old-age pensions, sickness insurance, primary and secondary education, relief programs, and the expansion of the civil service and of public control have necessitated ever mounting government budgets. And there has been growth in the variety as well as the amount of taxation—personal income taxes, company income taxes, death duties, inheritance taxes, stamp duties, customs duties, and many others swell the list.

The growing burden of taxation is felt by almost everyone, but it causes special difficulties to those engaged in international trade. Suppose that A has a factory in the United States; he sets up a branch factory in England, which nets him an annual profit of $10,000. If he has to pay income tax to both the English and the United States governments, he will suffer a double burden. If he lends money to a foreign country and is taxed on the income from it both at home and abroad, he will be put at a double disadvantage. The problem is complicated by the fact that it is not always easy to say precisely where income is earned. If A lives in one country and his money is invested in another, can we say with certainty just where the income arises? If his wealth is derived from foreign oil wells, it is obvious that the place is the important factor; but if he gains his income from profits derived from shipping between Canada and Japan, which government should tax him? The differences between tax laws in different countries have made the whole problem an extremely difficult one, although, generally speaking, foreign businesses are not specially taxed and they enjoy the same status in taxation matters as domestic companies.

But more is needed than an absence of discrimination in order to enable international trade to function satisfactorily, and governments have for some time realized the necessity of lightening the burdens which arise from double taxation. Unfortunately they have found it difficult to agree upon the general principles which should be adopted, and some have acted independently without reference to the policies of other countries. Great Britain, for example, granted certain exemptions to citizens who paid taxes on income earned abroad; and the United States in 1922 passed the China Trade Act exempting companies from paying income tax in the United States on profits derived from their business in China.

The Revenue Act of 1926 exempted Americans residing abroad from taxes on income which was earned abroad; and to Americans at home who paid income taxes to other governments it allowed that if the foreign tax were less than the American tax the United States government would merely collect the difference. Belgium taxed only one-quarter of the incomes derived from abroad if they had already been subjected to a foreign tax.

Such independent action on the part of governments, although in the right direction, did not go far enough. More systematic methods were required. The first step was for governments to enter bilateral agreements. For example, Great Britain and the United States, in an attempt to assist shipping interests which had suffered a heavy setback after 1918, agreed each to exempt the earnings of vessels registered under the flag of the other, thus adopting the principle of reciprocal exemption. Other countries followed suit. The bilateral method marked an improvement over the previous unilateral action; but, as Seligman points out, there are several basic differences of principle, and "it was high time that the matter should be taken up in a broad way." Various international conferences, private and governmental, adopted resolutions; and in 1921 the League of Nations instructed its Financial Committee to take up the problem. The committee appointed four experts to prepare a report, out of which grew a series of recommendations. Conferences of experts then produced model drafts of conventions to serve as a guide to countries contemplating the adoption of an agreement to minimize double taxation.

After the experts had produced their report and provided a theoretical basis for further action, the League Financial Committee collaborated with government experts whose practical experience in taxation made them valuable allies in working out the details, and also with the International Chamber of Commerce. It drew up four draft conventions covering income and capital taxes, succession duties, assistance in collection of taxes, and assistance in preventing fiscal evasion.

In October 1928 a Conference at Stockholm considered these matters at greater length and produced a series of model bilateral conventions. These were the first steps toward the realization of a multilateral convention which at the moment was not possible because of the great differences in national tax systems and the complexity of modern economic organization.

An analysis of the collection of international agreements and internal legal provisions for the prevention of double taxation and

fiscal evasion published by the League of Nations in 1936 shows
that, although taxation is one of the highest prerogatives of a sovereign state, modern conditions of economic life have rendered it imperative for governments to enter into international treaties so as to
limit the power of sovereign states to tax enterprises engaged in international trade and commerce. Theoretically national governments
may do as they please in the realm of taxation; in practice it would
be destructive of economic welfare if such theories were applied.

The document divides the international agreements into two
major groups—those concerning double taxation and those relating to mutual assistance in tax collection and the preventing of tax
evasion. Under the heading of avoiding double taxation are certain general agreements, including those between Switzerland and
Germany in 1931, between Belgium and the Netherlands in 1933,
between France and Germany in 1934, and between Sweden and
the Netherlands in 1935, and a number of agreements designed to
prevent double payment of succession duties and duties on gifts.
In addition there have been agreements concerning (1) profits of
commercial or industrial undertakings, the signatories agreeing not
to tax the profits or gains which arise through an agency of a commercial or industrial undertaking situated in their territory; (2)
profits of maritime shipping enterprises, governments agreeing to
exempt from income tax any profits which accrue from a shipping
business carried on by an individual or a company resident or registered in the territory of the other contracting party; (3) prevention of double income tax from air-transport profits; (4) prevention
of double taxation in the turnover tax and single or substituted
duties; and (5) exemption from taxation on motor vehicles from
the country of a contracting party while temporarily within the
country of the other party, on condition that the vehicles are used
only for the conveyance of passengers without hire or reward.

The second part of the collection of League documents dealt
with mutual assistance in collecting taxes and preventing fiscal
evasion. Between 1926 and 1935 eight such bilateral treaties were
signed; they form a complement to the measures designed to avoid
double and multiple taxation. It is important to avoid overtaxing
individuals; but it is equally necessary for governments to obtain
their revenues and to prevent individuals from escaping their just
share of national burdens.

The League of Nations Economic Section and the International
Chamber of Commerce also worked toward a multilateral treaty.
Bilateral treaties and domestic legislative acts are important; but

an international code to unify the principles of tax legislation is urgently needed. For this purpose the League Secretariat undertook a world-wide survey of tax law. An American official, Mitchell B. Carroll, directed the project, which finally resulted in a comprehensive five-volume report. The fiscal committee in June 1933 drew up a convention which was based upon the recommendations set forth by Carroll in the fourth volume of the survey and was designed to form the basis of a comprehensive system of principles of international taxation and of what Carroll calls a new field of "international tax law."

In 1935 Carroll wrote that "despite the incredible difficulties in the various systems fair concepts of fiscal jurisdiction were being established, uniform definitions were being formulated, the predominant kinds of income were being classified, and an international tax language was being developed." The convention accepts the principle that the signatory shall tax only the income which is directly "allocable to" a permanent establishment within its territory; it defines business income more carefully; and it embodies the principle of "treating the local establishment of a foreign enterprise as an individual enterprise and taxing it, wherever possible, on the basis of its separate accounts." It contains special provisions concerning the allocation of income of banking enterprises and prescribes that income from shipping shall be taxed only by the country in which the company has its fiscal domicile.

IMMUNITY OF STATE-OWNED PROPERTIES

According to the rules of international law, the courts of a country will not entertain suit against a foreign hereditary ruler, on the theory that to submit so exalted a personage to legal trial is inconsistent with his dignity and, in all probability, will produce political complications. The idea of the sovereign, moreover, expanded to include not merely a king but also a sovereign state or government. These and their instrumentalities, the most important of which are diplomatic representatives and a nation's warships, have enjoyed traditional immunities.

The growing preoccupation of governments with commerce and their entry into the carrying trade raise serious problems. Governments have assumed commercial, industrial, and banking functions also, and have claimed, by virtue of their sovereign status, the privileges and immunities referred to above.[31] These

---

[31] See *Immunities of State Enterprises* (League of Nations, Economic and Financial Section, 1927), II, 32.

claims place private enterprise at a serious disadvantage. If, to take only two illustrations, the state is exempt from the necessity of paying taxation, or if it will not submit to legal processes, should one of its government-owned commercial ships collide with a privately owned vessel and do it damage, it obtains advantages which, in the words of the 1927 World Economic Conference, "constitute an infringement of free competition by making a discrimination between enterprises carried on side by side." The Conference therefore recommended

That, when a Government carries on, or controls, any commercial, industrial, banking, maritime transport or other enterprise, it shall not, in its character as such, and in so far as it participates in enterprises of this kind, be treated as entitled to any sovereign rights, privileges, or immunities from taxation or from other liabilities to which similar privately owned undertakings are subject, it being clearly understood that this recommendation only applies to ordinary commercial enterprises in time of peace.

Not all governments have taken advantage of their theoretical legal rights. Some of them adopt a liberal view, and their national courts will accept suits brought by private individuals against government-owned vessels. The French courts have distinguished between government-owned ships used for "distinctly public purposes" and those used in "ordinary commercial operations," but they will not order the attachment of vessels which have had judgments rendered against them; thus it remains highly uncertain whether or not the judgment can be executed. The courts of Belgium have ruled that foreign ships engaged in ordinary commerce must submit to ordinary processes; but, like the courts of France, they have not been willing to order the attachment of vessels. On the other hand, the Italian courts go the full length and permit "both prosecution and execution of judgments." When the United States set up the National Shipping Board it apparently did not intend that its public vessels should at all times enjoy the traditional immunities accorded to the agencies of a sovereign power. To make the matter clearer, the Secretary of State sent instructions to American representatives abroad that they should notify foreign governments that the United States would not claim immunity for vessels of the Shipping Board engaged in commercial activity, although it might in exceptional cases claim exemption from arrest.

The courts of other countries, however, and the Supreme Court of the United States, have followed the customary rule. In 1880 the English Court of Appeals, in the famous Parlement Belge Case, refused to hear an action brought against a Belgian public ship which was used as a mail packet and also carried passengers and goods. In 1924, the English Court of Appeals, when the United States Shipping Board claimed that its ships should be immune from legal action in foreign courts, ruled that the Shipping Board was a department of the United States government and as fully representative of the United States as an ambassador himself. In 1926 the United States Supreme Court in *Berizzi Brothers Co.* vs. *S.S. "Pesaro"* took the same stand.[32] The steamship "Pesaro" had failed to deliver a consignment of artificial silk accepted by her at an Italian port for carriage to New York. The vessel was arrested and later was released after giving bond that she would return or pay the claim if the court had jurisdiction and the claim was established. During the trial the Italian ambassador to the United States testified "that the vessel at the time of her arrest, was owned and possessed by that government, was operated by it in its service and interest, and therefore was immune from process of the courts of the United States." The Supreme Court ruled that government-owned ships in the carrying trade "are public ships in the same sense that warships are." The ruling continued: "We know of no international usage which regards the maintenance and advancement of the economic welfare of the people in time of peace as any lesser purpose than the maintenance and training of a naval force." And the Supreme Court affirmed the decree of the inferior court which had dismissed the action for want of jurisdiction.

Professor J. W. Garner, in a comment in the *American Journal of International Law,* pointed out that the principle underlying the decision went counter to the practically unanimous opinion of jurists, the judgment of the International Maritime Committee, the subcommittee set up to deal with the question which later was to be submitted to the International Conference for the codification of international law, and the opinions of two judges of the Permanent Court of International Justice. He added that this judgment, coming from the highest court of a great power, "only serves to accentuate the necessity of an international agreement[33] which will remove the anomalous and unjust inequality which, in the opinion

[32] Manley O. Hudson, *Cases on International Law* (West Publishing Co., St. Paul, Minnesota, 1937), pp. 232–34.

[33] J. W. Garner, "Legal Status of Government Ships Employed in Commerce," *American Journal of International Law,* 1926, p. 767.

of the Supreme Court of the United States, is still the law of the United States, if not the law of nations. . . . ." Professor Dickinson in the following year expressed his disappointment that the Court felt constrained to adhere strictly to precedent, but suggested that he was "not entirely confident that the Supreme Court would have been well advised to embark upon a different course."[34] Like his academic colleague, he believed that it was essentially a matter for international action by governments.

Already many criticisms had appeared against the prevailing rule. Years ago, the great international lawyer, Bluntschli, stated that governments, by going into ordinary business, to that extent waived their sovereign dignity; if they could stoop to such ordinary activities, they should be prepared to accept the ordinary consequences and at least meet the claims of their creditors. Many private interests had suffered heavily from the governmental claims to immunity from suit. They were probably unimpressed by a United States Court judgment that it was "far more important for citizens of the United States to recognize the rule of international comity that an independent sovereign cannot be personally sued . . . . than it is to take cognizance of private rights, if by so doing that rule is violated." Both elementary justice and the future of private enterprise called for a reconsideration of a rule the expanded application of which was inflicting much injury.

Discussions took place at meetings of the International Maritime Committee at Gothamburg and Genoa. At the former conference it was proposed to abolish the immunity which state-owned and state-operated vessels and their cargoes had previously enjoyed and to place them on the same footing as privately owned vessels and cargoes. The conferences attempted to draw a distinction between public and private functions; but the effort failed, for there is no final line which can be drawn. What is private today may become public tomorrow. Accordingly the conferences accepted the principle that all vessels should have to appear before courts which were empowered to try cases against private ships. But several questions arose and were decided as follows:

1. Should foreign courts be permitted to try cases involving government warships and cargoes used for "governmental work?" It was decided that these vessels should appear only before the competent courts of their own states.

2. Should state-owned or state-operated ships be liable to at-

[34] Edwin D. Dickinson, "Immunity of Public Ships Engaged in Trade," *American Journal of International Law*, 1927, pp. 108–9.

tachment? One set of authorities believed that although state ships should be liable for damages they should not have to submit to arrest and attachment. The device of attachment originated to make certain that a private owner who might not otherwise have sufficient funds to pay the fine would at least be forced to use his vessel or his goods as a surety. A state would not be in such a position because it obviously would have sufficient funds to pay. Moreover, to attach a public vessel might seriously interfere with the public interest; for example, in an international crisis, a government would wish to have all its war vessels and mercantile marine in hand in case of outbreak of war. Other authorities believed that all ships should submit to the same legal processes without distinction, and that the reasoning cited was not conclusive enough to justify even the exemption of war vessels. The rule finally adopted by the Genoa Conference was that warships, state yachts, patrol ships, hospital ships, and their cargoes should not be liable to attachment but that other state vessels should be so liable.

3. The Genoa Conference added a further article to the effect that the proposed convention should not be binding on a belligerent state over claims arising during a period of war. That is, the convention was to apply only to peace time.

In 1926, after much thought and discussion, a Convention was signed at Brussels in which the principles described above were incorporated. The Convention, of fourteen articles, provides that all sea vessels owned or operated by states, and nongovernmental cargoes and passengers carried by the ships while engaged in commercial service, are to be subject to the same rules of liability and the same obligations as privately owned ships. Ships of war and vessels owned or operated by a state on noncommercial services are subject to a limited surrender of immunity. They may be sued for (a) collisions and other accidents of navigation, (b) salvage and general average, and (c) repairs, goods supplied, or other contracts relating to the vessel. If the court is doubtful as to whether or not the vessel or cargo is of a governmental and noncommercial character, a certificate from the diplomatic representative of the state will be sufficient to have the vessel freed from arrest, seizure, or detention. A state may suspend the application of the Convention in wartime, and is not required to take measures inconsistent with its rights and duties as a neutral.[35]

[35] Manley O. Hudson, *op. cit.,* p. 234. Also League of Nations, Economic and Financial Section, *Documents for the International Economic Conference* (1927, II, 32), pp. 10–14.

After several years, during which time the Belgian government was in communication with other governments which had declared themselves prepared to ratify the convention, the instrument came into effect on January 8, 1937. At that time it had been ratified by eight countries: Belgium, Brazil, Chile, Estonia, Germany, Hungary, the Netherlands, and Poland.

It is clear that if state-owned enterprises are exempted from taxation, they will have a great advantage in competition with private enterprise, and should be able to work at lower costs. Such an advantage, in the opinion of many people, constitutes an unfair form of competition. For this reason, some authorities and many business groups object to the claims of the state to immunity from taxation. For example, a state-owned butcher shop, which did not have to pay taxes, competing with a privately owned butcher shop, might be able to undersell the latter, not through more efficient organization, but by reason of its tax exemption. Or take competition between state-owned ships and privately owned vessels: The differences in cost by reason of state claims to immunity may be very great, and may work a hardship upon the private company, causing it to charge higher fares and cargo rates. The British Imperial Economic Conference of 1923 considered the Colwyn Report, which recommended: (1) that governments within the Empire engaging in trade should be liable to taxation in any other country of the Empire in which it owned property for trade purposes or in which it made trade profits, and such liability should be "coextensive with a liability of a private trading corporation in similar circumstances"; and (2) that foreign governments trading within the Empire, and Empire governments trading abroad, should not be treated "as entitled to any sovereign immunity from taxation, either directly or through the claim of superiority to the jurisdiction of Municipal Courts." The Conference agreed with the recommendations of the Committee, and invited the parliaments of Great Britain, the Dominions, and India to pass legislation to that effect, and favored opening negotiations with foreign countries with a view to reciprocal agreements calculated to bring the governments within the scope of taxation on the same footing as ordinary commercial and industrial enterprises. Several of the governments of the Empire passed legislation along these lines.

Other states might adopt similar legislation to resume jurisdiction over agents and property of foreign states within their borders, and thereby effect a needed reform.

PROTECTION OF INDUSTRIAL, ARTISTIC, AND LITERARY PROPERTY

To a degree not generally appreciated, modern trade and commerce depend upon protection guaranteed by law. It is doubtful whether our business civilization could long exist without the security afforded by patent rights, trade-marks, trade names, marks on goods to indicate the place of origin, and measures designed to insure fair competition. These things have become accepted as indispensable safeguards within nations; but, as trade and commerce become international in scope, the enterprising business man may find that an unscrupulous competitor is using his patent in a foreign country. The patent may be a simple device or it may be an invention which has involved the expenditure of millions of dollars. Or he may find his trade-mark and his trade name exploited by a foreign firm. Designs may be pirated, and authors find their books printed in lands where no copyright protection exists to give them a fair reward for their work. Firms of worldwide reputation find that their names (or ones very similar to them) are used on bottles and containers which contain inferior types of whiskey, gin, catsup, and a large number of other articles of consumption. Protection of economic rights has thus become an international question. As long as the world recognizes private property it should afford it adequate protection.

Trade-marks go back to very early days, but in the Middle Ages they were used rather to protect the consuming public against bad workmanship than to protect the producer against unfair competition. Modern patent legislation began in Great Britain in 1623 with the famous Statute of Monopolies, under which all monopolies except inventions were deemed null and void. The Act set forth the conditions under which a patent would be granted and the time during which the inventor might enjoy his patent rights. The first act to protect industrial designs on linens, muslins, calicoes, etc., was passed in England in 1787, and in 1862 the English Parliament enacted the first law of trade-marks. Other countries followed England's example in these matters, because their industrial and economic development necessitated similar legislative measures to curb the abuses arising from fraud and deceit in an age of rapidly developing impersonal competition.

Because of the variety of conditions and different rates of industrial progress, nations adopted legislative protection at different rates. In some countries the law was defective; in others the foreign merchant suffered discrimination, and enjoyed less protection than the nationals of the country. Moreover, the divergencies in laws relating to patents, trade-marks, trade names, and designs made it risky for a merchant to establish himself abroad.

Countries differed in their definition of patentable inventions and the conditions and formalities for granting patent rights. Some governments required a detailed preliminary examination of the proposed patent, while others were satisfied with no more than a registration of the invention. Patents were granted for periods ranging from three to twenty years; the amount of fees to be paid was seldom the same, and different rules existed concerning penalties for delinquency in tax payments. Some countries obliged the patentee to work his patent within a given time; others were more or less generous.

The combined effect of these differing regulations was to place great burdens upon the applicant. A foreign inventor had to obtain the services of a local attorney expert in patent law, to prepare his documents. The inventors were forced "to prepare as many different applications, drawings, models, etc., as the countries in which they wished to have their inventions patented. This caused them a great loss of money and time.[36] The obligation of a patentee to work his patent within a given period often worked much hardship because many inventions required "long experiments and many improvements which may require much time. . . . . These experiments, moreover, are very costly and may not result in anything worth while."[37] Few countries afforded any protection to foreigners in industrial designs and models. Laws were very diverse, and the risk correspondingly great. Trade-marks were freely pirated, and foreigners found it a tedious and costly undertaking to obtain adequate protection. Nor was the situation much, if at all, better in the matter of trade names and unfair competition.

The first steps in international protection of industrial property took the form of bipartite treaties. A signatory agreed, usually on condition of reciprocity, to protect the trade-marks and designs of the nationals belonging to the other signatory power. Most governments set up patent systems which gave protection to inventions, and (China, Persia, and Siam *et al.* excepted) signed international treaties and conventions which provided for

[36] Stephen P. Ladas, *The International Protection of Industrial Property* (Harvard University Press, 1930), p. 228.

[37] *Ibid.,* p. 330. I am greatly indebted to this work.

"the mutual protection of the patent rights of their nationals."
One instance may be given: the 1911 Treaty between Japan and
the United States provides that

the citizens or subjects of each of the High Contracting Parties shall
enjoy in the territories of the other the same protections as native
citizens or subjects in regard to patents, trade-marks and designs,
upon fulfilment of the formalities prescribed by law.

But such theoretical equality does not solve all problems. Donaldson notes that the patent laws of the United States are more
liberal, provide for a longer monopoly to the inventor, and have
fewer conditions attached than the patent laws of most other
countries. Whereas several foreign governments require that a
person must work his patent in order to retain it, the United
States does not have a compulsory working clause. Consequently
foreigners who take out patents in America may receive greater
privileges than Americans who take out patents in other countries:

For example, a foreign patentee may manufacture his product at
home, and, without manufacturing in America, hold a valid American
patent. The American patentee in order to insure the validity of his
foreign patent frequently must maintain an expensive factory in the
foreign country.[38]

So, with trade-marks. The purpose of a trade-mark is to
"insure a kind of fair play in trade." The United States has the
rule that anyone who wishes to use a certain mark may bring
forward proof that he has used this mark before anybody else,
even though the latter may have registered at an earlier time.
Other countries follow the contrary principle, that of "priority
of registration." From this difference of systems many hardships
may occur. To quote Donaldson again:

an American individual or concern may have employed a trade-mark
for many years at home and may even have used it in a foreign market
for some time, but if the precaution has not been taken to effect
prompt registration within such foreign country a coincidental or
piratical use of the same mark by a national of that country or a
national of a third country is possible without liability for legal procedure on the ground of infringement.

Sometimes nations included special clauses for granting patent
or other industrial property protection in their general treaties of

[38] J. Donaldson, *International Economic Relations* (Longmans, Green & Co.,
New York and London, 1931), p. 308.

commerce; these were liable to denunciation at the end of a given period, and in that case trade-marks, designs, and other matters lost the benefit of treaty arrangements and pirating could recommence.

Bilateral treaty methods were not adequate to meet the growing need of protecting property rights on an international scale. It became increasingly obvious, especially when the government of Austria-Hungary arranged an international exposition at Vienna in 1873, that more comprehensive steps must be taken. Foreign inventors believed that the absence of effective legislation would enable other people to copy their exhibits and, far from gaining extra markets as a result of the exposition, inventors would suffer at the hands of unscrupulous competitors. A special Austro-Hungarian law afforded temporary protection; but more permanent measures were necessary. In 1873 an international congress for patent reform was also held at Vienna; it laid down a number of general principles and appointed a permanent executive committee to study the question further.

An international congress on industrial property met in Paris in 1878, and discussed whether it was desirable to form a general union for purposes of industrial property protection or whether efforts should be made toward obtaining uniform legislation by various governments. One group held that uniform action was needed and that this end could be realized only by nations surrendering their independent policy-making powers and acting together as one body; the other group, more wedded to the ideal of national sovereignty, was unwilling to take even these small steps in the direction of international "government." Another conference at Paris, in 1880, paved the way for the famous international conference of 1883. Here was adopted a convention which forms the basis of the existing organization for concerted international action to protect patents, trade-marks, trade names, and marks of origin, and to eliminate unfair competition throughout the territories of the signatory powers.

The conference set up an international bureau which was to provide a permanent administrative organ. Its function was to gather information relating to protection of industrial property, to study the laws, legal decisions, and administrative practices of various countries, to supervise the working of the convention, and to propose improvements. During the half-century since then the bureau has done excellent work in publishing its monthly magazine, preparing conferences for revision purposes, and acting as a central office where trade-marks, etc., are deposited. We have seen elsewhere that international institutions have sometimes led the way toward more adequate national organization; and this phenomenon appears in the case of industrial property. For, by Article XII of the 1883 Convention, each of the contracting parties undertook to establish a special service to deal with industrial property and a central office to communicate to the general public and interested parties all information concerning patents, designs, and trade-marks.

Any international conference must make provision for alteration and revision in order to meet changing circumstances and to correct any defects which experience may show to exist in the original instrument. These conferences of revision have been held at Rome in 1886, at Madrid in 1890–91, at Brussels in 1897–1900, at Warsaw in 1911, at The Hague in 1925–26, and at London in 1933.

The conferences have established an important principle, namely, national and unionist treatment of industrial property within the countries that were members of the Union. Citizens of each signatory state enjoy within the other countries of the group a most-favored-nation position and, except for some slight "procedural discriminations," they enjoy a status of equality. In addition to the national-treatment principle (which may not give adequate protection to citizens of countries with more advanced legislation concerning industrial property protection) the Convention agreement affords other advantages:

By various provisions constituting a common legislation for all the members of the Union, it laid down a number of rules and principles purporting to furnish an equitable solution of the problems arising from the diversities of legislation and the need for protection of vested rights of industrial property having a really international character.[39]

Some examples, taken from Ladas' excellent work on which this section is based, will illustrate the "unionist" principle:

1. Applicants for patents, utility and industrial designs, and models or trade-marks within the Union have a right of priority for twelve months in the case of patents and utility models, six months for trade-marks and industrial designs and models. In this way a citizen of country A may be protected for a longer period of time in country B than the domestic law would have allowed. "Unionist" treatment thus gives more favorable privileges than "nationalist" treatment.

[39] S. P. Ladas, *op. cit.*, p. 210.

2. Applicants do not have to apply in all countries at once, and are thereby saved considerable anxiety and expense. Their application holds good throughout the whole Union.

3. An inventor will enjoy what is called "independence of patent." If he loses his patent right in one country, he does not forfeit it elsewhere in the Union. Thus he will not suffer universal loss by discontinuing his taxes on a patent in one land or in any other way ceasing to maintain its validity.

4. Inventors no longer forfeit their patent for importing into the country granting the patent patented articles manufactured abroad. They are thereby enabled to test out sales possibilities within a new country and to ascertain whether it would be profitable for them to market the invention there.

5. The convention considerably lightened the task of inventors by lengthening the time which may elapse before they must work their patents. Inventors are thereby permitted to experiment and adapt their inventions to the needs of the country and to overcome technical defects without the threat of immediate forfeiture.

6. The convention agreed upon a time of grace (extended by the 1925 Hague Conference) within which taxes may be paid in order to prevent forfeiture of patents.

7. By admitting a regularly registered trade-mark from one country into other countries of the Union, the convention and its subsequent modifications removed several obstacles to the acquisition of trade-mark rights in foreign countries, made easier a more universal protection of trade names, and provided for special measures to protect parties from the fraudulent use of trade names and marks of origin.

8. Finally, it made general reference to, but no specific provision for, measures which should be taken against unfair competition.

International problems have arisen from the desire to protect not only industrial property rights but also what has come to be known as literary and artistic property—a term which covers the copyrights of authors, the rights of translation of dramatic and musical performances, copyrights of mechanical musical instruments, moving-picture rights, radio-broadcasting rights, and articles in newspapers and periodicals. Within recent years the spread of education, the growing passion for the cinema, and the development of the gramophone and radio have extended the market for all kinds of creative cultural products; and authors and composers are naturally anxious that they shall obtain some benefit from the enjoyment of their works by people in foreign countries as well as in their own land.

In early days there was little question of protecting the author's rights;[40] rather the emphasis was placed upon the protection of the printers so that they would not suffer from piratical competition. Indeed, for some time it was debated whether or not authors really possessed property rights[41] in their creations and whether or not the government should give them a grant or privilege for what they had produced. Determination of the fundamental nature of literary and artistic rights involves abstruse philosophical and legal analysis which cannot be dealt with here,[42] except to note that in 1936 the French courts departed from the idea that authors had a property right and upheld the theory that they possessed a moral and pecuniary right based upon the idea of *droit d'auteur,* a concept *sui generis.*

In the first period before 1800 governments granted privileges to individual authors. Then followed a period of general legislation to protect authors' rights, begun in Great Britain in 1709, in Denmark in 1741, in the United States in 1790, and in France in 1793. In the nineteenth century a movement to protect foreign as well as national authors arose because the great spread of popular education had brought the need for copyright legislation on a wider scale. A number of Belgian publishers piratically reprinted French books, exported their products to foreign countries, and competed with books legitimately produced in France.[43] The United States was also the scene of much literary piracy. In 1852 the French government took a momentous step by declaring that the counterfeiting within France of works published abroad and the exportation and transportation of counterfeited works were unlawful. By its action France gained a strong moral position; other countries followed its example, and within the next ten years over twenty treaties for the protection of authors' rights were signed. Other bilateral treaties were entered into, and by 1886 thirty-three such agreements were in force. Un-

[40] See Stephen P. Ladas, *The International Protection of Literary and Artistic Property* (The Macmillan Company, New York, 1938) for an exhaustive treatment.

[41] F. Ruffini, "De la protection internationale des droits sur les œuvres littéraires et artistiques," *Académie de Droit International, Recueil des Cours,* Vol. II (1926), Tome 12.

[42] Ladas, *op. cit.,* chapter ii.

[43] Ruffini, *op. cit.,* p. 446: "La contrefaçon finit par constituer une véritable branche de l'industrie nationale dans certains pays ..."

fortunately, they lacked uniformity in the definition of the works protected, the amount of protection granted, and the length of the period of protection, and in several other detailed and technical respects. The time was ripe for a comprehensive attack upon the whole problem.

In 1858 a congress of authors and artists, attended by several hundred representatives from fifteen countries, met in Brussels. It resolved that there should be international recognition of copyright, and that foreign authors should obtain the same status as national authors and should not be required to comply with special formalities. Later congresses were held at Antwerp in 1861 and 1877 and at Paris in 1878. A conference at Berne in 1883 called by an international association (which had been created in 1878) paved the way to an official preliminary conference the next year and for a final conference at Berne in 1886.[44] Here the delegates drew up a comprehensive convention which constitutes a landmark in the history of literary and artistic property.[45]

The convention provided: (1) foreigners should enjoy the same advantages in each country of the Union as the nationals of that country; (2) no formalities were required except those prescribed by the country of origin; (3) translation rights were fixed at ten years; (4) newspaper and periodical articles might be reproduced unless reproduction was explicitly forbidden; (5) dramatical and musical works were protected on the national-treatment principle; (6) other detailed provisions too technical for treatment here.

Conferences of revision were held in Paris in 1896, in Berlin in 1908, and in Rome in 1928. The Union established an international bureau, which was placed under the administration of the Swiss government. Its functions were to collect and publish information relating to the protection of the rights of authors, make general studies, edit a periodical, and prepare conferences of revision. The same general problems of unanimity, reservations, and partial revision which confront international conferences in other fields concern conferences which deal with literary and artistic property.

Article II of the 1886 Convention prescribed the kinds of

[44] Ruffini tells how the Conference decided to form a Union rather than to try to obtain uniform legislation by governments: "L'exemple des Unions déjà fondées [Télégraphe, Géodésie, Postes] avait porté ses fruits" (p. 454).

[45] The Union, it was claimed, would cover territory inhabited by about five hundred million people, and would include all the principal European countries.

works to be protected. They included books and pamphlets, literary addresses, sermons, dramatic-musical works, pantomimes, musical compositions with or without words, drawings, paintings, architectural and sculptured works, engravings, lithographs, illustrations, geographical charts, etc. Works of art applied to industry and political discourses did not come under the obligatory protection of the convention. The successive conferences elaborated and refined the protection given; new inventions brought new methods of making public the results of an author's or composer's work, and further provisions for their protection were required. Some examples may be given: An author might find that a translator had rendered his work into another language. Can it be said that the translator has done an original piece of work? Could the author have had his book or article made known in a country using a different language had it not been for the translator? What would be a fair solution in the conflict of interests that arise? We have seen that the Berne Convention gave to an author the exclusive rights of translation for a period of ten years. This step constituted an improvement over the situation prevailing before that time. But not all governments were satisfied that ten years was long enough to be fair to the author, and in 1896 the Paris additional act provided that authors within the Union should enjoy the exclusive right of making or authorizing a translation of their works during the whole duration of the right of the original work; but if an author wished to enjoy the exclusive rights of translation, he must make use of it within ten years of the first publication of his original work. Some countries did not ratify the act, and in 1908 the subject came up for further discussion at the Berlin Conference and improvements were made.

The 1886 Convention protected dramatico-musical rights, and also protected authors against unauthorized representation of translations of their works; but they were required to give notice of reservation of the musical performing rights. This last condition, however, was omitted by the Berlin Conference of 1908.

With the growth of mechanical musical instruments, such as musical boxes, mechanical pianos, phonographs, and gramophones, the problem of protecting the rights of composers grew in scope. The 1886 Convention had stated that the manufacture and sale of devices for the mechanical production of musical works which are copyrighted should not be considered an infringement of musical copyright. Within the next few years so many developments had taken place that modifications had to be introduced, since it was not fair to exclude authors and composers from participating in the profits made from the use of their works on so large a scale. It was finally agreed that manufacturers of gramophones and phonographs, pianolas, etc., should be permitted to reproduce musical compositions on payment of royalties to the composer. The 1908 Berlin Convention provided that authors of musical works should have the exclusive right to authorize the adaptation of their works for musical reproduction, as well as the public performance of their works by means of such instruments.

The moving picture had not come into existence when the 1886 Convention was adopted. At Berlin in 1908 the Conference adopted the proposal of the French government that authors be granted the exclusive right to authorize the reproduction and the public exhibition of their works by means of motion pictures. Many technical problems arose—whether cinematograph work was mainly photographic or involved a creative element; what constituted reproduction and what constituted adaptation; whether cinematograph works could be circulated outside of a given territory with special authorization; the relation between sound and talking films, etc.—problems too intricate to be dealt with in this volume.

Radio broadcasting did not become a subject for international treatment until after many years had elapsed. An International Telegraph Convention had been signed in Berlin in 1906, and a new convention was adopted in London in 1912. These conferences dealt mainly with the more technical aspects of radio, and not until 1925 occurred the first international congress to deal with the rights of radio authors and artists.

At Rome in 1928 a proposal was made to recognize the author's exclusive right to permit his work to be broadcast by radio. The French and Italians led the delegations which supported this policy; but some countries urged that radio should be regarded as a cultural and social instrument for public welfare and that national educational objectives should take precedence over the rights of authors. They feared that monopolistic tendencies would develop and that excessive royalties might be demanded. The conference finally reached a compromise. Authors of literary and artistic works have since enjoyed the exclusive right to permit radio diffusion of their works to the public; but the national legislatures of the respective countries can regulate the conditions for the exercise of this right within their own territory, although they may not "adversely affect the moral right of the author." The

Rome Conference did not attempt to regulate rebroadcasting, an omission which Ladas believes to be "rather unfortunate."[46] He suggests that the Convention should be expanded to include regulation of the public diffusion by receiving sets and recording radio diffusion on mechanical instruments; this and the adoption of a rule that the author has the sole right to authorize the recitation of his literary works over the radio are desirable. Other technical problems too intricate to discuss here remain to be dealt with by international agreement.

The 1886 Berne Convention permitted the reproduction in other countries, by translation or in the original, of articles in newspapers and periodicals except when authors or publishers expressly forbade it. It did not prohibit headline news of the day and other material which did not possess the "character of intellectual creation," but it placed literary and artistic creations under copyright protection. At Paris in 1896 the conference made more specific provision for the protection of authors' rights. The Convention was revised to protect serial novels and fiction, including their reproduction and translation, to permit reproduction of current news and political discussion, and the reproduction of newspaper and periodical articles, provided that the authors or publishers did not forbid the reproduction. Other modifications were adopted at Berlin in 1908 and at Rome in 1928.

The evidence in this chapter should have made clear that the welfare of a growing number of people—merchants, bankers, investors, consumers, authors, inventors, performers, and many others—depends upon the development of adequate international machinery for the promotion and protection of their rights. The same kind of political and legal methods which have been found necessary within nations are becoming indispensable over a wider field of human intercourse. International organization is obviously a natural outgrowth of new conditions and not an artificial addition to national government.

[46] Ladas, *op. cit.*, p. 480. For protection of performers' rights, see above, pp. 159–60.

Chapter VIII

CONSERVATION OF RESOURCES

Somewhere H. G. Wells has remarked that the most urgent task which confronts the world today is to prevent the frightful wastage in the raw materials and resources of mankind. We are using up minerals, timber, and soil at an appalling rate, and are letting water power run to waste in a criminal fashion. The neglect is bad enough in time of peace; the intensified destruction is only too evident in time of war. It is true that the necessities of war impel men to better organization, even at the cost of liberty; but Wells is surely right in suggesting that mankind cannot go on trusting to the inventiveness of science to safeguard it against its follies. Fortunately, many nations have seen the necessity of engaging in programs of soil conservation, of reforestation, of preventing unjustifiable exploitation of oil, coal, and other mineral resources. The United States has undertaken remarkable schemes of hydroelectric power development, and undoubtedly Europe will have to engage in close international, and even federal, co-operation to make best use of its raw materials and resources, if it is to repair the damage done to its economic and social system by the present and the previous world wars. And in Lord Hailey's excellent *An African Survey* are several examples of the need for international co-operation to prevent soil erosion, to develop water supply, and to make mineral surveys.

We propose in this chapter to concentrate attention upon the resources of the sea, partly by reason of the accessibility of evidence and partly because of consideration of space. The same general principles, however, will apply to the problem of conservation of resources in other realms of human activity.

RESOURCES OF THE SEA

Until recent times, people assumed that the resources of the sea were inexhaustible, and the thought of conservation seldom troubled them. The spectacle of intensive fishing with modern gear aroused little or no apprehension. Fishermen obtained large catches and recklessly wasted the smaller fish and the parts not easily usable. Then unmistakable evidence of decline in the fisheries began to appear. The same catch involved greater effort per man and per unit of gear and an increased operating cost. The development of more efficient gear, of larger boats, and of better accessory equipment led to more intensive fishing. Because of the greater technical efficiency required, the better and more expensive ships came to be regarded as a normal cost, and this mounting cost of operations became a major factor in producing economic difficulties. According to Dr. W. F. Thompson, the 1914–15 crisis in the Pacific halibut industry and the general crisis in European fisheries resulted, at first, not so much from the lack in the quantity of fish as from the marketing of a poorer quality of fish which had to be obtained from a great distance at a high cost. The overhead expenses drove people farther afield in an attempt to avert losses, and the cost of expansion in turn became an extra charge against the fishing industry. Intensification of fishing led naturally to depletion of grounds and in some cases to their ultimate abandonment. It also was responsible for an international overlapping of zones of interest. Iceland, the North Sea, the Grand Banks of Newfoundland, the Bering Sea, the Arctic, and the Antarctic all witnessed the beginning and the intensive development of international competition, which hastened the depletion of fishing areas in those regions.

Unfortunately little or no preparation had been made to deal with the problem of international regulation and conservation. A rapidly developing crisis found the world unorganized, and unaware of the need not only for preventive but also for positive measures. Within national territorial waters and streams measures of conservation have been taken. But even here the decline of fish has been heavy, and national conservation policies have not yet been wholly successful. The decline has not been due merely to intensive fishing. Where industrialization has taken place many streams and rivers have become polluted, with disastrous consequences for the fisheries. Cities use rivers for sewerage purposes; ships discharge oil, and mills their waste products; factories pour out chemicals. Electric power projects, like Grand Coulee Dam and Bonneville Dam, place obstacles in the way of fish which proceed up stream in order to spawn. Irrigation projects have also had adverse effects. In order to meet these situations, governments have taken remedial action. In some cases special runways have been created for the fish. In other places, the authorities have set up hatcheries. Conservation measures now require better scientific investigation and economic regulation. The collecting of biological and statistical data will make possible an accurate determination of the amount of fish which may be caught, so that society may maintain a balance between the human need and the source of supply.

These measures on a national scale, excellent in themselves, are proving to be inadequate because fish which inhabit the ocean beyond the boundary limit of territorial waters (usually three miles) are *res nullius* and can be taken by anyone. Fishing by foreigners on the high seas may thus threaten national fisheries, and fishing becomes an international problem (1) when rival national fishing fleets meet on the same open-sea fishing areas, (2) when the intensive fishing depletes the supply and international conservation and regulation become recognized as a necessity, (3) when open-ocean fishing outside the three-mile limit has repercussions upon the national industry.

The North Sea.—In the Middle Ages fisheries had an economic importance which was traceable, in part, to religious influences. The fast days prescribed by the Roman Catholic Church led to a large consumption of fish in place of meat. Foreign fishermen plied their trade freely in British waters, under treaties signed by English monarchs guaranteeing them liberty of fishing. In Scotland the practice was somewhat less liberal; the home waters were reserved for the native people and foreigners were excluded. After the Reformation, English fisheries began to decline because people no longer observed fast days so rigidly, and because of the increasingly energetic competition from the Dutch, the problem loomed large in Anglo-Dutch political difficulties, which culminated in no fewer than three wars. Questions of maritime jurisdiction, of the striking of the flag, of the issuance of fishing licenses, and the general question of commercial supremacy at sea were involved. The decay of the Dutch fisheries followed the long wars which Holland found itself compelled to wage. Many ships were captured and burned; the States-General were unable to protect the fishing vessels from French and British cruisers, "and such interruptions told seriously upon a business which depended so largely on the export trade of the cured herrings. From these repeated blows, the Dutch fisheries never recovered and the fleets of busses gradually dwindled.[1]

[1] T. A. W. Fulton, *The Sovereignty of the Sea* (W. Blackwood and Sons, London, 1911), p. 534.

For over three hundred years Denmark asserted the right of exercising a monopoly over fisheries in the seas lying between Iceland and Norway. England recognized this claim under treaties signed in 1400 and 1523, and her merchants thereafter had to obtain licenses from the Danish king; this position, however, was challenged by the other powers, and Denmark had to relinquish its pretensions. We have noted elsewhere that governments in former times claimed sovereignty over large expanses of ocean; in the nineteenth century most of these claims disappeared and the question shifted to the extent of a country's jurisdiction over its territorial waters. The 1839 Anglo-French Convention was the first international bilateral agreement to fix the three-mile limit. It also provided for a ten-mile opening for bays, and a three-mile distance out to sea from that line, with special exceptions for oyster beds which extended for some miles. Fulton, while praising the treaty suggested that "the selection of so narrow a strip of the adjacent sea was in some respects unfortunate, and has probably acted injuriously on the interests of the sea fisheries."[2] The Anglo-French treaty did not end all disputes, because it did not settle the boundary limits relative to the fishermen of other nations. Belgians, for example, invaded the three-mile zone and even anchored vessels in the harbors and bays of Scotland. It was necessary to sign a convention in 1852 between Great Britain and Belgium to regulate the situation. These and other bilateral treaties helped to bring order into the realm of fisheries; but they proved to be insufficient. They could not deal with the banks in the North Sea where the fish spawned, because these banks lay outside of any national jurisdiction. Moreover, the fishermen of the various countries in the North Sea and elsewhere quarreled. They accused each other of cutting and stealing lines; the "Belgian Devil," a sharp instrument hung overboard to cut through fishing nets in the sea which impeded boats, created much discontent. The problem demanded a more comprehensive settlement than could be reached by bilateral treaty methods.

An inquiry by Mr. W. H. Higgin in 1880 revealed a most unsatisfactory state of affairs in the North Sea. British, Belgian, French, and Dutch boats operated under conditions which produced dissension and disorder, and Mr. Higgin suggested that some measure of international organization was urgently required. Great Britain thereupon invited France, Belgium, Holland, Swe-

[2] *Op. cit.,* p. 316.

den and Norway, and Denmark to consider possible remedies. Holland proposed the adoption of one joint convention instead of relying upon a series of bilateral agreements. A conference of the North Sea powers, including Germany, which had requested to come in, met at The Hague in 1881. Prolonged discussion ensued over the definition of territorial waters for exclusive fishery purposes. Britain and Belgium opposed, and France advocated, the adoption of three geographic miles from the low-water edge and a three-mile limit beyond the ten-mile wide bay. The French view finally prevailed. The German delegate showed praiseworthy foresight in urging that international measures be taken to prevent the destruction of small fish; but France and Great Britain objected, and this proposal, unfortunately, was not adopted. Nor did the suggestion that fishing vessels be regarded as neutral in time of war meet with approval.

The Convention was designed to regulate the policing of fisheries outside of territorial waters.[3] It stipulated the limits of the North Sea; made provision for the numbering and lettering of vessels; regulated the different methods of fishing, especially trawling and drift nets; prohibited the use of gear-destroying apparatus; drew up rules for the salvage of derelict gear and for freedom of navigation and anchorage in territorial waters; and empowered ships commissioned by the signatory powers to seize a fishing vessel found violating the treaty provisions and to deliver it to the government of its own country for trial. The Convention was to last for five years subject to one year's notice of termination. It was "an international document of high importance to the sea fisheries," and was followed by national legislative action. Norway and Sweden did not sign the treaty because they were not satisfied with the clause providing for a three-mile limit—they wanted a four-mile limit—but they were empowered to join later.

New methods of fishing which followed the introduction of trawling (dragging of huge nets along the bottom of the sea), improvements in marketing of fish, the use of steamships instead of sailing vessels, and the growth of the number of the ships engaged led to the impoverishment of the North Sea and other traditional fishing grounds. The trawlers thereupon sailed to more distant areas, and Iceland, the Bay of Biscay, the Moroccan Coast,

---

[3] C. B. V. Meyer, "The Extent of Jurisdiction in Coastal Waters," *A. W. Sijthoff's Uitgeversmaatschappij*, (N. V., Leiden, 1937), p. 109.

and even the Arctic Circle witnessed the invasion of the energetic foreigner. Governments passed measures to limit the use of trawl fishing; but the native inhabitants had to face the fact that trawlers could fish outside the three-mile limit and in this way threaten domestic supplies. Not only that, but the foreign vessels threw away "thousands of tons" of fish, mature and immature. One Iceland correspondent wrote that "the ground, which is valuable for fishing, is completely rotten with the refuse of the trawlers . . . . the ground is fairly poisoned."[4] Fishermen demanded international action to deal with the growing danger. They realized that the optimistic view concerning the unlimited resources of the sea was unjustified, and in 1883 and later attempted to find some remedy. English fishers petitioned Parliament after unsuccessfully trying the policy of voluntarily refraining from using certain areas. A select committee in 1893 recommended that an international conference of North Sea powers be called to extend the three-mile limit for fishery purposes. Little was done before 1914; and Fulton, at the end of his excellent volume, published in 1911, hoped that an international conference would soon be convened to consider how to make the regulation of fisheries more effective.

Several authorities warned that the species of fish most useful to man would soon become extinct if not safeguarded by regulatory and conservation measures. Accordingly Sweden invited representatives from the North Sea countries to meet at Stockholm in June 1899 and at Christiania in May 1901 to arrange a program of international scientific investigation of the North Sea, the Norwegian Sea, and the Baltic in the interests of the fisheries. The conferences set up the International Council for the Exploration of the Sea, which held its first meeting in July 1902. The Council gathered together much valuable scientific information, but at the time of the appearance of Fulton's book it had apparently produced no report concerning possible conservation and regulatory measures; and Fulton himself lamented that "meanwhile, the condition of the fishing-grounds in the North Sea is described as serious by those who ought to know most about it—the trawlers who are working daily there; and if no remedy is timously applied, the measures which will eventually be necessary will transcend those which are now proposed."[5]

The Permanent International Council for the Exploration of the Sea divided its investigations of the North Sea fisheries among

[4] T. A. W. Fulton, *op. cit.,* p. 714.   [5] Fulton, *op. cit.,* p. 738.

the member countries. Norway concentrated upon herring, cod, haddock, and coal fish; Great Britain, Belgium, Denmark, Sweden, and Holland concentrated upon plaice; while hake was assigned to France, which had some help from research vessels supplied by Britain and Ireland. Howell, commenting upon this international work of investigation, suggested that much of its excellent material was not made available in popular form to the owners and officers of the fishing vessels, and that it was necessary to take energetic steps to bring the findings of science to those most immediately interested.[6]

The development of steam trawlers, especially after 1911, "alarmed the herring-drifters," who found that their methods of fishing were being endangered by the new equipment. By 1913 nearly 80 per cent of the landings of trawled herring were made in the North Sea. Deputations waited upon governments and urged that the trawlers were using such small meshes that "large numbers of undersized herring and whitefish" were destroyed. Swedes complained that haddock and whiting were suffering as a result of the spread of the herring trawl, and in 1912 the International Council decided to investigate the herring trawlers, in so far as they affected the destruction of undersized fish of other species.[7] The World War of 1914–1918 led to an interruption of the Committee's work as well as of plans for co-operation among English, Scottish, Dutch, German, French, and Russian herring interests to protect the herring fisheries.

After 1918, efforts were resumed; and the International Council, in 1920, in view of the pressing nature of the plaice problem, suggested a temporary program of research and co-operation. Dutch and Danish representatives presented studies upon this problem which brought out the same principles as investigations elsewhere had revealed, i.e.: that restrictions upon vessels would be justifiable only if it could be shown that they would prevent depletion; that to be effective they must be enforced; that to be enforced the fishermen must believe that conservation measures were necessary.

In 1921 the United States, Canada, Newfoundland, and France founded the North American Commission for Fisheries Research. An International Commission for the Exploration of the Mediter-

[6] G. C. L. Howell, *Ocean Research and the Great Fisheries* (Oxford University Press, 1921), chapter iii.

[7] J. Travis Jenkins, *The Herring and the Herring Fisheries* (P. S. King & Son, London, 1927), p. 147.

ranean Sea had already been established in 1911.[8] But it was not until 1937 that the countries around the North Sea signed a general convention for the conservation of the fisheries in that area. In that year Belgium, Denmark, Germany, Great Britain, Iceland, the Irish Free State, Netherlands, Norway, Poland, and Sweden agreed to establish a permanent commission which was to have the power to recommend extensions and alterations of the Convention itself. The agreement limited the size of mesh to be used in the fishing nets and prescribed the minimum sizes of fish which might be landed and sold. The present war has undoubtedly interrupted the work of the Commission, and one may say that the intense political rivalries of Europe have been responsible for the lagging behind of the North Sea countries in international organization for the conservation of fisheries.

The following example will illustrate the need for international co-operation in the North Sea fisheries. Norwegian fishermen set out nets and lines which stretch underneath the water; the men leave the gear and come back next day to haul it in. The British, however, drag the bed of the sea with their trolls, and thereby frequently damage the Norwegian gear. Heavy financial losses ensue, and much bitterness develops. Much time is consumed in determining the extent of the losses, and if the men are arrested and taken for trial their catch is likely to deteriorate and be ruined. More efficient and rapid methods of settling disputes are urgently needed.

Such a method, it is hoped, is provided for by the agreement of November 5, 1934, which established a special tribunal to deal systematically and expeditiously with claims for damages. Each of the British and Norwegian governments nominates two persons on the tribunal, which possesses no compulsory powers but will consider any dispute submitted to it. The governments encourage the use of the Commission because it is quicker and less expensive than the ordinary law courts, to which, of course, parties can resort, if they so desire. The Commission is to operate in Norwegian waters; and, for purposes of formal equality, a similar tribunal has been set up to deal with disputes arising in British waters, although authorities did not anticipate that this second

[8] The Commission's first meeting was interrupted by the Italo-Turkish War of 1911; the World War of 1914–1918 prevented a meeting planned for 1915; but gatherings were held regularly during the postwar period. See P. Jessup, "L'Exploitation des richesses de la mer," *Académie de Droit International, Recueil des Cours*, Vol. XXIX (1929), p. 427.

Commission would be very fully occupied "as it is quite exceptional for Norwegian vessels to fish in English waters."[9]

Here we find another instance of efficient dealing with the fishery question from what has well been described the causal rather than spatial point of view, when national boundaries have become inconsistent with the essential needs of fisheries control both inside and outside of territorial waters.

Seal Fisheries.—Of the fur seal, which constitutes an important source of the world's fur supply, over 90 per cent are to be found in the herds which frequent the Pribilof Islands. In 1867, when the United States acquired Alaska, it was estimated that there were about 5,000,000 seals in the surrounding sea area. Some forty years later, the number had been reduced to approximately 150,000, and it seemed likely that the seals would "suffer the same fate of extermination at the hands of greedy hunters that had overtaken animals of similar species elsewhere."[10] Fortunately, an international agreement, which followed a long period of controversy, was at length successfully negotiated.

In 1868 Congress forbade the killing of certain fur-bearing animals "within the limits of Alaska territory, or in the waters thereof." Congressional acts of 1869 and 1870 proclaimed the Pribilof Islands a government reserve, and prohibited the killing of fur seals upon the islands or in adjacent waters except in June, July, September, and October; forbade the use of firearms; and authorized the Secretary of the Treasury to lease for twenty years the right of taking fur seals up to the number of 100,000 annually.

Two decades showed clearly that the measures taken were insufficient to prevent an alarming decline in the fur seals—the number dropped from over 3,000,000 in 1874 to 951,000 in 1890. The main reason was that foreigners from British Columbia, Hawaii, and even from the South Seas, attracted by the prospect of great earnings by reason of the increase in the price of sealskins (from $2.50 in 1870 to $30 in 1890), engaged in "pelagic" sealing, i.e., capture of seals in the open ocean. The newcomers, using spears and firearms, made no attempt to distinguish between the male and female of the herd, with the result that not only were mothers and potential mothers killed but thousands of young seals were destroyed through being left to starve on the rookeries.

[9] *British Yearbook of International Law, 1935.*

[10] L. M. Buchanan, "History of the Fur-seal Industry of the Pribilof Islands" (unpublished thesis, University of Washington, 1929), p. 3; J. H. Latané and D. W. Wainhouse, *A History of American Foreign Policy* (Odyssey Press, New York, 1940), pp. 461–72.

The United States, in an attempt to arrest the wholesale decline, had asserted exclusive jurisdiction over the waters of the Alaska Territory east of a line described in the Treaty of 1867. British sealers were subsequently seized and condemned and their masters and mates sentenced to fine and imprisonment. Immediately the thorny question of the freedom of the seas arose, and Great Britain championed the cause of her subjects. The United States suggested international action to protect the fur-seal fisheries, and France, Great Britain, Japan, and Russia signed a tentative agreement; then Canadian objections brought the proposal to an untimely end.

In 1889 American officials seized more British vessels, and controversy again broke out. Secretary Blaine argued that the taking of seals in the open sea was *contra bonos mores* and involved a "serious and permanent" injury to the rights of the United States, and that Russia had transferred its exclusive rights in the Bering Sea to the United States in 1867. The British reply of May 22, 1890, denied the American claim to property rights over the seals, and contended that fur seals were *ferae naturae* and *res nullius* until they were caught. It also denied that the Russian (and therefore the American) claim to exclusive jurisdiction over the Bering Sea had ever been acknowledged.

Fortunately, on February 29, 1892, the two governments agreed to a treaty of arbitration, under which a body of seven persons was to consider five major questions. The arbitrators decided that the United States did not have the "right of protection and property in the seal herd frequenting the Pribilof Islands"; but instead of stopping at a mere negative, legal decision, they authorized a tribunal to prescribe regulations for the protection of the seals outside the three-mile limit. This effort at Anglo-American co-operation to protect the seals on the high seas failed because the regulations were inadequate and cost a great amount of money to enforce. A further attempt by the United States to strengthen protective measures met with opposition from Canada, which asserted that the United States, in granting a monopoly lease to the North American Commercial Company, had assumed complete ownership of the fur seal, which the 1893 Convention had declared it did not have. Canada would not join in co-operative measures merely for the benefit of an American company. For several years the controversy dragged on; the seals were threatened with extermination, and the governments seemed to have reached an impasse.

A favorable opportunity occurred when the North American Company's lease expired in 1910. The United States government did not renew the privilege, and negotiations for an international agreement were resumed, finally resulting in a multilateral treaty, signed on July 7 between the United States, Great Britain, Japan, and Russia. The treaty provided that no person might engage in pelagic sealing in the North Pacific Ocean, and that anyone so doing might be seized by the proper naval forces. The signatories undertook not to permit any part of their territory to be used in connection with illegal sealing. The United States promised to hand over to Canada and to Japan 15 per cent of all the seals taken on the Pribilof and other islands belonging to the United States. Japan agreed to deliver to the United States 10 per cent of the sealskins taken on the islands of her jurisdiction. The Convention was to remain in force for fifteen years and thereafter, subject to twelve months' notice.

Congress ratified the treaty in 1912, and after an animated discussion suspended all killing of fur seals on the Pribilof Islands for five years. It prohibited vessels from being equipped for pelagic sealing within any harbor of the United States or its possessions; nor could skins obtained from pelagic sealing be sold in this country.

The seals increased from 132,000 to more than 400,000 during the closed period. Since that time careful conservation and protection measures have succeeded in rehabilitating the fur seals. The United States Coast Guard maintains a patrol during the spring and fall migrations. Cutters remain in the Bering Sea while the seals are in the Pribilof Islands. And the government stamps every sealskin which is sold in the markets of the United States. It maintains a medical establishment, schools, and other social services for the inhabitants of the Islands, who number approximately four hundred. The officials of the Bureau of Fisheries make elaborate tables concerning the number of seals, the annual killings, and the shipment and sale of the skins, and deliver the skins to the Fouke Fur Company at St. Louis, Missouri. In 1935, 57,290 fur seals were killed. It was estimated that the herd then totaled 1,550,913, an increase of 120,495 over the previous year.

In this area international agreement has succeeded in preserving an industry which unrestricted competition had been on the point of exterminating. Governments, instead of continuing to use the doctrine of sovereignty to prevent constructive measures, wisely adopted a quasi-international solution; the United States does the administrative and scientific work; the other countries share in the benefits.[11]

Halibut.—The halibut provides another of the fisheries problems.[12] This species, which inhabits the North Pacific and North Atlantic Oceans, has yielded about 90,000,000 pounds annually, of which the Pacific halibut accounts for about 60 per cent; its value amounts to perhaps $7,000,000 a year. In the Pacific active fishing operations began about 1888 near Cape Flattery and gradually reached northward along the coast until now it extends to a distance of about eighteen hundred miles. The area traversed in order to maintain the present output has thus increased enormously, and much more intensive effort is needed. The 1928 report of the International Fisheries Commission shows that the amount of gear then used on the older banks was about two and a half times the quantity previously required, but that the catch in the same area was only about 40 per cent of the previous yield. The Commission also noted that six times as much gear was necessary in order to maintain the catch of that year; it reported an increase in the number of undersized fish and concluded that the halibut fishery faced a serious situation. In 1930 it reported a fall in abundance on the older grounds from a yield of about 300 to 35 pounds per unit of gear.

The problem becomes an international one because it cannot be dealt with by one government alone. Most of the fishing is done beyond the limits of territorial waters; Canada and the United States might each impose restrictions on their own citizens or vessels operating on the high seas; but these restrictions would not apply to the citizens of the other country. Should only one government take action to limit its own fishermen, the rivals from over the border would be given an unfair advantage. Dr. W. F. Thompson, former Director of the International Fisheries Commission, well remarks: "The interests of Canada and the United States in this high seas fishery are too intimately related to one another. They cannot be separated."

At the 1918 conference on fisheries, Canadian and United States representatives recommended a closed season of three

---

[11] The agreement has been recently modified by the action of Japan.

[12] This section is based upon the *Reports of the International Fisheries Commission,* No. 1 (1928), No. 2 (1930), No. 5 (1930), No. 6 (1931), and No. 7 (1930).

months and a joint scientific investigation for the purpose of ascertaining more details concerning the life history of the halibut; it dealt also with questions of reciprocal port privileges and tariff duties on fish. The treaty, however, was too complicated and cut across too many interests. Authorities realized that it would be better to concentrate on fewer objectives, and especially to attempt to limit the fishing to a nine months' period and thereby provide an extended closed season. This step was successfully accomplished by the United States–Canadian Treaty of 1924.

The immediate purpose of the treaty was to offset the consequences of overproduction. From 1905, when gasoline engines were installed and vessels could go farther afield, until 1914, technical improvements revolutionized the fisheries. The installation of the Diesel engine, the adoption of electric lights on deck enabling fishing to take place twenty-four hours of the day, the utilization of steel cables for anchoring in great depths, and the further development of cold-storage plants gave a great impetus to fishing and led to overproduction. Prices were forced down at a time when the greater cost of the fishing boats and the decline in the yield of halibut made the expenses of production higher than ever before; these factors threatened heavy loss to the industry. The treaty was designed to curtail fishing during the most difficult and expensive time of the year, from November to February; its origin lay, then, in the desire not primarily to conserve the halibut but to lessen the costs of production.

The treaty, however, went further, and its terms may be thus summarized:

1. An annual closed season from November 15 to February 15, inclusive, which may be modified at the conclusion of the third season if the international commission set up by the treaty so recommends. Any halibut incidentally caught outside of this period during other fishing operations must either be used as food for the crew or be handed over to the public authorities of the United States and Canada to be sold for the public benefit.
2. Vessels of either United States or Canada may be seized by the public officers of either country, except that within their own territorial waters they are subject to the exclusive jurisdiction of their own national officials, offenders being handed over to their own country for trial.
3. A commission of four members, two from each country, is established in order to study the life history of the halibut and to make recommendations concerning its preservation and development.
4. The convention is to last for five years; and shall remain in force

thereafter until two years following the notice of denunciation by either party.

5. Both parties agree to implement the treaty by suitable legislation. This has been done and includes the closing of ports for illegal fishing or illegal preparation to fish, patrolling of all the fishing grounds, and penalties for violating the convention.

The international history of the halibut since 1924 centers largely in the work of the Commission which was set up by the treaty and the scientific investigations of the experts who work under the director, Dr. William F. Thompson. With Dr. Thompson have been associated scientific and other assistants, a librarian, and a captain and crew of the boat which is chartered for the purpose of making investigations at sea. The expenses of the staff are met by appropriations made by each government; the total has varied from $15,000 to $25,000 a year.

The scientific staff has done extraordinarily valuable work in determining the present condition of the fisheries by means of collecting as complete statistics as possible. Within the records of the International Commission are to be found the logs of fishermen operating for the past twenty to thirty years; and, although these statistical data were not complete, they helped to give results sufficiently accurate to enable certain tentative conclusions to be reached. It is impossible for a layman to reproduce the impression made upon him by the careful collection of statistics, the plotting of graphs, and the special studies of the distribution and mobility of the halibut. One small illustration may be given: Many thousands of small fish have been tagged and then thrown overboard. Several thousand have been recovered by fishermen, who collect a reward for each tag returned to the International Fisheries Commission. From an examination of the date, locality, depth, and total catch made at the time, the Commission obtained a history of the fish which revealed clearly "the tremendous growth in the amount of fishing, the great increase in total catch, and the resultant ominous decline from overfishing."

After nearly five years of work, the Commission concluded that any further increase in the intensity of fishing must be prevented. Dr. Thompson suggested the need of an additional control, which must be flexible and direct, based upon "constant and long-continued observation of rate of growth, abundances as artificially and naturally affected, and the yield of the stock." The 1924 Treaty, which gave the Commission power of investigation only, should be enlarged to give it power of control.

The International Fisheries Commission in 1928 recommended the limitation of the catch in certain defined areas to a predetermined percentage annually. The closed season provided by the 1924 Treaty had not resulted in a reduction in the total annual catch but had only made for less expensive operation costs. The decline in the halibut had been general, but it occurred in varying degrees on different parts of the coast. For this reason, and because it is necessary to keep enough young fish to produce spawning adults in each area, regulations to produce and protect such a spawning reserve must be adapted to different conditions in different areas.

No uniform protection of a single class of fish, such as the spawners, no closed season, no size limit or limit on gear, will be found to apply equally and efficiently, and while a limitation of area and catch is recommended, close study would be needed, and frequent revision of the rate of reduction, varying with the need in various areas, which implies the formation of such areas for administrative purposes.

Therefore, the Commission urged the permanent closure of small fish grounds, and the prevention of gear regarded as unduly destructive. The halibut varies from two or three pounds to over two hundred pounds, and it grows so slowly that at twelve years only about 50 per cent of the fish are mature; and since very small fish are of little commercial value, it is economically desirable to protect them. Of the various methods suggested toward this end, the Commission feels that the closure of young fish grounds is superior to imposing a size limit on catchment or to the prohibition of small-sized hooks, though the latter might help in certain cases.

The Commission recommended also: (1) the extension of the closed season by two weeks, with the right to alter the period if necessity should arise; (2) the licensing of vessels fishing for halibut in treaty waters, licenses to be granted under conditions which would enable the Commission to enforce the collection of statistical data necessary for its scientific work; and (3) drawing attention to "the very serious condition of this great fishery, and the necessity for prompt action to rehabilitate it."

The two governments embodied several of the recommendations in a second Halibut Treaty, which was signed in 1930. In 1937 a third treaty clarified some points. The results have been extremely gratifying. International scientific control has increased the abundance of halibut upon the banks. "The same amount of halibut is caught with just one-half the work that was required before regulation. This has tended to reduce the cost of production." The quality and size of the catch have improved. And yet the total amount of fish taken each year has not been reduced by the Commission from that which formerly was landed before regulation. On the contrary, it is considerably larger than it would have been had the decline been permitted to continue. . . . . Still more important from the standpoint of the future is the fact that the number of spawning fish is being gradually increased. This will ensure permanency and high productivity of the resource to the people of the United States and Canada.

In some respects, the methods and work of the Halibut Commission illustrate international organization at its best: (1) It has grown out of the needs of two countries, and it has been adapted to these needs. (2) It embodies a happy co-operation of political and scientific elements. Without the scientific data assembled by the experts there undoubtedly would have been a continual decline in the halibut; and without the prior political agreement, the scientific work would not have been possible, as is seen in Europe, where the scientist has been unable to do much in conserving the fisheries because of the failure of governments to reach a political understanding. (3) The successful outcome has been due also to the co-operation of the Canadian and American fishermen as well as their governments. The men have given considerable assistance to the Commission in the collection of scientific data and have supported each other in working out plans for the efficient marketing of the fish. "This voluntary control of the production by the industry is under the direction of the Halibut Production Control Board of the American fleet and of the Canadian Halibut Marketing Board for the Canadian."[13] In a highly specialized economic world, it would appear that the threefold co-operation of governments, scientific experts, and trade interests, including labor and capital, will produce the maximum results.

This international experiment has had a remarkable success within certain limits; but a number of awkward questions arise. What if other countries which have not been parties to the treaty come in, and attempt to fish in the open sea in such a manner as to threaten the whole conservation program which has been developed by American and Canadian effort? These two countries are building up the fisheries on the high seas, and establishing a

13 H. E. Gregory and Kathleen Barnes, *North Pacific Fisheries* (American Council, Institute of Pacific Relations, New York, 1939), p. 240.

right of ownership in which the moral claim can scarcely be disputed; but how may that moral claim be translated into effective legal form? The two countries have taken a step toward building up "sanctions," by refusing to permit the importation of halibut which is not caught in conformity with the treaty provisions. But will it be possible to say to Japan that her nationals cannot fish in these parts of the open ocean unless they observe the conditions prescribed by the International Commission? Gregory and Barnes put the matter thus:

The danger of possible interruption to the halibut conservation work cannot be too greatly stressed. At present the Pacific halibut banks are unquestionably being rehabilitated. This is a very delicate process, however; the reserve so far built up is small, capable of being swept away in one year of unregulated fishing. To bring the banks back to anything like their former state of abundance will require years of careful regulation.[14]

Sockeye Salmon.—In 1872 the German Emperor in an arbitration award drew the western section of the boundary line between the United States and Canada and gave the San Juan Islands in Puget Sound to the former country. His decision was later to give rise to the protracted problem of the sockeye salmon.[15] This fish comes from the ocean north of the boundary line, passes to the south of the boundary into American waters, turns northward, and re-enters the ocean on the Canadian side before going up the Fraser River to spawn. After their period of spawning the small fingerlings make their way to the ocean. In their wanderings the salmon come under two political jurisdictions, and from this fact arises an international problem which has lasted for fifty years.

The sockeye-fishing industry started in the early 'fifties at Point Roberts; by 1890 many people had come into the business. The development of more efficient gear, the increased use of machinery in canneries, the introduction of refrigeration, the growth of transportation facilities, and the extension of markets resulted in intensified fishing and the beginning of the decline of the sockeye. Even by 1899 warnings were sounded, but no regulatory or conservation steps were taken. Canadian and United States fishermen quarreled, each national group accusing the

[14] *Ibid.*, p. 242.

[15] See M. W. Cox, "The Sockeye Salmon Controversy, an International Problem" (unpublished thesis, University of Washington, 1922).

other of obtaining an unfair percentage of the catch. The state of Washington and the province of British Columbia each made regulations providing for closed seasons and prohibiting certain kinds of gear. In 1905–6 a joint conference worked out a possible solution, but opposition from fishing interests in Washington rendered the attempt abortive. American fishermen advocated enlarging the number of artificial hatcheries in order to increase the supply of fish rather than adopting restrictive regulation which would lessen the market supply. Canadians, however, held out strongly for conservation by limiting the time and the methods of fishing.

In 1908, after much discussion and dispute, a treaty was drawn up providing for an International Fisheries Commission with power to investigate the whole question of fishing in boundary waters, and especially the protection of the sockeye salmon in the Fraser River. The members of the Commission disagreed over measures which should be adopted. Dr. David Starr Jordan proposed cessation of sockeye-salmon fishing between 1910 and 1912; but the Canadian representative would not agree. Within four months the differences had been bridged and regulations were drawn up. Canada promptly ratified the treaty in 1910 and awaited action by the United States. For several years the matter dragged on, until 1916, when Canada, weary of the delay, denounced the treaty. Thus ended a determined effort to reach an international agreement on the sockeye problem.

In 1913 a great catastrophe occurred on the Fraser River. A rock slide caused the current to become so rapid as to prevent a fish from passing up the stream to spawn. The fish perished in countless thousands, and the economic loss was tremendous. Complaints of nonenforcement of regulations added to the bitterness between the two national groups, which a gentleman's agreement between the two states did not suffice to bring to an end.

At length commissioners were appointed to investigate the general problems. Once more the same differences arose: the time and length of the weekly and the annual closed season, the question of entirely closing the fisheries for a period of years, and the complicated problems of the use of traps and purse nets. A treaty was proposed which would have set up an international commission with effective powers to deal with closed seasons, gear, hatcheries, etc. Unfortunately, after Canada had approved the treaty, President Harding withdrew it, in August 1921.

So serious had the position become that the late Dean Cobb

wrote that only a total cessation of fishing for several years could have "the slightest beneficial effect," and that the closed season proposed in the treaty could do little to rehabilitate the sockeye salmon. Nevertheless nothing was done for several years, until in May 1930 Canada and the United States signed a Convention. It was to apply to the Fraser River, to certain streams and lakes, and to other defined parts. Both nations undertook to have charts prepared and buoys and marks set up. An International Salmon Fisheries Commission of six members, three from each country, was to be established, and to continue in existence during the life of the Convention. It was to investigate the natural history of the sockeye, hatchery methods, and spawning-ground conditions, and might stock the waters with the sockeye by methods it deemed advisable; it might recommend to the governments the removal of obstructions to and improvement of the conditions for the ascent of the fish in the waters covered by the Convention. It was to report annually to the two governments. The cost of the Commission was to be borne equally by both countries. The Commission might prohibit the fishing of sockeye salmon at any time between January 1 and August 20, and its ruling was to have full effect until the Commission itself modified or set aside its determination; and it could prescribe types of gear and appliances. Any proposal of the Commission must receive the affirmative vote of at least two commissioners from each country in order to be effective. Thus action affecting either Canada or the United States could be taken only with the consent of the majority of the respective national members. The two countries were to make joint efforts to establish and expand the fishery. The Commission was to regulate conditions so as to enable each nation to obtain as nearly as possible an equal portion of the fish. Each party was to be responsible for the enforcement of the regulations prescribed by the Commission. The treaty was to come into force after the exchange of ratifications and was to last sixteen years and for an additional year after notice of termination.

The 1930 Convention was held up first by Canadian opposition and then by the failure of the United States Senate to ratify until June 1936. At that time it inserted three reservations. Canada thereupon reconsidered the measure which it had meanwhile ratified. After further discussion the treaty entered into force in 1937.[16] A commission of three Americans and three Canadians

[16] "Sockeye Salmon Fisheries," *United States Treaty Series* (Washington, D.C., 1937), No. 918.

is to investigate the sockeye salmon for eight years and then issue regulations for their preservation. The Commission may then limit or prohibit the taking of sockeye in the convention waters between June 1 and August 20 in any year. During the fishing period, inhabitants of the state of Washington may use any gear that is legal in that state, and a similar privilege is to be enjoyed by the inhabitants of British Columbia. The Commission is granted power to improve the spawning grounds, to develop fish culture, and to recommend methods of improving conditions in the streams.

An advisory committee, including five Americans and five Canadians, is to assist the Commission, and the two committees will bear expenses jointly. Dr. W. F. Thompson, ex-Director of the International Fisheries Commission, has taken charge of the scientific investigation, which has already begun. It will be unable to regulate the sockeye salmon until 1945, and it is to be assumed that unless the governments of the state of Washington and of British Columbia issue effective regulations there will be a further decline in the salmon run. Nevertheless, an instrument capable of handling the problem has been created, and political theory has given way to economic need.

Alaska Salmon.—The Pacific salmon fisheries constitute one of the great natural resources of the world. The salmon pack is worth over $75,000,000 a year, of which Alaska's share amounts to nearly $45,000,000. The industry, which began in the 1870's and grew rapidly, was for many years unregulated, and canneries vied with each other in merciless competition. The intensive fishing and excessive numbers of traps had disastrous results on the fish which proceeded upstream to spawn; the resulting decline in the abundance of salmon forced the abandonment of several canneries.

In 1924 Congress placed the Alaskan fisheries under the Secretary of Commerce and gave supervisory and enforcement powers to the Bureau of Fisheries. It provided that at least 50 per cent of the salmon entering the rivers must be permitted to go upstream to spawn. The Bureau might close a badly depleted run for a period of years and might regulate the kind of gear, the time of the year, and the days of the week for fishing. Under these regulations it closed ninety-three fish-trap sites in 1934, and in 1935 prohibited commercial fishing in the Bristol Bay region. Gregory and Barnes called the Act "a landmark in conservation philosophy and technique."

The Bureau has undertaken a remarkable series of conservation measures, and spends thousands of dollars annually in clearing streams to enable the fish to proceed to the spawning grounds, in providing ladders to enable them to climb difficult streams, and in collecting and redistributing salmon eggs. As a result the Alaskan fisheries have been stabilized and given a permanency impossible under the old conditions of unregulated competition: "In short, salmon conservation has been raised to a fine art, and it is hardly to be wondered that the fish so conserved by the United States should be felt by some to be a possession of this country."[17]

Meanwhile the international aspects of the problem had come into prominence. Japan, "the most important fishing country in the world," has important fishing interests throughout the Pacific. Over one and one-half million people are engaged in her fishing industry; more than ten thousand vessels of over ten tons are used; and Japanese fishermen are active in their own waters and in waters belonging to the Soviet Union, and carry on their work in the direction of Mexico, Argentina, the Philippines, and Australia.

The Soviet fishing grounds are extremely important to Japan. In 1875 Japan received most-favored-nation-treatment fishing rights off Kamchatka, and under the 1905 treaty gained the right to "fish in Russian waters along the Pacific Coast." A 1907 Convention set forth the method of leasing fishery lots. This agreement expired in 1919, but in 1925 a general treaty was signed which provided that the 1905 treaty was to hold good. The Soviet Union recognized the right of Japan to fish in its waters. In 1928 a new fishery convention was signed:

The annual auctioning of the fishing lots which had been a feature of the earlier convention was continued. Fishing in the mouths of rivers and in the streams themselves was restricted to Soviet citizens, and some 37 bays and gulfs were likewise exempted from the provisions of the Convention.[18]

Many disputes arose over the payment for leases, the option systems, and other questions. Political difficulties after 1936 interfered with the fishing problem, and in 1939 no working arrangement was reached.

[17] Kathleen Barnes, "The Clash of Fishing Interests in the Pacific," *Far Eastern Survey*, November 18, 1936, p. 245.

[18] H. E. Gregory and Kathleen Barnes, *North Pacific Fisheries* (American Council, Institute of Pacific Relations, New York, 1939), p. 290.

The fishery question is entangled in the general mesh of Soviet-Japanese relations, which have grown progressively more strained since the end of 1936. While not denying Japan's rights to fish in its waters, the Soviet Union was not willing to conclude a new long-term agreement and also refused simply to extend the old one in 1939 as in previous years. A new temporary agreement was offered which restored the general auctioning of the fishing lots and closed about 40 grounds for strategic reasons. Japan for a long time refused to accept these terms and the opening of the season was in sight with no agreement as to how Japan should exercise its fishing rights. Finally at the beginning of April the agreement was signed.[19]

Gregory and Barnes point out that Japan's expansion in Soviet waters seems to have reached its limit, that Soviet fishing has increased, and that Japan's relative share has declined.

The application of science to fishing methods has given rise to a new and serious problem. Large floating factory ships have been invented which use nets several miles in length. They have been catching salmon in the ocean waters, and threaten to inflict permanent injury upon salmon runs. The Japanese government has used influence to consolidate several companies into one large concern. Coincident with this rapid centralization of control in the Japanese salmon fisheries has gone the evolution of new fishing techniques.

If these floating canneries station themselves a few miles outside of the territorial waters of, say, the Soviet Union or Alaska, they may do serious damage to the salmon runs in those parts. We have seen that the United States government has spent considerable sums in rehabilitating the salmon fisheries in Alaska. The question arises whether it is right for nationals of another country to take advantage of the doctrine of the three-mile limit, fish in the open seas, and by so doing threaten to ruin an important experiment in conservation.

In 1936 Japan appropriated 89,000 yen to investigate the fishing resources in Alaskan waters, and a ship proceeded to Bristol Bay for this purpose. The next year the proposal was made in Seattle, but without success, that American and Japanese capital join in open-sea canning of Alaska salmon, using Japanese equipment and cheap Japanese labor. Feeling ran high in Alaska and along the West Coast. The Diamond bill introduced into Congress in June 1937 declared that the United States had jurisdiction over all waters adjacent to the Alaska coast with a depth less than one

[19] H. E. Gregory and K. Barnes, *op. cit.,* p. 290.

hundred fathoms. In 1938 the Copeland bill provided for an extension of United States jurisdiction to the continental shelf around Alaska to the edge of a depth of a hundred fathoms.

These proposals did not become law, and the Department of State took the matter in hand. In November 1937 it sent a note to the Japanese government drawing attention to its own conservation efforts in Alaska and saying:

It is clear to all that if foreign nationals are permitted to carry on fishing operations off the shores of Alaska, the conservation efforts of the American Government would in a comparatively short period be completely nullified, whatever the intentions of those engaged in such fishing operations. Such an eventuality would be all the more deplorable for the reason that no conceivable economic gain would compensate the nationals of Japan for the probable destruction, however intentional, of resources developed through the general efforts of American citizens.

It reviewed the history of legislative action and reminded Japan of the large sums of money expended for the protection of the fisheries:

The American Government is confident that the Japanese Government will realize the seriousness of the problem involved in this situation and the urgency of there being taken early and effective action to dispose of it.

The American Government believes that the right or obligation to protect the Alaska salmon fisheries is not only overwhelmingly sustained by conditions of their development and perpetuation, but that it is a matter which must be regarded as important in the comity of the nations concerned.

Early in 1938 the Department of State announced that Japan had given assurances, "without prejudice to the question of rights in international law," that it would suspend the salmon fishing survey, that it would continue to suspend the issue of such licenses, and that it had disclaimed knowledge of fishing on a commercial scale in those waters.

Thus the present situation is one of compromise. Japan may claim under international law that it has the right to freedom of fishing in the open sea. The United States has traditionally upheld the three-mile limit on many occasions, and to demand its modification now might seem to be inconsistent. We have referred above to the view that under modern conditions the three-mile limit may not be conducive to the best conservation of fishery resources. The question is how to arrange for a new order of things which will enable conservation to be satisfactorily undertaken and at the same time do justice to the interests of all parties.

Recently the American Bar Association subcommittee on Pacific Coastal Fisheries considered the question and reported that the problem of fisheries was not to be identified with that of the extent of territorial waters as part of the domain of the state, and that several governments had insisted upon their right "to take action on the high seas adjacent to territorial waters for protection of . . . . vital interests," but that the United States had in the past taken positions which would make modifications now somewhat embarrassing.[20] Undoubtedly international action of some kind will be required.

Whales.—In recent years the necessity for international action in order to preserve the rapidly diminishing number of whales has been clearly recognized. The day of the whale may be almost over; for new methods have enabled vessels to kill many more of the great mammals than previously. The invention of the harpoon attached to a cord and fired from a cannon (the harpoon gun) made possible easier catches than with the old hand harpoon. The Norwegians invented a system of filling the body with air so that it could float more easily. The development of floating factories at sea enabled ships to treat many more whales and abstract more oil than was possible when they had to take the carcasses ashore for treatment.[21] The number of whales killed rose from about one thousand in 1900 to between twenty and thirty thousand in 1927 and to over forty thousand in the Antarctic alone in the year 1930–31.[22]

National measures to protect excessive whaling were made more difficult as pelagic whaling became widespread, because no nation had jurisdiction over the open sea. Many experts called attention to the need of international control, in order to prevent the "veritable butchery," to protect young whales, to create reserves for adults, and to insure full industrial utilization of all parts of the captured whale. M. Suarez, in his report on the "Exploration of the Products of the Sea,"[23] recommended the

---

[20] See also J. W. Bingham, *Report on the International Law of Pacific Coastal Fisheries* (Stanford University Press, 1938).

[21] P. Jessup, *op. cit.*, pp. 484–86.

[22] *Ibid.*, p. 491, and B. Bergersen, "The International Whaling Situation," *Le Nord* (1938), p. 113.

[23] Reprinted in *American Journal of International Law,* Vol. XX (1926), pp. 231–40.

calling of a conference of experts in marine zoölogy and in international law to draw up a convention which would embody general and local principles for rational control, such as the creation of reserved zones, the limitation of catches to certain zones in rotation, closed periods, and effective methods of supervising the measures adopted.

Jessup suggested that regulation could take place with respect to four matters: (*a*) the zone where whales might be killed; (*b*) the season during which they might be killed; (*c*) the kind of whales to be taken; and (*d*) the proceeds of the catch, involving insistence upon the complete utilization of the carcass.[24] The British Empire attempted some regulation in 1923 and Norway passed a whaling act in 1929; but the evidence showed conclusively that international action was required. Representatives of interested governments met at Geneva in 1931 and drew up a convention which, however, applied only to baleens, or whalebone whales. Under Article 5 the taking or killing of suckling and immature whales and female whales accompanied by calves was prohibited. Article 6 provided that the fullest possible use must be made of the carcasses of whales. The remuneration of gunners and crews was to depend not only upon the number of whales but also upon such factors as size, value, and yield of oil. Vessels must fly the flag of their country and obtain a license to engage in whaling. The signatory powers undertook to collect the most complete biological information on the whales and to communicate statistical information regarding whaling operations to the International Bureau for Whaling Statistics at Oslo.[25]

During the next few years intensified whaling developed. Expeditions carried out activities along ice barriers, and twelve companies were formed for pelagic whaling in the Antarctic between 1925 and 1930. Between 1932 and 1936 the number of whales killed increased enormously, and the number of immature Blue whales in the catch rose considerably.[26] Moreover, during 1936–37 there were indications that Germany, Japan, and the United States were about to engage in extensive whaling operations. "Under these circumstances it became a matter of urgent necessity to get an international whaling convention as soon as possible, in order that the previous years' efforts to preserve this unique source of raw stuffs for the world's market should not be thrown away."[27]

[24] Jessup, *op. cit.*, pp. 494–95.
[25] *League of Nations Treaty Series,* Vol. CLV (1934–35), No. 3586, p. 349.
[26] B. Bergersen, *op. cit.*, p. 118.   [27] *Ibid.*, p. 119.

Obviously a convention was needed which would protect most if not all species of whales instead of one only, and would stiffen up conservation measures. Such a step was taken by the interested powers, including South Africa, the United States, Argentina, Australia, Germany, Great Britain, the Irish Free State, New Zealand, and Norway, in an international agreement signed at London on June 8, 1937. It provided that the contracting governments would maintain at least one inspector of whaling on each factory ship under their jurisdiction. In this manner the supervision of the treaty was considerably strengthened. It was forbidden to take or kill Gray whales and/or Right whales, as well as Blue, Fin, Humpback, or Sperm whales below specified lengths, or to take or kill calves or suckling or female whales accompanied by calves or suckling whales. It prescribed a closed period of nine months per year for factory ships or whale-catchers in waters south of 40° South latitude, forbade the taking or treatment of whales in any area for more than six months per year, and set aside certain prohibited areas which need not be mentioned here. Article 11 directs that "the fullest possible use shall be made of all whales taken." By Article 12, ships must not take more whales than can be treated efficiently within a period of thirty-six hours after being killed. As with the 1931 treaty the signatory powers undertake to insure that gunners and crews are paid according to the total results of their work and not merely according to the number of whales caught, and that they will communicate to the International Bureau of Whaling Statistics all information possible.[28]

In 1938 a second conference, held at London, adopted certain amendments

in an attempt to tighten the restrictions. It added a one-year closed season for humpback whales in water south of 40° south latitude, forbade the use of a factory ship employed in antarctic waters in other waters during the same year, forbade keeping whale carcasses in the sea for more than 33 hours, and somewhat changed the territories closed to pelagic whaling.[29]

Nine countries signed the agreement; but Russia, Japan, and Chile abstained. Karl Brandt, in his able study, speaks of the limited results of the conventions, not because of the difficulties of law enforcement, or of ignorance of the steps which should be

[28] *League of Nations Treaty Series,* Vol. CXC (1938), No. 4406, p. 79.
[29] Karl Brandt, *Whale Oil, an Economic Analysis* (Food Research Institute, Stanford University, 1940), p. 99.

taken, but because of conflicting economic interests. He points out that a struggle exists between the interests of Britain and Norway on the one hand and those of Japan and Germany on the other. "While the Norwegian and British companies have to compete on their own account and can survive only with net profits, the German and Japanese industries are strongly fostered by the two governments and serve first of all the purpose of saving foreign exchange[30]—an interesting commentary upon the influence of power politics upon economic activities. Brandt is not hopeful concerning the future. He admits that certain technical progress has been made in avoiding unnecessary waste, but points out that the fundamental purpose, i.e., "the prevention of over fishing," has not been realized. But, given international stability, conditions may exist for better results in the future.

It may be that science will find a way to offset the disadvantages of the lack of political agreement among the nations. Professor Trevor Kincaid notes that the machinery provided for in the 1931 treaty, which came into effect in 1936, "operates so slowly that the whales may be gone before the red tape has been unwound and wound up again." He suggests that the following plan may afford a solution: Whales are of two kinds—those which strain from the sea great quantities of small sea life called plankton, and those that feed on the larger fish. The plankton obtains the oil from tiny plants in the sea, and Kincaid suggests that the oil "might be extracted directly from the plankton itself." If this were done, whaling would be rendered unnecessary. The amount of plankton is apparently almost inexhaustible, and the question is whether vessels can be equipped in such a way that they can pump in enough water, separate the plankton, and subject it to sufficient pressure in a battery of hydraulic presses so as to remove all the liquid contents. The remainder might then be pressed into cakes and made into animal food. The oily fluid could be piped to another section of the ship, where it would be filtered and processed to clarify the oil, which would then be stored in tanks pending its refining on shore.[31] The problem is one of cost, and Kincaid is carrying on his research to determine whether or not the scheme can be made commercially worth while.

[30] *Ibid.,* p. 81. See also L. L. Leonard, "Recent Negotiations toward the International Regulation of Whaling," *The American Journal of International Law,* January 1941, pp. 90–113.

[31] Trevor Kincaid, "Salvaging of Whales," *Tempo* (University of Washington), November 1939, pp. 14–16).

GREAT LAKES

Early in March 1938, representatives of the United States and of eight states of the United States, the government of Canada, and the province of Ontario met to consider measures to preserve the fishing industry of the Great Lakes, which was threatened with extinction. In Lake Ontario the annual production had dropped from 3,000,000 to 500,000 pounds; between 1924 and 1934 Lake Erie cisco production had declined from over 21,000,-000 pounds annually to a mere 135,000 pounds. Perch and white-fish of Lake Huron also suffered decline; the yellow perch "are only half as abundant in Lake Michigan and one-fourth as abundant in Lake Huron as they were a few years ago" and lake sturgeon are "virtually extinct."

The reasons are the same here as elsewhere in the world: improved boats, improved gear, increased number of fishermen, and movement of fishers from one area to another. Michigan complains that seven of the neighboring states, which control one-third of the lakes, take two-thirds of the fish. Little wonder that authorities on both sides of the boundary line met to consider remedies for this alarming state of affairs. The superintendent of Michigan fisheries, Mr. Fred A. Westerman, suggested to the conference the following regulations, which are typical of the measures adopted in other parts. He proposed: "(1) uniform methods of measuring fishnet mesh; (2) proper size mesh to prevent taking undersize fish; (3) closed seasons during the spawning periods; (4) regulations of the amount and size of gear; (5) control of the movements of fishermen; (6) complete statistics; (7) well-organized research; (8) control of marketing conditions."[32]

The principles which should govern the general policy of international conservation have been well set forth by Sir John Fischer Williams and Professor George Grafton Wilson in a report to the Institut de Droit International on *Les Fondements juridiques de la conservation des richesses de la mer*. They point out that the species of fish differ so much in their habits, number, and distribution that each of them requires a special study: "On ne peut pas légiférer pour les poissons en général." Their economic value differs, and species with a high individual value are in greater danger of extinction than those of a general mass value. The conservation of fish in the high seas is an international problem,

[32] *Christian Science Monitor,* March 9, 1938.

and the nineteenth and twentieth centuries show a slow but developing organization along these lines. The world now possesses enough scientific international organization for the study of the problem.[33] What it needs are rules for conservation which should be applied before the resources are too greatly depleted and some species disappear.

There are two problems: (1) To establish rules. These should be based upon scientific research carried out according to the highest traditions of academic work. That this is not merely a theoretical hope is seen in the work already being done by the United States and Canada under the auspices of the International Fisheries Commission. (2) The institution of sanctions to enforce the rules adopted. These can come about only by treaties and conventions ratified by governments and applied to their own nationals. There is the difficulty of what to do with countries which do not come into the agreement. Nevertheless, the rules should be drawn up, and it is not necessary to treat the questions of sanctions first. The history of the slave trade shows that the problem is not insoluble. "Ce problème de sanctions internationales contre un abus de la liberté des mers n'est pas insoluble." It will not be possible, or desirable, to draw up detailed legal rules in advance. The law must follow experience.

[33] Quoted in J. W. Bingham, *Report on the International Law of Pacific Coastal Fisheries* (Stanford University Press, 1938), p. 63.

Chapter IX

INTERNATIONAL AND WORLD ASPECTS
OF POPULATION PROBLEMS

Opinion on probably no other subject has changed with such rapidity in recent years as on the question of population. Within a short time experts and others who had been writing of the dangers of overpopulation, and painting gloomy pictures of international rivalries that must ensue, began to talk in terms of population decline and race suicide. Probably this new tendency will not eliminate the population factor as a cause of international friction, but it will at least considerably alter its emphasis.

Gunnar Myrdal would suggest that this sudden change of emphasis in population theory is not accidental. In his view the political element in political theory has been a basic, though often hidden, factor, and there has existed a close relation between the mercantilist theory and the seventeenth- and early eighteenth-century population doctrines, between the conservative reaction after the French Revolution and the theory of Malthus, between the growing radicalism of the nineteenth century and the reaction against Malthusianism, and today between (*a*) neo-mercantilism and the politics of force and (*b*) recent doctrines of the need of population increase: "Each population doctrine has in the main been correct only if we grant the major premises of those advocating it." "Population theory is part of the grand tradition of political economy." "I deliberately choose to discuss the problem of population frankly as a political problem of social goals and planned political action."[1]

The world's population increased but slowly before the seventeenth century. Carr-Saunders writes:

If we regard history as a whole, a stable rather than increasing population has been the rule . . . . during those periods when popula-

[1] G. Myrdal, *Population: A Problem for Democracy* (Harvard University Press, 1940), pp. 19, 24, 31.

tion was increasing, as when it was stable, there has always been some system in operation which has had the effect of preventing the inherent power of multiplication being realized to the full.

In the Middle Ages the relation between the number of people and the amount of arable land was a matter of great importance. Because communications were bad, certain areas seemed to be "overpopulated," and, when famines occurred, as they frequently did, little could be done to relieve them. It was natural that colonies came to be regarded as important as areas of settlement accommodating an adequate population necessary for political power.[2]

In a later volume[3] Carr-Saunders estimates that the world population was approximately 545,000,000 in 1650; 728,000,000 in 1750; 906,000,000 in 1800; 1,608,000,000 in 1900, and over 2,000,000,000 in 1933. A marked increase thus began less than two hundred years ago, since which time both Asia and Europe have gained heavily.

Within the last century populations have mounted with special rapidity, owing not to an increase in the birth rate, although this is observable in some countries, but rather to the lessening of the death rate. What have been the causes of the latter phenomenon? The establishment of political order has played its part, also each of the following: the development of social agencies to care for the sick and needy; the rise in the average provision of food and clothing and shelter; the development of sanitary organization, including the supply of pure water and the disposal of sewage; vaccination against disease; and generally the rapid advancement of medical science.

Even before the nineteenth century had given to the world the benefits derived from applied science, the prospect of overpopulation had concerned many thinkers. The theory of Malthus is well known. This clergyman in 1798—in opposition to Godwin and Condorcet, who claimed that a just distribution of wealth and the establishment of rationally conceived social institutions would permit indefinite population increase—argued that population would grow at a geometric rate of progression while foodstuffs would increase only in arithmetical proportion. Population would mount in the ratios 1, 2, 4, 8, 16, 32, etc., whereas foodstuffs would mount by only 1, 2, 3, 4, 5, 6, etc.

[2] A. M. Carr-Saunders, *Population* (Oxford University Press, London, 1925), p. 21.

[3] A. M. Carr-Saunders, *World Population: Past Growth and Present Trends* (Clarendon Press, 1936), pp. 17–45.

Ricardo preached the law of rent and the iron law of wages: Good land would become progressively scarcer, more and more marginal lands would have to be used, and an increasing effort would be necessary to get food from the poorer soil. Malthus did not believe that the great masses of people could, or would, progress morally, and considered that they must always exist near the level of poverty.

The next hundred years brought to light forces and theories which seriously challenged Malthus' theory: (1) Science revolutionized production and communications; it prevented the law of diminishing returns from operating with the intensity forecast by Malthus. (2) Despite the proofs of the pessimistic economists of the early nineteenth century, social legislation helped to raise the standard of living of the masses. (3) Karl Marx's theory that no "natural law" of population existed, but that its increase or decrease depended upon the organization of society, had a powerful influence. Capitalism, he preached, produces unemployment and overpopulation, and socialism, by providing a greater purchasing power for the people, would enable a population increase to take place. (4) John Stuart Mill enunciated the theory of optimum density, i.e., the maximum number of people which the most efficient combination of all wealth-producing agencies would enable to live at the highest average standard of life; three other economists—Cannan in 1888, Wolf in 1901, and Wicksell in 1911—further developed the theory. (5) The Belgian mathematician, Verhulst, in 1838, suggested that the rise and fall of populations obeyed "cyclical rhythms," and in the twentieth century Gini has also elaborated this idea. (6) Higher standards of living, rising levels of morality, and advances in the general values of society have resulted in a marked decline in the birth rate.[4]

Nevertheless, the nineteenth century continued to fear overpopulation, and an apprehensive state of mind continued even until after 1918. One prominent authority suggested that governments should conclude an international agreement to limit their populations and to spread information concerning methods of birth control. H. M. East published his *Mankind at the Cross Roads* in 1923, and a world population conference held in Geneva in 1927 considered possibilities of increasing popular knowledge concerning methods of limiting the size of families.

Curiously enough, the belief in overpopulation exerted two

[4] Imre Ferenczi, *The Synthetic Optimum of Population* (International Institute of Intellectual Co-operation, League of Nations, Paris, 1938), pp. 16–22.

distinct and diverging influences upon international relations. Countries which felt the threat of overpopulation seized upon the idea of colonization as a remedy. To fill the empty spaces of the New World seemed to them a necessary method of preventing excessive population and a decline of the standard of living at home. But the idea worked in another way: Population increase did not take place at the same rate in all parts, and countries with a smaller rate of increase became alarmed that a mounting population differential would menace their security. Large populations mean large armies, and a large army is important in dealing with neighboring countries. France realized that it had lost ground during the last hundred years in man power, a fundamental factor in the Franco-German problem. Most Frenchmen did not stop to think that the more rapid German increase was largely "justified by economic conditions"; they thought only in terms of security. As Clemenceau put it, "There are twenty million Germans too many." To offset her relative decrease in population and to acquire greater man power, France sought colonies.

Overpopulation is an easy term to bandy about.[5] It is far less simple to analyze scientifically. When *is* a country overpopulated? Is it merely a matter of area? Or can we say that there is overpopulation when there is a large amount of unemployment? It is obvious that the amount of territory is only one factor in the population problem. The development of superior methods of agriculture, the application of large-scale machinery and the specialization of labor, the improvement in communications of all sorts, the maintenance of a sound currency system, and the development of a high degree of technical, intellectual, and moral efficiency, all contribute to make possible a great increase in material resources. Conversely, a decline in the efficiency of national and world economic organization will affect the optimum density of a nation's population. Given an economic system whereby great fluidity of labor, capital, and goods is possible, the mere territorial factor becomes only one of many forces combining to affect human welfare. The optimum density, i.e., the density of population which will enable a country to make the best use of its resources in a world of international trade, depends upon a number of conditions, of which the extent of homeland and colonies is but one. Ferenczi writes: "The economic density of a country cannot, then,

---

[5] F. C. Wright, *Population and Peace* (International Studies Conference, International Institute of Intellectual Co-operation, League of Nations, Paris, 1939), chapter iv.

be studied in our day, generally speaking, without taking into consideration at least the total amount of national income much of which is obtained by international trade."[6]

In the early nineteenth century, before the economic revolution had led governments to seize colonies, a great amount of emigration took place in an unregulated fashion. Millions of people left Europe and went to the United States, Canada, South America, Australia, and New Zealand to seek their fortunes. These "empty spaces" provided a population outlet for several decades. Sauer writes that the last hundred years were part of the period 1492–1918 which witnessed the greatest migration of man and the most rapid population increase since neolithic times, and adds that the expansion was principally due to the invasion of lower and weakly resistant cultures by the overflow from higher, aggressive cultures. But recently, he says, a "marked stabilization of world population" has come and pronounced shifts in its relative density will become the exception.[7]

Without question, opportunities for unregulated mass migrations will be much rarer than formerly. International immobility has set in: (1) The new countries which have received immigrants have encountered labor and other economic difficulties. The United States, which grew from 8,000,000 in 1800 to over 130,-000,000 in 1930, now has serious unemployment problems. Other lands by reason of climatic and other factors are unable to support large populations. They all seek to raise immigration barriers against foreigners. (2) The question of assimilation has become more urgent. Immigration brought with it not merely the problem of economic but also that of cultural absorption. The United States toward the end of the nineteenth century realized that the task of welding millions of people from different cultures and historical backgrounds was enormous. Differences of race added to the difficulties of assimilation, and immigration barriers took the form of quotas, racial discrimination, health and dependence tests, and even inquiry into political convictions. (3) Sauer points to the decline in mineral prospects, and believes that, while there may be metallurgic advances, these are not likely to produce any great "relocation of industrial peoples" and that heavy industry

[6] Ferenczi, *op. cit.*, p. 40. Myrdal severely criticizes the "optimum density" concept.

[7] Carl O. Sauer, "The Prospect of Redistribution of Population," in Isaiah Bowman (Editor), *Limits of Land Settlement* (Council on Foreign Relations, New York City, 1937).

will remain in much the same geographic situation as now. The mining boom, he suggests, is largely eliminated "from major significance in future population shifts." (4) It is doubtful if the discovery and distribution of new crops will be sufficient to form the basis of large population changes. (5) There has been even a shrinking of resources because of destructive exploitation. Some countries have expanded agriculture at the expense of forest and pastoral lands; erosion has become a major problem and conservation a matter of urgency. The task is to preserve the basis for existing populations. (6) The spread of European colonization in the nineteenth century took place, in part at least, at the expense of native peoples, whose numbers declined because of imported diseases and cultural dislocations. With the spread of medical knowledge, sanitation, and sound educational policies, native populations will increase more rapidly than the whites, making it more difficult for the European element in colonies to hold its own as time goes on. (7) Technological invention may enable many of the new lands to support greater populations, and the revival of international trade based upon international order will serve the same end. Sauer writes that the areas of advanced technology will more rapidly benefit from technological advance than the more distant quarters of the world. And he adds the striking judgment, which should be deeply pondered, that "the areas of great accumulation of population are areas of great and persistent economic advantage and cultural energy."[8] Note the importance of the word "persistent." In a reasonable world the average European is "likely to benefit most by the elaboration of skill in his own land." Ferenczi remarks that owing to the growth of economic rigidities "men have become less and less mobile" and in consequence

there is a strong tendency for human migration to be replaced by migration of capital toward overpopulated countries, provided it is possible to create a local market in those countries or to ensure the exportation of the products of those countries at relatively low prices. In this sense it is possible to speak also of an optimum distribution of capital.[9]

If nations regain their sanity, lower international barriers, and restore confidence, Europe can perhaps still be "of all parts of the world the best suited to support a larger population." In the present economic and technological condition of the world, then, colonial settlement and migration may be less efficient methods of

[8] Sauer, *op. cit.*, p. 22.   [9] Ferenczi, *op. cit.*, p. 61.

solving population pressure than the restoration of unfettered trade, commerce, and capital investment, and the elimination of political tension.

In summary, there are serious obstacles to overseas settlement as a general solution for relieving overpopulation. We shall examine elsewhere how relatively unimportant are colonies as population outlets. To attempt to conquer and maintain colonies involves costly wars and enormous expenditures upon armaments; the result would not justify the effort.

The difficulties of mass migration in modern times were clearly revealed in the British Empire. After the World War of 1914–1918 Great Britain found in her unemployment position a heavy burden, and in 1921 she invited Dominion representatives to a conference to consider "the possibilities of state-aided settlement within the Empire." The conference recommended Imperial co-operation to secure a comprehensive policy of population settlement, especially in connection with land settlement. The Dominions possessed the land; the home country had the surplus population; the question remained, on paper, merely one of organizing transfer machinery. The recommendations were considered favorably by the 1921 Imperial Conference; the British government then passed an Empire Settlement Act in 1922, which gave it power to co-operate with any Dominion in mutually acceptable schemes. Britain was to be responsible for not more than one-half of the expense of any arrangement, which was not to exceed £1,500,000 for the first year nor £3,000,000 in any later year; nor was it to be liable for more than fifteen years after the passing of the Act.

The outstanding experiment under this agreement was the Western Australian group-settlement scheme,[10] under which, according to an agreement signed in 1923, the state proposed to settle 75,000 new immigrants there.

The first report was enthusiastic; but soon difficulties developed, due, according to Shann, to

(1) failure to select as group members those only who had proved their aptitude for farming; (2) degeneration of group clearing under

[10] For information on this scheme, see E. Shann, "Group Settlement of Immigrants in Western Australia," *The Economic Record*, November 1925, and *Report of Overseas Settlement Committee*, 1926. See also A. H. Charteris, "Australian Immigration Policy," *International Conciliation*, December 1927; A. B. Keith, *Responsible Government in the Dominions* (1928), Vol. II, p. 1213, in its general treatment of the Colonial and Imperial Conferences, gives a summary of the migration problem as it developed at each conference.

sustenance economy into "government stroke" on day wages, virtually unchecked by fear of dismissal; (3) the placing of a number of groups on unsuitable land; and (4) the attempt to do by mass action on the initiative of the State what has previously been done by individuals.

The result was disappointing; and, while the group scheme might encourage newcomers to work together, there was much more to be said for individual and family migration, with the result that the scheme was not energetically forwarded.

A new method was evolved in the form of an agreement in April 1925 between the Imperial and the Australian Commonwealth governments, by which £34,000,000 was to be loaned to the state governments at low interest rate for the purpose of furthering settlement on public works likely to assist in that direction: for each £75 advanced, one assisted migrant was to sail from the United Kingdom; and the scheme was intended to settle 450,000 people within a period of ten years. It was in furtherance of this plan that the Development and Migration Commission was formed in Australia in 1926, on the principle, as Mr. Bruce, the Australian Prime Minister, said, of the interdependence of development and migration: "We cannot develop unless we have more population, and we cannot absorb more migrants unless we develop." Keith, however, was not optimistic, and wrote:

The success of the agreement rests on the efforts of the States to carry it out: and the dislike of assisted immigration expressed by Labour in Australia, and resentment at the assurances contained in the agreement that assisted migrants are to be secured work, render the future of the agreement in actual operation extremely dubious.

In this sentence is contained one of the fundamental problems confronting Imperial migration. The Dominions, on the whole, need agricultural laborers and settlers on the land. Most, if not all, of the Dominions can do little to help the industrial unemployment in Britain, because they themselves have a similar unemployment situation; nor is Britain able to satisfy the Dominion needs for agricultural labor, for her supply for her own needs is inadequate and the absorptive capacity of the Dominions is limited by (1) the nature of the unoccupied lands (according to Professor Griffith Taylor about 42 per cent of Australia is arid, 34 per cent is good pastoral country, 21 per cent is fair, temperate farming country, and 3 per cent is suited for tropical agriculture); (2) climatic conditions (whether or not white settlement is possible in the Australian Tropics is a debated question, with many opinions on both sides) ; (3) the need of capital;[11] (4) resettlement, since the best lands in Australia are already alienated, as Charteris points out, "is not a question of unlocking new territory, but of subdividing and resettling existing occupied land," which is a costly and relatively slow process; (5) the finding of markets for increased agricultural produce resulting from increased settlement, which is by no means an easy task, in view of the growth of economic nationalism.

From these considerations, which only suggest in broad terms the difficulty of placing migrants on the land in Australia (and the same type of reasoning will hold for New Zealand, and in some measure for Canada),[12] it will be seen that anything approaching "mass action" in Imperial migration is out of the question.

This fact was definitely recognized by the special subcommittee on Overseas Settlement, set up by the 1926 Imperial Conference.[13] The Committee especially wished to disassociate itself "from the idea that the mere transfer of large numbers of people from Great Britain to the open spaces of the Dominions would afford a solution of the problem of overseas settlement." It affirmed, however, "the importance of accelerating the distribution of population" in the interests of the Empire as a whole and, while recognizing the obstacles, indicated a determination to press forward with the existing machinery.

It is clear from this account that, despite the advantages of a common Imperial sentiment and Empire organization, mass migration cannot be a solution of "overpopulation" under modern conditions.

[11] An economist writes: "Experience shows that in the absence of unprecedented opportunities, Australian capacity is not likely to exceed 35,000 per year. In order to absorb this number we require an equivalent in flow of new capital such as accompanied our immigration before the war. The present capital per head of population is about £300. To equip 35,000 people . . . . we need at least the same value per head, and we cannot do more than equip our own natural increase from our own savings. To absorb 35,000 a year we need at least £10,000,000 a year in new capital imports. The present unemployment in Australia cannot be disassociated from the fact that we have been accelerating our imports of men and retarding our imports of our capital." See J. B. Brigden, "The Limits of Australian Immigration," *The Economic Record,* November 1925, pp. 145–48.

[12] Charlotte Whitton, "The Immigration Problem for Canada, 1924"; Griffith Taylor, "The Frontiers of Settlement in Australia." Reprinted from the *Geographical Review,* January 1926. The Union of South Africa, owing to its peculiar situation in reference to its Negro population, can give little or no openings to labor.

[13] *Imperial Conference, 1926, Summary of Proceedings and Appendices,* Section X.

The popular habit of thinking of population problems in terms of agricultural extensity and of colonial expansion still persists. Into this mental climate has come a new factor of extraordinary importance. This factor is the decline in the rate of population increase. Northern and western Europe is failing to reproduce itself at the same rate as in former years; the surplus of 600,000 births over deaths is diminishing, and France, Sweden, Belgium, Germany, and Great Britain face a serious problem. In Italy, Portugal, and Spain there has been recently a surplus of 780,000 births over deaths, but this surplus is not being maintained, and a decline has set in. The reasons for the decline, which is causing great concern to statesmen and population experts alike, is the adoption of the small family; and this in turn is traceable to the fear of maternal mortality, the inconveniences incident to childbirth, the influence of writers on eugenics and others who have spread an anxiety complex concerning hereditary factors, economic insecurity, and the prevailing habit of thought which causes many married couples to regard larger families as an incumbrance. These factors and, above all, the spread of birth control have caused the reproduction rate to fall. The full effects will not be felt for some years; but unless some drastic changes occur to arrest the downward fertility trend, important sections of the world will experience a serious population decline.[14]

National governments today are therefore thinking, not in terms of international conferences to consider means of limiting population growth, but of devising methods to insure an increase in the national birth rate. Parliamentary and other commissions have conducted inquiries in Great Britain, Japan, Sweden, Denmark, etc. Italy has taken energetic action (especially after 1927), taxing bachelors and childless couples, giving preference in goverment positions to married men who have several children, and reducing taxes on large families. Germany has modified the law of inheritance so as to favor large families, giving preference in government employment to married men with children and by means of marriage loans encouraging couples to marry earlier than might otherwise be possible. France has adopted the family-allowance scheme in its wage scales, as have New Zealand and

---

[14] R. R. Kuczynski, "World Population"; H. D. Henderson, "Economic Consequences," *The Population Problem* (George Allen & Unwin, Ltd., London, 1938); Enid Charles, *The Twilight of Parenthood* (W. W. Norton & Co., New York, 1934); A. M. Carr-Saunders, *World Population (1936);* Jacques Marchand, *La Renaissance du mercantilisme* (1937).

New South Wales to a limited degree. Whether or not these attempts to raise the birth rate will be successful remains to be seen. Undoubtedly the threat of serious population decline hangs over many countries, pointing to the possibility of an underpopulation which will have profound effects upon the economic system (fewer consumers in an age of increased technological capacity, fewer renters for houses and offices, a greater percentage of old people, with a consequent increase in the burden of social services, etc.), and upon the political system (decline in man power, with its repercussions upon the problem of national defense), and all this at a time when the opportunities for mass migrations of the nineteenth-century type are not likely to recur.

Nevertheless, if the foregoing description is not to lead to overhasty conclusions, it is important to consider two qualifications: (1) The beginning of population decline does not mean that certain countries are not suffering from congestion. Even the more economically fortunate lands possess too many people who are undernourished, judged by the standards prescribed by social and medical authorities. But a number of other areas—India, Japan, Italy, Hungary, Poland, and southeastern Europe—show definite evidence of overpopulation in that a high percentage of their people "are unable, by any kind of economic activity, to secure the food supplies and other minimum conditions which are indispensable to physical life (i.e., for the maintenance of biological energy)."[15] Emigration would assist these countries in some measure at least to relieve the pressure, particularly if international tension continues to drive governments to still greater uneconomic expenditures on armaments. (2) Although many countries have increased their barriers against excessive immigration, there are still lands which need more people if they are to build their economic life to a plane of greater efficiency and welfare. If these countries suffer a decline of birth rate and insufficient immigration opportunities, they will be in danger of serious underpopulation.[16] For these reasons migration is still necessary. But in view of the closer-knit nature of modern society, and the

[15] Ferenczi, *op. cit.*, p. 39.

[16] J. E. Meade, in his *The Economic Basis of a Durable Peace* (Oxford University Press, 1940), pp. 153–54, writes of "the lack of balance which exists in the divergent trends of population in certain regions of the world. Some of the important countries in which there is relative overpopulation are still threatened with a considerable increase in numbers; in some of the important countries in which there is relative underpopulation the population will soon cease to grow and will probably decline."

interrelation of land, labor, capital, markets, and political sentiment, the matter requires consultation and co-operation among
governments and an accurate analysis of possibilities and conditions of settlement within each country.

We may summarize as follows: (1) Certain countries in
southern and eastern Europe are still congested and would be
helped by emigration of the right kind. (2) Some of the New
World countries, notably South America, the United States, and
to a lesser degree Canada, Australia, and probably some islands
of the Pacific, could receive more immigrants if international order
were restored and international trade resumed. (3) The conquest
of colonies is not worth the cost, and the attempt to plant families
in colonial areas may result in an uneconomic use of capital which
could be better expended in developing a more efficient economic
organization at home. (4) The day of mass migrations is over,
and the time for carefully regulated migration schemes has arrived. (5) Migration under these circumstances involves co-operation among governments; to allege the theory of sovereignty as a
justification for exclusive action is under modern conditions indefensible—immigration ought no longer to be considered merely
as a domestic problem. (6) The fundamental task is to place the
greatest number of people in the environment which will promote
the greatest amount of individual and general welfare.

A certain number of steps along these lines have already been
taken. The 1919 International Labor Conference adopted a resolution requesting its governing body to set up an international
commission "which while giving due regard to the sovereign rights
of each state shall consider and report what measures can be
adopted to regulate the migration of workers out of their own
states and to protect the wage earners residing in states other than
their own." The Commission, on which were represented nine
European and nine non-European countries, issued a report in
1921 outlining remedies for the many abuses which occur in relation to emigration and immigration. The Brazilian delegate suggested the establishment of a Permanent Immigration Commission
which might direct migration "in a reasonable manner from countries where work is scarce to countries where work is required;
it should act as a conciliator in the event of governmental disputes." The proposal was not adopted, because of the fear that
the existence of such a commission would constitute a threat to
national sovereignty.

The 1922 International Labor Conference recommended that

governments periodically send to the International Labor Office as much information as possible concerning immigration; and in 1924 the governing body of the International Labor Organization set up the Permanent Migration Committee.

These were the beginnings of an international organization to deal with migration problems. The organization was based on the assumption that, although the general world situation seemed to make impossible any great mass movements of the nineteenth-century type, the need for immigration and emigration still remained an important even though a less extensive issue. The International Labor Organization realized that its efforts to raise labor standards throughout the world by means of international labor conventions were rendered much more difficult by the existence of overpopulation in some countries and underpopulation in others. Declining standards of living due to either one of these factors constituted a threat to workers, employers, and governments alike. International policies to insure a better equilibrium of the factors of production by means of an organized redistribution of labor appeared to be an economic necessity.

The general truth was clear, but its application was less simple. Political and organizational difficulties arose between immigrant and emigrant countries. The latter desired to retain the citizenship of their departing subjects, while the immigrant countries naturally desired to assimilate them. In 1921 the emigration countries held an international conference; three years later immigration countries met to consider a general policy. Some uncertainty existed as to how far the International Labor Organization possessed the authority or competence to discuss emigration matters; because of this fact, and owing to the need for Italian emigration, the Fascist government called the International Emigration and Immigration Conference at Rome in 1924. The International Labor Organization sent representatives; at the same time it insisted that the conference could not in any way invalidate the right of the Labor Office to consider migration problems. It is interesting, in the light of subsequent events, to note that Mussolini in opening the conference urged that emigrants should not be considered as mere commodities and that they should be entitled to enjoy the same rights as nationals of the receiving countries. The conference drew up a number of resolutions recommending the adoption of "an international sanitary code, the insurance of emigrants, a thorough medical inspection, the laying down of minimum requirements for emigrant ships, and other means of safeguarding the interests of emigrants during the voyage."[17] It recommended that governments supervise lodging houses for emigrants and provide legal aid for them, and considered such matters as "undesirable emigrants, simplification of passport formalities, principles underlying labor contracts, measures against secret emigration, and the exchange of labor information." It also adopted principles "concerning equality of treatment of emigrants, and the admission of foreign workers to conciliation and arbitration committees."[18]

In 1928 a second emigration conference was held at Havana, in order to clarify some of the general principles adopted at Rome in 1924. Unfortunately, the number of delegates was smaller (only thirty-seven states were represented in contrast to fifty-nine states at Rome) ; Brazil, Canada, and Ireland refused to attend, and Great Britain sent only auditors. The Japanese delegates took a strong stand, and in general the emigration countries were found to be in opposition to the immigration countries. The conference had only a very limited success.

The economic depression which followed the slump of 1929, and the change in attitude of the Fascist government, which reversed its stand on migration and after 1927 adopted a policy of encouraging the birth rate and discouraging emigration, reduced the opportunities for international co-operation. National immigration restrictions were multiplied; foreign migrants found few opportunities to go abroad; and the unemployment problem, already intense enough in many countries, grew still more severe.

Nevertheless the International Labor Office and the economic committees which were set up in accordance with a resolution of the 1929 League Assembly continued their studies. They realized that the basic problem was to enable migration to respond quickly enough to economic changes in different lands, and to work out an efficient means of putting "the jobless man in touch with the manless job." For several years the League as an instrumentality in migration matters must have appeared dormant, if not dead. Such, however, was not the case.

Meanwhile a number of regional agreements had been made concerning labor and seasonal migration. France required a considerable amount of foreign labor, and had made several inter-

[17] R. L. Buell, *International Relations* (Henry Holt & Company, New York, revised edition, 1929), p. 173.
[18] *Ibid.*, p. 174.

national agreements for the regulation of collecting recruiting. We may note the Franco-Polish arrangement, which was similar to those made with Austria, Belgium, Czechoslovakia, and Italy. Under it the two governments agreed to afford "administrative facilities" to migrant workers, and to co-operate in the collective recruitment of workers. Each government undertook to advise prospective migrants of the economic conditions prevailing in the other country and, if necessary, to take preventive steps in unfavorable periods. It is manifestly important for the country of the emigrant to retain the right of deciding in what areas recruiting shall take place; otherwise serious labor dislocations may result. France and Poland therefore agreed on the number and occupation of the workers to be recruited. A special joint committee met in regular session to determine these matters. The Polish Emigration Office in Poland and the National Employment Office in France enrolled workers. The emigrants received medical examination before they left, and might be accepted or refused by either government. That is, the emigrant government might refuse to let the would-be emigrant go, and the receiving government might refuse to accept him. The agreements included the principle of equality of treatment of foreign and national workers in matters of social insurance, wages, and right of association. The governments drew up a standard application and a standard labor contract. These precautions guaranteed the French workers against competition from imported sweated labor, and at the same time insured to the Polish migrants a fair set of conditions when they arrived in France. D. Christie Tate writes that under this system nearly half a million workers were introduced to France in the postwar period from five different countries.[19]

The need of regulating seasonal agricultural laborers also led to international agreements between Czechoslovakia and Austria, Czechoslovakia and Germany, Poland and Germany, and Poland and France.[20] Germany and Czechoslovakia in May 1928 concluded an agreement concerning the recruiting of Czechoslovakian seasonal workers. The governments undertook to engage the laborers only on a "contract of employment" basis; and the contract, drawn up by experts of the two countries, was not to be

[19] D. Christie Tate, "The International Organization of Migration," *International Labour Review,* February 1930, pp. 202 ff.

[20] D. R. Taft, *Human Migration* (The Ronald Press Co., New York, 1936). Chapter 18 contains a useful summary of the measures adopted by Poland and France in bilateral agreements.

changed by Germany until the Czechoslovakian government had had an opportunity of giving its views. The workers were to be medically examined and vaccinated at governmental expense, and were to enjoy in Germany an equality of treatment with German workers in labor legislation, trade union membership, the right to public assistance, and regulation of labor conditions by conciliation arbitration. Under this system Germany could make certain of obtaining workers of known quality, and the migrant laborers were guaranteed certain standards and protection, and were better protected from the hostility of German workers. Because matters were regulated in systematic fashion, it was possible to examine the effects of the population movements more clearly.

The world-wide depression which followed the political and economic crises of the period following 1931 have lessened the number of foreign workers employed in European countries, as well as the amount of international seasonal migration. If, and when, the present political tensions ease, and mere economic movements function again, the methods already worked out will prove of valuable assistance in providing an orderly system of labor employment on an international scale.

The attempts of international organization went beyond the European continental scene, and included efforts to facilitate labor migration to South America. Poland and São Paulo in Brazil began negotiations and agreed upon certain general principles. The agricultural laborer was to be selected in Poland by a Polish emigration officer and a representative from the labor department of São Paulo. The conditions regulating transportation of the migrants were drawn up in detail. São Paulo agreed to grant the Polish immigrants equality with Brazilian citizens in labor legislation, social insurance, education, trade union organization, etc., and to set up societies and social agencies which would assist the newcomers. Standard contracts were adopted for workers engaged by the year and for those on a seasonal basis; the application of the agreement was to be supervised by two officials, one representing each government. The number of immigrants was to be determined by the São Paulo authorities each year; they would then notify Poland of this number and of the agricultural land available for settlers. If new areas were opened, São Paulo undertook to give priority to Polish families who had worked for two years on São Paulo plantations. Practical difficulties stood in the way, but the general lines of the agreement were sound.

Possibly nationalism commenced to yield a little to the logic of necessity in the field of migration when the American states held a labor conference in Santiago, Chile, in January 1936, and passed a resolution requesting the International Labor Office to undertake special inquiries into the possibilities of emigration from Europe to America, with particular reference to conditions necessary for successful colonization. The governing body of the International Labor Organization directed its experts to study the question, not merely from the angle of integrating the three factors of production—labor, land, and capital, but also as a regional problem. An International Labor Organization mission visited Brazil, Argentina, and Uruguay and joined the national authorities of these countries in studying the possibilities of migration settlement. The report of the mission and a general International Labor Organization report came before the Migration Committee in November 1936. They showed clearly that some of the American countries were ready to receive immigrants, but that it was necessary to work out carefully the financing of the transportation of emigrants, and their settlement on the soil. The Committee recommended that a conference of experts on migration for settlement investigate what practical measures might be possible; when their report was ready, another conference could be held. After a year's study the conference of experts met at Geneva, February 28 to March 7, 1938. Delegates from ten South American "immigration countries" and eight "emigration countries" (including Japan) and representatives of the governing body of the International Labor Organization, the Economic Committee of the League, and the Economic and Financial Sections of the Secretariat were present.

The Conference considered the International Labor Office report, a document of eighty-seven pages, and, on the basis of its findings and the evidence presented by the government delegates, unanimously adopted certain recommendations.[21]

It recommended that governments of immigrant and emigrant countries which desired to promote migration for settlement should exchange regularly and promptly all information possible. The former should make available information on the general conditions of admission of immigrants proposing to settle on the land, the facilities which would be granted (transport rates, customs dues, etc.), the land laws of the country, the types of settlers

[21] Technical Conference of Experts, *Technical and Financial International Co-operation with Regard to Migration for Settlement,* International Labour Office, Studies and Reports, Series O (Migration), No. 7 (Geneva, 1938).

which it desired, the conditions of acquiring land, what organizations exist to assist settlers, where suitable land is located, what taxes are due from settlers, etc. The emigrant governments should collect full information as to the number of families or unmarried persons available for migration, their technical qualifications, their farming experience, and the measures in force to facilitate migration for settlement. The governments should exchange this information and also communicate it to the International Labor Office which could serve as a clearinghouse. The governments should set up an official or semiofficial service to furnish information and to assist prospective settlers in the choice of land; these services in the emigration and immigration countries should establish "permanent co-operation"; and emigration countries might appoint emigration attachés to their diplomatic and consular representatives in the immigration countries.

Thus immigration countries should establish official, technical, financial, and other organizations responsible for immigration and settlement; but private organizations also might be set up to this end. Land intended for immigrants should "not be in litigation, mortgaged, or subject to any other charge." Before any group settlement by immigrants is undertaken, the government should take certain steps concerning

(a) the preparation and equipment of the land; (b) the organization of production and marketing; (c) the preparation, reception, and establishment of the settlers and their families; (d) the period of employment that the immigrant might serve on a farm in the immigration country before setting up as an independent farmer, in order to familiarize himself with the agricultural practices, language, customs, climate, food and other aspects of the country in which he intends to settle; the wage claims of immigrants so employed should take precedence over the employer's other obligations and the produce of the farm should serve as security for their settlement; summary judicial procedure should be available to the immigrant to enable him to recover his wages; (e) the financing of the expenses to be borne by the State, the settlement organization, and the individual settler respectively.

The Conference recommended that governments consider the possibility of affording free vocational and general training to prospective settlers, exempting them from consular dues, and their effects from customs duties, granting temporary relief to them and to settlement organizations from certain taxes. Governments might also pay part or all of the cost of the sea voyage, supply land, tools, and equipment free or at a reduced price, and perhaps grant subsidies; and grant loans and credits.

Because of the instability in national currencies the problem of transferring the assets of emigrants becomes a serious one, since the emigrants would probably have difficulty in obtaining the necessary foreign exchange. The Conference therefore recommended inter-governmental co-operation to facilitate the transfer of emigrants' assets "by means of exports of goods, including products needed for the preparation of the settlement . . . . and tools and equipment." It realized that perhaps further international financial co-operation would be necessary in order to permit a country to enable its emigrants to take their assets with them, and requested the officers of the Conference to study the possibility and desirability of setting up an International Credit Institution for this purpose. It concluded with a resolution instructing the International Labor Organization to continue its technical researches into the general problem and requested the governing body to "proceed with the consultations and other steps necessary for the establishment of a Permanent International Committee on Migration for Settlement."

It now remains for governments to act upon these excellent recommendations. Whether they will do so or will treat the migration experts as governments have treated the economic experts in the matter of tariffs, and substitute short-term expediencies for sounder principles, time will tell. The evidence given in this chapter should suggest the advantages of both bilateral and multilateral arrangements and the changing nature of population and migration questions. Whatever may be the legal theory concerning national sovereignty in these matters, the fact remains that today immigration problems have become international in scope and the population question will increasingly demand international co-operation. Government agreements can obviate frauds in recruiting, insure the quality of migrants, safeguard the workers of the receiving country, prevent the newcomers from getting into debt slavery, and save much confusion and disappointment. International organization, when more adequate and experienced, will be able to do something which unregulated individual migration and unilateral national regulation can no longer guarantee, namely, combine order with flexibility in the transfer of people from one land to another.

A heavy blow at immigration plans and policies has been dealt by the activities of "fifth column" agents of foreign powers. What country can now trust its foreign arrivals and assure itself that they really intend to become citizens devoted to the welfare of their adopted land? What guaranty is there that they will not be advance agents of a power bent upon ultimate conquest? The experiences of Norway, Denmark, and Holland may well make other countries pause before receiving people who may turn out to be "rats in the larder." In this, as in many other fields, German military methods which carry to a logical conclusion the implications of modern warfare will have had profound repercussions upon international life. The damage done to confidence upon which normal international activity depends has been tremendous.

Indeed, it may be confidently asserted that, unless the threat of war is abolished, international migration will practically cease. For if wars are to continue, and military action is to be merely the cutting edge of policies of conquest planned in all departments of modern life, then it is obvious that migration, like trade, intellectual interchange, propaganda, etc., will become primarily an instrument of war, a preliminary to the seizure of other countries, and not primarily a method of increasing human welfare.

Chapter X

MINORITIES

Human beings react to situations in different ways. A disappointed lover may give way to grief or indulge in hate. Opposition may call forth a man's determined will, or may crush his spirit. Individuals and communities may tolerate differences of opinion, or they may be roused to fear and hostility. And hostility may express itself in one of two ways: The orthodox will either attempt to convert the dissenter and bring him into the fold (for people seem to desire conformity and wish to "make people over") or else condemn him to endure discrimination and not infrequently segregation.

Tribal communities have insisted upon unity of religious observance because they fear that abstinence from tribal ceremonies on the part of even one person will call down the wrath of the gods. Individuals in a position of power find pleasure in making others bow to their will. Those with a sense of mission feel that they must save the doubter and the heretic. But if the conformist takes the other line and hates the dissenter, he will discriminate against him, ridicule him, impose legal and social disabilities upon him, isolate him as in a ghetto, and even burn or crucify him.

Political communities have had the problem of minorities for a long time, but the situation today has reached a stage of extraordinary tension. The reasons can best be appreciated by a brief reference to history. Under the feudal system the great majority of people lived in a subordinate and settled status and took little part in political affairs; hence the problem of minorities was of minor importance. When the modern state appeared the new monarchs had to assert their authority against the universal claims of the Pope and the supranational character of the Holy Roman Empire without and break the power of the nobles within, nobles who usually, though not invariably, spoke the same language and belonged to the same political group as their sovereign; while king and nobles fought, the minorities, who spoke a different language and professed a different faith, had a breathing space.

But the more the monarchs strengthened their power, the less room was left for dissenting minorities; all subjects, whatever their creed or language, owed obedience to their ruler. In the sixteenth century it was religion which first provided the great battleground between governments and dissenters. In Spain, the German states, England, Scotland, and elsewhere, monarchs attempted to impose religious uniformity, not only upon their subjects whose language, customs, and historical tradition were different, but also upon their own people. Since the monarch was an absolute ruler, all his subjects, whatever their language and customs, must profess his religion. The earlier form of the minorities question was therefore likely to be a religious rather than a political or "national" one.

When the idea of the state and of nationalism became more widespread, and when democracy arose, the problem of minorities began to appear in its modern form. If the majority of people were, say, German and insisted upon making the Poles into loyal Germans by enforcing the German language, German customs, and German law, they might treat the minority with more intolerance than an absolute monarch would have done. In short, the growth of the idea of nationality, with its emphasis upon similarity of behavior of all groups under a common flag, a national system of schools, (often) a national religion, and the attempt to translate this nationalism into a self-governing political state, sharpened the whole minorities problem.

Many parts of Europe had suffered from numerous wars in the course of history, and their conquerors had subjugated large areas and diverse groups of people. Turks conquered Bulgarians, Greeks, Albanians, Rumanians, and Serbs; Germans conquered Slavs; Hungarians conquered Czechs, Slovaks, and Slovenes; and so on. The fact of conquest meant national intermixture. Moreover, the dominant rulers undertook colonization: English kings planted Scotch Protestants in the north of Ireland; and the Hapsburg monarchs encouraged German colonists to settle in eastern Europe and invited Serbs to settle in lands which had been depopulated by Turkish armies. These colonists received certain privileges. They were a step above the conquered, as it were, even if they were not regarded as on an equality with their political masters. Now many of the peoples who had suffered defeat in war and had lost their freedom remembered their national history and dreamed of the glorious period when their ancestors lived in their "Golden Age." Greeks, Bulgarians, Albanians, Poles, Czechs, and Hungarians reawoke to self-consciousness in the nineteenth century and responded to the doctrine of nationality.

Here, then, was the problem: The dominant people, animated by feelings of imperialistic nationalism, insisted that their minorities adopt the national language, education, customs, and law; at the same time the minorities, impelled by the same type of nationalistic desires, demanded their own institutions and resisted assimilation by the majority. What was to be the outcome? Was the majority to be the hammer and the minority to be the anvil, as one German statesman put it, or could a number of self-conscious nationalities live peaceably together within a single state? The answer would depend upon the temper of the national groups and whether or not they could and would tolerate differences. While nationality remained of the liberal type no great problems arose, since the liberal state permitted cultural differences to exist; but, as historians point out, the French people, under the influence of an exuberant nationalism, set the modern example of attempting to assimilate minorities.

It was in Hungary, perhaps, that the most intense struggle of nationalities occurred in nineteenth-century Europe. The Hungarians, who had come under Austrian rule after their defeat by the Turks in 1526, attempted to regain their old political institutions. After three hundred years of struggle, they succeeded in 1867 in obtaining a position of equality in the Austro-Hungarian Empire. Now, the Hungarians themselves had to face the problem of their own national minorities, especially the Slavs. The question was whether those who had struggled for their own freedom would grant it to their subjects. The 1868 law of nationalities provided the answer. Macartney well points out that it was a not illiberal law, if one accepts the fundamental assumption that Hungary was a Magyar national state and the non-Hungarians were merely minorities; but this was precisely the assumption which the other nationalities refused to admit.[1] They desired their own way of life, and did not relish the thought of becoming assimilated to Magyar customs, and living a social and political life under Magyar domination. They resented many of the Hungarian actions, refused to conform, and obstinately clung to their own habits. The Hungarians in turn treated the recalcitrant minorities as traitors to the state, and coercion became increasingly common. The Hungarians were not alone in their methods. Prus-

---

[1] C. A. Macartney, *National States and National Minorities* (Oxford University Press, London, 1936), p. 120.

sia and, later, Germany attempted to assimilate the Polish minorities; Russia tried to "make over" many of the non-Russians, and other nations were more or less guilty of the same policy of assimilation.

Such action by the politically dominant national state against its minorities aroused the anger of outside nations which contained representatives of the oppressed groups. Over 50,000,000 people of prewar Europe lived as minorities; and their fate was a matter of deep concern to their brothers over the border. The Serbs in Serbia flamed up in indignation at the thought of the sufferings of their fellow Serbs in Austria-Hungary. Irishmen in America hated England because of its policy in Ireland. Jews all over the world were sensitive to the treatment of fellow Jews in various parts of Europe. Western Europe listened with increasing anger to tales of Turkish oppression of non-Turks. Deep calling unto deep, resenting the oppressive treatment of minorities, became a major factor in international relations, and a not insignificant cause of the World War of 1914–1918.

Prior to 1914 several attempts were made to provide machinery to deal with the question of the minorities. The first method was that of internal constitutional guaranties. The Austrian constitution of 1867 provided that each minority might preserve its nationality and language; the 1868 Hungarian Law of Nationalities permitted the use of minority languages in legislatures and schools; the United States, by the Fifteenth Amendment, provided that no person might be denied his freedom by reason of race, color, or creed; Turkey, by decrees published in 1839, 1856, 1876, and 1908 promised certain political rights to non-Turkish subjects. Unfortunately these legislative and constitutional safeguards often proved to be broken reeds, inadequate to withstand the passions of intolerant national majorities.

Hence it is not surprising that foreign powers frequently intervened on behalf of minorities. After the Reformation the Roman Catholic Church asserted its right to protect Catholics living in the new Protestant nations. Protestant rulers met this claim by opposing the principle of sovereignty, and the two contradictory principles met in seemingly irreconcilable opposition. Governments, however, signed Concordats with Rome which permitted the Papacy a certain amount of authority over religious matters within the states themselves. Such an arrangement embodied some limitation against the practice, even if not the theory, of absolute sovereignty, and bore witness to the difficulties which confront modern nations if they attempt to force men's life into a rigid monoloyalty. Tolerance was, in some measure, a national responsibility of the family of nations.

Sovereign states also agreed by treaty to observe the rule that a group of people "transferred from one sovereignty to another" through the fortune of war or otherwise "should be guaranteed freedom for their religious beliefs." Macartney notes[2] that the earlier treaties did not include the guaranty of linguistic freedom, because in all probability the language question had not yet become important.

As the nineteenth century developed, international treaties for the protection of minorities tended to become more extensive in number, and more detailed in character. In 1814 the great powers recognized the union of Holland and Belgium and required the new state to promise fair treatment to its minorities. In 1830 they sanctioned the independence of Greece, which promised to observe the same general minority obligations. In 1881 the Greek government was recognized as the ruler of Thessaly, and gave assurances that the inhabitants would enjoy the same civil and political rights as the rest of the nation. The Treaty of Berlin in 1878 prescribed that the governments of Bulgaria, Montenegro, Serbia, Rumania, and Turkey should not make religious differences "the basis of discrimination in civil and political rights." The 1858 treaty between Turkey and the great powers provided that in Moldavia and Wallachia there should be equality of taxation, and that Christians should not suffer discrimination in the enjoyment of political rights. Many years earlier, in 1774, Russia had claimed the right to protect Orthodox Christians resident in Turkey; and France had taken a similar stand on behalf of the Roman Catholics there.

The powers took other steps in the late nineteenth century to make Turkey honor its promise of fair treatment for its subject races. In a firman (or decree) of 1876 Turkey once again made fair promises, and the governments threatened that, if it did not translate these paper reforms into actuality within a short time, they would endeavor to devise international methods to protect the minorities within the Sultan's empire. The Armenian massacres in 1894–95 caused the powers to consider a proposal for "the European supervision of Christian minorities"; but the plan foundered on the rock of Anglo-Russian antagonism. Further

---

[2] C. A. Macartney, *op. cit.*, p. 159.

Armenian massacres in 1904–09 caused the Conference of Ambassadors to draw up a plan dividing eastern Anatolia into two parts. Each part was to have a foreign inspector-general with powers of control over the administration and police authorities in those areas; these two inspectors-general were to be appointed by the Sultan, but in reality they were nominated by the great powers.

Turkish repression in Macedonia in 1903 led to international activity. The European governments intervened and forced the Sultan to nominate a Christian inspector-general and two civil agents (one Russian, one Austrian). Foreign experts were to reorganize the police force, and a financial commission represented by six powers was to supervise her revenues. This international organization brought some improvements in conditions, although Colonel Lamouche, a member of the French section of the International Mission for the Reorganization of the Ottoman gendarmerie, wrote:

> La lutte entre les nationalités devenait de plus en plus violente et se manifestait jusque dans Salonique. ... Pourtant l'activité des réformateurs n'avait pas été absolument sans résultats.[3]

His judgment agrees with that of Schevill, who noted that the international institutions

> achieved only a comparative success, since the pestilential Greek and Bulgar bands stubbornly persisted. . . . . If it was a gain that the Turks were largely superseded as rulers of the country, the fact stands out that the animosities among the component ethnic groups had become so unbridled that reason and common sense were set at naught, while the whole population indulged in an orgy of self-destruction.[4]

The Young Turk revolution of 1909, which many had hoped would initiate a more liberal regime, proved to be the beginning of a more intense program of Turkification and oppression. The great powers again protested, and in 1912 the Balkan States demanded that Turkey permit a superior council of Christians and Moslems, under the authority of representatives of the great powers and the four Balkan governments, to supervise a reformed administration. War intervened before anything could be done, and the question remained unsolved.

The criticism usually leveled against the prewar system for the

[3] Colonel Lamouche, *Quinze Ans D'Histoire Balkanique, 1904–1918* (Payot, Paris, 1928), pp. 60–61.

[4] F. Schevill, *History of the Balkan Peninsula* (Harcourt, Brace & Co., New York, 1922), p. 436.

protection of minorities is that it lacked permanency. The great powers met as occasion seemed to demand but did not provide adequate continuity of supervision. Moreover, the right of intervention given to, or taken by, the great powers was frequently distorted to serve selfish political ends; national self-interest rather than solicitude for the minorities was the real motive for the seemingly altruistic championing of the cause of the weak.

In the absence of internationally recognized judicial institutions the powers were free to interpret the treaties as they wished; and self-interested governments obviously could not constitute a satisfactory and impartial tribunal. Finally, the prewar system provided no means of enforcing the treaties, many of which remained a dead letter; and the 50,000,000 people who lived as political and cultural minorities in Europe provided ample material for international strife in a civilization which lacked all but the most rudimentry international institutions and mentality to deal with situations which were growing daily more serious.

The position of minorities did not figure in the war aims of the Allied Powers in the early years of the World War of 1914–1918, and it was not until 1917 that the question came into prominence. In that year the United States entered the war, and President Wilson's public utterances rang with the challenging faith that the morality of states should conform to the morality demanded of individuals and that justice should be guaranteed to smaller nations and to subject peoples. Some months later, soon after the Bolshevist Revolution, the Soviet authorities proclaimed the freedom of dependent nationalities and recognized the independence of Finland. The Czechs and the Poles, meanwhile, carried on strenuous propaganda in their struggle for national freedom. These factors—Wilson's speeches, Soviet pronouncements, and Czech and Polish propaganda—brought the principle of self-determination into the limelight.

At the Peace Conference the statesmen redrew the map of Europe; they gave independence to Poland and Czechoslovakia, and agreed to the enlargement of Greece, Rumania, and Yugoslavia so as to include many of their compatriots who had previously lived under alien rule. But it was impossible to draw boundary lines so as to eliminate minorities entirely; and, in consequence, between 20,000,000 and 30,000,000 people remained in that unenviable category at a time when nationalist passions had been stirred even more violently than during most of the nineteenth century.

Under these circumstances a definite movement for the protection of minorities developed. The initiative came from some Jewish individuals and unofficial bodies which worked assiduously to have measures for the protection of their coreligionists incorporated into the peace treaties. Gradually their efforts, and those of others, bore fruit; the scope of the idea broadened to include other groups as well as Jews; and the League of Nations emerged as the new international institution for the protection of minorities. Within the next few years the following international arrangements were concluded:

1. Five minority treaties, signed by the Principal Allied and Associated Powers with Poland, Czechoslovakia, Greece, Rumania, and Yugoslavia
2. Four sections dealing with minorities in the Treaties of Peace with Austria, Bulgaria, Hungary, and Turkey
3. Five declarations made before the League Council by Albania, Esthonia, Finland, Latvia, and Lithuania at the time of, or soon after, their admission to membership in the League
4. Two special conventions, the German-Polish convention relating to Upper Silesia, and the convention for the Memel Territory

The General Minorities Treaties contained a list of rights which were guaranteed to minorities. They include the right to life, nationality, personal liberty, freedom of worship, also equality of all nationals before the law, equality of civil and political rights, and the use of minority languages. No persons because of racial, linguistic, or religious difference were to suffer discrimination in eligibility to public employment, and public honors, or in the exercise of their professions or industries or occupations. The minorities were to be permitted to establish their own charitable, religious, and social institutions and their own schools; and the signatory states solemnly promised (1) not to place restrictions on minority languages in commerce, in religion, in the press, or at public meetings and (2) that in areas where an adequate proportion of minority subjects resided they should receive an equitable share of state assistance in setting up their educational, religious, and charitable institutions.

In addition, certain special rights were guaranteed to minorities in special positions, such as the Jewish minorities in Greece, Poland, and Rumania, the Valachs of Pindus in Greece, the non-Greek monastic communities of Mount Athos, the Moslem minorities in Albania, Greece, and Yugoslavia, "the Czeckler and Saxon communities in Transylvania, and the Ruthene territory south of the Carpathians (Czechoslovakia)."[5]

The minorities treaties not only set forth certain rights; they contained guaranties from the League of Nations. The signatory governments recognized their obligations as "fundamental laws" which they undertook not to alter by unilateral legislative or administrative action; they agreed that these obligations were to be a matter of international concern and might be modified only with the consent of a majority of the League Council. A portion of the Polish Treaty is here quoted in full:

> Poland agrees that the stipulations in the foregoing Articles, so far as they affect persons belonging to racial, religious or linguistic minorities, constitute obligations of international concern and shall be placed under the guarantee of the League of Nations. They shall not be modified without the assent of a majority of the Council of the League of Nations. The United States, the British Empire, France, Italy and Japan hereby agree not to withhold their assent from any modification in these Articles which is in due form assented to by a majority of the Council of the League of Nations.
>
> Poland agrees that any Member of the Council of the League of Nations shall have the right to bring to the attention of the Council any infraction, or any danger of infraction, of any of these obligations, and that the Council may thereupon take such action and give such direction as it may deem proper and effective in the circumstances.
>
> Poland further agrees that any difference of opinion as to questions of law or fact arising out of these Articles between the . . . . Government and any one of the Principal Allied and Associated Powers or any other Power a Member of the Council of the League of Nations, shall be held to be a dispute of an International character under Article 14 of the Covenant of the League of Nations. The . . . . Government hereby consents that any such dispute shall, if the other party thereto demands, be referred to the Permanent Court of International Justice. The decision of the Permanent Court shall be final and shall have the same force and effect as an award under Article 13 of the Covenant.

This type of guaranty provided a threefold improvement over the prewar machinery: (1) a permanent control by the League Council, in contrast to the spasmodic interventions of the great powers in the nineteenth century; (2) a collective intervention instead of individual government action or interposition; (3) the introduction of a judicial procedure designed to remove the minority questions from the political sphere and so avoid a repeti-

[5] League of Nations, *Ten Years of World Co-operation* (Geneva, 1930), p. 360.

tion of the prewar experience in which minority questions had become entangled with power politics.[6]

The governments which were bound by the minorities treaties accepted their new obligations under considerable protest. The Polish representatives in particular expressed their opposition in a most emphatic manner. They claimed that these treaties introduced unprecedented conditions as a price of national recognition, constituted an unwarranted interference in national affairs and infringed Polish sovereignty, and placed Poland in an inferior position unworthy of its national dignity; international supervision, they maintained, would humiliate Poland without helping the minorities, with whom the Polish government could develop more satisfactory relations if they were not subjected to external interference. M. Clemenceau, the President of the Peace Conference, in his reply to M. Paderewski asserted that the minorities treaties did not introduce any new restrictive principle, and that during the nineteenth century several nations had accepted minority obligations in return for their recognition as independent governments; and he added that the principal Allied and Associated Powers "would be false to the responsibility which rests upon them if on this occasion they departed from what has become an established tradition." By their sacrifices in the war they had helped to establish Polish independence and consequently had a right to insist upon certain guaranties in order to prevent a recurrence of the prewar experiences. Such guaranties, he stated, however, did not cast any doubt upon Poland's desire to maintain the general principles of justice and liberty; but the minority guaranties were necessary because Poland and the other states were acquiring large populations

speaking languages and belonging to races different from that of the people with whom they will be incorporated. Unfortunately, the races have been estranged by long years of bitter hostility. It is believed that these populations will be more easily reconciled to their new position if they know that, from the very beginning, they have been assured protection and adequate guarantees against any danger of unjust treatment or oppression. The very knowledge that these guarantees exist will, it is hoped, materially help the reconciliation which all desire, and will indeed do much to prevent the necessity for its enforcement.

This statement disposed of the Polish claim that the best way of treating the minorities problem was to trust to the nation itself

[6] Julius Stone, *International Guarantees of Minority Rights* (Oxford University Press, London, 1932), chapter i.

and its own internal constitutional guaranties. Such a system had been tried in the nineteenth century and had been found wanting.

Sir John Fischer Williams suggests that the minority treaties were unpopular for the following reason:

Essentially, ... the movement for the international protection for Minorities is merely one example of the movement to secure good government, and that is perhaps why it is so much opposed and disliked, for no Government, and more than that, no People, likes having what it considers to be its domestic obligations pointed out to it by outsiders. There are analogies for this dislike in the ordinary relationships of private and family life . . . .

He sets forth a second fundamental difficulty:

The truth is that there is a certain artificiality in the separation of the treatment of a racial or a religious Minority from the general administration of a State. A State which has attained a high level of normal administration will treat its Minorities well as part of the ordinary functioning of the machine of government. The maltreatment of a Minority is as a rule an indication of a general disease; it is more than a separate and independent malady of one organ not affecting the whole of the rest of the body of the State.[7]

The new machinery thus attempted a very difficult task, namely, to effect some improvement in the position of minorities and afford them some guaranty against ill-treatment, and at the same time not to interfere unduly in the internal affairs of sovereign states. In order to succeed, the experiment would require: (1) an efficient League machinery, including not merely carefully devised procedures but also a fine sense of tact and a deep feeling for justice on the part of the League officials; (2) a favorable political temper in the governments which had undertaken minority obligations, since if they continually brooded over external interference and became more sensitive to their "sovereignty," "prestige," and "national unity" than to their international obligations, they would endanger the whole structure; (3) restrained conduct on the part of the minorities, for if they maintained a persistent attitude of hostility to their governments, and indulged in disloyal and even pin-pricking activities, they could easily wreck the fine balance of the new international experiment.[8] These three factors require further examination.

---

[7] Sir John Fischer Williams, *Some Aspects of the Covenant of the League of Nations* (Oxford University Press, London, 1934), pp. 194–97.

[8] The main minority groups in prewar Europe are described in L. P. Mair, *The Protection of Minorities* (Christophers, London, 1928). See also Dr. Otto Junghann, *National Minorities in Europe* (Covici, Friede, New York, 1932).

THE MINORITY MACHINERY OF THE LEAGUE
OF NATIONS

The League guaranteed certain rights to "persons belonging to racial, religious, or linguistic minorities," and in order to make the guaranty effective the League Council devised the following procedure: The minorities may send petitions to the League setting forth evidence that their rights have been violated by their government. Such a petition has no legal effect but is merely a document of information. The minorities do not obtain a legal personality, nor is the League to be an umpire between two equal parties—the government and its minorities.[9] To place the minorities in such a position would put the sovereign state on the plane of its subjects, a situation clearly not acceptable to governments.

Even so, the petition must fulfill certain conditions before the Secretariat of the League will "receive" it: It must have in view the protection of minorities in accordance with the treaties; it must not set forth a request for political separation, and must therefore accept the present political status quo; it must not be written by anonymous or unauthorized persons; it must not be couched in violent language; and it must not repeat information which has been recently dealt with by the League.

The Secretariat does not pass upon the substance or the merits of the complaint; its task is merely to ascertain that the petition is formally in order. Approximately one-half of the petitions have not satisfied these preliminary requirements; but one should not assume that the Secretariat rejects a petition on mere formal and technical errors, for that body has assisted petitioners to rectify small matters and has thus enabled them to have their petitions "received."

If the petition is in order, it is sent to the government concerned; for the League Council could not consider a complaint against a government without permitting the latter to examine and comment upon the charge made by the minority—otherwise the League would be judging a situation on inadequate evidence. By a 1923 resolution, the petition, after being examined by the government is circulated, together with the government's comments, among all the members of the Council. The petition is still only in the stage of being information, and does not yet set the judicial machinery in motion. Julius Stone notes that the documents at this point go to the individual members of the Council rather than to the Council as a body.

[9] Julius Stone, *op. cit.*, pp. 37–44.

In October 1920 the Council resolved that each petition should be considered by the President of the Council and two members selected by him. This procedure was adopted because, according to the minorities treaties, only members of the League Council possessed the right to bring before the Council any infraction or danger of infraction of treaty provisions. Now, if one state alone charged that a government had violated its minority obligations, it would lay itself open to the accusation of political interference, of ulterior motives, and even of unfriendly action. It is a serious thing for one government to accuse another of nonobservance or violation of treaties. Hence the Council agreed that each petition should be examined by a committee of the Council, which, in the words of Stone, juridically has no existence. There is no one permanent committee, but a new committee is set up for every petition that is to be considered. This committee of three, or perhaps five, is in reality a group of representatives of governments, which considers the evidence and decides whether or not the Council shall be formally "seized" of the question. The committee method overcomes the danger inherent in permitting one government alone to "seize" the Council.

The committee has first to evaluate the evidence contained in the minority petition; and for this task it relies heavily upon the Minorities Section of the League of Nations Secretariat, which has these important sources of information: (a) the minority petitions and the government comments, (b) a press information service which regularly receives a great number of newspapers, (c) a weekly bulletin summarizing articles which have appeared relating to minorities, (d) materials gathered by its special research department, (e) information gathered by members of the Minorities Section on their journeys to various countries, and (f) information gained from official and unofficial people visiting Geneva.

If the committee finds that the complaint is unfounded, it takes no further action. If the complaint seems well substantiated, it may attempt conciliation by entering into private conversations in order to persuade a government to remedy questionable policies; in this way it will avoid making a formal international issue of a minority complaint. It may suggest that the government refrain from certain actions relating to a minority which would clearly force the committee to bring the matter before the League Council, and may make specific proposals to remedy a difficult situation.

If the conciliation efforts of the committee break down, it may bring the matter before the League Council, which, after having considered a report submitted by the rapporteur appointed for the particular case, has several alternative courses open to it: It may refer legal questions to the Permanent Court of International Justice. It may attempt to persuade the government to modify its policy. Theoretically it may exercise the greatest pressure on behalf of the minorities by taking such action and giving such directions "as it may deem proper and effective in the circumstances."

How efficient has this machinery proved to be? What complaints have been leveled against it, and in what respects might it be improved?

1. Many people believe that the League guaranty should not be confined to specific complaints of minorities against their governments, but that the Council should undertake a "permanent supervision" over the minorities living under governments which have accepted minority obligations. Professor Gilbert Murray in 1921 proposed the establishment of a Permanent Minorities Commission along the same lines as the Permanent Mandates Commission. In 1929 Germany raised the same issue and proposed that a special permanent committee be set up which should meet at fixed intervals and handle minority questions upon a more definite and systematic basis. Those who favor a permanent committee assert that the committees of three lack continuity, and that the statesmen appointed to them are too busy to give their undivided attention to minority questions, some of which are not particularly important, and often send subordinate officials as substitutes. Also the committees of three have to judge on inadequate evidence; they are unable to interview petitioners, and in dictatorship countries where the freedom of the press is limited it is futile to rely upon the press as a supplementary agent of information.

Undoubtedly a permanent minorities commission could regularize and make more efficient the whole procedure. At present, delays and postponements are too frequent, and minority claims are apt to be pushed to one side; a group whose whole work was to consider minorities questions would build up an institutional permanency and a set of precedents of great value. The proposal, however, has not been adopted. A committee of the League Council decided that the minorities treaties "contained no provisions permitting the Council to exercise constant supervision with regard to the situation of minorities . . . . Modifications in the treaties require the assent of the Council [acting by majority]." Various commentators have severely criticized this judgment; but whether it be a satisfactory interpretation of the Treaties or not, it is undeniable that the attitude of governments has made the early appointment of a permanent commission out of the question, however desirable it may appear to liberal theorists or to the minorities themselves. Despite the assurance of the German government in June 1929 that it did not propose that such a permanent commission should have any power to interfere, or to investigate conditions, within the boundaries of any sovereign country, the prevailing national temper made impossible the acceptance of even this modified proposal.

2. Many critics have pointed to the undue amount of secrecy which has surrounded the working of the treaties. Until 1923 all the documents relating to minority petitions were circulated to all the League members. After that time, because of complaints from Czechoslovakia and Poland, the Council members alone received the documents, which were published in only exceptional cases. Lucy P. Mair writes that between 1922 and 1929 the Committees of Three did not even report to the League Council, which therefore exercised practically no control at all.[10] Moreover, petitioners had no means of ascertaining whether or not their complaints had ever been considered. As far as they knew, their communications might have been thrown into the wastepaper basket. And it was inevitable that the minorities would on this account lose faith in the League.[11] In 1929 the Council, in an attempt to remedy this obvious defect, ruled that the Secretary-General of the League should inform a petitioner when his petition was not receivable; send to all members of the League Council a report of all the letters sent by the Committee of Three to the Council; publish an annual statement showing (a) the number of petitions received by the Secretariat during the year, (b) the number declared nonreceivable, (c) the number accepted and referred to the Committees of Three, (d) the number of Committees of Three that had been formed and the number of meetings which they had held to consider petitions, and (e) the number of petitions which had been finally dealt with during the year. These

[10] L. P. Mair, "The League Council and a Minorities Commission," *The Political Quarterly*, July–September, 1930.

[11] Gustave Köver, *Non, Genève ne protège pas les minorités nationales* (Editions du Bureau Central des Minorités, Genève, 1938).

steps were designed to correct the unfortunate impression resulting from inadequate publicity given to minority petitions during the period 1922–1929.

3. Some authorities suggested that the League machinery would be considerably strengthened if resident agents of the League could be appointed to the most important minority areas for purposes of observation and conciliation. Several years ago Professor Gilbert Murray had urged this step for certain parts of Macedonia and Asia Minor; but the strong opposition of the Yugoslav delegate had caused the proposal to be dropped. C. A. Macartney believed that it was unfortunate that the League did not adopt some such method; he claimed that it was wrong to assume that impartial League observers on the spot would encourage restless minorities to multiply their grievances, "for if the agent is a responsible man, he will be able to detect the unreality of a complaint far more accurately than anyone in Geneva could do." Lucy P. Mair put the matter succinctly: "What is required is not so much more discussions at Geneva as more investigation on the spot." Minorities then will have confidence that their complaints are receiving attention; the method "ought also to reduce the number of frivolous petitions"; and it would make it possible "to verify the statements made." However, it was unlikely that governments which had unwillingly accepted minority obligations would agree to an extension of the investigating power of the League. The nationalistic temper abroad in Europe indicated that the powers would wish to weaken, and not strengthen, existing League methods.

THE ATTITUDE OF SIGNATORIES OF MINORITIES TREATIES

Indeed, several governments criticized the whole basis of international protection of minorities. They agreed with Poland in its plea to the Peace Conference that such measures were a violation of national sovereignty. Their attitude reflected a political fundamentalism which regarded sovereignty as so basic a thing as to be beyond external interference. To this objection was added the grievance that only a few states were obligated to the League of Nations in minority matters; other countries—Italy, France, Belgium, and Denmark—which had received territory after 1918 did not have to accept the system of international guaranty for minorities. Why, asked Czechoslovakia, Poland, and the others, should some governments have to accept, while others escaped, minority obligations? Why should not all states which possess minorities undertake the same international duties?

There is point to these questions. Undoubtedly there were historical considerations which made the minorities question more urgent in some countries than in others; but the British treatment of the Irish, the Italian methods in the Tyrol, and even French policy in Alsace-Lorraine suggest that minorities in all parts of the world are liable to harsh treatment and need international protection. Theoretically the case for generalizing minorities treaties was strong enough; practically the question arose as to whether or not it would be wise to attempt the difficult task of persuading the other governments to undertake international minorities obligations at a time when existing obligations were being so widely ignored. One might have argued that to generalize the obligation would remove the sting of alleged inferiority from the governments which make this complaint and cause them to liberalize their attitude and their policy toward their minorities. But a proposal to universalize minority treaties would, unfortunately, create resistance and tension. So strongly did Poland feel on the matter that Colonel Beck told the League of Nations, on September 13, 1934, that, "pending the introduction of a general and uniform system for the protection of minorities," Poland would refuse "all co-operation" with the international system for supervising minority protection. Representatives of the great powers insisted that a state could not release itself from its international obligations by unilateral action, and Poland consented, although unwillingly, to withdraw this threat, but in practice it continued to treat its minorities harshly.[12]

Critics of the minorities principle argue that the League treaties work against the realization of national unity, tend to create a state within a state, and encourage minorities to exaggerate their difficulties and to exploit their right of appeal to the League for selfish interests. We are rightly asked not to believe that the government is always wrong and that the minorities are always persecuted angels. Buell aptly observes that it is undesirable "to have minorities constantly appealing to an outside authority for redress of real or imaginary grievances." The Third Assembly of 1922 realized the force of the argument that the minorities treaties should be generalized, and passed a resolution expressing

---

[12] For a brief but effective summary of the plight of minorities in postwar Europe, see B. W. Maxwell, *International Relations* (Thos. Y. Crowell, New York, 1939).

the hope that states not bound by international legal obligations would accept the standards contained in the minorities treaties. But it also recognized the other side of the problem when it added a declaration to the effect that, while minorities should be protected from oppression, it was their duty "to co-operate as loyal citizens with the nations to which they belong."

As long as minorities give real or imaginary ground for the suspicion that they are using the privileges afforded to them by international treaties to weaken the state in which they reside, so long will governments feel the minorities treaties to be a liability and even a grievous burden. Czechoslovakia alleged that it could not treat the Sudeten Germans as an ordinary minority because they desired, not autonomy, but separation. How true the accusation was, time has shown. The mere fact that minorities may be used as a pawn in the game of power politics, or may wish to carry "self-determination" to a logical conclusion, i.e., separate statehood, will introduce a complicating and disruptive element into the working of minority treaties. For this reason the resolutions of the European Nationalities Congress were of great significance. This body, which represented many millions of minorities groups, accepted the existing boundaries as final and explicitly renounced any attempt to change their political allegiance. All they asked was cultural nationalism within the framework of existing political states. Such a declaration might have reassured the governments which had signed their minority treaties and encouraged them to adopt a more liberal policy toward their minorities. Unfortunately, such expectations were not realized, owing to deterioration of the general international situation.

In an effort to obviate, or at least lessen, the danger that petitions to the League might irritate relations between government and minorities, Count Apponyi proposed that the League Council should automatically consider petitions emanating from certain responsible bodies, such as supreme ecclesiastical organs or responsible cultural and economic institutions, which by reason of their acknowledged position would submit petitions to the League only after most careful consideration of minority complaints. This procedure, he claimed, would save the League from having to consider many small and trifling communications, and would introduce a greater element of responsibility in the submission of petitions. The Council felt that the proposal could not be accepted; for, although it would lessen the number of petitions coming before the League Council, the weight of accusation against a government would be increased by reason of the influential sponsorship on the part of ecclesiastical, cultural, or economic bodies and national authorities might find their authority more than ever challenged if well-known and respected bodies arraigned them before the bar of the League Council and of world opinion.

THE ATTITUDE OF MINORITIES

The restiveness of national governments which are bound by minority treaties and their dissatisfaction with the system are more than matched by the disappointment of the minorities themselves. The latter have complained of the long delay in considering their petitions, of the lack of notification to them of the fate of their petitions, and the tendency of the Committees of Three to sacrifice plain legal remedies required by the treaties to subterranean political negotiations with the governments concerned, which "makes possible various sorts of bargaining and hanky-panky at the expense of the minorities." The problem, however, goes deeper than methods. Macartney has convincingly shown that "no uniform treatment of the minorities as a whole is possible,"[13] because minorities range from numerically insignificant and culturally backward groups to self-conscious and politically minded peoples, and that their relations with their respective governments vary from deep-seated traditional hostility to relatively harmonious co-operation. No uniform pattern can embrace these varieties, which may be classified in four groups as follows:

1. The politically indifferent minorities, who maintain their national customs, celebrate their national holidays, and dress in the fashion of their forefathers. These groups, in general, constitute only a very minor problem, inasmuch as they have few or no political aspirations.

2. The numerically unimportant and geographically scattered minorities, who, even if they are politically self-conscious, are either too isolated or too small in numbers to have any political influence.

3. The numerically important, culturally and politically self-conscious minorities, such as the Germans in Czechoslovakia.[14] According to Macartney the Sudeten Germans in the early post-

[13] C. A. Macartney, *op. cit.*, p. 395.

[14] Arthur de Balogh, *L'Action de la Société des Nations en matière de protection des minorités* (1937), criticises the Treaties for guaranteeing only individual and not national rights. It will be necessary to end the distinction between majority and minority groups, he urges.

war period were not "fundamentally irredentist" but regarded themselves "as a natural and integral part of the historical units of Bohemia, Moravia, and Silesia." Their dissatisfaction arose from their being treated as a subordinate minority rather than as an equal partner. It can be seen that the borderline between a minority status and a partnership may be a fluctuating one, depending upon the temper of the various peoples within a state. That this is so, recent events tend to prove; for many of the Germans in Czechoslovakia, in a reaction against what they believed to be an unsatisfactory and unfair position, responded to the appeals of the German government, and afforded the latter a convenient excuse to pursue a policy of conquest, under the guise of protecting the rights of fellow Germans.

4. Finally, there are the frontier minorities. Because of their position, they have had to endure considerable suffering and even persecution, especially in times of crisis. They are close to their fellow nationalists across the border, and are bound to them by ties of geographical intimacy. They are normally characterized by an intense national consciousness and a desire for a reunion with their compatriots beyond the boundary. From the viewpoint of the country in which they reside, their attitude savors too much of irredentism, and threatens the security of the state itself; and Czechoslovakia, Rumania, Yugoslavia, and Poland watched with deep apprehension the national feeling among their German, Hungarian, and Lithuanian subjects, who lived near the boundaries of Germany, Hungary, and Lithuania. These illustrations suggest the general judgment that, in the absence of collective security, border minorities cannot hope to escape a policy of assimilation or at least pressure at the hands of their anxious governments. As long as boundaries possess military importance, and nations fear aggressive action from their neighbors, so long will the lot of border communities be an unhappy one. In this respect the position of minorities can hardly be improved merely by tackling their problem as such; it must form an integral part of a general settlement of more fundamental problems—disarmament, collective security, and peaceful change.

POSSIBLE REMEDIES

There were, however, several minority complaints which might have been remedied even within the existing framework. The minority treaties as they stood included several vague provisions. Some did not adequately define what minorities were. Some provided for educational facilities in a general way but failed to make specific provision for minority teachers; as a result governments might observe the treaty in some aspects of educational policy but fail to provide the most important element of a true minority school. The treaties provided for equality before the law, but in the opinion of several critics they did not prevent glaring discriminations in the enforcement of the law; and many instances occurred in which minority subjects suffered from land expropriation measures, did not receive a fair share of state agriculture credits, and had to endure unequal and unjust taxation burdens. More accurate definitions of rights, both substantive and procedural, should have been adopted. Minorities also asserted that there should be reforms in the treatment of their petitions,[15] and especially that there be more opportunities for recourse to the Permanent Court of International Justice;[16] and, of course, most of them urged the establishment of a permanent minorities commission.

Various private or semipublic organizations of an international character took up the serious study of the problem.[17] These organizations included: the International Federation of the League of Nations Societies, which had a Permanent Minorities Commission and made several recommendations to the League; the Interparliamentary Union, which in 1923 established a commission for "ethnic and colonial problems" and used its widespread influence to work for the improvement of the system of minorities protection; the Second International; the International Congress of Peace Societies; the International Law Association; the Institut de Droit International; and the Académie Diplomatique Internationale. The most important body has been the European Nationalities Congress, which first met in Geneva in 1925 and held annual sessions for several years. It consistently stood for a most important principle, namely, the frank acceptance of the present national boundaries and set its face against movements for territorial revision. Having thus unequivocally separated the minority question from the problem of security, which was necessarily bound up with the demand for frontier modification, the Congress

[15] See especially G. Köver, *Histoire d'une Trahison: le calvaire des minorités nationales et la Société des Nations* (Editions des Bureau Central des Minorités, Genève, 1939).

[16] Arthur de Balogh, *op. cit.*: "En resumé pour arriver à une protection réelle et efficace des minorités, il faudrait accorder des droits nationaux aux minorités comme entités collectives, assurer leur protection par un organe internationale, et leur permettre de saisir cet organe de leurs plaintes."

[17] Dr. Otto Junghann, *op. cit.*, p. 81.

proceeded to formulate the ideal of "free national-cultural development within the given state." This basic principle assumes (*a*) the existence of a multinational state under one political rule, and (*b*) the belief that full cultural economy will not result in a demand for political separation. But history has shown that political nationalism has frequently sprung from cultural roots. It may well be argued that this phenomenon appeared only because the minorities were mistreated and oppressed, and were denied a fair chance to develop their own cultural life. The Congress would doubtless contend that a free acceptance of the ideal of cultural autonomy, of a partnership of different groups in one single state, would suffice to create a genuine political unity and a strong and enduring loyalty. The Congress represented 38 minority groups embracing 27,000,000 people living in 15 countries, and its deliberations and findings were therefore of great significance.

The foregoing discussion has really shifted from the present relations of national minorities and League of Nations machinery to the consideration of another principle, that of the unnational state, that is, a state which comprises not merely one nationality, as the present-day national state tends to do, but a number of nationalities. Macartney has excellently written that it is the philosophy of the uninational state which is the basic flaw, in that it cannot be reconciled with the idea of national minorities. One does not leave room for the other. How true his statement is we are realizing today as we witness the determined attempts of the totalitarian states to assimilate their minorities, whether of nationality, party, or religion.

There can be, Macartney suggests,[18] only four possible solutions of the minority problem: First, the state may physically annihilate its minorities—a solution which has been tried in the past but which it is impossible to imagine as a practical policy in the face of from twenty-five to thirty millions of minority subjects in Europe.

Second, we may revise national frontiers so as to reduce the number of minorities to the minimum. To this proposal there are two objections: (*a*) Frontier revision can affect only the minority groups living along the boundary; it cannot alleviate the position of minorities scattered in the interior. (*b*) In the present temper of the world the alteration of boundaries would cause such international repercussions as to make any such attempt at minority amelioration far more explosive than remedial.

[18] C. A. Macartney, *op. cit.*, chapter xi.

Third, we may keep the existing boundaries and try to retain the national state by exchanging populations and transferring minorities to their "homeland." This method was tried in the early postwar period. After the disastrous Graeco-Turkish War of 1922, the two countries in January 1923 signed a convention at Lausanne providing for the compulsory exchange of their nationals as from May 1, 1923, except for those Greeks who had been established in Constantinople before October 1918 and those Moslems who were residing in western Thrace. The transfer was to carry with it the automatic exchange of nationalities; the people affected were to have the right of taking their movable property; and detailed provisions were elaborated for valuing and liquidating the property left behind. In order to execute the arrangement, Greece and Turkey each nominated four, and the Council of the League of Nations nominated three, members to constitute a mixed commission. The Commission was to prescribe and supervise the conditions for migration. In turn, it entrusted the actual details to eleven subcommissions, on each of which sat one Turk, one Greek, and one neutral chairman. By October 1924, 370,000 Turks had left Greece for Anatolia, and most of the Greeks in the new Turkey had been evacuated.

This great experiment, considering the temper of the time, may have been the lesser of two evils. But the remedy involved much suffering to the thousands of individuals affected. Not only were there many controversies over whether or not certain Greeks were really "established" in Constantinople, but the forcible separation of people from their home ties, the overriding of sentiment, the economic dislocation, the inability of professional people easily to establish themselves in new surroundings, the inevitable property losses through inadequate evaluations, the delays and complexities incidental to such a transfer, the agricultural problems arising from the transfer of farmers to new and unfamiliar areas, the peculiarly difficult position of Greece when inundated by a million refugees—all these and other factors combine to show that the experiment was one to be undertaken only as a last resort. In reality it involved the sacrifice of all other human associations and values to the one principle of nationality; the question arises whether or not, however exalted that principle may be, it is worthy of a sacrifice on so enormous a scale.

After 1918 about 150,000 Bulgarian-speaking people remained in Macedonia and Thrace under the Greek government, and many thousands of Greeks were living in South Bulgaria and in and around the Bulgarian Black Sea ports. The Treaty of Neuilly (1919) included provisions for the protection of minorities and for the reciprocal voluntary emigration of these Greek and Bulgarian people. Under a convention of August 1920 the two governments established a mixed commission, comprising two neutral members nominated by the League of Nations, one Greek, and one Bulgarian, to supervise the details. The experience of the next four or five years showed difficulties similar to those just outlined in the case of the Graeco-Turkish exchange, as well as one or two special factors. The Greeks living in Bulgaria were attracted to the rich soil of western Thrace in Greece and, being adversely affected by Bulgarian land legislation, were ready to move to Greece; but Bulgarians living in Thrace showed less enthusiasm at the prospect of being transferred to less fertile regions in Bulgaria. Soon scores of thousands of Greeks, refugees from Asia Minor, poured into Greece, and the Bulgarian settlers there now found their position growing increasingly perilous and begged the mixed commission to assist them to move into Bulgaria. So anxious were they to emigrate that many of them reached their new home in a state of destitution. Toynbee remarks that this situation was bound to lead to unfortunate incidents and to charges and countercharges of bad faith. In general, one may say that, while in theory the solution looks attractive, in practice the complexities incidental to large-scale interchange of population, especially compulsory interchange, make it highly unsatisfactory as a means of solving the minorities problem.[19]

Fourth, there remains the possibility of the "unnational" state. It is obvious that the League of Nations minorities treaties presuppose some degree of modification of national states, and that they are incompatible with the ideal of totalitarian nationalism; they presuppose tolerance, generosity, and the willingness of national groups to recognize and respect differences. They cannot work in an atmosphere of exaggerated political self-consciousness. They require a large degree of international stability. Political tension and the dream of power make for a warlike temper and war preparations; and freedom for minorities cannot flourish under these conditions. Until security is attained, minorities will be suppressed within and propagandized from without. They will become "cells" of disaffection and be made the excuse for inter-

[19] The policy of Hitler's Germany in forcibly uprooting minorities bears no relation to the experiments cited. The latter were designed to preserve nationalities as political and cultural entities; Hitler's aim is to destroy them.

vention. They cannot endure in an anarchical world, particularly in view of the methods of war which have now been developed. For who will any longer be able to say whether the complaint of a minority is a legitimate one or whether it has been artificially inspired in order to weaken the central government? If war is to be "total" war, there can be no room for differences of opinion even in the dominant nationality, let alone any possibility of equality of treatment for minorities.

It would be foolish to say that this factor was the only one in causing the failure of the minorities treaties. Maxwell writes:

> As has been shown the protection of minority rights were safeguarded in theory by the minority treaties and the machinery of the League. Now after nearly two decades it is possible to evaluate the effectiveness of such guarantees for the actual protection of minority groups.
>
> The story of racial and religious minorities in Central and Eastern Europe in modern times is a tale of blood and suffering. The savagery and refinement of cruelty exceeds anything to be found in the annals of the Dark Ages. The tale is worthy of an epic to be recorded by some great writer of tragedy. It is a story of broken promises, perjury, and betrayal. To the American or British student it is wholly incomprehensible since it is outside of his experience to apprehend such cruelty of human to human.[20]

The temper of postwar Europe, its unbridled hates and prejudices, and its excessive nationalism made compromise impossible, and would have wrecked any machinery.

THE SPECIAL REGIMES OF UPPER SILESIA AND MEMEL

Upper Silesia.—Under the peace terms handed to Germany on May 7, 1919, all of Upper Silesia was to have gone to Poland; but, as a result of strong German protests, the Council of Four decided to arrange a plebiscite, which was held on May 20, 1921. Despite a large majority who voted for Germany, the Inter-Allied Commission could not agree upon a line which would divide the Polish from the German share of the territory, and it was left to the League of Nations Council to formulate a solution. Its award, made on October 20, 1921, satisfied neither power. Germany in particular protested against a plan which placed some 300,000 Germans under Polish rule and gave to Poland the area which contained the larger part of the industrial wealth of Upper Silesia.

In order to afford guaranties to the German minority in Polish Upper Silesia and to the Polish minority in German Upper Silesia,

[20] Maxwell, *op. cit.,* p. 160.

a special regime was established by the Geneva Convention, signed on May 15, 1922. Under its terms, minorities, instead of appealing directly to the League Council, were to have access to regional machinery; the latter would by conciliation and mediation try to avoid a direct clash between the minority and the state. By its flexibility and immediacy, it would solve questions with less publicity and political friction. Both Germany and Poland enacted laws to make the convention municipal law, and the rules of procedure of the mixed commission were established in December. A regional minority office was set up in both Polish and German Upper Silesia. The German minority in Polish Upper Silesia could take its complaints to the minority office there (at Katowice), and the Polish minority in German Upper Silesia could take its complaints to the minority office at Oppeln. These offices examined the petitions and, if necessary, sent the matter to a president appointed by the League of Nations. The office was held by M. Calonder, a citizen of Switzerland.

In general, the regional machinery worked well; but it was discarded in 1937. Both Poland and Hitler's Germany disliked the League procedure for the protection of minorities and by treaty decided to settle their own minority problems. Julius Stone, writing in 1933, expressed the hope that the convention would be renewed, because in his opinion it was a definite guaranty for the peace of Europe and without it there was danger that trouble would again arise between Germany and Poland. Subsequent events have proved the accuracy of his analysis.[21]

One important development took place in the Upper Silesian experiment: Article 78 of the convention allowed the minorities the right of association there—as Stone puts it, it gave a wide charter for collective minority activity. Accordingly, the Poles in Germany formed a league with headquarters at Oppeln, and the Germans in Poland set up their Volksbund at Katowice. Stone believes that unless the convention had granted the minorities the right to collective activity it would have been impossible to protect them, because "legal modes of pressure" by the majority would have made the minority individual "very reluctant to take advantage of his legal right." He believed that these groups, like trade unions, would not injure the two states, but could render a valuable service of conciliation. The associations had the right to petition

---

[21] Julius Stone, *Regional Guarantees of Minority Rights* (The Macmillan Company, New York, 1933).

"as juristic persons," both on their own behalf, and on behalf of individuals, whether they were members of the association or not.

The advantages of the regional procedure were: (1) it was practically a nonpolitical method, differences being settled by a neutral president "quietly and in a spirit of justice and reconciliation"; (2) the personal element and more intimate contact with local conditions gave greater opportunity of persuasion and mediation; (3) it enabled the president to gather evidence much more easily than could be done at Geneva; (4) it did not preclude appeal to the League Council, which, however, was saved from having to consider many relatively small disputes.

Over a thousand cases arose. But scarcely more than 100 opinions had to be given; hundreds of cases were settled "in the quiet deliberate atmosphere of the able President Calonder." But the reign of reasonableness was of brief duration. National passions in Germany and Poland made justice to minorities increasingly impossible. Neither power was willing to exercise restraint in its dealings with minority groups, and each discarded the League machinery at the expiration of the treaty period in favor of a bilateral treaty. Today one of the signatories lies amid ruins; the other is its conqueror.

Without question the feeling on the part of the German people that the League Council's award of October 1921 represented, in substantial measure at least, a desire to weaken Germany by giving the rich industrial portion of Upper Silesia to Poland, rather than an impartial judgment on the merits of the case, helped to instill in their minds that the solution was a temporary and not a final one. Hence the regional machinery could play only a limited part: the stable foundations on which it might have built an enduring edifice were not there. However efficiently the international authorities on the spot might assist the minorities, the underlying political rivalries of Germany and Poland and, later, the ambitions of Hitler, as revealed in *Mein Kampf,* made its work one of limited usefulness. Instead of being part of a wider, harmonious Europe, it turned out to be an oasis in a political desert. But its experience remains as a valuable asset, available for the Europe of the future, should that continent be minded to make use of it.

Memel.—After the war a French High Commissioner administered the German city of Memel, situated on the River Niemen. The Allies had under consideration a plan by which Memel would become a "self-governing territory," perhaps along the lines of the free city of Danzig. In this way Lithuania would obtain special port facilities and an undisputed outlet to the sea. But many Lithuanians were not content with this prospect. They invaded Memel in January 1923 and forced the French troops to surrender. The Allies could not, or would not, compel Lithuania to retire and, after long and tangled negotiations, agreed to leave Memel under Lithuanian sovereignty. In 1924 a convention was signed by which Great Britain, France, Italy, Japan, and Lithuania guaranteed the city a considerable amount of legislative, judicial, administrative, and financial autonomy.

The desire to do justice to the Germans in Memel was no doubt praiseworthy; but the question was whether the Allies had not put the cart before the horse. Should they not have guaranteed Lithuania certain port facilities instead of separating a German town from Germany? Moreover, to allow a small nation to seize a town and confront the great powers with a *fait accompli* was hardly establishing a regime for protecting minorities on a sound foundation. The Germans could well argue that Memel constituted, not a genuine, but an artificial minority, and that a pretentious cloak of international organization had been thrown around an ugly act of violence.

Many difficulties arose, because, without any question, the majority of people in the city were German. Lithuania needed a port; but the sympathies of the people outbalanced the economic convenience to the Lithuanian state. By its very separation from Germany, Memel became more conscious of its loyalty and more determined to preserve its distinctive culture. On the other hand, Lithuania resented the restrictions imposed upon it, just as Poland resented the status of Danzig. Danzig had been placed under a League Commission, but not Memel, which therefore had less opportunity to appeal to the League.

The Memel legislature or Landtag, of twenty-nine members, was frequently at loggerheads with the Lithuanian president of the directorate; and between 1925 and 1927 three directorates had to resign because of votes of no confidence from the Landtag. After 1930, trouble became more intense and the Governor dissolved the Landtag again. Lithuania maintained martial law, to the great discontent of the German inhabitants, and tried to replace the German civic officials by Lithuanians. In February 1930 it refused to renew the permits of eleven German teachers, and next year matters came to a head involving an appeal to the World Court. The President of the Memel Directorate, Herr Böttcher, was dismissed by the Lithuanian government for going to Berlin without permission and interviewing the German Minister of Foreign Affairs and the Food Ministry. The Governor asked Böttcher to resign, but the German-minded chamber voted confidence in him. On February 6 the Governor dismissed him, and two days later the German government asked for an urgent meeting of the League Council. The rapporteur advised the four powers of their right of appeal to the World Court under paragraph 2 of Article 17 of the Memel Convention. The Court held that Memel's autonomy existed only within fixed limits, and that the Governor was therefore entitled to take appropriate steps to protect the interests of Lithuania but should do so only if an act was serious enough to prejudice Lithuania's sovereign rights. In reviewing the case the Court held that Böttcher, by going to Germany and discussing the question of agricultural exports which concerned foreign affairs, had exceeded his authority; and, therefore, in the opinion of the Court his dismissal was in order. At the same time it did not agree that the Governor's dissolution of the diet was in order.

After Hitler came to power it was only a matter of time before some pretext would be found to bring matters in Memel to a head. The German press was filled with stories of the ill-treatment of their fellow countrymen at the hands of the Lithuanians. The seizure of Austria and the acquisition of Sudetenland in Czechoslovakia in 1938 paved the way for exerting pressure upon the Baltic countries. In March 1939, Germany forced an agreement upon Lithuania for the voluntary return of Memel to the Reich. Germany claimed, and with considerable justification, that feeling in the Memel territory was so strong that cession to Germany was the only manner of avoiding collision. The treaty of March 22 provided that the Lithuanian military and police forces should evacuate Memel immediately and that a free harbor zone should be established in Memel for Lithuania. Each party agreed to refrain from applying force against the other.

Hitler visited Memel on March 22 and made a speech of welcome to the inhabitants of Memel. The experiment in minority protection had broken down because of the unsound total setting in Europe itself. In a reasonable atmosphere of mind it may not have made much difference whether Lithuania had formal sovereignty and German-speaking Memel extensive autonomy, or whether Germany had sovereignty over Memel, giving Lithuania undisputed harbor rights. But in an emotionally overwrought Europe the differences appeared to be profound. Exclusive nationalism and intolerance between national groups made a reasonable solution impossible. Both sides with their critical tempers could complain of grievances. Germany undoubtedly could point to injustices; but problems which should have been merely local in their importance became erected into issues of world-wide significance.

The attempt to protect "minorities" by international action also failed because the "minority" within Memel was a majority forcibly incorporated by Lithuanian military action. The theory of minority protection was unable to be genuinely tested, because the Memel Convention was merely a validating, in legal phraseology, of an act of force. The international machinery for protecting the German people could not make up for the fact that Memel had been torn from Germany in defiance of the principle of nationality for which the World War of 1914–1918 allegedly had been fought. Consequently the attempt to protect by "law" what had been seized by violence did not carry conviction; and, when stronger force appeared, it soon undid the work of sixteen years.

CONCLUSION

The rapid conquest of Europe by Germany brings into strong light the importance of minorities as a factor in security. In practically every country the Nazis have been able to foment discontent and disruption by working upon real grievances in some parts and imaginary grievances in others and by appealing to the latent or existing nationalist ambitions of certain groups in Poland, Czechoslovakia, Yugoslavia, and even France. All the conquered peoples and their governments have paid a heavy price for not living up to the minorities treaties where they applied or for failure to carry out the same principles even where no international treaty obligations existed. But the problem goes deeper than the observance or nonobservance of legal guaranties. Minorities may have a formal equality before the law and even enjoy a relatively great freedom from discrimination and injustice and yet not have a sense of "belonging" to the country in which they live. They may labor under what has been called "a devastating sense of difference": instead of being valued as representatives of the special genius of their culture, they may have been neglected, or even despised as culturally inferior; instead of being encouraged to develop a pride in their history, music, and handicrafts, and in their languages, instead of being given credit in educational institutions, many minorities (including immigrants into the United States) must have felt themselves to be a group apart from the main body of the nation and as a result have developed a heightened sense of self-consciousness, a marked sensitivity, and a feeling of inferiority alternating with a baffled sense of suppressed abilities.

Consequently these groups became easy targets for governments which were ready to use them as tools for their own ends but which had no interest in them as people in their own right. The German lure of autonomy promised discontented and ambitious minorities a glittering prize, which was soon to turn to ashes; but, as Sallust long ago wrote, there are men who prefer the unknown to the known; and if the known condition is unsatisfactory, they will be tempted to take a gamble and even to disregard the warnings contained in the fate of other minorities who had listened to the promises of the foreigner and then had been betrayed.

The lesson for democracy stands out clearly: Unless a country is made safe for differences, unless it encourages cultural diversity and at the same time inspires its groups to a richer unity, the probability is that in days of difficulty no ties of gratitude or sense of "belongingness"—whether nationalist, economic, political, or religious in nature—will call forth a common effort from both majority and minority groups on behalf of a creative all-inclusive civilization in which every person is regarded by everyone else as a precious unit of a community, as a "free" man valued for his excellences and cherished for his goodness, whatever the variety of forms in which that excellence and goodness expresses itself.

Chapter XI

MANDATES: THEIR STRENGTH
AND THEIR WEAKNESS

THE IMPACT of a more developed upon a weaker civilization invariably ushers in a period of stress and strain for the latter. Tribal peoples who have been brought into contact with Western life as a result of economic and political expansion have been subjected to profoundly disruptive forces. The first experiences with the white race were almost without exception disastrous. Many of the early traders were rough, unimaginative, and cruel. They introduced diseases—measles, dysentery, pulmonary troubles, and syphilis. The natives who had built up a resistance to endemic diseases died like flies when the new ailments spread throughout their lands.

Downright cruelty and exploitation in all parts of the world helped to produce depopulation. Tasmanian settlers formed shooting parties and shot natives in batches. African slave raiders carried off millions of people, of whom hundreds and thousands died en route to the coast. In South America, Indians perished in the mines and Peruvian natives suffered appalling cruelties. The atrocities perpetrated upon the Africans in the Belgian Congo became a world scandal. Recruiters kidnapped natives in the Pacific islands, carried them off by force, and held them in conditions of virtual slavery. From India thousands of men were taken as indentured laborers, with the ostensible acquiescence of their village chiefs. In Portuguese East Africa, frightful conditions prevailed. The Danish traveler, Holmboe, in his *Desert Encounter*, wrote that "Italian colonizing of Cyrenaica is such that any European who obtains a glimpse of it must feel ashamed to belong to the white race." Arabs were shot merely for being in certain areas, and for the offense of giving food to mountain tribes who were still trying to retain their independence. People were condemned to work in the salt lakes in the Libyan desert under shocking conditions.

Recruiting of natives for plantation labor disorganized native

459

society by removing large numbers of the young men who, had they remained at home, would have become the fathers of the next generation. Those who returned after having lived for some years on foreign plantations tended to grow dissatisfied with the old tribal life. They had seen the outside world; the tribal ceremonies lacked appeal, and appeared even somewhat amusing; they were disinclined to obey a chief who had seen so much less than they had. They became restless; they were "detribalized," and lived unhappily between two worlds—the native world which they had lost and the white man's world which they were unable to enter.

The white race, by introducing firearms to natives (whose warfare was often cruel enough even with their own primitive weapons), caused further demoralization. Many chiefs bartered personal and tribal wealth for the new weapons, partly from a desire to enjoy the delights of the white man's novelty, partly in order to gain additional power.

The introduction of liquor brought misery and ruin to whole groups of people. We have examined elsewhere the international efforts made to control liquor traffic in Africa. Here it will suffice to consider the fate of the New Hebrides. Despite the establishment of a joint rule, the Condominium, by Britain and France in 1906, Speiser, seven years later, wrote that Europeans, particularly the French, sold alcohol to the natives without hindrance from the government. He pictured the consequences as follows: The natives "drink in a senseless way, simply pouring down one bottle after another until they are quite overcome. Some never wake up again; others have dangerous attacks of indigestion from the poison they have consumed; still more catch colds or pneumonia from lying drunk on the ground all night. Quarrels and fights are frequent, and it is not a rare sight to see a whole village, men, women, and children, rolling on the sand completely intoxicated. The degeneration which results from this is all the sadder as originally the race on Ambrym was particularly healthy, vigorous and energetic. If the liquor is not speedily suppressed the population is doomed."

Rev. Frater in November 1928, fifteen years after Speiser, wrote of liquor as a growing menace in the New Hebrides. The Presbyterian Mission Synod concluded that the government must be ignorant of the extent of the liquor traffic, otherwise it was inconceivable that it would permit such conditions to continue. On some islands the traffic was increasing, and the Synod believed intoxication to be the great factor in native depopulation.

Changed methods of living played a part in weakening native society. According to several authorities, the introduction of Western clothing adversely affected the health of natives. Personal and social habits which were tolerably hygienic when people wore little or no clothing became risky, even dangerous, when they attempted to imitate the white man. For example, natives would get their clothing wet and neglect to change, with the result that they fell prey to serious colds, chest troubles, and even pneumonia. Native huts, which in the tropics admit fresh air from all sides, too frequently gave way to houses built on the European model, and the diminished ventilation had unfortunate consequences. The habit of spitting spread disease inside the new closed-in houses more rapidly than it had done in the old open huts.

The moral problem raised in the transition stage presented serious difficulties. With the abolition of the club law against immorality and the substitution of a religion of persuasion rather than compulsion, many backslidings occurred. It is not surprising that tribes (and nations) which have to face changing standards and social values normally experience a period of moral confusion.

In addition to the difficulties caused by a change of moral and social standards other factors helped to upset habitual lines of conduct. The missionaries, who preached the ideal of the family, did not approve the native practice of setting aside separate sleeping quarters for the men and encouraged youths to sleep in the homes of their parents. This innovation, combined with the contempt which the younger generation developed for the traditional tribal ideals, gradually produced a breakdown of the old moral restrictions. Young men and women thrown together under these circumstances were tempted to indulge in promiscuous sex relations.

The missions also opposed another Fijian custom, the separation of parents during the weaning of the child. The father, according to tribal usage, lived in the men's sleeping house for this period, which lasted from twelve to thirty-six months. The precaution was desirable, because, in the absence of artificial food for infants, the child had to be weaned over a longer time than in the case of Europeans. But the missionaries, believers in home life, encouraged fathers to return home, with the result that sexual intercourse took place too soon.[1]

In Africa, Christian missionaries tended to object to native

[1] Basil Thomson, *The Fijians* (1909), pp. 180–81.

marriage customs: (*a*) bride wealth, because it too nearly resembled slavery, and church councils passed resolutions forbidding native Christians to make such payments; (*b*) and polygamy, which they regarded as inconsistent with Christianity. Churches insisted that a native dissolve, for reasons that natives believe to be inadequate, what his society accepts as a legal marriage; and an extremely unfortunate position is thereby created for the dismissed wives. The clan may expect a man to marry his deceased brother's widow, even though he is a married Christian. As Westermann points out,[2] monogamy "is also made more difficult by the long continence which is expected of the man during his wife's pregnancy up to the weaning of the child." Nevertheless polygamy is gradually losing ground in Africa, and monogamy is producing a new problem for the unmarried women. The older African society had no such class to provide for; but under present circumstances many young women are forced into a life of prostitution, "especially where the clan life has been broken up and therefore gives no support to the independent women."[3]

THE PROBLEM OF COLONIZATION

The coming of the white man often had disastrous consequences for native political organization. Many of the new colonial administrators ignored the power of the chiefs, whose authority had possessed a divine or semidivine significance for the tribes. The continued disdain shown by the white settler or trader, coupled with the failure of the gods to intervene on behalf of the chief, served to weaken the ties of tribal solidarity. Sometimes it did the opposite, and created a longing in the soul of the native for his old ways of life and traditional forms of government. Many of them asked for the reintroduction of their chieftainship. Unable to understand the white man's ways, they were in danger of losing their own. In some parts of the world administrators have been wise enough to make use of the best of the native institutions; but in many colonies an unfortunate disregard of native foundations of law and order has characterized European colonial policy.

The economic life of native peoples suffered from the European invasion. We have already noted the disastrous results of recruiting. The presence of the white man has created other grave problems. Scarcely any native community has escaped the loss of

[2] D. Westermann, *The African Today* (Oxford University Press, London, 1934), p. 141.

[3] *Ibid.*, p. 143.

its land, much of which the white settler has robbed or confiscated. South Africa provides a tragic illustration of what can happen. The natives form two-thirds of the population of the Union, and about 85 per cent live in the country. Yet the area which has been assigned to them comprises only 8 per cent of the total, an amount entirely inadequate for their needs. Buell noted that the native areas are overcrowded, land is at the saturation point, water is scarce in many parts, and native health is adversely affected, malnutrition and tuberculosis being on the increase. Native renters and wage earners who live on European farms are in an unsatisfactory position, often having to work for rations instead of wages under the absolute control of the manager and with no security of tenure. The renters or squatters outside of the reserves also suffer from the same evil, and many live under conditions akin to those of the sharecroppers in the United States.[4]

In Kenya the Negroes have lost some of their most valuable land. White settlement there began in 1903 and the government made free 640-acre grants. The land policy which followed the Crown Lands Ordinance of 1902 was criticized by white settlers on grounds that it unduly restricted acquisition and transfer of property. The British government, which protected native land rights, in 1913 relaxed the rules as to land transfer by lengthening leases from 99 to 999 years. The land laws afforded progressively less protection to and permitted alienation of land with fewer safeguards from the Negroes. The Kikuyu tribe found some of their choicest areas passing under the white man's control; and the Masai tribe bitterly complained that they were forced out of their best land, receiving in exchange new areas, much of which was worthless.

Many white employers desired to dispossess the natives of their land, and thereby to obtain more native labor. They realized that if the native was permitted to retain sufficient land, he would not work for them. Land remains the great guaranty of native economic independence; deprive a native of his land, and he is at the mercy of the white settler. Few matters are more urgent, in the administration of native peoples, than the assurance that they will enjoy security of land ownership and that alienation of tribal lands to white owners shall take place only under most carefully regulated conditions.

In addition to the difficulties created by appropriation (some

[4] R. L. Buell, *The Native Problem in Africa* (The Macmillan Company, 1928), chapter v.

would call it stealing) of tribal lands, other economic problems arose. Many critics assert that native communal economic life is inefficient and that it is necessary to encourage the people to become more progressive—to increase their wants and raise their standard of living. Since the tribe is essentially a conservative institution which holds back its most progressive members, some European authorities are ready to introduce movements leading to individualism. An interesting attempt along this line was made in Fiji. If a Fijian worked for himself, the buli or tribal chief claimed part of his income for the tribe; and the loss of a considerable part of his earnings discouraged the would-be individualist native. Accordingly, a method was devised by which the Fijian paid a lump sum to the chief in order to liquidate his obligations to the tribal group. In West Africa native farms have been encouraged; there also the question arose: "If the farmers are confirmed in their holdings, what returns should they make to their chiefs?"[5] The problem is an extremely interesting one; for if the native becomes an individual producer, it is likely the tribe as a unit will be seriously disrupted. If the prestige of the chief continues undiminished, and he sets his face against the new methods which threaten his authority, he will make it difficult to educate the tribe in more efficient ways of production. In any case the question will arise whether or not the tribe can be maintained as a political unit and at the same time be very much modified as an economic unit; separating the economic and political bases of native society, unless the political authority of the chief is carefully maintained, will tend to weaken the whole tribal structure.

Where industrialism invades native communities, the labor problem becomes acute. Sixteen per cent of the South African natives work in factories. These men, separated from their tribes for periods of years, become "detribalized" and often pathetic beings. They probably live in overcrowded quarters, victims of poverty, exploitation, liquor, and disease. They are paid low wages, because the color bar exists (by either legislation or custom). In many occupations skilled labor is reserved for the white worker, and the Negro may work only at low-paid and unskilled tasks.

All these problems of adjustment are linked with the changing sense of economic and social values. In certain parts of Africa cattle have had an almost religious significance; in East and South

[5] A. McPhee, *The Economic Revolution in British West Africa* (George Routledge & Sons, Ltd., London, 1926), p. 157.

Africa, for example, the native enjoys an "extraordinarily close, almost personal relationship" with his herd, and each boy receives an ox which in a special sense is his own. "In these circumstances separation from a favorite animal is a real sorrow, and the idea of slaughtering it for a merely material purpose strikes the owner as cruelty."[6] The change to the modern, economic cash basis involves the transformation of this native religious, or semireligious, attitude to land, animals, and the products of the soil; there is danger that this transformation will be accompanied by greed, self-seeking, and unscrupulous competitive behavior, characteristic of much of the Western industrial world. Westermann wisely suggests that prolonged and intimate expert study of the processes and the effects of economic changes is needed in order to assist native society to make its adjustments with the minimum of suffering and exploitation.

The decline of the native's faith in his religion and way of life accelerates the disintegration of tribal culture. In Hawaii *kapu* was abolished in 1819. The people, at the bidding of their new ruler, threw their idols into the sea and at one blow destroyed the foundation of the old taboos and social beliefs. The Hawaiians could no longer call on their old religious formulas, which had provided them with a sense of certainty. Dr. Handy remarks that, with the abolition of *kapu,* the rule of the king or *moi,* who was regarded as an intermediary between heaven and earth, an incarnate god possessed of magical powers of prosperity, disappeared. The theocratic nature of the Hawaiian government ended. With it also went the organization of society based upon hierarchy and distinction of birth. The *alii,* or nobles, lost their religious and political prestige and could no longer demand tribute. Like the feudal lords of Europe they declined when their political functions were transferred to another authority. People abandoned the ceremony of consecrating their children. The *makahiki* ("harvest thanksgiving festival") languished; and the abandonment of this ceremonial, according to Handy, helped to disrupt the agricultural cycle. Disruption of agriculture resulted in neglect of the excellent Hawaiian irrigation projects and the passing of the fish ponds to the control of Orientals.

Fiji went through a similar experience. The missionaries performed a splendid service in converting the Fijian from habits of cruelty to the finer ways of life, and by 1876 the country had

---

[6] D. Westermann, *op. cit.,* p. 69.

become nominally Christian. But later heathen revolts broke out. Some of them were connected with revelations and prophecies of the end of the white man's rule and the destruction of his religion. Many Fijians secretly welcomed the new excitement and returned to their heathen practices, to devil-worship, and even to cannibalism. The movement failed, and the doom of the old gods was sounded. The effects went beyond the sphere of "religion," for their former faith had been closely connected with the arts and crafts and daily life of the people. In the Melanesian Islands, also, the abolition of head-hunting customs (connected with religion) had unfortunate effects upon the arts and crafts.

Mr. D. W. Hoodless in an official memorandum pointed out that the natives of Fiji had developed great skill in their manual arts but as they adopted European customs many of the old activities fell into disuse. The cessation of native warfare threw out of work the native artisans who had made clubs, spears, and war canoes; European articles replaced the native nets and fishlines; European dishes and plates took the place of the old wooden ones, and cotton clothes caused the abandonment of native methods of dress. Because no other hobbies grew up to take the place of the old manual arts, the Fijian "now finds himself with a large amount of leisure time for which he has little or no use."

In Africa the arts and crafts declined because the chiefs no longer had the same means of attracting artists, and the craftsmen who in earlier times would spend years on a single piece of work. Moreover, the chief has new duties. Under the white man's rule he collects taxes and acts as judge, supervises subordinate officials, and apparently gains more prestige by "filling his house with European things." He can hand down his image to posterity more beautifully by means of an enlarged photograph than by a wooden statue. Also European utensils are less beautiful, perhaps, but more "practical and durable."

Thus the passing of the old arts, and with them the spirit of satisfaction in creativeness, has produced an inner psychological void. It is difficult to bridge the gap between the life of the old and the life of the new. Native carving and industry are pushed aside by the modern machine, and the individual and the group are left with a sense of frustration and futility.

Several writers have noted the extreme importance of the psychological factor in native society. Some years ago W. H. R. Rivers drew attention to this element of "despair" which modification of, or interference with, native customs produced by depriving the people of many things which had given zest to their life. Natives die easily, he wrote. Their extreme sensibility quickly leads to loss of hope and to spiritual wasting away. The main question, then, is how to re-establish old interests, to modify old institutions and purge them of cruelty, and yet to preserve enough of them to maintain tribal interest and enthusiasm. Roberts asserts that population decline "is due primarily to psychological causes" and any effective remedy "must cope with the peculiar gap in native life—the gap between the old and new which gives rise to morbidity in the native mind." The native suffers from "psychological repression," from inadequacy of outlets, and "lacking interests and the means of expression, becomes first stagnant, then apathetic, even of life itself."[7] He adds that all over the Pacific there is a "dangerous void in the native mind" and quotes considerable evidence to support his contention. One has heard Marquesan poems of lament which reflect the hopelessness of some of the tribes, who feel themselves doomed because of the relentless advance of the white man's way of life.

PRINCIPLES OF GOVERNMENT OF DEPENDENT PEOPLES

What measures can colonial government adopt in order to meet the problems outlined above? What policies should they pursue, and what principles should guide them? The magnitude of the task will become clearer when it is remembered that the welfare of scores of millions of people is at stake. No minor question this, which affects the tribes of Africa, Indo-China, Ceylon, the East Indies and the many islands in the Pacific Ocean. The problem calls for the highest qualities of statesmanship.

In theory, governments may refuse to take any action; they may set their faces against the acquisition of empire and permit native society to work out its own salvation. Such a policy has been tried, and has failed. In Hawaii the native people sought vainly to maintain their freedom; in the course of the nineteenth century Americans and other settlers formed a bureaucracy which made native independence an illusion; finally, through annexation by the United States, the fact was recognized that Hawaii was no longer capable of ruling itself. Likewise in Samoa foreigners took part in tribal wars and irresponsible whites intensified native

---

[7] S. H. Roberts, *Population Problems of the Pacific* (G. Routledge & Sons, London, 1927), p. 139. Other authors do not emphasize the psychological factor so strongly.

rivalries, until at the end of the century the British, German, and United States governments stepped in and partitioned the islands. In Tonga, notwithstanding his efforts to imitate European political forms and methods, the native king could not maintain order, and power passed to a missionary, Mr. Shirley Baker. Difficulties developed into disorder, and disorder provoked struggle, until Britain finally intervened to restore settled government. Fiji and Tahiti, in turn, showed that the new forces which had been released by the coming of the Europeans could no longer be restrained by the natives themselves; and, tragic though it was for these tribal communities to see their traditional life and institutions threatened and then swept away, there was no longer any question of maintaining their independence. The only alternatives were to come under the brutal domination of irresponsible white traders or to be ruled by government officials of a European power. Roberts correctly judges that the theory of governmental nonintervention "was negative and an evasion of responsibility. It meant the sanctioning of a policy of drift rather than the definition of realities and the training of the natives."[8]

The European nations were tempted to go to the opposite extreme. Native kingdoms had proved their inability to stand alone; the white race, conscious of its superiority and proud of its power, tended to look down upon the "primitive" and "barbarian" people and to assume that there was nothing of value in their society and government. In an attempt to introduce "civilization" and efficiency, some of the colonizing powers abolished the rule of chieftains, destroyed native legislative and judicial methods, and imposed, with little or no modification, the political machinery used by themselves at home. This was "direct rule." In many instances, governments set up institutions which cut across tribal lines, took no account of tribal loyalties, and ignored the position and dignity of the chiefs. They attempted to apply conceptions of property and land-ownership to communities with fundamentally different economic ideas and tried to impose European theories of legal and social relations which violated native marriage customs, religious observances, and systems of periodic festivals. Such disregard of native habits, or mores, proved disastrous. It robbed the natives of their own mode of life, discouraged initiative, and even destroyed interest in life itself. It ignored deep-seated human sentiments, and produced instability and restlessness; it proved eco-

[8] S. H. Roberts, *op. cit.,* p. 148.

nomically burdensome, since the administration of widely differing tribes over large areas of territory involved heavy financial outlays. The theory of assimilation, of forcing natives into the European mold of life, on the assumption of universality of reason (as the French believed) or the superiority of Western culture, broke down badly.

The best-informed colonial theory today is summarized in the term "indirect rule," which postulates that natives shall be given the opportunity to develop along their own lines and to adapt themselves to the new forces of culture at their own pace rather than according to some preconceived Western plan. It recognizes value in the native way of life, its creative ability and cultural achievements. It recognizes the deep-seated differences, due to long centuries of environmental influence, between native and white civilizations, and attempts to preserve the finer aspects of native society, to purge it of its crudities, and to remedy its defects. In the political sphere it takes cognizance of the traditional power of the chief. The white adviser or resident stands behind the chief and advises him; on some occasions he will exercise pressure; but the tribal forms are maintained as far as possible, and respect and deference to the chief are encouraged. Native councils are permitted to pass legislative measures and, within prescribed limits, to make rules relating to the native community.

The theory is excellent. It is not always easy to put into practice. Many of the chiefs are inexperienced. Generally speaking, the elders, and the general body of natives themselves, cannot be expected to appreciate the need for some of the innovations desired by the European officials. One can imagine that they would question the need for a road here or for health precautions there, and conceivably might regard these newfangled things as economically burdensome and as dangerous to their old customs. Thus, inexperience, fear, and conservatism may combine unduly to delay the introduction and passage of necessary reforms and innovations.

Hence arises the need of encouraging the chiefs to be forward-looking and progressive. To that end schools for the sons of native chiefs have been opened in certain parts of Africa. There the boys are taught the elements of modern science and the organization of society but are still reminded of their chiefly rank and duties. While they thus retain the respect of their people, they come to appreciate the wider problems of modern government. It is important that Western governments do not make a

mere rubber stamp out of the chief; otherwise the native people
will soon realize that he is a creature of the white official with no
voice of his own. In that event the whole attempt at indirect rule
will be defeated; people will see through the pretense, and the institution of chieftainship will fall into decay.

A danger of the opposite kind also exists. Brown and Burt
in their *Anthropology in Action,* a study of the Hehe tribe in the
Iringa Province of Tanganyika, say that the fundamental lack is
one of insufficient internal checks on the authority of the tribal
ruler: In old days the chief dared not antagonize the tribe; today,
with the power of the British government behind him, he may
"proceed to seize such authority as is possible." They believe
that the great weakness is that "there is no adequate expression
of public opinion upon administrative affairs and thus no internal
constitutional check upon the tribal authorities." And the scale
of salaries is bad. The chiefs get too much and the head men too
little.[9]

Generally speaking, the system works well provided that the
ruling powers are willing to make haste slowly. The crucial point
is the speed of reforms; the power of assimilating new ideas and
habits cannot be forced beyond a certain rate. Patience and humor
are indispensable qualities for colonial officials, more valuable far
than mere efficiency.

Indirect rule finds expression not only in the legislative but also
in the executive sphere. In Buganda, for example, the native chiefs
have considerable administrative power. They may impose taxes,
maintain roads, and generally supervise native affairs. They control the machinery for collecting revenue, and keep their own books.
In some colonies, native taxes are put into a separate fund which is
used exclusively for native purposes. The assumption is that effective government implies not only the right of making rules but
also the power to carry them out, and that such a power necessitates the establishment of native treasuries. The estimates are
drawn up by the native authorities themselves, on the advice of
the tribal councils, under the general supervision of the resident
white adviser.

The policy of indirect rule may also apply in the judicial sphere.

[9] For a strong criticism of indirect rule, see G. Padmore, *How Britain
Rules Africa* (Wishart Books, Ltd., London, 1936), pp. 315–25.

The author describes it as a type of fascism which denies the blacks any
"voice in the affairs of state," "an autocracy backed up by British bayonets,"
which "lends itself to all kinds of abuses because it is difficult to fix responsibility upon those who operate the system."

In Tanganyika native courts of the first class may try civil cases involving sums up to 600 shillings, certain inheritance cases, and cases dealing with marriage and divorce under Mohammedan or native law. In criminal matters these courts may impose sentence up to six months' imprisonment or 200 shillings fine or eight strokes of the lash, and they may receive appeals from the lower native courts. Native courts of the second class have a less extensive jurisdiction in civil and criminal cases. Neither class of courts may impose the death penalty or life imprisonment, or punish witchcraft, or try cases where one of the parties is not a native. An appeal from the first-class or highest native court may be taken to the British administrative officer, who sits as court of appeal.

A system of legislative, executive, and judicial indirect rule presupposes the existence of well-established native tribal organizations. But where invasion and direct rule have impaired or even destroyed the basis of native institutions, as in Tanganyika and the Belgian Congo, or where distances between the native villages are great, and the villages themselves are small, as in Papua, the mandated territory of New Guinea, and the New Hebrides, it is difficult to proceed along the lines mentioned. In Papua no real chiefs and practically no system of public law exist, and the villages possess only men of stronger personality, whose influence is "often short-lived, too slight and fleeting to support even the most modest system of indirect rule." In contrast to West Africa, Papua had to adopt a modified theory of indirect rule. The administrative officials, having no hereditary chiefs to choose from, had to appoint village constables and village councilors from among the prominent men. Even so modest a degree of native authority was not easy to maintain, as the annual reports of the resident magistrates frequently show. Some of the councilors regarded themselves as above the law and exempt from taxation, or even possessed of authority to "corner the most attractive village maidens." The administration, in the absence of the system of chieftainship, could not set up native judicial institutions; it therefore established courts presided over by government officials. The question what law should apply gave rise to much difficulty. What we regard as murder may not be murder in the eyes of the natives. The taking of life may be due to a desire to achieve social honor, to avoid ridicule, or to win the favor of one's ladylove. To prove his merit a man goes out and kills someone; "returning in triumph, he is received as a hero and his suit prospers, almost beyond his hopes." "And then," adds Sir Hubert Murray, "we come along and put him in jail!" In some places natives wear a decoration of honor to show that they have killed a person; it is on record that a man once murdered somebody merely to oblige a friend. To apply European penalities in these cases would be grossly unfair. How then shall justice be dispensed? How punish those whose values are so different from those of their rulers?

It may be the mark of a wise administration to avoid undue interference with native custom; but what shall be done with murder, sorcery, adultery, and theft? These cannot be ignored. Murray suggests that the maintenance of order is the essential standard; native customs which tend to break down order must be discouraged and be punished according to the length of time the native has been in contact with white civilization. In Papua a native murderer is not sentenced to death unless he

was sufficiently civilized to realize what he was doing; and a native who has reached this stage very rarely commits murder. Still, if he does, he is hanged. A less civilized native might get a sentence of seven years, one less civilized still, five years and so on to three years or less; while the absolutely low savage from the frontiers of barbarism might escape with a merely nominal sentence.[10]

In the Belgian Congo the government ignored tribal organization for several years, but in 1914 a commission of inquiry recommended that the administration should recognize natural and not artificial chiefs. Since that time the government has attempted to reconstitute the tribes and to ascertain who were the traditional rulers. It has permitted the higher chiefs to invest subordinate dignitaries and thereby dramatize and reinforce their authority. Where a tribe was too small, the government took steps, in close co-operation with the chiefs, to combine these small groups into larger units. Also in Tanganyika the government has encouraged tribal amalgamation where tribes were "too small to finance projects large enough really to advance communal interests." In these cases, where tribal organization has been impaired, government has to do more than maintain a native system; it must restore, as far as possible, the traditional forms of native life.

The principles which should govern land policy among dependent peoples are the subject of much debate among colonial authorities and anthropologists. Some governments have proclaimed

[10] Sir Hubert Murray, *Native Administration in Papua* (Government Printer, Papua, 1929), p. 16.

unoccupied land as government land; others have permitted it to remain with the natives. In either case, the important thing is to forbid too extensive alienation of native land. Provided that it maintains adequate native land reserves, a government can permit a degree of white settlement; but security of native land tenure is a vital necessity.[11]

The question arises, should the white settlement be kept distinct from native reserves? Some people say that contact of native with white society is an education in itself, and that by learning modern methods of plowing and harvesting, seed cultivation, and fertilization, by acquiring habits of punctuality, cleanliness, and reliability, and by developing the skill to use machinery, natives will gain in experience and efficiency. Those who advocate separation of the races, though not necessarily absolute segregation artificially and legally imposed, insist that tribal life must be kept as intact as possible, and that sufficient land in compact areas should be reserved for the native population.

There is also much difference of opinion as to how far native cultivation should be encouraged. Those who are enthusiastic about modern methods point out that large-scale production introduces many economies.[12] Companies, such as Lever Brothers, Firestone, and the American Fruit Company, can clear land efficiently, introduce irrigation schemes, combat pests and insects on a large scale, build hygienic houses for laborers, introduce the benefits of modern medicine, and increase the yield of sugar, fruit, rubber, cotton, or coca. On the other hand, critics of large-scale white enterprise in the tropics argue that it is too impersonal; it breaks down tribal life by withdrawing too many natives from the reserves; potential fathers are removed from the villages; population suffers; white managers are prone to ill-treat native laborers, whose health is thus undermined; large-scale economic organization pulverizes the individual, breaks down his loyalties, and makes of him merely a "hand" or a laborer. Because of its dependence on foreign markets large-scale production is an economically unstable system: in periods of economic crisis the na-

[11] D. Westermann, *op. cit.*, p. 77. Also *Report of the Commission on Closer Union of the Dependencies in Eastern and Central Africa* (Cmd. 3234, 1929), chapter iii.

[12] As, for example, H. Martin Leake, *Unity, National and Imperial* (George Allen & Unwin, Ltd., London, 1935), Part III, "Colonial Agriculture." Dr. Leake was Principal of the Imperial College of Tropical Agriculture, Trinidad, 1924–1927.

tives are thrown out of work. Unemployment and demoralization thus more than offset the temporarily higher wages which they may have received in periods of prosperity.

One cannot be dogmatic on the question. Some crops are not suited for large-scale production; others are. But in general it is true that, wherever possible, native farming should be continued. In order to gain the best results, however, it is necessary to have white overseers and agricultural and veterinary specialists who can supervise methods of planting, cultivating, and harvesting, and can introduce measures to combat plant and animal diseases and to increase production.

Where native products are sent to outside markets it is desirable to afford assistance in the form of transportation and marketing schemes. Where shifting cultivation prevails, governments should encourage more intensive cultivation and closer settlement, realizing that sedentary life will lead to larger aggregations of people, more differentiation of labor, and greater economic complexity, with resultant specialization of skills. To improve cultivation, Williams suggests, government should encourage the improvement of tools; for imperfect tools tend to perpetuate a lower stage of economic and social development. The changes should not be too great. Any alteration should be of such a kind as not to offend the conservative prejudices of the native or make repairs too difficult to accomplish. New crops should be introduced to provide a more varied diet and to permit a greater diversity of, and wider interest in, gardening. To achieve this result teachers should instruct the native while he is young, before he has become accustomed to the traditional and antiquated tribal methods of cultivation.[13]

In many places the ideal of improved agriculture and better villages has not been easy to attain. Nevertheless, officials by awarding prizes for the best-kept villages and gardens have awakened in the people a feeling of village pride; natives are encouraged to keep their pigs away from the houses, to clean away rubbish, to install pumps, and to arrange their houses in better order instead of in the haphazard manner of older times.

Governments have also introduced other measures to encourage native cultivation. A system of taxation under which the native must pay an annual sum (say five dollars) is designed to force him to grow agricultural products and thereby learn the

[13] F. E. Williams, *Practical Education: The Reform of Native Horticulture,* Anthropology Report, No. 14 (Government Printer, Papua, 1933).

virtues of discipline and order. Some administrations put the revenue derived from native taxation into a separate fund which is used only for native purposes. Other authorities introduce an element of compulsion, and require natives to work a certain number of days each year for the government and/or privately owned estates.

We have now moved by degrees from a consideration of land to an examination of labor policy, for the two subjects are closely interrelated. The question of forced labor is dealt with elsewhere. Here we analyze the problem of free and indentured labor.

Under the indenture system natives sign a contract for a number of years; if they break their contract, they may be not only fined but also thrown into prison. Generally a breach of civil contract carries with it only a civil punishment; but natives have no wealth with which to pay damages, and mere civil prosecution would probably not deter them from attempting to run away before the expiration of their time. Recruiting is a costly business; and employers feel that, because it takes several months to make a newcomer into an efficient laborer, three years is not too long a period of indenture. Moreover, many employers believe that the indenture system gives them a greater control over their labor force, a greater certainty of an adequate labor supply, and a guaranty that the native, irresponsible and lacking in self-discipline, will not abandon his work and leave the plantation short-handed, often when it is necessary to gather the produce in the shortest possible time. A government official of Papua, Mr. O'Malley, in his annual report for 1927, admitted that most employers prefer to recruit labor under the indenture system even though they have to pay fees for recruitment, the cost of transportation of natives before and after indenture, and native labor-office fees. Mr. O'Malley questioned this view, and was of the opinion that free labor would be found more efficient in the long run and in every way more desirable. His reasons were: To take a Papuan native from his village where he has his family and may work according to the mood of the moment and hunt and fish and join in the tribal ceremonies, and to place him on a plantation with its strict hours of work, its discipline, its separation from the tribe, and its complete contrast to his old life, involves a tremendous strain. After the novelty has worn off, the new life of discipline and routine is likely to become irksome, the native grows discontented and resentful, and, in consequence, becomes inefficient. Under a one-year term many of these disadvantages do not arise; by the time the novelty of working for the white man has disappeared the laborer can look forward to returning home; after a short period there, he is more likely to re-engage; twelve months is not long enough to sicken him of plantation labor. Mr. O'Malley pointed out that of 200,000 native laborers in the mines in South Africa only about one-third were recruited natives, who averaged a twelve-month period of service; the rest were voluntary workers, who remained on average ten months and rejoined the mines after a short holiday at home. To the objection that it takes an employer six months to train a recruit into an efficient plantation worker, he answered that this is true of the native employed for the first time; if laborers are willing to re-engage, now being experienced hands, the problem no longer exists.

The wise employer, even under the indenture system, which provides for the imprisonment or the imposition of fines upon a negligent native, will not come to the courts if he can help it, but will attempt to reach a friendly understanding. A free laborer, if unsatisfactory, may be immediately dismissed; the threat of losing his job will act as a restraining influence because he will have to bear the cost of his repatriation.

The method of recruiting is most important. If the government does not exercise supervision, unscrupulous private recruiters use fraud and deceit to entice and even kidnap natives from their villages. If the government itself actively encourages recruiting, and an official even hints to the chief that men are required, his "request" is regarded as a command. Employers in East Africa believed that the government should promote recruiting; but several administrators hold the view that officials should remain strictly neutral and make no effort to influence the native, that each should make certain that the pay is adequate, that the native knows the terms of the contract and signs it of his own free will, and that conditions on the plantation are satisfactory. In the mandated territory of New Guinea, the 1922 ordinance permitted recruiting bonuses to be paid to chiefs, with two safeguards: (1) the intending laborer must testify before a district officer that he desired to work; and (2) bonuses were to be limited in amount.

Governments differ as to the indenture of women. Those who favor the policy argue that if women accompany their husbands the family will not be disrupted, the birthrate will not suffer as it would if the husbands were away for three years, and the presence of women will obviate the tendency to unnatural vice among the indentured men. Administrators who oppose the indenture of women minimize the importance of the foregoing arguments. They insist that to maintain the village as the center of native life is vital: "The men may go off and wander about the Territory, and stay away from home for three or four years, or more, if they can get the commissioner's consent; but, so long as the women are in the village, the men will, as a rule, come back again. But when once the women leave, the village life is dead."[14] For the same reason the government of Papua refused to consider the idea of native village settlements on European plantations. Such a system would enable a man to have his family with him and thus preserve family life; but it would also, in the opinion of officers in Papua, create a class of landless men, cause the loss of their tribal rights and status, and tend to separate them from the ways of their people.

Unmarried women should be recruited only under most exceptional conditions; and they should not be permitted to contract any marriage while in service on plantations, for "plantation marriages" have, in the past, given rise to serious abuses. Too often no cognizance was taken of any native customs, and as the marriage code in most of the native tribes is strictly defined, all marriages being exogamous, and any connection between members of the one clan being considered incestuous, it is easily understood that on return of the parties of the marriage to their district, there was much discontent and trouble. . . . . On the plantation marriages were frequently brought about between natives not even belonging to the same district. On the completion of the contract the man and his wife would proceed to the district of the man's house; in a few months, tiring of her, he would take a woman of his own district and the unfortunate native, who probably had been forced to marry against her will, would degenerate into the village prostitute.[15]

Colonial administration has become increasingly concerned with providing satisfactory conditions for laborers on plantations. The more enlightened laws provide that natives must be housed in quarters which have sufficient sleeping space and sanitary equipment; they must be given rations according to rules drawn up by medical officials; they must not be required to work more than a given number of hours a day. Some governments legalize Sundays and holidays as nonworking days; minimum wages, not high

[14] Sir Hubert Murray, *op. cit.*, p. 36.

[15] *Annual Report to the League of Nations on the Administration of New Guinea, 1921–22* (Canberra, Australia), p. 53.

according to our standards, are often prescribed. Governments have not a uniform policy of paying wages; some hold back a certain amount of pay until the end of the contract, so that the native may return home with something to show; others require employers to pay their laborers in cash and not in goods. Governments increasingly prohibit corporal punishment, and even prescribe fines or imprisonment for flogging.

Periodic inspection of plantations by government officials is common. In Papua, in 1925–26 officials visited 138 centers and examined over 13,000 natives. The officials have to submit a report which includes the name of the plantation or mine, the names of the owners and the person in charge, the number of indentured and casual natives employed, the hours of work, the amount of overtime and Sunday work, the type of work in each class, a description of the number and condition of the laborers' buildings, the supply of bedding and mosquito nets, the quantity of rations, the number and condition of cooking utensils, the source and quality of water supply, the condition of clothing, the state of the laborers' health, the sanitary arrangements, the accommodations for the sick, the provision of drugs and medical attendance, the machinery in use, the posting of native labor ordinances and regulations, the complaints of both managers and laborers, the recommendations made by the inspector to the manager, and observations by the inspector and his signature.

Authorities do not agree on the language question. Mr. Ormsby Gore and the Phelps-Stokes Commission claimed that in the early stages of education the native language should be the medium of education. Missionaries generally favor the use of the native language. There have not been lacking defenders of the policy of instruction in English.[16] But some authorities prefer to standardize one or more of the native languages.[17] These conflicting views are reflected in the Seminar-Conference of Educators and Social Scientists held at Honolulu in 1936.[18]

Opinion is not unanimous concerning the content of education for dependent peoples. Those who believe that truth and culture are universal minimize differences of culture and are more ready to have a system not fundamentally different from their own.

[16] F. E. Williams, *Native Education,* Anthropology Report No. 9 (Government Printer, Papua, 1928), p. 11.

[17] J. W. Burton, in *Studies in Australian Affairs,* p. 236.

[18] F. M. Keesing, *Education in Pacific Countries* (Kelly & Walsh, Ltd., Shanghai, 1937), pp. 164–80.

Those who believe that the "good life" and "self-realization" are conceptions too vague to be immediately applied to peoples deeply rooted in their indigenous culture say that education should assist in making native peoples more capable of the finest powers within them as native peoples. But education must also assist natives in adapting themselves to the new world forces which have touched them and are modifying their own social life. Such education must train them to esteem their own culture and not despise it. They must become "bicultural" and do what all peoples in varying degrees do, namely, adapt their beliefs and customs to life, the essence of which is change. In order to make them better members of a village, content to live in their village, and to obey their chiefs, education should be concerned with health, with improving agricultural methods, and with training the girls in duties of the home; it should aim at making the school the center of the community.

This utilitarian concept of education must also be combined with training of character and must provide for intellectual leadership; but the problem of higher education is difficult. If higher education is of a formal intellectual type, it may give "social polish" but will separate the educated native from his community, uproot him from his social setting, and isolate him from his fellow tribesmen. If he is given vocational training, he may, like many graduates in so-called civilized countries, be unable to find a position. The dilemma is serious. Holland has adopted a policy in the Dutch East Indies of strictly limiting the number of schools and the number of students who can be admitted to vocational and higher institutions. On the other hand, a well-educated individual may exercise a profound influence for good among his people. Sun Yat-sen of China, Booker T. Washington among the Negroes, and Sir Aparina Ngata among the Maoris are examples of educated men who have done extraordinary work in raising the life of their own people: "The production of one first-class anthropologist, doctor, or linguist of native blood and cultural backgrounds .... might well mean more to the future of such an indigenous area than the training of a whole army of minor native officials."[19]

These problems are alive and may be solved, given a deep sympathetic interest on the part of administrators, restraint on the part of the white settlers, and close co-operation of anthro-

---

[19] F. M. Keesing, *ibid.*, p. 140. Dr. Keesing's *The South Seas in the Modern World* (The John Day Company, New York, 1941), provides an authoritative study of the principles which should be followed in the government of dependent peoples.

pologists with government officials. The question calls for wise government, sympathetic education, and a limitation of the profit-seeking motive in the economic development of the countries in which the natives live. Under these circumstances it will be possible to carry out "the dual mandate" of governing in trust for both the native peoples and the white settlers. Culture contact may then bring enrichment and not disintegration. The next question that arises is, what agencies are best fitted to carry out these policies. We propose to examine the part played by imperialist powers and by the League.

CONSTRUCTIVE IMPERIALISM AND DEPENDENT PEOPLES

Although colonial powers have been guilty of ruthless exploitation of native peoples at different times and in many places, and although the record of the dealings of white nations with colored dependencies is marred by many black pages, happily other tendencies have manifested themselves and from earlier times in colonial history voices have spoken on behalf of the natives who have come under imperialist rule. Las Casas was an early champion of the Indians; and the Spanish throne, desirous of spreading the Christian faith, enjoined its officials in the New World to promote the spiritual and physical welfare of their Indian wards. Although the colonists disobeyed these praiseworthy instructions, the rulers of Spain had at least enunciated the ideal of trusteeship. The Church also did valuable work in protecting the rights of natives, and missionaries during the eighteenth and nineteenth centuries served as agents of a more enlightened imperialism.

Even colonial exploiters found that it did not pay to abuse the natives beyond a certain point; cruelty and neglect brought sickness and death to the laborers, and the plantations and mines were left shorthanded. Just as enlightened capitalism saw the wisdom of higher wages and shorter hours, of sanitary working conditions, and of freedom from anxiety over unemployment on the part of the workers, so the self-interest of imperial governments paved the way, although too slowly, for a better treatment of their native subjects. Toward the end of the eighteenth century, Edmund Burke and William Wilberforce raised their voices against colonial exploitation and slavery. Burke passionately pleaded for a finer concept of government in India. In his speeches, between 1783 and 1785, he drew Parliament's attention to the magnitude of Britain's task in that land, the problem of the clash of cultures and civilizations, and the danger of committing to the same men the functions of government and furtherance of trade; and he enunciated the principle of trusteeship and endeavored to overcome the apathy of the members of the House. Wilberforce and the antislavery groups carried out their splendid crusade, and explorers like Livingstone, missionaries of various denominations, Bible societies, and enlightened colonial administrators helped to bring pressure to bear upon their governments to correct or at least to mitigate the evils and weaknesses of their colonial policies.

Gradually higher standards of colonial administration were evolved and more efficient and humane methods were used throughout the colonies. We may here concentrate attention upon British colonial policy, which in some respects has gone farther than those of other countries. The Colonial Secretary administers "thirty-six different Governments each entirely separate from the rest, each administratively, financially, legislatively self-contained," with "its own administrative service, its own medical service, its own agriculture public works, and other technical services, its own scale of pay, its own pensions."[20] But, as Mr. Amery pointed out, such questions as scientific research and the problems of agriculture, of veterinary science, health, and transport necessitate more efficient organization. In 1927, therefore, the first general Colonial Conference was held and was attended by administrators from colonial possessions from all over the world.

The scope of the Conference is indicated by some of the problems here mentioned—recruitment and training of colonial civil servants, colonial pension legislation, nurses' retirement allowances, agricultural and veterinary research, the relation of technical to administrative services, the form and material of Colonial annual reports, the procedure and conduct of business in Colonial legislatures, colonial trade agencies in London, civil air developments, relations of road transport to railway development, developments in mechanical transport, wireless communication, forestry, medical and public health questions, education, and cinematograph films. The Governors of various colonies by coming together are enabled to discuss these major problems and policies, and return enriched in experience by the interchange of ideas. In addition to this, there have been other more limited colonial gatherings, such as an Agricultural Conference in Jamaica in 1924,

[20] Mr. Amery's opening address in 1927; see *Report of Colonial Office Conference,* Cmd. 2884.

conferences between Canadian and West Indian representatives in 1920 and 1925, a West Africa Conference of Senior Medical officers in 1925, of Railway Experts in 1926, of Agricultural Research Authorities or East Africa Law Officers and Agricultural Officers, and an East African Governors' Conference. In 1926 a conference of the main West Indian Colonies met in London to consider setting up a standing body to deal with matters of common interest to them.[21]

In addition to the general and regional colonial gatherings, other agencies exist to promote greater efficiency of administration and development of resources. The Crown Agents for Colonies purchase stores and raise loans for the colonial governments. They advise on several thousand miles of railway, manage over fifty colonial loans, make some 600 colonial appointments a year, and maintain various engineering and service offices. The colonies obtain cheaper materials, expert technical advice, and lower interest loans as a result of the crown agents' activities. The Colonial Survey Committee, established in 1905, assists the colonies in geographic and geologic surveys, the importance of which is very great; for upon the development of roads, railways, and other methods of transport depend efficiency of administration, the suppression of tribal warfare and slavery, the relief of famine, the education of natives in the interior, the improvement of health, and access to raw materials.

The Colonial Research Committee, appointed in 1919 administers a parliamentary grant for the assistance of poorer colonies in research on matters of local importance—agriculture in Tanganyika, coal in Nyasaland, insect pests in Sierra Leone, or the sponge industry in the Bahamas. The Colonial Advisory Medical and Sanitation Committee and the Tropical Diseases Bureau play an important part in the battle against disease. The Bureau publishes a monthly bulletin on hygiene, a monthly imperial disease bulletin, and a quarterly tropical veterinary bulletin. This involves a survey of over five hundred medical and veterinary publications. The Bureau has built up a valuable library and is thus well described as a "centralized intelligence service."

The Imperial Bureau of Entomology was reorganized in 1913 to encourage and co-ordinate, throughout the Empire, work on human and animal diseases. To its upkeep the Imperial Government, the governments of the self-governing Dominions, India,

---

[21] Linden A. Mander, "The British Commonwealth of Nations," *Proceedings of the Institute of World Affairs* (1928), pp. 96–97.

the Colonies and other Dependencies, the Sudan, and the North Borneo Company contribute. The Bureau publishes both a monthly and a quarterly review, identifies insects for official entomologists all over the Empire, and has set up a laboratory for the purpose of breeding beneficial parasites for export to the overseas Empire.

The Imperial Bureau of Mycology, founded in 1920, does a similar work on plant diseases. It is supported by the Dominions, India, the Sudan, and the non-self-governing colonies and protectorates. Its functions resemble those of the Bureau of Entomology, "distributing information in all matters connected with plant diseases, and undertaking the identification of specimens."

In 1899 the London and Liverpool schools of Tropical Medicine were founded, "primarily for the special training in tropical medicine of officers of the Colonial Medical services"; other universities followed their example by instituting courses and diplomas in the same subjects. Calcutta, in 1921, established its school of Tropical Medicine, and Australia built a similar institute in Townsville, Queensland. Schools for the training of a native medical staff have been founded in Ceylon (1870), Hong Kong (1887), and the Straits Settlements and the Federated Malay States (1905), while other measures, in this connection have been taken elsewhere.[22]

One can refer only briefly to the Imperial College of Tropical Agriculture at Trinidad, which, despite financial handicaps, has done important work in improving the quality of sugar cane, combating insect pests, stimulating research, and training experts for service all over the Empire. And only passing reference can be made to the first Imperial Agricultural Research Conference held in London in 1927 and attended by 150 delegates from all parts of the world. The Conference decided to become a permanent institution and recommended the establishment of central tropical and subtropical research stations, the foundation of new Imperial Bureaus, and other measures affecting all branches of agriculture. In the same year, a special committee under Lord Lovat presented a report (Cmd. 2825) on agricultural research and administration in the non-self-governing Dominions.

It may be objected that many of these institutions were set up primarily in the interest of the British, and only incidentally in the interest of the native people. The charge in large measure may be true; but if by such policies the dependent peoples do obtain a higher standard of health and economic welfare, the principle

[22] Mander, *op. cit., passim.*

of mutual welfare may be served. Both societies may gain from the application of science to the problems of the tropics. But there can be little question that the more recent attempts to develop native education are entirely praiseworthy.

National empires may become instruments of enlightened rule, just as governments at home may be expanded in purpose and function to serve the welfare of the many rather than of the few. Nor should one deny the devotion to duty on the part of thousands of colonial administrators, nor fail to appreciate the willing sacrifices of medical, educational, and religious missionaries who have frequently worked in close association with colonial governments. Nevertheless, the question may be raised whether this system should not merge into a wider, more comprehensive organization of an international character. Imperial trusteeship is unfortunately associated with imperialism, and with the theory that the colonial peoples primarily exist for the benefit of the home country.

An even more serious problem arises as to whether or not nations can combine their duty as trustees of native peoples with the necessity of using colonies as a part of a defense system in a modern fighting world. For, as we shall see, modern war has become so all-embracing that every other aspect of life must be sacrificed to it and colonies and native peoples will form no exception. Military requirements increasingly will supplant considerations of native welfare. To prevent exploitation is at best, and under the most favorable conditions, difficult; to permit this difficulty to be increased by having colonies drawn into totalitarian war may well prove fatal.

The real criticism of imperial rule is therefore not so much that the rule is bad as that (*a*) it lacks responsibility and publicity and (*b*) it is vitiated by the unsound international relations between the major powers, the disputes between haves and have-nots, and the pervasive element of strategic rivalry. A twofold modification must therefore be made: We must take colonies out of the arena of international squabbles; but if international cooperation of the great powers is designed merely to widen the field of exploitation and add to the number of exploiters, it will not mark any advance. We need therefore also to enlarge the idea of participation in trusteeship by associating all countries in the task of administrating dependent peoples.

The League of Nations mandate system represented an improvement over a previous colonial system of independent empires; we may now analyze its successes and failures.

THE LEAGUE OF NATIONS AND THE
MANDATE SYSTEM

The 1885 General Act of Berlin set forth certain principles which the powers agreed they should observe in their relations with the native peoples living in the Congo area. Unfortunately, international action did not equal international eloquence, and the control which was established remained ineffective. Nor did the Brussels Conferences of 1890 and 1899, which concerned themselves with the slave trade and the liquor problem, prove more successful. Some colonial administrations exhibited a more humane outlook, but in general the white race had sadly neglected its obvious duties toward the dependent and so-called backward peoples.

During the World War of 1914–1918 several British and American writers brought forward the theory that any postwar distribution of colonies should redound to the benefit of the international society as a whole rather than provide colonial enrichment for individual countries. Unfortunately the Allies during the course of the war had signed a number of treaties bargaining away the German and Turkish colonies. By treaties signed in 1916 and 1917, Britain and France and Italy were to obtain areas in Palestine, Syria, and Cilicia, and Japan was to acquire German colonies north of the equator.

These arrangements conflicted not only with ideas expressed by Hobson, Lippmann, Beer, Snow, and others but with those of two forward-looking statesmen. In 1918 President Wilson included as one of his Fourteen Points the free and impartial adjustment of all colonial claims, and General Smuts set forth a plan by which the principle of trusteeship could be put into effect. Smuts did not favor the establishment of a direct international administration—experience had demonstrated the failure of such a method—but that certain national governments should be nominated as trustees on behalf of the League.

The Peace Conference witnessed a battle between the two principles—outright annexation and the mandate system. French, Italian, Japanese, Australian, and New Zealand representatives argued in favor of the former. President Wilson championed the proposal of General Smuts. The British Prime Minister wavered, and after several days induced the Dominions to modify their attitude. By a compromise which applied to the German colonies in the Pacific and German South-West Africa, the objections of Australia, New Zealand, South Africa, and Japan were finally overcome. The "C" class mandates which these governments were to receive were to be administered "as integral portions of the mandatory state"; they would not have to observe the "open door" nor to afford equality of immigration rights to other League members, but must administer the colonies in trust for the League. The former Turkish colonies were allocated by the Supreme Council at San Remo on April 25, 1920, and after much delay, due in part to the opposition of the United States, the system came into operation in July 1922.

There are three classes of mandates:

"A" Mandates.—The Covenant of the League of Nations (Article 22, par. 4) provides:

Certain communities formerly belonging to the Turkish Empire have reached a state of development where their existence as independent nations can be provisionally recognised, subject to the rendering of administrative advice and assistance by the Mandatory until such time as they are able to stand alone. The wishes of these communities must be a principal consideration in the selection of the Mandatory.

These communities were Syria, Palestine, and Iraq; Great Britain obtained the Mandates over Palestine and Iraq, France the Mandate over Syria.

"B" Mandates.—Article 22, paragraph 5, of the Covenant provides:

Other peoples, especially those of Central Africa, are at such a stage that the Mandatory must be responsible for the administration of the territory under conditions which will guarantee freedom of conscience and religion, subject only to the maintenance of public order and morals, the prohibition of abuses such as the slave trade, the arms traffic and the liquor traffic, and the prevention of the establishment of fortifications or military and naval bases and of military training of the natives for other than police purposes and the defence of territory, and will also secure equal opportunities for the trade and commerce of other Members of the League.

The Supreme Council designated the mandatories on May 7, 1919. It awarded the mandate for the Cameroons and Togoland to France and the United Kingdom, and that for Tanganyika (former German East Africa) to the United Kingdom. After subsequent negotiations, Ruanda-Urundi (the northwest region of former German East Africa) was placed under Belgian mandate. The "B" class mandates are:

1. Cameroons under British mandate (administered by the government of Nigeria)

2. Cameroons under French mandate
3. Togoland under British mandate (administered by the government of the Gold Coast)
4. Togoland under French mandate
5. Tanganyika Territory (British mandate)
6. Ruanda-Urundi (Belgian mandate)

"C" Mandates.—Finally, paragraph 6 of Article 22 of the Covenant provides:

There are territories, such as South-West Africa and certain of the South Pacific Islands, which, owing to the sparseness of their population, or their small size, or their remoteness from the centres of civilisation, or their geographical contiguity to the territory of the Mandatory, and other circumstances, can be best administered under the laws of the Mandatory as integral portions of its territory, subject to the safeguards mentioned above in the interests of the indigenous population.

The Supreme Council awarded "C" mandates as follows:
1. South-West Africa (mandate of the Union of South Africa)
2. Western Samoa (New Zealand mandate)
3. Nauru (British Empire mandate)
4. New Guinea (Australian mandate)
5. Islands under Japanese mandate (the Marianas and Caroline and Marshall Islands)

Little enthusiasm greeted the establishment of the mandate idea. Some scholars and publicists and others realized that the new system possessed great potentialities for minimizing imperialist rivalries because freedom of access to raw materials and to colonial markets would (except in the case of "C" mandates) afford equality of economic opportunity to all nations. The system also promised to set a higher general standard for the government and protection of native peoples. The great majority of people, however, assumed either a critical, or a hostile, or an indifferent attitude. The United States, apparently fearing that the mandates meant nothing more than annexation in disguise, was concerned lest its trade interests should suffer from discriminating measures and took energetic steps to protect its cable interests in the Island of Yap. Australian and New Zealand statesmen would have preferred open annexation of Samoa and New Guinea. French nationalists spoke openly of their mandates as colonies; and British imperialists who distrusted the League and had been steeped in the traditions of British colonial policy viewed with disfavor a policy of divided control. It was in this atmosphere that the League of Nations began its work in the field of mandates.

The League supervises mandatory powers by means of the Permanent Mandate Commission, the Council, and to a lesser degree the Assembly. The Permanent Court of International Justice decides disputed legal matters concerning the mandates; while the health and legal sections of the Secretariat, the Standing Committee on the White Slave Traffic, the International Labor Office, and the Temporary Slavery Commission give valuable assistance in the various technical fields.

In order to exercise supervision satisfactorily the League must know fully what is happening in the mandated territories. Accurate information is indispensable. The question arises—what are the sources and are they adequate? The annual reports of the mandatory powers constitute the first and most important basis of information. Each of these undertakes to supply to the League each year a report which deals with main legislative and administrative developments, the general economic, social, and health conditions of the native population, the measures taken to insure their economic and educational progress, the conditions of labor, whether or not the prohibition of liquor, arms, and drugs has been faithfully observed, the financial position of the territory, and the main political events of the period.

The report is sent to the Permanent Mandates Commission, a body of individuals the majority of whom are citizens of non-mandatory powers. The members of the Commission, by reason of training or administrative experience, are expert in the problems of colonial administration. They examine the report and then call in the representative of the mandatory power in order to obtain from him fuller information on matters which the report does not make clear, or on conditions which seem to them to be unsatisfactory. Those who have read the minutes of the sessions of the Commission know that it has not been satisfied with perfunctory explanations. It has asked searching questions and has frequently stated its criticisms in no uncertain terms. When it has finished its examination it prepares a report for the League Council. The League Council considers the report and makes its observations, which go to the mandatory power concerned. The Assembly also may discuss matters arising from the report; occasionally it has passed resolutions criticizing the methods of the mandatories.

The Permanent Mandates Commission is at a disadvantage in having to rely so heavily on printed government reports. The information contained therein is likely to be weighted in favor of the mandatory, and in any case a written summary cannot take the place of personal observation. The Commission has often been unable to come to a conclusion because of the inadequacy of information at its disposal. In 1927–28 it had to consider the trouble in Samoa and for a time accepted the reports of the New Zealand government and of a Royal Commission, all of which defended the administration and condemned the opposition party under Mr. Nelson. It was not until after a New Zealand public commission had severely criticized some aspects of the administration in Samoa that the Mandate Commission realized that the information which it had received was not only inadequate but partial; then it did not hesitate to say so in strong terms. On the other hand, Japan claimed that the Commission was unfamiliar with the problems of the islands in the North Pacific under their mandate, as was shown by its alleged very vague and general questions.

The right of petition by the natives of mandated territories is held to be very important. They may send petitions to the League but must do so through the medium of the mandatory power. In the case of the "A" mandates, the Commission had to decide between what it called legitimate and illegitimate petitions; the latter were those which requested a revoking of the terms of the mandate itself, while legitimate petitions were those which pointed out alleged specific grievances. But the written petition suffers from the same drawback as the government report. It cannot give the whole atmosphere, and it was natural that petitioners should ask the right to send a personal representative. Certain individuals from Syria and Mr. Nelson from Samoa attempted to gain a hearing in Geneva, but the mandatory powers raised strong objections. They claimed that such a method would put government and subjects on the same level, and even place the ruling power in the position of defendant. The step would undermine the prestige of the government and make its task well-nigh impossible. Britain argued that the right of hearing was "based on misconception of the duties and responsibilities of the Commission and Council." The Permanent Mandates Commission rather cautiously suggested that in certain cases where it could not form a definite opinion "it might appear indispensable to allow the petitioners to be heard by it. The Commission, however, did not desire to formulate a definite recommendation on this subject before being informed of the view of the Council." And the right of oral hearing has not been granted.

It might be logically argued that if personal acquaintance is so important, the Commission, or some of its members, should be permitted to visit the mandated territories in order to supplement the information contained in their annual reports. Unfortunately this proposal arose not from responsible officials but from disaffected elements in Palestine, and however sound the view might be theoretically, it suffered from the circumstances of its origin. The mandatory powers opposed the idea, saying that the visits would make the task of government difficult by weakening their prestige and authority in the eyes of the inhabitants. Stoyanovsky suggests that a routine visit by members of the Permanent Mandates Commission need not have that effect, and proposed that the Commission divide the duties of inspection among its members, who would be designated as rapporteurs for the different territories under mandate. In his opinion the Council should ratify the appointments because the nationality and attitude of the candidates might affect the views of the mandatory power. A person who was not *persona grata* to the mandatory power should of course not be sent as a rapporteur. The person appointed should have the right of visiting the territory, examining the general situation, gathering all useful information, and presenting his report to the Permanent Mandates Commission at its ordinary annual session. The Commission would then have two reports, one from the mandatory power, the other from the inspector rapporteur, which together would enable the Commission more satisfactorily to form its judgments. Whatever the merits of the suggestion, the mandatory powers have shown the same objection to League inspection as have governments in Europe to the proposal to station League experts in their countries for the purpose of observing the condition of minorities.

Nothing has been done to strengthen the investigating machinery of the League, and the mandatory powers even opposed the suggestion of the Commission in 1926 that a more extended questionnaire be adopted in order to obtain more accurate and specific information concerning conditions in the mandated territories. The questionnaire adopted up to this time had fifty-one questions for "B" mandates and fifty for the "C" class, each divided into thirteen parts. Under the new arrangement, there would be 118 questions under 22 headings. Sir Austen Chamberlain claimed that the "immense questionnaire" now proposed was "infinitely more detailed, infinitely more inquisitorial" than that which was being used, and asserted that the Commission was threatening "to extend its authority to a point where the government would no longer be vested in the Mandatory Power but in the Mandates Commission." The vice-chairman of the Commission vigorously denied that that body desired to usurp the functions of governments, and insisted that the authority of the mandatory powers was supreme. The Commission, after obtaining further evidence on the attitude of the mandatories, passed a resolution that "it is entirely for the Mandatory Powers to decide whether they desire to use or not to use the 'List of Questions,' according to whether they share or do not share the Commission's opinions as to its usefulness." Dr. Kastl pointedly suggests that the rejection of the proposed questionnaire by the League Council "is symptomatic of the fact that in the eyes of many of the interested parties the international supervision of the Mandates Commission must stop at the point where it becomes inconvenient to the Mandatory Powers."

The Permanent Mandates Commission has had three major objectives—to make the mandate system a reality and not an excuse for outright annexation, to maintain the economic "open door" and commercial equality for all powers so that the mandated territories shall not be a source of political and economic profit to the mandatory, and to promote the welfare of the native inhabitants.

Despite the theory of trusteeship expressed in the mandate system there exists a temptation for nations to consider the mandated territories under their control as being under their sovereignty. One of the most baffling questions which has arisen out of the mandate system is that which concerns the location of sovereignty. The reason is obvious. A new form of international organization came into existence which could not easily, if at all, be harmonized with the traditional concept of sovereignty. The problem was further complicated by the fact that this much-used word has never received a universally accepted definition, and that its meaning has changed in the course of history.

Some jurists claim that the sovereignty is located with the Principal Allied and Associated Powers, in whose favor Germany renounced the colonies. Critics say that by Articles 119 and 257 of the Peace Treaty (this did not apply to the "A" mandates), those powers passed on their sovereignty to other hands. A number of writers believe that the mandatory powers themselves are sovereign. An Italian scholar, Giutio Diena, a Frenchman, M. Rolin, and an English author, M. F. Lindley, all believed that sovereignty had passed to the Allies, who in turn had handed it over to the mandatories, subject only to certain limitations.

A number of writers believe that sovereignty passed direct to the League of Nations. These include the German writers Schücking and Wehberg, and a Polish scholar, Beleski. Redslob, Kastl, Lauterpacht, and others support this view, and interestingly enough the German government in 1920 "advanced this theory." Critics say that an examination of the peace conference records shows that such transfer of sovereignty to the League was not intended; otherwise there would not have been a transfer of the territories from the Principal Powers to the mandatories without the interposition of the League. And others believe that the League is not a body which is capable of possessing sovereignty over territory. A few writers (including Millot and Stoyanowsky) believe that sovereignty exists in the mandated peoples themselves, even though for a time it is in suspense pending the achievement of their full powers of self-government. Critics believe that it is wrong to "attribute sovereignty to communities which do not exist," for "certainly in many of the mandated areas there is no organized community of all the inhabitants."

Finally, there are those who believe that we must find the sovereignty in both the League and the Mandatory Power and that, however distasteful it is to those who have hitherto claimed that sovereignty cannot be divided, the facts force the new theory upon us. Quincy Wright, Schneider, Freytagh-Loringhoven, Pearce Higgins, and P. E. Corbett have written in this strain. Critics claim that these writers have confused "the exercise of sovereignty with sovereignty itself." One may readily see that in the great variety of theories there is little unanimity, and he may sympathize with the view that the theory of mandates is in "complete chaos."

Jurists had raised the question whether a nonmember of the League could administer a mandate. In theory there seemed to be no reason why any government might not be nominated as a mandatory, whether a League member or not, provided that it observed the conditions of the mandate. Quincy Wright believed that the difficulties of such an arrangement "would certainly be almost insuperable"; but other authorities took a different view and maintained that it was merely a question of fulfilling the legal obligations of the mandatory power.

In 1933 Japan gave notice of her withdrawal from the League, and the mandates question at once came into the realm of practical politics. For the government of Japan did not relinquish its mandate and took the view that the Japanese withdrawal from the League did not disqualify it from continuing to act as a mandatory; but neither did it, as many Japanese nationalists claimed, absolve it from the obligation of continuing to administer the islands in accordance with the terms of the mandate. The legal reasons back of this action have been set forth by Dr. Tachi, whose general theory is that the League of Nations does not have sovereignty or even outstanding supremacy in the mandate system, that Article 22 of the Covenant provided a compromise between the desires of the British dominions to annex the German colonies and President Wilson's idea of the supremacy of the League, and that the League "has neither territorial rights in the mandated territories nor sovereignty over the Mandatories or over the inhabitants of the said territories, and as it has nothing to do with the choice of the Mandatories and assignment of the powers of administration to them, it must be deemed to have no power to deprive Mandatories of mandates."

The mandates problem is further complicated by the fact that mandatories are permitted in certain cases to administer the territories "as an integral part" of their own possessions; it is not easy to distinguish between "the administration of a country as an integral part of another country" and "the actual incorporation of the first country into the second."[23] The Mandates Commission has carefully examined the annual reports of the mandatories and consistently drawn attention to certain passages which might suggest that mandatory is thinking in terms of sovereignty: "The rights exercised by the mandatory Powers are dependent on the international texts. . . . . These rights can not be modified unilaterally by the mandatory Power by employing certain terms and expressions in its international legislation . . . . there should be no misunderstanding as to the precise value of these questions of internal legal terminology. The expressions employed are incapable themselves of affecting the real nature of the rights which from the point of view of the League of Nations the mandatory Powers possess."

The Chairman of the Permanent Mandates Commission em-

[23] E. van Maanen-Helmer, *The Mandate System*, p. 203. For a valuable treatment of the whole problem see Quincy Wright, *Mandates under the League of Nations* (The University of Chicago Press, Chicago, 1930).

phasized "that the Commission had the duty of seeing that the colonial administrations did not become influenced by the natural tendency to make use of the powers given them in order to convert mandated territory into a colony in full sovereignty."

The Commission questioned the view of South Africa, which, on the occasion of a frontier agreement between Portuguese Angola and South Africa, claimed that the Union, "subject to the terms of the said mandate, possesses sovereignty over the territory of South-West Africa," and criticized phrases used by Belgium and Great Britain which suggested that mandated territories were under their sovereignty.

The question of the status of the inhabitants also involved the problem of sovereignty. If it were decided that a person resident within a mandated territory were the subject of the mandatory power, that would confirm the tendency to regard the territory as a colonial possession. The question was connected with the problem whether or not inhabitants in a mandated territory can be naturalized and become citizens of the mandatory power. It was generally agreed that they could be naturalized as individuals; but could they be naturalized *en masse?* The Commission considered that a compulsory collective naturalization would infringe the principle of the mandate system, for a general naturalization would simply convert the mandated people into subjects. The League Council in 1923 agreed in these words: "the status of native inhabitants of mandated territory is distinct from that of nationals of mandatory Powers and cannot be identified therewith by any process having a general application."

The League Council was approached by the Union of South Africa to grant an exception to this rule which forbade "collective naturalization." The Union had over 30,000 white settlers in the mandated territory of South-West Africa, and wished to give them all the same nationality. It claimed that there was no substantial difference between admitting people to voluntary naturalization one by one and collectively. The latter would be simpler and involve less trouble. Two laws in 1924 and 1928 provided for collective naturalization of the whites, "but in the latter case without allowing them individually to decline to become Union nationals." This forcible naturalization, Kastl declares, has "almost completely obliterated" the distinction of nationality "between the inhabitants of the mandated country and the nationals of the Mandatory Power."

The mandatory power should not use the mandated territory

as a source of military strength. The Covenant forbids the establishment of fortifications or naval and military bases and military training of natives for other than police purposes and defense of the territory. The question arose as to whether it was legitimate to enroll men within the territory if they were to be put into units organized for service beyond the frontier; the Permanent Mandates Commission decided that it would violate the spirit, if not the law, of the mandate to enroll any men for service in a unit "which is not permanently quartered in the territory and used solely for its defense or the preservation of order within it," except that, in a general war troops might be used beyond the territory in order to repel an attack, or for the more effective defense of the territory itself.

The Permanent Mandates Commission in 1932 inquired whether or not Japan had fortified the mandated islands in the Pacific Ocean, north of the equator. The Japanese representatives assured the Commission that Japan would loyally observe its undertakings.

The Chairman was anxious that there should be no ambiguity on this point. A naval base might not be self-evident, since harbour works permitting of the entry of ships could be used by submarines. He preferred therefore to ask M. Ito to state quite frankly whether the works undertaken were intended only to promote mercantile navigation.[24]

The Japanese Government, on December 1, made this unambiguous reply:

it has never contemplated and does not propose to plan in the future the establishment of a naval base in the islands under mandate; the additional expenditure on port construction is solely due to the increase in the cost of improving the port of Saipan for economic purposes.[25]

If a mandatory is not a full sovereign power it would logically follow that it has not the independent right to mortgage mandated territory as security for loans. In fact, however, the Council has not required that such transactions obtain its prior consent but has insisted that any treaty which affects the boundaries of a mandated territory, or which modifies the mandate, must receive its approval before being ratified. Quincy Wright noted that Britain and France in their agreement of December 23, 1921, which dealt with their mandated territories, Iraq and Syria, may

[24] League of Nations, *Permanent Mandates Commission* (Minutes of the Twenty-second Session, Nov. 3 to Dec. 6, 1932), p. 115.   [25] *Ibid.*, p. 319.

have gone beyond their power, because if mandated territories come under the sovereignty of "the mandatory acting with the consent of the League Council" the mandatory cannot, strictly speaking, make a treaty on its own account.[26] The mandatory has the right of extending diplomatic protection to mandate inhabitants abroad and the right of intervention so as to maintain order within the territory.

The League has attempted to make a reality of the open door and the principle of economic equality in mandated territories. The late nineteenth century witnessed the revival of neoimperialism and the building of tariff walls around colonial possessions, and the recent controversy between the so-called "have" and "have-not" powers has brought the question of colonies into renewed importance. Gerig writes that colonies and colonial enterprise are today mainly in the hands of ten nations, and that the open door provides an important remedy "for these inequalities incidental to this unequal distribution of markets and resources of the undeveloped territories." The mandate system, he believes, may be "the most effective instrument yet devised to make the open door effective" and, if honestly carried out, would be "irreconcilable" with economic imperialism.

What is involved in attempting to keep the open door in mandated territories? First, that the mandate shall not be a source of profit to the mandatory power. The Permanent Mandates Commission raised the question when its 1923 annual report relating to New Guinea showed that 12,000 pounds had "been paid into the Commonwealth [of Australia] Revenue as the profit from a government trading organization in Sydney." The Australian representative pointed out that the Commonwealth had lost a considerable amount each year and asked whether the Commission expected that a mandatory must "necessarily incur losses on its administration." Phillips notes that, while a trustee normally cannot profit from administering a trust, "there is a growing modern tendency to permit such a trustee to receive compensation for his pains and troubles" and quotes Charteris, who "likens the mandatory to a trustee who has himself a beneficial interest, and who may reap a profit so long as he observes the limitations of the trust instrument."[27] Even if this qualification were allowed, there would

26 Quincy Wright, "The United States and the Mandates," *Michigan Law Review*, Vol. XXIII, May (1925), pp. 746–47.

27 P. D. Phillips, "Some Legal Aspects of the Mandates," in F. W. Eggleston (ed.), *The Australian Mandate for New Guinea* (The Macmillan Company, Melbourne, 1928), p. 32.

still be a great difference between a mandate which permitted re-muneration for services and the use of a territory for purposes of colonial exploitation.

The theory of the open door in mandated territories needs qualification. In the "A" mandates economic and commercial equality is guaranteed, but not necessarily economic and commer-cial freedom. Palestine might wish to build up its own industries and could therefore erect tariff duties. In one sense this would not be an open door, but in another sense the principle of equality would be observed provided that Palestine applied the duties equally to goods coming from Britain and from elsewhere. Palestine, therefore, by its mandate is precluded from "according a prefer-ence to British Empire goods." Stoyanovsky suggests that be-cause the tropical areas under "B" mandates are more important to world trade and industries by reason of their raw materials, the interested governments have insisted upon "a wider application of the principle of economic equality in these areas as compared with Palestine and the other territories under 'A' mandates."[28]

Under Article 22, paragraph 5, the open door applies only to the "B" mandates; with reference to the "A" class, provision was made for equality of treatment to League members. The United States was naturally anxious concerning the policy to be followed for non-League powers. In December 1924 it concluded a conven-tion with Great Britain which read in part: "the United States and its nationals shall have and enjoy all the rights and benefits secured under the terms of the mandate to Members of the League of Nations and their nationals, notwithstanding the fact that the United States is not a Member of the League of Nations." In the "B" mandates it is clearly provided that customs must not be im-posed against foreign countries. Does the prohibition extend to a customs union between the mandatory and its mandated territory? At first sight it would seem that such a union would violate the guaranty of equality to other nations. France, however, estab-lished such a customs union in the French Cameroons, and be-cause the French Congo did not afford preferential tariffs to the French nation the Permanent Mandates Commission did not ob-ject to the union. For similar reasons it acquiesced in the customs union of the Ruanda-Urundi district and the Belgian Congo and adopted a favorable attitude toward the proposal to incorporate Tanganyika and Kenya colony for tariff purposes. But in the

[28] J. Stoyanovsky, *The Mandate for Palestine* (Longmans, Green & Co., London, 1928), p. 312.

event of a customs union, the Commission requires a careful division of customs receipts so that the colony and the neighboring mandated territory shall each obtain its fair portion of the receipts. The customs union must be designed to serve the purposes of administrative efficiency, and not to constitute a step toward converting a mandate into a colony.[29]

Financial loans to small and insecure powers have often led to economic absorption, and the question arises whether similar loans to mandated territories might not gradually threaten the status of the mandated territory and pave the way to complete absorption. In 1923 the French government negotiated a loan for the development of a railroad in the Cameroons. If the customs receipts of the territory did not suffice, would France mortgage the railroad and, in the event of default, assume the guaranty? The danger of "veiled annexation" might be a real one. On the other hand, mandated territories require capital for their economic development, and investors desire, and are entitled to, adequate guaranty for the regular payment of interest and sinking funds upon their loans.

Theoretically, a mandatory might transfer its mandate or, in case of "A" mandates, the dependent peoples might obtain their independence and the security for investments might be considerably weakened because the new mandatory power or the emancipated mandated territory might not be so efficient in its internal finances or so conscientious in carrying out its repayment obligations. Hence the importance, as M. Rappard pointed out, of a clear statement by the League Council that no change could be legally made in the mandate system without the consent of the Council. That body therefore adopted a resolution to the effect that a new government which took over a mandate should respect all prior rights, and that the Council would exercise its influence to insure the fulfillment of all obligations. We shall see that both the Permanent Mandates Commission and the Council carefully considered whether or not Iraq and Syria, after the cessation of the mandate, would be in a position to repay its external debts.

The Council has also attempted to insure that, except in the case of essential public works and services in the "B" mandates, concessions are granted only after public notice has been given. The Mandates Commission urged that governments should exercise great care in granting concessions and monopolies. Railroads and quasi-public utilities, by their very nature, involve a degree of

[29] These sections are based upon Benjamin Gerig, *The Open Door and the Mandates System* (Allen & Unwin, London, 1930).

monopoly; but, as Gerig notes, it is not always an easy matter to ascertain what degree of publicity is effective publicity, and some difficulties have arisen with reference to concessions and monopolies.

The Permanent Mandates Commission has also had occasion to discuss what is called the purchase clause, under which a borrower must purchase his goods from the country which makes the loan. For example, in 1926 Britain passed the East African Loans Guaranteed Bill with this purchase clause attached. Mr. Amery, the Colonial Secretary, justified the measure on the ground that a country which took the risk and loaned money had a right to promote its legitimate interests, that such a step could not truly be described as "profiting" by the mandate, and that the materials were necessary for "essential public works and services." Mr. Amery's argument did not convince all parties. It was suggested that the Permanent Mandates Commission might pass upon loans for public works before they were made instead of having to decide later whether or not they were justifiable.

In 1925–26 Great Britain granted reduced postage rates from Tanganyika to British possessions. Could this step be regarded as "profiting" by the possession of the mandate? The Permanent Mandates Commission was divided in its opinion. Some members believed that the question was not important enough to raise the principle of economic equality, which they believed was intended to apply only to articles of commerce, and that in any case non-Britishers as well as British subjects in the mandated territory could take advantage of the cheaper postage rates to the Empire. The majority of the Commission took the opposite view—that the open-door principle should be liberally interpreted and that postal rates might conceivably have commercial effects.

On the whole, substantial economic equality has prevailed in the "A" and "B" mandates; but this does not hold true of "C" mandates. The British Dominions had desired to annex the German colonies, and only unwillingly accepted the "C" mandate on condition that the territories were to be ruled as an integral part of their own country. Their stand involved a denial of the open door and soon brought international problems. In 1919 and 1920 Australia restricted Japanese immigration and prohibited Japanese ships from carrying copra from Rabaul to Sydney. Japan asked why it should be shut out from New Guinea by its allies, particularly as its ex-enemy Germany had in prewar days granted more generous treatment.

Professor Bailey wrote in 1928 that the Australian policy since 1920 was little calculated to allay Japanese discontent: "One by one, limitations upon equality of economic opportunity within the Territory itself have been placed upon the Ordinance Book."[30] Among these were the 1923 fisheries regulations (rescinded after a period of fifteen months), which prohibited non-natives from pearl fishing upon certain of the reefs. In 1924 the Companies' Ordinance provided that no agricultural, pastoral, mining, or forestry company shall be formed unless two-thirds of the shares are held by British subjects; in 1924 the Land Transfer Control Ordinance and the Mining Ordinance limited foreign rights in these activities; and the Navigation Act gave British shipping preferential position, although in September 1925 the trade between New Guinea and Australia "was declared not to be coastal trade within the Act."

The United States protested against the "C" mandates on two grounds: (1) that it had not ratified the Versailles Treaty, and (2) that the mandate system was "a sacred trust for civilization" and should be regarded as a trust not only for the natives themselves but also for the world at large, and hence that a policy of economic exclusiveness was inconsistent with the principle. As Bailey points out, the United States did not raise any difficult questions with reference to New Guinea. It did take strong action over the island of Yap, which contained a cable and radio station of great importance.

In very many respects the mandates system has worked very well. The Permanent Mandates Commission and the Mandates Section of the League have served to collect information and focus world opinion upon the mandatory powers. They have constituted an organ of continuous supervision, and thereby have supplied an important element in good administration. The standards of colonial government have undoubtedly been affected; for it was not easy for Britain or France to continue ruling their colonial possessions in one way and their mandated territories in another, especially as some of these areas were contiguous and comparison could easily be made by native groups, missionary bodies, and others. Moreover, the explicit recognition in some detail of the rights of dependent peoples, embodied as they were in a document (the League Covenant) signed by most of the nations of the world,

[30] K. H. Bailey, "Foreign Powers and the Mandate," in F. W. Eggleston (ed.), *The Australian Mandate for New Guinea*, p. 17.

marked a distinct advance, comprising at least an international acceptance of principles of colonial administration.

The mandatory powers experienced many difficulties in their efforts to carry out the provisions of the mandates. Australia had trouble in New Guinea; New Zealand and South Africa had to face native uprisings in Samoa and German South-West Africa; and Britain and France faced even graver problems in the "A" mandates. In part the difficulties in the "B" and "C" mandates were due to: (a) the appointment of inexperienced administrators to take the place of the German officials who had been sent back to Germany; (b) the preference awarded to returned soldiers, whose claims of military service played a larger part in their appointment than should have been the case; (c) the attempt, in Samoa at least, to change too rapidly the native ways of living; (d) the economic consequences of expropriating experienced German settlers from plantations, settlers who had built up much expert knowledge of tropical industries and agriculture; (e) the interruption to scientific research resulting from the temporary closing of the Amani Institute in Tanganyika.

Nevertheless, as years went by, the new administrations became more efficient, and the difficulties which arose from the newness of the task were gradually lessened. But in the "A" mandates of Syria, Palestine, and Iraq a new kind of problem was presented, namely, the problem of ruling an area inhabited by people predominantly Mohammedan in their religious outlook. This Mohammedan world, which carried its faith into every aspect of daily life—the position of women, the rules concerning marriage and divorce, the status of children, the laws governing the inheritance of property, etc.—had been profoundly shaken by contact with Western society, its scientific outlook, and its political and economic forces of expansion. At first the Moslem peoples tried to withstand the West by strengthening their own religious foundations, and then by turning to nationalism in an effort to drive out the West by using the methods of the West.

The attempt to apply the mandates system to Iraq and Syria, whose intelligentsia and merchant class were rapidly developing national self-consciousness, would have been a difficult matter, even under the most favorable circumstances, for no people likes to be branded as too immature or lacking in capacity to be able to rule itself.

Unfortunately the mandate system which was adopted was a compromise between the aims of those who wished to take the

former German and Turkish colonies in full sovereignty and those
who wanted a genuine system of administration and trust for the
world. Moreover, in the case of the "A" mandates applying to the
former Turkish colonies, Palestine, Syria, and Iraq (the last one
modified), one of the victorious Allies had promised the Arab
peoples the establishment of an Arab nation. Other conflicting
commitments had been made, and the most fundamental difficulty
in the "A" mandates was that they could not be developed according to the inherent principles of trusteeship, because the situation
was already poisoned by the belief on the part of the Arab people
that Britain and France as mandatory powers did not have clean
hands or a genuine desire to assist them to gain independence.
They believed that the mandate was simply imperialism thinly
disguised. Even under the most favorable conditions it would
have required largeness of vision, considerable patience, and administrative skill on the part of the mandatory, and a trust and
restraint on the part of the mandated people if the system were to
work; the former would have to be sincere in encouraging self-
government at every step; the latter would have to avoid rashness
in claiming full independence before it had the strength or training to maintain its status and security unimpaired in a world inhabited by imperialist powers and doctrines of force.

The history of the "A" mandates, especially, shows as much
the conflict of commitments on the part of the mandatories, as the
problems arising from the relations of a single-minded mandatory
and the mandated territory, although Iraq forms a partial exception to this judgment.

We cannot review in detail in this volume the many complicated questions which arose to plague the administration of Syria,
Palestine, and Iraq, but must limit our observations to one important fact, namely, that the war which is being waged in the Near
East as these lines are being written bears witness to the fact that
strategic considerations have increasingly dominated the whole of
this region and have made impossible the normal workings of the
mandates system. Nevertheless, one important fact stands out—
that Iraq in 1932 was granted its independence and became a
member of the League of Nations.

In 1930 Great Britain initiated a move to terminate the treaty
by which she controlled Iraq and urged that country's independence. The League of Nations had to decide whether or not a mandated country was capable of fulfilling the requirements of an
independent state before it felt justified in agreeing to the step.

In June 1931 the Permanent Mandates Commission set forth the conditions which it believed to be necessary for the termination of a mandate. A country, to qualify for entry to the League, must possess a stable government, be capable of operating the essential government services in a regular manner, be able to maintain its political independence, to guarantee and maintain internal peace and order, be financially strong enough to meet normal governmental expenditures, and possess a system of law and a judiciary capable of dispensing equal justice to all. It must guarantee protection to minorities, freedom of conscience and worship, and legal rights to foreigners. It should undertake not to denounce existing financial obligations, and should grant to members of the League most-favored-nation treatment in trade and commerce.

The League Council considered the Permanent Mandates Commission report on Iraq at its January 1932 session, and Iraq was admitted to the League at the September meeting.

Toynbee, commenting upon these developments, stated that the political emancipation of Iraq represented a "reversal of Western imperialistic expansion" and demonstrated the error of cynics who had preached that the mandate system was merely "veiled annexation." Trusteeship, remarked Toynbee, really meant something. Indeed, it seemed as if Britain had been more anxious than the Permanent Mandates Commission to end its mandatory control, perhaps because Britain felt that imperialism in Iraq no longer was worth the costs involved, perhaps because adequate safeguards for British interests could be gained by less obvious control; while the Permanent Mandates Commission regarded the mandate as "a responsibility rather than a privilege" and therefore scrutinized the proposed arrangements in order to see that the responsibility was not prematurely discarded.[31]

The future of the mandate system will depend upon the future of international organization in its larger setting. One cannot expect the mandatory powers to be effectively supervised by the Mandates Commission of the League if in the fields of security, minorities, and disarmament world organization is ignored and flouted. Dr. Kastl remarks that the system will depend upon the success of the League in excluding the application of physical force, in overcoming the policy of alliances, and in creating equality and an atmosphere of peace and mutual toleration in the world. If these things can be achieved, "the mandate system will have

[31] Arnold J. Toynbee, *Survey of International Affairs, 1934* (Oxford University Press), pp. 109–15.

some chance of fulfilling its purpose." But the system must in the meantime prove itself superior to the former colonial policy from the standpoint of both the colonizing country and the colonized.

Dr. Kastl has well said that:

if the present mandate system remains what it is considered by a very large number of people to be, namely, a way to camouflage and conceal the confiscation of certain provinces and colonies from their former owners, and if the undeniable desire of certain Mandatory Powers to annex or at least to prepare the annexation of the territories entrusted to them persists, the mandate system will certainly lead to failure and world solidarity will suffer a grievous blow.[32]

Benjamin Gerig, who has considerable knowledge of the mandates problem, has recently proposed the following measures, which, in his judgment, should be the minimum international organization required for the efficient government of the so-called backward areas:

1. The Permanent Mandates Commission should be continued, with power to make inquiries on the spot. The native communities should be enabled to send petitions to the Commission more easily than has been the rule. And the mandatory power should be required to utilize administrative officials "drawn in part from among nationals of States other than the mandatory power."

2. Other colonial territories, especially those held by Britain, France, Belgium, and Portugal in Central Africa, should be added to the mandate system.

3. An International Colonial Commission should be created "with powers to exercise direct administration in certain specified territories, the class B mandates to begin with and others added later." The Commission would govern the colonies, raise international loans, appoint administrators from other states, provide for the welfare of the communities, supervise private or public funds already invested there, and guarantee equal economic opportunities to all countries, subject only to the welfare of the native people. It should also be empowered to adjust boundaries to "eliminate all . . . . barriers to the natural tribal organizations now existing."

4. An international development fund should be created to be administered jointly by the Permanent Mandates Commission and an international bank. This fund, Gerig believes, might help to

---

[32] L. Kastl, "Colonial Administration as an International Trust," in *Problems of Peace, Fifth Series* (Oxford University Press, 1931), p. 166.

ease the change from war activities to peace-time requirements "and to take up the shock which would result when millions of demobilized men seek normal reemployment."

5. "Colonial territories contiguous to metropolitan States such as South-West Africa, and other class C mandates, as for example New Guinea, Samoa, and Nauru, should perhaps be recognized as subject to the special charge of the powers now exercising the mandate. The similarities of regimes and certain economic and social reasons of a special character seem to indicate that these territories could best be developed by recognizing the responsibilities of the present mandatory powers subject, of course, to international supervision and to the possibility of transfer if necessary. The benefits of the international development fund might, of course, accrue also to these territories."

6. Gerig foresees the time when all peoples of noncolonial countries will participate "fully and equitably in the enlightened development of the so-called backward areas of the world." In the meantime, the machinery which is set up should be "on an elastic and flexible basis" because of the growing importance of the problem and the need of proceeding carefully and wisely.[33]

What would be the position of colonies and mandates in the event of a world or a European federation? Professor Jennings suggests that it might not be wise at first to transfer all colonial territories to the federation because of such difficult problems as the nationality of inhabitants, the language of administration, the recruiting of the civil service, the possibility that colonial issues will cause difficulties in federal elections, and that a European federal legislature might be prevented from effectively discussing European questions, by the undue intrusion of colonial problems.

Jennings would therefore prefer a united federal control with power on the part of the federation to disallow laws made by a federated state for a colony. He would strengthen the principles of trusteeship for native races and open the colonies "to the capital and enterprise of all Federal citizens without discrimination in favor of the citizens of the colonial empire."[34] He would have the

[33] Benjamin Gerig, "Colonies in an Eventual World Settlement," Commission of Study and Organization of Peace, Preliminary Report and Monographs, *International Conciliation*, April 1941, pp. 519–25. The passages quoted are all taken from Gerig's article.

[34] W. Ivor Jennings, *A Federation for Western Europe* (Macmillan & Company, Ltd., Cambridge, England, 1940), p. 55.

colonial services open to all federal citizens, and would establish a colonial commission the members of which should hold office for a six-year term. The commission would have the power to recommend to the federation: (1) the disallowance of any measure passed by a member of the federation relative to its colonies, (2) grants for colonial development, and (3) the establishment of a colonial defense force under careful safeguards; and it should fulfill the same function as the Mandates Commission now does in examining annual colonial reports; "this alone is a function of considerable importance because it would compel the colonial power to disclose information and justify its administration."[35]

Once again we see that the future of native peoples depends upon the soundness of the wider international organization. On the fundamental reconstruction of the world after this war will rest the fate of dependent peoples.

[35] W. Ivor Jennings, *op. cit.,* pp. 61–62.

Chapter XII

INTELLECTUAL AND RELIGIOUS CO-OPERATION

INTELLECTUAL and spiritual advance has been largely the achievement of individuals, groups, of societies and peoples who in their search for scientific, artistic, and philosophic truths have been only incidentally members of a political community. Furthermore it is important to remember that all peoples of the human race have contributed to mankind's cultural heritage.[1]

Can the world forget its debt to the poems of Homer, the dramas of Sophocles, Aeschylus, and Euripides, the philosophic wisdom of Socrates, Plato, and Aristotle, the religious genius of Buddha and Jesus, and the medicine, mathematics, and general scientific spirit of the scholars of ancient Greece? Did not the Romans give to the world a long period of order, build remarkable roads, bequeath the gifts of Roman law, the poetry of Horace, the history of Tacitus, and the thought of Epictetus and Marcus Aurelius? During the period of the European Dark Ages the Arabs preserved and developed learning and culture, restored science to life in Alexandria, made discoveries in mathematics, physics, astronomy, and chemistry, were apparently the first people to make and use soap, improved the practice of medicine, provided a stimulus for the first universities of Europe, increased the scope of the science of geography, formed schools of music, built baths, aqueducts, palaces, and embankments, planted orchards and gardens, influenced architecture, and encouraged poetry and philosophy.

In Europe the clergy slowly rescued Europe from the Dark Ages. Missionaries from Italy and from Ireland journeyed to various parts of the Continent in a noble effort to instill the habits of peace, industry, and goodness. The building of churches developed into the building of great cathedrals in the north of Italy

[1] C. Delisle Burns, *A Short History of International Intercourse* (George Allen & Unwin, London, 1924), Preface.

507

and in France. Although these originally were in the Romanesque
style, the French in the thirteenth century introduced the Gothic
pointed arch and made a lasting contribution to architecture. The
expanding influence of the church enabled different people under
its sway to give their separate gifts to human needs. The famous
medieval universities of Bologna, Paris, and Oxford, to name but
three outstanding ones, cut across local divisions. The monasteries
all over Europe and the reformed orders—Benedictines, Cluniacs,
Carthusians, Cistercians, Franciscans, and Dominicans—originated in different countries and labored in all lands. Medieval
cities developed, and from their trade and commerce grew the
beginnings of maritime law. Italian painting and music stimulated
similar cultural arts throughout the rest of Europe.

During the Renaissance the great art of printing took hold of
the Western continent. Carter has shown how it moved westward
from China, and then from Germany and England, to play its
profound part in the following centuries. The Italians, drawing
upon old Greek manuscripts, led the world into a new intellectual
life; in painting, literature, art, sculpture, and architecture, they
placed the world under an eternal debt. And English, French,
German, and Spanish scholars responded to the stimuli, and in
turn gave to humanity their distinctive contributions.

The discovery of the New World by Spanish, Portuguese,
and English explorers opened a new era in the life of Europe.
Soon the gold of the Americas, the tea, coffee, and spices of Asia,
the silks, prints, and designs of China began to make their way
into the West. Lest it be thought that this survey is merely
Europacentric, one should hasten to add that the artistic and cultural triumphs of China and the religious and intellectual contributions of India and the Middle East must be included in their own
right and not as mere appendices to European culture. These
countries had enjoyed many of the amenities of refined culture
long before Europe began its discovery of civilized values. In the
succeeding centuries the West brought many new things to the
Orient, but the Orient was also to modify the life of the West.[2]

In the seventeenth century, the so-called Age of Enlighten-
ment witnessed the growth of the great academies and scientific
societies in many lands. The eighteenth-century developments in
political theory, in scientific investigation, and in literature were
European in scope; the great names which fill the pages of history
belong to every country.

[2] A. Reichwein, *China and Europe* (A. Knopf, New York, 1925).

Is there any need to do more than point to the obvious fact that since the industrial revolution the thousands of inventions in every walk of human life have been due to learned men and women from every country and every nation of the world? The mere catalogue of famous individuals in science alone would suffice to fill pages. In the light of these facts, surely it is superfluous again to stress the point that compared with the contributions of "nations," the peaceful arts have been overwhelmingly indebted to individual, group, and supranational forces.

The history of civilization "is a history of peace, because peace is the name for the common cause of all this growth, namely the transfer of ideas from one race to another. The flower of civilization grows in one locality or another; but it is fertilized by those who travel in body or mind. The history of peace is not, indeed, the whole of human history. Wars and revolutions are important and have sometimes promoted liberty or secured order."[3] But the history of the arts and the sciences and of commerce cannot "be explained by a history which deals mainly with war and opposition between peoples." And at the conclusion of his volume Delisle Burns writes: "Civilized life is not and never has been a private possession or the achievement of one nation. Intercourse between nations is essential to it; for if one nation conquered all others and destroyed them utterly, in one generation the conquerors would sink back into barbarism."[4]

The universities for many hundreds of years have embodied this tradition, that learning knows no frontiers and that truth is independent of boundaries; they grew up when central and western Europe enjoyed a unity of civilization based upon Greek thought, Latin literature, Roman law, the Latin tongue, and the Christian faith. In the sixteenth century the growth of national languages, the decline of Latin, the appearance of the modern state system, and the disruptive effects of the Reformation dealt heavy blows to the unity of Western life. During the next few centuries national cultures tended to displace the common European outlook; their laws and educational systems, and the religious divisions, bore witness to the centrifugal tendencies at work. By the eighteenth century, however, the pendulum began to swing somewhat slowly toward a European cultural unity, and this phenomenon was due largely to the growth of toleration and the decline of religious persecutions: men could travel more freely on the Continent.

---

[3] Delisle Burns, *op. cit.*, p. 8.   [4] *Ibid.*, p. 153.

Mowat writes that during this century "the universities were recognized as centers of a knowledge which was common to all, and of methods of instruction which were universally familiar." They assisted scholars to retain a broad cultural outlook, and linked the various countries in a fine fellowship of learning. And he draws attention to Oliver Goldsmith's *The Present State of Polite Learning in Europe,* published in 1759, wherein the famous writer speaks of a "Commonwealth of literature" which had existed in Europe since the days of Virgil and Horace, and of a European culture which still drew its inspiration from the classics. As Mowat puts it, "for the purposes of learning, Europe was a unit; a student could choose any university he liked,"[5] and a cosmopolitanism of outlook marked the educated classes of the time. Hayes has shown how even the national patriots of the century—men like Rousseau in France, Herder in Germany, and Bolingbroke in England—thought of their nations as harmonious parts of a great cultural internationalism wherein each people would contribute its own special genius to the totality of civilization to be enjoyed by all. Diversity of cultures, yes; but also a unity embracing those diversities.[6] And yet to many scholars of that time the idea of the nation or state appeared too narrow and limiting for the free spirit of man who not merely inhabited a particular country but dwelt in the realm of thought which knows no bounds. Man is a part of the universe, and must be permitted to follow truth unhampered by the petty restrictions of political states. Schiller wrote to Körner in 1789:

Es ist ein armseliges Ideal, für ein Nation zu schreiben: einem philosophischen Geiste ist diese Grenze durchaus unerträglich. Dieser kann bei einer so wandelbaren, zufälligen und willkürlichen Form der Menschheit, bei einem Fragmente (und was ist die wichtigste Nation anders?) nicht stillstehen.

And he proposed to be a citizen of the world "who serves no prince. I lost my Fatherland, to exchange it for the great world." To Lessing, the ideal of humanity seemed so much finer than that of one's country that the latter appeared "at best but an heroic vice." "To be praised as a zealous patriot is the last thing I desire—a patriot, that is, who would teach one to forget that

    [5] R. B. Mowat, *England in the Eighteenth Century* (R. M. McBride, New York), pp. 14, 15.
    [6] C. J. H. Hayes, *The Historical Evolution of Modern Nationalism* (New York, 1931).

I must be a citizen of the world." And Goethe could say, "If we find a place where we can rest with our belongings, a field to support us, a house to shelter us, have we not a Fatherland?"

During the nineteenth century the centrifugal forces of Europe gathered strength. Not that the universities and the aristocracy lost a great deal of their cosmopolitan outlook, but rather that the spread of nationalism into the middle classes and later among the workers paved the way for national systems of education. No longer were the great majority of children permitted to go to private schools or remain illiterate. They were made to attend national schools in order to learn to read and write and to absorb the national versions of history; and they acquired a greater sense of prejudice against foreigners or a heightened sense of national importance than a consciousness of being part of a supranational system of culture or faith. Newspapers tended to heighten the daily interest of millions of people in local or national affairs, and propaganda even in the nineteenth century started on its ominous career which was to realize fuller possibilities during and after the World War of 1914–1918. Thus the university traditions of the past, and the declining respect for the intellectual on the part of a business-minded age, resulted in a growth of serious intellectual "gaps" between nations.

Even before 1914 a number of agencies were formed with the object of bridging some of these gaps and of strengthening the bonds among scholars of different countries. The Consular Academy of Vienna, founded in 1754, as the Oriental Academy for giving special training in Oriental languages and history, was reorganized in 1898 for more specifically Austro-Hungarian consular preparation. The American Society of International Law, established in 1906, had as its object to "foster the study of international law and promote the establishment of international relations on the basis of law and justice." Over thirty years earlier, in 1873, a group of scholars had founded the Institute of International Law at Ghent, and another group established the International Law Association at Brussels in the same year. In 1889 began the important International Parliamentary Union, which held regular conferences of members of Parliament, worked steadily for international arbitration, made important studies, and published the inter-Parliamentary bulletin every two months at the headquarters of the bureau in Geneva. Of the other prewar agencies the most notable was the Carnegie Endowment for International Peace established by Mr. Andrew Carnegie in 1910. In the course of thirty years it has done striking work, to which further reference will be made presently.

At the conclusion of the war in 1918 men turned to the building of a political organization which would minimize, if not eliminate, the danger of war. Out of the discussions and differences came the Covenant of the League of Nations, which represented the first world attempt to bring political and economic forces within a system designed to promote world co-operation rather than world rivalry. However, a world which is closely knit by economic and scientific forces but is divided by mental barriers stands in a precarious position. Intimate political and economic relations unaccompanied by a corresponding development in intellectual relations will soon break down. Without a League of minds, a League of political nations cannot long endure. This truth was appreciated by M. Hymans of Belgium, who proposed that the League Covenant include a clause providing for intellectual co-operation. He was unsuccessful, but the first Assembly of the League considered the matter and passed a resolution. The Council thereupon proposed the appointment of a committee, whose activities were defined by the second Assembly to include questions of intellectual co-operation (but not of education, be it noted, since the latter field was deemed to be within the province of the sovereign state).

The problems which confronted the newly constituted Intellectual Committee were extremely numerous and complex. In the nineteenth century scholars had been generally drawn from the middle and upper classes; they lived relatively detached lives, and experienced little fear of unemployment. Only a small number of people went to the universities and engaged in the professions. By 1920 the situation had radically changed. The intellectual class had been called by governments to assist in the application of scientific knowledge to social, industrial, and military affairs. No longer were biologists, chemists, economists, geographers, and bacteriologists able to work in comparative isolation; nor were university and high-school teachers of social sciences permitted to enjoy a cloistered detachment from the influences of everyday life. Instead, all were subjected to the propagandas and pressures of political forces, popular prejudices, and state interference and domination. Finally, the fear of unemployment, intensified by the dislocation of war and economic crises, now confronted the intellectual as well as the manual classes.

In facing these urgent questions, the Committee had little

support, either moral or financial. Indeed, it was difficult for the League to obtain enough funds to pay even a small staff; and, in 1924, the situation was extremely discouraging. The French government then offered to the League the services of an institute in Paris and an annual income to enable the Committee to carry on its work. In one respect the offer was timely, for without it the work on intellectual co-operation would have been seriously delayed. On the other hand, many League officials felt that to accept the French offer would constitute a dangerous precedent: other governments might offer headquarters in their capital cities for League activities, and thereby gain undue influence over organizations supposed to be international in character. In 1928 the League agreed to the establishment of an International Institute for the unification or assimilation and co-ordination of private law, to be under the direction of the League and with headquarters at Rome.

ORGANIZATION FOR INTELLECTUAL CO-OPERATION

As then established, the organization for intellectual co-operation comprised (1) the Intellectual Committee, which was the advisory organ to the Council and Assembly, consisting of nineteen members appointed by the Council. In 1930 the Committee established an executive committee to supervise developments between sessions. (2) Committees of experts for special purposes. Fourteen permanent committees have dealt with arts and letters, principles and facts of intellectual co-operation, science, architecture, international museums, institutes of archaeology and of the history of art, higher education, libraries, archives, the publication of a Japanese collection, the publication of an Ibero-American collection, intellectual rights, historical monuments, and folk arts. In addition to the permanent committees there were committees which were established for special purposes and which disbanded when they had accomplished them.

The organization had two main executive bodies: (1) The Intellectual Co-operation Section, which was the administrative secretariat of the international committee; this body had to do with the League Council and the Assembly, and was the channel for official communications with governments and certain other international organizations. (2) The International Institute of Intellectual Co-operation at Paris, which was the executive organ of the committee. It arranged the meetings of expert committees, provided for inquiries, and published results. In addition there were forty-five national committees in countries in every continent of the world, whose function it was to serve as a connecting link between the international organization and the educational and intellectual groups within the member states.

In 1938 fifty states sent delegates to a General Conference of National Committees in order to adopt an international act concerning intellectual co-operation. It was designed to improve the original statute and to strengthen the organization of the national committees themselves.

The methods and subjects embraced under the heading of intellectual co-operation are so numerous that only the most general summary can be made here. One important fact should be kept in mind: The aim of all human and especially of intellectual activity should be directed to life's *summum bonum*. Knowledge has become so specialized and scientific research so technical that no one person, institution, or nation can dispense with the findings of other individuals and other national institutions. Truth knows no national boundaries, and the infinite possibilities open to human creativeness within the limits of mortal life demand that national boundaries be minimized as far as possible, and that the utmost be done to co-ordinate the efforts of educators, artists, writers, scientists, and inventors in all fields of scholarly endeavor.

First we find that there have been great movements for the scientific study of international relations. Only by a widespread accurate knowledge of the political, economic, and social bases of international affairs can passion and prejudice be overcome. Accurate knowledge is a necessary bulwark against irrational emotion. Many national institutes and centers for the study of foreign policy have been set up in different countries—the Council on Foreign Relations in the United States, the Royal Institute of International Affairs in Great Britain and the Dominions, Institutes at Milan and Madrid, a study center in Paris, and the Institute of Pacific Relations with branches in the countries bordering upon and directly interested in the Pacific. Sometimes these institutes are assisted by the Rockefeller Foundation, the Carnegie Endowment, and other bodies. They are gradually but surely developing new methods of international co-operation.[7]

These include international studies conferences, which meet about every two years and are attended by experts from different countries after a period of preparatory study upon a carefully

[7] See also p. 527, below.

prepared agenda. Thus far the studies conferences have considered such subjects as the state and economic life, collective security, and peaceful change,[8] the papers and studies which have been published are valuable contributions to these problems, while the several conferences of the Institute of Pacific Relations in the last fifteen years have dealt with practically every important phase of the affairs of the Pacific world. Also limited meetings and personal visits are arranged among members of the studies conferences.

Something more than conferences is required if the maximum result is to be obtained from widespread study. Hence the League Committee has sponsored the preparation of directories of research and institutions which teach international affairs. From a comparison of methods followed in different countries, teachers are enabled to improve their own knowledge and methods.

One of the most interesting developments has been the arrangement of a series of "conversations." Each year the Committee invites some outstanding scholars to meet and discuss an important cultural question. Twenty, or perhaps thirty, world figures are enabled to overcome the obstacles of distance and for a few days engage in stimulating and provocative exchange of ideas. The conversations thus far held include discussions of Goethe on the occasion of the one hundredth anniversary of his death, the future of European culture, art and reality, the relation of art to the state, the development of modern man, toward a new humanism, the present relation between Latin-American and European culture, the future destiny of letters, and "quality and life."[9]

At first sight these conversations may appear to have little bearing on the question of international relations, but no one who has read any of the published volumes can fail to appreciate the value of having great minds brought together in a process of mutual inspiration. They help to lift the problem of international affairs above the merely political, and assist one in realizing the limitations of politics in the development of human culture.

Sometimes it has been impossible to bring scholars together; in that case the Committee arranges for two or more eminent men of letters to write to each other in an exchange of views. Thus far

[8] The International Studies Conference which met at Bergen in September 1939 had to be abandoned a few days after the opening on account of the war which had broken out between Poland and Germany.

[9] The series was designated *Entretiens* and is published by the Institute of Intellectual Co-operation.

published volumes of these include: *A League of Minds, Why War?, Culture, Ethics, and War,* and *East and West.*

Co-operation is highly desirable in the exact and natural sciences as well as in the social sciences. In 1925 a proposal was made to draw up an agreement between the Council of Scientific Unions and the International Organization for Intellectual Co-operation in order to avoid unnecessary duplication of work. After twelve years the agreement was signed, and since 1937 the executive committees of the two bodies have met to consider the best method of organizing scientific research. Plans are under way for the study of phytohormones and for the publication of old scientific works in the form of facsimiles of very rare manuscripts or reprints of fundamental classical works in the development of science. A study committee for the determination of molecular atomic weights of gases has been set up, and it is proposed to join with the International Council of Scientific Unions and the International Union of Physics and Chemistry in the study of such problems as new vitamins, nomenclature of genetics, new theories in modern physics, etc. It is desirable also to make readily available reports on the progress made in each branch of science and to prepare scientific bibliographies.

The committee has arranged conversations in the field of science. The first meeting was held at Warsaw, May 30 to June 4, 1938. Outstanding scientists contributed to the discussion of "The New Theories of Modern Physics." The Committee has also organized study meetings to consider "The Fundamental Principles and Methods of the Mathematical Sciences," "Magnetism," "The Philosophical Consequences of New Theories in Physics," and "Two Specialized Problems in Biology."

It is important to preserve for succeeding generations the outstanding achievements in human history. Many priceless works of art and science have perished through neglect, ignorance, and lack of organization. Hence the importance of the Draft International Convention on the Protection of National Artistic and Historical Possessions which is being prepared by the executive committee. The International Museums Office and the Committee on Intellectual Co-operation have also drawn up a convention for the protection of monuments and works of art in time of war, a question of profound importance to the world in view of the great destructiveness of modern warfare.

In March 1937 an international conference on excavations was held at Cairo, succeeding other conferences which had been held at Rome, Athens, and Madrid. The experts there considered the technique of excavations and field research, and problems of a legal character which were involved, and drew up an international charter concerning antiquities and excavations. The charter was considered by the League Assembly in September 1937 and communicated to the respective governments. In this field, which is revealing to the world the hitherto hidden evidences of human culture in other ages and is deeply influencing our ideas of history, we find the great scholars of many nations joining their efforts in an attempt to widen the horizons of the human mind.[10]

A beginning has been made on the collection of ethnographical and historical works on the origins of American civilization and on the publication of outstanding literary and artistic Japanese works. Since 1932 the Institute has published an international bibliography of translations. This publication enables scholars to gain more adequate knowledge of foreign works. An international committee for folk arts has been conducting research into the documents of folk art "in order to establish scientifically the popular sources of esthetic and affective expression, and to inform nations concerning their distinct or common origins." Studies include documentary sources, popular music and songs, the symbol in folklore and folk art, and means of using gramophone and cinema to record "traditional techniques still in use by artisans today." The department of arts, archeology, and ethnology of the Institute is engaging in many technical tasks which lie beyond the province of the amateur, who must be referred to the official publications for further details. The International Committee for Folk Arts has organized several congresses—in Prague, Brussels, Liege, and Antwerp.

It is important to preserve the results of human discoveries, and therefore libraries, archives, and museums are of the highest importance to mankind. In 1931 a committee of scientific advisers drew up a plan for the co-ordination of work among science museums. Under the direction of an International Museums Office, established in 1926, conferences of experts have been arranged on specialized subjects; they have considered questions involved in international exhibits, the preservation of historic buildings, and the principles of construction and equipment of museums. The International Museums Office publishes a quarterly magazine and

[10] The International Museums Office has published extensive and attractive volumes on the *Conservation of Monuments* and *Museographie* (1934), of great value for specialists working in these fields.

monthly supplements which review the administrative and technical studies connected with museums and the preservation of ancient monuments, together with a survey of current activities of museums in all countries.[11]

In 1937, the International Congress of Architects passed a recommendation aiming to raise the intellectual and professional standard of architects. In the International Centre for the Study of Architectural and Town-planning Questions, a subdivision of the International Committee on Intellectual Co-operation drew up a report dealing with international aspects of architecture and town planning.

As learning becomes more specialized it is impossible for city, state, and even national libraries to carry more than a small proportion of the books which appear. Nor can they afford to purchase more than a limited number of documents which form the basis of much historical and scientific research. Not only for these reasons is it important to effect a great measure of international co-operation but also because the purely technical questions involved in an efficient library system require an improvement of library methods and facilities equal to those of the most advanced countries. In 1929 there was formed an International Federation of Library Associations, which has dealt with such questions as the professional training of librarians, facsimiles of manuscripts, the principles of planning and constructing libraries, the relation of central libraries to branches, the use of slides and films in reproducing old documents, and many other matters.[12] Important questions have arisen over archives, and the Committee of Archives Experts has supervised the compilation of an international guide to archives, some volumes of which have already appeared. The exchange of lecturers on the technique and science of archives has been arranged, and technical problems have been considered.[13]

The more immediate and popularly appreciated tasks of intel-

[11] See, for example, *Les Dossiers de L'Office International des Musées*. No. 1 contains the Conclusions of the Conference on the Conservation of Artistic and Historical Monuments (held at Athens, 1931). No. 2 contains the documents relating to the Conservation of Paintings and the general conclusions of the Rome Conference of 1930.

[12] Société des Nations, *Mission Social et Intellectuelle des Bibliothèques Populaires* (Institut International de Coopération Intellectuelle, Paris, 1937); see also the Institute's *Rôle et Formation du Bibliothécaire* (1935).

[13] The League of Nations Library publishes a monthly list of selected articles on all phases of League work. Abstracts of about 1,200 periodicals are made, and are extremely useful for scholars working in the fields of politics, economics, social welfare, education, etc.

lectual co-operation refer to international collaboration among universities, schools, and higher institutions of learning. The Committee has assisted in promoting more than forty centers of educational information and documentation in different countries, and has set up a committee of directors of higher education comprising representatives from Great Britain, France, Italy, Hungary, Switzerland, and the United States. National committees on intellectual co-operation have been formed and have been active. Representatives of these committees met in a general conference at Paris in July 1937, and the American Committee held a conference in Santiago in January 1939. The Baltic and Northern National Committees have also held regional conferences. These committees have encouraged universities to re-examine the fundamental principles of higher education, the relations between the state and universities, how far academic freedom and administrative autonomy are desirable, the problem of budgets and other such questions; also the internal organization of institutions of higher education, including the relations between the boards of trustees, the president, the faculty, conditions of appointment of professors, etc.; examinations, degrees, and tuition fees, including the relative value of the university degrees of one country compared with those of another; scholarships and student welfare organizations, including reduction of tuition fees for needy students, organization of loans, and the establishment of houses, hostels, restaurants, clubs, and sanitoria for students. The League Committee has attempted to find the most efficient ways of enabling the major research institutions in different countries to co-operate in scientific, industrial, and social science research. It has worked for the co-ordination of national university statistics so as to obtain a clearer picture of national university life and also to serve as a basis for international comparison. It has undertaken inquiries into the organization of biological studies and the teaching of modern languages. Efforts have been made to have international collections of textbooks used in schools, and to organize permanent and temporary exhibitions of gramophone records for teaching foreign languages, and to make lantern slides and educational films. It has arranged conferences of educators who specialize on educational aims and methods. The British national center arranged for English teachers of modern languages to teach a year abroad as auxiliary professors.[14]

[14] See Société des Nations, *L'Organisation de L'Enseignement Supérieur* (Institut International de Coopération Intellectuelle, Paris, 1938).

In 1926 the Committee of International Student Organizations was set up, and in 1936 reviewed the results of ten years of co-operation among such student organizations as the International Confederation of Students, the International Students Service (at first organized for student relief and later for promoting self-help in university circles), the International Federation of University Women, the World Student Christian Federation, the International University League of Nations Federation, the Pax Romana (an organization to promote religious, social, and corporate activity of Catholic students in all countries), the World Union of Jewish Students, and others. In the recent past, hundreds of students have gone to Europe each year to take holiday courses. In 1936, there were given 154 such advanced courses for foreigners in nineteen countries. From 1933 to 1939, a semiannual bulletin, *Students Abroad,* published information on all that concerns international travel of students.

One of the greatest obstacles to world peace is the existence of national histories which, by distorting or at least overemphasizing or underemphasizing incidents and policies, perpetuate and intensify international prejudice and misunderstanding. For several years national groups have worked toward eliminating objectionable phases and biased historical judgments, particularly as they deal with responsibility for wars and seizures of territory.[15] In 1934 the Institute was asked to undertake an examination of history textbooks used in certain countries. Several national committees investigated a large number of volumes and brought together valuable information. In 1935, several French and German professors made forty recommendations "concerning certain controversial questions in the history of France and Germany, with a view to indicating the general lines to be followed by the authors of textbooks in the two countries." The resolutions were adopted and later published. The Pan American Peace Conference in December 1936 adopted resolutions concerning the revision of school textbooks and civic instruction. A number of governments voluntarily made corrections, and a great step forward was taken with the Declaration on the Revision of School Textbooks which was submitted to the 1937 Assembly for approval. It came into force November 1937, when it was signed by Belgium and the Dominican Republic. Perhaps the greatest advance in this connection has been made in the Scandinavian countries as a result

[15] See Société des Nations, *La Révision des Manuels Scolaires* (Institut International de Coopération Intellectuelle, Paris, 1932).

of the work of the Committee for the Teaching of History of the Norden Association.

Broadcasting has become an important instrument in primary and secondary education and in the controlling of public opinion. The future of the world depends in large measure upon the wise control of so powerful a force. The League Committee set up a body of experts to study the whole question of the possibility of promoting better understanding by means of international broadcasts devoted to programs describing the civilization, attitudes, and policies of foreign countries.[16] In 1936 the League convened an intergovernmental conference to draw up a convention on the use of broadcasting in the cause of peace. Twenty-eight states signed the Convention, which had two ends in view: (1) to prevent deterioration of good relations by "misleading or simply inconsiderate broadcasts" and (2) to encourage programs which would increase understanding. The Convention provided that broadcasts which might incite the people of a country to violence shall be prohibited, and the signatories agreed to stop any such transmission. They undertook to intervene when obviously false statements were broadcast. Each signatory promised to furnish other states on request with program items designed to provide a better knowledge of the civilization and conditions of life in its own country. In case of dispute, the Convention permitted appeal to arbitration or judicial award or to the good offices of the Committee on Intellectual Co-operation. According to the annual summary of the Institute the Convention did not impose new obligations on the contracting parties but merely defined their mutual responsibilities in a field where almost daily incidents pointed to the need of regulation.

It is needless to add that the methods pursued by the German and Italian and other governments show that there is considerable room for improvement in this field of effort, and that while broadcasting is regarded as an important instrument of war, its use for genuine cultural appreciation will be seriously impaired.[17]

Within the last few years a large number of agreements on intellectual matters have been signed among governments. A few such accords existed before 1914—among Mexico, Chile, and

[16] League of Nations, *Broadcasting and Peace* (International Institute of Intellectual Co-operation, Paris, 1933).

[17] See Harold N. Graves, Jr., *War on the Short Wave* (Foreign Policy Association, New York, 1941). For a discussion of the cinema, see J. E. Harley, *World-Wide Influences of the Cinema* (University of Southern California Press, 1940).

Peru (1831), Costa Rica and Honduras (1895), both concerning the exercise of liberal professions and the equivalence of studies and examinations; also the Franco-Swiss convention of 1887, and the 1912 Franco-Italian agreement regulating the exchange of professors of modern languages. After 1918 the need for intellectual agreements grew as new problems arose and new tendencies appeared. After 1926, intergovernment intellectual accords became more numerous.[18] They may be divided into three types: those which concern practically all intellectual questions relative to the two contracting parties, those which refer primarily to questions of teaching in universities and schools, and those which deal with other matters such as the creation of scientific institutes and artistic exhibits. The agreements provide for the exchange of information, the exchange of teachers engaged in higher education, creation of chairs for foreign professors, instruction in foreign languages (illustrated by agreements between Italy and Austria, Bulgaria and Czechoslovakia), radio and cinema programs dealing with the history and culture of the other country, gatherings of artists and musicians from the country of the other signatory power, student exchange and encouragement of student travel abroad, vacation courses, the revision of textbooks of history and geography, the exchange of official publications, etc. Some agreements contain certain of the provisions here outlined; other conventions contain other items; but they all were ostensibly designed to improve intellectual relations, which become increasingly important in an age of political uncertainty. Unfortunately, some academic exchanges were designed to serve political ends and, as appears elsewhere, this form of "co-operation" is becoming increasingly menacing.

The movement for international intellectual co-operation has made headway on the American continent also, and Pan-American conferences have devoted much attention to the question.

In 1933, at the seventh international conference of American states held at Montevideo, the governments initiated a Pan-American convention relating to the teaching of history. The matter had been considered at previous nonofficial conferences, notably at Lima (1924), Montevideo (1928), Buenos Aires

[18] In Europe, Germany–Hungary, Germany–Italy, Austria–France, Austria–Hungary, Austria–Italy, Belgium–France, Belgium–Holland, Belgium–Poland, Bulgaria–Poland, Denmark–France, Spain–Great Britain, France–Italy, and several others; see Société des Nations, *Recueil des Accords Intellectuels* (Institut International de Coopération Intellectuelle, Paris, 1938).

(1929), Bogotá (1930), and Rio de Janeiro and Montevideo (1931). At the international conference held at Buenos Aires (1936), the representatives adopted a convention for the encouragement of inter-American cultural relations. It provided that every year each government would grant two scholarships to students from each of the other countries for the following academic year, a provision based upon agreements concluded between Argentina and Chile (1935), Argentina and Peru (1935), and Chile and Peru (1936).

At the Lima Conference in 1938 the twenty-one republics recommended the following measures for the purpose of promoting intellectual co-operation: (1) The governments which had not ratified the 1936 Convention for the promotion of inter-American cultural relations should do so, and make provision for the interchange of graduate students and professors. (2) The Pan-American Union should study the possibility of establishing a center for the exchange of works of American composers. (3) National committees of intellectual co-operation should promote a close association of American writers and artists. (4) American governments should assume their obligation to send to the Columbus Memorial Library of the Pan-American Union a copy of all works published in their respective countries, and should promote greater interlibrary co-operation in order to facilitate loans of books, documents, and other materials. (5) Signatories should encourage the teaching of democratic principles in their respective countries. (6) School texts should be revised and the study of pacifism, "with special reference to the progress of International Law, the ideas of the great thinkers on universal solidarity, the experiences of the past in intellectual co-operation, the creation of institutions which tend to strengthen the bonds which unite all peoples, and to agreements outlawing war," should be encouraged. (7) Mutual recognition of degrees from institutions of higher learning should be given. (8) As far as possible, school curricula should include Spanish, Portuguese, English, and French languages. (9) Vacation courses in the languages, literature, history, and social sciences for foreign teachers and students should be established. (10) Co-operation in scientific, technical, and social welfare research should be encouraged. (11) An institute of co-ordination of geographic sciences, to be called the Inter-American Geographic Institute, should be set up in Buenos Aires. (12) The governments should give moral support to the ethnographic and historic collection dealing with the origin of American civilization, a work to be published by the University of Buenos Aires. (13) Radio broadcasting should be used to promote closer continental bonds of culture by means of lectures, artistic programs, and courses in teaching.

The executive committee of the Institute of Intellectual Co-operation has spent much time in the study of unemployment among intellectuals. With the support of the International Labor Office, which has had great experience in dealing with unemployment problems, it has undertaken inquiries as to measures adopted in different countries to provide work for the intellectual class. The steps taken in France, especially in the United States (which has provided work for over 72,000 unemployed teachers, artists, and writers), also in Germany, Poland, Switzerland, and other states have been described in reports which are now available for study. Centers of university and professional information have been established to publicize each national situation, and inquiries are being conducted into the possibility of finding work for intellectuals in overseas countries.

Intellectual co-operation has extended also to the field of rural life. The Institute of Intellectual Co-operation sent to the Health Section of the League a number of questions to be considered at a projected European conference on rural life which has been postponed on account of the war. Considerable anxiety has been felt at the exodus of farmers and peasants to the city, and authorities realize that rural rehabilitation involves not only economic and medical action but also improvements in primary, secondary, and adult education and encouragements of social life. Consequently experts have experimented in the use of radio for rural schools and adult groups. Already thirty-two countries have special rural broadcasting programs. The use of the cinema and of libraries is important.[19] Rural museums might form the center of a general institution devoted to rural meetings, lectures, films, and entertainments of various kinds.[20]

In 1931 the Institute of Intellectual Co-operation published *Art populaire,* comprising the papers and exhibits presented at the First International Congress of Popular Arts (held at Prague in 1928). It is impossible here even to summarize the list of contents. Suffice it to point out that 42 experts gave papers dealing with the popular arts of their respective countries, and

[19] See League of Nations, *International Institute of Intellectual Co-operation* (Paris, 1938), p. 77.

[20] *Ibid.,* pp. 78–79.

that over one hundred and twenty papers on architecture, world sculpture and designs, metals, ceramics, textiles (including costume design and tapestry), music, the dance, and the theater were given. The volumes breathe a civilizing atmosphere in strange contrast to the war which was to follow.

At Prague in 1928 the Congress urged that steps be taken to prevent the disappearance of popular songs and melodies in all countries. At the Second International Congress of Popular Arts it was decided to establish a Bureau to draw up lists of archives, museums, etc. The study of comparative folk music demands the services of experts who by means of the film, the disk, or the Edison records can preserve some of the most beautiful efforts of peoples to make life happier.[21]

Private agencies have done even more than governments and the League to develop the idea and machinery of intellectual co-operation. J. Eugene Harley in 1931 brought together a great amount of information on this question, and the following paragraphs are based upon his volume.[22] International houses for the purpose of permitting students from many lands to live under the same roof or in adjacent buildings were founded in New York in 1923 and later in the University of California at Berkeley and at the University of Chicago; in Paris, the University City was commenced in 1925, designed to accommodate over a dozen different national groups; the International Quaker Student Hostel was opened at Geneva to provide accommodation for the growing number of students attending Geneva for educational purposes.

Many universities and other institutions of higher learning promoted summer or vacation schools and institutes. Chief of these were the University of Chicago's Norman Wait Harris Memorial Foundation, which has held institutes since 1924 and has published a number of important volumes. The Institute of Politics, begun at Williamstown in 1921 and lasting till 1932, was a gathering for one month every year at which outstanding authorities appeared to lead round tables and deliver public lectures. The Institute of International Relations at Riverside, California, began its annual weekly sessions in 1926 and is still active. The Geneva School of International Studies, established in 1924 under the direction of Professor (now Sir) Alfred Zimmern, gave spe-

[21] Société des Nations, *Musique et Chanson Populaires* (Institut International de Coopération Intellectuelle, Paris, 1934).

[22] John Eugene Harley, *International Understanding, Agencies Educating for a New World* (Stanford University Press, 1931).

cial fortnightly courses and offered scholarships. The Geneva Institute of International Relations was established in the same year to devote intensive discussion to current international problems during one week in every August. The Institute of Pacific Relations, which developed out of the initiative of the Y.M.C.A., held its first conference at Honolulu in 1925. It was attended by men and women from the Pacific Basin countries, and was a forerunner of several biennial conferences and a wide range of research projects and publications too extensive to be described here. The Academy of International Law began in 1923 at The Hague with the support of the Carnegie Endowment, and promoted the higher studies of international law and cognate sciences.

What Harley calls special institutes or associations of a permanent nature developed rapidly after the World War of 1914–1918. Chief of these, with their founding dates, were the Foreign Policy Association (New York, 1918), the Council on Foreign Relations (New York, 1921), the Chicago Council on Foreign Relations (Chicago, 1922), the American University Union at Paris, London, and Rome, the National Student Federation of America (1926), which became a member of the International Confederation of Students, the National Federation of Business and Professional Women's Clubs (St. Louis, 1919), and the American Association of University Women, which is part of the International Federation of University Women.

Other postwar international agencies include the Students' International Union organized at Geneva in 1924; and the International Confederation of Students founded at Strassburg in November 1919, with a central office at Brussels, which publishes an annual yearbook, a monthly bulletin of information, and other material. In 1921 the Catholic Students formed the International Secretariat of Catholic Students' Unions; and the World Students' Christian Federation, which was established in 1895, continued to carry on a great amount of work in many branches of student life. The World Federation of Educational Associations was formed in San Francisco in 1923, has held biennial conferences in various cities of the world, and has attempted to carry forward the ideal of peace through education. In 1925 the International Bureau of Education was founded at Geneva and has carried on a similar program of distributing information and carrying out scientific research and forming international conferences.

The Royal Institute of International Affairs, which held its inaugural meeting in July 1920, aims to advance the study of international politics, economics, and jurisprudence; it has done a splendid work in publishing the *Annual Survey of International Affairs* as well as several authoritative studies on special subjects. It has co-operated with other institutes such as the Institute of Pacific Relations and the Council on Foreign Relations in New York, has built up an extensive library, and issues every two months a report on foreign affairs and a journal, *International Affairs*. Affiliated institutes have been established in Australia, New Zealand, and Canada.

Finally, brief mention should be made of the major endowments and foundations. The Carnegie Endowment for International Peace has continued its wide range of activities. Its Division of Intercourse and Education has published a valuable but inexpensive series of studies under the title *International Conciliation*. It has established international relations clubs in many colleges and universities in the United States and abroad. It has sponsored travels by professors of international relations and editors of newspapers. Its Division of International Law has taken an active part in the movement for the codification of international law, has published several volumes of the important classics of international law, has granted fellowships for the study of international law, and has assisted in conferences dealing with international law. Its Division of Economics and History, under the directorship of Dr. James T. Shotwell, undertook the 150-volume economic and social history of the World War of 1914–1918 and is engaged in other studies. In 1912 the Endowment established its European Center, which carried on until interrupted by war in 1939.

The World Peace Foundation was established before 1914 but has done its greatest work since 1917. It maintains a library and a research staff, until recently has been a distributing center of official and semiofficial documents, and has published much valuable material in its pamphlet series. We have referred in chapter i to the health work of the Rockefeller Foundation. In addition to this service, the Foundation in 1923 established the International Education Board, which has devoted its efforts primarily to awarding several hundred fellowships in the pure sciences, in agricultural research, and in education. The Institute of International Education, which began in February 1919, has engaged in a wide range of activities—promoting personal interviews, arranging itineraries of visiting professors, arranging the study programs of foreign students in the United States, granting fellowships and scholarships, publishing volumes dealing with higher education and international fellowships and scholarships, and maintaining representatives and offices in several countries abroad. The John Simon Guggenheim Memorial Foundation, incorporated in 1925 to "promote the advancement and the fusion of knowledge and understanding, and the appreciation of beauty, by aiding without distinction on account of race, color, or creed scholars, scientists, and artists of either sex in the prosecution of their labors," carries out its purposes by awarding fifty fellowships each year, including in its later programs a number of Latin-American exchange fellowships.[23]

The foregoing list does less than justice to the admirable work carried on by these institutions, but it serves to indicate how indebted modern scholars are to the generosity and vision of their founders and to the ability and devotion of their directors and officials. Although they have not succeeded any better than the other sections of modern civilization in preventing war, they have enriched contemporary life by assembling information, promoting research, putting scholars in contact with one another, and in many other ways promoting the economic, physical, mental, and moral welfare of hundreds of thousands of people all over the world. In terms of welfare there is not a scholar in the field of international relations who has not directly or indirectly benefited from the work of these foundations and institutions.

Unfortunately, the hopes of intellectual co-operation which the establishment of the League and the many private agencies had raised to a high peak of expectancy have been seriously disappointed by reason of two factors: (1) the growing political anarchy of the world; and (2) the official backing on the part of Germany, Italy, the Soviet Union, and other countries of a "revolt against reason." These two factors require some explanation.

Now that war has become all-embracing in its character, making use of economic resources, scientific inventions, popular attitudes, and propaganda instrumentalities, the conditions for intellectual co-operation beyond national boundaries have become, if not impossible, at least most risky and inexpedient. For what scientists can present the results of their research to international gatherings if their discoveries are likely to be translated into strengthening the military power of another government? What welcome can be given to foreign students and professors if there is a suspicion that these men are not primarily seekers of truth but are, like

[23] J. E. Harley, *op. cit.*

Herr Abetz in Paris and many another German scholar abroad, political agents working to undermine the unity of the countries in which they sojourn? Given the modern German theory of war and the planting of cells abroad as the advance agents of a policy of war and conquest, the outlook for international intellectual co-operation is indeed black.

These obstacles operate in a direct manner, and Staley notes that because of the threat of war "certain aspects of geology, geography, chemistry, and other sciences have become dangerous political subjects, which it is not everywhere safe to discuss in frankness with a foreigner."[24] He adds that if the present temper continues very long, it may be necessary to censor scientific periodicals before they can be sent abroad, and that "delegates to international technical congresses will have to be as tight-lipped as diplomats, for fear of revealing national secrets." At a Pacific Congress held some time ago, delegates suspected that the inquiries of one national group concerning resources in the colonies of another were made with military rather than scientific objectives in view.

Some economic nationalists claim that it is desirable to limit the amount of international trade but to encourage the free interchange of ideas among the scholars of various nations. However, as Grebler points out, historically

economic exchange has always blazed the trails for cultural exchange. When commercial exchange dries up, the exchange of products of the intellect, of science, of art, is bound to be reduced.

Organized exchange of students selected according to political principles, and the swamping of foreign countries with propaganda material, are no substitutes for this free and spontaneous use of science and arts that was the pride of bygone days. If goods and finance are homespun, ideas and culture too become homespun.[25]

The importance of international economic investigation is enormous. The Washington navel orange was brought from Brazil in about 1870; and barley, rice, oats, rye, sorghum alfalfa, soya beans, cotton have since been brought from Turkey, Egypt, Formosa, Italy, Sweden, Africa, Peru, Japan, and elsewhere.

In 1928 United States scientists explored for three months in Papua and New Guinea to see if they could find a new variety of sugar which would resist disease in the United States. They

[24] Eugene Staley, *World Economy in Transition*, p. 47.

[25] Leo Grebler, "Self-sufficiency and Imperialism," *Annals of the American Academy of Political and Social Science*, Vol. 198 (1938), p. 7.

shipped home 160 different varieties. In 1898 an American official found a wheat in Russia which would resist rust in the United States, and 4,000,000 acres are now planted with this wheat on the American continent. Two years later, Carleton revisited Russia and found a hard red winter wheat, which is planted in over 2,000,000 acres in the United States. Who can deny that these everyday articles have enriched not merely the material life of the United States but have also given an impetus to further scientific investigation? Staley quotes evidence to show that the development of mathematics and of printing has followed trade. And undoubtedly the influence of the Orient in silks, prints, and the decorative arts would not have taken place without the fertilizing influences of trade.

It is a mistake to think that ideas can be divorced from the achievements of economic life. What limits the freedom of the latter threatens to destroy the creativeness of the former. Human life in its varied aspects is closely interrelated, and what adversely affects one may cripple another. Man cannot be half-slave and half-free—the mind cannot explore untrammeled in the realms of philosophy and science if the scholar is to be regarded primarily as a citizen dedicated to the task of merely making his country militarily strong or secure.

On the other hand, it must be admitted that the challenge of national self-sufficiency, both economic and military, has intensified the scientific search for the most efficient use of raw materials. Without question war and the threat of war have produced inventions which later have made for progress. To this degree, the condemnatory judgment must be modified, but there can be no doubt that the benefits along these lines are more than outweighed by the losses sustained through the limiting of the findings so made to one group and by preventing scholars from as freely stimulating one another as would be possible in a more stable and less politically divided world.

The second outstanding obstacle to contemporary international intellectual co-operation lies in the widespread revolt against reason. During the nineteenth century several thinkers had criticized reason, alleging that it could not supply a dynamic to effective human action, that it could not penetrate to the ultimate mysteries of truth, that abstract generalizations were removed from the pulsating rhythmic reality of things, that static concepts could only act as pointers, that social morality was little more than social "myths," that a thing did not work because it was true but was true because it worked. Nietzsche preached the doctrine of the superman with emphasis upon power and will. Darwin was popularly interpreted as preaching the survival of the fittest in a world of struggle amid a nature red in tooth and claw; Marx urged the revolt of the proletariat and talked of "bourgeois" truth and "bourgeois" system of ethics; Sorel advocated violence instead of reason as an instrument of social change; D. H. Lawrence substituted sex for the pale gray matter of the brain; and in these and other ways scholars concluded that reason had either failed, or that it had proved man's unimportance in the universe. Modern psychology, with its alleged emphasis upon instincts, the subconscious, rationalizing, and behaviorism, helped to produce a spirit of skepticism and in certain quarters a cult of irrationality.

But all these movements were private, and the influence which they exerted was either directly upon relatively small groups or indirectly upon a wider public. When, however, the Fascist and Nazi governments came to power in 1922 and 1933, following the advent of the Bolshevist government to control in 1917, a new situation developed. In these three instances governments liquidated intellectuals and erected into a government policy affecting over two hundred and fifty million people the ideal of conscious indoctrination. Communist truth was proclaimed in the Soviet Union, national truth in Italy, and racial truth in Germany. The evidence is too voluminous to summarize at this point, but it is impossible to deny the truth of the judgment expressed by Hamilton Fish Armstrong when he wrote that, whereas previously educated people did agree on certain terms for describing general things, so that ideas could be exchanged—"Our minds can meet, even in disagreement, because the words we use have meanings accepted in advance"[26]—now a great gulf is being deepened between the dictator countries and the democracies. Armstrong asks, "how are we to talk to people who say familiar words but mean something else? . . . . who say 'art' and mean 'propaganda,' to whom music by Mendelssohn is not music, and poetry by Heine is not poetry . . . ."[26] How can we send our students to German universities when their greatest scientists—Einstein, Franck, Hertz, Meyerhof—have been expelled? He goes on: "Shall we go there for art . . . . shall we go there for historical research," when the German authorities denounce "the false ideal of objectivity" and affirm that "we will never approach history impartially

[26] H. F. Armstrong, *We or They* (The Macmillan Company, New York, 1937), p. 7. Quoted by special permission.

but as Germans"? How reach an understanding with those who assert that law arises out of race and that cancer comes from the conflict of races within the body? "Could Pasteur engage in profitable discussion with a man who says that?" We need give no more examples. The tragic truth is well expressed in the words: "A great gulf indeed is fixed between the two conceptions of life. Nor does there seem a way to bridge it with words, because on the two sides words no longer have any commonly accepted meaning."[27]

The difficulties in the way of intellectual co-operation appear from a consideration of the League's attempt to persuade governments to revise their school textbooks in order to eliminate from them passages offensive to peoples of other countries. Take, for example, the question of responsibility for the World War of 1914–1918 and the justification or condemnation of the resulting peace treaties. One can readily see that even trained scholars might passionately differ on these questions. But if emotion can distort the judgment of university people supposedly trained to approach the social sciences in an analytical spirit, how much greater will be the tendency of national governments to influence history writing so as to make good citizens of their growing children.

The French and German textbooks contained material of a particularly offensive nature; in them education and propaganda became hopelessly mixed. One or two examples may be given at random. German storybooks for little children contained versions of the Mother Goose story in which a Jew is made the ogre and the pictures are of an appalling and insulting character. German mathematical textbooks contained problems designed to instill in the minds of the children a consciousness of Germany's losses during the war. For example: "How much territory would have to be taken back by Germany . . . . ," "if Germany retained her coal mines . . . ."—around statements like these were framed simple mathematical problems. The Committee on Intellectual Co-operation did good work and helped to persuade French and German authorities to make considerable revision of their textbooks between 1920 and 1930. When Hitler came to power these revised texts were destroyed and others of the type of propaganda just mentioned were introduced. After his Rhineland occupation of March 1935, the Führer said that he was ready to agree to a permanent French-German committee operating under the aegis of the League to consider the whole question of textbooks. But critics believed that Hitler's action was designed to stop all French

[27] H. F. Armstrong, *op. cit.,* p. 25.

criticism of what the Nazis were doing in internal and international affairs, of its policy toward Jews, liberals, trade unionists, Roman Catholics, and of National Socialist philosophy.

Here, then, is the problem: Is intellectual co-operation to mean that other countries cannot subject the policies and actions of a country to criticism? Is it to be a colorless agency which must permit nations to go their own way? Or is it to be allowed to bring the light of reason to bear upon the abuses and extravagances which may exist in national curricula? Rational criticism depends upon basic values, and today there is a widespread reaction against reason. To tell Hitler or Mussolini that a thing will not stand the test of reason will bring the retort "Whose reason?" What intellectual co-operation is possible with those who allege that truth is not universal, that right is what is right to an Aryan, and that there is no such thing as objective science? How much co-operation is possible between the liberal mind which believes in analysis and experimentation, trusts in reason, and believes in obtaining as much evidence as possible and arriving at an a posteriori judgment, and the fundamentalist mind which accepts certain fundamentals on faith, believes that reason and analysis are inadequate to solve the deeper problems of the universe and its meaning, and proceeds according to a priori methods? The believer in reason will claim the right to analyze things which the fundamentalist would regard as beyond the province of reason.

Even in social affairs one does not have to go far to ask whether in our liberal society one would find much sympathy for the view that we should dispassionately analyze with children the pros and cons of free love, stealing, murder, lying, and other actions. No; we assume that these things are wrong, and our defense is not necessarily a "rational" one. Suppose, however, that the same attitude is carried over into racial matters and that apologists say that these things cannot be discussed by merely rational methods. Suppose that Fascist and Nazi leaders deny the claims of the intellect and preach the desirability of force, saying that violence, noble violence, is necessary, and that in a nation there is a mystical unity between a people and its soil. What then?

Suppose they say that there are limits to intellectual co-operation, that history shows the tragic breakdown of certainties when traditions and values are unduly and too rapidly undermined by new ideas. The Indians in Central and South America lived a life reasonably adapted to their environment, but when the fighting, individualist Spaniards arrived and mingled with the communal

Indians, the result was chaos to their children, who socially inherited mutually contradictory values. Their minds became confused and their purposes uncertain, and instead of the richness of variety they suffered from the consequences of the cancelling-out process induced by the meeting of incompatible values. What is the limit of synthesis? And how much can the average mind absorb and assimilate?

Moreover, if the state be regarded as the great instrument for truth, or if its leaders and people believe that the security of the state is the highest duty of its citizens, then the outlook for intellectual co-operation today depends upon the solution of this security problem. If security is to be obtained by the nation arming itself to the utmost, if war is normal and desirable, then the state must prepare the minds of its citizens for warlike purposes. The greater the danger of war, the more definitely must all values be made subordinate to this purpose. But to make human minds the instrument of national war is to limit the scope of intellectual co-operation to a small compass.

It may be argued, of course, that the educated soldiers of various countries can meet on common ground and that, although their ultimate purpose may be to destroy one another, they can attain the chivalry and the nobility of character which military tradition at its best inspires. The educated military man probably does not hate his brother officers of other countries, and the spirit of sacrifice engendered by a willingness to die for one's country may be compatible with a high spirit of culture and of tolerance for difference of beliefs.

Unfortunately popular attitudes toward other countries do not reach this level. In order to make the nation into an efficient fighting instrument it seems necessary to arouse the spirit of hate, and the present propaganda methods throughout the world seem to require the indoctrination of millions of people with crude and distorted ideas of other countries.

Today there is a progressive limiting of human interests by more than one state; and in order to maintain an emotional unity of an uninformed kind, the thoughts, contacts, and speculations of scholars are being confined within dangerously small limits. Thus it is not unjust to say that emotional nationalism, and especially the totalitarian state, is not compatible with any substantial intellectual co-operation in social, political, scientific, and philosophic matters. Nor is a unity of temper in which different beliefs are held easily attainable under conditions of present political rivalry.

A scholar can help to enrich and even revolutionize the life of his generation and of generations to come—witness Pasteur, Faraday, and many others—but if war kills him, or political or economic chaos starves him or deprives him of the opportunity of unfettered thought, he cannot make his contribution. Intellectual advance presupposes a minimum of world order; without it, scientists face the prospect of becoming primarily adjuncts to rival national-defense machines. Only with the defeat of the doctrine of anti-reason and of the fallacies of the superman and the superior race can rational progress be insured; and the prevention of future aggression in turn can be achieved only by the establishment of adequate international political and economic institutions.

How close is the relation between intellectual co-operation and the development of agriculture, industry, health, and other matters pertaining to general welfare one may see from the subjoined list of international scientific congresses held or announced between 1930 and 1939. The list was compiled in the Library of the National Research Council, Washington, D.C. When one remembers that these meetings were held during the continual breakdown of international political society, he realizes the divorce between the political organization of the world and its economic and intellectual requirements. A more eloquent description of common interests transcending national boundaries could scarcely be given.

INTERNATIONAL SCIENTIFIC CONGRESSES HELD OR ANNOUNCED BETWEEN 1930 AND 1939

Academies
Acetylene
Acetylene, oxy-acetylene welding, etc.
Acoustical
Actuaries
Administrative sciences
Aerial safety
Aeronautics
Agricultural economists
Agricultural engineering
Agricultural industries
Agricultural press
Agricultural teaching
Agricultural technicians
Agriculture
Agriculture, forestry and animal industry, Inter-American
Agriculture, instruction

Air navigation
Alcoholism
Alimentation
Americanists
Anatomists
Anesthesia
Anthropological and ethnological sciences
Anthropology and prehistoric archaeology
Apiculture
Applied mechanics
Archaeological excavations
Archaeology
Archaeology, Iran
Architects
Architecture, modern
Asthma
Astronomical Union

Fever therapy
First aid on roads
Fishery
Forensic medicine
Forest research organizations
Foundry
Fruit as food
Fruit juices, unfermented
Fruit tree culture and pomology

Gas
Gastro-enterology
Genetical and cytological nomenclature
Genetics
Geodesy and geophysics
Geographic pathology
Geographical
Geographical Union
Geography and history, Pan American Institute
Geological
Geometricians
Glacial epoch
Glass technology
Goat breeding
Goiter
Gout and uric acid
Grain
Grape and juice of the grape
Grasslands
Gynecologists

Health
Health, national directors
Health service of students
Health technique and communal hygiene
Heating and ventilating
Heating and ventilating exposition
Hepatic insufficiency
Highways, Pan-American
Hispanic-American history
Historical geography
History and geography of the Americas
History of medicine
History of pharmacy
History of the sciences
Home economics
Homeopathic

Homeopathic medical, Pan-American
Hormones, Sex
Hormones, standardization
Horticultural
Hospital association
Hydraulic laboratory association
Hydrographic
Hydrology, climatology, and medical geology
Hygiene

Illumination
Immunology
Indian life
Individual psychology
Industrial accidents and occupational diseases
Industrial chemistry
Industrial property, protection
Industrial psychology
Infantile psychiatry
Intellectual unions
Intellectual workers
Inventions, exhibition
Inventors
Iran, art and archaeology

Leather trades chemists
Leprosy
Letter symbols, heat and thermodynamics
Librarians
Libraries and bibliography
Light, investigation
Lighting applications
Limnology
Locust
Logopady and phoniatry
Lubrication and lubricants
Lymphatism

Magnetism
Malaria
Management
Masonry and reinforced concrete
Massage
Mathematical recreation
Mathematical sciences
Mathematicians
Mathematics, teaching

Mechanics, general
Medical advisors for athletes
Medical assistance by air
Medical education
Medical education, advanced
Medical, Pan-American
Medical post-graduate (Tomarkin foundation)
Medical practitioners
Medical public health officers
Medical week
Medicinal plants and essences
Mediterranean hygiene
Mental hygiene
Mental hygiene, Inter-American
Mental prophylaxis and hygiene
Meteorological
Metrology, applied
Microbiology
Military medical information office
Military medicine, documentation
Military medicine and pharmacy
Mining and electricity
Mines, metallurgy, and applied geology
Montessori
Municipal sanitation
Museums, directors

Naval architects and marine engineers
Navigation
Neohippocratic medicine
Neurological
New education fellowship
Nitrogen
Nuclear physics
Nurserymen
Nurses
Nutrition

Odontology
Olive growers
Ophthalmological
Orientalists
Ornithological
Orthodontic
Orthopedic surgery
Oto-neuro-ophthalmology
Oto-rhinolaryngology

Pacific health
Pacific science
Papyrology
Pediatric
Pediatrics, preventive
Petroleum
Pharmaceutical
Philosophy
Philosophy, scientific
Phonetic sciences
Phonographic industry
Photogrammetric
Photographic and cinematographic documentation
Photography, scientific and applied
Photoluminescence
Physical chemistry
Physical education
Physical medicine
Physical therapy, x-ray and radium
Physicians
Physicians, postgraduate and graduate education
Physics
Physics, chemistry and biology
Physics, pure and applied, Union of
Physiological
Physiotherapy
Phytohormone
Plant breeders
Polar exploration
Population problems
Population, studies regarding
Postgraduate medicine
Poultry
Power
Pre-Cambrian
Pre- and protohistorical sciences
Prehistorical research in Far East
Protection of nature
Protection of savants, etc.
Psychical research
Psychiatry, infantile
Psychoanalytical
Psychology
Psychology, individual
Psychopathology and psychology
Psychotherapy
Public health workers
Public hygiene
Pulmonary radiography

Quaternary period

Radiation, solar, terrestrial and cosmic
Radio, Inter-American
Radio consulting committee
Radio telegraphic convention
Radio, Union
Radio-aesthesia
Radiobiology
Radiology
Rail assembly
Railway
Railway fuel
Rat and plague
Rectors, deans, and educators
Refrigeration
Religious psychology
Renal insufficiency
Rescue and first aid
Rheumatism
Rheumatism, chronic progressive
Rheumatism, League
Road
Road tar
Rubber
Rural engineering
Rural hygiene, Far Eastern

Sanatoria
Sanitary, American republics
Sanitary material
School medicine and physical education
Scientific, Pan-American
Scientific management
Scientific press
Scientific unions
Sea
Sea, exploration
Seed crushers
Seed testing
Serological
Sex hormones
Sex research
Sexual reform
Short waves in physics, biology, and medicine
Silicosis
Silviculture
Snow and ice

Snow survey
Social sciences
Sociology
Soil mechanics
Soil science
Spectroscopy
Standards
Statistics
Steam, properties
Steel construction
Steel development
Stomatological
Stratosphere
Students, health service
Sugar
Sugar analysis
Sugar cane technologists
Sugar council
Surgical, Pan-American
Surgery
Surveyors
Syphilis and venereal diseases
Syphilis, serotherapy

Teaching
Technical aviation
Technical education
Telegraphy
Telephonic
Telephonic, telegraphic, and radio
Testing of materials
Thalassotherapy
Theory of probability
Therapeutic light
Therapeutics
Throat, nose, and ear specialists
Timber production
Timber utilization
Tobacco
Topology
Toponomy and anthroponomy
Trachoma
Tropical and subtropical agriculture
Tropical medicine, Far Eastern
Tropical medicine and hygiene
Tuberculosis
Tuberculosis, Pan-American

Undulant fever
Unity of science
University conference

RELIGIOUS CO-OPERATION

Although the saints of Christian history spoke of being one in Christ, the last nineteen hundred years have little to show of this lofty ideal. For centuries the East and the West, Protestant, Catholic, and a bewildering number of other sects have argued and fought with each other over doctrinal questions, ecclesiastical jurisdiction, and the more self-regarding quest of who should be first in the Kingdom of God both on earth and in Heaven. In fact, disunion has become so habitual as to make the dream of Christian unity scarcely more than a vague wish on the part of millions of people.

Yet a few leaders and thinkers have long grieved over hair-splitting theological controversies and narrow sectarianism, and have believed that true religion can unite all creeds and classes in the pursuit of lofty social and spiritual ideals which will lift the churches out of their petty bickerings and limited vision, and some progress achieved by them can be recorded. Before 1914 little progress was made in that direction beyond a few conferences, the Student Christian Movement, and a number of missionary enterprises. And during the years 1914 to 1918 German, Austrian, Russian, British, French, and other Christian nations prayed to God for support in waging war and for military triumph. God received a chaotic babel of nationalistic petitions, and looked down upon human beings using the Cross for the purpose of intensifying national hatreds. Some Christians realized the utter tragedy of it all, and saw that the disunity of Christendom had in no small measure contributed to the world cataclysm.

In November 1914 a number of outstanding church leaders issued an appeal for peace. The Archbishop of Upsala, Soderblom, a noble ecclesiastic who was later to play a decisive part in the Ecumenical Movement and was to receive the Nobel Peace Prize in 1930, took the initiative in reminding the world, then amid the clash of arms, "that war cannot sunder the bond of international union that Christ holds in us." In 1917 five neutral Protestant countries issued a declaration setting forth the unity of Christendom; they deplored the fact that the church had frequently stressed that which divides and not that which unites, and urged that it should work for the settlement of international disputes through mediation and arbitration. After the war had ended, the World Alliance for Promoting International Fellowship met at The Hague in 1919, and approved the proposal of Archbishop Soderblom for an Ecumenical Council which should strive for a common doctrine so as to realize an organized unity of nations for the application of Christian principles to social and international life within an international brotherhood.[28]

In 1920 the Lambeth Conference of Anglican Bishops issued an appeal to all Christian people, and passed a resolution on the desirability of Christian unity. Their action paved the way to later "conversations" between these bishops and the leaders of other Protestant denominations in order to see how far there could be "unity with variety" among Christian churches. Meanwhile a committee of the Hague Conference proceeded to organize the first ecumenical conference at Stockholm in 1925. During these years the Eastern Orthodox Church had also realized the need of a closer unity with other Christian churches, and in January 1920 the Patriarchate of Constantinople issued an appeal to that end. In addition to supporting the idea of the League of Nations in the political sphere, he suggested a pan-Christian conference to deal with questions of vital importance to all persons of the Christian faith.

The committee working for the Stockholm Conference must have had almost as mountainous a task as the statesmen who set out to build the League of Nations! In both cases differences of doctrine, of long-settled habits of thought, of material interests and selfish purposes stood in the way of realizing the clear and sensible vision which might have delivered mankind from its suffering. The committee itself realized that it would be impossible to achieve an immediate unity of faith, and doctrinal differences would die hard. And the committee concluded that it would be wiser to separate the movement into two parts: (*a*) Life and Work, which should confine itself to co-operation in social, na-

---

[28] Bishop George Bell, "The Stockholm Conference," in Percy Dearmer (ed.), *Christianity and the Crisis* (Victor Gollancz, London, 1933).

tional, and international relationships; and (*b*) Faith and Order which should consider "the ultimate but more remote goal of unity in Doctrine and Church Order."

The Stockholm Conference, the first world-wide Christian conference for almost sixteen hundred years, met August 19–30, 1925. Over five hundred delegates attended. They represented all Christian churches except the Roman Catholic, and came from thirty-seven nations. The Conference considered six main subjects, including: God's purpose and the duty of the church; the church in relation to (*a*) economic and industrial problems, (*b*) social and moral problems, (*c*) international relations, and (*d*) Christian education; and also methods of co-operative and federative action by Christian churches. The Conference passed a number of resolutions. It realized that its work would not end with one gathering but needed constant and consistent effort; accordingly it appointed a continuation committee, which met each year from 1926 to 1930. In 1930 it became the Universal Christian Council for Life and Work, comprising one hundred members, divided into the Orthodox, Continental European, British, and American sections, each with a president holding office for two years. The Council has its headquarters at Geneva, where there has also been established an International Christian Social Institute with a research department and a general secretary. The Institute has important contacts with the International Labor Office and the Economic and other sections of the League of Nations. It has arranged conferences on various social problems, such as the economic crisis, unemployment, and opium; it publishes a quarterly newsletter in English, French, and German; and it sponsors the meeting of international commissions dealing with youth, the press, etc.

In 1930 over three hundred bishops gathered at Lambeth and again appealed to "all Christian people" for an agreement on the fundamental bases of Christianity, which they believed was consistent with considerable national and regional variety of creed and worship. They again invited nonconformist churches to participate in joint conferences with the bishops for the purpose of further exploring the possibilities of reunion.

Within each of several countries the union ideal is making headway. There is the United Church of Scotland; the Wesleyans and Methodists of Canada have joined forces; Baptists, Congregationalists, and Presbyterians in England are striving to find a basis of unity; and other movements are taking place in Persia,

China, Japan, Nigeria, India, and elsewhere. These movements are not unimportant.

As J. H. Oldham well reminds us, the church has been for many years content to fit into the framework of the modern political state. But can it be true to its spiritual mission and accept such a subordinate role? Can the church which claims to be the instrument of God be satisfied to allow the world to become increasingly dominated by secular, national, "this-worldly ideals and loyalties"?[29]

The research department of the International Christian Social Institute organized in 1934 a preliminary international conference, which decided to convene a world conference of churches to deal with the problem of "Church, community, and state." The work of preparation for the universal gathering occupied over two years; several subsidiary conferences were held for purposes of preliminary study; over one hundred papers by outstanding scholars were circulated; and, as a result of these thorough preparations, the Oxford Conference of July 12–26, 1937, proved to be an event of first importance. One may find in its *Proceedings* a description of the common worship each morning, the brilliant garb of the delegates, and the addresses and reports. Here it must suffice to point out the main conclusions:

The Conference made an important distinction between ecumenical and international. The latter term presupposes the division of mankind into separate nations "as a natural, if not a final, state of affairs"; the former term emphasizes the fact of unity in Christ. Now, because the church has an ecumenical spiritual character, it can, or should, bring to international questions "an insight which is not to be derived from ordinary political sources." To those who doubt man's capacity to overcome the divisions of nationalism through an effort of will, the church offers "not an ideal but a fact, man united not by his aspiration but by the love of God."

The Conference came to a conclusion which, if Christians take it seriously, has tremendous consequences for the modern state: A true conception of international relations, it asserted, "requires a recognition of the fact that the state, whether it admits it or not, is not autonomous, but is under the ultimate governance of God." The delegates realized that international relations are still considered in terms of power. This evil they claimed must be reme-

---

[29] "It seemed plain that Christian thought must be directed with the utmost energy to the problem of the state."—J. H. Oldham, *The Oxford Conference, Official Report*, p. 7.

died. The source of the evil is to be found "in the claim of each national state to be judge in its own cause," and the church has the duty of urging upon nations the abandonment of the claim of absolute national sovereignty. The Conference, while admitting the failure of the League of Nations in many respects, asserted that "no alternative conception or method of comparable range has come to light in the intervening period, and the need for an agency of international co-operation is as great as ever." It supported the Permanent Court of International Justice, and strongly condemned war, which it described as "a particular demonstration of the power of sin in this world and a defiance of the righteousness of God as revealed in Jesus Christ and Him crucified. No justification of war must be allowed to conceal or minimize this fact."

The delegates noted that Christians are not agreed as to what they should do in the event of war. Some accept pacifism; others will support a "just war," provided that judgment is given against an aggressor by a third party on the basis of international law and organization; and a few, believing that war is rooted in human nature, accept the view that a Christian's duty is to obey the state as far as possible, because it is the duty of the state to maintain order within and defend its people against enemies from without. These contrasting views, the Conference suggested, bear witness to a perplexity which itself "is a sign of the sin in which its members are implicated" and urged that through prayer and study the problem should be still further examined. A profoundly challenging statement is contained in the words: "the Church should remind its members that the principle of the unconditional supremacy of the state or nation, advanced either in time of peace or war, is incompatible with the Church's faith in Jesus Christ as its only Lord, and is therefore unacceptable as the final norm of judgment or action."

A close examination of the declarations of the Conference reveals that in them the participating Christian churches have taken a stand in general terms against the excessive claims of the most dominant political institution, the state, and the most powerful idea, sovereignty, which together have ruled the political world since the Reformation.

In December 1938 the International Missionary Council of the Christian Church held an important meeting at Tambaram, near Madras, in India. With 471 persons from about seventy countries in attendance, for the first time in history the younger churches of Asia, Africa, Latin America, and the Pacific Islands had the same representation as the older churches of Europe, North America, Australia, and New Zealand. Hundreds of proposals which of course cannot be mentioned here were considered by it. The Madras Conference may usher in a new era of co-operation because of the profoundly inspirational character of its proceedings and the universality of its representation.[30]

Although students have been subjected to the dividing influences of nationalist and secular education, the Student Christian Movement for nearly fifty years has striven to maintain the ideal of unity throughout the world. It has branches in nearly three thousand universities and a membership of 300,000. It has held world conferences in Tokyo (1907), Peking (1922), and India (1928) for the purpose of binding Occident and Orient more closely together; and the latest world conference in Holland in 1939 endeavored to set the Christian ideal of brotherhood above the intense nationalisms rampant in the world—but with apparently doubtful success, even among its own members at the Conference.

The future of these efforts will depend largely upon a clari-, fication of the relations which should exist between religion and the state in the present-day world.

Conferences have also taken place between representatives of Christian and non-Christian religions in order to see if the great religions of the world which derive inspiration from infinitely greater sources than human political organizations can co-operate to preserve the finest values of the various civilizations which are now being threatened by the reign of war and barbarous destruction. A typical gathering was that held in England in 1938, when services and discussions were led by profound scholars of the Moslem, Buddhist, Christian, and other religions. By using a common terminology they were able to realize the essential unity of purpose underlying the respective faiths and the relatively small importance of the differences in their expressions of faith.

But religions like nations are not all willing to forego their claims to exclusive loyalty. Some of them claim to be the special medium through which God reveals his will and purpose and are unwilling to co-operate with other religions on a level of substantial equality. Admirable is the ideal of interreligious co-operation; but it will involve a much greater knowledge of comparative religion, a deeper appreciation of the best in all religions, and a

[30] See J. R. Mott, *Five Decades and a Forward View* (Harper & Bros., New York, 1939).

sense of the appalling gap between theory and practice which characterizes practically every organized religion.

It is relatively easy to make a declaration that absolute sovereignty belongs to God alone and for the churches to take a theoretical stand against the doctrine of political sovereignty claimed by the modern state. Admittedly such a step bears witness to some advance in recent religious social thought. But if nothing more than a vague general statement is made, little will be done to arrest the processes of disintegration, because no procedures will be established to translate the general ideal into practice.

If it was simple enough for governments to appeal to the Kellogg Pact, which renounced war as an instrument of national policy, in order to justify wars allegedly defensive in character, it will be even simpler, in the absence of appropriate institutions to determine the aggressor, for war-minded governments to preach a defensive war in the name of morality, of religion, and of God himself. The question is whether it is possible to devise procedures by which the religious values of peace and good will can be combined with the ideal of preventing the aggression of a war-minded state. The church is right in denying the claims to absolute sovereignty on the part of the state; but that alone will not prevent men from fighting for the defense of their country if it is attacked by an invader. The church must therefore support the institution which can best stop aggression. It must ask itself what form of society will prevent governments from making war, and it must transfer its sense of civic duty and loyalty to that form of society. Sooner or later it would seem that the church must take a determined stand against the present exaggerated claims of the state, if it is to be true to the loftiest ideals which gave it birth.

To wait until war breaks out is of course futile, and a broad program of studies and sermons on the relations of church and state must be undertaken. The emphasis must be on the devotion to the institutions (especially as they go beyond the state) which will best prevent war. The church is not to conceive its duty in terms of accommodating itself to the state. There are values beyond those which the state is at present serving. Christians are more than citizens of a state, and if they are to be loyal citizens of the wider community of God they must set up expert committees to study the technical problems involved in the prevention of war. Many such committees have already been established and are working in co-operation with laymen's committees.

Their findings need to become part of the everyday active values of the whole body of Christendom and other faiths.

One important method is suggested at this point, namely, that the international obligations of the states within which churches reside should be transformed into constitutional obligations. The religious groups should insist that international treaties entered into by their governments should in all cases be binding upon them. How far the churches are from being ready to take so determined a stand, and to subordinate the sovereign state to wider ends, may be seen by asking the question how many churches would be willing immediately to remove the national flags from above their altars.

A happy reconciliation is possible between the claims of the state and of the church and of other forms of society, but at present the everyday emotional loyalties are in the service of the national state. If, however, the latter continues to exhaust itself by unceasing turmoil and warfare, and to reveal its inadequacy to satisfy the deeper needs of man's nature, we may well witness a widespread renewed sense of the fact that basically man is a creature of the universe and only secondarily a citizen of a state. When this sense of proportion returns, loyalties may fall into truer perspective and a better balance be struck between the claims of the immediately political and the ever-present universe which religion, however imperfectly, attempts to interpret. No final answer can be given. The outcome depends upon the kind of religion and the kind of nationalism.

Chapter XIII

INTERNATIONAL LAW AND ORGANIZATION

THERE has been a persistent tendency to oversimplify the description of political societies. Scholars write of tribes bound by blood ties, and about city-states, feudal communities, nations, and empires; but it is important to realize that these names do not describe entirely different entities with nothing in common. In reality, all groups of people must meet common problems; and although a thinker may err in the direction of finding too much similarity among different types of groups, he may also exaggerate the element of difference; differences then become magnified into near absolutes and the intellectual superstructures tend to monopolize theorists and others, blotting out the common foundations upon which all societies must exist.

CHANGES IN THE UNITS OF GOVERNMENT

Many tribal communities have been bound together chiefly by blood ties and myths, but even they did not and could not entirely discard the territorial factor. Tribes live on the land, and there grows up a vested interest in land. The soil is sacred to many tribes, and it would be strange if legal or political claims to it would not come about. Moreover, Indian tribes formed major federations; and these must have had some kind of territorial foundation. Unless a tribe is purely nomadic or engages in nothing but a shifting cultivation, if rivers or water holes are important to them for drinking purposes, there must be agreements as to their use. Thus the tribe cannot be considered apart from the place in which it lives. A tribe's concept of boundaries may have been far less exact than ours, but tribalism does not imply total lack of territorialism. One principle alone does not govern this or any other form of society.

The Greek city-state was not merely a geographic unit; it was also a tribal state, a community of persons, united by tribal ties and religious bonds; and blood, brotherhood, and birth entered into its concept of worship. Moreover, these cities had a large element of the country in them and were less sharply separated from rural life than are many of our own metropolitan centers. Thus, although the political unit in ancient Greece was the city-state, it was not wholly divorced from tribal organization and myths and ceremonies connected with the tribal attitude to life. The same holds true of Rome. Now, as an instrument of government, the city-state may appear to have little in common with the modern nation; but the political groups of that time, like our own, had to live together and work out orderly intercourse. Were the rules which governed them intermunicipal rather than international relations? It may be, but the term "international" has been freely and appropriately applied to them. In some respects the ancient city-states had the essential characteristics of a modern state, and the inter-city relations bore a resemblance to present-day international relations. Otherwise, why the designation "state"?

Federations of city-states grew up under the threat of invasion from the Persians in 479 B.C. The Delian League enabled Sparta and Athens and the others to defeat the Persians; but the united Greece did not last, "for what centuries have put asunder two summers cannot bind fast." Athens tried to transform the Delian Confederation into an Athenian empire, just as some great powers today have tried to twist the League of Nations to their imperial ends. For over one hundred years the Greek city-states dissipated their energies in foolish and fruitless warfare for the sake of petty leadership. Arbitration helped to settle minor disputes but was unable to prevent major conflicts in the political sphere. The cities combined into another confederation against Philip and Alexander of Macedon about 340 B.C.; but the Achaean League failed in its purpose and was dissolved by Rome in 146 B.C. For a time the Greek city-states were permitted to retain some self-government, which greatly diminished until the fiction of independence gave way to an explicit recognition that they had become Roman provinces. Civic strife within the cities helped toward their downfall.

The civic patriotism of the Greeks was only partial, and their essential weakness was twofold: they could not or would not develop an adequate inter-Greek-city organization; and they could not or would not develop an adequate internal unity. The unit of government of the city-state was not strong enough to solve the wider problems of defense or to settle the differences within the

city arising between its social classes. Thus the excessive desire
for absolute state independence, the failure to form larger political
units which the changing times and needs demanded, the declining
power of the god Apollo, the ravages of plague, and the failure to
solve the problem of war led to the fall of the city-state or rather
its transformation into a subordinate entity. Alexander formed a
great empire, and in the light of this the fights between the little
Greek states at home "for a strip of meadow land seemed mere
ebullitions of jealous folly."[1] What were once struggles in the
balance-of-power system of Greece became in the new and wider
perspective absurd local squabbles and bickerings.

The destruction of Greek political independence did not mark
the complete eclipse of the city-state. As a form of government, it
was to play an important although not an independent role in European history for several centuries. Alexander, the Seleucids, and
Rome preserved the city-states as political units, superimposing
upon them a wider imperial form of government. The Roman
Empire comprised in large measure a union of city-states under
the control of a premier city-state. The new government was not
merely an empire excluding the city-state; the two types co-existed,
each fulfilling certain purposes.

In the days before Rome became master of the Mediterranean
world, and while she was yet a city-state of the same character as
her neighbors, her relations with other peoples went through developments similar to those of the earlier Greek city-states. The
Romans developed an elaborate procedure in declaring war. The
priests of the Fetial College made an exhaustive inquiry concerning the dispute and set forth their reasons when they decided that
a conflict was necessary. Detailed provisions concerning the an-
nouncement of war were developed; these show that the Romans
made a clear distinction between legal war undertaken by public
authorities and unauthorized social strife. The Romans also limited war to certain times and places, forbidding the waging of
hostilities in the region of temples, sanctuaries, and certain specified cities.

As Rome pursued her path of conquest and brought more and
more cities and peoples under her sway, she modified her attitude
toward the doctrine of equality of states. Having become the
dominant power, she forced her neighbors into special relations
with her, relations which were not those of equality in peace time
and did not permit their neutrality during war. If they did not

---

[1] C. Oman, *A History of Greece*, p. 545.

choose to be her "allies," they must run the risk of being regarded as her enemies. When Rome reduced the Greek cities to a condition of dependence, the relations of the latter with one another "became only pseudo-international in nature, being subject to the increasing overlordship of Rome." Arbitration was then not truly international in nature, but rather a form of civil regulation, since Rome made it almost mandatory. Vinogradof designates the international law of Rome "private international law."

The concept deserves further analysis. In the early days of the city of Rome, the people drew up laws which were local, rigid, and formal, applying only to the citizens themselves. Legal actions were based upon the Twelve Tables, which were interpreted by the Pontifical College. But such laws were too local and too inelastic to be applicable to the great variety of peoples which came under the rule of Rome after its conquest of Italy in 260 B.C. The praetors gradually developed a body of law which applied to disputes between the citizens of Rome and "foreigners." They did so because of the sheer needs of commerce. Economic life on a wider scale could not develop within the framework either of the rigid local law of Rome or of the conflicting rules of different cities. Some law comprehensive enough to embrace the subjects of all the groups was required. And so the praetors expanded the law (1) by the use of "fictions," (2) by the use of "equity," and (3) by their control over legal procedure (especially the praetor's edict).

Gradually what was called the *ius gentium,* which comprised the rules for regulating relations between different peoples, grew in importance. It owed not a little to the Stoics, who were impressed by the great forces of the universe which were common to man and transcended the relatively small differences between human beings. The "law of nature" was to have a long history.

Nevertheless, the old *ius civile,* which applied only to Romans, continued to exist and the *ius gentium* stood out in contrast to it. For some time there was duplication of institutions. For the Roman Empire as a whole the *ius gentium* became a great instrument for uniting the peoples which came under its rule. It was not that this *ius gentium* involved the extinction of local autonomy and institutions. In fact, the provinces developed a peculiar relation with Rome, a relationship of a "peculiar semi-international character." Roman law by resolving conflicts between different regions according to equitable principles more or less common to all made an extraordinary contribution to the unity of Europe.

The Romans permitted a great variety of status and a large amount of self-government in their provincial towns. They dissolved those political leagues and unions which threatened military resistance, but at the same time they permitted the traditional forms of city life to continue. There were different ranks for different cities—those with full Roman franchise; those which possessed the rights of Latins; the free or federate cities, which enjoyed freedom and immunity from taxes; and stipendiary towns, which were subject to taxes at the pleasure of Rome but were administered by their own magistrates and enjoyed considerable autonomy. Undoubtedly the Roman rule brought peace and order to the outlying provinces. The administration of justice under the Empire improved, and economic prosperity followed in the train of public law and order. The Empire maintained communications on land and sea; "it confined war to the frontiers"—itself a remarkable boon—"and removed a variety of checks and hindrances." It substituted an imperial currency for the multitude of monetary systems; it lessened the scope of war and politics, and encouraged industry. The Roman Republic, the Pax Romana, in the words of Vinogradof, "marked a new period in the history of the world, broke down the barriers of internecine hatred, gave a real meaning to the conception of civilized mankind, made possible an era of prosperity and economic progress."[2] This peace, which embraced many different peoples, produced the Roman roads and a great economic area in which countries could exchange goods, engage in economic specialization, and obtain the benefits of better economic organization. The "narrow restrictions and prejudices of the municipal laws of the various communities which came to be included in the empire gave way before wider conceptions of justice and humanity."[3]

On the frontiers the Empire maintained a number of dependent kingdoms, permitting the people to live under their native rulers on condition that they paid tribute and supplied soldiers. Gradually, however, it was found desirable to bring these dependent peoples under more uniform administration. This organization of the Empire kept the peace of the Roman world for almost a century, and enabled its inhabitants to enjoy a happiness which according to Gibbon has been seldom equaled in human history. Thus the Romans advanced their "private international law" to a higher stage than the Greeks.

[2] F. S. Marvin (ed.), *The Evolution of World Peace,* p. 26.
[3] *Ibid.,* p. 34.

The fall of the Roman Empire did not take place in sudden catastrophic fashion. Many of its ideas and much of its organization lingered on. But, as the central power weakened, local units grew up. They took the form of feudalism, manorial in the country and civic in the towns. As the Church grew to power, another unit of government grew up; and between the Church and the local feudal units, many struggles developed. After several centuries the idea of universal government based upon Christianity and the inherited traditions of the Roman Empire reasserted itself.

The "universal idea" which captured the imagination of medieval thinkers was essentially religious in nature. Men sought guidance and authority from the Holy Scriptures; they contemplated the universe and saw society and the individual in relation to it. They saw that God had made the world and created harmony between its many parts, and believed that each individual reflected something of the universe in himself—he was a microcosm in the macrocosm. It followed that all the individuals who composed mankind formed a "unity" which came under the operation of God's law and that the government of this mankind logically should be a "unity." Now human life is both physical and spiritual, and its unity must therefore embrace both these aspects.

It was at this point that the medievalist saw that Church and State each had a part to play: God rules in Heaven over the heavenly spirits, and the Pope as his representative on earth should rule over the souls of man. But God is also Lord of the earth and consequently has "a second earthly viceroy," the Emperor, to minister to the civil needs of man's present life. Both Pope and Emperor therefore have high functions to fulfill; each must help the other in the furtherance of the Kingdom of God on earth.

This noble ideal of two universal representatives working in alliance for the purpose of establishing justice and happiness on earth demanded extraordinarily high qualities on the part of Pope and Emperor—skill and insight, tact and devotion, and readiness to co-operate. It presupposed a fairly clear dividing line between spiritual and temporal matters, and that the duties of the Pope and the Emperor could be easily delimited so as to avoid disputes concerning the scope of their respective jurisdictions. Unfortunately, human life seldom presents mankind with such obvious classifications; and the Middle Ages found that the divisions of human behavior into "sacred" and "secular" involved it in as much legal argument as the modern attempts to separate the political powers of state and federal governments. Is a bishop first and foremost a citizen of the King or Emperor, or is he primarily subject to the Pope? Is Church property a temporal or a spiritual thing, and should it be taxable by secular authorities? Are priests accused of crimes against laymen to be tried by the Church, or should they, like any other person accused of illegal conduct, submit to the secular courts of law? Is education a matter for the Church because the fear of the Lord is the beginning of wisdom, or should the state control educational policy for the purpose of training citizens? These and other questions show that even on the plane of theory the idea of co-ordinated universal powers is likely to break down, because of the extreme difficulty of accurately defining the spheres of Pope and Emperor. And when personal rivalry, self-interest, and ambition likewise appeared, when each of the authorities indulged in pretentious claims (backed by quotations from Scripture) at the expense of the other, the two universal champions, instead of co-operating in the maintenance of peace and the promotion of justice, exhausted themselves in bitter warfare and paved the way to the ruin of both. The first cause of the breakdown of this so-called Universal Holy Roman Empire in its attempt to organize society was therefore the transformation of the Pope-Emperor relationship from a condition of co-operation to one of irreconcilable hostility.

Logically the clash began when the theorists of the Church began to develop the argument that the Pope was superior to the Emperor. Was not the spirit more precious than the body, Heaven incomparably greater than earth, and the eternal more important than the present? The Papal protagonists elaborated this theory, and claimed for the Pope an overlordship which came to include anointing the Emperor, correcting the mistakes of secular authorities, and deposing and even excommunicating an unworthy Emperor and releasing his subjects from their allegiance to him. Nor could any secular law challenge this paramount sovereignty of the Church, argued these theorists.

Such claims denied all possibility of an equal status to the Emperor and relegated him to the position of a subordinate. It is not surprising that his defenders opposed the clerical theories and pretensions with all the energy at their command. They combed the Bible for texts to show that the kings of ancient Jewish times were divinely chosen and that in the New Testament the divine character of their office was recognized. Thus their apologists set up what they asserted to be the right of kings against the pretensions of the Papacy. Most of the emperors did not attempt to meet the Pope's assertion of power over secular matters with a counterclaim to sovereignty over church affairs; nevertheless, they did, in practice, nominate Popes and they exercised considerable influence over church organization. The Emperor regarded himself as an instrument for the propagation of Christianity as well as the builder of a worldly empire. When Charles the Great fought the Saxons he undertook a war of religion as well as one of conquest—he carried relics of the saints with him, he made his enemies submit to baptism as "the seal of their allegiance," and he and his successors regarded a "relapse into heathenism" as a crime against the state. The German people, moreover, passionately held to the principle of legitimate succession and resisted the Papal claim to depose their rulers. To them their old tribal customs were more powerful than the command of a distant Pope. It is clear that unless Emperor and Pope behaved with moderation and restraint, and refrained from extreme claims for their position, the attempt at what might be called "joint universalism" was not destined to succeed and Church and State would find themselves competing, and not co-operating, for men's allegiance.

But neither Pope nor Emperor behaved with moderation and restraint, and for several centuries they fought each other in bitter conflict. They looked for allies and intrigued with cities and bishops and local bodies to gain more power. The ideal which had begun as a co-operation of two universal authorities bound together in a mystic unity degenerated into little more than a medieval struggle for the balance of power; and the representatives of God, both civil and spiritual, succumbed to the typical methods of common political bargaining. Both Imperial and Papal agencies forgot their duty as shepherds, and called religion into play as a servant to their material ambitions. For a time (1056) Emperor Henry III triumphed over the Pope; but soon after his death the Papacy turned the tables and developed the remarkable power and organization which for several hundred years was to dominate European politics. This was largely due to Pope Gregory VII and his successors. They asserted the supremacy of the spiritual over the temporal. Gregory went so far as to declare that kings and dukes were unworthy beings, claimed the right of deposing political rulers, and threatened with the direst penalties those bishops who accepted investiture at the hands of lay authorities. The Empire must abandon all claims to invest prelates; it must release Church property from all feudal charges; it must be prepared to receive rebukes from the Pope, and must accept the Pope's dictates in matters of peace and war.

With the defeat of Emperor Frederick II (1250) the Empire fell and ceased to be a universal agency of real power. It was to continue as an ideal and a theory, but its great days had ended. The Papacy seemed to have won an unqualified triumph. The Church became the great center of European life and the controller of its destiny. Pope Innocent III placed France under interdict until the King restored his wife to her legitimate place. He also put England under interdict and excommunicated King John. He nominated and deposed emperors. He set in motion various crusades, and claimed the right to mediate disputes between monarchs and between rulers and their subjects.

But the Church was not the only unit of government. There was the Emperor. There were the feudal lords, many of whom looked with fear and suspicion upon the claims of the Pope, many of whom disliked the sending of so much revenue to Rome. They opposed the claims of the Pope to be supreme arbiter because of the absence of a universally recognized system of international law.

Moreover, feudal law varied from state to state, and there was no authoritative code; nor was there any guaranty that the Pope, a nonexpert, would be qualified to settle points of feudal law. Nevertheless, the Papacy continued to make its exclusive claims and asserted that the Church might give and take away from subjects the right of citizenship, and that religious consecration was necessary before accepting temporal authority. Thus the Pope could use a doctrine to support rivals of an irreligious or anti-Papal King.

Note, too, that the Church had in reality become engaged in an amazing amount of legislative, administrative, and legal activity. Canon law covered a wide field. Rome exercised a universal appellate jurisdiction. The Church claimed the right to excommunicate and interdict and could denounce heresy and make the confessional obligatory. These religio-political powers clashed with the growing system of state or national law and, as already mentioned, with the feudal law. Another factor also appeared. The extension of trade and commerce revived ancient customs and rules which gradually developed into a cosmopolitan system, the Law Merchant, enforced by the merchant courts of various countries. Economic life was developing its own organization, methods, and scales of value.

Moreover, national law was beginning to grow up, in England

from the twelfth century and in other parts of Europe more slowly. The growing power of the princes and the national states took place at the expense of the feudal lords below and the Emperor and the Pope above. A new unit more extensive than the feudal and more suited to economic needs grew up. Whatever the theory of European unity under Church and Empire, the practice was frequently deplorable. Disorder was rampant. The new national units were in many ways not efficient instruments of government; but the King and the state which developed in opposition to feudalism on the one hand and to the Pope and Church on the other did serve a real need, and their growth challenged the whole basis of medieval society.

In the earlier years princes and Papacy had combined when the imperial power had threatened to become too strong and oppressive. Ranke remarks that they advanced in parallel steps—both in opposition to the Empire. Gradually the princes developed the doctrine that headship of the Universal Empire should not remain within a hereditary house but should be regarded "as residing in the collective body of the princes rather than in the person of the emperor." And in this attempt to limit the power of the Emperor the princes carried their appeals to the Papacy. But it was always open to the princes to join the Emperor against the Pope in case the latter became too powerful and threatened their position. When Innocent III claimed the right to nominate the Emperor, the princes realized that his claim, if successful, would negate their theory that the headship of the Empire resided in themselves collectively. And as the princes increased their own power, they also realized that a victory of the Pope over the Emperor would mean that the Pope's universal claims would be soon turned against them. Later history justified the fears of the princes and kings: the Papal pretensions which had successfully triumphed over the Empire now threatened the new national states, whose rulers naturally then turned against the Pope, who had formerly been their supporter against the Empire. A new conflict appeared on the European scene—the King and his State versus the Pope and the Church.

Pope Boniface VIII issued the Bull of 1296 that monarchs had no power to tax the clergy or even to accept voluntary grants. Such a measure seriously imperiled the whole basis of national existence, and national opposition was not slow in appearing. The English had already passed the Statute of Mortmain in 1279 forbidding any further alienation of knights' fees to the Church. Parliament insisted that Edward I should not submit the question of his conquest of Scotland to the arbitration of the Pope, to whom the Scotch had appealed on the ground that they were his fief. Philip of France burned the Papal Bull of 1302; he refused to permit the export of precious metals from France; and he summoned the Estates-General in 1303 hoping to unite all classes in a national resistance to the Papal claims.

At this time the Papacy suffered a well-nigh fatal blow. It had become a battleground of factions, and in 1305, following a period of confusion, Pope Clement V withdrew from Rome to Avignon in France and began the so-called "Babylonian captivity," during which the Papacy was, in the eyes of Europe, a tool of the French.[4] Thus had the destruction of the Empire involved the Church itself in ruin; for while the Empire existed the new nationalism had hesitated to attack the Papacy, but with the Empire gone the new national states were free to challenge the authority of the Pope more openly. And the Pope, removed from Rome and the tradition of Rome's universal greatness, lost both prestige and independence. The princes and kings feared that France would use the Papacy to increase its power in Europe. The other countries increasingly opposed the financial claims of the Pope; for he not only was living in France but was actually lending money to the French kings! And what nation desired to strengthen its political rival? In 1372 the Rhineland monasteries resisted a Papal levy; Bavaria in 1367 had forbidden the clergy to pay tribute to the Pope, saying that "their country is a free country"; the English Parliament passed several acts to limit the amount of money which could be remitted to the Papacy; in 1363 by the Statute of Praemunire it restricted the right of legal appeal to the Papal Court and increased the power of the English Crown over the judicial rights of the clergy. Undoubtedly the action of England, betokening a weakened allegiance to the Pope, arose in no small measure from the transfer of the Papacy to Avignon, which lay in the territory of France, England's traditional enemy. The same principles were to clash in the League of Nations over five hundred years later.

Public opinion in Europe in 1367 forced Pope Irwin V to return to Rome; but the influence of the French Cardinals and the weariness of the Pope himself caused him to go back to France in 1370. This step dismayed the Italians, whose reaction was so strong that eighty cities formed a league to induce the Pope again

[4] Just as the League of Nations, a universal institution, was later regarded by many critics as an agency of French designs.

to reside in Rome. And in 1377 Gregory re-entered the Holy City. National rivalries mounted higher and became so unrestrained that for almost forty years Europe had two Popes. The Great Schism, as Workman suggests, marks the triumph of the spirit of nationalism over the spirit of European solidarity which for centuries had formed the basis of Catholicism. French, Gastons, and Italians were now attempting to reduce the Papacy to a national institution and make it serve political ends. The Church, instead of being the ruler of Europe and maintaining its spiritual and cultural unity, was becoming a unit in international diplomacy. Its "universalism" had been unable to withstand the centrifugal tendencies of the growing national states. In denying a measure of independence to the secular rulers, it had evoked a national feeling which was to reject the claims of the Papacy and reduce the Church to subordination and impotence.

The condition of the Church and its drastic need of reform caused many Catholics to consider the possibility of improvement by curtailing the power of the Pope and placing authority in a representative council of the Church. Such a council would check any waywardness or misjudgment of the Pope, and would bring together different sections of Europe which were objecting to the extreme supra-national claims of the Papacy. Why should there not be a federal council which could represent the national groups in a Catholic Europe? Cardinals could then be representatives of their nations, and would meet in ecumenical conference. Christian unity would thus be combined with national self-consciousness and Christ's Kingdom be strengthened. These proposals were made at the Council of Constance in 1415.

Unfortunately the attempt failed.[5] The liberal-minded Catholic leaders could not restrain the conservative policy of the Popes, who, despite and perhaps because of these nationalist challenges to their traditional authority, intensified the all-embracing claims of the Papacy. In turn the universal pretensions of the Church were later to call forth heated claims of absolute sovereignty and independence on the part of the state. The failure of the compromise at Constance in 1415 led to a "hardening of temper," the development of uncompromising attitudes, and a head-on clash between the "secular" state and the "spiritual" Church!

[5] Will the attempt to build a European federalism on secular foundations in 1940–1950 succeed, when it failed long ago to reconcile religious unity and national autonomy?

The Reformation movement completed the disunity of Christendom. Luther opposed the Church and exalted the power of the German princes. He claimed divine origin for royal power, insisted that subjects give absolute obedience to their rulers, and condemned the peasants for revolting against lawfully constituted secular authority. He set the divine right of kings against the divine institution of the Church, and even advocated giving control over religion to the sovereign princes. He gave a tremendous impetus to the state, and encouraged a policy which was to repudiate the ideal of the Church Universal and to become closely identified with the growing national states.

Machiavelli was also expounding the all-importance of the ruler and the state. His teachings struck a further blow at the Church and at religion as the unifying agency of Europe, and intensified the forces making for political and social disunity.

Meanwhile Europe was experiencing a curious confusion of religion and politics, similar to the confusion which we find in the modern world. For more than a hundred years people were torn by the conflicting loyalties of religious faith and the growing nationalism. Was a person primarily a Frenchman, owing allegiance to his king, or was he above all a Catholic, bound by indissoluble ties to the Church? The question became a real one to the people of Christian Europe, and the religious wars from 1500 to 1700 showed that men had not yet finally chosen nationalism as their god, for Catholics and Protestants still fought each other to the death within the bosom of a single state. The universal idea of the Papacy was still the living politico-religious faith of millions of people; and many Protestants, too, who did not think in political terms but merely desired peace and salvation for their souls, fought and suffered for religious freedom, and opposed the claim of the state to mediate between God and man.

Others attempted to reconcile religion and nationalism, or tried to separate the spheres of politics and religion.[6] Many Catholics believed that they could remain good Catholics in religion and be good Frenchmen in politics; many of them were willing to support a foreign Protestant prince against a foreign Catholic ruler if such an action would strengthen the political power of France, even though it meant weakening the influence of the Church by weakening its political allies. Nor did this confusion of loyalties complete the picture. The Emperor still claimed a paramount position and watched the mounting claims to inde-

[6] The same forces are at work in the Moslem world today.

pendence of kings and princes with deep concern. Each of the units—Church, Empire, and nation—became engaged in a contest to gain and preserve as much power as possible for itself. The Reformation unloosed these criss-cross emotions and produced a veritable chaos of tangled forces. For thirty years, the struggle continued: Emperor versus nation, Emperor versus Pope, Pope versus nation, shifting alliances, and confusion of purposes. It is not surprising; for Europe was engaged in changing its fundamental basis; and changing fundamentals necessarily produces doubt and confusion.

The Treaty of Augsburg (1555) provided a temporary peace for Germany and for Europe. It set up a confederation of German states and permitted some of the princes to secularize their lands. But the Treaty satisfied few people in an age of rising tempers and incompatible ideas. The Emperor desired to maintain his old position of supremacy, and continued to resist the thought of surrendering power to the national princes. Some of these national princes, on the other hand, were dissatisfied because they still had to submit to certain Imperial limitations upon their independence. The Pope disapproved because the treaty had been signed without his sanction—the first treaty in the history of Europe to dispense with religious approval. Moreover, the Pope and the Church viewed the loss of their lands with considerable alarm. Thus the compromise between the Emperor, the princes, and the Church did not endure; and at the Council of Trent, 1545–1563, the Church organized a great counter-reformation to win back for Catholicism the ground which had been lost and to restore the Church to its position of universal authority.

The Counter-Reformation is extremely important in the development of the modern state. The Church, in trying to regain its religious supremacy, used political and social methods which had tremendous political consequences. The forces on the side of the Church were the Jesuits, the Catholic monarchs, and the Inquisition. The Jesuit order sent its members all over Europe to work for the restoration of the universal Catholic faith. They worked in Ireland against the Protestant English King Henry VIII; they participated in the 1571 plot against Elizabeth and the Gunpowder Plot to blow up King James I in 1605; they influenced the German Emperor and the King of Poland; and they sided with the Guise faction in France. The Church also utilized outstanding political leaders like Philip II of Spain, the Emperor Ferdinand II, and King Sigismund of Poland; it established the

Inquisition to punish heretics, and through the Jesuits set up educational institutions in various parts of Europe to train leaders to carry the banner of the Church and push forward its policy.

To the Church, heresy was one of the greatest sins. To permit men and women to dwell in mortal error and so imperil their eternal souls was terrible. To overthrow heretics who sat on the thrones of nations and controlled the destinies of millions of individuals was vital. To the orthodox Catholic, nationalistic ambitions were as dust in the scales compared with the overwhelming importance of maintaining the unity of the Christian faith. But when in order to maintain religious unity such political methods were adopted as the Spanish Armada against England, the use of fire and sword by Spain in the Netherlands, and plotting and intrigue against national monarchs, it is not surprising that in the defense of their own country Protestants became still more nationalist: They were fighting for their faith, but they were fighting also for their hearths and homes.

To countries like France which had both Protestants and Catholics this hundred-year period brought grim tragedy, as Frenchmen fought Frenchmen in the name of religion. In other lands the same bitter conflicts occurred; and it was not until the political loyalty of subjects had grown stronger than their religious faith that the modern state was established on its present foundations.

When the state had become more firmly organized, what happened to the all-embracing claims of the Pope and the assertion of the Church universal? No longer could the Papacy ignore the existence of the sovereign state, however much it might deplore it. It was obvious that there was no longer a united Christendom, and that the Pope no longer stood as the supreme head of one great assembly of the faithful. At the conclusion of the great religious wars of 1618–1648 the Treaties of Westphalia revealed that the Pope had suffered an irreparable loss of power and prestige, and that Europe had rejected his claim to unlimited authority and had turned to the ideal of the modern state. The new settlement, by depriving the Catholic Church of its universal power, opened the way to what we know as "modern international relations," i.e., relations among sovereign states. Territorialism and Protestantism had gained a permanent place in Europe. The religious and civil powers were no longer two aspects of one society; Church and State had become two different institutions. International politics had become secularized.

But the Papacy did not submit to the "secularization" of European and world politics without protest. The Treaties of Westphalia threatened the whole basis of Catholic supremacy which had been so patiently built up during the centuries. Wangereck, and other apologists, protested against the Treaties because (1) the princes had granted the right of worship to heretics, but only the Pope, as the guardian of men's souls, could exercise such a power; (2) the princes had wrongly set aside the jurisdiction of the Church when they had extinguished "certain bishopries and other ecclesiastical rights or decrees." Wangereck protested also against the general formula which had been inserted in the Treaties in order to override and nullify any Papal protest.

Here stood the signpost marking the change from the medieval to the modern system of international relations. The Pope's protest might enable a state to break its treaty obligations, on the plea that the Pope's superior command ordered it to do so; in that event there could be no guaranty of treaty observation and stability. Therefore, the princes deemed it important to guard against the possibility of permitting Papal interference. They did this by inserting a most remarkable clause:

That there shall never be alleged, heard, or allowed, neither against this Treaty nor any of these articles or clauses, any canon or civil law, nor any general or special decrees of councils, whether privileges, indults, edicts, commissions, inhibitions, mandates, decrees, rescripts, pendencies, sentences, rendered at any time whatsoever, [any] verdicts, imperial capitularies, or other rules or exemptions of religious orders, whether former or future protests, appellations, investitures, transactions, oaths, renunciations, all sorts of pacts, still less the edict of 1629, or the Transaction of Prague with its appendixes, or the concordats with the popes, or the interim of the year 1548, or any other statutes, whether political or ecclesiastical decrees, dispensations, absolutions, or any other thing which can be imagined under whatever name or pretext; nor shall there anywhere ever be decreed against this transaction indictments or commissions either from the side of the seeker or possessor.[7]

The Treaties of Westphalia did not end the conflict between Church and State. The Papacy has made many protests against treaties between secular powers during the last three hundred years. One may note especially the protest against the Treaty of Vienna in 1815, both for its secularization of German ecclesias-

[7] Quoted in Carl Conrad Eckhardt, *The Papacy and World Affairs* (The University of Chicago Press, 1937), p. 138.

tical lands and its failure to restore the Holy Roman Empire, described by the Papal nuncio as "the center of political unity consecrated by the august character of religion." But the protests and threats of the Church were of no avail and were merely noted.

Nevertheless, arrangements had to be made between the new secular states and the Papacy, because, although the states claimed the exclusive loyalty of their subjects, the fact could not be denied that millions of men and women were devoted to the Catholic faith. They had two loyalties; moreover, a sovereign state which ruthlessly attempted to uproot the religious loyalties would run the risk of having its own foundations overturned, and the Catholic Church could not force its own religionists to forego their political loyalties. A compromise was reached in the form of the Concordat, an arrangement between the Papacy and the state which regulated the rights and privileges of bishops and other officials of the Church and of the body of people themselves. The Concordats are in a sense a truce between two irreconcilable views of life. The fundamentals of the Catholic Church cannot be reconciled with the fundamentals of the modern sovereign state. The two instruments may compromise their differences, but a compromise only it will be. Basically the same is true regarding the Protestant and other religions.

The state system set up in the seventeenth century was largely absolutist in character. The French Revolution challenged the social foundations of the absolutist order and attempted to take charge of the state and to change its internal nature. In 1814 a conservative restoration took place. Within the formal framework of the state, many variations were possible: Theoretically, it made little difference who controlled the state, seeing that the state was a sovereign entity; but in practice differences of social complexion had far-reaching consequences.

The earlier state system was not synonymous with the modern nation, and, indeed, nationalism arose as a rebellious movement against the established state order. Almost no modern nation has arisen to power except by war. The Turkish, Austrian, Russian, Spanish, and, in a sense, the British empires, were each transformed, having to give independence to their nationalities at the point of the sword. But the new nations transformed themselves into states. In a theoretical sense, the state remained unaltered. It was still sovereign, but only in the most formal sense could the sovereignty of the hitherto subordinate fragments be the same as the sovereignty of the empires of which they had been a part.

The establishment of the national state did not end the loyalty of many of their subjects either to the Catholic Church or to local institutions, some of which retained a distinctively feudal flavor. But the theories of sovereignty and the exclusive devotion to the new political theory of nationality obscured the fact that many rule-making agencies outside of the state remained effective and that many groups which had amalgamated retained their special interests. The theory of monoloyalty tended to hide these other deep-seated factors.

The state and the later nationalist societies came into contact with other forms of government, and the impact had momentous results. The Sultan of Turkey was not only the political ruler of the Turkish Empire but also the caliph of the Moslem faith; in the latter capacity he exercised a great influence over millions of Mohammedans who lived outside his political domain. Europe was to have plenty of evidence that the Moslem society could not be easily fitted into or reconciled with the modern sovereign state. But after 1918 the Moslem unity of religion gave way to the new political fashion of nationalism, although much of the Middle East still is in a condition of confused loyalty similar to that of Europe in the seventeenth century.

The history of the Far East shows the results of the impact of the European sovereign-state system upon the Chinese society with its principle of suzerainty, and we need do no more at this point than emphasize the fact that part of the difficulty of international relations lies in the fact that some countries have adopted the theory and practice of sovereignty while others have not. The rise of Communism and of Nazism as supra-national phenomena for a time (and perhaps that time is not yet finished) constituted a threat to the whole of the Western state system, because they substituted for the state, which they regarded as an instrument of economic exploitation of the poor by the rich, the doctrines of a unity of workers irrespective of national boundaries or of a superior race whose destiny it is to rule other races. We have still to see whether or not the theory of Communism will itself not be transformed into a nationalist pattern as Christianity in so many cases has been transformed.

An analysis of nationalism shows there is no one variety of nationalism—that it is a mistake to consider it a static phenomenon—for one of the characteristics of most nationalisms is their desire to expand, and the line between nationalism and imperialism is a difficult one to draw. Moreover, in a sense any group which chooses to regard itself as a national group may be justified in doing so, and the minority problem of Europe shows that whatever the theory of the sovereign state may be there are minority groups which spoil the beauty of the structure so neatly imagined by theorists. Why should not the Croatians be regarded as a nation if they can in turn throw off the rule of the dominant Yugoslavian government and become a nation-state? They have a common history and tradition. (But what is a common history and tradition? A moment's reflection will show that it is by no means a simple conception.) They have a desire for independence. The question arises, what kind of independence?

Finally, the new developments of applied science and the rapid expansion of economic life have shown that, whatever meaning be attached to the word sovereignty, the modern state or, if one prefers, the modern nation cannot, except in a purely formal sense, control its own destinies. Whether we wish it or not, the evidence forces us to conclude that the manifold complexities of modern life necessitate new forms of government.[8]

SUMMARY

The survey just given should make it clear that there has been no single pattern in government at any one time, that although there has been a predominant tendency in any given age there have always been survivals of other forms of government which, in varying degrees, have been combined with or incorporated into the new form. But the new form has also been in continual process of transformation. Often theories that have grown up and have largely reflected the temper of the time in which they developed have been carried forward to dominate the thinking of the next generations or even centuries. These theories may conserve values; but in a rapidly changing age like our own, they may do much harm, because they may cause an excessive rigidity of attitude in a civilization which above all requires elasticity.

There have in fact been many societies, but theory tends to pick out one or more of them and ascribe undue prominence to them. With the development of international trade and other contacts, new systems grow up which promise solidarity between individuals belonging to distinct political groups.[9]

The greater the inter-social relationship and solidarity, the

[8] See W. A. Robson, *Civilization and the Growth of Law* (The Macmillan Company, 1935).

[9] See G. Scelle, "The Law of Peoples," quoted in Zimmern, *Modern Political Doctrines* (Oxford University Press, 1939), pp. 291–92.

greater will be the need of restraints, because only by restraint and agreement to act consistently according to agreed-upon rules can society exist.

The fluctuating nature of units of government and the shifting content of law can be seen in an analysis of the changing relations between state and federal governments within a federal nation. The United States may be cited as an outstanding example.

Congress took action in the control over rivers, over radio, and over white slavery when the facts demanded adequate laws, but there were many fields in which the national legislature could not take so direct a step. In agricultural research the federal and state agencies co-operate in a close manner. Agreements are drawn up with states to prevent the spread of animal diseases. Co-operation exists in the sphere of food and drug acts. The two types of authority work together to control narcotics, to provide more efficient vocational education. For nearly forty years, annual conferences of state public health authorities have taken place; state and federal labor departments co-operate to collect statistics on employment and wages and other matters. The Federal Bureau of Mines and the Federal Bureau of Reclamation would be much hampered unless they had the co-operation of the states. The same holds true of fisheries.

Every year a national conference of commissioners on uniform state laws meets to consider the problem of lessening the differences which exist in the laws of the forty-eight states. Some progress has been effected in connection with bills of lading, negotiable instruments, partnerships, aeronautics, automobile traffic, motor registration, divorce, etc. Much remains to be done before the law is brought into line with the requirements of continental economic and social life. In the executive sphere the National Convention of Insurance Commissioners is at work to standardize many requirements. The National Board of Fire Insurance Commissioners is attempting to develop more uniform requirements in the regulations which govern building throughout the country. Few of us realize the great importance of uniform weights and measures and the bewildering complexity within the United States. Taxation problems are legion, not the least being the problem of double taxation. Interstate agreements have made possible the construction of great bridges and tunnels and the use and distribution of waters from rivers flowing in more than one state. Some states have reciprocal agreements for the exchange of insane persons. Agreements are necessary for the extradition of persons of one state from another for judicial purposes. These are only a few of the ways in which states and federal authorities co-operate in order to meet the growing needs of trade and commerce within the country. The rules which grow up are, in Scelle's word, "secreted" in order that the solidarity may be maintained and developed.

It is only a matter of degree, and not of kind, when such co-operation spreads beyond the boundaries of a national state. The elimination of obstacles between nations in their trade and commerce has the same purpose as the elimination of obstacles within a federal union. Double taxation is an inter- as well as an intranational problem. Weights and measures, co-operation in health, labor standards, joint use of international rivers, measures to control narcotics, greater uniformity in negotiable instruments and bills of lading, agricultural co-operation, the prevention of the spread of animal diseases, extradition problems—all extend beyond the boundaries of every nation and constitute a series of concentric circles, as it were, an ever widening sphere of activity, in which common rules must be drawn up. The more extensive the national circles become, the more they intersect other national circles, and the more rules must be developed so that intercourse will take place in an orderly fashion; else, owing to the excessive rigidity and exclusiveness of national law, or national emotion, or both, the wider relation must be hampered and run the risk of being destroyed. To a large degree government is government by co-operation; it is not only that, because the suppression of crime and the enforcement of order require restraints. But Scelle's major conclusion remains unassailable—that for the maintenance of sound and efficient life every inter-social standard "must take precedence of every conflicting internal standard" and must either modify it or invalidate it.

In the light of this analysis one can see why some scholars claim that international law began with the writings of the Spanish jurists and of Grotius in the sixteenth and seventeenth centuries and why other scholars go much farther back in history. Some are more and others are less impressed by the sharpness of outline of the modern state, and upon this attitude will depend their judgment upon several matters now to be discussed.

INTERNATIONAL LAW AND THE MODERN STATE

After the breakdown of the feudal system and the political authority of the medieval Church, as we have seen, the modern state arose and developed the theory of sovereignty presently to be examined. Nevertheless, intercourse between peoples did not cease and rules to govern that intercourse gradually evolved. These rules constituted the beginnings of modern international law as we know it. They were helped by the spread of Roman Law throughout Europe during the Middle Ages and by the rules or regulations developed in order to serve the needs of medieval trade and commerce. Towns and cities had to work out rules in order to regularize conditions under which ordinary peaceful trading between relatively independent towns might take place. Indeed, they formed leagues, the most famous of which were the Hanseatic League, the League of the Rhine, and the Swabian League, which set up arbitration methods and united for the defense of the interests of their members.

The growth of sea trade led merchants from different cities to work out codes which dealt with many complicated problems arising in ocean transportation. The formation of the British and Dutch East India Companies and other similar organizations, often under government auspices or at least with official encouragement, assisted in the same direction. Grotius' famous work, *Mare Liberum,* which deeply influenced the course of international law, was written to assert the right of Dutch merchants to participate in the trade of East India.

The century-old habit of sending official representatives with diplomatic status led to rules of official intercourse which regularized the ways in which governments transacted business with one another. Men realized that rules of war must be adopted if conflicts between communities were not to degenerate into irresponsible massacres; if war was to be an appeal to force in order to obtain rights or to remedy wrongs, and not just wanton destruction of human life, it must be fought according to methods agreed upon by the different peoples. Scholars did not lose the ideal of the intellectual unity of Europe; and the Church and theological writers kept alive the intellectual and spiritual background which formed the inspiration for many scholars in their endeavor to build a more orderly society in Europe.

The jurists played an important part by their appeal to the law of nature.[10] The concept of natural law is not so easily expressed

[10] The factors which contributed to the development of international law are dealt with in G. A. Finch, *The Sources of Modern International Law* (Carnegie Endowment for International Peace. Washington, D.C., 1937), chapters 1–3.

in nontechnical language, but perhaps for the general reader it can be put thus: Human beings cannot disregard the natural world in which they live. They must have food and water, warmth and shelter. If they wish to build a house or a road or a harbor, to sail a ship, to paint a picture, to play an instrument, or to construct a machine, they must follow certain rules. If they are to be efficient they must adapt themselves to the requirements imposed by the nature of the materials with which they work; and they must take into account the nature of human beings; the society which ignores or violates some of these fundamental facts of life must pay the penalty.

Political law cannot ignore certain fundamental natural conditions. The weakness of the naturalist school of jurists lay in their too easily identifying so-called physical laws with human laws. Nevertheless, it is basically true that human standards must be built within certain limits of natural forces, and mankind does well to remember the earth-bound and nature-bound conditions of its existence. It is in this sense that natural law forms the basis of international law. Sheer necessity requires that individuals and peoples in their dealings with one another shall observe restraint, promote order, and live within a considerable measure of routine.

The development of international law was profoundly influenced by the rise of the modern state. One might even say that its very existence was challenged by the new theories which grew up, and especially by the concept of sovereignty, which, from relatively humble beginnings, came to dominate much of the legal thinking of the West. Originally *sovrain* (from the Latin *superanus*) meant "superior" and "superiority"; it is a relative term, which implies that there are persons subordinate to the "superior," and was used in the sixteenth and seventeenth centuries (1) to justify the separation of the state from the medieval Church and free it from ecclesiastical interference; and (2) to centralize power in the monarch in order to bring unity to the state from within and break the independent power of feudal lords, cities, and other local authorities. From that meaning, it grew until today states use it to justify their absolute independence and their right to do anything in international life which they will to do.

Luther helped to expand the idea of sovereignty by calling upon the secular princes to reform the Church. Since the Church was a divinely ordained institution, the prince had to have a correspondingly divine status if he was to exercise power over it; and Luther used theological arguments for the purpose of freeing the state from external interference at the hands of the Roman Church. Bodin in 1556 published his *De Republica,* in which he argued that in every state there must be a central power, the sole creator of laws, yet not bound by them. Bodin had not cast off certain medieval ideas; hence he did not carry his theory to a logical conclusion; "his sovereign, though not bound by the law of the land, was bound by divine law, by the law of nature, and also by the law of nations," and even by certain fundamental laws. Nevertheless Bodin had "laid the foundation of national sovereignty."

Gentilis (1551–1608) took the important step of separating international law from theology and ethics and made it a branch of jurisprudence.[11] In contrast to the Spanish writer, Victoria, who based international law upon medieval religious foundations, Gentilis turned to the actual practice of states in order to find out what was the nature of international law.

During the sixteenth century the state was mainly concerned in establishing its internal sovereignty and preventing interference from without. When Spain, England, Portugal, and Holland began to found their colonial empires, the state began to assert sovereignty in its external relations. It was to be free from restraints imposed by any other authority in its expansion abroad; no other human institution could limit it. Sovereignty thus grew in meaning. This transition was accomplished by Grotius (1583–1645), who wrote his *De jure belli et pacis* in 1625. He attempted to do two major things: (1) He attempted to prove that the independence of states must be accepted, and that the idea of sovereignty must be conceded. The ruler must have power over his subjects, but he must use his power to promote justice. Because man is a rational being, he must obey natural law or "the dictate of right reason." The sovereign therefore was not free to act without a view to right conduct. (2) He also attempted to mitigate the barbarities of war. He wrote during the great Thirty Years' struggle (1618–1648), which evoked terrible passions and cruelty "as if a single edict had released a madness driving men to all kinds of crime." So, while accepting sovereignty, he tried to make it compatible with distinguishing between a lawful and an unlawful war. A sovereign must indulge only in lawful or just wars. He is not free to abuse his sovereign rights but must obey the law of nature.

[11] See E. D. Dickinson, "Changing Concepts and the Doctrine of Incorporation," *American Journal of International Law,* April 1932.

Unfortunately the law of nature was not a clear-cut system of specific rules; and the very vagueness of the concept enabled rulers to do it lip service, if they so desired, and yet go to war. Nor did Grotius' attempt to distinguish between a just and an unjust, a legal and an illegal, war fare better. In the absence of any third party to judge between two states in a dispute, each could claim that it was fighting in a just cause. Grotius had made it possible for later princes and theorists to use his idea to give a cloak of legality to their aggressive designs. His attempt to clarify the distinction between a legal and an illegal, a just and an unjust war failed because of the absence of satisfactory international machinery to give an impartial and authoritative verdict. Perhaps he was too close to the days of the medieval Church to be able to propose any supra-national machinery.

Despite his great service, Grotius gave an emphasis to international law which was in one respect unfortunate. He was so preoccupied with the problem of war that he gave it a disproportionate share of attention and did less than justice to the necessity of building up everyday rules to make possible the smoother functioning of the peaceful relations between peoples and states. Sovereignty thus became increasingly associated with the right to make war, and the restraints imposed by the law of nature dissolved under the critical thought of the eighteenth and nineteenth centuries.

For, given the idea of sovereignty or independence, some thinker was bound sooner or later to develop the concept to its logical conclusion. That thinker was Thomas Hobbes (1588–1679), who with incisive skill argued that if the state is supreme, if it is to give orders to all and accept orders from none, then there is no way in which its will can be bound except by its consent or by its being conquered by another. Relations between states cannot therefore be permanently organized except by treaty—an agreement between sovereign states—and a state, being sovereign, may break off the agreement when it so wills. The belief in natural law as a source of international law was therefore weakened and gave place to the idea that only positive law had any validity. Despite Pufendorf (1632–94) and Bynkershoek (1673–1743) the fashion of legal thinking turned toward regarding international law as no more than the rules by which sovereign states agreed to abide. Ideas of natural law were regarded as "metajurisprudence" or were relegated to the domain of philosophy or theology and therefore of no concern to the jurist. Vattel (1714–

69), who accepted the positivist view, wrote that sovereign states must be regarded as so many free persons living together: men are by nature equal and states are therefore equal; "strength or weakness produces in this regard no distinction . . . . a small republic is no less a sovereign state than the most powerful kingdom." From these premises the doctrine of the equality of states naturally followed; and, because states are sovereign and cannot be bound except by their own will, a unanimous vote is necessary before a multilateral treaty can come into effect. If unanimity is required, even a small state can legally prevent a proposal which other sovereign states have agreed to from applying to itself.

John Austin and others in the nineteenth century continued the same line of reasoning, with the result that a modern doctrine of sovereignty, far more pretentious than in its original form, became enthroned in modern international relations. Its main ideas may be summarized: (1) Law is the command of a sovereign. What is not commanded by a sovereign cannot truly bear the name of law. (2) Law must be enforced. Without enforceability, there cannot be law in the true sense. That which distinguishes law from other rules in society is the power of the state to enforce it. (3) A sovereign state is legally and politically independent, and owes no habitual allegiance to any other human superior. Should, by any chance, a sovereign agree to a limitation of its authority, such action is no more than an autolimitation, a choice of its own free will which may be altered at its own pleasure. (4) Since law is a command, there can be no limitations imposed by "natural law." Things, values, and actions rooted in the very nature of life itself which lie beyond the commanding power of the sovereign state there may be; but there are not laws to which positive law must be subordinate. (5) From this viewpoint international law cannot be true law: It has no sovereign power, no enforcing power behind it. So-called international law may represent convention, agreement, or morality; but it is not true law. (6) Consequently no external power has any right to interfere with the internal affairs of a sovereign state which cannot admit any legal restrictions on its freedom of action in foreign affairs. It may disregard treaties, declare war, and carry out national policy, without legal let or hindrance.

The theory of sovereignty did not remain unchallenged. Many jurists criticized it from the viewpoint of legal science. They asserted that: (1) Law is as much the result of consent and agreement as it is of command, perhaps more so. Even a dictator must rule in accordance with public opinion. (2) A law is an expression of man's "material, intellectual and moral needs."[12] There are many factors which contribute to giving power to a government, which "it seems clear can only maintain itself in any durable fashion through the belief of its subjects that the rulers perform their functions." The basis of public law then becomes a matter of organization. If laws are passed to regulate and operate public services and facilitate private services, government and its officials "are no longer the organs of a corporate person issuing its commands. They are simply the managers of the nation's business." (3) Merely to say that law is a command and to disregard its purpose and its material aim is to "distort" one of its most essential factors, namely, the ideal of justice.[13] Law is not merely the instrumentality or expression of a command; it is an agency of justice. This justice, difficult though it may be to define, is or should be superior to even the authority of the state. (4) Historically, law existed for long periods before the advent of the sovereign state. The Mosaic Law, Hammurabi's Code, the Code of Manu, and Medieval Canon Law illustrate the close connection between law and religious belief. Hundreds of tribes have regarded law as the embodiment of tradition; and custom administered by the old men or the chief or the priest is the law for these societies. In Europe, from the days of Greece and Rome, the concept of natural law, the work of philosophers and jurists, profoundly influenced legal systems.[14] The historian would therefore claim that to regard law as nothing more than a command is to ignore its historical development and to overstress the merely modern period. Indeed, the critics go further; they say that the doctrine of sovereignty arose from an assertion of national independence at a time when society was reacting against the universal claims of the Church on the one hand and disorderly, quarrelsome, local and feudal groups on the other, and to erect a theory developed in response to particular conditions into a general rule for other times is unscientific in method and mischievous in practice. (5) Despite the claim that sovereignty is one and indivisible,

[12] Order or law "of any kind is preferable to anarchy." It is rooted in sheer necessity, if life is to be livable. See Charles Fairman, "Sovereignty and War." in *Proceedings of the Institute of World Affairs* (University of Southern California), 1941.

[13] See "International Ethics," preliminary (1928) report of the Committee on International Ethics of the Catholic Association for International Peace.

[14] See Lon. L. Fuller, *Law in Quest of Itself* (Foundation Press, 1940).

it is impossible to locate sovereignty in many nations, especially those with a federal system, where power is divided between the central and state governments and neither is finally supreme. In modern government, where division of powers increasingly takes place and delegated legislatures and administrative law are expanding,[15] one can speak of law as command only in a purely abstract and formalistic fashion. (6) The theory of sovereignty is based upon an artificial conception of society. Men and women are not merely citizens of the state but also producers and members of special groups, i.e., trade unions, employers' associations, churches, clubs, professions, etc. It is incorrect, critics say, to assume that these nonpolitical associations are created by the state and depend upon the will of the state. Rather, these groups arise spontaneously and carry out their group activities essentially independent of the state. The state therefore cannot in any important sense be said to be sovereign in its relation to these "independently originating and functioning groups." (8) Not only is the state one of a number of groups within its own territory, or at best an association of associations; it is also only an association among associations. To ignore the interrelationship of nations, merely to speak of the independence, and not to consider the interdependence, of nations is to look at them in an entirely formalistic manner. To talk in theoretical terms of absolute sovereignty when the nation is in fact not thoroughly independent is highly misleading. To concentrate attention on one group, the nation, and to disregard the many groups inside and outside its borders is to see one part of the picture only.

From the viewpoint of international organization there are also serious reasons for doubting the soundness of the theory elaborated by the more eloquent and extreme defenders of "supreme or absolute sovereignty." The so-called sovereign state comes into the family of nations only by reason of the recognition accorded it by the society of nations, which may require the fulfillment of certain international obligations. Most of the nations which gained the recognition of their independence in the nineteenth century and since 1918 did so concurrently with acceptance of certain responsibilities. Belgium and Holland undertook to grant religious equality; Greece was recognized as an independent power on condition that it grant civil and political equality to its new subjects. In 1858 Rumania made certain promises, especially

---

[15] See Karl Olivecrana, *Law as a Fact* (Oxford University Press, 1939).

undertaking not to impose discriminatory legislation upon Jews. After 1918 several of the new governments, some of them under protest it is true, accepted the Minorities Treaties, under which they promised to afford civil and religious liberty to minorities living within their borders.

These obligations of an international character cannot lightly be dismissed by a gratuitous assertion that a sovereign state has freedom to do just what it likes. It cannot by mere unilateral action, or by adopting a particular constitution, free itself from its international commitments. The Permanent Court of International Justice has put it thus: "A state cannot adduce as against another state its own constitution with a view to evading obligations incumbent upon it under international law or treaties in force." A treaty embodies a solemn obligation; and it is not enough to say that merely because a society claims to be sovereign it can violate promises and in the name of independence disregard the rights of others.

What do sovereign states claim as their fundamental rights? They claim independence, the right to be treated as equals; they claim respect, and the power of jurisdiction within their own borders; they claim, above all, the right of self-preservation, which carries with it the right of defense against attack and aggression. But it is clear that if one nation has these fundamental rights the other nations have the fundamental obligation to respect these rights, and that if all nations possess these fundamental rights they must all accept the fundamental obligation mutually to respect each other's rights. Thus, sovereign rights within the society of nations can be only a relative matter; respect for rights means fulfillment of obligations, and therefore national sovereignty becomes a condition of relativity and not of absoluteness. It also follows that if nations do not exercise their rights in the light of correlative obligations they may be guilty of what is called an "abuse of rights." Logically there can be no absolute sovereignty; for, if that were so, all states would have rights in a world where no state had any obligation to respect rights—which would be chaos.

The problem may be approached from another and less theoretical angle. Since the Industrial Revolution the world has become so closely knit that nations are no longer in fact "independent"—they are intimately bound together in a thousand ways. They no longer have absolute control over their own destiny, whatever the legal theory may be. A political assassination in Sarajevo in 1914 leads to a world war; the failure of an Austrian bank in 1931 forces a world financial crisis; the armament program of Hitler's Germany has caused repercussions all over the earth; Great Britain goes off the gold standard and carries other nations with it. Capital, labor, tariffs, opium, armaments, security, immigration, and health present problems which go beyond any one nation. National governments can no longer solve them. They require inter- or rather supra-national action. Whereas, two hundred or even one hundred years ago, nations could look inwardly for the solution of many of their problems, today such is not the case. The welfare of the nation itself and that of the community of nations require the common action of nations. And "what touches all must be decided by all." From this principle follows the conclusion that sovereignty, the claim to unfettered national action, is no longer to be regarded as the norm by which rights and duties are to be judged. Where the action of the one will endanger the welfare of the many, its actions must be restrained. The facts of modern life are forcing mankind to extend the concept of "abuse of rights" to the international sphere. In a closely knit world where the power to do evil to others has immeasurably increased, how a nation uses its sovereignty is a matter of urgent and common concern. Because interdependence, and not independence, is the fundamental characteristic of world society, interdependence and not independence must be recognized as the fundamental premise on which political and legal thought and organization must be built.

What becomes a matter of concern to the whole world obviously introduces standards of behavior which must be prescribed by world society. The mere plea of exercising sovereign rights no longer suffices; it has to undergo international examination in order to ascertain whether or not the act of a sovereign power can be justified. The Covenant of the League of Nations has applied to international relations the principle already accepted within the nations themselves. They had adopted a system of collective national action against individuals or groups found guilty of infringing the rights of others and disturbing the social peace; as long as persons indulged in a legitimate exercise of their individual desires, they were unmolested; but beyond a certain point they were liable to social control and social correction. In a similar way the League of Nations carried with it the implication of a hierarchy of values. Nations might still claim to exercise sovereignty; a declaration of war, despite a League judgment that the Covenant had been broken, would still produce a legal situation of war, and to that degree nations might still be sovereign powers able to wage war. The Covenant, however, provided methods of enabling other nations to express combined disapproval and condemnation such that it would not pay states to exercise certain so-called sovereign rights. Certain consequences might then gradually come about. Traditions would grow up and rules become more precise; they would introduce clearer distinctions between legitimate and nonlegitimate expressions of sovereignty. International control over abuses of sovereignty might develop; a struggle in principle over the question whether the nation itself or international society should be the judge of certain actions hitherto regarded as the accepted legal right of a sovereign state would become important. Over a long period of years it might be expected that a modification of practice would bring in its train a modification of theory. "Sovereign" actions disapproved by the nations acting in a collective manner would tend to be recognized as "abuses"; what is an abuse would be deemed illegal and no longer the expression of a sovereign power in the absolute sense, because the action had become judgeable by some other human superior. Thus the Covenant contains the evidences of an attempt to build a society of "sovereign" nations; and if *human* society is really to function, a considerable modification of the practice and theory of "sovereignty" must come about.

The history of the British Empire supplies an interesting illustration of the manner in which legal theory changes to fit into a world of changing facts. One hundred years ago the British Parliament legislated for the Empire; its laws were supreme. After the American Revolution it agreed not to tax a colony without that colony's consent, but its legal power to do so undoubtedly remained. In time the colonies and the Dominions gained more and more effective self-government until they reached virtual international status. But the British Parliament retained a theoretical legal supremacy which did not square with the new situation; and the contradiction could not persist without creating much confusion. Sir Robert Borden of Canada attempted to narrow the gap between theory and practice by claiming that, although the Imperial Parliament possessed the "legal power," it did not have the "constitutional right" to pass laws binding the Dominions in certain respects. When the Dominions entered the League of Nations the theoretical legal power of the British Parliament had not yet disappeared, but as an effective power it had ceased to exist. Practice had outstripped theory; and it was only a matter of time before the theory itself would have to go. The Imperial Conferences of 1926 and 1930 and the 1931 Statute of Westminster gave explicit expression to the fact that the legal power of the British Parliament no longer existed over the Dominions except with their consent.

Unless we are to witness the breakdown of international society there must be a similar development in the international world. For many years there will be passionate appeals to sovereignty; but, if international order is to come, abuses of sovereign power must be curtailed, "sovereign" actions must be tested by the standards of common international good, and sovereignty must become subordinate to a higher principle. The concept may continue to exist, with a changing connotation, until it comes to signify no longer the supreme legal power of an irresponsible state, but to designate an independent state subject to restraint if it abuses its power. We shall then have returned nearer to the original meaning of the word *sovrain*. If, however, the word is still to mean absolute sovereignty, the sooner it is discarded the better.

The history of politics is thus largely the history of units of society and government which have existed for the preservation of order, the promotion of justice, and the enforcement of rights and duties. These units have changed in the course of history. There have been the tribe, the city-state, the feudal system, the medieval Church, the modern state, and, to a limited degree, the League of Nations. These units may have different purposes and they may overlap. In discussing law, we must realize that there has been no law except in association with institutions. In a sense, it is beside the point to discuss the abstract nature of law when law is never met with except as embodied in some form of government.

The law is not an abstraction. It cannot be understood independently of the political foundations on which it rests and of the political interests which it serves . . . . Every system of law presupposes an initial political decision, whether explicit or implied, whether achieved by voting or by bargaining or by force, as to the authority entitled to make and unmake law.[16]

Now institutions awaken a certain attitude of mind, and this psychological attitude is important in considering law. One's con-

[16] E. H. Carr, *The Twenty Years Crisis, 1919–1939* (Macmillan & Company, Ltd., London, 1940), pp. 229–31. Quoted by permission.

ception of law is not of law *in vacuo* but of law embodied in institutions. Law has been part of government, and government cannot be maintained without rules of law. And as units of government change in response to new conditions, law must change.

Moreover, there may be laws on the statute book which have become out of date, or they may be inadequately enforced. The distinction will then arise between weak law and strong law. Similarly, in the international field there may be rules which are generally accepted and toward which there is an attitude of mind favorable to their operation, and there may be other laws or rules which are frequently if not freely broken. International or national law may be strong in some respects and not in others.[17] The significance of this approach appears when we consider that there may be a distinction between the ultimate power of the state and its everyday power. If an ultimate power such as is claimed for the sovereign state cannot be efficiently wielded, what then? If we assume that law must be enforced and yet a habit grows up by which two independent units join in enforcing rules, what then? Theoretically, they may break their agreement, but in practice they may so consistently enforce the agreement that it becomes for all practical purposes a rule of law. Note that a modern state cannot merely command by force for any length of time. If so, the state would be unmitigated tyranny, and many people today complain that dictatorships by abolishing older rules of law have wielded naked power. But even dictatorships must conciliate minorities, and must wield power through propaganda, through conciliation, through symbols, and perhaps ultimately through the sword. To say that law is a command and that what is not a command is not law is to neglect consideration of the actual methods by which laws are made and enforced.

What is the purpose of the modern state? If it is to keep order, the question then arises whether or not it is doing so. Internally it may have an efficient police force; but if externally the international disorder is so great as to threaten the very foundations of society, what shall we say of the state whose final justification is supposed to be that it can keep order? If the state,

---

[17] Note Hall's interesting phrase "the rough jurisprudence of nations," quoted by R. Jennings in the *British Year Book of International Law, 1939*. Commenting upon Janowsky and Fagan's claim that Germany had incurred a conventional pledge to treat her minorities justly by making the promise in its "Observations on the Conditions of Peace," Jennings admits that the argument may be in accord with strict theory, but is too refined for "the rough jurisprudence of nations."

therefore, is the law-making institution but the problems upon which it must legislate are too wide for it to encompass, then it can no longer be the sole legislating authority except in a purely formal sense. The standards must be drawn up by an agency which is extensive enough to encompass the whole problem (opium control, prevention of slave raiding, etc.). If the state exists for law enforcement and claims to be the supreme agency but cannot efficiently enforce a law (e.g., double taxation) without outside assistance, it would seem that a dangerous gap between the formal concept and the changing basis of law is likely to grow up; only by ignoring the real basis can the facts be fitted into a formal framework. If law is a set of rules,[18] we need a wider basis than the state, as several chapters in this volume attempt to show. If law is a command with a penalty for disobedience, the question will arise as to whether it is the command of an absolute authority or an authority which is in fact only substantially or partially independent. If law is a combination of both force and rule, of obedience and power, it is conceivable that rules may be drawn up by agreement and enforced by a local or national agency.

Admitting that force may be a component part of law in practically every instance, it does not follow that force is the essence of law any more than hydrogen, being a part of water, is the whole of water. Arbitrary force may give a kind of law, but it will be an inferior kind and not a superior kind. The federal power may intervene in the United States in many ways but itself is bound by the Constitution. It may bring in many laws, but there are fields which it may not touch. If the state is a corporation, the juridical personality of a nation, if all its common purposes fall within the sphere of state activity, the question arises as to what are common purposes. We have seen elsewhere that a state or a nation is a state or nation for certain purposes, and it is unreal to assume that states can exist for all purposes.

Law depends upon the conviction that it is a valid thing. A state is relatively powerless to impose mere force except for a short time. There must be a prior condition existing before a legal

---

[18] The concept of law as rules includes the idea of rules to make rules. A dictatorship must have a large number of rules if it is not to degenerate into anarchy. But if the dictator can alter rules at will, an inferior kind of law results. Democracy attempts to safeguard against tyranny by introducing regular methods for making, enforcing, and interpreting rules. Constitutional restraints, and provisions for due process of law, the conduct of the legislature, political parties, martial law, elections, etc., bear witness to the importance of "rules to make rules."

system can evolve, and Jellinek is right in saying that the state obligates itself to its subjects, in creating a law, to apply and execute the law. To that extent it is bound by the law. Otherwise, there is pure arbitrariness. If this is so, then even on Jellinek's theory the state will oblige itself to apply and execute the law which it has created along with other states. In a real sense, "law is legally limited force, even though in another sense law is a continual threat of physical force."

But, it may be objected that the state is a unity, is "one," and international society is not such a commonwealth. The question then arises, what is a unit? It has been pointed out before that anything may be a unity. A drop of water, a hat, an atom within the hat, a person's finger, a person, a family, a city, a state, the world, the universe—each is a unity from a certain point of view. To say that the state has unity may mean much or little. It has unity for certain purposes, but no more. These purposes may change. The more purposes there are in common, and the more agencies there are, the stronger will be the unity. If the state is an agency to co-ordinate the other agencies which are building a unit of society, then the state loses its absolute character and takes on a relativist character. As Duguit points out, public law is then grounded not in the command of a state but in organization. Many groups may co-operate to produce statutes and decrees, and theoretically these groups may be within or without a given unit of society; and theoretically the decrees and statutes may be enforced by the state or any particular branch of a state. If inter-independence is necessary in order to create law, and if the violation of the law "provokes a social reaction," there would seem no valid reason for denying to many rules drawn up by international society the character of law. It is, as Duguit points out, not the existence of coervice force which is needed but the consciousness of the need for coercive sanction that suffices to transform national or international social norms into law. International law, therefore, comes from relations which have grown beyond the boundaries of the state or nation, and international public services are growing up which demand the adoption of rules that become laws when, and if, sufficiently accepted.

Just as national law has expanded in response to the needs of national society and its agencies have increased, so the growing complexity of international life necessitates more rule-making bodies, a greater number of judicial agencies and administrative bodies. Moreover, the content of international law is changing, albeit more slowly than some theorists would desire. Until now, and even at the present time, international law has dealt with states and not individuals or groups. Grotius claimed that international law should govern relations between states and individuals, but the doctrines of sovereignty of the 250 subsequent years left little room for the individual in international affairs. Within the last generation economic and professional groups have become more important and more organized, and have taken an increasingly important lot in initiating enforceable rules of conduct within nations. And it would be shutting one's eyes to obvious facts in a blind devotion to mere formalism to ignore the number of rules which international organization has made on behalf of individuals.[19] It is true that many of these rules can become effective only through the intermediary of states members and that they must be ratified by states; but it is also true that national laws depend upon the intermediary actions of national officials who may seriously affect the application of law by their inefficiency or negligence; and while they may be ultimately called to account in a manner not yet possible in international affairs the question is whether or not such accountability is a matter of degree rather than a difference of kind. Unquestionably the difference of degree is at present most pronounced. In the International Labor Organization, government, workers', and employers' representatives take part in drawing up rules. According to treaty arrangements, minorities and certain international unions and mandated communities have been given a standing in international relations. Piracy is now a crime against the law of nations and remedies for it are available against individuals. The attempts to make slavery also a crime have thus far failed but may some day succeed. A convention has been signed to set up an International Criminal Court to try individuals.

Without question the great number of conventions and agreements—how many there are can be seen from a perusal of the legislative treaties as published by Judge Manley Hudson[20] or in the League of Nations treaty series—shows that international conferences are filling a basic need of the modern world. Although we do not have a world international legislative body similar in constitution and power to national legislatures, nevertheless, inter-

[19] And the content of law will change if the individual's position in society undergoes substantial alteration, and if revolution introduces new social purposes and new instrumentalities.

[20] M. O. Hudson (editor), *International Legislation* (Carnegie Endowment for International Peace, Washington, D.C., 1931), p. xiii.

national law-making has become an extremely important part of
the law of nations today.

Despite the theory that international law is not true law, the
fact remains that national courts on thousands of occasions have
applied what they consider to be international law, and that governments have so far recognized its existence as invariably to attempt to justify a course of action which seemed to be irregular
by appealing to the principles of international law or to the fact
that an opponent had violated international law. Judge John Bassett Moore has pointed out that international law in times of peace
is on the whole as well observed as municipal law, and that, considering the great amount of international intercourse which takes
place, there is little need to have recourse to claims—contracts and
agreements in normal times are not broken. That international law
covers a great variety of peace-time service can be seen by referring
to any textbook on the subject.[21]

International law also dealt with forceful measures short of
war: (*a*) retorsion, which Oppenheim defined as "retaliation for
discourteous, for unkind or unfair or inequitable acts, by acts of
the same or similar kind"; (*b*) reprisals, i.e., illegal acts against
a state which is alleged to have also acted illegally; (*c*) intervention
by single states or by states acting collectively; and (*d*) pacific
blockade in peace time as a means of compulsion. Typical textbooks discuss at length the laws of neutrality as well as the laws
of warfare. True, these rules have been frequently broken; but
in the majority of cases they are observed and serve useful purposes, despite an urgent need of reform which now exists.

The question arises as to how these rules came into existence
and what gave them whatever obligatory character they possess.

1. Textbook writers usually regard custom as one of the most
important sources of international law. Out of long experience
certain rules are so uniformly observed and are felt to be so binding that they acquire the force of law. Custom is in no sense "a
less working origin of law than actual conventions or specific
declarations," writes Sir John Fischer Williams, who quotes from
Pascal: "Custom is the creator of all equity, simply because it is
accepted; that is the mystical foundation of its authority." Pascal
also wisely stated that "it was custom and example more than
certain knowledge which persuaded us, and the things of which

[21] For instance, see C. Howard-Ellis, *The Origin, Structure, and Working
of the League of Nations* (Houghton Mifflin Co., Boston, New York, 1929),
pp. 294–95.

men are persuaded are the stuff out of which they make their law."
In the Paquete Habana case, 1900, the United States Supreme
Court declared: "By an ancient usage among civilized nations,
beginning centuries ago, and gradually ripening into a rule of international law, coast fishing vessels, pursuing their vocation of
catching and bringing in fresh fish, have been recognized as exempt, with their cargoes and crews, from capture as prize of war."
Many other examples might be quoted of how national courts have
appealed to custom.

2. Treaties are likewise sources of international law. Ordinary
bilateral treaties which resemble contracts bind only the particular
parties, but certain multilateral conventions have been commonly
accepted as law-making because the signatory powers thereby establish certain general rules of law. And "when a solemn declaration of this kind is made, the world at large is surely entitled to
take it seriously and by acting in the faith of the declaration to fix
it as binding on the declarant." Most writers agree that the Conventions of Vienna in 1815 which established the principle of freedom of navigation and that of international rivers and regulated
the status of diplomatic agents, and the Declaration of the Powers
in 1858 which adopted rules governing the relations of neutrals
and belligerents in naval warfare, and the 1864 Red Cross Convention which was revised several times, concerning the sick and
wounded, and also the Covenant of the League of Nations, the
Washington Conference, and other major multilateral treaty arrangements all are sources of international law.

3. Judicial decisions made by international tribunals, by prize
courts, and by national courts have contributed to building up international law.

4. The writings of eminent jurists have frequently been quoted
by national and international tribunals and have played their part
in the development of international law and practice.

5. There was also fairly widespread agreement that the general
principles of law recognized by civilized nations are another source
of law.

THE WEAKNESS OF INTERNATIONAL LAW
AND ORGANIZATION

The weaknesses of the prewar system of international law
(which cannot be considered entirely apart from the organization
of international society) will now be apparent:

1. There was profound disagreement as to the nature of inter-

national law. Some scholars claimed that it was superior to national law, even though it had no enforcing agencies. Others claimed that it was inferior to national law because it was not a command and had no enforcing agencies: it was merely the expression of a number of agreements. Still others took the view that international law was law, but of a different kind from national law. These theoretical differences had important consequences because they led to the second difficulty.

2. Many jurists and statesmen took the view that treaties were the expression of the will of a sovereign state. Other jurists claimed that treaties were legal obligations which limited the sovereign action of the contracting parties. In critical times governments usually acted upon the first assumption even though they may have given lip service to the second. It is noteworthy that while international courts considered an act of a state invalid which went beyond the authority of international law, national courts accepted the legislation of the state in question as constitutional, although they attempted to reconcile, as far as possible, the legislative act with the provisions of international law. Treaties as an act of a sovereign will conflicted with a fundamental doctrine emphasized by many legal writers that *pacta sunt servanda*—"agreements must be kept"—and until the confusion existing in this matter was cleared up there could be little hope of genuine progress. If sovereign states could not or would not bind themselves, or if there was mere "auto-limitation," international law was merely a precariously existent set of rules. But if obligation comes from law which is something outside the will of the state, the consequences will be fundamentally different. Until this uncertainty is removed there will under present conditions continue to be confusion in international affairs. Both doctrines cannot co-exist. One or the other must go.

3. The doctrine that treaties must be observed, while true in most fields of international endeavor, confronted an almost fatal obstacle in that international law recognized the validity of treaties imposed by force. Presumably war could be ended only by treaties of peace; but if nations took advantage of their victory to impose a punitive peace and did not observe the doctrine urged by Vattel in the eighteenth century that peace treaties should be acts of equals, it followed that the defeated power would not regard such a punitive treaty as sacred and would await the first opportunity to overthrow it by force. It may be too much to say that to give a punitive treaty the effect of law is to legalize anarchy; but to

admit such a practice tends seriously to divorce law and justice. Difficult as it may be to define justice, it is relatively easy for the injured party to feel that it suffers injustice, particularly when the victorious power is both judge and party in imposing the conditions.

4. There is further what Professor Dickinson calls the "tyranny of arbitrary rules which have outlived their reason." The doctrine of the three-mile limit of the territorial authority of a national government is "developing a deceptive certainty and illusory advantage of an arbitrary rule" at a time when the rapidity of communications and the need of conserving resources at sea demand new methods; nevertheless governments have insisted upon maintaining the three-mile limit. Inconveniences and injustices follow also from a rigid devotion to the rule that foreign states should be immune from suit in national tribunals unless they expressly waive their immunity. Today, with governments going into businesses on a large scale, this immunity results in widespread injustice; but national courts are powerless to alter the rule. Another tyranny is that of the right of nations to use the high seas unhindered. The discussion of slavery, narcotics, and liquor as international problems has shown what frightful abuses can be committed in the name of the freedom of the seas. Other instances might be quoted to show that international law possesses "inadequate means for change and adaptation."

5. Many scholars have pointed to another serious obstacle in the attempt to apply law to international relations, i.e., the diversity of legal systems throughout the world, and the consequent difficulty which an international court would experience in knowing which law to apply in a particular case.

The English word "law" means law and nothing else; on the Continent it means not only law but also right and justice. English jurisprudence tends to exclude, and Continental jurisprudence to include, the ethical. And Continental jurisprudence is more metaphysical in character than English.[22]

The common law is deeply concerned with the principles of public law or justice for the individual; whereas the Roman law, which passed to the Middle Ages, was derived from the Corpus Juris of the Emperor Justinian—"the law of an imperial dictatorship"—and established "no institutions of independent judicature . . . . no guarantees for personal liberty, or for the due

[22] Sir John Salmond, *Jurisprudence* (Sweet & Maxwell, London, 1924), p. 9.

process of law."[23] The common law places more emphasis than does the civil law upon "questions of fact" and therefore examination and cross-examination of witnesses and the whole law of evidence are much more highly developed in Anglo-Saxon countries. Continental law has permitted judges a much greater use of "inquisitorial" methods in finding out evidence against accused persons in criminal matters, although in civil matters the ratios appear to be reversed. Continental law is much older than the common law, the former having been about twenty-six hundred years and the latter about six hundred years in existence; with the result that the older system has abandoned more of the formalism and substantive institutions based upon rules of jurisdiction and procedure than has the common law. Anglo-Saxon jurists make a clearer distinction between law and right than the Continental legal thinkers, and Anglo-Saxon law is based more definitely upon the doctrine of precedent. "Nowhere else than in England and in countries which have derived their legal system from England have the decisions of judges been systematically treated as authoritative"; indeed, the fifth article of the French Civil Code "expressly prohibits judges from pretending to lay down general rules when giving their decisions."[24] For these and other reasons some of those who have been trained in the so-called Anglo-American school of law fear that to give a permanent international court jurisdiction over all legal questions "would subject Great Britain and the United States in advance to decisions of a tribunal most of whom have been bred in and wedded to the Continental doctrine."[25]

Perhaps, so Alvarez maintains, the international law which developed in western Europe does not contain principles of universal validity, and countries of the New World have faced new conditions, have a different outlook on life, have attempted to create new values, and have rejected certain elements of the public law of Europe.[26]

In 1908 the first Pan-American Scientific Congress declared that there were American problems which were *"sui generis* and of clearly American character" and had "not been found susceptible of world agreement." After 1918 a movement arose for the codi-

[23] Sir Morris Ames, in Harvard Tercentenary Lecture, 1936.

[24] W. Markby, *Elements of Law,* p. 17.

[25] H. Lauterpacht, "The So-called Anglo-American and Continental Schools of Thought," *British Year Book of International Law, 1931,* pp. 31–62.

[26] Alejandre Alvarez, *Le Droit international Americain* (1910).

fication of an American system of international law, not for the purpose of detracting from the authority of universal law, but to add "principles and rules which are found to relate to the special exigencies of the American Republics." In 1925 a committee of the American Institute of International Law issued a report defining American international law as "all of the institutions, principles, rules, doctrines, conventions, customs, and practices which, in the domain of international relations, are proper to the republics of the New World." It did not intend to create an international system separating "the Republics of this hemisphere from the world concert," but recognized regional systems which in some respects go beyond the general world order. The Panama Conference of September 1937 actually established certain new rules of neutrality which may well be regarded as international law principles for the Western Hemisphere.

Thus the content and method of law vary according to the kind of society which has been evolved. Law exists in order to promote human welfare. If, therefore, law is directed to the achievement of certain ends, it follows that the quality of the laws adopted, as well as the general spirit of the law, will reflect the purposes of a community. Law in a predominantly capitalist society will differ in content and method from law in a communist society; and both the capitalist and the communist systems of law will differ from the Fascist and the National Socialist systems.[27] The rules vary, and affect the individuals and classes differently because the ends or purposes vary.

It follows that until a sufficient number of problems are common to different societies the amount of law which they will accept as binding upon them all will be limited. Until that time comes, the differences will be more obvious than the common factors, and law will develop in uneven and even in contradictory fashion. As the communities come into closer relation, there will be conflicts of laws. As long as the major part of life is dominated by internal concerns, the emphasis will remain upon the local or national source of law; and new rules will tend to be regarded as something extra, something added to the central body of national law.

When science and communications bring regions and even con-

[27] T. A. Taracouzio, in *The Soviet Union and International Law* (The Macmillan Company, 1935), writes that international law for the Soviets is a provisional interclass law aiming to further the interests of the proletariat in a struggle for world supremacy.

tinents into increasingly intimate relationship, there will develop
an urgent need for still further rules for certainty.[28] Those who
have been accustomed to think in national terms will regard the
new rules as less authoritative than the old rules which have gained
the sanction of time and custom; those who look to the future and
conceive of society in dynamic rather than static terms will be impressed by the need of expanding the agencies of making rules or
laws binding upon all countries.

Because estimates will differ as to the importance of preventing war or establishing a world currency, or in some other way
adopting definite and unambiguous rules, estimates will vary as to
the need for and the method of creating the new rules or laws.
Some thinkers will stress the requirements of the new and will
minimize the differences existing between the various systems in
the light of the greater problems to be solved. We shall examine
this view presently.

6. International law has had a relatively small scope and the
most serious conflicts between nations have arisen over matters
concerning which international law has laid down no precise rules.
For example, immigration and tariffs have been regarded as "domestic" questions reserved to the sovereign states, despite the fact
that immigration and tariff barriers may have profound effects
upon the welfare of other countries. Some writers claim that there
are "gaps" in international law. Others assert that international
law forms a complete system, and that there is no question which
cannot be settled according to the rules of international law; if
particular rules do not exist, the international courts have recourse
to the more general principles of law common to civilized communities. Others write that there are no "gaps," because tribunals
can definitely ascertain whether or not a rule exists, and if it does
not exist the plaintiff has no action; it is therefore easy for the
judges to establish the line between domestic and international
jurisdiction. Still others admit that, although international law
may be theoretically complete, there do not exist enough specific
rules to guide international courts or tribunals; if the latter had
to decide on the basis of very general rules, then they might be
applying equity, or giving the judgment of a "good man," but it

[28] L. Oppenheim, in *The Future of International Law* (1911), writes of the
progress of the law of nations: "Much, if not all, depends on whether the international interests of individual states become stronger than their national interests, for no state puts its hand to the task of international organization save
when, and so far as, its international interests urge it more or less irresistibly
to do so."

would not be law, for there would be too great an element of discretion.

7. Another aspect of the limited scope of international law is seen in the problem raised by what are called "justiciable and non-justiciable" matters. Many theorists assert that in international law, there is a definite limit to the judicial processes, that there exists a great difference between political and legal disputes, between legislative and legal methods. They say that the law declares what are existing rights but cannot alter existing rights; legislatures alone can create or modify rights.

In a broad sense, this judgment is true, although readers will recall the age-old controversies whether judges declare or make law. When a common law judge gives a decision on a particular case, it is based upon precedent; the judge applies existing law. But the application of existing law to a present situation where conflicts of principle are involved is influenced in close decisions by the general legal philosophy of the judges. The subordinate and quasi-judicial powers exercised by administrative bodies suggest that the line between law and politics is not clear and unalterable. Australian and New Zealand arbitration courts apply legal methods to decide matters of wages and hours, a procedure which some critics believe tends to discredit law by bringing it into the controversial area of economics. The League of Nations machinery for the protection of minorities was an attempt to shift the question from prewar political to a postwar legal basis. These illustrations show the difficulty of drawing a sharp division between political and legal disputes in domestic and international affairs.[29] The essential point, however, is that the realm of the unquestionably political so dominates the international sphere that the realm of law has been considerably limited. Policy still remains overwhelmingly dominant. This fact was recognized in Article XIV of the League Covenant (as amended in 1924), embodied in the statute of the Permanent Court of International Justice, which limits the legal processes to a small category of questions:

Disputes as to the interpretation of a treaty, as to any question of international law, as to the existence of any fact which, if established,

---

[29] E. H. Carr, *op. cit.*: ". . . . no definition of disputes recognised as justiciable can be universally or permanently valid; for political agreement (which makes the law and which treats it as binding) is a factor which varies from place to place and from time to time." See especially, H. Lauterpacht, *The Function of Law in the International Community* (Oxford University Press, London, 1933).

would constitute a breach of any international obligation, or as to the extent and nature of the reparation to be made for any such breach, are declared to be among those which are generally suitable for submission to arbitration or judicial settlement.

Moreover, at one time certain matters may be regarded as political and at another as legal; and governments have on occasions refused to submit certain disputes to arbitration even though the matters at issue were susceptible of judicial determination, as in the case of the foreign powers in their dispute with Venezuela in 1902 and the United States in several disputes with Caribbean nations. It may be objected that no country can permit a group of judges to decide concerning its vital interests and its self-defense. To this it is replied that "resort to force must be a matter for the state concerned" but that a determination as to whether the exercise of the right of self-defense is justified may be a matter for judicial determination; the attitude of states makes a given issue nonjusticiable; a nonjusticiable question is one which governments choose to regard as nonjusticiable.

Other jurists believe that it would not necessarily follow that an extension of the rule of courts would be an extension of the rule of law. The mere existence of a court or tribunal may not be sufficient to guarantee justice on the basis of law, although it may provide justice according to discretion. They say that to hope too much from law is to ignore the lessons of history: An English judge gave a decision in 1637 that ship money was legal, but it led to Hampden's resistance and paved the way to the English civil war. The American Supreme Court in 1857, in the Dred Scott case, gave a judicial decision on the slavery issue, and thereby helped to precipitate civil conflict. Judicial decisions by themselves do not settle questions; they only enable a settlement to take place if the parties are sufficiently united in viewpoint to accept the judgment.

8. The limits of international law are seen in another direction. Normally only states are subjects of international law, and individuals have no standing in international courts; indeed, by Article 34 of the Statute of the Permanent Court of International Justice, "only states or members of the League of Nations can be parties in cases before the Court." There are a few exceptions to the general rule in that pirates, counterfeiters, and blockade-runners are punishable under international law even though the national courts normally impose the penalty.

We have seen that individuals or corporations who wish to

lodge claims against a foreign state must have their case taken up by their own government and that this procedure is open to many criticisms. Individuals have suffered inconveniences and hardships by having their claims presented by their own government, for they may become, to use Borchard's phrase, the "plaything of politics and of their accidents."[30] Before 1914 the question of awarding protection to the individual on international law was discussed and the Central American Court, which lasted from 1907 to 1916, had authority to consider a legal action of an individual against a state; and the second Hague Conference in 1907 discussed the possibility of establishing a prize court to assume jurisdiction over individuals.

The judgment of Sir John Fischer Williams in 1939 might have been written before 1914:

But however this may be, the present limitation of "subjects" of international law to states in the sense that, before a legal or arbitral tribunal administering international law, states alone, in the absence of some special provision, can enforce international rights or be required to implement international duties, can hardly be destined to remain in force for an indefinite period of time. States are human creations, and they are only one form of the organization of men.[31]

It still holds good, although, as hinted elsewhere, new tendencies are at work. In surveying these tendencies, Politis writes:

International law will not really become the law of individuals until relations between peoples have lost their international character and have become properly speaking universal. At present they are still, in principle, international. They are carried on through the intermediary of States. But as the universal society comes into being, there are some relations which, by way of exception, are already world-wide, being maintained directly between the citizens of the various countries. What is now the exception will one day become the rule.

Until that day comes the modern conception of the right of peoples will remain in rivalry with the old conception of the right of States, but with an increasingly manifest tendency to supplant it.[32]

Thus the weaknesses of international law may be regarded as

[30] See also C. Eagleton, *International Government* (The Ronald Press Co., New York, 1931), pp. 181–85.

[31] Sir John Fischer Williams, *Aspects of Modern International Law* (Oxford University Press, London, 1939), p. 21.

[32] N. Politis, *The New Aspects of International Law* (Carnegie Endowment for International Peace, Washington, D.C., 1928), p. 31.

the effect as well as the cause of the lack of a closely knit international community. Is international anarchy (if the term be
permitted) the result of inadequate law-making and law-inter-
preting institutions, or is it the cause? The lack of institutions
made it impossible to have efficient international relations, but the
lack of international institutions in turn came from an inadequately
developed international society. Sir Frederick Pollock has defined
law as "a rule of conduct binding on members of a commonwealth
as such." If there is no commonwealth, no sense of common welfare, there will be no sense of the binding force of rules. Law is
strong when the sense of social unity is strong, and weak when the
sense of social unity is weak.

How inadequate international institutions have been we may
see by comparing international law-making and law-modifying
agencies with national legislatures. The national-sphere legislatures convene at definite times as a regular practice. They have
agenda, they possess adequate fact-finding bodies, and they enjoy
the benefit of a permanent civil service which carries on in the
intervals between sessions. By contrast, international conferences
are not easy to convene. Some government has to take the initiative; and because of the lack of continuity, the same things have
to be done over again. Much time is consumed and many disputes arise in the preparation of the agenda. After the conferences have met, resolutions can be passed only by a unanimous
vote; and, because of the theory of equality of states, a small power
has the right (theoretical, at least, and occasionally in practice)
to block general international legislation. Except in a few cases,
such as the Copyright organization and the Postal Unions, there
exists no permanent secretariat to continue the work begun by
conferences and to translate general resolutions into practical
achievement, to collect information, and to encourage ratification
of conventions. Because of the doctrine of sovereignty, international agreements cannot bind the participating states without their
ratification. Ratification, however, is frequently a difficult thing
to obtain; some states will not ratify; other states ratify condition-
ally, and consequently those who do ratify impose obligations upon
themselves which others fail to undertake. Other governments attach reservations to international agreements, and many confusions result. The revision of international conventions is a matter
of great difficulty and has hindered the effective development of
international organization. The Hague Conferences of 1899 and
1907 showed the possibility of periodic meetings; but the intervals

between them are too long to enable the gatherings to be efficient legislative bodies, and the same general criticism may be made of the Pan-American Conferences, which meet only every fifth year. *Ad hoc* and infrequent periodic conferences, even annual League Assemblies, are insufficient for the needs of a complex world.

We have already suggested that the solution of international disputes by legal methods has been confined to a small area of international relations. International arbitration had a long and honorable history in ancient times, but fell into disuse in the early part of the modern period of European history. In the nineteenth century it was revived and a great number of disputes were arbitrated. There was, however, no obligation to arbitrate; nor did any permanent institution exist until almost the close of the period. If two nations had a dispute, they had first to agree to establish an arbitral tribunal for the purpose of giving a third-party judgment. They had to agree in defining the scope of the question to be arbitrated, and each government insisted on nominating one or more arbitrators, who then chose an impartial chairman not a national of either of the litigant parties. The states thus participated in the selection of their own judges; moreover, it was a very general practice for these arbitrators to act, not as judges, but as negotiators.

The establishment of the Permanent Court of Arbitration at The Hague represented a distinct step forward. It provided for a more definite procedure in the selection of the umpire or chairman, and it emphasized the appointment of persons of highest competency in questions of international law. Nevertheless, the Hague Court, was, as Ralston puts it, "neither permanent nor a court" but "merely a panel of possible arbitrators who may to the usual number of three or five be called together to act in a given instance."

Law does not act in a vacuum. It is indissolubly connected with organization, and rules short of law likewise need organization and institutions if they are to be effective. Whatever one's view about the theoretical nature of law, or the relation between law and government, the fact remains that before 1914 society did possess some international institutions. States had to have intercourse, and required agencies for the discussion, communication, and negotiation of agreements.

Consuls existed many centuries ago and their rights and duties were the occasion of treaties between states. After the modern nation appeared, the consular service was adapted to its needs.

Today there are over thirty thousand consular agents in the world; their business is to promote and protect trade, to investigate trade opportunities, to report upon market conditions, to issue certificates, to issue invoices of goods, to administer regulations relating to quarantine, to settle estates of citizens who have died abroad, to issue bills of health, to issue passports, and to give advice. They certify births, marriages, and deaths, protect their fellow citizens against injustice in local courts, and inspect those who are preparing to migrate to the country of the consular agent. Consular practice rests upon many bilateral treaties and conventions, and is evidence of a high degree of international solidarity. Consuls do not receive diplomatic immunity, although they enjoy certain other privileges. They do not play an important part in settling disputes, but upon them has long rested a great deal of responsibility for the smooth working of daily international intercourse.

In former times envoys were sent from one country to another, but there were no permanent embassies and no career diplomats. With the establishment of the modern national state under the European monarchies, rulers sent diplomats to foreign countries. By the seventeenth century the diplomatic corps had become an intimate part of the modern international system but remained relatively unorganized and dependent upon usage and custom. In 1815 and 1818 the Congresses of Vienna and Aix-la-Chapelle adopted a classification of diplomats which substantially holds good today: The envoy is the representative of his state; his person is inviolable; he is exempt from the civil and criminal jurisdiction of the country to which he is accredited, and from customs duties and personal and property taxes. His correspondence and archives are likewise inviolable and his residence cannot be entered without his permission. The diplomat supplies information to his government so that it may more efficiently develop its foreign policy, and upon his skill and uprightness the good relations between governments to a considerable degree depend. Before 1914 the diplomat had almost exclusive charge of negotiations. Policy was determined by the foreign office at home and only seldom did a minister of state meet in direct conference with other foreign ministers.

The prewar diplomacy system has been the subject of considerable discussion. Its critics have denounced it because of the element of secrecy it involved, saying that cabinets could commit their people to war without any check from the public in absolute monarchies, and with little control from parliament in democratic countries. Even the British Cabinet was under no obligation to submit treaties to the House of Commons unless they contained clauses which required financial implementation.

Many stories exist of the deceitfulness, bribery, and corruption of diplomacy, too numerous to summarize here. On the other hand, some writers have defended the old system by pointing out that, although it was wrong to have secret treaties committing a country to a military alliance or even to war, there was a defensible and satisfactory type of secret diplomacy, i.e., diplomacy of negotiation. The prewar diplomats who lived abroad came to know one another very well. Diplomatic intercourse was "leisurely and polished"; the most important communications took place by means of written notes, so that there should be no misunderstandings of what was said between diplomat and minister. Many crises were averted by the calm deliberations of professional diplomats removed from the public gaze. They were enabled to discuss matters more easily than would have been possible had their deliberations taken place in public. The major criticism of prewar diplomacy lies not in the institution itself, for diplomacy is essential, but in the fact that it was part of the balance-of-power system which prevented the best elements in diplomatic life from operating to the fullest extent and accentuated the bad effects of its evil side.

Before 1914 the royal courts were not unimportant in international intercourse. What Mowat called "the international of monarchs" helped Europe to maintain a certain unity. Although most rulers had lost at least some power to parliaments or to cabinets in domestic matters, they still exercised considerable influence in foreign affairs. Indeed, Mowat suggests that the balance-of-power system was able to function as well as it did in Europe because of the existence of a few great monarchs who maintained the habit of communicating with each other and who could write to each other more intimately than could their ministers of state—who usually were not acquainted with other foreign ministers. The World War of 1914–1918 destroyed the international of the monarchs, and with it an institution which, with all of its defects, did something to offset the growing anarchy of a Europe divided into sovereign states.

Whether or not legalists admitted the existence of international law, international society had to find some means of settling disputes unless it was to live in a condition of perpetual disorder. Before 1914 various methods were used. First was diplomacy—

many differences which never became headline news were settled by discussion between foreign offices, and upon the tact and ability of diplomats and foreign ministers depended the efficient working of international relations. If diplomacy failed to reach a settlement, a third state might tender its "good offices" to the disputants in the hope of inducing them to come to an amicable agreement. The third party did not make an award or give a decision or even participate in negotiations.

Mediation constituted a further stage. In this case the third party took more active steps by offering suggestions and proposing a solution. The 1907 Hague Convention for the pacific settlement of international disputes formally recognized the method of mediation. Before this time, a third party which attempted to mediate was theoretically open to the suspicion of intervening in a dispute to serve its own purposes; but the Convention provided that states should "have recourse as far as circumstances allow to the good offices or mediation of one or more friendly powers" and that the offer of mediation was not to be regarded as an unfriendly act. The mediator could not give a judgment; nor were the disputants obligated to accept his proposal. The method was useful on several occasions generally confined, it must be admitted, to disputes between the smaller powers.

Commissions of inquiry constituted another method of pacific settlement of cases where disagreement existed as to facts. The Hague Conferences accepted this method; but unfortunately the convention covering it did not apply to disputes which involved the honor and vital interests of the signatory powers. Moreover, each commission of inquiry was limited to the facts and could not give an award, and the powers involved retained full freedom of action. This method was used in settling the Anglo-Russian dispute which arose as a result of the attack by the Russian fleet upon some English fishing vessels operating off the Dogger Bank in the North Sea. In 1911 Secretary Knox negotiated treaties providing for a mixed high commission of inquiry which should make recommendations for the settlement of disputes; but the Senate rejected his policy. In 1913 Secretary Bryan signed a number of "peace commission" treaties under which certain states agreed to refer disputes for investigation and report to a permanent international commission of five members, two selected by each state, one of whom must be a national of a third state, and the fifth to be selected by agreement between the two governments. Each such commission was to be allowed one year for the completion of its investigations and the presentation of its report; the disputants agreed not to declare war or begin hostilities during that time.

The theory behind the commission of inquiry is that if the facts of the controversy were clearly established, the possibilities of peaceful settlement would be improved. Under the Hague method, there were three disadvantages: (*a*) delay through having to reach a special agreement on the constitution and appointment of the commission; (*b*) loss of time between the nomination of the commission and the beginning of inquiry, during which the temper of the disputants might rise and the situation become worse; (*c*) the exemption of disputes involving national honor and vital interests—a dispute could be excluded from inquiry simply by designating it so. The Bryan Peace Commission Treaties represented an improvement: The commissions were permanent; they were established in advance; they did not except questions of honor and vital interests; and they provided that no war or hostilities should be undertaken during the year in which the report was being prepared. But the machinery was cumbrous and has not proved practicable.

The method of conciliation marks a further advance in the pacific settlement of international disputes. A conciliation commission not only conducts impartial inquiry in order to establish the facts of the dispute but also makes proposals which may be used by the parties as a basis of settlement. The proposals are not binding upon the disputants, but they may have considerable effect in providing at least a starting point for specific constructive effort. Treaties of conciliation became frequent only after 1918. Brazil and Great Britain in 1919 signed such a treaty, and Sweden and Chile in 1920.

The many other bilateral treaties which followed represented an advance in that nations began to assume the obligation to submit quarrels to pacific settlement. They improved the machinery by having a permanent commission of conciliation established, and they reduced the number of questions which might not be dealt with by conciliation commissions. Questions of national honor and vital interests were no longer excepted. Three major lines of development may be noted: the bilateral treaties just referred to; multilateral conventions such as the inter-American conciliation treaty of 1929, which established two permanent commissions, one at Washington and one at Montevideo, and under which the parties are obliged to submit all disputes which cannot be settled by diplomatic means of conciliation;[33] and the Locarno settlement of 1925, which included a number of treaties providing for conciliation as a process of settlement and for the establishment of permanent conciliation commissions. In the event that these commissions failed to produce proposals satisfactory to the disputants, the latter were obliged to submit the matter either to the Permanent Court or to a special arbitral tribunal. In 1922 the League of Nations Assembly adopted a resolution recommending that states should "conclude conventions with the object of laying their dispute before conciliation commissions formed by themselves" and suggested nine rules for the creation of these commissions. Clearly much effort and energy would be conserved if states could agree upon multilateral conventions for conciliation instead of having to rely on bipartite treaties. If forty or fifty nations each signed a separate treaty with every other nation, the number of resulting instruments would be enormous. A general treaty to cover all states would constitute a great economy of effort. From a recognition of this truth came proposals which resulted in the 1928 General Act for the pacific settlement of international disputes, under which states might accept each or all of the obligations to conciliate, to arbitrate legal problems, or to arbitrate all problems even of a nonlegal character.

Conciliation treaties have been considered sometimes as supplementary and sometimes as alternative to the method of arbitration by which a binding judgment is given by a third party. Those who emphasize the value of conciliation with its nonbinding recommendations do so because they are impressed by the limited scope of international law and the strength of national sovereignty. For these reasons they desire to encourage friendly agreement, and believe that in the present state of world society, peace, stability, and good feeling are more important than legal awards. Conciliation leaves the way open to compromise, whereas arbitration by a final decision may create ill-will in its endeavor to fulfill the letter of the law. In so far as individuals and communities can settle disputes on a friendly basis, so much the better. If they can avoid prolonged legal controversies and settle disputes in an amiable spirit without the costliness of legal proceedings, they have rendered a great service to the cause of peace.

The weaknesses of conciliation, however, must not be over-

[33] This convention was in fact a continuation of the Gondra Treaty of 1923, which provided for commissions of inquiry modeled upon the Hague Convention and the Bryan Treaties.

looked. The obligation not to move troops or take hostile action during the period of investigation rests entirely upon the good faith of the members, and the Italo-Ethiopian and the Sino-Japanese crises showed that one of the parties could alter the essential problem by taking military steps which themselves weakened prospects of successful conciliation. After the report has been issued, either disputant may accept or reject any proposals; it regains complete freedom of action. The great number and variety of conciliation treaties leads to overcomplexity; public opinion cannot clearly follow negotiations unless there is a reasonable simplification of machinery. Conciliation processes work satisfactorily if national security is not at stake and if general conditions do not threaten the existence of either signatory; but neither party can afford to make concessions if it has reason to believe that a concession, once granted, will be the occasion of further demands on the part of the other state. If a dispute cannot be entirely separated from the problem of security, then what appears to be even a relatively unimportant matter will not be susceptible of treatment by conciliation. On the other hand, if fundamental security is guaranteed, incidental and also not unimportant differences may be settled by mediatorial or conciliatory action. The more intensely the problem of security looms up, the less chance there is for mediation and conciliation to be successful; a state dares not run the risk of wasting time if its safety is in the balance. Or, if it does submit to conciliation processes, it will do so with its tongue in its cheek and will continue to trust in God and keep its powder dry; but such attitude and action destroy the confidence which is necessary for the pacific solution of disputes. Conciliation treaties have been able to eliminate questions of honor and vital interests. Until the fundamental question of security also has been eliminated, by some means or other, conciliation will not possess the adequate foundations on which to build peaceful settlement of disputes.

Another characteristic of prewar international organization was the acceptance of the doctrine of neutrality. In ancient times India and Greece recognized a degree of neutrality status. Rome did not; communities were either her allies or her enemies; and the Romans had no word which conveyed the precise meaning of our word "neutrality." Public opinion during the Middle Ages accepted the principle that war was a matter of general concern; the Church recognized the distinction between a just and an unjust war, and even applied sanctions or penalties against those who broke the peace. With the advent of the modern national state the theory developed that, because war was the act of a sovereign, a neutral power was no longer even morally bound to pronounce on the justice of the act. This concept did not win easy acceptance. In the seventeenth century there were different degrees of neutrality—"natural, strict, perfect, imperfect, qualified, conditional, conventional, etc."; and for some time the rights and duties of neutrals were ill-defined and inadequately respected. Belligerents marched over the territories of neutrals and seized men and goods. Gustavus Adolphus, King of Sweden, asked, "What then is neutrality? I do not understand. It means nothing."[34] And for a long time nations had to negotiate special agreements in the absence of which their right to enjoy the benefits of neutrality depended upon the good will of the belligerents. Neutrals had ill-defined duties as well as uncertain rights. They could help one or the other of the belligerents without losing their status of neutrality. In 1630, for example, Charles I of England, while at peace with the German Emperor, allowed 6,000 men to join Gustavus Adolphus on his expedition against Germany.[35]

In the eighteenth century, maritime powers increasingly adopted the policy of blockading and thereby interfered with the trade of neutrals. With the growth of modern commerce and the extension of the area of modern warfare, the interests of the belligerents and of neutrals began to clash more and more definitely. It was therefore necessary to attempt a clear definition of the rights and duties of neutrals in their relation to states engaged in war.[36]

Grotius had already laid down the following rules: (1) articles useful in war are always subject to capture; (2) articles not useful in war are always free; (3) those which may be useful in both war and peace ("conditional" contraband) must be classified by reference to existing facts.

The declaration of the neutral powers in 1780 asserted that (1) neutrals should be free to continue their trade as far as possible, when other nations were at war; (2) noncontraband goods

---

[34] N. Politis, *La Neutralité et la Paix* (Librairie Hachette, Paris, 1935), p. 33.

[35] *Ibid.*, p. 39.

[36] Although Christian Wolff in 1749 wrote that a state must help a state which fought a just war, must not support an unjust war, and must remain neutral only where the justice of a war was doubtful, Westlake much later claimed that there was no general duty of remaining neutral. Some other writers have doubts concerning neutrality.

of an enemy should be free from seizure if carried by neutral vessels, and neutral noncontraband goods should likewise be free from seizure if carried by enemy merchantmen; (3) only munitions of war should be regarded as contraband liable to seizure; and (4) no port should be regarded as blockaded unless the belligerent power had sufficient ships near at hand to shut off the port from normal trade. The United States fought the War of 1812 against Great Britain over the question of neutral rights. Jefferson had already enunciated the principle that international war should be fought in such a manner as to disturb the normal life of the rest of the world as little as possible. His theory is admirable; international and domestic strife undoubtedly should be subordinate to the normal peaceful life of society, and Americans were justified in demanding that their neutral trade and commerce should be subjected to the minimum interruption. The theory assumed that war could be waged between major powers without infringing upon the rights of neutral countries, and that the belligerents would respect the neutrality of others even though it acted to their disadvantage. The World War of 1914–1918 showed the hollowness of this assumption. The methods and conditions of war had so developed as to make the needs of belligerents increasingly incompatible with the rights of neutrals. Belgium, Greece, and Persia found their neutrality violated; and the United States entered the war because its neutral rights were outraged. The doctrine was to be considerably modified in the Covenant of the League.

POSTWAR ATTEMPTS TO STRENGTHEN INTERNATIONAL LAW AND ORGANIZATION

Rule of unanimity.—The doctrine of sovereignty led logically to the doctrine of unanimity. A sovereign state cannot be bound by another, and it must therefore agree to any measure which may affect itself. A small state had the same "independence," legally speaking, as a large state, just as a small circle is as round as a larger circle.

The rule of unanimity was often regarded as constituting a serious obstacle to international organization. Critics pointed to the fate of eighteenth-century Poland, which suffered irreparable loss from its unity-requiring constitutional provision, the *liberum veto*. They said that no society could progress if it had to wait upon the unanimous verdict of its members.

It was not surprising that an attempt was made to modify the rule of unanimity when the League of Nations was established. Considerable discussion took place, and some advance was made. Yet Article 5 of the League Covenant seemed to consecrate the principle, which, if strictly carried out, would render international government difficult, if not almost impossible. The Article reads: "Except where otherwise expressly provided in this Covenant or by the terms of the present Treaty, decisions at any meeting of the Assembly or of the Council shall require the agreement of all the Members of the League represented at the meeting."

There are, however, several exceptions to the rule of unanimity contained in the Covenant. Two-thirds of the Assembly may vote the admission of new members. The majority of the Assembly and a unanimous Council may name further permanent members to the Council. A two-thirds majority of the Assembly may fix rules dealing with the election of nonmembers of the Council. Matters of procedure in both Council and Assembly may be decided by a majority vote. The successor to the first Secretary-General was to be appointed by the Council with the approval of the majority of the Assembly. In the event of a dispute investigated under Article 15, the Council may either unanimously or by majority vote make a report of the facts of the dispute and submit its recommendations, and may adopt a unanimous decision apart from the votes of the disputing parties. Should the dispute be referred to the Assembly, an Assembly report, if accepted by all the Council members and a majority of the other League members (excluding the disputants), shall be equally binding. A nation may be expelled from the League by a Council vote exclusive of the vote of the nation involved. And, finally, amendments to the Covenant take effect when ratified by all the nations which comprise the League Council and a majority of the Assembly members.

These exceptions to the rule of unanimity are not unimportant; in fact they make rather a striking list. Nevertheless, had this been the whole story, the outlook for the future would have been unpromising enough, because in matters of essential policy (except Article 15) the requirement of unanimity seemed sufficient to enable a nation to obstruct any measure which it regarded as adversely affecting its interests and ambitions, whatever the requirements of world society.

The Council and the Assembly when given duties to perform cannot take action but can merely recommend to member governments a policy for their adoption: Under Article 8 the Council formulates plans for reduction of armaments; but the governments must adopt them. Under Article 10 the Council merely advises how the obligations contained therein are to be fulfilled. Under Article 16 it proposes steps and recommends what military forces the members shall contribute for action against a state which has violated the Covenant. The Assembly under Article 19 "advises" the reconsideration of treaties which have been inapplicable. Voluntary association is still the basis of the League of Nations.

A number of modifications have been adopted in the rule of unanimity during the generation of the League's existence and at one time they promised to open a wider door to more effective international government. It has become the practice that nations which do not vote on a given matter are regarded as absent. That is, a nation which does not vote against a measure but abstains from voting at all is held to have accepted the result of an otherwise unanimous vote. "No one against" (*nem. con.*) is translated to mean "unanimously accepted." This procedure was not accepted without debate; but its acceptance means that a nation not positively in favor of a measure does not definitely have to oppose it—it can avoid the embarrassment of voting unwillingly for, and it need not force a deadlock by voting against, a proposal. A serious question arose when a state claimed that, by not voting, it was reserving its decision and was not committing itself in favor of the measure. Such an interpretation would have led to endless confusion; a subsequent plea to be released from obligations accepted by other nations on the ground that the nonvoting nations had not expressed positive agreement would introduce universal uncertainty of obligations. The League members rightly rejected so dangerous a claim.

The Covenant provided that questions of procedure might be settled by majority vote; but, in the absence of a clear definition of "procedure" as against "policy," the League later faced serious problems. It was agreed that the order of business in the Council and the Assembly and the election of officers and of nonpermanent members to the Council were procedural. In the 1931 Sino-Japanese dispute, the Council unanimously agreed to keep the United States informed of proceedings by means of written communications. A later proposal was made to supplement this action by permitting a representative of the United States to be present at the Council debates. The Council members, apart from Japan, maintained that such an action was merely an extension of the procedural step already taken; but Japan asserted that to ask a non-League nation to sit on the Council was clearly a matter of policy, since the decision to associate nonmembers with members involved a drastic departure from League principles. The President of the Council disagreed with the Japanese view and ruled that a matter of procedure and not principle was involved. Several authorities questioned the correctness of the verdict; but M. Briand's action constituted an important step, in that by an extended interpretation of "procedural" questions many important international problems might be settled by majority vote.

It has been generally accepted that commissions of inquiry may be appointed by the Assembly or the Council by majority vote; and in the 1920 Albania-Jugoslavia dispute, the Greco-Bulgarian quarrel (1925), and the Polish-Lithuanian dispute (1928), committees were so appointed—not without protest from some of the interested nations, on the ground that their national sovereignty was being infringed.

The League has attempted to overcome the need of a unanimous vote by distinguishing between "decisions," in which all voting members must concur, and "recommendations," which may be adopted by a majority of the members. The latter course is pursued when it is clear that there is little chance of reaching a unanimous verdict—the Assembly, for example, failed to obtain unanimity of decision upon the budgetary limitation of armament expenditure; it therefore adopted, by majority vote, a recommendation which, although it possessed no legal validity, would, if the majority were a decisive one and included the major powers, carry great moral weight. A danger exists in that the powers may be tempted to side-step definite decisions and immediate action in favor of pious recommendations, which may be merely a verbal substitute for effective deeds. Thus far the danger has remained a theoretical one, and the constitutional power to adopt recommendations has not been abused. The government of Colombia proposed that a two-thirds majority should suffice to decide whether or not a proposal merely developed a principle or introduced a new one; but the idea was rejected because the dividing line between a principle and its particular application is not an easy one to draw. The Council preferred to retain the distinction between recommendations and decisions.

Although the Covenant by Articles 15 and 16 excludes the parties to a dispute from voting, it makes no similar provision in the important Articles 10, 11, and 13; a party to a dispute may claim under Article 11 the privilege of voting, although President

Wilson and others urged that disputants should not vote under Article 11. The League moved uncertainly in this matter. The whole spirit of the Covenant, of course, suggests that no party should be a judge in its own cause; and yet Article 5 specifically states that, unless otherwise definitely provided in the Covenant, unanimity is essential for a decision. In some instances the Council has taken action apart from the vote of the interested parties, as in the Mosul boundary dispute between Great Britain and Turkey and the Greco-Bulgarian dispute in 1925. However, this procedure was not followed in the Polish-Lithuanian or the Sino-Japanese disputes, Lithuania voting in the one and Japan in the other. In the Far Eastern crisis Japan by its vote was able to block several proposals. It would seem that an effective organization must insist upon the right, should mediation fail in serious crises, to take decisions to override the "sovereign" objections of the disputants.

Committee work in the League is of great importance. Although the Assembly rules of procedure apparently require unanimity, the sixth committee has frequently made decisions by majority vote. And often states which have opposed a matter in committee have withdrawn their opposition in full Assembly and in that way facilitated unanimous action.

Provisions for constitutional amendment are extremely important to subsequent legislative development. Article 26 of the Covenant provides that a proposed amendment to the Covenant must be ratified by the members of the Council and a majority of the Assembly; but it indicates no method of proposing the amendment. The question therefore arose whether a unanimous or a majority vote would be necessary to take this initial step. The advocates of the latter method argued that unanimity requirements would make amendments almost impossible; that it would be ridiculous to insist upon a unanimous vote in order to propose an amendment and yet require merely a majority to ratify it; that a proposal was only a proposal, and a state could withhold ratification later, and therefore unanimity was not necessary to protect the "sovereignty" of nations, each one having the right to secede from the League in case it disapproved the amendment. The advocates of the unanimity rule replied that Article 5 of the Covenant laid down that unanimity was required in League decisions unless specifically mentioned to the contrary. It should be held to apply to proposals for amendments. It was misleading to assert that a nation could effectively protect its sovereignty by withdrawing from the League, because a state must balance its general interest against a particular proposal for amendment and therefore, however much it might disapprove an amendment, it could not afford on that ground alone to break the many ties of interest which bind it to the League. In practice, amendments to the Covenant have not been introduced with the reckless rapidity which a mere majority rule might seem to imply; and it would seem that the Assembly was wise in considering this problem from the point of view of substantial purposes and probable consequences rather than from the viewpoint of a narrow and restrictive legality.

Several other international instruments provide for decision by majority vote, especially where the matters are of a technical rather than a political character. Although unanimity is theoretically required, practical considerations lead to some modification. Provided that the great powers are in agreement (and there is the rub!) it is likely that substantial action will be taken. Smaller nations may, by obstinate behavior in their treatment of minorities, render effective action difficult; but, given anything like the will to compromise, the unanimity rule need not present an insuperable difficulty. (The general problem is considered at length by Cromwell A. Riches in *The Unanimity Rule and the League of Nations,* and *Majority Rule in International Organization.*)

In the Italo-Ethiopian crisis the unanimity rule came to the front. It will be recalled that "recommendations" of the Council or the Assembly can be made by a majority vote, and that under Article 16 the Council may "recommend" to governments what contribution they should make in order to uphold the Covenant. After the Committee of the Council had reported that, in its judgment, Italy had violated its obligations, the President of the Council asked each representative on the Council to give his opinion. This was done, and only the Italian member dissented from the judgment of the Committee. Hence the Council as a whole passed no resolution; the individual members gave their "separate expressions of view." The President of the Council then noted, not that the Council itself had adopted a resolution or decision, but that fourteen members of the League of Nations represented on the Council considered that they were in the presence of a war begun in disregard of the Covenant.

Next day the Council report was presented to the Assembly, which followed substantially the same procedure. It adopted no formal resolutions, and avoided any procedure which might have necessitated a unanimous decision. The President of the Assembly significantly stated:

> It must be made clear that no organ of the League has power to decide, in such a way as to bind all the Members, that one of them has violated the Covenant. . . . . I was anxious to make it clear at the outset that, in the present case, this is not a resolution in the strict sense of the word, but an invitation addressed by the Assembly to the State members.

The Italian representatives, Baron Aloisi, objected to this procedure and argued that the Assembly's vote must be unanimous in order to be effective. Italy had hoped that Poland would vote on its side during the Council proceedings, but had been disappointed. In the Assembly it relied upon Austria, Hungary, and Albania to prevent a unanimous vote of condemnation against Italy. But M. Beneš, President of the Assembly, announced that "the members of the Assembly are invited to express an opinion. . . . . What is required is the assent of each Government individually. We are not going to propose a vote. . . . . I shall give to those who desire to express a contrary view an opportunity to speak," or to abstain from voting. Silence was to imply agreement. Over the protests of Baron Aloisi the Assembly upheld its President, and its members individually (with the exception of Austria, Hungary, Albania, and Italy) concurred in the findings of the fourteen members of the Council that the Italian government had violated its obligations under the Covenant. The Assembly thus acted upon the theory of substantial unanimity.

In spite of the failure of sanctions against Italy, the constitutional significance of the crisis cannot be ignored. At the time the international organization worked out a procedure which effectively overcame the obstacles imposed by the doctrines of sovereignty and unanimity, and enabled fifty nations to join in measures against an aggressor. The action may prove to be a precedent of extreme importance in world affairs.

The Permanent Court of International Justice.—We have referred to the establishment of the Permanent Court of Arbitration as a result of the First Hague Conference in 1899. Under the convention each signatory power may select four persons, whose names are sent to the Bureau of the Court at The Hague and are included upon the panel of judges. About one hundred and fifty persons constitute the panel, and from them the members of tribunals are selected when a dispute arises. Each party then signs a *compromis* which sets forth particular questions to be decided, the number of members of the tribunal, and the method of choosing the judges from the panel. It can be seen that the Court is not a permanent court. It has tried relatively few cases, averaging indeed less than one a year. And it suffers from several defects: The tribunal is overweighted by members selected after the dispute has arisen by governments which perhaps will have an eye to the known views of the judges on the panel concerning the principles at stake. There are too many representatives of interested parties compared with neutral judges. A court which sits only once cannot build up continuity and prestige, which come from long experience; its judgments will not carry so much weight (since the next tribunal will be selected from the one hundred fifty members on the panel) as if the same members sat year after year.

Consequently an attempt was made at the Second Hague Conference to remedy the defects, and the American delegates were instructed to urge the establishment of a permanent tribunal of judges "who are judicial officers and nothing else, who are paid adequate salaries, who have no other occupation, and who will devote their entire time to the trial and decision of international causes by judicial methods and under a sense of judicial responsibility." The movement failed because of the difficulty in finding a method of electing judges satisfactory to both the small and the great powers. If the former each had one judge, the court would be too large; if the latter each had one judge, the small powers would be in danger of being excluded. A move to confer a degree of compulsory jurisdiction upon the Permanent Court of Arbitration failed because of the opposition of Germany. And a similar fate befell the attempt to create an international prize court to be composed of fifteen members, including judges chosen by eight of the great powers.

In 1907 a Central American Court of Justice was established comprising five judges, one nominated by each of the five participating states. It was given wide jurisdiction, including the right to hear suits brought by an individual against a foreign state. The charge has been made that it failed because it attempted to try cases which had too great an element of the political in them. It sat upon the 1916 Bryan-Chamorro Treaty between the United States and Nicaragua which granted to the United States an option for constructing an interoceanic canal and establishing a naval base in the Gulf of Fonseca. Costa Rica and Salvador appealed to the Court, claiming that the treaty violated an 1888 treaty with Costa Rica and that the Gulf was owned by the three countries. The Court decided in both cases against Nicaragua. The latter refused to admit the jurisdiction of the Court, and the United States ignored the decision as well. Resentment ran high, and the Court ceased to exist after 1918.

In 1922 the Court was theoretically re-created. A panel of thirty names was drawn up, and three judges were to be chosen for each case. Its jurisdiction was to be obligatory, but it could not deal with problems affecting sovereignty and independence. However, it has not been called upon to try any cases.

After 1918 another move took place to build a more adequate institution. Article 14 of the Covenant provided that the League Council should formulate and submit plans to the Members of the League for the establishment of a Permanent Court of International Justice. An advisory committee met and drafted plans which, after considerable discussion and modification, were adopted by the states and became the Statute of the Court. The major problem which had remained unsolved in 1907—the election of judges—was now successfully solved by the method suggested by Mr. Elihu Root. From the panel of judges nominated by the national groups in the Permanent Court of Arbitration, the Council and the Assembly elect the Judges, each body sitting separately. Such a method gives the small powers a voice but reserves a special voice for the great powers.

The Court was inaugurated in February and held its first session in June 1922. At first it comprised fifteen members—eleven judges and four deputy judges. In 1929 this provision was modified to read that the Court "shall consist of fifteen members who are chosen regardless of their nationality for their high legal and moral qualifications." Article 9 provided that the Court should represent the main forms of civilization and the principal legal systems of the world. The judges hold office for nine years and are eligible for re-election. They thereby enjoy independence, and the nine-year period enables changes to be made so as to avoid the danger of a judge becoming too old in his office. A judge may be dismissed only on the unanimous vote of the other members of the Court. Thus the institution is freed from the danger of political interference. The judges elect their own president for a three-year term, and also the registrar of the Court. The Court is situated at The Hague, and the original statutes provided that it must meet at least once a year, although the President could summon extraordinary sessions when necessary. By the revised Article 23 the Court is to remain permanently in session except during the judicial vacation. Nine judges form a quorum.

Article 34 prescribed that only states or members of the League can be parties in cases before the Court, with special provisions for cases involving the International Labor Organization. Although several of the Committee of Jurists believed that individuals ought to be able to appear before the Court, this provision was not inserted. Nonmember states by making a declaration accepting the conditions laid down by the Court may appear before it. Much discussion took place as to whether or not the Court should exercise compulsory jurisdiction, i.e., whether states against their own will could be summoned before the Court. The Committee of Jurists decided in favor of this principle, but the Council and the Assembly refused to accept it and instead approved Article 36, which provides that the Court has jurisdiction over all cases which the parties refer to it and all matters especially provided for in treaties and conventions in force. There are many treaties which confer compulsory jurisdiction upon the Court, and the Covenant itself requires that certain questions shall be submitted to judicial settlement. Disappointing as the rejection of its compulsory jurisdiction was to many legal experts, they found some consolation in the compromise known as the Optional Clause. Article 36 also provides that states may agree to recognize as compulsory the jurisdiction of the Court in all or any of the classes of legal disputes. The Scandinavian countries led the way, and other countries followed, signing the Optional Clause, usually for a period of five years. The reason for the limited period and for the unwillingness of some powers to accept the principle of compulsory jurisdiction is to be found in the difficulty of clearly establishing the line between a legal and a political dispute, a question which is here dealt with elsewhere.

We have discussed earlier in this chapter the question of differences in the legal systems of the world. One can imagine that countries living under the Anglo-Saxon common law might hesitate to submit their cases to a Court dominated by judges brought up under the Roman law. Because of the alleged gaps and uncertainty and contradictions in international law, it was a matter of importance to decide what law the Court would be authorized to apply. Its statute provides that it may apply international conventions, whether general or particular, established rules expressly recognized by states, international custom as evidence of general practice accepted as law, the general principles of law recognized by civilized nations, and judicial decisions and the teachings of publicists. The Court may also, if the parties agree, render a decision *ex aequo et bono,* i.e., according to equity and good conscience. (Fachiri suggests that this clause was inserted to enable parties having disputes of a political character, or which were otherwise not suited for decisions on strictly legal grounds, to have recourse to the Court as a "purely arbitral party untrammeled by rules of law.")

There is a special chamber to consider labor cases, comprising five judges appointed by the Court every three years. If the parties to a dispute involving labor demand it, the chamber will hear and decide them; but if there is no such demand the full Court sits. A similar chamber for transit cases is provided. And Article 29 provides for a third chamber, that of summary procedure, comprising three judges with two substitutes, elected annually by the full Court.

Under Article 14 of the Covenant the Court "may give advisory opinions upon matters referred to it by either the Assembly or the Council." These two bodies have had frequent recourse to the Permanent Court for advisory opinions, which, because of the thoroughness with which the Court considers the questions, "are practically equivalent to regular judgments" and have on many occasions been of great assistance in determining the legal position in matters involving political problems considered by the Assembly or the Council.[37]

States were unwilling to submit to judgment of the Court without having a national representative sit on the bench. Fachiri points out that there were three possible situations relative to the question of the nationality of judges; on the bench there might be a judge of the nationality of each party, there might be a judge of the nationality of one of the parties only, or there might be no judges belonging to the nationality of either party. Under the circumstances it would have been possible (1) to make no alteration in the membership of the Court at all, (2) to have the judge belonging to the nationality of one party retire, (3) to appoint an *ad hoc* judge if

---

[37] Practically every volume on international organization contains a general summary of the World Court, its structure, and procedure. Three works may be mentioned here: A. S. de Bustamante, *The World Court* (The Macmillan Company, New York, 1925); A. P. Fachiri, *The Permanent Court of International Justice* (Oxford University Press, London, 1932); M. O. Hudson, *The Permanent Court of International Justice* (The Macmillan Company, New York, 1934).

the nationality were not represented, or (4) to appoint national assessors with advisory powers but with no vote on the decision of the case.

The Committee of Jurists, after much discussion, recommended the inclusion of judges representing the nationality of the parties. It was felt that perhaps the national judge could explain more authoritatively the legal position of his own state, and that if the verdict went against his state he could assist to form the judgment of the Court in a manner less calculated to give offense. In Fachiri's words: "It is not sufficient that justice should be done; it must also appear to have been done."

Many, however, criticized the provision for *ad hoc* national judges. They asserted that the function of a judge is not to represent his own nationality or state, or to advocate a particular point of view. His vote might be sufficient to change the decision or at least to prevent unanimity. The very presence of national judges may change the character of the deliberations of the Court, and the argument that they may defend national interests is unconvincing because the national representatives who appear to plead the case, and the long written opinions which are submitted, serve amply to present a national viewpoint. Lauterpacht suggests, as a compromise, that for a time, pending their abolition, there should be a panel of national judges who could act in an *ad hoc* capacity; at least this method would provide a permanent list and would eliminate the political appointment of a national judge on the occasion of each appearance before the Court.

What has been accomplished by the new institution? Already the Court has done important work in building up international case law.[38] Theoretically the Court is bound by Article 59 of the Statute to limit its decisions to particular cases; but in practice it has referred to previous decisions and, while not rigidly observed, the doctrine of precedent has necessarily not been ignored. In the interest of continuity and stability the Court must maintain a strong element of consistency. Most of its work has been concerned with the interpretation of treaties; but in the course of its decisions it has made many authoritative announcements on many aspects of international law, not by way of *obiter dicta* but in the course of a judgment which must be fully sustained by

[38] H. Lauterpacht, *The Development of International Law by the Permanent Court of International Justice* (Longmans, Green & Co., London, New York, 1934).

sound legal reasoning. The Court is limited to cases which national states consent to bring before it and to cases which are submitted to it under the provisions of a great number of post-war treaties. Except for the Optional Clause, the Court has no compulsory jurisdiction over states. Consequently, it must proceed with extreme caution in applying international law. If it attempted to lay down general statements and did not confine itself strictly to the particular case at issue, governments would refuse to submit disputes to it or to renew their obligations under the Optional Clause at the expiration of the stated period. Lauterpacht well puts it that if governments will not transfer legislative functions to a League, they will certainly not transfer them to a tribunal. The Court, therefore, will not deal with purely hypothetical questions; it avoids statement of general principles; it has shown great caution in assuming jurisdiction; and it has been particularly on guard against making pronouncements upon certain highly controversial aspects of international law, such as the doctrines of servitudes and *rebus sic stantibus*.

The Court must remember that states are still jealous of their sovereignty; on the other hand, if it is to be true to its task of declaring the law, it must assert the binding nature of law. In its Twelfth Advisory Opinion, it had to decide whether a unanimous verdict was required in the application of certain disputed passages of the Treaty of Lausanne. Article 5 of the Covenant had stated that except where expressly provided otherwise in the Covenant there must be a unanimous vote on the League Council or Assembly; but the Court held in this case that justice required that the interested party could not judge its own cause. It has regarded the Covenant as a legal and not a mere political document; therefore, "as a matter of judicial duty, it must be interpreted so as to be effective." In the Danzig Railway case, the Court ruled that Poland could not release itself from treaty obligations by failing to enact municipal legislation to give effect to those obligations. Its decisions in minority treaties have been to the effect that nations must observe the obligations which they have undertaken in those treaties. It has ruled that states cannot evade their international responsibilities by an appeal to their domestic constitutions. It has proceeded upon the principle that its judgments should give finality to questions under dispute and shall not be interpreted in such a way as to prolong the issue. It has not rigidly insisted upon rules of evidence, if, by so doing, the demands of essential justice would be defeated; and in one case it did not refuse to accept jurisdiction because of defects in formal presentation.

It has upheld the rule that private rights do not cease when sovereignty changes, and found in favor of the German settlers in Poland. It has awarded damages for actions taken in disregard of international obligations. It has refused to admit the plea that a state can disregard its international obligations by asserting that the measures which it took were applied also to its own nationals and to other aliens.

Although the Court has not been a major instrument in preventing international strife, it has made a notable contribution in building up international institutions for the settlement of legal disputes. Its high standard of judgments, its careful and thorough work, its impartiality (despite the criticisms made of the Court when a bare majority of the judges in the Austro-German customs regime case found that the proposed Custom Union was contrary to treaty obligations) have combined to enhance its prestige, and the mere fact that the Court exists makes it possible for states (if they desire to do so) to agree more easily to submit their legal disputes to an authoritative tribunal. Whatever be the outcome of the present international crisis, it is difficult to believe that, unless political chaos completely triumphs, the Court will not continue its work and strengthen and expand the scope of international judicial activity.

Attempts at Codification of International Law.—In most countries the time comes when the great bulk and complexity of the massive body of law which has been created by custom, statutes, and judicial decisions causes men to ask if this material cannot be sifted, analyzed, and put into logical order. Every year legislation grows in volume, the number of judicial decisions increases, and the task of judges and lawyers becomes more difficult. Codification seems to provide an obvious answer, and history affords many examples—the Code of Justinian, the Prussian Code of 1751 (replaced by the German Civil Code of 1900), the Napoleonic Civil Code, and many others. In the international field the problem appears to many people to be even more urgent. We have seen that there are conflicts of laws and that the binding force of some rules is by no means universally admitted. Would not a clearer statement and elimination of inconsistencies help to encourage recourse to international arbitration?

A number of scholars deny that codification can be applied to the international sphere as it can in the national sphere. In a relatively undeveloped system, premature codification would arrest the growth of law. Many cases will arise for which the code will have made no provision, and difficulties will ensue in the attempt to incorporate new laws into the code. Codification will destroy flexibility and elasticity. Further, the most serious disputes likely to lead to war arise not from conflicting views of international law but from divergent interests. Nor can we expect that codification conferences are the best method, because national representatives are frequently hampered by precise instructions which cause them to overemphasize the national views of their government instead of taking a broader view of the law.

Again the international courts have developed rules to deal with conflicts of laws and, provided that these rules are known in advance, no hardship is encountered. Also a state would probably accept the verdict of an international tribunal, whereas it would "not be prepared beforehand to accept the view of the law which the tribunal in fact adopts." It is better to allow law to grow out of the needs of communities rather than to attempt by governmental action to force the process. Finally, codification has a double meaning: (a) merely to express the law in a clearer and more precise form, and (b) to restate the law in such a way as to eliminate substantive differences, which really involves legislative activity. It is argued that codification of international law involves much more legislation than codification of national law, and for that reason the statesman rather than the lawyer is required: "What is being attempted in fact is to arrive at agreement, not so much on what the law is, but more especially on what it shall be in the future."

Proponents of codification allege that customary law grows too slowly and must be supplemented by more rapid case law, which codification would encourage. International law stands in need of restatement and precision and "it needs also the authority of treaty obligation, and the confidence produced through agreement, and the elimination of conflicting interpretations." If laws are more definite, nations and governments will be more willing to resort to international tribunals, which would then "have more opportunity, through judicial interpretation, to develop international law and give to it necessary elasticity." Moreover, codifying need not destroy the elasticity of developing law, as is seen in the United States, where a rigid Constitution has not prevented the growth of conventions which have become powerful. Codification has been successful within nations, and success attended the efforts of the Committee of Jurists who drafted the Statute of the Permanent Court of International Justice, which was in effect a codification of the sources of international law.

During the nineteenth century a number of unofficial efforts were made to promote codification. Jeremy Bentham, Bluntschli, who produced his code in 1868, David Dudley Field, who published his draft outlines of an international code in 1872 and 1876, and the Italian jurist, Fiore, whose work appeared in 1899, were outstanding individuals in the cause. The Institut de Droit International founded in 1873, the International Law Association, the American Institute of International Law, and other organizations, and the Harvard Research in International Law (begun in 1926) have worked consistently at the problem.

On the American continent several official conferences have devoted their energy to the same ideal. At the 1906 Pan-American Conference a committee of jurists was appointed and formed six commissions, whose work was interrupted by the World War of 1914–1918. After the restoration of peace, the work was begun again. In 1928 the sixth Pan-American Conference at Havana adopted seven statements of the law dealing with the status of aliens, the duties of neutrals in the event of civil war, the position of diplomats and of consular agents, the problem of maritime neutrality, and the right of asylum.

In Europe discussions took place at the two prewar Hague Conferences, but after 1918 no mention was made of codification in the League Covenant. The British representative, Lord Cecil, in the first League Assembly, opposed codification; and not until 1924 did the Council, at the request of the Assembly, set up a committee of experts for the gradual and progressive codification of international law. After some time it produced several recommendations. Out of these recommendations and the labors of a preparatory committee came the first Codification Conference, attended by representatives of forty-eight states. It met at The Hague on March 30, 1930, and considered three subjects: nationality, territorial waters, and the responsibility of states for damage caused in their territory to the person or property of foreigners. The conference had only a most limited success, if, indeed, it may not be described as a failure. The committee on nationality, instead of being able to adopt a code to abolish multiple nationality, produced an instrument which "rather consecrates its existence." The attempt to overcome the differences in laws dealing with the nationality of married women found the conference divided into two groups—that which wished to maintain the unity of the family, and that which advocated an equal choice for men and women. The conference was able to adopt two protocols: one providing that a person of dual nationality who habitually resides in one country be exempt from military obligation in any other land in which he also is a national; the other eliminating to a certain degree the condition of statelessness. Fundamentally, the conference was able to do so little because the problems of nationality are more political than they are legal. The states which lose people by emigration desire to have laws enabling them to retain their original nationality; immigrant-receiving countries wish to have laws making it easy to acquire the new and renounce the old citizenship.

The attempt to codify the law of territorial waters was even more unsuccessful. Two fundamental questions were the extent of national jurisdiction in marginal seas and the legal rights of a state to enforce its laws outside of the limits of territorial waters. Norway, with its rich fishery resources, was anxious to keep the four-mile limit in order to reserve the fishing rights between the third and fourth miles to its own citizens. Russia, Italy, Portugal, Sweden, Denmark, and Greece also claimed jurisdiction over marginal seas for a distance greater than three miles. Some states (France and certain Latin-American countries, for example), which generally accept the three-mile limit, claimed the right of extending their jurisdiction beyond the three miles for specific purposes. The need of conserving the resources and of preventing criminal activities has led to serious questioning as to the utility of the three-mile doctrine. Little wonder that the conference could not reach an agreement. A subcommittee which attempted to devise methods of determining the limits of territorial waters in bays, around islands, and within archipelagos and straits met with no success.

The effort to codify the laws dealing with the responsibility of states was also fruitless. Questions of delays by judicial tribunals, of the acts of officials, and of armed forces, of insurrections and riots, and whether foreigners should or should not enjoy a more favored position than nationals could not be resolved because of conflicting political and economic interests.[39]

[39] For a general summary of the Hague Conference for the Codification of International Law, see *The American Journal of International Law,* 1930, pp. 467 ff.; also J. L. Brierly, "The Future of Codification," *British Year Book of International Law, 1931,* pp. 1 ff.

620   Foundations of Modern World Society

Perhaps the inadequate technical preparation and the lack of experience were factors contributing to the failure of the Codification Conference, which itself made a number of observations urging the need of more detailed preparation.

The "sanctity" of treaties: a dilemma.—We have seen that from one point of view a treaty is merely the expression of the will of a sovereign state and is binding only so long as a sovereign state so desires, and that from another point of view a treaty is a solemn contract entered into by two states and therefore inviolable. Those who hold to the strict Austrian theory of sovereignty will adopt the first view. Those who believe that the foundation of all order lies in the keeping of promises and the observance of treaties and that law is more than the command of a sovereign will accept the second view.

It is significant that in spite of the record of broken treaties—and the list is a long one—the tradition of the inviolability of treaties is even more impressive. Space does not permit reference to the great number of examples which might be drawn from scholars, law courts, statesmen, and governments of many countries and ages. It is also significant that a government in breaking a treaty seldom claims that international law is not binding, although some new theories seem to be growing up along this line. Governments which break treaties usually plead that they do so because another country has already violated its obligations or because the necessity of self-preservation impels them to such action. In everyday life the great body of treaties has been observed as well as people respect their national law.[40] But two great weaknesses exist: (1) the fact that a peace treaty imposed by a victor upon a vanquished nation is held to be sacred, whereas domestic contracts entered into under duress are not legally binding; and (2), because of the change in conditions, certain treaties are felt by one of the signatories to have become inconsistent with its national welfare.

The first problem is of fundamental importance. A war cannot end until a peace treaty has been signed. The kind of peace treaty will depend upon the temper of the victors and the severity of the terms judged necessary to disarm the vanquished power.

---

[40] J. B. Moore, *International Law and Some Current Illusions and Other Essays* (The Macmillan Company, New York, 1922), p. 300, states: "In respect of actual observance, I venture to say that international law is on the whole as well observed as municipal law. Perhaps one would not go too far in saying that it is better observed, at any rate in time of peace."

The development of modern war is making for harsher peace treaties and rendering more difficult the kind of peace urged by Vattel in the eighteenth century and by Woodrow Wilson in 1916. Military security will demand that the defeated power be disarmed in all potential fields which constitute a threat to the victor, and such wholesale disarmament must in these days of totalitarian warfare impose heavy economic and social disabilities. The more thorough the military disarmament the less satisfactory the political peace, because the defeated power will observe the treaty only so long as it has to do so and, like Germany, will repudiate it at the earliest possible moment. The sanctity of all treaties, therefore, becomes part of the problem of eliminating war by means of collective or some other form of security. After a modern war it is growingly impossible to devise a peace which is both politically and militarily sound.

This question requires further elaboration. The world has witnessed the fatal consequences of attempting to reconcile the idea of a League of Nations based upon the principles of common consent and collective responsibility and such peace treaties as in 1919 were imposed upon defeated countries based upon the principle of keeping those countries in a position of essential inferiority. The League of Nations did not have an opportunity to function according to its own inherent principles. Collective security required conditions of substantial equality and of nondiscrimination among the nations of the world; but the peace treaties were based upon force. The enemy powers had to accept extremely harsh conditions; the "Carthaginian" peace emphasized the distinction between victors and vanquished. Now the contradiction between the peace treaties based on force and the League of Nations based on the ideal of collective guaranty of substantial equality of rights had to be resolved before the League could function in its own right, free from the distortion of a punitive peace. The time came when it was no longer possible simultaneously to move in these divergent directions, and hence the confusion and deadlock in Europe.

The source of this contradiction must be found in the history of the last two hundred years, and its full significance must be adequately appreciated. The Italian historian, Ferrero, has called attention to a fundamental concept of Vattel, who in his *Law of Nations*, written in 1758, urged that, inasmuch as both countries at war believe themselves to be right, and because no impartial tribunal exists to give an authoritative verdict, a peace treaty must represent an agreement which is accepted by both sides as substantially just or at least as substantially not unjust. A peace treaty, if it is really to end a war, must liquidate the causes of the war in such a way as to be "fully and honestly accepted" by the defeated power. But the victorious nation imposes the treaty by force; how then can a defeated power accept it "freely and honestly"? Only if the victor acts with sufficient restraint and combines two objects—obtaining satisfaction for himself by appropriating the object for which he fought, and at the same time avoiding what will appear "an intolerable exercise of compulsion" upon the defeated party. Only in this way will the treaty be sacred or at least tolerable to the loser as well as to the winner. The war must therefore be concluded before the weaker power is so exhausted that it cannot exercise a fairly wide degree of free choice in preferring "a certain and immediate loss but of limited extent" to a later overwhelming defeat and exhaustion. It must feel that it has suffered an honorable defeat at the hands of an honorable opponent whose respect it still enjoys. A peace treaty should be essentially a matter of compromise between two nations which have resorted to arms in order to gain what they believe their rights. Now a compromise is inconsistent with the application by the victor of harsh penalties, especially if they are imposed in the name of justice. Vattel insists that nothing in war "is more opposed to moderation than the judicatory spirit" on the part of the winner; to use his victory to assume the role of a judge when he has been one of the contending parties is fatal; and to inflict unnecessary punishment upon a defeated enemy is a licentious action condemned by the law of nature.

Only on the principle of "peace without victory" could the treaties of Versailles, St. Germain, Trianon, and Neuilly have the essential spirit of compromise so eloquently urged by Vattel. Yet the very developments of war itself made this kind of peace difficult if not impossible to achieve. During the eighteenth century armies were small—Marshal Saxe claimed that an army of 42,000 men was sufficient. The object of war was to execute "skilfull maneuvers" rather than to "annihilate the enemy." The French Revolution destroyed this conception of war and introduced the idea of a nation in arms and organized conscription. It aroused popular emotion by the use of symbols and propaganda. Passion replaced professional training, and military writers began to advocate the application of sheer force and numbers, instead of avoiding battles and indulging in chess-like maneuvers. The military restraints of the small professional armies were destined to disappear.

A new era had begun, writes Ferrero, an era in which national wars were to assume an increasingly devastating character because of the overthrow of this principle of restraint, the growth of propaganda, and the increased application of science to warfare. The World War of 1914–1918, because of its unprecedented proportions, the fury of its character, and the unleashing of passions on a world-wide scale, became a conflict which lost all relation to any specific objectives. It became its own end, and it is significant that war aims were not even discussed until 1916.

Here we find the essential cause of the great contradiction between the requirements of modern war and the necessities of modern peace. In order to maintain a military victory the general staffs must insist that the enemy be rendered as helpless as possible. Because of the rapidity of modern inventions in the field of armaments, the victorious nation feels that it cannot adopt a peace without victory. The defeated power might recover so rapidly as to endanger the advantages of the victor. Hence the enemy must be disarmed. The Peace Treaties gained this objective to an unusual degree; but the military requirements contradicted the fundamental conditions of a sound political peace. There could be no political compromise along the lines suggested by Vattel or President Wilson.

The World War of 1914–1918, because of its very intensity, led the victors to impose a punitive peace designed to keep Germany, Austria, Hungary, and Bulgaria in a position of military and economic inferiority, not a peace of compromise but a Carthaginian peace, a peace of "woe to the vanquished." It was not merely the severity of the material terms but also the imposition of Article 231 with its judicatory tone which caused such resentment. In vain did the defeated powers ask for an impartial commission to examine the responsibility for the world conflict. The Allies determined to be both parties and judges in their own cause. Consequently the treaties which became sacred to some (though not all) of the victors represented an unfair and intolerable burden to the defeated Central Powers.

It is here that the tragic dilemma of the present time appears. Germany and the other defeated nations could have the peace treaties modified only if the Allied Powers adopted the Vattelian principle of compromise and essential equality; otherwise the latter had to maintain the unequal treaties by force. It is true that some modifications were grudgingly made. Finding it impossible to extract by force the astronomical reparation figures demanded from the vanquished peoples, the Allies then asked them to consent to pay sums of a lesser magnitude. The Dawes Plan and the Young Plan are interesting examples of the way in which consent, not force, enabled the victors to gain some payments from the losers. The futility of a treaty of force was hereby excellently illustrated: Within five years of a complete military victory, the victors were agreeing with the vanquished.

Similarly in the realm of security, in 1926 Germany was admitted to the League of Nations, following the Locarno Pact. The loser, Germany, voluntarily agreed to observe the western frontier as an inviolable boundary—another illustration of the need of obtaining from the defeated power a full acceptance of a situation, an acceptance freely assented to and not forced at the point of the sword.

Unfortunately these two adjustments did not suffice to solve the contradictions within the Peace Treaty—the element of victorious force on the one hand, and the ideal of genuine collective action on the other. The defeated powers demanded a restoration of essential equality in armaments, colonies, elimination of the so-called war-guilt clause, and self-determination. They were met by the reply that, according to international law, the peace treaty imposed at the end of the war was legal and any modification of the situation created by it must come through the assent of all the signatory powers. The only other legal way was for the vanquished to modify the situation by armed force, or by the threat of armed force to gain concessions. Thus Germany and the other defeated powers confronted this problem; an international situation, extremely distasteful and humiliating to them, had been imposed by force and was now to be maintained by law. What one set of nations, rightly or wrongly (and in the absence of a third-party judgment who could tell whether rightly or wrongly?), believed to be an unjust and immoral treaty became for them a legal obligation. Such a condition is most serious. When a people comes to regard the overthrow of a legal situation as its most pressing moral duty, trouble must ensue.

The League of Nations and the ideal of collective security could not, therefore, develop along sound lines while they were called upon to guarantee the status quo which itself was the result of war. To make Articles 10 and 16 serve the purpose of perpetuating provisions of a forcible treaty, and not to enable

Article 19 (and other Articles) providing for the reconsideration of existing treaties to come into play, was to invalidate the whole claim that in preventing aggression by collective sanctions the League was engaged in "police power." Within nations themselves, police power is not used to enforce contracts imposed by threat or violence by one person against another. And until nations agree to modify treaties in favor of those countries which lose in war, sanctions must appear as a collective instrument of the victors against the vanquished, and the latter will use the threat of force or go to war, as Germany did in 1939. And this is no solution, because there is no guaranty that Hitler is not using a past grievance as an excuse for future conquests as unjust as he complains the Treaty of Versailles to have been.

Thus the question of sanctions presents a dilemma. Strong sanctions cannot develop until there is fairly universal feeling among people in favor of using them to maintain peace. But rigid definition of aggressors and schemes for automatic sanctions are dangerous until flexibility in treaty arrangements comes about. Otherwise, sanctions mean collective immobility and resistance to change in a changing world.

Peaceful changing of existing treaties carries with it profound implications. If in a threatened war no party should be a judge in its own cause, if the international community claims the right of restraining the aggressor and later of inquiring into alleged grievances, it must follow that the international community is bound to take cognizance of treaties which are the source of irritation and danger. If that be the case, international organization must be in a position to pronounce that certain parts of certain treaties stand in need of modification. Thus the claim of the defeated powers to treaty revision must be examined and must be subordinated to the good of the world as interpreted by collective judgment; but victorious powers in a past war must also realize that their desire for treaty perpetuation must be subordinate to the general good as interpreted by collective judgment. The fact that treaties contain no provisions for revision or denunciation cannot be made the basis of a claim against the superior rights of the international community.

How can a system be devised to prevent treaties from militating against "peaceful change"? For we need a system which will permit stability on the one hand and change on the other. Punitive peace treaties make peaceful change a most difficult matter. They intensify the argument of the "have" and the "have-not" nations. Germany has been a "have-not" largely because of the peace treaties. Japan and Italy are so-called "have-not" nations because of the damming up of world markets, the collapse of currency, and the struggle for adequate reserves of raw materials in case of war. Peaceful change cannot take place in a world which is building armaments at a feverish pace, and in which military preparedness dwarfs all else. Peaceful change in a war world is a senseless statement. There cannot be peaceful change until there is peaceful routine. Peaceful change must grow out of a more basic order in international as well as national society. But, given the fundamentals of order, steps must be taken to prevent order from becoming solidified into a static political system and to prevent treaties from becoming instruments of political rigidity.

To this end it will be necessary to establish some independent body which can supervise the performance of treaties. Obviously neither of the signatory parties should have the final right to say that a treaty is no longer observed because conditions have changed. A treaty should remain binding until a court or tribunal, after hearing an appeal from the parties, shall determine that modification should be permitted.

Certain principles[41] would assist in maintaining the sanctity of treaties: (1) They should be signed for a fixed but not over-long period, and should contain a clear statement of methods by which the signatories may denounce or modify them. Short-term treaties will be less liable to denunciation than those of indefinite duration. (2) The signatories should agree to submit any dispute arising from the interpretation or application of the treaty to the Permanent Court of International Justice or some other tribunal. (3) As described above, any pleas that conditions have changed should be submitted to a third-party judgment and should not provide the excuse for either signatory to denounce the treaty. (4) Because some treaties exist which no longer express a common interest, a system of peaceful revision is necessary. At present the only practicable solution is to encourage the parties to come to a voluntary agreement. International organization can do little more, although, in Whitton's judgment, "an impartial investigation and report . . . . made under the auspices of the community of nations, may be useful." (5) The codification of the Stimson doctrine of nonrecognition should be made

[41] John B. Whitton, "The Sanctity of Treaties," in *International Conciliation* (Carnegie Endowment for International Peace, New York, October 1935).

into "a universal rule of international law," so that every treaty which results from a violation of the League Covenant or the Kellogg Pact or any other conventions for the prevention of war and aggression should be deemed to be "contrary to international public order" and therefore *"invalid ab initio."*

The United States in revising the permanent treaty with Cuba in 1934 and the unsatisfactory treaty with Panama in 1939, in order to carry out the Good Neighbor Policy, has provided an example of treaty revision by diplomatic action which merits consideration as another means of peaceful change.[42]

The Enforcement of Treaties.—The enforcement of treaties in the service of peace and international order meets two further obstacles: (1) treaties, including the League of Nations Covenant, "are in principle of equal status" and (2) because of this theoretical equality of treaties, international society suffers from "such a paucity of forms available that obligations of many sorts must be compressed into the common treaty mould." The two points require elaboration.

During the Italo-Ethiopian crisis an American authority on international law in a letter to the *New York Times* claimed that if the United States imposed an embargo on the exports of oil to Italy for its alleged violation of the Kellogg Pact, it would violate a United States–Italian commercial treaty signed in the late nineteenth century. If Borchard's argument was sound, a commercial treaty of relatively minor importance could still stand in the way of a subsequent treaty of major significance. On the other hand, if the international community could successfully claim that the obligations of the Kellogg Pact (under which signatories renounced war as an instrument of national policy) were more binding than those of a prior but minor treaty, a long step forward would have been taken in the development of a sense of constitutionality in world organization.

Another example shows the difficulty of effecting a multilateral convention in the face of a pre-existing treaty. In 1932, Holland and Belgium signed the Ouchy agreement to lower tariff barriers until they had been reduced, as between the signatory powers, by 50 per cent. Great Britain announced that it would claim the most-favored-nation treatment accorded by earlier treaty arrangements, and by its assertion of a legal claim helped to ruin

[42] See Graham H. Stuart, "Diplomacy as an Adequate Procedure for Treaty Revision," *World Affairs,* September 1940, pp. 159–63.

a regional attempt to arrest the rising tide of economic nationalism.

At the 1933 Montevideo Conference several American states signed a multilateral convention for the lowering of duties and, in order to obviate any subsequent doubts, pledged themselves not to claim the privileges of any existing bilateral treaties containing the most-favored-nation clause. (Belgium declared that she did not think it necessary to make such a pledge, in that, in her opinion, the multilateral treaty took precedence.) The League of Nations, the Permanent Court of International Justice, and other international bodies, it is hoped, will "help to systematize the world's conglomeration of treaties by regarding certain covenants as fundamental, and by declaring invalid, or in need of revision, engagements contrary thereto,"[43] and in this manner build a system of constitutionalism in international affairs.

International law has contained two startlingly inconsistent doctrines, the sovereignty of nations and the sacredness of treaties. From one view a treaty is only the expression of the will of a sovereign state to act in a given manner, without, however, surrendering its subsequent freedom of action; from the other view, a sacred treaty implies an obligation on the part of a so-called sovereign state which must limit its "sovereignty." Also, a later treaty signed by a nation which is inconsistent with an earlier treaty is deemed to be nonbinding to the extent of its inconsistency (a curious comment upon so-called sovereignty). How may nations build a system of international obligations and at the same time make and unmake agreements in the name of unfettered sovereignty?

The League of Nations Covenant as a treaty may be regarded as no more binding than any other treaty, but it is an extremely comprehensive instrument in which are included many obligations concerning war, armaments, minorities, labor, mandates, health, and social questions. Within the whole range of these matters the members of the League declare, in Article 20:

. . . . that this Covenant is accepted as abrogating all obligations or understandings *inter se* which are inconsistent with the terms thereof, and solemnly undertake that they will not hereafter enter into any engagements inconsistent with the terms thereof.

2. In case a Member of the League shall, before becoming a Member of the League, have undertaken any obligations inconsistent with the

[43] Payson S. Wild, *Sanctions and Treaty Enforcement* (Harvard University Press, Cambridge, 1934), p. 6.

terms of this Covenant, it shall be the duty of such Member to take immediate steps to procure its release from such obligations.

But Article 20 does not explicitly state that treaties which are inconsistent with the Covenant are by that fact null and void. Wild makes the following comment:

Apparently, if states do not take steps to release themselves from treaty obligations which are incompatible with the Covenant [who is to be the judge in such a case?] such obligations are still binding as between the contractants, and no powers under the article are given to the League to bring about the termination of treaty commitments of this character.[44]

In 1920 M. Seferiades of Greece suggested that the League could refuse to register a treaty between two or more powers if in the unanimous opinion of the Council its provisions were contrary to international public order, the treaty therefore being deemed to be nonexistent. The Italian representative argued that to give the Council power to decide upon the validity of treaties would tend to cause evasion of the registration provisions, and the League took no action at that time.

The Italo-Ethiopian conflict brought the problem to the fore. League members were determined in this case to regard the Covenant as the "higher law," having a constitutional priority over previous treaty engagements. A legal subcommittee set up by the Co-ordinating Committee of the Assembly decided that the application of sanctions against a state guilty of breaking the Covenant suspended the operation of prior treaties, providing for the execution of a commercial treaty and the reciprocal enforcement of judgments. Nor could a state member of the League which did not take part in sanctions legally claim the benefits of a most-favored-nation treaty. In accordance with these and other findings, Turkey informed Italy that its obligations under the Covenant to the League were paramount to its obligations to Italy under the Turco-Italian Treaty of Friendship of 1928; and other nations took similar action. The precedent established may or may not (according to the future fate of collective society) have decisive importance. Article 20 may yet come to be, in the words of Lauterpacht, "a perpetual source of legal energy possessed of a dynamic force of its own."[45]

---

[44] *Ibid.*, p. 7.

[45] H. Lauterpacht, "The Covenant as the 'Higher Law'," *British Year Book of International Law, 1936.*

National constitutions and international order.—A rapidly changing world has transformed the majority of national constitutions from relatively effective to comparatively inefficient instruments of government. A constitution should be framed with a view to assisting toward the fullest life of the citizens of the nation. If, however, it does not include adequate provision for dealing with many forces which affect the people living under it, it does no more than part of its work. In older days the major problems originated within the national boundaries, and international relations did not necessarily touch the everyday life of the inhabitants. Such a state of affairs no longer holds. The chapters of the present volume which have dealt with communications, currency, tariffs, migration, slavery, health, social questions, colonies, security, and armaments show that a high degree of continuous interpenetration takes place among nations. National constitutions which fail to take these facts into consideration are out of date, unfitted to serve their fundamental purpose. Constitutions which make difficult the effective execution of treaties dealing with matters which vitally affect the daily welfare of citizens of national groups are a hindrance and not a help, and they should be revised in order to increase the common national good which results from international co-operation as well as from internal effort.

No longer can constitution makers merely turn their eyes inward. They must look outward, because forces which originate from beyond a nation's boundaries must be dealt with in orderly fashion if disappointment and disorder are not to ensue. There are two main fields of effort in this connection: (1) adaptation of national constitutions to the international machinery designed to stop war, the modern crown of thorns; and (2) revision of national constitutions to enable more rapid adoption and ratification of international agreements, so that in the fields of labor standards, currency, tariffs, etc., expensive and irritating delays may be obviated.

In a chapter[46] entitled "Constitutional Sub-structure of the Collective System," C. W. Jenks deals with this problem of harmonizing national constitutions (many of which were drawn up in the prewar period, the age of "international anarchy," as he calls it) with the League Covenant, the Kellogg Pact, and other

[46] C. W. Jenks, "International Aspect of the Indian Constitution," in F. M. Houlston and B. P. L. Bedi (ed.), *India Analysed* (Victor Gollancz, London, 1933).

collective instruments of the postwar period. He points out that practically all constitutions begin with a recital of national sovereignty and independence; they indicate which branch of the government may declare war, but make no reference to obligations undertaken to exhaust peaceful remedies before resorting to war. It is true that some countries have incorporated provisions requiring municipal courts to respect rules of international law; in the very vital questions of war and peace, however, modern national constitutions show little or no influence of the tremendous principles embodied in the League of Nations Covenant and the Paris Pact.

The 1931 constitution of Spain, now displaced, is a notable exception. Its Articles 65, 76, 77, and 78 provide that (1) Spain may declare war only after having exhausted all the remedies of the League Covenant, (2) its government may not give notice of withdrawal from the League until the step has been approved by vote of the Cortes, (3) treaties and international agreements shall be registered with the League of Nations in accordance with Article 18 of the Covenant, (4) secret treaties and agreements shall not bind the nation, and (5) "all the international agreements ratified by Spain and registered in the League of Nations, and having the character of international law, shall be considered a constituent part of Spanish legislation, which shall be in accord with the terms of such agreements." Although some of the provisions are loosely drawn, and certain principles are formulated in too general a sense, the Spanish example is a significant one which other nations should follow. The government of Siam adopted a constitution on December 10, 1932, of which Article 54 "limits the right to declare war to cases in which such a declaration will not involve violation of the Covenant."

Jenks proposes four ways in which national constitutions may be given an "international orientation":

1. Governments should be empowered without waiting for special enabling legislation to take immediate steps to give effect to Article 16 of the Covenant providing for sanctions against an aggressor. This proposal is of interest in view of the Italian-Ethiopian crisis. An appreciable delay occurred after the League decision to enforce a boycott against Italy because many governments by reason of constitutional requirements had to wait for their legislatures to enact special measures.

2. Nations should adopt a constitutional provision that their membership in the League of Nations is permanent and that a

constitutional amendment is required in order to give notice of withdrawal. At present the possibility of a nation's retirement from the League on two years' notice is a distinct handicap to collective security and makes it possible for governments not thoroughly representative of public opinion to take precipitate action by means of threats or actual withdrawal. Each constitution should therefore contain a declaration to the effect that League membership is an essential part of the national constitution system and that the government shall not withdraw from the League while the constitution remains in force.

3. War should be prohibited constitutionally as well as internationally. At present a government which declares war may violate its international obligations but does not thereby violate its own constitution. Were it possible to insert in a national constitution such a prohibition, the group of people who support peace would be strengthened, in that their opposition to war would no longer be open to the charge of disloyalty to the government, nor be interpreted as lack of patriotism, as is so often the case at the present time.

4. Constitutions should secure the supremacy of international over municipal law in case of conflict between the two; unregistered treaties should not be regarded as valid by a municipal court; treaties once ratified should have constitutional force until denounced in a regular manner as provided for by international authorities.

It will be seen that the fourth proposal deals with the problem of reforming national constitutions so that the way to more effective action in matters that require international legislation may be cleared of the difficulties that obstruct progress. Treaty law is progressing at an extraordinary pace. Several hundred international conventions adopted within twenty years bear witness to the new needs of the modern world. If constitutions are adopted, or continued, with little or no reference to fundamentally important factors which have their origin beyond national boundaries, human life will suffer from added difficulties and complications.

The first essential step is to bridge the gap between international and domestic law and to insure the supremacy of the former over the latter in case of conflict. One doctrine is that within an independent nation, should a conflict occur or appear to occur between a treaty and an act of the competent national authority, the latter shall prevail. The Permanent Court of International

Justice has given a different emphasis to the whole problem in two important judgments, which lay down that treaties are sources of legal obligations and are not mere political instruments which safeguard a nation's freedom of action; treaties are not to be interpreted restrictively by artful devices of municipal legislation; nor should their effectiveness be limited by deliberate ambiguity of terminology. It is probable that the influence of the Permanent Court of International Justice will gradually make headway against the overriding claims of sovereignty,[47] but it would materially assist in improving the daily conditions of the mass of mankind if states would incorporate into their constitutions explicit provisions along the lines suggested by the Permanent Court.

Federal governments have experienced difficulty in ratifying conventions. The Austrian nation, under Article 16 of its first postwar constitution, obliged provinces to take measures to give effect to treaties and authorized the federal government to pass the necessary law or laws in the event that one or more of the provinces failed to act. But the United States, Canada, and Australia do not find it easy to ratify international labor conventions. Jenks expressed the hope that India would not adopt its new federal constitution (1935), "inadequately equipped to join in the development of international legislation" and suggested methods by which that nation might avoid error: (1) by giving the federal legislature full powers to legislate on matters of international importance or (2) by giving to the federal legislature full power to implement international engagements or (3) by developing machinery for consultation among the provinces, the Indian native states, and the federal government.

Many states do not ratify treaties and conventions which have been signed by their representatives, or they delay ratification for long periods. At a time when the world needs rapidity of international legislation it finds a tendency to slower action by national authorities. In the earlier part of the last century, ratification often occurred within two to six weeks; today, if a time limit is imposed,

---

[47] C. W. Jenks, "The Authority in English Courts of Decisions of the Permanent Court of International Justice," *British Year Book of International Law, 1939*, pp. 1–36. The author argues that the assertions of the judges in three cases quoted that a decision of the Permanent Court of International Justice is not binding on English courts do not necessarily hold true, that the question is "still an entirely open one," and English courts should under certain circumstances consider themselves bound by a World Court decision.

it may be from one to three years. To no small degree the situation has changed for the worse.[48]

1. Modern life is extremely complex and national parliaments have so many domestic issues before them that action on so-called "international" matters is relegated to the background and postponed. The growth of democracy has added to the difficulties of ratification; for however great is the advantage of government by discussion, it almost necessarily invites delay. Sometimes, indeed, governments have to wait for some months until Parliament is called into session.

2. International legislation has expanded in scope and amount to an enormous degree. Hundreds of treaties are now signed, whereas in the nineteenth century there were only dozens, and these newer instruments contain much more than the merely political matters usually contained in treaties of fifty years ago. Only two international labor conventions resulted from one hundred years of international effort; between 1919 and 1939 the number has increased to about fifty. Considerations of health, currency, labor, opium and drugs, slavery, etc., complicate the subject matter of present-day treaties, and many more administrative agencies in the respective nations must be consulted, because the detailed application of the conventions will rest with the executive and administrative organs of government.

3. Many treaties now require modification of the domestic law, and, in view of the detailed and specialized character of much of the legislation, prolonged study is frequently required.

4. Still more important is the financial aspect of the proposed conventions. Raising labor standards, providing workers' leisure, unemployment and sickness insurance, lessening workers' hours, establishing protection for married women in industry, conducting health campaigns and nutrition experiments (to mention only a few of the hundreds of proposals made in international conferences) involve heavier governmental expenditures, and extra taxation worries governments—although one must add that all the costs of the internationally proposed social and economic reforms would not approach within measurable distance the appalling expenditure at present incurred in competitive armaments.

5. Several governments, anxious not to be put at a disadvantage by reason of undertaking heavier obligations than other

---

[48] F. O. Wilcox, *The Ratification of International Conventions* (George Allen & Unwin, London, 1935), pp. 110–22.

governments, wait and see, or adopt the policy of conditional ratification or of ratification with reservations.

6. Some conventions are loosely drafted, and their meaning is ambiguous and perhaps obscure. Naturally enough, as Francis O. Wilcox notes, "states hesitate to assume the obligations imposed until they have a definite assurance of what they really are. Unfortunately there is no easy method of obtaining official interpretations of questionable phrases or clauses."[49]

When all these difficulties are adjusted, delays in ratification would still proceed in no small measure from the neglect of national governments and the indifference of national public opinion. Accordingly, several attempts have been made to overcome governmental inertia and to speed up the ratifying process. Wilcox has summarized the efforts of the League of Nations and its associated bodies: The 1921 Barcelona Conference proposed that ratifications should go to the Secretary-General of the League; he should keep a record which League members should be free to inspect, and the list should be published from time to time. Later the League Council ordered publication once a year; and in 1924 a 27-page report appeared, the modest beginnings of "a steady publicity campaign." Two years later M. Beneš, then President of the Council, re-emphasized the urgency of the question of ratification. The Assembly at length adopted a resolution requesting the Council to call for a report on the progress of ratification each six months and to consider means of speeding up the process. From that time the question has regularly come before the Council, which has thus become an important agency in reminding governments of their obligations.

In addition to the League Council, the Assembly has concerned itself with the problem, especially after the failure of many governments to ratify conventions adopted by the Work Economic Conference. In 1930 the First Committee announced that indifference to ratification was "liable seriously to affect the authority and prestige of the League. It was dangerous to arouse year after year hopes which were not realized"—for ten years the League had sowed, and the time for reaping had come. A special committee was therefore set up to investigate the causes of delay in ratification and to suggest remedies. Although it did not produce any novel ideas, the committee brought together the following proposals: (1) that the Secretary-General request from states which

[49] *Ibid.*, pp. 115–16.

had failed to ratify the reasons for their delay and word as to whether or not they yet intended to take action; (2) that states which had not acceded to League conventions within five years should be requested to give reasons; (3) that revision conferences be called to reconsider League conventions; (4) that states bind themselves to submit a convention to their suitable national body for ratification within a stated time; (5) that attempts be made to enlarge the number of international agreements which might be adopted without the necessity of ratification; (6) and that the League publish adequate tables and diagrams in order to afford substantial publicity.

Generally speaking, the "follow-up work" of the League has helped to speed up ratifications and consequently to facilitate international legislation.[50] Other suggestions include: (1) that the time limit for ratifications and final signature be reduced; (2) that if an insufficient number of ratifications are forthcoming within a given period, another conference should be held to inquire into the reasons for failure to act on the part of signatory powers; (3) that national constitutional requirements be modified.

Wilcox notes that thirty states require that the legislature approve all treaties which are negotiated by the executive. This condition he believes to be undesirable and unfortunate, and he proposes that nations adopt one of the following methods: (a) that the legislature be empowered to approve certain important classes of treaties (involving peace and war, finance, cession of territories), but that the executive retain power to ratify all other international engagements; (b) that the cabinet or executive retain treaty-making and ratifying power but be always responsible to the legislature; (c) that the legislature delegate to the executive the power to conclude and ratify treaties, retaining control by its power of withdrawing the delegated powers if in its opinion the executive abuses its position or endangers the welfare of the country.

Wilcox further suggests (4) that the League of Nations machinery be strengthened by the creation of an advisory committee on international legislation for the purpose of studying means of facilitating ratification. Noel Baker has proposed (5) that ratification should be taken for granted unless nations within a given time specifically reject a treaty which their representatives have already signed. But such a proposal would materially change the

---

[50] F. O. Wilcox, *op. cit.*, pp. 158–60.

present emphasis; the signature of a treaty in international conference would then not be in the nature of a preliminary step as it now tends to be; instead of requiring further action for its completion, it would necessitate positive action for rejection. In many cases the latter would be sufficient to insure the acceptance of a treaty if only on the principle of inertia. But even more it would emphasize the factor of international legislation, since national groups likely to be affected in an adverse manner would be forced to raise the issue in a defensive way, whereas at the present time, unless the government is wholeheartedly behind a treaty, it may not be able to find the necessary support to insure ratification. G. E. Toulmin urges (6) that ratification should take place in international conference so as to avoid the danger of delayed ratification on the part of some nations and of nonratification on the part of others. Eagleton and others have even raised the question (7) as to whether it would not be possible and desirable to dispense with ratifications altogether.

Conclusion.—What of the future of international law? No precise answer is possible, because we do not know what the outcome of the war will be. But one may predict with some confidence that international law must either go forward very much, or be quite discredited. It cannot remain in its present position, containing as it does so many contradictions. If law is defined as a set of rules obeyed by a given society, then the set of rules that world society will adopt in the coming years will depend upon what principles and purposes triumph in the present struggle. We have already seen that the Catholic theory of international law differs from the Austinian theory, and that certain proposals have already been made for the strengthening of international law based upon theories which do not accept the position of the Austinians. We must also recognize that the Soviet theory of international law bears little resemblance to the theories at present in operation. To the Communists, international law is the outcome of capitalistic society with its intra-capitalistic struggles and agreements on the one hand and its hostilities to the workers on the other. A complete realization of communist international law would involve the suppression of capitalism, the elevation of the proletariat, and the dethronement of the "bourgeoisie state" throughout the world. The victory of Nazism would bring a new international order with its own rules based upon the Nazi racial conception of law, the suppression of minorities, the elimination of small sovereign states, and the undoubted hegemony of Germany. The law which would then be in operation may not correspond to what we consider law, but it would provide rules which would have to be accepted by the conquered as well as by the victorious peoples.

If it be true that international law as we have known it has proved inadequate, because it has recognized the legality of war and the validity of treaties imposed by force, because it has not had legislative and executive organs suitable for its development, because it has not determined whether international law is primarily an act of agreement between sovereign states in the exercise of their will or is binding unequivocally upon member states; and, finally, because it disregards changing functions of groups and states in modern life—then there is much ground for Niemeyer's claim that "political reality has become unlawful, because the existing system of international law has become unreal," that the traditional law of nations is no longer adequate "to check the action of political units, to hamper governments, to restrict states," and that today it is used, or rather abused, as a weapon "in the struggle between states."[51]

We have seen that modern war has become so transnational in character that it cannot be kept in bounds by the existing state system, and that sovereign communities can no longer by themselves guarantee the conditions necessary to maintain their health, commerce, and culture. The new continental or world unit of government which will be the minimum necessary for controlling and harnessing the great forces of modern life, the new rules, which must be considerably more far-reaching than those at present in existence, will constitute a new international law, built upon the experience of the past but enlarged and modified in accordance with new purposes and conditions.

Chief of the new requirements will be the maintenance of order without which all other rules rest upon foundations of sand. The new international authority must have sufficient power, as does the United States government within its borders, to guarantee peace and order.

But this political power must be used in accordance with rules which can be legitimately described as rules of law. The new international society, if it is to be a genuine society, will have an international law which will closely approximate constitutional law. The constitutions of the respective states must be geared to the

[51] G. Niemeyer, *Law without Force* (Princeton University Press, 1941), p. 98.

constitution of the larger regional and world unit, so that an infraction of international law or what will be transnational law will at the same time be an infraction of both national law and the new society's fundamental law.

Whether the new constitution (which, to repeat, is nothing more than a formal setting forth of the rights and duties of individuals, groups, and communities and the methods of prescribing, enforcing, and interpreting those rights and duties) should contain a sharply detailed division of powers, such as obtains in the American Commonwealth, with a judiciary to decide on disputed points of jurisdiction, or whether it should incorporate the principle of federal disallowance as in Canada, or the principle of paramountcy which Great Britain exercises over the Native States of India, will depend upon the deliberations of the statesmen of the world and public opinion throughout the nations. What seems to be unquestionable is the need of eliminating the obstacles at present placed in the way of international government by the existence of the claims to exclusive domestic jurisdiction by the sovereign states. Under modern conditions there are no such distinctions as "domestic affairs" and "international affairs." The "domestic" or "international" relevance is not inherent in affairs or matters as such. "The criterion of difference between the two categories lies in the functional objective toward which the operation of the states is directed."

Since a state or a nation is, in the words of Mommsen, a society for certain purposes, the kind of nation or state will depend upon those purposes; if problems arise within the boundaries of a state which intimately affect the welfare of other states, and new and wider purposes come into being, a new society for those purposes will result. And rules must be adopted to meet the changing circumstances; the more actions take place across boundaries the greater must be the growth of rules to channelize these actions to constructive ends. There is nothing surprising, therefore, in the contention that international law must be tremendously expanded in scope and in institutions if the modern world is to regain some degree of order.

If it be objected that law must grow out of the organic life of a people, the answer clearly must be that the intensive development of applied science has forced mankind to quicken its power of adaptation. Radio, not a generation old, has become so intimately a part of our life as to be called organic; and the same holds true of automobiles and airplanes and of most of our material culture.

Only by ignoring the world in which we live can we refuse to make out a case for changing the scope of government and of law.

If a small percentage of the energy and propaganda which are used to divide men's loyalties were used to enlarge them, the problem would be relatively simple. Indeed, it must be pointed out that the fall of France, Yugoslavia, and other nations has been due to the fact that the boasted organic unity of these countries has not existed (even in the case of France) and that in each the more local purposes and interests triumphed over national interests. It follows that only if there is a wide enough understanding of, and enthusiasm for, the forces which are continental and world-wide in character, can international law and organization be expanded sufficiently to minister adequately to the needs of the contemporary world.

Today international society is at least so interdependent (whatever men's attitudes may be) that civil wars have immediate international repercussions (as in Spain); international wars produce national revolutions, as was witnessed on a large scale at the end of the World War of 1914–1918; tariffs, although allegedly a domestic matter, may affect the economy of a foreign country to its very foundations; minority problems within a state cause international strife; and arbitrary action by a government may ruin thousands of foreign investors. If, therefore, the world refuses to give political and legal expression to this interdependence, the consequences will be disastrous.

Chapter XIV

THE DEVELOPMENT OF WAR AND ITS
EFFECT UPON THE SOVEREIGN STATE

IN FEUDAL days there was no permanent army. At the end of a campaign, after having performed his military service, the knight returned home. To him fighting was a privilege reserved to the upper classes and woe betide the commoner who dared usurp his prerogative.

The growth of cities and the Protestant Reformation brought burghers and peasants into the fighting line. Frequently townspeople in their struggle against feudal lords for their liberties hired and armed mercenary troops to wage their battles for them. The use of the bow and of gunpowder put the knight at a disadvantage and dealt the landed class a heavy blow. Noblemen protested against the new, unfair methods of war! The rise of a new class and the introduction of new weapons thus had important consequences for European society.

The freedom due to the absence of any standing army, which seems so extraordinary to our modern world burdened with the cost of maintaining millions upon millions of men under arms, was offset by the danger of roving bands which came into existence when mercenaries were disbanded at the conclusion of hostilities. And, indeed, standing armies as we know them arose in order "to liquidate bothersome military groups seeking to perpetuate their existence by marauding."[1] The remedy was effective; but in turn it threatened the new middle class, which found that the standing army, called into being as its protector, was likely to become a greater menace than the disorderly marauders had been. The standing army enabled the feudal nobleman, who had been displaced by the new mercantile economy and the rising power of nationalism, to find a new vocation. Nobles monopolized army positions; they obtained prestige; in return for their readiness to serve on the field of battle they gained the privilege

[1] Alfred Vagts, *A History of Militarism* (W. W. Norton & Co., New York, 1937), p. 45.

of tax exemption; they boasted of their peculiar code of "honor," in defense of which they fought duels; and they banded together to resist even royal interference. Their honor did not extend to those of lesser rank, who found that decorations for bravery were reserved to the nobility. In this way the national standing army, officered by post-feudal noblemen, carried into the eighteenth century. At that time war was waged according to a well-accepted set of rules: Armies were small. Indeed, one outstanding leader, Marshal Saxe, claimed that an army of 42,000 was quite adequate in size, since the fundamental object was to execute skillful maneuvers, not to annihilate the enemy, and that an able general could all his life wage war effectively without fighting more than a few battles. War was essentially a game between sovereigns, characterized by restraint and the concept of honor.[2]

The eighteenth-century concept of peace, as set forth by Vattel in his *Law of Nations,* showed similar elements of restraint. A peace treaty must end a war by removing the cause which had given rise to the conflict. The victor must take only what he strictly needs. If the treaty is to be sacred to loser as well as winner, the latter must observe moderation. He must not exercise "intolerable compulsions" upon his defeated rival; he must accept an honorable compromise, and must avoid "punishing the loser in the name of justice." There must be a peace among equals.

However, new ideas appeared which were to destroy the eighteenth-century conceptions of war and peace. Military thinkers began to ask whether a nation in arms instead of a small professional army would not be more efficient and less expensive. Guibert, the Duke of Brunswick, and others urged that national armies trained in virtue and patriotism would be much more effective than the traditional standing army. But conservatism had its way until the American Revolution proved to the world that common soldiers taking cover and firing from behind natural ambush were more than a match for professional soldiers fighting in the conventional fashion.

The French Revolution and the Napoleonic Wars completed the destruction of the old military system. In 1793 France called up 300,000 men, and next year French regular troops and volunteers were amalgamated. The artillery became an important element in warfare. The French used propaganda on a wide scale and inspired their mass armies to great enthusiasm. They relied upon

---

[2] The difficulties of communications, due to poor roads and the problem of supplies, of course had a decisive influence upon the nature of warfare.

numbers to overwhelm theoretically better-trained troops, and despite terrible losses they won battles. The leaders developed, and acted upon, the theory of mass offensive. The great aim was to destroy the enemy forces and not, as in the eighteenth century, merely to entrap them. Napoleon carried the system still further. He introduced a new type of military honors designed to gratify the pride of the common soldier. He defrayed the costs of his campaigns as far as possible by making the conquered countries pay, and exacted hundreds of millions of francs from Austria, Prussia, Italy, and North Germany. He insisted upon the element of speed, cutting his baggage train to the lowest limit. In spite of enormous losses in manpower, his earlier wars were profitable.

The attempt to maintain mass warfare over twenty years, however, brought disaster. Napoleon gradually lost the sense of the relation of war to sanely realizable objects, and he called forth against him in other countries the very type of organization and methods which had brought him such brilliant initial results. Prussia in the face of poverty and exhaustion created a national army, which was strengthened by means of economic and political reforms, the establishment of the *Tugenbund* (League of Virtue), and the inculcation of liberalism from above. Prussia rebuilt its whole life so as the more efficiently to fight its enemy, France. Great Britain reformed its military system more slowly, and Austria continued conservative, fearing that nationalism and nations in arms would ruin her whole empire.

The 1815 treaty which was imposed upon France was, judged by the standards of 1919, not unduly severe. The inflamed masses urged the typical penalties against the defeated enemy. They would have hanged Napoleon and seized territory and money from France by way of reparation. But the statesmen were still under the influence of eighteenth-century ideals and concluded what was on the whole a relatively mild treaty between equals. Talleyrand, the French representative, took part in the peace negotiations, and the political requirements of peace were not sacrificed to the wholesale demands of the military conquerors. The statesmen, realizing the danger of national war based upon popular passion, tried to abolish conscription. Instead, France adopted a seven-year term of military service, and the Bourbons restored what they could of the classical system.

Nevertheless, the die had been cast and the nineteenth century was to witness a continuation of the violent methods and mass organization which the Revolutionary and Napoleonic Wars had set in motion. Military writers leaned heavily upon the doctrines of Jomini and Clausewitz.[3] The latter writer, in particular, had great influence. He regarded war as nothing but a continuation of state policy by other means and developed the idea of "absolute war." The greater the development of nations, he urged, the more definitely will war become absolute in character, and the leader who uses force unsparingly will gain the advantage over one who is less vigorous. "To introduce into the philosophy of war a principle of moderation would be an absurdity. War is an act of violence pushed to its utmost bounds." Although Clausewitz qualified his statements in some respects, he preached the necessity of superiority in numbers and the need of great masses of men.

Overwhelming superiority of manpower became the great goal of military leaders. The mechanical inventions of the nineteenth century assisted them, for the coming of the railway and the telegraph enabled them to combine armies of men into numbers beyond those previously dreamed of. Moltke was thus enabled to bring the supreme command to a focus and "to direct from a single center, through fan-like controls, enormous bodies of men and operations covering hundreds of miles . . . . Larger armies, concentration of forces and command, and delegation of authority to subordinate commanders with managerial responsibility were signs of a new stage in warfare."[4]

The Crimean War (1854–1856) and the Prussian-Austrian War (1886) ended in peace treaties which were marked by restraint. But the Franco-Prussian War witnessed the triumph of military romanticism. In it the German numbers inflicted disaster upon the French, who relied upon their professional army trained in the traditional manner. The Peace of 1871, compared with those of 1815, 1856, and 1866, was not marked by moderation. Military necessity demanded that all, and not part of, Alsace-Lorraine go to Germany (the military men triumphed over Bismarck); and France, smarting under the blow, adopted the principles of the victorious enemy, and "since numbers were the most easily measurable feature of armies, the decision of the French Assembly of 1872 to have an armed force as numerous as Germany's set going the competition in which each increase of peace-time effectives induced every potential enemy to follow suit, arguing in terms of balance of power politics."[5]

---

[3] See Liddell Hart, *Ghosts of Napoleon* (Faber, London, 1933; Yale University Press, 1934).

[4] Vagts, *op. cit.*, p. 215.   [5] *Ibid.*, p. 232.

Captain Gilbert claimed that France had lost because it was satisfied to remain on the defensive; and at length Marshal Foch, accepting Clausewitz's ideas, wholeheartedly wrote: "Modern war knows but one argument: the tactical fact, battle." The will to conquer, the belief that an improvement in firearms would help the attack, led to an excessive devotion to the offensive à outrance. Colonel deGrandmaison wrote:

The French army, returning to its traditions, no longer knows any other law than the offensive. . . . . All attacks are to be pushed to the extreme . . . . to charge the enemy with the bayonet in order to destroy him. . . . . This result can only be obtained at the price of bloody sacrifice. Any other conception ought to be rejected as contrary to the very nature of war.[6]

The theory of mass armies and mass attack carried with it the logic that war would be short and dramatic. Schlieffen and others believed that great armies maintained at great cost and operating in a world of shattered trade and commerce must strike quickly and decisively.[7] Victory would fall to those who were strongest in attack. Unfortunately, the facts did not bear out these hopes. Even in the nineteenth century it was becoming increasingly difficult for the attacking army to overcome the defensive army, and battles were becoming less and less decisive. Fundamentally this fact was due to the growth of mechanism and the improvement of firearms, which enabled defenders in trenches to withstand far superior numbers of attacking soldiers. The 1866 war between Prussia and Austria and the Franco-German war of 1870 both proved that tactical defensive had acquired a great advantage over the offensive. In the Boer War, and especially in the Russo-Japanese War, the same factor came into prominence, "the paralyzing power of machine guns, the hopelessness of frontal attacks, and the consequent relapse of armies into trenches."

But the idea of the necessity of superiority in numbers and of the offensive à outrance persisted. Under the influence of these theories the French made mass attacks the basis in Europe of their policy during 1914 and 1915 and lost hundreds of thousands of men in gallant but suicidal exhibitions of personal bravery. Mechanized warfare brought on exhaustion, and for months hundreds of thousands of men on both sides were unable to make any effective advance. Artillery attack proved less efficient as an offensive

---

[6] Quoted by Liddell Hart, op. cit., p. 137.

[7] Alfred Vagts, op. cit., p. 379. Also Max Werner, Military Strength of the Powers (Modern Age Books, New York, 1939), pp. 145–46.

weapon than had been hoped, because resulting damage to the terrain made it difficult for the infantry to advance; it also removed the element of surprise, which had become increasingly important if armies were to overcome the tactical superiority of defense made possible by the machine gun and the rifle. Moreover, industrialization brought to the World War of 1914–1918 a powerful factor, and the naval blockade (underestimated by many military leaders) helped to make the war one of attrition and exhaustion. This result had been foreseen as early as 1897 by a Polish banker, M. Bloch, who wrote:

The war, instead of being a hand-to-hand contest, in which the combatants measure their physical and moral superiority, will become a kind of stalemate, in which, neither army being willing to get at the other, both armies will be maintained in opposition to each other, threatening the other, but never being able to deliver a final and decisive attack. . . . . That is the future of war—not fighting, but famine, not the slaying of men, but the bankruptcy of nations and the break-up of the whole social organization . . . . Everyone will be entrenched in the next war. It will be a great war of entrenchments. The spade will be as indispensable to a soldier as his rifle . . . . All wars will of necessity partake of the character of siege operations . . . . Your soldiers may fight as they please; the ultimate decision is in the hands of famine.[8]

The World War of 1914–1918 not only outstripped previous wars in the intensity and extensity of its operations; it differed from others because it lost all relation to particular ends. Nations went on fighting because they had begun and did not know how to stop.

At the end of the war, the political needs of peace were sacrificed to the military needs of victory. Propaganda had roused passions on all sides, and the restraint of the eighteenth century was no longer possible. No chivalry, no code of honor, no supernational sanction existed to restrain nations which had allowed their hate to dominate them for four years. Warfare no longer could be restricted: the sacrifice bore no reasonable proportion to the questions at stake.

In the postwar period military authorities attempted to devise means of overcoming the stalemate which had developed during the years 1914–1918. Their problem was to strengthen the offensive in order to offset the advantage which mechanization had

---

[8] Inter-Parliamentary Union, *What Would Be the Character of a New War?* p. 55.

given to defense. At first it seemed as if air power would supply the answer. In 1921 the Italian, Douhet, advocated the creation of an invincible air force which would be essentially the offensive arm, the army and navy to be relegated to supplementary and defensive operations. He claimed that a large fleet of bombing planes would always "get through" and that no anti-aircraft or fighting planes could provide an adequate defense. Many authorities supported his view.[9] They alleged that ten planes would be needed against each armed bomber; that within a few hours bombers could reach the capitals of the European cities and drop explosive and incendiary bombs and poison gases over large cities; that dull weather conditions would still further facilitate air attack; and that because of the rapidity of attack and the impossibility of defense the only course open would be to retaliate by counter raids upon enemy cities. Other critics alleged that airplanes, the submarine, and fast surface craft had reduced the value of battleships, which even during the war of 1914–1918 had been unable adequately to protect English commerce; that the long narrow Mediterranean could not be kept open for British shipping; and that, even though the major battleships could withstand attack in the Mediterranean, English commercial ships would have to be routed around the Cape. They further argued that, aviation being yet only in its infancy, greater attacking possibilities must still be expected and that, with the increasing conversion of civilian into military planes, the next war would witness a conflict of thousands upon thousands of machines which, by taking advantage of the law of gravity, would do incalculable damage.

The eloquent claims made by those who pictured the new air force as constituting an offensive weapon against which defensive measures would be of little avail did not remain long unchallenged.[10] Military experts pointed out that a plane can remain in the air for only a relatively short time; it must make a sudden attack, but cannot maintain its bombing for long periods because of two major difficulties—the airmen cannot stand the strain of so

[9] To cite a few only: Brigadier-General P. R. C. Groves, *Behind the Smoke Screen* (Fabian, London); Air Commodore Charleton, *War from the Air* (Thomas Nelson and Sons, 1935); Captain Philip S. Mumford, *Humanity, Air Power and War* (Jarrolds, London, 1936); J. M. Spaight, *Air Power in the Next War* (Geoffrey Bles, London, 1938). Spaight admits the seriousness of air power but is perhaps more conservative in his conclusions.

[10] Brigadier-General O. L. Spaulding, *Ahriman: A Study in Air Bombardment* (World Peace Foundation, Boston, 1939); R. E. Dupuy and G. F. Eliot, *If War Comes* (The Macmillan Company, 1937).

intense an experience beyond a few hours at the most, and when the supply of bombs has been exhausted they must return to their base of supplies. Thus the plane may produce terrible destruction but it cannot hold a country.

Military opinion tended to accept the view that the plane, as an instrument of terrorism, had been overrated. Experience in the Spanish Civil War seems to show that the civilian population is not demoralized but rather stiffened in its emotional resistance after the shock of the first raids is over. In any case the diversion of energy occasioned by attacking civilians is a weakness from the military point of view; energy should be concentrated on attacking strategic areas, such as railways, roads, junctions, factories, etc. Both sides, perhaps, will be advised to concentrate on strategic objectives and not indulge in indiscriminate civilian bombings.

Under the stress and strain of war bombers are not likely to be as accurate as under the favorable conditions of peace, where meteorological information is much more readily available. Bombers also must flatten their course before they drop their missiles, thereby giving to anti-aircraft guns, which have been developed to a high pitch of efficiency, a greater opportunity to fire upon them.

To those who believed that planes might drop gas bombs over cities and so wipe out whole centers of population, the reply was that the fear was largely unjustified. There appeared to be no gases which combined the property of deadliness and persistency. Gases which remain a long time are not deadly, and deadly gases seem to be easily dispersed by wind and readily diluted by the air. It was suggested that tons of gas would be needed to cover a large city to a depth of three or four stories (one part of gas to 10,000 parts of air) and that people would have to breathe this poisoned air continuously and without protection for at least one hour. The population could, it was claimed, obtain protection by staying in an ordinary closed room for some hours, and if they used gas masks there would be relatively little danger. The chief problem, according to one school of thought, was that of panic on the part of a city population, which might become stampeded by its fear due to its ignorance of the relatively limited potency of poison gas. Proper drill with gas masks and education in the effective measures to take would be of major importance. But it was difficult to say how much of the writing on both sides had the element of propaganda in it; and the world had to wait for the future to bring an answer.

In sea power similar attempts to develop new weapons took place. In the last war it was a battle between the British blockade and the German submarine. Britain won by the barest margin. After 1919 discussion took place as to whether or not the great capital ship had seen its day, being vulnerable to air force or submarine, and, if still effective (as was generally agreed), whether or not British ships of the line could so bottle up the enemy's fleet as to prevent raiders from sinking merchant ships in such numbers as to starve Great Britain. Today, as in the last war, we witness Germany's attempt by mines, air raids, and raids upon commerce by pocket battleships, cruisers, and submarines to bring England to its knees. Britain replies by the blockade, increasing the list of contraband, and putting pressure upon neutrals. Germany can obtain supplies from Russia, the Balkans, Italy, and Switzerland: in some respects she has developed self-sufficiency. But she badly needs iron and oil and fats (especially butter, lard, vegetable oil, and whale oil). Two questions were asked: Will her railroad system stand the congestion? Can she pay for her purchases? There is not a great deal of gold, and to send exports would strain her war economy. The present war has afforded partial answers; but the issue "blockade versus blitzkrieg" is not yet settled.

Determined postwar efforts were made to strengthen the power of attack on land so as to be able to break through the stubborn defense which had been developed by 1918. The offensive had to increase its power and its mobility and yet maintain the element of surprise without losing the co-operation of the many units involved. The answer seemed to be found in mechanization. Great hopes were placed in the tank. In 1917 tanks had proved to be instruments of great striking power able to overcome the most formidable obstacles placed in their way. Since then great improvements have been made; today tanks weigh from three to one hundred tons and travel from four to sixty miles an hour. Motorization and mechanization have produced "cavalry" squadrons without horses; the infantry can be carried great distances in vehicles; artillery has become more mobile; and amalgamation of the various types of arms has developed. Highly mechanized units with great offensive striking power operate in co-operation with the air army.

These developments have led to a new theory of the importance of mobile warfare. Some experts believe that a veritable revolution has occurred and that Europe, which in 1939 had about 25,000 planes, 30,000 tanks, 50,000 guns, and 200,000 machine guns, will not again see the trench warfare which characterized the period 1914–1918. War was to be dominated by mobility and rapid movements which would surprise opponents and compel them to sue for an early peace. Especially in Central and Eastern Europe, an area of immense plains, would a war of movement take place. The two-weeks' campaign in September 1939 which sufficed to vanquish Poland seemed to confirm the prophecy of proponents of blitzkrieg, or the strategy of annihilation.

Yet conservative critics detected weaknesses in these arguments. The tank was not a final weapon of offense, but had several limitations. It lacked mobility, was readily visible, and would be an easy target for special anti-tank guns. Cannon were dangerous to it. Anti-tank mines could stop it. All kinds of artificial obstacles can be created: the Chinese swamped the dirt roads and fired from behind cover at the huge machines stuck in the mud; deep trenches and rows of stumps or concrete pillars would serve similarly.[11] Flame is a potent defense against tanks. Troops may set fire to brush and burn the men inside; gasoline may be spurted through the eye-slits of the tank. Other difficulties of the tank are its noise, which both warns the enemy and hinders the crew within from hearing where anti-tank guns are, the poorness of vision due to the small eye-slits, the difficulty of communicating with other tanks, and the danger of being isolated from them. Tanks, like automobiles, may break down and they require skilled mechanics; they use enormous quantities of gasoline and must therefore be supplied by large gasoline trucks, which, if traffic becomes congested, may be bombed by the enemy. And tanks were said to be only the spearheads; the infantry must finally conquer and hold the country.

Experts also pointed out that mechanization had served to increase the power of defense. A man behind a machine gun can defend positions with deadly efficiency. The defending force can use rapid transport to resist attack, and defenders have the advantage in view of their more intimate knowledge of the terrain. They can destroy bridges and block defiles and engage in other methods of obstruction. The advancing enemy may engage in bombardment in order to cover the advance of his infantry, but bombardment tears up the ground over which the troops must go, making infantry attack much more difficult. The offensive army must

[11] Major E. W. Sheppard, *Tanks in the Next War* (Geoffrey Bles, London, 1938), p. 143.

concentrate sufficient troops to strike with power; but it must also make use of the element of surprise. If the men attempt to advance under cover of darkness or smoke screens there is great danger of confusion. And progress in anti-tank defense has been so great that in the future it will not automatically bring victory.

These technical considerations of attack and defense were to be placed in an entirely new setting after the outbreak of war in 1939. Within twelve months Germany had conquered and subjugated Poland, Norway, Denmark, Holland, Belgium, Luxembourg, and France; within the last few months, after dominating Rumania and Bulgaria, it has conquered and subjugated Yugoslavia and Greece, taken Crete, and invaded Russia. How could such an amazing result have been achieved? The answer lies in three directions.

First, the six- or seven-year intensive preparation within Germany was a preparation in which all aspects of life, economic, military, and psychological, were directed toward one supreme end—conquest. The philosophy of power which had been preached by many thinkers and acted upon by many statesmen was there harnessed to an efficiency and a comprehensiveness of aim unparalleled in history. Both Germany and Italy inculcated the military attitude for a long period before the outbreak of hostilities. They also accomplished an economic mobilization, directed toward war preparation, with a thoroughness which commands admiration even if not approval. Hitler turned all idle plants and labor to use. Capital, labor, and industry had to submit to fixed prices, limited profits, compulsory investment in nationally important enterprises, prohibition or control of new plants according to their usefulness in the military scheme of things, absolute control by priority of government orders, absolute government control of foreign exchange, government domination of the capital market for government loans, and limited salaries for the heads of government corporations. Labor had to accept fixed wages, and complete government direction as to where and when to work and the suppression of all strikes and independent labor unions. Consumers were forced to accept food rationing and directed consumption, eating and using less of what was short and accepting the regulation of specified control agencies. The government tried to solve the raw materials question by a strict control of foreign trade, a rationing of materials for war purposes according to the urgency of their use, and the creation of substitute or *ersatz* goods. It obtained capital by defaulting on foreign debts, by issuing public securities, and by a heavy program of taxation. It is estimated that 47 per cent of the national income has been returned to the government by drastic taxation.[12]

The second method whereby Germany was able to obtain such startling success was by weakening the morale of the potential enemy by a long period of subtle undermining.

Hitler learned as a result of his abortive putsch in Bavaria in 1923 that a head-on attack upon a government in power is foolish and wasteful.[13] Only when a government has lost the confidence of the people is it wise to show one's forceful hand. He therefore set to work to divide the German people by making promises to discontented groups, by playing upon the prejudices of parties and classes, and by skillfully using every person through an appeal to vanity, disappointed ambition, or genuine desire for a better social order. The fact that many of these promises were hopelessly contradictory in character seemed to many to doom his program to failure; but the Nazi leader showed his superior knowledge of human beings by appealing not to their rational logic but to their subrational desires.

When he had finally gained control of Germany Hitler continued the same policy on the international stage which had brought success within his adopted country. He realized that there are discontented people in every nation, and by playing upon the forces of discontent and division he hoped so to demoralize his opponents that when the shooting phase of the war began the enemy's morale would have been undermined and even destroyed. Bloodless war has thus been raised to the highest efficiency. In this new technology of war, psychology and economics are called into play to strengthen Germany at home and to weaken nations abroad. Invisible war precedes visible war, and in some respects the former is more deadly than the latter because fighting with guns is more spectacular and attracts popular attention, but subtle destructive penetrations go on for years before their purpose is realized. In contrast to the Communists, who preached hostility from the start, the Nazis take steps as follows:

First, offer terms that appear advantageous to certain groups and propose mutual business.

[12] Otto D. Tolischus, *They Wanted War* (Reynal Hitchcock, New York, 1940); Frank Munk, *The Economics of Force* (G. W. Stewart, New York, 1940).

[13] See Francis Williams, *War by Revolution* (Viking Press, New York, 1941).

Second, conclude clearing and barter agreements tending to make the respective countries depend on your business.

Third, accumulate large blocks of frozen credits within your own country.

Fourth, use your economic domination to install a government willing to take orders from you.

Fifth, under the cloak of regular business, plant agents, spies, provocateurs, members of the secret police, and army officers in important positions in the enemy country.

Sixth, prevent normal economic or military preparations for adequate defense. If they cannot be prevented altogether, apply every measure to slow down economic and military rearmament.

Seventh, couple economic pressure with threat of arms. Conclude alliances that will squeeze your enemy and prevent him from concentrating defenses in one direction.

Eighth, strike.[14]

More than any other group the Nazi leaders made skillful use of psychological insight. They showed uncanny skill in exploiting deep-seated tendencies in human beings and in making people serve Nazi ends. They took advantage of the freedom of political discussion and of the press, and the freedom of association, whether of employers, trade unions, or national minorities in the democracies. As a crisis developed they encouraged groups to push their own interests irrespective of national unity; thus capitalists whose markets were threatened by the prospect of a war with Germany were appealed to and their desire for immediate profit caused them to become appeasers.

In the campaign to undermine France the Bretons received propaganda leaflets which spoke of Breton nationalism and asked why they should sacrifice themselves for the Poles; also agents encouraged the Communists to redouble their criticism of the democratic governments and, by taking advantage of an already weakened unity, helped to intensify domestic dissension. The press was subsidized, and false rumors were spread. Great headlines cast doubt on the efficiency of the government, and contradictory reports appeared to bewilder an already anxious people. Radio broadcasts from Germany daily alternated peace offers and veiled or open threats. Hundreds of personal letters were received by private individuals in which the national leaders of democracy were denounced or the Jews blamed or some plea was made for an understanding with Germany. Pacifists were encouraged to op-

[14] Munk, *op. cit.*, p. 176.

pose any foreign policy that aimed to strengthen the national armament or to oppose Germany's seizure of Austria, Czechoslovakia,
or Danzig and her demands upon Poland. Within France division
and disintegration spread apace. Meanwhile the controlled press
in Germany concealed genuine differences of opinion at home and
excluded propaganda from abroad.

After the war had begun, the German methods of breaking
the enemy's morale continued with admirable success. Hundreds
of agents with small radio sets directed German movements, and
the French were able to find few of the culprits. False radio reports created terror and helped to create panic among the civilian
population, which blocked the roads and prevented French army
movements. Germany renewed peace offers in order to perpetuate
and deepen the division within the enemy camp. The so-called
fifth-column group of Germans and German sympathizers in foreign lands in the same way secretly prepared the way for the invasion of Denmark, Holland, and Norway, as records eloquently
testify.[15]

The third method by which Germany was enabled to gain such
rapid victories was by a remarkable use of blitzkrieg methods
when it finally did strike. In previous wars generals always strove
to compel their opponents to fight under adverse conditions, but
in the blitzkrieg the enemy was prevented from arriving at the
fight. Britain's great sea power and her reliance upon the blockade in traditional fashion proved no match, at least in the early
phases of the war, for the lightning thrusts of German air power
working in perfect co-ordination with mechanized forces.[16]

The Allies persisted in regarding Norway as a side show,
whereas Germany, by obtaining control of the air bases and by
landing troops from planes, made the British position untenable.
Having gained Norway, Hitler's forces were thereby brought two
to three hundred miles nearer to British naval bases and were enabled to protect German's Baltic flank. The seizure of Norway
was the first step in the advance. Air power and a savage attack
upon the Dutch cities sufficed to conquer Holland in a few days—
even the Dutch attempt to halt the Germans by flooding the
country impeded Dutch mobility far more than it hindered German movement. The succeeding campaign against Belgium and

[15] Edmond Taylor, *The Strategy of Terror: Europe's United Front* (Houghton Mifflin Co., 1940); Francis Williams, *op. cit.;* M. W. Fodor, *The Revolution Is On* (Houghton Mifflin Co., 1940).

[16] S. L. A. Marshall, *Blitzkrieg* (W. Morrow, New York, 1940), p. 54.

France showed the remarkable co-ordination of mass air attack, massed tanks, and successful flanking movements. The tank was now revealed as an instrument perfected in Germany to such a degree that existing methods of defense were helpless against it. By the utmost concentration upon given points, by taking the bold initiative on the assumption that the British and French could not, or would not, the Germans were able to seize key positions and then dominate the surrounding country. They then put civilians and prisoners to work for them and thereby strengthened the German war machine. In this way Germany has tended to become stronger with time and to expand its economy with relatively small military losses.

With the prestige thus acquired Germany has been able to conquer some of the smaller dependent nations, the Balkans for instance, "by telephone." All the while Britain could use little but the slow method of the blockade, a method which has revealed serious defects. Over a dozen seaports have changed hands in the last six years through the co-operation of air and land forces, and at Crete the British navy was unable to take the initiative because of limitations of speed.

The outcome of the war is still uncertain; but it would seem that the advantage has passed to the nation which has developed the greatest striking power, the most complete mobilization, and the most efficient methods of weakening the enemy's morale by preliminary propaganda and economic conquest. Undoubtedly total war can be met only by total war, and the question arises as to whether or not democracy can solve the dilemma: If it organizes for total war over a long period of time, can it survive within? If it does not organize for total war, can it survive attack from without?

The foregoing analysis is confirmed by the findings of Dr. Edward Mead Earle and Dr. Alfred Vagts, of the Institute of Advanced Study, Princeton University.[17] Both of these authorities urge that the liberal democracies in the past have underestimated, and are still underestimating, the psychological aspect of war, and suffer from "a curious want of military thinking" on the part of the civilians. They urge the introduction of military history and military policy into the curriculum of the universities and widespread co-operation of civilians and military men in build-

[17] E. M. Earle, "National Defense and Political Science," *Political Science Quarterly,* Vol. LV, No. 4, December 1940; Alfred Vagts, *War and the Colleges* (American Military Institute, 1940).

ing up a total defense: "We are slowly gaining consciousness that Total War can be met only by planning for a Total Defense and are therefore entering upon an era which will bring radical alterations in our attitudes as regards military and naval power. This is not of our choice, nor, judging by contemporary evidence, is it likely to be a transitory phase in the history of the world." The two scholars are anxious lest, at the end of the war, democracy, if it still survives, should lapse into a period of apathy and even hostility toward the need of defense. They say the pattern stands out clearly: Instead of concentrating attention upon international institutions which have broken down, we should increasingly use schools and universities as instruments of preparedness.

Now, if it is certain that nothing can be done to substitute some other form of political life for embattled nations facing each other in ever increasing military and naval array, such advice as Vagts and Earle give is correct. But let us also recognize something of the consequences. For the principles already discussed above concerning the balance-of-power system hold true here. The two authors advocate bigger and better and more total preparations, including psychological, for defense; if other nations do the same thing, we shall have no limits to the process. From a few courses on military affairs which in themselves are unimpeachable, we will come, as a democracy, to the same total mobilization of economic and human resources, materials, human bodies, and minds, that we lament in Germany and Italy today and to eliminate which is the real motive of our help thus far to Great Britain.

The authorities cited assume the finality of the modern sovereign state, and suggest that the continued study of international relations as conducted during the last twenty years should be considerably modified to adapt our thinking and methods to the political fortunes of today—to beat a masterly retreat as it were and to cease studying the possibility of more adequate forms of political organization required by the present-day world. They may be right; and perhaps for some time, whatever the outcome of the war, the widespread study of military matters may have to be continued. But let us not mistake the significance of this course, if that is the only thing left to us. It means increasing the scientific study of still more terrible conflicts that must occur under the anarchical balance-of-power system. It means the more skillful use of propaganda, whipping up emotion and ultimately destroying the very basis of scientific thought itself. It means the last word in counseling despair.

It is submitted that the two authors have swung too far under the influence of the tragedy of the present war and that, grim as the outlook now is, an urgent need exists to study the most efficient means not only of building preparedness but of exposing the deep contradictions which underlie the whole of the present international situation.

It must be emphasized and re-emphasized that, should the present international anarchy continue and a limitless increase of armaments take place, not only will our economic systems be ultimately disrupted but the whole basis of democracy will be threatened. For Nazi Germany has introduced a new principle of warfare: that of psychologically undermining the unity of its potential enemies by undercover encouragement of pacifists, Communists, business men, religious groups, intelligentsia, and others interested in opposing war and in promoting international co-operation. The evidence of this kind of action is overwhelming, and the point to be remembered is that in the future it will be difficult for a democracy to decide whether those who oppose continued increase in armaments, or who criticize government policy in other fields of effort, do so in a desire to preserve and strengthen democracy or direct their criticisms against the government for the purpose of discrediting it and the institutions which it represents. Already during the present war we witness rising tempers and a questioning of motives on the part of those who have argued for and against the Lend Lease Act. Now a democracy stands or falls by the quality of its differences, and the quality of its differences depends upon a sufficiently common purpose and sufficient internal unity. Continued international anarchy and mounting defense costs may well cause well-disposed people to question the wisdom of indefinitely piling up armaments and to advocate a new form of collective security or some kind of world or regional federation. But who shall guarantee that fifth columnists will not be behind such measures, supporting such policies so as to divide the country? One can easily imagine that under these circumstances independent and nonconformist attitudes of mind will become increasingly impossible and the democracy will rest upon most precarious foundations.

We must admit, however, that if the balance of power, with all its weaknesses as an instrument of security, is to continue, then we must choose the less of two evils and seek power above that of any potential enemy. Under present circumstances many people who have supported the League of Nations, and have criticized

Britain's and America's foreign policies of the last twenty years, are compelled to face a situation which they believe would have been avoided by the acceptance of the principles of the League of Nations or a stronger international organization. At the moment they have to choose between the possible consequences of a German victory and those of a British victory.

There is good reason to believe that a German victory would bring a new order in Europe which would end the possibility of reasonable treatment for minorities, political parties, religious organizations, liberal thought, and business and labor organizations; the theory of force and militarism would be carried over a wide area, and would compel the United States and other nations to intensify their armed preparations. There would be no possibility, even, of international collaboration. On the other hand, a British victory might result in the kind of postwar confusion and half-hearted devotion to the principles of collective security which marked the period 1919–1939. In this event the world would witness another melancholy breakdown of hope. If, however, a victorious Britain, profiting from her mistakes of the last generation, and if other nations, including the United States, accepting their responsibilities, will begin a bolder and more determined effort to rebuild the world, some ground for optimism will still remain. On the future policy of a victorious Britain, therefore, depends the ultimate justification for extending American aid to her at this time, and for temporarily advocating the adoption of power politics, which, as the foregoing analysis shows, cannot permanently provide the essential conditions of world stability in a modern mechanical age.

One thing should be clear: Modern war has revealed that the sovereign state is an inefficient instrument for achieving national security. The nation today is as little able to defend itself without sacrificing an overwhelmingly disproportionate share of its wealth, leisure, and man power as were the feudal castles after the invention of gunpowder. It will be futile to resurrect Holland, Belgium, and the other nations as sovereign powers with their own armies, navies, and air forces; for within a short time they will fall victims to larger nations bent upon aggression. And the so-called great powers will bankrupt and ruin themselves if they continue to try to solve the problem of war by their independent sovereign efforts. The following chapter should strengthen this conclusion.

The main objective and the subject matter of this book would seem still to be in line with present world needs.

Chapter XV

SECURITY: THE PROBLEM AND ATTEMPTED SOLUTIONS

Analysis of the institutions of war thus makes clear that security is today the all-absorbing and urgent question. By what means shall it be attained? The methods examined in this chapter are: (1) national power; (2) alliances and the balance of power; (3) the League of Nations; (4) a strengthened League, with special agreements closing the gap in the Covenant; (5) the Kellogg Pact; (6) regional agreements; (7) federation; (8) neutrality; (9) pacifism; and (10) reduction of armaments.

Each of the methods has its strengths and weaknesses. Some may be more unsound in principle than others. Some which are sounder in principle may be difficult to realize in practice owing to technical differences, unwillingness to give up national prejudices, or incapacity to exercise the moral restraint and intelligence necessary to control the vast resources of power unloosed by modern science.

Security rather than peace is the essential problem; for people will seldom listen to the plea for peace unless they are convinced that their country is guaranteed security. Without security, there is no peace. The search for security is the condition of the realization of peace.

NATIONAL POWER AND THE BALANCE OF POWER

Many people claim that the best means of obtaining national security is to develop national power. A nation must be strong enough to defend its territory; weakness invites attack. But if any one nation becomes too strong, other nations run the risk of being defeated. A balance of power is therefore desirable. In this sense, a certain plausibility attaches to the doctrine: "If you wish peace, prepare for war." Power is necessary to defend one's self, but excessive power in the hands of any nation may be abused.

The American Constitution provides for a division of powers within the nation; the founders believed that over-powerful governments tended to become corrupted. On similar reasoning, nations attempt a division of powers in a somewhat different sense (and with profoundly different consequences, as will later appear); they would prevent any one member within the family of nations from being able to threaten the security and independence of the rest. The greater the armaments of another nation, the greater must be one's own armaments if the balance of power is to be maintained.

The modern state system which grew out of the breakdown of the European medieval unity quickly adopted the balance-of-power idea. The concepts sovereignty and balance of power go together; one implies the other. A nation's "sovereignty" can endure only if it has the power to maintain itself; and nations can have the power to maintain themselves only if there is a certain balance among them, the ideal being that each state can keep what it already possesses and no state or group of states is able to coerce the rest. In dealing in turn with Louis XIV, Napoleon, and Germany in 1914, the balance gave way to armed conflict; and after considerable loss of life and property a new balance was achieved.

We have now to examine whether the system is inherently sound and the wars which occur within its framework are the more or less necessary accompaniments of human change; or whether it has fundamental defects which are themselves productive of chronic instability and inevitable conflict. If the former judgment be true, then the great cost of armaments will be justified, since peace and security will have been obtained, albeit expensively; if the analysis should show that the latter conclusion is correct, no amount of sacrifice and expense can achieve the desired end; in fact, the heavier and more complicated the problems, and the greater the effort put into an unsound system, the more rapidly and decisively will its organic weakness be revealed.

Without question, if one nation is stronger than another it will be safe from immediate attack, and by building up its armaments beyond those of its rival it will gain a measure of security for itself. But only for a time. For if nation A outbuilds nation B in weapons of war and thereby gains "security," B feels itself in danger and in turn speeds up its armament construction. The two nations, therefore, if they have reason to fear each other, can both have security only by each being stronger than the other! When many nations are involved and the theory of national power is

held by every one of them, the situation becomes still more illogical.

The nations must then attempt to overcome this impossibility—
of every one being the strongest—by alliances and understandings.
A and B will combine against C, and obtain security; whereupon
C joins D; E becomes partner to A and B; and F hastens to the
side of C and D. The race is simply transferred from single nations to combinations of powers. If the Triple Alliance is stronger
than the Triple Entente, the latter in alarm hastens its armament
preparations in order to become the stronger, which involves,
when achieved, the automatic inferiority of its opponents. And
so the seesaw goes on, with both alliances piling more and more
fighting material on the ends of the plank; sooner or later the
plank is bound to break under the intolerable load. The truth is
that nobody really wishes a *balance* of power: everybody wishes
to be the strongest, and in the attempt to reach that impossible
goal tension increases with every increase in armaments. It is important also to note that the greater the power of armaments the
greater the tension, because people know that modern implements
of destruction can inflict infinitely more damage than the simple
weapons of previous years. Modern tanks, bombers, dreadnaughts,
poison gas, machine guns, and submarines endanger peoples to an
extent undreamed of in the days of feudal armor, spears, bows
and arrows, and old-fashioned muskets.

The logical outcome of the balance-of-power system with its
ever-mounting armaments is that war and preparation for war lose
all relation to particular ends to be gained. The balance-of-power
system has led to preparations so gigantic that they have little or
no relation to the problems to be solved; they increasingly involve the subordination of all aspects of life to the institution of
war. The theory of totalitarian war means that in peace as well
as in war nations must be placed on a war footing. Thought, as
well as economic and military power, will be mobilized and regimented for one purpose only—power. But since all nations will
have to pursue a similar policy, the essential problem will remain
unsolved. The struggle for power grows fiercer, tension increases,
the sense of insecurity mounts—until the system (or lack of it)
must collapse either in open conflict or in exhaustion because of
the unlimited burdens which nations are forced to carry.

Even before 1914 the system was so unstable that it was possible for a dispute over a small nation to involve a whole world,
just as powerful forces if sensitively enough balanced may be set

in motion by the slightest event. Hence when Austria presented its demands to Serbia after the murder of the Archduke in June 1914, Russia intervened in order to prevent Austria from weakening Serbia, and thereby threatening Russian plans in the Near East. Russia and Serbia together could have defeated Austria; Germany then would have been surrounded by France and Russia; in order to prevent such an outcome, Germany came into the struggle. Germany and Austria combined would have beaten Russia and Serbia, leaving France in a precarious situation. Therefore France for reasons of "defense" was dragged in, and the British Empire could not remain aloof. Like mountain climbers tied together, the European nations were dragged into the abyss when one of them fell. If the system of power politics, mistakenly called the balance of power, is so unstable and is becoming more so, there would seem little reason for claiming it as an instrument of security.

The system sacrificed the independence and integrity of small nations. The urgent need of obtaining a temporary advantage led governments to take the "offensive defense"; if Belgium or Greece stood in the way, so much the worse for them. Military necessity could not wait upon the niceties of international law. The greater the forces engaged in struggling for predominance, the less the chance that weak nations will obtain justice. Germany seizes Sudetenland, Italy takes Ethiopia, Spain is sacrificed, and China is overrun. The more feverish the race for armaments, the more ruthless the political behavior of the great powers.

The piling up of armaments does not solve the problem, because both sets of potential rivals believe that the armies and navies are for "defense" and the forces of their opponents exist for "offense." In prewar days and in recent times, statesmen of all countries claimed that they were arming "in case" other powers should attack. While each group proclaims that it is preparing for defense, it regards the "other side" as the danger point, the potential aggressor, the ambitious one. Under the balance-of-power system there is no satisfactory method of ascertaining who is the offender and who is the defender in the matter of increasing armaments.

We have only to imagine what would happen in daily life if every village lived under the suspicion that the next village might attack it. If no national law courts and no police systems existed to which individuals in the last resort could refer their differences and have impartial judgments enforced, and if there were no legislatures to make new rules, there would be no security; each village would try to be stronger than every other village, and general fear and suspicion would result.

No clear-cut test of aggression would be possible. One cannot prove aggressive and defensive designs from perusing armament figures. One cannot compare two nations separately and decide that one is more peaceful than the other. One must compare two sets of nations. Those who say that prewar Britain spent only 28 millions on the army, whereas Germany spent 68 millions, and that Germany had aggressive designs, miss an essential point: They forget Russian and French military expenditures. For the Entente armed over one and a half times as heavily as did Germany, Austria, and Italy. When one considers that Italy's alliance was regarded as "doubtful" by some and practically "valueless" by others within Austria and Germany, the Allied preponderance takes on an even greater significance.

Under the balance-of-power system it is thus not only impossible to allocate responsibility for an increase in armaments but equally impossible to reduce armaments. Lord Haldane visited Germany in 1912 in an attempt to reach an understanding with the German government. He insisted that an agreement concerning armies would be "bones without flesh" if Germany began fresh shipbuilding and so "forced us to do twice as much." But the question was one of Germany's naval competition not with Great Britain alone but with France and Russia as well. Moreover, between 1900 and 1914 German naval expenditure at no time reached one-half the amount spent by Great Britain. If A has 10 guns and B has 5, and A asks B that each destroy two guns, the result will be A, 8 guns, and B, 3 guns—the reduction will have operated to the disadvantage of the weaker party. In 1913–14, France and Russia, potential enemies of Germany, spent more on their navies than Germany. While danger of war existed between either France and Germany or Russia and Germany, it was folly to expect an Anglo-German agreement to limit naval construction. So with armies. Mr. Lloyd George, not nine months before July 1914, declared the German army "a vital necessity" to the German nation, and the Kaiser's remark to Lord Haldane in 1906 had a great degree of truth: "A splendid machine I have in this army, Mr. Haldane . . . . And what could I do without it, situated as I am between the Russians and the French?" The amount of armaments a nation has is no final gauge of its pacific or aggressive intentions.

Nor can one decide who is the aggressor merely by pointing to the nation which declares war. If two nations believe that hostilities will come, the weaker may declare war and strike quickly in the hope of dealing a decisive initial blow. There is an "offensive defense" which may apply in the political as well as in the military and naval sphere. The Boers declared war on Great Britain; but who will assert that they were solely, or even mainly, guilty of provoking the conflict? Certainly the Boers thought that they were fighting a righteous and defensive war. The British, they claimed, put obstacles in the way of agreements; the Milner negotiations had broken down; and Britain was pouring troops into Cape Colony. There seemed to be no hope of agreement; and, since war appeared inevitable, the Boers claimed that they, the weaker power, must seize every advantage while time permitted. Because there were faults on both sides, and no third-party decision was invoked, the world lacked the conditions for a definite test as to which side wanted war. France declared war on Prussia in 1870, but historians are still estimating the relative degree of responsibility for the outbreak of hostilities. Germany declared war upon Russia in July 1914, after having given Russia twelve hours to demobilize its army.

For all but emotional partisans, it is impossible in the balance-of-power system to prove a particular nation responsible for a war. The system provides no test to distinguish between "offender" and "defender." The one who declares war is not necessarily the offender.

Is there no other way? Must mankind aways remain in the condition that each nation passionately believes itself to be in the right? Must inadequate international organization always permit the aggressor-minded statesmen to take advantage of the plausible excuses which the anarchic principle of the balance of power provides, enabling them to take shelter behind the confusion of evidence and the absence of precise methods which could clearly point to the aggressor? If we are limited to the balance-of-power system, we can never find any such tests, and humanity will have to endure ever increasing armaments and increasing tensions. There exists no principle of limitation in the struggle for power. The more effort nations devote to a system which can give only the most temporary protection to those who happen to be stronger at the time, the more unsound becomes the total situation.

The problem may be approached in another way. The balance-of-power system and the doctrine of national sovereignty stand in intimate relationship one to the other. If nations are sovereign, and owe no habitual obedience to any other determinate human superior, if international law is not true law, governments are free to take any action which they deem desirable. Under this system all wars are legal, however immoral, wrong, and foolish they may be.

A system which had no provision for a hierarchy of political values, which made no distinction between legal and illegal action and possessed no means of preventing the abuse of sovereign powers, had some day to suffer the consequences of political anarchy. Within nations it had long been recognized that orderly life required rules operating within the framework of a constitution, and that law must prescribe limits beyond which individuals and corporations were not free to act. National welfare depends upon the ability with which citizens maintain order and harmony by preventing the abuse of power through the exercise of rules which clearly draw the line between legal and illegal conduct. Until international society adopts a similar principle of legal restraint, there must be anarchy. As long as war can impose conditions which when embodied in treaties are called "sacred," so long will the world suffer from a grotesque caricature of international law. And to the degree that international law recognized the forcible conquests of war, to that degree it was contradicting the essential nature of law.

Another characteristic marks the balance-of-power system, namely, that nations insist upon being judges in their own cause. Within the nation itself it is accepted as the indispensable prerequisite of law and order that, when a dispute between two persons goes beyond a certain degree of seriousness, the state will step in as a third and impartial party and render judgment. No permanent basis of order exists unless this simple but fundamental rule is observed. For frequently the problem is not one of right versus wrong but of right versus right, of conflicting conceptions of rights. It is not enough that each party believes itself to be right and moral and just. Each may be perfectly sincere and yet be mistaken. Civilized states accept the principle that social progress is wrapped up with the reign of law, requiring third-party judgments given by courts and legislatures which can hear grievances, devise new rules to remedy them, and lay down laws for future behavior.

The system was further complicated by the recognition of the right of "forcible measures short of war" which arose from conditions which must be traced far back into history.[1] After the fall

---

[1] See especially A. E. Hindmarsh, *Force in Peace* (Harvard University Press, Cambridge, 1933).

of the Roman Empire, disorder became widespread in Europe. The anarchical conditions of feudal times and the great differences in the feudal laws of different areas necessitated a considerable degree of self-help on the part of merchants engaged in commerce. Foreigners had difficulty in obtaining justice and were inclined to take the law into their own hands. Private reprisals, although immediately effective in some cases, did not prove to be compatible with the advance of commerce; and during the thirteenth and fourteenth centuries the rulers were able gradually to impose regulations which limited the right of self-help. Definite methods were prescribed which grew into "legally recognized practice." Thus if a foreigner could not obtain legal redress abroad after having suffered injustice, he might petition his ruler for authority to seize goods from any individual who belonged to the community of the offending person; government A would then grant a letter of marque or reprisal to its subject "a," who could then attack subject "b," subject of government B, for an injury committed by "b."

As piracy declined, the need for private self-help became less urgent. The growth of national states led governments to take a stronger hand in imposing order. Gradually the custom grew of regarding an injury to a foreign individual as an offense against his state or government. Rulers considered it inconsistent with their sovereign power to allow individuals to take independent action; sovereigns acquired the habit of dealing with sovereigns, and direct state action on behalf of an individual superseded the practice of self-help under letters of marque and reprisal. This transition from private to public reprisals spread over a long time, but by the eighteenth century the practice of national self-help and reprisals had replaced the medieval practices.

Thus conceptions of self-help which originated in the rules of earlier days became implanted in modern international life, and under international law nations frequently took forceful action against other nations without declaring war. No legal status of war resulted from this action, and no problems of the rights and duties of belligerents and neutrals which are incidental to the legal situation of war.

Such forcible methods included the use of pacific blockade of one or more ports of another country; embargoes; landing troops to protect citizens or restore order or even to collect duties; the temporary seizure of property; the occupation of territory; the declaring of certain areas to be neutral, thereby preventing a government from invading areas over which it claimed sovereignty. These measures were frequently regarded as necessary to enforce law and order in weak and backward countries. Doubtless the stronger governments endured many provocations. But national self-help and reprisals were often quite arbitrary; they confused "law and vengeance," power and justice, might and right. Frequently the powers refused to appeal to impartial judgment and no principle or organization existed to decide whether a government's forcible measures short of war constituted unjustifiable aggression or a legitimate protection of its citizens abroad who had been denied justice.

Just as the balance-of-power system made it impossible to distinguish between an aggressive and a defensive war, so it made it difficult to decide whether forcible actions short of war were essentially offensive or defensive in character. War itself is but the logical development of the principle of national self-help, and the balance-of-power system had evolved no adequate organization to prevent either the major self-help called war or the minor self-help called forcible measures short of war.

In 1918 Germany imposed the Treaty of Brest-Litovsk on Russia and the Treaty of Bucharest on Rumania. The terms were of the utmost severity and showed that Germany would give little mercy to her vanquished enemies. President Wilson had enumerated his Fourteen Points before this time; but the revelation of Germany's temper caused him to modify his position, and he increasingly spoke of the necessity of crushing German militarism. This fact must be kept in mind as part of the explanation of the harsh terms meted out by the Treaty of Versailles. Hitler's Germany denounces these as monstrous; but the Allies retort that Germany herself pointed the way by her action at Brest-Litovsk and Bucharest, and that the peace treaty was not based upon the Fourteen Points only.[2]

The Treaty of Versailles contained both the Covenant of the League, based upon co-operation, and the punitive sections based upon the need of crushing Germany as a military power. The two principles were incompatible, and one or the other had to give way. As recent events show, it was the League Covenant which fell and the politics of power which triumphed. France dared not let Germany have a fair chance, fearing that Germany would make use of that fair chance to pursue the policy of conquest. But to deny

[2] J. Wheeler-Bennett, *The Forgotten Peace* (Wm. Morrow & Co., New York, 1939), pp. 363–69.

a nation a fair chance, on the assumption that it will abuse its opportunity, is dangerous; for the vanquished nation will think more of the injustice it suffers than of the fact that its enemies believe that it would use an equitable settlement to act unfairly. The dilemma was complete from the beginning but took nearly twenty years to stand revealed in the final bankruptcy of war.

Until about 1930 it seemed possible that the principles of the Covenant would triumph and that Germany would be re-admitted as an equal. France in the early days after the Peace had signed military alliances and kept Germany in a position of inferiority, but one by one concessions had been made. By 1932, however, the tide had turned: Japan violated the Covenant successfully; the Disarmament Conference opened inauspiciously; and by March 1933 Hitler had come into power. His speeches and writings alarmed the French, and what he regarded as a reassertion of German rights was viewed by the French as a renewed threat to them. He denounced the military clauses of the Treaty of Versailles in 1935—another step toward equality, but to France another manifestation of the possibilities of German aggression. Hitler occupied the Rhineland in 1936. From Germany's point of view it was just; from France's point of view it weakened her in Europe by making it impossible for her to give as effective help to her allies in Eastern Europe, who began to desert. Hitler invaded Austria in 1938, invoking the principle of self-determination and of national unity, which the Treaty had denied. To France it meant power added to Germany, which would strike when the time was ripe.

Meanwhile, the balance-of-power system had been complicated by Italy's desire to gain what she thought had been denied her by the Treaty. Mussolini's troops invaded Ethiopia. The imposition of sanctions against Italy drove that country into partnership with Germany, and the two Axis powers now confronted France and Britain and to a degree the Soviet Union. Hitler demanded the Sudetenland, again appealing to German rights. His action there, however, further upset the balance of power in Europe. Collective security was dead; and a scramble ensued. The Munich Accord was an attempt on the part of Chamberlain and Daladier to reconcile the German claim to equality and national rights with the peace of Europe based upon equilibrium of the great powers. The ink was scarcely dry when the equilibrium was disturbed: Hitler accused Czechoslovakia and the Soviet Union and Great Britain of organizing to encircle Germany, and proclaimed a protectorate over the rest of Czechoslovakia. His assertion that this action was taken in reply to aggressive action by the other powers was indignantly repudiated by the latter, who argued that Germany made use of its new strategic strength in Europe to take what the Allies could or would no longer prevent him from seizing. To them it was an unjustified act of aggression.

Soon after came Poland's turn. Poland, in fear that Germany would attack her, signed an alliance with Britain. Hitler chose to regard this step as indicative of hostility toward Germany, and he canceled the 1934 German-Polish nonaggression pact and the Anglo-German naval agreement of 1935. Matters went from bad to worse, and Hitler demanded of Poland that Danzig must be German and the Corridor returned. From the point of view of nationalism, there was much to be said for returning Danzig to Germany; but Hitler had made and contradicted so many statements that nobody believed him when he said that this was his last demand. When Poland stood firm and the outbreak came, the typical phenomena appeared—each side accused the other of provoking hostilities, of perpetrating atrocities, and of bombing open towns. These tactics are familiar to the student of international politics, and are inseparable from the balance-of-power system.

Each side had some right and some wrong in its policy but each side blamed the other entirely. Further, it was not only a particular action but the purpose behind it which led to misunderstanding. Hitler spoke of one purpose. His opponents believed that he had another. They said that his methods were destructive of international law and order; Hitler replied there was no other way in which he could obtain German rights, since under international law whatever he did to obtain German rights violated the law. The truth is that both sides had a certain logic, but it was an inadequate logic which did not take into account the total situation. Each side pointed to the other's faults and ignored its own. Hitler's opponents talked of the persecution of Jews in Germany; Hitler talked of the persecution of the Germans in Poland; and the Poles might have retorted by reminding Hitler of the prewar Germanization policy in Posen. Neither side possessed an adequate sense of justice; and the world has witnessed the consequence of accumulated inadequacies of policy on the part of all powers until the contradictions have become so complete that there seems to be no way out. The balance-of-power system has led to intensified armaments, intensified propaganda charges and countercharges, a deplorable decline of public manners and morals, and an elevation of lying into a principle until no government's word can be trusted; and the modern state which demands mankind's supreme loyalty even unto death threatens to destroy all culture and goodness in the mere effort of survival and seizure of power.

Plainly the balance-of-power system will not do, is not worth restoring.

COLLECTIVE SECURITY—THE LEAGUE OF NATIONS

The inability of prewar institutions to deal efficiently with the rapidly increasing number of international problems—security, communications, health, finance, intellectual co-operation—led to the establishment of the League of Nations. The League was to guarantee order and stability which the balance of power had failed to maintain; its economic and financial sections were to help national governments collectively to draw up more extensive rules in all branches of economic life and its other sections were to fulfil the same task for other fields of human activity; the International Labor Organization was to specialize in labor relations; the World Court was to provide a more adequate instrument for interpreting international law. In so far as the failure of prewar society was to be traced to the lack of political institutions, it was to be remedied by the new order of the society of nations.

The movement did not stop with the League. Within the British Empire conferences and secretariats grew up in order to deal with problems, internal and external, which affected the welfare of one-fifth of the world. The countries of the American continent strengthened the Pan-American machinery; the Scandinavian countries adopted many measures of international co-operation; and the Little Entente and the Baltic and Balkan States built up regional organizations. The significance of these new rule-making, rule-enforcing, and rule-interpreting agencies must now be examined, particularly in relation to the problem of security.

The Covenant of the League of Nations sets forth the principles and instrumentalities of the new organization. Article 1 deals with membership. The original members are named in the annex; other states, dominions, or colonies may be admitted by two-thirds vote of the Assembly after giving evidence of good faith and intention to observe the conditions laid down by the League relating to armaments. Three things may be noted: (1) The defeated powers, Germany, Austria, Bulgaria, and Turkey, the Soviet Union, and Mexico were not original members. Thus the

League suffered from lack of universality at its very inception. (2) Provision is made for the entrance of self-governing dominions or colonies—a breach in the theory hitherto held that international relations are between "sovereign states." (3) The article contains an exception to the normal rule of unanimity, since a two-thirds vote of the Assembly is sufficient to admit new members.

Articles 2 to 7 deal with the instruments of the League: The Assembly, the Council, and the Permanent Secretariat. The Assembly consists of representatives of all the League members and is to meet "at stated intervals and from time to time as occasion may require"; it may deal with any matter within the sphere of action of the League or affecting the peace of the world. At its meetings each member has one vote and may not have more than three representatives. The Council is to comprise representatives of the Principal Allied and Associated Powers (the United States, the British Empire, France, Italy, and Japan) and four other members selected by the Assembly "from time to time in its discretion." The Council and a majority of the Assembly may add to the number of both the permanent and nonpermanent members of the Council; and the Council is to meet from time to time but at least once a year. Like the Assembly, it may deal with any matters within the League's competency or affecting the peace of the world. Each Council member has one representative and one vote. The Assembly was thus to be the less important body, meeting less frequently than the Council but able to deal with essentially the same matters as the Council. A majority of the Council was to have derived from the great powers; but, for reasons discussed later, this hope was not realized; the nonpermanent members outnumbered the permanent members, and the small powers were thereby enabled to occupy a stronger position in the League than had been intended.

Under Article 5, Council and Assembly decisions must be by unanimous vote "except where otherwise expressly provided." Matters of procedure are regulated by majority vote of members present at the meeting. Article 5 thus consecrates the principle of national sovereignty in matters of international policy.

The Secretariat is the civil service of the League. At its head is the Secretary-General, who, with the approval of the Council, appoints the secretaries and the staff.

Council, Assembly, and Secretariat comprise the rule-making agency and the civil service of the League. They were designed to provide a set of organs more adequate to the needs of the modern world—regularity of conferences, opportunity for both great and small powers to participate in rule-making, and a set of permanent officials whose duty it was to carry on correspondence, prepare the agenda, supervise finances, and prepare for conferences.

Article 8 deals with the reduction of armaments. It reads: "Members of the League recognise that the maintenance of peace requires the reduction of national armaments to the lowest point consistent with national safety and the enforcement by common action of international obligations." It may seem surprising that the first article concerned with policy should have had reference, not to legislative activity, but to the question of armaments. In reality the priority of this clause is quite natural: No society can hope to build a structure of law and order if the units that comprise it have great military, naval, and air forces. Until international society has more force at its disposal than the respective nations possess, peace must remain uncertain and fragile. Excessive armaments put force in the foreground of a dispute instead of keeping it in the background. In the attempt to restore a better balance in the distribution of force within international society, the Council was to recommend plans for the reduction of armaments and League members promised to attempt to regulate the evils of the private manufacture of arms and to exchange full information on their armament programs. Under Article 9 the League was to set up a permanent commission to advise regarding the foregoing provisions.

A society's first concern is to control and direct force so that it may become the instrument of order and not of anarchy. Its next concern is to guarantee the security and property of its members. From this standpoint, Article 10 logically follows the article dealing with the reduction of armaments. The League "guarantees as against external aggression the territorial integrity and existing political independence of its members." In the event of aggression or threat of aggression, the League Council is to advise upon the manner in which the League shall fulfill this obligation. Note that the Council can only "advise."

Here is a serious problem. What if the League members do not choose to accept the League's "advice"? What assurance will a threatened nation have that the League will live up to its guaranty? This question was asked during the drafting of the Covenant, but states would not surrender their sovereignty and agree in advance to place their military and naval forces at the disposal of the Council, should the latter decide to impose sanctions against the aggressor. Article 10 remained an uncertain guaranty, and did not supply the complete assurance of security desired by nations which stood in fear of attack by other nations. On the other hand, the obligation (incomplete though it was, at least in provision for practical application) to respect and defend the territorial integrity and existing political independence of member states proved too much for the United States, which rejected the League Covenant, largely because of its unwillingness to guarantee the permanency of the political situation created by the Peace Treaties.

Article 11 writes into the law of nations a principle which challenges the traditional right of sovereign states. It asserts that war or threat of war between two nations, "whether immediately affecting any of the Members of the League or not, is hereby declared a matter of concern to the whole League," which "shall take any action which it deems wise and effectual to safeguard the peace of nations." War is no longer a matter which sovereign nations have the right to claim as their exclusive prerogative: they are sovereign nations, but they must not abuse their sovereignty. War concerns the greater society within the League, and that society now claims the right to propose measures for its prevention.

The article also declares that any League member has the "friendly right" to draw the attention of the Assembly or Council to any matter threatening the peace of the world, thus emphasizing the method of conciliation. The Council or Assembly vote, to be conclusive, must include all members, including the disputing parties. The general, although not unanimous, view is that Article 11 does not enable the League to override the vote of a disputant and is likely to be invoked when the international dispute is not of a grave or urgent nature. The quarrel must be settled, if at all, by means of persuasion and mediatorial effort.

Under Article 12 the members agree to submit disputes "likely to lead to a rupture" to arbitrators whom the disputants themselves may appoint, to arbitrators provided for by a previous treaty arrangement between them, to judicial settlement by the Permanent Court of International Justice, or to inquiry by the League Council if the matter is primarily a political one. Members further agree not to go to war until three months after the award is given. The award of the arbitrators or the judicial decision must be made "within a reasonable time," and the Council must give its report within six months. Thus in both legal and political disputes there is a definite promise to submit to the judgment of a third party.

Article 13 deals with legal disputes more in detail. If League members have a dispute which they themselves recognize to be suitable for legal determination and which has remained unsettled by the ordinary diplomatic methods, they agree to appeal to suitable agencies—to the Permanent Court of International Justice (provided for in Article 14) or to any other tribunal. The article mentions four types of legal disputes which admit of settlement by recourse to judicial decision.

First are disputes over the interpretation of a treaty. On many occasions nations have disagreed as to the meaning of a treaty provision. China and Japan had serious differences of opinion as to the meaning of a 1905 treaty by which Russian rights in South Manchuria passed to Japan; the Italo-Ethiopian dispute arose in part from controversies over treaty matters. The second type is any question of international law. Authoritative pronouncements by a Permanent Court will do much to encourage recourse to judicial settlement. Third is the existence of any fact which if it were proved to be true would constitute a breach of international obligation. In most disputes there is a difference of opinion as to the facts themselves; and adequate development of law requires the existence of tribunals which can determine the facts and ascertain whether or not the law has been broken. And the fourth type is the extent and nature of damages to be awarded for the breach of international obligation. The reign of law requires that judicial agencies shall have the power not merely of declaring the law but of prescribing penalties. Should any member not carry out the award, the League Council may propose the necessary steps to give effect to the decision.

The Permanent Court provided for in Article 14 may hear disputes submitted to it by states and may give advisory opinions at the request of the League Assembly or Council. The latter bodies, in attempting to settle a political dispute between two members, may be confronted by an intricate question of law, and may desire more influential, though not necessarily more able, opinion than the legal advisers in the League Secretariat can give. In this case it is important to have a body which can speak with widely recognized authority. As we have seen, some jurists wished to confer compulsory jurisdiction on the Court; but, after much discussion, the founders refused to take the step. The Covenant, therefore, contains no reference to compulsory settlement of legal disputes.

Article 15 provides that League members will submit to the

Council any dispute likely to lead to a rupture provided that it has not already been submitted to arbitration or judicial settlement. If the Council succeeds in settling the dispute by conciliation methods, it is to publish a statement setting forth the facts and explanations; but, if the dispute is not thus settled, the Council "either unanimously or by majority vote shall make and publish a report containing a statement of the facts of the dispute, and the recommendations which are deemed just and proper." If the Council's report is unanimously agreed to by all the members other than the disputants, the League members undertake not to go to war with the party which complies with the recommendations in the report. If the Council does not reach a unanimous verdict (the disputants not being permitted to vote), the disputants may then take such action as they deem necessary to maintain their rights. If the Council finds that a dispute arises out of a matter solely within the domestic jurisdiction of either party, it will make no recommendation as to settlement. The Council may also refer the dispute to the Assembly, and either disputant may within fourteen days after the dispute has been submitted to the Council request that the matter be brought up before the Assembly. If the Assembly adopts a report "concurred in by all the Council representatives" and a majority of the other members of the Assembly, it shall be deemed binding.

This article is most important. It provides for the compulsory arbitration of international disputes of a serious nature. And the disputants may not vote. A decision may be reached over their heads. But as a concession to the principle of sovereignty, it was agreed that unless the nondisputant Council members unanimously (all the Council members plus a majority of the other representatives of the League in the case of the Assembly) come to a decision, the disputants resume their liberty of action. Here is a gap in the Covenant, for what assurance is there that unanimity will prevail? What if a disputant has an ally who is a member of the Council?

Article 16 provides that if a member of the League resorts to war in disregard of the Covenant, it shall be deemed to have committed an act of war against the other League members, who undertake "immediately" to sever trade and financial relations. The Council will have the duty of "recommending" to the governments "what effective military, naval or air force" League members shall each contribute to assist in military sanctions. The League members also agree to support each other in the financial and economic measures taken under the article in order to minimize the losses and inconveniences occasioned thereby. Note that the League members undertake immediately to impose economic sanctions but that only the League Council can recommend military sanctions. Here was another gap in the Covenant. There was no assurance that the Council's recommendations of military action against an aggressor would not be disregarded by the League members. It is clear that a nation relying for its security upon a mere recommendation of an international body would be running a great risk, and we should expect to see later efforts to strengthen this article. Note also that the Covenant-breaking member which resorted to war—a difficult word to define—was deemed to have committed an "act of war." The question arose as to whether or not an "act of war" against members of the League involved a "state of war," and upon the interpretation of these phrases a great deal depended.

Article 17 provided that the League would take cognizance of a dispute between a member of the League and a state not a member of the League, or between states not members of the League. The theory was that war was a matter of international concern, and that the League of Nations could not witness aggressive action by nonmembers without taking steps to prevent it and, if necessary, applying the sanctions provided for in Article 16.

Articles 11 to 17 constitute the part of the Covenant devoted to the settlement of disputes and the prevention of war. Article 18 provides that all treaties entered into by League members must be registered with the Secretariat and that no treaty or international engagement shall be binding until so registered, a provision which looks straightforward enough but which contains many snares.

Article 19 reads: "The Assembly may from time to time advise the reconsideration by Members of the League of treaties which have become inapplicable and the consideration of international conditions whose continuance might endanger the peace of the world."

This article provides for peaceful change and should, in the opinion of many statesmen and scholars, have been included in Article 10, which guarantees the security of nations, so that security and change could have been linked together. Obviously, in a changing world, security must be consistent with change; if no provision for change is made, an international guaranty of security will be no more than an international guaranty of the status quo. But postwar France, preoccupied with security and fearing change, insisted upon placing the two principles in separate articles instead of incorporating them in one article. Note the limited character of Article 19: The Assembly "may" advise, not "shall" advise; the Assembly may only "advise"; it may not "prescribe," and the members are to do no more than "reconsider." These words are very general, and do not foreshadow energetic action. Notwithstanding these defects, the principle of change was written into an international document of the first importance, and while no specific machinery was provided in Article 19, Articles 11 and 15 did make it possible for the League to consider disputes which might arise from the continuance of treaties which, in the opinion of one or more states, had become "inapplicable" or of conditions which were endangering the peace of the world. Article 19 provided a multilateral statement of general principles; given the will to make it work, it could become an instrument of great importance. It should not be considered in isolation but in conjunction with Articles 11 and 15, which contained provisions for procedures to consider means for peaceful change.

Article 20 provided that League members must abrogate obligations or understandings *inter se* which were inconsistent with the Covenant, an article of apparent simplicity but in reality of peculiar difficulty. Article 21 reads: "Nothing in this Covenant shall be deemed to affect the validity of international engagements, such as treaties of arbitration or regional understandings like the Monroe Doctrine, for securing the maintenance of peace."

This is an incorrect definition of the Monroe Doctrine and was inserted primarily to secure acceptance of the Covenant by the United States.

Article 22 establishes the mandate system which is described elsewhere. Under Article 23 League members undertake to establish the organizations necessary to improve conditions of labor, to secure just treatment to native peoples, and to supervise traffic in women and children, and traffic in opium and other dangerous drugs. The League is to supervise the trade in arms and ammunitions, to provide for freedom of communications and transit and equitable treatment for the commerce of League members, and to take steps in matters of international concern for the prevention and control of disease. Articles 24 and 25 provide for the establishment and direction of international bureaus. And Article 26 states that amendments to the Covenant shall take effect when ratified by a unanimous vote of the Council and a majority of the Assembly, but that no amendment shall bind a League member with-

out its consent; if it refuses to accept the amendment, it shall
cease to be a member of the League.

The foregoing summary of the League Covenant will show
that it contained six main principles: (1) war as a matter of international concern; (2) pacific settlement of disputes; (3) joint
responsibility for preventing aggression; (4) general limitation
and reduction of armaments; (5) peaceful change of the status
quo; (6) establishment of machinery for the prevention of social
and economic ills and the promotion of social and intellectual and
economic welfare. The successful working of the Covenant would
demand advance on all six fronts. Failure to give effect to any
one of the six principles would constitute a threat to the other five.
In a word, the success of the Covenant depended upon comprehensiveness of policy in all fields, and the acceptance of the need of
comprehensiveness by the majority if not, indeed, all the powers,
and especially the great powers of the world.

PRINCIPLES AND PROBLEMS OF COLLECTIVE SECURITY

The essence of a collective system is that no party shall be a
final judge in its own cause. If this principle were carried to its
full length nations would be finally bound by the decisions of
other agencies and each would therefore definitely have submitted
to a curtailment of its sovereignty. The governments and peoples
of the world were not willing in 1919 (or in 1939) to accept so
far-reaching a limitation. The doctrine of sovereignty was (and is)
dominant, and some compromise had to be made. The original
American plan at the Paris Peace Conference proposed a modification of the principle that only a unanimous decision of an International Conference could bind the participating states. Colonel
House hoped that a three-quarters vote might suffice for a decision; General Smuts suggested that the League Council be enabled
to make decisions if not more than two states opposed; President
Wilson was also willing to see the unanimity rule set aside. National feeling proved to be too strong, and Article 5 of the Covenant embodied the general rule of unanimity. In case of disputes
brought before the League Council under Article 11 decisions of
the Council must be unanimous (including the votes of the disputants) in order to adjudge a nation guilty of having violated
the Covenant by resort to war or unjustifiable aggression. It is
clear that the evidence would have to be most convincing, especially
in an age of political rivalries and alliances, to bring about a unani-

mous verdict under Article 11 or even under Article 15 (which excludes the vote of the disputants). Should the decision not be unanimous, the disputing nations would be free to resume their hostilities after a period of three months. The Covenant thus embodied a compromise system which was to suffer all the disadvantages of trying to mix two principles—national sovereignty, and third-party judgment.

The Covenant did not abolish all right to make war, but did attempt to establish a method of distinguishing between a defensive and an offensive war. Under Article 13 League members promise to submit disputes to arbitration, which "they recognize" as desirable; should "they" not agree, but only one nation desire to submit a dispute to arbitration or adjudication and its rival refuse, Article 15, paragraph 1, gives to the League Council compulsory jurisdiction. Not even reasons of self-defense and of sudden attack against it by an invading force permit a League member to escape its obligation, under Articles 11, 12, and 15, to submit the dispute to the League Council.

A League member, even if not a party to a particular dispute, may under Article 11 bring it up before the Council. Great Britain took such action on two occasions—the Swedish-Finnish dispute over the Aaland Islands, and the Jugoslavia-Albania dispute. Nonmembers of the League have not a right directly to ask the Council to intervene in a dispute; in consequence Germany in 1921 (at that time not a League member) was unable to bring the Allied occupation of the Rhineland before the League.

In what ways did the League Council put into operation the principle of international intervention in a dispute between two nations in an attempt to effect a peaceful settlement? After some experimenting it worked out the following procedure: If hostilities had already broken out, it tried (1) to separate the combatants and (2) to find remedies for the causes of the dispute. The theory was that the League's first duty was to restore the peace, because the machinery of justice could not work satisfactorily in an atmosphere of violence. The President of the League, if the matter were urgent, was to send a telegram to both disputants, calling their attention to their obligations under the Covenant. The aim was to concentrate attention on the one important thing—the cessation of hostilities—without raising the many issues at stake and without bringing up then the difficult question of who was the aggressor. The League Council might meet to support the action of its President, or might initiate action if the President had not already taken the first step, the aim being to induce the disputants to refrain from military action.

This procedure was successfully tried in the Greco-Bulgarian quarrel of 1925. Theoretically it could designate as "aggressor" either side which insisted upon continuing hostilities in the face of the League Council's proposals. The assumption here was that by bringing two disputants together before the attention of the whole world, and by what Conwell-Evans called a League "dictatorial interference," the aggressor could be easily identified as the one which refused to accept a unanimous decision concerning methods of ending hostilities.

The second stage in the settlement of a dispute began after hostilities had been suspended. The League then appointed a commission to inquire into the causes of the rupture and suggest the remedies. These commissions were selected by neutrals and were to consist entirely of neutrals, whereas under the prewar treaties of arbitration and conciliation each disputant was to choose one or more members of a commission, who then together selected a fifth person as chairman; the interested parties in each case were to choose the personnel and largely to determine the procedure of the commission. The League method marked a distinct advance toward impartiality and third-party judgment. An independent commission (as, for example, the Lytton Commission in the Manchurian dispute) prepared an impartial report of the facts leading up to the dispute and submitted its recommendations. The Commission's report, which was purely advisory, came before the Council with the two disputants present. The disputants were asked to comment, and full opportunity for frank discussion was afforded. The Council, after considering the report and the comments by the interested parties, drew up its final report, which, if unanimous (apart from the disputants under Article 15, including the disputants under Article 11), acquired such binding force that its rejection and resort to war were construed as evidence of an actual breach of a member's obligations under the Covenant. "The varied resource at the Council's command is thus manifest, and must give in most cases an almost irresistible authority to the report of a Commission of Inquiry whose conclusions the parties must find difficult to reject."[3]

Despite the breakdown in the collective machinery of the League, world opinion has largely accepted the principle that re-

[3] T. P. Conwell-Evans, *The League Council in Action* (Oxford University Press, London, 1929), p. 163.

jection of recommendations impartially reached affords substantial evidence of aggression. Most people in neutral countries have no doubt that Japan and Italy were aggressors in China and Ethiopia; and they base their beliefs upon the fact that the Japanese and Italian governments were adjudged guilty by the League after hearing evidence collected and weighed by neutral investigations. But public opinion, even if theoretically favorable to the principle of third-party judgments in quarrels of other countries, was often not prepared to accept a judgment against its own nation, and came to realize the inability or unwillingness of international organization to make its judgments felt and recognized. Internationally the world appears to be at the stage reached in the United States a hundred years ago when President Jackson said: "John Marshall has given his verdict; now let him enforce it if he can."

The prevention of aggression requires an adequate police force, so that the law-abiding peoples may be guaranteed security against attack and injury. Within a nation security is guaranteed by the inviolability of the home, the institution of habeas corpus, the law courts, the police force, and, ultimately, if required, the armed forces of the realm. Such manifold protection is so taken for granted that only when crime, gangster rule, rioting, and social revolution occur do we appreciate the conditions created by civilized life for the maintenance of order. Within stable countries more force is at the disposal of the state, which is the judge, than is at the disposal of the litigants. Even if the private citizen or certain groups may have their rifles and other instruments, their force is so small compared with the force behind the law that the latter is able to function satisfactorily. Unless this condition is maintained, the unity of the state is imperiled. Postwar Austria illustrates the fate which befalls a nation wherein two rival and armed political parties can challenge the government of the day. And within nations we witness the need of a strong police force, with all the skill which modern science can put at its disposal, to outwit the master criminals who use scientific knowledge and weapons for anti-social ends. How far can the analogy be used in international affairs?

The theory of sanctions and their application will be discussed later. Here it is sufficient to note that under Article 16 the League Council could only "advise" what military and naval forces might be used against the aggressor. And what guaranty was there that its "advice" would be accepted?

Another difficulty of a most serious character soon arose in connection with the application of the Covenant. Although international law has been classified under the headings of the law of war and the law of peace, the division between war and peace is not so sharp and well defined as the two titles might suggest. We have seen that international society recognized forcible measures short of war. Not only that, but it was difficult to decide when war actually existed. Some authors believed that it was necessary for a state to make an explicit declaration of war or to give an indication of an *animus belli gerendi*. Others believed that if a state committed an act of force without the *animus belli gerendi,* and the state against which the act was committed treated the act as initiating a state of war, then war would exist. In other words, did war exist when one of the states intended and declared it to exist or did it arise when certain things were done? And, if so, what were these certain things? Was war a legal condition, or merely the existence of the exercise of force?

These questions became even more urgent after the establishment of the League of Nations. Article 16 of the Covenant condemned "resort to war" and prescribed penalties if such war resulted from a violation of the Covenant itself. Italy in 1923, Greece in 1925, and Japan in 1931 declared that, although they exercised force, they did so without the intention of making war; and the Secretary-General of the League in 1927 reported that war between two states depended upon their intention, and not upon the nature of their acts, however drastic they might be. But such a doctrine ran the danger of condemning merely the word "war" and permitting actions as cruel and extensive as war itself.

In 1921 the Blockade Committee reported to the League Council that the state which undertakes armed action against another state is regarded as having committed an act of war against all the Members of the League, but that this action could not create a state of war. The Second Assembly in 1921 resolved that the action of the defaulting state could not create a state of war but merely entitled the other League Members to resort to actual war or to declare themselves at actual war with a Covenant-breaking state.

In 1923 the Italian representative on the League Council claimed that the League Covenant did not forbid "peaceful means of repression" and that therefore the occupation of Corfu by Italy was a peaceful reprisal and a measure of guaranty permitted by international law. M. Branting claimed that this argument was not convincing and that there was a great difference in what states might do before and after signing the Covenant. A body of jurists was set up to deal with the question as to whether or not measures of coercion which were not meant to constitute acts of war were consistent with Articles 12–15 of the Covenant, if taken without recourse to the procedure laid down in those articles. The reply of the jurists was not conclusive. They said that such coercive measures might, or might not, be consistent with the Covenant; and it was for the Council, when the dispute had been submitted to it, "to decide immediately, having due regard to all the circumstances of the case, and to the nature of the measures adopted, whether it should recommend the maintenance or the withdrawal of such measures."

Many of the states were disappointed at the findings of the jurists, but one must note that they did suggest that forcible measures short of war might be incompatible with the Covenant.

In 1932 the League Council solemnly reminded Bolivia and Paraguay that they were legally and morally bound by their obligations to the League not to have recourse to "armed force, but should refer the matter to arbitration, judicial settlement, or to the Council." Yet if a full declaration of war is not needed to bring a state of war, what will be the objective facts which will produce such a condition? In a rapidly changing world perhaps one cannot define in advance what particular actions will have this result.[4] Presumably a third-party judgment must be given, as the jurists in 1924 decided.

The question also arises whether or not hostile measures short of war are contrary to the Kellogg Pact; and here, too, opinions differ. For if nations renounce war as an instrument of national policy, and agree to settle disputes only by pacific means, and yet continue to make use of armed force, on the ground that these are pacific means sanctioned by international law, then the Pact becomes almost useless. Obviously international society must expand the meaning of the word "war" and take over the authority to enforce peace in the larger sense, or else resign itself to witnessing all the essential miseries of war without their being so christened. Changing circumstances have permitted hostile acts to be so drastic and effective as to wipe out the independence of another state or to reduce it to impotence. Unless new methods

[4] Sir John Fischer Williams, *Some Aspects of the Covenant of the League of Nations* (Oxford University Press, 1934), p. 310.

can be devised to circumvent mere technicalities, international society will have done no more than create a verbal defense against war; and words are ineffective agents against determined leaders and armies. One can see why France and some other states wished to "close the gaps" in the Covenant, and why, in the early years of the postwar period, so much discussion took place to find means of overcoming the problems caused by the inadequacies of international law and defects within the Covenant itself.

Moreover, the League did not possess a force capable of immediately acting against an aggressor. The Covenant did not completely guarantee security; it contained "gaps," and under certain circumstances permitted war; in any case it was extremely doubtful if the League Council would come to a unanimous decision against an aggressor quickly enough to stop actual invasion (even if it were possible for it to come to a unanimous agreement at all); too, the League was a young and untried institution. For these reasons France demanded additional guaranties. At first, Great Britain and the United States promised to come to the aid of France in the event that she was attacked; but when the United States rejected the League, and the Anglo-American guaranty failed to materialize, the French hastened to gain security in other ways. They did so by a series of alliances with Poland and the Little Entente, and by attempting to strengthen the League of Nations.

The Covenant was, in theory, an admirable thing; it made war a matter of concern to all member states wherever they were. Unfortunately, numbers did not guarantee strength. Many of the nations were scattered and far distant, and their guaranty to uphold collective security promised to be of little practical value. If Germany should attack France, it would be important to know if Great Britain, Italy, and other nations near by would afford immediate assistance. It would be small comfort to know that Persia, Haiti, Chile, and other distant and militarily insignificant members of the League would send troops, who might (or might not) arrive many months later. The wide League membership did not of itself make for sufficient security. A general guaranty was inadequate; continents should be able to reach an agreement along the lines of regionalism to provide mutual help, immediate and certain, against an aggressor. Why should not the European nations bear the first responsibility for enforcing peace within Europe? Why should American lives be endangered every time a European crisis breaks out? The desire of apprehensive nations for immediate help from states near by; the reluctance of distant nations to be involved in "foreign" disputes, together led to attempts to harmonize extra commitments along regional lines with the general obligations already undertaken by members of the League of Nations.

ATTEMPTS TO STRENGTHEN THE COLLECTIVE SYSTEM

THE DRAFT TREATY OF MUTUAL ASSISTANCE

The first proposal, the Draft Treaty of Mutual Assistance, which was prepared during the years 1922–23, showed the influence of this regional idea: (1) In addition to the obligations which League members had already assumed under Article 16, the Draft Treaty provided for the possibility of "supplementary defensive agreements." For example, states A and B could work out plans to come to each other's aid immediately if another state attacked either one of them. The League Council would examine these agreements to make sure that they did not conflict with the League Covenant, and might, if necessary, suggest changes in the text. (2) The treaty went beyond the League Covenant, by providing that

if the League Council believed that there was reasonable ground for thinking that a menace of aggression had arisen, it could apply economic sanctions against the aggressor State; call upon any of the contracting parties whose military assistance was required; determine the forces which each State furnishing assistance should place at its disposal; prescribe measures for the communications and transport connected with the operations; prepare a plan for financial co-operation so as to provide for the State attacked, and for the States furnishing assistance, the funds they required for the operations; appoint the higher command and establish the object and nature of its duties.

This measure was of extreme importance. Under the Covenant the League could take such action only after the outbreak of war; under the Draft Treaty it could take action before, in order to prevent war. Instead of waiting until the damage was done, it could take steps to prevent the infliction of damage. (3) The Draft Treaty made more precise the method of determining the aggressor. If actual hostilities had begun, the Council could decide which of the parties was the victim of aggression and whether or not it was entitled to the assistance of League members. The Treaty did not attempt the extremely difficult task of defining an act of aggression; it suggested that the Council might fix "neutral zones which the parties would be forbidden to cross." Should the armed forces of a state cross that neutral zone, such action would be one (and an important) factor in helping the Council to determine the aggressor. The Council might also propose an armistice and invite the disputants to put their claims before the League Council or the World Court, and refusal to accept this invitation would provide additional evidence of aggression. Had such a clause bound Japan and Italy in the Manchurian and Ethiopian crisis, the situations might have been considerably modified. (4) The Draft Treaty proposed that governments might agree with other governments to establish a number of demilitarized zones. (5) The Treaty provided that an aggressor must bear the whole cost of military, naval, or air operations undertaken by the powers to prevent aggression and all reparations for damage caused by its aggression; in this way it was hoped that a financial deterrent would be added to the fear of combined military action by the signatories. (6) The signatory powers were to co-operate in a general disarmament scheme which the Council might propose. It is interesting to note that a reduction of armaments was to have taken place within a period of two years! Mutual assistance "was to be given only to parties which had reduced their arms."

The Draft Treaty failed. Eighteen governments accepted it in principle; but the opposition of Great Britain and the unfavorable attitude of the United States and the Soviet Union sounded its doom. Great Britain asserted that the scheme was too complicated, and contained clauses the practical effect of which was extremely unpredictable. It claimed that "it was rarely possible for plans of assistance to be arranged in advance"—because situations changed so rapidly that detailed plans might soon be rendered out of date (although this difficulty does not seem to prevent close collaboration in military alliances). It criticized the clause dealing with special regional agreements. And here Great Britain was on solid ground. An agreement between two states to take precautions against a third might easily degenerate into little more than a military alliance of the old type. They might attack the third party, claiming self-defense. Subsequent inquiry by the League Council might prove that the attack was not justified. But a retrospective inquiry would not have stopped the war; nor might the Council thereafter be able to exact adequate reparation from the powers which were found to have wrongly used the plea of self-defense. Other critics added that the plan did not define the aggressor in sufficient detail, and advocated the adoption of more definite criteria by which to determine international aggression. Moreover, the Treaty required a unanimous vote of the Council before its judgment could go into effect, and unanimity would have been just as difficult to obtain in the case of the Draft Treaty as in the case of the Covenant.

Some governments criticized the scheme because it went too far and created too many obligations. Others claimed that the plan did not go far enough, and desired to strengthen still more the international guaranties of assistance. The first attempt to create a supplementary regional security plan in addition to the League Covenant thus met with defeat.

THE GENEVA PROTOCOL

After much detailed consideration, the Procotol for the Pacific Settlement of International Disputes appeared in 1924. In some respects, it resembled the Treaty of Mutual Assistance; but its fundamental basis was different, for it returned to the theory of general or universal security, and rejected the principle of special regional pacts. The Procotol, like the Treaty of Mutual Assistance, denounced aggressive war, and declared that no signatory power should be entitled to make war against any state which had undertaken the obligations laid down by the Protocol. It set forth a complete sytem of compulsory arbitration. Under the Covenant, it will be remembered, the disputants were to submit their quarrel to the Council but were not bound to keep the peace in case the Council failed to reach a unanimous decision: within three months they might have resort to war. The Protocol was designed to remedy this weakness by providing that should the Council fail to come to a unanimous decision, it was then to refer the matter to a Committee of Arbitration, "without any intervention" by the disputants. That is, once the matter had come before the Council, the contending parties under no circumstances would be permitted to resort to war. They must submit to a verdict of the World Court, or to a Council decision, or to an arbitral award. The dispute must be settled by peaceful means. This procedure was popularly known as "closing the gap" in the Covenant; it was designed definitely to limit the sovereign right of states to resort to war.

It was realized that any attempt to define aggression in advance was likely to fail, simply because under modern conditions there are many forms which aggression may take. The matter must be left to the Council, which would have to decide whether or not aggression had taken place. The question arose whether its decision was to be by unanimous or by majority vote. If the former, the country that feared attack might well despair of a unanimous Council vote (as in the Covenant). If the latter, countries would hesitate to send troops to support international order on, say, a 7 to 6 vote of the League Council. Such a vote would mean that a state's armed force would be put at the disposal of the League as a result of the single vote of a foreign government. In the Protocol, the proposals adopted were five:

1. There would be a presumption of aggression until proved to the contrary by a decision of the Council. If a nation refused to accept the procedure of pacific settlement, or to accept a decision of a recognized third party, including the Council, or violated provisional measures laid down by the Council, it would be deemed the aggressor. Should the Council, however, not be unanimous, the Protocol provided that it could require an armistice of belligerents by a two-thirds' majority vote, and "the party which rejects the armistice or violates it is to be held" the aggressor. The rule of unanimity was therefore modified in order to require states to observe an armistice, during which discussions could be carried on. If this procedure had been in operation during the Sino-Japanese or the Italo-Ethiopian disputes, Japan and Italy would have been obligated to withhold their military movements in China and Ethiopia, respectively, and to observe the interim conditions imposed by the Council. This might have had important consequences.

2. After the Council had designated the aggressor, it might invite the signatory states to apply immediate economic and military sanctions. But, whereas the Treaty of Mutual Assistance provided that the Council should have a voice in directing these measures, the Protocol provided that each signatory power should remain in control of its own forces. The states, therefore, were to remain judges of the manner in which they were to carry out their obligations.

3. The Protocol defined in more detail the steps to be taken in imposing sanctions and in giving the economic and financial support outlined in Article 16 of the Covenant.

4. The Protocol, as already suggested, paid far less attention to special regional treaties, although they were not entirely ruled out.

5. It provided that the signatories were to take part in an international conference on June 15, 1925, for the reduction of armaments and the Protocol was to come into force only after the conclusion of a disarmament convention.

This far-reaching proposal came before the League Assembly on October 1, 1924, and was unanimously adopted. But the British Labor government went out of power, and the Conservative cabinet later announced that Britain must reject the scheme. First, Britain considered it unwise to erect an overambitious organization imposing obligations beyond those which nations would accept in practice. Better be content with modest workable schemes than indulge in pretentious paper constitutions which would be ignored when the test came. Better trust to the logic of experience than rush into methods which were the mere creations of theoretical reasoning and in advance of present public opinion. Second, Great Britain believed that it would be dangerous to adopt the sanctions contained in the Protocol without knowing in advance what the attitude of the United States would be. If Great Britain were called upon to put its fleet at the disposal of the League, and that fleet tried to shut off United States supplies from the aggressor, a serious controversy involving the United States and Great Britain, as well as the United States and the League, might develop. Until the United States made clear that it did not intend to defend its neutral rights in the event of the imposition of sanctions, British reluctance had at least some plausibility. Third, Britain argued that for the League to be preoccupied with penalties and sanctions would alter its character, transforming it from an institution of co-operation to one of coercion. International society must develop along other lines by taking disputes in hand before they had reached the breaking point; by promoting friendly co-operation it should seek to maintain a spirit of mutual adjustment rather than to bring force and restraint into the foreground and to encourage peaceful change by conciliation and compromise rather than to introduce legal and forceful methods.

The British Dominions—Canada, Australia, South Africa, and New Zealand—and India were largely responsible for the rejection of the Protocol. They feared two things: (1) that, under the Protocol, international authority might override their sovereignty (especially in the matter of immigration, about which they exhibited considerable concern); and (2) that they might again become involved in a European war. In this respect they reflected a New World attitude similar to that of the United States, whom they, with curious inconsistency, blamed for not joining the League.[5]

Despite the pleas of many continental nations, the Protocol was doomed. The British method of favoring one step at a time, its distrust of large general commitments, was successful in torpedoing a comprehensive and what may yet come to be regarded as a necessary plan.

It may be asked whether the Protocol would not have imposed an excessive rigidity upon the world, in that many inequalities imposed by the Peace Treaties still remained. Would the Protocol have perpetuated the conditions of the Versailles Treaty? The French would probably have replied that if they had been given the degree of security provided by the Protocol, they would have allowed Germany to resume its place as an equal among the great nations. Yet there was no guaranty that such an enlightened temper would prevail, just as there has been no evidence that Germany, having thrown off its inequalities by force, has observed moderation and restraint. Theoretically, French security, attained through the Protocol, could have led to wider co-operative temper, just as German equality granted freely by the Allies could have led to the same spirit in Germany itself. Unfortunately, no nation was willing to take an adequate initial step and make the gesture of generosity. The dilemma remained inescapable, and no solution was reached.

THE LOCARNO AGREEMENTS, 1925

The next attempt at security was again regional in approach. Great Britain had advocated solving the more difficult immediate problems which threatened the peace of the world rather than attempting to draw universal blueprints. And of the immediate problems, none appeared more urgent than the relations between France and Germany. As long as the boundary between these two countries was not regarded as final, so long would security and peace remain unattainable. It was the great merit of the Locarno Pact that it embodied a declaration as to the finality of this boundary and thereby seemed to make a great contribution to European stability.

In the first place, Germany, Belgium, France, Britain, and Italy "collectively and severally guaranteed the maintenance of the territorial status quo" of the Rhineland. Germany and Belgium

[5] See G. M. Gathorne-Hardy, *A Short History of International Affairs, 1920–1934* (Oxford University Press, London, 1934), p. 63.

and Germany and France undertook "in no case to attack or invade each other or resort to war against each other" except (*a*) in resistance to a flagrant breach of Articles XLII and XLIII of the Versailles Treaty which would justify immediate action and unless (*b*) the signatories each agreed to "come immediately to the assistance of the Power against whom the act complained of is directed." In case of a flagrant breach, each party "hereby undertakes immediately to come to the help of the party against whom such a violation or breach has been directed as soon as the said Power has been able to satisfy itself that this violation constitutes an unprovoked act of aggression." The League Council, however, was later to decide whether such defensive, immediate action had been necessary; and the parties agreed to accept its view, provided that the decision was unanimous, the disputants having no vote.

The other Locarno agreements comprised German arbitration conventions with Belgium and France which provided that all disputes not amenable to amicable settlement by normal methods of diplomacy should be submitted for decision either to an Arbitral Tribunal or to the World Court, and similar arbitration agreements between Germany and Poland and Germany and Czechoslovakia.

The Locarno agreements, which temporarily eased Europe's situation and opened the way for Germany's admission to the League, emphasized local and regional agreements instead of the general or universal commitments of the Geneva Protocol. Its proponents convincingly argued that states would accept the more limited but specific obligations of a regional pact. Unfortunately, the problem of peace was not as simple as that. The World War of 1914–1918 had its origin in Eastern Europe and in problems arising from outside Europe, as well as from the Alsace-Lorraine question. The Locarno agreements were of limited value, because the general diplomatic situation might so develop as to reduce the Rhineland problem to a secondary factor. Suppose that Germany joined Austria without getting the consent of the League Council, or made war on Poland? Would France be justified in invading Germany in order to fulfill its treaty obligations, despite its undertaking at Locarno not to attack, invade, or resort to war against Germany? If relations deteriorated, and the general framework of security were weakened, could the Locarno pacts be expected to survive? In reality was it more than a limited step, depending for its continual usefulness upon a strengthening of the wider foundations of international society? Could the whole be achieved by a successive solution of the parts? Or was a more organic and comprehensive answer necessary? Time was to provide an eloquent answer.[6]

AFTER LOCARNO. FURTHER ATTEMPTS TO STRENGTHEN THE LEAGUE SYSTEM

For a time these questions remained dormant, and the Locarno agreements seemed to mark an important turning point. Between 1919 and 1925 nations had been concerned to erect a system of penalties against the aggressor. The World War of 1914–1918 had left men's minds preoccupied with the task of preventing a repetition of military invasion. The League Covenant had not been strong enough to satisfy the demand of states for security, and for six years attempts were made to strengthen the Covenant to close the gap, and to make provision for the more specific application of sanctions.

The years of 1925 to 1931 witnessed a remarkable change in emphasis. The idea of sanctions fell into the background, and less discussion took place concerning Article 16. Crises were less frequent. European hostilities seemed to be diminishing: Germany entered the League in 1926; Japan seemed loyally to be observing the Washington treaties of 1921–22. An era of good feeling appeared to be at hand. Statesmen emphasized Article 11, the article of conciliation, rather than Article 16, the article of threat and punishment. General Smuts announced that the League must not be made into a world policeman; the world must not use the method and temper of war to kill the institution of war. The whole spirit of the League was at stake—it must be a League of spiritual endeavor and not one besmirched by the war spirit. Common consent and not collective repression must be the dominant ideal.

The Seventh Assembly, in 1926, devoted much attention to extending the type of Locarno agreements to other regions and urged the Council to offer its good offices toward this end. The Eighth Assembly adopted a resolution that provided: "all wars of aggression are and shall be prohibited," and "Every pacific means must be employed to settle disputes of every description which may arise between states."

---

[6] E. H. Carr (*op. cit.*, p. 136) emphasizes that power politics played a dominant part in the Locarno Treaty: "Ten years after its conclusion, the delicate balance on which it rested had disappeared." Carr fails to analyze the ultimate consequences of the balance-of-power system and the effects of the modern methods of waging war.

But how give effect to these ideals? Some delegates wished to revive the idea of the Protocol; but general sentiment went the other way, and finally the Assembly decided to recommend the appointment of a Committee of Arbitration and Security which should survey methods by which League Members could perform their obligations under the Covenant and take further steps to support the Council with military, naval, or air forces in stopping conflicts.

The Committee prepared a number of model conventions and treaties, which formed the basis of the "General Act for the Pacific Settlement of International Disputes," adopted by the Ninth Assembly in 1928. They provided for the establishment of conciliation committees, methods of judicial settlement, general procedures of arbitration. The Ninth Assembly also approved three model bilateral conventions dealing with conciliation, arbitration, and judicial settlement, and three model treaties of nonaggression and mutual assistance. They were:

1. Bilateral Convention for the Pacific Settlement of All International Disputes (Convention a).
2. Bilateral Convention for Judicial Settlement, Arbitration and Conciliation (Convention b).
3. Bilateral Conciliation Convention (Convention c).
4. Collective Treaty of Mutual Assistance (Treaty D).
5. Collective Treaty of Non-Aggression (Treaty E).
6. Bilateral Treaty of Non-Aggression (Treaty F).[7]

In 1926 Finland had proposed a scheme by which states which were victims of aggression could receive financial assistance. It pointed out that small states which accepted disarmament proposals would be placed at a disadvantage in the event of being attacked; that their limited financial resources would make it difficult for them to make rapid purchases abroad; and that they should therefore receive the benefit of "special arrangements" in the form of financial assistance to enable them to withstand an aggressor nation.

After four and a half years of discussion the proposal became a convention. The scheme as finally drawn up provided for a loan, guaranteed by all the powers which signed the convention.[8] To avoid delay in raising credit, the convention provided for special guaranties by some of the great powers whose stronger

[7] *Documents on International Affairs,* 1928.
[8] *Annual Survey of International Affairs, 1930,* p. 84.

financial position would enable a more rapid flotation of the loan. The loan would therefore be secured by (1) the credit of the borrowing government, (2) the ordinary guarantors, and (3) the special guarantors. During 1929 the scheme evoked wide discussion; opponents argued that such a scheme involved the promotion of peace by "financing war" and would perpetuate a "war mentality" instead of promoting a "peace mentality"—the argument that had been used against sanctions in general.

Many British people believed that their Empire would be called upon to make overheavy contributions to the loan, because the amounts guaranteed were to be determined "according to the scale of contributions to the budget of the League." Others felt that the special guarantors would undertake unjustifiably heavy financial risks. Proponents defended the scheme by arguing that an aggressor-minded state would be discouraged from attacking another nation if it knew that the latter would receive not only the moral support of the League but also sufficient financial help to insure adequate supplies of armaments.[9] Advocates of the measure met another objection by saying that a unanimous decision of the League Council was necessary before the loan could be granted; and, since the special guarantor nations were likely to be members of the Council, they would be fully protected against being bound without their consent. Some critics believed that for the League Council to vote financial help in the event of the threat of war would endanger, or even destroy, the Council's value as a mediator, to which it was replied that "if the council were to be debarred from granting financial assistance until war had actually begun, the Convention would lose its chief value, since it would no longer provide an additional means for the prevention of war." A final compromise was agreed upon— that the Council might use financial grants in order to prevent the actual outbreak of war, but only after it had exhausted all reasonable efforts at mediation.

The convention adopted by the 1930 League Assembly, and signed by twenty-eight states on October 22, contained 36 articles. The details may be omitted on account of their complexity; it is sufficient to note the general principle underlying the proposal, namely, that the collective guaranty of security to a state threatened by an aggressor should not be confined to measures provided

---

[9] It is interesting to speculate how much longer Ethiopia might have held out against Italy, if it had been able to receive help under this convention instead of having been deprived of arms.

in the Covenant but, in addition to penalizing the aggressor, the League members should grant financial help to the victim.

The convention did not come into effect; it was to wait upon the conclusion of a general Disarmament Convention. It therefore suffered the same fate as the Disarmament Conference itself.

The German representative on the Arbitration and Security Committee, appointed by the Eighth Assembly in 1927, urged that a treaty be drawn up by which states would promise in advance to accept as binding any recommendations which the Council might make in the event of an international dispute. The Committee accordingly framed a Model Treaty for Strengthening the Means to Prevent War. The 1928 Assembly submitted the text to the various governments for examination; and a draft general convention was drawn up in 1930, submitted to the Assembly, and signed at Geneva on September 26, 1931. It was to come into force on deposit of ten ratifications or accessions.

The signatories undertook to accept and apply any nonmilitary measures which the Council might recommend to prevent the aggravation of a dispute. The Council might prescribe the evacuation of a territory, or territorial waters, or of a demilitarized zone; and the signatories promised to carry out without delay the measures so prescribed. If circumstances should threaten war, the Council might "fix lines which must not be passed by . . . . land, naval, or air forces and, where necessary, in order to avoid incidents, by their civil air craft." The signatory states promised to accept these recommendations, and to give strict orders to their commanders, if the Council so recommended, to take all necessary precautions to avoid incidents. The Council might appoint commissioners to verify on the spot the execution of the measures it had prescribed; and resort to war in violation of the Council's recommendations was to be regarded as "prima facie" evidence "that the party guilty thereof has resorted to war within the meaning of Article 16 of the Covenant."

A convention by which contracting parties promised in advance to carry out the provisional recommendations of the Council, and to abstain from all measures which might aggravate or extend the scope of the dispute, might have had important results. Had it been accepted by Japan and by Italy, Japan, for example, would have been bound to accept the Council's recommendations of September 30, 1931. Failure to do this would have been interpreted as prima facie evidence of aggression. Perhaps strong collective pressure at this point would have made Japan desist from its forward policy in China. If the League had been successful then, perhaps the debacle of the following years could have been avoided. But the Convention was not accepted, and therefore failed to play any part in stopping aggression.

THE KELLOGG-BRIAND PACT, 1928

A great event in the post-Locarno years was the signing of the Kellogg-Briand Pact on August 27, 1928; it gave hope to those whose trust lay in conciliation and moral suasion rather than in collective coercion.

M. Briand, in 1927, had suggested that the United States and France should celebrate the one hundred and fiftieth anniversary of American and French friendship by signing some kind of anti-war treaty. The suggestion, though good in theory, was not easy to carry out. France had advocated a comprehensive international organization capable of acting quickly enough to restrain aggression and guarantee security; during the postwar period it had supported the establishment of an international police force, the abolition of military airplanes, the internationalization of civil aviation, and the creation of a permanent international commission to supervise the execution of a disarmament convention. The United States, however, anxious to avoid becoming entangled in the League of Nations, had certainly been opposed to participating in any kind of international police system. The question thus arose as to how far an agreement would be possible between two countries holding such diverse views.

The Kellogg-Briand Pact did not bridge the gap. On the other hand, what began as a suggestion for a bilateral treaty became a multilateral instrument signed by most of the nations of the world. The text is:

The High Contracting Parties solemnly declare in the names of their respective peoples that they condemn recourse to war for the solution of international controversies and renounce it as an instrument of national policy in their relations with one another.

The High Contracting Parties agree that the settlement or solution of all disputes or conflicts, of whatever nature or of whatever origin they may be, which may arise among them, shall never be sought except by pacific means.

The Pact of Paris thus embodied an attempt to obtain peace by mobilizing world opinion (by "invocation," its critics argued); but it provided no machinery by which the renunciation of war as an instrument of national policy could be enforced against a violator, nor any method of determining whether or not a particular act was a violation of the Pact. Yet a solemn declaration accepted by the majority of states was not unimportant. Its success would depend almost entirely upon the good faith of the contracting parties. Unfortunately, too many suspicions remained abroad in the world, and almost immediately controversy arose as to the exact meaning of the two relatively short clauses of the Pact.

Even during negotiations, France made several reservations:

1. The Treaty should not become effective until "universal adherence" was given, unless special agreements provided to the contrary.
2. Each signatory should retain its right of legitimate self-defense.
3. If one signatory violated its pledge not to engage in war, all others would be automatically released.
4. The Treaty should not interfere with the previous obligations of France under the League of Nations, the Locarno Treaties, or her neutrality treaties.

Mr. Kellogg, on April 29, 1928, agreed that nothing in the American draft restricted or impaired the right of self-defense, that there was "no necessary inconsistency between the Covenant and the idea of an unqualified renunciation of war," or between the Locarno obligations and the Pact, and that if a state violated the Pact by going to war its action would "automatically release the other parties from their obligations to the treaty-breaking state." He was not willing to jeopardize the success of the proposal by making universality a condition of its coming into force.

What precisely is meant by the phrase "to renounce war as an instrument of national policy"? Suppose that a state is attacked and fights to defend its territory. Is that a war of national policy? Or is it only a defensive measure against a war of national policy undertaken by another nation? When Mr. Kellogg pronounced that defensive wars were permissible under the Pact, critics said that this was to give the whole case away, since all nations have claimed that their wars have been wars of defense, and to reduce the Pact to a mere pretentious illusion.[10] Others feared that it would constitute a backward step because, in contrast to the League Covenant—under which nations cannot plead self-defense and take the law into their own hands, but must

---

[10] This is the basis of the charge that the Pact was designed to stop all wars except those which were likely to occur.

submit their disputes to international judgment—the Pact, according to Mr. Kellogg, would permit a defensive war; if this were so, it would tend to weaken the Covenant.

Great Britain added another reservation which caused additional misgivings. It proclaimed that "certain regions of the world the welfare and integrity of which constitute a special and vital interest" for its peace and safety must be exempted from the operations of the Treaty. The Soviet Union pungently observed that the British reservation carried "an invitation to another signatory to withdraw from its operation still other regions," and added that it would not recognize as binding a reservation which was nothing but an attempt to use the Pact "as an instrument of imperialistic policy."

After the Treaty had been signed, the United States Senate added another interpretation—that the United States included the maintenance of the Monroe Doctrine within the right of "national defense," which statement seemed still further to limit the scope of the Pact. In these ways, then, the Treaty became complicated and obscured by interpretation—an "Instrument of International Confusion," as some cynics designated it.

It was not unnatural that an attempt should be made to harmonize the two most universal documents—the Covenant and the Pact. War was not entirely renounced in the Covenant, but it was renounced as an instrument of national policy in the Pact. The latter treaty by interpretation permitted defensive wars, which were not admitted by the Covenant. The original negotiators, it was said, saw no conflict of obligations on the part of the signatories, but rather a conflict of rights; i.e., a private war between one government and another was renounced for at least a period of nine months under the Covenant, but was renounced completely under the Pact (except for Mr. Kellogg's right of defensive war). At the Ninth Assembly of the League, Lithuania suggested an inquiry into the relations between the Covenant and the Pact; the Assembly decided not to take any action at the time because several nations had not yet ratified the Pact. The next year, 1929, Peru brought forward a similar proposal. It favored alteration of Article 18 of the Covenant so as to prevent any recognition by the League of a treaty resulting from an illegal war; it would recast the rule of neutrality, and modify the requirement of unanimity so as to permit the League in certain cases to act against the threat of war or aggression without having to obtain a unanimous judgment. The Scandinavian countries objected that the Assembly could scarcely take upon itself the task of interpreting the Kellogg Pact, because some of the signatories of the Pact, the United States and Russia, for example, were not League members.

The Assembly appointed a committee of eleven to study the question. After much discussion it proposed to alter Article 12, Section 1, of the Covenant so that instead of renouncing war for a period lasting until three months after an arbitral award or a Council report, the nations would make an unlimited renunciation of war. The Committee also proposed to modify Article 12, Section 4, so that an award could be made by the Council without permitting the disputants to vote as at present they may do (except in the case of Article 15) ; and to strengthen Article 15, Section 6, so as to force the disputants to agree to carry out the recommendations of the Council report, if unanimous, instead of, as now, only agreeing in a negative manner not to go to war with the nation which complies with the recommendations of the report. Finally the Committee suggested that in Article 15, Section 7, the Council should be empowered to order other procedures in case its own recommendations were not unanimous—reminding one of the provisions in the unsuccessful 1924 Protocol.

The proposals of the Committee brought to a head the opposition between those who desired to strengthen the Covenant so as to prevent all wars and thus harmonize it with the renunciation-of-war clause contained in the Kellogg-Briand Pact, and those who did not wish to place more specific obligations upon the League members.

The Swedish representative warned against the attempt to extend sanctions, saying that to outlaw all war by means of sanctions would add to the commitments, and impose an unduly heavy burden upon members of the League. Lord Cecil agreed that theoretically the objection appeared valid but that, in practice, the more definitely wars were outlawed the less need there would be to use sanctions. To make all wars illegal, he said, would have a deterring effect; the greater the collective unity against war, the less need there would be to use collective force. Japan opposed amending the Covenant, saying that (*a*) it was unnecessary; (*b*) to harmonize the League Covenant and the Kellogg Pact would require a definition of the difficult phrase "war as an instrument of national policy"; (*c*) since some nations had signed the Covenant but not the Pact, and vice versa, it would be difficult to harmonize the two treaties, neither of which had been universally accepted. The attempt at harmonization, in short, did not succeed; and the two instruments of peace continued to exist side by side.

In 1929 came the first test of the Paris Pact. A dispute between China and the Soviet Union resulted in a movement of Soviet troops into Manchuria; fighting and loss of life occurred. Secretary of State Stimson appealed to both parties as signatories of the Pact to settle their differences by peaceful means. The Soviet replied with some asperity that it was strange that the United States, which had not recognized the Soviet Government, should address an appeal to it and strongly hinted that Mr. Stimson's action was dictated by other and less worthy motives than a single-minded desire to promote peace. The charge no doubt was unfair; but Mr. Stimson's attempt revealed the weaknesses of the Pact in several respects: (1) the disadvantage of having no recognized machinery and procedure for calling upon disputants to desist from hostilities; (2) the danger of misunderstanding if any one government took the initiative in reminding states of their obligations, the Treaty having conferred upon no government the explicit right to do so; (3) the lack of recognized procedures of investigating the causes of the dispute and of proposing remedies. The Kellogg Pact as it then existed seemed to lack "teeth"; it had stated principles, but did not contain machinery for putting those principles into operation; it required "implementation."

Mr. Stimson took a step in this direction when on January 7, 1932, some months after the outbreak of Sino-Japanese hostilities in Manchuria, he sent a note to the Chinese and Japanese governments containing the famous nonrecognition doctrine. The United States, he wrote,

does not intend to recognize any situation, treaty, or agreement which may be brought about by means contrary to the covenants and obligations of the Pact of Paris of the 27th of August, 1928, to which treaty both China and Japan, as well as the United States, are parties.

Mr. Stimson reaffirmed the doctrine in a letter to Senator Borah on February 23, 1932, in which he suggested that similar action by other governments would "effectively bar the legality of any title or right sought to be obtained by pressure or treaty violation." On March 11, 1932, the Assembly of the League voted a resolution declaring that "it is incumbent upon the members of the League of Nations not to recognize any situation, treaty, or agreement which may be brought about by means contrary to the Covenant of the League of Nations or to the Pact of Paris."

Mr. Stimson declared the next day: "This action will go far toward developing into terms of international law the principles of order and justice which underlie those treaties . . . ." and on August 8, 1932, in an address to the Council of Foreign Relations he made a lengthy analysis of the implications of the Pact and the significance of the nonrecognition doctrine:

. . . . Under the former concepts of international law, when a conflict occurred it was usually deemed the concern only of the parties to the conflict. The others could only exercise and express a strict neutrality alike towards the injured and the aggressor. If they took any action or even expressed an opinion, it was likely to be deemed a hostile act towards the nation against which it was directed. . . . . But now under the covenants of the Briand-Kellogg Pact such a conflict becomes of legal concern to everybody connected with the Treaty. . . . . Moral disapproval, when it becomes the disapproval of the whole world, takes on a significance hitherto unknown in international law. For never before has international opinion been so organized and mobilized.

CONSULTATION AS A MEANS OF ATTAINING SECURITY

Many people in the United States supported the Kellogg Pact, because they believed in the efficacy of consultation as a means of promoting international peace.[11] It is obvious that intercourse between governments necessitates some form of consultation. The more frequently problems arise, the more frequent will be the need of exchanging views. In the nineteenth century, the great powers often consulted, particularly in times of crisis; but the mechanism had failed to prevent the World War of 1914–1918, in part at least because consultation was not regularly organized. Under the League of Nations, consultation became a regular thing: the Assembly met annually, the Council met at frequent intervals, and the Covenant (in Articles 4, 10, 11, and 15) provided for consultation under certain conditions.

As the United States had become more involved in world affairs, it had had to consult other governments. The question arose whether the occasional prewar consultations, undertaken as occasion demanded, should not be replaced by a more definite and systematic arrangement. On the theory that the combined influ-

[11] See R. M. Cooper, *American Consultation in World Affairs* (The Macmillan Company, New York, 1934).

ence of a number of powers might suffice to bring two disputing powers together, the Washington Conference of 1921–1922 had drawn up the Four-Power and the Nine-Power pacts, which provided that in the event of any controversy which could not be settled by diplomacy, the parties would communicate fully and frankly with each other. But neither treaty established any machinery which could be employed by the contracting parties; consultation was obligatory, but no means by which it could take place had been provided.

In order to make certain that consultation did not imply an obligation to take further action, the United States Senate added the reservation that it understood that under the terms of the treaty there was no commitment to employ armed force, no alliance, and no obligation to join in any defense. Under these treaties the United States for the first time accepted the obligation to consult; the obligation, however, was limited to the Pacific area, and did not extend to Europe.

Subsequent events were to show that it was not easy to combine effective consultation and effective neutrality. Mr. Stimson's efforts to strengthen the Kellogg Pact by giving it an extended interpretation had failed to gain general support. Japan denied that his version of the Pact was an accurate portrayal of the international legal position, drawing a wide distinction between his and its understanding of the Pact, and added that his rendering could not be taken as the universally accepted judgment of the world.

Thus neither the Kellogg Pact nor consultation proved to be an effective instrument in major crises. We have seen that in the 1929 Sino-Soviet Manchurian dispute Mr. Stimson's efforts were unsuccessful. Neither the Pact nor the Covenant restrained Japan during the 1931–1932 and later Sino-Japanese hostilities. In 1935 Ethiopia appealed to the United States during the Italo-Ethiopian dispute, asking it to use its influence under the Kellogg-Briand Pact to restrain Italian aggression; but the appeal was in vain.

The optimism of those who between 1925 and 1931 had believed that consultation, mediation, and moral suasion would prove sufficient to solve international disputes likely to lead to war had been rudely shattered. Discussion had failed; reason had been ruled out; recommendations for peaceful change both in Manchuria and Ethiopia had been rejected. It was becoming clear that war resulted not merely from the clash of rights, or from inadequate machinery for investigation of grievances, but also from a will to war, a glorification of force and a militant philosophy of life which no amount of reason could check. It seemed that the founders of the League and those who had argued that force must be used in international as well as in national life, by the community against members who threatened the independence of other members, were right. Sanctions which had gone out of fashion in 1925 reappeared in 1935, and the League applied penalties against Italy after judging that the Italian government had violated its obligations under the Covenant.

SANCTIONS

The idea of sanctions, "measures for securing obedience to law," is not new. Law must be obeyed, and means to that end have been sought and adopted by national authorities for many years. Two things are necessary: (1) The police whose duty it is to suppress disorder must use only that amount of force required to preserve the peace; their action "must not be indiscriminate . . . . punitive . . . . vindictive"; and (2) they must not assume the right to "punish the criminal, or to settle disputes that may arise," for these functions belong to the courts. Within the international sphere the difficulties are greater. There law is less developed and police power is practically nonexistent. However, collective, if not international, measures to enforce peace are not unprecedented. In the Middle Ages, under the influence of the Church, there grew up the Truce of God, "la trève de Dieu," and the Peace of God, "la paix de Dieu." The Church also arbitrated differences, and promoted the law of nations. These "sanctions ecclésiastiques" comprised maledictions, excommunications, and the interdict, the last involving refusal of the Church's holy offices: christenings, marriage ceremonies, and funeral services might not be held.

Unfortunately these measures also proved ineffective. They encouraged the formation of "associations for peace," whose duty it was to punish those who had violated their oath or had refused to accept the decisions of the "judges of peace." The system had many successes, but only too often its efforts failed against the great barons and states.[12]

With the development of the modern state and the doctrine of sovereignty, the international doctrines of the Church became a

---

[12] See Frederic Duval, *De la Paix de Dieu à la Paix de Fer* (Paillard, Paris, 1923), p. 34.

thing of the past. Grotius tried to maintain the distinction between just and unjust wars, but even that disappeared, and in the eighteenth and nineteenth centuries international law accepted the doctrine that sovereign states have the legal right to make war, and that other nations, except in so far as war affects their vital interests, should observe neutrality as a legal right and duty.

The establishment of the League of Nations reintroduced the idea of just and unjust wars: war was declared to be a matter of concern to the whole of the international society organized in the League. Under Article 16 members of the League were immediately to apply economic sanctions against a state which violated the Covenant, and the Council was to recommend "what effective military, naval or air force the members of the League shall severally contribute to the armed forces to be used to protect the covenants of the League." Members were to support each other in order to minimize the loss resulting from the imposition of sanctions.

Almost immediately the nations began to weaken the effect of their obligations by a series of resolutions. In February 1920 the League Council appointed an International Blockade Commission to consider the application of sanctions under Article 16, since the article itself provided no machinery to apply the sanctions which it enumerated. The Committee concluded that because "the League of Nations had not yet attained a world-wide or nearly world-wide character, a rigid application of Article 16 might not only meet with very great obstacles, but might also place the States Members . . . . in very difficult situations." It was therefore desirable to "make allowance for the facts as they are." The Assembly was guided by the Report and drew up four amendments to Article 16, and a number of interpretative resolutions which were to serve as "rules of guidance."

The amendments and resolutions incorporated the principle of progressive sanctions—just sufficient force was to be used to prevent an aggressor from efficiently waging war. (1) Unnecessary sacrifice on the part of both the boycotting and the aggressor state should be avoided. The purpose being to prevent, and not to punish an aggressor, diplomatic sanctions should first be tried, then economic measures of a restricted nature; if necessary, these could be "gradually increased and intensified, culminating in cutting off food supplies in obstinate cases." (2) In order that sacrifices should not bear more unfairly on some states than on others, Resolution 9 provided that "it may be necessary to recommend the execution of special measures by certain States," and to postpone, wholly or in part in the case of certain states, the effective application of the economic sanctions in order "to reduce to a minimum the losses and embarrassment which may be entailed." (3) A resolution made it clear that it was for "each member of the League to decide for itself whether a breach of the Covenant had been committed." (4) Resolution 3 weakened the effect of the phrase in Article 16 that a League member which resorted to war in disregard of its covenants under Articles 12, 13, or 15 "shall *ipso facto* be deemed to have committed an act of war against all other Members of the League" by stating that "the unilateral action of the defaulting State cannot create a state of war." League members could now avoid the inconveniences of a state of war if they so wished.[13]

The 1921 amendments remained unratified but were generally, although not universally, regarded as an authoritative interpretation of Article 16. The League made no attempt to apply economic or military sanctions during the next decade; especially after 1925 did it place its trust in collective moral suasion and appeal to world opinion. The hope that these methods would suffice to prevent aggression received a severe setback in the Sino-Japanese crisis over Manchuria, which broke out on September 18, 1931. The Lytton Report and the League Assembly (on February 24, 1933) judged that Japan had violated its obligations under the Covenant. Conciliation had failed to stop Japan's aggression; but the next step, the application of sanctions, was opposed by the great powers and especially Britain, acting upon the nineteenth-century practice of trying to localize hostilities and claiming that the moral and diplomatic influence of neutral powers to induce the disputants to humanize and limit the extent of the conflict would be more effective than to make a quarrel in Asia into a war of world-wide magnitude. Such a view, of course, denied the very foundations of collective security and constituted a disregard of obligations under the Covenant. The active sin of commission by Japan was different only in degree and not in kind from the sin of omission by Great Britain, France, Italy, Germany, and other League members.

In the war between Bolivia and Paraguay over the Chaco region the League Council belatedly, on May 19, 1934, recommended an arms embargo against both powers; after a ruinous delay, twenty-eight governments acted upon the recommendation. Later

[13] See Bruce Williams, *State Security and the League of Nations* (The Johns Hopkins Press, 1927), pp. 120–50.

twenty-one countries lifted the embargo against Bolivia. The League Assembly did not take stronger action because of the opposition of the South American countries, Argentina, Chile, Peru, and Uruguay, and later handed over the problem to the nations of that continent for solution. The danger of conflicting with the Pan-American peace machinery led to caution on the part of the League, a caution which doubtless fitted into the lukewarm attitude of several of the member states.

The Italo-Ethiopian crisis witnessed the first (and thus far only) attempt by the League to impose a superficially impressive but actually not comprehensive system of sanctions. The Council adopted committee reports to the effect that Italy had violated the Covenant without determining whether or not "war" in a strictly legal sense had begun. No declaration of war had been made; but the Council and later the Assembly took action on the ground that Italy had sent troops into Ethiopia and commenced hostilities before the Council had issued its final recommendations. In thus establishing the existence of war on the basis of objective facts and without reference to any preliminary declarations of war, the League created an important precedent. Henceforth, any form of organized hostilities or invasion of a country may be regarded as war within the meaning of the Covenant.

The Co-ordination Committee, a Committee of Eighteen, and several subcommittees by October 19, 1935, had considered the following sanctions: (1) an arms embargo; (2) financial measures; (3) prohibiting the importation of goods from Italy; (4) an embargo on certain exports to Italy; and (5) the organization of mutual support. The detailed consideration and adoption of these measures within a period of nine days (October 11–19) was a remarkable international achievement. The Italian representative complained that the League revealed lamentable inconsistency in taking action against Italy when it had applied sanctions to only a limited degree in the Bolivia-Paraguay dispute and not at all to Japan. "Why two weights and two measures?" he asked. The reply was that many states members feared that the League system of collective security could not withstand a second blow; it "had barely survived the Japanese breach of the Covenant and the Italian breach was still more flagrant." Great Britain realized that its imperial interests coincided (temporarily and selfishly, as events showed) with its obligations under the Covenant, and for a time acted firmly.

The sanctions were accepted by approximately fifty governments in each case (numbers 1–5) and were put into force by over forty. They included embargoes: on the shipments of arms, ammunition, and implements of war to Italy and its possessions; on direct loans and credits (though not the transfer of funds, as for example, remittances by Italian emigrants, payments of Italian shipping services, and proceeds from Italian holdings of foreign securities and the foreign assets); on imports from Italy and the colonies (except gold and silver bullion and coin, printed matter, maps, and sheet music); on exports to Italy of goods which the League members controlled or supplied wholly or in part, together with measures to insure that "these articles, which were exported to a country other than Italy, would not be re-exported directly or indirectly to Italy."

The sanctions failed; and with the Italian victory over Abyssinia the League of Nations and the whole policy of penalties collectively imposed against an aggressor received a deadly blow. The reasons are clear: (1) The League refused to adopt a complete economic embargo. Toynbee and others have shown that an oil embargo adopted in November 1935, especially if the United States had co-operated, would have sufficed to cripple the Italian campaign. Other important raw materials were not included. (2) The United States and Germany were not in the League; Austria and Hungary refused to join in sanctions; Albania and Paraguay took no action. (3) Some of the League members claimed that their special position entitled them to be freed from the obligation to assist in imposing sanctions upon Italy. Switzerland, especially, pleaded its traditional neutrality and its Italian-speaking population as an excuse. Its refusal to act enabled Italy to maintain a market which accounted for 8.1 per cent of its exports in 1933. (4) Other League members, particularly those from Latin America, made reservations: Argentina pleaded constitutional difficulties in the way of prohibiting imports from Italy. Venezuela, Uruguay, and Peru failed to take measures. And Litvinoff, speaking for the Soviet Union, said that twenty-five per cent of the League members did not apply one or more of the sanctions. (5) Behind the scenes many controversies raged among the sanctionist powers concerning the compensation due some of them (especially Jugoslavia, Greece, and Rumania which suffered severe economic repercussions because of the interruption of their extensive normal trade with Italy); Great Britain opposed the idea of financially compensating these powers unless commercial negotiations and adjustments proved insufficient. Their losses, disproportionately heavy in their eyes, must have dampened their enthusiasm for collective security, especially in view of the miserable diplomatic double-dealings of France and Great Britain. They might well ask why the small countries should again undertake economic sacrifices only to be betrayed by the great powers whose resources could have enabled them to bear much heavier burdens had they so desired.

Another factor in the failure of sanctions was not the principle underlying them but a fundamental error in their application. It will be recalled that in 1921 the Assembly, basing its action upon a report of the International Blockade Commission, adopted the theory of progressive sanctions: They should be preventive and not punitive in character. Restraining measures should be just strong enough to keep the aggressively minded government from gaining its object of conquest. This method, to be successful, required an accurate estimate of the total situation; a miscalculation of the resources and temper of the aggressor and of the ability of the invaded nation to defend itself might result in failure. It rested upon the mistaken theory that the threat of progressive sanctions would suffice to prevent the aggressor from taking steps. Nor was this all. Instead of warning Mussolini before his preparations had gone very far, neither the League nor its individual members took any steps until he had committed himself so deeply that he could not stop without loss of prestige.

Progressive sanctions completely overlooked the factor of national feeling. They were psychologically unsound. They merely served to strengthen Mussolini's determination and to arouse in his followers a persecution complex. The only justification of sanctions was a successful vindication of a third-party judgment; anything short of that was stupidity. If sanctions are to be employed in the future, they must be ready for application at the very moment the aggressor moves troops, planes, or warships beyond his boundaries and refuses to immobilize his forces pending international investigation. Halfway sanctions have failed. The failure has not proved the unsoundness of a more efficient application or of the general theory of sanctions.

Underlying these causes of failure were others. As Toynbee wrote with eloquent indignation:

the criminal act of military aggression against a primitive African community, which was being executed by Italian hands, presents itself on a larger view, as the common crime of Western Christendom. . . . . Europeans and Americans beyond the borders of Italy were deliberately and eagerly making commercial profits out of the will and the power of an Italian dictator to wring from an already ruined Italian people the purchasing power that he required for buying abroad the material means for waging war on the almost defenceless people of Abyssinia. This world-wide purveyance of supplies to Italy and to the Italian colonies in East Africa was carried on crescendo during the months immediately preceding the outbreak of war. . . . . though it was manifest all the time that these supplies were going to be used by Italy for the purpose of committing an act of military aggression against a neighbor who was her fellow member of the League of Nations, and after the outbreak of the war this ghoulish traffic did not cease.

In other words, English, French, Americans, Scandinavians, Austrians, Poles, Turks, Czechs, and others assisted Italy to overthrow Ethiopia. They did not merely not stop Italy; they actively assisted that nation to violate the League Covenant. Glasgow supplied a large distillation plant for drinking-water supply; the United States sent scrap iron; Northamptonshire sold boots for the Italian soldiers; Poland shipped blankets and coal; cereals, coal, oil, and timber came from Russia, cereals, dried fruits, and olive oil, coal, and cattle from Turkey, and dozens of articles from other countries. Commenting upon these and other illustrations which he has collected, Toynbee adds:

At the scent of war-profits, men of business had lifted up their hearts, all over the world. The random illustrations of this war profit-making that have been given above are sufficient to show how widely "the civilized world" of the day had implicated itself in advance in the blood-guiltiness for the innocent blood that Italian hands were to shed. The Italian military campaign in East Africa could be described in economic terms as a world-wide business transaction.[14]

Forces were at work in the sanctionist countries, which were legally bound by solemn obligation to restrain aggression, actively to help Italy to violate the Covenant and destroy its victim. They assisted in destroying a system which otherwise might have worked successfully.

A fatal confusion of the processes of conciliation and sanctions persisted. It is true that conciliation should be used as far as possible; when, however, it has failed, and definite action has been deemed necessary against an aggressor whose troops continue to pour into the territory of its opponents and whose behavior gives no evidence of desiring genuine conciliation but only evidence of

[14] Arnold J. Toynbee, *Survey of International Affairs, 1935*, II, 220–21.

playing for time, it is the height of folly to continue to revert to conciliatory processes.

The confusion can be traced to a still more deep-seated cause, namely, the unwillingness or inability of France and Britain to realize that peace is indivisible. Hitler knew how to profit from this attitude of mind. As he wrote:

A shrewd victor will, if possible, keep imposing his demands on the conquered by degrees. He can then, in dealing with a nation that has lost its character—and this means every one that submits voluntarily— count on its never finding in any particular act of oppression a suffi- cient excuse for taking up arms once more. On the contrary, the more the exactions that have been willingly endured, the less justifiable does it seem to resist at last on account of a new and apparently isolated (though to be sure constantly recurring) imposition.[15]

The problem may be expressed in another way. Theoretically Article 11, under which every war or threat of war in any part of the world is to be deemed a threat to all members of the Interna- tional Society, is open to criticism. If states must take collective action every time a dispute breaks out, especially if the aggressor is determined and angry, the world will be in constant turmoil and nations will be continually sending troops abroad in quarrels which seem to be no concern of theirs. To Great Britain and France and the other powers it did not seem a matter of urgency to risk a war to save Lithuania from being attacked by Poland in 1923—why should they be interested in so unimportant a country? Or to save Greece from being attacked by Italy in 1923—why make a world crisis out of a local incident? Or to protect China from being invaded by Japan in 1931—why defend a weak, dis- united, Oriental people, far distant and hostile to foreigners? Why save Ethiopia from Italian aggression—a colored people, back- ward, who still indulged in slavery and were uncivilized? To save Spain from the intervention, cynical and boastful, of Mussolini and Hitler—why should Britain or France risk her safety for the sake of a scrap of paper, the Covenant, and to save "Reds"? Better keep the peace by a compromise between the great powers, by appeasement, which, although involving a sacrifice of other people, would prevent a major catastrophe. As to the seizure of Austria by Germany—again, what interest did Great Britain have in Central Europe? Did not the Germans and Austrians wish to come to-

---

[15] Adolf Hitler, *Mein Kampf* (181st German edition), p. 759. R. C. K. Ensor has a slightly different version in *Mein Kampf*, Pamphlet on World Affairs (Farrar & Rinehart, New York, 1939), p. 27.

gether in 1920? Why keep them apart? The surrender of the Sudetenland in Czechoslovakia to Germany under threat of war— was it worth drenching Europe in blood for the sake of three million people, many of whom wanted to join the Reich?

There is a certain plausibility in this line of reasoning, but the cumulative effect of permitting at least seven successful aggressions in twenty years was catastrophic. One by one the foundation stones of the temple of the collective system were loosened; and the world witnessed after the event what it should have known in advance, had its sense of justice not been dulled and warped— that a wrong committed against the least one of the nations constituted a danger to the whole world. Why do national and state authorities so zealously hunt down a murderer or a kidnaper and immediately discharge a judge found guilty of accepting bribes? Men know that to allow murder to go unpunished in one instance or to allow a judge to accept even one bribe is to encourage other people to feel that they can indulge in murder with impunity, other judges to relax the high standards of conduct becoming to their office, so that the ultimate result will be universal insecurity and judicial corruption. Hence the crucial importance of the great historic instances when men stood for a principle on the ground that a small hole in the ship of state threatens it with disaster and ruin. Justice was and is indivisible, applying to the poor as well as the rich, the weak as well as the strong.

The international world has had eloquent testimony of these profound truths. Failure to defend the integrity and independence of the small nations one after the other progressively weakened confidence in the orderly settlement of disputes. Because Britain, France, the United States, and other states would not guarantee justice in all parts, but would intervene only when their "interests" were at stake, the aggressor could base his calculations upon collective disunion. Two aggressors together, and especially three, could play a beautiful game of threatening A at one time, stripping one leaf at a time from the artichoke in the belief that B, C, D would not move; the second then demanded something of B knowing that A, C, and D would remain immobilized.

Why did not the League intervene? Because some of the great powers which are now most threatened did not, in the early days, lead the nations of the world in insisting upon respect for the rights of the small nations. In turn, the small nations which joined in sanctions against Italy (and they comprise the majority of the European nations) deserted the ideal of collective security which the major countries had already betrayed. Their desertion, entirely natural under the circumstances, took two forms: (1) They reasserted their neutrality. Belgium, Holland, and the Scandinavian countries gave notice that they intended no longer to join in sanctions against an aggressor and run risks and undertake burdens for international society; they would attend to their own houses and keep them in order. The more they did this, the more the aggressors were strengthened in their policy of peace "piece by piece": the disunity of the small powers was now added to the disunity of the great powers. (2) The smaller powers climbed on the bandwagon. When France failed to take an effective lead in the application of League sanctions, and showed itself unwilling to keep Hitler out of the Rhineland and Austria, the nations of southeastern Europe knew or believed that they could expect no assistance either from France as an ally or from the League as a collective institution. They, therefore, being unable to stand alone, made arrangements with Germany and Italy, preferring to run the risk of being satellites to strong powers of imperialist tendencies rather than to be "allies" and "friends" of France and/or the League powers whose defense of small nations was confined to brave words and pious gestures.

Thus the basis of collective action grew narrower and narrower until, when the Czech crisis broke out in 1938, only a few nations were ranged up on either side. Nevertheless, despite a superiority in resources (whatever the military situation), Britain and France preferred to give way and follow a policy of appeasement.

It may be objected that Austria should have been joined to Germany and that the Sudetenland should not have been given to Czechoslovakia. The objection may well be sound. In that case the powers should have remedied the situation earlier by a policy of peaceful change and not later at the point of the pistol. The method of change was fundamental. If it was right, it should have been done in an orderly manner; if wrong, the powers should not have given way. This question opens up a wider issue which must be treated later.

When all is said and done, one fact stands out clearly, that the prime cause of breakdown of collective security and the peace of the world lies in the attitude of the great powers. The problem of international peace is the problem raised by the rivalries of Great Britain, the United States, Japan, Italy, Germany, France, and the Soviet Union. None of these powers has genuinely and consistently supported the principles of collective security. The evidence is clear enough; and, to repeat, the active sin of commission by Italy and by Japan and to a degree that by Germany is different only in degree and not in kind from the sins of omission of the other great powers. All in some degree are responsible for the present situation.

PROPOSALS TO REFORM THE LEAGUE

The inner development of the League before 1935.[16]—Even before the collapse of collective security following the failure of sanctions against Italy several voices had been raised in favor of reforming the League from within. Some advocated the modification of certain articles in the Covenant. Others desired to make a radical change in what might be called the constitutional relations between the great and small powers which were members of the League which had developed in a somewhat unexpected manner between 1920 and 1935.

The founders of the League of Nations intended that the great powers which had dominated international politics in the prewar era should retain considerable power and influence. Not only was the League Council to be more powerful than the Assembly, but within the Council itself the great powers were to form a majority. Article 4 of the Covenant reads: "The Council shall consist of Representatives of the Principal Allied and Associated Powers, together with Representatives of four other Members of the League. These four Members of the League shall be selected by the Assembly from time to time in its discretion."

At the time there were five principal allied and associated powers; it was thus expected that the four smaller powers elected by the Assembly would be in a minority. To be sure, a Council decision must be unanimous and the mere possession of a majority by either great or small powers might therefore seem to be a relatively unimportant matter. From the angle of discussion and moral influence it would be a very different thing for five great powers to deal with nine or ten small powers instead of only four. The larger number could speak with more weight, and their combined will could not be so easily ignored. It was not surprising that the issue of great versus small powers would find expression not

[16] I am indebted to Felix Morley, *The Society of Nations* (Washington, D.C., 1932), for much of the material in this section.

merely in the relations of the Council and the Assembly but also over the question of the number of seats within the Council itself.

But the refusal of the United States to join the League altered the whole balance of the Council and from the beginning prevented the great powers from obtaining a majority. Representatives of four great and four small powers attended the first meeting. Within the next few years the Assembly had enlarged the number of the nonpermanent members on the Council from four to six (September 25, 1922) and from six to nine (September 8, 1926). The admission of Germany raised the membership of the Council to fourteen—five great and nine smaller powers.

This alteration in balance was due not only to an attempt of the weaker to curb the stronger nations on the Council but also to a struggle among the lesser powers themselves. The Covenant provided that the Assembly should select the four nonpermanent members "from time to time in its discretion" and that, pending the first election, Belgium, Brazil, Spain, and Greece should fill the positions. Now these four powers, once selected, were unwilling to vacate their seats; they succumbed to the normal temptation to retain the power which they had gained, and felt that their prestige would suffer by a surrender of their privileged position. The problem was to formulate rules by which the Assembly might conduct its elections. The first Assembly proposed that no permanent member should hold a Council seat for more than two years. But the proposal was rejected because it would "limit the discretion of future Assemblies" and the Assembly had no constitutional power to bind its successors.

Some members wished to establish the principle of rotation of nonpermanent seats on the Council in order that the smaller nations might be sure of an opportunity. But this proposal would need an amendment to the Covenant (requiring a unanimous vote in the Council). In 1921–22 Spain used its vote to prevent the adoption of the principle of rotation. The Assembly, thus balked, had recourse to a compromise by increasing the number of nonpermanent members in 1922 from four to six. In 1926 the proposal to admit Germany to the League and to a permanent seat on the Council brought matters to a crisis over the nonpermanent seats, for the Assembly found that only two of them had been vacated in seven years.

Meanwhile it had become clear that the traditional classification of nations into great and small powers no longer accurately described the facts. Several states which could not truly be called great powers were, by reason of population, economic resources, and area, easily distinguishable from small countries like Haiti, Albania, Latvia, Siam, and others. Argentina, Czechoslovakia, Spain, Poland, Rumania, and Sweden could each justly claim the higher status of intermediate powers. Some of these took advantage of the proposal to admit Germany to a permanent seat on the Council to press their claims to a similar permanent occupancy. Spain, Brazil, and Poland made eloquent pleas to be classified as great rather than small powers. But it was rightly felt that unduly to enlarge the number of permanent seats would make the Council unwieldy and would alienate the great powers which claimed that their voice should have more influence because of the interests which they had at stake.

A compromise was reached in 1926 by which Germany alone received a permanent seat on the Council; for nonpermanent seats the principle of rotation was established, the Assembly electing three members each year for a period of three years to nonpermanent seats on the Council, thus enlarging this group to nine; and the special position of the intermediate powers was recognized by "the doctrine of re-eligibility for non-permanent seats." At the conclusion of its three-year term a nonpermanent member might be re-elected to the Council for a further three-year period, provided that (1) the Assembly in a preliminary vote agreed by a two-thirds' majority to permit the retiring member to stand for re-election, and (2) not more than three of the nine nonpermanent seats should be occupied by such "re-elected" members.

The solution to the problem of representation on the League Council was reached at the cost of much bitterness and the resignation of Brazil and Spain; and it brought to light a further problem, that of regional representation. The nine nonpermanent members, it was realized, should be elected so as to enable the different continents and civilizations to be represented. Complaints had frequently been made that the Council was predominantly European in character and unduly occupied with European matters. Hence the proposal for a regional distribution of nonpermanent seats on the Council. Brazil had unsuccessfully urged that Latin America should be adequately represented by a permanent seat; it was now agreed that three of the nine seats should go to Latin-American states. Other regions or groups which obtained a seat (to be occupied successively by the regional or group members) were the Little Entente, the Scandinavian countries, the countries of Asia (apart from Japan), and the British Dominions. Thus seven of the nine permanent rotating seats were assigned. Spain and Poland were re-elected; consequently, certain countries, as Austria, Bulgaria, Greece, Hungary, and Portugal, had no opportunity to be elected to the Council. This situation was bound to cause dissatisfaction, and Portugal at the Eleventh Assembly expressed its disappointment at its practical exclusion by giving notice that it would not seek re-election to the Council "as long as the present state of affairs endures" and would "use every effort to introduce into the system in force those amendments which are indispensable for safeguarding the essential principle of the equality of states."

The small states were not satisfied; nor did the increase in the number of states on the Council please the great powers. They met the growing power of the Assembly relative to the Council by holding discussions and reaching understandings outside the formal deliberations of the former body. And the presence of the small powers on the Council encouraged great states to develop an "inner circle" and what was called "bedroom diplomacy." An overlarge Council, hampered by the rule of unanimity, made for unwieldiness and delay. The great powers therefore tried to reach previous understandings on problems which affected themselves. It is true that, if major countries can settle their disputes without the complication of public debate and the intervention of the smaller states, peace may be strengthened (for, after all, it is the quarrels of the great and not the small powers that lead to war). Nevertheless, private bargains and agreements between great powers were open to objection: (1) they tended to disregard the League procedure and machinery; and (2) secret diplomatic settlements were likely to be at the expense of the small members of the League, as the diplomacy between France, Britain, and Italy with reference to Ethiopia, and between these powers and Germany concerning Czechoslovakia, illustrated only too well.

The small powers gained relative to the big powers within the Council in another way. The original intention was to have a President of the Council elected for one year by its members. The jealousy of the smaller states led to the practice of having that office filled according to the rule of rotation. The small powers thereby obtained equality of chairmanship with the larger nations. The action, however, served to intensify the lack of continuity of the Council; it meant that in the four (later three) Council meetings a year, different statesmen took charge of important proceedings. Delegates who were relatively new to League problems had therefore to rely upon the expert services of the Secretariat and especially the advice and judgment of the Secretary-General. Later, nations tended to make use of the Assembly in view of the greater publicity and dramatic appeal possible by calling together representatives of nations from all parts of the world. The Covenant in several articles conferred powers on the "League of Nations," and there was always a possibility that either the Council or the Assembly would take action according to circumstances.

As the World Court developed, and particularly after the adoption of the Optional Clause (under which many states agreed to submit justiciable disputes to the Court), appeals to the Council on these matters tended to decrease. This factor illustrates Felix Morley's judgment that, as international organization becomes more developed and its agencies gain in experience and efficiency, many of the problems which in the early days of the League went to the Council would be considered by other League agencies at Geneva.

Despite the loss of some of its powers, the Council yet remained a body of supreme importance. Its ordinary meetings were reduced from four to three a year; but these relatively frequent gatherings of the important statesmen of Europe bore witness to the great advance made since prewar days when the departure of a foreign secretary from his own country was the occasion of diplomatic excitement and rumor.

Articles 2 and 7 of the Covenant provided for the Permanent Secretariat. It grew to become a body of over five hundred officials drawn from practically all the nations of the world. These specialists, representing every phase of administrative activity, conspicuous for skill and devotion, gradually developed the Secretariat into an important institution. What was intended to be little more than a recording and classifying body became an instrumentality with considerable discretionary and advisory power. (In part, the growth of civil service influence reflects the general tendency in government; because of the complexity of modern life, the need of expert judgment, the importance of continuity of administration, the unexpert nature of amateur cabinets, and the impermanency of legislatures, administrative officials come to play an increasingly important role.) So with the Secretariat. The Council and the Assembly met infrequently; the representatives of the member states were continually changing; statesmen were necessarily preoccupied with their own national tasks and had to depend, even more than in national legislatures, upon the research and judgment of the permanent officials. The increase in the prestige and power of the Secretariat, therefore, need occasion no surprise.[17]

It strengthened its position in three ways: (1) It set up a liaison bureau with Latin America in order to strengthen League relations there. (2) It established an information section in the capital cities of states, permanent members of the Council. (3) Several of the League members maintained permanent delegations at Geneva whose day-to-day contacts with Secretariat officials had important results.

The Secretariat had a strong influence in formulating policies. When Costa Rica requested from the League a definition of the Monroe Doctrine—a step which threatened to embarrass the League in its relations with the United States—it was the Secretary-General (and Lord Robert Cecil) and not the Council which drafted the reply. Thus "the formulation of the most far reaching policies" occurred in the Secretariat, and both the Council and the Assembly were influenced by its findings. Many of its technical activities had important political consequences. When China was not re-elected to the Council in 1928, the Secretariat took steps to offset what might have been regarded as a political rebuff by encouraging a permanent Chinese delegation to Geneva and by organizing technical co-operation between the League and China in order to assist the latter in its task of national reconstruction.

The Secretariat, because of its position as "a permanent adviser on international affairs," acquired considerable influence. Its effectiveness derived from its international character, its impartiality and detachment. This truth was recognized in the early years of the League. The Balfour Report of 1920 described members of the Secretariat as servants of the League of Nations. They were to enjoy diplomatic privileges and immunities and, by the Council Resolution of June 1920, were not to accept honors or decorations.

The staff regulations adopted by the League Assembly on October 2, 1930, put the matter beyond doubt and made more explicit the principles contained in the Balfour Report. But the ideal of a truly international civil service was difficult to maintain for a number of reasons. First, French and English were the official languages of the League, and that fact alone tended to provide the larger number of officials from France and Great Britain. Secondly, the high posts were regarded as "plums" for

---

[17] M. Beer, in *The League on Trial* (1933), criticizes Sir Eric Drummond, the Secretary-General, for not pursuing a stronger course of action.

diplomats "who temporarily leave their respective services for a time at Geneva." It was originally intended that outstanding non-official national representatives should be chosen, and without question the appointment of diplomats was contrary to the spirit if not the letter of the regulations.

Political rivalries arose over appointments, especially those of the under-secretaries-general. If nation A received an appointment to one post, nation B insisted upon a *quid pro quo*. Because the Secretary-General was an Englishman, the Deputy Secretary-General had to be a Frenchman; other great powers then claimed an under-secretary-generalship. When Germany entered the League the question came up again and a German under-secretary had to be added. These political appointments caused considerable friction between the small and the great powers. Why should the most important offices be a preserve of the latter, asked the smaller nations. Finally, the appointment of a Committee of Thirteen to inquire into the whole problem was arranged. In 1930 the Committee presented its report, which reflected the conflicting views. A special committee was ordered to report to the Twelfth Assembly, which in turn evaded the issue by adopting a compromise measure, and the situation remained substantially unaltered. Despite the temptation to governments to dishonor the truly international purpose of the Secretariat by diplomatic appointments— a temptation to which Germany and Italy, before their withdrawal from the League, had succumbed—that body proved itself to be one of extraordinary ability and devotion.

The Assembly within a few years had gained an important place in the League system, and was able considerably to alter the relations between itself and the Council. Those who drew up the Covenant anticipated that meetings of the Assembly would take place only occasionally (perhaps once in four years) and that its position would be inferior to that of the Council. In the Covenant the role of the Assembly "was indefinite, its duties undetermined, its authority severely restricted."[18] Moreover, the Council was in active operation, and had met no fewer than eleven times when the Assembly first came together in November 1920.

The Covenant provided no clear separation of powers, and in an early report the Council suggested that, inasmuch as the functions of the Assembly and the Council not only overlapped but in many respects were identical, it would be undesirable for the one

[18] Morley, *op. cit.*, p. 502.

organ to interfere with a matter already under consideration by the other. Since the Council was already holding frequent sessions, and the Assembly was intended to meet only on occasion, the effect of the resolution was to emphasize further the subordinate character of the Assembly.

The Assembly, however, early showed a disposition to protest against the Council's assumption of priority. The Swiss representative proposed a resolution to make the committees of the Assembly "whose mandates have not been exhausted during the course of the session of the Assembly" permanent until the next Assembly meeting. Owing in part to the opposition of the great powers, the resolution was not adopted; but the Assembly did claim to be "the sovereign but intermittent power of the League."

Under Article 3 of the Covenant the Assembly was to meet only "at stated intervals and from time to time as occasion may require." When the Assembly decided to meet every year it exerted more continuous influence, exercised greater control over League finances, and developed a more continuous policy through its regular meetings than would otherwise have been possible. The problem of security could not have been so comprehensively examined, nor could sanctions against Italy have been so quickly effected if the annual sessions of the Assembly had not developed a routine which made rapid concerted action possible.

The story of the Assembly's control over the finances of the League is too intricate to be summarized here. Students of constitutional history familiar with the importance of the power of the purse in the development of parliamentary government will readily appreciate how important to the Assembly was its assumption of financial supremacy. It has been well said that the liberties of Englishmen were won not by the blood of Englishmen but by their money; Parliament waged a long and persistent struggle for the power over appropriations, knowing that this was the road to political control over the Monarchy and the House of Lords. The League Assembly gained its victory over the budget in much shorter time and was successful even in taking from the Council the last vestiges of control over the supervisory commission which had been appointed by the Council in May 1922 for the purpose of watching over the finances of the League. The commission became in effect a standing committee of the Assembly—an interesting commentary upon developments since 1920, when a similar proposal had been rejected.

The two great crises, the Sino-Japanese dispute and the Italian invasion of Ethiopia, showed most clearly the growing importance of the Assembly. When the latter body met on March 3, 1932, to consider the Manchurian situation after the Council had played an undistinguished role, it opened another chapter (albeit a short one) by asserting a vigorous leadership in handling disputes of an international character and considerably modified the hitherto accepted practice of leaving to the Council the problem of attempting to maintain world peace. The smaller powers took almost immediate action, led a forceful analysis of the more fundamental principles involved, and within a few days had passed the resolution of March 11, which resulted in more action than had come from several months of the Council's deliberation. In the Italo-Ethiopian dispute, the crisis was scarcely two months old when, under auspices of the Assembly, a far-reaching program of sanctions was adopted.

To the great powers the new developments were not pleasing. They preferred the atmosphere of the nineteenth century, where, by the exercise of their power, they could dominate the European scene. They had fought the World War of 1914–1918 ostensibly for the rights of small nations, but now that they had enthroned them in a League of Nations they regretted their action. They complained of the obstructive tactics of the small governments, of the disadvantages of the rule of unanimity, of the folly of giving responsibility to general conferences which had failed to "get things done." The League may have been too much the instrument of some of the great powers, but the restraints which the smaller nations were able to impose proved to be too irritating for the ambitious leaders. Mussolini proposed the Four-Power Pact in 1932–33, and talked of a reformed League. After the failure of sanctions (and even earlier), statesmen emphasized the limited nature of their obligations under the Covenant. They preferred to return to the theory and practice of the balance (or unbalance) of power, inadequately appreciating the magnitude of the revolution which had taken place in the problems of war and security.

Proposals to reform the League after 1935.—The failure of sanctions against Italy led to a re-examination of the League by its members during the period 1936–1939. The government of Chile took the initiative, and, although immediate action upon its proposal was postponed for a short time, the Assembly on October 8, 1936, set up a Special Main Committee to examine "the application of the principles of the Covenant and all problems connected therewith." The committee decided to constitute a

Committee of Twenty-eight, which in turn began its labors in December 1936.[19]

The first major problem discussed was "the League and universality." Lord Cranborne, the rapporteur, made the following observations: (1) The present rules governing admission to the League did not constitute an obstacle to an extension of League membership; and any alteration of such rules would not be likely to attract any states which on other grounds did not desire membership. (2) No advantage was to be gained by adopting the principle of automatic membership of all states; membership in the League should be a privilege carrying obligations, rather than a right automatically existing merely because a state was a state. (3) It was undesirable to create a special category of members with a position and obligations different from the rest of the members; such a procedure would raise difficulties and confusion owing to a "multiplicity" of relations. The same end, closer association with nonmembers, would be better attained by promoting more intimate technical co-operation between the League and non-League states. The real difficulties of the League, Lord Cranborne pointed out, were political, and would not be solved by admitting to membership nations which wished to avoid or weaken political obligations imposed by the League. (4) Three types of League, i.e., coercive, non-coercive, and intermediate, might be distinguished. And the stronger the collective obligation to coerce an aggressor state, the more likely it was that fewer nations would accept membership in the League. But to universalize the League by making it a non-coercive institution would reduce it to an instrument of consultation instead of an instrument to prevent war. On the other hand, the League was called into being to "supersede the old system of alliances and rival armed camps." Because of its present lack of universality, however, it was "in danger of degenerating into something corresponding to an alliance of its Members against non-Members; . . . . this alliance is . . . . one of those who are satisfied with the status quo against those who are not; and . . . . this tendency, unless corrected, must lead to the very war which it was the purpose of the League to prevent." Hence, the importance of making the League an instrument of peaceful change. (5) The attempt to universalize the League met with the difficulty that some countries objected to the very principle of international co-operation and some which accepted the prin-

[19] S. Engel, *League Reform. An Analysis of Official Proposals and Discussions, 1936–1939* (Geneva Research Centre, 1940).

ciple objected to the particular commitments involved in League membership and desired reform of the Covenant accordingly. Such reorganization would not attract those countries which object to the fundamental principles of the League.

Thirty-two governments sent their judgments. Some urged that unless the League were more universal it could not, and should not, be coercive; that its character was likely to deteriorate from an association to develop and defend international law into an alliance; and therefore that the League must attempt to become more universal by making the Covenant more flexible and its obligations less severe. Other states argued that under no circumstances must the League weaken its obligations in an attempt to attract members. Merely to gain more states would not render the League a more effective instrument of peace. To forego its political functions would be to emasculate the League, to "commit suicide in order to preserve a semblance of life." No advance would take place by changing rules of international law "into mere precepts of international morality."[20] From the beginning the League had lacked universality, and even in 1938 its members could have prevented aggression if they had been sufficiently united, M. Litvinof asserted. Thus, defenders of the Covenant in its existing form urged that it would be preferable to have a "League without universality than universality without League principles."

The second major question discussed by League members in their search for means to remedy the defects and strengthen the sound principles of the Covenant was the separation of the Covenant from the Peace treaties. Many people claimed that the League existed primarily to enforce punitive measures against Germany and the defeated powers of the World War of 1914–1918, and they pointed to the fact that within the Covenant itself such expressions as "the High Contracting Parties" and the "Principal Allied and Associated Powers" bear witness to the connection of the Covenant with the Peace treaties. During the postwar period Germany urged that the Covenant be separated from the treaties and the stigma of inferiority thereby be removed from certain nations. After Germany's withdrawal from the League in 1933, and especially after its declaration in 1937 that it would never return to the League under any circumstances, the question seemed to some people less important than it had formerly been. Nevertheless the Assembly adopted a resolution embodying the recommendations of ten jurists which, by altering certain expres-

[20] Quoted in Engel, *op. cit.,* p. 84.

sions in Articles 1, 4, and 5, were designed "to give the Covenant
. . . . an independent existence."

The question of co-operation between the League and nonmember states produced considerable discussion. The Covenant
provided for a certain amount of co-operation in both political and
nonpolitical matters (Articles 16, 17, 23, 24, and by interpretation
Articles 10, 11, 18–21) ; and in practice quite a little technical
co-operation had taken place between Geneva and governments
outside the League. Moreover, the United States in 1934 had
made a special agreement with the League concerning the publication by the latter of treaties subsequently to be signed by the
former.

M. Pardo reported upon the problems arising out of the existence of three instruments designed to prevent war—the League
Covenant, the Paris Pact, and the Argentine Treaty. The League
Covenant does not condemn all wars but does provide for sanctions. The Pact of Paris contains a more comprehensive renunciation of war but has no "teeth," no provision for procedures
to carry its general principles into effect. The Argentine Treaty
provides that members will adopt a solitary attitude but makes
no provision for diplomatic or armed intervention by the signatories against the aggressor; in fact it forbids such action. The
difficulties of harmonizing these three instruments are overwhelming, and in consequence all that the Assembly could do was to
pass a general resolution on October 4, 1937, urging the League
to associate with its own efforts the nonmember states bound by
either or both of the other Covenants, i.e., the Paris Pact and the
Argentine Treaty. The resolution did no more than describe what
was becoming the practice.

Encouraged by the replies, the Assembly set up the Bruce Committee, which proposed the establishment of a Central Committee
for Economic and Social Questions,[21] partly to enable nonmembers
to co-operate more closely with the League in economic, financial,
health, and social matters. By giving to the proposed Central
Committee a large degree of autonomy in nonpolitical matters
and separating the political from the nonpolitical budgetary and
other obligations it was hoped to strengthen international organization on the technical side. Nonmembers would be freed from
the danger of political involvement arising out of the political
disputes of League members.

[21] See above, pp. 247–49.

To consider possible improvements in the League's nonpolitical relations with nonmembers, the Assembly on September 30, 1938, passed a resolution inviting comments or suggestions from non-member states "for the wider development of . . . . technical and non-political collaboration." The United States replied, on February 2, 1939, that it hoped for "the development and expansion of the League's machinery for dealing with the problems in those . . . . fields and . . . . the participation of all nations in active efforts to solve them" and undertook to "continue to collaborate in those activities . . . . and . . . . consider in a sympathetic spirit means of making its collaboration more effective."

The Assembly on December 13, 1939, adopted a draft resolution approving the report and requesting the Bureau of the Assembly

to take the most appropriate steps for setting up the Central Committee proposed in the Report to unify the economic and social work of the League and perform the other functions indicated in the above mentioned Report, co-ordinating its work where necessary with that of the International Labour Office, which retains its present autonomy and competence, and hopes that the Central Committee will proceed as rapidly as possible with the study of the conditions under which all States desiring to do so may participate in the work of the League relating to economic and social questions.

The international situation thereafter deteriorated so rapidly that the resolution remained on paper: Military factors dominated Europe, and made all thought of economic and social co-operation appear foolish; no constructive international organization along these lines was possible, while political anarchy became daily more obvious. Modern civilization cannot at one and the same time plan for welfare on an international scale and prepare for war at an ever accelerating pace on a national scale. Did the trouble perhaps lie in the fact that the League of Nations, by its very nature, lacked power to enforce order, and therefore lacked the conditions to insure welfare? Those who answer this question in the affirmative must take the next step—toward an international force and toward federalism. Those who had to act quickly reverted to neutrality.

RETURN TO NEUTRALITY; ITS FAILURE

This breakdown of the League was followed by a return of the theory and practice of neutrality on the part of several of the smaller powers. If the big powers wished to "reform" the League in order to play power politics more freely, the small powers did not wish to remain bound by their obligations. Under the League of Nations and the distinction it created between a just and an unjust war, there seemed to be no place for a neutral policy in the face of aggression. Under Article 11 of the Covenant, war became a matter of concern to all members of the League which undertook to impose sanctions against a state which violated its obligations under Articles 10–16. A complete system of collective security seems to be incompatible with neutrality. One may or may not quarrel with the whole principle of collective security; but, once the principle is adopted, the basis for prewar neutrality is gone.

Several countries, however, did not draw this conclusion, and attempted to combine devotion to the theory of collective security with the maintenance of a degree of neutrality. The Scandinavian states, which had had a remarkable tradition of neutrality before and during the World War of 1914–1918, opposed Article 16 of the Covenant in so far as it imposed the obligation to use military sanctions. They were willing to take part in an economic blockade against the state which had gone to war in violation of its obligations under Articles 11, 12, 13, and 15 of the Covenant; but they refused to support a movement to strengthen the League Covenant by employing more definite and extensive sanctions against the aggressor such as had been proposed in the Treaty of Mutual Assistance. The northern countries supported economic sanctions against Italy in 1935 and bitterly opposed the Hoare-Laval plan, which would have sacrificed part of Ethiopia to the Italian aggressor. Whether or not the smaller countries did the League and themselves a disservice in trying to restrict the scope of Article 16 may be open to question; whether or not their early support of more extended sanctions would have really affected the subsequent issue may be doubted.

Whatever the "might-have-beens" of 1920–1934, the fact remained that sanctions against Italy had failed and the League had collapsed, leaving the smaller powers in the unenviable position of realizing that once more they were at the mercy of the great powers and that collective security would not suffice to protect them. Naturally, they did not see why they should continue risking their own resources, and even safety, on behalf of other nations by upholding a collective system, when the great powers themselves had so feebly and even hypocritically played with sanctions against one of their number—Italy. If the great powers would not genuinely support the League, why should they? When the balance-of-power system was revealed again in its nakedness after 1935, it was to be expected that the small powers would attempt to return to the theory and practice of neutrality which had provided a measure of safety in the years before the war. In July 1936, just before sanctions against Italy were lifted, Belgium, Denmark, Finland, Norway, the Netherlands, Sweden, Spain, and Switzerland each issued a declaration stating it to be unjust that certain articles of the Covenant, especially Article 8 (which dealt with reduction of armaments), should be ignored while others were enforced. They had grave doubts whether or not the premises on which their obligations to the League rested were still in existence, and by implication they criticized "the incomplete and inconsistent manner" in which the Covenant was applied. In October 1936 the King of the Belgians announced that Germany's re-occupation of the Rhineland, by ending the Locarno Pact, had brought Belgium back to its prewar international status and that Belgium would now have to follow a policy of neutrality. In March 1937 the Dutch foreign minister stated that Article 16 could not obligate members of the League to participate in sanctions which might injure their own vital interests; and the Swedish statesman Sandler that November even declared that Article 16 was no longer legally valid and that "a law which is not binding for everybody and on every occasion has ceased for the present to be a law." M. Unden, at a League committee in January 1938, stated that "sanctions were now in fact suspended"; that "the League no longer possesses the characteristics of a coercive League corresponding to the provisions of Article 16 of the Covenant," and that "League members did not consider themselves bound to take coercive action against an aggressor." In 1937 Switzerland decided to resume its neutrality, and in May 1938 the League Council took official notice of the Swiss declaration. During the same month, the governments of Denmark, Finland, Iceland, Norway, and Sweden signed a declaration stating their intention of applying rules of neutrality in the event of a general war, each country specifying the rules which it had adopted. The northern countries requested the League to make a formal recognition of their declaration concerning nonparticipation in sanctions, and in July 1938 went on record as favoring the "non-compulsory character of sanctions" for all League members. The League Assembly did not take action upon the question but made note of the declaration.

The reversion to neutrality on the part of smaller powers received the praise of those international lawyers and students who believed that the institution of neutrality, built up since the sixteenth century, had been a vital factor in preserving peace. Professor Borchard, a pronounced critic of the League Covenant, and of what he called the jargon of collective security, lamented the "unfortunate disparagement of neutrality" implied in the philosophy of the League of Nations and advocated the return to conciliation and arbitration methods of prewar days. Professor Padelford praised the Scandinavian countries for their "sane and correct interpretation of the status and the duties of the neutral" and, in effect, congratulated them for not becoming "bogged in the morass" of trying to unite "legal neutrality with an unneutral politico-moral condemnation and sanctions against aggressors."[22] Theoretically there is much to be said for this view. If collective security is a dangerous illusion, then it is better for nonbelligerents to be entirely neutral than to be dragged into hostilities under high-sounding titles which merely mask the ugly realities of nationalist and imperialist rivalries.

Perhaps the issue is not so simple. Even in prewar days small powers enjoyed their neutrality on sufferance; in no small measure their rights depended upon the grace or expediency of the major nations. Today the conditions which induced the great powers to respect the neutrality of small powers during the nineteenth century seem to be fast disappearing.[23] We have seen that contemporary warfare is far different from warfare a century or even a generation ago. War has become increasingly totalitarian. Goods which once were clearly noncontraband today become necessary for military purposes. The clash between neutral rights and belligerent needs grows more pronounced. The expanding nature of war jeopardizes the peaceful trade and even the existence of neutrals. The fate of Denmark, Poland, Norway, Holland, Belgium, Greece, and Jugoslavia, and the practical absorption of Rumania, Bulgaria, and Hungary by Germany confirm this view, and suggests that to rely upon neutrality is to lean upon a broken reed.

Nations are exercising less restraint than in the nineteenth century. They wage "undeclared" war so as to avoid the obligations of the laws of belligerency and neutrality. Repudiation of international contracts has become so commonplace as to excite

[22] See E. M. Borchard, "Neutrality and Unneutrality," and N. J. Padelford, "The New Scandinavian Neutrality Rules," *The American Journal of International Law,* October 1938.

[23] I have left this passage as it was written before 1940. Events have confirmed the general judgment it records.

little indignation. With these elements of international law being thrown overboard, it seems idle to believe that the great powers will respect neutral declarations of small powers, should it become militarily disadvantageous for them to do so.

It is wrong to suggest that this development of nonrestraint is an outcome of the idea of collective security. It is the outcome of the type of warfare which the modern age has evolved, and against which carefully worked out paper schemes of neutrality will be powerless. Such consideration makes the suggestion of a new Hague conference to define neutral rights somewhat unreal. The institution of war has grown too great for such restraints.

Thus the small nations, and indeed the so-called great nations, face the breakdown of both systems, collective security and neutrality. They can expect little safety from the latter alternative which they have chosen. It may be that a hastily snatched neutrality may save them from immediate attack by the powers which hate the League and may provide a precarious short-term immunity. That it will suffice to save them from the ambitions of expansionist nations is more than doubtful.

The evidence provided by the events of 1940 and 1941 conclusively supports this judgment. Does it, however, apply to a great power like the United States?

NEUTRALITY AND UNITED STATES SECURITY

We have seen elsewhere the changes which took place in the theory and practice of neutrality in international affairs. The United States had a considerable influence upon the nineteenth-century doctrine. Not merely did it adopt the theory that one sovereign nation should remain aloof from wars waged by other sovereign nations, but it laid additional emphasis upon the theory by connecting with it the idea of nonentanglement. If the United States hoped to keep Europe from spreading to the American continent, it must keep out of Europe's wars and give no occasion for retaliation by European governments. Nonentanglement, the Monroe Doctrine, and neutrality spring from the same root. But effective neutrality demands the observance of duties as well as the assertion of rights; and the United States clearly saw this truth.

Under the 1794 Act, it forbade its citizens to accept commissions, to enlist for foreign service, to fit out American vessels for either belligerent, or to arrange any military expedition against a foreign power with which the United States was at peace. Later acts (1797, 1818, and 1838) tightened up the requirements. It was not an easy matter to enforce these measures; during the early and middle nineteenth century many armed men left the United States to take service in Cuba and Central America, and Spain had reason to complain that the American government was failing to observe its duties as a neutral. These difficulties of application, while not unimportant, were minor matters compared with the outstanding contribution made by the United States to the theory and practice of neutrality. For a long period it helped to limit the area of war and to assist in widening the scope of legitimate commerce.

Unfortunately, new forces were at work transforming the institution of war. It became increasingly difficult to separate war from nonwar materials, and the doctrine of contraband became more difficult to apply to the satisfaction of all parties. Nonmilitary factors came to exert a more decisive influence, and the greater the ramifications of war the greater were the losses to neutrals likely to be and the more their "rights" were likely to be sacrificed by either belligerent.[24]

The World War of 1914–1918 brought into sharp relief the serious clash between belligerent and neutral in modern times; it showed that any conflict was likely to develop in two directions— belligerent against belligerent arising out of irreconcilable differences, and belligerent against neutral arising out of the desire of the belligerent to shut off its enemy's trade as far as possible and the desire of the neutral to maintain its normal trade to the utmost limit. The more modern war develops the more is the neutral driven to assert his claims at the risk of war or to resign a great part of his commerce in order to avoid the risk of war.

How this arises is quite clear. During 1914–1918 Great Britain early extended the list of goods which it regarded as contraband. The United States protested, saying that international law had laid down a certain definite list which belligerents were not at liberty arbitrarily to alter. Great Britain replied that it had not signed the Declaration of London of 1909 and, in addition, claimed that, since modern science had caused many hitherto harmless articles to be used in the making of war materials, Great Britain was justified in interpreting contraband according to later developments. Thus the United States and Britain clashed over the question of the extent of contraband.

[24] See Philip C. Jessup, *American Neutrality and International Police* (World Peace Foundation, Boston, 1928).

By means of its naval power Britain applied an effective blockade, with disastrous results to neutral trade. Moreover, belligerents claimed the right of visiting and searching neutral vessels suspected of carrying contraband goods.[25]

Neutrals found their trade ruined in other ways. Under the doctrine of continuous voyage, the Allies seized vessels destined for neutral ports and placed upon the trader the burden of proving that his goods would not be transferred from the neutral country to an enemy power. Not only that. In 1915 Great Britain passed an act extending the principle of punishing persons attempting to trade with an enemy by drawing up a blacklist. American traders doing business with enemies of Britain might find themselves on this list; if so, they were liable to boycott by British firms even though they were engaged in legitimate neutral trade. The United States opposed this measure, saying that it was an arbitrary interference with neutral trade; Great Britain claimed that it was domestic legislation. When the United States entered the war, it adopted the very blacklist policy which it had denounced as a neutral.

The clashes between the United States and Britain were frequent, and, had it not been for the German submarine campaign, the controversy might have developed to most serious lengths. But Germany began a policy of unrestricted submarine warfare to offset the advantage which the Allies enjoyed by having control of the seas and because the Allies were gaining a great advantage by their interfering with neutral rights and by preventing non-contraband goods from reaching Germany. The military party, therefore, believed that it was necessary to blockade Britain effectively and thereby starve it out. Unfortunately for Germany the submarine campaign involved the lives and not merely the property of American citizens; this basic difference, in the opinion of the American historians Seymour[26] and Paxson, and that of Newton D. Baker, was sufficient to change the policy of the United States from one of verbally defending neutral rights against Great Britain to a condition of war with Germany. Walter Millis[27] and others, however, claimed that economic forces and not the question of loss of American lives drove the United States into the conflict.

[25] Clyde Eagleton, *International Government* (Ronald Press, 1932), p. 595.
[26] Charles Seymour, *American Neutrality, 1914–1917* (Yale University Press, 1935).
[27] Walter Millis, *The Road to War: America 1914–17* (Houghton Mifflin, 1935).

It is important to note that the Peace treaties did not settle one question concerning neutral rights, and that after the war no neutral power took action to submit its claims arising from violation of neutral rights to international arbitration. Indeed, in 1927 Secretary of State Kellogg, in correspondence with Great Britain, deliberately gave up any such attempt. Whatever the specific causes of America's entrance into the conflict, the basic fact was that belligerents and neutrals clashed because of the growing difficulty and ultimate impossibility of reconciling their interests after the war had reached a certain intensity.

The advent of the League of Nations created a new problem for the United States. If the world was now to organize against aggression, and war was a matter of concern to all the members of the League and not merely the exercise of the sovereign will of a state, if collective security was really to work, there would exist no place for neutrality within the League. When the United States refused to join Geneva and resumed its policy of isolationism, a serious question confronted the League of Nations in dealing with the problem of aggression. The American government might claim that the imposition of League sanctions did not create a state of war and that, therefore, there being a state of peace between the United States and the "aggressor," American commerce must not be molested. If it took the view that League sanctions meant a League war against the aggressor, it might still insist upon its neutral rights of trading with a belligerent within the limits laid down by international law. Could the League hope successfully to impose sanctions in the face of such a view? If the United States traded with the aggressor it would destroy the efficacy of a League blockade, and if the League combined to resist the United States' economic intercourse with the aggressor it might become embroiled in hostilities with the United States, which conceivably might go to war to defend its neutral rights against the League. Either course was open to grave objection. The fact remained that as long as the United States did not make it clear that it would not trade with an aggressor, the League as an instrument of preventing aggression was considerably weakened.

In 1928 the United States signed the Kellogg Pact renouncing war as an instrument of national policy. Many individuals and organizations believed that, even if a case could have been made for maintaining its traditional neutral rights in the face of League sanctions against an aggressor, the United States, now that it had signed the Kellogg Pact, could no longer insist upon the advantages of trading with a country which had violated the treaty to which the United States had attached its signature. Others believed that the country should be neutral to both parties, and should not discriminate against the alleged aggressor. A number of measures were introduced into the House of Representatives and the Senate which illustrated the conflict of views. In January 1928 Mr. Burton introduced a House resolution that the United States should prohibit the export of arms, munitions, and implements of war to any nation engaged in war with another nation; the President, when he recognized the existence of war, should proclaim a state of neutrality, and it would be unlawful except by consent of Congress to export arms to either belligerent. Here we find a new idea at work, i.e., that the United States give up its traditional right of trading with the belligerents in contraband goods, and by preventing this trade lessen the chances that the United States would become involved. Note that the Burton resolution made no distinction between the belligerents, aggressor or victim.

Senator Capper's resolution of February 1929 provided: that when the President announced that a country had violated the Kellogg Pact, it should be unlawful, unless otherwise provided by Congress or by proclamation of the President, to export to such country arms, munitions, implements of war, or other articles for war use; that nationals of the United States would not be protected by the government if they gave aid and comfort to the violator of the treaty; and that the President should negotiate with other signatories to the Pact to obtain their agreement that their nationals also would not be protected if they gave aid and comfort to the aggressor. The Korell House Resolution was along similar lines; the theory was that a country which had violated the Kellogg Pact had broken an agreement with the United States and could therefore not be justly entitled to claim the equal treatment given to both belligerents under the normal rules of neutrality. Mr. Stimson, before the House Committee on Foreign Affairs, claimed that if the League or other important body of states had agreed that one side or the other was the aggressor, the United States should participate in a general arms embargo, not only for practical reasons, but "to preserve their national dignity and standing as a peaceful nation."

On May 24, 1933, Mr. Norman Davis declared before the general commission of the disarmament conference at Geneva that the United States would be prepared, in the event of a breach or threat of breach of the Kellogg-Briand Pact, if certain disarmament steps were taken, to consult; and if a decision were taken by a conference of the powers in consultation determining the aggressor and if the United States independently agreed with that judgment, it would "undertake to refrain from any action and to withhold protection from its citizens if engaged in activities which would tend to defeat the collective effort which the States in consultation might have decided upon against the aggressor."

Until now the proposal to enable the President to declare an arms embargo against an aggressor had not attracted a great deal of public interest; but the government's declaration at Geneva aroused much controversy. Opponents alleged that the power to declare an embargo was almost equivalent to the power of declaring war, and that the executive should not be entrusted with the heavy responsibility of naming the aggressor in an international dispute. The Senate Committee on Foreign Relations added an amendment to Mr. Davis' statement to the effect that the President must place the embargo against all parties in a war and not merely single out the aggressor nation. Professor John Bassett Moore expressed the fear that if the resolution were passed, various groups would attempt to influence the President to make an unneutral application of the law against the nation which they disliked. Professor Borchard criticized the resolution as unconstitutional and dangerous because it gave the President power substantially to make treaties with foreign countries without the consent of the Senate and because to prohibit goods from going to one belligerent and not to another would be to violate neutrality; such discrimination would be an unfriendly and hostile act of the gravest character, and against a strong power "might very readily be a prelude to a war. It is, indeed, a warlike act, if not itself an act of war." The alternatives[28] thus seemed to be as given in twelve paragraphs following.

1. The United States might adopt a policy of complete isolation, withdrawing from all intercourse and thus avoiding any risk of a clash with the belligerent powers in a dispute over neutral rights. Such a course would be within its power. In practice it is doubtful whether the people would accept the sacrifices involved. In 1807 Jefferson adopted this policy in promoting the famous Embargo Acts—a magnificent experiment in pacifism, two writers have called it—but the result was failure. Many groups protested violently and even talked of secession because of the losses which

[28] See especially A. W. Dulles and H. F. Armstrong, *Can We Be Neutral?* (Harper & Bros., New York, 1936).

they sustained. Today the people desire to avoid being drawn into war but are not willing to give up their trading rights. Complete isolation undoubtedly would dislocate the economic life of the United States and perhaps produce economic crisis.

2. The United States might seek an international agreement for a very strict definition of neutral rights, or might itself decide what minimum concessions it will make to belligerent claims, or by agreement with other neutrals it might bring collective pressure to bear in the defense of neutral rights. All these policies are designed to preserve neutral rights; however, should a belligerent enlarge its list of contraband goods and interfere with the neutral trade, one of two things must result: either the neutrals, singly or jointly, must be strong enough to persuade the belligerents to back down; or they must fight for the defense of their rights, in which case, they cease to be neutrals. It is at least open to question whether the cost of enforcing so-called rights is not too great to be worth attempting.

3. The United States might forbid the shipment of war materials to both belligerents, each of which would therefore know that its enemy was not receiving instruments of war. To that degree the scope of possible disputes between neutrals and belligerents would be curtailed. But, should a belligerent power extend the list of contraband goods, the same problem would arise as was indicated above. The risks would be lessened but not eliminated. Moreover, it is a question of definition. Should oil and cotton, for example, be regarded as war materials? The National Munitions Board, set up under the 1935 Act, decided against including these two commodities. What will happen if belligerents include them?

4. On the assumption that the loans and credits which were extended to the Allies helped to drag the United States into the World War of 1914–1918, the nation could forbid a repetition of this development. Belligerents will then realize that they cannot hope to finance war with American help and, unless they can pay in cash, they will be unable to buy ordinary materials from the United States. The diminished trade, in turn, would lessen the chances of submarine attacks on American vessels and the endangering of American lives, and would make a war boom in industry less likely.

5. Some people urged the cash-and-carry policy, under which belligerents must take title to goods in this country and transport them in their own ships. This policy would undoubtedly eliminate controversies arising from submarine attacks on American shipping, but it would also deal a heavy blow to the shipping interests,

which would lose their carrying trade. It would not solve the problem of the United States' relations with neutral powers; if American ships sailed for neutral countries, they might still encounter belligerent submarines, and the problem would then emerge in another form. To go farther and put both the neutral and the belligerent trade of the United States on a cash-and-carry basis would amount to such an extensive embargo that the country would be unlikely to adopt it; and "those nationalistic elements of the population which now deny the importance of foreign trade would be among the first to cry out against an abandonment of lucrative neutral rights."[29]

6. The rapid growth of trade between the United States and Italy during the Ethiopian crisis—for example, the 600 per cent increase in oil exports to Italy in August and September, 1935, over the amount exported in the corresponding period of 1934— and the augmented sales of nonmetallic minerals and of materials, manufactures, machinery, vehicles, and chemicals led many people to advocate limiting trade in these materials to normal peace-time quotas. A belligerent, seeing the abnormal increase of trade between its rival and a neutral, might claim that by engaging in this trade the neutral has in reality violated its neutrality by giving more help to one side than to another; and it might attempt to redress the balance by submarine or other activities. While a normal quota would undoubtedly remove some difficulties and risks, it would involve much governmental machinery and be extremely difficult to apply. Complexity does not mean that the principle is unsound, and Assistant Secretary of State Moore suggested that to keep shipments down to normal would lessen controversies with belligerents, restrain war profiteering, and make possible a more effective neutrality.

7. Some experts, believing it unwise to attempt too intricate a policy and that shifting factors in warfare make any such attempt futile, advocated the principle of "trade and travel at your own risk." There is no reason, from this point of view, why American passengers and seamen who travel and work on belligerent ships should not do so at their own risk and why traders should expect national protection. The insurance companies have enabled traders to spread their risk, although admittedly at higher premiums. However, traders charge higher prices to cover their risks; and if private trading activities endanger the peace of a nation, the

[29] P. C. Jessup, *International Security* (Council on Foreign Relations, New York, 1935), p. 143.

safety of which can be guaranteed only by some sacrifice of private trade, there should be no question as to the right course. If the principle of "trade at your own risk" had been in operation in 1914, perhaps the United States would have been able to keep out of the conflict. One must not imagine the policy would be an absolute guaranty. If persistent submarine attacks against American vessels and repeated loss of American lives took place, it is possible that popular emotion would become so great as to demand war. Trading at your own risk, while lessening danger, does not eliminate it.

8. Charles Warren added other restrictive measures which would be necessary to keep the United States from being involved in controversies with belligerents. The government should (*a*) take over all high-power radio stations, probably forbid the sending of any secret code or cipher messages, and possibly even forbid any ships in United States ports or waters from using radio so as to avoid the possibility of their directing belligerent fleets at sea by wireless messages; (*b*) forbid the entrance into American waters of any belligerent armed merchant ship or at least treat these ships as belligerent auxiliary cruisers and force them to leave American waters within a given time after the outbreak of a war; (*c*) treat merchant ships chartered by belligerent governments as adjuncts to belligerent navies and intern them if they remain in American waters longer than the time permitted to armed belligerent vessels under international law; (*d*) forbid any ship from entering American ports which had been guilty of flying the American flag for purposes of deception; (*e*) strengthen the law so as to forbid any kind of foreign enlistment by citizens of the United States.[30]

9. Belligerent powers might be forced to pay for goods taken from American ships after the United States had confined its non-contraband shipments to neutral countries and to prewar quotas. Thus in the last war Great Britain could have purchased the whole of United States shipments to the Scandinavian countries and the Netherlands for a sum equal to the costs of from four to seven days of war—the amount of the trade was out of all proportion to the business created by British interference with it. "An agreement on these lines would have been a cheap price to pay for the avoidance of serious friction with the United States and possible alienation of that country. The statesmen of the two nations must

---

[30] Charles Warren, "Troubles of a Neutral," *Foreign Affairs,* April 1934.

be sorely lacking in common sense, ability, and vision, if they cannot devise some means of preventing the renewal of such a situation as arose, relative to neutral trade, during the World War."[31]

10. It was debated whether a neutrality law should be mandatory in character or not. Those who believed that the President had been subjected to a great amount of pressure by vested interests to force him to declare war against Germany in 1917 advocated a law which would prevent him from exercising much discretion. On the theory that clearly defined rules of law would tend to prevent actions which would involve the United States in war, the isolationists worked for an extensive act with specific provisions to cover as many eventualities as possible. Opponents of the mandatory principle claimed that because the President had more information on foreign affairs than members of Congress he must be trusted to make decisions in moments of crisis. They pointed out that a neutrality act which imposed unnecessary sacrifices upon the nation would soon become unpopular and lead to demands for its repeal or modification. The trade restrictions to be applied should depend on the kind of trade with belligerents which would be likely to cause controversy. Obviously, it would be foolish to impose rigid restraints in advance unless the danger were real; but the difficulty with an inelastic act to be applied to all circumstances was precisely that. Therefore, it should be left to the President to decide what goods, if any, should be placed upon the forbidden list. Isolationists countered by arguing that it would be better to run the risk of over-rigidity than to experience a repetition of 1917.

11. The Ludlow proposal represented an extreme manifestation of distrust of presidential discretion. Representative Ludlow proposed a constitutional amendment by which the United States could not be committed to war abroad without the approval of the people obtained by means of a national referendum. The main reasons were: (a) In a democratic country the supreme issue of peace or war should be decided by the people. No official, however high-minded or able, should have it within his power to send hundreds of thousands of people to their death. History shows that secret diplomacy has often permitted wars to start on trivial provocation. (b) The United States went into war in 1917 because of the financial interests, and a referendum would permit adequate discussion of these and other factors. (c) In 1917 the general public was much calmer and more in favor of staying out of war

[31] Charles Warren, "Congress and Neutrality," in *Neutrality and Collective Security*, p. 150.

than members of Congress, who were subjected to pressure from the Executive to vote in favor of war. (*d*) Members of Congress would be less open to pressure from war-mongers than the President.

Opponents of the Ludlow amendment assert that members of Congress are much more likely to be influenced by popular jingoism than the President, because of the biennial elections which place them at the more immediate mercy of the electorate. They deny that the President is more susceptible to propaganda than members of Congress. They fear that the necessity of holding a referendum on issues of war would tie the hands of the President and prevent him from exercising mediatorial functions in international disputes; and that, should a popular referendum be held and a fairly close vote ensue, the result would be added bitterness and division within the country, because opposite views would have been much more crystallized. The Ludlow sympathizers denied this last point, and claimed that the example of a great country taking the issue of war and peace into its hands would stimulate a like movement in other countries and strengthen the popular will for peace, because it would enable public opinion to become effective instead of remaining frustrated as now.

12. Finally, there were those like Secretary Stimson who claimed that neutrality was a secondary issue; that the main problem was to keep the United States out of war by helping to prevent war from arising. The United States had a fundamental interest in law and order throughout the world, and should therefore cooperate to maintain peace. But if it felt that it did not wish to participate in international organization, it should at least serve notice that it would adopt a neutrality act which would not permit supplies to reach the aggressor. The United States should not hinder the efforts of the League of Nations to stop aggression and should therefore pass an act giving the President power to lift the embargo from the nation which had been declared the victim of aggression. This type of proposal had been made from 1927 on, and had met with opposition on the grounds that collective security was an unsound principle, that the League of Nations was not a real League but was an instrument for maintaining the status quo of the defeated powers, and that the United States had no right to pass moral judgment upon the alleged aggressor in view of the injustices of the Peace treaties and the inadequate instrumentalities for the promotion of peaceful change.

The foregoing survey indicates the great division of opinion in the United States concerning the question of neutrality. The outbreak of the Italo-Ethiopian crisis led the country to take practical steps to meet a situation which seemed not unlikely to develop into a general European struggle. Out of the conflicting views reflected in public opinion and Congress alike came the 1935 Neutrality Act, which provided that when the President should decide that a state of war existed between two belligerents there should go into effect an embargo on the export of arms, ammunition, and implements of war. The President might also withdraw protection from United States citizens who traveled on belligerent ships, and might at his discretion extend the arms embargo to other states if they became involved in war.

When Congress met in January 1937 it realized that the Act did not apply to civil war, but only to war between "two or more foreign states." Consequently the government was unable to refuse licenses for the export of war materials to Spain, then in the throes of a conflict between the Loyalists and the forces of Franco. Hurriedly, on January 6, the House and the Senate adopted a joint resolution to prevent the export of arms and war munitions for "the use of either of the opposing forces of Spain." It was felt desirable to expand the particular prohibition into a general rule, especially as the existing neutrality law was to end May 1, 1937.

After considerable discussion, in which the House favored a greater degree of discretion for the President, the 1937 Neutrality Act was passed, providing that, when the President finds that a state of war exists between two or more foreign states, he shall issue a proclamation to this effect. Thereupon there are automatically prohibited (*a*) the export of arms and munitions and implements of war to belligerents, (*b*) the purchase or sale of securities of belligerents, (*c*) the solicitation or receipt of contributions on their behalf, (*d*) transport of implements of war in American vessels to belligerents, (*e*) travel by United States citizens on belligerent vessels, and (*f*) arming of United States vessels. In addition the President has authority to prohibit transport of any commodity on United States vessels to a belligerent, the export of any goods to a belligerent until "all right, title, and interest" have been transferred to a foreign government (this "cash and carry" provision was limited to two years), the use of the ports of the United States as bases of supply for belligerent ships, and the use of these ports by submarines and armed ships.

A comparison of the 1935 and 1937 acts shows that the sentiment of the American people had moved further toward isolation in the event of a foreign war. The 1935 act dealt only with arms, ammunition, and implements of war; the 1937 act might be extended at the discretion of the President to other commodities. Under the 1935 act the President might withdraw protection from American citizens traveling on belligerent ships; the 1937 act specifically forbade such travel except under emergency conditions. The 1935 act imposed no restrictions on financial transactions with belligerents; the 1937 act prohibited loans and credits except those necessary for normal commerce. The 1935 act provided that the President *might* extend the arms embargo to other states when they became involved in warfare; the 1937 act made it imperative for him to do so.

Undoubtedly the acts did diminish the risks of war for the United States, by reducing the possibilities of contact between neutral and belligerent. They were based upon the principle of neutrality and abstention from certain types of trade. This was in contrast to the prewar neutrality, which was based upon the principle of insistence upon neutral rights. Instead of following Jefferson's theory that war should be limited to the greatest extent consistent with normal neutral trade, the acts accepted the view that neutral commerce should be reduced to the greatest possible extent in order to avoid a clash with belligerents in an age of almost totalitarian warfare. Nevertheless, the attempt to legislate the country out of war ran into many difficulties:

1. In the view of some critics the acts were inconsistent with several of the multilateral treaties signed with the South and Central American states in the 1923, 1928, 1929, 1933, and 1936 conferences, which provided that the American states would attempt to discourage aggression and would consult with a view to preserving peace. The neutrality acts made no distinction between aggressor and victim; therefore they might be considered as having weakened the Pan-American peace machinery.

2. If put into effect the neutrality acts would apply to members of the League of Nations applying sanctions against an aggressor and, therefore, might be construed as weakening the League organization. However, it was argued that the League had no prospect of imposing sanctions in the near future, but even so fifty nations applying sanctions against one or two Covenant breakers would suffer far less from an embargo placed by the United States upon arms than would the aggressor.

3. Although the 1937 act provided for embargoes on loans, it excepted short-term credits for normal commerce. But the experi-

ence of 1914–1918 showed that it might be difficult to withstand pressure for the renewal and extension of these loans and continued renewal might be the equivalent of loans; moreover the purpose of the clause could be defeated by extending loans and exporting arms to neutrals, who, in turn, might lend to belligerents.

4. If countries likely to be involved in war could not obtain raw materials and other materials in war time, they might divert their peace trade to other channels in an attempt to build up supplies and regular channels in case of national emergency and, in that event, Mr. Hull's trade policy would be injured.

5. The acts, to some extent, took the control of foreign policy out of the hands of the United States; for, if two countries began fighting without a formal declaration of war, either one could, at a later time, declare war and by that action compel the President to bring the neutrality act into effect, at a time most advantageous to itself.

6. Munition-makers who would be unable to supply belligerents with arms during a foreign war might be encouraged to transfer their plants to Canada; such an action would reduce the amount of capital and labor employed in the United States, even though it would lessen war-time risks.

7. Critics claimed that it was unwise to legislate in times of mental calm for periods of intensive emotional stress; and certainly the experience of the Spanish civil war gave some ground for such criticism. Senator Nye, who vehemently preached against foreign entanglements, expressed strong opinions against Franco's "rebels" and criticized the application of the neutrality act in the case of Spain on the ground that it injured Loyalists more than it injured Franco.

8. Armstrong and Dulles asked whether, if the act really did lessen the risk for the United States, all provisions should not be put on a cash-and-carry basis. They urged this course because they believed that the trade in arms could not really be separated from trade in other materials useful for war, and that to substitute a cash-and-carry policy for a mandatory embargo upon arms traffic was more logical.[32] This view was shared by Mr. Hull, who on May 27, 1939, proposed the abolition of Section 1 of the 1937 Neutrality Act so as to permit the sale of arms on a cash-and-carry basis.

9. Dulles and Armstrong criticized Congress for its distrust

[32] H. F. Armstrong and A. W. Dulles, "Legislating Peace," *Foreign Affairs,* October 1938.

of "every move which implies positive co-operation for peace." This distrust, they believed, arose from an inability to appreciate the real position of the United States in the modern world. They pointed out that it is the most powerful single nation, and could, if it expressed its position "clearly and resolutely," exercise incalculable influence in preserving peace. To do this, it would not have to take joint action with other powers; it could take independent yet powerful action—not for sentimental and vaguely idealistic reasons but actually on behalf of American vital interests, which were endangered by the spread of lawlessness throughout the world.

The years which followed 1933 bore witness to the essential uncertainty of United States policy. It tried to avoid political entanglements on the one hand and yet could not keep out of world politics. Frequently the President and the Secretary of State spoke out strongly against aggression and asserted the sanctity of international treaties and the need of law and order, but almost in the same breath they were at pains to emphasize that the United States would not use its forces to help police the world. Sometimes official statements went in the direction of suggesting action against the aggressor, as when President Roosevelt in his Chicago speech of October 1937 talked of quarantining the aggressor; but almost immediately, because of the pressure of public opinion, the administration reverted to the idea of strict neutrality, and the United States refrained from taking an active lead against Japan at the Brussels Conference in November. In 1936 at Buenos Aires the President attempted to form a bloc of neutral American powers who would refuse to trade with warring nations in Europe; but he and Mr. Hull were unsuccessful in their efforts.

The United States attempted to maintain a middle course. Mr. Hull in March 1938 again stated that "we are fully determined to avoid the extremes whether of internationalism or of isolationism"; the former would mean "undesirable political involvements," and the United States would not join in "policing the world." It would not retire from the Far East, for it would be absurd for it to stand for international law and the sanctity of treaties in that area and yet surrender those principles in the other half of the world. Hull denounced the seclusionist viewpoint and asserted that the government would participate in international, scientific, technical, and other conferences, would push its reciprocal trade program, but would not become involved in political or policing efforts. The United States would co-operate in the tasks of peace but would fight not to prevent war in general but only if its own vital interests were affected.

In September 1938 President Roosevelt in an appeal to Hitler and Mussolini reminded them of their solemn obligations under the Kellogg-Briand Pact to solve controversies only by pacific methods and urged upon the Fuehrer that "a general war is as unnecessary as it is unjustifiable"; nevertheless he stressed that the United States had no political involvements in Europe and would assume no obligations.

In November 1938 the United States recalled its ambassador from Germany as a protest against the shocking treatment meted out to the Jewish people there; and in March 1939, after the annexation of Czechoslovakia by Germany, it imposed a further 25 per cent duty on German imports. Thus it followed a policy of moral appeal, combined with an assertion of political non-entanglement, and a policy of penalties imposed as protest after certain things had been done. It has been well suggested that merely to protest to Germany against the treatment of the Jews and to reiterate verbally certain principles which are derided by dictator countries only serves to aggravate sentiment and does no good. On the other hand, defenders of the Administration's policy claim that the persistent devotion to the principles of international law, such as was expressed by Mr. Hull in July 1937, has a great value even though these cannot be implemented in practice during days of dark uncertainty—better uphold the ideal, even though practice falls short, than allow principles to be overthrown without protest.

In April 1939 Secretary Hull asserted that the forcible and violent seizure of Albania was unquestionably an additional threat to the peace of the world and would destroy confidence and undermine economic stability everywhere. On April 14, 1939, when rumors were abroad that Hitler intended to attack another small country after absorbing Czechoslovakia, President Roosevelt sent a remarkable communication to Hitler and Mussolini. He pointed out that four independent nations had had their independence terminated, and that it was desirable to have from Germany and Italy an assurance that their armed forces would not attack or invade thirty nations which he named one by one, and suggested that they guarantee an assured period of nonaggression for at least ten years, or even for a quarter of a century. In return, he promised to call international conferences to deal with the prob-

lem of the crushing burden of armaments and of economic relations. Unfortunately, Roosevelt, while asking for specific
commitments, offered in return no more than a promise of international discussion; and it was easy for Hitler to point out the
failures of conferences within the last ten years to effect any
substantial improvement and to sidetrack the essential issues.

Anarchy increasingly engulfed Europe, and opinion in the
United States expressed itself in favor of neutrality as long as
Britain and France followed an appeasement policy. When once
they began to arm against Germany the Administration and
later Congress modified their policy in order to supply the democracies with arms with which to fight the dictatorships. The
middle course based upon the assumption that neutral powers in
the twentieth century still could stand aloof and exercise a marked
influence upon the course of events between potential or actual
belligerent powers was still open to question. Would the United
States later experience the bitter proof, already brought home to
Great Britain and France, that in a closely knit world a rapid
succession of piecemeal attacks against small and apparently distant nations would result in a cumulative strength to the aggressor
so great as to threaten all neutrals?

After the outbreak of the European War in September 1939,
American opinion underwent a remarkable change. Sympathy
for Britain and France led to demands for co-operating with
democratic states as far as possible. A renewed emphasis was
placed upon national rights and interests and the Administration,
even before war had broken out, urged a modification of the
Neutrality Act by a repeal of the Arms Embargo, which Mr.
Hull suggested was illogical and played into the hands of the
aggressor states and against the peace-loving nations. The President announced that American territorial waters extended as far
as the interest of the United States required, and Secretary Hull
proclaimed that this country had not abandoned any of its rights
as a neutral under international law. After considerable debate
Congress passed a revised neutrality law which repealed the Arms
Embargo and placed all materials on a cash-and-carry basis but
gave to the President relatively little discretion.

The new act was based upon the assumption that, by permitting Britain and France to have access to the American market,
even under the limitations of the Neutrality Act, they would be
able to defeat Germany. By July 1940 this assumption was shown
to be highly doubtful, and the rapidity of German conquests led

the United States to think more in terms of security and of aiding democracy, hoping, of course, that these two objectives might be attained within the former framework of neutrality. The plea that American security was bound up with Germany's defeat led to such remarkable steps as the Lease-Lend Act, the extension of jurisdiction over the three-hundred-mile ocean area, the proclamation that Greenland and Iceland came within the scope of the Monroe Doctrine, openly expressed governmental views on the international situation and the assurance of the President on May 27, 1941, that military supplies must, can, and will reach Britain, his assertion that this country will interpret its own needs of preventive measures of defense, and his proclamation of an unlimited national emergency.

American neutrality has failed primarily because war under modern conditions has become so international in character and so comprehensive in method that the old simple formulas of contraband and noncontraband, of neutral and belligerent rights, have completely failed to describe the situation. The smaller nations have succumbed to the piecemeal penetrating tactics of a strong, efficient, and determined power, and no democracy, however strong and powerful, can long witness such tactics and still remain indifferent to them.

PRIVATE BOYCOTTS

The failure of governments to arrest the forces of aggression led to a widespread movement in favor of private boycotts against Japan and Germany. Private organizations, including trade unions, co-operatives, peace societies, employers, and women's organizations in almost twenty countries called upon their members to refrain from buying goods which would provide the aggressor with the foreign exchange necessary to purchase munitions of war and other goods. The movement was essentially a voluntary one of private individuals, unconnected with governmental action. It arose from the conviction that, whether or not the failure of governments was due to legitimate causes, the moral conscience of mankind could not stand aloof and watch countries become invaded and innocent people suffer in violation of treaties providing for the peaceful settlement of international disputes.

In so far as the private action followed the third-party judgment provided for by treaties, it was an affirmation of the sanctity of international engagements and a challenge to governments to live up to their commitments. Although foreign policy is sup-

posed to remain in the hands of official authorities, the people
have a strong moral case in taking action against a government
which has been declared an aggressor by recognized international
methods.

Proponents of the private boycott urged that it was immoral
for countries to condemn an aggressor and at the same time to
supply it with arms and munitions and to buy from it other materials and thereby enable it to continue the war. They claimed
that in the case of Japan the boycott would be peculiarly effective
because Japan depends upon foreign supplies for its nickel, tin,
rubber, cotton, wool, and most of its oil, pig iron, and lead. The
United States and the British Empire purchase more than 40
per cent of Japanese exports; and a general boycott by the citizens of these two countries would seriously disrupt Japan's economy. Because the United States purchases all of its raw silk
from Japan, amounting to one hundred million dollars a year,
and since Japan exports only a few commodities, the boycott
would be relatively easy to organize. The boycott, while damag-
ing Japanese trade, would not deprive her civilian population of
foodstuffs, over 90 per cent of which are grown at home or
within the Empire. Thus a boycott, while inflicting some suffering upon Japan, would not produce suffering comparable to that
inflicted upon the Chinese by the Japanese military invasion.
Moreover, it savors of hypocrisy to raise a few hundred thousand
dollars for Chinese relief and at the same time to provide Japan
millions of dollars' worth of scrap iron and other materials which
make possible the infliction of such terrible damage.

Opponents of the private boycott urge that such action takes
the conduct of foreign affairs away from the government and
places it in the hands of private organizations, which do not have
the responsibility of conducting foreign policy in all its complicated relations. And unless public opinion is very careful it may
be led away along bypaths and indiscriminately indulge its emotions; it may lead to further misunderstanding and hostility and
conceivably produce a permanent or a long-term enmity and even
induce war. Proponents of the boycott deny that Japan, for example, would dare run the risk of indulging in retaliation against
this country and American interests in China, because it already
has its hands full. Opponents also claim that the boycott could
not act quickly enough, even if adopted by the majority of private
individuals in a dozen countries, to force Japan or any other
country to cease fighting. Aggressor-minded governments have

surplus stocks in hand and do not undertake a war unless they are certain of being able to carry on for an extended period. Also, a private boycott would seriously affect the industries within the boycotting country which have relations with the aggressor nation. To this charge it can be replied that, whereas war penalizes many industries in neutral countries, a private boycott, by selecting the industries ministering to the war activities, would more effectively threaten the success of a war campaign. To the argument that a boycott may assist to derange world currents of trade the answer is made that war tends to do this very thing, and it is better to capitalize necessary and calculable derangement in order to serve organized efforts against aggression.

The arguments on both sides have considerable force; but it may be suggested that one most important consideration is that the private boycott comes too late in the day. Energy should be exerted earlier to build up international organization to such a point that national aggression is rendered impossible. To wait until a war is declared and then expend emotion and idealism seems like waiting until the horse has escaped before locking the stable door. Private boycotts bear witness to the persistence of the ideal of human justice in an age of international anarchy, but their very necessity shows the desperate condition into which organized society has fallen. If they can impress governments with the determined and deep and ceaseless desire of people for international law and order, they may prove to be a starting point for a renewed effort toward adequate international organization. But to be effective they must be merely a foretaste of actions to come; they can never hope by themselves to be a sufficient instrument for lasting peace. If enthusiasts for the private boycott do not see the larger issues of comprehensive organization to prevent war, but are satisfied to make passionate protests after wars have started, they will attack only the manifestations and not the causes of war.

PACIFISM

In opposition to all these plans for obtaining security which are based upon the utilization of force, either by national governments or by some form of collective international or supernational organization, the pacifist urges that security and peace are better obtained by the practice of nonviolence. His belief may be derived from religious or philosophic sources, or from an analysis of the failure of both power politics and collective security as hitherto practiced to bring stability to the world.

From Christian teaching he learns, "Thou shalt not kill," and that Christ commanded Peter to put up the sword, saying that they that take the sword shall perish by the sword. To pacifists the example of Jesus is indisputably clear, for He who might have called upon legions of angels to help Him refused to do so and went to the Cross in order to demonstrate His ideals and love for men. The Jains in India believe that no life at all should be taken, and Hindus carry the principle of nonviolence to the point of refusing to kill animals for food.

Some pacifists use a philosophic or even a biological argument, saying that the survival of a species depends upon its adaptability to new conditions and that the dinosaur succumbed to other forms of life less gigantic than his own because the new forms developed along directions other than mere physical size. Now mankind too is threatened with extinction unless it can rise above the purely inventive and intellectual, and can live by a principle loftier and more embracing than that of power gained through the discoveries of science. Love is therefore not a mere indulgence in vague sentimentality; it is an active principle of finding greater truths which may embrace and include the lesser truths discovered by the intellect. It develops a creative ability denied to the merely wise, and the greater the development of mechanism the greater must be the development of restraint based upon love; otherwise man's discoveries will be turned against him, and the machine which he has created will destroy him.

Undoubtedly the pacifist who advocates his philosophy is right when he asserts that wars are a clumsy and inefficient means of settling disputes, that the World War of 1914–1918 especially left infinitely more problems unsolved than existed before it began— that war is no solution.

There is something grand and sublime in the highest teachings of pacifism. They show that it is not the fear of death but the horror of taking life which is its foundation. It is not a cowardly or self-seeking creed. It is not a negative thing but is a living faith in the power of love and nonviolence.

Another type of pacifist argues that, whereas the people profoundly desire peace, government leaders, because they lack trust in other governments, build up armaments and prepare for war. Finally the pacifist can point to outstanding examples of those who through their love of peace have changed the destinies of nations and built the foundations of a better life. Jesus is one outstanding example of ancient history. Gandhi, so his followers claim, has altered the whole political consciousness of India and England's relation to that land by his preaching and practice of nonviolence. William Penn dealt with the Indians kindly and refused to use force against them.[33] These are only three of dozens of examples which pacifists might quote.

The critics of these positions may well pay tribute to the goodness and nobility of the ideal they reflect and the inspiring lives led by the great exponents of pacifism, even though they doubt whether what has worked on many occasions and in individual cases can prove a consistent and universal guide for the complicated affairs of millions of people in their everyday life. The pacifist ideal assumes that man is fundamentally a spiritual being, to whom lofty spiritual ideals will ultimately appeal and convert to active goodness. Nevertheless, many thoughtful people cannot help believing that man is also a biological being, and that to ignore certain deep-seated tendencies is to refuse to see human beings as they really are. Even if one claims that man's quarrelsome and fighting behavior comes not from unalterable instincts but from conditioned behavior, or even from the existence of sin, there is, they assert, no clear reason why methods of prevention should not be adopted so as to stop criminals and aggressors, liars and cheats, from having uninterrupted freedom to do damage to other people. To those who say that force should not be used, the answer might well be that in a sense all life involves some kind of force or power. To move stones and build houses or to drive automobiles means to channelize human energy. The important question is for what purpose the power is used. If one person misuses his energy so as to endanger others, may it not be right to restrain him? If he attempts to murder another person, should not force be exerted to stop him? If he runs amuck and kills three or four in a crowd, and is liable to murder a dozen more, is it not wiser to kill him rather than to let twelve others die? If we are consistent in renouncing force, we shall have to forego the police force within nations, and few people would be prepared to support this step. The pacifist criticism of collective security on the ground that a collective use of force against an aggressor is essentially the same thing as war leads logically to the denial of police activity.

It is true that law by its very nature is unlikely to touch the

---

[33] Although Penn advocated collective sanctions against a war-making government.

deepest motives of human life, and that beyond a certain point man cannot be legislated into goodness. But laws are rules of behavior which human experience has found to be necessary and wise. Although laws may, and often do, inflict hardship and restraint upon many, nevertheless, in a world of almost bewildering social complexity, they are essential and must be enforced. Once more, the question is how to harness force to the widest and most constructive human ends. Ideally speaking there is no reason why force may not be used as an ally to noble purposes; the more universal the acceptance of justice, the less crude will be the type of force required to save them from danger.

The pacifist believes that the example of tolerance and love will serve to convince the wrongdoer and even the criminal of his unworthy behavior and persuade him to alter his ways, that one may win an enemy by nonresistant goodness, and that if the Allies after 1918 had shown more restraint and justice there may not have been a Nazi Germany today. To no small degree these ideas may be true. But as things stand, it is very doubtful whether even the highest type of pacifism would not be interpreted by the military-minded leaders of the Reich as weakness and decadence; for these men have frequently proclaimed their contempt for what they think is the nonheroic and effeminate nature of pacifism. They have control over radio and press and it is doubtful how far the German people as a whole could profit from the example of even a widespread pacifism in other lands, since their leaders would probably use propaganda methods to hide or distort the real situation.

No one can prove whether or not, if all people of a country laid down their arms and offered no resistance to an invader but met him in love and charity, the latter would be inspired to throw away his arms and embrace a similar lofty ideal. Nor is it altogether clear that it is the people who desire peace and that governments are the agencies that lead the masses to war. There are many examples to show that diplomats and governments would have gone farther toward the peaceful solution of disputes had they been permitted so to do. There are also many examples of governments and diplomats plotting and scheming to bring about war for the sake of attaining certain economic, political, and cultural objectives. Millions of signatures of ordinary people poured into Geneva at the opening of the disarmament conference in 1932; hundreds of peace societies, League of Nations Unions, fellowships of reconciliation, student-movement groups, and many other organizations exist for the promotion of peace; and to this degree it is true that the people wish peace. On the other hand, millions of people who wish for peace wish also for things which are inconsistent with peace. And it seems impossible to draw a generalization which will hold true for all governments and all peoples.

It may well be that mankind will perish if it cannot exercise restraint in the use of the great forces unharnessed by science. But one may ask whether or not the only alternative to unrestrained force is the non-use of force, and whether or not a wider political community which can control national force is logically ruled out and in practice unattainable. It would seem that if mankind is unwilling or unable to harness force in the service of the larger community, it is not likely to renounce it altogether. If it cannot do the lesser, it will probably not do the greater.

Paradoxical as it may seem at first sight, it may be true that the answer lies in neither force nor pacifism, but in a sound combination of both. Undoubtedly more of the pacifist temper, which would go to great lengths to avoid inflicting injury and injustice, would benefit the world today. There is too much quarrelsomeness abroad, making the peaceful solution of disputes almost impossible. But, granting the need of a widespread spiritual and moral change in individuals, the question of law still remains. Ideals and their application are subject to many changes of mood and interpretation. Over nineteen hundred years of Christianity as an ideal have shown that, whatever it might accomplish if universally practiced, it has not been accepted sufficiently to enable society to dispense with law and order. Unless one deals in absolutes (and one's conception of an absolute may be a very faulty affair), he may have to choose between the lesser of two evils rather than between adulterated wickedness on the one side and untarnished purity on the other. To inject more charity and more living goodness into legal forms is a major task; to work toward the minimization of armaments and other forms of coercion is desirable; but to erect force and peace into two incompatible elements may be an error of the greatest magnitude. A more pacific temper, a sounder system of law, and a wider set of political institutions able to enforce order should not be impossible to combine.

TOWARD FEDERATION?

The question whether or not the League of Nations and sanctions are sound in principle remains to be discussed. Ever since the adoption of the League Covenant, their philosophic basis, as well as the practicability of their application, have divided individuals and groups into opposing camps. Many people confuse sanctions with the mere application of force; but if we remember that the word means "an authorized enforcement of legal obligations," we shall be saved from one serious error. The problem then is who shall define and enforce legal obligations—a self-interested state? a group of self-interested states? a community of states? or an international federal unit applying the judgment of a third party?

Discussion usually centers on collective sanctions applied by League members under Article 16 of the Covenant. Those who favor sanctions say that history shows law to have been respected only when it has been supported by force, that it is foolish to rely upon mere voluntary obedience to international law. Pacifists who oppose the use of force (although many of them accept the policeman) and nationalists who dislike international organization and prefer national strength agree on this issue. Both deny that there is any analogy between enforcement of law within the state and enforcement of international law by international coercion of sovereign states. To a considerable degree the point is well taken. But to argue that sanctions are merely another kind of war against a state by a number of states, other scholars urge, is clearly an error. There is a world of difference between force placed at the disposal of a third-party judgment and force as an instrument of national aggression; in the one case the end sought is social justice, in the other, national aggrandizement is the objective. True, the more successful war is, the more a nation is likely to engage in war; but the more successful sanctions are in restraining aggression, the less need there will be for sanctions in the future. It is also true that there may be an external resemblance between war and sanctions, just as there may be an external resemblance between a policeman and the courts, who take life in the service of law, and a robber who shoots his victim; but the difference of purpose entirely separates one action from the other.

The principles are clear enough; but in their application we meet with further objections. Some say that it is impossible to enforce sanctions against a great power. But surely this objection has little validity. If it is possible for one alliance to defeat another alliance, it should be possible for the combined forces of a League to prevent aggression on the part of one great power. Obviously one power against fifty can have no hope of victory. What critics often mean to say, although they do not say it, is that the League members will not or do not want to apply sanctions honestly and effectively against an aggressor; but this is a very different question.

Again, it is no final criticism to say that nations will support sanctions from motives of self-interest. During the Ethiopian crisis, many people accused Great Britain of supporting sanctions for selfish purposes, and in no small measure the charge may have been justified; but we all support the law from a mixture of motives, and in the early days of a new system, it is to be expected that self-interest will be much to the fore. Undoubtedly, in the rise of the national state a strong feudal lord often invoked the ideal of national unity as a cloak for his own self-interest; but, as law and order extended over a wider area and the importance of general welfare increased, the scope of self-interested action was correspondingly diminished; and in the development of international organization we may expect the same general evolution to take place.

Another variant of the same charge is that sanctions are merely a device of the "haves" to keep what they have from the "have nots," an instrument to perpetuate the status quo. Within the national community there is a similar division of interests, and groups struggle to gain control of the national legislature largely to serve their own as well as the national interest. But the degree of national unity is measured by the extent to which the different groups will subordinate group interest to general welfare. So in international affairs sanctions undoubtedly will be supported by certain states more enthusiastically if they minister to the immediate interests of those states. Without question, in the early stages of the League, national interests have played a disproportionately heavy part.

Yet to say that the whole question is merely one of maintaining the status quo is to ignore facts. The two countries which dealt the heaviest blows to the League between 1931 and 1936 by overt acts were Japan and Italy. Both of them, allegedly "have not" powers, were offered substantial changes by the League of Nations, the one in Manchuria and the other in Ethiopia. They rejected the proposals, not because the League did not propose change, but because the changes did not go far enough. Thus, unless we are prepared to say that any "have not" nation should be able to get just what it asks for, and unless we deny that a third-party judgment is a fair way of deciding upon peaceful change (in case the two disputing parties cannot agree), we must admit that international organization does allow the possibility of change. True, the change may not be fast enough; but at present (1941) it may be that what is required is a less rapid rate of change and that more stability rather than less is desirable in international politics! Nor can it be asserted that only the "have" powers favored sanctions. The truth is that Great Britain and France, so-called "have" countries, made little genuine effort to apply sanctions against Italy. It was the small countries (many of them "have nots") which were the most enthusiastic upholders of the principle. To identify the "haves" with the sanction-supporting powers does not square with the evidence.

Some object to the application of sanctions because they accept Edmund Burke's aphorism that it is impossible to indict a whole people, and that many innocent people will suffer in the application of sanctions against an aggressor government. But many innocent people (in the country which is attacked) likewise suffer as a result of unrestrained aggression and thus, in facing the problem of preventing or permitting war, one must choose between evils. Unless a determined and successful application of sanctions will discourage further aggression, the suffering of innocent people living within an aggressor country will be less than the suffering of innocent people living in a country attacked by the aggressor, particularly if aggression multiplies in a lawless world. It may well be that we need to undertake further study on police action, both national and international; but at present it is not easy to avoid treating nations as units when it comes to war even though there may be many people within the nation who do not want war.

We have seen in the discussion of slavery that in the middle of the nineteenth century many British people asked why British lives should be lost in enforcing standards of civilized conduct upon the slave traders in the African waters. Today similar questions are asked: Why should one country send troops or make other sacrifices when its own immediate interests are not threatened? Why should American lives be jeopardized in enforcing peace in Europe or English lives jeopardized in stopping German aggression in Austria or Czechoslovakia? The answer to this question is not easy, because what seems not to be an immediate interest today may become an immediate interest tomorrow. To the average Englishman there seemed to be little connection between his interests and preserving China against Japanese aggression in 1931. He saw no immediate British interest threatened when Italy invaded Ethiopia in 1935, or when Germany seized Austria and Czechoslovakia, or when Italy took Albania, or when Italy and

Germany intervened in Spain. Today we realize that the loosening
of foundations of orderly procedure in 1931 did threaten British
security, even though not immediately. But so rapid are the developments of the modern world, owing to its interlocked character, that the merely remote interests of 1931 became immediate
and even urgent interests in 1939. A wise precaution in ample time
may well serve an immediate self-interest.

AN INTERNATIONAL POLICE POWER AND AN INTERNATIONAL EQUITY TRIBUNAL

The principle of collective security had to confront a stubborn
fact, namely, that under Article 16 of the Covenant the League
Council could only "advise" what military sanctions were to be
applied. It rested with the member states individually to decide
whether or not they would accept the Council's recommendation.
Clearly a law-enforcing agency which is at the mercy of units free
to help enforce a decision or not according to their pleasure is an
unsound one, because the states will be more than tempted to apply
sanctions only when and in so far as they coincide with what they
believe to be their immediate interest. Therefore they will be less
likely to consider the essential justice of the case than the effect of
proposed sanctions upon their own political power.[34]

Because national sovereignty was not seriously challenged in
the League it appeared that collective security did not greatly differ from the old alliance system. League members still trusted
primarily to their national forces, and the more they relied upon
themselves the more they moved away from the fundamental requirements of genuine international security. Moreover, each of
them was able to justify its rearmament program, saying that it
was "in defense of loyalty to the League."

These considerations led the New Commonwealth Institute to
the judgment that security can come only when the world is willing to establish two important organizations—an international
police force and an equity tribunal. The group led by Lord Davies
claims that there can be no rapidity of preventive action while
world society depends upon separate and independent national
forces. Only a supra-national force which can be brought into
action quickly against an aggressor can prevent the type of thing
which happened in Manchuria and in Ethiopia.

[34] See Introduction to C. van Vollenhoven, *The Law of Peace* (Macmillan
& Co., London, 1936), pp. xi–xii.

But why an equity tribunal? For the simple reason that international law has accepted the fruits of conquest. If Hitler asks for the return of the German colonies, he is told that according to international law Germany gave up those colonies and that the Treaty of Versailles must be held sacred. It follows that there may be a great gap between international law and international justice; but until there is international justice there can be no hope of international peace. It follows, therefore, that until international disputes are solved along the lines of equity rather than of legality, especially a legality based upon conquest, we must expect a continuation of strife.

Undoubtedly until international society can command more force at the disposal of law and command it more rapidly than governments which would make war, there can be no guaranty of stability. Without doubt, too, there must be provision for change. The question arises as to whether an international force is desirable and feasible. The history of the Disarmament Conference would suggest that the ideal, though difficult, is not impossible and that international society will not find stability or security until the modern state gives up its armies and navies and air forces.

Whether or not an equity tribunal is sound in principle is also open to question. By what rules would such a tribunal be guided? Would it have power to alter boundary lines, modify tariffs, dispose of colonies, or take any other major step to remove the fundamental causes of war? If the world ever reaches the condition of being willing to hand over to international organization powers of this nature, it will be ready to go much farther and entrust these things to more representative and widespread institutions. The Lytton Commission made recommendations along the lines that one imagines an equity tribunal might have followed; but other institutions will be required, and it seems correct to point out that the complexities of international change will require more representative and diversified organs than the equity tribunal envisioned by the New Commonwealth group. Carr well writes that equity tribunals must base their decisions on well-defined political presumptions if they are not to be capricious. Within national communities such presumptions may exist: in international society they do not. There is no political agreement even of the vaguest kind as to what equity and common sense mean in relation to such questions as Britain's interest in Egypt, the problem of Danzig, etc. Carr adds that "no responsible tribunal cares to commit itself on any important issue of an authoritative pronouncement as to what is 'equitable' or 'just' in international relations."[35] The problem will involve legislative action rather than action by such tribunal. But who will be the legislators? Representatives of sovereign nations, or of regional or world units of government? The New Commonwealth has now accepted the logic of the situation and has come out in favor of federation as a necessary condition of world peace.

FEDERATION PROPOSALS

Much of mankind's judgment upon the future form of society will depend upon whether it believes that we have or that we have not reached a turning point in world history comparable in significance to the breakdown of the Roman Empire, or the emergence of the modern state system at the end of the Middle Ages, or the foundation of the American federal form of government replacing the system established by the Articles of Confederation. If we accept the principle that political institutions are primarily made for men, and not men for political institutions, we must fearlessly face the question whether or not the sovereign state has already overlived its usefulness. The evidence brought forward in this volume seems to point conclusively to the fact that it can no longer defend itself or feed itself or keep itself in health or be an extensive agency of cultural and religious excellence.

Without question, new political institutions of a more comprehensive character are required, and the failure of international cooperation to overcome the struggles of the balance-of-power system suggests that the power system can be remedied only by being absorbed by something more adequate to human needs. This something an increasing number of scholars, statesmen, religious leaders, industrial and labor representatives, and average citizens believe must be nothing less than federalism. It will be impossible to refer here to the many plans and the large number of writers. All that can be done is to suggest the main lines of thought and the bases of the proposals.

One may ask if a federal form of government can evolve out of what remains of the League of Nations, if the League's organization can be adapted to the new requirements, or if the League idea must be rejected and a constitution for the world, or for continents, be adopted *de novo*. But the line of division among these different views is not hard and fast. The principle is clear: the machin-

[35] E. H. Carr, *The Twenty Years' Crisis, 1919–1939*, pp. 262–63.

ery will have to be worked out by widely diffused and energetic thought and action. It is appropriate to examine a few of the outstanding and more representative specific proposals.

FROM THE LEAGUE TO FEDERALISM

Oscar Newfang[36] notes that a successful government guarantees security and peace, maintains order, keeps the area of unrestricted trade free and open, and promotes social welfare. Tested by these standards both the League of Nations and its member states have failed. International conferences have not been able to prevent a staggering increase in armaments and a catastrophic breakdown in currency standards and trade. Yet have the sovereign states by their own efforts done any better? Their attempts to gain security, political and economic, by building up their own national military strength and by adopting economic autarchy have led to increased confusion, to war and to anarchy. The League of Nations failed because the member states insisted upon retaining their sovereignty. The Disarmament Conference failed; collective security broke down because the sovereign states could not or would not co-operate quickly enough; consultation consumed too much time; and the great powers would not submit their quarrels to the League. Nor would they accept a compulsory jurisdiction for the Permanent Court. The League was unable to reconsider treaties which had become inapplicable to present conditions. The Covenant under certain circumstances recognized the existence of legal war. The unanimity rule made the League cumbrous and unworkable. Sanctions could not be applied efficiently because the procedure was too complicated and because they were not compulsory. And delegates to the League, the Assembly, or the Council had no authority to act, but had to refer matters back to their governments. Further, the League had no independent financial resources; and it was unable to impose freedom of commerce.

In order to make the League work, Newfang suggests that it must be transformed into a world federation, possessing a legislature able to make laws, a court to interpret laws, an executive to carry them out. In order to do this, he further proposes: that Article 5 be expanded to permit the League instead of the member states to pay the Assembly members; that Article 8 be revised to permit the gradual transfer of armed forces to the League; that

[36] Oscar Newfang, *World Federation* (A. F. Barnes, New York, 1939).

every decade one-tenth of the military, naval, and air forces of each member state shall be handed to the League of Nations and the military budget of each state reduced by one-tenth; that Article 10 should be strengthened to make an explicit guaranty to preserve the independence of the members; and that the League as a whole and not the member states should give the guaranty. He would revise Articles 14 and 15 to give the Permanent Court of International Justice compulsory jurisdiction in the event that the League Council fails to reach a unanimous decision. He would eliminate Articles 16 and 17, providing for sanctions and for action against any power outside the federation, because sanctions will not be required in a federation. He would amend Article 19 to give the Assembly authority to take action upon and not merely to advise upon treaties which have become inapplicable and international conditions which threaten the peace of the world. He would amend Article 20 to make the Covenant and the laws of the Assembly and the decisions of the Permanent Court of International Justice the supreme law of the world, and would insert a new paragraph providing that every executive officer of a member state must take an oath of allegiance to the League. He would strengthen Article 23 in order to give the League power to regulate labor conditions, to tax individual citizens of member states, to maintain armed forces on land, sea, and air, to establish a world monetary or banking system, and by a two-thirds vote to take over any other subject which it considered desirable.

This ambitious program, which many people regarded as utterly unrealizable in practice, to Newfang is the minimum condition of peace and security throughout the world. In his final chapter, he puts the alternatives without qualification: Either transfer the armed forces to the League or continue the armaments race until war and collapse result. Either give power to a world federation to remove tariff barriers and remove the main economic cause of war, and thereby make possible a rise in the standard of living, or permit economic barriers to continue to increase with a resultant decline in the standard of living and insecurity. Either establish a world monetary or banking system or have a continuance of increasing currency wars and mounting national debts.

Newfang's analysis is challenging because it reminds us that within the national communities political order and economic security depend upon power of taxation, control of armed forces, and authority to limit internal tariff barriers. In many respects the countries of the world are economically closer than districts within the present nations were one to three hundred years ago. Materially Newfang's world federation is not impossible; psychologically, it may be impossible. We should realize, however, the clear distinction between the material conditions which may or may not make possible a political order and the mental attitudes which may or may not prevent the adoption of a new political system.

Newfang might agree that the world will not take this step. He does not necessarily claim that the method will be adopted. He does say that it is necessary, and that it is a minimum condition. Nothing less than this will work. This new division of powers between world authority and national units is indispensable for orderly and efficient government. But mankind may prefer to retain its political myths rather than face social realities. It may not be prepared to do the necessary thing. Newfang describes what he thinks mankind must do for its political health; he does not claim that mankind will do it.

FEDERATION INDEPENDENT OF THE LEAGUE

All advocates of federalism agree that the fundamental obstacle which stands in the way of peace is the sovereign state.[37] In opposition to those philosophers who have spoken of the state as the highest expression of law and of spiritual values, many thinkers, including Clarence Streit, maintain that the state in its external relations lacks the elements of a moral being: it has no sense of moral obligation to the great majority of mankind, but only to the few million people within its borders; even to its own subjects, the fulfillment of its obligations is too often a matter of caprice or arbitrariness. Consequently, the world cannot hope to survive in an age of increasing interdependence if sixty or more states are to continue to confront each other in a condition of nonmoral relationship. The only solution then is to abolish the nonmoral state and replace it by a more comprehensive form of society in which political organization does express moral obligation to the people of other states as well as of one's own state.

The problem goes even deeper. The state has not merely been endangering the peace of the world by virtue of its nonmoral external relations; it has been sacrificing the freedom and welfare of its own subjects. Streit is outspoken on this point on his book,

[37] W. B. Curry, *The Case for Federal Union* (Penguin Books, Ltd., Harmondsworth, England), especially chapter iv, "Does Nationalism Make Sense?"

Union Now. We should, he says, cease sacrificing the freedom of individuals to the freedom of sovereign states. Democracy has waned because states have grown in power and pretension and have become absolute, and democracy is incompatible with the absolute state. Only by eliminating the state which has enslaved the individual can the latter find again his true self. Only in such manner can he, in the words of Berdyaef, cease from becoming dehumanized and being sacrificed to an impersonal thing.

To those who believe that a strengthened League can work while at the same time "leaving the states in possession of their sovereignty," Streit answers that patching simply will not work. We have tried to patch the world's currency system and failed. Big collective alliances and small regional pacts have failed. World wheat, sugar, and textile conferences have failed. Disarmament conferences have broken down. Nor can organizations halfway between sovereign states and universalism such as Pan-Americanism and the British Empire solve the problem. Leagues, whether universal or regional, cannot work. They cannot act quickly enough. The unanimity rule despite some minor modifications in practice still prevents them from becoming efficient international legislative bodies. They cannot enforce the law. First, they lack coercive power. Second, the attempts to apply sanctions must fail because the state (or nation) is an immortal body and one cannot punish a people in the same way as an individual or a corporation: "It is one thing for the immortal state to brand as a criminal one of its millions of mortals, and quite another for a few moral statesmen to attach the stigma of guilt to an immortal nation. It is an appalling blunder, a monstrous thing, inherently indefensible."[38] Third, whereas one can lock a person up pending trial, he cannot do so to a nation. "What law and order would any nation enjoy if the police could not arrest even a flagrant offender before they had convicted him in court? Yet this is just what any league must do."

The result is that a league cannot provide the essentials of order. It is a hybrid product and must give way to a much more comprehensive form of society. In Streit's view, this society must be nothing less than a union of peoples, a union which will absorb states, "put individuality back on the throne that nationality has usurped,"[39] eliminate excessive government, and enforce the law

---

[38] Clarence Streit, *Union Now* (Harper & Bros., New York, 1939), p. 145.
[39] *Ibid.,* p. 12.

upon the individuals and groups within its boundaries because of its overwhelming power.

But how step from national sovereignties to Union? Both Curtis[40] and Streit advocate the method of growth around a political nucleus. Nations with the greatest common interests and the greatest devotion to the principle of human freedom must recognize the need of surrendering sovereignty and must combine to form a new unit. These nations, Streit suggests, to begin with, will be the fifteen democracies which he names: the United States, the United Kingdom, Canada, Australia, New Zealand, South Africa, Eire, France, Belgium, the Netherlands, Switzerland, Denmark, Norway, Sweden, and Finland. The number is not final and no country should be excluded which wishes to join. These are the nations which should lead the way to form the new Union.

The Union should have the sole right to grant citizenship and admit new states to control all foreign affairs and defense measures, to regulate commerce within and without the Union, to control all monetary matters, and to own and operate communication services. It should guarantee a democratic form of government to each of its component parts. It should work through a bicameral legislature: a House of Deputies based upon population, and a Senate to which each state of less than twenty-five million should elect two senators and those above twenty-five million two extra senators for every additional twenty-five million people. The executive power should be vested in a board composed of five citizens—three elected directly by the Union, one by the House, and one by the Senate. And the judicial power of the Union should be vested in a High Court.

This barest of summaries will indicate the line upon which Streit would proceed to a world government. It is based upon two fundamental ideas: (1) the conviction that international legislation and the prevention of war are both impossible under present world conditions, in which the modern state is a fatal obstacle; and (2) a belief that the League of Nations and regional organizations do not provide an adequate modification of the sovereign state.

That new political institutions are required to serve the means of modern mankind must be obvious. That some form of world government is necessary in the interests of legislative efficiency

[40] Lionel Curtis, *Civitas Dei* (Macmillan & Co., London, 1937), Volume Three, pp. 77–81.

and national security must undoubtedly be granted. That a state or nation is a society which exists for certain purposes and should be modified in response to new conditions is undeniable; and that no progress can be made until the modern state relinquishes its sovereignty is evident from the survey made in this volume. The modern state can no longer efficiently serve its own interests in health, security, communications, prevention of crime, intellectual development, and economic amelioration. It must give way to institutions more appropriate to modern world needs.

That the ultimate ideal is one along the lines advocated by Streit may well be. That it is possible to persuade fifteen democracies (more or less) to abdicate their sovereignty when they have been unwilling to strengthen the League of Nations in less fundamental ways may be open to question.[41] Moreover, there are many other serious problems: What would be the character of the international relations of the new unit? Streit points out that the Union would have overwhelming economic strength. But what guaranty is there that it would base its foreign policy on the foundations of true freedom? Would it engage in a new balance of power to struggle with the nonmembers, or would it offer to submit disputes to third-party judgments? Would it take sufficient steps to reduce tariffs to the outside world or to internationalize colonies? Do not the United States and the British Empire dominate the Union under his plan? In his House of Deputies the United States and the British Commonwealth nations would have 198 seats, the other democracies—Belgium, Denmark, Finland, France, Netherlands, Norway, Sweden, Switzerland—only 89; of 42 Senators the former would have 24 members, the other democracies 18. These figures are not fatal. But they occasion pause for reflection.

Would it tend to degenerate into a military alliance, or be so interpreted by the Fascist powers? Is it so certain that the modern state cannot submit to adverse decisions? Is the state more immortal than the Church of Rome or the respective states of the American Union?

Streit asserts that people must again enthrone liberty and democracy and that we must begin with the peoples who are most given to liberty. The United States founded a remarkable and a new principle of government when it subordinated the state to the

---

[41] The present war has eliminated, temporarily at least, several of the democracies. Advocates of "Union Now" now counsel Anglo-American Union. See below, pp. 766–68.

welfare of its people and discovered the device of federalism to serve the cause of freedom in a modern world. This form of government, Streit says, permitted the expansion of the United States from 3,000,000 to 130,000,000, from thirteen to forty-eight states, embracing many different kinds of people. And yet this United States was near bankruptcy and ruin when it changed its political organization and adopted federation. Critics of Streit say that his use of historical analogy is faulty. They point out that the thirteen states had been British colonies and subjects of the same king for about one hundred and fifty years; they had had a common culture and language, and enjoyed much the same conditions of life. But the nations which Streit suggests should federate have had (in some cases, at least) histories reaching back hundreds of years; they have lived under different rulers, speak different languages, and exhibit cultural and other values marked by great variety.

We must leave it to historians to decide whether or not American history presents sufficient parallel to justify the strong claims made on behalf of a world federal union beginning with the fifteen democracies. Critics of Streit say that the American Civil War involved sanctions of the most complete kind, and that President Lincoln not only called out the state militia and proclaimed a blockade of Southern ports but appealed for volunteers, suspended the writ of habeas corpus in certain areas, and thereby coerced not merely a number of people but a number of states. For it was primarily states and not individuals which fought the American Civil War. And, despite the bitter feeling which remained in the South against the Yankees, the Confederate States again took an honored place in a united America.

Streit and others claim that the League has failed, that one cannot imagine that Germany, Italy, and Japan will return to this organization, but that they are more likely to join a union. Critics suggest that it would be the height of folly to throw away an existing organization which has had a generation of knowledge and experience and which in spite of its failures to prevent war has developed institutions for co-operation on a wider scale than the world has yet seen. To Streit's contention that the United States would be more ready to join a Union than a League, they answer with a flat denial. Moreover, they point out, the British Dominions during the postwar period have refused to join even a British Commonwealth Federation; and it is not likely that they will join a still wider federation in which they would have still less voice as to foreign policy and the direction of armies, navies, and air forces manned by their citizens.

Streit opposes the ideal of federation based upon continentalism because in a rapidly shrinking world it would be too small to handle fundamental problems and because, without the United States, such a scheme would be doomed from the beginning. A European federation must include Great Britain, which is a worldwide and not merely a European power. If the totalitarian states were not included in the European union it would not be strong enough; if it did include a democratic Germany and/or Italy after the present war, it would still lack sufficient mutual trust among its constituent people, and sufficient experience in self-government on the part of many of the new units.

In 1941 Streit issued a modified version of his plan to meet the situation caused by the rapid German conquest of several of the democracies which were to have formed a part of his original union.[42] Streit recognized that the ideal of federation would have to take the altered conditions into account, but claimed that recent events had demonstrated the soundness of his principles and the greater urgency of their adoption. He now proposed immediate union with Britain, first in order to insure British victory, and second in order to guarantee a sound peace. True, he says, an alliance with Britain would be an unsatisfactory means of dealing with the present war; it would promote national disunity and partisanship in America, would cause Britain and America to drift apart at the conclusion of hostilities, and would thereby cause a repetition of the errors made between 1917 and 1920. However, a union would provide a tremendous moral force comparable with but superior to the great appeal made by Woodrow Wilson twenty-five years ago. Its appeal would go farther than awakening hope and faith through the enunciation of principles; it would provide a threefold guaranty—to the American people that the peace would not be lost after the war, to the British and Canadians that we would not withdraw from the task of reconstruction at the conclusion of hostilities, and to the German people that in the event of a revolution against Hitler we would this time live up to our promises. The moral decline of the world, Streit believes, has been disastrous. Those who have heard him speak will recall his impressive statement that this is the first American generation to have suffered a reverse in economic

---

[42] Clarence Streit, *Union Now with Britain* (Harper & Bros., New York, 1941).

progress, a decline in a vital faith in democracy, and the conviction that its dead have died in vain.

A new comprehensive ideal worthy of men's devotion being required, Streit proposes two steps: First, a limited provisional union with Great Britain, Canada, Australia, New Zealand, South Africa, and Eire, based upon the principles of the Declaration of Independence and the great fundamental rights of man; a supreme government of the Union in the form of an intercontinental congress; and suitable executive and judicial organs as its political instruments. At first the congress would comprise forty-nine members (twenty-seven from the United States, eleven from Great Britain); and Streit paints a glowing picture of the galaxy of great men who would be available as representatives—the Union executive would comprise three men, including Churchill and Roosevelt. Second, when the time was ripe the provisional union would give way to a broader permanent union, under a federal constitution drawn up by a Federal Convention.

Streit undoubtedly would be the first to admit the many difficulties and omissions which critics may adduce. But he has been concerned to emphasize the fact that, difficulties or no difficulties, nothing less than federation can possibly work, and that defects in the mechanism of the plan he proposes are of minor significance compared with the great task which lies ahead. He calls for great qualities to meet an overwhelming crisis—will, idealism, faith, political inventiveness, release of energy, and conquest of doubt. These are the essential things, rather than whether Streit has or has not meticulously worked out the relations between the Union legislature and the Union executive and many other technical problems. The political science experts may pick flaws in the plan, just as the economic experts proved that Hitler's economic system could not work. But experts work within the framework of a social faith and a set of political and philosophical values; change that faith and those values, and the experts may have to concede that their fundamental technical problems have changed and that their logic which was valid upon a certain plane of conduct no longer binds with the same inexorableness as before.

Streit answers several objections to his proposal. To those who ask whether Britain would accept a numerically inferior position in the Union he replies that the Union Senate will in part offset the disparity in numbers and that the party divisions within the Union will help to offset the sense of separateness. To those who doubt whether or not Britain would be willing to join the

Union, he points to the fact that Churchill made a similar offer to France in 1940 and that this offer indicates a receptive frame of mind at least. He discounts the argument raised above that a union of democracies would call a "counter bloc" into being, and claims that the stronger the democracies have grown the less arrogant they have become. Nor does he believe that his scheme would endanger the pan-American experiment; he thinks that the two aims are not contradictory but rather supplementary. He hopes that some of the Latin-American states will apply for admission, but asserts that thus far they have shown little genius for federal union and cites, as examples, the failure of federal schemes during the past century and the criticism aroused by Senator Smather's recent proposal.

Many other details must be passed over, for the outstanding question which emerges from Streit's plan is whether or not anything less fundamental than federalism can politically control the vast forces of present-day society, whether or not the world has become so closely knit in economics, politics, and culture that any organization less integrated than federalism will mark a fatal divorce between the political and the nonpolitical aspects of human life. We have already suggested elsewhere why the very development of war and the necessities of even a tolerable peace necessitate a federal union in Europe. Streit would carry the logic farther and say that to restrict federalism to Europe would give rise to the same disintegrating forces as between Europe and the rest of the world as we have witnessed within the League of Nations itself.

THE LIMITATION AND REDUCTION OF ARMAMENTS

The problem of armaments in its present acute form is of relatively recent origin. Until the last hundred years or so the progress of invention had not reached such a stage as to make the instruments and the institution of war the overwhelming factors which they now are. The terrible destruction of life and the financial burdens imposed by the preparation for and the conduct of modern war mean that there is no longer any reasonable relation between the matter of dispute and the method of settling it. War has become the most inefficient method of international change; the continuous preparation for it threatens to ruin the foundations of modern life. Some method of lightening the burden is urgently needed. Limitation and reduction of arms seemed an obvious remedy, and millions of people have had high hopes in this direction.

The whole question, unfortunately, bristles with difficulties.[43] There are baffling technical problems; but, before even considering them, one must take into account certain more general factors: (1) Nations differ considerably in their attitude toward life; some have a martial tradition and glorify war; others preach the virtue of peace. What can disarmament mean to a Mussolini or a Hitler who proclaims the cleansing power of war and its role in producing heroes and rousing peoples to noble and glorious action? (2) The lag of social thought makes nations reluctant to put aside armaments which they imagine constitute their only means of defense; they do not realize the changing nature of the international world; their "stereotypes" prevent them from seeing the growing strain and the ultimate impossibility of gaining security by separate national action. (3) Democratic national governments change. Elections upset cabinets; and an incoming Prime Minister and his colleagues may introduce a foreign policy with an emphasis very different from that of their predecessors. International agreement is thus frequently at the mercy of domestic political instability. (4) The rapidity of modern invention brings the danger that the discovery of new weapons will render a disarmament agreement useless, for how can armaments not yet invented be limited by treaties in advance?[44] (5) A nation's fighting strength rests not merely in its men and war materials, but in its total economic and military power, its resources, manufactures, geographical position, communications, constituting its "war potential"; one may limit guns and men, but how measure the compensation which a country should receive in the form of armaments to offset its poverty of raw materials, or its unfavorable geographic situation? (6) A question which has handicapped every postwar disarmament conference is whether security or disarmament should come first. On the one hand, the French argued that it is dangerous for any people to lay down their arms until the total police power of the world is sufficient to guarantee the safety of individual countries; within nations, the willingness of private citizens to forego guns and pistols in daily life has followed and not preceded the establishment of an adequate judicial and police system. On the

[43] See S. de Madariaga, *Disarmament* (Coward-McCann, Inc., New York, 1929), chapters, i–iii.

[44] See P. J. Noel Baker, *Disarmament* (Harcourt, Brace & Company, New York, 1926), pp. 37–47.

other hand, governments which are unwilling to commit their countries to further international security arrangements claim that a general reduction of arms of itself will serve to increase the general feeling of security: the less the armaments, the less the damage that can be done; people cannot create such havoc with pickaxes as with bombs.

Four problems arise at the outset in discussing the more technical problems of disarmament.

1. Should limitation be direct or indirect, by reducing the number and amount of men and materials or by reducing the amount of money which each nation may spend on its armaments? Advocates of the latter method claim for it the merit of simplicity—reduction of military and naval budgets would effect far-reaching economies, deliver the world from staggering expenditures, give relief to taxpayers of all nations, and free economic life from ominously increasing burdens. Budgetary limitation, it is asserted, would involve few if any of the technical difficulties connected with the attempt directly to limit men and material in land, naval, and air services. Opponents of budgetary limitations argue that differences in national systems of accounting and standards of living make adequate comparisons between nations impossible, and that it is not easy to decide whether certain roads, bridges, and harbor works within a country are primarily of civil or of military importance.[45] League of Nations experts attempted to meet some of these objections by drawing up a uniform method of accounting. Undoubtedly a successful disarmament scheme should contain provisions for budgetary limitation; but it would also have to contain detailed technical plans and to exist within a framework of general political agreements providing for security as well as disarmament. Budgetary limitation alone, unless extremely far-reaching, would not suffice.[46]

2. Governments became involved in protracted controversy over another general question of method. Should disarmament be effected separately for land, naval, and air forces, or must a successful scheme embrace all three services? The French and others held that it would be impossible to make progress by limitation or reduction in one service only: an agreement to reduce air forces alone would lead to intensification of rivalry in land forces; naval

[45] Baker, *op. cit.*, pp. 66–73.

[46] Paul Molden-Hauer, "The Budgetary Limitation of Armament Expenditures," in *Disarmament and Equal Rights* (Carl Heymans Verlag, Berlin, 1934), by Schmidt and Grabowsky (editors).

limitation alone would result in greater competition in the air. Great Britain and the United States claimed that the problems of the three services were distinct enough to warrant separate consideration, and that less complication and delay would result from considering them separately. The Washington Naval Conference, they said, had been successful, and the outlook for further naval reduction was not unpromising. If navies were susceptible of such treatment, why not armies and air forces?

3. If a Disarmament Conference were successful in reaching a comprehensive agreement, should each government be trusted to carry out the provisions, or would it be dangerous to rely upon its good faith? If a government should break its word and secretly arm, or skillfully conceal weapons which it had promised to destroy, the security of states which had honestly fulfilled their obligations would be endangered. France therefore advocated a Permanent International Commission with power to make investigations within the boundaries of the signatory powers, just as, after 1918, the Allies set up an Inter-Allied Commission to supervise the disarmament of Germany. If international inspections were required at that time for the few defeated and relatively helpless countries, similar methods would be necessary for the heavily armed great powers with their huge armament factories and highly integrated politico-economic arrangements. Great Britain and the United States took the opposite view. They believed that a Permanent International Commission would involve an excessive interference in national affairs, and that unless the world could trust to the good faith of the signatory powers no disarmament agreement would succeed.[47]

4. The danger of having heavily armed forces confronting each other with only a boundary line to separate them must be obvious. Enemy troops can strike immediately, and the smallest border incidents may provoke hostilities. It is natural, therefore, to ask whether it would not be possible to lessen the chances of war by providing demilitarized or neutralized zones which could act as "insulators" or "cushions."[48]

The experiment of neutralized territories has often been tried. Witness the neutrality of Switzerland, Belgium, and Luxemburg, and, although less known, Cracow (neutralized in 1815) and

[47] Major General A. C. Temperley, *The Whispering Gallery of Europe* (Collins, London, 1938), pp. 65–66.

[48] J. H. Marshall Cornwall, *Geographic Disarmament* (Oxford University Press, London, 1935).

Albania (neutralized in 1913). A similar role was played by buffer states in Asia and in Africa. They were somewhat useful in preventing hostile powers from coming into close contact; but without a definite guaranty they were likely to become objects of intrigue by neighboring great powers, as the British wars with Afghanistan and the British expeditions into Tibet attested.

In addition to neutralized and buffer states it may be possible to establish demilitarized zones within sovereign states. In these zones military preparations may be prohibited in times of peace and the powers may agree not to fight within them in time of war. The former conception, i.e., restrictions upon fortifications and maintenance of troops, involves a restriction on the sovereignty of the state. Some international lawyers believe that they would approximate international servitude; but this last term is a highly disputed one. The demilitarized zone, to be effective, might be the result of voluntary agreement by all powers, and in this case the limitation on sovereignty would not be externally imposed. Before 1914, there were certain parts of the frontier between Russia and Persia which had been demilitarized by the 1881 Treaty, a zone between Peru and Colombia was established by the 1889 Treaty, an area between Abyssinia and Sudan was agreed upon in 1902, and a neutral zone was established between Sweden and Norway by the 1905 Convention.

After 1918, the Rhineland was demilitarized, Czechoslovakia agreed not to erect military works on the right bank of the Danube to the south of Bratislava, Danzig was not to serve as a military base or erect fortifications or manufacture munitions, and the Soviet Union signed demilitarization agreements with Esthonia and Finland in the Baltic, and with Turkey in Transcaucasia. By the Washington Treaty in 1922 five naval powers agreed to refrain from increasing their fortifications and naval bases in the Pacific Ocean; and in the same year Iraq and the Nejd agreed to establish a neutral zone between their territories. By a 1923 agreement the Tangier zone was placed under a regime of permanent neutrality. And in 1921 the Aaland Islands in the Baltic Sea were demilitarized and placed under the supervision of the League of Nations.[49]

At the Lausanne Conference, 1922–23, the frontier zone of

---

[49] For the demilitarization of the Aaland Islands in 1856, and the subsequent history of attempts to obtain disarmament in the Baltic, see C. R. Pusta, *Le Statut juridique de la Mer Baltique à partir du XIXe siècle* (Librarie du Recueil Sirey, Paris, 1936).

Thrace was demilitarized to a depth of thirty kilometers along certain sections of the Turkish, Greek, and Bulgarian boundaries. Greece undertook not to establish a naval base at or to erect fortifications on or to permit military aircraft to fly over the islands of Mytilene, Chios, Samos, and Nikaria. The Conference agreed to demilitarize certain defined areas on both shores of the Straits of the Dardanelles and the Bosporus and certain islands in the Sea of Marmora and in the Aegean Sea.

These examples and others which might be quoted indicate that demilitarization and neutralization of specific areas have been frequently tried. Within certain limits the experiment has been successful. But the facts that within the last few years the Rhineland has been reoccupied and fortified, the Turkish Straits have been remilitarized, and permission has been granted to fortify the Aaland Islands show that regional demilitarization is a subsidiary solution depending for its effectiveness upon peace within the larger framework of international society. As a method of reducing the possibilities of war in minor disputes it is invaluable; but it does not touch the root of major differences between the great powers. If war between the latter is to be stopped, the solution must be of a more extensive and far-reaching kind.

Discussion of geographic disarmament brings out one fundamental truth—the concept of a frontier as a line is an anachronism. The basic interests of a country are so many-sided as perhaps to demand different frontiers. Why should there be but one frontier for customs, trading, military, and maritime purposes? The majority of countries have extended their frontiers for purposes of crime prevention, and there is no valid reason why in a highly integrated world nations should not have a number of frontiers, each serving its own purpose. Marshall-Cornwall makes a noteworthy suggestion: "In future we must think of frontiers, not as lines, but as zones, which, in effect, they really are."[50] If this is done, national frontiers will cease to inconvenience travelers, traders, and others, and may come to resemble the boundary lines between the states of the American Union.

In the light of the more general considerations just outlined

[50] J. H. Marshall-Cornwall, *op. cit.*, p. 175. The author quotes (p. 174) from Paul de Lapradelle: "Le phénomène politique de la frontière n'est pas un phénomène simple ... C'est une zone de services publics, distincts des services de l'intérieur, et dont chacun porte le nom de frontière. La frontière douanière, la frontière militaire, la frontière maritime, sont autant de services dont l'organisation et le fonctionnement ressortissent au droit administratif interne."

we turn to consider the special problems of reduction of armaments on land, on the sea, and in the air.

LAND ARMAMENTS

The Preparatory Commission of the League held its first session in May 1926. When it came to consider land armaments, it had before it the work of the Allied military experts, who after careful study had drawn up a plan of disarmament which was imposed upon Germany and the other defeated powers at the conclusion of the World War of 1914–1918. In order to insure that Germany and her ex-allies would be in no position to wage future war, they took comprehensive measures. (Since Germany was the most important power the Treaty of Versailles may be taken as a model.)

In regard to manpower the treaty (1) limited the effective troops to 100,000; (2) provided in detail for the organization of the army by prescribing the strength and character of every unit; (3) limited the number of officers to 4,000, not more than 5 per cent of whom could be released before the conclusion of their term of service; (4) prohibited the sending of any German military mission abroad; (5) abolished conscription; (6) forbade all measures of mobilization; (7) limited the number of auxiliary forces, such as customs officers, coast guards, and police, and forbade them to receive any military training; (8) denied universities, schools, and clubs the right to engage in military exercises; and (9) abolished Germany's military air forces.

In the sphere of armament and materials the Allies prohibited Germany from having any military aircraft, armored cars, and tanks, and permitted only relatively few of the smaller weapons. The amount of ammunition was rigidly prescribed—400 rounds for each rifle, 8,000 for each machine gun, and 1,000 for each field gun—and had to be kept at specified places. A few designated factories were permitted to manufacture arms and munitions; the others were dismantled. Germany might not export or import military supplies. Her fortifications were limited, and on the Western front an extensive demilitarized zone was established.

In order to see that these provisions were carried out, the victors set up an Allied Commission of Control, with headquarters at Berlin. When it was satisfied that Germany had fulfilled the disarmament provisions of the treaty, it handed over its supervisory duties to the League of Nations.

When the Preparatory Commission tried to adapt measures which had been imposed upon a nation defeated in war to a disarmament convention which should bind a large number of sovereign states, it encountered many obstacles. It had to deal with governments, most of which did not operate under the externally imposed limitations of a peace treaty, but were free to pursue their national programs unhindered except for agreements which they might voluntarily accept or had accepted. Obviously under these circumstances the Commission could not adopt a peremptory solution such as the Allied experts had done in 1919 when they had had the power of victorious armies behind them. Nor could the world perpetuate the sharp contrast between the armaments of the Allied Powers and those of the nations defeated in 1918 if it was to reach a genuine settlement. Not only were the League members bound by Article 8 of the Covenant, but they were obliged by dictates of highest expediency to treat Germany, Austria, Hungary, Bulgaria, and Turkey as partners in a common task—that of finding methods of reducing the number of armed men, the amount of war material, and the cost of war preparations.

The first difficulty concerned the length of military service for land forces. The Peace Treaty had prescribed a twelve-year period for private soldiers in the German army. The French, however, had a conscription system which applied to all men for one and one-half or two years. In attempting to effect a disarmament plan the experts had to consider how far they could compare the military value of a German professional soldier and a short-term French conscript. Unless they could reach some agreement on this matter it might be necessary for Europe to agree to a general reorganization of the various national armies along lines of greater uniformity by reducing the German and lengthening the French period of military service.

The question of reserves proved to be the next stumbling block. Should only the military forces on a war basis be reduced in number, or should those in reserve but still subject to a short period of annual training be included? The Treaty of Versailles had forbidden reserves to Germany; now, Germany in turn demanded that France and the other powers limit their reserves. The French objected; whereupon the German representatives pointed out that reserve forces could for some years at least be rapidly transformed into first-class fighting troops and that a scheme without a limitation of reserves would favor France and penalize Germany.

The problem of colonial troops aroused prolonged controversy. Germany had been deprived of its colonies and therefore no longer possessed colonial troops; consequently it advocated restrictions upon nations which could draw upon their colonies for manpower. France asserted that it needed large numbers of soldiers for local defense purposes in North and West Africa and in the Far East. Germany replied with much force that to limit peace-time effectives and leave to nations which possessed colonies an unrestricted number of colonial troops would place Germany in an unfair and unfavorable position in the event of a European War. It did not wish a repetition of the Black Troops on the Rhine.[51]

No clear-cut line separates military from non-military organizations. Boy scouts, civil air pilots, youth camps, and other organizations give training in discipline. The question of this type of training came before the Preparatory Commission. Some governments claimed that the Fascist and Nazi youth organizations received instruction which served military as well as civil purposes and should therefore be limited in numbers.

After four years the Preparatory Commission produced the Draft Convention of 1930. This document revealed how basic were the differences of principle (apart from the baffling problem of application, once the principles had been agreed upon) which separated the governments. The items which met with general agreement included budgetary limitation of war material, a limit to the period of active military service, the establishment of a Permanent Disarmament Commission, limitation of land, sea, and air effectives, acceptance of naval limitation by categories as exemplified in the 1930 London Naval Treaty, and renunciation of chemical and bacteriological warfare. Unfortunately, the omissions were more noticeable than the inclusions. The Convention failed to abolish conscription, to provide a solution to the problem of trained reserves, and directly to limit and reduce war materials. A state would therefore be free to supply its limited army and trained reserves with an unlimited amount of war material. The Convention was thus of little worth and the few principles embodied within it were hedged about with enfeebling reservations.

Despite the high hopes of the people of the world, the Disarmament Conference, which met in Geneva on February 2, 1932, was soon in difficulties. So great was the pessimism in certain official quarters over the atmosphere resulting from the economic collapse of 1931, the abandonment of the gold standard, the Japa-

[51] Dr. Karl Megerle, in *The Problem of the Native Soldier in Disarmament and Equal Rights* (C. Hymans, Berlin, 1934), by R. Schmidt and A. Grabowsky (editors), pp. 119–29.

nese invasion of Manchuria, and other matters that some officials believed that the Conference should be postponed.[52] Indeed, its opening was delayed owing to the League preoccupation with the Sino-Japanese dispute.

Three major methods were proposed in the opening week, the French plan for internationalization and security, the British plan (later elaborated by President Hoover in June 1932) for qualitative disarmament, and the German demand for equality. We need not follow the melancholy story of the next two years. The French increased their demands for security as the Germans the more loudly proclaimed their need of equality. Especially after the advent of Hitler to power did France insist upon more absolute guaranties of international security. Proposals and counterproposals followed in dreary succession. They served to change the emphasis from disarmament to rearmament. On June 11, 1934, the General Commissions of the Conference adjourned sine die. Thus

after two and a half years of discussion the disarmament problem was as barren of solution as it had been at the opening of the Disarmament Conference in February, 1932. By the summer of 1934 the deadlock was complete. All hope of disarmament had vanished, that of limitation of armaments had grown tarnished and faded, and the fear of general rearmament and its possible ghastly results had become a threat and a nightmare before the mind of the world.[53]

AERIAL DISARMAMENT

The problem of limiting or reducing aerial armaments is complicated at the outset by the difficulty of drawing a clear line between military and civil planes. Civil aviation has become an indispensable part of modern life, and will continue to grow in importance. It follows that if experts cannot devise aircraft on which a machine gun cannot be mounted or from which bombs cannot be dropped, the very progress of civil aviation carries with it an ominous increase in military strength.[54]

Four schools of thought appeared at the Preparatory Commis-

[52] Temperley, *op. cit.,* pp. 188–89.

[53] John W. Wheeler-Bennett, *The Pipe Dream of Peace* (W. Morrow & Co., New York, 1935), p. 238.

[54] In the attack upon Holland in 1940 Germany was able to use the element of "surprise" in its Blitzkrieg by transporting parachute troops in converted commercial airline planes "obsolete in design." See S. L. A. Marshall, *Blitzkrieg* (W. Morrow & Co., New York, 1940).

sion of the Disarmament Conference. The United States and Great Britain advocated the abolition of the bomber only. The delegates from Denmark, Norway, and Sweden urged total prohibition of military aviation and of the manufacture of military planes and the internationalization or strict control of civil aviation—the abolition of military planes alone would cause an increase in the construction of commercial planes, which could in turn be used for aggression. Germany, Hungary, and Turkey, forbidden by the Peace treaties to possess military planes, favored abolition of military aviation for all nations but would have left civil aviation unregulated. France, Belgium, Czechoslovakia, and Poland urged the establishment of an international air force equipped with bombing apparatus and proposed the internationalization of civil air forces.

Is it possible to measure the offensive and defensive qualities of a military plane? Those who answered in the affirmative proposed to limit the size of the plane. Some authorities suggested two tons, without fuel and other load. Great Britain proposed a maximum of three tons. Critics said that these figures were too high. They proposed to limit engine horsepower to, say, four hundred (as suggested by the Soviet Union), and to limit the wing space to, say, two hundred square feet. The last two proposals brought to light differences between governments. Several years ago the German and Dutch machines possessed less wing area than those belonging to other nations. Germany and Holland therefore urged limitation by wing-area measurement! Great Britain used a lower horsepower in the engines, and naturally preferred limitation by horsepower! Others proposed to limit planes to single-seaters. It was claimed that a large plane required more than one person for effective observation and bombing purposes, and that the single-seater would therefore be essentially a defensive machine—a view which meets with much criticism from pilots. Still others would build sufficient single-seated planes to resist any attack by the civil aircraft of another country. Some proposed to prohibit government subsidies to commercial aircraft on such conditions as would permit them to be used easily for military purposes and also wished to prohibit military training of pilots engaged in commercial aviation, and to limit the money to be spent each year for military aircraft construction and possibly to limit the total budget for the whole air service.

Some years ago, E. P. Warner suggested that it was possible, by limiting the weight, the horsepower, the wing area, the seating capacity, and the number of military planes, to effect a substantial reduction (up to 80 per cent) in aerial armaments. Since that time the progress of invention, the rapidity of building, and the very close integration of military and civil aviation seem to have rendered these palliative measures much more difficult, if not impossible, of attainment.

The Draft Convention prepared for the Disarmament Conference had provided for the limitation of effectives in air forces but not for any direct limitation of air material. France early in the Conference submitted proposals which closely resembled the fundamental ideas presented to the Paris Conference in 1919 and the Geneva Protocol Conference in 1924, i.e., the internationalization of civil aviation. These provided that nationals belonging to signatory powers might build nonmilitary planes below a prescribed tonnage, but machines above that figure would be assigned to organizations—continental, intercontinental, and intercolonial—under the authority of the League of Nations. Only the League should possess heavy bombing machines, which should form part of an international police force. Unfortunately, no agreement was reached, and another failure had to be recorded.

The Air Commission appropriately, and most unfortunately, found itself unable to take off, and in consequence never did more than bump about the ground. It became involved in a discussion as to whether the control of military aviation or the internationalization of civilian aircraft should be dealt with first. Spain proposed a scheme for the international organization of civilian aviation on the lines of the Universal Postal Union, which proposal received a certain amount of support from France and Sweden. The Germans wished to see military aircraft abolished entirely, but this received only the votes of Italy and the U.S.S.R. The British were concerned in trying to devise a plan which would prevent the use of civil aircraft for military purposes. The United States delegates were of opinion that the problem was an exclusively European one, and were prepared to agree to any scheme which was adopted.[55]

The present war would seem to show beyond doubt that Europe is too small to permit the existence of national air forces. The destruction wreaked upon cities bears eloquent testimony to the fact that, although a country may not be conquered by air power alone, the effects of air bombardment upon civil life and upon the possibilities of postwar reconstruction are so great that we are justified in asserting that modern nations are as inefficient instru-

[55] John W. Wheeler-Bennett, *op. cit.*, p. 37.

ments of defense against present-day weapons as the feudal castles became after the discovery of gunpowder, and that a new unit of government to guarantee peace and order is urgently required.

In the light of these developments it is of interest to examine the practicability of the proposal made by France in February 1933 to the Disarmament Conference for the establishment of an international control over civil aviation—the major air routes to be managed by an international company organized by the League of Nations, and the lesser lines to be controlled by subsidiary companies under the general supervision of a permanent disarmament commission. Many students of the question supported the plan, believing that it was technically feasible and economically desirable to establish an international directorate of aviation comprising the ministers of transport of the member states and the Secretary-General of the League of Nations. The Directorate would meet twice a year and adopt decisions by majority vote; it would be responsible for the policy of an International Aviation Company which would have exclusive ownership of all civil planes, airdromes, and other equipment. The company would be administered by a board of directors, chosen not as government representatives, but as acknowledged experts. Jonathan Griffin's scheme provided for a board of twenty members, eight selected from countries which lead in civil aviation. The members would hold office for three years and be eligible for reappointment by the directorate mentioned above.

The personnel of such an international world airways company[56] would thus transcend national boundaries. Administrators, pilots, and ground staff would be drawn from all parts; vacancies would be filled by examination after wide publicity had been given, and only 10 per cent of the positions could be filled by men from any one country. The scheme would necessitate a central technical college for air mechanics, for these men would have to be familiar with airplanes and airplane parts from every country. The aviators would be formed into an international guild of air pilots. No one country should have more than, say, 25 per cent of the pilots, wireless operators, and ground staff from its own nationality operating within its own borders.

In order to finance the scheme the money would be raised through the Bank for International Settlements. Stockholders would have no voting powers, and would be guaranteed a standard

[56] Jonathan Griffin, *Britain's Air Policy* (Victor Gollancz, London, 1935).

rate of interest, which after a given period could be altered by common consent. Each country would be permitted to own only a certain percentage of the stock. One great difficulty would be the allocation of orders for material and employment, for different countries would exert pressure on their own behalf. But although the problem appeared difficult, it did not appear incapable of solution. The international company should have "compulsory option on aviation inventions of all kinds." It would run the main airlines of the world, holding a complete monopoly of them, but would probably hire out planes to governments or other units, to operate the secondary and less important lines.

The scheme would involve the disappearance of civil aviation subsidies, except to the international company, which would, within a short time, be independent of such help. To the objection that this type of monopoly carried with it the danger of bureaucracy and inefficient service the answer was that the European sleeping-car monopoly had not tended in this direction, and that in any case a desperate situation required a comprehensive remedy even though some dangers might attend it.

The plan could come into operation only after the abolition of national military air forces. Even then, it would be necessary, in addition to an international civil force, to have an international air-police force in order to prevent a strong country from indulging in aggression. Could a practical method be devised for such an international police organization? The technical difficulties seemed not insuperable.

Noel Baker proposed the following plan: The chief of staff of the international force would be chosen by the League Council, and he and the Council would select other members of the high command. The officers and men would be engaged under conditions of pay and service equal to the most favorable conditions prevailing, because the efficiency and morale of the force would depend upon the prospects of a highly paid career with ample opportunity for promotion. The force would use two official languages, French and English. It would possess bases and repair shops scattered throughout different countries in Europe, most of them in the smaller countries so as to obviate the danger of the establishments being seized by one of the great powers. The bases and repair shops would be thoroughly defended by the most modern methods, and would possess adequate supplies of all kinds. They would doubtless function in the manner of the present repair shops which serve the European sleeping-car organization.

They would require the most up-to-date design and research equipment, and would be in the forefront of aeronautic investigation. Baker estimated that an international force of a thousand machines would not cost more than a hundred million dollars a year, whereas even in 1934–35 nations were paying many times that amount without gaining security.

The new air organization would not lack work; it could be fully employed to advantage. The pilots, Baker suggested, could assist in supervising the observance of disarmament conventions by making periodic tours of inspection. They could engage in many civil tasks of unquestioned value, such as the "meteorological service, the air ambulance service, the extermination of locusts with poison gas by airplanes," and similar work. They could transport national delegations to the meetings of the Assembly, Council, and commissions of the League, the International Labor Organization, and the Permanent Court of International Justice. They could be put at the disposal of national ministers and, by reducing the time consumed in transportation, contribute much to the efficiency of international government.

Finally, the international air-police force could be used under strictly defined rules of procedure to take action against a government guilty of aggression. The important principle to be observed must be the minimum use of force in order to prevent the spread of war. It may be difficult to define aggression, but any convention should include a special clause which "must make it clear that there is no provocation so serious that it would justify aerial bombardment." Aerial bombardment is *ipso facto* aggression, and the international air force should be "empowered to begin at once to deal with it, even before the Council could be consulted." Along every frontier there should be a demilitarized zone under the patrol of an international air force which would be able to prevent armed trespass. A disarmament convention should confer two definite emergency powers: (1) the resources and personnel of the international air force should immediately withdraw from the territory or vicinity of an aggressor nation and (2) the high command of the international air force should be permitted to "take immediate action to intercept an air attack."[57]

These ideas were lost sight of in the mounting tide of international anarchy, and each nation preferred to trust to its own air force for security. The present position in Europe with its ruined

[57] Griffin, *op. cit.*, p. 139.

cities and ports suggests that the "practical" solution of national defense adopted by a number of the rival nations has turned out to be highly impractical, and that the continent might have been spared many needless horrors by the use of more imagination and insight.

NAVAL DISARMAMENT

Theoretically, naval disarmament should be easier to accomplish than military disarmament. Warships can use only a certain number of men; their weapons are in definite locations (i.e., in the ships themselves) and cannot be concealed; governments cannot maintain as much secrecy in building ships as in manufacturing armaments for land warfare. Naval forces cannot be used in peace time as freely as army units for civil purposes; nor is it possible to train as many men for supporting duty in the navy as in the army. Naval disarmament, though not a simple technical matter, is thus by no means as complicated as land disarmament; and one might expect it to have a better record.[58]

Under the Treaty of Versailles, Germany had to destroy all vessels under construction, disarm or destroy her cruisers and fleet auxiliaries, refrain from building submarines and naval aircraft, and destroy the fortifications and the naval bases by which she had dominated the sea routes. Very little replacement was permitted—a serious restriction because of the rapid obsolescence of modern ships of war. Germany was also forbidden to have naval conscription, and was therefore unable to build up a naval reserve. The Allies had effectually crippled German sea power.

Meanwhile two new forces had emerged—the United States and Japan. The United States had embarked on a great naval building program in 1916, partly because Great Britain had interfered with what America considered to be its legitimate neutral trading rights and because during the war Japan had extended its influence on the mainland of Asia and threatened European and American interests in China. Moreover, the Anglo-Japanese Alliance, formed in 1902 and renewed in 1911, was due to expire. Some parts of the British Empire were in favor of its renewal; other parts, especially Canada, believed that to continue the Alliance would seriously injure Anglo-American relations. The new situation which had arisen in the Pacific, as well as a possible naval rivalry resulting from the Anglo-American controversy over neu-

[58] A. Engeley, *The Politics of Naval Disarmament* (Williams & Norgate, London, 1932), has a good general discussion of the question; also, Benjamin H. Williams, *The United States and Disarmament* (McGraw-Hill Book Co., 1931).

tral rights, induced the Secretary of State to summon the Washington Conference, which met on November 12, 1921.

At the first session Mr. Hughes startled the delegates by the definite and far-reaching proposals which he made; and the relative success of the Conference was largely due to the fact that a detailed scheme had been prepared beforehand. The United States based its plan[59] upon four principles:

1. Abandonment of all capital-ship building programs.
2. Scrapping of a number of the older ships to permit still further reduction.
3. Maintenance of existing naval ratios as far as possible.
4. Reduction of auxiliary ships in the same proportion as reduction in capital-ship tonnage.

After considerable discussion the Conference agreed to limit capital ships to 35,000 tons and guns to 16 inches (with two exceptions); aircraft carriers (limited in most cases to eight-inch guns) were not to exceed 27,000 tons. It drew up rules for the replacement of these types of vessels; these rules were important in limiting naval expenditure, because the rapidity of inventions threatened to render warships quickly obsolete. The control of the rate of replacement was, therefore, a success of the first order.

The attempt to abolish the submarine failed. Japan was willing (reluctantly, it is true) to accept the ratio for submarines which had been adopted for capital ships, i.e., Great Britain, 5; United States, 5; Japan, 3; France, 1.75; Italy, 1.75. But the French refused. They realized that during the World War of 1914–1918 the submarine had challenged the battleship and that "auxiliary craft" were no longer merely auxiliary but were "vitally important." Had not the German submarine campaign brought Great Britain, despite its superiority in capital ships, almost to defeat? Moreover, France expected a *quid pro quo* in the form of a security arrangement for Europe, in return for its participation in naval limitation plans. But Mr. Hughes refused to link naval questions with the European problem. France therefore would not agree to accept an inferior position in submarines, and failure to limit submarines ended the hope of limiting destroyers and cruisers.

The Treaty also provided that no new fortifications and naval bases were to be established in the Pacific (excluding Hawaii and Singapore); it prohibited any increase in facilities for the repair and maintenance of naval forces; and it forbade any increase in

---

[59] Hugh Latimer, *Naval Disarmament* (Royal Institute of International Affairs, London, 1930), p. 5.

coastal defenses. Japan would accept the 5 : 5 : 3 ratio only on condition that Great Britain and the United States agreed "not to add to their existing fortifications and naval bases in those areas in the Pacific in which they might have constituted threats to Japan's existing spheres of influence."[60]

The Treaty was to last for ten years. At the same time the Nine-Power pact, a political agreement in which the powers agreed on policies relating to China, and the Four-Power pact, in which Great Britain, France, the United States, and Japan agreed to consult each other in the event of a crisis in the Pacific, were signed. Most authorities agree that the success of the naval limitation program at Washington was closely connected with the successful political agreement; limitation of battleships and aircraft carriers bore a close relation to political stabilization in the Far East. Failure of limitation in submarines, destroyers, and cruisers was not unrelated to the failure to provide security guaranties for France. In so far as the powers agreed upon the fundamentals of policy, they surmounted the technical obstacles which confronted the naval experts; but where they could not agree upon policy, they reached no technical agreement.

By failing to limit *all* categories of vessels, the Conference left the way open for an Anglo-American "cruiser race," which began to strain relations between the two countries, especially by the year 1926. To remedy the situation, President Coolidge invited the Five Powers to a conference at Geneva in 1927. At the outset France wished to discuss security, but the Anglo-Saxon powers insisted upon confining the Conference to technical problems of reduction and limitation. The French therefore refused to take part; Italy, which was demanding Franco-Italian naval equality, also absented itself. Only three powers therefore attended the Conference, which opened in an unfortunate atmosphere and soon was in difficulties over cruisers.

The United States desired to keep the 10,000-ton cruisers with eight-inch guns in order to offset the disadvantage under which it labored by reason of its small number of naval bases. Britain was anxious to limit the number of 10,000-ton cruisers with six-inch guns. The United States delegates opposed the British proposal because the six-inch gun would permit Britain to arm its merchant vessels by strengthening their decks—merchantmen could take six-inch but not the larger guns. Because Britain had the largest

[60] Latimer, *op. cit.,* p. 8.

merchant marine, both the United States and Japan felt that the abolition of the larger cruisers in favor of smaller type would give Britain the advantage of being able to utilize merchant vessels for war purposes. Great Britain denied that "converted" merchant ships would give any great advantage in "combatant effectiveness."

The British then argued that because the British Empire was so widespread, and its lines of communications were so extensive, it would need at least seventy cruisers in order to safeguard its essential sea routes in time of war, whatever the number possessed by the other powers. The United States replied that if Britain insisted upon this figure, the other two powers must arm accordingly and the result of a Conference called to limit armaments would be to increase them. The only way to effect a genuine limitation was to set a maximum total tonnage in auxiliary vessels (cruisers, destroyers, and submarines) of 400,000; otherwise, there would be no point in signing a treaty.

The failure of the Conference was occasioned by the following: (1) the cruiser problem, (2) the Anglo-American difference over six- and eight-inch guns, (3) the propaganda of large sections of the press and the activities of the armament firms, as revealed by William B. Shearer, who confessed his part in attempting to wreck the Conference, and (4) the inadequacy of diplomatic preparation. There had been little or no prior discussion of political objectives, and the experts who attempted to find a basis of technical parity were unable to do so. The difficulties confronting the Conference were, as the French had insisted, primarily political, and not technical and arithmetical. The real aim was security; and mathematical ratio alone bears no necessary relation to the needs of national security. The experts tried in vain to match a cruiser with eight-inch guns against a cruiser with six-inch guns. Preoccupation with "mathematical parity" necessarily led to disappointment—the world could not be saved by "faith, hope, and parity," because total resources and political objectives and alliances had to be taken into account. Norman Angell pertinently commented:

I am rather less interested in the caliber of guns than in the direction in which they are finally going to shoot . . . . it really makes a difference . . . . who is going to be with us and who against us is important, and that depends upon policy. Merely to equate weapons, and to leave undecided the question of their use, does not solve the problem.

The failure of the Geneva Conference induced, as a natural reaction, the reassertion of the political factor. The French view that security must precede disarmament had been in large measure vindicated. The wide acceptance of the Kellogg Pact in 1928 provided a more hopeful political atmosphere and encouraged a new move for disarmament, despite a serious complication which arose out of the Anglo-French Naval Compromise of 1928.

President Hoover and Premier MacDonald discussed the cruiser question, and decided provisionally that the United States should have a "superiority in large cruisers and the British a superiority in smaller cruisers." This agreement on a subject which had wrecked the 1927 Geneva Conference was a great step forward; but no success attended the other important question—the French demand for security. On December 20, 1929, France reiterated its fundamental position, and announced that the Kellogg Pact did not effectively increase the amount of collective security against aggression beyond that already guaranteed by the League of Nations. The French again questioned the validity of merely applying "mathematical ratios" to the problem of limiting navies, and claimed that the strength of their navy must be based upon national requirements, including the colonial empire and the length of lines of communications to be guarded.

Moreover, the French position was complicated by the problem of the Mediterranean. Italy announced that it would reduce its navy to any figure provided that no other Continental power exceeded that total. The French, however, asserted that Italian mathematical naval equality with France would in fact put France in a position of inferiority; the latter had to protect not only its position in the Mediterranean but also its colonies in West Africa and the Far East. Should France be engaged in an overseas war, her navy would be dispersed and Italy with her navy concentrated in the Mediterranean would be able to endanger French security. Italy argued that if France were permitted a larger navy because of her colonies and extended communications, Italy would be reduced to a position of permanent inferiority in the Mediterranean. The French alliance with Yugoslavia made Italy realize the danger of having two potential enemies, one in the west and one in the east, especially in view of Franco-Italian rivalries in southeastern Europe. A Mediterranean "Locarno Pact" by which the Mediterranean powers would guarantee the security of Italy and France, much as the Locarno signatories had guaranteed the security of Germany and France, might have solved the problem.

Britain, however, would not undertake added responsibilities in this region, because, in its opinion, the Mediterranean problem could not be separated from the more general question of south-eastern and central Europe; it did not intend to increase its obligations beyond those incurred under the League Covenant.

The London Naval Conference opened on January 21, 1930. France almost immediately demanded a total of 724,479 tons, and would lower its level only provided that it could obtain added political guaranties of security. The 1929 Sino-Russian crisis had revealed the inadequacy of the Kellogg Pact and the need of further machinery. France accordingly asked Britain if it would clarify its obligations under Article 16 of the Covenant and be willing to use the British fleet against an aggressor named by the League. The British would make no commitments until they knew that the United States would modify its neutrality policy or, at least, join in consultation in the event of a crisis. Secretary Stimson would not bind his country to a consultative pact, and his stand seemed to preclude any possibility of a political agreement which would induce France to join in further disarmament plans. A breakdown occurred: France and Italy withdrew, leaving the three major naval powers once more to wrestle with the problem of cruisers, destroyers, and submarines.

The Treaty as finally adopted provided, first, for no new battleship construction before 1936; the signatories agreed to extend their "capital-ship holiday" for another six years. Certain battleships were to be scrapped, so as to enable the three nations to reduce the number and tonnage of ships of the line. Great Britain undertook to scrap five ships, the United States three, and Japan one; this step would bring the three navies nearer to the 5 : 5 : 3 ratio provided for in the Washington Conference of 1921. Secondly, the Treaty provided for maintenance of the Washington Treaty arrangements concerning the tonnage level of aircraft carriers in opposition to a British proposal to modify them, and a redefinition of the aircraft carriers to include ships under 10,000 tons. It also provided for limitation of the other categories in large and small cruisers, destroyers, and submarines. The United States received a larger tonnage in large-gun cruisers, Britain a greater tonnage in smaller-gun cruisers. In this manner, the obstacle which had wrecked the Geneva Conference in 1927 was surmounted. The United States in agreeing to a 150,000-tonnage in cruisers accepted a considerable reduction, having over 290,000 tons when the Conference met. Great Britain and the United

States had favored the abolition of the submarine on the plea that it was essentially a weapon of aggression. The French and Japanese delegates claimed that it was a defensive instrument and far less costly than the battleship, which Japan proposed should be abolished. The Treaty gave Japan equality with Britain and the United States in submarines. Japan, in return, accepted an unequal position in cruisers and destroyers but obtained a modification of the 5 : 5 : 3 ratio (applied to capital ships) to 10 : 10 : 7 for cruisers and destroyers. The ratio was not to constitute a binding precedent, and Japan's action was to be "entirely without prejudice to our attitude at the Conference to follow." Finally, the Treaty contained the so-called "escape clause," by which a signatory power, if it deemed its security threatened by the naval construction of a nonsignatory power, could give notice of the increase that it would require in its own tonnage.

Defenders of the Treaty hailed it as a noteworthy achievement; they emphasized the importance of an agreement among the three major powers on all the categories of armed vessels, the settlement of the dispute between the United States and Great Britain over the cruiser question, the extension of the Washington Treaty relative to capital ships, and the great financial economies effected. Their opponents fastened attention on Article 21, the escape clause, which, they feared, would give the signatory powers an excuse to take advantage of a general situation to scrap the Treaty and renew the naval race. On the whole, optimists were right; the Treaty held good until 1936; but by that time any hope for further disarmament had disappeared.

The events after 1930—Japan's invasion of Manchuria, the breakdown of the World Economic Conference, the failure of the Disarmament Conference, the economic crisis and its accompanying emotional stresses and strains, the Italian aggression in Ethiopia—together chilled the political climate in which the London Naval Conference of 1935 had to meet. At the preliminary conversations in 1934 Japan demanded naval equality, and thereafter refused to modify its position.

The Japanese viewpoint was that (1) Japan did not accept the 5 : 5 : 3 ratio as final at Washington in 1921; the ratio had been modified in 1930, and Japan had served notice that it would reserve the right to re-open the question; (2) the progress of naval science had altered the situation in the Pacific by increasing the radius of action of naval vessels; Japan therefore had to strengthen her defensive equipment; (3) Japan had to reckon with the growing power of the Soviet Union, which had submarines and fighting planes concentrated in Vladivostok only 500 miles from Tokyo and Osaka; and (4) prestige and national honor required that Japan enjoy naval equality.

Accordingly, Japan proposed an all-round reduction on a 2 : 2 : 2 ratio; on this basis she was prepared to scrap approximately 250,000 tons in capital ships, 70,000 tons in aircraft carriers, and 100,000 tons in big cruisers. Japan would reduce her naval strength to about one-half its existing tonnage if Great Britain and the United States would make similar reductions. Japan again urged the abolition of offensive weapons, saying that a navy should be sufficient for defensive purposes only, that governments should agree to abolish capital ships, aircraft carriers, and big cruisers, and in this manner lessen the burden upon their taxpayers and at the same time diminish international tension.

The American viewpoint was admirably stated by Admiral Pratt as follows:

It has been stated openly in the press that Japan at the next naval conference will ask for an increase in the naval ratio assigned her. Is the request logical on the ground of security? It is not, and technical men know it. . . . .

Let us ask ourselves certain questions.

In time of war, does Japan have the seas of the world to cover as a necessary part of her own security, as does the British Empire? She does not, and in addition she has a secure line to the mainland which England has not.

Does Japan have two great ocean fronts and one of the main water arteries of the world to defend in case of war, as does the United States? She does not.

As a neutral in a great war, would the obligations and responsibilities imposed upon Japan put as heavy a burden on her shoulders as they would upon either Great Britain or the United States? They would not.

Is there any nation in the world, which, after taking care of its essential obligations at home and elsewhere, could lay successful blockade to the coast of Japan? There is not.

In the last half century has there ever been any action taken against Japan on the part of the two leading sea Powers which legitimately could be called aggressive? The writer thinks not.

Is a Japanese claim for increase of ratios justified on the grounds of national income? Japan's national income is approximately 16½ times less than ours, yet in the eleven years following 1922 her expenditures for new naval construction exceeded our own during eight of those years, and the ratio of her naval budget to national income is 5½ times greater than our own.

No, the Japanese claim for an actual increase in her naval ratio will not further the purposes of peace, and must find other reasons than equality and security.[61]

The London Naval Conference which met in December 1935 thus had little hope of success from the beginning. Great Britain wished to invite Germany, but France refused to assent, on the ground that such a step would be equivalent to condoning Germany's violation of the Treaty of Versailles in unilaterally rearming in March 1935. The European nations were already busy with rearmament on land and in the air, the British Parliament being about to vote huge sums for military and aerial preparations. The Hoare-Laval Plan, which dealt a further blow at collective security and intensified international unrest, appeared on the day the conference opened; and Italy announced that it would not sign any naval agreement until sanctions had been lifted and her position in Ethiopia recognized.

No new arguments were brought forward during the ten days of discussion, and no amount of effort on the part of the other nations could persuade Japan to modify her position. On January 15, 1936, the die was cast: France, Great Britain, Italy, and the United States rejected the Japanese claim for equality, whereupon Japan withdrew from the Conference.

On March 25, the British, French, and United States delegates signed a Treaty which reflected the growing anarchy in international relations. Compared with the Washington (1921) and London (1930) treaties it appears as a pale, ineffectual ghost. Although it provided for a measure of qualitative limitation, it omitted the most important matters. No limitation remained on the number of battleships, aircraft-carriers, cruisers, destroyers, and submarines which the nations might build and no mention was made of ratios. Nor was that all. The few agreements which the Conference had been able to reach were weakened by an "escape clause." Any signatory on grounds of national security requirements might notify other parties that it would no longer observe the restrictions imposed by the Treaty. This step was taken by Great Britain on September 3, 1939, when it informed the United States that in consequence of the war with Germany it suspended "all of the obligations of the said treaty."

[61] Admiral William V. Pratt, *Foreign Affairs,* July 1934.

ATTEMPTS TO LIMIT THE PRIVATE MANUFACTURE OF ARMAMENTS

Many people believed that the private manufacture of armaments has been and is an outstanding cause of wars, and that international security might be strengthened if the munitions industries were nationalized or their profits drastically reduced. Undoubtedly armament firms have materially added to the world's fear and unrest, and it is significant that the statesmen and experts who drew up the League Covenant included in this document Article 8, which reads: "The Members of the League agree that the manufacture by private enterprise of munitions and implements of war is open to grave objections." And the Temporary Mixed Commission in its 1921 report condemned the system of private manufacture of arms because firms had been active in fomenting war scares, had attempted to bribe government officials at home and abroad, had disseminated false reports concerning military and naval expenditures of different countries so as to stimulate further armament expenditure, had sought to influence public opinion through control of the press, had organized international armament rings to play off one country against another, and had created international armament trusts to increase the price of armaments sold to governments. Ample evidence exists to support these charges,[62] but unless one remembers that armament firms are government-sponsored and government-encouraged he will misunderstand the basic problems.[63] As far back as 1887 a British cabinet minister had claimed that armament firms were an important element in the nation's defense. Nearly sixty years later the Minister of War said substantially the same thing—that these private firms were part of Great Britain's reserves and to abolish them would be to deal a fatal blow to British security. The United States War Department has defended the private system and has opposed the nationalization of manufacture of armaments. And governments permit private firms to fill orders for foreign governments, even though the guns, ships, airplanes, and munitions which they make may later be turned against the manufacturing country and thousands of men may be killed by the armaments made in their own land by their fellow nationals. War departments justify the system by saying that national security requires

[62] Details are necessarily omitted from this volume.

[63] P. J. Noel Baker, *The Private Manufacture of Armaments* (Oxford University Press, 1937, New York), pp. 56–81.

that private firms keep operating, which they can do only by also catering to foreign markets.

Governments award honors and titles to important persons in the armament business. They grant direct and indirect subsidies. They give contracts to different firms and not necessarily to those who produce most cheaply, so that in wartime they may have a sufficient number of producing units to take care of the tremendous expansion in output required. They give private firms the results of their research into complicated and technical problems of armament and munition manufacture. They even encourage banks of their own country to finance orders abroad, and have gone so far as to provide guaranties from national treasuries. For example, the French government supported loans to Russia, Bulgaria, Poland, Yugoslavia, and other countries in order to enable these nations to buy munitions from French firms.

Governments have assisted private companies by releasing the latest designs of war materials in order that firms may supply foreign countries with the most up-to-date products. In April 1934 an American firm wrote to the government of Peru that it could furnish "the most modern fighting unit of its type ever developed—a type furnished only to the United States Army Air corps. . . . . Provided that we have a contract for at least ten planes we will be able to secure permission from the United States government to build for Peru."

The Nye Commission found that the United States War and Navy departments permitted private companies to sell to foreign countries planes and engines which were being constructed for the United States government so that the American manufacturers could "make prompt delivery" and thus keep their factories in operation. It is charged that some companies "may have supplied military secrets in order to secure foreign orders." Governments lend their experts to foreign governments in order to enable the latter to modernize their navy, army, and air forces. They permit private firms to make use of their own army and navy officers or ex-officers to serve as agents. We have the curious spectacle of men who as high military and naval officials have been entrusted with important military secrets later serving as commercial agents to sell armaments to foreign markets. The United States government even permitted some of its vessels to demonstrate the guns of the Driggs Company to the Turkish government. The private manufacturers of armaments therefore have grounds for grievance when public opinion accuses them of being villains, profiteers, and traitors. However unethical and corrupt many of their practices may be, they can claim that governments regard them as important and even indispensable elements in national security. Yet there must be something fundamentally wrong in the world when governments defend an armaments system which national and international commissions and responsible statesmen have condemned.

ATTEMPTS TO LIMIT THE PROFITS OF ARMAMENT FIRMS

If it is necessary to use private firms for national defense, may not some of the evils be overcome by taxing excessive profits made from the expansion of industry in war time? Unfortunately, the problem is simpler to answer in theory than to remedy in practice. Take for example the bill introduced into Congress to take away supernormal profits by a 95 per cent tax on the difference between war-time and peace-time profits. Critics claimed that taxing war profits would not prevent war booms, and that there was no evidence to show that any such taxation could be effective. They pointed out that after the last war interminable controversy developed over "valuations." If a company valued its plant at one million dollars, and the Bureau of Internal Revenue valued the plant at $400,000, there was endless controversy. Companies increased their depreciation figures in order to avoid paying taxes, and probably exaggerated their overhead costs and padded their estimates. Tax evasion seems to have been comparatively easy. Some companies increased their costs by paying extra salaries and even by making extraordinary allowances for such pleasantries as cigars, liquors, and "entertainments." For these and other reasons the Senate Munitions Committee reported: "We must guard against a blind belief that all profiteering can be ended by proposals for wartime taxes and industrial control."[64]

Finally, as the War Department had emphasized, it is more important to win a war than to save money, and unless a country is prepared to accept wholesale regimentation, it must resign itself to permitting wars with profits to war industries or boldly face the alternative of nationalization.

NATIONALIZATION OF MUNITIONS INDUSTRIES

Proponents of nationalization of munitions plants claim that governmental control would eliminate the undesirable activities—

---

[64] Quoted in Stephen and Joan Raushenbush, *War Madness* (National Home Library Foundation, Washington, D.C., 1937), p. 148.

bribery, propaganda, false rumors, international trusts, high costs and excessive profits—associated with private manufacture, decrease the international traffic in arms, and reduce lobbying for heavier armament expenditure. Most of them admit that the government-owned plants could supply the military and naval requirements in peace time but that it would be uneconomical to have "publicly-owned establishments adequate for war-time needs." They add that nationalization would materially reduce the causes of war, especially if shipment of arms to belligerents were forbidden.

Critics of nationalization proposals assert: (1) Group pressures would not be eliminated, because the communities in which government plants were situated would resort to lobbying in order to maintain the establishments at full capacity. (2) Governments could not expect the close co-operation of private industry which it now enjoys if it turned away from private firms and, unless the government is prepared to regiment most if not all of the hundreds and thousands of processes which are involved, it must to a considerable degree depend upon the goodwill and co-operation of private enterprise. (3) The record of countries in which the government maintains control over the armament industry—Japan, Soviet Union, Germany, and Italy—does not support the view that the private control of arms is a major factor in promoting wars. As Shepardson and Scroggs put it, "the totalitarian states of Europe . . . . were closing in on the private profits of war industry, and at the same time they were making themselves the greatest known threat to the peace of the world." (4) Most nations do not produce their armaments but depend for their supplies upon ten manufacturing countries, and any step which deprived them of the right to buy armaments would constitute a serious threat to their security. The problem of nationalization thus merges into the problem of controlling the international traffic in arms.

ATTEMPTS TO CONTROL THE INTERNATIONAL TRAFFIC IN ARMS

Benjamin Williams lists three main reasons for attempting to meet this evil: (1) Means must be provided to safeguard colonies, mandates, and other possessions from disorder and revolution. (2) A successful disarmament treaty will require measures to limit and supervise the amount of war material in each country, involving a supervisory body to see that governments fulfill their obligations and do not obtain munitions from other countries. (3) Shipment of arms from neutral countries in war time must be controlled. The important question is whether neutrals should refrain from sending arms to both belligerents or should shut off supplies for the aggressor nation only.

The international conventions signed at Brussels in 1890 and at St. Germain in 1919 need not be reviewed here. The 1925 Convention, signed by forty-four governments, designated five categories of arms: "(1) arms, ammunition, and implements of war exclusively designed for warfare; (2) arms and ammunition capable of use for both military and other purposes; (3) war vessels and their armaments; (4) aircraft and aircraft engines; and (5) gunpowder and explosives, except common black gunpowder; arms and ammunition without military value."[65] Under it, government licenses were necessary for exports; normally shipment might be made only to governments, though in certain cases they might go to private manufacturers; and the government of the importing state must give its consent in a signed order. A special regulation was adopted for particular zones in Africa and in the Near East; and more technical matters were included in the Convention.

For several years the United States held aloof, the Senate refusing to consider the Convention until 1934, when it voted a conditional ratification. In the same year the American government proposed a far-reaching Draft Convention which provided for: (1) strict inspection and supervision of manufacture and trade; (2) licenses, renewable every five years, for private manufacture; (3) licenses, for export and import of arms; (4) a Permanent Disarmament Commission at Geneva, which should receive from the signatory powers lists of state armament factories, copies of licenses to private manufacturers, lists of orders received by the state and licensed factories, information as to manufactures and copies of all import and export licenses issued; (5) empowering the Commission to examine the information, set up a publicity system, make special investigations, and establish a permanent and automatic system of inspection within the boundaries of the signatory powers. The Nye Committee also made several far-reaching recommendations to prevent companies from shipping arms in violation of national embargoes and treaty obligations.

It should be obvious that little success will attend efforts to

[65] B. H. Williams, *op. cit.*, p. 378.

reduce the international traffic in or the private manufacture of arms while the danger of war still exists. The traffic and the manufacture, attended though they are by heartless greed and callous indifference to human suffering, are the outcome of the prevailing international anarchy. It betrays a poor sense of proportion to condemn the armament firms and at the same time permit governments to organize for and to precipitate war. Until the political conditions of the world improve, talk of controlling traffic in arms will remain ineffective.[66]

SUMMARY

The foregoing analysis should make clear that only when a substantial measure of political agreement had been reached did any success attend the Disarmament Conferences. The progressive deterioration of political relations in the last decade made technical limitation more and more impossible. Subsequent experience has shown that without much more effective security arrangements, any disarmament agreements must have been of a very fragile character. If shooting is now the last stage of a carefully planned psychological, economic, and political offensive, if arms come into play just to administer the *coup de grâce,* then measures must be taken to prevent the long, preliminary aggression in the nonmilitary fields.

We are therefore driven to conclude that until economic and psychological power cease to be instruments of war, the limitation of armaments will prove to be impossible of attainment or at best superficial in its achievement. And economic and psychological power cannot be divorced from military power while the modern sovereign state system remains.

[66] Engelbrecht and Hanighen, *Merchants of Death* (Dodd, Mead & Company, New York, 1934), p. 8.

Chapter XVI

REGIONAL INTERNATIONAL ORGANIZATION

UNCERTAINTY exists, as stated above, as to whether the enforcement of security in a particular area should be a matter of equal concern for all members of the League, irrespective of their geographical setting, or should be subject to special regional agreements by which the countries most immediately affected would assume major responsibility in maintaining peace. The Draft Treaty of Mutual Assistance and the Locarno Pact were based upon the latter idea. A series of graded obligations has been suggested:[1] the countries nearest the area of aggression would undertake the heaviest responsibilities, and those in outlying parts would assist by renouncing their neutral rights of trading with an aggressor nation.

In 1933 an attempt was made to save the Disarmament Conference by working out a plan of concentric circles, as it were, of forceful opposition to aggressor countries. It was suggested that in the event of a successful Disarmament Conference the United States would not insist upon its neutral rights with an aggressor; in continental Europe the land-powers would immediately use armed force against the aggressor; Great Britain, occupying an intermediate position between the outermost and innermost areas, could impose economic sanctions without sending men to fight; and the United States, by surrendering its freedom of the seas in the interests of world peace, would enable Great Britain to place its blockading power at the disposal of the defenders of peace on the European continent without becoming involved in the thorny question of neutral rights. Unfortunately, the Senate rejected the proposal.

In 1934 the French government proposed what might be called

---

[1] James T. Shotwell, *On the Rim of the Abyss* (The Macmillan Company, New York, 1936), chapters vii and xii; see also Eduard Beneš, *Democracy Today and Tomorrow* (The Macmillan Company, New York, 1939), pp. 126–27.

a refined system of regional security pacts. The weakness of the universal system of guaranties lay in the fact that distant members could not be expected to undertake the same burdens as near-by nations in stopping an aggressor. American countries might well ask that European governments accept the first major responsibility in preventing aggression in Europe. The French plan provided for regional agreements within Europe: the Locarno Pact would take care of Western Europe; certain nations were to sign a Mediterranean pact; others would join in a Central European pact; and some would accede to an Eastern European agreement. That there would be overlapping is obvious. But the French hoped that these subcontinental schemes would be sufficient to prevent aggression.

These attempts were not successful; but the future may yet see the adoption of some such plan.

During the postwar period other attempts were made to form regional organizations within Europe. Most, if not all of them, were designed to supplement and not compete with the League of Nations; they included the Little Entente, the steps toward a Balkan Union, the co-operation of the Scandinavian countries, and the Baltic Pact.

THE LITTLE ENTENTE

The Little Entente was formed in order that Czechoslovakia, Rumania, and Yugoslavia might co-operate to retain what they had won in the World War of 1914–1918 and to safeguard themselves against the domination and encroachment of the great powers.[2] At the Peace Conference the three nations were referred to as "Powers with limited interests," a disagreeable reminder of their dependent position, and later were told to "reach no decision" and "undertake no action" before consulting the Conference of Ambassadors. Accordingly, the three governments during the next few years worked out methods of co-operation. At Genoa in 1922 they agreed upon a common policy and joined with Poland in order that one of their representatives might sit on all the commissions which were considering different aspects of the European economic problem. They gained here the right of continuous representation on the Council, and thereafter continued the method of rotating representation at the Hague Conference. They began

[2] See John O. Crane, *The Little Entente* (The Macmillan Company, New York, 1931), pp. 3–15.

periodic meetings of their foreign ministers, and thereby introduced a measure of routine into co-ordinating their foreign policies.

The advent of Hitler to power in 1933 caused the Little Entente to enter into still closer relations. The members signed a new pact of organization on February 16, 1933, the object of which was "the complete unification of their general policies" and the "establishment of an organization by which this common policy shall be directed." This organization comprised a Permanent Council of Foreign Ministers, a Permanent Secretariat at Geneva, and an Economic Council. Politically the Little Entente thus showed a remarkable degree of international co-operation for several years. But political co-operation was only one side of the picture; the question arose how effective could they make economic co-operation in the face of the extraordinarily complicated problems which confronted them.

The three partners inherited a terrible economic situation after the collapse of the Austro-Hungarian Empire, which in prewar days had formed an extensive economic unit. After the Peace of 1919 this economic unity had given way to a number of passionately self-conscious national groups; the lines of international trade were broken, and the desire for national self-sufficiency and national security caused the nations of southern and eastern Europe to build many uneconomic industries.

The difficulty of putting the economic "humpty dumpty" together again may be seen from the fact that Czechoslovakia had no tariff treaty with either of the other members of the Little Entente until 1930, almost a decade after the political agreement had been signed. The reason is clear. The Little Entente powers formed an ellipse-shaped group partly surrounding Austria and Hungary, which separated them; and Austria and Hungary were a necessary element in any real economic integration of the Little Entente.

The Little Entente found that it could not solve its economic problems in regional isolation because they extended beyond the territories of its component parts to embrace central and eastern Europe. In turn the economic problem of central and eastern Europe formed part of the general European question, which was linked up with the economic situation of the whole world. Such are the limits of regionalism: it may solve certain problems both political and economic; but when more fundamental questions are involved, a solution upon a wider basis becomes indispensable and without such a solution the achievements of regional co-operation rest upon precarious foundations and may collapse at any moment.

Recent history has confirmed the truth of this judgment. For the Little Entente collapsed when the League of Nations and Great Britain and France failed to check the onward march of Hitler's Germany and Mussolini's Italy.

THE BALKAN CONFERENCES

The Balkan peninsula has an area equal to the combined area of France and Germany and contains between fifty and sixty million people. The six nations within its confines have likewise attempted to build a regional organization in order to gain political security and promote economic and social well-being.

The idea of a Balkan Union is not new. It had been suggested as early as the latter part of the eighteenth century, and proposals along the same general line were made in 1888, 1905, and 1910. Several events subsequent to 1918 helped to advance the idea of a Balkan regional organization: the example of the Little Entente; the 1925 Locarno Pact; the settlement of the Greco-Yugoslavic dispute in 1929 over the Yugoslavic demand for an enlarged free zone at Salonika; the pact of Greco-Turkish friendship signed in the same year which ended the long and bitter rivalry between those two countries; the general influence of the League of Nations in the Balkans; M. Briand's plan for the United States of Europe; and several bilateral Balkan agreements. Individuals threw their energies into the Balkan movement. The most prominent was M. Papanastassiou, a former prime minister of Greece, who did a great deal to bring about the first Balkan Conference.[3]

At the twenty-seventh Universal Congress of Peace held at Athens in October 1929 representatives of the Balkan countries prepared the ground for later developments. At this Congress arose the major difficulties which were to confront the conference during the next five years. The Greek group advocated a confederation and a Balkan pact to outlaw war. Yugoslavian representatives were not enthusiastic about the political approach, which, they felt, would bring up the awkward question of minorities and lead to serious disputes concerning sovereignty over internal affairs. They wished to consider matters which promised the maximum amount of immediate co-operation, and therefore urged the

[3] A. P. Papanastassiou, *Vers l'Union Balkanique* (Centre Européen de la Dotation Carnegie, Paris, 1934).

consideration of economic questions, arguing that if the Balkan countries attempted to raise the standard of living by economic means the political questions would become less acute. The Bulgarian representatives insisted upon considering the problem of minorities, saying that no real progress could come in inter-Balkan relations until the several million Bulgarians who were living under the rule of other governments obtained more humane and just treatment and respect for their political and economic and social rights.

The Congress drew up an agenda for the next year and proposed the organization of a Balkan Union, the holding of conferences, and the adoption of particular measures to promote political, economic, and intellectual co-operation of the Balkan countries.

The need for economic co-operation stood out in clear relief. A committee report showed that inter-Balkan commerce amounted to only 9 per cent of the total foreign commerce of the member states. High tariffs blocked trade between the Balkan countries, and communication facilities were poor and travel was difficult.[4] Unofficial conferences between 1930 and 1934 made many recommendations, which dealt with a customs union, the unification of tariff nomenclature so that exporters could more easily calculate duties payable on imported goods, agricultural credit societies, the encouragement of co-operatives, the creation of a Balkan Chamber of Commerce, and a Balkan Tourist Federation, the establishment of a Balkan Bank, and measures to improve the cultivation of cereals and tobacco.

Other proposals included the building of railways, motor roads, telegraph lines between the capitals, the "construction of two main trunk lines (rail and road) through the Balkans," the building of bridges over the Danube, and improvement of existing railroad lines. Without doubt many of these recommendations were sound, but since the Balkan countries were all agricultural in character, produced much the same commodities, and had relatively little to export to each other, the question arose as to the fundamental basis of economic co-operation. Nevertheless tobacco conferences and conferences of co-operative societies were held. It was hoped that relations between capital and labor might be improved by extending the methods of conciliation and arbitration to industrial disputes. The proposal to set up a regional customs union met

[4] See N. J. Padelford, *Peace in the Balkans* (Oxford University Press, New York, 1935), p. 19.

with serious difficulties, for Bulgaria preferred to sign bilateral commercial treaties. Many of the recommendations remained recommendations only, and constructive action failed to materialize, owing in part to the fact that the proposals would involve the expenditure of money, which in turn would necessitate the imposition of more taxes—not an easy thing to do in a time of economic depression.

In what might be called the social and intellectual arena of human life, the conferences made many recommendations. Members realized the importance of attempting to lessen the amount of international friction caused by the teaching of a kind of history which often served merely to confirm national prejudices. They therefore proposed that a Balkan historical institute be formed which might assist in a revision of history textbooks and emphasize the common heritage of the countries in the Balkan peninsula. The conferences drew attention to the desirability of reaching a greater measure of uniformity in the laws of the respective Balkan states and reducing the element of conflict in them. Other proposals looked to the exchange of teachers, professors, and students, the establishment of a Balkan press association, the adoption of a children's charter based upon the model charter of the League of Nations, the development of inter-Balkan athletic contests, the translation of the finest works of Balkan literature, and the inauguration of "Balkan Weeks." In November 1932 a free dispensary was founded in Athens "for the treatment of nationals of any Balkan state who suffered from tuberculosis."[5]

Moreover, a number of important measures were undertaken, including the establishment of the Balkan Chamber of Commerce and Industry, a Balkan co-operative office, the Oriental Tobacco Office, the Balkan Tourist Federation, and the maritime section of the Balkan Chamber of Commerce and Industry. These, it is suggested, are not negligible achievements if one considers the short period of time which elapsed before the collapse of Europe took place. The general deterioration in the European situation was to make any further progress impossible. As with the Little Entente, so with the Balkans. It was clear that regional co-operation could play a limited part, but, if the wider foundations of society were unsound, no amount of effort on the part of a few nations, especially small nations, to strengthen their own portion of the edifice of human association could hope to succeed.

---

[5] A. J. Toynbee, *Annual Survey of International Affairs,* 1934, p. 509.

SCANDINAVIAN CO-OPERATION

The Scandinavian countries—Denmark, Norway, Sweden, Iceland, and Finland—developed a fine regional international co-operation, and their experiment is one of considerable interest. These nations in past centuries fought one another about as frequently as other independent powers. Their close cultural relationship did not prevent bitter national wars. Norway was arrayed against Sweden and against Denmark, and the Swedes fought the Danes. Norway and Sweden were united from 1814 to 1905; but after their separation they maintained a cool and critical attitude toward each other.

The World War of 1914–1918 forced upon the Scandinavian countries the realization of the advantages of closer co-operation. During it the King of Sweden invited the King of Denmark and the King of Norway, and their foreign ministers, to meet him to consider problems arising out of the war and affecting the three countries in their neutral status.[6] The statesmen accordingly met in frequent consultation. Especially notable was the meeting in Oslo in 1917 when King Gustav at a banquet remarked that the Scandinavian countries were realizing a new unity and extended his right hand to the King of Norway, and his left hand to the King of Denmark in a gesture which made a lasting impression.

The political co-operation begun during the war was continued in the postwar period. When the Scandinavian representatives came to Geneva they held joint meetings to consider their mutual problems and invited neighboring countries to join in a frank interchange of views; and Dutch, Luxemburgian, Belgian, Swiss, and (before the civil war in Spain) Spanish delegations frequently met with them. Belgian and Dutch foreign ministers were invited to attend the meeting of Scandinavian foreign ministers to explore the possibilities of further political co-operation. Especially after the depression in 1931 co-operation became more intimate. For some years the meetings of foreign ministers had been discontinued; but they were revived in 1932 and in 1934 Finland entered the group and Iceland followed.

Co-operation went beyond political consultation. The countries attempted to unify their legal systems, with the result that there are probably more difficulties confronting the several states of the United States in legal co-operation than there are between

[6] C. J. Hambro, "When Kings and Foreign Ministers Meet," *Le Nord*, 1938, pp. 9–28.

the five Scandinavian countries. In matters of trade, banking, bankruptcy, divorce and marriage, insurance, minority protection, joint-stock companies, the recognition and enforcement of legal judgments and award of damages, the laws are identical in the five countries. Thus, a bankrupt cannot cross a border and create extradition difficulties.[7]

The unification of national laws did not depend entirely upon official action. Bar associations, judges, and committees of experts met and framed their recommendations. What were called neighborland committees, or executives in industry, trade unions, fishing, and farming, met to discuss practical matters and to prepare identical laws. These neighborland committees appointed their permanent secretaries. Teachers and even political parties had similar organizations and methods.

Expert committees met and analyzed the raw materials and natural resources of the Scandinavian countries and exchanged information and worked out plans, so that in case a European war might again subject the northern countries to blockade they would be able to stand the siege for at least two years.[8] In social questions, co-operation went far. If a Norwegian laborer in Sweden became unemployed, he received the same unemployment assistance that a Swedish worker would enjoy; and this mutual treatment held good throughout the countries—at the end of the year the amounts were totaled up and a country out of pocket for the support of unemployed nonnationals within its borders was reimbursed by the benefited countries.

Intellectual co-operation was not lacking. The governments took a forward step in the matter of school textbooks by appointing a committee from the five countries to examine the whole problem. As a result of their report the authorities undertook to eliminate from the textbooks expressions which might hurt the feelings of neighboring countries, and to present historical facts in the same way to the children of all the Scandinavian countries. The experiment aroused the interest of the International Institute of Intellectual Co-operation at Paris.

In economic and political matters the Scandinavian countries

[7] Birger Ekeberg, "Die Nordische Zusammenarbeit auf dem Gebiete der Gesetzgebung," *Le Nord,* 1938, pp. 82–91. Also, *The Northern Countries in World Economy,* published by the Delegations for the Promotion of Economic Co-operation between the Northern Countries (Johan Grundt Tanum, Oslo, 1937), chapters xiii and xiv.

[8] H. J. Procopé, "Economic Co-operation between the Northern Countries," *Le Nord,* 1938, pp. 48–58.

tried to fit their regional organization into the wider world society.
Regionalism was not an exclusive matter. They co-operated with
the League of Nations and were members of the Permanent Court
of International Justice, by which the important eastern Greenland controversy between Denmark and Norway was peacefully
determined in 1933. The relations of the northern countries to
the League of Nations and their attempts to stem the rising tide of
tariffs have been dealt with elsewhere.[9]

The Scandinavian regional organization did splendid work in
matters affecting the everyday life of its inhabitants. But like the
Little Entente, the Balkan Union, and the Baltic Pact, it was confronted with problems too great for it. The organization was not
powerful enough to be an efficient instrument of defense against the
great powers; and the greater the spread of disorder and insecurity
in Europe after 1935, the greater were the obstacles placed in the
way of peaceful co-operation for economic and social welfare in
the Scandinavian countries. When Russia invaded Finland, it
confronted the other members of the region with a tragic conflict
of loyalties. They saw one of their number ruthlessly treated, but
nevertheless each felt constrained to consult what seemed to be its
own immediate interest. They could not have both peace and continued co-operation with Finland.

THE BALTIC PACT

In 1918, M. M. Piip and C. R. Pusta published a plan for a
Baltic League which was to embrace three groups—the Scandinavian, the East Baltic, and the South Baltic (Lithuania and
Poland)—for the purpose of safeguarding the freedom of the
Baltic Sea. A number of conferences, beginning with one at Riga-
Bulduri in 1920, were subsequently held and several treaties of
political accord, conciliation, and arbitration were signed.[10] The
attempt to develop a regional organization did not meet with much
success in those early years, partly because of the bitter dispute between Poland and Lithuania. Nor could the position of the smaller
nations be entirely independent of the balance-of-power struggle
among the great powers which were interested in the Baltic. The
neutralization of the Aaland Islands, and of the islands in the Gulf
of Finland, the grant to Danzig of the status of a free city, the
award of autonomy to Memel, and the opening of the Kiel Canal

[9] See above, pp. 211–13.
[10] See C. R. Pusta, *Le Statut juridique de la Mer Baltique à partir du
XIX siècle* (Librairie du Recueil Sirey, Paris, 1936).

as a result of the Peace treaties and subsequent settlements were too much intertwined with the position of Germany to enable the Baltic countries to do more than play a minor role; an attempt at closer relations would not make a major contribution without a settlement of international relations on a wider basis. The history of the years 1934–1940 was to illustrate the truth of this statement.

In 1934, after extensive negotiations, Esthonia, Latvia, and Lithuania signed the Baltic Pact. This experiment in regional co-operation was designed to enable the three countries more confidently to meet the troubled situation in Europe created by the development of German military power under Hitler. The dictator in *Mein Kampf* had written of attacking Russia; and, unless he were to go through Poland, he must go by way of the Baltic. Moreover, the three countries possessed an influential German minority, among whom were descendants of the Baltic baron-landlord class which had suffered from the land reforms after 1919. The 1934 treaty between Poland and Germany made the three countries realize the need for common action. In February 1934, Latvia and Esthonia signed a close agreement by which they were to be represented at international conferences by common delegations. They were to meet at conferences at regular intervals, and a permanent joint council was to be set up in order to co-ordinate legislation and, it was hoped, political and economic action as well.

Overtures were made to Lithuania; but Esthonia and Latvia were anxious not to become involved in Lithuania's quarrel with Poland over Vilna and in its quarrel with Germany over Memel. Accordingly the threefold pact signed in August and ratified in November 1934 excluded a united front on these two questions. The three powers, however, agreed that their foreign policies were to be a matter of common concern, and their foreign ministers were to confer at least twice a year. The first conference was held at Tallanin (Reval), November 30–December 1, and in January 1935 a bureau for the promotion of co-operation in economic and cultural matters met at Riga and drew up a program. The Union was to be open to other states, if the three parties agreed, and the treaty was to last for ten years.[11]

This regional experiment, like the others already surveyed, was of only limited importance. For their successful development

[11] *Annual Survey of International Affairs, 1934,* pp. 404–15.

regional agreements require a stable continental community. In so far as they attempt to combine military force against the great powers, they must fail. They can succeed as regional groups only in the economic and cultural fields; they cannot be effective instruments of defense and security. This truth was clearly revealed when Russia, which in 1934 had unsuccessfully proposed to Germany to give a joint guaranty to Finland, Lithuania, Latvia, and Esthonia, forced Esthonia to grant it facilities for naval and military action in the Baltic, undertook military operations against Finland, and finally absorbed the Baltic countries. The major problem of security can be settled only in the wider framework, because the major problems, although they may be touched off to war in the Balkans or the Baltic, in reality exist between the great powers. Regional agreements, to be successful, must be secondary; they must follow substantial agreement within the wider international community before they can play their subordinate, but not on that account unimportant, and creative part.

EUROPEAN UNION

The spectacle of a divided Europe with more than thirty customs barriers and twenty monetary systems, several thousand kilometers of boundaries, fragmented economic life, political rivalries, and accumulated national hatreds has caused political scientists, philosophers, and statesmen to ask whether this division is inevitable or whether the separate national groups have not been the result of mere political events. Geographically the great European plains offer few obstacles to communication and to concerted economic efforts; race differences are small; and Europe's natural wealth is great. Nevertheless Europe has lost its commanding position as the world's financial center and as the dominating political and cultural influence of the world. It has lost a large part of the world's markets, not merely because of the rise of manufactures elsewhere (involving a permanent loss) but also because its internecine struggles are ruining its economic efficiency. Culturally Europe is threatened by a submergence of the intellect and the subordination of the scientific spirit to political doctrines and warfare. The question is whether or not Europe can now preserve its finest political, economic, and cultural achievements without a transformation of its political institutions.

The Church, the Holy Roman Empire, and the scholars of the modern period have striven to maintain an adequate European unity. In 1464 King George de Podiebrady of Bohemia proposed to Louis XI of France an alliance of all Christian nations against Turkey; and, as M. Herriot writes, one cannot help asking if the course of history would not have been completely changed if the French king had accepted the invitation to join in forming the first federation of Europe. In 1593 Sully sent his Grand Design to King Henry IV. In 1716 l'Abbé Saint-Pierre published his Plan of Perpetual Peace. In the eighteenth century Voltaire wrote on the subject, proposing a European diet and a code for the settlement of disputes. The French financier, Necker, in 1784, criticized the balance-of-power system. Eleven years later, Immanuel Kant wrote his *Perpetual Peace,* in which he described the futility of treaties between independent nations. Kant criticized the idea of a Europe with small and great states and emphasized the need for abolishing permanent armies and for establishing a federation of free nations. Spiritual ideals he regarded as most important— the moral imperative must hold sway.

The French writers, Lamartine, Michelet, and Victor Hugo, wrote on the problem of Europe. Hugo in 1869 claimed that the idea of the frontier is the first of the enslaving conceptions.

Qui dit frontière, dit ligature. Coupez la ligature, effacez la frontière, ôtez le douanier, ôtez le soldat; en d'autres termes, soyez libres; la paix suit.[12]

Godin saw the need of extending European organization to economic problems and suggested that the kind of international organization set up to supervise the navigation of the Danube should be applied to all kinds of transportation, and proposed a treaty of peace in a document of forty-six articles.

The World War of 1914–1918, Europe's civil war in the eyes of many people, did not kill the idea of unity. In 1923, Count Coudenhove-Kalergi began preaching Pan-Europa: Europe's ills were political and not biological in nature, and could therefore be remedied by political means—by a European Federation. Under his plan England would not be included because of its overseas empire and its world interests—a Pan-Europe including England would "gain in power but lose in cohesion." The Soviet Union was not to be eligible because it was not democratic. Kalergi did not regard the League of Nations as a satisfactory instrument for European unity because in his opinion it was inorganic and was joined together "mechanically like bricks, large and small states,

---

[12] Quoted in E. Herriot, *Europe* (Les Editions Rieder, Paris, 1930), p. 34.

Asiatic and European, neighboring and distant, without regard to geography, history, culture, or economics." In 1925 the French Prime Minister, Herriot, announced, "If I have devoted my energies . . . . to the League of Nations, I have done so because in this great institution I have seen the first rough draft of the United States of Europe." And in his book published in 1930 he analyzed the political, economic, health, and intellectual needs of Europe, and concluded, at the end of a study, *"simplement pré-liminaire,"* with a number of principles: (1) The European union could be realized only within the framework of the League of Nations. (2) It should respect both the national and the international framework of society. (3) It should be open to all the European nations, including Great Britain, which had interests at the same time universal and European. (4) It should have representation of the nations on the basis of absolute equality. (5) It should work through periodic conferences and a permanent secretariat. (6) It should strive for the eradication of customs barriers and the establishment of a European credit organization. It could endure only under a régime of arbitration, disarmament, and security.

Other proposals have included those of M. Loucheur, who was particularly concerned with Europe's economic problem and analyzed European federation from the point of view of nationalization of production and the formation of cartels. But it was M. Briand's plan which aroused the greatest interest. On May 17, 1930, he sent a memorandum to the governments of Europe, proposing "some kind of a federal bond," some system which would permit Europe to "study, discuss, and settle problems likely to be of common interest." The new institution should operate within the League of Nations and be subordinate to it. There should be a regular European conference, a permanent political committee, special technical committees, and a secretariat. Nevertheless the union was not to infringe upon national sovereignty.

He proposed nine questions for discussion: (1) European economic reconstruction, through the development of cartels and the reduction of tariffs; (2) co-ordination of motor roads and canals; (3) improvement of intra-European traffic; (4) establishment of international financial credit for certain areas in Europe; (5) European labor problems, including migratory labor; (6) special application to Europe of the Health Organization methods developed by the League; (7) intellectual co-operation; (8) utilization of the Inter-Parliamentary Union; (9) the development of European sections within the more general international bureaus.

The replies to Briand's proposal, as one would expect, were by no means unanimous. All states agreed that a greater amount of European co-operation was desirable; but they differed in their views as to the methods to be pursued. First, what was Europe? Could one say that Russia and Turkey were within Europe or within Europe and Asia? And if within Europe, why should M. Briand propose to exclude them just because they were not members of the League of Nations? Some feared that the proposed organization would weaken the League of Nations by duplicating its machinery at a time when Geneva was endeavoring to establish itself on firm foundations. They denied that security was so exclusively a European problem that it could be settled purely along European lines. British interests in the Far East and its naval relations with the United States obviously prevented Great Britain from ignoring the armament strength of America and Japan; and Britain's military and naval strength would influence the policy of France, Italy, Germany, and Poland. The development of Russian military power would influence armament and security arrangements within the framework of M. Briand's new organization. Clearly if the United States were a member of the League of Nations, Europe's security would be increased.

Subsequent events have shown that the fundamental basis of security and disarmament is world-wide and not continental, and that European union is therefore a secondary, although not necessarily on that account an unimportant, problem.

Nor were economists satisfied that Europe possessed such a degree of economic interdependence and independence as to be able to dispense with the great amount of trade which had grown up with the rest of the world.[13] Mere contiguity, it was said, counts less for economic purposes now that sea traffic and air traffic have become so important.

Still other critics questioned whether one could speak of European union and national political sovereignty in the same breath: The terms seemed to be incompatible; it would be possible to have one or the other, but not both. Finally, Briand's proposal aroused the suspicion that France was exploiting the concept of European unity in order to maintain the status quo, and with it, French supremacy. Was the European Union to be used as the League of

[13] F. M. Russell, *Theories of International Relations* (D. Appleton-Century Co., 1936), p. 469.

Nations had been, to perpetuate the disabilities of the powers defeated in 1918? So asked Germany, Bulgaria, Italy, and Hungary.

Several committees were established and proceeded to conduct inquiries into European needs. A League Committee presented a report to the Stresa Conference on the agricultural situation in Europe and the proposal to establish a system of European credit. Investigation into transportation and other phases of life might have led to useful results had it not been for the fatal obstacle imposed by political rivalries. For the proposals for a United States of Europe failed primarily because of the foreign policies of the great powers, which preferred to trust to their own armed might, despite the fatal flaws which time was to reveal in that choice, rather than subordinate their traditional methods to a more comprehensive organization. They continued to act as if they could still perform the tasks which they had been able to fulfill in the nineteenth century, and refused to adapt themselves to new conditions. Consequently they all were to stagger under overwhelming burdens imposed by another war which broke out in 1939 and which threatened not only their national welfare but all European civilization. The following survey should reveal the tragic inadequacy, the shortsightedness, and lack of comprehensiveness of the policies carried out by the foreign offices of Britain, France, Italy, and the Soviet Union, which paved the way for the rapid conquests of Hitler's Germany and threatened Europe with a union based upon force rather than consent.

GREAT BRITAIN

Great Britain is an island; it is situated near Europe; is the center of a far-flung empire; and is a nation dependent upon world trade. This fourfold character makes the determination of Britain's foreign policy one of peculiar difficulty, and may explain the many hesitations and contradictions which have marked its governments' actions.

Traditionally Britain has striven to keep the Baltic Sea open, to maintain the freedom of the English Channel, to prevent the Irish Channel from coming under foreign dominance, to maintain the independence of the Low Countries (including the guaranty of Belgium's neutrality since 1839), to secure the maintenance of uninterrupted communications around the Cape of Good Hope (and therefore the maintenance of close relations with Portugal), also the safety of the Mediterranean route by control of Gibraltar,

Malta, and Cyprus, and the safety of the Suez Canal by international convention and Britain's special position in Egypt. It supported the policy of free trade so as to afford the fullest opportunity of developing its world-wide commerce.

The rapidly changing nature of the modern world has confronted Great Britain with a series of sharp challenges to its traditional policies. After 1900 the effort to combine relative isolation from Europe and occasional intervention to maintain the balance of power there, without becoming involved in alliances, grew increasingly difficult. In 1905 Britain signed an agreement with France in which it attempted to provide against a possible German aggression and yet keep a free hand. It engaged in military conversations with France and Belgium, and brought its Mediterranean fleet to the North Sea. Although its government regarded Britain as not bound to France in July 1914, it was unable to refuse assistance when France was attacked. The war which broke out in Eastern Europe in 1918 showed the artificiality of the British policy of limiting its obligations to Western Europe on the assumption that Western European affairs could be separated from those of Central and Eastern Europe: Continental peace was indivisible, once it was threatened by any of the great powers.

After 1918 the British people were not united on the methods to preserve the security and welfare of the empire. One school preached isolation. Despite the coming of the airplane and the progressive conquest of distance, its adherents believed that Britain could and should reduce her interests in Europe to an absolute minimum. The second school still believed in the limited-liability idea. In 1925, its objective was somewhat realized by the signature of the Locarno Pact, under which Great Britain, France, Germany, Belgium, and Italy agreed to a collective defense of the boundary between Germany and France; several powers also signed a number of conciliation agreements. A third party believed in pacifism and opposed both a renewed armament program and the collective security idea of the League as long as the latter included the imposition of sanctions against an aggressor. The fourth group were the collectivists. They believed that Britain, in reality, had no frontier, because the far-flung nature of her empire made the conception of a frontier artificial or unreal, and that, in a closely knit world, peace was sufficiently indivisible to warrant support of the League of Nations as the only organization comprehensive enough to deal with disputes all over the globe. They also pointed out that the rapidity of modern invention made almost any small and hitherto unimportant place a point of potential vulnerability, and that it would be increasingly difficult for a statesman to keep his fingers on all the threads in such a complicated world. The greater the number of points of vulnerability or attack, the more impossible it would be to be militarily prepared at each of these points. They argued, therefore, that such a world empire, even with its diversified resources and naval power, was no longer able to guarantee its own defense by means of partial agreements, and that security had ceased to be exclusively an imperial problem and had become primarily an international one. They also said—and their assertion had considerable validity—that Great Britain was no longer able to intervene with the necessary decisiveness and strength to maintain the balance of power in Europe. A generation earlier Britain had had the ability to intervene with decision; now it was unable to do so because of the increasingly high-powered nature of the modern world. Modern science and industry had created new centers of effective resistance. There were too many strong powers situated at great distances apart to enable Britain any longer to throw her whole energy into any one part. The postwar history was to show which of the four schools of thought had most correctly gauged the new international situation.

In the early years after 1918 some events occurred which necessitated considerable modification, or at least questioning, of Britain's policy. At the Washington Naval Conference, 1921–22, Great Britain had to give up its two-power naval policy and admit the United States to naval equality. The question then arose what would Britain do to find an equivalent for the security which had been lost by reason of the progress made by other countries, by reason of their advances in applied science. Economic changes in the direction of economic nationalism were threatening Britain with the loss of many of its postwar markets and rendering its economic position much less secure. Would Britain be able to make the transition from the nineteenth-century free-trade era to a twentieth century marked by intensified nationalism all over the world? In what way could Britain halt these tendencies? Were they inevitable in the law of economic growth, or were they in large measure the outcome of a struggle for political security? If the latter, what was Britain to do about it?

One other important influence affected Britain's policy. In the nineteenth century England was master of a political empire;

but gradually some of the colonies grew to Dominion status, and after the war Canada, Australia, New Zealand, South Africa, India, and later the Irish Free State became members of the League of Nations, thereby gaining international status. Great Britain could no longer make decisions involving the whole of the empire; and for several years most of the Dominions, situated as they were in the New World, did not desire to be entangled in European affairs. Thus there was a definite pull in British policy: the Dominions wished to keep out of European politics; but Europe, being so close to Britain, knocked with insistence at its door. Could Great Britain reconcile these opposing tendencies? Austria-Hungary had failed to maintain its power because the effort to face eastward toward the Balkans and westward toward Western Europe had proved too great a task. It was open to debate whether in the absence of effective international organization to maintain peace Britain could reconcile her position as the center of a world commonwealth and her position as a European power.

A conservatively minded government dominated British policy for most of the postwar period. Many of the conservatives accepted the League with ill-concealed dislike. Whereas France wished to have a strong League which could act with decision against an aggressor, the British government preferred to make haste slowly. It opposed the 1922–23 Treaty of Mutual Guarantee and Assistance which would have strengthened the League by providing supplementary regional guaranties. It rejected the 1924 Protocol, which was an even more far-reaching effort to close the gaps in the Covenant. It supported the Locarno Pact in 1925 and thereby guaranteed the finality of the frontier between France and Germany. It thus limited its obligations to Western Europe and refused to consider extending this type of commitment to the Mediterranean. It insisted upon interpreting its League obligations under Article 16 of the Covenant in a restrictive manner.

In the Sino-Japanese crisis the British representative opposed any strong League collective action and urged that Japan and China be permitted to work out a solution on a conciliation basis. The attempt to combine the collective guaranty by League members with the nineteenth-century theory of isolating a dispute betrayed either a curious lack of logic or a deliberate self-blindness. The government failed to give a strong lead in the Disarmament Conference which opened on February 2, 1932. In the Italo-Ethiopian dispute which broke out in December 1934, it

betrayed the same inconsistency of attitude. It wavered between
advocating some satisfaction to Mussolini and applying sanctions.
Even after sanctions had been applied and hostilities had gone
on for some time, it attempted conciliation by means of the
famous Hoare-Laval plan.

After the failure of the League, British prestige dropped;
and in the Spanish Civil War the government advocated a nonintervention policy, while Italy and Germany continued to pour
troops into that country. It sacrificed Czechoslovakia in 1938;
but by 1939 it had become evident that the British policy of appeasement, of limiting its active obligations to the Western part
of Europe, and of restrictively interpreting its League obligations,
had broken down. In March of that year it took the unprecedented step of giving guaranties to Eastern Europe, pledging
help to Poland, and later to Greece, Rumania, and Turkey. The
guaranties came too late, and the war which broke out in September 1939 revealed the fatal weakness and inadequacy of British
policy. Its government had failed either to support a genuine
system of collective security or to build up sufficient armaments
in the face of Nazi Germany. A world empire had talked in
terms of limiting its commitments to Western Europe—a curiously
tragic spectacle. Britain might have gone out wholeheartedly for
power politics, or have put itself wholeheartedly behind a new
world order. It might have supported a policy of more rapid
peaceful revision of the Versailles Treaty, while insuring that
Germany should not use the revision for war purposes. It refused to be strong and generous; it gave way grudgingly until it
had weakened its whole position. Instead of realizing that time
had rendered necessary a transformation of the British Commonwealth into an intimate part of a new world system, instead of
expanding the principles of equality which it had applied to its
own Dominions, it preferred to think in terms of nineteenth-
century methods, which were to prove their catastrophic weakness in the short period 1939–1941. Today it is obvious that
Britain must become a part of a larger political unit—either an
Anglo-American federation, or a United States of Europe, or
something approximating a world unit. The days of its power
politics are over, even if with American help it can win this war.

FRANCE

During the later half of the nineteenth century France attempted to prevent the unity of Germany, and after its defeat in

1871 it refused to accept the Franco-German frontier as permanent. Although it undertook colonization, the specter of Germany was ever before it, and pre-1914 French diplomacy was primarily concerned with the possibility of German attack. The War of 1914–1918 cost France nearly one and a half million dead, seven hundred thousand crippled, and more than two and a quarter million wounded; in the northeast of the country cities, mines, and farms were destroyed on a colossal scale. It is therefore no matter for surprise that after the victory France should have demanded a Carthaginian peace, for Germany had invaded it twice within less than fifty years: Germany must be completely vanquished, never to be a threat again.

The Peace treaty disappointed France, which regarded it as unduly lenient and as affording less than the minimum of security. With renewed energy it sought security in an Anglo-American guaranty backed by a League of Nations and in a policy of extracting the utmost reparations from Germany. When the United States and Britain refused to confirm the treaty of guaranty, France was driven to sign treaties with the small nations of Europe—Poland, Czechoslovakia, Jugoslavia, and Rumania. In this way it hoped to encircle Germany and thereby keep its enemy in a position of inferiority.

The policy of exacting huge reparations failed because it conflicted with the economic interests of Great Britain and other powers whose economic welfare was dependent upon re-establishing economic relations with Germany, and because only a strong industrial Germany could pay reparations and a strong industrial Germany was potentially a dangerous military power.

France's policy of supporting a strong League of Nations and of filling in the "gaps" of the Covenant so as to provide an international organization which would completely guarantee immunity from aggression failed also. The reasons for the breakdown of the League and of proposals to strengthen the League have been examined in the chapter dealing with security. In addition to these factors, certain forces within France were also responsible. Many of the right-wing supporters did not approve the League, and some even advocated an understanding with Hitler after his advent to power. Even more serious were the deep-seated class divisions, which prevented any continuity of a constructive foreign policy.

The economic collapse in 1931 helped to weaken the French position in Europe; the rise of Hitler to power caused France to seek allies elsewhere, and to make bargains, notably with Italy in January 1935, whereby Italy was to assist in opposing Germany's threat of power in return for acquiescence in its territorial expansion in Africa. The Ethiopian crisis ruined the hopes of France. Public opinion in England finally demanded the imposition of sanctions upon Italy, and France was impaled upon the horns of a dilemma. If it took decisive action against Italy, Germany might begin hostilities; if it did not stand behind Britain, it would alienate its strongest friend. In the end France suffered from the worst consequences of both policies. It had helped to drive Italy into the German camp, and by its joint responsibility for the collapse of the League had helped to drive the small powers to reaffirm their precarious policy of neutrality.

Hitler reoccupied the Rhineland in 1936 and thereby did much to prevent France from giving effective help to the Little Entente. The countries of southeastern Europe naturally began to make terms with Germany. From now on until 1939 French policy was opportunistically on the defensive. It did little beyond engage in an ineffective noninterventionist policy in the Spanish Civil War. Neither it nor Britain did more than verbally protest when Hitler took Austria in March 1938. Six months later, France's ally, Czechoslovakia, was betrayed at Munich, and France's other ally, the Soviet Union, was not even consulted. The Franco-German declaration contained the promises of peaceful settlement; but it deceived very few people and served merely to furnish a precedent for the Soviet Union, which in turn signed an agreement with Germany in September 1939.

French postwar policy undoubtedly had a breadth of conception and a logic superior to that of the other powers in the matter of security and disarmament. But its superior logic relating to instrumentalities required to attain security was vitiated by the suspicion that France intended to use international organization not only to guarantee its security but also to preserve its hegemony. Had France been able to obtain security, it might well have adopted a more generous policy toward Germany; but many people had their doubts as to whether France would do so, and this lack of faith poisoned French attempts to strengthen the League. Men suspected that it was not devotion to League ideals which animated France, but rather the exploitation of the League for national purposes. Comprehensive in certain directions, French policy was inadequate in other directions; and the present tragic position of the country, under the heel of Nazi Germany, is a sufficient commentary upon the lack of comprehensiveness in its international policies and of internal unity.

THE SOVIET UNION

The Bolshevist Revolution constituted a challenge of great magnitude to the Western-state system. State sovereignty, political loyalty, and the dominance of the nation comprised the fundamental belief of the West. To the Bolshevist leaders the state was an instrument of class oppression; it was an undesirable thing, and should give way to a classless, nationless society. Both international law and the League of Nations were regarded as mere extensions of the capitalist technique of exploitation. There seemed to be no compromise between the Western national states, which were instruments of capitalist rule and exploitation, and the Soviet Union based upon fundamentally incompatible ideas.

It is not surprising, therefore, that in the early postwar period the two systems clashed in uncompromising hostility. The Allies supported the counter-revolutionary forces in the Soviet Union, and their intervention gave the appearance of a capitalist world united against Communism. The Soviet Union struck back by promoting international revolution through the encouragement of civil wars within Germany, Austria, Italy, and Hungary and by attempting to organize the colonial peoples of Asia in a move to oust their Western imperial masters. By 1921 it was clear that capitalism was more tenacious and had a degree of resistance and a capacity for recovery which Communism had underestimated. The internal difficulties of the Soviet Union and its need of foreign capital and the desire of capitalism to find new markets and new investment opportunities paved the way for an era of uneasy compromise, which lasted roughly from 1922 to 1933. During this time most of the Western powers recognized the Bolshevist regime, commercial treaties were signed, and the Soviets negotiated several bilateral treaties of friendship and neutrality and co-operated with some of the technical organizations of the League.

The rise of Hitler and the threat of the Nazi movement to Communism as well as to democracy led the Soviet to join the League of Nations, to sign an agreement with France, and to take part in sanctions against Italy in 1935. Litvinov on behalf of the U.S.S.R. repeatedly stated before the League that aggression must be stopped in every case, otherwise movements against smaller powers would occur again and again. After the invasion

of Austria in 1938, the U.S.S.R. proposed that immediate practical measures be discussed. When the Czechoslovakian crisis
broke, the Western powers did not consult the Soviet Union,
despite the existence of the Franco-Soviet alliance. The Union
repeatedly assured France and Czechoslovakia that it would
honor its military obligations both to France and to Czechoslovakia. Great Britain and France chose to believe that the Soviets
either would not or could not grant effective aid to the Czechs,
and negotiated directly with Hitler and Mussolini. At the Munich Conference decisions were taken without consulting the
Soviet. France and Britain now sacrificed Czechoslovakia, and
completed the ruin of the collective security system. The result
was to throw Europe into the utmost political confusion.

What was the Soviet to do under the new circumstances? As
the German threat grew apace, Great Britain and France, realizing that at some point resistance must be offered to Hitler, sought
to retrieve their shattered position. Britain made guaranties to
Poland, Greece, and Turkey, and entered into negotiations with
the Soviet Union. That the latter now had little enthusiasm to
join the movement against Hitler with those who had so readily
bargained away their allies was understandable. Why not adopt
a hands-off policy and let the democratic and Fascist countries
cut each other's throats? As it turned out, the Soviet signed a
trade agreement with Germany in August 1939 by which Germany was to acquire raw materials and Russia would obtain
heavy machinery and manufactures. A nonaggression pact which
provided that in case one of the signatories became "the object
of warlike acts by a third power, the other party would in no way
support this third power" created consternation in the democratic
countries—which did not ask why, if the Allies could appease
Germany, and France could sign a treaty of understanding in
1938 with Hitler, the U.S.S.R. should not sign a treaty in 1939?

It is unnecessary here to describe in detail the Soviet moves
after the outbreak of war in September of that year. The occupation of part of Poland, the attack on Finland, the absorption
of the Baltic countries, and the seizure of Bessarabia may be interpreted in different ways. The basic fact is that Moscow was
placed in a most serious position by the rapid advance of Germany
during 1940. If Britain fell soon after the surrender of France,
the Soviet Union would probably be next in line for German
invasion. If it attacked Germany in the rear the Union might
suffer rapid defeat; or, should it prove successful in withstanding

Hitler, it might drive Britain and Germany into a compromise at the expense of the U.S.S.R. The least risky thing to do at the moment was to play for time, remain neutral, and hope that the future in some way would deliver the Soviet Union from its precarious situation.

The Bolshevist Revolution set up by proclaiming freedom to the workers of the world had now become enmeshed in the bewildering intricacies of the balance-of-power system; and, like Britain, France, and Italy, the Soviet Union was suddenly to realize that a new force had risen which, taking advantage of the unstable equilibrium produced by the policy of mutual obstruction of these powers, was to use the reawakened energy of a united Germany to threaten democracy and communism alike.

The truth of this judgment was dramatically revealed when the German invasion of Russia began on June 22, 1941, in violation of the nonaggression pact which had been signed between the two countries. Hitler had once more succeeded in dividing his potential opponents, waiting until it suited his purposes to attack. Nazism had made evident what many thinkers had already proclaimed— that it stood for a set of values based upon power which denies the primacy of economic welfare, whether under a capitalist or a communist regime. Both the Soviet Union and the Western world found that their economic organizations, based upon incompatible principles though they were, faced the prospect of being eliminated by reason of the enormous growth of military preparations required by the sovereign state; even more grim was the prospect of military defeat.

ITALY

The tradition of the Mediterranean as an Italian sea dates back to the distant past, even though modern Italian national unity was attained only in 1870. After that date Italy undertook some African campaigns and attempted to strengthen its position on the European mainland. Italian neutrality in the opening months of the World War of 1914–1918 proved of incalculable value to France. As a result of the Treaty of London, in April 1915 Italy entered the struggle in return for the promise of territory in Europe, a share of Asiatic Turkey, and compensatory gains in the event that Britain and France increased their colonial possessions in Africa.

Italy was considerably perturbed by the 1916 Anglo-French agreement which partitioned the Turkish possessions between those two Allies, thereby, according to Italians, violating Italian rights under the Treaty of London. By its protests it was able to obtain the acceptance of the Treaty of St. Jean de Maurienne (April 17, 1917), which it believed re-established its rights in the Levant. But Britain and France made the Bolshevist Revolution an excuse for denying that the 1917 Treaty had legal effect, and this action the Italians regarded as a clear breach of faith. Two of Wilson's Fourteen Points—that there should be a readjustment of the Italian frontier along clearly marked lines of nationality, and that the Austro-Hungarian people should be given the freest chance of autonomous development—roused much opposition in Italy on the ground that they conflicted with provisions of the 1915 Treaty.

At the Paris Peace Conference President Wilson opposed several Italian claims and, by appealing to the Italian people over the head of the Italian government, caused considerable bitterness. The Treaty itself greatly disappointed the Italian nation. Although formally a victor in the war, Italy received no territory in Asia Minor or in Africa and had become engaged in a quarrel with Yugoslavia over Fiume. Moreover, France denounced the Tunis agreement of 1896; and it is not surprising, therefore, that on several occasions in subsequent years Italy sided with the revisionist powers which were dissatisfied with the Peace.

When Mussolini came to power in 1922, a new note appeared in Italian foreign policy. Il Duce appealed to Italy's past, its prestige, its vital interest, the heroic quality of its life, its disdain of the merely academic, and its unwillingness to have its affairs at the mercy of a "lifeless academic organization of no importance," as he described the League, which he denounced as an Anglo-Saxon institution. He also spoke of treaty revision, of colonial expansion, and of freedom from the domination of Western Europe, and insisted that the Mediterranean must again become an Italian sea, and Rome once more the center of European civilization. His actions suited his words. In 1923 Italy bombarded and occupied Corfu, and Mussolini dared the League to intervene. In the same year he demanded Italian participation in the international government of Tangier. He protested against the policy of France in sheltering anti-Fascist refugees, even though Fascist provocateurs engaged in unsavory plotting abroad. For some time, it is true, Mussolini spoke in terms of co-operation with the League of Nations; but after 1929 and 1930 his tone changed and he spoke of a future Fascist Europe, of "we

or they," and of the necessity that the great powers should dominate. More openly he scoffed at the ideal of peace, and praised
war as a means of bringing human beings to a state of highest
tension.

Italy refused to sign the Naval Treaty of London in 1930
because it could not obtain parity with France. Its dictator proposed a reform of the League of Nations so as to increase the
position and power of the leading nations; for he did not relish
the growing influence of the small powers in the League. Fascism,
which denied democracy within a nation, was not likely to promote democracy among nations. The same philosophy of leadership dictated Mussolini's advocacy of the Four-Power Pact in
1932 on the ground that if the major powers—Britain, France,
Italy, and Germany—could agree on their fundamental policies
Europe would be better off. Whatever the merit of this view, it
met with opposition from the small powers, which feared that it
was no more than a revival of nineteenth-century imperialist
control. (That their fears were amply justified was shown by the
manner in which France, Britain, Germany, and Italy settled the
Czechoslovakian crisis in 1932.) In 1934 Italy opposed Hitler's
move toward Austria. The murder of Dollfuss deeply shocked
the nation, and Mussolini hurried his troops to the Austrian border. Both France and Italy believed that their security was threatened by the prospect of German control over Austria. To France
it involved an immediate threat to its ally Czechoslovakia. To
Italy it meant a united Germany adjoining Italian territory. The
two powers therefore signed an extensive agreement in January
1935 settling many questions in Africa and making concessions to
Italy so as to bring the latter into the nonrevisionist camp. On
April 16, 1935, Britain, France, and Italy issued a joint com-
muniqué at Stresa, announcing that they would oppose any treaty
repudiation which might endanger the peace of Europe.

The invasion of Ethiopia in 1935 profoundly changed the
whole course of European politics. Mussolini had reason to believe that Britain and France would not object to his new "colonial venture," and was infuriated when Great Britain led the
League of Nations in employing sanctions against Italy. The
attempt threw Italy into the arms of Germany, and weakened
Britain's prestige to its lowest point during the present century.
Having made one blunder, Mr. Chamberlain attempted to retrieve his position by signing a gentlemen's agreement with Italy;
but its only result was to help re-establish Mussolini's position,

which was somewhat damaged by the striking successes of his
Axis partner, Hitler. Italy, which had recognized the Soviet
Government in February 1924, had signed an economic agree-
ment with it in 1930 and had entered a pact of friendship, non-
aggression, and neutrality in 1933, signed the Anti-Comintern
Pact with Germany and Japan against the Soviet Union in 1936.
Such were the confusions in an age of demoralized power politics.

We need not analyze the later developments of Italian foreign
policy since it has become subordinate to the general plans set forth
by Hitler. The invasion of Albania and the attack upon Greece
were incidental to the larger ambitions of Germany. The serious
reverses suffered by Italy in Greece and in Africa have dimmed
whatever prestige it may have had, and it is generally agreed
that the junior partner of the Axis will play a relatively minor
role at the end of the present war: In the event of a German
victory the determination of policy will obviously rest in the hands
of Hitler. If Germany's opponents win, Italy will be reduced to
a condition of military impotence along with Germany.

GERMANY

It is unnecessary to describe postwar German policy in detail.
Germany's disappointment over the Treaty of Versailles, the collapse of the mark in 1922–23, the ruin of the middle class, the
temporary restoration of economic prosperity after 1924, the Indian summer which followed the 1925 Locarno Pact, the gradual
economic deterioration after 1928, and the bitter disappointment
of Germany at the failure of the Disarmament Conference to grant
her a measure of equality have been told often enough.

In part they explain Hitler's rise to power, but it is difficult to
believe that they alone account for the peculiar dynamic quality
of Hitler's foreign policy. The source of that energy must be
found elsewhere. In the chapter dealing with war we have discussed some of the methods which Hitler has used in his rapid
conquests, and it is sufficient to note at this point that Nazi Germany has been able to take advantage of the precarious equilibrium existing among the other great powers and also to drive a
wedge between hostile groups within the respective nations.[14]   In

[14] The Nazis were more skillful than the Communists in that instead of attacking religion and property in advance they promised to protect them, "only
to whittle down both of those institutions through economic restrictions and
racial discrimination" after their advent to power. See Vera Micheles Dean,
"Hitler Resumes Crusade on Communism," *Foreign Policy Bulletin,* June 27,
1941, p. 2.

other words, it has exploited international and class and group rivalries. It has taken advantage of the capacity for mutual obstruction, which nations and classes have exhibited in so striking a manner, to isolate nations one by one for the purpose of conquest. The effect of its policy has been to weaken the idea of nationalism and to make possible a military expansion unparalleled in modern times. It is doubtful if nationalism can ever be reestablished with its former emotional intensity.

Thus Germany has confronted the world with two alternatives: either a German-organized world, or a world integrated in another fashion. The old order cannot hope to be brought back to life. If Germany should win, the small nations will not have the rights which they might have enjoyed under a successful League of Nations and which they may still hope to possess under a Europe sufficiently organized to promote and guarantee political, economic, and cultural freedom.

A EUROPEAN FEDERATION?

One cannot too strongly insist that the development of new methods of waging war makes urgent the task of federalizing Europe. The restoration of smaller sovereign states would be sheer folly in the face of modern problems. But the difficulties which were pointed out in connection with Briand's plan of European union will still remain: What shall be the scope of this federation? What nations will it include? What will be the relation of the European federation to other larger units? What will be Britain's position? Can the Soviet Union be admitted?

However, it is not sufficient merely to point out the difficulties, for difficulties have confronted every attempt to reorganize society. What must be emphasized is the absence of any genuine alternative. The extent of the new European federation in the event of a British victory will depend upon circumstances; but, whatever area it embraces, the new federation must be very closely connected with other larger units of government if a further armament race and economic and propaganda rivalry are not to take place. It may be well argued that undue attention has been paid to nomenclature in recent discussions and that, whether the League of Nations be so strengthened as to guarantee an international force or whether a new series of continental units closely linked will emerge, the outcome must be more international or supra-national government, whatever its name may be.

One cannot ignore the problem of what units should comprise

any proposed European or World Federation. At first sight the question seems simple—the existing nations should form the basis for the new political organization. But are they to be the nations which existed as of 1921, or those of 1940, or are they to be states which give a full independence within the new scheme to minorities which have been part of multi-national states? For example, will Czechoslovakia be a unit, or will Bohemia and Slovakia be separate political individualities? If we give separate representation in the federal system to Bohemia and Slovakia, will these two be joined in a Czechoslovakia as an intermediate agency? If Czechoslovakia is retained, we will have a three-dimensional federalism, as it were. If Czechoslovakia disappears, we will then have an independent Bohemia and an independent Slovakia. So with Poland. Shall the reconstituted Poland be the same as it was in 1921 when it had about one-half of its population consisting of non-Poles? In the new federation, should Ruthenia have an independent status or representation both in the federal system and a new or reconstructed Poland? So with Yugoslavia. Are the Croats to have direct representation in the federal system or to be part of a Yugoslavia in which Serbia, Croatia, and the other units are primarily a part of a multi-national state, which in turn will be a part of a European federal state? Macedonia has been clamoring for independence for many years. Will the European state declare an independent Macedonia? The Catalonian autonomous movement in Spain may demand direct representation in the new federal Europe and not be satisfied with being merely part of Spain, even if granted considerable regional autonomy. We can see that nationalism provides a very uncertain basis for units in the new federal government. Indeed, one can see that a federated Europe based upon states as they existed, say in 1930, would be a very different affair from a federated Europe based upon wholehearted acceptance of the theory of nationalism. One may go even farther and say that it may well be impossible to devise a federated Europe based upon the extreme theory of nationalism, because this theory carries the logical conclusion resulting in groupism. Who is to say whether the Bretons are really part of France, or whether the Flemish or Walloons are integrally part of Belgium? Mommsen was right when he said that the history of every nation is a vast history of amalgamations. On this basis, there is nothing final in the theory of nationality to provide a clear-cut basis for a reconstituted and federal Europe.

Ultimately the question comes down to this—whether the individual owes prime allegiance to his nation or to a larger unit. In the present deadlocked condition of the world it may be that both the ideas of a strengthened League and a "Union Now" labor under the difficulty that any immediate application of them would appear to be only a manifestation of power politics in another guise. So it must have appeared centuries ago to many feudal knights who saw one of their number talking in terms of himself as national king. To them the aspirant to royal honors must have seemed to be only a pretentious feudal knight trying to subordinate others to his power. The test was, and still must be, whether or not power is to be used in the service of law and order. Ultimately a strengthened League of Nations able to apply sanctions against an aggressor must lead to a form of society wherein currency, raw materials, tariffs, security and armaments, and the prevention of crime on an international scale must be looked at alike as problems involving world organization. The fundamental question is whether Streit is correct in saying that this condition cannot be realized by a gradual and progressive modification of the modern state but must come through a definite and drastic transformation of political institutions.

THE PACIFIC

During the eighteenth and nineteenth centuries the Western powers strove to gain a status of equality with China in their dealings with that country and to force it to give up its pretensions of superiority. Singly and in co-operation they imposed the so-called unequal treaties upon China and made a united stand when the Boxer Rebellion broke out against the hated foreigner. There was little genuine regional co-operation in these actions, rather, a struggle of one set of powers against another power. Their common action did not prevent a great deal of rivalry among their members. For a time, at the close of the century, compromise won the day and provided a temporary breathing spell; Germany, Russia, Great Britain, and France mapped out spheres of influence, and divided China into areas of economic exploitation. This action also was not an example of regional co-operation but a type of power politics which was soon to create many difficulties.

The Open-Door policy, implied in principle by the United States as early as 1843, was reasserted by John Hay at the end of the century, and superficially suggested the principle of international co-operation. But it clashed with the growing Japanese policy which became more pronounced after the Russo-Japanese War of 1904–05, presaging Japan's insistence upon a special position in eastern Asia. The proposal of Secretary Knox in 1909 that the Manchurian railroads be neutralized had a flavor of regional co-operation; but Russia and Japan chose to see in it a method of blocking legitimate Russian and Japanese interests. A similar objection was raised to the proposal for an international consortium made just before August 1914.

In none of these proposals did China appear as a partner. The arrangements which were suggested came from foreign powers alone, and therefore lacked the fundamental requirement of a genuine regional policy which would have included China.

Between 1914 and 1920 Japan made considerable advance on the mainland. The Twenty-one Demands of 1915, the campaign in Siberia, the many loans to China during 1917–18, and Japan's further attempts to obtain acceptance of her special position in China—witness the Lansing-Ishii conversations of 1917—caused the Allies to take steps to protect their interests, which they believed to be endangered. Moreover, the threat of an Anglo-American naval race was creating considerable anxiety.

Such, in brief, is the background of the 1921–22 Washington Conference, which for some time appeared as an effort to substitute regional agreement and consultation for the prewar system of the balance of power. We have now to see whether it did substantially modify the balance-of-power system in the Orient or whether the new institutions were, in reality, a new expression of old forces at work.

The Conference adopted a four-power pact (by which Great Britain, France, the United States, and Japan agreed to maintain the status quo in the Pacific), a five-power naval pact limiting battleships and aircraft carriers, and a nine-power treaty (February 6, 1922), which dealt with the position of China. The signatory powers agreed to respect China's sovereignty, independence, and territorial integrity and not to support their respective nationals in seeking special commercial or economic rights or any monopoly or preference which would "frustrate the practical application of the principle of equal opportunity." China agreed not to permit unfair discrimination on her railroads, and the other powers undertook to respect China's rights as a neutral in case of a war "to which China is not a party." The treaty was designed to prevent any country from making any future claims to a monopolistic economic position in China; any "general superiority of rights" was forbidden.

It was the first international treaty recognizing the Open Door, which as originally conceived was limited to trade and did not apply to concessions. The effect was substantially to offset the advantages which Japan had obtained in the years 1914 to 1922; but in so far as it concerned itself only with the future and did not modify the position of existing interests, it may now be regarded as having been less far-reaching than at first sight appeared.

The Washington Conference attempted to solve two sets of problems: (1) that of naval limitation and the maintenance of the status quo as to naval bases in the Pacific; and (2) that of giving China an opportunity to achieve a national unity uninterrupted by the imperialistic rivalries of the great powers. The Nine-Power Treaty was intended to remove the fear of territorial aggression from China and to give to the Open Door doctrine — essentially a doctrine of fair competition — the added strength of a formal treaty. It placed a limit upon Japan's action in China, and to that extent must have appeared to the more forward-looking group in that country as an irksome restraint. But the naval agreement gave Japan a large measure of political security in return for its acceptance of a co-operative policy in China. The 5-5-3 arrangement in battleships and aircraft and the promise not to construct naval bases in the Pacific removed the fear of a successful naval attack upon her. Moreover Japan, being close to the Chinese market, had a substantial advantage in developing its economic interests in Manchuria and the rest of China. The Naval Treaty and the Nine-Power Treaty were therefore interrelated documents. The Japanese later denied this contention, and claimed that the Five-Power and the Nine-Power conferences were entirely separate and the Five-Power and the Nine-Power treaties not interdependent. The consequence of these divergent interpretations was seen in the troublous times after 1931.

The Washington treaties seemed to be an important addition to the peace machinery of the world. The United States had not joined the League of Nations, and the League Covenant therefore did not adequately cover the Pacific area. It was hoped that the new agreements would fill the gap. Undoubtedly they worked well for almost a decade; but they were subjected to increasing strain in three ways. First, the treaties were based upon the assumption that China, once freed from aggression, would turn its energies to internal construction and would continue to observe and respect the remaining foreign privileges, which had been obtained, by force, the Chinese insisted, from former Chinese governments, and which the Washington Conference had only modified in some respects. But the promise to give China an unembarrassed opportunity to set its house in order implied at least enough political stability to enable foreigners to continue there and to develop their business relations with substantial guaranties of safety and justice.[15] Unfortunately, disorder within China continued on a large scale, and in order to protect their own interests the foreign governments disregarded, or at least appeared to disregard, China's integrity, and by so doing produced an intense nationalist reaction which took an aggressive form in a determined campaign against the so-called unequal treaties.[16]

The campaign was not confined to legal agitation. Disorders broke out, attacks on the lives of foreigners became frequent, economic boycotts dislocated business and caused heavy losses, and customs revenues were seized. This nationalist reaction helped to break down the regional co-operation envisaged in the Washington treaties, and it showed that the statesmen in 1921 and 1922 had assumed too complete an identity of the political and economic interests of the foreign powers in China. In reality, Great Britain and Japan had by far the greatest economic stake, the United States possessed potential rather than immediate interests on a large scale, and the other nations accounted for relatively little. The Chinese anti-foreign activity was therefore felt most by Japanese and British interests, which experienced the heaviest losses through economic boycotts and disorders.

For a time the United States joined in forceful demonstrations against the Chinese; but during 1926 and 1927 American public opinion grew more unfavorable to the policy of dispatching warships to protect the commercial and economic interests of foreigners which had been erected under the so-called "unequal treaties." The Porter Resolution in favor of treaty revision passed the House of Representatives, although it was lost in the Senate Committee on Foreign Relations. The United States therefore found itself in the position of being unable to co-operate

[15] See George E. Taylor, *The Struggle for North China* (Institute of Pacific Relations, New York, 1940), p. 8.

[16] G. F. Hudson, *The Far East in World Politics* (Oxford University Press, London, 1939), p. 204.

with the other powers in a repressive policy, but equally it could not neglect its own nationals in China. It tended to adopt an independent line by giving to its naval officers on the spot considerable discretion in deciding whether or not force was required to protect the interests of American citizens and if so how much. Even this type of action provoked criticism at home, with the result that the United States was the first to conclude an agreement, in July 1928, which acknowledged "the principle of complete national tariff autonomy." In a sense, this action revealed the weakening of the united foreign front postulated at Washington in 1921 and 1922. Japan and Great Britain now had to face serious disorders in China, and the two governments came to an understanding to the effect that inasmuch as they had much greater interests in China than the other powers they would co-operate as far as possible to defend those interests. Already by 1928–29 the unity had been, if not broken, at least badly impaired. After long negotiations the Chinese Nationalist government gained control of its own tariff, and by 1930 the new trade treaties based upon the principles of equality and reciprocity were in operation. Nevertheless the numerous incidents and the tensions which had been created proved to be a powerful factor in strengthening the hand of the militaristic and expansionistic party in Japan, which demanded stern measures in China in order to protect Japanese rights and which for a time under the Tanaka government adopted a more "positive policy," a policy which was to be resumed in 1932. And Great Britain found that its agreement with Japan in 1928 was to interfere with its support of strong League action. The Chinese Nationalist movement had borne undesired and complicating fruit.

The second factor which led to increasing strain upon the peace machinery set up by the Washington Conference was the rise of the Soviet Union to power. In 1922 that government was a relatively negligible factor in Far Eastern politics and did not even take part in the Nine-Power Treaty negotiations. Soon afterward Communist activities developed apace, and for five years the Chinese Nationalist movement owed much to the technical assistance and emotional driving power of Soviet emissaries. Not only that; the Bolshevist government resumed its railroad rights in Manchuria and, in contrast to its assistance to China in other directions, resorted to coercion in 1929 in maintaining the status quo on the Chinese Eastern Railway. The failure of the Kellogg Pact in this connection showed that at least one of the peace instruments could not be relied upon in the event of an international crisis; and the lesson was not lost upon the leaders of Japan.

The third force disintegrating the Pacific situation was the growing economic difficulty of Japan after 1929. Its rapidly mounting population and its industrial program necessitated a ready access to the raw materials and markets of the world. Yet the economic depression in the United States lessened the American demand for Japanese silk, the growth of tariffs everywhere seriously damaged the export trade, and the collapse of the silver market lessened Chinese buying power. The Chinese boycott and China's demand for tariff autonomy combined to subject Japan to increasing economic pressure. The Washington treaties had afforded Japan political security against Great Britain and the United States but not economic security in a world of economic nationalism.

Meanwhile, conditions in China had become more unsettled, and a series of incidents culminated in the explosion on the railroad near Mukden on September 18, 1931. Japan immediately moved its troops, and within a few days had seized a considerable area of Manchuria. The matter came before the League of Nations, and for several months the statesmen at Geneva attempted to find a solution. In December 1932 it was decided to send the Lytton Commission to inquire into the whole problem.

The Commission sailed in February 1932, and after an exhaustive inquiry issued its report in October of that year. After giving a historical summary of the difficulties which had arisen in Manchuria and of other problems which existed between China and Japan, it set forth as its main conclusions:

1. China was a nation in evolution. It had not fully attained unity, and its international relations, therefore, involved a number of particularly difficult problems. Its reconstruction was hindered by three or four major factors—lack of communications, civil wars due to the rivalry of war lords, and the existence of banditry. These difficulties had been somewhat overcome, but, at the time of writing, Communism threatened the unity of China, and had actually become a rival of the central government. All foreigners, but especially nationals of Japan, had suffered from China's unsettled condition.

2. Manchuria, although largely independent of the central government had never been an entirely sovereign entity. The Commission thus denied Japan's contention that Manchuria did not form a part of China, but agreed that corruption and maladminis-

tration had been rampant and that Japan had legitimate grievances on these scores.

3. The growth of communistic influences in the northern part of Manchuria added to the problem of security for Japanese interests.

4. The Commission dealt with the railroad and other issues between China and Japan in Manchuria, and with the position of Korean settlers, analyzed the disputes which preceded the incident of September 18, 1931, and decided that both China and Japan had grievances against each other.

5. The explosion on the South Manchurian railroad on the night of September 18 did not justify military action, nor did the military operations of the Japanese troops constitute a legitimate measure of self-defense.

6. The newly formed Manchukuo was not a spontaneous creation of the local inhabitants. The Commission believed that the new state could not have been formed without the presence of Japanese troops and the activities of Japan's civil and military officers, and doubted whether or not it could carry out many of the reforms which it had advertised. It concluded that the new state did not have general Chinese support, but was primarily an instrument for Japanese purposes.

7. As to the Chinese boycott of Japanese goods the Commission considered that Japan was commercially vulnerable, and the Chinese boycotts, which had been stimulated and co-ordinated by the Kuomintang, therefore, might constitute a serious blow to Japan. It suggested that all states should co-operate to consider the problem of the boycott and draw up rules of international law to determine its limits.

8. Manchuria was a country of great importance to the economic development of Japan, which had to depend upon further industrialization in order to meet its population and agrarian problems. But industrialization required further markets; and Asia, and especially China, offered the "only large and relatively sure markets" that Japan could expect to find. The Commission doubted whether Japan's military expedition into Manchuria, however definitely it may have been undertaken for reasons of national security, was the right solution, and suggested that peace based upon effective international organization would best serve Japan's interests abroad.

On the basis of these findings, the Commission set forth ten principles which, in its judgment, were necessary for a comprehensive solution. It rejected the idea that the status quo ante could be restored, and believed that "the maintenance and recognition of the present regime in Manchuria would be equally unsatisfactory." The solution should: (1) serve the interests of China and Japan; (2) take into account the interests of the Soviet Union; (3) be consistent with the existing multilateral treaties (the Covenant of the League, the Nine-Power Treaty, and the Kellogg Pact); (4) recognize Japan's interests in Manchuria; (5) establish a new set of treaty relations between China and Japan; (6) provide for the effective settlement of future disputes; (7) provide for a large measure of Manchurian autonomy consistent with the sovereignty and administrative integrity of China; (8) provide for the internal order of Manchuria and its security against external aggression, and to this end there should be established an effective local gendarmerie, other armed forces having been withdrawn, and a treaty of nonaggression between the interested countries should be signed; (9) encourage close economic relations between China and Japan; and (10) promote international cooperation in the reconstruction of China, pending a strong central government there. In Manchuria the principle of the open door should be maintained, "not only from the legal point of view, but also in the actual practice of trade, industry, and banking."

These principles should underlie a general settlement, embodied in four separate instruments: (a) a declaration by China constituting a special administration for the three eastern provinces, after a Sino-Japanese advisory conference had been held; (b) a Sino-Japanese treaty dealing with Japanese interests; (c) a Sino-Japanese treaty of conciliation and arbitration, nonaggression, and mutual assistance; and (d) a Sino-Japanese commercial treaty.

The Lytton Commission and the Assembly thus denied Japan's claim that her action in Manchuria was one of national self-defense and asserted that in their judgment the amount of force which Japan had used in defending its alleged rights was out of all proportion to the injuries it had received. True, there had been bandits, and Japan had suffered from the delay in the settlement of disputes; but these things, however exasperating, could not possibly justify the military occupation of so extensive a territory.

Japan had claimed that the new Manchukuo government was a spontaneous movement of the people of Manchuria. This claim was unqualifiedly rejected by the Commission and the Assembly. In their opinion Japan had created a puppet state and the new regime owed its existence to Japanese military initiative and military support. The League of Nations, therefore, had no difficulty in following the lead of the United States in the "nonrecognition" of a situation which had been brought about by the use of force.

The Japanese representatives had argued that Article 10 of the Covenant (i.e., that League members undertake to preserve as against external aggression the territorial integrity of members of the League) did not apply to Manchuria, because Manchukuo had arisen as a result of a purely internal movement within China itself and Japan, therefore, had no obligation to defend China against what was essentially a secessionist movement. The Lytton Commission and the League Assembly, having denied that Manchukuo was the result of a spontaneous movement within China, could not accept the Japanese view that Article 10 of the Covenant did not apply in this instance.

During the debates Japan had repeatedly asserted that China was not a state or nation in the Western sense of the term; that China had not yet developed the unity necessary to enable the central government to exercise sufficient control over Chinese territory or to guarantee the protection of foreign rights and interests there. China at best exercised only imperfect sovereignty; Manchuria was not truly a part of China and the existence of so many limitations, such as extraterritorial rights, leased territories, and foreign customs control, bore witness to the abnormal political condition of Japan's neighbor. Therefore, concluded Japan, it was manifestly impossible to apply the League Covenant to the disputes of a country which did not meet the test required for a League member, i.e., fulfillment of its international obligations; the government of China had not the machinery to carry out any treaty arrangements, and Japan therefore was compelled to take forceful measures to safeguard its rights: to arbitrate disputes with so undependable a government would be useless.

Japan's claim was rejected. For several years China had been a member of the League, and even had had a seat on the League Council. Moreover, at the 1921–22 Washington Conference, the signatories of the Nine-Power Treaty had undertaken to permit China the fullest opportunity of developing its national unity. Until the League decreed that China was unfit to continue its membership, and the states which had signed the Washington Conference Treaty had modified the status which had been accepted, China must be regarded as the possessor of rights which could not be extinguished by unilateral action on the part of Japan.

These differences proved to be insurmountable, and in March

1933 Japan gave notice of its intention to withdraw from the League, having been led, to quote its own words, "to realize the existence of an irreconcilable divergence of views dividing Japan and the League on policies of peace and especially as regards the fundamental principles to be followed in the establishment of a durable peace in the Far East." Japan complained of the "exasperating" inability of the League to understand its views and its problems; the League found itself equally unable to appreciate Japan's attitude and reasoning.

Having resigned from the League, Japan adopted an independent policy toward China. Two distinct aspects of this are to be observed. The first was an attempt to induce China to recognize the new regime in Manchukuo by promising co-operation and compensation. Had China accepted the offer, and given recognition, it would have gone far to nullify the League's report and its policy of nonrecognition. The second aspect was the forward and aggressive policy of the militarist group, which, claiming that China was not a unity but was divided into regions of clearly marked political and geographic characteristics, undertook to set up autonomous governments detached from the capital, Nanking.

By the Tangku truce of 1933 a demilitarized zone was created between the Great Wall and a line drawn from east to west a few miles north of Tientsin and Peiping. Japanese forces were to withdraw behind the Wall, and Chinese police were to keep order in the zone. Agreements were later made for the opening of customs offices, railway through traffic, postal communications, and air routes between Manchukuo and China. A tenable view is that these arrangements reduced China's policy of nonrecognition to a fiction.

During 1934 Japan made several proposals to China looking toward co-operation. Foreign Minister Hirota in January said that Japan sincerely hoped "for the political and economic rehabilitation of China," and that China "will be enabled to unite with Japan in performing the obvious mission of both Japan and China to contribute through mutual aid and co-operation to the peaceful development of their part of the globe." But what kind of co-operation? Was it to be the co-operation of equals, or a co-operation involving the coercion of China? Was it to mean that China was to renounce all significant relations with other powers? The answer to these questions was of fundamental importance, and was supplied by Mr. Amau of the Foreign Office, who on April 26, 1934, said:

Owing to the special position of Japan in her relations with China her views and attitude respecting matters that concern China may not agree in every point with those of foreign nations; but it must be realized that Japan is called upon to exert the utmost effort in carrying out her mission and in fulfilling her special responsibilities in East Asia. Japan has been compelled to withdraw from the League of Nations because of their failure to agree in their opinions on fundamental principles of preserving peace in East Asia. . . . . Japan at all times is endeavouring to maintain and promote her friendly relations with foreign nations, but in East Asia we must even act alone on our own responsibility, and it is our duty to perform it. . . . . there is no country but China which is in a position to share with Japan the responsibility for maintenance of peace in East Asia.

We oppose, therefore, any attempt on the part of China to avail herself of the influence of any other country in order to resist Japan; we also oppose any action taken by China calculated to play [off] one Power against another. Any joint operations undertaken by foreign Powers even in the name of technical or financial assistance at this particular moment after Manchurian and Shanghai incidents are bound to acquire political significance.

. . . . supplying China with war aeroplanes, building aerodromes in China, and detailing military instructors or military advisers to China, or contracting a loan to provide funds for political uses would obviously tend to alienate friendly relations between Japan, China, and other countries and to disturb peace and order in Eastern Asia. Japan will oppose such projects.

The Japanese paper, *Asahi,* described the statement as "an epoch-making departure whereby Japan abandons her former policy of co-operation with the West in China" and inaugurates "a policy based on the principle that East Asian affairs should be settled by Japan and China alone." Several proposals were made, which included the following: (*a*) There should be no anti-Japanese demonstrations or boycotts by China; (*b*) China should resign from the League; (*c*) China should co-operate with Japan, lower her tariffs on Japanese goods, concentrate upon developing raw materials, borrow money and utilize financial advisers only from Japan; and (*d*) China should co-operate in a military way by restricting instructors in her army to Japanese officers. These proposals confronted China with a difficult choice. If it agreed, it would seriously compromise, if not actually surrender, China's independence. If it refused, Japan could assert that China was obstructive, anti-Japanese, and obviously hostile to Japan's legitimate offers of co-operation. China's policy, therefore, was to accept some of the demands for co-operation but to sidestep others in order to gain time for military preparations for a conflict which to many of the leaders seemed inevitable. It passed laws forbidding the boycott of Japanese goods and demonstrations against Japan. It lowered some of the tariffs on Japanese goods and appointed some Japanese naval officers to the faculty of the Chinese naval college to instruct in affairs of the practically nonexistent Chinese navy! But it refused to desert the League of Nations, or to promise to confine its economic development to raw materials, or to restrict its borrowing to Japan; and it rejected the other proposed forms of military co-operation.

China's attitude was revealed in a statement of April 19:

China is always of the opinion that international peace can be maintained only by the joint efforts of all members of the family of nations. . . . . No . . . . state has a right to claim the exclusive responsibility of maintaining international peace in any designated part of the world.

Nevertheless, as hinted above, it expressed willingness, given equality, to co-operate in a friendly way. In May 1935 Japan raised its legation in China to an embassy, and the Nanking government in June issued a good-will mandate. Unfortunately the Japanese military party was now deciding upon stronger action. It supported a movement for autonomy in the five northern provinces—Hopei, Chahar, Suiyan, Shansi, and Shantung, with a population of over 90,000,000 and an area of over 400,000 square miles. It demanded that Japan should be permitted to establish military bases, and to build roads and construct airplane bases in Inner Mongolia. It indulged in considerable smuggling in North China.

Although the move to set up the autonomous provinces failed, Japan insisted in 1935 that Chinese troops in Hopei be transferred, and it forced the Peiping branch of the National Military Council to dissolve. In 1935 it expanded its control into Chahar and attached part of it to Jehol. Under Japanese auspices Prince Teh set up an autonomous Inner Mongolian government in February 1936.

Nevertheless, negotiations directed toward a Sino-Japanese understanding did not cease. China offered Japan co-operation, if the latter would treat China as an equal and cease from aggressions. Foreign Minister Hirota announced in January 1936 that he desired China's "active and effective collaboration with Japan" and urged China to recognize Manchukuo and to suppress Communism, for Japan desired to co-operate with China in the eradication of that doctrine. But Hirota's principles, although expressed in conciliatory form, were either too vague for immediate co-operation or else implied that China would have to accept the loss of Manchuria, "forsake the world and make common cause with Japan against Soviet Russia"—a policy which Nanking could not accept.

In February 1936 the army extremists in Japan attempted to overthrow the government by force. For a time the outcome was uncertain there, but Sino-Japanese tension began to mount. Japanese troops poured into North China in May. Until now China had been passive, because of military weakness and lack of political unity; but a new temper had arisen. Chiang-kai-shek in July had stated that China was determined to maintain its territorial integrity and that "if any nation should seek to violate our territorial sovereignty it would be absolutely impossible for us to endure. We . . . . shall definitely refuse to endure actual violation thereof . . . . when that time comes we shall not hesitate to make sacrifices."

The kidnaping of Chiang-kai-shek at Sian in Shensi Province in December indicated the strength of the national feeling, and the willingness of the Communists to forego their revolutionary agrarian program so as to form a united national front against Japan. A pact signed in January 1937, between Nanking and the generals who had led the rebellion, provided that the Communist armies were to occupy northern Shensi; later the Kuomintang voted to incorporate the Communist forces into the national army. Despite official statements and efforts of some business leaders, conditions grew worse until in July 1937 the Lukouchiao incident was sufficient to set going the vast forces of war even though the name was not officially used.

Japan had feared either one of two possible developments in China. Anarchy would have endangered Japanese investments and provided a standing menace to its security. On the other hand, a united China might have enabled the country to oppose Japan on the field of battle. The only way out of the dilemma was to obtain Sino-Japanese co-operation. But the question was how? Japan attempted to combine the principles of the imperial way, the doctrine of a special mission, the theory of trusteeship, with its definition of co-operation; and when China refused to accept what to it was the surrender of Chinese independence, Japan was forced to fight to impose it.

The Japanese advance into China led to the reassertion by foreign powers of their rights and interests based upon international treaties. Japan's claim that the Nine-Power Treaty no longer held good brought forth protests from other signatory powers which saw their own interests being progressively squeezed out by Japan. The elimination of American oil companies, the obstacles placed in the way of other foreign business, the Japanese protests against an American loan to China for the purchase of wheat, the League of Nations health program in China, and contracts for the delivery of American airplanes showed the direction in which forces were tending during the years 1933–1937.

After the outbreak of hostilities in the latter year, foreign rights and interests were subjected to new dangers. In December 1937 the U.S.S. "Panay" was sunk and three other American vessels were destroyed by Japanese forces. The attack of civilian populations endangered foreign lives and property, and both the League of Nations and the United States lodged strong protests against indiscriminate bombing of innocent civilians. Japan insisted that its policy was to respect as far as possible the interests and lives of third parties; but the record of twenty-three bombings of American property between January 15 and June 12, 1939, seemed to suggest that they were the outcome of a deliberate policy rather than mere accidental by-products of legitimate military action. In January 1938 the United States formally protested against the repeated illegal entry of American property and the removal of goods and employees by Japanese forces. The Japanese explanation seemed unsatisfactory. In the lower Yangtze Valley American business men and missionaries were prevented "from returning to their places of business and mission stations and . . . . denied even casual access to their properties." The American Chamber of Commerce and the American Community Committee at Shanghai appealed to the Department of State. They expressed alarm "over the steady progress of the realization of Japanese plans to oust Americans and other trade from China by means of monopolies, trade and travel restrictions, control of commodities, exchange control, currency manipulation, as already in effect in North China." They demanded restoration of the Shanghai municipal council to full authority and control in the settlement, restoration of American homes and businesses to their owners, discontinuance of Japanese censorship and interference with mails, telegrams, and cables, also restoration of trade rights in the Yangtze Valley, North China, and elsewhere, and due respect for and observance of all American treaty rights.

In May 1939 Japan suggested that, in view of changed conditions, a remodeling of the Shanghai municipal council was imperative, and that Japan should have a greater voice by reason of its large increase of citizens and in order more thoroughly to prevent anti-Japanese propaganda within and near the settlement. The United States replied that the present time of disorder was not conducive to an orderly readjustment of the situation in Shanghai. In 1939 Japan claimed that the international settlements and concessions at Kulangsu, Shanghai, and Tientsin were merely administrative limitations on China's sovereign rights, and that, since Japan was fighting to place the sovereignty of China under Japanese control, it should have the right of sending armed forces into such concessions to clear them of enemy forces.

What of relations between China and Japan? The result is still in doubt. If Japan had calculated upon a speedy victory against a disordered China in a distracted world, it was disappointed. In 1894–95 Europe had been strong enough to prevent Japan from intervening decisively in Asia; but in 1937 Japan hoped that the European opposition could not effectively prevent a successful military campaign. It had wavered between the ideal of uniting Asia in a partnership against the West and of dominating Asia. The latter ideal now triumphed. After four years, the countries appear to be in a condition of military stalemate. Foreign observers say that, although Japan controls coastal cities and the railroads and major lines of communications, and has established an efficient blockade, it does not hold China, which now has enough military strength to permit it to wage a war of economic attrition, and that Japan will not be able to placate, or probably to conquer, China. The question arises whether or not China can win. Military experts point out that, although there is in China military unity, the efficiency is low, and much remains to be done in order to modernize China's military life. In civil branches of government the disunity is most pronounced. Vested interests, personal rivalries, and inadequate development of personnel and resources still characterize the country. It is by no means certain that China can emerge victorious.

This reasoning leads to the conclusion that the decisive factor in any constructive solution will be the international one. Unless Japan can win outright and succeed in developing China with China's consent, and can gain some relief from the exhausting international tension, which is most unlikely, peace along the following lines would seem to be necessary: (1) a renewed opportunity for China to build its unity, free from foreign attacks, and from the remaining unfair, unequal treaty provisions; (2) agreement between China and Japan for co-operation on a substantial level of equality; (3) international economic assistance to China with recognition of Japan's important interests at stake there; (4) sound international peace throughout the world with greater opportunities for Japan in world markets.

Merely to suggest these principles is to suggest the need of a complete volte face in Japan's present policy; and at present, there seems to be no indication that they will receive a moment's attention. The contradictions are too deep, and one cannot expect a solution without a settlement of the general world situation. For the problem of the Pacific turns out to be not exclusively a regional problem. Whatever doubts there may have been as to the truth of this statement should have been dispelled by the events of the last five years. In 1936 Japan and Germany signed the Anti-Comintern Pact, and from that time Japan was able to exercise an increasing pressure upon the democratic powers of Europe by threatening their possessions in Asia. As Germany and Italy advanced in Europe, so did Japan attempt to advance in Asia. Demands upon France increased throughout 1940, culminating in the Vichy-Tokyo Pact of September 22, under which Japan was permitted to establish three air bases in northern Indo-China and to send troops to the French colonies. The United States replied to the attempt to upset the status quo by President Roosevelt's proclamations in July licensing exports of various products useful for war and embargoing exports of aviation gasoline to countries outside the Western Hemisphere. The Axis counter-reply came on September 27, 1940, with the signature of the Triple Alliance under which Japan recognized the leadership of Germany and Italy in establishing a new order in Europe, and Germany and Italy recognized Japan's leadership in establishing a new order in Greater Asia. The three partners agreed "to assist one another with all political, economic and military means when one of the three contracting powers is attacked by a power at present not involved in the European war or in the Chinese-Japanese conflict."

The year 1941 was to provide additional evidence of the world implications of events in Asia. Japan moved south, occupying Indo-China and threatening the Dutch East Indies and British Malaya. The United States realized, late in the day perhaps, that Japanese control over these areas would place the American defense program in extreme danger, in view of the fact that the greater part of two essential elements—rubber and tin—are obtained from Southeastern Asia. The national security of the United States and the possibility of a British victory in Europe might well turn upon events many thousands of miles away from either country.

Without question the re-establishment of peace and order in the Pacific will depend upon the outcome of the present war, which is a world-wide matter; and the new order in Asia will reflect the triumph of either democracy or dictatorship in Europe. Regional organization in the Pacific, like regional organization elsewhere, must be a subordinate part of a peace system which embraces the whole world.

PAN-AMERICANISM

After the Central and South American peoples had obtained their independence from Spain, a number of thinkers hoped that they would form an organization for mutual assistance and welfare. The Monroe Doctrine of 1823 served notice that the New World was to be free from the historic disputes, accumulated passions, and political struggles of Europe. It was natural for the Americas to wish to do more than live upon a somewhat negative policy of keeping other people away. A positive policy of building a nobler society through the co-operative efforts of the newly liberated American nations—was such a dream to be only an illusion?

There was ground for believing that Pan-American ideals might succeed. The Americas had a common heritage of political freedom gained by casting off the restraints and restrictions of European empires. North and South America are on the same continent, and people assumed that this geographical factor would prove to be a unifying force, forgetting that distances between many American states are greater than those which separate some of them from Europe, and that the sea may provide fewer obstacles to trade than a difficult terrain. It was hoped that devotion to democratic ideals would promote unity; unfortunately, democracy was not to prevent sovereign nations from fighting, and many of the Central and South American countries, though democratic in name, were ruled by oligarchic and military dictatorships. Nationalism of a jealous kind soon reared its head, and in 1839 the Central American Federal Republic, established in 1821, broke down. Many of the state governors had refused to obey federal officials, and civil war broke out, resulting in the substitution of five independent states for one larger unit. In later days many of the Central and South American peoples feared that a Pan-American ideal was but another name for North American imperialism. The United States had enunciated the Monroe Doctrine, and for a time the Latin-American nations were grateful. Later they suspected the expansion of the Doctrine in every United States advance into the Caribbean and elsewhere. First there was the "Manifest Destiny" period; then the United States undertook military intervention in Nicaragua, Haiti, and the Dominican Republic, imposed the Platt Amendment upon Cuba, and adopted a nonrecognition policy toward revolutionary governments. President Theodore Roosevelt's "big stick" and Secretary Knox's dollar diplomacy were poor instruments with which to promote a genuine Pan-Americanism. Until the Americas could find some means of eradicating the fear of the great northern power, and until the United States would consent to modify its forward policy, the outlook for continental solidarity did not appear bright. A United States Monroe Doctrine and its extension could not easily harmonize with a Pan-Americanism based upon essential equality of states.

Nor was that all. The United States was a creditor country, and most of the Latin-American states were debtors. The former desired to strengthen compulsory arbitration for the settlement of claims; the latter were unwilling. The United States adopted a high-tariff policy and shut out goods from abroad, and the greater the consequences of the postwar economic depression the more resentful grew the Central and South Americas against a policy of commercial exclusion. They in turn adopted policies of economic nationalism, making Pan-American international co-operation still more difficult.

Finally there were profound cultural differences. Many of the peoples to the south regarded North American civilization as materialistic, sacrificing spiritual values to the acquisition of economic wealth and power. North Americans tended to regard their southern neighbors as backward, inefficient, and unsanitary, and lumped them together in one confused category, not realizing the growing national differentiation that was taking place.

For these reasons the Pan-American ideal did not make great headway. In the early nineteenth century Bolívar had preached it with noble eloquence, and in 1826 inspired a Pan-American Conference, at which, unfortunately, the United States delegates arrived late and exercised little influence. The next sixty years witnessed scant progress, until in 1889 the first of the modern Pan-American conferences took place; and from that time meetings have been held periodically.

In the meantime other difficulties arose in the form of rival schemes for the wider allegiance of the Central and South American peoples. There was the Pan-Hispanic movement. After the bitterness of the revolution against Spain had died down, the new nations began to revise their attitudes toward their former mother country. New histories appeared which reinterpreted the old Spanish colonial policy in a more favorable light. Newspapers and books preached the value of maintaining, instead of excluding, what was precious in the Spanish heritage. As early as 1856 the Spanish minister at Washington held conferences with diplomats from Latin America and discussed Pan-Hispanic projects, but with limited immediate results. At the turn of the century a new spirit appeared. In 1910 the Hispanic-American Congress met at Barcelona; historic and geographic congresses were held, and numerous institutions came into existence for the purpose of promoting Pan-Hispanic friendship and unity. After the revolution of 1931 Spain incorporated in its constitution a clause permitting double citizenship for people coming from Latin America on condition of reciprocity. No great practical results have come and no great increase in trade between Spain and the Americas.

A movement known as Latin-Americanism also arose. In some respects it was a negative force, deriving strength from a consciousness of the need of defense against North America. Intellectuals who regarded Paris as their spiritual home and others preached that their Latin culture must be preserved at all costs. A number of conferences were held, visits from Europe were arranged, and a committee on co-operation in Latin-American universities and colleges arranged special university courses. Recently President Cardenas of Mexico made an appeal for Latin-American economic solidarity, and the labor groups in some of the countries have taken up the cry.

INQUIRY AND CONCILIATION

In spite of the obstacles mentioned above, and the competing regional, political, and cultural organizations, Pan-Americanism has made headway. The main achievements between 1881 and 1938 may be summarized as follows:

The first logical step in the development of peace machinery is to strengthen the means of inquiry and conciliation to deal with more general questions. In many international disputes it is difficult to know just what the facts are. If both sides will agree to a commission of inquiry and thereby obtain fuller evidence, a more accurate appraisal of rights and wrongs is possible. In 1923 the Gondra Treaty provided that controversies which cannot be settled by diplomacy or by arbitration means shall be submitted to inquiry, and set up two permanent commissions of diplomats to be situated at Washington and at Montevideo, which can set the machinery of inquiry in motion. Either party to a dispute can request an inquiry, and the commission must immediately notify the other disputant. The Commission of Five must report its findings within a year, and the parties undertake not to mobilize their troops near the frontier until six months after the report has been issued. The Commission in its report of the facts may propose a settlement, but its proposals are merely advisory and do not bind the respective governments.

The Gondra Treaty thus follows the Bryan Peace Treaties of 1913–14, which included an undertaking to submit all disputes to inquiry and conciliation and made provision for a "breathing spell" during which the disputants promised not to resort to force, pending the report of the Commission. Its weaknesses are obvious: the treaty excepted disputes which affect constitutional provisions; the machinery was clumsy and slow to put in motion; it assumed that the publication of facts would suffice to establish clearly the rights and wrongs of a dispute, whereas such is often not the case; it presupposed that an aggressive-minded government would wait and would not use propaganda and other methods to rouse its own people; it even minimized the importance of conciliation.

In 1929 the general convention of inter-American conciliation marked a step forward "by specifically adding conciliation to inquiry"; the persuasion of other governments was to be added to the "logic of facts." The permanent commissions of diplomats at Washington and Montevideo, provided for in the Gondra Treaty, were empowered to act as commissions of conciliation, and might even on their own motion take action when it appeared that there was "a prospect of disturbance of peaceful relations." But the proposals of a conciliation committee are not binding: no judgment is given; the parties do not have to be "persuaded"; they retain full liberty of action; no legal judgment restrains them. The aim of the 1929 Convention was "to amplify rather than to replace the Gondra Treaty." It added to the functions of the Permanent Commissions, and did away with the cases which under the 1923 treaty were excepted from the process of peaceful settlement. Nevertheless the commissions were still to be *ad hoc* bodies, of which there would be 210 in existence! Truly a clumsy arrangement. A further advance in Pan-American organization had been theoretically made when several American states had signed the Kellogg Pact renouncing war as an instrument of national policy, and later when nineteen governments on August 3, 1932, by adopting the "nonrecognition" principle agreed not to recognize the fruits of aggression. Several American states signed the Argentine Anti-War Pact of nonaggression and conciliation at Montevideo, October 10, 1933, under which they agreed to submit their differences to a conciliation commission of five members comprising one national from each country and three nonnationals, or else to a court of justice. *Ad hoc* commissions were to be replaced by "permanent, but dormant commissions"—a theoretically important advantage.

Such a commission's report is to have only an advisory force, and parties may reject the proposed solution; nevertheless they must observe the breathing spell. Two types of disputes are excepted, those arising from purely domestic questions and those which affect "constitutional precepts." The first two articles of the Pact condemn wars of aggression and pledge the states to settle disputes by pacific means. By Article 3 the states undertake, should a signatory fail to live up to the above-named obligations, to exercise the political, juridical, and economic means authorized by international law and to adopt as neutrals "a calm and solidary attitude," also to bring the influence of public opinion to bear upon the disputants; but in no case will they resort to intervention, either diplomatic or armed, "subject to the attitude that may be incumbent upon them by virtue of other collective treaties to which such states are signatories."

The 1936 Buenos Aires Conference adopted a convention to co-ordinate, extend, and assure the fulfillment of the existing treaties among the American states. The convention standardizes the procedure to be adopted but does not set up "any important new devices"; it reiterates obligations rather than creates new ones. The existence of several treaties tends to produce confusion, especially as many of the countries have not ratified all of them. Despite the increase in the number of ratifications, the situation is not yet satisfactory; moreover, only six of the signatory powers have nominated the permanent conciliation commissions provided for by the Montevideo Conference.

There is some reason, therefore, for the proposal of the Mexican government of a code of peace under which the American states would undertake to refer all disputes to permanent commissions of conciliation or arbitration or to an Inter-American Court of Justice. The plan is that, unless an appeal is made to either of the other bodies, the commissions of conciliation will function. The sole advantage is that it would establish a body with more explicit power to initiate conciliation proceedings than the present diplomatic commissions now possess.

In two recent international disputes mediation has had some success. Honduras and Nicaragua in 1937 quarreled over a region of land bordering the Caribbean. The United States government sent a telegram to the disputants and notified the other American republics. Fortunately, Nicaragua and Honduras accepted the tender of good offices; but it would appear that the dispute has not yet been finally settled. The United States acted in accordance with the normal procedure of diplomacy, in that the treaty did not provide methods by which third parties could set the conciliation machinery into motion, although it did not exclude such procedure.

The dangerous crisis occasioned by the massacre of many Haitian people at the hands of some Dominican soldiers in 1937 tested the Pan-American conciliation machinery much more severely. After an anxious period the matter was referred to the permanent diplomatic commission at Washington. Happily an agreement was reached; the Dominican government expressed regret and paid an indemnity of $750,000; and other outstanding issues were settled. The Pan-American peace machinery had rendered fine service in preventing what undoubtedly would have developed into a bitter war.

ARBITRATION

The next step in advance of mediation or conciliation is that of arbitration; in this case the disputants undertake to accept the award of a third party. The United States had submitted many particular disputes to arbitration during the nineteenth century; but the Senate refused to consider adopting general treaties of arbitration providing in advance for the submission of agreed-upon classes of disputes to third-party determination. The Central and South American states signed over two hundred arbitration treaties by 1910, and negotiated over one hundred in the next decade, of which many remained unratified. In 1902 Argentina and Chile signed an agreement providing for compulsory arbitration of all disputes except those dealing with constitutional questions.

In 1907 the five states of Central America established a Court of Justice with jurisdiction over all disputes without exception which might arise among the five states concerned. Individuals might bring suit against a state. The Court was given power to determine its own jurisdiction and might even hand down a judgment in the face of a refusal by one party to appear. In the ten years of its existence it rendered eight decisions, some of them involving political issues; unfortunately, in attempting to decide upon the action of Nicaragua in granting certain privileges to the United States under the 1913 Bryan-Chamorro Treaty, it ran into difficulties: Nicaragua refused to recognize the decision, which had gone against it, and in 1917 denounced the Court, which ceased to exist.

Several American states signed a claims convention in 1910 and thereby took an important step in developing continental machinery to deal with an extensive set of international problems. The United States had advocated compulsory arbitration of disputes arising from pecuniary claims, and at the Second Pan-American Conference a treaty to this effect was signed and ratified by nine governments. Further action was taken at the Rio de Janeiro Conference in 1906; but the 1910 convention replaced the earlier treaties. Under its terms the signatories agreed to submit to the Permanent Court of Arbitration at The Hague or to a special tribunal all claims for pecuniary loss or damage that could not be adjusted by diplomacy and were sufficiently large to justify the expense of recourse to arbitration.

For several years nothing worthy of note was done to further inter-American arbitration until the Treaty of Inter-American Arbitration was adopted in 1929. Under this instrument the signatories agreed to submit to arbitration juridical disputes such as the interpretation of a treaty, any question of international law, the existence of any fact which if established would constitute a breach of international obligation, and the nature and extent of the reparations to be made for the breach of such an international obligation. There were two exceptions: the parties were not obliged to arbitrate domestic questions or questions affecting the interests of or referring to a state not a party to the treaty. If the disputants are unable to agree as to the arbitrator, a procedure is available to overcome the difficulty. If within three months of the establishment of such a tribunal the disputants have been unable to formulate the special terms of the controversy, the tribunal itself may take action.

In addition to the 1929 treaty the Conciliation and Arbitration Conference of 1929 drafted a Protocol of Progressive Arbitration, Article I of which reads: "Any party to the general treaty of Inter-American Arbitration . . . . may deposit at any time with the Department of State of the United States of America an appropriate instrument evidencing that it has abandoned in whole or in part the exceptions from arbitration stipulated in the said treaty or the reservations attached by it thereto." In effect, the Protocol of Progressive Arbitration resembles the Optional Clause of the Permanent Court of International Justice.

The General Arbitration Treaty has been ratified by all American states except Argentina, Bolivia, Paraguay, and Uruguay. The United States Senate ratified the Protocol of Progressive Arbitration in 1935, but that measure has thus far been ratified by only eleven of the twenty-one republics. Some questions have been dealt with under the arbitration treaties; but the most serious of them, the dispute between Mexico and the United States over the expropriation of American property, still remains within the realm of diplomatic negotiation, Mexico having rejected Secretary Hull's proposal that the matter be referred to arbitration.

ADJUDICATION

The advantages of having a permanent court to which judicial matters can be referred are obvious; and several American states have felt that the arbitration process, while commendable, does not go far enough but that efforts should be made to build up a consciousness of the need for institutions which by their permanency can create a consistent and extensive body of international legal decisions. All of the twenty-one American republics with the exception of the United States joined the World Court at The Hague; but it was felt that steps should be taken to set up a similar court for the American continent. In 1923 Costa Rica made such a proposal, and five years later at the Havana Conference Colombia submitted a similar plan. The Mexican Code of Peace, considered at Montevideo in 1933, had a chapter dealing with an American Court of Justice comprising one member from each state and a Canadian member as well. The Court would have compulsory jurisdiction over the so-called legal or justiciable disputes and general jurisdiction over others. The Court would act as a court of first instance and also as a court of appeal in certain defined cases. And it would also be empowered to give advisory opinions.

At Buenos Aires in 1936 Panama and Peru again broached the subject and Costa Rica, Salvador, Guatemala, and Nicaragua reported favorably upon the proposal. Thus far no practical steps have been taken and it is difficult at this point to see clearly whether the project will go beyond the realm of theory for some time. It would be unfortunate if such a court operated to weaken the World Court at The Hague; on the other hand, it can be reasonably asserted that if the habit of submitting international disputes to judicial settlement is to become sufficiently widespread we shall need the services of several international courts of a permanent character.

CONSULTATION

The theory of consultation is that, if disputes of an international character arise, the interested states by meeting together to discuss problems and difficulties may be able to find a peaceful solution. Informal consultation dates from prewar days, but there were few provisions pledging states in advance to take concerted action of this character. Consultation was rather of an *ad hoc* kind. The Washington Conference in 1921 provided for "joint conference" in the event of a dispute arising over the insular possessions of the United States, the British Empire, France, and Japan with which the Four-Power Treaty was concerned. The Nine-Power Treaty dealing with China also made provision for "full and frank communication between the Contracting Powers," but neither instrument outlined the procedure to be followed; and procedure is an important thing.

Consultation among the states of the American continent was not emphasized until the Montevideo Conference in 1933, and the prolonged and bitter dispute between Bolivia and Paraguay over the Chaco region was well under way before the Saavedra Lamas Anti-War Treaty of Non-Aggression and Conciliation was adopted at Montevideo. This instrument provided for consultation in the event of disputes, condemned wars of aggression, approved the nonrecognition of territorial gains obtained by use of force, provided for a "common and solidary attitude by the neutrals," and proclaimed that intervention would not be resorted to. The treaty "implied rather than stated" the use of consultation.

The ominous situation in Europe and the Far East and the breakdown of the peace machinery of the League of Nations led the American states to consider whether they should not strengthen the Pan-American organization and thereby save themselves from the anarchy which was spreading elsewhere in the world. A special conference called at Buenos Aires in 1936 at the suggestion of President Roosevelt considered the whole problem of peace not merely in relation to the American continent but "against a background of world affairs." The United States took the initiative, and because of the popularity of Mr. Roosevelt and the influence of Mr. Hull the North American delegation possessed a strong advantage.

Out of a sharp clash of ideas came the convention for the maintenance, preservation, and re-establishment of peace, which explicitly provided for consultation when the peace of the American republics is menaced. Consultation is also to take place in case of war in another part of the world, should that conflict threaten the peace and security of the American continent.

The members of the Conference agreed to file with the Pan-American Union the names of eminent jurists from whom mediators could be selected in case of an inter-American dispute, to set up a permanent commission to study plans for the elimination of the causes of war, and to take steps to put the existing inter-American agreements into effect. At Lima in 1938 the Eighth Pan-American Conference specified more definitely that in order to facilitate consultation the foreign ministers of the republics or their representatives at the initiative of any one of them will meet in the various capitals "by rotation."

MODIFICATION OF THE UNITED STATES FOREIGN POLICY

During this period Pan-Americanism made considerable headway by reason of a threefold change of emphasis in the policy of the United States affecting the Monroe Doctrine, the right of intervention, and the scope of Pan-American co-operation. During the course of one hundred years the Monroe Doctrine had been variously interpreted, but by the twentieth century it had been given an expanded meaning. Originally it was designed to prevent political penetration by European powers, and then to prevent European economic expansion from being converted into political control. But the United States found itself in the position of having to guarantee the economic stability of Central American republics in order to insure that American nations fulfill their obligations to their European creditors. The policy of supplying financial advisers, of limiting borrowing, and of interfering in elections aroused resentment in Latin America, and charges were made that the United States was using the Monroe Doctrine as an instrument of expansion. Critics pointed out that Pan-Americanism could not flourish as long as the United States took it upon itself to define the Monroe Doctrine and to apply it without consulting its southern neighbors. A unilateral Monroe Doctrine seemed to be inconsistent with genuine Pan-Americanism. Nevertheless, in 1923, Secretary of State Hughes adhered to the old position; and it was not until President Roosevelt had enunciated the good-neighbor policy and the United States government accepted the principle of continentalizing the Monroe Doctrine that the way was clear for further progress in Pan-Americanism.

For many years the United States clung to the doctrine that under international law it had the right of intervening in countries to the south of its borders in order to protect its own citizens. We have discussed the general problem of protection of national interests abroad in another chapter. Here it is sufficient to point out that the right of intervention was strenuously opposed by the Latin-American states, and only after Secretary Hull informed the Montevideo Conference in 1933 that his government renounced the right of intervention did the full possibilities of Pan-American co-operation open up.

For a long time after the first Pan-American Conference in 1889 the United States attempted to restrict the scope of discussion in these gatherings to nonpolitical objectives, and its insistence in this matter also hindered the development of Pan-American relations. As political conditions grew worse throughout the world following the economic crisis of 1931, the invasion of Manchuria by Japan in the same year, and the breakdown of the Disarmament Conference by 1933, the United States realized the necessity of expanding the scope of Pan-American activity; and at Montevideo in 1933 it consented to discuss political questions, which, indeed, had now come to the front and within a few years were to dominate the scene.

PAN-AMERICANISM AFTER 1933–36

During the period following the advent of Hitler to power the whole question of inter-American relations became complicated by the rise of new and the intensification of older methods of penetration on the part of Germany, Italy, and Japan. Not only the interests of the United States but also the future of Pan-Americanism stood in jeopardy, and considerable thought was given to the problem of how to meet policies which seemed to menace the security of the Western Hemisphere.

Foreign settlers in large numbers had come to South America. Several hundred thousand Japanese and millions of Germans and Italians formed centers of national influence and became instruments of economic, political, and cultural penetration. There is nothing new in this phenomenon as such; but the German and Italian groups developed techniques which, it was alleged, were beyond the activities normally regarded as legitimate for foreigners living in other lands; they brought extreme pressure to bear upon their fellow countrymen to make them join Nazi and Fascist societies; if anyone was bold enough to refuse, his compatriots boycotted his business and submitted him to social ostracism and even to bodily harm; they supported local Latin-American political parties which favored dictatorship methods, and threw their influence against the democratic forms of government. It is true that imperialist powers have frequently supported anti-governmental forces in return for the promise of economic advantages; but it was charged that recent Italian and German methods constituted a much greater and more unjustifiable degree of interference in domestic affairs, because the ordinary German and Italian citizens had become part and parcel of a continuous long-term political objective which contrasted with the more limited objectives of the older imperialisms. It may be that the difference is one of method and of degree rather than of kind; but in many situations affecting human relations the problem is primarily one of degree and not of kind. Thus, although the skeptic might assert that the English settlers in Egypt and the French settlers in Morocco were also centers of political penetration, the reply was that the latter were not concerned with spreading a particular kind of "ideology" and were not consciously or unconsciously tools of a proclaimed new world order.

The totalitarian regimes conducted active sales campaigns within Latin America. Their agents pushed German and Italian goods. Trade missions visited the various countries; trade exhibits made known attractive wares which were available for purchase; and the art of appealing to the peculiarities of the various peoples of America was raised to a high point of efficiency. These methods, however, had not been peculiar to Germans and Italians. British, American, French, Japanese, and other nations also have sales agents, trade missions, and trade exhibits, which are the normal instruments of gaining new customers. Do we witness here only another typical instance of imperialist rivalry? And are the so-called democracies complaining because the other powers are more efficient in salesmanship? Or do other forces enter into the situation? British and American interests charge that it is not the competition to which they object but the methods, which are essentially unfair. · For example, some Germans living in South America were agents for United States firms and did excellent work in selling American goods. Under pressure from their consuls they were forced to take the agency for German products. They then pushed the German and kept the American goods in the background. They had built up a considerable degree of business and good-will, and American interests assert that they suffered as a result of the political interference by German officials. American consuls are said to maintain a strict neutrality; they provide information concerning business houses and conditions within their areas, but refrain from putting any political pressure upon American salesmen or American residents in order to gain markets for goods made in the United States.

Italy and Germany signed commercial treaties which differed from the traditional type in that they were placed upon a barter basis. After the breakdown of the prewar methods of relatively free international trade, the development of postwar economic nationalism, and the disruption of foreign exchanges, the agricultural countries of Latin America were unable to pay their debts abroad or to mobilize exchange sufficient for buying extensively in foreign markets. Consequently, foreigners who had hitherto enjoyed markets in the southern continent found their trade falling off as a result of the profound currency disequilibrium.

Out of the resulting economic confusion the totalitarian powers were able to extract an advantage which added to the difficulties of traders from the less regimented countries. Because dictator governments could control and direct trade, they could offer goods to Latin-American countries in return for goods. Germany, for example, might take wool in exchange for agricultural machinery because its government could so arrange matters within Germany that the wool could be disposed of; an American exporter would have been placed at an obvious disadvantage if he had had to accept wool in return for his agricultural machinery, for he would have had little chance of selling wool on the open market and, in any case, he was not an expert in wool. The many independent American traders had no co-ordinating agency, as had the regimented German groups; and in the absence of adequate foreign exchange facilities they found themselves losing ground. Moreover, the German government could agree to buy the wool at a particular level of currency; it might accept five milreis to the mark for the transaction in question, whereas the normal rate might be ten milreis to the mark; under the circumstances the German manufacturer was able to undersell the American manufacturer. Although Germany might make little if any profit on the transactions, its government could distribute the loss among the employer, the worker, and the general public. The same government, by skillful manipulation, might recoup its losses elsewhere; and if it could succeed in weakening its competitor, and so obtain a monopoly control, it might subsequently charge higher prices. Viewed from this angle, the German methods constituted a species of dumping; and dumping has been traditionally regarded as an unfair trade practice. Moreover, the German trade successes were designed to serve as instruments for obtaining political advantages and later political control.

By negotiations Italy and Germany were able to obtain the lifting of currency restrictions in their favor. Such actions led to strenuous protests to the Latin-American countries from the United States and Great Britain, which claimed that such discrimination was inconsistent with commercial-treaty obligations and constituted an unfriendly act. In the struggle for political power on an ever wider basis, progressive intensification of so-called unfair methods took place because the more strenuous and all-embracing become the competitive activities upon which may rest the fate of countries in a major conflict, the more will nations, as political rivals, take advantage of every possible opportunity to obtain security and ultimate victory by weakening their opponents. The more closely trade becomes tied to military objectives, the less chance will there be for the preservation of fair trade methods. International political security is the prerequisite of international commercial integrity.

The competitor nations all indulged in campaigns to sell munitions to the Latin-American countries; and it is open to question whether the armaments rivalry of itself affords any ground for criticism that some countries do and some do not engage in unfair practices, in view of the revelations of the Nye Committee and other bodies which have investigated the methods of the armament salesmen.

Communications also have entered into the struggle. Italian, German, United States, and British shipping have engaged in a battle of freight and passenger rates, and charges and countercharges of unjustifiable state subsidies and mergers were frequently made. The airplane is playing an increasingly important part. The need of frequent service in an age of increasingly rapid tempo in commercial affairs is obvious enough, and a great deal of economic penetration may depend upon the efficiency of the air services. In countries where railway and road building involve enormous expense on account of distances and the difficulty of the terrain, the airplane assumes an added importance as a means of promoting national solidarity. As an instrument both of commerce and of war, it cannot be neglected. The Latin-American market provides great scope for competition among the leading airplane manufacturers of the world, and the major countries have been very active in trying to sell their machines.

The world today, for commercial and other reasons, has become dependent upon daily and even hourly information, so rapidly do events change. National governments are increasingly concerned with molding public opinion, and in consequence the radio has been added to the instruments by which nations attempt to further their interests and defend their security. The German and Italian governments have maintained almost uninterrupted radio programs which have contained a large element of propaganda, and have been so organized as to give Germany a considerable advantage; moreover, international friction has developed because British and American programs have suffered from interference and important speeches have been made unintelligible to listeners by the deliberate employment of static and by the more powerful sending stations drowning out other stations which are on a particular wave band. More technical developments in radio may be able to prevent such interferences, but in all probability the battle of the air waves will continue. Until the major problem of political security is settled we may expect a refinement and intensification of the radio struggle in an attempt to win support from the Latin-American people.

The totalitarian countries were particularly active in courting Central and South America by an appeal to cultural understanding. They formed societies to promote good-will, established and paid for lectureships in universities, offered scholarships to enable

Latin-American students to travel abroad, and attempted to interest influential business people in key positions so that out of cultural friendships business advantages might accrue. The Japanese,
Germans, and Italians took into account the sensibilities of the
Latin-American people more successfully than did the North
American and British traders and residents. They were less exclusive and more willing to enter into the cultural interests of
the people among whom they lived. In all this activity there need
have been little or nothing open to legitimate criticism. In North
America, the psychology of salesmanship and the art of making
people buy through appealing to their personal pride or weakness
have long occupied business executives. Normally these methods
can be regarded as incidental to either a genuine desire for cultural understanding, or to an attempt to make cultural relations
a handmaiden to economic advantage.

Critics claim that the methods of the totalitarian regimes go
far beyond the bounds of legitimacy. Especially do they draw
attention to the existence of press attachés within the totalitarian
diplomatic services operating in Central and South America. They
assert that the Italian and German governments give free news
to editors who must pay for the services of the United Press,
the Associated Press, Reuter's, and Havas. Naturally newspapers
are anxious to cut their costs as much as possible and will take
news furnished to them gratis or at little expense. In consequence
their readers are thereby exposed to a continuous stream of pro-
German and pro-Italian news, and their sympathies develop along
those lines. One official states that without doubt this method of
news distribution was a major cause of the pro-Franco attitude
of most of the Latin-American people and that had the Loyalist
government possessed the same propaganda facilities the viewpoint of Central and South America might have been very
different.

The United States watched the introduction of European
political rivalries on Latin-American soil with anxiety, because a
continent hostile to democratic institutions might ultimately endanger the security of the northern power. The traditional policy
(enunciated in the Monroe Doctrine) of excluding European politics from Central and South America, as well as Pan-Americanism, seemed to be threatened. The question arose whether or not
a more positive policy along political, economic, or cultural lines
should be undertaken in order to combat totalitarian influences.

The problem was most difficult; it necessitated an attempt to separate the genuinely economic and cultural forces of a peaceful kind from those which were primarily the instruments of political penetration and aggression. If the United States, under the guise of protecting the Monroe Doctrine or promoting Pan-Americanism, should lay itself open to the charge of shutting out legitimate trade and commerce of non-American nations, it would invite charges of hypocrisy and would promote ill-will instead of good-will. The same result would ensue if cultural relations were promoted, not as ends in themselves, but merely as a "handmaiden of commerce and a servant of international power politics." Despite the close connection between the political, economic, and cultural phases of life, it was necessary that an attempt be made to keep them as distinct as possible, unless they all were to become part of a general totalitarian rivalry. The Fascist, Nazi, and Communist regimes made politics, economics, and culture serve one supreme purpose, the power of the nation or class. This condition made and still makes for confusion and misunderstanding in foreign relations. If the democratic nations should attack every move, cultural or economic, of the totalitarian powers on the plea that the latter have aggressive political objectives, every small incident is likely to become a major issue of diplomacy. If they acquiesce in the "piece by piece" tactics of Germany and Italy, they might find a repetition of the German methods which proved successful in Austria and Czechoslovakia. Is there any way out of the dilemma?

POLITICAL DEVELOPMENTS

We have referred above to the beginnings of continentalizing the Monroe Doctrine in 1933 and the pledge of consultation by the American nations at the Buenos Aires conference in 1936. At the Eighth Pan-American Conference held at Lima in 1938 the governments discussed in considerable detail what should be done to meet any attack on American security. The League of Nations had broken down, and it was generally realized that some stronger steps would have to be taken on the American continent to meet the dangers which were rapidly growing more obvious. Secretary Hull urged biennial meetings of the foreign ministers of all the American nations; but Argentina, suspicious of the United States, would not agree to a permanent consultative machinery. Consequently the Declaration of Lima provided only for consultation by foreign ministers when they deemed it desirable. The "Declaration of American Principles" also adopted at

Lima, while general in character, was of great importance psychologically, and gave assurance to the Latin-American states that their northern neighbor had accepted the three principles of equality, independence, and voluntary co-operation. The way was clear to further common action should events abroad dictate its necessity.

In September 1939 an Inter-American Consultative Conference was held at Panama in accordance with resolutions passed at Buenos Aires in 1936 and at Lima in 1938. It was designed to discuss the situation brought about by the outbreak of war in Europe. The meeting was attended by the foreign ministers (or their representatives) of twenty-one American states. The Conference drew up measures designed to increase economic co-operation by the creation of an inter-American financial and economic advisory committee. It made a general declaration of continental solidarity and reaffirmed the resolutions of Lima. It reasserted the doctrine of neutrality and emphasized the rights and status of neutrals, and declared that the participants would prevent their territories from being utilized as bases of belligerent operations, would prevent their subjects from engaging in unneutral acts, and in other ways would uphold the general principles of neutrality as prescribed by international law. The declaration of Panama read in part as follows: "There can be no justification for the interests of the belligerents to prevail over the rights of neutrals causing disturbances and sufferings to nations which, by their neutrality in a conflict and their distance from the scene of events, should not be burdened with fatal and painful consequences." The European war, it went on, "would not justify any destruction to inter-American communications." The Conference then declared that the waters adjacent to the American continent must be free from the commission of any hostile act by a non-American belligerent and defined the geographical limits of the zone of security. The governments also agreed to consult together if necessary in order to determine the measures to be taken to secure the observance of the provisions of this declaration and, if the need existed, to patrol, either individually or collectively, the waters within the defined zone adjacent to their respective territories.

The twelfth resolution suggested that there should be a second meeting of the foreign ministers at Havana on October 1, 1940, unless special circumstances demanded another meeting in the meantime. Another section provided for consultation in the event that it was necessary to determine what measures should be taken to secure the observance of the provisions of the declaration; still another resolution provided for consultation in case any region within the American continent at present a colony or dependency of a non-American state "should be obliged to change its sovereignty" and if from this action "there should result therefrom a danger to the security of the American continent." For example, should Germany defeat Great Britain in the present war and demand the cession of Jamaica or Trinidad, it would seem likely that the American states would meet in consultation under the provisions of the above-mentioned section.

In claiming a zone of security the American republics asserted "what is intended to be a new rule of international law"; the "inherent right," according to Fenwick, should be taken as meaning not a rule of law already in existence but "that the American Republics believed that the new rule they were announcing was inherently reasonable and should be accepted by the belligerents."[17] The governments did not announce that they would use force to secure the immunity of the zone from warlike operations, but the suggestion that the American states deny the use of their ports to the vessels of any warring power which violated the zone was frequently made. Britain, France, and Germany, however, each made objections based upon its self-interest as a belligerent; each was anxious lest the security zone would afford a greater advantage to its opponents than to itself. And in the last resort it appeared the American republics might even have to go to war to protect their neutrality!

The Inter-American Neutrality Committee, which met January 15, 1940, at Rio de Janeiro, soon confronted a number of problems relating to the maintenance of neutrality—the activities of the German merchant ship "Tacoma," which had helped to scuttle the "Graf Spee"; the desirability of excluding submarines from ports and territorial waters; the use of belligerent merchant vessels; the use and abuse of postal correspondence (a question which involved the question of inviolability of mails); the use of automatic contact mines; the control of radio broadcasting; and the blockade of foodstuffs and clothing intended for civilian populations within belligerent countries. The Committee had been asked to formulate a codification of the law of neutrality "which would seek to unify the practice of the American States in many matters which, for lack of a clear rule of international

[17] Charles G. Fenwick, *American Neutrality: Trial and Failure* (New York University Press, 1940), pp. 130–31.

law, had hitherto been left to the decision of the individual state."[18] The task in itself would have been very great if indeed not overwhelming, but even more serious was the implication "that the mere acceptance of such an objective for the proposed code involved acceptance of the legality of war in the framework of international law." To attempt to codify the law of neutrality "was an implied recognition that international law was unequal to the task of distinguishing between right and wrong, between good faith in the observance of treaty obligations of peaceful procedure and the recourse to violence for the attainment of national objectives."

Events in 1940 rapidly revealed the inadequacy of the neutrality policies adopted in the Pan-American conferences at Buenos Aires, Lima, and Panama. The German invasion of Norway, Holland, and Belgium, the fall of France, the Italian attack on Greece, and the desperate position of Great Britain brought out clearly that a new problem had arisen. Before June 1940 most of the American nations believed that "this was the war of 1914 over again . . . . and there was little need to take positive and drastic action."[19] Now, with Hitler the conqueror of Europe, and in view of his ambitions set forth in *Mein Kampf,* the New World realized that something new had entered the stage and that organization for neutrality was not enough; organization for defense had become vital. The foreign ministers of the American republics who met at Havana in June 1940 decided (1) to put under an Inter-American Commission on Territorial Administration any territory which one non-American state should directly or indirectly seize from another non-American state; (2) to co-operate in preventing subversive activities of foreign agents who had been encouraged and abetted by diplomatic and consular officials of certain European countries; and (3) to adopt a policy of special economic co-operation to meet the disruption of world trade created by the European war and to prevent the possibility that totalitarian governments in the postwar period might attempt to use commerce as an instrument of political penetration. The Emergency Committee for the Provisional Administration of European Colonies and Possessions in the Americas was to be set up as soon as two-thirds of the American republics had appointed

[18] Charles G. Fenwick, "The Inter-American Neutrality Committee," *The American Journal of International Law,* January 1941, p. 38.

[19] W. Stull Holt, "United States and Western Hemisphere Defense," *Pacific Historical Review,* March 1941, p. 36.

their members. Fifteen American states also signed a coffee agreement to regulate the export and import of that commodity and established an Inter-American Coffee Board with headquarters at Washington, D.C., to regulate quotas for the United States market. The agreement was to last from October 1, 1940, to October 1, 1943, and was designed to steady the market and to prevent the serious disorganization of prices which undoubtedly would arise if any large part of the ten million bags normally consumed by, but now shut off from, Europe were dumped on the world market.

In September 1940 President Roosevelt announced the destroyer deal under which the United States acquired the right to lease naval and air bases in Newfoundland, Bermuda, the Bahamas, Jamaica, Santa Lucia, Trinidad, Antigua, and British Guiana. Whatever be the correct view of the legality of the step (if indeed events have not made the concept of neutrality almost meaningless), it met with general approval in Latin America. Similar approval greeted the passage of the Lend-Lease Bill by the United States Congress in March 1941, although unofficially some Latin-American countries criticized the provision which authorized the United States to open its ports to the war vessels of Great Britain, a step which some writers believed conflicted with the inter-American agreement made at Panama in October 1939. Perhaps early further consultation with representatives of other American republics is in order.[20]

The deepening crisis in Europe led to further steps in continental American co-operation. Panama announced that it would permit the United States to erect defenses in Panama outside the Canal Zone: Panama was to retain jurisdiction over civilians within the area and would receive compensation for the land occupied; and the United States agreed to vacate the region at the end of the war emergency. Equally important was the United States–Mexican agreement by which the two countries undertook a joint program for common defense in accordance with the resolutions drawn up at the Havana Conference of foreign ministers in 1940. The plans included the development of naval bases in Mexico and the improvement and use of Mexican airports by the armed forces of the United States. Suggestions were also made for the establishment of a permanent joint board similar to that set up by Canada and the United States.

[20] W. T. Stone, in *Foreign Policy Bulletin,* February 7, 1941, p. 4.

The growing unity of hemispheric policy expressed itself in dramatic fashion when the United States seized German and Italian merchant vessels anchored in its ports. Several of the other American republics followed suit, thereby giving evidence of a common determination to prevent sabotage by the totalitarian powers.

ECONOMIC AND CULTURAL CO-OPERATION

Political and military co-operation alone cannot insure safety, and the American republics have realized the great importance of working out an adequate economic policy. As the years have rolled by, the scope of economic co-operation has widened, and only after some time has the pattern become clear. From earlier *ad hoc* measures, the American nations have proceeded to long-term objectives, and while realizing the importance of dealing with emergencies they have attempted to see beyond the immediate needs of the moment.

Between 1937 and 1939 the United States and Brazil set up two joint committees, one at Rio de Janeiro, the other at New York, to study the best means of encouraging trade between the two countries. The members were to serve for two years and to report on the operation of the United States–Brazil trade agreement. The Secretary of the United States Treasury and the Minister of Brazil signed an agreement by which the United States undertook to sell gold up to $60,000,000 to Brazil, and make available to it dollar exchange for the purpose of promoting exchange equilibrium. Brazil was to free the exchange market for commercial transactions which would permit transfer of funds to repay obligations due to United States citizens who had made investments in Brazil; and, in order to help eliminate exchange fluctuations and remove restrictions on foreign trade, the United States in March 1939 agreed to assist Brazil in establishing a central reserve bank. It also announced that the Export-Import Bank had agreed to consider the arrangement of suitable longer-term credit to finance Brazilian purchases of economic equipment in the United States. The latter would co-operate with Brazil in studying and developing the agricultural products which would complement production in the United States.

The interdepartmental committee on co-operation between the American republics in November 1938 reported that there was a wide range of activity in which the governments of these republics could co-operate. Thirteen departments and agencies were already at work and the committee approved projects from every agency: public health, public administration, economic, commercial, and fiscal matters, labor, agriculture, etc. In May 1939, Congress enlarged the scope of an Act of May 1936, to enable governments of the American republics to obtain the services of experts "in such matters as highway construction, public health, control of plant and animal contagious diseases, fisheries, and other technical or scientific problems." United States experts have since then aided in Brazil, Colombia, Argentina, Nicaragua, and Paraguay.

On August 16, 1940, the President of the United States approved an order issued under the authority of a 1916 Act establishing the office for co-ordination of commercial and cultural relations between the American republics and appointing Nelson A. Rockefeller as Co-ordinator.[21] Mr. Rockefeller's duties are to establish and maintain liaison between the advisory commission and the several departments of the government interested in inter-American relations, to be a member and chairman of the inter-departmental committee on inter-American affairs, and to formulate and carry out the policy of co-operation in the fields of "the arts and sciences, education and travel, the radio, the press and the cinema," with the end, it is interesting to note, of furthering national defense and of strengthening the bonds between the nations of the Western Hemisphere.

On November 14, Mr. Rockefeller announced the appointment of several advisers for the cultural program of the Co-ordination Office, which is a subsidiary of the Council of National Defense. The advisers who acted in a voluntary capacity served on the following committees: Policy, Scholarship, Literary, Publications, Music, Art.

Meanwhile the Inter-American Development Commission had been established on June 3, 1940, "as a working unit of the Inter-American Financial and Economic Advisory Committee organized following the Conference of Foreign Ministers called at Panama in 1939. While the parent body is composed of representatives of the 21 American Republics, the Commission consisted of only five members," whose duties were to compile basic information, to establish contacts between interested parties especially in the

[21] The following sections are based upon publications of the Co-ordination Office.

fields of Latin-American mineral resources and agricultural and forest products and to encourage the establishment and development of industrial plants. On December 30, 1940, it was announced that Brazil had established the first of the twenty-one national councils which were to be set up by the Inter-American Development Commission, and it was hoped that at a later date similar groups would be formed in the other American republics.

The European War had confronted the United States with several emergency problems in its attempt to build a continental solidarity. The closing of the European markets involved an annual loss of six hundred million dollars to the Latin-American countries, and the necessities of war forced the United Kingdom to adopt clearing arrangements which in turn resulted in a further loss to them of three hundred million dollars of exchange. The combination of loss of markets and serious restriction of free exchange with which to buy manufactured articles threatened to produce a catastrophic decline in the standard of living and hence the possibility of economic crises and political upheavals in Central and South America. Both short-term and long-term policy therefore indicated the desirability of exploring means of alleviating the present distress and of building the foundations of wider inter-American political and economic co-operation. The United States took the lead in the following activities.

1. It made loans to Latin-American Central Banks in relation to surplus commodities as well as loans direct to governments.

2. It made large purchases of strategic materials for defense purposes.

3. It led in loans to Latin America for the development of basic industries of a noncompetitive nature such as rubber, hemp, chromium, and asbestos, and a loan of twenty million dollars was made by the Export-Import Bank to Brazil to produce simpler steel articles formerly purchased from Europe.

4. The development of better business relations was attempted by (a) an investigation as to whether or not American business firms were too frequently represented in Latin America "by firms and individuals now known to support objectives contrary to the best interests of the American Republics," a mission which made an extensive tour having found that there were a sufficient number of cases to arouse "a serious concern from a defense point of view" but that many of the businesses were co-operating in order to remedy the situation; and (b) the creation of a merchant advisory service with headquarters in New York to give

expert advice on merchandising to exporters of products from Central and South America and thereby "to broaden the United States market for products from these nations."

5. Co-operation in broadcasting was realized to be of great importance, and two systems planned to inaugurate programs dedicated to inter-American understanding. It is interesting to note that the recent (1941) change in wave lengths which affected more than eight hundred stations in the United States resulted from an agreement between the United States, Canada, Mexico, and Cuba.

6. Improved news distribution was offered. In an endeavor to strengthen American press relations several of the important newspapers including the *Herald-Tribune* opened new offices in South America, the *Reader's Digest* issued a special edition in Spanish at low cost, and *Time* now offers South American subscribers the service of air-mail distribution.

7. The Motion Picture Producers and Distributors of America have appointed an expert on Latin-American customs and languages to guarantee authenticity in films and "to advise on language and historical problems." A number of companies plan to send outstanding actors and actresses to South America to appear in person. The industry also proposes to increase the amount of news reels and short subjects dealing with Central and South America and has appointed a number of committees to consider such questions as visits to South America, South American film facilities, short subjects, art direction, and story material.

8. Athletic relations have been established. Mr. Rockefeller in an address delivered before the *New York Herald-Tribune* Forum on October 23, 1940, announced that his office planned to increase the number of athletic interchanges between the American republics, and mentioned specifically baseball and soccer teams. One wonders if a type of pan-American Olympic games and Davis Cup contests may not develop.

9. Tourist facilities have been enlarged. The authorities are also hoping to stimulate tourist traffic and are being helped by the fact that the war in the Far East and in Europe is making travel in those continents impossible. Already many thousands of tourists are visiting Mexico and other parts of the American continents.

10. Better transportation is being developed. A Committee for Co-ordination of Inter-American Shipping, created early in 1941, proposes to co-operate with shipping companies to ensure

adequate transportation facilities for inter-American trade during 1941.

In developing its policy of extending loans, the United States has been confronted with over three thousand million dollars of Latin-American loans which were outstanding on December 31, 1939. A considerable proportion of these loans were in default, either by abrogation of the gold clause or by reduction of the whole or part of the interest and sinking-fund payments. The development of the international crisis in Europe, however, caused economic security to take precedence over the debt adjustment.

While some economists warn that Pan-American economic co-operation cannot proceed far independent of the restoration of world trade, other scholars urge that a considerable amount of multilateral trade is possible within the Americas, and that many countries on the American continent produce raw materials and handicraft goods which could find markets within neighboring states if adequate commercial and advertising facilities were developed.[22]

Successful inter-American economic co-operation must take into account the growth of economic nationalism and the reaction against economic colonialism in the countries to the south of the United States. Any policy which aims to maintain the nineteenth-century status of these countries in the sphere of international trade will be doomed to failure, and the measures just outlined would seem to indicate that the United States has accepted a modified economic nationalism on the part of Latin-American countries as a permanent factor in its future relations. Also the United States must accept the existence of a social-reform movement in the other American states, a movement which finds expression in a desire to improve the condition of the poor and dispossessed and to curb the wealth and profits of the rich. Because most of the important companies in Central and South America have a considerable amount of foreign capital invested in them, a movement of social reform in those parts inevitably involves international considerations. Upon the restraint of the United States and its sympathetic understanding will depend a great deal of the future development. If foreign investors in Latin America show too conservative an attitude they may do much harm to inter-American relations, and if Latin-American countries are

[22] See Frank Henius, *Latin-American Trade* (Harper & Brothers, 1941-; also, M. Ezekiel, "Economic Relations between the Americas," *International Conciliation*, February 1941, No. 367.

unreasonable in their policy toward property rights it cannot be expected that Pan-American harmony will be easily maintained.

The suggestion may be ventured that just as within the United States the people have had to expend millions of dollars for social purposes without seeing any immediate economic return, so the United States may be willing to undergo financial sacrifice in an attempt to build up a sounder civilization on the American continent. Ultimately, the question of values dominates the whole question and upon the devotion to the highest human ideals the success of political and economic policies will depend.

Pan-Americanism may now be summarized: First, it must take into account the Spanish heritage of Central and South America. The Spanish character is one which differs essentially in its scale of values from that of the people of North America. Madariaga writes that the Spaniard lives against a background of eternity, that he is an individual stripped of all but essential tendencies, and that, although at home in essential things, he is apt to evade things merely necessary or useful. Unfettered by a sense of social pressure, he shuns abstractions. He is not a citizen of an equalitarian state nor a partner in a national society nor a subject of an empire. He is a *Man,* who does not easily co-operate in social affairs but who leaves uncultivated what Madariaga calls the middle stretches of political and economic life.[23] In another volume[24] the same author notes that Spanish thought is concrete and is applied; that its interest is in man as an individual, in the person of flesh and blood who eats and drinks and plays, not the man who lives a public life or engages in organized society. A Spaniard has great passion, spontaneity, and penetration, but is weak in speculative vigor; in him the creative triumphs over the critical. Unamuno notes that the Spanish emphasis on personality is connected with his strong desire for immortality and his peculiar preoccupation with death.[25] To the Spaniard, as several writers have pointed out, work is evil; he prefers to lessen his wants rather than to continue his labors. Leisure is a precious value. He does not like organized and routine labor, but is nevertheless capable of great outbursts of energy when his enthusiasm is aroused. Morente, in a series of lectures[26] given in 1938, said

[23] S. Madariaga, *Spain* (Scribners, New York, 1931).
[24] S. Madariaga, *The Genius of Spain and Other Essays on Spanish Contemporary Literature* (Oxford University Press, 1930).
[25] M. de Unamuno, *Essays and Soliloquies* (A. A. Knopf, New York, 1925).
[26] M. G. Morente, *Idea de la Hispanidad* (Espasa-Calpe, Argentine, S.A., 1939), especially pp. 104–8.

that what the Spaniard chooses to do comes not from written codes or customs or human conventions but proceeds from his own conscience, his own inner law; that the Spaniard thinks of people in terms of private relations, and the public relations of which Anglo-Saxons make so much are to him abstractions lacking in reality and compelling power.

Moreover, to Spaniards law as law has no great appeal unless it is embodied in persons. This concept has great consequences for any plan for Pan-American relations. United States people talk of government by laws but not by men, and put their trust in institutions and organizations. But this is not the Spanish way. Much of the corruption in Latin America derives from the claims of friendship and the feeling that laws do not possess the all-embracing character which Anglo-Saxon jurisprudence assigns to them. Thus Pan-Americanism must emphasize personal relations and awaken personal and group enthusiasms. It must not trust merely in public organizations. Such a method is not easy, because the Spaniard is a self-contained person. His pride is dominant, and he must be appealed to largely along the lines suggested above, namely, personality. Nevertheless, this Spanish ideal of the wholeness and intensity of the individual has led to anarchy on frequent occasions, because it has not been balanced by an adequate sense of social responsibility, of routine, and of administrative efficiency; and the United States can offer much to supply a corrective in these matters, as well as to learn of the qualities that enhance personality and deepen inward culture.

The second factor to be taken into account with respect to Latin America is its Indian heritage. The Indians are of various tribes, and their differences cannot be ignored but must be taken into account and woven into a larger pattern of life. The blend of Spanish and Indian culture has taken place at different rates in different countries,[27] but without doubt the clash of two such opposing cultures as the highly individualized Spaniard and the communal Indian begot in the *mestizo* confusion and uncertainty. The new civilization which the *mestizo* must find will have some elements of the Spanish and some elements of the older Indian life; the question is how much of each. And at present the struggle centers in the realms of religion and education. Some wish to emphasize the Catholic faith with its values; others believe that the deep-seated ways of the Indian population should be sought

[27] Consequently it needs special regional studies, as Dr. Manuel Gamio has convincingly shown.

out, incorporated fully into the new life, and encouraged to creative effort under modern conditions; still others, under the influence of modern economic doctrines, apply Marxist principles to
education and social organization.

These problems of education and its fundamental objective
complicate the question of Pan-Americanism,[28] as does the problem of land. In Mexico, particularly, the restoration of land to
the Indian villages—the *ejidos*—has created many difficulties. The
present struggle is to decide whether or not the Indian communal
lands shall be individualized. In the background the old feudal
owners watch, probably in vain, for signs of a restoration of their
power. In other parts of Latin America considerable feudal
property still exists and the social struggle will no doubt follow
the general Mexican pattern. Wherever foreigners own land in
Latin America, these struggles will have international repercussions.[29]

The American countries to the south have emerged from a
colonial status and from their subordination to Spain only to go
into a semicolonial economic status due to the penetration of the
United States and Europe with their capital investments, their
search for concessions, and other activities. In their reaction
against that economic imperialism the new nationalism has attempted to take strong measures against foreign economic interests. As we have pointed out elsewhere, the foreign interests
demand that at least a minimum international standard of justice
be meted out to their citizens in Latin America, whereas Latin-
Americans talk in terms of national sovereignty and of putting
foreigners upon the same legal status as their own people.[30]

The Latin-American people have a keen sense of injustice
arising out of a hundred years of struggle against the dominance
of the European powers and the United States, and the present attempt at Pan-Americanism must take this deep-seated suspicion
into account. The recent new Good Neighbor policy is only a few
years old and must bear itself with considerable restraint and
patience if it is to offset the feelings aroused by the preceding
century when the power, political and economic, of the United

[28] See the effect of the anti-religious program in Mexico upon Roman Catholic opinion in the United States, and its influence upon Mexican–United States
relations.

[29] This question can be only mentioned and not analyzed here.

[30] See above, chapter vii, dealing with the protection of nationals, their property, and investments abroad.

States was much in evidence. Nationalism and socialist criticism of imperialism combine to render precarious the continuance of international trade along the lines suggested by Mr. Hull. If the United States takes strong steps to protect what it believes to be the fair rights of its citizens in Mexico in connection with the oil problem, the cry will be raised in Latin America that United States imperialism is showing itself in its true light and that the Good Neighbor policy is merely a cloak. If the United States does not protect its interests against national emotion and Marxist doctrines which are in intimate alliance in Mexico, other South American countries may be tempted to follow the same pin-pricking policies, and the cumulative effect of such actions may be to destroy much of the spirit and method of the Good Neighbor policy. If the State Department tries to escape from these dilemmas by offering to submit the oil dispute to arbitration, Mexico is likely to reply that this is a matter involving national sovereignty. In reality the attempt to transform Pan-American relations from a condition in which the United States was the dominant force, using its power to forward policies not always distinguished for their tact and understanding, to one of genuine co-operation, will require extraordinary skill, a rare quality of patience, a willingness to take several rebuffs, and, at the same time, a clear demonstration that patience and restraint connote strength and not weakness.

Intellectual co-operation will be a matter of the utmost importance, for Latin-American scholars value culture for its own sake and welcome the fellowship of those devoted to the ideals of culture and truth. Without close-knit intellectual interchange and friendship, the purely political understandings will have but limited success. But the utmost care must be taken to avoid giving the impression that intellectual co-operation is merely a device to serve the purposes of continental defense and international power politics. Pan-American intellectual co-operation cannot be exclusively continental; to be really successful it must be part of the larger world system.

A warning should be sounded against the optimistic belief that American trade can be switched from Europe so as to make this continent relatively independent of the Old World. The idea sounds reasonable and in these days of European anarchy has a certain attraction. Closer examination reveals that it will be impossible to build up anything like a closed Pan-American economy, because the major exports of countries of the south compete with many of the products raised in the United States. Argentinian beef and cattle, Cuban sugar, many of the tropical fruits, South American wheat, and other items can in normal times find markets more readily in Europe than in the United States. On the other hand, if multilateral trading arrangements can be re-established, the products mentioned above may go to various European countries which in turn can send other goods to the United States, and the United States in its turn can export its manufactures to Central and South America. We should by all means encourage the greatest amount of regional international trade, not at the expense of and as a rival to world trade, but rather as a factor supplementary to it.

Pan-American machinery for the promotion of security should be strengthened. Within the continent at present the danger of civil war tends to be greater than that of international war. Nevertheless, the idea of nationalism is rapidly gaining ground in Central and South America, and international jealousies combined with the growth of communications and armaments may unloose upon the American continent the same evil passions and intensity of war which are now devastating Europe. It is therefore important to take time by the forelock and to strengthen the security pacts and to systematize plans for action against aggression. Yet within the Americas, as within the world at large, there is still no unanimity, and indeed very little agreement, upon the principles which should be followed and the organization which should be adopted to stop war. The Americas are as uncertain as the European nations, whether it is best merely to consult in the case of emergency, to declare their neutrality, to impose moral or economic or military sanctions, or to limit their armaments in some fashion.

Moreover, it is by no means certain that the danger of war exists merely within the American continent. Time has yet to show whether or not there are forces and interests which so transcend continents as to make it impossible to localize a war in Europe or in Asia. Up to a point, a continental declaration of neutrality may serve to keep the Americas out of a war which originates elsewhere. But if it should appear that the very developments of war itself, owing to the growth of science and the application of mechanical principles, cause belligerents so to infringe upon the rights of neutrals that the latter are finally driven forcibly to defend them, we shall perceive the futility of a purely continental approach to the question of war. It may be that the wide expanse of ocean, the strength of the United States, and the determination of the other American countries to resist being drawn into what began as a European war will serve to keep the two Americas at peace. On the other hand, the judgment arrived at in reference to the Little Entente, the Balkans, and the Scandinavian countries may also apply to Pan-American efforts to attain security: Regional co-operation in the absence of a sound world system rests upon uncertain foundations.

The Pan-American foundations may not be as precarious as recent years have shown other regional foundations to be; but they may be less secure than some advocates of an exclusive Western World imagine. For however closely knit the Americas may be they will still be drawn into an unlimited armaments race, an intensified economic struggle, and all the fears of fifth-column penetration unless an American security system is so closely interlocked with other regions of the earth as to make aggression impossible in any part. Continental security must be part and parcel of the larger world security; it cannot be attained by continental exclusiveness.

Chapter XVII

THE PRESENT WAR AND THE
PROSPECTS FOR WORLD ORDER

PREVIOUS chapters reveal a fatal contradiction within modern world society. Whereas, owing to the developments of science, the economic and cultural relations of the peoples of the world have become ever broader, necessitating wider forms of political organization, men's minds have been shrinking in their outlook. Under the inspiration of the doctrine of nationalism, popular loyalties grew more restricted and allegiance was given to a form of society which was increasingly incapable of providing security and welfare for its people. Something has had to happen. Either national institutions must be modified to meet the new realities, or the new forces must be pressed and distorted into an inadequate national framework. There cannot be a conflict in political and economic tendencies for a long period of time without some kind of revolution.

In recent years the nations of the world have taken the course of sacrificing many aspects of life to the dominant political emotion, nationalism. At the end of the World War of 1914–1918 this nationalism appeared to have triumphed, and the failure of the disarmament conferences, the breakdown of the League, the growth of tariff barriers, quotas, and currency restrictions, and the prodigious rearmament programs indicated that the national ideal was firmly in the saddle. Several years ago the writer ventured to predict that despite appearances nationalism was in such a precarious condition and was

confronted with forces so menacing that one may not unreasonably prophesy that the modern nation as we at present know it will in large measure have disappeared within the next fifty years unless in the meantime the League of Nations becomes a tower of strength among the peoples of the world. Insofar as the situation of the League is precarious nationalism is threatened with collapse, for the weakness of the League reflects not the strength of modern nationalism, but its fundamental weakness, masquerading it is true as power and energy.[1]

At that time I suggested that just as the religious wars of 1618–1648 marked, not the reassertion of religious faith, but its eclipse in the public life of Europe, so the World War of 1914–1918, which apparently marked the enthronement of nationality, really indicated its approaching decline. It was obvious that most of the nations of Europe had no real unity, that some of them were little more than a collection of hostile minorities, which soon came under dictatorships because their lack of a common faith made democracy impossible, and that many groups within the new states by carrying self-determination to excessive lengths were threatening Europe with a chaos of sectionalism which in turn was calling forth the iron rule of repressive nationalism. A spurious unity was being enforced upon political parties, trade unions, Jews, Communists, and churches; and many legitimate and necessary expressions and forms of human life were rendered impossible.

Meanwhile events were showing that the apparently irresistible ideal of nationalism had neither clarity nor dominance. For in truth there exists no one kind of nationalism. Cultural nationalism, Jacobin or radical nationalism, conservative nationalism, liberal nationalism, integral nationalism, racial nationalism, religious nationalism, socialistic nationalism, and even communistic nationalism are all possible, just as there exist many religious sects within Christianity, Mohammedanism, and Buddhism.[2] Among the various kinds of nationalism there may be little in common; the nationalism of a Darlan is poles apart from the nationalism of a Leon Blum, and Harold Laski's conception of what constitutes true British nationalism bears faint resemblance to that of Neville Chamberlain! Indeed many civil wars have occurred because of the divergent views within a country as to what the nationalism of that country should connote.

Many people suffer from having a wrong mental picture of their nation. They assume a finality of outline, a too clear-cut line of distinction between the nation and the other units of society, and ignore the many divisions within the nation itself. The United States is far different from the image which a map

[1] Linden A. Mander, "Nationalism: Ascendant or in Decline?" *Proceedings of the Institute of World Affairs, Twelfth Session* (The University of Southern California Press, 1935), p. 180.

[2] See C. J. Hayes, *The Historical Evolution of Modern Nationalism* (Richard R. Smith, New York, 1931).

calls to mind. Its history, its foreign commerce, its citizens abroad, and a thousand other factors go to make up the bewildering complexity called America. But the picture of America, the visual image, plays a large part in overemphasizing the separateness of the country from other countries and in obscuring the many differences, social, cultural, political, and economic, that exist within its borders. Such a nation appears to be a more timeless and changeless entity, and to possess a more unalterable "essence" of its own, than actually is the case.

In reality, a nation is a unit of changing content, and we are mistaken to assume that it is a final entity. Initial regional and local differences persist in a nation.[3] They are not obliterated. The Catalans, the Basques, and the Andalusians retain many of their historical differences in contemporary Spain. The Tuscan accent is still to be noted in Italy. Flemish and Walloons still form contrasting groups in Belgium. One may note differences of accent in the various counties of England and in regions of the United States. Nor is this surprising. The character of the nation depends upon the compelling power of the uniting ideal. What holds people together is the consciousness of a common factor or factors which transcend their everyday economic and social life—loyalties which bind them into a wider fellowship without destroying the more intimate associations.

From this it is clear what happens when a nation declines. National disintegration takes place because groups cease to feel themselves as part of a whole.

There are always centrifugal tendencies at work in society and in nations. Personal ambitions, class rivalries, sectionalism, international affiliations, inertia, local habits, resentment against overcentralizing tendencies of government, burdens of taxation, exhaustion through war, disease or famine, a subtle "loss of nerve" (as Gilbert Murray puts it in describing the change in ancient Rome), the growth of the philosophy and practice of personal pleasure, the desire of the cultured man for the delights and harmonies of his world of books free from the hurlyburly and crudity of politics, the longing of the mystic to withdraw from the world, the appeal of nature to the nonpolitically minded—all these and many other things can weaken the bond or bonds which make the sense of nationality a living, all-pervading factor, transcending

---

[3] See José Ortega y Gasset, *Invertebrate Spain* (W. W. Norton & Company, New York, 1937), pp. 20–29.

personal and group interests and lighting them up with the enthusiasm of a comprehensive and creative ideal.

The nation, like any other form of society, is an unstable and changing thing. Today, however, millions of people think and act as if the state or nation were an institution of fixed form and content. Yet nothing seems more futile than discussion of the abstract questions of loyalty, of the relation of the individual to the state or nation, or of the international relations of states themselves. The truth is that these relations must vary because different ages impose different tasks on society and individuals.

The matter is even more complex. Individuals may be loyal to some aspects of their national life and at the same time oppose other aspects. They may willingly submit to taxation for military purposes but object to fiscal measures designed to alleviate unemployment or to provide for social insurance. The state and nation are particular manifestations of society existing for particular purposes; when they cease to serve those purposes, they begin to decline.

A factor common to most nationalisms has been fear and hate of the foreigner. Just as the individual becomes highly self-conscious when threatened, so the nation has been frequently held together despite internal differences by an appeal to national security and to the necessity for national defense. In turn, the preparation for military strength becomes associated with the thought of past glory and national greatness, and the flag as symbolic of that national glory comes to play an important part. Symbolism, however, must express a living unity; if it becomes a device to cover up internal rivalries, if it is nothing more than a social "myth" created by propaganda, it will soon reveal its inadequacy. Unless a reasonable balance is struck between social justice, economic welfare, devotion to daily duty, and a spirit of devotion to right conduct, men and women will not defend what they consider to be present injustices against the dangers which may arise from without. Internal decay will then proceed apace until internal revolt or conquest by the foreigner (either by military victory or by use of fifth-column methods) reveals the collapse of inner unity.

During the last generation in particular the growth of group and class self-concern took place at the expense of men's wider interests. Despite an intellectual appreciation of the interdependent character of the modern world, men's deeper desires were concentrated upon private gain and group advantage. The poor and dispossessed had little reason to feel many ties binding them to a community which was content to let them remain in hunger and loneliness. It has been well said that the despair of the masses under a certain kind of leadership becomes the revolt of the masses. With effective faith in the nation undermined by reason of the selfishness of the rich, the resentment of the poor, and the indifference of disillusioned intellectuals and others, quite naturally the sovereign state, already outmoded as an instrument of defense against a powerful enemy which had mastered new techniques, fell before the onslaught of a new political faith armed with the latest weapons which modern science had devised.

It is not too much to say that the modern national state collapsed because it neither adapted itself to the scientific requirements of a new age nor maintained sufficient inner vitality to bend modern inventions to the service of its professed ideal. The way was therefore open to a new conqueror able to combine unity of purpose with technical and military efficiency. This new purpose was supplied by Hitler, and to a less degree by Mussolini. These two dictators substituted power for reason, discipline for consent, conquest for equality, and dreams of a new world order based upon the superiority of the elite peoples for what they considered outworn equalitarian and national society. Hitler by preaching the doctrine of race made a deeper appeal to man's irrationality than Marx had done in his call to class war based upon economic motives.

Like Machiavelli, Frederick the Great, Nietzsche, Bismarck, Gumplowicz, and others, Hitler claims that power is the dominant factor in human life. The philosopher of power exalts the pagan virtues of courage, heroism, and daring, and disdains the Christian virtues of humility and resignation. He glorifies strength and applauds the will to be free from the tyranny of the weak, whose rules cramp and confine true genius and distort its creative ability. He argues that it is not justice but power and armed force which secure the objects of man's desires. What conservative, he asks, will forego his privileges by being reasoned with?

The philosophy of power is generally based upon a distrust of individuals: only force can guarantee the unity of the state or nation. From this viewpoint it is easy to regard all civilized society as engaging in a perpetual struggle for power and territory.[4] This doctrine asserts the superiority of an individual, or race, or nation

[4] See F. M. Russell, *Theories of International Relations* (D. Appleton-Century Company, New York, 1936), p. 266.

over the others, and according to nineteenth-century apologists the fortunately endowed races have a mission to perform.

Now this philosophy has been seized upon by the leaders of perhaps the most efficient war machine which civilization has yet confronted. The Nazi government has ridiculed the concept of humanity, of peace, and of reason. It has elevated strife and war to the highest goal of human endeavor, and has identified the good life with the masterful control of the dominant race. It superadds the doctrine of race to the doctrine of power in a fanatical fusion, and a tremendous driving force results. A people or nation bound together by a common history, culture, or linguistic similarity possesses only uncertain bonds of unity. History reveals many changes in political fashions and thought; and geography and language are not final. What is needed is something more permanent to insure that a nation or "Volk" shall be an entity independent of time and change. It is here that the idea of race plays an important part, for its proponents call in biology to their aid: blood rather than mere thought is the first and foremost thing; the rest, culture and civilization, are but incidental by-products of purity of race. On the basis of the assumption that there exist fundamental differences of race which environment cannot change, that some races are born superior to others, that the decline of empires has been due to the intermingling of races, that God reveals himself through the laws of race, blood, and soil, and that law, art, literature, science are dependent upon race, the German leaders have built their claims that Germany should rule the peoples of other countries.

Scientists may easily disprove the doctrines of power and of race; but we have only to look into our own midst to appreciate how the skillful use of propaganda has persuaded people to buy all kinds of things which have been advertised by the most absurd and unscrupulous methods. And Nazidom has merely carried into the field of war and politics the methods of propaganda-persuasion in an effort to swamp reason and reflection. The future has yet to reveal whether reason can hold out against the force of prejudices and passion marshaled with consummate skill by men in charge of the great instruments of social control—radio, press, and military power.

The doctrine of race, leadership, and power clashed with the theories of nationalism, sovereignty, and a League of Nations based upon independent states. Nazi theories were incompatible with traditional international law or such modifications of it as a league might have introduced. More than that. The Nazi way of life is hostile to the type of liberal nationalism which the so-called democratic countries accepted, and is able to attack the sovereign state and liberal democracy because the two latter ideals have become incompatible with each other.

Sovereign nationalism had lost the capacity of self-defense by reason of the developing of modern military science. But most people still cherished the illusion that freedom could be preserved within the confines of the national sovereign state. In vain did Norman Angell and others point out twenty years ago that democracies would have to band closely together if they were to preserve their freedom, that sovereignty and freedom were no longer compatible, and that a determined military power might pick off independent nations one by one. Men and women persisted in the illusion that freedom could coexist with political sovereignty, because they recalled that in the nineteenth century nationalism had been a means of winning freedom from the older empires. They forgot that times had changed. Consequently, when Nazi Germany unloosed its relentless power upon the world many people saw in the event merely another war between the great powers; others saw in it a threat to democracy. Few realized that Hitler was challenging both sovereignty and freedom, and was being helped by the very fact that many people were still trying to attain both purposes, which in reality had become incompatible. Today the danger exists that men and women will misread the evidence, state the problem wrongly, and try to restore both democracy and the national state. If they do so, they must inevitably fail. It is necessary therefore to emphasize the two questions (1) dictatorships versus democracies, and (2) the kind of international order which must be established so as to provide the minimum condition under which freedom can be restored and maintained.

It is difficult to deny that democracy has its back to the wall and that its external foes are more numerous and more convinced of the superiority of their values than has been the case for over a hundred years. Democracy is the avowed enemy of dictatorship. One system or the other will triumph. This war is fundamentally a war between two different political faiths, an issue between two worlds, a struggle between two issues, a struggle between human beings who believe "conflicting things."[5]

[5] See Archibald MacLeish, *The American Cause* (Duell, Sloan & Pearce, New York, 1941); also Henry R. Luce, *The American Century* (Farrar & Rinehart, Inc., New York, 1941).

In the international sphere there can be no return to the old order. Something more comprehensive is needed. Democracy has been content to serve the national state without realizing that the defense of freedom has long since demanded a more efficient instrument than sovereignty. Whereas in the early nineteenth century democracy and nationalism may well have been allies, in the twentieth century democracy and sovereignty have become incompatible ideals, and the disunity of the democracies has marked either the decline and fall of the nationalistic era of the last two hundred years or the eclipse of both. The price to be paid for the survival of democracy is international reorganization.

It would be the height of folly to restore the small nations as sovereign entities with their own armies, navies, and air forces. Of what use to re-establish even a sovereign Britain or France? Almost immediately the new methods of war, psychological and economic, would be subtly at work and, as we have indicated above, democracy would be completely destroyed because it would be no longer possible in the future to decide whether in a balance-of-power system criticism of the government is designed to strengthen or to weaken that government and the country over which it rules. The alternatives are clear: There must be either a world dominated by the philosophy and practice of totalitarianism with its doctrines of leadership, discipline, power, and conquest, or a world genuinely devoted to the ideal and practice of freedom organized under an adequate system of international government. We here suggest policies which must be followed if the fruits of victory are not once more to be thrown away in the international sphere as they were after 1918.

In the first place, the possibility of an enduring peace depends upon a widespread appreciation of the enormous scope and complexity of the task. It will be of little value to make grudging adaptations here and there, only to realize that remedies which do not reach to the roots of the difficulties are no remedies at all.[6]

There is serious danger that people will underestimate the task of peace, as they did in 1919–20.[7] Once again men may be led to assume that a treaty has settled matters and there is no longer need for continuous study and planning for adequate and workable

[6] See Vera Micheles Dean, "Toward a New World Order," *Foreign Policy Reports,* May 15, 1941, p. 51.

[7] For a general discussion of this question, see Henry M. Wriston, *Prepare for Peace!* (Harper & Brothers, New York, 1941).

institutions. To begin with, the negotiators of the peace must have sufficient expert information at their disposal, and to this end countries should at once set out to make as detailed a study as possible of the many problems which will arise—at Paris in 1919 there were no fewer than fifty-eight committees and twenty-six commissions. Since one of the essentials is to obtain a treaty in a relatively short time, because nations are war-weary and are anxious to get back to normal, the utmost precision of thought and accuracy of information will be indispensable. Close collaboration is required among officials and the best of the laymen drawn from universities, industry, labor, and the professions if a many-sided peace involving health, government of dependencies, restoration of economic life, re-establishment of intellectual co-operation, and similar objectives is to be achieved.

Not less important will be a comprehensive program of public discussion. After the World War of 1914–1918, the American people reacted violently against President Wilson's plans. They had made considerable sacrifice during the war, but too many mistakenly assumed that the peace could and would take care of itself. Consequently a generation later the country faces the possibility of another war and sees freedom endangered as never before. Only if the general public understands the kind of world in which man now lives will it see the inevitability of reforming and enlarging political institutions in order to channelize the great energies released by science so as to insure law and order.

One may suggest that the work being done by the Carnegie Endowment for International Peace in publishing the findings of experts in an inexpensive pamphlet and the publications of the Foreign Policy Association and the studies being prepared by various churches are all steps in the right direction; but much more is needed. The universities should become centers of public forums the country over. Thousands of groups should be regularly discussing the political, economic, and social bases of the new peace and of the methods that will be required to make provision for peaceful change in a peculiarly dynamic period. At present there is too much indifference and far too little appreciation of the extraordinary demands which will be made upon every citizen if the world is to escape complete breakdown of institutions.

Two important phases of the peace negotiations must be kept in mind. First, the treaty to be successful must not repeat the fundamental error of 1919 when at Paris two conflicting principles, namely, collective security and power politics, were embodied in the same instrument. How to overcome this difficulty will be discussed presently. The other phase is the procedural phase.

Perhaps, after the negotiators know clearly what kind of new world they wish to create, they should draw up a preliminary treaty and impose it upon the vanquished; this treaty should deal only with the immediate military situation—the withdrawal of troops, the surrender of arms, and the demobilization of armies. Not until a year has elapsed should the negotiations for the final treaty begin. The conference should be held in the capital of a neutral state, some of whose citizens should comprise the secretariat of the conference; in this way the abnormal atmosphere of Paris in 1919 would be avoided. Both government and opposition parties should send delegates to the conference, which, therefore, would be a meeting of people's representatives. The congress should last for at last twelve months and the public should be warned that no hurried final solutions are possible or desirable. The people should be kept completely informed of the proceedings.[8]

For without doubt a period of immediate emergency reconstruction will follow the war and attention must be given to this vital work; otherwise it will be impossible to build an enduring peace upon sound foundations. If Europe is to be left in a condition of prostration, if epidemics break out and starvation confronts many sections of the Continent, there will be little or no hope to enlist enthusiasm for far-reaching plans of political and economic reorganization.

Thus the delivery of food and the prevention of disease will be an urgent necessity. Fortunately, the world has a great deal of experience to build upon; but it will have a much greater challenge at the end of this war than at the conclusion of the last. The wholesale destruction of cities, ports, and railroads, and the great dislocation of transport services generally will make the problem of material reconstruction a much more difficult one than it was twenty years ago. Financial and psychological reconstruction needs will be grave.[9] At the end of the present war we may expect to see civil war within France, Germany, and Italy because of the bitternesses that have been engendered. Emergency problems must be faced the day the armistice is signed, and on their solution will

[8] See Harold Nicolson, *Why Britain Is at War* (Penguin Books, Ltd., 1939), p. 147.

[9] See Arthur H. Sweetser, "Our Future International Society," *War and Society, Proceedings of the Institute of World Affairs, Eighteenth Session* (The University of Southern California, 1941), pp. 273–74.

depend whether or not international society gets off to a good start in its attempts to solve the more fundamental problems of reorganization now to be discussed.

The suggestion has been made that at the conclusion of the war Great Britain and the United States should impose peace upon the world by their superior military, naval, and air power. This Anglo-Saxon peace, it is assumed, would be relatively magnanimous and would serve as a prelude to a more complete international order based upon consent of all powers.

The proposal, attractive at first sight, has most serious limitations. The two powers simply could not afford to ignore the other peoples—the Norwegians, the Belgians, the Free French, the Greeks, the Yugoslavs, the Dutch—who have joined in the fight for freedom. These nations have sacrificed much and must be admitted to a new order on terms of equality. Otherwise they will regard themselves as pawns in another mere fight among the great powers. An Anglo-Saxon–imposed peace would give a handle to those who would charge the nations with imperialism. The "have" and "have-not" controversy would take on a new lease of life. The step would disillusion the Latin-American countries and would threaten with ruin the whole structure of Pan-Americanism which has been built up within the last decade. The United States has been able to win the confidence of the countries to the south of it only by using its power in the name of a larger international organization. And Great Britain and the United States can achieve and maintain their moral influence over all the rest of the world only if they in turn use their power for larger world purposes. In any case, the task will be difficult enough. France and Great Britain were freely charged with using the League for their own ends, and not a few people will repeat the accusation against Britain and the United States even if they do sponsor a new world order. It follows that the two powers must use their strength with considerable restraint. They must make plain that they mean what they say when they assert that they have fought for freedom and democracy. The world may survive one generation of disillusionment; it is more than doubtful if it would survive a second shock comparable with the first.

If as a result of United States help Great Britain and its allies win the war, and the victors draw up a peace based upon inadequate international organization, we shall witness a continuation of essentially the same kind of balance-of-power system which has resulted in an increasingly militarized world. Such a peace will be no peace, but merely an interim of progressively anarchical relations which will lead to further strife and suffering. If the world is to have an enduring system of peace and order the following minimum conditions must be observed: (*a*) An international or supra-national society which can immediately prevent war and hostilities short of war must be achieved. (*b*) The force at the disposal of this society must be so great that any national forces permitted (to serve essentially police functions) would have no chance of waging a successful war. (*c*) The treaty, unlike the Treaty of Versailles, must reconcile security and equality, probably within a federal system or something very closely approximating to federalism. (*d*) Under such a system no national unit will be able to be the final judge in its own cause; each will become primarily an administrative unit within a more comprehensive political system, and will be compelled to submit controversies for final decision to international or supra-national tribunals. (*e*) The treaty must establish on firm foundations cultural and human rights of national groups and of minorities within those groups, and these rights must be incorporated into a stronger system of world law. (*f*) If anything short of a federal system is adopted, provision must be made for international supervision of treaties so as to permit peaceful change. (*g*) Should an aggressor succeed in defying international authority, it must be met by the Stimson doctrine of nonrecognition of annexation resulting from war or the economics of force. (*h*) In order to guarantee the continuance of such a world order, mankind must develop a system of world constitutionalism and a loyalty to it, so that international obligations which will override the present sovereign claim of nations to break agreements in the name of their sovereignty will be acknowledged. Only then will the contradictions which at present exist in international law be removed.

If these things are done, the treaty will have established, not an international order in the present sense of the term, but something much more resembling what may be called loosely a federation. As pointed out elsewhere, it will be undesirable to make a hard and fast separation of powers between a Regional (or Continental) or World Authority and the component national states. In a rapidly changing world, new powers may have to be assumed by the central body and a rigid federal system would make such transfer difficult. Obviously, the old division between domestic and international affairs will have to be seriously modified. In a case of internal war, the international authority must be able to intervene decisively by means of blockade or munitions control or outright suppression of disorder. Such a development implies the rejection of the traditional doctrine of sovereignty, and the acceptance of a much greater development of organization to provide actual means and machinery for the peaceful settlement of internal disputes.

This power of the International Authority, which may be defined as paramountcy, may well vary according to the needs of different continents. It has been suggested above that a much closer form of "federalism" will be necessary for Europe, because it is in Europe that the greatest dangers of world wars lie, whereas in the American continent international disputes are not so likely to involve world-wide conflicts. The adoption of this principle will mean that Europe at least will have to have an international police force. European national armies, navies, and air forces must cease to exist. The Continent is too small for the existence of such armies and, as we have seen in the chapter dealing with war, it will be useless to maintain them. But, obviously, if European nations hand over their defense to an international European force, the evils of the balance-of-power system will be repeated as between continents unless the American continent and Asia, either as units or as made up of subunits, have so close an agreement with the European federation that no aggression can possibly succeed, and unless it is known in advance that no aggression has any chance whatsoever of success.

The International Authority must, therefore, have sufficient power to guarantee order; unless it can do so, nations will be justified in refusing to give up their sovereignty. It is a serious thing to urge countries to make such revolutionary change; and the only justification lies in the fact that the certainties of the good that will eventuate will so far outweigh present advantages that the change will appear to be overwhelmingly desirable. If the International Authority is to have sufficient armed forces and is to possess the power of distributing these forces throughout the world, and is to have bases, arsenals, factories, etc., for the technical equipment which will be necessary for such a force, the question will arise whether the nations which grant these forces will retain control over them and be able to withdraw them (if so, the International Authority will rest on a fragile foundation and will soon collapse) or whether the International Authority itself will possess the constitutional right and power to determine the size and effectiveness of the force. If it is to do the latter, it must have financial resources; and the further question then arises by what means the money is to be raised. Is the International Authority to have taxing power, and, if so, what will be the nature and extent of that power? Is it to rely for collection upon the instrumentalities of the national states, or will it have its own taxation authorities? If the former, and the national states default in payment, will the International Authority have power to seize property? These problems are extremely difficult; but they are not impossible of solution.

The question of loyalty raises serious problems. It has been pointed out that national states have been able to rely upon common interests within their borders, particularly upon the common fear of potential foreign aggressors. A world federation will have eliminated the latter element and therefore will need a very lively and continuous appreciation by the millions of people throughout the world of their common welfare. The task of enlisting the enthusiastic support of the great masses of people throughout the world, a task truly mountainous in nature, should stir the imagination and call forth the creative energies of scholars, publicists, religious leaders, and, indeed, of all thinking people.

The legislative, administrative, and judicial machinery of the world will be matters of utmost importance. One or two general observations may be made: (*a*) The world assembly, if it is to function efficiently, must not be bound by the rule of unanimity. On the other hand, the majority vote may be difficult to adopt, particularly in the early stages, and certain matters perhaps may have to require a two-thirds or a three-fourths vote. (*b*) The units of a federation will be difficult to prescribe. In the chapter on regional co-operation it was suggested that the problem would arise in Europe whether Yugoslavia and Czechoslovakia would be represented as a unit, in addition to having representation from their respective "national" groups. Not only that, but within Europe the problem of Germany will be a most baffling one. This strong, virile, and efficient nation has to find a place within the system; and yet in some way it must be prevented from exercising the dominance over a European federation which Prussia exercised over the German federation, before and after 1914. (*c*) Undoubtedly a much greater and more extensive civil service will be required. Where dozens of men and women were employed in the League, thousands will be required in the new International Organization. And over a period of years international-civil-service training courses will be necessary, even though vast numbers of people already have the technical ability to serve as international civil authorities. (e) The same general truth holds for the judiciary. More institutions will be needed, and probably divisions of the Permanent Court of International Justice should be set up either on a continental or on a functional basis, or both. (f) Finally, the world must make much more adequate financial provision for international government than it has hitherto done. The work of the League of Nations cost considerably less than ten million dollars a year, a tiny fraction of the amount spent on national armaments. There simply can be no peace while this appalling disproportionate expenditure exists. A relatively modest percentage of the sums now being expended on war will suffice to set up the new international institutions of government. While the expense for government will be much greater than it has been, it will be infinitesimal compared with the enormous amounts which have been expended upon wars of destruction.

As for the fundamentals of economic policy, they should include these things: (a) A more co-ordinated international investment policy which would place greater supervisory powers in the hands of a world Bank for International Settlements or the financial section of a greatly strengthened League or Federation is required. (b) In the absence of an international currency, which lies beyond the realm of probability (and yet would seem to be demanded by a federation), there will be required an International Monetary Authority to assist in maintaining reasonably stable exchange rates. (c) Although a certain amount of uneconomical manufacturing in all countries will undoubtedly continue, because the policies of the last generation cannot be entirely wiped out, nevertheless a considerable reduction of tariff barriers must be effected if trade is to be resumed in sufficient amounts to permit the world to enjoy the full benefits of the law of comparative advantage. Great Britain and the United States must give a strong lead in freeing the world from excessive tariff duties, customs formalities, and other obstacles. (d) The world will need close co-operation in maintaining labor standards during the most difficult years which lie ahead; after the cessation of war industries the most careful planning will be necessary if we are to avoid a catastrophic dislocation of the labor market. (e) International public works, particularly in the years immediately following the signing of the peace treaty, should perhaps be inaugurated. In all probability the countries of Europe will have been so impoverished by the destruction wrought by the present war that their reconstruction will be an international undertaking. (*f*) International institutions for co-operation in conservation of resources must play an ever more important part. The work of the International Halibut and Sockeye Salmon Commissions should provide an excellent model for other international commissions in the methods by which governments, scientists, and the professions can work together toward a common end. Conservation of hydroelectric power, the prevention of soil erosion, and efficient utilization of coal, oil, timber, and many other raw materials all will call for concerted efforts. (*g*) Migration problems are likely to present serious difficulties. In Europe the compulsory transfer of many hundreds of thousands of people by Germany during the last few years will have to be remedied by affording those who desire to do so an opportunity to return to their homes. This task will call for the highest statesmanship and for the creation of bodies with ample powers to deal effectively with the problem.

These and many other tasks will necessitate more international institutions. It will be impossible to carry out policies which will be comprehensive enough unless the machinery is adequate for the purpose. Not only will the agencies of the League, which dealt with economic and social problems, have to be revived and expanded (at Geneva or elsewhere), but in addition to the cluster of departments centering in one city there must be continental decentralization of international institutions. There is no reason why close co-operation should not be maintained between the regional and the central authorities. The Pan-American institutions have co-operated to some degree with the League and should continue to do so; the International Labor Organization will probably have to have enlarged branch offices throughout the world; and the Far Eastern Division of the Health Organization of the League provides an example for the kind of associated institutions which the world will need in the future. A combination of close co-ordination of policy with the maintenance of sufficient continental, national, and local initiative will be necessary. Such a happy combination will not be easy to achieve, but in the United States experience is showing that centralization of policy is consistent with a great amount of consultation with state and county officials. The requirements of an international order will simply enlarge this process and make it more complex; but in this age of ready communications it should not be impossible to devise adequate methods of effective consultation combined with responsibility of decision.

The world faces a great choice, perhaps unprecedented in its complexity and in the consequences which will flow from that choice. At the moment considerable doubt and pessimism have spread over many countries as to man's capacity to find a solution of the baffling questions which now confront him. And yet great reasons exist for optimism. Never has the human race enjoyed the fruits of scientific discovery to so great a degree. We are indeed a fortunate generation if we could but realize it. Medical discoveries have placed health within the reach of the great majority of mankind; and applied science has made comforts possible to every man, woman, and child, if the nations will only turn their attention to the production of goods which will serve human welfare.

Nor should the magnitude of the task of international government appall us. The League of Nations has shown that people can organize on a world scale. Previous chapters should have made clear that extensive international organization has been at work, all for a few million dollars a year. The League and other organizations have shown also that it is possible to depoliticize many problems and to bring to them the technical experts who can point the way to solutions. Moreover, the League experience has revealed that international government can grow from within and can appreciate the tasks which unfold before it. Nevertheless, these institutions have been sacrificed temporarily because they were not properly appreciated; they did not enter into the everyday consciousness of the average man and woman nor become a matter of importance to them.

It is sometimes said that events will force mankind to make adjustments. To a degree this is true; but in a complicated world people may misread the meaning of events; they may misinterpret the direction in which society is moving; prejudice and ignorance may cause men to see things out of perspective. Thus one of the great tasks of the immediate future is to make certain that men and women can adapt themselves psychologically and intellectually to the changes which have occurred, that they appreciate the nature of the world in which they live, and that they cease living in a past which cannot return. To enable them to do so, a vast program of political education will be required. For several years it should be the major consideration of the statesmen and leaders of democracy to make possible, over the radio and in public forums, town meetings, the universities, high schools, clubs, churches, and all other associations, the widest discussion of the fundamental problems which confront the world in its effort to obtain peace, order, and good government.

The great political and economic changes demanded by the international conditions today require a mental change which may well amount to a mental revolution. Not only must our political concepts be radically revised but our views on economic organization must be greatly expanded. It will be impossible, however, for these two things to take place unless also there develops a much graver attitude toward life as a whole. People do not change their political and economic values as they would change a suit of clothes. Changes in values arise from philosophies; and what is required today is a more comprehensive philosophy to take the place of the confusion and uncertainty which beset men's souls.

It does not lie within the province of this book to attempt to outline what should be the nature of the philosophic changes which alone would be adequate to encompass the necessary political and economic adjustments. But it may be suggested that one of the deep-seated causes of present contradictions and conflicts is the fact that mankind has allowed the merely intra-human and political things to come so close to it and absorb its attention so exclusively as to block out all but the immediate foreground of our human activity. As a penny held close to the eye may shut out the universe, so excessive preoccupation with economic and political rivalries has impaired our philosophic perspective.

We have not seen life steadily nor have we seen it whole. We have become unduly preoccupied with the pressing tasks of organization and have made politics and economics almost completely the objects of our attention. We have thought of man as primarily a citizen, when in reality he is primarily a creature of the universe. Without heat and light and gravity, the rain, the soil, the trees, and the foodstuffs which nature provides, man could not exist, and his relation to these things which are part of the universe is fundamental. But in political and economic theory we take little account of these obvious facts; we abstract man from his total setting, and then think it is possible adequately to place him in a stable political order. Not until we evaluate the personality of man in the light of his whole environment can we escape the consequences of seeing life in false perspective. Today men seem politically hypnotized. Yet much of that which is necessary and good for us goes on irrespective of our political strivings— the sunshine, the rain, the blossoming of the flowers, the ripening of the harvests, the passing of the seasons. The hills still stand, friendships remain precious, men and women fall in love, children play and dream, and the stars look down on human life. It has been said that we cannot argue ourselves out of a dilemma and, given many of the values that are commonly held today, there may be no way out of the international dilemma. We can, however, raise ourselves above the dilemma by considering problems from a new level of comprehension, imagination, objectivity, and insight. A deeper appreciation of the totality of life may permit us to have the mental ability and restraint necessary to control the vast forces unleashed by science, which today have revealed the bankruptcy of international political institutions as they are and the insufficiency of man's purpose to channelize them. Dominating all the international problems of today may be the problem whether or not man can control the great things which he has invented, whether or not he has the morality to use what he has created or must succumb to his creations.

The answer may well depend upon whether or not we can discover better understanding of the wholeness of life and the sense of perspective mentioned above. If we can see our human problems in their wider setting, we will indeed not find simple solutions to the grim political complexities which now beset us, but we may consider them in a spirit and temper which will deliver us from undue pessimism and cynicism. We shall not be overimpressed by man's achievements, knowing that, although he has recently made airplanes to fly at 400 miles an hour, the Author of light has been causing light waves to travel at 186,000 miles per second for what may have been an infinite period of time, and that man's great engineering and architectural feats are as flecks of dust compared with the majesty and silent wonder of the mountains, the planets, and the stars.

We shall not overestimate man's goodness, nor fall prey to the romantic belief in inevitable progress, but will take into account his propensity to evil. We shall see that many human pretensions —individual, social, and national—are vain and foolish and that they deny many essential relations of man with man and man with nature. Deeper insight will reveal the creative power of the moral ideal; the restraints of law are not mere inhibiting conventions but the source of man's entry into the kingdom of larger personality and values; freedom from prejudice—religious, racial, economic, and national—opens up the friendship of men of different race, class, and creed and stimulates mental and spiritual growth, while intolerance closes the gates of mutual inspiration. One's

freedom is not insured until all men are free : the employer is the
slave of anxiety as long as his workers are hostile ; the teacher is
not free while his students remain indifferent ; and the culture of
the scholar has no guaranty that it will not be destroyed unless
antirationalism and bigotry cease to dominate human souls. Few
people in the world today are free from the scourge of war, and
their condition has arisen because some leaders in distant lands
were enslaved by resentment and ambition and because millions of
common people are bound by national pride and prejudice and
class fear and hate.

Fortunately there are signs that the deeper aspects of man's
nature are demanding legitimate expression and the adoption of
political methods and institutions which will permit the development of truer values than at present can be realized. It is reasonable to hope that an age which has produced its Faradays, Pas-
teurs, Einsteins, Brantings, and Woodrow Wilsons may develop
its Platos, Goethes, and Michelangelos, and that its failure to
make the best use of its inventions will cause it to re-examine the
ethical and spiritual truths uttered by the great religious leaders
of the past and the philosophers of the present, so that by insight
and discipline it may draw upon the inexhaustible resources of the
universe which lie ready at hand to serve the constructive and
creative purposes of human life.

Today the sounds of armed conflict ring in the ears of mankind and the urgencies of self-survival compel men to make a
choice between tragic evils. It is to be hoped that they can maintain the fight and yet keep a clear vision of the greater values at
stake, that they may hold steady during the battle in order to return to more human and cultured ways in happier days ahead.

INDEX

A

Aaland Islands, 679, 772
Abyssinia, 61; *see* Ethiopia
Academy of International Law, 526
Achaean League, 549
Adjudication, Pan-American proposals for, 850–51
Advisory opinions, 613, 615
Africa: colonies, 463–64, 469–71; control of liquor traffic, 44–47, 485; land and labor problems, 463–64; "open door," 222; rivers, 287; slave trade, 54–65; traffic in arms, 796
Aggression, 663; sanctions as penalty for, 675, 682–86
Agreements: bilateral and clearing, 209–11; regional, 211–13
Agriculture: in crisis of 1931, 215; Imperial Bureau of Tropical, 483; international co-operation for control of industries, 232–41; plant and animal quarantine, 204–5; *see* Imperial College of Tropical; International Agricultural Mortgage Company; International Institute of Agriculture
Air, jurisdiction over, 308–9; transportation, 307–11; *see* Air law
Air forces: invincible, proposed by Douhet, 647; proposed international control of, 778–83
Air law, codification of private, 311–15; International Conference of Private, 312
Airmail, 319–20
Airplanes: disarmament proposals, 777–83; doctrines of Douhet, 647; effects of, on modern life, 307–8; success in warfare, 654–55
Air Navigation Convention, 309–10
Air Navigation, International Commission for, 310; Sanitary Convention for, 313–14
Alaska salmon, 398–402
Albania, 744

Alexander the Great, 548–50
Alliances, and international organization, 659–65
Amau, E., on Japanese Monroe Doctrine, 836–37
Andrews, John B., 138
Anglo-American co-operation in postwar world, 885–90
Anglo-American school of law, 588
Animal diseases, international co-operation to prevent, 33–37
Anti-Comintern Pact, 824
Anti-tank weapons, 650
Appeasement policy, 710–12, 816, 818
Arbitral tribunals, 608, 609–10
Arbitration: commercial, 352–58; compulsory, 844; General Treaty of Inter-American (1929), 849; Hague Permanent Court of, 595–609, 849; in modern times, 609; Protocol of Progressive (1929), 850
Arbitrators, national interest in the selection of, 609
Argentina, and League of Nations, 707–15
Argentine Anti-War Pact (1933), 847
Armaments: aerial, 777–83; attempts to limit international traffic in, 770, 795–97; attempts to limit private manufacture of, 792–94; land, 774–77; limitation and reduction of, 768–73; limitation of profits of armament firms, 794; nationalization of munitions industries, 794–95; naval, 783–92
Armies, development of, 641–51
Arms, convention on traffic in (1925), 796; proposed convention (1934), 796
Arms Embargo, 705–6
Ashley, W. J., *The Economic Organization of England*, 3
Assembly of League of Nations, 671–77, 692, 699, 704, 706, 708, 713–25
Assessors, for labor cases, Permanent Court, 613

eignty, 830–31; communism in, 833, 839; consortium, 828; customs autonomy, 831; dispute with Russia, 831; Eastern Railway, 851; Japanese policy in, 832–42; Manchuria, 832–36; "Open Door" in, 827–29; Shanghai municipal council, 840–41; silver question, 112–14; spheres of interest in, 827; suzerainty system, 565; unequal treaties, 830; and the Washington Conference, 829; and Western culture, 508

Cholera, 4

Christianity, 540–47; and pacifism, 752; *see* Religious co-operation

Church: Concordats, 564; Counter-Reformation, 561 (*see* Religious co-operation); influence on medieval international law, 553–59; in the Middle Ages and Reformation, 553–59; protection of rights of dependent peoples, 480–81; sovereign state, opposition to, 561–62

Cinema, influence of, 521 n.; other inter-American co-operation, 857

City-state, Greek, 548–50

Clausewitz, Karl von, 644; doctrine of war, 644

Clayton-Bulwer Treaty, 266

Coal, 235–37; *see* World Economic Conference

Collective security, 670–85; attempts to strengthen, 685–713; British policy toward, 815–16; distinguished from balance of power, 670; French policy toward, 817–18; principles of, 678–85; sanctions and, 675–76, 682; Soviet policy toward, 819–20; weakness of, 684–85; *see* League of Nations

Colonial Conference, First General (1927), 481

Colonial policy, British, 480

Colonial Research Committee, 482

Colonial Survey Committee (1905), 486; emergency committee and Pan-American co-operation, 862

Colonies: and capital investments, 220–21; raw materials resources of, 219; relief of population pressure through, 218; trade and commerce with, 221–22; weakness of concept of "have" and "have not" powers, 218–23; *see* Dependent peoples, Mandates, Minorities

Colonization, problems of, 462–67

Comité International Technique d'Experts Juridique Aériens, 312

Commerce: balance of trade, 166–67; bilateral and clearing agreements, 209–11; Brussels financial conference, 193–95; customs penetration and nomenclature, 199–206; economic nationalism, 181–84; and imperialism, 217–28; imperial preference and, 213–17; mandates, 496–500; and most-favored national clause, 207–9; Peace Treaties, 170–71; regional agreements, 211–13; reparations and, 171–73; United States reciprocal trade agreements policy, 228–32; United States tariff, 177–81; World Economic Conference, 196; World War, 168–70; *see* International trade

Commercial arbitration, 352–58

Commercial treaties, 167, 209–11

Committee of Jurists, 614

Committees of Three, in League Council, for minorities questions, 440–41

Commodity control schemes in international trade, 232–40

Communications, 263–328; effect upon national and international life, 263–64; international, *see* Cable, Radio, Telegraph, Transportation

Communications and Transit Organization of the League of Nations, 276, 289; Secretariat on, 327

Communism, and international organization, 819

Conciliation, 599–601; inter-American, general convention in (1929), 599, 847; and League of Nations, 673, 692–93; and Locarno, 600; methods of, 598–99; and sanctions, 709–10

Condliffe, J. B., 134, 136, 137, 249

Conferences: Barcelona, on Communications and Transit, 292; Brussels, International Financial (1920), 193–97; on customs formalities (1937), 199–201; disarmament, 776–77, 779, 784–92, 797; on migration, 420–21; Pan-American, 844; on textiles (1937), 197–98; on wheat (1931), 233; World Economic (1927), 195–96; World Economic (1933), 198

Congo, Belgian, conditions in, 66; mandated territory, 471

M